D1231573

FARBER ON FILM

THE COMPLETE FILM WRITINGS
OF MANNY FARBER

FARBER ON FILM

THE COMPLETE FILM WRITINGS
OF MANNY FARBER

EDITED BY
ROBERT POLITO

Hillsborough Community
College LRC

A SPECIAL PUBLICATION OF THE LIBRARY OF AMERICA

Distributed to the trade by Penguin Group (USA) Inc.

This book is set in Caslon 540, with Americana headings.

Library of Congress Control Number: 2009928058
ISBN 978-1-59853-050-6

First Printing

Printed in the United States of America

Contents

INTRODUCTION

Other Roads, Other Tracks

Criticism is very important, and difficult.
I can't think of a better thing for a person to do.
—Manny Farber

"One of the most important facts about criticism is obvious," Manny Farber once advanced in an interview. "It's based on language and words. The desire is always to pursue: what does the word mean, or the sentence, or the paragraph, and where does it lead? As you follow language out, it becomes more and more webbed, complex. The desire is always to find the end. In any thought you put down, what you're seeking is truth: what is the most believable fact and where is the end?

"It's the idea of writing about the film as commensurate with the way the filmmaker's mind is," Farber continued. "The work's qualities should influence the structure of the piece. . . . I don't think you can be mimetic enough."

Farber's insistence on criticism as language—his insistence, too, that his critical language arise from the volatile particulars of the films he writes about—makes him the most adventurous and original stylist of the mid-century El Dorado of American film criticism that spans Otis Ferguson, Robert Warshow, James Agee, Andrew Sarris, and Pauline Kael. At the start of the 21st century Farber also proves the film writer with the deepest enduring influence among that distinguished generation. Provocative traces of Farber's style can be registered in contemporary figures as various and persuasive as Greil Marcus, Luc Sante, Geoffrey O'Brien, J. Hoberman, Jonathan Rosenbaum, Paul Schrader, Jonathan Crary, Ronnie Scheib, A. O. Scott, Meredith Brody, Jean-Pierre Gorin, Kent Jones, and Howard Hampton. As far back as 1963 Susan Sontag, in her essay "Against Interpretation," called for "acts of criticism which would supply a really accurate, sharp, loving description of the appearance of a work of art. This seems even harder to do than formal analysis. Some of Manny Farber's film criticism . . . are among the rare examples of what I mean. These are essays which reveal the sensuous surface of art without mucking about in it." Recently, novelist William Gibson speculated that "if

America were Japan, Farber would long since have been declared a National Treasure." As Schrader concluded, "In the beginning was Manny Farber."

Farber on Film collects for the first time all of Farber's film investigations, his coruscating forays as a featured, often weekly or monthly reviewer for *The New Republic, The Nation, Artforum, The New Leader, Cavalier,* and *City,* among other magazines, as well as the landmark pieces of his only book, *Negative Space* (1971, and reprinted in an expanded edition in 1998). He is legendary for fierce, serpentine essays that shun movie-criticism commonplaces like character psychology, story synopsis, and social lessons. *Negative Space* accents Farber's extended performances of the late 1950s and '60s, "The Gimp," "Hard-Sell Cinema," "Underground Films," and "White Elephant Art vs. Termite Art," reprinting only a dozen full or partial film columns from *The Nation* (where he started reviewing in 1947 and published over 65 film pieces) and just a single film column from *The New Republic* (where he started reviewing in 1942, and published almost 175 film pieces). The wonder of these early reviews is how impressively his *New Republic* and *Nation* columns deliver both as traditional criticism and innovative Farber prose, as he elegantly focuses acting, plot, even entertainment value, the very moves his monumental essays resist. The present volume returns those later essays to the movie occasions that prompted and sustained them, and one of its pleasures is tracking precarious notions like "termite art" or "the gimp" or the "underground" across three decades. *Farber on Film* also sweeps up his important film pieces after *Negative Space,* including crucial looks at Scorsese and Altman.

Farber and *Negative Space*

The Farber equation is never simple. That sentence is a variation on a Samuel Beckett line I've wanted to adapt for an essay, review, biography, even poem, ever since I read the original in college. As the opening sentence to his first book Beckett wrote, "The Proustian equation is never simple," and from the outset I was comforted by the promise of persistent, accelerating, perhaps eternal difficulty and puzzle. But as over the years I repeated to myself the sentence, "The Proustian equation is never simple," at the blind start of any obstinate piece of writing, I found myself startled by Beckett's conflation of "Proustian" and "equation": his brisk juxtaposition of involuntary memory and the painstaking working through of quantities and variables.

I never found a space for the sentence because the bewilderment the arrival of Beckett's six words in my head customarily signaled turned out always to expose only a lack of preparation or confidence, a private anxiety that refused to intersect the subject at hand. But for Manny Farber's film criticism and paintings, the introductory oddities, muddles, crises, contradictions, dead ends, multiple alternatives, and divergent vistas spiral along "chains of rapport and intimate knowledge" (to quote his essay on Don Siegel) into still more tangled and intractable mysteries; following Beckett on Proust, the Farber equation creates "a sustained, powerful, and lifelike pattern of dissonance" (to quote his essay on Preston Sturges) that insists on insinuating the steeped-in-time personal and sensual alongside the abstractly intellectual, formal, and conceptual.

For much of his writing life Farber was branded an advocate merely of action films and B-movies—as though it might not be distinction enough to have been the first American critic to render serious appreciations of Howard Hawks, Samuel Fuller, William Wellman, Raoul Walsh, and Anthony Mann. Yet Farber resisted many noir films of the 1940s as inflated and mannerist— "over the past couple of years, one movie after another has been filled with low-key photography," he complained in 1952, "shallow perspectives, screwy pantomime, ominously timed action, hollow-sounding voices." Farber also was among the first critics to write about Rainer Werner Fassbinder, an early champion of Werner Herzog, and an exponent of such experimental directors as Michael Snow, George Kuchar, Andy Warhol, and Chantal Akerman. *Village Voice* film critic J. Hoberman told me that upon discovering Farber in college, he was "stunned by how eclectic Farber was, how wide-ranging his references were. I wasn't that interested in commercial films. I was interested in underground movies, the French New Wave, and such B-movies as existed. I would read Andrew Sarris, I would read Kael, but I felt they were operating from a different perspective—whereas Farber seemed to me to be a much hipper intellect." As Hoberman quipped in the introduction to his collection *Vulgar Modernism*, Farber played "both ends off against the middlebrow."

Still, Farber's notoriety as a film critic largely resides in his B-movie-steeped, careering slams of the 1950s and '60s—"The Gimp" (for *Commentary*, 1952), "Underground Films" (also for *Commentary*, 1957), "Hard-Sell Cinema" (for *Perspectives*, 1957), and particularly "White Elephant Art vs. Termite Art" (for *Film Culture*, 1962). The termite/white elephant essay cashiered "masterpiece art, reminiscent of the enameled tobacco humidors and wooden lawn ponies bought at white elephant auctions decades ago." White elephant directors "blow up every situation and character like an affable inner tube with recognizable details and smarmy compassion" or "pin the viewer to the wall and slug him with wet towels of artiness and significance." Farber instead tracked the termite artist: "ornery, wasteful, stubbornly self-involved, doing go-for-broke art and not caring what comes of it." Termite art (or "termite-fungus-centipede art," as he also bottled it) is "an act both of observing and being in the world, a journeying in which the artist seems to be ingesting both material of his art and the outside world through horizontal coverage." Against the white elephant "pursuit of . . . continuity, harmony," termite art mainly inheres in moments—"a few spots of tingling, jarring excitement" in a Cézanne painting where the artist "nibbles away at what he calls his 'small sensation'"; John Wayne's "hipster sense of how to sit in a chair leaned against a wall" in *The Man Who Shot Liberty Valence*; and "one unforgettably daring image" in *Jules et Jim*, "kids sniffing the bicycle seat just vacated by the girl in the typical fashion of voyeuristic pornographic art."

Farber's attention to vivifying details and gestures rather than the encrusted masterwork reminds me of Robert Frost in his *Paris Review* interview. "The whole thing is performance and prowess and feats of association," Frost asserted of his poems. "Why don't critics talk about those things—what a feat it was to turn that that way, and what a feat it was to remember that, to be reminded of that by this?" Farber similarly personalized his termite/white elephant division for the introduction to *Negative Space*: "The primary reason for the two categories is that all the directors I like . . . are in the termite range, and no one speaks about them for the qualities I like." As termite artists he indicated a diversity of painters, writers, photographers, producers, and actors, which encompassed Laurel and Hardy, Otis Ferguson, Walker Evans, Val Lewton, Clarence Williams, J. R. Williams, Weldon Kees, Margie Israel, Isaac Rosenfeld, sometimes James Agee, and film directors Howard Hawks, Raoul Walsh, William Wellman, Samuel Fuller, Anthony Mann, and Preston Sturges.

Farber published his last film essay, "Beyond the New Wave: Kitchen Without Kitsch," in *Film Comment*, in 1977, a few years after he moved from New York to San Diego with his wife, the artist Patricia Patterson, to paint and to teach film and painting at the University of California. Among his reasons for abandoning criticism, as he told me: "I no longer wanted to be viewed as the film critic who also paints." In New York Farber traveled among the late 1930s generation of New York writers and critics, many aligned with *Partisan Review*—Clement Greenberg, Agee, Saul Bellow, Jean Stafford, Mary McCarthy, Kees, and Ferguson, among others. For his reviews and essays for *The New Republic*, *The Nation*, *Time*, *Commentary*, *Commonweal*, *The New Leader*, *Cavalier*, *Artforum*, and *City*, Farber manifested overt and enduring affinities particularly with Ferguson, Agee, and Greenberg. Yet his approach to the actual writing could not be more divergent, incongruous, maverick, perverse. Where Greenberg aimed at what might be styled a fastidious lucidity, even as he traced the destruction of representation, and Ferguson and Agee offered distinctive variations on conversational lyricism—Ferguson tilting toward 1920s jazz, Agee canting into rhapsody—Farber is perhaps the only American critic of modernism to write as a modernist. He emerged as the boldest and most literary of film and art critics of the 1940s and '50s by coursing along almost stridently anti-literary tangents. Farber advanced a topographical prose that aspired termite-fashion through fragmentation, parody, allusions, multiple focus, and clashing dictions to engage the formal spaces of the new films and paintings he admired.

Farber once described his prose style as "a struggle to remain faithful to the transitory, multisuggestive complication of a movie image and/or negative space." No other film critic has written so inventively or flexibly from inside the moment of a movie. His writing can appear to be composed exclusively of digressions from an absent center. One of his standard moves is a bold qualification of a qualification, in a sequence of vivid repositionings. His strategies mix self-suspicion, retreat, digression, and mulish persistence, so that Farber (once more Beckett-like) often proceeds as if giving up and pressing on simultaneously. There are rarely introductory overviews or concluding summaries; his late reviews in particular spurn plot summaries and might not even name the director of a film, and transitions seem interchangeable with nonsequiturs. Puns, jokes, lists, snaky metaphors, and webs of allusions supplant arguments. Farber wrenches nouns into verbs (Hawks, he writes, "landscapes action") and sustains strings of divergent, perhaps irreconcilable adjectives such that praise can look inseparable from censure. *Touch of Evil*, he writes, is "basically the best movie of Welles's cruddy middle peak period." He will cast prickly epigrams—"Huston is unable to countenance the possibility of every gentleman being a murderer at heart, preferring instead every murderer being a gentleman at heart." His sentences will dazzle through layers of poise and charm:

> What is so lyrical about the ending [of Don Siegel's *The Lineup*], in San Francisco's Sutro Museum, is the Japanese-print compositions, the late afternoon lighting, the advantage taken of the long hallways, multilevel stairways, in a baroque, elegant, glass-palace building with an exposed skating rink, nautical museum, and windows facing the sea with eye-catching boulders.

But Farber *qua* Farber typically arrives at a kind of backdoor poetry: not "lyrical," or traditionally poetic, but original and startling. This is Farber on *How I Won the War*: "At its best, it has a crawling-along-the-earth cantankerousness and cruddiness, as though the war against fascism were being glimpsed by a cartooned earthworm from an outhouse on a fake hillbilly spread somewhere in the Carolinas." Or here he invokes the "underground" theaters along 1950s Manhattan's 42nd Street:

> The hard-bitten action film finds its natural home in caves: the murky, congested theaters, looking like glorified tattoo parlors on the outside and located near bus terminals in big cities. These theaters roll action films in what, at first, seems like a nightmarish atmosphere of shabby transience, prints that seem overgrown with jungle moss, sound tracks infected with hiccups. The spectator watches two or three action films go by and leaves feeling as though he were a pirate discharged from a giant sponge.

Many of these writerly aspects are on display in Farber's magnificent Hawks piece, originally published in *Artforum* in 1969. The essay manages neither a welcoming preface nor a resolving conclusion—the start and finish are all canny abruptness. The first four long paragraphs compose a docket, or roster—one Hawks film for each paragraph. Farber situates Hawks inside a vast allusive complex—Piero's religious paintings, cubist composing, Breughel, F. Scott and Zelda Fitzgerald, Tolkien, Muybridge, Walker Evans, and Robert Frank; almost a kind of collage of allusive appropriation. Many phrases describe Farber's own writing practice and anticipate the complex, tangled surfaces of his future paintings: "secret preoccupation with linking," "builds detail on detail into a forbidding whirlwind," "each one bumping the other in an endless interplay," "many plots are interwoven," "the idea of topping, outmaneuvering," "intricately locked humor," "the ingenuity of its pragmatic engineering," and "the geography of gesture." And, rare for Farber's prose, there is an explicit autobiographical reference—to the border town of his birthplace. The seaport in *Only Angels Have Wings* might be good, he proposes, for a Douglas, Arizona, high school production.

Farber Before *Negative Space*

You don't necessarily think of Manny Farber as your *Baedeker* to the shadings of mainstay American movie acting, as a dab hand of the concise plot summary that uncoils into deft film critique, or associate him with audience recommendations and words like "marvelous," "sensitive," "poignant," and "sparkling." You particularly don't think of Farber this way if your experience of his writing is confined to *Negative Space*. Yet consider three short illustrative moments from his many, sometimes weekly film columns of the 1940s and '50s.

This is Farber on Frank Sinatra & Co. in *From Here to Eternity* for *The Nation*, August 29, 1953:

> The laurel wreaths should be handed out to an actor who isn't even in the picture, Marlon Brando, and to an unknown person who first decided to use Frank Sinatra and Donna Reed in the unsweetened roles of Maggio, a tough little Italian American soldier, and Lorene, a prostitute at the "New Congress" who dreams of returning to respectability in the states. Sinatra plays the wild drunken Maggio in the manner of an energetic vaudevillian. In certain scenes—doing duty in the mess hall, reacting to some foul piano playing—he shows a marvelous capacity for phrasing plus a calm expression that is almost unique in Hollywood films. Miss Reed may mangle some lines ("you certainly are a funny one") with her attempts at a flat Midwestern accent, but she is an interesting actress whenever Cameraman Burnett Guffey uses a hard light on her somewhat bitter features. Brando must have been the inspiration for Clift's ability to make certain key lines ("I can soldier with any man," or "No more'n ordinary right cross") stick out and seem the most authentic examples of American speech to be heard in films.

Or here he is on Jerry Lewis in *That's My Boy*, two years earlier on September 1, 1951, also for *The Nation*:

> The grimmest phenomenon since Dagmar has been the fabulous nationwide success of Jerry Lewis's sub-adolescent, masochistic mugging. Lewis has parlayed his apish physiognomy, rickety body, frenzied lack of coordination, paralyzing brashness, and limitless capacity for self-degradation into a gold mine for himself and the mannered crooner named Dean Martin who, draped artistically from a mike, serves as his ultra-suave straight man. When Jerry fakes swallowing a distasteful pill, twiddles "timid" fingers, whines, or walks "like Frankenstein," his sullen narcissistic insistence suggests that he would sandbag anyone who tried to keep him from the limelight. Lewis is a type I hoped to have left behind when I short-sheeted my last cot at Camp Kennekreplach. But today's bobby-soxers are rendered apoplectic by such Yahoo antics, a fact that can only be depressing for anyone reared on comedians like Valentino, Norma Shearer,

Lewis Stone, Gregory Peck, Greer Garson, Elizabeth Taylor, or Vincent Impellitteri.

Last, listen to the opening of his review of *The Best Years of Our Lives* for *The New Republic*, December 2, 1946:

> For an extremely sensitive and poignant study of life like your own, carrying constantly threatening overtones during this early stage of postwar readjustment, it would be worth your while to see "The Best Years of Our Lives," even at the present inflated postwar prices.
>
> The sparkling travelogue opening shows three jittery veterans flying home to up-and-at-'em Boone City, a flourishing elm-covered metropolis patterned after Cincinnati. They are too uneasy about entering their homes as strangers to eat up the scenery. The chesty, down-to-earth sailor (Harold Russell), whose lack of sophistication and affectation furnishes a striking contrast to his two chums, is hypersensitive about his artificial hands and is afraid his girl (Cathy O'Donnell) will marry him out of pity rather than love; the sergeant (Fredric March), whose superiority rests in his being old and experienced, a survivor of the infantry and before that a successful banker and father, feels he has changed too much for his old job and his family; the bombardier (Dana Andrews), who has about him that most-likely-to-succeed look of the Air Forces, got married on the run during training and hardly knows what to anticipate.

Despite the journalistic nimbleness and surprises inside these sentences, or manifold tonal differences from the famous essays of *Negative Space*, you still witness emblematic Farber strokes in these early extracts from *The New Republic* and *The Nation*. Observe throughout the stubborn, graphic detailing as he tabs various personality-revealing gestures: Sinatra, for instance, "reacting to some foul piano playing," or Dean Martin "draped artistically from a mike." Farber's later commemoration of the "natural dialogue" and "male truth" of action films is a recasting of his appreciation here of Montgomery Clift's "authentic . . . American speech" in *From Here to Eternity*. Note too the distinctive seesaws of contrary adjectives and nouns ("grimmest," "fabulous," "success," "masochistic mugging"); the bouncy slang ("up-and-at-'em," "sandbag anyone," or "short-sheeted my last cot"); and the rollick of his self-consuming cadences on Lewis. Topical allusions (the blonde model-actress

Dagmar graced the cover of *Life* the previous July) bump against deadpan, likely fictive citations ("Camp Kennekreplach"), much as that initial reference to Brando dangles, a tease, nearly a nonsequitur, even after Farber ostensibly resolves it later in the paragraph. Observe especially that signature Farber list of "comedians" that concludes the impish Jerry Lewis swipe. Valentino, Gregory Peck, Elizabeth Taylor . . . all comedians? The final name belongs to the then-mayor of New York City, Vincent Impellitteri, aka "Impy," appended to the litany—I'm guessing—as much for his Tammany Hall affiliations and betrayals as for his public welcoming a few weeks earlier of Martin and Lewis to the Paramount Theater on Broadway.

By his "Underground Films" essay of 1957 Farber would flip over his fiesta for Sinatra and *From Here to Eternity*, the crooner-turned-actor by then evincing only "private scene-chewing," and you will uncover in the *New Republic* and *Nation* columns analogous complications for his later appraisals of Preston Sturges, John Huston, and Gene Kelly. Farber initiated his career as an art and film critic at *The New Republic* early in 1942, and co-wrote his last essay with his wife, Patricia Patterson, in 1977; that's a 35-year arc. Of the original 281 pages of *Negative Space*, roughly 230 emanate from a 12-year stretch, 1957 through 1969, directly prior to the book. Farber titled a magnificent 1981 "auteur" painting, rooted in the films of William Wellman, *Roads and Tracks*. *Farber on Film* can advance alternate routes—other roads, other tracks—into, through, and around Farber's familiar trajectory as a critic and writer.

Occasionally in interviews he will present himself as a sort of natural critic, steeped in opinions and argumentative strategies. "An important fact of my childhood was that I was surrounded by two brothers who were awfully smart, and very good at debating," Farber once told me. "We averaged three to four movies a week, sometimes with my uncle Jake. There was a good library, and in the seventh grade I started to go there and read movie criticism in magazines. I would analyze it and study it." Then, at other moments, Farber suggests that ultimately only words matter to him. "When I'm writing I'm usually trying for a language. I have tactics, and I know the sound I want, and it doesn't read like orthodox criticism. What I'm trying for was a language that holds you, that keeps a person reading and following me, following language rather than following criticism. I loved the construction involved in criticism."

Manny Farber was born on February 20, 1917, in Douglas, Arizona, his house at 1101 Eighth Street just five blocks from the Mexican border. His parents ran a clothing store, La California Dry Goods, on G Street, Main Street in Douglas, across from the Lyric Theatre and also near the Grand Theatre. He followed his older brothers Leslie and David to Douglas High School, where he played football and tennis, wrote about sports, and contributed drawings of Mickey Mouse to the school yearbook, *The Copper Kettle*. After his family moved to Vallejo, California, and then to Berkeley, Farber enrolled in the University of California, Berkeley, for his freshman year, before transferring to Stanford. At Berkeley, Farber covered sports for *The Daily Californian*; his earliest signed article, a spirited forecast of the upcoming track and field season, appeared on January 25, 1935, under the headline BEAR WEIGHT MEN RATED AS STRONG GROUP. As he concluded his journalistic debut:

> Further joy was added to the track outlook with the announcement that big Glen Randall, Little Meet record holder, will again heave the discus this spring. Seriously hurt in an automobile accident last October, Randall is again ready to hurl the platter out to the 150 foot line. Aiding him in this event is Warren Wood, a potential first place winner but an erratic performer.

Farber often claimed sportswriters as an influence on his criticism, and routinely injected sports metaphors into his columns, surprisingly for art as much as film. Richard Pousette-Dart, he suggested in *The Nation* (October 13, 1951), "is something close to the Bobby Thomson of the spontaneity boys," while Ferdinand Leger, he contended in *The Magazine of Art* (November 1942), "reminds me of a pitcher who can throw nothing but fast balls, and his fast balls so fast you can't see them." Reviewing sports-film features, he stressed that the games be represented as convincingly as any other profession. On Gary Cooper as Lou Gehrig in *Pride of the Yankees*:

> No matter that Gary doesn't like baseball, is right-handed, lazy and tall-skinny, whereas Gehrig was left-handed, hard-working to the point of compulsion, and his one leg was the size of two of Gary's. So they taught him to throw left-handed, but they could never teach him to throw with any muscles but the ones in his arms, like a woman, nor could they make his long legs run differently from those of someone trying to run with a plate between his knees, nor could they move his body with his bat swing.
>
> All of which meant cutting the baseball action to a minimum —montage shots mostly from long distance up in the press box, and the picture was shot to hell right there. (*New Republic*, July 27, 1942)

After taking drawing classes at Stanford, Farber enrolled at the California School of Fine Arts, and then at the Rudolph Schaefer School of Design. Around San Francisco, he supported himself as a carpenter, until he joined his brother Leslie in Washington, in 1939, and then in New York, in 1942. Both Leslie and David Farber found callings as psychiatrists; Leslie, notably, was the author of *The Ways of the Will: Essays Toward a Psychology and Psychopathology of Will* (1966), and *Lying, Despair, Jealousy, Envy, Sex, Suicide, and the Good Life* (1976). Leslie Farber's psychoanalytic essays track curious affinities with his brother's film writings; Leslie's "distrust" for "any psychological doctrine . . . [which] requires the repeated fancying-up of some item of experience—memory, dream, feeling, what have you—to give it an epistemological razzle-dazzle it couldn't manage on its own" inevitably recalls the "wet towels of artiness and significance" of white elephant art. Overall his brothers' immersion in the human inner life appears to have prompted Manny's contempt for psychology, whether on screen or in his own writing. "I moved as far away as I could from what Les and David were doing," Farber told me. "My whole life, the writing, was always in opposition to Leslie's domain, his involvement with psychology, brain power, etc. But there was never any quarreling between brothers. It was just competing, that's all." Under the title "Paranoia Unlimited" (*New Republic*, November 25, 1946), Farber joked:

> In answer to the demand for movies that make you suspect psychopathological goings-on in everyone from friend to family dog (yesterday's heroes killed Indians, today's are associated one way or another with psychiatry), MGM has reissued a pokey oldie called "Rage in Heaven." This relic starts at a lonely asylum with a comic-opera escape by an unidentified inmate (Robert Montgomery) who is known to be paranoid only by the asylum doctor (Oscar Homolka, who gives an embarrassing rendition of a Katzenjammer psychiatrist).

Still, as with football or baseball, he would notice the "fairly accurate" rendition of an analyst's questions in Hitchcock's *Spellbound*, even as he dismissed the Dali dream as "a pallid business of papier-mâché and modern show-window designing" (*New Republic*, December 3, 1945).

With a characteristic mix of the flip and the canny, Farber bamboozled his way into *The New Republic* with a "smart-aleck" letter to editor Bruce Bliven, indicating that "I could do the job better than anyone else who was doing it." His earliest art column appeared on February 2, 1942, a review of the MOMA show "Americans 1942—Eighteen Artists from Nine States" that featured a postage stamp–sized sketch by Farber of artist John Marin. His next art column two weeks later delineated the face of Max Weber, then in a Whitney Museum watercolor exhibition. "I planned to do a drawing to go along with every article," Farber told me, "but I just couldn't keep up." After Otis Ferguson enlisted in the Merchant Marine as a seaman, Farber took over the film column, publishing on March 23 a round-up review of three war films, including *To Be or Not to Be.* As an art critic, Farber sounded like Farber from his premiere column, accenting "action" and "flexibility," denouncing "stylization" and "dogma." With movies, he took longer—perhaps also piling on at first too many films at once for a short review; not until May would he learn to fixate on a single film and wrap up the others in a codicillary paragraph.

As I suggested at the outset, *Farber on Film* can be read for both continuities and departures, especially toward or away from the key essays of *Negative Space.* Looking back from the vistas of "The Gimp," "Underground Films," and especially "White Elephant Art vs. Termite Art," Farber can be viewed as implacably progressing into his galvanizing notions. In "The Gimp," for instance, published in *Commentary* in 1952, he imagined a "gimmick," a device with a string that a director might jerk any time he wished to insert some "art" into a film. As far back as 1945 he was propounding a sort of protean mask for the same purposes:

A device will soon be invented in Hollywood that will fulfill completely the producers' desire to please every person in the movie-going public. The device will be shaped like a silo and worn over the face, and be designed for those people who sit in movies expecting to witness art. It will automatically remove from any movie photographic gloss, excess shadows, and smoothness, makeup from actors' faces, the sound track and every third and fifth frame from the film in the interest of giving the movie cutting rhythm. It will jiggle the movie to give it more movement (also giving the acting a dance-like quality). To please those people who want complete fidelity to life it will put perspiration and flies on actors' faces, dirt under their fingernails, wet the armpits of men's shirts and scratch, flake and wear down the decor. It comes complete with the final amazing chase sequence from "Intolerance" and the scene from "The Birth of a Nation" in which the Little Sister decorates her ragged dress with wads of cotton, which it inserts whenever somebody is about to conduct an all-girl symphony. The gadget also does away with all audience noise. (*New Republic*, August 20, 1945)

Throughout the 1940s and early 1950s Farber memorialized the 42nd Street itch-house hippodromes he would tag "caves" in his 1957 essay "Underground Films." This, from 1943:

> Who builds movie theatres? If you seek the men's room you vanish practically away from this world, always in a downward direction. It is conceivable that the men's room is on its way out. At the theatre called the Rialto in New York the men's room is so far down it somehow connects with the subway: I heard a little boy, who came dashing up to his father, say, "Daddy! I saw the subway!" The father went down to see for himself. Another place that lets patrons slip through its fingers is the theatre in Greenwich Village where the men's room is outside altogether. (*New Republic*, June 7, 1943)

That same year he observed of the action films he would eventually ticket as underground: "It is an interesting Hollywood phenomenon that the tough movie is about the only kind to examine the character's actions straight and without glamor" (*New Republic*, January 11, 1943).

The dynamics of white elephant art were fully in place at least nine years, maybe even more than a decade before Farber's 1962 essay "White Elephant Art vs. Termite Art." He attached the word "elephantine" to the concept for an October 17, 1953, *Nation* column, and defined it recognizably in his recapitulation the previous January of his ten best films. "The only way to pull the vast sprawl of 1952 films together is to throw most of them in a pile bearing the label 'movies that failed through exploiting middle-brow attitudes about what makes a good movie.' . . . It is difficult to say whether I liked or disliked a number of films that will appear on most other lists, since it was usually a case of being impressed with classy craftsmanship and bored by watching it pander to some popular notion about what makes an artistic wow" (*Nation*, January 17, 1953). But white elephant art loops back through the years, accruing linkages and implications. A 1952 review of *Carrie* positions underground films against white elephants without naming either:

> Hollywood films were once in the hands of non-intellectuals who achieved, at best, the truth of American life and the excitement of American movement in simple-minded action stories. Around 1940 a swarm of bright locusts from the

Broadway theaters and radio stations descended on the studios and won Hollywood away from the innocent, rough-and-ready directors of action films. The big thing that happened was that a sort of intellectual whose eyes had been trained on the crowded, bound-in terrain of Times Square and whose brain had been sharpened on left-wing letters of the thirties, swerved Hollywood story-telling toward fragmented, symbol-charged drama, closely viewed, erratically acted, and deviously given to sniping at their own society. What Welles, Kanin, Sturges, and Huston did to the American film is evident in the screen version of Dreiser's "Sister Carrie," which is less important for its story than for the grim social comment underscoring every shot. (*Nation*, May 17, 1952)

Such fledgling evocations of white elephant art render explicit, as his 1962 essay never would, the intimation that Farber, who as a carpenter in San Francisco tried to join the Communist Party, was specifically dethroning the vulgarities and hypocrisy of liberal New Deal Hollywood as much as any other inadvertently comic bourgeois correctness. As he wrote of *Come Back, Little Sheba*, "You will half-enjoy the film, but its realism is more effective than convincing, and it tends to reiterate the twisted sentimentality of left-wing writing that tries to be very sympathetic toward little people while breaking its back to show them as hopelessly vulgar, shallow, and unhappy" (*Nation*, November 8, 1952). Other reviews connect elephantitis with films that would be dubbed noir (*Murder, My Sweet*; *Farewell, My Lovely*; *Laura*; and *Double Indemnity*) with European films (*Miracle in Milan*), Japanese films (*Rashomon*), Oscar aspirants (*Mrs. Miniver*), and Disney cartoons (*Bambi*). As a category, if not a punchline, white elephant art was vital to Farber's thinking about movies and paintings from his first months at *The New Republic*.

Termite art of course is *everywhere* in his *New Republic* and *Nation* columns, though fascinatingly never via the urgent termite metaphors ("tunneling," "burrowed into," "excavations," "veining," "nibbles away,") that stitch together both "Underground Films" and "White Elephant Art vs. Termite Art." You twig termite art in Farber's 1940s valentines to B-movies and B-directors, his early assertion that "there is not a good story film without what is called the documentary technique" (*New Republic*, July 12, 1943), his recurrent application of the adjectives "honest" and "accurate" for his highest praise, his emphasis on scrupulous history in allegedly historical movies, and in phrases like "the details of ordinary activity" (*New Republic*, February 8, 1943), and "actual life in actual settings" (*New Republic*, March 13, 1944). His dazzling invocation of late-night New York radio talk-jocks for *The American Mercury*, "Seers for the Sleepless," similarly would italicize their fidelity to the "sounds of real life."

These columns also comprise a sort of anthology of the infinite ways of scaffolding a mixed review. Early and late, in his writing and for his paintings, Farber would demand multiple perspectives. As he ultimately lamented about popular arts criticism, "Every review tends to become a monolithic putdown or rave" (*Cavalier*, June 1966). Here he leads off a 1942 *New Republic* art column being wisecracking and caustic toward Thomas Hart Benton:

> A bush-league ball player never gets beyond the Three Eye League, but a bush-league painter can be known coast to coast, especially if he has the marvelous flair for publicity that is Benton's. When Mr. B paints a picture, almost like magic the presses start rolling, cameras clicking, and before you know it everyone in East Orange is talking about Tom's latest painting.

Yet, by the next paragraph he is already back-pedaling—he admits that "Benton has painted war as it actually is" and concludes, "Mr. Benton may be strictly a lightweight as a painter, but he is nevertheless honest and wise enough to paint the war as war, and not as pattycake pattycake" (April 20, 1942). By 1945, reviewing *The Clock*, Farber could insinuate all his contrary responses into just one paragraph:

> The movie is dominated by the desire to be neatly pleasant and pretty, and truthful only so far as will not basically disturb the neatness, pleasantness and prettiness. The furlough without an empty, disappointing, lonely, distasteful or fearful moment is as hard to believe as is the portrait of New Yorkers as relaxed, daisy-faced, accommodating people who send champagne to soldiers in restaurants. Most of the story is the sensation-filled, laugh-hungry, coincidence-ridden affair a gag writer would invent, and probably the hardest fact to swallow is the film's inability to show anything in its lovers that might indicate that their marriage would ever turn out to be any less blissful than their two-day courtship. Mainly because of the direction of Vincente Minnelli, "The Clock," though, is riddled as few movies are with carefully,

skillfully used intelligence and love for people and for movie making, and is made with a more flexible and original use of the medium than any other recent film. (*New Republic*, May 21, 1945)

By 1953 Farber would require just a single mixed sentence. "*Stalag 17* is a crude, cliché-ridden glimpse of a Nazi prison camp that I hated to see end" (*Nation*, July 25).

Ultimately, though, for all its intersections with *Negative Space, Farber on Film* inscribes alternatives rather than correlatives. For the first time it's possible to shadow Farber as a professional chronicler of new films, and he emerges as thoughtful and skillful precisely where his reputation predicts he might be careless—actors, plots, judgments, even annual best lists. Alongside his reviews, he also wrote an alluring motley of "think pieces" on such topics as "The Hero," "Movies in Wartime," "Theatrical Movies," independent film trends, screwball comedies, documentaries, newsreels, hidden cameras, censorship, 3-D, and television comics. Farber moonlighted away from both his beats—smart, resonant essays on Russel Wright dinnerware, Knoll furniture, jazz, and Pigmeat Markham. Part memoir, part prescient anatomy of the exaltation of talk radio in American experience over the coming decades, part midnight hallucination of "disembodied" voices, "Seers for the Sleepless" approaches the everyday visionary art of his Greenwich Village friends Weldon Kees and Isaac Rosenfeld. His early pieces during World War II routinely entail vivid social history, and Farber always proved alert to racial affronts and offenses in Hollywood films. From 1942: "Behind the romantic distortion of Negro life in 'Tales of Manhattan' is a discrimination as old as Hollywood" (*New Republic*, October 12). Or 1949: "The benevolent writers—working in studios where as far as I know there are no colored directors, writers, or cameramen—so far have placed their Negroes in almost unprejudiced situations, presented only one type of pleasant, well-adjusted individual, and given him a superior job in a white society" (*Nation*, July 30).

As a regular reviewer, Farber also turns out to be *funnier* than you'd calculate, not just caustic or cranky, but witty. Early on he complained about overcrowded museum exhibitions of two, maybe three hundred paintings. "Something like it would be reading *War and Peace*, two short stories and a scientific journal in one sitting" (*New Republic*, February 16, 1942). "All kinds of hardships have to be endured in wartime," Farber confessed. "Some of them could be avoided. One of these is the war poster that plays hide-and-seek with art and our times. I don't think the lack of aesthetics is anything to carp about at this stage, but I do think they ought to mention the war above a whisper"

(*New Republic*, March 16, 1942). Reviewing a three-and-a-half-million-dollar film about Woodrow Wilson called *Darryl F. Zanuck's Wilson in Technicolor*, he observed, "For several reasons, one being that Wilson had a 'nice' tenor voice, there are 87 songs blared or sung in the picture from 1 to 12 times and as though the audience left its ears in the cloak room: come in at any time and you will think 'Zanuck's Sousa' is being shown" (*New Republic*, August 14, 1944). Still, Farber could also sound caustic and cranky—"The closest movie equivalents to having a knife slowly turned in a wound for two hours are 'Tender Comrade' and 'The Story of Dr. Wassell'" (*New Republic*, June 26, 1944).

Once Farber quit New York and moved to San Diego with Patricia in the fall of 1970, he abandoned criticism for painting and teaching. Although he wouldn't entirely stop writing until 1977, Farber ended—at least he set in motion the steps that would lead him to end—his three-and-a-half decade stint as a critic as whimsically (or craftily) as he had started it with that wise-guy letter to *The New Republic*. During a drunken dinner—and Manny rarely drank—after a 1969 show of his monumental abstract paintings on collaged paper sponsored by the O.K. Harris Gallery, he found himself talking to another artist, Don Lewallen, a UC San Diego professor in painting, on leave in Manhattan and wishing to stay. Somehow, by the end of the night, Farber had traded his loft on Warren Street for the professor's job at UCSD.

He joined the Visual Arts faculty, teaching small painting classes and large film lecture courses. "It was hell from the first moment to the last," Farber recounted in an interview. "We came for me to teach painting, which was fine. I'd been doing that once a week in New York. I was very comfortable, and it was a nice thing to do. But someone had the idea that I teach film appreciation, since I'd been writing criticism. And it seemed OK. We didn't realize it would become such an overwhelming job. The classes in film would have 300 students, instead of the 15 you'd have in a painting and drawing class. I was swamped." The UCSD faculty mixed artists, poets, critics, and art historians, and included David Antin, Jehanne Teilhet, Michael Todd, Ellen van Fleet, Newton Harrison, Gary Hudson, Allan Kaprow, and eventually J. P. Gorin.

Farber taught a "History of Film" class—one opening week he screened *The Musketeers of Pig Alley*, *Fantômas*, *A Romance of Happy Valley*, and *True Heart Susie*, while his week three spanned *Sunrise*, *Underworld*, *Scarface*, and *Spanky*. He also taught "Third World Films" and "Films in Social Context" and created a class in "Radical Form" called "Hard Look at the Movies" that moved from Godard-Gorin and Andy Warhol through Fassbinder, Marguerite Duras, Michael Snow, Miklos Jancso, Jean-Marie Straub, Alain Resnais, and Ernie

Gehr. "Manny's film classes," as Duncan Shepherd, later film critic for the *San Diego Reader*, recalled, "were the stuff of legend, and it seems feeble and formulaic to call him a brilliant, an illuminating, a stimulating, an inspiring teacher. It wasn't necessarily what he had to say (he was prone to shrug off his most searching analysis as 'gobbledegook') so much as it was the whole way he went about things, famously showing films in pieces, switching back and forth from one film to another, ranging from Griffith to Godard, Bugs Bunny to Yasujiro Ozu, talking over them with or without sound, running them backward through the projector, mixing in slides of paintings, sketching out compositions on the blackboard, the better to assist students in seeing what was in front of their faces, to wean them from Plot, Story, What Happens Next, and to disabuse them of the absurd notion that a film is all of a piece, all on a level, quantifiable, rankable, fileable. He could seldom be bothered with movie trivia, inside information, behind-the-scenes piffle, technical shoptalk, was often offhand about the basic facts of names and dates, was unconcerned with Classics, Masterpieces, Seminal Works, Historical Landmarks. It was always about looking and seeing."

Farber's exams and quizzes demanded his students see all the films, and then remember everything they saw and heard—"Describe the framing (composition) and use of people in the following: a. *McCabe and Mrs. Miller*; b. *Walkabout*; c. *Fear Eats the Soul*; d. *Mean Streets*"; "Identify the movie in which this unforgettable scriptwriting appears. . . ." He directed pitiless essay questions—"MOUCHETTE emphasizes the existence of contradictory impulses succeeding one another (more rapidly than is admitted in our culture). Describe this transiency in either the stream edge fight between poacher and warden or the rape scene between Arsene and Mouchette (camera, framing, etc.). BROKEN BLOSSOMS is gravely different; using any of the scenes between Lucy and Battling, show how these two characters are locked into a single emotion in relation to each other." (This was one question.) Sometimes he asked for storyboards:

> Draw one frame from each of the following scenes:
> a. the dancehall scene in "Musketeers" when Lillian Gish is first introduced to the gangsters.
> b. The subway scene in "Fantômas" with the detective and the woman he is shadowing in an otherwise empty car.
> c. The scarecrow scene with Lillian Gish in "A Romance of Happy Valley." Indicate in words alongside each frame how

close the actors are to the screen surface, the depth of space between figures and background, the flow of action if there is any.

Farber retired from teaching in 1987.

Farber After *Negative Space*

Farber's 1969 Howard Hawks essay—as hinted earlier—lodges a wry double self-portrait: as he summons his own birthplace for a joke about small-town provincialism, his praise of the filmmaker's mobility and speed conjures his own termite activities as a writer and painter. His film criticism is personal, even autobiographical, though of a deflected sort that edges into allegory and fever-dream.

In *A Dandy's Gesture* (1977), one of Farber's two "auteur" paintings focused on Hawks, he glances at—often through toys and miniatures—images from the director's films: a plane crashed into a chocolate candy mountain, from *Only Angels Have Wings*; a tiger, from *Bringing Up Baby*; an elephant, from *Hatari*; a boat, from *To Have and Have Not*; and newspaper layout pages, from *His Girl Friday*, with gangster Johnny Lovo (from *Scarface*) in the headline. But following the train careering down the track on the left of the painting to a notebook, we discover Farber slyly inserting himself into the painting. A little reporter's pad quotes his own notes for his film class on Hawks at UC San Diego. What might be the lines connecting a director at work in the Hollywood studio system and a painter at work in a university—here, cramming for a lecture; or, perhaps, not cramming, but painting *A Dandy's Gesture* instead? Who is the gestural dandy of the title? Howard Hawks? Or Farber himself?

His friend the late Pauline Kael condescended slightly to Farber during a *Cineaste* interview, remarking, "It's his analysis of the film frame as if it were a painter's canvas that's a real contribution." Farber could direct painterly thoughtfulness to issues such as color in Disney cartoons or slackness of camera in Hollywood features as far back as his first *New Republic* reviews, and always in his criticism references from film and art crisscross and trespass. Still, the correspondences in Farber's film criticism and his paintings are more radical and strategic. During nearly all the years he actively wrote criticism Farber worked as an abstract artist—as a painter, sculptor, and the creator of gallery installations and monumental oils on collaged paper. But after he moved to San Diego, Farber shifted to representational paintings—a profusion of candy bars, stationery, film titles, film directors, and domestic still lives—and soon discontinued his film writing. Characteristically these new paintings are multi-focused and decentered. Intense detailing arrests the eye amid spiraling chains of association: visual, cultural, or personal. They sometimes imply narratives, but without positing the entrances, exits, and arcs of any particular pre-existent story lines. Despite their subjects, these works can hardly be mistaken for Pop—yet for all their conceptual focus on the medium, or on art history, they aren't abstract either.

Farber's paintings import film dynamics, but paradoxically. The controlling intelligence of an auteur director atomizes into a profusion of stories and routes; much as with an interactive e-book, a viewer can enter a painting only by realigning the givens. But in Farber's film criticism, I want to suggest, is a prediction of the painter he would become. Certain reverenced film directors—Hawks, Wellman, Sturges, Lewton, Don Siegel, Jean-Luc Godard, Robert Bresson, Warhol, Fassbinder—arise from the essays almost as self-portraits of that future painter. The painter Farber will be is forecast in his observations and descriptions of his favorite directors, actors, and film moments, but also (and vividly) in his writing style.

Hawks is only the most courtly of these projections of Farber's future paintings. From his inaugural review for *The New Republic* on February 2, 1942, Farber insisted on a multiplicity of expression and form, criticizing a Museum of Modern Art exhibition where each artist "has his one particular response to experience, and no matter what the situation, he has one means of conceiving it on canvas. . . . Which is all in the way of making a plea for more flexibility in painting and less dogma." Long before he started to collaborate with Patricia Patterson on his film writing, Farber managed to insinuate a sense of multiple perspectives, even multiple voices into his critical prose—his *New Republic* and *Nation* columns often found him so insistently mixed as to suggest (at least) a pair of contrary authors; subsequent pieces review disparate films, and discuss them all at once. Among Farber's last solo pieces was his anti-auteurist "The Subverters" for *Cavalier*, in July 1966, the summer photographer Helen Levitt introduced him to Patricia:

> One of the joys in moviegoing is worrying over the fact that what
> is referred to as Hawks might be Jules Furthman, that behind
> the Godard film is the looming shape of Raoul Coutard, and that,
> when people talk about Bogart's "peculiarly American" brand of
> scarred, sophisticated cynicism they are really talking about what
> Ida Lupino, Ward Bond, or even Stepin Fetchit provided in
> unmistakable scene-stealing moments.

His Preston Sturges essay (*City Lights*, 1954, co-written with W. S. Poster) etches a variant on Farber's nostalgia-for-the-future self-portraits. Remarking "the almost aboriginal Americanism" of the character actors in Sturges's comedies, he celebrates the director for his "multiple focus," "fragmented action," "high-muzzle velocity," "easy handling of multiple cinematic meanings," and "this modern cinematic perspective of mobility seen by a mobile observer." Echoing his first *New Republic* article, he surmises, "It is also probable that [Sturges] found the consistency of serious art, its demand that everything be resolved in terms of a logic of a single mood, repugnant to his temperament and false to life." Still more closely intuiting his own distant paintings, Farber wrote: "Basically, a Sturges film is executed to give one the delighted sensation of a person moving on a smoothly traveling vehicle going at high speed through fields, towns, homes, even through other vehicles. The vehicle in which the spectator is traveling never stops but seems to be moving in a circle, making its journey again and again in an ascending, narrowing spiral until it diminishes into nothingness." Farber would eventually quote fragments of his Sturges essay on a note pad he sketched into his "auteur" painting *The Lady Eve* (1976–77).

Raoul Walsh materializes as another stand-in for the painter—"Walsh's style is based on traveling over routes"—as do other such "underground" filmmakers as Wellman and Mann, who open up a scene "by road-mapped strategies that play movement against space in a cunning way, building the environment and event before your eyes." By the early 1970s and his joint productions with Patricia Patterson, Farber's surrogates are not limited to action directors, nor are the directors only American. On Godard: "His is basically an art of equal emphasis. . . . Dissociation. Or magnification of the molehill against the mountain, or vice versa . . . The words becoming like little trolley-car pictures passing back and forth." On Herzog: "The awkward framing, unpredictable camera positions . . . the droll, zestful, looming work of a filmmaker still on the prowl, making an exploratory work each time out." On Fassbinder: "A kind of lurching serpentine. . . ." Buñuel conjures Farber's future paintings, but acidly, from inside a dark mirror:

> Each movie is a long march through small connected events (dragged out distressingly to the last moment: just getting the movie down the wall from a candle to a crucifix takes more time than an old silent comedy), but it is the sinister fact of a Buñuel movie that no one is going anywhere and there is never any release at the end of the film. It's one snare after another, so that

the people get wrapped around themselves in claustrophobic whirlpool patterns.

Many of these directors, along with Sam Peckinpah, Wim Wenders, Budd Boetticher, Jean-Marie Straub, Marguerite Duras, and Eric Rohmer, would prompt "auteur" paintings from Farber during the late 1970s and early '80s. The witty, devastating *Roads and Tracks* (1981) that issues from films of William Wellman shadows inversions and reversals. At the top of the canvas, the staid women falling (or jumping?) from airplanes, for instance, are from *Wings*; they immediately transform into angels, probably in a punning reference to Hawk's *Only Angels Have Wings*. In a counter-image to the angels, near the bottom center of the painting, a modern pop-tart woman in a bathing suit pops up from a glass. The cowboy stomping the man on the tracks at the lower right is from *The Ox-Bow Incident*, while the tracks themselves arrive courtesy of a favorite Wellman film of Farber's, *Other Men's Women*, a love triangle among railroad roustabouts, with many scenes set in a kitchen (hence the butter, the corncob, the lettuce, and bottles). The appearance of James Cagney with a grapefruit on his face is a twist on the famous scene in *Public Enemy*.

Throughout, crisscrossing tracks and roads frame—and force—an impression of stuttering immobility; for all the alleged motion, they don't go anywhere. They're blocked, and destructive. Besides figures from action and war films, the painting is full of cliché, often toy reproductions of '30s small-town, working-class life—a milkman, old advertisements, the houses, cars—and also teasing intimations of a world outside that life: most notably, the art book open to the Indian tantric sex painting at the lower left.

Along and inside the tracks Farber races trains of associations, historical, cultural and private. *Roads and Tracks*, like all of his "auteur" paintings, refutes the notion of any single authorial consciousness—the multi-perspectives of the winding allusions, their various knowledges, visual textures, and experiences are at once too public and personal for that.

Farber's "auteur" series flaunts conspicuous links to his film criticism which other paintings will probe ingeniously and boldly. An explosion of the notion of a still life, *Domestic Movies* (1985), likely derives its smart title from the suggestion of time and motion through a tilted perspective and the film leaders that take the viewer up and down the painting. Farber got rid of the object in the center, and the perspective is almost vertiginously multiple—the overhead view of the bowls of lemons, for instance, is distorted by the upward push of the various potted flowers. The flow along the film leaders and up the stalks is checked by other forms of verticality—the donuts, for example, or subtly raised objects, such as the dead bird on what looks like a book, or the plant on a rectangle of blue cardboard on the left. Movement also is checked by the intensive detailing of the lemons and the half-eaten bowl of oatmeal. The film leaders contain titles of films Farber was teaching at the time, such as Yasujiro Ozu's 1962 *An Autumn Afternoon*, and there are scattered written notes, one a snatch of movie dialogue: "I want this room filled with flowers."

Over and over Farber's film writing prizes the detail—"the real hero is the small detail," he observes in "Underground Films," and termite art radiates "walls of particularization," "focusing only on a tiny present area," and "bug-like immersion in a small area without point or aim, and, over all, concentration on nailing down one moment without glamorizing it." Decorous, overwrought white elephant art, "tied to the realm of celebrity and affluence," accents (as noted above) "the continuity, harmony, involved in constructing a masterpiece." Yet Farber also will argue for the subservience of all parts to a flowing totality—"Everything in a good movie is of a piece," he affirms in the introduction to *Negative Space*. Other essays criticize directors and actors who indulge electric, illuminating "bits" instead of a "panoramic unfolding," a "continuously developing, forming personality," or "an inevitable train of events." Farber's paintings, no less than his film criticism, operate along a stress, maybe a contradiction, that sometimes honors a grace note over the whole, and at other times exalts organic form over the niceties of any incandescent moment.

Hacks (1975), from the "American Candy" series, is one of Farber's earliest representational paintings, and my favorite of his oils on paper. Against overlapping gray-silver planes, Farber arrays networks of circles and lines. The circles: a lollipop at the bottom, a candy tin at the top left, the corks. The lines: various candy bars—Tootsie Rolls, Black Crows, and the wondrous Hacks. All these candies would have been familiar to Farber from the movie concession stands of his childhood, much as the ground colors cue the silver screen, and it's tempting to stroke some of the associations. The childhood movie candy vies with icons of adult life—the chocolate cigar at the right, the corks by the Tootsie Rolls. There is the sense of "hack" as in cut or bludgeon —a number of candy items are chopped off by the frame, or already half-eaten. During 1975 Farber also was writing movie reviews for Francis Ford Coppola's *City* magazine, and he was roughly 18 months away from his last article. Inevitably, given all the film hints, might the notion of the "critical hack" surge as well from the wily web of resonance? Farber hardly can expect a viewer to complete more than a few of the circuits he has coiled into his paintings like springs inside a jack-in-the-box. But as in Beckett's confounding of "Proustian" and "equation," it's the snarl of mechanism and memory that Farber is chasing here, the way the formal dynamics of multi-perspective slide against the instinctive disclosures of a life.

Manny Farber died at home in Leucadia, California, on August 18, 2008, at the age of 91, just months after his final solo art exhibition, "Drawing Across Time"—no longer able to paint, he had created at a table in Patricia's garden some 68 mixed media on paper drawings: a reinvigorated proliferation of last looks, obsessive, commemorative, sensuous, vertiginous, his variations on a wall, window, path, flowers, bushes, trees, hypothetically at least, inexhaustible, infinite.

The Farber equation, as I said, is never simple.

Robert Polito

1942–1947

With Camera and Gun

Now that Congress is leaving Hollywood alone to make war movies, the only question is when there is going to be a good one. For war comedy, Ernst Lubitsch's "To Be or Not to Be" is mildly amusing. The story is complex as hell, but undoubtedly has to do with the adventures of a Polish Shakespearean troupe and the German Gestapo during the fall of Poland. There is a lot of maneuvering of people and scenes to get laughs which sound more like titters. Such manipulation leads to the kind of laugh that comes from a gag-line and not from something inherently funny in the situation. Also they haven't decided yet whether to make Jack Benny a comedian or a juvenile, and there is nothing so perilous and uncertain as Benny walking seriously across the screen. Still, as a Shakespearean tragedian he makes a nice stooge for such things as "What you are I wouldn't eat." After developing into one of Hollywood's best actresses, Carole Lombard wasn't given much to bow out on, being there for the Lubitsch touch and to fall in love with the bomber pilot because he's the only man she ever knew who could drop three tons of dynamite in two minutes. Funny lines, with people moving into position to say them.

On a more serious level, the latest English epic, "The Invaders," attempts to incorporate all the evils of Nazism into an exciting adventure film. It takes two hours in the telling, a superb cast of male actors, most of eastern Canada to chase around in, and behind it the London Philharmonic Orchestra for noise written by Ralph Vaughan Williams. And after all of that, it is still an elongated educational film without excitement, which wanders too far for any sustaining interest or unity. The idea is to show the Nazi menace from every conceivable angle; to accomplish so much message "The Invaders" comes up with an ingenious story technique—six German submarine survivors fleeing across the democratic lands of Canada to reach the neutral (before Pearl Harbor) United States. How they got into such a pickle seems very unwarlike—their submarine ran out of oil and supplies and was blown up in Hudson's Bay.

For propaganda purposes this set-up is just the thing, what with the endless situations it affords for showing the contrast between Nazi and democrat. As for making a picture, the technique defeats itself by having to use the Nazis as the central characters. It cannot have the audience's sympathies with the Nazis, who therefore must lack humor, warmth and daring—the qualities that make adventurers fun to watch. So it adds up to a pretty dull cops-and-robbers routine. In addition, the continual change of locale and characters wears out your pleasure. Situations like that at Hudson's Bay are built carefully and well, with regard to environment and people. But no sooner is it all set up and you get to like the place than the Nazis have to move on. And you keep wishing you were back in Hudson's Bay where you left Laurence Olivier, French-Canadian trapper, dialect and all, acting all over the place. This touch-and-go procedure becomes very embarrassing when, at the three-quarter mark, you come to a lake in the wilderness of Canada, and who should be rowing on the lake but Leslie Howard as big as life—fishing. Still, the picture tells the Nazis off, and that's worth doing when the telling is as adult as this.

"Churchill's Island" is a superb documentary two-reeler, the first in a series called "The World in Action," dealing with war strategies as they affect the United Nations. This one has to do with the British and their defense against invasion. Very honest presentation, with incredibly fine photography and newsreeling. Here you see the real thing—both inside a fighting Spitfire and an attacking German submarine (this from German sources), grim shots of sea casualties. In other words, the war as it really is.

March 23, 1942

Three's a Crowd

Considering how hard Hollywood finds it to get all of its departments on one track when they make a movie, you are grateful when even one department manages to be good. This is the kind of movie RKO's "Joan of Paris" is. The good department is the action. The story is concerned with five English fliers grounded in France and trying to escape the Gestapo long enough to get back to England. If the script had made things a little more exciting and the people more substantial and less like Hollywood actors, the movie might have been good enough. As it is, Director Robert Stevenson deserves all of the credit for making a zero script into something which is presentable, if not much else. Stevenson is the director who is up to his ears in dramatic tone. For him that means turning the lights down low, having the people whisper intensely and filming the action very deliberately and slowly. And no other director is so slow. When someone walks downstairs, Stevenson almost shows you his footprints. This time how could he help it if the script wasn't exciting and nothing happened after all of his pains? At least he made it *look* harrowing.

This is the picture to introduce the French actress, Michele Morgan, and unfortunately both for the story and herself it's one of those flubbed introductions that force you to say Pardon me, I didn't catch the name. As usual,

Hollywood was more concerned with making sure she held on to her glamor through everything than in getting a character with significance for story and credibility for you. Then there are Laird Cregar and Paul Henreid who seemed intent on proving they could act. They could, just like Laird Cregar and Paul Henreid.

I don't know why Columbia called its latest effort "Bedtime Story" unless they figured to put you to sleep with it. But in that case everybody talked too noisily. This noise was intended as satire on the love life of a famous playwright and his equally famous stage-acting wife, and satirically enough, Loretta Young is the actress. If you can manage to fall asleep, wake up for the last few situations, which are funny.

The Russian film "Tanya" is about the Cinderella who "exchanges her humble station, not for the perfumed languor of a shining palace, but for the dignity of free labor." Quite a sermon. The moral is that the greatest pleasure is for her who turns the most looms. Tanya starts as a household drudge who looks like a butterball and acts like Charlie Chaplin. From there to school; from school to janitor; from janitor to loom worker—first one loom, then two, eight, sixteen, and finally a record, 150 looms at once. Running out of loom room, she becomes an engineer, and on an off day finds time to get married. A working woman's "Yank at Oxford" and no better.

Breaking in a new Deanna Durbin on the movie-going public is almost certain to call for the soft home-cooking of "You're Always in My Heart." This movie, better known as what is home without a father, is the one about the separated parents brought together again by their children. As usual, Kay Francis has to be Mother; Walter Huston is Father because Lewis Stone belongs to MGM. The villain says, "Kay, you've been a widow long enough, and I'd like to take over the burden." Whereupon the governor paroles father Huston in time to save Kay from marrying into wealth, his son from going to the dogs, his operatic daughter from drowning; to make a happy ending happier he achieves radio fame with a harmonica band. And meanwhile the reason for all this, Gloria Warren, turns out to be a good actress in spite of what you're thinking, likable and professional. But this one is not even recommended for harmonica-lovers.

April 6, 1942

The Little Fellow

A MAN with a forlorn and wistful face sits down at a table, takes two forks in his hands, plunges the forks into two rolls, bows, and begins the most memorable scene in movie history. It is the dance of the rolls from Charlie Chaplin's "The Gold Rush." Back again after almost two decades, this picture is still the most satisfying of all movies, and seeing it again now, with all those miles of reels in between, makes Chaplin's art look better than ever. Actually, "The Gold Rush" is so perfect you wonder how he did it.

Something might be said for the simplicity of the theme—those long expanses of plain snow were perhaps the best foil he ever had. The character he created is the puniest of living creatures, a pushover for a puff of wind, forever in search of love, either born too soon or in the wrong world or both. Put him in the wide-open spaces of Alaska, surrounded by starving, burly prospectors, beautiful dance-hall girls and assorted Alaskan animals, and anything can happen, any of the absurdities that can assault Charlie and bring forth his inimitable reactions. "The Gold Rush" is full of them, and offers, along with more fun than anything, a good chance to look the man over again.

You see things that are so peculiarly a result of his genius you can't explain them. The way comedy comes indescribably from the hitch and shuffle in his walk, his surreptitious kick at an assailant; or the fleeting, tentative expressions on the most mobile of faces that project an almost impossibly elusive feeling. On this mastery of pantomime, and on his exact knowledge of what he wants and of what is humanly moving, he builds a character, then fits it into a situation, and it comes out all of a piece.

These situations begin with something absurd: a dancer's feet represented by two rolls, a house half on, half off a cliff, a meal made from a shoe. But Chaplin's pantomime changes the absurdity into something significant with human feeling—the rolls come alive with the personality of a dancer, the house, for all the triteness, becomes a stirring reality, and what happens to the shoes is unbelievable. An absurdity has been made real and enormously significant; this is where you feel whatever emotion was intended by Chaplin. But at the same time, shoelaces aren't spaghetti, and so you're laughing. It is this interwoven double play that constitutes the complex genius of Chaplin.

The only thing you didn't get out of "The Gold Rush" back in the twenties that's there now is a musical score and narration by Chaplin in place of the old subtitles. His talking along with the picture is more of the Chaplin spirit, taking it even further. There's the same doubling of the ridiculous on the grave; when a wind carries away the cabin with Charlie and the frustrated heavy, Big Jim, asleep inside, the voice gets both contemplation and hysteria into the cry "Fate—it's *always* Fate!" Or as Charlie, who has been rapturously watching over the shoe in the stew pot, turns to the unconvinced Big Jim, the voice echoes the spirit in the pantomime as it says briskly, "Just two more minutes!"

Along with all this, Chaplin brings a craftsmanship that has probably never been surpassed. He has a grasp of every aspect of the moving picture, and by doing it all himself has brought acting, direction and camera work into the unity necessary for great art. The virtues of this kind of movie making are being rediscovered by men like Sturges and Welles. The photography in "The Gold Rush" of twenty years ago has a natural, effortless grace easier on the eyes and sensibilities than the heavily posed artfulness of this day. The scene in which Big Jim, who has been starving for days, sees Charlie as a plump chicken is still a beauty of camera manipulation—a rare thing, fantasy used with utter straightforwardness.

So go and forget all the headaches Hollywood's been giving you lately.

May 4, 1942

Gabin in Hollywood

"Moontide" mixes human warmth and love with homicidal brutality, serves them straight and simple by way of some actual, living people named Tiny, Bobo and Anna, and an inferior plot doesn't keep it from being a superb moving picture. Which is really gravy, because you pay your money to see the French importation, Jean Gabin, prove the rumor that he is screen actor number one and sex-appeal champ besides. Since he has the rare gift of pantomime, meaning the exact grimace and gesture for the feeling needed, along with a face which is both tough and soft, somewhat punched up like a prize-fighter's, thin lips, innocent wavy hair, and a precocious underlip which drips words off in a personal sort of way, he probably wins on both counts. Despite this, he is no better than the girl, Ida Lupino, or the villain, Thomas Mitchell, or the direction of Archie Mayo. A picture moving and good.

The screen play is John O'Hara's, and it has all of his clarity and feel for ordinary people living, talking and usually drinking. Something got at Archie Mayo—maybe it was Producer Mark Hellinger—and he directs it that way. But slowly. He has trouble getting the picture away, what with side, front and upside-down shots of Jean Gabin to introduce him to American audiences.

Gabin in highlight or in shadow is vital and real to watch, even on such long solo spins. Mayo's slowness focuses the interest on the people, and that's where it belongs. You get to know each of them: Bobo the wandering, good-natured dock worker with a tendency toward getting drunk and choking somebody, his buddy Tiny, weak and ugly, the night-watchman Nutsy who doesn't sleep, hasn't since 1936. Around them all is a quality of human goodness and fraternity. There is a minimum of talk; the feeling comes from fine understanding of the personalities and their interrelationships.

After Gabin is thoroughly looked over, there is some trouble getting him drunk; they go on almost indefinitely showing you a drunken world through a tipsy camera. But once this is out of the way, the picture is started with one man choked to death and nobody knowing who did it except Bobo and Tiny, who have a good idea. Bobo then falls for the girl he has saved from suicide—that is Ida Lupino—they make wonderful movie love, get married, and Tiny tries to break it up. He almost breaks Ida instead; Bobo does Tiny in; and it ends somewhat as usual, the husband carrying the crippled bride into their renovated home.

The material sounds hackneyed, but it doesn't look that way. Sincerity of feeling in acting and direction gives it an honest tenseness, with always the fear of a choking to destroy the gentle happiness. The climactic violence in which Anna is attacked will really startle you—Mitchell's skillful performance of his bad man and the direction which has made it a forcefully dramatic value have built a suspense beautifully resolved in this scene.

There is a genuine performance turned in by Ida Lupino, the "Oh leave me alone, will you" girl, with less of the neurotic quality she usually relies on. Instead of acting with vivid tightness she makes Anna very ordinary and loving, and I haven't seen such warmth since Elisabeth Bergner played Gemma Jones in "Escape Me Never."

You're getting off cheap just going for Jean Gabin.

"The Tuttles of Tahiti," a Nordhoff-Hall story adapted by James Hilton, achieves nothingness with the same attitude and technical facility of a slick magazine story. Nobody was sincere here; it's a string of dull incidents, banal acting and uninspired direction. The island is swarming with actors but the only living people are Charles Laughton and Victor Francen, and even they can't rise above the material.

There isn't even Laughton in a picture called "Twin Beds."

May 11, 1942

Blaboteur

T̲HE latest adventure movie directed by Alfred Hitchcock is "Saboteur" and it has the craftsmanship of "The Lady Vanishes," except for one thing. It's not exciting—not even mildly. Unfortunately that's the very thing it needs, and the thing Hitchcock is famous for. In his earlier masterpieces the quality he achieved by making danger constantly real and imminent was an overwhelming horror unsurpassed for getting the last subtle and delicate turn of the screw. In "Saboteur" they talk things over. Actually, in place of suspense, it is conversation, and when it's Robert Cummings and Priscilla Lane it is worse than that.

The film is constructed on that basic pattern for movie excitement, the chase. The cops are after Robert Cummings for burning an airplane factory and Robert is after the real criminals, a ring of Fascist saboteurs. And don't think Hitchcock can't chase. Across the continent from San Diego to the Statue of Liberty by way of a ghost town, Boulder Dam and Radio City Music Hall, he chases. Wherever there is a deserted shack, a winding stairway, or any like hazards conducive to thrills, there is Hitchcock, breathlessly followed up by Robert. But still with plenty of wind left to talk. Of course this destroys the suspense, or what was the point? And there is not even a suggestion of the smooth, fast continuity Hitchcock once achieved. It gets to such a state that the final excitement of Cummings out on a limb of the Statue of Liberty, risking his neck for the most vicious criminal in the United States, is the last grab at a straw for thrills, and as such silly.

So the only virtues of this emasculated adventure are the small displays of Hitchcock technique. He is one of the sharpest and most adult of movie satirists, one who doesn't have to resort to pie throwing to make fun of people. His formula is to confine this skill with genre to bit players; the important players he leaves to get along the best they can, and when it was Michael Redgrave or Robert Donat it worked. Even "Saboteur" has these mordant sketches, which are among the most excellent things in movie history, people caught at a moment of speech or pantomime that defines their characters to a pitch completely beyond the reach of ordinary character handling. In "The Lady Vanishes" this talent was used to contribute to the total effect of horror, not simply, as in "Saboteur," as a sideline to hide inadequacies of movement. The man who rediscovered the movie value of the Western and gangster film lost his grip completely in this one.

The propaganda against the Fascists in this film is as neat as you like, and illustrative of the Hitchcock invention, which never falls for the hackneyed.

There are telling bits here about the significance of democracy, treated intelligently and not tacked on, and an actor only once turns flush to the audience to deliver an oration.

But for all of these bits, and for all of the clear, dramatic camera work, there is nothing to make the film stand up and move. And in spite of the propaganda subtleties, the best chance yet to show the brutality and horror of the Nazi character is lost in a patter of words.

"We Were Dancing" is a motionless picture in which two faces, Norma Shearer's and Melvyn Douglas', talk to each other at dull length about whether they should go on living together. The last thing they were interested in was making you care. Sometime they'll find that Melvyn Douglas has been made to play this role just once too often. It starts off by following a one-act play by Noel Coward and carries on like "My Favorite Wife," to the shame of both.

May 18, 1942

The Naked Truth

Two non-Hollywood movie makers, Paul Strand and Leo Hurwitz, were almost three years getting enough money and film together to screen a story of America's working man called "Native Land." But if their picture gets into enough of our theatres, it may be just the thing to wrench the movie industry out of its lingering adolescence. "Native Land" is the first American picture of its kind, and everybody who is interested in movies or democracy or almost anything at all should see it. The film is a violent and forceful indictment of the men who paraded as righteous American citizens while making a mockery of the workers' constitutional rights. Based on findings of the Senate Civil Liberties Committee, it describes the outrages of the Ku Klux Klan, the labor spies and the blacklist—all of the methods of intimidation used against American workers who exercised their right to organize.

The story starts in 1934, at Custer, Michigan, where a farmer leaves his plow to talk with visitors. Ten minutes later his wife finds him beaten up. The night before he spoke at a farmers' meeting. In Fort Smith, Arkansas, sharecroppers wanted ten cents more for picking cotton, and a posse raided their meeting place, hunted them through the swamp, wounded one Negro and then killed him and the white man who tried to help him get away. Outside of Tampa, Florida, in 1935, the union organizers Shoemaker and Poulnot, and a minister, were released by police into the hands of the Klan, who flogged and tarred and feathered them. These are the things "Native Land" shows, the things most newspapers didn't print and the movie industry wouldn't touch with a ten-foot pole.

This is an important social document. But as a movie it has shortcomings which impede its effectiveness—faults of taste and over-all comprehension that a good Hollywood director like John Ford or Fritz Lang would not make. Its failings have to do with a general too much of everything; for all the exciting camera interpretation of growing, building, and moving, this was not meant to be a nature study, and one wave, one tree and one mountain would have got the idea across, even to the most urban customer. There is an overdependence on Paul Robeson's narration and a tendency to not quite explain the action on the screen so that you have to wait for him to tell you what happened. There is repetitious use of symbolic babies and weeping women. By implying that " 'Native Land' is a document of America's struggle for liberty," when actually it is only the story of the fight of the labor unions against fascism, the directors sacrificed some of its force. Moreover, they tried to back up their claim, which meant generalities put into the narration of specific events and a reliance on the camera to encompass America.

But these are esthetic considerations and the importance of the film is greater than its art. It is honest where Hollywood is always dodging, it tells a story which too long has been distorted through the mouths of congressmen and newspapers.

"The Maltese Falcon" is a good story which Director John Huston told brilliantly on the screen. Ellen Glasgow's prize novel, "In This Our Life," also has its good points, but Director Huston didn't get any of them into his picture. Instead he stripped a complex novel of the frustrations of Southern family life down to just another custom-built vehicle for its star, Bette Davis. The action is as dull and static as a bad stage play, the kind that takes place over a telephone or by letter. People phone in to say the heroine has been married or divorced or killed. The players around her never emerge as real characters.

May 25, 1942

Not by the Book

THERE are certain stories that even Hollywood is reluctant to dress primly in long skirts and send to Will Hays. "Tortilla Flat," by John Steinbeck, was a tough problem of this sort. Its author is famous and its message is noble and philosophical, but its episodes are entirely about sex and drinking. Three years ago MGM tried to make it but gave up. Now its author is more famous than ever, so this year they finished the job of extracting the philosophy out of Steinbeck's *paisanos* by conforming with the episodes but garbling them into something of astounding bad taste. They did it by changing the emphasis. In place of the story of Danny and Pilon who love everything in sight that you can drink or sleep with, a trite business with strong religious overtones was substituted. There is a great deal of praying by Spencer Tracy and Frank Morgan— few scenes have been as tortuous as these. Finally, in a forest, bells toll and everything lights up like a Christmas tree. John Garfield and Spencer Tracy play Danny and Pilon in the hard-boiled tradition of Sergeant Quirt, replete with Brooklyn accent, and whenever Hedy Lamarr opens her mouth the wrong words with the wrong feeling invariably come out. Victor Fleming directs in a kind of dreary conservatism that doesn't turn up one emotion in eighty minutes.

In keeping with everything else, the film of this movie was dunked in sepia, which means general softening and blurring. After all these years of hankering after the stage the movies are now on the trail of oil painting. They think. The effect in "Tortilla Flat" is oversentimentalization of nature to produce an idyllic sham in the manner of the worst Umbrians. If they want some camera innovations why don't they go back to that radical, D. W. Griffith?

Joan Fontaine's eloquent portrayal of an English girl in love is all that you see in Darryl Zanuck's production of "This Above All," and considering the pretensions of this movie, her performance isn't enough. The picture ostensibly sets up a problem (whether it is worth while to fight a war that will merely end in preserving the existing order and the class system in England) and then gets out of all responsibility for resolving it by ducking into a love affair. A one-sided one at that, because the man is the one who has the problem—a personal one, involving his psychological workings as well as his interpretation of facts— and the movie leaves all that out of the character Eric Knight put it into.

Tyrone Power is given things to do like grinding his teeth in his sleep, but he's never allowed an explanation. His last scene, where he is in the hospital with a smashed head, has its tragedy considerably damaged because he and his girl have previously waked up in separate beds so often you can't be sure they ever slept together. But "This Above All" is worth seeing because Joan Fontaine is an actress of fine sensibilities for a special kind of aristocratic delicacy, and she achieves a poetic quality good enough to repay you for being otherwise hoodwinked.

June 1, 1942

War Horses

PROBABLY "Mrs. Miniver" will be called the best picture of 1942. It has all the things that win Academy awards. "The Great Ziegfeld" and "GWTW" were miles long and Miniver is so long it gets lost. Also it has Morality. So it is in the way of being an epic and I can't remember an epic that didn't win something, or why do they make them? But most of all this picture is not very good and was made by MGM and that clinches the argument, because the publicity department at Metro has already started the campaign.

"Mrs. Miniver" is about an English family which is prissy and fake like all screen families. The five Minivers are all very pretty and behave according to Will Hays and whoever wrote "Little Lord Fauntleroy." Greer Garson makes motherhood seem the profession of impeccable taste and Walter Pidgeon acts a wise father by smoking a pipe, nodding his head knowingly and saying nothing (thereby losing every scene to Miss Garson). The older son is in the smiles tradition of Robert Taylor, a mother's delight from Oxford, and the two little Minivers make those irritating and unchildlike smart cracks because it's the one device known these days for comedy relief in family pictures. The difference between these people and their originals in Jan Struther's novel is the difference between marshmallows and human beings.

The picture is entertaining enough, but its cloying goodness will make you yourself feel like a problem child. It is well acted, well photographed and well everything, technically. William Wyler directed and he is seldom in bad taste. If there is nothing in the scene to work with, he manages small details so that there is something to fill in the gap. Given a good script like "The Little Foxes" or "Wuthering Heights," he will make it look good, on the solemn, deep side, somewhat uninspired. But the crowd of writers who worked on Jan Struther's quiet and unmovie-like novel had nothing happen for the first hour of the film—Mrs. Miniver walking and talking but without the acute perception and feeling for living of the original woman. For the second hour these writers had a burst of invention that would fill two ordinary pictures: the son flies off to war, gets married, the father goes to Dunkirk, the mother captures a German aviator, the son's wife is killed, the family house is bombed and a Mr. Ballard wins a prize for the best rose. It seems too much and too late.

There is a wonderfully exciting episode in which all of the small craft of England are commandeered for Dunkirk. First only a few boats are seen moving down an English river toward the Channel; others join in, and soon there is a huge flotilla of small boats. It is a director's dream, with everything moving across the screen toward one mass scene, and that of great and thrilling heroism. Wyler gets the last bit of grandeur from it, with good camera work but particularly with as fine use of sound as we've had for a long time. Dunkirk itself isn't in it, and the let-down is terrific as we return home to Mrs. Miniver. Perhaps it's just as well, because Dunkirk will some day make a great moving picture.

The picture ends on a minister's plea that this is a people's war, and there is some effort to show why. But it's hardly sincere. The commoners simper without really wanting a change, and the one who speaks of injustice is shown to be a fool. As in "This Above All," the feeling is of someone shouting "Change!" while running to hell and gone away from it, and nothing like the kind of thing Vice President Wallace gives us.

From Warner Brothers comes another epic called "Yankee Doodle Dandy" which is an ear-shattering flag-waver that thunders like a Sousa march, jerks like a buck-and-wing and behaves like Jimmy Cagney, which adds up to a rather likable way of saying it's American. It is a field day for the dynamic Cagney, whose volatile, cocksure toughness provides everything cinematic. He is in the film-acting tradition of Chaplin, with the athletic grace and gesturing of Fairbanks. There are no vacancies in his acting; whenever he is on the screen he is expressive. It is the mimicry of doing, in the way he uses his hands, even his fingers, and the strange, pugnacious thrusts of his body, with the sensitive use of the face of Chaplin and Gabin. Most essentially his is the sudden jerk into unexpected action, which makes him the screen's unique aggressor. This is what makes the film entertaining for all of its two hours of mediocrity. It is indicative of Cagney's vitality that so much tripe could seem so fresh.

"Yankee Doodle Dandy" is one of those he-could-do-no-wrong biographies, based on the life of George M. Cohan, that Warners hand out. It is even more Horatio Alger than the various lives of Paul Muni, since Cohan had complete censorship powers over what went in. There is the inevitable wise and tolerant everybody—wife, mother, father, friend, etc., and it is possibly the most repetitious picture ever made. It is so full of Cohan's mouthy songs and stiff-legged, loose-armed, crazy tap dancing that halfway through you can't recall anything of a plot. That may have been the intention, because the plot is mainly Jimmy being good to his family and situations that wind up with a gag having to do with quaint stage vernacular. It gets pretty wearisome at times, especially during the childhood and the talks with the President, and it sings "Mary" and "I'd Rather Be Right" four choruses too often. But before it kills you off there are exciting moments, as in the first half of the Yankee Doodle Dandy routine, which is a combination of Cohan's style and Cagney's go. There is a whirlwind scene among Cagney, Sam Harris and Mr. Schwab, the latter a comedy gem contributed by S. Z. Sakall as a dazed producer with a flabby, thick accent and that weird, inverted phrasing. The songs are good Tin Pan Alley, as they always were, with a nice roll to them and a simple brightness. But the thing that makes the picture fun in the early parts is the producers' surprising integrity in capturing the spirit of the early razz-matazz stage show. It's a change from the elegant grace of Astaire and Draper, and even more from the Busby Berkeley chorus colossals.

June 15, 1942

Hollywood Blues

For esthetes there is nothing so much fun as kicking the movies around. It is the obscenity of the arts, they say, and it's been that way since the day Griffith's "Intolerance" failed at the box office. The esthetes are usually pale, one-sided people, who, if they can't see the perfect, see nothing at all. But the movies don't do much to prove them wrong. Take the picture "Syncopation." It is the third Hollywood attempt to explain and express hot jazz—"Birth of the Blues" and "Blues in the Night" were the first two. Your total experience of jazz from all three of these pictures is negligible compared to what you get from any good record. The esthetes would say these movies are inartistic, shallow and dull, and they would be right.

At least this "Syncopation" gives the credit for hot jazz to the Negroes. It's this that makes the film more honest than the one Bing Crosby made, or the one Johnny Mercer's song made. To give the Negroes their due, and still not make a picture *about* them, called forth some unusual acrobatics from the script writers. They managed the problem by focusing the story on a little white girl. She is living in New Orleans and loving the early jazz that was then rocking the honky-tonks. Because of the family fortunes, she is taken to Chicago, and it is she—the dainty, aristocratic Bonita Granville—who introduces New Orleans rhythm style to Chicago. It seems she played a light-fingered boogie-woogie. The rest is easy. She marries Bix Beiderbecke as Jackie Cooper; he tries to make money by playing the symphonic sweet of Paul Whiteman, goes crazy from reading notes instead of improvising, and finally finds himself with his own band.

All this is very convenient for tracing some of the history of true jazz, but it fails to get close to the music it eulogizes. Bonita Granville's importance, for all her natural ease and warmth, merely hides the music, the men who make it, and why. This is typical of Director William Dieterle: so to mix history and fiction as to forget that his pictures must have action and pace, his people be as honestly right as his historical facts. The result here is a dull, incoherent parade of dates, facts and ambiguous fiction. First show the African jungle to get the importance of the tom-toms for jazz, next a slave ship, then a few measures on the cornet by King Oliver and Louis Armstrong, then up to Chicago to catch the next jazz development with Bix, Whiteman and war, and while the pages are turning manage some way to work in the girl-boy plot. What you get is a calendar procession of static episodes—Adolphe Menjou poeticizing about New Orleans, Cooper about Walt Whitman, Todd Duncan pointing his cornet at the sky and saying he's going to pull down a star—that neither moves nor is it jazz.

The acting is quite distinguished. Both Granville and Cooper have the naturalness child actors seem to start with and keep when they grow up. Cooper is especially convincing as a cornet player, he even holds his arms like one. Adolphe Menjou continues to be wasted in this, as he has been for years, and Todd Duncan mugs too prettily in the Armstrong role. I can't for the life of me understand why they didn't use Armstrong himself, since he's a natural-born actor, and was that, in his early Bing Crosby pictures. We wouldn't have had all that one-handed playing Duncan tries, nor all the grimacing behind the cornet, nor a blues number with valve-pushing that looks like a fast passage in a Sousa march.

And what was this about crediting the Negro jazz musicians and their kind of music? The picture contradicts itself at the end by naming and showing "the great men of jazz," *i.e.*, Barnet, Rey, Jenney, Goodman, Krupa, Venuti, and so on. It seems they forgot Armstrong, Morton, Bechet, Higginbotham, Hines, Singleton, and so on, or they remembered these people are colored.

June 22, 1942

Saccharine Symphony

THE new Disney cartoon "Bambi" is interesting because it's the first one that's been entirely unpleasant. The robust irrationality of the mouse comedies has been squelched completely by the syrup that has been gradually flowing over the Disney way. In an attempt to ape the trumped-up realism of flesh and blood movies, he has given up fantasy, which was pretty much the magic element. Mickey Mouse and Donald Duck lived in a beautiful escape land, where they flew through the air, swam under water, died a thousand deaths and lived to see the end of each picture. These comedies were perfectly suited to a moving camera; held down by nothing human, they had terrific pace and action. It was a wonderful movie shambles.

But not "Bambi." The animals here behave just as Hollywood thinks we do, and behaving that way it's old stuff and boring because of it. Everything is straight-faced, with feet flat on the ground. The animals give birth, grow up, fall in love, get shot at and killed. Besides, it is moral, starched heavy. The hero is a deer named Bambi, whose mother is killed by the villain, Mr. Man, whose sweetheart is attacked by Mr. Man's dogs, whose terrestrial paradise is destroyed by Mr. Man's fire. There's no harm in Disney's being righteous, unless, as in this picture, the accent is on the cute and pretty rather than on the comedy invention which produced the righteous Donald. Only so much amusement can come from fairylike naïveté, after that it's just one long squirm. Along the way "Bambi" has all the stereotyped mechanisms of the formula movie—the heavy side to the love triangle, the fight for the doe's ("Faline") affections, the wise old king deer whose place Bambi wins over in the closing shots.

In keeping with this new spirit, "Bambi" talks itself dizzy to the exclusion of movement and action. The animals are horribly equipped with human voices, not the neuter piping of Mickey or the incoherent gabbling of Donald, which were so perfectly right, but the cuddly or waspish voices of ladies and gentlemen. Like their counterparts in the regular movies, the animals here gather round and trade chitchat, very sweet, and it is grotesque. And there are songs everywhere, coming out of the mountains, from under the trees, flooding you with the most maudlin sounds a director ever let happen. Example: "Drip, Drip, Drop, Little April Shower."

The bogus art which has been creeping into the Disney pictures is really hammered at you in this one. Again, it is an affectation of reality, like a Maxfield Parrish painting. No more the flat house-paint colors of the early comedies, in which there were no half-tones or dull intensities, with every red the same hot, pure scarlet, every black like coal, and nothing flimsily grayed. The films are now doused in sweet sugary tints, flowery violets, fancy-pants pinks, and he'll waste ten minutes if he can end up with a gold-splashed sunset. Whereas the early color was fresh, simple and in the comedy spirit, this new development is a synthetic reveling in vulgarity. The worst effect of all this artiness is the preference now for cheap painting, the Vanishing American kind you buy in Kress's, in place of the movement which was the main thing before. No longer do the trees and flowers carry on like mad: they are there for pretty;

and as the camera moves slowly over them and you drink up all this tinseled
loveliness, there is the lone deer on the distant hilltop, a gold aura around him.

Mickey wouldn't be caught dead in this.

June 29, 1942

The Grapes, Alas

CONTRARY to what the producer would like to imply, "Juke Girl" isn't about a
loose woman. It was called "Juke Girl" to get more people through the turn-
stiles to see Ann Sheridan, and since she had to be there once they got in, the
script had to be jimmied around to take care of her. But actually it is a movie
that wanted to be brave and forthright about the rotten farming conditions in
the South, which also wasn't exactly what the producer wanted; so it's coated
over with the cheap glazing of any horse opera. In fact, it is a sort of Florida
"Grapes of Wrath," with farmers and their land, their working and sweating on
it and never getting anything for it, and the search of migratory workers for
employment which at best pays them off in squalor and hunger.

You'd think all that was needed was a camera turning on a small town and
some people. But instead it's on a juke joint that could have been the saloon
out of the last picture about Tombstone. There's the saloon brawling, the grim,
silent, two-fisted Bill Hart type, the pretty girl in a tight dress, the buddy who
wasn't really bad, just got in with the wrong crowd—a gang of rustlers—a wisecracking child and a pop-eyed superstitious Negro for laughs (make the white
people laugh, the Negroes don't have many theatres anyway).

The picture is paced wrong. It ends in the middle and then starts over
again. The packing-house owners, who have been cheating the farmers, are
beaten, but Miss Sheridan has to be accounted for and made happy, so off we
go again. She was in love with Ronald Reagan but left him because she was
tainted with jukism. So a murder happens in the end to reunite them. Then
they are nearly lynched.

Here in this last episode is a good example of the cheap mind and the lazy
camera behind the picture. The frenzied mob moving on the jail house is
straight from Fritz Lang's great movie "Fury." In that picture Lang achieved
a terrible reality of ordinary people united for human destruction. It was done
with a camera that moved as a person within the mob, showing bits of significant action—ringleaders, bystanders there for fun being swept up into the hysteria, little boys acting big, righteous women, and on the inside the terror and

panic. The same thing takes place in "Juke Girl," except that the camera is set down stock still on the steps of the jail and shows 500 movie extras walking toward it. On the inside are Ann and Ronald, cool as cucumbers, babbling something about how funny life is. The crowd comes in, takes them out, and that's all. Nothing was tried and nothing was gained (though Forbstein's musical accompaniment really got mad). It's the difference between illustration and expression.

The picture is the most belligerent thing you've ever seen. Seven main bouts, two prelims, and a snarling, loudmouthed atmosphere. The funniest fight is one with Gene Lockhart up against the wall and someone whaling the living daylights out of him with the palms of his hands.

As for the players, they did creditably what they were told to do. Mr. Reagan and Miss Sheridan, who made "Kings Row" feel inside your stomach, are fine to look at, with the natural freshness that makes good movie playing a joy to see. Stage-actor Richard Whorf still does most of his acting with his mouth, and there is a repeat performance for Gene Lockhart's cowardly villain.

The thing is, what do juke girls, cowboy stuff and murders have to do with a social study of farmers? It's a cheap way of avoiding something especially important at the same time that you're facing it.

July 6, 1942

True and False

"United We Stand," a documentary film intended to cover political history from Versailles to Pearl Harbor, is worth seeing by anyone, but especially I would advise it for the people who made the newsreels from which this picture was culled. The average person will find nothing in it that he didn't know, see or hear of before, but the conquests of Poland, Czecho-Slovakia, Ethiopia, Spain and the partial conquest of China should be seen again if only to get sick and revolted at what we allowed. Whereas much of the film is seriously lacking in detail—the results without the causes—the Chungking sequence, with all of its human slaughter, the people working to protect themselves from bombs without the tools to work, a child breaking up stones for mortar and nothing to use except other stones, has details that will upset you. So will the scenes of Dunkirk, which lack the heroics of rescue but show the acres of shells, railway guns, airplanes which were left behind—enough to supply an entire army. As illuminating are the scenes during the French retreat: roads choked with refugees and soldiers trying to get past, and always walking with packs and seemingly without aim. Of course there is the complete destruction which is like another world.

The rest is pageantry. The marriage of Juliana to Bernhard, Sir John Simon walking hurriedly into Number 10 Downing Street, the coronation of at least a dozen puppets, glimpses of important people's faces, which are disappointing because they are too negligible to be informative. The only illuminating portrait is that of Mussolini, with theatrical bombast and hand gestures so oddly unsynchronized. A few shots of Hitler are also interesting but more familiar.

But so much of this film is on top of the headlines, where it is misleading, that if people who saw the original newsreels had had no other information, and many of them undoubtedly had not, they must have formed grotesquely inaccurate ideas of what was going on. For instance, the coverage of the Spanish war in this picture contains only the statement that there was dissension within the country—nothing of the meaning of the dissension. A mere shot of Gandhi and no mention of what he stood for, nor of any other part of the Indian problem. Appeasers are simply labeled men who wanted peace, which they did, but other things as well, and of these things there is no mention. The French and British statesmen are shown leaving the 1939 negotiations with the Russians, with no pertinent information given about who held out for what. This presentation throughout the whole picture of results without causes argues very well the theory that disunity, which is a result, brought on the present war. It would seem more appropriate to have shown the bases of disunity. It always has seemed inevitable in newsreels that if something was to be said about Rumania, for example, it was said about Crown Prince Michael, who was only one of several million Rumanians, and with perhaps less significant problems. So that this particular resumé of world history is just who happened to be wearing the crown when.

Walter Wanger's movie, "Eagle Squadron," is so timely it has Quentin Reynolds in it for the first few minutes. According to Mr. Reynolds, this movie is the story of the Americans who went over to England a year ago to fly for the RAF, "the boys who didn't wait for the stab in the back." Following Mr. Reynolds there are some shots of these Americans, and then the movie gets off—no more surprises, just typical movieland blah.

July 20, 1942

Gehrig to Cooper to Chance

Before seeing "The Pride of the Yankees" you may or may not know that the Yankees referred to are the ones who win the World Series each year. After seeing it you will find that the reference is indirect.

Deep down inside it's the baseball story of Lou Gehrig, the silent strong boy, who went from Columbia to the Yankee Stadium to hit home runs. It was at the start of the fabulous Yankees, when the manager was a runt-sized baseball genius named Miller Huggins, and "Murderers' Row" meant Gehrig, Ruth, Combs and Meusel. For fifteen years Gehrig played first base, with something keeping him there in spite of broken toes and fingers and a sprained back. There was finally a tragic end: when Gehrig was thirty-four years old, disease ruined his perfect muscular control, and shortly he died.

That was the story before the star system moved in. Gary Cooper had been Mr. Deeds, Wild Bill Hickok, Alvin York and Marco Polo, so why not Lou Gehrig? No matter that Gary doesn't like baseball, is right-handed, lazy and tall-skinny, whereas Gehrig was left-handed, hard-working to the point of compulsion, and his one leg was the size of two of Gary's. So they taught him to throw left-handed, but they could never teach him to throw with any muscles but the ones in his arms, like a woman, nor could they make his long legs run differently from those of someone trying to run with a plate between his knees, nor could they move his body with his bat swing.

All of which meant cutting the baseball action to a minimum—montage shots mostly from long distance up in the press box, and the picture was shot to hell right there. It is pretty good, but so little of what it could have been. There is none of the artistic grace and coördinated power that is great ball playing, the thing that makes a lightning throw from short to first as thrilling as Koussevitzky conducting Sibelius, or an unbelievable one-handed catch out of the dirt as fantastic as a leap by Mickey Mouse. The acrobatic genius of Doug Fairbanks, which was partly trick camera but thrilled us anyway back in the twenties, comes a dime a dozen on any major-league ball field—and real. All that was needed was a natural ball player, and there are plenty around. There's one in this picture—Bill Dickey—who seems right at home before the camera. But instead they chose Cooper, cut the baseball, and used their old clichés for excitement: a boy in a hospital for whom Lou has promised to hit two home runs, or the last inning with the home team behind, two out and two on base and the idea of Gehrig being walked intentionally and disobeying the manager's orders by trying to hit (turn over in your grave, Huggins).

If the writers of this movie know what it is about a baseball player, why he does it, and how, they didn't use their knowledge in the script. In place of this, which is as exciting and marvelous as anything can be, there are the usual fillers-in they use for any movie. A dance by Veloz and Yolanda, a song by Ray Noble, with one hand playing the piano and the other directing the orchestra like a fairy wand, Bill Stern and his radio claptrap, lots of Lou Gehrig in college among such standard collegisms as the snotty fraternity boy who doesn't want hard-working Lou in Alpha Alpha, and the jokes played on the bashful boy, a couple of idiotic newspapermen, one childish and the other villainous. I long ago lost interest in all funny-but-good mothers and fathers, and the movie is stuffed with these.

The picture, as a result, wastes its first two-thirds. They couldn't miss on the ending, and you will cry plenty. Actually, this man's picture was held together by a girl, Teresa Wright, as Mrs. Gehrig, who is good, no fooling. Since "The Little Foxes" and "Mrs. Miniver" she has added warmth and cuteness to talented plainness, and is still finely unlike a movie actress. Gary Cooper was directed to be modest and youthful in the first half, in other words to act—he's awful. Badly timed goofy smiles, blinking and popping eyes, hands with the coördination of a moron. Later on, after Lou grew up, they left him alone and he is, as always, plain and easy, a perfect movie player. But the best thing, outside of Miss Wright, is the camera work of Rudolph Maté, the finest I've seen this year (and when are they going to give the movies back to the camera?). Maté achieves exhilaration from his angle shooting and the feeling throughout out of a concave screen. Whatever feel of baseball this picture has is the result of his running camera. He uses a simple clarity of dark and light values without any of the thousand and one trick shadows seen in movies these days, and none of the murk of Rembrandt gone mad. When there's a fight the camera seems to be doing the punching. And with Maté, an expressive shot is never something that whams you over the head.

Well, all right, but it looked as if they even had to teach the child actor to bat left-handed.

July 27, 1942

Twice Over Heavily

Orson Welles's second I-did-it should show once and for all that film making, radio and the stage are three different guys better kept separated. "The Magnificent Ambersons" is one of those versions of the richest family in town during the good old days. Front and center of the Ambersons is the Oedipean situation between Dolores Costello and son Tim Holt, which, according to the movie, started when Dolores married the wrong man. All her frustrated love went toward smothering her son, and sure enough he grew up to gloriously rotten manhood. When the father dies, Sonny Boy keeps Mother from marrying her first love, who for some reason is still hanging around (from what you see you wouldn't think she was worth the fuss). As a result, limpidly pretty Dolores shrinks up and dies.

While telling this story, haltingly and clumsily, the movie runs from burdensome through heavy and dull to bad. It stutters and stumbles as Welles submerges Tarkington's story in a mess of radio and stage technique. The radio comes in those stretches of blank screen when the only thing present is Welles's off-screen voice mellifluously setting the period and coyly reminiscing, talking and drooling, while you sit there muttering let's get on. And at the times when something *is* on the screen and Welles tells you what for. Meanwhile, for something to do, you count the shadows. Theatre-like is the inability to get the actors or story moving, which gives you a desire to push with your hands. There is really no living, moving or seeing to the movie; it is a series of static episodes connected by narration, as though someone sat you down and said "Here!" and gave you some postcards of the 1890's. The first ten have to do with costume. Then some on the many-gabled architecture. Then the first automobile, the second, the third, and you wait for somebody to say "Get a horse," and finally somebody does. Eventually the main people come on and act mostly on a dime (Welles, off-screen, says Isabel Amberson is rejecting a suitor and you see the suitor rejected). Then, cut, and you're on Main Street with the average man. Now back for another fond look at the Amberson mansion with the camera ostentatiously snailing its way into corners and crevices until finally a face turns in out of the stage-muddy murk, looks or talks or walks upstairs or, if it's Agnes Moorehead, has hysterics. The pace of the camera (Stanley Cortez') is too slow for movie eyes, and the pace of the story (Orson Welles's) too labored to create any emotion but boredom.

Aside from all the dead spots the story is told as badly as would seem possible. The incidents selected don't explain themselves sufficiently to be there, and moreover, are ineptly chosen to get across the psychological workings of the Ambersons, which is the main concern of the movie. Repetitious display of Aunt Fannie's hysteria is good theatrical bombast, but every fit after the first is irrelevant as far as the story's concerned. Toadying like this to melodramatic effect strips the other roles, particularly the two older lovers', to almost nothing. So that you feel that you're looking at the main plot—the triangle of son, mother and lover—through the wrong end of a telescope. There are long awkwardly handled scenes that add up to nothing. Their are some plain cheap effects: Richard Bennett as old Major Amberson is finally given his due when they set his face to the camera and Welles tells you he's scared to die. The two minutes you've seen of him before wouldn't prove it (in fact you wonder who the old geezer is), but even if you accept this fact what have you got? The transitions are handled miserably, and in the midst of all the redundancy the story thuds suddenly into situations without any reason that you can see. Just before the end, pace, characters and feeling change abruptly and sprint to a hearts-and-flowers finish. Much of this seems the fault of blundering editing.

In keeping with this eclecticism are photographic tricks from everywhere, so unintegrated you can't miss them. These aren't as objectionable as the general theatrical use of the camera, which subscribes to the theory that six shadows are six times as dramatic as one and the blacker the better. This eighty-eight-minute dim-out negates nearly everything a camera can do.

On the credit side is Welles's drive, as in "Citizen Kane," toward three-dimensional characters and away from standardized movie types. He wants realism and there's no one in Hollywood to touch him in its use. He directs his actors in more meaty portrayals of neurotic people than any other Hollywood director. But even this, which is so admirable, suffers from the general clumsiness, and from the fact that stage acting is more boring than not on the screen.

August 10, 1942

A British Movie Biography

Though it is badly named, an unpretentious, mild and serious-minded English movie—"Wings and the Woman"—is uncommonly truthful for a screen biography. More simply and logically than in any other movie for years, Director Herbert Wilcox got its point across: women have come out from the home to such an extent that now they ferry bombers. It's done with the story of Amy Johnson and Jim Mollison, at one time "The Flying Mollisons," or a man and wife who grew up in aviation trying to beat each other's time through the air. Aggressive and businesslike Yorkshire Amy flew a rickety second-hand Moth in 1930 from London to India, at eighty-five miles an hour, but faster than anyone before her. She was also fastest from London to Tokyo, from London to Cape Town, and the first woman to fly the Atlantic. Extroverted Jim Mollison, who calls himself the playboy of the air, and writes more proudly of that than of his flying, flew the Atlantic one way or the other four times and is alive today ferrying bombers from English factories to RAF flying fields. In the same service, Amy was drowned in the Thames a year ago.

Unlike so many screen biographies, this one is not glorious with haloes nor embarrassed with melodramatic clichés of the "I did it all for Mother" type. The Mollisons are human if not so pretty. Amy breaks Jim's record from London to Cape Town partly to settle a grudge against him; at the end of their flight across the Atlantic Jim's stubbornness crashes them needlessly at Bridgeport, Connecticut; Amy divorces Jim, and Jim doesn't go to pieces nor is he shown the light five seconds before you go home. Amy's father is one of the best for feeling ever in movies, since he bears no resemblance to the wise Judge Hardy or the brave Mr. Miniver, and he isn't funny at all.

This straightforward approach is not in the tradition of the best English movies, but its creation in terms of visual movement is, and ranks with Hitchcock, Rotha and Reed for that reason. Done in a world of miniatures, newsreels and canned airplane shots, it still seems more up in the air than most cockpit sagas. Careful documentary filming is combined with skillful montage and double exposure to achieve exact dramatization of early flying conditions. When Jim tries his first Australia-to-England flight, the Port Darwin airfield looks like the Dakota Badlands, has a ground crew of one, and is dangerously bounded by telephone wires. Even Jim's vanity can't get his overloaded plane high enough to clear and the take-off ends in a mess of wires. On Amy's initial flight to Australia you experience the physical lashing a flyer took in one of those open cockpits, with the feeling that flying in 1930 was as close to nature as you could get. There are some breath-taking bits—the roll of clouds and sky, and what land looks like to the aviator who has set his heart for months on being the first to see it that way. Some things are the highest kind of movie expression, as a shot of the father standing in the wake of Amy's plane, which in purely visual terms sums up—without slopping over—the emotions of such a moment. In a montage of three shots the divorce is accomplished.

With its rigid purposefulness the movie ran into some dead spots. The Mollisons were one record flight after another, so there's a good deal of repetition, particularly of cheering throngs. Obviously difficult is filming in the air and capturing the movement of the plane while yet holding onto the individual inside. The picture is slow to get off, and to get Amy out of pigtails, and since most of the thrills happened early in her life, it rises fast, then levels off and finally sneaks out like a stowaway.

But this is a good movie and I wish there were more like it. The playing is thoroughly English, and the best English movie players know their business as well as any today. Robert Newton, who plays Jim Mollison, is one of these—he was the pugnacious bum of "Major Barbara." Moving with loose slouchiness, his evil, ingratiating face suggestive in every shot, his speech carelessly foggy, he is in complete control of his medium and gives precisely the feeling of Mollison. Anna Neagle, with the square, hard face and thin lips, as Amy Johnson is polished and competent but less spontaneous and brilliant. All of the minor roles are cast and played with a careful sense of proportion. Still, it is less an actor's picture than it is a director's and cameraman's.

August 24, 1942

Real War

WHEN you have seen the movie, "Wake Island," you will realize that finally, and it's about time, Hollywood has gone to war. Up till now the movies have been fighting a limited dream war of their own: one which took place in some conquered nation, and showed any one of fifty Hollywood stars outwitting and escaping the Gestapo. At best this movie war was exciting—"Underground"—or mildly charming—"The Pied Piper." At worst, and in either case, it overestimated the comic capacities of the Gestapo and grossly underestimated its capacity to think and to kill. At its prettiest moments—"Mrs. Miniver"—it showed the heart of England's aristocracy to be with the poor people. At its lowest point, the man of the United Nations, Leslie Howard in "The Invaders," was portrayed as a passive, able-to-take-anything flimsy intellectual who could only be aroused when the Nazis tore up his Matisse. And in "The Pied Piper" there is a Nazi general who gives his captives a sumptuous meal and free passage across the Channel. With apalling thick-skin, the movie "To Be or Not to Be" facetiously thought that Nazi-dominated and cholera-ridden Poland was a world of laughs.

The picture these Hollywood morale-builders gave the millions of movie goers was dangerously misleading and almost entirely negative.

If the idea had been to soften up the people with bright adventure dreams, the movie industry couldn't have done a better job.

"Wake Island," I hope, will mark the start of a new attitude. There is no fantasy in this war. Here the enemy kills unmercifully and unerringly and with no questions asked. The side that is prepared with the most men and guns and planes is the side that usually wins, and it is a larger issue than the escape of one gallant soul from the Gestapo. The 478 Marines and the 1,100 AFL construction workers on Wake didn't have a chance of coming out alive. After the first surprise attack on December 7, they had six five-inch guns and four planes left to fight with. The Japanese sent over wave on wave of bombers, destroying everything, and were ready to land on December 11. So the Americans played dead while the Jap fleet was sucked in to 4,700 yards, and the Americans opened fire, sinking four Jap ships and wiring the War Department to "send us some more Japs."

The enemy finally got the island on the 21st.

Director Farrow and writers Burnett and Butler stuck close to the facts. Only about a third is fiction but it is a costly third. It represents the human element, the often tried Sergeant Flagg and Corporal Quirt comedy skit, the stooge saying "sez you" and the smart aleck saying "sez me." There are two pairs of these in "Wake Island." So strangely enough, great human tragedy, of which Wake had plenty, is missing. When Sergeant Quirt dies in this it's no sorrow; you know he'll be back in the next one. Then there is the odd type of Hollywood thinking, which imagines that a funeral is moving even if you hardly know who died, and has the bad taste to try to draw tears with a letter announcing the death of a soldier's wife you haven't seen.

Nevertheless this movie, a human slaughter house, neither under- nor overestimates the factors involved in this war. The main point about it is that it is war at last and adventure no longer.

September 7, 1942

The Logic of Lunacy

ONLY sourpusses and unbending esthetes aren't thankful for screwball comedies. At their best these comedies have more actual invention in situation and character and more turbulence and energy than nine-tenths of the seriously intended, pretentious movies. The recipe was invented by director Frank Capra and writer Robert Riskin in 1934, and it fails only when it isn't followed. In screwballs, relentless common sense is imposed on a lunatic situation which has come out of and continues to operate in a realistic American atmosphere. The comedy depends on someone like Jean Arthur, who sums up in her person all the characteristics of these movies: she is both an ordinary girl with ordinary reactions and a scatterbrain who wears birds' nests on her head and at normal times is out of breath from running or screaming or hitting someone on the chin. No one less cockeyed than Jean could negotiate the situation that makes you laugh. She serves also as stooge to the smart cracks of the hero, and this is what the hero is for—smart cracks. When Gary Cooper or Henry Fonda plays the Jean Arthur role, the girl supplies the bright banter. The main thing is the gag and the laugh, and the butt is always conventional living. But the social criticism is only a foil for the laughs, except in Frank Capra's worst moments, when preaching takes seriously Christmas-card sentiments. Screwballs magically please and criticize in one picture everybody, from tory to radical, the people who laugh most at prat-falls and those who laugh most at Noel Coward. They are apt to have a high level of invention in characterization and observation of contemporary life. And in any case they are a triumph of the gag-writing art.

"Talk of the Town," the latest example, is in between the best and the worst, but follows the formula closely enough to be good. One reason is that Jean Arthur is in it, not only to talk through her nose but to hide Leopold Dilg (Cary Grant) from the police. Eventually, with the help of a Supreme Court Justice (Ronald Colman), she saves Dilg from being lynched. Unfortunately, I found it hard to believe in Cary Grant as a soap-box orator and impossible to take Colman for Felix Frankfurter.

The playing, then, in all the main cases, is more stereotyped than fitting; but the big blanks that this draws are the long waits in between laughs and action, when Dilg and Grant become involved in the interpretation of the law. Director George Stevens directs, and not for the first time, at a pace which is more thorough than funny and shows his usual predilection for sentimentality. For some reason, the regard of Colman's valet for his master and the fondness between Colman and Grant turn out to be a little morbid. And somehow I can't take my lynching so lightly, even in a screwball. Still, I am all for this kind of comedy, for reasons noted earlier, and for players like Arthur and Grant, who can mug more amusingly than most script writers can write.

September 21, 1942

Memorandum for Hollywood

To the makers of documentary war movies:

Take it easy, boys, we get the idea. When the title of your latest movie said "The Battle of Midway," and you showed a Pacific island with American soldiers and equipment on it, and then our anti-aircraft firing at planes in the sky, you didn't have to tell us. But you did: in the midst of rapidly changing action, the noisy din of gunfire, airplane engines and bombs, there was Donald Crisp's voice, out of key, rhythm, feeling, telling us that this was Midway and those were Japs we were firing at. If you'd ever looked at this movie of yours it must have occurred to you that it is self-explanatory. That's the idea of movies—you show people, you make with the pictures. A film document is analyzing the facts in visual images. For a word document we stay home and read books. But your movie documentaries are like the Beethoven Fifth with Deems Taylor talking alongside, explaining each sound as it is heard.

You're too zealous. You aren't content to move us simply with pictures and sound, you have to throw a voice in to wrench some more emotion out of us. For extra bad measure the voice of a famous movie star—so plus everything else, it's a quiz you give us: who belongs to the voice? Up till now one voice would do you. In "Midway" you have most of the Joad family, in addition to a character actor I haven't guessed yet. Donald Crisp, Henry Fonda, Jane Darwell and Mr. X. A symphony of discord. When a bomber takes off, the squeaky, matronly voice asks, "Say, is that one of those Flying Fortresses?" "Shore is, ma'am." "Is Junior Finney going to fly that big ship?" "Shore is, he's the skipper." And when the wounded are shown over the screen, quaveringly from Miss Darwell: "Take those pore boys to a hospital. Oh hurry, please."

I can understand why you might feel that your documentaries aren't getting across the idea by their pictures alone. That's to be expected, since up to the war hardly any documentaries had been made in this country, and the newsreels got lazier with each year—more Lowell Thomas than pictures, and what with censorship, more Bronx Zoo and Lew Lehr than social commentary. It's no wonder that when war came you needed a narrator to explain such documents as "This Is War" and "The World at War." Especially since so much of both films was originally from incoherent newsreels or from the German picture "Sieg im Westen." The idea of documentaries is that they show you something you haven't seen before, or something you have seen but in a more illuminating way. I've seen some of these shots four times now, in four different documentaries.

But no matter how feeble your camera work, it is still true that hardly any visual images can be made to jibe with an added-on narrator's words. Donald Crisp's voice won't express the take-off of a plane any more than the Andrews Sisters could express the Hallelujah Chorus. The only way you can heighten the effect of a take-off is by heightening the effect of the visual images with music or sound that is the same in abstract feeling. Even so artistic a commentator as Carl Sandburg produced in your short "Bomber" an overwhelming emphasis on words that completely obscured visual effect. In the places where you must use words, use them with a feeling for the moment. When you show an airman's face just after he has been up and in battle, take a look at the mood on the face before you pop off with your high-school dramatics. If it's tired, nervous and distraught, don't be so brisk and phony: "How many more today, Skipper?" But why not try making a documentary without words for a change? You might turn up with your first war documentary.

"The Battle of Midway" was made, of course, on Midway itself and during the battle, with all that implies of difficulty and heroism. A very large part of it was necessarily censored by the navy. But John Ford attempted in it the one thing most obviously lacking in past documentaries—an expression of the human element. There is, in his film, as much expression for the soldier in battle as there is for smoke, bombs and airplanes. His fighting sequences continually refer back to the men who are doing the fighting, and the shots of the men after battle, with the emotions still on their faces, are inspired. In such passages where the emotion is so passionately present, the commenting voices are little less than indecent.

October 5, 1942

Black Tails and White Lies

BEHIND the romantic distortion of Negro life in "Tales of Manhattan" is a discrimination as old as Hollywood. The Negro life is the last section of a six-part Cinderella story which traces the life of an evening coat. At the end, while being worn by a gangster, the coat is accidentally dropped from an airplane, and picked up by two Negro sharecroppers. The coat has the gangster's fifty thousand dollars in it; the two distribute it among the poor Negroes of their village.

This episode superficially seems harmless enough. Its Negroes are gentle, persevering, comical people, who love to sing religious songs in glee-club formation. The atmosphere, costuming and intent, as in all Negro movies, is quaint and charming. Of course, the Negroes are *segregated*. There are no white people in the whole scene, just as there are no white people anywhere that the Negro plays a leading role. If the movies want to give a Negro front billing, it has to be an all-Negro picture or nothing. The segregation in "Tales of Manhattan" is complete. The village they live in is in deep wilderness, not a white man in sight. After segregating them, the movie shows the Negro his place in the social scale. In the earlier parts of the picture the white people are lawyers, directors, actors and composers. The Negroes are either sharecroppers or nothing. Elsewhere in movieland they may be servants, comical fellows or members of the Hall Johnson choir. However, once the Negro recognizes his place in movies, he is treated with a great love. The roles he is given to play are always likable. We take everything away from them, stick them off by themselves or make men-servants of them, and then are terribly fond of them. In "Tales of Manhattan" we drop fifty thousand dollars to them.

In the same picture with this episode are five others having to do with white people, and it is really not much fairer to them. To start with, Charles Boyer gets shot at for playing around with another man's wife. You think he's dead, but since he is wearing a lucky tailcoat, he isn't. Among the failings of this scene are unoriginality, a hoked-up quality about the people, and too much talk to get through. Mr. Boyer of course brings out that incredible vein on his forehead, and Rita Hayworth shows herself. The next scene is worse, since it doesn't even have the movement of a bullet. Henry Fonda and Ginger Rogers here spend the longest half-hour in their picture life. As everyone must now know, Charles Laughton bursts the coat at the shoulders while conducting the next sketch at Carnegie Hall. His audience in the movie, unlike the audience I was in, laughs itself dizzy over this, while Laughton sits down on the podium to cry. The picture audience then apologizes to him by taking off their own coats, and Mr. Laughton proceeds—an inspired player even here, with his mobile face, which, some people only now are finding, overacts. I also like his wife, Elsa Lanchester. Following this, Ed. G. Robinson, an alcoholic tramp, wears the coat to a college reunion and is given a helping hand by his former college mates (all leaders in the industrial world), a chance to become once again a respected member of society. This scene carries the most obnoxious load of pseudo-Christian teaching since "Mrs. Miniver," a picture MGM made this year.

Without considering esthetics, this is six of the ten worst pictures of the week.

October 12, 1942

Fiction and Fact

THERE is more of method in "The Moon and Sixpence" than there is of Charles Strickland, whose life it pretends to be. Instead of going directly to Strickland (George Sanders), the movie sends a writer (Herbert Marshall) around to ask about Strickland, and intermittently, by word of mouth, you get a bare outline of his life. He was a dull, middle-aged stockbroker who suddenly got a compulsion to paint, and felt he had to break completely with society to do it—going as far as Tahiti, where he married an underslung, sloe-eyed native girl, caught leprosy, went blind and died. Mostly, though, you get a lot of Herbert Marshall and some rather interesting people to talk to you; some of them new movie faces: Strickland's white wife and his mistress, Molly Lamont and Doris Dudley, both strikingly cold, tense women; three Tahitian personalities, Eric Blore, Florence Bates and Albert Bassermann.

The method, though, is artifice, since it doesn't show why such a stick-in-the-mud stockbroker suddenly became so brave an artist, nor why he had to break with society to do it, nor why he suddenly changed from being an iconoclast to someone who went through a marriage ceremony, nor, and most important, what kind of man he was beyond the superficial vocalization and the fact that he looked like Robinson Crusoe. His whole life on Tahiti, for instance, is no more than Hollywood's familiar cliché of South Sea life—hula dances, alcoholics and Dorothy Lamour characters. Behind the evasion, of course, is censorship, which makes direct biography almost impossible, and cuts all the vitality out of movies like this one.

The little it does show is done to a crisp, good-looking if stilted, adequately played, and made for grown-ups. The mere outline of Strickland's life is interesting, but the best moments have nothing to do with anything except the acting virtuosity of the several minor characters. Then, at the end, you are finally shown what kind of paintings Strickland made; it is no worse than the Technicolor, but there aren't many good paintings being done this year or ever, and those not for the United Artists Movie Co.

The twelve war documentaries from England called "Inside Great Britain" are worth seeing, even beyond the educational implications and despite the superfluous commentaries. The English get more variety into their documentaries than we do. There are studies here of a troopship, a railroad, a shunter, a bricklayer, and a funny one which is just the animation of abstract color patterns to "The Bugle Call Rag"—and even so carries a message. Also there's a nicely done regeneration of a file clerk into a toolmaker, starring, among others, Ernest Bevin. The English prove here again that they know more about photography and editing than Hollywood, and that the documentary is better than the star-system ever will be (the worst one here is a glossy, sluggish, hoked-up one starring Leslie Howard). Incidentally, twelve is too many.

There are a number of laughs in "My Sister Eileen," depending on what you laugh at and whether you want to, and if you can stand seventy minutes of wisecracks. The laughs in these revamped stage comedies are no excuse for what goes with them: the characterizations are awful, because everyone is either, without rhyme or reason, a stooge or a wiseacre, the situations are always ending woefully short of the time and space needed for screen humor, and the technique, which isn't far from the two-line Pat and Mike joke, gets stale and obnoxiously obvious.

October 19, 1942

The Movie Art

Aʙᴏᴜᴛ movies, playwright Elmer Rice, in the magazine Soviet Russia Today, says "It seems highly improbable that the motion picture, synthetic in its construction, and heavily dependent upon technological paraphernalia for its production, will ever make manifest that human breath and those human thumbprints which characterize all great works of art."

Like all chestnuts which art-lovers fall back upon when they go witch-hunting into the fields of esthetics, this one diverts attention from the real villain, which in the case of the movies, is Censorship. That, Mr. Rice, is what keeps the movies in the "protracted infancy" you mention, not any disease of technology within the medium itself. Every art is defined by the nature of its mechanics: painting has to do without time and sound, writing without color and line. But such limitations aren't the weaknesses Mr. Rice makes them out to be. The very boundaries of an art produce its most basic advantages. In the movies the basic advantage is the movement of visual images, which the cameras, players and technicians make possible—the technological paraphernalia that worries Mr. Rice.

In the peculiar quality of each image, and the movement created by their succession, exists the particular expression of each artist, the human breath and thumbprint Mr. Rice says isn't there. Compare the camera images of Tisse ("Alexander Nevsky"), Bissert ("Intolerance") and Ivens ("Zuyder Zee"), and see the human breath of these men, the cool nobility of Tisse, the sentiment of Bissert, the expressionistic violence of Ivens. Behind every shot in an Eisenstein movie is the cold, exacting sensibility of that artist with a compulsiveness like Cezanne's that will plan every last piece of metal in a bit-player's costume so that it will be within the expression of Eisenstein's idea. Even when Chaplin is not on the screen in his movies, his thumbprint is: the innocent man killed by the greedy "Black Larson," the trek of miners across snow, both scenes carrying the unrewarded search and isolation that are Chaplin's expression.

Elmer Rice seems to think that art is incapable of happening when two or more people take part in its creation, but no one is complaining that it takes Koussevitsky and a hundred others to complete what Mozart wrote. In "Young Mr. Lincoln" there is an equal grasp of the idea in the direction of John Ford and the acting of Henry Fonda. The same unity occurs in "Alexander Nevsky," with Prokofieff's music, Tisse's photography and Eisenstein's conception. Nor can one discern who is more responsible for "The Passion of Jeanne d'Arc," cameraman Rudolph Maté or director Carl Dreyer. Obviously the terrible, prying realism of this picture can only be the result of their collaboration.

The tendency in talking about art is always to pigeonhole rather than to judge a thing for what it tries to do. Cezanne lovers cannot stand Velasquez; it is easy to see why, if you choose to judge Velasquez by the standards of Cezanne. I have listened to esthetes roar with laughter at a Chaplin movie, and come out criticizing it for its lack of movement or its sentimentality, forgetting that they have seen Chaplin, not Eisenstein. Mr. Rice is looking at one art through the eyes of another, or he would not be blind to a real spontaneity peculiar to movies, the lack of which he insists on. There is no step I can think of in the process of making a movie where a signature is not cut into the film. Directors like Griffith, Chaplin, Welles, Sturges impose themselves everywhere; players like Cagney and W. C. Fields overcome any director. And so on, too obviously. Can Mr. Rice discern the thumbprint of Frank Lloyd Wright, in a house designed by him, unsmudged by those of the intervening plasterers?

October 26, 1942

Between Two Worlds

"Now, Voyager" (title from W. Whitman) is a mixture of Olive Higgins Prouty, who also wrote "Stella Dallas," infantile fixation and Bette Davis, with the last two carrying the most weight and making the movie good. The appealing quality of this movie is the accuracy and extent to which it shows the relationship between a daughter (Bette Davis) and her mother (Gladys Cooper), and later, there being quite a few movies here, another mother-daughter relationship. It's about the repressed daughter of Back Bay wealth, who is cured by a psychiatrist (Claude Rains), falls in love with a married man (Paul Henreid), whose wife and children keep Bette and him separated, apparently forever. Bette is compensated by the happiness of taking care of her lover's neglected daughter.

In between the two solidly conceived mother-daughter relationships, which carry the tension that comes when the movies get down to life and behind the Hays office, there are some moth balls straight from Mrs. Prouty. This accounts for the feeling that you've seen this movie before—the tragic lady movie, in which girls like Bette Davis, Barbara Stanwyck, Helen Hayes and Irene Dunne can't marry the man they love but achieve a loftier happiness. Other moth balls are the ineffectual, doomed man married to an impossible woman, the tabu on divorce, some high-school psychotherapy, and that trip on a pleasure steamer to a foreign paradise where the ill starred lovers meet to the tinkle of contract bridge. Consistency is sacrificed for the sake of hokum drama: you might well ask why, if a psychiatrist got Bette safely out from under her mother, one was not used to get her lover untied. It leads to such things as the noble renunciation at the end. As Paul Henreid, who has kept his love on a high plane for eight long reels, makes one last grab at Bette, she holds him off yet saying, "Let's not ask for the moon, we have the stars!" and out and up goes the camera to a starlit sky—no moon. What it seems is always lacking in the movies is a person with some sense and a pair of scissors.

But cutting in and out of this silliness is the frank intelligence about dominating mothers. The interacting relationship of mother, daughter and psychiatry (which should have been the whole movie instead of a springboard for a frustrated love affair) is exceptionally accurate. The scenes in which average people are faced with a neurotic illustrate reactions and conversational responses which are emotionally exact. One scene is perfect: a flashback to a repressed adolescent's idea of love. There is a vitality in the playing, emanating mostly from Miss Davis, who is more vivid than hysterically mannered here. Gladys Cooper as the mother is genuinely upsetting as well as genuinely Back Bay, and Claude Rains, who is accustomed to rolling around in his characterizations as though they were bathtubs, rolls around some more but always with a knowledge of the part. (This is not a vote for the kind of typing that makes every neurotic Bette Davis, every psychiatrist Claude Rains, every younger sister Bonita Granville and every Ilka Chase type an Ilka Chase type.) The movie has fineness in spite of the distortion toward gentility given by its love affair.

"For Me and My Gal" is the backstage life of a vaudeville team, Gene Kelly and Judy Garland, and how it was never good enough to play the Palace.

It includes things like tap dancing before the last war. I think Judy Garland is too young to be playing in pictures.

November 2, 1942

The Journey, Cont.

"One of Our Aircraft Is Missing" is the second lap of a walking tour being conducted by Michael Powell and Emeric Pressburger. On the first lap ("The Invaders") six survivors from a destroyed German submarine were killed while walking across Canada. This second time six British fliers from the bomber called B—for Bertie—are seen sneaking through the Dutch underground back to England to fly again. After they bail out they are discovered hiding up in a tree by some likable Dutch farmchildren, who take them to Else Meertens, underground leader and pretty woman. She takes them through a church and a rugby game to Jo de Vries, underground leader and pretty woman. Then in a canoe to the North Sea and home again.

Mr. Powell is no Hitchcock. The entire journey is unmarred by casualties to the British fliers, danger to them, or by anything else that might break the ice (even the sixth flier, who got separated from the others, is come upon playing in a rugby game). Then they row down a Dutch river in the middle of the morning. The picture runs like a train schedule. Mr. Powell is obsessed now with making things look real, as in parts of "The Invaders." This means he uses natural settings and lightings, and players, who if they can't be natural don't do anything, which mostly happens plus some not too glistening photography, composed brilliantly in dark and light, and you have the correct, undecorative decor for movie-making—what Hollywood will need when it cleans house—besides a commendable plainness.

But the furthest this movie gets emotionally is to note impersonally some striking views: the high-lighted flight of a night bomber across the land, the pastoral effect of children gathered in a sunlit glade, looking up at the fliers in the tree, and a complexity of noble-looking people. What must come finally in Powell's pictures is some humanity, from either a closer examining of his people or from a closer examining of his essentially romantic ideas. His design is still to make a highly adventurous structure look utterly believable, and it still has a bolt missing. I suspect that, since Powell's adventure lacks adventure and his realism is merely negative reporting, the very romantic structure of his pictures is an evasive device, a way of bowing both to realism and romanticism without actually meeting either. The overindulgence in beautiful still-life photography rather than the achievement of any kind of emotional vitality in terms of movement shows the same lack of coming to grips with his material. Still, he has logically left Leslie Howard and other anomalies of "The Invaders" behind, and has made a clean, handsome film.

Mr. Powell's journey is rightly cast. Alongside of our own jobs, these British actors seem wonderful. The reason partly has to do with the fact we don't see a British player like Hugh Williams so often as we see Don Ameche, nor do we hear that kind of accent. But beyond this, the British producers do not cast to rigid beauty patterns (compare the complexity of people in this with those in "Eagle Squadron"). Finally, their directors insist on cutting all the scenes that show an actress looking unnecessarily silly. I liked all the Dutch people, and Miss Googie Withers, who stood, in this picture, for indomitable Holland.

November 16, 1942

Witches' Brew

Two-THIRDS of the way along in René Clair's "I Married a Witch" nothing of much moment has happened—it is half-hearted, slick Clair bounded by a Thorne Smith story. Two witches have cursed all Wooley marriages because of a witch-burning in Salem in 1690. (Historical note: Witches were hanged, not burned.) The successive generations of Wooley have been flashed back— failures. Fredric March has been wooden, Veronica Lake has threatened to take off all her clothes, and Robert Benchley has done his usual. Comes a modern election day with a Wooley running for Governor, and Veronica Witch, as a bit of smoke, passes through the voters' minds, changing them all to Wooley supporters. Bands play for him, babies cry "Wooley!" Madison Square Garden goes crazy, Wooley wins—2,684,922 to 0. (Even the rival candidate didn't want to vote for himself.)

The pace and sustained humor in this latter passage are the picture's saving grace. There are, to be sure, some small niceties that indicate M. Clair: a new variety of sophisticated pratt fall, the reaction to waffles of a woman who has been dead for 252 years, what two witches look like riding on one broomstick, what smoke sounds like on entering a bottle, and so on, mostly in dialogue.

What happened—because, including me, a lot of people liked René Clair at least up to his surrender in "The Ghost Goes West"—to René Clair? Mostly there is laziness through the whole production. Clair showed the story the easiest way he knew how—being in Hollywood. The photography is glossy, the settings elegant fallacy and the people millionaires. Nor does Clair try to make you laugh out loud, nor is he unduly original. The great society wedding which goes awry while Miss Van Horseface sings "I Love You Truly" is very familiar. So is Robert Benchley and the bedroom humor. An artist like Clair, who loves to comment on sex as much as anything, is restrained dreadfully by our puritan ideas, and reduced to dabbling—Racy Dialogue. This second American effort of Clair's is no different from the initial performances of most foreign directors in that the treatment of American people and customs seems to be confined to what Hollywood showed them, plus the most notorious Americana: graft at the polls, political bosses, etc.

The laziness of the direction is most evident in the playing. Fredric March looks as if he were rehearsing the part for the first time, contrary to the unrehearsed Pierres and Alberts of Clair's French films. Cecil Kellaway looks more like a director's prank than a witch—a disheveled, gray-haired business man. Miss Lake, on the other hand, makes the turn from fantasy to real without leaving a question in your mind. She uses her mellophone voice well, and gets plenty of chance to. Noteworthy are two unidentifiable jailbirds who make much of small chores.

Hollywood comedy, with the exceptions of Preston Sturges and the Schlesinger satirical cartoons ("Hiawatha's Rabbit Hunt"), has recently been tending toward the genteel, with writing teams dominating the picture. The more it gets like this the less good it is, and more especially, the less funny. This dependence on charm seems to be altogether on the wrong track, when you think how thoroughly you used to laugh at the early Disney, the Marx Brothers, Chaplin and Clair himself. It used to be that characters were inherently funny, now they just say funny things. It seems, remembering his old simplicity, fatuous to have tied René Clair up in the complicated plot of Thorne Smith and to have destroyed the free play of his naturalness, which, when it was comic naturalness, was truly comic.

November 30, 1942

The Warner Boys in Africa

Probably just as much hokum is turned out for circulating libraries, record albums and art galleries as for double bills, but movie hokum is easier to take.

One reason for this is that Hollywood often uses its best players, writers and directors for its epic phonies; and phony or not, something at least vivid results from so much talent. Each studio has its preference: Metro's is a James Hilton romance with its sprinkling of good works and roses round the door, starring Greer Garson and a suitable male; Columbia's is the Riskin-Capra comedy with its moral catch—but more important, Gary Cooper and Jean Arthur; Paramount's is a comedy of wacky millionaires written by Sturges, Wilder or Binyon; Warner's is "Casablanca." Before Allied troops made it more famous, Casablanca served as a jumping-off spot to America for many of Europe's refugees—therefore a timely place to carry on Warner's favorite cops and robbers.

Besides having to be timely, "Casablanca" had to have a prominent place in it for all of Warner's famous stars. That meant a Grand Hotel picture, a human crossroads. Humphrey Bogart will own one saloon (Rick's), Sydney Greenstreet another (The Green Parrot). Bogart will get hold of two precious passports, whereupon the leader of the vast European underground movement, Victor Laszlo, and his wife, Ingrid Bergman, who once ran out of a love affair with Bogart, will appear looking for passports. The saloon locale will take in all of Warner's character gems—the Mischa Auer character, the pickpocket, the fat waiter with the funny accent, the corrupt chief of police, the cabaret girl, and seven or eight song interludes.

The "Casablanca" kind of hokum was good in its original context in other movies, but, lifted into "Casablanca" for the sake of its glitter and not incorporated into it, loses its meaning. Thus, Sydney Greenstreet's velvet gesturing and suave cruelty were vitally necessary to "The Maltese Falcon," even potentially in "Across the Pacific," whereas in this picture he's not even needed. He's there merely for Sydney Greenstreet. So that whenever he finishes a superfluous conversation by sadistically swatting a fly it can be chalked up as hokum. Peter Lorre played his birdlike whimpering to Bogart's tough manhood effectively in "The Maltese Falcon." He repeats it here, wrinkling and unwrinkling his forehead faster than ever, but without effect, since there were so many other things there was no time to develop his character with sharpness and credibility. The Mischa Auer (Leonid Kinskey) skit has often been funny, mainly in "My Man Godfrey," but it misses here. Bogart's humanitarian killer, who was disillusioned apparently at his mother's breast, has to say some silly things and to play God too often to be as believably tough as he was in his last eight pictures.

Actually the picture has more acts than it knows what to do with for truth and beauty—and gives too much time to less important ones, such as the

Bulgarian couple whom Bogart allowed to win from his roulette table so that they would have money to pay their fares to America. The emphasis on everything, big or little, makes for a kaleidoscopic effect. Neither the story nor characters are firmly set in their environment save for a glance or two at a native market and one at a painting of the town.

Yet the people in Hollywood don't project their hokum without reason. They know very well the pleasure one gets from seeing Ingrid Bergman, so noble and utterly clear, Mr. Bogart's mouth, which seems to be holding back a mouthful of blood, the contrast in villains of Veidt, Greenstreet and Lorre. If, as this is, it is from Warner's, it is full of political intelligence. In addition there is an album of jazz classics, with a Negro (Dooley Wilson) singing them. Finally, there is one good sequence where intuitive feelings prevailed over script writers' unconcern and Director Curtiz' incapable scissors—the scene in which the fighting Frenchmen drown out the Germans' "Horst Wessel" by singing their "Marseillaise." "Casablanca" is as ineffectual as a Collier's short story, but with one thing and another—like Bergman, Veidt, and Humphrey Bogart—it is a pleasure of sorts.

December 14, 1942

Preston Sturges: Satirist

Preston Sturges has made six satirical movies famous for their ability to make you laugh out loud and at length, with comedy that is a modernized sophistication of Mack Sennett—but no daintier. Sturges trips his characters just as hard, sticks as big pins in them, throws as much food at them as Sennett ever did, but unlike him, Sturges uses the slapstick technique to point up their personalities; it is not so completely a matter of getting to the nearest cliff to fall off. In his continuous invention, and especially his somersaulting pace, he recalls Sennett, and also in his unconcern for the niceties of screen art (in contrast to the delicacies of Chaplin or Clair). Sturges' potential position as a screen creator becomes really important, I think, on a lesser known movie, "Christmas in July," and his poorest one, "Sullivan's Travels." The former didn't have a cinematic moment in it but it was a startling movie. Camouflaged by a Cinderella story, it had as hard and clear thinking in social criticism as has come out of Hollywood, when, at intervals throughout, representative victims of industry delivered sincere, warmly human monologues on what success meant to them, their chances of getting it, their bewilderment and their fear.

"Sullivan's Travels," unlike his other movies, was immature in its philosophy, formless, and without a single discerning characterization; but it had an astonishing display of film technique. Taking the best qualities of all his movies, it is apparent that Sturges is the most progressively experimental worker in Hollywood (aside from the cartoon-makers) since the early days.

He is essentially a satirist without any stable point of view from which to aim his satire. He is apt to turn his back on what he has been sniping at to demolish what he has just been defending. He is invariably mean, with few of the human overtones that give poignancy to Chaplin and Clair, contemptuous of everybody except the opportunist ("The Great McGinty") and the unscrupulous little woman who, at some point in every picture, labels the hero a poor sap.

This explains a lot of the freedom that Sturges has fortunately been allowed. He champions nothing, and he gives his employers enough of what they want in the way of box office—his pictures always have their full share of leg art, strip tease and Hays-office morality to pad his own idea of life. That the invariable fairy godfather of each picture is not only expressive of his own cold-blooded cynicism but of typical Hollywood fantasy is an example of how this works. Another phase of his attack is shrouding in slapstick the fact that the godfather pays off not for perseverance or honesty or ability but merely from capriciousness.

His latest comedy, "The Palm Beach Story," has scenes as wholeheartedly funny as anything can be, most of them coming in the first third of the picture. It is a freshening up of some old movie characters, a worn-out plot, and a number of ancient laugh-getters like the burp, all of which Sturges manages to carry just a step past their usual treatment. For instance, his deaf man either hears nothing or the wrong thing, and asks "What's that you say?" as all deaf men do in the movies; but Sturges gives him the quality of a disembodied spirit, believably a pixie—or "The Wienie King." When the heroine tries to climb into an upper berth, she *does* step on Lower Berth's face. The difference Sturges gets is that the injured party only asks that she pick the pieces of broken spectacles out of his eyes. The puppets for Sturges' satire range from John D. Hackensacker III ("tipping is un-American") to Rudy Vallee ("you have a *nice* little voice"). Vallee plays the Rockefeller role (so deftly under Sturges' direction that he will probably be the most talked-of movie birth for sixty days), but it is indicative of Sturges' frivolity as well as invention that part of the time the satire of this character is aimed at Rudy Vallee, not Rockefeller.

The moth-eaten story for this movie causes the comedy to drop after the first third; after that Sturges' smartness only partially relieves it. Very irritating is a latter-day failing of his, an unbounded delight in his ability to write witty dialogue, not one line of which he will forgo. It is important to see "The Palm Beach Story" from the beginning: as an experiment Sturges does a miniature movie while the credits are being shown. This brief business, it seems to me, is as funny as anything that comes afterward up until the last shot.

December 21, 1942

Movie of the Year

THE importance of "In Which We Serve," the movie of British sailors which Noel Coward wrote, directed, produced and acted in England, is that it contains the vitality noticeably absent in most films. Coward is trying continually to keep the screen expressive. In the shipbuilding scene at the start, he gets exactly the rhythm of construction, and especially the individual's importance in it, some of the energy, danger and craft. The important battle scene on the ship in last year's battle at Crete brings out progressively the increasing pressure on the men, which never undermines their complex teamwork behind cannons and below the decks; the direction of action here is something any director would be proud of. When the screen is expressive in this sense, something of significant content is being shown, keyed to the pace of the action, and having the right camera angle, the right gestures and sounds to produce an experience the audience participates in, as emotion defined by movement. Even the description of sailors' shore leave, which censorship and the established mores of popular art kept at a "naice" level, are given a kind of vitality by the right casting, timing and dialogue. There is unusual respect for the ordinariness of people's behavior; so that they come out stronger, more admirable for being natural.

The final episode, when the captain says goodbye to the men—a scene so common everyone understands its sadness and dignity—is done without any drama at all, without any pointing up of any particular man, without condensation; the men walk by one by one, shake hands with the captain and say goodbye. The scene is extraordinarily moving because the farewell is said by each man in his own way, and because there is no dramatic elaboration. This simplicity and fidelity to the individual's natural response is in control of most scenes. I think only thirty minutes of this year's movies have been similarly expressive, though certain players, like Cagney, Ida Lupino, Ann Sheridan and

Ronald Reagan (in "Kings Row") were that by themselves despite what happened around them.

The movie is the story of HMS Torrin, sunk at the Battle of Crete. As its survivors cling to a rubber float, each man's thoughts are shown on the screen in a series of flashbacks. Their thoughts are conveniently, for purposes of morale, always for their good wives, their good ship just sunk and their good captain, also riding the float and thinking back. The movie goes out of its way to show what a perfect captain this Kinross—Noel Coward—is; more sensitive, more intelligent and more mature than any of his men. First comes the sailor's Christmas dinner at home, then the chief petty officer's, then the captain's; and each time the conversation rises a notch in sensitivity and discernment. Though Captain Kinross certainly makes too many paternal pep talks to his men, saves too many lives and is too omniscient for a man who is only Noel Coward and not Nelson and St. Francis in one, the picture, above almost any other, is painstakingly accurate in showing the ability, strength and stake in the war of all the men.

As for the movie's form, there are too many flashbacks of thoughts and Kinross for the raft to carry—you have a tendency to worry about what is happening on that float while you are meandering all over England inside someone's mind. The deletion of the word "bastard" in one scene has deleted the sense of the next one: it is depressing to be more priggish than the English, to need to cut a movie they saw with equanimity. In spite of its length and overindulgence in captains, this picture is alive all over, notably in the scenes in middle-class homes where there is jawing over the dinner table and rasping mothers-in-law. It is cast the right way—or the other way around from Hollywood. A face, body and voice were found to fit each part, rather than a part to fit Thomas Mitchell, Claude Rains, etc. For the sailor's mother, Kathleen Harrison has a bounce, a loud screech and great charm. The chief petty officer has a face as strong and honest as Abe Lincoln's and the ring of the middle class in his voice—with corny overtones ("The whole of civilization is trembling on the edge of an abyss"). Celia Johnson has the necessary sensitivity to be the captain's wife, which is pretty sensitive. The feeling that her voice will crack at any moment keeps most of her scenes extremely tense. Coward is too stiff even for the loftiness of this particular captain, especially in the petrified way he holds binoculars. The most compelling performance, as well as the picture's most important one, is John Mills's sailor, Shorty Blake, who is a small pert redhead with every sailor's face and voice. There is an amazingly fine scene on the raft when Sailor Blake, wounded, gets his shirt cut away from the wound.

Examining the movie further, you find that Coward did some obvious things that have been wanting for a long time. He made a picture of average people in war instead of the exclusively Harper's Bazaar set of "Mrs. Miniver." He made a picture of war rather than cops and robbers, as were "Casablanca" and a score of others; and a picture of numbers rather than those two fun-loving soldier boys of "Wake Island." Even his movie's structural center is that widely reproduced and most moving news picture of this war, sailors clinging to a raft in an oily, heaving sea.

One is aware from the start of this movie that it is something new, not done before, that it has behind it artistry and intelligence and an authentic desire to make a moving picture. The content of each shot was conceived in a film sense rather than any other, and no other picture this year has equaled it. Not even nearly.

December 28, 1942

Children's War

In American films of the past year there has been a sturdy trend toward a more mature appraisal of personality and behavior in our society. It probably started with the unhoneyed treatment of Citizen Kane's life. "Kings Row," for all its indulgences, treated sadism in medicine as well as insanity. "The Moon and Sixpence" showed the clear superiority of a social rebel over the convention-bound lives around him. "The Male Animal" glossed it over, but it was against the Gene Talmadges in the scholastic world and recognized the feelings of an intellectual. "Now, Voyager" considered the mother as the root of a severe neurosis and advocated a kind of psychoanalysis. This brave new movie world continues in "Journey for Margaret," which attempts to show the appalling psychological effects of a war on small children, not as poor little things and sure box-office, but as ill human beings.

The children are seen in a nursery during the height of the German raids in 1940. War correspondent Robert Young comes to get a story, meets the refugee doctor, Fay Bainter, standing probably for Anna Freud, the child psychiatrist. Miss Bainter shows him her roomsful of shocked children: the little girl who screams at the sight of a man, the boy who retreats from the world to his woolly lamb, the girl who constantly jerks her head up and down, Margaret, who has a compulsive gesture of wiping the corners of her eyes and cannot be parted from her "imagesium" bomb. The scene of the little boy, clutching his lamb and saying over and over, meaninglessly, some magic phrases, is pretty subtle for movies. Mr. Young is impressed, and so are you, for the most part. The two central children have some difficult assignments—the writing here is good—and they almost reach the convincing physical and emotional derangement demanded of them, though stealing glances at the director often enough and walking so painstakingly as to keep you jittery. In some of these scenes the camera acts as an interested onlooker and a sustained one; so that you can watch the child's behavior for long sequences. Margaret O'Brien, a professional seven-year-old, with a dark, oval, fiery face and a wonderful hat like Picasso's clowns, has a way of blurting her words suddenly and emphatically, like a delayed bomb. The other child, William Severn, is better when he is not just being cuddly.

As a rule, in psychiatric movies, the further the picture gets from the hospital and case histories the worse it is, and "Journey for Margaret" is excruciatingly true to this form. It has a love story about Robert Young and Laraine Day, which is ghostlike in comparison to the children's home. They and their subplot do strange things the movie doesn't prepare you sufficiently for. Miss Day has a way of turning on smiles, intoxication or pain so extremely and fast as to leave you behind. The psychology of the husband and wife is all right, except that it is shown as inadequately as a mountain-climb would be by showing the climber at the top of the peak. The writing of their speeches is terrible ("Oh, God! Gimme the strength and wisdom to stay mad!"). That one was so embarrassing for everybody they pityingly turned the light off Young's face when he said it.

The intentions of this movie are admirable, but it has the unforgivable fault of talking down to the audience. One's natural response to the bombing, if only for its effect on the children, is substantial enough without the set speeches about Rotterdam. But worse is the tendency to turn aside from the serious effect of the movie with something easily recognizable, perhaps to be laughed at, such as Young's four chair-squeaking scenes and the Japanese envoy, in fear that you might forget that movies are your best entertainment. It is a good movie only when it is about the children.

January 4, 1943

Mystery Movie

Tough murder movies bear the same relationship to the great movie epics as detective novels do to the latest best-seller: they are sometimes more worth spending time on. In the case of the tough movie, characterizations are often studied with more insight and originality than they are in the epics, action is better timed and sustained, behavior and environment are less given over to superficialities and gentilities, and the dialogue is good. "This Gun for Hire" had a couple of episodes in it—the opening on a flophouse with action concerning a killer and a chambermaid, and the entire, exciting chase at the end—with more drive and invention than anything in such best-sellers as "One of Our Aircraft Is Missing." In the same way, "The Glass Key," with many inadequacies, has some splendid scenes, and one portrait which should be noted.

The portrait is that of a hulking, good-natured killer named Jeff, resembling Steinbeck's Lennie and played by William Bendix. The director and Mr. Bendix, who is a more bulky blond-curled version of Louis Wolheim, create this irresponsible murderer without reserve. He loves to knock people around—he calls them bouncing balls—or choke them to death. While choking one victim thoroughly and viciously he explains that his trouble has always been a lack of aggressiveness, that anybody can work on his soft nature and get him to do anything. The light of understanding that Mr. Bendix projects in this scene is remarkable. In fact, the whole thing is a brilliant portrayal of a man proud and at the same time doubtful of his great strength, using it beyond ordinary social bounds since he hasn't the same conception of boundaries as other people.

The good scenes have usually to do with Jeff—one vivid drunk sequence that starts with a good bleary shot of a cabaret singer, proceeds through a strange mixture of sadism and affection between Bendix and Alan Ladd, and finally to a murder; another which ends in the season's most nervewracking fall, which should startle you considerably. It is an interesting Hollywood phenomenon that the tough movie is about the only kind to examine the character's actions straight and without glamor, a close appraisal of personal habits being too coarse for our Mrs. Minivers. As a result the tough movie captures a descriptive power common to the other arts. For instance, the way the political boss brushes his teeth or puts on his socks, the way Mr. Bendix spits or hugs a future victim, or how someone else fondles a bottle he is about to crack over a skull, or Mr. Ladd's speculative glance.

The film is a striking example of good movie making, which was no accident, and an equally conscious but conflicting desire to ring the box-office cash register by throwing away great hunks of film to emphasize Alan Ladd's sex appeal, and also Veronica Lake's. For Mr. Ladd, action stops while lights soften to a woolly texture on his face, and without blinking a lid or moving a muscle of his just-parted lips he mutters a virile monosyllable. Aside from this obvious and cheap exploitation he gives a rather nice, studied performance, though his every grimace, or lack of one, seems keyed to the memory of Rudolph Valentino. Many of the movie's ailments are the result of a disease common to tough detective stories, where the mystery, its detection and the unity of the story are sacrificed to sensational but irrelevant data: near-seductions, sub-rosa characters, scenes of strange violence, especially the indecent mauling the hero can and always does take.

It should be said that Brian Donlevy plays his Great McGinty again, affably as always, and that the direction of Stuart Heisler is exceptionally good in the scenes cited.

January 11, 1943

Our Town

NOWHERE is movie censorship and the effect of a box-office control on art so apparent as in the second half of a double bill, where one might expect to find the movies' practice fields and proving grounds—new talent, unconventional stories and ways of showing them. Instead one finds a macabre and grotesque thing like "The Great Gildersleeve." This is a typical "B"—about an American family, the Gildersleeves, in the American town, Summerfield—made for the suburbs and the towns; so that the theatres there can coax their public with two pictures for the price of one. It merits discussion because it is typical.

Since we find that the B picture is not experimental, we might then expect, because censorship and box-office decree that no one's feelings be either examined or hurt, that it at least be a fairly innocuous picture of an average American family. However, this is not it either; for up pops so gross a misrepresentation of American life that it might almost be a revulsion on the part of the producer at the kind of people and culture which made for the forces that made this picture. These "average" Americans in "The Great Gildersleeve" are all of the idiot variety, and the sole concern of each is to outtrick the rest by deceit, lie or practical joke.

The Great Gildersleeve is a huge, glutinous, moronic fellow, who moves about without aim, purpose or profession, yet rides in a fine car, to a fine home, in which there are two adopted children, a maid and a grand piano; his radio trademark seems to be an ability to get into trouble and when there to give an unconvincing laugh. His daughter leads around a five-piece orchestra of collegiate adolescents, who carry their trumpets and saxophones uncased; so that they can break into music at any place or moment, whereupon the daughter becomes a high-stepping drum majorette. The county judge is a disreputable version of the man with the pitchfork in Grant Wood's "American Gothic." His one concern is to marry off his homely sister and turn her room into a den for himself. The rest of the citizenry tag along after the judge or Gildersleeve to see which one will best the other.

The judge threatens to take Gildersleeve's children away from him unless he marries the judge's daughter. The children figure out the solution: they will make Gildersleeve more famous than even the judge, by covering the town with pictures of his face and titled only—The Great Gildersleeve. The idea being that fame and position depend—as the children explain—not on "What you do, but on what people think you did."

Just as repellent is the picture projected of the American scene: the county court in session with only two people present, the recorder playing solitaire and the judge kibitzing; the great banquet where the town's important citizens play their pranks on the guest speaker (the microphone squirts water in his face, there is a hidden buzzer in his chair); the footrace between Gildersleeve and the judge to decide which is the better man; and finally, those two vicious gossips, who get into all American-town-life movies as the trademark.

In everything, then, is ruthless disrespect for ourselves and our lives. It bears no resemblance to the French satires on European provincial life ("The Baker's Wife," "Carnival in Flanders"), nor to Alfred Hitchcock's great displays of humor in his secondary characters. In these the criticism starts from essential love and respect for the people, and even more, from knowledge. The French movies take pride in their people, in their sexual potency and freedom, in the cleverness and bravery of the women, in their good looks, in the artistry of the craftsmen, in the pleasure instinct of the Jouvets, the independence of the Gabins. When the French movies poke fun it is at the mishaps caused by a too eager enjoyment of life. "The Great Gildersleeve" is absolutely without standards, its humor exterior to life.

I think "The Great Gildersleeve" is less the fault of Hollywood's workers than it is of censorship, box-office and a lack of indignation from the movie public. The movie code decrees that the showing of actual love is indecent; in "The Great Gildersleeve" love becomes a matter of juggling for prestige, of how one person can trick the other into marrying. Pressure groups and box-office insist that actual American life not be examined closely; Americans' activities in this movie consist entirely of childish pranks and conceits. Honest failure is considered shocking; instead success is shown, even if it is only a matter of advertising that fools the public. But also it is felt that real intellectual success is un-American, and so all leaders in the community are made plain, down-to-earth idiots. Finally, it is inacceptable for the characters in the movie to react with real emotion; the substitute for this warmth and human feeling is the defeat of the other person, roses round the door and money.

In B pictures the worst elements in Hollywood production run wild. There is neither time nor inclination in the production of B pictures for the invention and hard work that in A pictures overcome the codes and prejudices. Obviously there are too many pictures; there should be no B's at all, unless they are used as experimental cinema, where the errors of inexperience, new and untried attitudes could be made and learned from. Perhaps the most deadly thing about "The Great Gildersleeve" is that it has no errors.

January 18, 1943

History and Hollywood

In spite of its infinite pains to tread lightly among the delicate issues, "Tennessee Johnson," the movie life of the underestimated and misinterpreted Andrew Johnson (which was first called "The Man on America's Conscience") has a warmly human quality, a lack of pretense and a fine spirit. In some places the movie is intense with emotion, and otherwise is almost always interesting in showing famous figures of American history in famous or infamous moments. One scene is a great movie episode—Jefferson Davis' secession speech to Congress. It is spoken amazingly well by Morris Ankrum, with all the rigid formality of the speech and the cultured superiority and dogmatism of the man dominating the first half; but the end, in the quivering lips and body, is full of the terrible effort he was making to keep his emotion within the bounds of his speech.

Its Johnson is a passionate, mulish fighter for the underprivileged, the Union and the Constitution, but because the movie is afraid, it hardly mentions slavery, states' rights, the problems of reconstruction, the war; that Johnson hated the Abolitionists as much as the Secessionists; that he believed in emancipating the Negro but had no plan for rehabilitating him. Instead it concentrates on two freak incidents that are more sensational than indicative of the man and his times. One is the crazy circumstances that brought an upright Vice President to his inauguration maudlin drunk (he was never known to be so before or after) and led to Johnson's reeling, extemporaneous speech about his youth. The other has to do with the famous, hoked-up impeachment proceedings (in the movie Johnson shows up at his trial). And while it gets stuck in slow, long-winded debates in Congress and the White House it misses the tragic era outside and a great deal of the man—especially what he was most interested in, the poor white.

It has the hard luck to be intelligent, interesting and unpretentious without being convincing. For instance, the Tennessee scenes of Johnson's youth are fair enough to his early life: he *was* a runaway tailor's apprentice whose wife *did* teach him to read and write, his first speeches *were* given in meetings that broke up into gun fights, as a Jacksonian Democrat he *did* fight bitterly Lincoln's election—but all these scenes seem too custom-made and familiar, just as its people are too easily recognizable as Regis Toomey, Marjorie Main and Grant Withers rather than Tennessee settlers, and their speech more contrivance than Southern.

The picture looks to have been pretty thoroughly censored, so as not to rake up any coals still burning. There is one telling long-shot of Thaddeus Stevens which shows him wearing an ugly, black wig similar to the one he actually did wear and to the one that "The Birth of a Nation" Stevens wore. Elsewhere there is no wig but softly flowing brown locks. To please the OWI, Director Dieterle reshot several sequences to make Abolitionist Stevens a more sympathetic character. In my opinion, censorship is a disgrace, whether done by the Hays office and pressure groups, or by liberals and the OWI. Certainly it is a comedown from the unhypocritical, cynical, dictatorial, powerful Stevens to the indefinite Stevens Lionel Barrymore projects, using only the material considered safe, which is a bundle of gestures and grimaces rather than a personality.

Van Heflin plays Johnson with knowledge, and makes him a grim, humorless, somewhat puzzled personality, who seemed never to get over the knocking about he took in his youth; not given to tact, but a proud, courageous President who faced the post-war chaos that would have fallen to Lincoln. Heflin's was a difficult job, with the camera almost never away from him and a lot of long talks to be given, but he makes it, and lifts the picture generally, giving the portrait more dimension than is actually written into it.

It is certainly one of the less obvious pictures in a year of obvious ones. Its hero is not a box-office figure, and at least it tackled a controversial period. For these reasons it deserves respect. And it is a thoroughly interesting movie.

January 25, 1943

Hitchcock in Stride

"Shadow of a Doubt" has a good deal of the peculiar, almost revolting emotion movie director Alfred Hitchcock tries to capture by suggesting that the most ordinary circumstance may turn up something sinister—the census takers at your door may be part of a widespread plot, the next time you cross the street somebody may push you in front of a truck. Hitchcock threatens your very possible world with the impossible so often in this movie that at the end, in addition to the emotion mentioned, you are not sure of anything.

This feeling of ambiguity is introduced immediately, though obscurely, after some accompanying music has worked the "Merry Widow Waltz" into a terrifyingly psychotic state and Joseph Cotten is seen wondering if the two men outside have anything on him. Mr. Hitchcock has contrived to give them the vague air that may belong either to gangsters, Nazi spies or murderers, just as undefined in activity and character and mission as Cotten himself. So that, as Cotten slowly unwinds himself, leaves the house and walks toward them, you expect something catastrophic. Later Cotten takes his questionable identity to Santa Rosa, California, to visit his sister Emmy's family. Here he arouses progressive feelings in Emmy's daughter, Teresa Wright, of adoration, hope, perplexity, doubt, fear and terror, and an appreciable amount in you.

The movie depends largely on the ability of Joseph Cotten to project horror within his passive, old-world-gentlemanlike behavior, and on Teresa Wright's giving her role the eerie, half-suspended disquiet of adolescence. But there is often an unfocused quality in their acting, especially Cotten's, which loosens the tension a good deal, though Miss Wright has two lyrical love passages, one mystic and latent with Cotten, the other awakening with Macdonald Carey, in which her beautiful projection of the innocent's perceptiveness and terrible unguardedness creates much the same feeling as do Elizabeth Bowen's heroines. In contrast to the two leads, Patricia Collinge gives a sharp, clear tenseness to a character less important in the action. Since she has this ability, however, her performance tightens many of the scenes, and she can turn on that abrupt, bubbling laugh as often as she wants to for me. The young upright

American that Carey portrays lacks the prettiness the role usually gets and has instead a restrained, believable sensitiveness; and though Cotten is quite slow and rather awkward, he does have a rich, ingeniously used voice.

Unfortunately, Mr. Hitchcock's people here tend to resemble figures on a Saturday Evening Post cover or actors in a stock-company production of Tarkington. Not that they are made silly or have to say silly things; but rather that the treatment of the family and friends is corny and superficial, lacking insight and seriousness. They are homespun, clean, gentle people, but they do nothing, say nothing and inflict nothing that is telling. His comic characters, Pa and Herbie, the detective-story fans, are disappointingly obvious and a long way from the satirical sketches of the English days. What flavor they have— and especially the children—comes probably from Sally Benson and Thornton Wilder, the writers. There is one odious, moral bit with what is supposed to be the American high-school girl gone bad—fallen to waiting on tavern tables.

The direction of the people in an environment is more like it. In photography (Joe Valentine), pace, costume, everything is very unlike Hollywood and more like Santa Rosa, California. It is Hitchcock's ability to make these scenes—the street, the library at night, people strolling in warm California evenings and on the lawn before Sunday dinner, the family meeting the train —seem so real that it is like the unaware awareness of living. His English movies always had some of the most perceptive, unglossed photography anywhere, and here he took his company away from the studio on one of those unheard-of, breath-takingly pioneer excursions by Hollywood into an American town.

Hitchcock has adapted Orson Welles's realistic dialogue techniques—the three-dimensional kind where a voice floats on and on from somewhere else while the people on the screen are talking, and the incoherencies of several conversations going at the same time—so expertly that it fills in for some lack of event.

Hitchcock shows here that sensationalism is not necessary to every part of a movie if the details of ordinary activity are examined for their fullest suggestiveness. His most expressive moments are the sudden switches in emotion in midstride of an activity: the abrupt change in the pace of a walk or the tone of a voice, the sudden hurrying of people into position. As a result he is producing movies of high quality. As for his famous horror and suspense, they are here, and better than in any other of his American movies so far.

February 8, 1943

Wartime Documentaries

FUTURE historians will find that aside from the Russians, who had only to send their movie-makers into their front yards, the most informative documentaries of the war, up till now, shown in the United States were made by the National Film Board of Canada. America's fact films are produced by the OWI, Hollywood and The March of Time. The OWI's purpose is to show how perfectly American industry, government and people work together in this war. It does the best job technically, but it uses a formal, coldly passive camera that seldom catches a spontaneous action. The OWI soldier in "Troop Train" is well combed and brushed, rehearsed in his lines and directed in his actions until there isn't much left of him. "Troop Train," however, has the fine distinction of trying it alone without a narrator. "Paratroops" has the narrator back, but has also some good music and the photographic nobility of an Eisenstein picture, where man is shown large, daring and efficient against the vastness of nature. Hollywood's most informing documentary is a Pete Smith two-reeler which describes in detail the brutal but effective hand-to-hand fighting techniques being taught our soldiers.

The Canadian films, "The World in Action" series, written and edited by Stuart Legg, have material from the vital zones of the war, material that hasn't been prepared, set and posed in a studio nor sterilized by overzealous censorship, nor conceived in the pseudo-realism of Luce, Inc., or Mr. Metro. These shorts are intelligent editing jobs on film gathered from every available source in the world; so that their value is dependent on the vitality of the individual shots rather than on progressive development. The most terrifyingly beautiful scene I've seen of this war is in their latest release, "The Invasion of North Africa," of an early dawn populated by General Montgomery's tanks, each tank fuzzily discernible in the less than half-light, but jutting out of desert sands on all sides as far as the eye can see. It is this shot and others (the horizon full of the 850 ships that made up our convoy to Africa, the grotesque Brobdingnagian quality of a German railroad cannon being moved up to the Russian front, a bird's-eye view of the Libyan desert's cobweb of dirt roads, every foot jammed with motorized transport) that achieve the sense of quantity in this war. This short would be worth seeing if only for the one shot of Casablanca's French citizenry saluting the captured German officers with a gesture of four-letter implication.

Many of the early films of this series were marred by too long and complex a story structure, which called for excessive cutting and extended explanation by Lorne Greene. They attempted a detailed analysis of Haushoferian geopolitics, of the civilization of the Japanese in two reels, or ten minutes. Yet their material, in contrast to that of the OWI, was unconventionalized: the opening sequences of "The Mask of Nippon" are as revolting as anyone will ever see—they include a Japanese soldier throwing a child into the air and catching it on his bayonet, and whole groups of Chinese being buried alive. "North Africa" and "Fighting Freighters" are neither so all-encompassing in structure nor so ear-shattering in talk as were the earlier ones ("Our Russian Ally," "Inside Fighting China," "Food for Conquest"). "Fighting Freighters" is a fair account of the merchant marine, with a rough, thorny feeling that Coward's "In Which We Serve" lacked. The Canadians have been criticized for juxtaposing German as well as Allied film, because, it is said, one didn't know which side was winning in a "World in Action" war. Obviously, however, enemy film which showed some of the 2,000,000 tons of Allied shipping they sank in six months of the war is necessary to a discussion of the merchant marine.

Behind our American shorts there is the unpleasant sense of meeting a quota; proving that we are doing our part. There is too much dwelling on obvious facts—that our army is well fed ("Army Food"); that the universities are taking part in the war ("The Universities in Wartime") and that the railroads are moving our troops efficiently, but not nearly enough of the actual documentation seen in Russian and Canadian films. This war is being thoroughly filmed by our government, and it seems to me that releasing at least some of this action film along with OWI food talks would create a better understanding.

February 15, 1943

The Heroes of the Mary Ann

WHILE Americans in the islands of the Pacific were trying to deal with surprise and superior numbers in the first days after Pearl Harbor, an American flying fortress, the Mary Ann, was making a harried, four-day flight through the same area, unable to reach a safe airfield, fleeing because unarmed, or crippled, or out of gas, finally landing on an Australian shore. Warner Brothers have put a good deal of zeal, honest effort and integrity into "Air Force," the story of this flight. They have also put ten stock Americans taken from the drawer marked "Service Picture Types" to man the Mary Ann (whether Warners know it or not, all ten are the same person). But the players instil into their ancient characters an earnestness and belief and enjoyment in the things they say and do. Most of all, the picture is full of wonderful views of air warfare: planes taking off, coming in on wheels or without, exploding by the dozen if they're Japanese, a hectically cut—the best spot in this picture—airplane attack on a Japanese fleet, which is mostly wooden miniatures in a studio tank but enough newsreel as well to communicate the bedlam of battle as though it all took place in the center of an explosion. It is the best, most interesting, movie record to date of the Pacific war theatre.

In contrast to the English war films, there is no end to the heroism and the rewards for it that an American soldier can produce and earn in a Hollywood film. Each take-off of the Mary Ann is conceived as a great victory, pulled from the fire by the pilot. Each time the navigator plots a course, anxiety stacks up in great layers through the whole crew, the navigator himself almost goes to pieces, and his ultimate success is the occasion for backslapping and official wonder. Even the rear gunner, who flunked out of pilot school, gets his chance finally to fly the ship, the other men having bailed out, as he would have too had not the motor unexpectedly started kicking over. This goes along with his wonderful feats as a gunner. English movie fighters, with the exception of course of Captain Noel Coward, do their movie warfare as though it were only what was expected, which is probably more like the truth.

Of the players, John Ridgely has the tall, unbothered efficiency and respectable good looks of a pilot or a bus driver; the navigator, Charles Drake, has the blond passive largeness of a right tackle, and something that didn't have to be there, a pensive quality. The rest fill out the portraits that the McLaglens, Lowes, Cagneys and O'Briens started: the tough, cocky little man, down on the service and his commanding officer, the Irish and Jewish comedians, Harry Carey, and the soft, good-looking Southern aviator that used to be Johnny Mack Brown and now is capably and graciously James Brown.

The photography of James Wong Howe, like the job he did on "Kings Row," has great vigor. It is unwashed by the usual lacquered shadow, and uncentered in the old sense taken from painting, so that it seems to spread out in all directions past the boundaries of the screen. This technique, plus expensive accuracy and concern for details of décor and action, make the picture look as it should—like a newsreel, and a good if not profound record.

February 22, 1943

To What Base Uses

WITH war nerves and prosperity sending more and more people to the movies, the studios are creating good films like "Shadow of a Doubt" and also slapping together any old thing, but in either case seeing the movie breaks attendance records wherever it is shown. For instance, on one of New York's stormiest mornings this winter a line of people four abreast was wrapped like a bracelet around a square block, waiting in a heavy rain to see the most maudlin movie of any year, "Random Harvest." There is one now, called "Star Spangled Rhythm." Its musical numbers alone seem to be the last gasps of a form even the producers are at their wits' end about: the first one opens on Dick Powell wearing the most insipid little smile ever forced on a singer, then breaking into a song that starts "Twinkle, twinkle, twinkle"; the second one, the factory swing shift, is so grotesque you almost have to think the singers and dancers are sleepwalking; the third, a number by Vera Zorina, is to the ballet what the old-fashioned calendar cutie is to painting.

"Star Spangled Rhythm" also has the weirdest sexual emphasis of any movie I ever saw. In one skit the four male actors, Milland, Tone, MacMurray and Overman, show how they would act if they were women, which is such watered-down female impersonating that it is nothing but pointless vulgarity. Further on, the Misses Goddard, Lake and Lamour describe their boredom with their sex appeal and are followed with a rather better female parody by three of Paramount's homeliest males. Finally, at the picture's end, Zorina steps down from her photograph on a soldier's table, to stand before him ten inches tall but alive. The soldier wakes up, making with his eyes, mouth and hands like Boris Karloff, and grabs at her, the movie producer implying indescribable rape and strangulation at the same moment. Talk about your horror.

Even worse than all of these distortions of decent vulgarity (which would be a creative female impersonation, for instance, or an honest burlesque joke that is funny as well) is the obscene—there is no other word for it—rush the movies are now giving Negroes, with a part set aside in each musical for an (all) Negro act. Now we are going to be democratic; it's the fashion. This is not in any way to say the movies have changed their attitude toward Negroes; there is just more of it. As witness the wholly objectionable caricature of Negro dress and dancing in the zoot-suit number, in which Rochester and Katherine Dunham sing and dance something you could spend all your life in Harlem and never see the like of. Then there is the complete cancellation of the talent for rhythmic singing of the Golden Gate Quartet by putting them into a silly song and negating whatever effect their voices might have had by making the men clown.

This movie blatantly misuses more talents than any other picture in recent history, giving the most stupid and ordinary turns to Bing Crosby, Jerry Colonna, Victor Moore, Mary Martin, besides those already mentioned.

It has some good laughs. Sterling Holloway's long-legged zany parody of Veronica Lake is one. A skit in which Alan (Quiet—death approaching!) Ladd takes out of that sinister overcoat a small bow and arrow and shoots the rival gangster dead in a nice parody on the décor of the American pool room, is another. The third and choicest is a shower scene between Bob Hope and William Bendix that is entirely wonderful. If you manage to see just this sequence, which comes about three-quarters of the way through, you should be so lucky. Otherwise I hope I have made it clear—and the people and newspaper critics standing in line are at least half as much to blame as Hollywood—that this movie would scare Dracula.

March 1, 1943

Native Fascist, MGM Style

At one point in the new Spencer Tracy–Katharine Hepburn movie the widow of the great American patriot, Robert Forrest, floats angelically into a room and poignantly places lilies before her late husband's portrait. At the end of the picture she tells you she had hated her husband so thoroughly and was so sure he threatened the freedom of a whole nation, that she murdered him without a pang.

"Keeper of the Flame" is disconcerting and irresponsible in this way. There is before you throughout the movie the bewildering paradox of Spencer Tracy, an ace reporter: stern and compassionate in his search for truth; yet actually blind as a bat and taken in at every turn. As a reporter he had witnessed the rise to power of the Fascists in Italy, Germany and Spain, and he was determined to fight to prevent the same thing from happening in this country. But he couldn't recognize an American fascist when he was shown one with all the trimmings. He was writing a hero-worshiping biography of Robert Forrest, without a suspicion that Forrest was not quite another Lincoln. He was oblivious of the fact that Forrest, at the moment of his death, was about to stage a good old Nazi *putsch* and set himself up as a dictator with storm-troopers, youth groups and race laws. There is then, behind the movie, this tricky proposition: that our native fascists hide their fascistic ideas from the people in order to rise to powerful positions, that such ideas can be hidden, and that when they are there is no way of telling a fascist from a democrat, since no one in this picture (not even The New Republic) suspected what Forrest was up to.

This MGM portrait of a native fascist starts at his death. What you find out about him comes out after an hour and twenty-five minutes of fencing, in a sort of formless, impotent detective story. Steve O'Malley, the just reporter, in nosing around Forrest's estate to get material for his biography, finds a sullen gatekeeper who limps and knows something; Forrest's insane mother, whom no one knew about and who had been hidden away by someone for some reason; the gatekeeper's boy, who was ill because he thought he had killed Forrest; the gatekeeper's daughter, whom someone had put into a sanitarium; a sulky brother-in-law who threatens to thrash O'Malley; and the wife who murdered her husband so as not to destroy the nation's illusion that he was their hero. At the end, with most of these not ordinary lives full of sinister behavior unaccounted for (the disturbing personality enters the picture, threatens to disclose something and vanishes, leaving a cloud behind, and another such personality appears), there is a long and boring monologue which does explain Forrest, but in the dullest movie way possible. The picture then immerses itself in Grade-C melodrama; the Hays Office has a ruling that the wife who murders her husband doesn't live: so Miss Hepburn doesn't live.

Cinematically, most successful are some shots taken during Forrest's funeral, which strike close to the more frigid, lifeless parts of American life in the same way some Grant Wood paintings do. Margaret Wycherly's performance as Forrest's insane mother, who hears her son's voice, does more in its brief span to indicate what kind of man Robert Forrest was, and why, than all the rest of the characters, who always threaten to but never do. The part of Forrest's secretary, who is about six miles past being a mere opportunist and a mere hypocrite, is written well, and with insight.

The movie throughout gets into interesting situations which don't materialize or stay interesting either; nevertheless it keeps you in your seat, and it is justified in cautioning us against the kind of person Forrest was. But such a vital problem as an American fascist and the reaction of the people to him would seem to call for less romanticizing and more attention to what an American fascist really is, and how he gets there.

March 8, 1943

The Too Beautiful People

IF you tried to imagine the most gruesome result of a collaboration between William Saroyan and MGM, to both of whom life tends to be a chocolate soda made out of words, you couldn't have approached the disaster of "The Human Comedy." Its humanity and its comedy never get past its sermons, its hymns and the overwhelming proportion of Dale Carnegie in Saroyan, but even more in MGM.

The movie's most serious error is in stripping the Saroyan world of its main charm—the humor, the zaniness and the mishap—and in playing it straight for its homely morality: sing your troubles away; every cloud has a silver lining; love thy neighbor and the devil take the hindmost; it's not what you do, it's how you say it. All this is right back in the smooth old MGM groove, with the best Saroyan nowhere in sight. In other words, the movie hasn't produced Saroyan in anything like the proper spirit: in a medium like the movies, with an impact of visual realism that the printed page does not possess, there must have been a touch of fantasy to achieve any of the wonder Saroyan insists is everywhere, occasionally well enough to achieve conviction, as in the stories of his own people. In "The Human Comedy," Saroyan has written about some people whom the movie presents as inexorably *average*. Both he and the producers, using the heaviest realistic approach, have tried to settle on their ordinary shoulders the burden of godhood. These average Americans, lacking utterly the exoticism and the life-is-but-a-song spirit which, in the "Aram" stories, gave real being to goodness and innocence, are people whose wonder and happiness, this film would have you believe, can be had just by saying it's there; and Saroyan has made no attempt to go deeper than that. To believe this movie, American life is wondrous when you sing constantly, pray out loud and explain your prayer, see no evil and hear none (naturally you don't do any yourself), and at intervals make sure you tell someone at length the secret of a beautiful life. There are a few exceptions to this kind of behavior: the one villain, the high-school track coach, who turns up a drunken spectacle in the town saloon, demonstrating the humiliating prospect in store for all liars and fascists; and that good fellow, the rich man, whose worth is indicated in the simple way he greets his fellow man with "Hiyah!"

The idea is to tell you how wonderful the Macauleys of Ithaca, California, are. The trouble is that their goodness is so flashy and exaggerated and their real goodness, as it would come out in behavior instead of sermons, so ignored, that even the promising situations die hideously from marmalade poisoning. An example of this sham occurs in the scene in which a returned soldier stands on a corner and rhapsodizes about the town, while nowhere in the picture were you shown the wonder that really is there, and in every town. The straight realism makes it so much hogwash—you can't get an emotion on the screen by simply using the words that describe it.

The production is strictly MGM in its weird pseudo-realism. The girls have that ravishing Hollywood beauty that makes you cringe when you first see it. Ulysses, who acts like three years old and very cute for that age, turns out to be five, and you wonder, is he an idiot? His pal, twice his size and eleven, first appears to be unpopular because he is a bookworm, and then it develops that he can't read, and you must ask the same question, getting no answer. The students in Homer's high-school class have nothing to do with the awkward, chaotic personalities you would find in your own high school. The photography outlines each head with a halo and deadens the outdoor shots with painted backdrops, usually forgetting to put occasional people into the street scenes or the telegraph office (except when a stooge is needed on whom to demonstrate the Boss's beautiful character), making these scenes look like those of a play without the money to hire walk-ons. When the three soldiers and their two girls go into a theatre there isn't an empty seat in the house except five on the aisle.

The actors, Mickey Rooney, Jack Jenkins, Fay Bainter, James Craig, Van Johnson, Frank Morgan, play the characters with every capability, trying in some cases, especially Rooney's, to understand and project people that are beyond understanding. And so they are inevitably unable to capture a warmth that was never in the character. If something had loosened up somewhere, if it were all less trite, if the picture had shown a real understanding of beauty and wonder instead of trying to impose it, these actors could have made it sing.

March 15, 1943

Young Mr. Pitt

THE English film, "Young Mr. Pitt," is a costume piece of the late 1700's, featuring the dress of the time but hardly the life inside it, and presenting the historical parallel between England's first defense against a dictator, Napoleon, and the one going on now. What the picture hasn't got most of all is a bloodstream or a heartbeat, either of its own or of William Pitt. It is, actually, hundreds of good-looking, accurate stills, put together with considerable art. Among them are some telling things: the senile vegetables who composed Commons, who could carry on like chattering monkeys when the twenty-four-year-old Pitt showed up as their Prime Minister, and who otherwise ate peanuts when they weren't asleep. There is the elder Pitt's speech in defense of the American Revolution—the only one of a dozen in the movie which catches fire. There is Charles Fox halting his speech to Parliament to ask the hulk next him, "Milord, how's your gout?" and then hurrying on to denounce Pitt without finding out. Best of all, there is that very shrewd, stupid man, George III, taking a bath in a small roped-off square of water at Weymouth (Pitt said that telling George anything was like blowing porridge through a blanket).

The picture, like so many English films, suffers from overrestraint. Billy Pitt, as played by Robert Donat, has a frozen, wide-eyed, pained expression, and a pair of heavy-set legs—and little more. Neither the writing nor the acting here is enough to fill up a biography or make it very much alive. Pitt, it is said, was austere and dignified, but he must have had an occasional fling, depression, period of doubt, boredom or desire (at least it would seem so, considering that his indebtedness for hats alone was six hundred pounds). On the other hand, the picture restrains itself from pointing up any frigid zones in the man, using his only indulgence, an incredible avidity for port, to make him seem more human. The love affair enters the picture with the gutlessness of a Gainsborough painting and then evaporates. Such inconsequence makes the picture fall away throughout. Lord Nelson, though played with a threatening, exciting spark by the late Stephen Haggard, is seen hardly at all, and his battle none.

It is undoubtedly true that drawing parallels in movie histories between a past era and our own negates a lot of important life that was going on outside the strictures of the imposed parallel. (The movie tries to show that England learned, at the time of Napoleon as well as Hitler, that isolation was impractical, and that a conqueror must be stopped some time.) In fact, an important part of Pitt's life, and a part important to audiences now—the about-face of his government from its pre-war liberalism to a wartime reaction, one that squelched all reforms and reformers, the habeas-corpus act, trade unions and anti-slave movements, and permitted child (six-year-old) labor—has been left out. The movie leaves you with the feeling that Britain's war and her troubles stopped at Pitt's death and the battle of Trafalgar. The completely ignoble portrait of Fox—who fought for the civil liberties Pitt repressed—as simply a loose-living, evil man, is inexplicable in any light, historical or otherwise.

But if the picture is somewhat impotent in nearly all ways, it does show Director Carol Reed's eye for pictorial expression, his care and intelligence as to details. The playing, in the cases of George III, Napoleon, Nelson, Fox and Talleyrand is very good. The whole thing proves that Director Reed, who can be superb, as in "The Stars Look Down" and "Night Train," can never be wholly bad, but sometimes dull. And though on the whole dull, this one is interesting in detail.

March 22, 1943

"*The Hard Way*"

For the first half-hour, a movie called "The Hard Way" is the best moving picture I've seen in a long time. It takes place in Greenhill, Pennsylvania, which wasn't named for its coal-town grime and slums, and concerns a bitter woman (Ida Lupino), her coal-mining husband (Roman Bohnen) whom she left once and who in all sincerity wishes she would again, and a younger sister (Joan Leslie), who would like more than anything else a white graduation dress but instead falls in love with the clumsy half of a vaudeville team. These people are terribly plain and blundering; they are caught at unflattering moments— the high-school boy trying to get in some necking at the theatre with his stage-struck girl, who won't relax until the acrobats replace her favorites, or the husband, who is the essence of tired living, trying to be the stern father and being laughed at. Underneath this part of the picture is a bubbling, unpredictable vitality, which moves you through grimy Greenhill into its homes and lives, which are made up of minor crises, inconsequence and cursing, the people neither all villain nor all angel but somewhere in between. These early sequences have been conceived in a true cinematic manner.

After the two sisters and the vaudeville team, which one sister married into (the other saw to it that she did), leave the nondescript railroad station at Greenhill, their life stories settle grimly into the backstage movie plot in which the girl rises from sad rags to sadder riches, while her not so talented husband mopes through one-night stands, finally to shoot himself in despair. The characters now divide off into either full villain or full angel, and become people caught in a plot which will never slow down and which is always riding rough-shod over them to get to the next turning point. The two people who have shown no signs of a suicidal tendency commit suicide; a perfectly ordinary singer and dancer rises from the bottom of the ladder to the status of Katharine Cornell; a woman who you've been shown can only love her sister suddenly turns up in love with Dennis Morgan, a hoofer suddenly transformed into a famous orchestra leader.

"The Hard Way" lacks the emotional drive it seeks to show, of a relationship in which one woman controls and lives through the life of another. Unlike this movie, the nature of such an affair is neither so obvious nor so cold as a barber-shop pole. Watching the actions of the aggressive sister, to quote one of the actors, "is like watching the maneuvers of the Atlantic Fleet." That is to say, her character is presented with none of the sexual prompting or the over-layer of social acceptability that should be there; she rules her sister not with an iron hand in a velvet glove but with an obvious sledgehammer.

There is still, inside some of these later situations, a little of the fine directing and writing that went into the first quarter of the movie, as well as the photography of James Wong Howe, who can give substance even to trite situations. There are genre sketches, such as that of the soused actress being knocked into shape for a play reading, which are powerful in construction, and throughout there is the director's knowledge—Vincent Sherman—of the ways of the stage. Dennis Morgan, in a plum-pudding part as a minor-league philosopher, has lines which are neither obvious nor meaningless, and a spirited ability to make them tell. I would like to point to a raucous, vulgar nurse, played wonderfully by an actress whose name is not given. Much might have happened had Joan Leslie had the dancing-singing ability her part called for, or a face which didn't change so drastically from view to view. Ida Lupino, a fine player, has the same difficulty breathing life into that straitjacket role of villain as Bette Davis had for years.

March 29, 1943

Zanuck at the Front

"At the Front in North Africa" is a fact film made by Darryl Zanuck during the first stages of the African campaign. It follows American tank troops into their landing at Bone, through an undecipherable air attack, to a routing of Mark IV tanks at the battle of Tebourba. With thirty-four men under his supervision Zanuck still couldn't erase the impression that these were shots taken by an amateur photographer who found himself turning a camera on doings he never expected to see. Like a scared rabbit, the film runs out of the middle of one event smack into the tail-end of another, stays strictly away from people and glances nervously at airplane and tank battles out of the corner of an eye. Mr. Zanuck doesn't, in this manner, get inside of facts.

To explain deficiencies in films like this one, army and newsreel people have some valid excuses. Censors allow scarcely any battle film to get to the public (one commander, for instance, was just swerved from destroying all the film on Pearl Harbor). The terrain and the kind of light in the jungles of Guadalcanal and other tropical battle areas called for the kind of camera work of which most Service crews are not yet capable, and much of the fighting in such areas is at night. Modern warfare is immensely difficult to photograph because air battles are too fast and cover too much distance during their course for a camera to hold in focus, and in engagements of tanks and infantry there seems little for the camera to get hold of. Cameramen, while allowed to take reels and reels of soldiers eating and tanks disembarking, are frequently barred from the battle zones. Such reasons as these would seem to explain a good deal.

The main historical value of "At the Front" will be the officially posed pictures of Gens. Mark Clark, Cunningham and Anderson with Darlan and our own Pétain man, Robert Murphy. The view of the terrain our men are fighting in is interesting, since it definitely does away with the picture of darkest Africa most of us grew up with. The narrative for the movie is excellent because there is so little of it and because of the words at the close of the battle: "This morning when the battle started this was a conquered valley in the hands of the enemy; now it is a free valley." "At the Front," like "The Battle of Midway," is in bleary technicolor, mostly hazy blue atmosphere in which details can only be approximately picked out. These only film records of our troops at war are hardly the place to use such an imprecise medium.

In addition to the physical difficulties, there is something else behind the ineptitude of films like "At the Front." This is the fact that Americans know very little of how to make movie documents. Americans who made fine ones before the war, like Flaherty, Lorenz and Strand, aren't making war documentaries, and their earlier work had no effect on Hollywood. While Hollywood in its story films depended entirely on cast-iron plots of flashy incident to get their pseudo-life and pseudo-movement, no one, not even the newsreel companies, examined human actions and behavior in detail with the motion-picture camera. Whereas Eisenstein in Russia, Ivens in Holland and Grierson and Legg in England were watching the daily life in fields, factories and coal mines with their cameras, not only in documentaries but in story films as well. So that American directors generally, without their preconceived plot to use, are unable to film actuality and get from it its meaning and emotion, a technique which can't be acquired in a day.

In Canada, in England and in Russia experienced workers are, to quote Dovzhenko, "recording the visual aspect of war completely and unflinchingly," consequently outranking the Americans. This is apparent in any Russian film. One of their most powerful jobs is one out now called "A Day of War—Russia, 1943," which was shot by 150 cameramen, some sixty of whom were

killed doing it. In every part of it there is just what American documents lack—
the pinprick in each episode that makes it something more than ordinary.

April 5, 1943

One for the Ages

THE British government's documentary, "Desert Victory," is a pleasure and an
excitement. It is a real documentary, not a newsreel assembly that jumps from
one minute part of one event to another minute part of another event until two
reels are over. "Desert Victory," in fact, puts you inside the North African campaign where it was last October, and allows you to see it as it progresses, from
the beginning to the end. At the start the British Eighth Army was barely
holding a thirty-mile front between the Quattara depression and the sea, and
at the end British tanks are passing, thirteen weeks later and 1,300 miles further west, through the gates of Tripoli.

This is the first time a movie has been the original source for the clearest
account of an event. The film-makers of the British government were obviously as well prepared for the attack that came in the night of October 23 as
was the Eighth Army under Montgomery. The photographing of this attack is
so successful that the soldiers come as close to being movie players, without
being, as is possible—this while clawing their way forward through barbed
wire, or fishing anti-tank mines out of the sand, or as their bagpiper plays while
walking with the Highlanders, stiff-legged and sweating, through their own
land mines. Seconds before the signal for attack is given the screen goes bare
and silent, and then explodes in your face as British artillery laid down the barrage that shook buildings outside of Alexandria, sixty miles away. So that here,
for the first time, is a sustained record on film of an attack, as it was being
made—the entire scope of Montgomery's plan is studied as it unfolds. Incredible photography was almost underfoot of the advancing Highlanders, up
ahead clearing the way with the heroic sappers, with the air force that was
strewing the desert with Axis wreckage. There was even a photographer to run
around with the dour, angular-faced Montgomery. Everywhere the event is
examined with the completest curiosity of which the camera is capable (from
Rommel's viewpoint as well).

"Desert Victory" contains the two great ingredients of the English movie
tradition: slow, lucid, beautifully modulated photography, and nearly perfect
film editing. The photography sees the outside world of texture and light

values in the same way as the human eye, leaving the business of drama and working up of emotions to the content of the event itself. (The opposite of this method, of course, is that of Orson Welles, whose camera is used to fix mood artificially.) While English photography seeks the clarity of the eye, English editing tries to follow the demands of human instinct, that is, to approach the heart of an event and to stay with it as long as one's curiosity holds out. This technique, as applied in "Desert Victory," is in contrast to the flickering, choppy aspect of the Russian war documentaries, where the heavy hand of moral and purpose is always teaching you your lesson—this scene is to show that the Nazis destroy art, that one that the Russian pianist raises morale, the other that Russian women work in coal mines, etc., and never is the continuity controlled by the unpredictable progress of the event but by a program of secondary meanings. This is not in any way to condemn the brilliant work the Russians are doing in covering their war, but only to say that emotion and interest in a film have more chance of taking hold when the event is shown at such length that it can speak for itself.

The longest chase in history, that of Rommel from El Alamein to Tripoli, is in the film sketchily, mostly signposts and a touch at each stop—Tobruk, Bengazi, El Agheila—to watch the crowds lining the street as the British go through. But the main purpose of the film has already been accomplished, to a thorough degree, and that rare thing, a perfect movie, has been made. Col. David McDonald, of the Army Film and Photographic Unit, directed twenty-six men in making "Desert Victory"; four were killed, six wounded, seven captured. It is a fact that Tobruk was actually taken by the British film unit, which arrived some hours in advance of the fighting forces.

April 12, 1943

The Trouble with Movies

THE trouble with the movies is that they so seldom get below the surface of a story and its characters, that their whole is rarely as good as the parts, and the characters of their players—Gary Cooper or Margaret Sullavan, for instance—are usually more powerful than the characters they play. The movies don't have any Tom Joneses, Raskolnikovs or Natashas. What you remember about Sergeant York is Gary Cooper. Script writing has been rare that could make the whole equal to its good parts, as were "Alice Adams," "Wuthering Heights" and "The Lady Vanishes." The reason I mention this now—it being always true—is that I have seen four movies in the last week dealing with the resistance to Nazism in the conquered countries, none of which came anywhere near to revealing the nature of such resistance.

They missed the point because they were governed by the traditional attitude of characters subordinated to plot. There are three fundamentals of a traditional movie plot: it is composed of spectacular events, the spectacular part is all that's shown of the event, the events run on one level only, and in one direction as far as time is concerned (the flashback is a beginning toward breaking down this attitude, but it too has become stylized).

It is the use of the literary writer's technique of storytelling (rather than a technique developed especially for movies) which results in scripts that miss the essential fact that the camera medium is enormously fluid: having a voice, eyes and legs, it is more fluid than any other medium. Like the mind, it is physically unbounded and can paint; the least thing mentally ill Charlotte did in "Now, Voyager" was to suffer the symptoms of mental illness; the least thing first baseman Lou Gehrig did in "Pride of the Yankees" was to play first base. Necessarily, when so little real character is written into their roles, the actual personalities of Sanders, Davis and Cooper must make up the difference.

"Shadow of a Doubt" is an example of what the movies might do in breaking with the idea that the story is more important than the movie. It was not the *plot* that Hitchcock projected, it was the sense of doubt seeping through a certain number of people. He was solely concerned with their behavior and effect on one another as shown by their actions within this doubt. Hitchcock has stopped being dictated to by the necessities of a plot, as he was in "Foreign Correspondent," and is filling his movies with what he is really interested in, and what is interesting to an audience—the use of the camera to tell more about people and a situation than that a muddle arose and was straightened out at the end.

April 19, 1943

Writers as Producers

"This Land Is Mine" is a good example of a writer's movie (Dudley Nichols) and of a trend—the graduation of the better Hollywood script writers from typewriters into producers' chairs. Some other writers who now have full say over what they have written are Nunnally Johnson ("The Pied Piper"), Albert Lewin ("Moon and Sixpence") and Michael Powell ("One of Our Aircraft Is

Missing"). According to Leo Rosten's survey of Hollywood, that control is what they wanted most. The evidence of their work so far points to movies of a greater seriousness in intention, more social comment and a clearer, less gingerbread form. But this type of movie has also shown serious lacks. "This Land Is Mine" hasn't any romantic chases, or love affairs—the one chase ends in the hero's death, the two love affairs are minute and unresolved—and there are no jokes. Its plot concerns the regeneration of a cowardly schoolteacher in an occupied country. It is a tribute to the movie that there is nothing silly about it as it does what it sets out to do: instruct our schoolteachers in their spiritual task during wartime; condemn overzealous mothers who hoard milk; show the grocer, the mayor and the station master the price they pay for collaboration with the Nazis. One of its best passages is an ironical scene showing the entrance of the Nazis into the city against and around a monument to the Unknown Soldier in the city square. It is concise and well thought out, and the differences between the Nazi and democratic ideology are completely discernible.

But all of these first writer-produced movies have propelled their ideas out of the intellectual idiom of the writer rather than the visual one of the movies; so that in spite of their wisdom, lack of sentimentality, straightforward, formal clarity, they have been, as yet, unemotional and powerless. Most simply, it is a matter of attitude toward a story, of telling rather than showing it. The ideology of the free peoples is expressed in "This Land Is Mine" by giving the schoolteachers the Bill of Rights to read to their classes, which they do, from the first article through the last. The character of the resistance as it affects the middle-class shopkeeper is one in a long, wearisome speech from a witness stand. Essentially the method's weakness is in straitjacketing behavior to the written word instead of seeking the idea in the visual world of action and movement, which is the more suitable, and so more emotionally vital, manner for the movies.

There is a pseudo quality pervading the city in this movie where the people are regulated neatly and logically and mechanically. The character of the resistance cannot be that simple, to judge from the scraps of information that seep through to us from such places. The people of Czecho-Slovakia, France and Holland are starved and terrorized, and what they accomplish must happen quickly, with little time to show a change of heart or to explain motives to the whole populace. A Quisling is poisoned or an Underground hero is blown to bits, with little of the ordered logic, the individualistic momentousness, that attaches to each event and person in this movie. To this extent it reads more like a commendable textbook in civics than a movie, and misses the life in occupied countries, its tragedies, accidents, unknown deaths, complete horror.

The picture just about hits the jackpot as far as miscasting goes. Since the author implies no definite country or people, no dialect or national custom, the cast becomes pretty much a hodgepodge of unmatched actors, who also suffer from the superficialities that go with all talk and no play. Charles Laughton seems to be unable to do anything at all with his role of schoolteacher.

These writer-produced movies have without exception been commendable jobs. They are the necessary wedge of integrity and earnestness which must first break through the wall of Hays Office and producers before there will be the freedom which is essential to artistic expression, in the movies as well as anywhere else. And they are bound to reexamine their movie-making methods when they find that their good works are coming forth somewhat stolid and unemotional.

April 26, 1943

The Nazis Again

Fʀɪᴛᴢ Lᴀɴɢ's "Hangmen Also Die," which is as badly named as most movies, is a grim, awkward film having to do with the murder of Reinhard Heydrich, the Reichs-protector of Czecho-Slovakia, and the failure of the Nazis either to capture the murderer or to break the spirit of the Czech people. The movie fails to do for Czecho-Slovakia what other occupation films have failed to do for Holland, France or Norway (twice), and that is, capture the spirit of the Czechs. Like all the others, it didn't even try. It is a Hitchcock man-trying-to-get-away-from-the-police plot, but unlike Hitchcock, it has no suavity, suspense or fluidity. Most of its success comes from the complete hate with which it goes after its Nazis, drawing each portrait in thick black line. Heydrich the Hangman flounces around with his wooden hatchet face lipsticked clumsily enough to make sure you get the idea, the other Nazis squeeze pimples, crack their knuckles and slobber over fat sausages or fat prostitutes.

The style used here is the healthy one of the silent movie days, when you had to prove visually the evilness of the villain. So the savagery is more grueling than in other propaganda films: victims are smothered under coal piles, killed in groups, kicked to death. By far its most successful scene is the one in which the heroine is set upon by a mob of Czechs, who have been told she is an informer. Here, if nowhere else, the fierce, unalterable nature of mass resistance to the Nazis is allowed to develop within the scene, and the emotion of the crowd played against the terror of the girl works up to something real.

The plot's windings are endless and sometimes fantastic. Much of the playing is beginner's stuff. The lighting is awful. The dialogue contains such clumsy "German" as "Stay right where you are or you get a slug in the guts," and such weird "Czech" as "Don't let yourself get snowed under at Valley Forge." Nowhere are human beings examined deeply enough to find the ideologies this movie is presumably about. The whole thing is as stagey as its murder of the Quisling, who manages to fall near enough to a cathedral to try to drag himself up the steps and inside while the organ plays. Also, it does seem as if not every scene need be made a device of propaganda, or if it has to be, the dialogue should be at least pronounceable and the players rehearsed in how not to sound like radio announcers.

Near the end a subplot gets going, which draws all of Prague into a plan to convict a rich Quisling beermaker—Gene Lockhart—for the Heydrich affair. The way they all gang up on Mr. Lockhart, who sobs convulsively as usual, is both funny and ingenious, and the thing in general unwinds with more vitality than the main bout. This, with the Nazi portraits and that scene between the girl and the crowd, get it in for my vote as good, in spite of all the ineptitude—but it's close.

Another occupation film out now is Warner Brothers' "Edge of Darkness," in which everything is twice as bad.

May 3, 1943

Mishmash

Now I'm ready to vote for the booby prize: I have seen "Mission to Moscow." Before the movie starts Ambassador Joseph E. Davies says, "There was so much confusion and prejudice about Russia that I felt it was my duty to tell the truth about the Soviet Union as I saw it." Any truth that has ever been told about Russia heretofore now has this obstacle to face. We didn't deserve that Mr. Davies should have met the Warner Brothers.

At no point does this truth about the Soviet Union show what communism is as an ideology, a way of living, what victory in this war would mean to it and to those of us who are allied to it. The movie can only condemn fascists because they gobble up neighboring territories and make soldiers of their children. This is a peculiar picture, because it makes no effort to have you understand the things it talks about. Its two revelations about Russian communism are that Soviet women use cosmetics and that Soviet workers get paid extra for extra work—hurrah for the Revolution! Nowhere do you get any idea of Russians who refuse to be conquered either by Hitler or by purges, and one of the most ingenious oddities of the film is that it can make one-sixth of the earth's surface seem like a cranny at Warner Brothers'. Not one character emerges. The faces are expensive, finicky duplicates of famous faces and still not any good (not nearly so good as Madame Tussaud's). The only character who comes off at all is Oscar Homolka's Litvinov, and that as potently as a characterization of Babe Ruth would if it barely got across the idea that he played baseball. The ideas the characters mouth are banal, unlikely and crude.

There are many interpretations, right, left and indifferent, as of the period of 1937–38 in Russia, which were two years of the purges and the Moscow trials. It's indicative of this movie that for the history of the period it makes up its own facts. For instance, "Mission to Moscow" says that on his way to Russia for the first time Mr. Davies presented Roosevelt's disarmament plan to Schacht, whereas this actually took place much later. It crams what were four main trials into one trial at which there is the preposterous spectacle of Radek, Bukharin, Yagoda and Tukhachevsky confessing cheek by jowl. The illusion created is that the bloodiest purge in the history of man consisted of one trial at which sixteen men were convicted. It has Krestinsky, at the trial of Radek and Pvatakov, accused as their go-between with Trotsky, replacing the actually accused Romm, possibly because Davies interceded in Romm's behalf—take it easy, Mr. Dewey. So you have the police chief (Yagoda) being convicted at the trial for which he had produced the evidence; the general (Tukhachevsky) who was arrested, tried secretly and shot within forty-eight hours, telling the world and Mr. Davies about his crimes; and the main thing all of these men were tried for—the assassination of Kirov—not mentioned. The movie's reason for all this distortion is to prove that the trials, terror and bloodletting were entirely a fifth-column plot among Trotskyites, Germany and Japan: Davies wrote in his book in 1941, "None of us in Russia in 1937–38 were thinking in terms of fifth-column activities. All of us paid comparatively little attention to that side of these cases."

Mr. Davies' book was a stale, innocuous melange of the fewest and most obvious facts that Soviet interpreters, left, right and center, had been reporting on Russia for years. Its perceptions were on a level with a Fitzgerald travelogue: everyone was "attractive and a fine type of," everything in Moscow was beautiful, old. I mention this because the movie fights continuously and always to its death to make Davies out a major-league prophet in a minor-league world. There wasn't an event of the years 1937–42 that Davies didn't predict, understand or analyze for the world, while around him everything was intrigue, doubt and confusion. It manages to do this at the same time it perpetuates the appalling caricature of "naïve American abroad." Those wonderful types of ambassadors—Lord Chilston, Shigemitsu, Coulondre, Grzybowski—that Davies found, and wrote about in his book, he finds in the movie are wasting their time at billiards and misinterpreting everything.

The movie, as a movie, is the dullest imaginable. The extent of its device is to have Davies talk or be talked to. There is a prologue five minutes long, pompous and queasy, in which the real Davies explains his motives in writing his book and authorizing the movie; the first incident of the movie itself is the identical situation, but now with the Huston-Davies explaining his motives for, etc. The mechanisms are as redundant throughout. To describe Davies' tour of Russian heavy industry, one device is used five times without break— Davies talking to a mechanic, a coal miner, an engineer, a farmer—until you expect a flashback to the October Revolution and Davies talking to Lenin (obviously like this: "Just what do you think of your chances, Mr. Lenin? I'm a capitalist myself. . . ."). President Roosevelt chats at his desk with Davies as though he were trying to make himself heard over the uproar in the Yankee Stadium. The movie is even incapable of expressing the wonder and excitement of Russian singing and dancing, something which should be about as easy as falling off a log. Perhaps worst of all is to see the Warners, in need of a Polish figure, asking themselves what Pole Americans know; that is why you will learn in "Mission to Moscow" that *Paderewsky* was the Pole to see about peace in 1938.

This mishmash is directly and firmly in the tradition of Hollywood politics. A while ago it was Red-baiting, now it is Red-praising in the same sense—ignorantly. To a democratic intelligence it is repulsive and insulting.

May 10, 1943

Let Us Now Praise Movies

In "The Oxbow Incident," which is not a horse opera, a dreadful side of human beings is portrayed in a magnificent film. It marks a break in Hollywood's ugly movie career because the people behind it—William Wellman, Lamar Trotti, Walter Van Tilburg Clark—director, producer and writer—and Henry Fonda, Frank Conroy and Henry Morgan, the players, had their say without losing a scene, a character or a line of dialogue to the Hays Office, the studio or the box office. As the work of unhampered artists, it is for the audience a thrilling experience.

The movie is an examination of an incident—the lynching of three men at The Oxbow, Nevada, in 1885. Aside from its extraordinary indictment of lynching, it shows the failure of liberal men, inspired by justice, when they are opposed by irrational and powerful men of anger. The men of the town, and one woman, were led willingly toward the hanging by an ex-soldier, Colonel Tetley, who dressed his fanaticism in his old Civil War uniform for the occasion, and brought the thing off with the aplomb of a born leader. The few who rebelled against the hanging were too weak to oppose this man's will, or too scared for their own skins—this includes the hero. The leader who fought for justice could not find the emotional key to the situation and lost every trick to Tetley for that reason.

But its soundest, most original declaration is its realistic, pedestrian view of violence, that there is nothing unusual about it in our society, that the men who participated in it did not regard it as violence. The main reason offered by the movie for the success of the lynching is that the majority of the people were either irresponsible, ignorant or moronic, the lynching a form of self-esteem, and a natural product of such characters as the film had already built. There was no hysteria. Several hours elapsed between the decision and the fulfilment, the victims were allowed to plead their case, write last letters and share a meal with their hangmen.

The introduction to this situation is an example of perfection in movie techniques of camera work and acting. Free for once to play into the character without being pushed around by unlikelihoods, Henry Fonda is magnificent in his projection of an unremarkable, bored, sexually frustrated cowboy, who has been on the range too long, analyzing a nude painting over the saloon mirror, getting drunk fast and beating someone half to death just out of mean-ness. Alongside, his buddy, Henry Morgan, creates an insensitive, moronic cowboy by a masterpiece of restrained playing.

The camera pace is slow, monosyllabic and stolid, it drills persistently into the scene, seeing the event as less important than the behavior of the people making it. Its violence is blunt and dreadful, its details beautiful to watch—details such as the exchange of smiles between the tyrannized and sickly, appalled son of Colonel Tetley and the Mexican he is forced into helping to lynch, or the scene at the end between the Colonel and his son, with the laugh which the son wrenches out of a hysterical sob. More than anything I would like to emphasize the psychological tension built out of visual movement, which is the movies' own baby. It is overpowering in such scenes as that of the Negro preacher walking toward the hostile crowd, the pace so felt that the air into which the man walks seems to be pressing him back. I tell you this is a movie.

On its way "The Oxbow Incident" destroys all kinds of puritanisms that have been strangling movies for years. The ex-soldier makes his sadism respectable by a uniform which personifies justice; a housewife—moreover, that cliché of Mother Earth, Jane "Ma" Darwell—is shown as the most extreme sadist of the crowd, and lewd in the bargain; a son is shown in wild joy when his father commits suicide; the hero is actually no hero; the Negro is treated as a human character not a side-show freak, his religion a detached mysticism. The idea it implants that the Mexican is the only man on a grand scale among the just and the unjust is the most surprising departure of all— unless it might be the fact that none of these points is hammered at you *à la* Carry Nation.

The movie is so fine that its faults are on an astonishingly high level. It chose to accent the nobility of the victims, in preference to depicting the individual reactions of the murderers. But the nobility of the lynched men is actually of no consequence so far as the morality of lynching is concerned. The main impact is frittered away in an ending which shouldn't have happened, since the audience has already felt the guilt of the deed: everything after the revelation of the men's innocence is merely slugging away at empty air; the opponent has already gone down.

It is an American legend that Hollywood cannot produce a serious work of art because of censorship, the role of the movies as the entertainer of the masses and the synthetic, mechanical quality of the medium, which esthetes say makes it incapable of personal expression. For the good of everyone, that legend can now be called extinct. "The Oxbow Incident" is a significant moment in our culture. Cheer for it and hope it will not stand alone.

May 17, 1943

Less Talk and More Mail

THE remarkable fact that the English are making better films than anyone else is the result of their movie makers' faith in the ordinary—ordinary behavior, ordinary people and small talk. It is true that the English scrape no further below the surface than other people who make movies, but they are the only ones who consistently show the surface the way it really is. Whatever they achieve in movie effects comes from their acute perception of the walk, look and manner of speech of their characters. The action of their plots is always within the possibilities of the characters they create. The first Hitchcock pictures capitalized superbly on the willingness of an audience to accept the fact that horror can be latent in an ordinary situation. In an English film the psychological factors are made visual, and to do this and keep the audience from snickering at the far-fetched, the characters and environment of the movie have to be honestly handled.

Two of their latest pictures, "Next of Kin" and "Letter from Ireland," trade on this attitude and owe their success to it. "Next of Kin" is a feature-length admonition against loose talk in wartime; "Letter from Ireland" is a twenty-minute glimpse of American soldiers in Ireland, a mild heartwarming for the folks back home.

"Next of Kin" impresses the whole weight of war on its audience by using inconsequential people and endowing them with the greatest responsibility for the prosecution of the war. A frightened soldier tells a burlesque performer where his division is training. An overworked, petulant, ordnance man bemoans the fact that so much is asked of him—for instance, that two divisions need outfitting, etc., etc. These details themselves are insignificant and unrelated, but the Germans put them together—a raid on the French coast is anticipated and half a division is lost. The important point is that these people do not realize the importance of the information they possess. The hard lesson is that a superhuman effort to be careful must be made by people who are overworked and overwrought; for the odds lie with the enemy. And the lesson is made grimly moving. The visual character of the people who count most in the picture is made depressingly real, their faces have a pinched quality, a lack of charm and humor; their deadly seriousness, combined with the knowledge of their responsibility for any number of lives far removed from them, makes you sense the extraordinary pressure under which they live.

This is purely an instruction film, but the intent is to present the case in its precise nature, no tin schoolroom form. Giving vital information is something you usually do unwittingly, and that is how this movie shows it is done. It is a small masterpiece of skillful education. It set out to turn war-poster reading into movie entertainment, and came out with a great deal more—a good picture of wartime England.

The twenty-minute letter from two American brothers stationed in Ireland to their parents could have been as distressing as one of Eddie Cantor's serious oratoricals on what you should do that people should love you. But the movie has been controlled to a sensible degree and is actually heartwarming. The idea is said to have been suggested by an actual incident, but it could have been figured out by anyone with a head on his shoulders. An officer in an artillery regiment notices that two boys haven't been getting any mail. He finds that the reason is they don't write any; so he makes them turn out some fifty pages, etc. To be exact, the boys write about Carrickfergus Castle, the printing shop of Thomas Gray and Son at Strabane, and a Catholic church in Londonderry. You don't learn much about castles, printing or the boys, and the war seems far away. But the movie achieves what it set out to achieve, a small human warmth: the dry, reticent humor of the Americans, their lack of interest in what they are visiting, their unhurried walk in an unhurried country. The effortless dialogue is the most commendable thing about it. The two heroes are Private Wally Newfield and Sergeant Don Prill, not brothers but both from Minneapolis.

May 24, 1943

Education for War

"Prelude to War," made by the government specifically to educate men in the armed forces, is an assembly of newsreel clips arranged to show the events, and some of the causes, leading up to the war. The army unit under Col. Frank Capra made the film so well that it is Capra's best film as well as the government's. Its exceptional quality only highlights the fact that no film like it came out when it could have done the most good: that is, before the war began, when the events it shows were happening. In 1939 Will Hays was striking out of movies any hint that Hitler was evil; until that year, and "Confessions of a Nazi Spy," the industry hadn't condemned fascism—if you got your news from movies you might not have known fascism existed.

The cause for the war, "Prelude" says, was Axis aggression and militarism. The film contrasts the freedoms we have in this country with the destruction of freedom in Italy, Germany and Japan, accents the regimentation of children and marriage to further the ends of militarism, and shows that the people of the Axis nations were the pawns and victims of small groups of men. The newsreels it uses to show its hatred of these men are familiar, but it is still worth seeing Mussolini mugging to sell a line of oratory two minutes after the line is spoken, or Hitler simpering in his own you-can't-do-this-to-me fashion. Its most surprising departure from earlier films of this type is its determined branding of all the Fascist leaders, saying "Remember these faces!" as it shows careful close-ups of everyone from Hess to Dietrich. It is interesting to note at this time that wherever the movie boasts of the brightest gains made by democracy, it shows a contribution of the New Deal—the FSA Housing project at Greenbelt; the amazing Grand Central Parkway in Queens built by the PWA; the CCC; the wages-and-hours bill being signed by Roosevelt.

It is a masterful job of clear, effortless story-telling from stray scraps of disconnected shots, which are put together to catch secondary meanings beyond mere news data. The finest part—a symphonic arrangement of dictators' armies marching—keeps enlarging, Bolero-like, on the grotesque sleepwalking quality of these armies, yet never loses sight of their concentrated power and breadth. The effortlessness of its story-telling is got by compressing incidents to their barest essentials, and then overlapping or double-exposing them. In this way it runs through its calendar of the war in a tenth of the time earlier films took, with more power and a pace adapted to the explosiveness of blitz warfare. Moreover, it captures to a poignant degree the particular tragedy of each conquered country. If the movie does not go very deeply into the reasons why whole nations of men and women would sacrifice individual liberty for the sake of being mothered by the state, the dissolute vacuity on the faces in the scene of Nazi mass marriages is one revealing shot.

Ease of thought and technique is a main ingredient of all Capra films. It is a little too easy here. The psychological and economic reasons for the rise of fascism are quickly and effortlessly glossed over. The hope of the United Nations is never wholly presented; the impression the movie leaves is that we fight for the survival of such freedoms as we have had—the right of Americans to continue voting, the right of the Chinese to their own country—but the dynamic kind of freedom we haven't had before, freedom and growth of people everywhere, doesn't emerge. Not that the interpretation of events is wrong, but that it is not carried far enough. The film makes the very human mistake of holding idyllic Greenbelt to be a not uncommon American neighborhood, which is as excusable as thinking of your Sunday best as your characteristic dress. In terms of the American people's ambitions, of the surface aspects of fascism, of recent history, its interpretations are accurate, intelligent and, above all, brilliantly translated into a visual language. As a limited but discerning mirror of civilization in the thirties the movie manages a rough, clumsy vitality, which makes the Hollywood versions of the same period seem bloodless and inconsequential.

May 31, 1943

The Trouble with Movies: II

Much that is wrong with the movies can be blamed on what I call the terrain —the cashier in her glass house, the difficulty of reaching one's seat, the location of the men's room, the poor quality of the candy—if something isn't done about removing such obstacles between you and the movie, television is going to be brought back.

The management gives you no satisfaction all along the line. You are made to look like a fool before you're even inside. I don't think you are supposed to know what time the feature goes on; they make it so hard. The cashier, who doubles in Information, never hears your question because she is cut off from the world on all sides by glass, and either you are forced into sign language or that right-angled stance that goes with talking up through the ticket slot. Meanwhile the attendant is prodding you—"Move along; have your money ready," and blotting out whatever the cashier feels up to telling you. This, however, is preferable to asking the attendant himself, because he knows you are going to wait a long time, and, insufferable character, he enjoys this. The theatres are showing so many movies, featurettes and trumpet players these days that it's impossible for anyone to know what is on at a particular hour—I hope you are not foolish enough to believe the newspapers. The ticket-taker has recently become another obstacle. He no longer holds out his hand for your ticket, making your passes at him seem forward.

Who builds movie theatres? If you seek the men's room you vanish practically away from this world, always in a downward direction. It is conceivable that the men's room is on its way out. At the theatre called the Rialto in New York the men's room is so far down it somehow connects with the subway: I heard a little boy, who came dashing up to his father, say, "Daddy! I saw the subway!" The father went down to see for himself. Another place that lets patrons slip through its fingers is the theatre in Greenwich Village where the men's room is outside altogether.

Then, in the gold-leafed Carlsbad Caverns type of theatre there are the stairways, sweeping up and around and down and under, and since there are no signs telling you where to go I advise you not to stir a step until you can get hold of the manager. Something should be mentioned about managers, but aside from the one who said he personally would get me a seat in the center and sent me three separate times to the left wall, I am willing not to say it. Speaking of the left wall: do they think you can see from it? You find yourself looking so far to the side you are apt to be watching your neighbor instead of the picture, and is he a sight.

What is wrong with the candy? It comes in little boxes for five cents, and there are five kinds of it. They are all the same—gum drops; this includes the caramels. I have never seen these pebblelike candies sold anywhere except in movie theatres, where there is nothing to talk back to but the machine. The distinguishing feature of these candies is that they neither chew up nor melt away but remain in your mouth long after their function is over.

It used to be, but is now no longer, a courtesy to stand up when a person wanted to get to his seat. I don't know how else you are expected to get in. The average hurdle course of spectators' knees is well nigh impregnable. "Lady, I can't get by, you don't give me enough room," is usually answered by sotto-voce imprecations out of which one phrase, something like "You're pinching my flesh, damn you," is audible. And so you go, pinching, shoving, stumbling or actually falling, as the case may be. The unsportsmanlike attitude of every-one concerned in this is absolute. You must take care not to curse back, because they will pass the word along the line to stiffen up. I have found out that if the first person arises, all accordingly rise—otherwise, they all stay put. Therefore I suggest that before you enter the row you say politely, "Pardon me?" and *wait*—on no account go forward before the first person has had time to show his colors.

If it is winter, everybody is holding his overcoat, which warns you that soon you will be getting out of your own. If you try to do this quietly and with no hysteria, you soon find yourself in danger of strangulation, and in the end you will have to stand up anyway, having cut off the circulation and nearly throttled yourself. (Note: It is impossible to get out of your coat while you are sitting on it.)

There is an increasing tendency among women to keep their hats on, arm-rest hogs have become more vicious and the people who plant their knees against the back of your chair to make it rock are riding you for a fall.

It sometimes seems to me that movie-goers do not understand very well, and have, at the same time, a brotherly urge to help one another out by ex-plaining what is happening on the screen. With those of you who do not under-stand I would like to have a word. The person in front of you is practically a nervous wreck now from having gone through the movie terrain. Every word you speak, no matter how small, how friendly, how inconsequential and of interest to no one but yourself, may be just the thing to make that person crack. So I will repeat what I have often said in the past: "Quiet, please! Shhh!"

June 7, 1943

The Sea Without Salt

"Action in the North Atlantic" (Warner Brothers) is an overdue tribute to the fighting merchant marine of this war, one of the series "in praise of a branch of the service" which is based on action and wisecracks and expresses nothing at all. The action is piled up in great layers. In a Warners' picture it becomes of supreme importance. The ship is blown up for the sight it makes and for the jazzing it gives the plot. So when one ship is blown up, six or seven follow it, and then six or seven submarines get theirs. The action is emotionless because it is without order, pace or rhythm, because the people concerned in it are so utterly alike, and characterless, and because bombs and killing cease at a certain point to concern human beings and become mere spectacles. Yet, this is one of the more efficient versions of the action-wisecrack formula. It moves right along without a hitch, the audience waits for each line of dialogue to turn up its laugh, the action is the last word in technical verisimilitude—they have learned to make like a newsreel with the photography.

There is no mood nor personality of the sea, of being on it, in it or of it. If the merchant seaman finds a kind of security off land that he doesn't find on it, if he is surly and boastful of his ability, if his living quarters on the ship are any different in feeling from those in the locker room at the Athletic Club, if the engineer differs from the mate and if either of them differs from the airmen in "Air Force" or the marines in "Wake Island" or the sailors in "Crash Dive," there is nothing in this movie to indicate it. It is lacking in character, because our war movies are plagued with a Boy-Scoutish conscientiousness that makes them hopelessly good and hopelessly bad, and eats them out of body and soul. They must answer first to God, country, American mothers, the producer, the recruiting branch of the merchant marine, people who come to see Bogart knock someone's teeth in, people who come for laughs, for action, for love, etc., and they never get a second chance to be warm, human or anything real. In deference to seamen, Bogart goes to the first saloon and blonde that he sees; but when he walks out of the bedroom door in the next scene he must, for American mothers, I suppose be married and a loving husband forever after. If the mate gripes, traditionally, about the food on board, it must be hurriedly pointed out, for the recruiting service, I suppose, that the mate may be out of sorts that morning. It hardly seems possible that Pulaski, six years an A.B., would aspire to wear a cadet's cap, but it is presumably desirable to show that seamen move up the ladder to success.

As a result of the movie's double duty of citizenship and entertainment, everybody on board gets terribly articulate. It is not the articulate felicity of workmen about the bungling of their superiors, their own facility with their work and their women, the wonders of every job but the one they're on. Nor is it the symbolical volubility of an O'Neill character. This is talking to keep you laughing, and everyone from God to a Liberty Ship happy.

The visual incuriosity of this film is amazing. The implication is that the field the camera covers is so barren that it must be artificially blown up. It is typical that the union-hall sequence is taken up entirely with Pulaski's shouting at the top of his voice that he either is or isn't a coward, and someone's tearing his union button off and putting it back on again. Here, where a completely male world runs over in poker, pool and talk, and the phrase "brotherhood of man" is inherently present to an overwhelming degree, where seamen are as serious about their card games as anyone else, the movie relies on moompitcher drayma. The inner world of a ship and the men's duties on board are confined to an occasional wheel rotating and talkative watches. Half of the visual power of any image is in the differentiated appearance of the players—such as the lean, open-faced quality that makes Henry Fonda a working stiff before the story-writer has even put pencil to paper. But "Action in the North Atlantic" is so unconcerned with character as seen, that you could reshuffle all the characters and nothing would be gained or lost. The one interest, visually, of movies of this kind is the violent-action image; they do it well, and it moves right along from one spectacle to another with that smooth-surfaced vitality which is always interesting, and which gives you everything but human beings—the loneliness, and clear joy of it, the suffering and the complete excitement of sea life.

June 14, 1943

The Expendables

THE movie "Bataan" is a skillful condensation of the original battle of Bataan Peninsula. It is Hollywood's best war film to date and, as a movie, an experience worthy of the battle itself. The film manages to capture the values of the original: the artfulness of the American-Filipino forces, who were so overpoweringly outnumbered; and their heroism which thwarted the whole weight of the Japanese Empire on a pinpoint of land, causing this empire to pour more and more men into the tiny area—to win it finally but only after hideous slaughter. What the movie does is to reproduce on a small scale the action of intensified warfare. This is done by concentrating on a makeshift American patrol covering the final retreat from the Peninsula, its duty being to blow up one bridge as fast as the enemy rebuilds it. Small, isolated groups like this one (it was composed of twelve soldiers and one sailor), hopelessly unprepared, with only their own pack animals for food, bedeviled by malaria, actually held off the enemy for many months instead of the expected few weeks.

The situations the film uses to present these thirteen expendables have a pulp-story insufficiency. Probably its most antiquated war sequence is that in which the wounded aviator uses his dynamite-laden plane to crash into the bridge. But George Murphy's enactment of this, in which there are no heroics but only a man gruesomely ill and in pain, supremely disgusted with the pain and the world that caused it, makes this sequence anything but silly. And the whole preparation for this flight, which is so marvelously played and cut, gives it a humanity far from the cliché it could have been. The corny conflict of the two old enemies, Robert Taylor and Lloyd Nolan, reunited on the battlefield, is made digestible by the admission that a man—Nolan—can hate most things and most people and still not apologize. Hollywood romanticism gets out of hand ultimately, in the last half-hour, with Pickett's charges of Japanese and the inevitable dying off of the patrol, which leaves Sgt. Bill Dane (Taylor) alone, pouring bullets into the oncoming enemy while standing in a grave marked with his own cross. But the success of the movie has already been established, and for keeps. Inside the grotesque pockets of the plot is an emotional honesty got by Tay Garnett's direction and the good human quality of the playing.

Technically, "Bataan" is that rare American movie which watches an event patiently from moment to moment and from all sides. Of a tree-climbing episode the vital part is the craftsmanship of the climbing and an onlooking soldier's wonder at it, making the result what it should be—the climax of an action. The psychology of the director is best evidenced by his care in showing the route through the jungle that Taylor and Nolan must take to blow up their bridge, so that when they come back, under attack, the audience knows every painful turn of the course and suffers with them. The accidents are brought off with the greatest sharpness—the death of the Negro, Wendell Epps (Kenneth Spencer), will throw you out of your seat, and the moments of waiting are made interminable—the one in which the men nervously hold their gunfire until the moment arrives to cover the take-off of the airplane is an intensity of acting and cutting. Major credit is due Robert Andrews for his script, which he wrote with the camera rather than the pencil in mind, and for his dialogue, which is meaningful, original and good throughout.

For the most part the players project a definite integrity into their roles; the faults are all minor—the cornet-playing sailor is a caricature, and like the hep-cat Mexican, is embarrassing. The new Negro player, Kenneth Spencer, creates a figure of soft nobility and a great deal of presence. Lloyd Nolan, who has been knocking around B pictures for years (because by Hollywood's standards he is not handsome enough for hero parts and not ugly enough for character roles), gets back with a vengeance. He twiddles his thumbs distractedly, pantomimes impatience, disgust and obscenities, and produces a trombonish Brooklynese for the ugly surliness of his romantic Mister Boins. Robert Taylor offsets his collar-ad handsomeness with poise and sincerity.

"Bataan" is a picture I like, and recommend as intelligent, where human emotions were, for once, considered appropriate material for the screen.

June 21, 1943

Columbia Cooler

COLUMBIA Studio's freshener, which annually features Jean Arthur, wholesome comedy and a part of the American scene, is this summer called "The More the Merrier," and is getting frayed at the edges. This product is like an air-conditioner, in that on the hottest day of the year it is better than no conditioner at all. There is a certain foolproof quality about it: each line produces some kind of smile, even if it takes all the smart dialogue writers in Hollywood; the people who play in it are invigorating, and all fitted out to look their handsomest. There is nothing in this formula that is vulgar or unnecessarily trite.

"The More the Merrier" takes place in Washington, D. C., but utilizes few of the farcical possibilities of living there. As a patriotic gesture, Miss Arthur, formerly of the Office of Facts and Figures, rents half her apartment to a housing man, Charles Coburn, who rents half of his half to a propellor man, Joel McCrea, for six dollars. Mr. Coburn does this because, aside from being a millionaire who wants factory workers' houses built closer to factories and a man who says, "Damn the torpedoes—full speed ahead!" over and over again, he is a Cupid.

Anyone who has lived in Washington can tell you it is a joke on the human race (where government buildings are of a hugeness beyond comprehension, like the nebulae; where one stenographer is known to have moved twenty-three times in six weeks in a mistaken search for privacy; where millions enter the city daily, and the city, to accommodate them, has the millions already there move over a little bit—it is beyond the worst anxiety dream of a sardine before reaching its can). In deference to this exaggerated place of habitation, a comedy about it should have been a huge, frenzied belly laugh: but "The More the Merrier" is little more than a smile and much too light treading.

The movie cuts along quickly, at its best, when it is directly concerned with its scene. The apartment Miss Arthur splits with Coburn is four-square and barren in the true Washington interpretation of the Colonial style. Inside it, Miss Arthur, more spinsterish than usual, arranges out of her background of facts and figures a schedule to get both her and Mr. Coburn out of the house by seven-thirty. This ends up, as it deserves to, with Mr. Coburn on the fire escape (newspaper picked up at 7:01 in one hand and the coffee pot, to be put on at 7:03 in the other) begging to be let in again. Next Mr. McCrea appears, with his propellor from California, some bright lines to trade with Coburn, and a nice parody of a man practising the rumba. All of this, though not boisterous, is decidedly not unfunny. After this point the picture starts running contrariwise to its title, slugging poignancy and Miss Arthur to a bad end. This new train of thought is brought on by a need to prove Miss Arthur, who marries McCrea after only two days' acquaintance, truly in love, and not promiscuous.

It is also brought on by the incompatibility of Director George Stevens' real talent with the requirements of farce. His flair is for directing people so that they come out as natural, warm, bright, middle-class Americans, whose lives have tact and poignancy and not too much laughter ("Alice Adams," "Penny Serenade"). It is shown in this picture in his concern for the small, compassionate moments such as the one in which the young man gives Miss Arthur, after she has kicked him out, the hundred-percent-all-leather-double-duty traveling bag, and her legitimate dismay, on returning from her honeymoon, to find she has forgotten to take it. Director Stevens' troubles always arise in a comedy of this sort where his compassion collides, head-on, with slapstick. This gums the last half of the picture with tendernesses that fall flat, and laughs that break wrong.

But inconclusive as "The More the Merrier" is, it has a buoyant quality; it is definitely engaging and not at all a waste of anyone's time.

June 28, 1943

The Great White Way

HOLLYWOOD's latest example of segregation, "Cabin in the Sky," is the usual religious-comic handout that is given the Negro by a white studio whose last thought is to make a movie that is actually about Negroes. This is like trying to make a Christmas tree by bringing together all the tinsel, lights and candy canes you can lay your hands on but leaving out the tree itself. "Cabin in the Sky" misses the heart of the idea, although it is played solidly by Negroes, and has all the guaranteed (by white men) Negro-folk fixtures from Heaven and Hell walking around in pants to Hall Johnson Choir music. There is going to be no movie made about the Negro until one is made about him in relation to the rest of the country of which he composes ten percent. His blues, dress, his whole attitude, do not exist in a vacuum but have meaning only as they are seen inside the society that made them.

"Cabin in the Sky" first cuts itself off from everything white and then constructs a niggertown—out of jimcrack architecture, stage grass and magnolia trees—to look like Paradise. In this state of unreality the only course is to fill the movie with God's messengers and make the struggle one between Heaven and Hell for the hero's soul. In the midst of this, the story line is no different from the more superficial movies made about white people. The wife loses her husband to the charmer and wins him back again, the approach being from the snickering, genteel side of sex. The characters are merely tags marked "Gambler," "Temptress," "Wife," which is what you have left after you have stripped the character of all emotions and qualities that would arouse comparison, perplexity, feelings of inferiority or admiration in a white audience. The preacher in this movie is just about what the Tuesday-afternoon bridge club would like for a Negro preacher—a broad-shouldered, clean-cut young man with perfect manners, clothes, and a suitably unprofound religion, a man who is not too much a Negro because he has all the manners of a white man. Compare him with the Negro in "The Oxbow Incident," whose presence bespeaks a life that has endured much hatred and violence, and whose religion, by forgiving everything, has become a mysticism beyond the understanding of the townspeople. Moreover, the visual quality of this man has a roughness, irregularity and unprettiness that I have seen achieved so well and in the same spirit by two Negro painters, Horace Pippin and Jacob Lawrence.

Hollywood, in its position of greatest public influencer, solidifies racial prejudice to an enormous degree by its "Cabins in the Sky," which are an insidious way of showing the Negro his place. The all-Negro film is no less Jim Crow than a bus where whites sit in front and Negroes in back, because the film is owned, operated and directed by whites, even to the song writers. (The story that is always going to be written by Duke Ellington is always tripped up somewhere and never gets written.) On the surface a whitewash, but really a stab in the back, these religio-comic treatments rob the Negro of a self and a place, relieve the whites of any necessity to realize that the Negro is really a person who lives next door, goes to work on the same bus to the same factory in Detroit. (Even the place society has given him inside the noose of a lynching party is given to whites in the anti-lynching movies.) Hollywood, in sound treatments of Negroes like those in "The Oxbow Incident" and "Bataan," has shown maturity and intelligence, but it will have truly merited respect only when it brings out a movie where the central figures are Negroes living in a white majority.

The one value of all-Negro films lies in giving Negro artists an outlet for their talents. And the one value of "Cabin in the Sky" is the talent of Rochester, Lena Horne and Louis Armstrong, irrespective of anything in the movie script. Rochester gives just the right emphasis to his innocence and guilt and tops everything with his wonderful dance concocted out of a minimum of movement. Lena Horne, despite her voice, has some truly marvelous equipment and ability to use it, and Louis Armstrong, without his trumpet and song, is still at home. Their offerings are well turned decorations on something which is a stale insult, cheap, and growing daily less innocuous.

The tragic fact is that the Negro artists are in no position to bargain with Hollywood, because if they refuse to play in bad movies they only bring Hollywood closer to its goal, as shown in "Cabin in the Sky"—the complete negation of the Negro in American society. As long as Americans accept the all-Negro film, it is obvious that they can take it or leave it, and Hollywood is more than willing to leave it.

July 5, 1943

Between Two Words

"Documentary" is a word that has always been used loosely in the movie vocabulary, and since the war has brought English, Canadian and Russian documentaries to our attention, the term has been taken up and really flung around. It has got to the point where anything good in movies is called documentary. Actually, the difference between the documentary and the story film in the final esthetic evaluation is unimportant. There is not a good documentary without a story, and there is not a good story film without what is called the documentary technique. All the qualities of that technique—photography that is consistent with the nature of the subject in value, intensity and design, movement in images to parallel in rhythm the idea being expressed, the dependence on showing a story rather than telling it, people straight from everyday life in dress, talk and manner, and the environment as a living, natural part of their life—are all qualities that started in the story film and appear wherever a good movie, called documentary or otherwise, appears. While the story film over the past decade has depended more and more on superficiality and less on art, the documentary has hit a much higher average in quality, a fact which may be responsible for the wide gulf imagined between the two kinds of film. But either the documentary or the story film, to be any good, will express the essential nature of the subject, which is human life in one form or another. Whether the start is from actuality or from the imagination, there is only one way to photograph a mail box, and that is the best way in terms of the desired end, and there is only one way to show an idea or a story in the movies, and that is also the best way. As soon as either kind of film means to be art, the distinction between them becomes very unimportant.

Two short movies (not equally, but both called, documentary) sent to this country by the British government, "World of Plenty" and "Silent Village," are of good quality, but on the thin side emotionally. Made with the coöperation of the Czecho-Slovakian Ministry of Foreign Affairs, the South Wales Miners' Federation and the people of the Swansea and Dulais Valleys, "Silent Village" reënacts the martyrdom of Lidice, using the people and civilization of the town of Cwmgiedd, South Wales, as the medium. With the neatness and dispatch of "The 39 Steps," most of the story is left to your imagination and previous experience, the movie merely giving you the necessary directives. A prohibitive order over the loudspeaker by a raucous voice implies that the Nazis have come (repeated symbolically by the village brook, which had been running quietly in traditional brooklike manner, but now churns violently and noisily). The failure of that order to change the expression of the bleak, uncommunicative face of a Welsh washerwoman, shows a stony determination to resist any tampering with the traditional Welsh life. It is a lyric, satisfactory business for its twenty-five-minute length, and as a memorial to the people of Lidice, it has a fitting love and dignity.

"World of Plenty" is commendably composed out of newsreels, maps and advice from statesmen, farmers, doctors and housewives, to show that the right control of the production, distribution and consumption of food is helping us to win the war and will lead us to a world of plenty unlike anything we have had. It uses all the film lying around from pre-war years that showed starvation in this country, India and Britain, while food surpluses were dumped into the sea. Invariably there is not enough of this shown for the audiences to be left with any kind of guilt. For the edification of American audiences, there is plenty of room given to the beauties of Britain's point rationing, the level of health the English are sustaining, blitz or no, and a great pat on the back for us for our help.

"World of Plenty" is on the lecture side of movie-making. It is as diligent, clear and all-inclusive as a schoolteacher, and as stiff, prim, dry and long-winded. Like a very neat but complex outline, it tends toward big A, little a, and 1, 2, 3, 4, rather than people, happy or sad, starved or stuffed. None the less there is a good deal of quiet humor in the selection and direction of people who talk to you as well as in the dialogue of the late Eric Knight, especially in one bit where a question is popped abruptly at a housewife as she is walking to the store: "I say! You did give me a fright!" she says. The graphs and maps are accompanied by an African drum played by a Gene Krupa fan—how this combination was arrived at I don't know, but it is certainly entertaining. The movie pounds home the four freedoms, when that conception is embarrassingly and noticeably absent from our own films.

July 12, 1943

Tinkle

DOING nothing that would disturb a Fascist, the Hays Office or the State Department, and doing what is left listlessly and ineffectually, "For Whom the Bell Tolls" will ring nothing but the box-office register, and may not ring that. There is nowhere in it the slightest attempt to justify or explain why a school teacher from Montana was blowing up a bridge in Spain in 1937, with the help of Spanish guerrillas, or why the Loyalists were fighting the Rebels, what the Loyalists stood for or what their enemies stood for, what Robert Jordan stood for, or Pablo or Pilar. After this failing, it fails to project any feeling of love— and the love between Maria and Jordan is half of the movie's physical content. Nor is there any greatness of scene: the environment of mountains and snow country seems if anything to make the thing more phlegmatic. And finally the characterization is smudged, almost inconsequential. The movie is full only of badly made-up and costumed character actors from the world over, brought together into one room without any key to their relationships, so that the inside of the main setting, a cave, is too much like a café and too little like a place that a half-dozen people have inhabited. The talk between people seems too loud, or too fast, or too florid; everything jerks slam-bang, comes and goes abruptly, without order. The most amazing fact is that the hero, Gary Cooper, is not in the picture, not a character at all, but someone standing outside the story watching it.

Yet it was a film which above all others had the chance to show feelings and ideas that are alive today. The essence of its theme is the fight against fascism, the fight "for all the poor in the world, against all tyranny, for all the things that you believed and for the new world you had been educated into." And it not only had the chance, it was the chance: it was a picture that had been allotted millions of dollars, which shot an immense amount of material and used one of the most striking arrays of talent ever brought to a film.

I have never felt that a picture suffered more from the restraints and frustrations of movie-making in Hollywood—not only from censorship, which came from all quarters, but from the pressure of having to get a thing done before you felt right about it, of hurrying to make what had to be long, tedious and expensive. Add to this the astounding ballyhoo and the anxiety therefrom that pursued the picture, making it almost a public property, from the day Hemingway published it as a book. Censorship killed the theme. It is Spain, 1937, the civil war; but the movie takes no side, no one is called right or wrong (the word "Fascist" isn't even mentioned), there is the ignoble impression that these people are seriously, intently, killing one another for no discernible reason at all. Authorities on decency ruined the love story. It is almost more than one can stand to see how this love is turned into talk, into undercover manipulations of scene in an attempt to say both that Jordan and Maria slept together and that they did not.

The over-all incapability—whatever its roots outside the movie—is due inside to the ineffective showing of anything, of its heart particularly. Most of it is talk, uninspired and delivered erratically, and where the event is shown it is presented in a half-hearted way, almost unwillingly. The reason for this, I think, is that the picture fails to switch the word images of the book into completely told screen images. For instance, the battle of El Sordo and his men on the mountain top is, as a part of the movie, so little explained, so badly cut, that its place in the story is unjustified; likewise, the flashback to the guerrillas' early days is again insufficiently shown and completely useless to the film, since it not only failed to get across any great image of the first day of a revolution, but failed to explain Pablo, ostensibly its reason for being there. The situation which builds to the climax is a major one. It involves two separate events: that of Maria and Jordan making love and that of Andrés making an anxious journey to get a vital message from Jordan through enemy lines to his general—and it is done by cutting back and forth from one event to the other in the manner of "Intolerance." But in one event there is no love-making, and in the other there is no anxiety, and in the whole there is no quickness, no sparkle in editing, to carry the thing along.

I am not sure how much of the picture's peculiar lack of effect is the result of its technicolor. I myself find it difficult to take seriously a movie made in technicolor: profundity seems out of key with the carnival spirit of the color, which is always gay and bright, masklike, without substance. Nor am I sure how much of its stiffness and unmaneuverability is the product of technicolor. For a picture of Sam Wood's direction, it has a strange lack of ability to move in and out of and around a scene to get everything clear and full. It either shoots the image long or close, but never in interrelation. This is apparent in the laying of the dynamite at the bridge, which is a good thing in this movie, but too meager in documentation.

The moments that are good come out sporadically in the playing. Ingrid Bergman brings luminously to life her ecstatically satisfied love, which has a soft, blossoming loveliness, making Cooper's seem something thin, hard, almost not there. Her projection of Maria's parting from Jordan is so magnificent it at last creates the extremity which such a foreshortened love affair as theirs demanded. Katina Paxinou as Pilar has some good moments, particularly in explaining the love life of an ugly woman and in expressing a knowledge of the new love between Maria and Jordan. Lilo Yarson, as Joaquin, is perfectly cast as a sensitive Spanish boy. Mikhail Rasumny gets in some hurried examples of a gypsy, and Konstantin Shayne as the Russian, Karkov, lights up everything before and after him with a studied, deliberate intensity of good acting. But in the main the playing is deviled by the anxiety to be like the character in the book without any of the necessary time to do it in: so that such things as Paxinou's deep, hard laugh, Rasumny's gleeful glances, Bergman's ecstatic smile, are so concentrated, in such heavy doses and so precipitately, as to give the effect of desperate people trying to create something, anything, before the camera turns away. Cooper is an enigma in this movie. By cutting all that Hemingway put into his mind and replacing it with nothing, they obliterated him. And unfortunately the Cooper failing is always present: the special speech, one fancy with thought and idea, comes out of his mouth with almost hysterical unreality.

So "For Whom the Bell Tolls" is a failure—perhaps Hollywood's most exasperating refusal to fulfill any of its obligations.

July 19, 1943

When the Pie Was Opened

"Stage Door Canteen" is an extravagant vaudeville-movie in which the few actors left in the world who aren't in the movies get half a chance not to murder themselves on the screen, and millions of people who aren't in big cities or the money get half a chance to see them. It is full of fine, enjoyable performances by famous stage people, a plot which is interesting in the same way a carnival freak is, and individual concerts by approximately 352 bands, including Guy Lombardo's. Clearly, about the second hour, it will remind you of those Mack Sennett automobiles into which an endless, unbelievable parade of people enter. It is, however, one of those rare times when stage actors are sufficiently taken care of by the screen—their material well prepared as movie material, the camera remembering that stage actresses are here movie actresses and must be shot in a movie way (the fact that stage actresses do a lot of talking has never been a reason that the camera must stand there and listen to them), and their acts given enough screen time to get over.

Gypsy Rose Lee steals everything without removing anything but a garter belt and derolling her stockings neatly, expertly and with one finger. It isn't burlesque, but Miss Lee projects as much rare and gracious femininity by face, timing and voice as Katharine Hepburn projects the opposite at the end of the film with the same means. Miss Lee's is the most excellently turned, buoyant and delightful movie playing I've seen this year. Equally surprising is Katharine Cornell in quite a tough spot: she is dishing out the desserts over the Canteen counter when a piquant rosebud of a soldier breaks into Romeo and Juliet and they go to it over the chocolate cream. Hers is much more grimacing and mouthing than one associates with movie playing, but it is one of those singular times on the screen when it comes off as love, sadness, desire, and not facial gymnastics called Shakespearean. Ethel Merman's is a much smaller chore, but even this she swells out into something that is the best part of joy, getting full bounty from the worst lyric of the war.

The finesse of these actresses and the way the movie uses them raises doubts as to whether the screen has explored the emotional depths to be achieved with plain acting, the voice in the foreground. The technique of movie playing lately has been toward the negative side of the physical demonstration of emotion. It is obvious from this film that stage acting, if correctly timed and integrated into the movie image, needn't come out at all theatrical and blown up as in the early days of Lionel Barrymore. There is, to take the voice only, an enormous difference between what is done by these actresses and, for instance, Gary Cooper in "For Whom the Bell Tolls." The Misses Lee,

Cornell and Ina Claire project a certain emotional state, while Cooper's natural speaking of lines, if not properly directed, denudes situations of their particular meaning. I am making not a plea for theatricals but for a retreat from the path of barrenness the movies are increasingly pursuing. If the spoken word need not necessarily be fruity, it might at least get clear of the state it has been put in by the Lamour contingent.

Another thing that is clear from this movie is that the jazz band will replace the movie player and the jazz singer the jazz band. Perhaps it is a conspiracy to swell the sales of aspirin.

Tossed in with the abandon of Diamond Jim Brady is a plot. Several unpleasant people have been gathered together to impersonate several unpleasant characters around the theme that a soldier won't get past the porters in New York without being hooked by a Canteen girl. What happens is that the movie, with lots of boys and girls, unable to be free and easy sexually and still wanting sex to be its theme, falls way over on the most unpleasant side of sex— the tongue hanging out, straining after, grasping for the kind of love which never reaches its goal. If this technique were used for a theme that was actually concerned with sexual teasing it would be perfect, but here it leads to such distorted idiocies as the boy writing the girl who gave him one very small kiss, "You made a man out of me."

The picture offers a number of suggestions for round-table discussions, such as why a good war song has such a powerful effect on the screen in spite of almost any degree of terrible accompaniment in acting. Also, if producers feel that audiences won't take Menuhin whole, why do they have him at all (he is here to play "The Flight of the Bumble Bee")? And is there such a thing as an average type of person from a section, state or city, and must the movies, to establish this, go on calling such a person "Kansas," "Dakota" or "Jersey"?

Whatever you want to see, in this movie you'll see it.

July 26, 1943

The Production Line

W HEN several newspaper critics in New York were hard put to find something good about the movie "For Whom the Bell Tolls" they dug up *production* and called it fine. Production to them means any technical element that remains after discussing the subject matter, acting, directing and editing, and it is something on which they feel their readers should concede Hollywood's excellence. The critics' belief that Hollywood has production all wrapped up and put away is based on the infinite money, pains and time Hollywood spends on a movie production, the infinite money, pains and time it spends telling the public how much it has spent, and the knowledge that Hollywood production techniques have changed little since the late twenties, and that therefore what has become a standard technique must be either a good one or a bad one. They would rather think it is a good one. They feel it is a minor item to be taken for granted the way you take a paint job on a new automobile. It is obvious from the rigidity of production that they and Hollywood's producers have one standard for production goodness: actual-looking sets furnished with actual-looking furniture, costumes that seem accurate as to time and place, photography which is not cracked or blurred and which centers properly on the players' faces, and sound which does credit to American mechanics. This, what they feel is excellence, is actually the lowest mean requirement of a movie, like the lumber you haul up to the building site. It is what can be accomplished in a movie without recourse to the mind or the sensibilities, and it has neither significance nor merit until the moment arrives at which it is integrated with the movie idea. Hollywood stops too often before this moment is reached and consequently too often its production is not excellent at all but inferior.

The main thing about Hollywood production is that Hollywood no longer uses photography to any advantage. Its photography is characterized by a tone of watery gray, by an abuse of artificial lighting and by the paltriness of its detail. This puts it in exactly the opposite state from that in which its founding fathers—Griffith, Sennett, von Stroheim, Chaplin—left it. It no longer has any particularity of person, place and thing. Particularity (the personality of a given image) is a matter of texture, detail and warm and cool tones. The gray monotone has distilled all the warm tones from the image, the all-over glossiness has negated textural differences, and the theatrical lighting which producers have substituted for natural lighting either blacks out too much of the detail or splatters too many highlights over it so that light is divorced from form and a pattern or embroidery of light is placed in front of the detail, removing its character. This photography is banal compared to the work of the early days. Today the main effect is one of pretense or shallow sophistication; the Chaplins and Sennetts were beholden to the power of the scene around them and believed with idolizing patience that the camera's creative function was to integrate that power with their picture's story.

Modern movies approach nature and human affairs with the same insecurity as the merchandiser who gives you two pairs of pants for the price of one. The producer must add ten more shadows to each forest glade, three more crags to each mountain, five more turns to each road, yards more chromium to each interior. Thus, a picture like "For Whom the Bell Tolls" approaches a scene loaded; there is not one iota of wanting to understand it and use it significantly, the feeling that comes first, before it can be sifted, selected and clarified for art. Instead, "For Whom the Bell Tolls" has the single purpose of making nature a wow, and you get such a fantastically cheap scene as the one in which Pilar and Jordan pose amid falling snow, a scene false and meaningless, utterly without reference to anything.

At the bottom of most production errors is an underestimation of the camera eye and its ability to make apparent the slightest value, texture or form, combined with a grandiose attitude toward make-up, sets and costuming. "For Whom the Bell Tolls" may serve as evidence of what this leads to. Here was pulled the characteristic trick of advertising character actors as character actors by covering their faces with so many age lines, chin whiskers and skin shadings that whatever relation the actors might have held to the movie idea is destroyed in the beginning. So much did the director relish the whites of eyes against a leathery face that Pablo and Pilar were like nothing so much as oncoming automobiles at night. How much of the personality of Bergman's Maria was diluted by leaving her clipped hair long enough to be beautiful by Hollywood standards is an interesting speculation. And the velvet quality of her skin and the whiteness of her teeth were so accented as to take your mind completely off the after-effect of mass rape on her, and off the action of the moment, be it love or talk called love, and to make you think instead of candy and Sunbonnet Sue. Equally, the dress of the guerrillas is accurate in detail, but the effect of each detail on the whole is disregarded and there is no arrival at the idea of "guerrilla," but only at a certain kind of costume.

The goal of production, in costume, sets, make-up, is the creation of a scene out of which the story and character drama will directly emerge. The coal-mining environment of "The Hard Way" poetically expressed the lives of the characters, and whatever they wore, whatever they moved in, was added up to a single movie idea. The environment of "The Stars Look Down" seemed the main determinant of its people's look and soul. One recalls Emlyn Williams sprawled on the low roof of a dwelling, where he, his clothes, the way he wore them, the dreary smallness of the dwelling, were a unit expressing the idea which each of them aimed at alone. It is a curious fact that Hollywood is very often done with environment after the first few moments of the picture;

after you have spiraled up from the street, up the side of the skyscraper, into the big shot's office and on to the face of his secretary, you have left environment for good.

August 2, 1943

Method in Its Badness

THE interesting fact about "Mr. Lucky," a movie worthlessly concerned with a gambler and his war problems, is that it is as creative technically as it is uncreative in all other ways—intellectually, morally and emotionally. Its unacademic approach to its disgusting story, like hitching Count Fleet to a garbage truck, does not, on the whole, lead to much. Besides the vulgarity of its story, there is a wanton trading on the talents of its star, Cary Grant, and since the technique is only grafted on to the first part of the picture, the total effect is of a bad movie. But there are some things about this technique that can be called exciting and important.

Mainly the technique takes advantage of geography—the position of a person in relation to his environment and the people occupying it with him—using distorted photography, sound and acting, and some symbolism. This produces an intrinsically cinematic form, and a three-dimensional one. For instance, when the gambler (Grant) gets entangled with the ladies and bankroll of War Relief, Inc., the entangling is a combination of architecture, pantomime and movie devices used with almost acrobatic invention, which is quite a different thing from just making speeches about entanglement. The partitions of War Relief, Inc., being of glass, you see the people talking behind them; when a door opens their voices come on the sound track, a key word or sentence is heard, disappearing with the shutting of the door; the ladies' old-hennish tendencies are shown by looking at them through the partitions as their gestures and mouthings are stylistically exaggerated. Handled like this, a situation uses all the components of a fluid medium, and the effect is a real movie one, neither theatrical nor literary.

The best and funniest things, like some business with knitting, take place inside these useful partitions, but the most interesting spots are where the action and the means of showing it are distorted not only to carry on the story but at the same time to comment on it. When Grant first makes his appearance, his walk, whistling and finger-flipping are all stepped up to the tempo of exaggeration, while the scene is shot at such an angle as to show him really cutting a swath through his world; so that we have Grant getting from one place to another and a caricature of him as Joe the Greek as well. Later there is a scene on a bench, Joe at one end, his girl at the other, with people between them. As the two of them talk, the people's heads turn back and forth rhythmically from one voice and face to the other, and while the story is carried in their dialogue, the silliness of the moving heads gets an effect of kidding the story, Joe, the girl and the people. Much of the interpretation is made with acting that is a caricature of itself (in the case of the two leads badly so, the trouble being that the smiles and eyeing extend past the idea), and with George Barnes's camera work. The latter is as good as a fine, distorted view of Grant against his slot machines, or the distortion of props and atmosphere around Charles Bickford to express, symbolically, the switchback in time from him to the story he is narrating. It is as bad, too, as a horrible moment in a cathedral when Joe kneels to pray and the lighting on his face, to show he is turning over a new leaf, changes four times.

It is possible that the awfulness of the story is what drove the producers into the rashness of using a fancy method, and at that a method which is something a movie maker can get his teeth into. In "Mr. Lucky," although H. C. Potter, the director, must have had fun, this technique fails, being wrapped around the first half of something that is very cheap, a movie which uses war and the Greeks as glibly as a socially acceptable solution to its glib story of a gambler.

There is some very nice supporting work from Florence Bates, Charles Bickford (a welcome return), Gladys Cooper and Vladimir Sokoloff, as you would expect from any of them, and a promising performance from the vaudeville mimic, Alan Carney, as Joe's henchman, wonderfully named Crunk. Also, Hollywood has a discerning ability to hunt out the best of Tin Pan Alley that has been buried under the years to use for its ballroom scenes or incidental music: here it digs out "Something to Remember You By," which is a valuable service. Admirers of Cary Grant will be shocked; but after they have hardened themselves against the indecent exploitation of him, they will at least find "Mr. Lucky" interesting, like a bad salad with an intelligent dressing.

August 9, 1943

Tessa's Last Stand?

THE defense, in the latest form of "The Constant Nymph," of composers and nymphs against philistines (or, Margaret Kennedy's idea of the opposite of the English gentry against her idea of the English gentry) has been very nearly slugged to death by delirious earnestness. Once more we are at that romantic Alpine chalet where the great composer Sanger is going to seed and his blonde, horsey daughters are carrying on the Sanger tradition of spirit that cannot be quenched. The Warner Brothers have attacked the idea literally, in flying-wedge formation. To express the wild freedom of the Sanger personality, the daughters scurry around, ever constant, in a heavy lope (for instance, Tessa wakes her sister by grabbing her by the ankle and flinging her halfway across the room). To express Sanger's musical turn the fruity music is approached with a fearsome solemnity that comes from knowing music is dissonance when it doesn't have melody and full of genius when it does. Miss Joan Fontaine has missed being the nymph by littering her portrait with all the standard nymphisms—the spread-legged squats and stances, the fiddling with the skirt, the walking on tiptoe, arms outstretched, the constant look in the eyes as of hearing far-off birdsong—all that goes with an unrestrained love of acting. Director Goulding has not cautioned her at all, and has weighted the role even more by advertising every flurry with special gauzed lighting to imply purity.

"The Constant Nymph" has, in all of its four previous versions as movie or play, been a plot which after much detailed maneuvering accomplished the fact that a young girl who had loved a composer since childhood died of a valvular lesion just as he was coming around. Warner Brothers have added several more overloud conclusions to it, thereby stepping it up to an event-a-minute clip, meanwhile deleting much good criticism of English manners and musicians' personalities.

In Hollywood this kind of movie is called an "art picture." The term, like some other words Hollywood uses, for instance, montage, is closer to meaning fancy than to what it usually means. Art pictures are usually taken from a novel or play which has been stamped heavily on the public's mind as an impressive creation, and in them the current queen or near-queen of the films is given every right of way to prove her claim to the movie-acting championship. The main characteristic, though, is that the production is given an expensive and flamboyantly artistic setting. In "The Constant Nymph" this takes the form of fancy lighting effects, a wallowing in the scenic splendors of the Tyrol, a whipping-up of wind when terror strikes, and a lot of gaudy touches like turning the highlight on an andiron into a small fire and thence into a sunset when Tessa dies. But the more exotic innovations are to weave the hero-composer's work in with his love life. When he is with his cold English wife his music lacks heart and melody; when he returns to Tessa his music becomes good and melodic. And Tessa's death, to make a supreme heart tug rather than just any old heart tug, has been speeded up to happen when she is listening to her lover's début over the radio.

The movie is best when it forgoes its lush lyrical curvings and gets down to something more substantial. The character of the composer's English wife—Alexis Smith—is undecorated in its selfishness and fears; the hate which exists between her and her husband is hard and rough, and as a result gets across as clear and vital. The satire on English manners is entertaining but standard. Miss Fontaine occasionally breaks through her mechanics, the dialogue turns up its good lines, and Charles Boyer is excellent as the composer and never looks silly while pretending to be a musician. On one occasion, with Miss Fontaine mauling the scene in the background, he does a masterful job of leading the Sanger girls' orchestra. As a whole, however, "The Constant Nymph" is rather like that chromo you've seen every time you pay your yearly visit to your elderly aunt; only on this visit you find she's taken out her water-colors and added a few strokes herself.

August 23, 1943

Seeing Zero

ONE of the things wrong with movies today is that the images movies use to show their stories are very dull, unimaginative and conventional simply as pictures. The producers and directors spend all their time figuring out a novel story idea, constructing a series of events which will adequately tell that idea, directing the players so that they won't look odd or silly, getting the dialogue to sparkle, the leading lady to look glamorous, the sets to seem real—then the thing is shot with the imagination of a cow. Either you have been inside the same room, at the same angle, with the same people a hundred times, or the amount of stuff to look at in proportion to the amount of stuff to hear is about one to six, or, finally, there is nothing put in the props, costuming or acting that will intrigue your eye enough to keep it focused on the story. The story goes along in the dialogue or by the bare resumé that is got from a related progression of events. In contrast to this, whenever memorable scenes are recalled, they are always scenes which provided images of a special nature. When Hitchcock's adventurer finds himself between the audience at a political meeting and the police, when Clair's funny-faced nature lover lies majestically on the spring grass, gazing up at a flower that then breaks into song, when Wellman's cowboys discuss the painting of a nude woman in a saloon, the pictorial content is vital and rich enough to seem the exact point of the idea.

The dismaying spread which exists between the nature of the script and the nature of the pictures used to show that script is well exemplified by Ernst Lubitsch's latest film, "Heaven Can Wait." The movie undertakes to show the more daring escapades in the life of a wolf, and while showing them, to point the moral that heaven smiles on such a life because it affords so much pleasure both to the wolf and to the ladies. Whether Lubitsch wanted it that way or not, Henry Van Cleve is a sheep in wolf's clothing. Even if you take the numerous hints that are dropped about his pursuits for their most licentious possibilities you will still feel he led a mild and familial existence. But even his small handful of escapades are shown in a blank movie way. In retrospect the most devilish thing Henry did was to go out with the family's French maid while he was still in short pants and still Dicky Moore: but all we see of this is little Henry in bed the next day with a hang-over. Midway in his happy married life his wife, Gene Tierney, leaves him because of his philandering. His philandering is shown by his wife's confronting him with a bill for an expensive bracelet which she had never seen. As descriptions of a man's love life, these meager images are about as informative as a picture of the Davis Cup would be in telling the story of the Davis Cup Matches. The remaining events on "Heaven Can Wait's" string must seem academic stuff to you—the society musicale in which a shrieking and ugly soprano is singing and being interrupted; the visit of the father to the gold digger who is milking his son and his attempt to buy her off; the hero's illness and his getting sicker with his ugly day nurse and reviving with his beautiful night nurse; the hostile man and wife at the dinner table and the table so long and cluttered they needn't look at each other and can communicate with each other by way of the waiter. Academic as all these incidents are they are made even more so by being visualized with the zest of the Dormouse. That is, to get the camera off ten or fifteen feet, to center the people square and at eye level and then watch them discourse.

Besides the stringency of Hollywood censorship, there are other reasons for the pictorial sterility of this movie or any of Hollywood's recent products. Wherever movie making approaches the efficiency, speed, and volume of the factory, its visualization is set before it reaches the shooting stage and necessarily frozen to certain conventional poses, angles and ideas. There is less creating off the cuff, fewer accidents of camera angles, lighting, movement or pantomime occur, environment is nullified, and players are made to look more and more alike. It is startling to recall the movie "Citizen Kane" and see how little effect it had on Hollywood. It was made with the one driving desire to construct each scene as a vigorous, new visual experience. Photographically and orally it was the most acrobatic American movie since Griffith, and whatever its success or lack of it in anything except method, the method itself demonstrated shatteringly the visual sterility of the standard Hollywood film.

August 30, 1943

Not So Sound as Furious

In its animated form, Major Alexander de Seversky's argument, called "Victory Through Air Power," is the least imaginative cartoon Disney has made, as well as the most naïve and brutal view of the war anyone has taken. The film's procedure is to show a sketchy, half-whimsical airplane history, emphasizing the advance we have made in two world wars in the science of demolition by airplane, after which de Seversky comes on in person (businesslike, with a good movie manner, in a streamlined office that would give any good architect nightmares) to present an illustrated lecture of his idea. The final impression is of a conglomeration of animated cartoon styles, mostly bad, which take so delighted an interest in the destructive possibilities of the airplane that they seem like the dreams of Buck Rogers' creator.

There is a disparity between the cartoon's aim, which is to sell to anyone yet unsold the idea of a great big air force, and the real effects of the salesmanship. Though the film raises certain critical objections to de Seversky's plan—as, why is it too costly to bomb Japan from the Pacific Islands, China, Russia, aircraft-carriers? (and answers them before most screen audiences will digest the answers)—it obviously doesn't raise enough such questions to give the Major a good run for his money. Audiences can wonder how long it will take to build so many Armadas of ocean-jumping Leviathans, what is to stop the Axis from building them or from inventing just as elaborate anti-aircraft devices, whether it is possible to demoralize a large city completely by air power, whether long-range bombers can defeat short-range fighters—and they will go on wondering for all the film cares. Because the film has the appearance of an educational project, it is obligated to care. In not doing so the pleasant feeling of learning something that the picture gives you is displaced by the unpleasant one of feeling propagandized. You find it is a hurdle race with only one man running, and hardly any hurdles on the track. Because all the forces operating in the war, enemy planes and operations, for instance, remain in the movie frozen at their present state, the Major's phantom airforce of the future shows to marvelous advantage—which is like someone in 1923 saying that the V8 of 1943 will beat the Model T.

Both Disney and de Seversky were carried away with the damage the airplane (of the future) could wreak. When de Seversky's dream comes true at the end of this movie, his airforce of super-bombers bristling with cannon, carrying monster loads of local-earthquake bombs, and armor-piercing rocket bombs with auxiliary charges, rend the screen with super-destruction. It is a carnival of destruction, relieved of all such imponderables as human beings, ideals and causes and effects. On de Seversky's part the overindulgence in knocking everything to pieces is merely that of a man who has an idea and wants to show it persuasively, and it is an idea he thinks will win the war. On Disney's part it arose when he undertook to illustrate the idea realistically: to equal the intensity of real life destruction his cartoonists exaggerated their explosions to a degree more appalling than any news reel. There is no reason anyone should leave this film feeling his life in any way safe from airplanes. The picture drives home the fact that, just as the automobile replaced the horse, the airplane will replace the human being.

It is true that the animated cartoon is the only medium that could pictorialize "Victory Through Air Power's" argument, which is largely still argued on the drafting board, but it is anything but malleable subject matter for Disney's art. His contribution to de Seversky's argument doesn't make a good movie nor does it come close enough to grappling with any of its ideas to be called serious.

There is an interesting job around now called "The Fallen Sparrow," which has some good acting and is not disconcerted by its jimcrack plot. The plot's motivations and conflicts are unbelievable, and the characters are unclassified bodies on which have been hung such exotic matter as tics, twisted legs or names like "Pagan" and "sadist," but the director, Richard Wallace, has taken that for granted and by doing a good job with close-ups and acting has knit the thing tightly and excitingly together. It shows, in its love affair and in the playing of its star, John Garfield, plenty of resemblance to "The Maltese Falcon." It lacks, however, the striking detail and vivid contrast in people that the "Falcon" had, and Garfield proves that Bogart's grimace in which the lips are pulled back from the teeth doesn't mellow with use. The movie has vitality and there is a fine supporting contribution by John Miljan as a very average dour detective. In the movies, one element, in this case acting, can make a picture worth your time, which may only mean that the movies are in such a state they are easily redeemed.

September 6, 1943

Parting Is Such Sweet Sorrow

"Watch on the Rhine" has arrived where all successful things one day arrive—in the movies, where it is still a good play and one of exceeding intensity. It faces its task of showing a veteran anti-Fascist's mind, as well as that of a Rumanian ne'er-do-well who took up with the Nazis, with unusual frankness and purpose, but operates in a conflict which is inadequate to bringing out a conclusive expression of the problem. A picks B's briefcase, proceeds to blackmail B with evidence of anti-Fascist activities found there and gets shot by B—but even so it achieves far more seriousness than the usual reworked Superman script. In the conception of the hero the noblest realization of anti-Fascism is achieved. He is of such stature and humanity that through him or in conflict with him the war's purpose for both the Allies and Nazis can be felt.

Nothing will bring out the handkerchiefs in a movie audience in such number as a scene which shows someone returning to his mother after years of separation, or the same thing in reverse, some one leaving, perhaps forever. "Watch on the Rhine" repeats this mechanism of returning or parting and its overwhelming sadness a good many times. In the course of her returning, the long absent daughter, Bette Davis, is shown in her reactions to her childhood home, her mother, to her brother and to her old nurse. Later her husband takes leave of her, of his children individually and together, his brother-in-law and mother-in-law, and the thing ends up with the son telling his mother he too must soon leave. Its clearest illumination of its problem is in this parting-returning sadness; you are made to feel that Fascism is worth fighting against if such noble people who deserve only happiness are willing to go through such pain.

The filming of Lillian Hellman's play was put under the too reverential care of Herman Shumlin, who directed it, and Dashiell Hammett, who adapted it, and an odd bundle turned up. Their aim (through an introduction and coda have been clapped fore and aft the orginal structure) was to have you see an exact version of the play, but not a static movie—and they succeeded exactly on both counts. It is the dialogue and acting taken straight from the play which are so damaging to the movie. The dialogue has a cold, precious, triple-duty nature, that doesn't seem to come out of the people who deliver it, and it is enunciated as to an audience that might not hear in the back rows of the gallery (not loudly, but explicitly). One of Miss Hellman's greatest virtues is an ability to spread a rich, human group of characters over her plays, but where her lines may have developed the character sufficiently on the stage they are, as movie lines, so overpacked that they exist as a thing apart from the characters. The children, for instance, have lines to say which advance them nowhere either as children or as adult-children, which the three Muller kids are supposed to be. Their speeches achieve, as do so many speeches in the movie, a certain monumentality simply as speeches, but leave the character stranded behind.

The major part of the playing gets this same woodenness, or lack of connection, between any or all of the following—the look of the person, his pantomime, the character he is supposed to be, or the nature of the particular lines he is saying. The one exception to this, and the reason for much of the movie's success, is the performance of Paul Lukas as Kurt Muller. His portrait is the only one that is sufficiently mobile for the screen, and where the mobility, as expressed in pantomime, is always natural and understandable for the character played. In the case of Lucile Watson, Donald Woods and the children there is not enough mobility, and in the case of Beulah Bondi, Geraldine Fitzgerald and Miss Davis there is too much.

"Watch on the Rhine" is on the whole a satisfactory movie which holds its interest tightly and achieves considerable compassion.

September 13, 1943

Short and Happy

SOME of the best movies of the year are seven-minute cartoons called by names like *All This and Rabbit Stew* or *The Fighting 69th 1/2*, which come on as unheralded transitions in the double bill and feature the notorious Bugs Bunny, a rabbit that not only performs physical feats of a Paul Bunyan magnitude but is equally sharp with his mind. They come from Warner Brothers, are produced by Leon Schlesinger, made by Chuck Jones, Friz Freleng, Bob McKimson, and called *Merrie Melodies*; ten of them are being reissued this fall still as *Merrie Melodies* but with the addition of a Blue Ribbon.

One reason for the brightness of *Merrie Melodies* and for their superiority over Disney's product is that Jones is out to make you laugh, bluntly, and, as it turns out, cold-bloodedly. This runs him against the grain of the several well-worked grooves down which the animated cartoon has traveled under the belief these grooves will never wear through. However, it no longer seems funny to see animals who talk and act like human beings, who do all sorts of ingenious tricks—most of them superhuman—who go through lives of the highest excitement and reward, but have no inner, or mental, life. The complex emotional life and three-dimensional nature of Jones-McKimson characters allow their makers to poke fun at everything in sight, or out of sight—especially if it is something familiar and well loved, like McKimson's *Hiawatha*, a kind person, or any bad actress's great moments. It is an illusion of most cartoon-makers that they must have a moral, or do good, if it means only killing the villain; Warner's crew isn't under this illusion. The masterpiece, *Inki and the Lion*, is also a masterpiece of amorality—so far the other side of goodness that it is a parody of *Bambi*. In this version of forest life, man is the likable spear-thrower, preyed on by animals, and the king of the forest is a supernatural horror called the Myna bird, who hates man and beast alike.

The artistic method in Warner cartoons is neither in Disney's top drawer (at his best) nor Popeye's bottom one, but, even so, it has gone off at a tangent lately that may open up new paths to the cartoon method. It is a change from the straight, insipid realism to a sophisticated shorthand, made up of flat, stylized, posterlike representations, using a sort of Persian color of fancy tones like dusty pink. It is a much simpler style of cartoon drawing, the animation is less profuse, the details fewer, and it allows for reaching the joke and accenting it much more quickly and directly: it also gets the form out of the impossible dilemma between realism and the wacky humor.

The goal in heroes is a comic figure with a temperament and behavior as peculiarly his own as those of a Chaplin or Fields, which goal is never achieved; but it leads to several rewards, like the Myna bird, who appears in the *Inki* (little African boy) series. The Myna bird is like a toucan, shaped like an acorn, coal black, who moves inscrutably in an atmosphere of overwhelming supernaturalism, to the tune of Mendelssohn's overture to *Fingal's Cave*. At the end of each musical phrase, he gives one prodigious, syncopated hop, thereafter moving forward indomitably. The Myna bird is inevitably followed by a passive three-year-old individual named Inki, who loves to throw spears, and by a lion (the lion is Jones's least successful creation—he looks like Robinson Crusoe). The famous Bugs Bunny is Avery-Jones one-animal advertisement of the moral that unadulterated torturing of your fellow men pays off.

Despite the various positions on humor (Tex Avery is a visual surrealist proving nothing is permanent, McKimson is a show-biz satirist with throwaway gags and celebrity spoofs, Friz Freleng is the least contorting, while Jones's speciality, comic character, is unusual for the chopping up of motion and the surrealist imposition: a Robin Hood duck, whose flattened beak springs out with each repeated faux pas as a reminder of the importance of his primary ineptness), the Warner cartoonists are refreshing iconoclasts because they concentrate on so many other humor antecedents besides brutal mishaps, cultural punning, balletlike sadism. One of Jones's key inventions is the animal who is a totally invulnerable, can't-possibly-be-stopped adversary, a mysterious force like rain that is always surrounded by a hush that is a mixture of the awe, revelation, instinctive reverence of a soon-to-be-victim just before he is maneuvered off the cliff or into a distant puff of smoke miles away in the desert. Ridiculousness is behind every Jones gag, but it is labyrinthine in effect because of how much gentleness is mixed in along with an infinite response to one animal's brass, hunger, manipulative power, or blinding speed. Disney's boredom-encased drawing, Barbera's cat-mouse drag, and the smugly "mature" Hubley works are incapable of this Warner's lightness: that there should be no end in defining the human quality of hunger (an animal fated from birth to be a scrawny piece of meat trying to eat tin cans, blindly grabbing at flies in a hostile environment of doomful rocks) as long as the metaphorical elaboration is kept within lighter-than-air feats of quick, fractional wit. The never-stop, pushing-on insistence in Warner's cartoons is important: having eaten some Earthquake Pills from a little bottle, the effect on the victim's body is a tremor that has the insistence and unsolvable disaster of hiccups.

Because of the twenty-six-issues-per-year rate at which they are thought up, the *Merrie Melodies* are bound to vary greatly in quality. The surprising facts about them are that the good ones are masterpieces and the bad ones aren't a total loss. For instance, the poor *Rabbit Who Came to Dinner* (Freleng) is given a tremendous lift when, in the midst of the inevitable and tedious chase of the rabbit by Elmer, the clock strikes twelve and Bugs breaks into one of his typical emotional upsets, roaring out *Auld Lang Syne*, kissing Elmer, flinging confetti in the age-old tradition of New Year's Eve—Elmer being as easily diverted in July as in any other month.

Jones-McKimson-Freleng are in the Sennett tradition, which uses the whole sphere of man's emotion and behavior simply as a butt for humor, no matter what it leads to. The aim is purely and simply laughter. Schlesinger's men are rich and inventive humorists, and their smart-alecky freshness has turned what is meant to be an interval on the program into the moment when the whole audience brightens up.

September 20, 1943

Love in the Foxholes

"So Proudly We Hail," a movie which shows what it is like to make love in the foxholes of Bataan, on the decks of troop transports and in the rocks of Corregidor, is so rotten and the two millions which Paramount spent on making it so obviously distributed in the right directions to get it all back in paid attendances, that the film's only importance is in indicating certain attitudes of the commercial mind. In war pictures the exhibitors ask, and presumably the audience, "Where is the love interest, leg art and comedy?" By deciding to make a war movie with women protagonists (nurses) Paramount found the answer, ably assisted by the snide movie attitude toward women. The lives of women in the movies are almost exclusively confined to love careers of a dreams-come-true nature. So that whereas audiences wouldn't stand for a movie which showed Bataan's soldiers spending half their time making love, they feel it is perfectly natural for movie women to do so, especially if the women are Claudette Colbert, Veronica Lake and Paulette Goddard. War or no war, then, the Misses Colbert, Lake and Goddard can devote their nursing life to the fulfilment of their love.

Given this premise, the theatre owners get this cheesecake in hunks so great that much of the movie hinges on Miss Goddard's black nightie; Miss Colbert's difficulties as commanding officer become exactly those of a headmistress in a school for young ladies; and the sex resides in Sonny Tufts's kiss, which Miss Goddard kicks back from as though he had a firecracker in his mouth.

This is the kind of movie that gives me the shakes. It is teeming with varieties of one woman, whose looks, personality and talent for acting are strikingly unsuited to passing instruments in a caesarian operation in the Marivales jungle, or for throwing herself on her stomach under ambulance cars to escape enemy bullets, or speaking of the way the Japanese treated women in Nanking. She has that hard, vacant map that Max Factor could produce on Orphan Annie, and which hides implacably anything out of the way or natural like a thick eyebrow or an underslung jaw, or skin that doesn't reflect the sun of Bataan like steel plate. Her acting is like Drama Day with the Camp Fire

Girls—Now we are in an airplane, girls, now we are tired and distraught, etc. The material she is given to act is a stale romanticism of Dolly Dawn, and her pal, Dolly Dawn, who went on a cruise to Hawaii, and while one falls in love with the handsome doctor who teaches laboratory technique at the University of Hawaii the other, more playful, falls in love with the comical All-American football player named Kansas. This used to be barely acceptable as the plot to display the merits of Bing Crosby's singing, the Marx Brothers' comedy or Fred Astaire's dancing: here it is for serious—for describing Bataan. Accompanying it is a running commentary composed of solid cliché (". . . after a nerve-wracking trip through the jungle . . .") spoken off-screen by relays of nurses.

"So Proudly We Hail" is admirably filled with stuff to earn money, but even so the writer shouldn't have been allowed to get away with murder. He has built a whole movie on the fact that Lt. Janet "Davy" Davidson has been in a coma ever since she was told her lover was given up for lost on a raiding trip. At the beginning of the movie a psychiatrist walks in with a letter from said lover, takes one discouraged reading of Davy's pulse, and then informs the seven nurses of her unit that he may be able to bring Davy to if they tell him—the doctor—absolutely everything that happened on Bataan. So the nurses tell what being in love on Bataan was like ("after a nerve-wracking trip through the jungle") in an hour-long flashback, and at the end the doctor says he thinks he can bring her to. He then reads Lieutenant Davidson the letter and she wakes up. I contend a really good psychiatrist would have read Davidson that letter without a flashback.

There are three good things, which seems hardly a fair trade for two million dollars; but anyway, they are: a mother who says to her daughter's friend, "I like you; you eat so much"; a performance by Sonny Tufts, who has been coached too well to use his hands like Cary Grant but gets his pantomime over with a rather tricky sense of timing; and a meaningful bit by a Filipino doctor (Ted Hecht) who ruminates aloud while he operates.

September 27, 1943

Exterior Decorating

"Holy Matrimony" is a typical job of carpentering by the producer-writer, Nunnally Johnson, who takes rather mediocre, clumsy frameworks and reworks them into adequate movies, which look nice, function well and stop just short of significant movie expression. The virtues of a Johnson-hammered film arise from a considerable talent for surface effects, which includes using extra players to advantage, an awareness and control of the environment so that it can be made either realistic or satirical, and a facility with dialogue. His productions are graced with a raft of experts like Alan Mowbray, Melville Cooper and Eric Blore. The ailments in the original scores of such things as "The Moon Is Down," "Life Begins at 8:30" and this one, are still in after Mr. Johnson finishes with them, but they are not so noticeable.

"Holy Matrimony" is a pleasant, gray-haired comedy, which Arnold Bennett first thought up in 1905, about an English painter who palmed off his dead valet as himself so he could live quietly and unknown in London. Later he is found out on the strength of two moles he has on his left collar-bone—the papers scream "Shame! Painter not in Valhalla!" and one carries the headline "American Claims Record—105 Moles." The painter has a tendency to confuse his assumed name of Henry Wadsworth Leek with Henry Greenleaf Leek. The picture seems to be spoofing Paul Gauguin, since in this case an English painter leaves his palmy Tahitian paradise for a quiet married life in the heart of the London suburbs with a practical, middle-aged matron. Mr. Monty Woolley plays the painter; he is still an inert performer covered by a beard, with an irascible voice that snaps the ends of his sentences off in a cold fury, even when he is conversing contentedly. Miss Gracie Fields plays his wife with much more talent. She has a good face and a good voice for movies, and only rarely does the professional impersonator show through her performance.

For a movie based on such an incredible occurrence as this one is, it is the most lethargic and restrained of comedies, which gets by on meager helpings of understated humor and quiet life, for which elderly people will go quietly crazy. It is no doubt Twentieth Century-Fox's intention, now that they have helped lower the age of the most frequent movie-goers to 18 with Betty Grable and Flicka, to try to lift it to 58 with Woolley and Fields.

In "Holy Matrimony" the laughs are always the result of commendable secondary effects brushed over situations which are unrealized, anemic and often vague. In the Westminster Abbey episode the diversion is in the interest of the ceremony and spectacle of Abbey burying. The hat-fitting episode has a brief, beautiful parody of the way a hatter swipes the felt smooth, and then, after clamping the hat on his customer's head, intimidates him into liking it. One of the finer episodes has the dead valet's first wife showing up to claim Mr. Woolley, who is now living in middle-aged seclusion and paradise with Miss Fields. The scene produces nothing that is new or remarkable: the artist, who has never seen the woman, is horrified; his practical wife gets him out of the way and then convinces the other woman that Mr. Woolley is crazy, a pauper, and will bring disgrace on her and her three sons. The scene's humor is in the spinsterish dress and posing of the family—middle-class and puritan in their coal-black Sunday best, except for a third son, who hulks sourly in the background, looking like a woodchopper in his working clothes, clearly the bastard son.

There are many scenes that make you feel the thing wasn't grasped too well. Mr. Woolley's breaking down and crying at his funeral seems odd, because till then he had seemed to understand his part as requiring no emotion; his refusal to admit his identity at the end is as unconvincing as was his urge to admit it earlier in the picture. It is never clear just what personality Mr. Woolley is going to try to be; he is a three-way light connection which the plot and director switch as they see fit. Nevertheless, the film is sufficiently sprinkled with laughs, like a papier-maché sundae with real nuts. Also, it is the first American movie to show paintings that were executed by a painter rather than a sign painter. Mr. Woolley's art—Eakins-like paintings of non-surgical or non-rowing scenes—could very well be considered quite good by all the people who so considered them.

October 4, 1943

Russian Victory

THE first part of the newsreel-assembly called "The City That Stopped Hitler: Heroic Stalingrad" is identical with any preceding battle-front portrait containing Fitzgerald-travelogue views of a city, the pastorals of harvesting farmers, and the blitz roaring down someone's highway in captured enemy newsreels. But in the latter half of the film is an irony that will make it one of the more grimly poetic descriptions of the war, as different from the usual war documentary as the battle of Stalingrad was from any other battle of the war. It is an irony occasionally intended but mainly the result of the inveterate Russian sense for cinema realism at work on the material of Stalingrad, the very nature of which would make any film of it a kind of Bible in the extremes of fighting techniques, destruction, death and heroism.

Scorn, irony and satire have usually been rendered in war movies as meaningless and embarrassing devices of name-calling (like the continual reference to the Japanese as rats). But in this film there is an unmistakable, grim savor, implicit in the visual content, and its effect would be there, with or without

Mr. Donlevy's narration. For instance, the mockery is Breughelesque when the most unfortunate, stricken German prisoner, an Ichabod Crane of a person whose frozen feet are burlesqued by the enormous woolen bundles wrapped around them, is walked off into the barren Russian landscape as a symbolical allusion to what awaits the ambitious army that invades Russia. There is a similar shot of a decapitated, frozen body at the very edge of the Volga, showing that the Germans actually did reach the river, as they swore they would, but in an utterly useless condition. The entire sequence at the end, which juxtaposes examples from the most glorious moments of goose-stepping German militarism in the West, with its frozen, humiliated and hopeless state after the surrender at Stalingrad, is a valid monument in scorn.

This Amkino-film is not as lucid, clean and exact as the British film of the North African campaign, "Desert Victory," but it is closer to the actual grain of war. It treats of two factors—death and destruction—which are usually glossed over in movies for the more successful details of a battle, such as the raising of the conquering army's flag over the conquered town, or for the more active periods, such as airplane dogfights. The fact of death in movies is seldom equal to the solemn look and stance of the spectators at the funeral, the words of the preacher, and the little Passion Play that the director has figured out to make you cry. But here death is treated as a physical, visual fact, with unusual curiosity and quiet. The person's deadness and the condition he was left in by the bullet, bomb, or in this case the freezing cold, are the most important elements of the death scenes and achieve, as a result, the strength of compassionate dignity. I can remember no American or British film which expressed the destruction of war so honestly and well. Some of the most important contributions of this movie are the comparisons it repeatedly makes between the peacetime city and its present ruins. There is a sardonic reality in views of the rubbled city behind a gaunt, rickety horse, in Apocalyptic reference, and again behind a statue, somehow left standing in all the ruins, of a frolicking circle of children. Even a view of the victorious Russian army marching through the beleaguered city after the siege had been broken was made less romantic than usual by the grim nature of the scene around the marchers, who are indeed victorious but not in the deathless, destructionless vistas conquering movie armies usually march through.

Completely contrary to the existing, close-mouthed war-document tradition is the appearance here of a new secret weapon called "Katushka," which was first used by the Russians to relieve the siege on Stalingrad and which I find impossible to describe except by saying that it is a series of multiple cannon which explode a ceaseless, spraying avalanche of rocket charges. Finally there is the climaxing scene in which the Soviet armies of the north and south joined at Kalach, trapping the entire German siege force of 330,000 men around Stalingrad. Their meeting has been somehow completely caught on film, two white-clad armies approaching each other in a line stretching for miles, and finally falling joyfully into one another's arms. (It is an inspiring scene which could make Eisenstein's or Griffith's mouth water, with their love of crowds or armies which move in lines and, if possible, come together.)

After the war all but a few war films will be permanently retired because they were too pretty. Because it contains more sides of the war and more humanity, "Stalingrad" will be an important record. Its candor and simplicity make its account of the battle so moving as to be a rare experience in documentaries.

October 11, 1943

The Hero

THE hero in American movies fluctuates between two idealized personalities, whose common bond is an allegiance to Superman. One, the older, is a mixture of Abe Lincoln, Dick the Chimney Sweep and a cowboy, in which goodness and lonesome bravery are the main ingredients. The other is a belligerent, egocentric character who is as malevolent and aggressive as the other is pure of heart and backward; in the gangster-movie days he was called Blackie, now he is called by names like Rick, Joe Rossi and Sam Spade. He is acted mainly by Humphrey Bogart, but also by John Garfield, Alan Ladd, Brian Donlevy and George Raft.

The older-fashioned hero is a long-bodied, long-armed man whose air is one of troubled silence, and who grew up in the bleaker parts of the country to be shy, honest and not given to excesses. He doesn't seek success, but because he is a physical genius he reaches the hero class and performs there as a good honest man would. He is probably the most likable person to see winning so many rewards, especially when his person is that of Gary Cooper (who had as much to do with shaping this movie personality as anyone else), Jimmy Stewart or Henry Fonda. His career, which the earliest pioneer first hacked out and which Hemingway revived by opening new worlds for him to conquer, is apt to be an untroubled one of physical superiority; but the faint tinge of tragedy latent in his personality sometimes leads at the end of the picture to the fact that he or his wife will die or that he must leave her in some far-off desert oasis, singing in a cabaret, to prove that the twain of East and West cannot meet for very long. Though he seems made for lonely nights out on the range, the picture of his love life is always one of wholesome, perfect, physical compatibility, and he is a conscientious, non-professional lover. He is seldom bothered about money, since he works outside the civilized world of business, and his few excursions into that world are in the roles of philanthropist or savior ("Mr. Deeds," "Mr. Smith").

The hero played by Mr. Bogart, which grew out of the gangster film and Dashiell Hammett detective novels, looks as though he had been knocked around daily and had spent his week-ends drinking himself unconscious in the back rooms of saloons. His favorite grimace is a hateful pulling back of the lips from his clenched teeth, and when his lips are together he seems to be holding back a mouthful of blood. The people he acts badly toward and spends his movie life exposing as fools are mainly underworld characters, like gangsters, cabaret owners and dance-hall girls (and the mayor whom he puts into office every year). Everything he does carries conflicting quantities of hatred and love, as though he felt you had just stepped on his face but hadn't meant it. His love life is one in which the girl isn't even a junior partner in the concern, his feeling about life is that it is a dog kennel, and he believes completely in the power of the money which he steals or works everyone else's fingers to the bone to earn. He is the soured half of the American dream, which believes that if you are good, honest and persevering you will win the kewpie doll.

The character of this hero, who is the spit and image of hate-thy-neighbor, and who only milks human kindness, is nevertheless as popular as the nobler hero played by Gary Cooper. His mutilated good looks, plain, unbecoming clothes and slight stature are easier to project oneself into than the cowboy godliness of Mr. Cooper, and his vicarious, purple screen life is closer to one's own day-dreaming of the most pleasurable kind of existence than the rigidly plain, pure one of Messrs. Deeds, Smith and Doe. Also Bogart lacks the forlorn pensiveness which, in Cooper, Fonda and Stewart, has a subtle poetry far less reassuring to movie audiences than his own noisy violence in which nothing is hidden. And in a world where so many people are doing things they dislike doing, Bogart expresses the hostility and rebellion the existence of which the Cooper tradition ignores. What the characters share are successful lives of extreme action, free of the routine matter of existence, which are carried out in dramatic places like a night club in Casablanca, in a cave in Spain or on the baseball field at Yankee Stadium, and which contain the untroubled string of physical victories that Hollywood feels Americans need and desire.

For the basic likeness is that both are men of action, with as little emphasis as will make sense on thought and emotion. Cooper's screen life is taken up with proving his efficiency as a soldier, cowboy, baseball player, explorer, sea captain, adventurer and lover, and he seems unnatural only when he has also to stand for a message to mankind, as he did in "For Whom the Bell Tolls," or as a father, or when he has to show something lush or heartfelt in the way of emotion (the response being equivalent to tickling the mountain faces Gutzum Borglum carved). The main factor in all of Bogart's careers of daring is his toughness—at one point in each movie he takes a horrible beating, but like a wrestler bounds back as good as new—and his ingenuity in a brawl. His movies are the ultimate in evil fighting methods, and he is a master of the surprise hold or kick, which takes a minimum of muscle and energy. For both of them it is the doing of the thing rather than the thinking it up or reacting to it that is important.

The anti-intellectual, anti-emotional and pro-action life of these heroes is in the historical American pattern, and perfectly suited to the movies, where movement and gesture are of so much importance (it is one that the Hollywood producer has embraced so wholeheartedly that he sees it as the only definition of cinematic movement). It is interesting to note that though the heroes have always been active, they have not always looked that way. D. W. Griffith's heroes had sensitive, wistful faces, probably because Griffith dealt in stories whose heroes were hurt by society; then came an era when the gigolo face of Valentino or Novarro or Gilbert was thought appropriate both for lovers and adventurers; in the early thirties producers discovered that their stage-adopted habit of using cosmetics on the actor's faces devitalized them, and the eye-penciling, hair-greasing and lipsticking was given up, with the result that the faces suggested aggression rather than passivity, the great outdoors rather than the boudoir.

Cooper and Bogart, the champions of their particular weights, are the reverse and obverse sides of the biggest, the most golden medal Hollywood has for heroes. Whatever may be said about the *type* of personality they play, they, as particular personalities, override any conventional facts in their screen life because they have the rich, visual vitality of which the greatest movie heroes will always be made.

October 18, 1943

The Perils of Tartu

"The Adventures of Tartu" are the same ones that happen every morning in the funny pages to Vic Jordan, Race Riley of the Commandos and Flyin' Jenny, but they have been transformed into a movie of surprising freshness and enthusiasm. The hero is the English chemist, Captain Stevenson (or Robert Donat in need of a haircut), who is sent by the British Intelligence to destroy a German plant that is perfecting a most deadly poison gas, and Mr. Donat goes through Europe evading the bullets of Nazis and saving the lives of many people, until he locates the hidden gas plant inside a mountain near Pilsen. There he places four highly concentrated grenades into important parts of the gas works, blowing them up, then steals a Messerschmitt from several soldiers and flies home, with the sweetheart he picked up in Pilsen. The American director, Harold S. Bucquet (who made the Dr. Kildare series), and everyone in this otherwise English production went to a good deal of honest, talented effort to make you believe in and enjoy these incidents: half of the time you do.

This is the occasion of an odd marriage, in which the English way of making movies by starting with an idea and proceeding to make the idea out of the materials of the art, is unfortunately united to Hollywood's, which starts with a dozen or so formulas for pleasing every showgoer in America and then figures out a script to contain them all. The marriage is immediately indicated in a scene during the bombing of London in 1940. There is a two-ton bomb which has failed to go off but is about to, the bomb-disposal squad is called, and it turns out to be Donat, who must take the engine out of the bomb. Up to his entrance the film has had all the visual strength of character the English demand of their films, and as he straddles his bomb, looking for all the world like a mermaid riding an iron fish, he does as neat and pretty an operation of removing detonator from bomb as you could wish from the documentary-conscious British. However, just next to the crater in which Mr. Donat is doing his dismantling, a bed is seen, containing an injured child who cannot be moved, though the bomb may go off, and beside him, his courageous nurse, who won't leave him for any bomb. The dramatic nature of their presence along with their brave conversation as they carry on with Mr. Donat, moves the picture bodily to Hollywood.

To attract one's belief and emotions to material as obviously romantic as Tartu's adventures are, the director must enforce the most exact sleight-of-hand realism (which Hitchcock made famous), or turn the movie frankly into fantasy, satire or comedy. The directors of Tartu do it the realistic way, trying to show the problems, moods and transitions of the story in their most significant, concise and plausible way. Mr. Donat's adventures with the bomb, his airplane flight over Europe and parachute jump into Hungary (realized beautifully as a movie problem), the action at the construction job in Hungary, and Mr. Donat's whimsical transformation into the person of Tartu, a precocious Rumanian with a sing-song voice, have the true richness of scene and action to make them believably heroic and wonderful. And in an occasional place—where it shows a fear-crazed adolescent's face, or the war nerves of a wild-eyed young Czech—it does what no other war-fiction film has wanted even to try, and that is the showing of war emotion with all the power of the medium turned on, and so well it is no longer an attempt but an accomplished fact. But from the moment the love story starts the movie relaxes its hold, the affair itself is much too complicated and slow-paced to enter the picture in mid-passage, and it has not the virtue of being different from any average love affair in the movies, as far as acting, photography and material are concerned. The events that follow—the capture of the Messerschmitt, and the flight through the Wellsian gas works—are insufficiently original, believable, and deliberated on to be more than mediocre.

The playing consists almost completely of Mr. Donat, who has enough accents, characters and duties to perform to please a Barrymore, and Mr. Donat plays them like a Barrymore of the movies, the result being a clever performance of a chameleon character rather than a convincing, artistic one. The chain of events in Tartu has both too many links and some of Hollywood rather than English make, but it is constructed with a flair for and delight in adventure and in movie-making.

October 25, 1943

Whimsy Gets the Whammy

"Flesh and Fantasy," Charles Boyer's first movie as producer-actor, is a picture with the theme that dreams, the occult and any wishes you may have floating around you are big as life and twice as handsome, and with some morals like faith in yourself will drive the pixies away; do evil things and you will look as ugly as Hitler; you can make your dreams come true if you try—none of which, unlike Lassie, comes home. It is a chaotic smorgasbord of meshed-geared thinking and bad movie-making but it is also interesting. Movies with deep thought, morals and the occult, or anything except physical action, are as rare this year as hen's teeth, and especially so when containing the gushing energies and naïveté of Mr. Boyer's film.

"Flesh and Fantasy" is one of those four-in-one movies, which Boyer's director, Julien Duvivier, continues laboriously to love, where four little movies are hung from the thread of one of those awesome ideas you get in the middle of the night, such as, it just goes to show what funny tricks life can play, and in which Mr. Duvivier plays Mr. Fate or fairy godmother to the studio's star list. Here the thread—read in three stories by David Hoffman (the gnomelike man who played Radek in "Mission to Moscow") to dream-fearing Robert Benchley—is the idea that dreams and palm-reading aren't to be tossed off frivolously, nor, on the other hand, accepted wholesale. In the first one, a mean, ugly slavey, who is about to commit suicide, is given a dose of Lloyd C. Douglas oil—do good and you'll look good—and a beautiful mask to wear to the Mardi Gras for two hours. So she shelves the meany role for the time, has a beautiful spirit for two hours, and gets a real, live fella and a beautiful face (Betty Field's). In the second act a talented palm reader, played by Thomas Mitchell, tells the lawyer, played by Edward G. Robinson, that he will eventually be a murderer. And after Fate robs the lawyer of two likely prospects who will not be missed by anyone and by their death would have relieved him of his Fate, he gets hysterical and murders the palm reader! The third act concerns a tightrope walker (Charles Boyer) who has a dream in which he falls from his rope. For the next three reels he has quite a time with his tightrope walking.

The main thing about the movie is its chaos. Actually the idea of the validity of the corporeal and non-corporeal as expressed in the title runs consistently enough through all the stories, but it has been used as a gullible, unimaginative person would use a patent medicine he has been told will work on everything from the common cold to rickets if he uses it often enough and doesn't ask any questions. The first episode, except for a couple of early, noisy dashes somewhere, is a straight, if trite, moral fable; the second and third, which are better simply from being more than a radio skit accompanied by scary, watery snapshots, have only a touch of morality, but enough to confuse everything, and their strokes of fate occur unrestrainedly whenever they are needed to keep a superficial story going. Then the clever ending turns up, and you are left, having witnessed two long, dull stories spiced with heavyweight sleight of hand, with nothing at the end and having been neither surprised, enlightened nor excited in transit. The material it uses, which is so old and undistinguished, is not heightened by its supernatural jazz, and the result of the jazz projects no meanings, emotionally or intellectually.

Mr. Duvivier's movies, which are so intoxicated with whimsy, are in themselves extremely pedantic affairs, unimaginative, and lacking in lightness, taste or charm. When the palmist tells Lady Mildred Platz that she will soon hear from her husband whom she hasn't heard from in seventeen years, the radio answers immediately that someone bumped into the missing Arctic explorer, Harold Platz, at the North Pole and that Platz would now address his radio audience. You can't blame Lady Platz for fainting. The material of the movie is the prim, stuffed-shirt elegance of an era even Hollywood has forsaken, when heavy, obvious sentiments were expressed with extreme seriousness and enthusiasm. The shipboard romance between the tightrope specialist and the reformed diamond thief, which ends with the girl being led off to prison and her tightrope lover beamingly awaiting the day when she will be paroled, will make you feel old. Betty Field contemplates suicide with the persistence of an air drill and Mr. Robinson does his victim in with enough force and perspiration to kill a battalion of palmists—yet not for one second do you feel you are seeing anything but a particularly enthusiastic character actor's rehearsal. At no place is the treatment imaginative enough to justify whimsy. Mr. Duvivier's wand is like a crank.

November 1, 1943

The Cardboard Star

"The North Star" is a movie I admire for the effort, patience and talent—all sincere—that went into the making of it; but it is one that I feel is too careful of how it walks and what path it takes. This in spite of there being no shoddiness, that it is a grateful, compassionate tribute to the Russian people, projected cleanly and with that elegance of craftsmanship that Sam Goldwyn manages by obtaining the best material and artists available to satisfy his idea of a well tooled product; that Lillian Hellman wrote the script, the first she has done directly for the movies; Lewis Milestone did the directing, James Wong Howe the photography and Aaron Copland the music.

"North Star" is the name of a Soviet coöperative farm and village on the Bessarabian frontier. Its life is shown during the two peaceful, unsuspecting days before June 20, 1941, and during the next two days when the villagers go through the first horror of the German invasion, lose their village to the Germans and return as guerillas to destroy both. There is a freedom evident in its material; whether it is singing, dancing, going to school or a walking trip of four

young Russians to Kiev, it has an unhampered mobility that is free of all pater-
nalism. The Russian life it projects (any part of which could be used to adver-
tise Sunkist oranges) is a fount of gayety and brightness and people who are
free of all rancor or selfishness. But the movie does not express the ultimate
freedom in which individuality or differences in people are respected—its
characters are so undifferentiated (unusual for a Hellman script) that they are
not only uninteresting but are difficult to keep apart. Here again coöperative
life, or communism, is adolescently denatured. And there is no great figure of
fascism presented, to accent, or put a strain on, freedom. It is simply another
picture in which the ideas more difficult of expression are evaded by being
taken for granted as known already to the audience.

The fault at the heart of the movie, and of almost every other modern
Hollywood movie, is in a usurpation by the artist of the spectators' brains and
sensibility, in order to make the action of the film perfectly clear and understandable to them. The producers have carefully removed all the foreign
bodies, diluted the idiosyncrasies or left them out altogether, and simplified
what is left into slow, rounded, general statements. The food has not only been
cooked for you but eaten and digested. There is no shock left, none of that
magnetism which picks the spectator up and deposits him inside the story.

This kind of cleaned and plucked movie art, which is to the spectator what
a prefabricated house is to the carpenter, is the result of the overomniscience
that is the perpetual trap to the director of a medium as encompassing as the
motion picture—especially to those who overestimate how much of an
encounter can be shown before straining the spectator's sense of the pace,
duration and undeliberate quality that makes the artistic projection of an
encounter living rather than merely explained. This turning of the spectator
into a receiver rather than a co-worker occurs in the conception itself of the
subject matter: the too-fortunate and conscious view that the camera takes of
events, so that you feel the artist is merely copying an action he thinks of as
already accomplished; the manipulation of characters into patterns of action, so
that you feel the ostentation; and the lack of individuality in the texture of the
photography, so that you feel it is not expressing the spirit of the idea but
merely making a clear reproduction of a reënactment of the idea. The result is
that no matter what you are shown—the folk dance, the strategy of the guerilla
attack, the school commencement exercises—your feeling is that you are
seeing a posed, not a spontaneous, action.

After reducing the characters to saccharine strait-jackets tagged "old man,"
"young girl" and "intellectual," putting starched oratory into their mouths,
giving them the latest college-cut looks and refusing them the right to have

some sentiment that is native, unpampered and free, there is little that acting can save, and except for certain irregularities presented by Ann Harding and Eric von Stroheim which still interest me, as far as I am concerned, nothing is saved.

Near the end of the picture there occurs one exception to the general tidiness, one which finally scratches your emotions and understanding. The villagers have successfully carried through their counter-attack, and the Russian surgeon faces the Nazi surgeon, the proud liberal who has put up with Nazism and makes such statements as, "I do not like much what I have done for the past nine years." The Russian answers, "I have heard about men like you. The civilized men who are sorry. Men who do the work of fascists and pretend to themselves they are better than those for whom they work. It is men like you who have sold your people to men like Hitler." And the Russian shoots this Nazi. Whatever has been lost by making this picture's only important Nazi a "civilized man," it is the only moment in the picture when the uneasy and the unconventional has been dared—it is what you entered the picture to find. The fault of "The North Star" is a failure of the kind of nerve that produced this incident and the inability to attach the little that it does say to the emotions of the spectator.

November 8, 1943

Two Shorts and a Wrongo

A BRITISH Ministry of Information short movie titled "I Was a Fireman" accounts for a spectacular night's activity in the life of a Fire Service unit as it sets about stopping a London waterfront fire during a particularly heavy Luftwaffe raid in 1940. The men involved are real firemen. A good part of their film has been cut severely to fit in between double bills when it is shown in this country (it is almost impossible to place government films in theatres here when they run beyond forty minutes—and it is hard enough to place them then, even for free). But the film is very fine anyway.

I think that the sequences in which the men go through their fire fighting on the roof of a warehouse, where one of them is injured by a falling beam and tied to the top of the hook and ladder and so lowered to the ground, while another is killed when the building's roof caves in, are in the best sense emotionally true. (Hollywood's version of the same action would have lost all the detail, the uneven, hazardous movement and the spontaneity by lackadaisically following the hero around. Reason—the hero is what's popular at the box office, not the fire.) The direction and photography of this Humphrey Jennings film are extremely loving and sensitive. There is a morning sequence where the exhausted men, who have struggled against the fire all night and have now been relieved, slowly and wearily go about getting their gear together to leave the scene, while they talk to Londoners going to their jobs in the early morning, that has a bright, warm movie way (Hollywood would have skipped it to get to another fire, funeral or medal-pinning). But the real virtue of the movie is its exact respect for the instinctive behavior and responses of men working. This is the kind of thing that gets lost in the movie attitude that treats an action as though it has happened already and is now being reënacted—so the hero uses the action as a foil rather than interacting with it.

The tension set up by the problems in all violent work, which have to be answered effectively and immediately, produces a surliness and aggressiveness in the relations between workmen that usual movie scripts do not realize. This one does. The fire chief is dictatorial, exasperated, he yells the same orders over and over, forgetting what he has been yelling from moment to moment—"Get it down! Get it down!" he shrieks at two of the men and pushes down the hose they have been aiming too high over the fire. The men take orders or give them to one another, and the need for hurry, the anxiety that the job will get away from them, cuts all the niceties away from the action and leaves it tense and raw. Such incidents, which construct a movie character in depth faster than any amount of polished heroics, are something every moviegoer should see to find out all the things the movies are not in the habit of giving us.

"Before the Raid" is a British short of equal length, which retells a tale that many films have already told—about a Norwegian village people's bravery (with a neat variation: the Norwegians lure the German officers off to fishing grounds and then pen them up in the middle of a forest of small fishing craft). Like "The Silent Village," which retold the Lidice story, this film is lyric and economical, but suffers from depending solely on real-life actors and half-good photography to carry a too pat story. But its early sequences on board a raiding Commando ship are good, and non-actor Norwegians give it an invigorating native grain; and there is a very worth-while bit of symbolism in a scene that cuts abruptly from a pleasant fishing genre to the German soldier idly throwing rocks into the water.

In case you didn't see "Action in the North Atlantic" and Noel Coward's "In Which We Serve," but are interested in seeing a picture like them, "Corvette K-225," made by Howard Hawks, will provide you with the plot of the former and some of the plot of the latter and more besides. In addition to being a picture about a convoy's itinerary, and a stiff-jointed captain who is in love with a ship, this movie's captain also needles his girl's brothers, who are sub-lieutenants, because he doesn't believe sparing the rod helps at all, and this leads to some arguments between the captain and his girl, and the boys turn up nasty. (You may have seen this new material somewhere else during your life, in pictures with Pat O'Brien.) This is a stock contraption all the way, with evidence that Hollywood has its eye but not its mind on films like "I Was a Fireman." It has one good scene during a convoy conference, which adds a wrinkle to other film convoy conferences, some minor characters who do very well, and there is a new lacquered Canadian actress, Ella Raines, to look at and hear speak platitudinous matter in a cello voice.

November 15, 1943

Newsreel

THE newsreel film is a superficial, inconsequent mirror of world affairs which inevitably comes in a poor third to the radio and the newspapers in its news coverage. Two weeks ago the newsreel program offered in movie houses contained the de Marigny trial, the bombing of the Naples post office by delayed-action mines the Nazis had left there, the Moscow Conference, Notre Dame's football victory over Navy, a war-plant fire in New Jersey and an article titled "Swim for Victory" (which had no swimming or even water in it, but showed the new bathing suits to be worn presumably during the winter months). Football fans saw a few scattered touchdown plays, the Moscow Conference consisted in a brief snapshot of Cordell Hull getting out of a plane at some airport, almost a third of the newsreel of what is supposed to be actuality in the making was posed, and the storm, the fire and the football game followed such old, conventional newsreel patterns that they could have been a thousand other storms, fires or football games that the newsreel has covered, and no one would have noticed.

The attitudes in newsreel making parallel those that go into making story films, because they are produced at the same impossible rate of speed and in the same exorbitant quantities (the newsreel produces two complete changes of program weekly), in the same kind of vacuum, inside of which there are half a dozen different newsreel companies but not one whose product is appreciably different from the others, or tries to be, and they command the same complete popularity. The newsreel, like the story film, is more conscious of its audience than of its reason for being, and will vary and modulate each of its programs until it has an item in each for every taste—polar bears, the Apple Queen, the President's speech and the latest-style mink jacket. It is just as afraid of a subject that is controversial as the fiction film is, just as afraid of the instinctive, individual and characterful, and of showing a subject that is short of being the height of pleasure (the terrible nature of the Naples bombing, in which you can see the injured trying to escape the explosion and fire, and a man covered with blood lying stunned against a lamppost, is ended with a shot of some town where the Italians rejoice at the arrival of American troops). The newsreel is so rushed for time it loses all sense of timing in its individual shots and, like Hollywood, invariably falls back, as a result, on certain well worn patterns of newsreel presentation.

Since it involves so much more complicated a process than the other news-gathering agencies which have only to set type or put mouth to microphone, it becomes ever more questionable whether the newsreel should attempt keeping abreast of all the news, and not instead concentrate on presenting a more comprehensive digest of fewer events. During the last decade, and especially since the war, the documentary, which also treats of actualities but examines the idea or event in all of its references, has made the newsreel look more and more functionless and its content less valuable. This was never more apparent than in the four-reel film, "Desert Victory," which gave audiences a greater knowledge of the event it covered than anything that has been written or broadcast about it, let alone all that has been sprinkled haphazardly about the event through a hundred newsreels.

Whatever its future direction and task, there are definite ways of improving the newsfilm in its present form, and the most apparent way is to limit its coverage by at least cutting out those events that are of no importance as far as one's knowledge of anything is concerned, for instance, the way in which Mr. Hull descends from an airplane. A shortening of the field covered would release more cameramen to each event, and would necessarily counteract the spottiness of present-day coverage. What is most needed is more curiosity and imagination on the part of the cameramen, or perhaps it may be the editors. Consider how little we know of the actual visual character of personages that we have been seeing over and over in newsreels, like Hull or Roosevelt or de Gaulle, and you will realize how uninterested and sterile the newsreel camera is. There is nothing candid about this camera. The personality that is interviewed by Fox Movietone, Paramount or RKO-Pathé is invariably prepared with his most presentable or least spontaneous manner.

The only truly unposed and disarming and significant portraits we get in our newsreels are either of military enemies, like Mussolini, or of little people who have no social prestige who are allowed to go to pieces or get along as best they can in front of the camera, and as a result appear natural and human. The medium's laziness is also shown in its inability to stay with a good thing in an action, but to be moving forever away from it, and unable to alter the speed of the moving so as to make the material more easily grasped. At present it employs few of the newsreel's resources, especially slow or fast motion, still photography, microscopic lens, divided screen and montage. What seems most characteristic of the modern newsreel is this lack of imagination or even interest in what it is doing; people run for touchdowns, soldiers walk through cheering throngs, storms lash countless seaboards, and the newsreel streaks past with the attention of an eight-day bicycle rider, showing neither less nor more interest for any part of what it sees, though the announcer is always enthusiastic and happy, and only different when he is more so.

November 22, 1943

Heaven, American Style

"Happy Land" is one of the sweetest numbers of the Goody Two Shoes series, the one that is so comfortably certain that it is *the* portrait of American life. Since not one thing occurs here that is short of being the contented cow's idea of what she would like her milk to grow up to be, it becomes ever more amazing to me that the people in Hollywood can go on presenting this fantasy that makes sugar seem sour as typical American life. It is the fantasy that every American is schooled in from his first school day, and there should be a New Republic supplement on why we feel it necessary to uphold it, as though it were the flag itself. It makes the soap operas of the radio and "Mary Worth" of the comics look like "Tobacco Road"; and Saroyan's "Human Comedy," which it has ghost-written, or vice versa, seems like a rich, full life.

The central problem in "Happy Land" has to do with a son's death in the war, and his father's being so broken up about it that Old Gramps descends to earth out of Heaven to show him that suffering and pain are also a part of life, and that "as long as American kids can be Boy Scouts and aim to do a good turn every day—as long as they can eat ice cream—go to high school (go to movies like this)—play football—have a picnic in Briggs's Wood—then it'll be worth while. The whole thing . . ." Then the boy's pal returns from sea to take the dead son's place in the family. It manages to include other American points of interest along with the ones Gramps noted. There are the first day of school, block "H" sweaters, the hurdle race (in family movies the hurdles seem to be the great American pastime), graduation exercises, train whistles, a drug-store, not the pool hall or masturbation. I think you will find little in these points of interest that will recall anything to you, since they seem to have been made to satisfy the most suspicious, narrow-minded upholder of American goodness in the world, which I don't suppose you are.

"Happy Land" is a movie in which each face is the empty, good-looking one that is associated only with other movie faces, because only they can be so bare of emotional states, can call up so little of the environment (and I don't mean Max Factor) that developed them, can be so inhumanly uninspired and unmoving. Everyone is so careful to be gentlemanly and in good taste that you feel they walk around in dancing pumps. But mainly there is not one moment of it that will strike you as the actuality. When it experiences death it is with a face that is not nearly ugly or terrible enough (though Mr. Ameche's is certainly a pain). And what it does to the Boy Scouts is inhuman.

Now, to turn a sharp corner; because this is, I think, an important movie for how it does what it is saying, as well as for what is said. It is a good movie technically, and even an important one, as far as Hollywood's development goes. It has a great deal of undecorated, solid honesty in its visualizing, and it looks at and paces its material with a homely, unromantic, plodding spirit that the material itself lacks completely. Its refusal to jazz things up by cutting makes it even dull, a monotone. There is continually a promise in this picture—that the same eye and attitude directed at an adult experience of reality will some day turn out American movies that haven't been seen since the silent days.

This picture is like nothing so much as a particularly terrible women's baseball team managed with the Puritan perfection and lack of compromise that could only be Joe McCarthy's. There is an early episode of the father in the garden just after he has received news of his son's death; as he miserably moves back and forth, the camera resolutely moves back and forth with him, keeping stolidly dead center on his face, and achieving a fascinating quality by its exact realization of the movement. Later, as the picture flashes back to the son's growing up, he and his father walk home at night from the city, and again the people are looked at with almost blind devotion, till you get tired of their faces and start watching the night-dark city buildings passing very slowly behind them, a scene that in spite of what they are talking about, is exciting for being so purely as it would actually be. The last episode, which brings the dead son's sailor pal home, and the only face with any character that has yet appeared, indicates what this technique could produce if it had more faces as natural as his. There are others: several tours taken with the wife (Frances Dee, who has a particularly marvelous quality) through her house; a brief one on the train with a college boy returning home, where the sound image and the visual image combine for one brief moment to catch the exact reality of train-ride rumination.

Like so many recent movies, "Happy Land" has noticed that the people in the English pictures, notably Coward's and "Desert Victory," talked softly, and it therefore has all its members talk softly. It can drive you crazy. Other Hollywood Americana are the fact that, unlike Saroyan's Uticans, "Happy Land's" HEARTfieldians of the male sex may tipple—their intoxicant is loganberry wine, the loganberry being undoubtedly the thing that gets it across as in the soft-drink class; it is okay for Heartfield's upright sons and daughters to kiss one another's foreheads. The only thing I can say is that you can take your choice of not seeing a custard pie, or of seeing an interesting technical performance.

December 13, 1943

"The Cross of Lorraine"

"The Cross of Lorraine," which is based on Hans Habe's novel "A Thousand Shall Fall," is a grueling movie and a good one. It is an exposition essentially of the horrors of life in a Nazi prison, though it undertakes many—too many— other things, like the attempt by the Nazis to break a man's (Gene Kelly) spirit, the glory of the Free French movement, portraits of the Nazi character, a traitor, and various sides and aspects of the Frenchman. It projects its overwhelming horror by cumulative use of brutality, produced with the most exact reality at its highest effectiveness and force. These brutalities, which are necessarily restricted to one classification (since such effects as that of starvation are beyond the reach of even Hollywood's make-up people, the filth of the prison yard and the dysentery of the prisoners beyond the reach of what isn't censored), include careful reproductions of a man's face being kicked in, another's stuck with a knife, bodies being riddled by bullets, burned up, or dropped from the roof and bounced across the street. These are pictured as they seldom have been in the past, and I advise no one to see the movie who is sickened by such things, as well he might be. But it is one of the few films to come out of Hollywood this year that has been emotionally effective, has got close to the more unpleasant aspects of the war and has used anything like the means that are at the disposal of film directors. It is, I think, close enough to what it must be like in Nazi prisons, and important enough, to be seen by everyone.

All this is due to the ability of Director Tay Garnett, who is invariably way-laid by his writers and by the mores of Hollywood movie-makers; so that in this picture, as in "Bataan," he has to create realism out of something that was in the beginning purposefully less sincere. For instance, the script presents him with the job of projecting a traitor who is obviously stagey, too foolhardy for belief, and too quickly characterized to seem more than planted. He is given a minimum amount of screen time to build substantial portraits of his Nazis, situations that immediately strike you as implausible, and a story that turns about-face in the last thirty minutes to make a headlong rush toward morale-building in the bad sense. (This thirty minutes adds nothing to the picture save insincerity.) After successfully stating a Nazi's homosexuality or the castration of one of the heroes, Mr. Garnett is made to waste several minutes taking it all back. He has, though, the ability to make these facts as believable as possi-ble, and is able to get the highest emotional effect from them by projecting on the screen rich, volatile realizations of the ideas that are contained in the script.

Mr. Garnett's greatest talent (shown in miniature by the climactic brutali-ties noted above) is to realize action with striking pictorial truth, complexity and force. He is always forcing the emotion of an action by getting the clear-est, most direct views of it, by cutting his film so that the action continually strikes out at the audience and by constructing pictorial images of the action that are exciting and full of illumination. All of the action episodes: the trans-fer of the soldiers from train to camp, the life of the prison yard and particu-larly the bedevilment of the guard, the attempt at escape, the prisoners' murder of the traitor, the chase, and even the final romanticized struggle between some villagers and some Nazis, are fine motion-picture realizations, and full of intense feeling. Garnett's film vocabulary is to my mind the most extensive, most imaginative and aggressive one operating in Hollywood at a moment when others just as good as his or better are hibernating. His pictures contain the most imaginative use of cutting, an exact eye for a visual fact and the greatest effort to bring the audience into the picture of any being released during this period.

Since I seem on the point of crowning Mr. Garnett Hollywood Ace of 1943, this is a good moment to do the same for Sir Cedric Hardwicke as the finest film player of the year for his performance as Colonel Lanser in "The Moon Is

Down" and for his Father Sebastian in this picture. His performances should be a constant lesson to all those movie players who feel that projecting vitality on the screen calls for ever constant machinations with the hands and the features; for his technique is a subtle, quiet use of pantomime and voice, and exacts—as witness the prayer he gives in this—the finest, most human and adult response from the spectator (for the same sort of thing I mention Henry Morgan, for his cowboy, Fonda's partner, in "The Oxbow Incident" and for his sailor in "Happy Land," who in my review last week was named only a face). There are flashes of playing that are emotionally true, from the other actors in this movie, like Ford's sudden fear before his attempt to escape, some of Kelly's playing and all of Joseph Calleia's. But Garnett has been waylaid by actors as well as by writers, and mainly by the two leads, Pierre Aumont and Hume Cronyn, whose stiffness he tried to offset with an intricate, planned pantomime but didn't.

December 20, 1943

Movies in Wartime

THE problem that faced American movie producers from the moment the United States entered the war, which pushed the reluctant industry into declarations as to the nature of the times, was to make clear to movie audiences as much of the problems of fascism and democracy and the struggle between them as can be handled by movies. Since December 8 the movie people have been pecking away at the problem, mostly at the outside of it, but diligently and without stint. In order to show a fascist demagogue, they presented some of his mannerisms, like his salute, a great deal of theatrical brutality and hot temper, a few of his desires for a Nazi world, a small part of the psychology and background that produced him. The movie battlefield has been without exception a neat, heroic and orderly corner of what a real battlefield must be like; one that has exploded realistically enough but never very unpleasantly. Their Americans have been trouble-shooting automatons, licking a hundred times their weight in Nazis and Japanese; the other fighters of the United Nations haven't been so ingenious, but they have been friendly, industrious and uncomplainingly good people. Everything else that the movies have shown as part of the Allied war effort can be summed up as highly complimentary to it, and anything that has had to do with the fascists, highly uncomplimentary.

The war movie today is appreciably less mawkish, melodramatic and naïve than the films that were made in the First World War. But this progress is only an advance in degree; the house has essentially the same framework, though its surface appeal is less silly, more direct, fresh and simple. Inherent, though, is still the melodramatic attitude, patriotic narrowness and glibness all around, no problem or character ever being encountered in all of its aspects or implications. To understand why this framework must remain, no matter who is building it—Dudley Nichols, William Wellman, Nunnally Johnson or Howard Hawks (who are obviously just as aware of the problem as any of us are)—will demand all the well worn facts of the Hollywood business. Let it suffice to say that it is a whole set of effects and counter-effects arranged to produce films that needn't say—in fact almost never do say—what anyone actually, sincerely believes to be the truth.

The technique that has been used to present the problem has been, in the majority of cases, that of the Western film, where psychological, economic and social factors are subordinated almost out of sight to chase-fight, chase-fight, chase-fight, and final victory for the hero over the villain despite insurmountable odds. To have discussed fascism on any higher level than this would have made things more difficult than Hollywood likes them, and would, moreover, have brought into play all the forces of which it is most in fear, among them censorship and the supposed feverish resentment of the paying public for anything other than entertainment. The intense activity and heroics of the Western provided Hollywood with a camouflage in which there was a great deal of milling about. It abounds in villains, and so offers a convenient receptacle for Nazis; it gives a pleasant illusion of war, in which killing and destruction, in the midst of mystery, love and shenanigans, seem hardly real. If you decide, as the movie people did, that all you are going to show of fascism is its military aggression, then the Western offers a simple, black-and-white-version of what happens to people who take what doesn't belong to them.

What has been most lacking is a forthright, informing portrait of the authoritarian character. The Nazis in movies have been either all black or all white, and in either case unsubstantiated. The common soldiers are unmitigated thugs and killers; the highest officers often have been, amazingly, brave, independent, civilized men, who were just barely distinguishable from the highest type of democrat. This interesting case of the Good Nazi is no doubt the result of a feeling that an all-black Nazi is too much of a stock type, too unbelievable and too inhuman. But in making the Nazi more humanly complex, the only psychological construction they could rearrange him into was one composed of the qualities which made their heroes, and he came out simply a good man. Their aim in making a more human Nazi was to make a more rational human being, whereas the Nazi, in fact, is most understandable as a human being acting on his irrational drives. Hollywood has always been averse to exploring or admitting the irrational aspects of human beings, and especially averse to discussing the kind of society that will force those irrational traits into dominating the entire character. This refusal to supply the Nazi with an adequate framework has led to a general vagueness as to just what a Nazi is, a fact strikingly brought out in the only movie Hollywood has made in which there is admitted to be such a person as a homegrown fascist—"The Keeper of the Flame." The astounding fact about the fascist in this movie is that no one knew he was a fascist, and he was the most renowned person in America.

In an anxious relationship like that of Hollywood to the public, which is rather like the one between a child and the parent whom he wishes to please, the level of Hollywood's behavior will approximate the level of the public's response. The public's response has often been disastrously irresponsible. This was apparent in the most important of wartime movie polls (that taken by Film Daily), in which the nation's movie commentators were asked whether they thought Hollywood should deal with controversial issues. More than a third of them (38 percent) thought not—"No," said one, "let's keep controversy away from our shores as long as possible." Or, one thought the screen should treat controversial issues of the day "if the facts are presented in such a way as not to influence the opinions of moviegoers one way or another." In a medium that is so delicately tuned not to provoke its audience, this 38 percent of the nation's film authorities can sometimes become the voice of the majority—the voice that is echoed by the vice-president of Paramount when he says, "My company carefully avoided injecting any political or controversial material into this picture."* The picture, "For Whom the Bell Tolls." But as a rule the effect of expressed opinions is more insidious than this, for it usually causes the producers to demand of their writers and directors just the amount of the sugary element that will in each picture flavor whatever of reality the writer or director would like to express. It is the denaturing ingredient that changes the castor oil into orange juice with a slight castor-oil flavor.

The movie audience's desires are to a great extent that of the school teacher who would really like to let her students use their own ways of working out a problem, but is unable to leave them alone for fear they won't all get the right answer. Mrs. Edna R. Carroll, the chairman of the Pennsylvania State Board of Motion Picture Censors, warned the movie

---

*For this and other quotations, as well as for many facts and figures, I am greatly indebted to Variety.

people that "'Desert Victory' and 'Prelude to War' must both be considered from the angle of spreading a particular doctrine or a system of principles—in short, they are propaganda films, and all such excursions into the field of propaganda via the movies are part of a pattern of regimentation which is diametrically opposed to representative, free government." This is the voice of the censor, one of Hollywood's biggest problems. Then there is the exhibitors' voice, another practical concern of the industry, which is continually rancorous, querulous and doubtful. Their chorus is that there are "too many war pictures; we want more musicals and comedies." But their remarks are always mixed with uncertain statements like this: "In spite of too many war pictures, this one, 'Commandos Strike at Dawn,' was an exception and drew a fairly good crowd. It is queer that once in a while a war picture will draw a good crowd, and I can never guess ahead of time which one it will be."

Also, above the exhibitors and the censors, are constant threats from die-hards in Congress that the country should do something about these "propaganda movies"—the last one being the Ploeser resolution demanding a congressional investigation of such pictures. Variety's statement was that the resolution "should make the men in pictures realize that Congress does not recognize for the industry the same rights of free expression and free opinion which newspapers, radio and other businesses have."

In trade journals ominous notes appeared. From The Hollywood Reporter: "Dies, Tenney and others who have taken the trouble to look deep into the activities of many of our writers and the groups that surround them are of the most definite opinion that those boys and girls are out to get communism on the screen, IF they can. BUT whether they know it or not, there are a lot of hands that handle the script before it goes to the production stage and there are more executives and producers to stop such writing than there are writers to write it." The confusion as to what movie artists can or cannot say ended in such travesties as that surrounding "The North Star" in which the producer censored his writer's script for mention of communism, the Hearst press excoriated the producer for mentioning communism, and the film's most ardent upholders praised it for not having any communism whatsoever.

The war movie comes in four shapes: the in-praise-of-a-branch-of-the-service film; half-fiction, half-historic accounts of actual battles; a kind that in the early part of 1943 threatened to swamp the exhibitors, which shows the resistance of native populations in Europe to the conquerors; and home-front films. The first and second produced the best pictures, the fourth the worst and the third the most.

The ingredients of all servicemen films are identical psychologically. The central character, whether he is a bombardier in a Flying Fortress or the captain of a United Nations ship sailing supplies to Murmansk, has by the end of the picture become a hero of the war no matter how he started—as a sulker, the brother of the captain's hated rival, or an idiot. These heroes are treated in groups rather than as individuals, and though they are given a democratic texture of names like Winocki, O'Doul, Feingold and Ramirez, they are given only one personality. Winocki-O'Doul-Feingold-Ramirez is a man of average looks, on the handsome side, very friendly, short on ideas and emotions, philosophically on the Saroyan side of the street and capable of trading you a wisecrack. At an early point in the picture the hero finds he is fighting a righteous war, because he sees the Germans or the Japanese taking blood from children to use for their own soldiers, firing on survivors of ships they have torpedoed, behaving ruthlessly in Pearl Harbor or Czecho-Slovakia, ripping up a painting by Picasso or the house that Tolstoy lived in.

The only conflicts in the pictures arise out of someone's discontent with the way things are going, e.g., that he should have been promoted instead of flunked out of pilot school, that he is too conceited, surly and know-it-all to be liked, or that he is asked to be officer of the day too many times in a row. And all this has a rotten effect on the group's morale. This conflict is resolved during the first battle, when the unruly one awakens to the fact that the Germans or the Japanese are bestial, that he would rather be fighting them than leave the service for a shore job, or when he finds that the captain is not the hard-boiled egg he supposed, because the captain asked him to play parchesi. The tolerance of this American is exhibited by his love and care for a dog, which he finds or is given by another group, and which he often calls Tojo or Hirohito. Usually there is a father in the battle whose son is killed, or has to have his leg cut off, which is meant to imply that the war is as grim as could be imagined; and there is a mother, wife or sweetheart at home to read a letter from one of the soldiers, to show that the home front is behind the boys and to show the importance of the family tie. Death and destruction in war are diluted almost out of sight by various devices. Only one of the group would be killed, and so the death was hardly noticed, or the emphasis turned from individual dying to mass slaughter so that it became no longer a matter of men dying but endless streams of extras running wildly out into the open and falling down. Death would be further sterilized by switching immediately to more heroics, intense activity or scenes with a merry note.

This does not add up to saying that all the war movies are bad. It would be closer to say that they are all slight. Their scope in no way admitted all of the material that should be encountered in dealing with the problems they set up. Many of the best films took original material that was superficial and tawdry and made the best they could out of it—this was the case with "Bataan," "Air Force" and "Sahara," which gave a good idea of the nature of the fighting and of the terrain. In them the living from moment to moment in war was splendidly realized; there were pieces of good dialogue and the beginnings of fine characterization. Yet it was all like a cheap watch that is kept running by expert attention but is doomed nevertheless to a short and not too happy life. There were films that started with sincere grasp of an actuality, but for one reason or another saw fit to erect an artificial, inadequate structure around it. Still, in films of this nature, like "Wake Island," the main procedure—the nature of one battle in the war—is still discernible and informative. The work of expert hands was always noticeable: the production handling of Nunnally Johnson on "The Moon Is Down," that of Hawks and Tay Garnett on everything they direct, the writing of Dudley Nichols, Robert Andrews and Lillian Hellman. Players like Humphrey Bogart, Sir Cedric Hardwicke and Lloyd Nolan projected in look and gesture a strength of character that made up for much of the content lost in the script, though naturally their talents projected only humanity and not ideas. The virtue of an otherwise dull movie of how the Czechs struck back at the Nazis and their mad hangman Heidrich was that the producers of "Hangmen Also Die" stated forcefully how much they hated Nazis and the weight of this emotion was, within its scope, completely convincing. Despite everything, Hollywood's mass of film will leave to posterity the greatest mirror of a kind that has ever been left of a war.

Though there was muttering in various quarters (including this one) about the quality of war films, and though the public itself was heard to complain, it at the same time encouraged what it was getting. When, in the poll of the movie commentators mentioned before, the question was asked as to whether too many war pictures were being made, there were 42 percent who thought not, but did think, with Archer Winsten of The New York Post, that there were "not too many but too many routine ones." The 58 percent who thought there were too many war pictures had often the same thing to say: "Yes [no war pictures], but principally because there have been so many shoddy, cheap, downright bad war pictures." In spite of these judgments and the constant pleading of the motion-picture exhibitors to please stop making war films, the fact is that few war pictures of better Hollywood quality have failed since the war started to be what the box-office statisticians label an outstanding hit. In 1942 alone, this included twenty-one pictures. "Mrs. Miniver" made $5,000,000 in 1942,

"Sergeant York" had made $4,000,000 in 1941, and "So Proudly We Hail" was on the way to doing that well in 1943.

In fact, the confusion of criticism and suggestion was further confused by the fact that "Mrs. Miniver" and "Wake Island" were the public's favorites last year, the latter by the men, the former by the women and the children. (The children are extremely interesting: in the poll of the National Board of Review of Motion Pictures they caused consternation by voting "Kings Row," which was a grim movie concerning psychiatry, sadism and incestuous fathers and daughters, as the fourth-best picture of the year, after the newspaper critics had roundly upbraided it: what they say about war pictures is well summed up by a conversation about a typical film of this kind. Eleven-year-old girl: "Little children in 1A, 2A, 3A are afraid of war pictures"; thirteen-year-old boy—"If they see these pictures they will learn not to be scared—five, six years old, they got to learn some time.") Obfuscating the enormous popularity of "Mrs. Miniver" were the nation's soldiers, who went to thirty other films more often than they went to "Mrs. Miniver," which they seemed to dislike violently, but no more so than "In Which We Serve," which the New York Film Critics judged the best of the year.

The agitated perplexity of the exhibitors is understandable; but there seemed no reason in the war years for them to take their perplexity seriously. People went to see anything. The figures for the 1942 year of the war shows that four and a quarter million more people went to the movies *weekly* than went in 1941, for five and a half cents more on an average for a ticket. In 1941 the seven major film companies had made $36,000,000 more than they had in 1939 (when the foreign market was still there). For every twelfth American there was a movie seat—the others stood outside and waited for him to get up. The hardest time to get in was at 7:30 p. m. on Sunday.

The character of the movie audience has changed radically during the war years. It no longer seems to be the silent, rapt mass it once was: there is a noticeable quality of more or less cynical detachment, it has become a little more like the audience at a ball park where the crowd is broken up into pockets of people who do not give up their personality wholly to the spectacle but in one form or another express their own reactions—moviegoers nowadays are running conversations with one another, criticizing the film while watching it, taking the whole thing far less seriously than formerly. The reasons, and there are many, must have largely to do with the war: people have more money and are less fiercely intent on getting the most for it; they are living outside the settled equilibrium of home existence; they are going more frequently, less to see the movie than to get somewhere simply to sit down (this is particularly sadly applicable to servicemen and their girls); the crowds are younger and less frozen; longer hours of work for parents make the movie theatres improvised nurseries; and perhaps most of all, a curious atmosphere that wartime is to some extent vacation time, a transition period in which life is not quite the same as it has been before.

The attitude of the audience showed itself in many odd ways. Prices could be raised as much as twenty cents in some cities and attendance would still increase. As people made more money, the attendance at neighborhood houses fell off, because the people preferred theatres showing the latest movies and charging the highest admissions. The plight of the small theatres, it was said, was equally the result of the blackout—an inability to see such theatres as well as the fear of housewives to venture into less frequented, dimmed-out streets. Vandalism hit a peak in ferocity. One man was stopped in a New York theatre who had an upholsterer's knife on him; when questioned by the police, he said he was going to rip up all the seats. Drapes were being hauled down and pushed into toilets, in some cities it became popular to put lighted cigarettes into the seats—which was so successful in the Campus Theatre in Berkeley, California, that it burned to the ground. Smoldering chairs were found in the State Theatre in Oakland on four successive nights, and the manager of an El Paso, Texas, theatre strode the aisles with a shotgun to keep order. People in Boston complained that young males removed their hats less and less. The theatres' position in the morality of the community was equivocal: the United Automobile Workers wanted them to stay open from one to five-thirty a.m. so that defense workers would be kept away from drink, while the Good Government Club of St. Louis moved that they close at ten p.m. so that the residents would buy more war stamps, get more sleep and stop drinking.

In Hollywood itself the war has made many changes. By 1943 one of the most peculiar and important wartime effects was that some thirty former scriptwriters had become directors and producers. Their first efforts proved to be serious undertakings which were more like novels or plays than the movies had ever been before. Once more the stage and everything in it came to Hollywood; from Broadway came stage producers, the entire Theatre Guild and every play and musical comedy in sight. Leading men were scarce as hen's teeth, and actors who had been in retirement for years were coming back. The studios were having trouble getting enough Japanese-looking males for battle scenes—you were seeing the same little man die five times in one movie—and enough extra men who looked big enough and strong enough to act American soldiers. In the confusion of the question as to whether or not to make war pictures, musicals became more popular than they had been in the peak year of the early talkies, and dancers were at a premium. Any orchestra venturing into Hollywood came out minus half its members, who stayed behind at good pay to dub in music. Hollywood also met the mysterious demand for horror pictures, but no one surpassed Universal, and no one surpassed Variety in describing what Universal was doing: "Universal to toss Wolf Man and Ghost of Frankenstein into one horrendous grapple. Lon Chaney Jr. who played monster in both pictures to clinch with himself."

The contribution of the movies toward entertaining troops, selling bonds and instructing newly recruited factory workers, was of a size that only Hollywood achieves. By June, 1943, 2,000 actors had made 13,000 camp appearances, 3,000 bond-selling tours, 300 special films for the government—the first on sex hygiene, the last, "Battle Formations"—the "Rifle Platoon." Twelve hundred 16mm. prints of current pictures were circulating to troops overseas, which made 7,000, all told, in circulation. The Hollywood canteen had entertained approximately 1,000,000 servicemen since its opening; motion pictures were training aircraft workers faster than they had ever been trained before.

The most significant work in motion pictures during the war has been contributed by official government information services in England, Russia, Canada and this country which have communicated the actual life and temper of the war in factual films. Even this documentary arm, which is the only one on the movie body that is alive and comparatively free, is forced to function within the social and political boundaries that prevailing opinion in each country sets for it. But within these boundaries the artist is given the freedom and means to express his subject matter with all the power and persuasion he possesses, and on the whole the limits have allowed material that is more adult and sensible than what is permitted in Hollywood. In the documentary film there is a quality of straight, level communication with the audience on as high a level as the makers of the film know and it is this direct honesty that marks the principal difference of the documentary from the Hollywood film.

The documentaries have been made in England, Canada, Russia and by the Signal Corps in this country. Among the finest have been the Russian "Moscow Strikes Back" and "Siege of Leningrad." There have been a great number of significant English films, the prize specimens probably being "Desert Victory," "Target for Tonight," "Listen to Britain" and "The Silent Village." Documentaries in Canada have concentrated on an editorialized newsreel compilation ("World in Action" series) which has been the only one to view the war consistently as a worldwide affair rather than a narrow, nationalistic one, and the only one to interpret its patterns as they progressed. Here, the Signal Corps, under the direction of several Hollywood artists like Capra, Litvak and Keighley have produced what many people feel is the best American work in years ("Prelude to War," "Battle of Britain," "Battle of Russia"). For the first time the importance of the documentary has been brought home to the great mass of moviegoers, and it must certainly be the most significant assault so far on the myth that surrounds movies—that there is one and only one kind of movie of any worth, Hollywood's. It provides, too, as witness the sudden swerve to naturalism taken by recent Hollywood war films, the competition that Hollywood so long needed. This information-film production has trained thousands of new movie technicians, whose entrance into the field indicates that we may expect a wider, more varied postwar movie world.

The war has once more pointed up the need for complete freedom from repression for the movie artist, and also the incongruous fact that in a war where freedom is the most prominent word, the most popular medium of expression is nowhere free. Censorship, as always, has been the real villain of the war-movie piece, and it is responsible for the war movie that seems never to start from inside the individual but from a filing cabinet of accepted forms. My own idea is that the movies cannot well remain exactly as they are now; the balance that has been maintained among the forces of big money, censorship and artists is becoming an imbalance, and one that I think is being affected predominantly by the striking importance of the war documentary. Hollywood artists who were not supposed to care for or want to work in anything but the accepted style of commercial cinema have shown that when given a chance at anything else they take it and produce work far above their Hollywood average. I do not think it likely that all of these artists will return to Hollywood and take up contentedly where they left off; nor do I think it probable that the movie world will be so completely dominated by Hollywood after the war. Meanwhile, the coming attraction is going to be pretty much like the one you saw last week.

January 3, 1944

Earth on Heaven

"A Guy Named Joe" is a film-malted that is mostly cloying, sometimes quite amusing, and so rich and plentiful in certain Hollywood attitudes that it is also educational. The picture features Spencer Tracy as Joe and Irene Dunne as

Dorinda Durston, in a story about a flier who is killed and returns to earth in almost the same state he left it, to help student fliers learn to fly. He can "get through to them" but they can't see or hear him. Hollywood has been fighting a tremendous battle with the problem of death in the war and this is the most elaborate statement of its conclusions on the subject.

Immediately after Joe dies in a bombing dive on a German aircraft-carrier, he is seen, jovial and as good as new, walking and whistling his way across the same expanse of clouds that another transcendental wonder named Joe walked across in "Here Comes Mr. Jordan." He meets an old buddy who was killed in a bombing raid over Brest, and the two of them walk on to God's headquarters. This is an airfield, and God is a World War I ace, or Lionel Barrymore, who has given this type of advice often on earth but never before in heaven. He shows Joe that the freedom he feels when he flies high in the clouds alone as an air-man is the same kind of freedom as is being fought for on earth—"the freedom of men to breathe the very air they fly in." He tells him that he will pay his debt to the past by teaching young fliers, and Joe proceeds to pay his debt for the rest of the picture, as a kind of spiritual *alter ego* to a young flier named Pete and his girl, who used to be Joe's girl, Dorinda (Dorinda is a girl who at various times is called "pretty as a new pair of yellow shoes, pretty as a P-38, pretty as a new propellor, pretty as a dream and the prettiest girl in the world"). The moral to draw from this movie—besides the one that life after death is, if possible, a narrower state than the life before death shown in Hollywood movies—is that death is so like what comes before it that it shouldn't offer any problems to Americans. You may be bored with it if you're not a flier, or even if you are, because it is taken up completely with good works ("there is plenty of work up here," says one contented messenger), but it is not one—the movie insists—that will be a drastic change for you. And so the movies take yet another load off the mind of mankind.

This picture is also an example of the prime attitude of Hollywood toward war films: that they are going to try to keep public morale up first (in the hearty slap-on-the-back way), and second, make movies. "A Guy Named Joe" is literally a handbook of do's and don't's for airmen, and for their relatives when the airmen die, which is given a somewhat more human slant than most handbooks by wisecracking, fantasy, warmth. The essential imperfection of this and other textbook movies is that of forcing the audience to accept more coincidence, unbelievable speech-making and success-story progress than it likes to take in a picture standing for life. But the advice will do you no harm and I am going to give you as much of it as I can remember: don't tighten up at the controls, have hero hunger or lone-wolf it; think for yourself; don't take chances;

while you're up in the clouds, feel what it is like to be up there; go out with girls, or at least eat and dance with them; and pay attention to your instincts, sixth-sense—which, I take it, is your spiritual helper, Mr. Tracy, who is, never doubt, always there, trying to get in to you.

This movie is also full of a hero type who is the more average, less eccentric and less popular relation to the tall, shy cowboy-like hero and the shorter, tough men who operate in the underworld. Films like this refer to him warmly as a guy, a lug, or old boy, name him Joe, Pete, Dan or Bill, and put him into less exotic, more pedestrian jobs than the ones that Cooper and Bogart are put into. In this job he progresses, by hard, honest, uncomplaining work, from the lowest rank to the highest, even taking him, as this picture does, to Wing Commander God in heaven. He is not, for a change, anti-talk. His line, like his face, is a good, unvarnished, pliable one, that says for a name like Sanderson "Sanuhson" out of a mouth that is generally used as though full of tobacco juice. He is the movie ideal of the family man, beyond sin, but he is apt to spend the picture, as Gable did in "It Happened One Night," treating and teasing his girl as if she were a dumb little child. His life with his girl is usually, besides a continual stream of banter, cute. This hero's existence is consciously intended to be a more rounded one, and his personality capable of responding with greater elasticity to that existence than were the heroes personified by Cooper or Bogart, but, unlike them, he is usually sugared to death.

There is a speech at the end of "A Guy Named Joe" that is the finest description of this kind of film. Part of it runs, "Everything's going to be prettier, you're not to have any more bad dreams, you're going to have all the things people have, your life is going to be living, laughing, fighting and loving. . . ."

January 17, 1944

Among the Missing: Hitchcock

"Lifeboat," the new Alfred Hitchcock movie, is a kind of ersatz film that both irritates and holds you effortlessly to its exposition for more than two hours, though it hardly ever moves outside the radius of a rather large-sized lifeboat. The film enacts the story of ten people in this boat, somewhere off Bermuda, nine of whom are survivors from an American freighter sunk by a U-boat, and the tenth is a Nazi from the submarine which the freighter sank just before going down. The film's design is to show how this Nazi (beautifully played by Walter Slezak), by taking advantage of the others' humanity, sense of fair play, divided aims and general physical and mental debility, gains control of their boat, their minds and bodies and stabs them all in the back. This intended parallel to the way the Nazis came into power leaves a number of points in doubt, proves itself by some rather flat-footed dénouements and is never essentially convincing. It is an intellectual preconception that never seems to come out of the natures of the people involved, but happens like a shotgun wedding. This inevitability is no doubt just what the authors wanted, but it is their inevitability, not the film's or its people's; one of its failures is that you get no idea of what passes in men's minds and in their relationships during an event that is one of the most strikingly odd, awesome and important occasions of this time. You will come out of this movie knowing no more of what it is like in a lifeboat with a few people in mid-ocean than you did when you went in.

Hitchcock and the two authors (John Steinbeck wrote the original and Jo Swerling did the screen adaptation) have performed a major-league trick of entertainment and concision in keeping you comfortably and completely interested in their story, though it is solid talk in rather close quarters. They have jolted the voyage from one bewildering event to another (each event made compulsively ironical), left out all transitions or passive moments, achieved a certain realism on a theatrical level and rightly concentrated on the arresting looks of the cast. It is a strange voyage: no one is silent or discomforted, or hungry, or cold, or afraid, nor are you supposed to feel much of that. The events pile up ineffectually one on the other; they give you no intimation of the characters' personalities; there is a great deal of old scenario baggage in the boat, yet the picture never lets go of you.

The cast is the most invigorating one to look at—person for person—that I have seen in years, and it is a capable one directed by a man who seldom leaves any bad acting on the line. Personally, I could only marvel at William Bendix's capacity for following the director's orders to the letter (his drunk scene is the best thing in the picture), have nothing but praise for Hull, whose jovial capitalist is beyond my analysis, like Hume Cronyn best, Bankhead least, and feel that Mary Anderson is a twin of Teresa Wright's and a good one.

But this film contains less of the original Hitchcock quality, before it got caught in the Hollywood assembly line four years ago, than any of the American films Hitchcock has made since. He still exercises a good hand with his players, though the acting here is much broader, more theatrical and showy than anything he made use of before, and his sense of pace still operates: these two talents make the picture as much as the melodrama, the flashy dialogue or the actors themselves. There is no longer the intent or the need on his part to make his material, no matter how romantic it is, seem perfectly real and natural in appearance—the quality that made his English films light but rewarding experiences of the manners, classes of people, architecture and prejudices of our time.

He indicates this naturalism in the very opening scene of "Lifeboat"—but never again after that—when he realizes the whole emotional effect of the freighter's sinking by concentrating solely on the movement of the smokestack as it passes into and out of sight under the water. Then he makes a characteristic, sardonic visual comment on the fact by passing some of the freighter's wreckage in the water before your eyes: a crate of oranges, a copy of The New Yorker, some currency, a deck of cards slowly fanning out, and a Nazi's dead body. It is the satirically edged naturalism of an intelligent, highly inquisitive creative talent from which emotion is largely lacking, which uses nothing but the means of the cinema to tell its story and has an exact eye and ear with which to do it. Everything else in this movie is theatrical or posed—when a person or group sits in the boat you feel instinctively that they were arranged there a moment before and aren't going to do anything that isn't in the script. The lifeboat gives less the illusion of a lifeboat, for all its pitching and tossing, than of an expansive, well protected stage, and the actors, in spite of their caked mouths and peeled, sunburned skin, seem the best fed, most rested and secure actors in the war movies. It is this lack of belief in or concern for the actual event in the picture that makes you most distrustful of what it tells you.

Hitchcock's working vocabulary—before the death-dealing pressure in Hollywood hit him—was one of the most natural and complete that I know of in contemporary movie-making; but that vocabulary dwindles more and more as the number of his films increases. There is no indication in "Lifeboat" of his talent for getting the most startling effects with sound, nor of his use of screen silence to build the highest tension into a moment. But sometimes here, as in the playing of Hume Cronyn, he realizes that peculiar Hitchcock manner with the player, in which the actor seems to be concentrating mentally on what he is about to do but never quite does it; so that his pantomime takes on a kind of sinister spontaneity. At one point where Alice (Mary Anderson) is telling Mrs. Porter (Tallulah Bankhead) of her fear of becoming an adulteress, the crossed feet, which belong to the man sitting above her, and which stick into the top of the scene, suddenly fall apart, making one of those typical symbolic allusions that were always possible in Hitchcock's early films. At another point, in the siesta of the young lovers, the man repeats an action that has occurred before—undoing the ribbon around the girl's hair—and she asks, perplexed and somewhat irritated, "Stanley, why must you do that?" It is the highly surprising and spontaneous statement that was also more likely than not in the early films.

I hope that "Lifeboat" is only an aberration and not the solidifying of a destructive trend in Hitchcock's work, and also, if it is a result of pressure, which seems likely, someone will have the sense to remove same.

January 24, 1944

Pow, Bam and Sock

"The Miracle of Morgan's Creek" is Preston Sturges' most gag-concentrated comedy, his smoothest, most artificial, cautious and showmanlike one, his most consciously Mack Sennett-modernized, and his most entertaining film.

Sturges has realized his trademark in this movie better than in any of his other films—that is, to keep a picture exploding from scene to scene with a great frenzy, excitement and energy, by gagging anything either for a laugh or to keep the pace and nature of the movie close to a rout. The most endearing quality of Sturges' roughhouse is that it is pulled off with speed, positiveness and pleasure; there is no pettiness, innuendo, or the puss-in-boots naughtiness that one finds in the comedies of Lubitsch, or the bored, effortless kind that is so popular everywhere today in which the person is paid to be funny and does so—ennui and all. Sturges enters a film like a runner starting a race—to have a good time for his money, to do the best he can under the circumstances, and under no circumstances to allow anything to slow down. Nothing is smooth or exact, but it is all full of spirit. Even his slynesses—his maneuvering of leg-art into most scenes or his mere aping of sincere movie art—are good-natured, clean, vigorous and in character. Sturges' films come very close to the energetic sadism of primitive comic strips like "The Katzenjammer Kids," and they are a fine pleasure.

He has two essentially funny facts in this movie. The first is Norval: played so well by Eddie Bracken, who is beaten to his socks because of his humility, fine nature and dependability by his girl (Betty Hutton), her sister, a fifteen-year-old brain (Diana Lynn) and their father (William Demarest). The story of this picture—the policeman's daughter who has a child but no father for it and picks out Norval to be the father—is only incidental to the main theme, which is to kick Norval around the movie. Norval is a fine character because he has more than one terrible malignancy to suffer from: he has three to be exact—a stutter, high blood pressure, which he calls "the spots" and which choke him up at important occasions, and the gesture of slapping his hands together to stop his stuttering. Along with that he is a likable youth whom Sturges has dressed well, given a good upbringing and made as ingratiating as possible (by his choice of Mr. Bracken to play the part), so that you don't feel he is just another punching bag for a slapstick comedy—even though the film amounts to a complexity of slow takes, humiliations, falls, agonized screams and speechless apoplecticisms by Norval. Norval's humanity and wholesomeness give a roundness and likableness that is extremely important to the movie because no other character gives them. The other funny fact is the relationship of unrestricted loathing that exists between the very smart younger sister and her father. This is a nice clean affair; they hate each other—and rightly so—and this isn't confused.

A Sturges player must have the same bounding energy as the movie he is in and provide a face and personality that are (save for the hero's) quite striking but devoid of humanity. The characters he has chosen and directed in this picture are perfect fits—for instance, the dowdy fat hen who plays the blues trombone at the social, Porter Hall's justice of the peace, who enters the film looking through a stereopticon, the Louise Fazenda character who serves as witness for the young people's wedding, and the brief but wonderful performance by Akim Tamiroff as the state political boss—all have the great clarity and bizarre provincialism that is demanded. The playing is generally more vigorous than perfect—for instance Bracken's stutter almost never seems right, but the roughness of pace, speech and manner is all part of the conscious primitivism.

There is a catch to all of this. While Sturges forces his roughhouse as fast as he can from one gag to another, somewhere very far distant and very faint is the story—the movie is in other words hollow. It is a business completely of surface and you are always conscious of both its lack of insides and the extreme forcing that goes on. Unlike the comedies with Chaplin, Keaton or Fields, or those of Clair, the gags are seldom the natural product of the type of character involved, but are set-ups that the character is pushed headlong into. There is always in a Sturges film the feeling that he is above most of his comedy effects and that he is stooping quite far to make use of a comedy of which he realizes the entertainment value, as well as the fact that he realizes that a more profound, devastating satire (which he is more capable of in movies than anyone I know) is impossible in Hollywood and slapstick is a formula to rest comfortably in. It is the difference between feeling that Sennett or the man who draws the Katzenjammer Kids is right in his own back yard while Sturges is actually slumming. Everything comes out extremely well because he has an amazing talent for comedy and moving pictures; he gives a film every ounce of his energy and attention, and he is quite irresponsible anyway, so there is no confusion. This is, in other words, a good movie.

February 7, 1944

Theatrical Movies

LIKE many words used in talking about movies, the word "theatrical" is vaguely and loosely applied, usually as a term of disparagement. Since I use it often myself and since I think it is an important term in movie criticism, I would like to give my definition of it.

The use of "theatrical" as a movie description depends essentially on the way the events of the film are related to the camera eye. If the events are arranged to progress as though there were no camera present, if the camera merely watches and records what those events look like, the movie is to my mind the true nature of a movie: that is, it is non-theatrical and by way of being an anomaly in these days. In this case the acting and procedure of the event will be seen propelled solely by factors within the event itself, irrespective of the camera. Therefore, if the events are not treated as spontaneous, unalterable happenings witnessed by an impersonal camera, but are arranged before it as though it were the eye of the audience and the events developed in order that they may be seen by the camera in the role of an audience, the process is essentially a theatrical one. Then it is a reënactment toward an audience—the process is no longer that of watching an action but of acting it toward those who watch it. The difference between a theatrical and non-theatrical film is most closely felt when, in seeing a true movie, one senses that it has been watched by the camera in such a way as to have left it with a life of its own, which takes place without reference to an audience—clearly not the attitude of the stage. The whole complexity of relationships (actor to actor, actor to environment, etc.) is consistently interwoven, proceeding as though unaware of director, writer or cameraman. The best pictures of Clair, Hitchcock's English work, von Stroheim's "Greed," the best Russian work, Griffith's films, the French "Crime and Punishment" are examples of movies that proceed unmolested by the idea of the audience.

When a movie is called theatrical it is conventionally inferred to be either static in regard to its locale, or talky, or both. Yet Donat's extemporaneous speech to the political society in Alfred Hitchcock's "The 39 Steps" is both, and is still essentially cinematic because the attitude in filming it was that of watching impersonally, with the strictest adherence to the inviolable course of a train of events, of finding from moment to moment the most significant thing to watch: that is, the relationships within the event were never sacrificed for a relationship between the scene and the audience. On the other hand, Hitchcock's latest movie, "Lifeboat," is eminently theatrical, but not because it is dialogue-heavy and confined to a single set. Its theatricality lies in the fact that it is entirely an arrangement in which the audience does not, as it should, seem outside of the event, but is the main person in the boat, the person everyone speaks to and for whom everything is happening. The event that is supposed to be taking place falls away from conviction at every point for this reason—it simply is not taking place in a lifeboat in the middle of an ocean but right in front of you on a stage. The characters are constantly stepping past the boundaries of the scene into an oration that is divided from the scene by the fact that their words are no longer driven and provoked by the situation but by the audience. That is why this movie, and most Hollywood movies, are visually enormously inadequate to the content of the plot.

The fact that a movie is least theatrical when the attitude in constructing its action is "What does the event look like?" is dependent on the initial factor in the movie process, the camera, which in simplest terms is a machine for recording the visual diary of an event. The movie that disrupts and designs events to make a play of them before the camera immediately destroys the felicity of the camera: there is no event left, only representations of it, and the preservation of the purity of the event is the reason for being of the camera. Equally, the movie which is seen topsy-turvy, through a complexity of spectacular camera angles, is no less theatrical for, again, destroying the main function of the camera in order to make it the chief entertainer in the movie process—besides being vulgar.

Most scenarios are written today with so little regard for displaying the events sufficiently that the amount of story and character considerably outweighs the final visual product; after you have heard this kind of movie's sound track once you will never again be influenced by its ideas because those ideas are so little equaled, proved or synthesized with the picture's visual record. There is actually an abnormal Hollywood confidence in how well they can project any emotion or event in visual terms: so that in movies like "Lifeboat" or "Casablanca"—the two most theatrical popular movies I can think of at the moment—you find the directors and writers attempting a visual realization of everything from jazz to pronouncements on the history of the last decade, throwing in on the way several counter-plots of love, intrigue and the nature of war, and actually giving only an inaccurate, flashy hint of these things and never meanwhile coming anywhere near a movie truth. It is my opinion that the fascination of these two films lies in a visual fact, that of watching vital, invigorating-looking people, but not in anything they are doing or saying.

February 14, 1944

The Happiness Boys

AMONG movie-goers there is a sect whose members prefix all discussions of films with the statement: "I only go to the movies to be entertained." The statement implies that the rest of us, who are serious about the films, go to them as we would to castor oil. Any appreciation of art is a satisfaction of an emotional need and therefore a pleasure; the people who go to the movies *just* to be entertained are not referring to this pleasure but are implying that the movies aren't art and if taken at all ought to be taken frivolously, and that those who do think the movies are an art go to them in a vain pursuit of nonexistent esthetic values. All the implications of their statement seem to me snobbish and silly.

The main trouble with their proposition is that it actually supposes that a person can consciously leave all of his experience of life and his desire for new experiences behind him when he goes to the movies, and can present to the movie a kind of third-rate part of himself that is interested only in being diverted by what he believes are third-rate representations of life. Short of blind self-deception or a peculiarly affected attitude toward esthetics, I don't know how this can be done. It might be comfortable if one could leave at home when he goes to the movies his convictions of actuality, his instinctive sense of harmony, rhythm, balance and unity, his dislike of the spurious, the academic and the unimportant; that is what Hollywood's press agents might desire most. It's a nice idea, but it won't work, because there is hardly a movie in which at least one person wasn't passionately and earnestly involved in his performance—as soon as you can detect the area of this person's activity neither the press agent nor anyone else can be frivolous with a clear conscience. In spite of which the people who go to the movies just to be entertained defend their kind of movie-going with the statement that the movies today are made with no serious intent. And yet last year movies like "Watch on the Rhine," "The Oxbow Incident," "The Hard Way," "The Moon Is Down," were meant in their entirety to be taken completely seriously no matter how well their aim was achieved—to look at them just to be entertained was to be foolish.

The argument for movies only as entertainment (a less offensive way of saying the movies are a place for slumming) implies that the more seriously one takes the movies, the less pleasurable they become. The serious-minded, though, go to be shown the movie-maker's idea, the best the movie-maker can do with his idea. To be shown anything less than the best is to be given that much less pleasure—unless one is more entertained by artifice and bad performance than by its opposite. To differentiate in movies, as in any art, really enlarges the pleasure to be got from them, whether the movie turns out to be good, bad or indifferent. The bad, in this way, takes on more meaning and definition, and therefore serves a wider purpose. To seek merely entertainment in movies seems to me to be an aim toward misinformation and ignorance rather than toward the avowed aim of pleasure—merely an aim toward not understanding the full context of a movie fact. There are people who don't confuse the qualities of pleasure in Irving Berlin and Bach; yet meanwhile they are degrading the concept of pleasure in art by lumping all movies, good, bad and indifferent, into a category labeled "something by which to be entertained." The reason for this standardlessness is often that the entertainment-seekers think a good picture is the pretentious idiocy of the so-called serious film which is a slugging match of trick camera angles, heavy shadows, stagnancy, pompous dialogue and deep thinking (for this kind of "art film" see "The Voice in the Wind"): the people who have this kind of movie concept have actually little idea of what a good movie is. A really great movie like "Greed," with the rich exactness of the material it shows in pursuit of its theme, has no relation at all to the "art film" and makes the "entertainment film" seem flimsy and eminently unsatisfying solely on the grounds of pleasure.

I believe that in some quarters the question is still being battled as to whether the movies are art. Battle or no battle, that the movies are an art is a fact: the movies are a medium for human expression and differ from poetry only as poetry differs from painting or from music, in having a different set of technical instruments.

I am not making out a case for every movie as a work of art. I too have heard the Hollywood slogan—"The movies are your best entertainment," and I have seen my share of junk. My case is, however, that if you go to the movies for the diversion offered by an exhibition of junk, Hollywood, in more ways than one, has put something over on you.

The Great Cardboard Event

"The Song of Bernadette" is an overwhelmingly careful failure to present the religious career of Bernadette Soubirous, who in Massabielle, France, in 1858, saw a beautiful Lady who called herself the Immaculate Conception and produced a healing spring at the place of the vision. The script for this modern religious movie epic is uninspired to the point of tedium, and has been produced as though the entire picture were on trial before the Catholic Church. It is so cautious that near the end the whole production appears to be turning to stone: when people bend they creak, lifetime associates meet and come together with all of the recognition of ambulating sculptures, and they look at each other with paralyzed faces. It is actually one of the most sick, wracked films I have ever seen: there are several people who talk as though they had nasal catarrh, most of them look as if they were wearing deathmasks, and the heroine (Jennifer Jones) has been directed to be retiring to the point of evaporation. Everything is very delicate. I think that in general woodenness has been confused with seriousness, sensitivity and piety, that almost childlike idiocy has been confused with the goodness and the religious passion of a young girl, and that an arrangement of tableaus is confused with a movie.

"The Song of Bernadette," besides lacking grease for its joints, is dry of situations, movie devices and character insight. It has two basic images—both static: Bernadette kneeling in a grotto watching the beautiful Lady, and a talk between two or more village people or Church people to try to disprove the fact. Neither Bernadette nor the villagers and the Church are characterized sufficiently. The villagers, who are the leading performers, have been done more humorously, exactly and richly by a dozen prewar French movies.

The difference between the French prewar products and this, as far as showing French people is concerned, is that we seem to stop our characterizations with the casting and the costuming, and thereafter take our characters out of their environments and events to exhibit them in show-off fashion like prize hogs. Even the air seems to be on exhibit in "Bernadette," as the freshest, most real, pearly air in captivity, along with the other fixtures. There is no relationship to a period, a richly differentiated manner of life or a defined environment. Our films have a baldness, while those that the French made had a definite pigment, texture and substance. The talk, which here is the one device, is sprung out of great, devouring close-ups, each of which has been designed as a masterpiece of painting. The production of a Hollywood epic is pushed to such a level of pretentiousness and is so thorough that nothing can escape it: even Marcel Dalio (the remarkable player who accompanied Gabin in the escape in "Grand Illusion"), who of all the people in the picture is aware of the temperament of a petty bourgeois and did present its idiosyncrasies in his policeman in "Bernadette," is nevertheless just as much a museum piece as the rest of the players.

I doubt whether the producers knew much—or dared to—about Bernadette's life. Her movie biography, as scant as it is, is standard for famous movie biographies: she came of poor but honest people—a baker and his wife who had four children and lived in the basement of a prison which was too cold to serve as a prison; she was ridiculed and harassed by society until she died for believing in her vision; everyone who had ridiculed or doubted her was punished or apologized; she died—of a tumor and tuberculosis of the leg—but happily in sight of her Lady. The discussions as to whether she was the real thing or not—as in all movie biographies—take up most of her life and get the picture nowhere except in length and conventionality.

Bernadette is characterized in the film by giving her a strangely unsure, mincing walk, a baby voice and a completely passive nature. She is portrayed in general as very pretty and doll-like in the manner of a children's book child-saint; the entire movie to my mind is conceived on the terms and for an audience that reads children's books. It is consecrated to not analyzing anyone's ideas, character or profession beyond an insufficient hint, a cliché characterization or a light tap on the wrist hurriedly followed by a hearty slap on the back. The atheist, Vincent Price, is slapped a little harder, but the slap is so belated and insincere that it is one of the worst moments in the movie.

For whatever service it may be to movie-goers, I should like to list fairly often what I think are the best of recently released films. At the moment they are "The Miracle of Morgan's Creek" and "Phantom Lady."

March 6, 1944

Two Phantoms

"Phantom Lady" is a mystery movie about a New York engineer, Alan Curtis, who is convicted of strangling his wife, Marcella, to death but is saved from the chair by his secretary, Ella Raines, who at the last minute finds the real murderer. This is a likable thriller that works much harder than most modern movies to turn up some actual life in actual settings, and to project the psychological states of both its people and its events in a genuine movie way. As a mystery it leaves you with more riddles than it solves: for instance, the murderer seems to have been in two places at the time of the crime, the hero was convicted, first degree and all, though he was witnessed everywhere but at the scene of the crime—nor is the case history of the phantom lady cleared up by your finding her at the end of the picture in her home on Long Island under the care of a psychiatrist. Being generally unhampered by circumstantial evidence, the picture is able to construct a convenient movie chain of events, such as a jam session, a seduction scene in a hotel room and the trailing of a barkeep home from work. Simply by trying to show the main visual facts of these events, the film achieves a certain degree of lust and frenzy on the part of the jazz drummer, of discomfiture on the part of Miss Raines, who has to endure his advances, and the clammy fear of the barkeep. The producers, for once, were interested in the psychological tone of each event and as a result they got hysteria out of the jazz bit, a stalking quality into the trailing episode, and lust in the seduction. Despite all this, which is likable, and despite the realism of the decor and photography, the scenes for one reason or another seem contrived, not going deeply or exactly enough into their realism, winding off to keep on the right side of the Hays Office, or being stiffened by the ham nature of the casting, acting and dialogue. Everything might have been better had the actors been closer in looks to New York bars and theatres than they are to their Hollywood studios, or had their playing been less stereotyped. Its chief attribute is that where it has had an incident to project, it has actively entered the event and tried to get over to the audience the heart of the moment instead of relaxing into the lazy evasiveness that bogs down most movies.

Some of the important features of "Jane Eyre" are that it tries for a gloomy, passionate spirit, which it achieves in only the secondary effects of the film; that, though it threatens time and again to pursue some one of its events into the depth, subtlety and significance that are demanded by each event, it never actually does, and remains a meager, chaotic résumé of itself; that it has had the common movie difficulty of transcribing the events of a novel with equal significance into the time limit of a movie. Little occurs in "Jane Eyre" beyond two barely adequate conversations between Jane and Mr. Rochester and abrupt, hectic and invariably second-hand allusions to events—nor are these allusions made better by doing them so brown in painting-like compositions which achieve a pretty obviousness inappropriate to the stark emotional moods they are intended to present.

Jane Eyre herself in movie language is confined in characterization to that uptilted head and that heartsore expression that are becoming Joan Fontaine's trademark. She is glimpsed so whenever the directors can find a place for her in such a complexity of material and only two hours to present it all—usually in or around Orson Welles's blanketing performance of Rochester. That performance presents Rochester in three versions, one given by Welles's toasty-crackle voice, the second by his face, and the third by his second face, which is composed of make-up and the shadows of photographer George Barnes. Charlotte Bronte's or the adapters' words are never so important as Mr. Welles's voice, and the character of Rochester is what you can piece together out of the indications of humanity washing around in the flood of his unregulated and unbashful talent. Along with his two faces and Joan Fontaine's one, the real visual matter of the film consists in a pot-pourri of gloomy paraphernalia—scenes on the moors and inside Thornfield, sudden moans, screams and candles coming out of the blackness, music full of foreboding, and every minute or so a lonely carriage and four traversing the moor. All of these Gothic splashes hint of things that never quite materialize, including your interest.

March 13, 1944

B Plus

"The Curse of the Cat People" is a Val Lewton-produced B-picture about a problem-child which is a sound educational aid to parents, an occasionally delicately exact portrait of a child, and so sincerely adult-minded in its whole approach as to make it the least Hollywood-like film from Hollywood this year. Its problem has a startling dignity and human significance for a Hollywood movie—being about a child (Ann Carter) who worries or antagonizes the people around her with her day-dreaming: the more she antagonizes them the more she is forced back on the people of her fantasies for "friends." When she finds an old photograph of her father's deceased, psychopathic first wife, she sees her as one of her fantasied "friends," and the father is afraid his daughter has become mentally ill and is under a curse. His insistence that she stop day-dreaming brings about the climax, and the film's conclusion is that he should have more trust and faith in his daughter and her visions.

The entire writing and production of the film are surprisingly devoted to the interests of a sincere understanding of its problem. It is no textbook on the reason and development of childhood day-dreamers, but its ideas, I think, are unusually adequate and its motivations logically and subtly developed. The box-office connection it makes to the earlier "Cat People" and its use of a conventional plot-enlivener about a haunted house are too melodramatic for the picture's needs, but even with these there has been a real effort to work them into the theme with convincing psychological presence and relationship. Much of the characterization is lacking in the usual synthetic trappings and romantic aids, and technically the picture was produced with sensitivity and thought. On its naturalistic level, "The Curse of the Cat People" lacks sufficient life in the significance of its insights into reality, and the playing, which is on the stiff, precarious side of naturalism, doesn't compensate for this sterility with enough vitality to make it an artistic dream movie. But it has so much more dignity than the other Hollywood films around that it seems at this moment inordinately wholesome.

Besides its general respect for intelligence, it has the ability to convey at times the exact quality of certain states of childhood. It is especially good in getting across the delicacy and warm enchantment surrounding the girl in her day-dreaming, through close-ups and the lighting of her face and blond hair. There are a few extraordinary moments in the treatment of these episodes— one of them when the girl sits by the pond in her yard, friendless and in the first stage of reverie, and dips her hand idly through the water: the symbolized view of her arm in and out of the water produces a very strange, almost macabre, visual impression. At another time there is a fine use of sound and constructions of shadows that build a very convincing accompaniment to the child's nightmare. The lyrical use of people, sound and light when the child's daydreamed friend appears, and the scenes between the two, in spite of the burleycue discordancy of the treatment of Simone Simon—in an amazing garment—are excellent compared to some similar vision-producing in "The Song of Bernadette." The performance of the girl in "The Curse of the Cat People," which is not remarkable, is still less wooden and more passionate than Jennifer Jones's in "Bernadette." They do, for instance, some fine things here with the small girl's walks toward and within the haunted house—capturing the right degree of fascination and fear.

The quality of these moments throws the sterility of the characterization of a number of other important items of the picture into an even more pronounced light—the un-Hollywood-treated parents are also uncharacterized —beyond their looking exactly like the young married pair that used always to come on in small-town movie advertisements for the local grocer or shoe store; also their home, their daughter's school life and her schoolteacher have the same ideal innocuousness. Still, whatever its lack of vitality, it hasn't the sickly green cast of the usual superficial Hollywood product.

March 20, 1944

Hate for Sale

"The Purple Heart" is a very efficient Hollywood production, produced by Darryl F. Zanuck and purportedly written by him under the pen-name of Melville Crossman, which shows the trial by the Japanese of the eight American fliers who were captured in China after they had taken part in the bombing raid on Tokyo. The fliers are tried—in violation of international law—for murder because they are accused of having bombed non-military objectives. The real aim in trying them seems to have been to get them to disclose where and from what they took off on their mission. After the fliers have been horribly tortured and still refuse to tell the Japs, they are executed. "The Purple Heart" has a bill of goods to sell, concerning the cruelty and inhumanity of the Japanese as opposed to the humanity of Americans, which it sells very crisply and effectively. But I dislike it thoroughly.

There are ways and ways of presenting the enemy's bestiality; the way of this movie—especially with its provocative use of a trial of war prisoners as a bloodthirsty hint to those courts which, after the war, will try war criminals— seems to me to be the most inhuman, dangerous and short-sighted way. "The Purple Heart" is not interested in making you understand or in enlightening you about the Japanese character, nor in any facts that would account for such cruelty. Rather it has to offer an endless number of similar, one-dimensionally-examined examples of Japanese brutality, the effect of which is to narrow and solidify hatred of a group of people into hatred of a whole people. Besides treating an enormously complicated subject—the Japanese personality— which has a whole complexity of causal factors that "The Purple Heart" doesn't make the slightest effort to uncover, it treats an enormously delicate subject, which can have the severest, most tragic repercussions, with the care and foresight of a mad bull. I don't see a great deal of difference between the Japanese court that this movie shows and whose injustice it hates, and its own creative attitude: the movie says that the court was thoroughly biased against the fliers, while the movie's own attitude toward its every fact is completely biased; the Japanese court in this film is accused of every sort of perjury and malevolence, yet this same film sets itself up as the historical image of an event whose every detail it fashions to its own bias; it is horrified at the inhumanity of the Japanese, yet its own attitude toward them is without human feeling. Whether or not what this film shows is true, it is still, because of its narrowness and restrictiveness, to me an irresponsible picture.

"The Purple Heart," which stars as its fliers Dana Andrews, Sam Levene and Farley Granger among others, is directed by Lewis Milestone with his usual crispness and conviction, but with a more flexible turn than he showed in either "The North Star" or "Edge of Darkness," where every happening seemed a stylized, metallic proposition of an original event. There is somewhat more naturalness and give here: in the volatile energy of the fliers' responses at the trial, in Greenbaum's self-mockery, and in the imaginative and delicate rendition of youthful love that occurs in a flashback over a water-pail. There is more screen invention and quality in the way events are shown (that of the bailing out of the fliers), in the way they are introduced, and joined. I still think "The Purple Heart" is too much a device solely for allotting models to Americans for bravery and medals to the Japanese for deceit without finding out enough of the characters of the men underneath the medals.

It is a minor point—but worth bringing up after so many repetitions in war movies—that some football-players don't make All-American, and if they do, aren't necessarily characterized by that fact, nor are they always so large-sized and of middle-European parentage; some Jews do not come from New York, nor need they always be of the half comic, half wise-guy street-car conductor-type; while we're on it, why can't the Jew for once be the villain, or the pilot and leader of the airplane crew; the "Red River Valley," wonderful as it is, can't be made to fit all visual images. The Brooklyn Dodgers aren't used again in this film, but what has been said above applies to them (there are some people who go for the Giants).

As far as I know, the best of the recently released films are "The Curse of the Cat People," "The Adventures of Mark Twain" and the government release, "With the Marines at Tarawa."

The address of Blue Note Records, mentioned in "New Orleans Survival," February 21, is 10 West 47th Street, New York City.

March 27, 1944

Men in Battle

"With the Marines at Tarawa" (shot by Marine Corps photographers and assembled by Warner Brothers) is the most descriptive account of American men in combat that has been issued this war. If any film has got into the heart of battle, it is this account of one of the more dreadful engagements in the Pacific, in which some 3,000 Marines were killed or injured in taking a 22-mile-long island. None of them is shown being killed or injured; there is only the one glimpse which has been reproduced in newsreels and magazines of the dead floating in the water along the shoreline. But the nature of the fighting is indicated throughout the film's 19 minutes—in the moment where some Marines warily move forward to finish off a blasted Japanese pillbox and in every halt, doubt, erratic movement that marks their walk into possible enemy bullets; or in the unending way a machine-gun crew pours bullets straight ahead, and in the way one of the crew turns as though he had been doing this for hours and was due to go on doing it, and lights a cigarette; or in the look of the men who leave the island or those walking in across that deadly, exposed expanse of water from ship to beach. Besides the intensity of its image of men facing death at every instant, it gets over an equally meaningful one of the special state to which modern fighting has progressed. You never see the enemy because he is hidden behind incredible concrete defenses, but you realize his deadliness by the way the Marines inch their way up to these defenses until they can blast out the occupants with flame-throwers, grenades and mortars. There is a constant haze of smoke over the island from gunpowder, and by the fourth day Tarawa looks as if it had been shaved.

The producer of fictional war films, as well as everyone else, would do well to watch this short, where nothing is ever as direct, orderly and bald as it is in fiction films, and everything is full of strange idiosyncrasies and unpredictable movements that make every scene tremendously significant. He would learn that grenade-throwing isn't something as flowery as a wind-up by Buck Newsome, that the nature of a battle might be captured wholly by a glimpse of a face that has been through it, that there is something queerer and much more moving in the walk of a really injured person than in, say, the way Thomas Mitchell walks in "Bataan." "With the Marines at Tarawa" is a film I strongly advise everyone to see.

The continuity of "Tunisian Victory," which is a joint effort by the government film units of Great Britain (under Hugh Stewart) and the United States (under Frank Capra) to record the latter part of the North African campaign as well as "Desert Victory" did the earlier part, has been chopped practically to confetti. The film seems to have been worked by several thousand cooks, each of whom decided to throw in another commentator, some more maps and some business he found exciting in another documentary. Or else the original material was spotty, or the attempt to show all of the parts of a complicated campaign in clear, scholarly manner squeezed everything down to evaporation. Whatever the reason, "Tunisian Victory" will prove, even at its level of interest, more exciting than some future schoolbook accounts of the campaign, and maybe as accurate. It has undoubtedly established a record for the number of different commentators used per second and for the number of maps used per inch.

"Chip off the Old Block" amiably intertwines several stock movie situations solely as an excuse to show the complete working vocabulary of Donald O'Connor, who was seen as a smaller boy several years ago in "Sing You Sinners," and now, after a vaudeville career and more movies, is a candidate for Mickey Rooney's role of most precocious film juvenile. O'Connor has some of the looks and vitality of a cricket, dresses like orchestra leaders or crooners, and tries everything—this includes the dancing of Fred Astaire and Don Hartman, the mugging of Mickey Rooney and some of Ben Blue's goon-like comedy. He is best without any of these influences, having a soft, unsullied and friendly quality plus an extremely cagey, vaudevillian's talent, which permits him to make use of almost any kind of material and to give it a certain charm and originality. This ability to brush off a stock gag without waving it at you will surprise you: for instance he even gets by with that business of eating the girl's powder puff instead of the marshmallow. I'd like to see him in straight roles. The picture has much of his lightness and grace when he is around doing straight non-singing, non-dancing comedy. There are a number of rather famous older people interspersed in the doings, among whom Arthur Treacher and J. Edward Bromberg enjoy themselves most with material that might kill them otherwise.

April 3, 1944

The Lady and the Belle

"Lady in the Dark" is a three-million-dollar enameling job on the Moss Hart musical play in which a woman's magazine editor (Ginger Rogers) is psychoanalyzed into marrying a younger man (Ray Milland) rather than an older one (Warner Baxter), and into becoming a less mannish female. The story has to come through the kind of technicolor that makes each shot look like the domestic interiors in linoleum ads and through the kind of costuming, interior decorating and make-up that occur most frequently in the higher-priced department stores' windows. The task of filling his scenes with color seems to have driven the director to filling them with more furniture and clothes of a spectacular nature. Scenes like the ones in the analyst's office amount to displays of what the well dressed analyst and analyzee should wear, what the one should write with and the other lie on: a special pencil gadget that unhooks from the belt, and a great green-leather monster that curves so you don't need pillows. Anyway, it is all the people can do to carry around the clothes, and the furniture seems to be sitting in their laps. The spade work of getting color into movies has to be done, of course, but I think the people who see "Lady in the Dark" will be pulling for the kind that will produce a less livid variety of neutral color, more atmosphere and more color affected by the atmosphere.

Underneath the decor, it is mainly a business of hearing the lines, and not being very much affected or convinced by them. Miss Rogers, for instance, seems just as mechanical and hard after her analysis. I thought her choice among the three men was the worst possible one. She chooses the man whom several perceptive players in the show call a heel and a stinker and who uses words like "boss-lady." The movie has her going to pieces when he is around clowning as an indication of how ill she is, whereas actually it is one of the more intelligent reactions in the picture. However completely the film disregards actual dream imagery in its dream sequences, this can be managed with extreme conviction and emotional power, as was indicated in a good B movie several years back called "Blind Alley."

"Memphis Belle" is a smart, effective job of filming by photographers of the United States Eighth Air Force, and records the nature of one of the bombing missions over Germany. The twenty-fifth trip by the crew of the flying fortress, Memphis Belle, is used for the added drama that goes with every twenty-fifth mission, the one which, if successful, sends the crew home to be flying instructors. The tip-off on the experimental attitude that put this film together comes possibly a moment before the plane's take-off, when a glimpse of a chaplain praying with four of the fliers is followed immediately by a shot of a rack of bombs being wheeled across the field to the plane. But despite this imaginative cutting, done principally by William Wyler, the first stark, clear color shots of the English countryside going underneath the plane indicate in their strength the chief attribute of the film. The photography that makes up the flight sequences is exactly chosen for what it shows, and has the added emotional impetus of the best realistic color that I've seen in films. It includes startling images like that of the plane rushing up to and through flak, a terrible scene in which the impossibly huge form of a disabled fortress is seen lazily and drunkenly falling to earth, one in which the mushrooming shapes of the first bomb-hits on Wilhelmshaven turn into a great massing and boiling up of smoke. It is much more descriptive of what is seen on the outside of the plane than on the inside, though an extremely canny use of sound and dialogue makes up for some of that.

"Memphis Belle" and "Lady in the Dark" resemble each other only in that they are both color films. The former was made by the rather odd procedure of processing already colored film in technicolor. Without losing the rough actuality of the original film, this added coloring process seems to have been used successfully in clarifying and dramatizing forms, also in composing them. "Lady in the Dark" works along on about the same opulent level that characterizes Hollywood black and white photography of recent times. Its underlying principle seems to be never to trust anything in its native state.

April 10, 1944

Up from Slavery

THE more the conventions of movie ideas and technique petrify, the more tempting buffoonery becomes as an antidote. The conventions in painting which drove the Dadaists to their burlesque were as nothing compared to the conventions the movies have built up. For the first Hollywood film Dadaist I have a few suggestions. For instance, I have always thought that the best way to film a famous novel would be to let the audience read it word for word off the screen; at the end of each chapter a list of suitable questions could be asked to see if the audience was getting it. My suggestion for the most worthwhile newsreel would be one that ran for three hours and consisted solely of horse races—the newsreel people could thus see for themselves how alike one horse race is to another and perhaps see so many of them as to get their fill once and for all.

As an antidote to the Bogart and Cooper pictures, a picture should be made in which all the people who were beaten up by Bogart or defeated by Cooper were given a chance to say why they made such a bad showing. My favorite thirty-second movie would open on an idyllic forest glade, with the faithful little boy—played by Roddy McDowall—nuzzling and petting a gentle collie dog, named Lassie: suddenly the dog would turn on Roddy and bite his head off, and the last scene would show Lassie as she was at the start but Roddy would be without a head. And then there would be an Orson Welles movie in which the camera mucked around on a dark stairway for two hours looking for Welles. I'd like to see a movie in which one never saw the faces of the players, and the idea would be that those people in the audience who could identify the actors from their bodies would be given free tickets to next week's show, in which only the legs of the players were shown; whoever could name the actors this time would be given tickets to a final performance where nothing was shown, and those who could name the actors this time would be made life-long members of those actors' fan clubs.

Just a little nonsense has gone a long way lately toward making hash of some of Hollywood's pet conventions. Much was mentioned in "The Miracle of Morgan's Creek" that was supposedly unmentionable in movies. A good deal of the value of Sturges' films in general has to do with his kidding of the more precious film conventions, and with his kicking over a few technical clichés now and then. For instance, his starting his movies from the moment the credits start has got rid of the bore of slugging through endless credits and of listening to the terrible music that is played for them. The Bugs Bunny cartoons have got a good amount of humor out of letting the rabbit manipulate the working of the film to suit his convenience, by making asides to the audience and by relaxing the seriousness of the film everywhere. Paramount News has rejuvenated a couple of its recent reels by playing around with the cutting and editing of an Australian rodeo, and using Zero Mostel for its story on the income tax.

The injection of more nonsense into the movies would no doubt lead to playing up many of the great Hollywood exaggerations by a process of worse exaggeration. The tears would well up in such torrents out of actors' eyes as to cut gorges in their faces; actors would put so little food on their forks when they ate in films that by the last reel they would have shrunk away to skeletons; they would write so fast when there was a need to write in a picture that they would finally be able to wave their hand at the sheet of paper and a five-page, closely packed letter would be the result; a new cigarette, suitable for only one puff, would be discovered; the reshaping of lips would push past the nose and eventually do away with the need for false eyelashes, and the rise in breasts would do away with the need for faces. No male actor over Dickie Moore's present age would ever be seen without his trenchcoat, and there would be trenchcoats made that intertwined so complicatedly that no man could ever be taken alive out of one. There would be movies in which the music was kept at the same deafening pitch it has when the credits are being shown, so that not a word of what any one was saying would be heard throughout the entire film.

Theatre owners and the movie public would undoubtedly take their cue from this Dadaist phase of movie making. Theatre owners would provide each seat with a noisemaker so that the audience would make some real noise; the spaces between each row of chairs would be done away with entirely so that there would be no chance of your walking to your seat. A way would be found to run four movies simultaneously and spectators would be imported from Central America to make the wait for seats a day or two longer. The public would retaliate just as playfully by merely going to the theatre to buy their candy, then going home to eat it.

April 17, 1944

The Great Brain Robbery

"The Lady and the Monster" is a horror movie made by George Sherman for Republic Pictures which gets into gear at about the three-quarter mark and comes home, if not a winner, a film that is imaginative and effective. The story has essentially to do with a crippled scientist (Erich von Stroheim) who discovers a way to keep a brain alive after the rest of its owner has died. The brain is kept alive in a solution that contains adrenalin and it records its aliveness through an invention of the scientist's assistant (Richard Arlen) called the encephalograph. The encephalograph looks and acts like the mechanical arrangements for fountain-pen displays that show how long and nice a line the pen can make. When they have succeeded in keeping the brain alive and making wiggly pen lines, their problem is to find out what the brain is thinking or wanting to do with itself. After what I thought was a frivolous suggestion of Arlen's— that they get to the brain with Morse Code—they hit on a plan of keying the brain up with more adrenalin and having Arlen empty himself of all thought and action so that the brain can use him as a telepathic agent.

At this point the picture and Arlen pick up wonderfully. Arlen is changed by the brain into the person the brain belonged to and goes to Los Angeles to finish up some of that person's unfinished business. The change in Arlen from his usual tendency to be a piece of sculpture to his being an aggressive, dominating person is managed with real film imagination and talent. The people and environments he gets involved with under the brain's direction are far less corny and more believable than those around the laboratory, and the main problem that turns up—about a misdirected murder trial—contains real interest and even suspense.

All of "The Lady and the Monster's" troubles have to do with what are considered horror-movie fixtures. The real interest of the film is in what will come of the murder trial Arlen gets involved in and, for some reason, your concern over what the movie will decide is the social end of the brain discovery. But this is all evaded by bringing in two conventions. The scientist has to be a monster and there has to be a lady he is after; she finally influences Arlen to destroy the scientist and his work because Arlen is not himself any more, and she is afraid the scientist is in love with her, and that the whole business is illegal because the brain was stolen from a dead body, which is against the law. There are also the other conventions of horror movies: the wind ripping up outside a spookhouse, which looks like a Mongolian idiot produced by the marriage of a French castle and a Spanish bungalow in Los Angeles; the evil-eyed, crippled scientist puttering with glass retorts; a burlesque-proportioned blonde sliding in at every moment in a new silk gown and fearfully handing him a hemostat; in the background a mean-looking household drudge stands unnamed and untalked to; and then the scientist ominously calls for the "Jiggly-saw" to rip open someone's skull.

But in spite of all this whirling around of cliché, it is a good example of the low-budget picture that is sometimes apt to take an unpromising script and a set of conventions and by really commendable work on the actual filming give it dignity and intelligence.

On the other hand, there is no reason to go to see another quickie made by the Pine and Thomas firm for Paramount, called "I Live on Danger." But if you catch it on a double bill you will find it is not bad at all, and for many of the same reasons. The B's have generally a more convincing actuality than the expensive films, probably for the fact that they have less money to spend building sets and lighting them so they shine and sparkle, and designing costumes that almost walk by themselves. With less money and time to inject spurious entertainment angles into his film, the B director is more likely to spend his time making what he has real rather than classy. There is not nearly so much need for him to make a box-office miracle of his film, so there is less selling of popular attitudes and less jazzing up of ordinary circumstances. B films are also an inevitable refuge for players who are no longer pretty or handsome enough to meet expensive film standards, or for those who are just hard up for work, and many of them are seasoned players. For instance, the film mentioned above, which is concerned with a radio reporter's adventures, has Chester Morris, for my money a very capable and ingratiating actor.

May 1, 1944

Fathers and Songs

"Going My Way" is Producer-Writer-Director Leo McCarey's surprising movie that presents the Catholic Church with a method of gaining recruits and Paramount Pictures with what should be a box-office miracle and probably the next Academy Award winner. It has just the right amount of bright eventfulness, moral purposefulness and the kind of movie smartness that can sell a very sugary business, with enough sophistication, good direction and playing to win almost any popular poll. The story is about a young priest called Father Chuck O'Malley, played by Bing Crosby, who is used by his Bishop to revive religion in parishes where the church membership and finances seem to be dwindling. The one he revives in this picture is St. Dominick's in New York City's slums, presided over by an ancient receptacle of old man's crotchets, Father Fitzgibbon (Barry Fitzgerald), who is driven to distraction by Crosby's dress—a baseball outfit given him by the St. Louis Browns—his choir, which sings "Three Blind Mice," and his ability to leap the rectory hedge and sing college songs over the telephone to his old roommate. At the end of two hours and ten minutes everything is rosy and Crosby leaves to take the sag out of another church.

The basic pattern of "Going My Way" is an ancient and irritating one, though it is reworked here with some unusual weave and has enough well perceived human touches and real movie talent to make it pleasant. Its pattern is that in which something bountiful, delightful and exciting is forever happening to everybody, supposedly because of their moral right-doing and because that's the way things happen in real life; but actually it is because the producers are afraid their movie will be too dull, or too morally unpalatable or subtle for audiences in any less jazzed-up form. Five minutes out, you can see the rest of the movie coming, the kind of tone that will be achieved in each event, the attitude and success with which Crosby will meet each one, the narrow kind of provincialism that the parish people will bring against him, and, more unpleasantly, the realization that, once started, the piling up of one kind of event must repeat itself until at the end nothing seems sincere; and the moral tags and realism turn more and more sour as the obvious entertainment ideas keep cropping up regularly in the plot.

But though "Going My Way" is continually jazzed up with obvious entertainments and too-fortuitous circumstance, there are a number of fine things done within the circumstances, the most commendable being the natural, informal way that the people are allowed to go about. There is a lazy quality about the procedure of the events that makes you feel the people did not realize they were in a movie: they are rather slow getting to the dramatic business on hand; they walk and eat as though they were in the picture only to do that; then when the drama has occurred, they are allowed to go on for an unusual amount of movie time—ruminating about what has happened, strolling in the rectory, or finishing their meal. It provides the plot-skeleton of this movie with just the life that it needs. More of this kind of humanity is gained by also allowing an unusually large number of the people the freedom and footage to make themselves into characters, and talented players like Barry Fitzgerald, Gene Lockhart and Porter Hall produce the richer humanity of which they have always been capable. I thought Fitzgerald quite wonderful in his presentation of the pets, lapses and stubbornnesses of a man close on senility, though the picture trades too obviously on his comedy talents: every so often it stops like a jazz orchestra, and Fitzgerald, the star performer, produces the improvised break. Crosby and Fitzgerald do the touchy interpersonal relationship of a younger priest nosing out an older one with a good amount of the exploring and adjusting that gives the relationship a continual tension and soreness.

Add to all of these extraordinary virtues, good photography, better settings —well littered by the right textures and patterns (one of the best being Fitzgerald's night shirt)—a likably offhanded way of getting the songs in and out, nicely achieved realism, such as allowing the choir boys to react as they boyishly would before celebrities like Risë Stevens or Crosby instead of stiffening them with prepared actions, and you have a good many virtues. I wish the vehicle that carried them weren't so hoary and sugar-coated.

May 8, 1944

Personnel Department

Hollywood's supply of players has been affected in two ways by the war: a large number of familiar and experienced performers have been taken out of the studios and put somewhere in the armed forces; and an equally large number of new players have been replacing them. The following people strike me as being notable additions.

Gene Kelly, Keenan Wynn and Percy Kilbride were all recruited from the theatre. Kelly, whose most recent picture is "Cover Girl," has been cast either as the smart, tough young hero or as the unfortunate half of the song and dance team, but his progress and accomplishment have been far more unusual than the stock characters he has played. No other young player to my knowledge gets over a particular attitude and response with as much clarity and sharp effect, or with as much uncorrupted feeling, and I have seen him do a variety of characterizations with equal success. He plays up the smaller responses of his part without killing the character they are part of. The two things he does least well—singing and dancing—are what he is given most consistently to do.

Wynn and Kilbride are both supporting comic performers who invariably make the parts of the picture they are in very bright and exciting. The former is the son of a fine influence, Ed Wynn, and provided two corrupt, cynical notes for two otherwise completely sweet shows—"See Here, Private Hargrove," and "The Lost Angel." In the latter he helped Margaret O'Brien, who is also good, and new, and only seven years old, relieve a basically terrible moment where she is supposed to teach him better than to be a gangster, by doing a bored, enigmatic kind of gangsterism, and by his virtuosity in capping and explaining situations with some business with his hands or face. In the sophomoric "See Here, Private Hargrove" he has a more unusual screen character to play, the young man (found in every college dormitory) with a passion for promoting small business on the side as he goes through basic training. He fills the role well, with the necessary amount of sinister, thick-skinned greediness that responds with a mildly disfavoring blankness to anything except the success or failure of one of his business deals. Kilbride is the character with the Buster Keaton kind of face and the absurd caricature of a New England farmer's voice, who is usually inserted into films to whip them up somewhere and does it in a clear, wonderful manner. It turns out that along with the comic quality of Kilbride's face and voice, he is one of the most subtle and inventive comic spirits to hit Hollywood in years. It seems to me that Kilbride is capable of becoming a great movie comic, directly in the great line of Keaton and Chaplin, if he is given the necessary featuring and freedom.

I also recommend any performance by Roman Bohnen, Henry Morgan or Alexander Granach, William Eythe's in "The Song of Bernadette" and Bill Phillips' in "See Here, Private Hargrove."

By far the most unusual phenomenon in the advent of new players is the type of heroine being introduced simultaneously by most of the studios—girls with a spectacular amount of breeding, intelligence and acting ambition. Some of their names are Jean Sullivan, Jean Heather, Eleanor Parker, Susan Peters and Mary Anderson. I think the idea is for rival studios to cash in on the success of the styles of Ingrid Bergman and Teresa Wright, and to show soldiers the kind of girl they should wait for, look for or expect when they get back. To be a good fit as this soldier ideal these young film heroines have something from all the former Lady categories. This includes the ambition of the great acting ladies like Bette Davis, the body of the bathing beauty, the face and wholesomeness of the girl who plays Sister in family movies, and the free-swinging, sexual lustiness of the vampire women. But they have also the added jigger of sensitivity. For that jigger they are indebted to Bergman; also they use her worst cutenesses, and that eager kind of acting intelligence which in some of the actresses makes you feel that they read and understood the script and then hid the hero's before he could read his. I think they have also been influenced by Teresa Wright, the kind of face she has and the respectable clothes she wears, which are sold in Junior Miss departments. They are also usually hung in that troublesome state between girlhood and womanhood that Miss Wright plays so well. There is no denying their interest in acting, their intelligence about what they are supposed to be doing and their desire to be better than anything.

There are other new heroines, fashioned along more traditional lines, including Ella Raines, K. T. Stevens, Donna Reed and Marsha Hunt. Miss Hunt has a good amount of talent, drive and sincerity, and has decided to follow the Davis-Lupino road, which is founded on the basic realization that life is hard, severe and bitter. As a result she shows little in the way of softness or relaxation, even when there is no great demand for her tense, belligerent manner.

Perhaps Paramount's Gail Russell, who was introduced in "The Uninvited," has the greatest effectiveness of the new crop of heroines, because of her unusual kind of screen beauty—that which gets lost in fairy tales, or is saved by a Knight of the Round Table—but she has carefully turned all of her mannerisms into a pure demonstration of that beauty.

May 15, 1944

Creep House

"Gaslight" presents the creepy plot, taken from Patrick Hamilton's play, "Angel Street," of a wife (Ingrid Bergman) being systematically driven out of her mind by her husband (Charles Boyer) while he looks for some precious jewels that he failed to find when he murdered her aunt years before. The method of the husband, who is himself unconvincingly insane in his attachment for precious jewels, is to undermine his wife's belief in herself in every way—he steals her jewelry and then accuses her of having absentmindedly lost it; he proves to her that she is also capable of stealing from him; each night the gaslight in her room peters out and noises start which scare her out of her wits but which she has been told are her own hallucinations; he keeps her penned up, friendless, in a depressing London apartment and then hires a maid to plague her to death. The effect of his treatment is just about to do the trick when a kind detective (Joseph Cotten) steps in and saves her sanity.

Up to about the time that the detective starts dogging the husband's footsteps, the picture builds a good, convincing, morbid relationship between the man and his wife out of a series of conversations, and acting bouts within them, among Boyer, Miss Bergman and a maid, who is acted at a fine, surly, unbecoming level by Angela Lansbury. The quality of the Victorian rooms where these bouts occur is such as to give you the right feeling that the wife is also being buried alive; the pace is a dreary, lifelike one, and the complications of the husband's Iago-like maneuvers and his wife's being caught by them— somewhat too accommodatingly—are worked out with an unusual degree of emotional subtlety for the movies. A lot of the credit for the quality of these scenes is due to Miss Bergman, who is able to strike variations of hysteria, perplexity or love that make actually static episodes seem more than adequately flexible and meaningful. It is true that she is one of the few actresses who are expected—and allowed—to do this in films. Her acting zeal and ability sometimes run her on unnecessarily, like a runner who is unable to stop immediately after finishing a race, but she gives a nice rendition of an unwary and unworldly woman being hurt and bewildered, and, in the first part of the picture, her more notorious ability to portray the most adoring and lovely of wives makes the nature of the tragedy and the cruelty seem even more extreme.

As the film progresses, it is loosened up to include a stock detective mystery involving sterotyped mystery problems, people who act the oldest kind of detective-fiction personalities, and devices that are supposed to be hair-raising but are only reminders of what may have scared you in your childhood. The melodramatic turn events take is in the interest of bringing out Miss Bergman's character alive, but it turns what had been a moving duel of two people's wits into a laboring, distraught organism which will remind you of the kind of mystery stories Earl Derr Biggers used to write. For the most, however, it is morbidly successful and has a good deal of intelligent writing and direction—plus, of course, Miss Bergman.

May 22, 1944

Boys in the Back Room

"The Hitler Gang" is an attempt by Paramount to show the nature of the Nazi leaders, their careers between the First and Second World Wars, with special emphasis on their methods of gaining power. It is very likely the most conscious and complete attempt made in a single film by Hollywood to reproduce history. It has been put together with a good technical efficiency by Producer Buddy DeSylva and Director John Farrow and is diverting enough for one reason or another in the tight, jolting manner of gangster movies. The value of its history is a different matter.

This neat, slick simplification of history narrows everything concerned in the careers of the Nazi leaders down to the gangsterlike facts that they were all irresponsible men who wanted power and used any means to get it. Their fascist ideology is shown coming to them by a sort of catch-as-catch-can route: at one time or another they needed an idea, so they chose the first likely one that presented itself and seemed capable of winning them power. Their fascism, according to the producers of the picture, had no deep roots in these people: Hitler hires himself out as a political speaker and gives the speech about the supremacy of the German army that he is told to give, though he seems never to have thought of it before; when Himmler suggests making the Jews a Nazi scapegoat and using their money to strengthen the party, he and the other leaders contemplate the proposal as though it were the first anti-Semitic thought or feeling any of them had ever had. Someone advises Hitler to write a book setting forth his ideas, and he begins doing this, picking ideas out of other people's writings as though he had little previous awareness of or feeling for them. The problem arises of breaking the power of the church, and they sit around once more mulling over the best way to achieve that end; finally one of them thinks of educating the children against the church, and another Nazi idea is born as though on the spur of the moment for some need of the moment. While the film makes an unbelievably flimsy connection between the men and their ideas—fascism seems as little inherent in them as the politics of a political boss is in the gangsters he hires—it makes practically no connection at all between the leaders and the people around them, or with any economic, social or psychological force that may have propelled them into power.

The characterization of the leaders is also on the extra-simple, extra-naïve side, but it has the decided movie virtue of having actors who are sharply delineated in physical look and a director wise enough to take advantage of it. This virtue is pretty well canceled out by a number of things. The players themselves act more like their usual screen selves than the people they're impersonating, and seem generally far too mild and inconsequential to have accomplished what their real-life counterparts did.

Every now and then the picture takes a moment out from the usual back-room meeting of the masterminds and the brief out-door glimpses of their gangsterism that composes the most of the film to note in a sentence or a single shot that Roehm was a homosexual, Hitler a paranoiac, Goering a drug addict and a patient in an insane asylum; and that is supposed to make them seem as awful as anything in your minds—homosexuality, drug addiction and having been a patient in a hospital for the insane being in the movie mind synonymous with complete evil. At any rate, there is no attempt to make any of the accused act in a paranoid or homosexual way, so that the effect of the disclosure is only momentary, if indeed it amounts to anything at all. In their back-room conferences, every member takes a turn advising some villainy, and this makes it difficult to tell just what each one was particularly like. For some reason, the producers chose to make Hitler the most virtuous and least capable, and characterized him merely as a puppet used and driven by his colleagues. Whether or not he is, and whether or not Himmler is the party's brain, the main idea of the movie still seems to be that the way to prevent millions of people from becoming wholehearted fascists is to keep political gangsters out of office—which is no doubt partly true.

May 29, 1944

Quick Dissolve

RENÉ CLAIR's art has disappeared in Hollywood with as much speed as that of Hitchcock, Lang or Renoir, but in Clair's case the disappearance has been so neat and complete as to seem magical. At the same time that his films have become increasingly empty of any kind of statement or attitude about anything, his technique has become dominantly dependent on dialogue, and the visual aspects of his films are confined to what are, admittedly, both tasteful and smooth renditions of stock movie situations. Though the characters in his newest film, "It Happened Tomorrow," are treated with gentleness, dignity and love, in a spirit that has a little of the folk-love that he exhibited in his French movies, they have far too little folk manners and pursuits. The difference between what Clair used to say and what he says now in a movie can be easily seen in the difference between the song in "Sous les Toits de Paris" and those used in "It Happened Tomorrow." For significance of every kind, the former has it about 200 percent over the latter.

Clair's newest movie was a "Short Short" story years ago in Collier's and has since traveled the rounds of the studios, being worked and reworked until it now bears half a dozen writers' names, including Clair's, Dudley Nichols' and even Lord Dunsany's. It is still, however, about a reporter, Dick Powell, who gets his wish to see tomorrow's newspaper 24 hours early. With this foreknowledge of the news, he becomes an ace reporter and is able to win $600,000 at the races. Then he gets the premature newspaper that announces his death, and much of the latter half of the picture is spent watching Dick Powell's sophomoric demonstrations of anguish over this fact. In the meantime he meets and marries Linda Darnell, the assistant of a magician, Jack Oakie.

Whatever enjoyment you can get out of the bare idea of a man being 24 hours ahead of everybody else, the events that are caused by the idea have happened in a lot of other movies in just about the same way, and often much better. It is told in a flashback from an anniversary celebration that you've seen before, where the little girl has trouble learning the little speech she has to give. There is also a chase across rooftops, and a struggle on the edges of various buildings. There are several scenes in which one comic detective, Edgar Kennedy, displays his irascibility. The situations would be all right if they illuminated any kind of character, manners or environment, but they don't, humorously or otherwise: the deficit is partly hidden by setting the time in the nineties, under a lot of costumes and period architecture—but Jack Oakie, and Edgar Kennedy, Powell and Darnell come through pretty clearly as what they have always been.

The events aren't much, but Clair does put them together very neatly, and manages some slight, tasteful humor in each one. For instance, the man who gives the reporter the magical newspapers is a nice, gentle sort, John Philliber, whose toothless kind of intonation and clear indication of sincerity and kindness, and a talented kind of rickety, precarious acting, make his scenes quite charming. An equally slight humor is managed at the horse races by recording their progress in Oakie's pantomiming as he bewilderedly watches his friend predict one race after another. There are some cute pieces of business, especially by various people's hands—the old man's manner of pawing and dusting off his newspaper file, Oakie's non-professional habit of gesturing at the audience while he is doing his magic tricks, the disarming way that Miss Darnell pushes at the knot of the man's tie she has to wear in one scene. The attempt, of course, is at a mild, warm little picture. But these amusements and whatever other slight charms the film has are so tenuous as to make it vacant rather than mild, and all that is indicated of Clair's personal expression, beyond taste and ease, is a faint echo of his former anarchic movie attitude and method; so that when gangsters shoot policemen the atmosphere of make-believe overrides that of realism and the seriousness of consequence disappears. There is also, but in a worn-out way, a kind of laughing at people's cowardice. But altogether there is so little to be identified with the old René Clair that it is like looking at a new one.

June 12, 1944

Andersen's Fairy Tale

No matter how earnest and wholesome its intentions, "The Eve of St. Mark" turns up a disconcerting number of war-film clichés, and presents with irritating, recruiting-poster purity a picture of wartime American civilians and soldiers leading prettily heroic, contented and richly rewarding lives. The movie tries to show the more important attitudes and experiences of a soldier named Quiz (acted pallidly by William Eythe, in a quick reverse from what he did in "The Song of Bernadette") as he moves through his training period to the heroic stand he makes with a gun crew on Bataan, as well as showing those felt by his family and sweetheart back on their idyllic farm in upstate New York. As it turns out, the soldier scenes are less insipid and funnier than the family's; but the latter make up the difference by being the worst in the war films. The picture's theme for both is to show people either aggressively proud and happy to have their sons fighting in the war or sons aggressively proud and happy to be fighting, and its way of explaining their 100-percent affirmation and satisfaction is to show them living in as pretty a way as possible, which doesn't lead to a significant understanding of anything.

Still, if you can get through the farm scenes where the father and mother and the sweetheart (Anne Baxter) go around with a pleased-as-Punch look, as though they were eating each other and finding they were all made of delicious candy, you will find some good comedy, some provocative feints in the direction of realism, and a script that is rather tightly packed with one thing after another.

The comic business, which should be mentioned first because it is the best, hardly rubs anyone or anything in a wrong direction and is always performing the hoary task of showing how wonderfully amusing every minute of camp life is, and how marvelously friendly everyone is with everyone else—there is never a hitch in the relationship between the rowdy, tough Irishman and the Southern aristocrat-scholar, nor between either of them and the pure hero, nor between those three and the sulking, aggressive Jew. Still, there are amusing things: a scene in which five soldiers mimic their sergeant drilling recruits, which is done as a less obvious caricature than it usually is; a scene at a camp-town soldier-hangout, which is a chaos of opposing intentions—but in which someone had the bright idea of injecting a truly wacky character, a horribly overworked waiter who moves deafly and dumbly with a terrible limp and a punchdrunk expression. There is a touching moment filled with wonder when the veteran sergeant nostalgically tells the story of the greatest crap game in history, which took place simultaneously on all the ships returning the soldiers home from Manila, and ended with an entire army payroll in the hands of the seven winners, who were then escorted by armed guard down Market Street. The film has a good comic named Michael O'Shea, who adds an unusual degree of rough, sprawling lewdness to the age-old Irish soldier comic. By comedy I don't mean the three reels of comically intentioned rhetoric and verse droned out by the Southern scholar, but I thought Vincent Price did a good job of droning.

The film has the habit of threatening something commendably more realistic, or subtle, or significant, and then of shrinking back into its normal and rosy attitude. On both of the son's furloughs home he and his sweetheart show the strain of unrealized love one moment and in the next are blissfully free of any such agony. When the boy, surprisingly for the movies, picks up a girl in the camp town and shows the logical amount of enthusiasm for her, the film writers hurriedly attribute it to his imagining he is with his true sweetheart and have him leave wholesomely early to mail a letter home. A hand is shown moving toward someone's knee but is forgotten about in mid-passage. The soldiers, for the first time, I think, in this war in films, are shown drinking worse than beer. But they don't get out of hand. A soldier smacks his buddy with real hostility, but the flare-up is magically doused.

This one-third now-you-see-it and two-thirds now-you-don't becomes more serious in the final scene when the heroes are making a hopeless stand somewhere on the Bataan Peninsula, and a vote is taken as to whether they should make an honorable retreat or fight on to inevitable death. They vote unanimously to stay, fight on heroically until their gun is knocked out, and then escape anyway. Also, in the process of the voting, one of them who has already cast his vote vehemently argues for retreating, but when his vote is read it turns out he has voted to stay. His argument for retreating had to do with his dissatisfaction with the prewar poverty he had lived through. Then the picture has someone cow him by saying he wasn't the only one who suffered during the depression, which is supposed to be an answer.

June 19, 1944

The Unholy Three

THE closest movie equivalents to having a knife slowly turned in a wound for two hours are "Tender Comrade" and "The Story of Dr. Wassell." The latter is Cecil B. DeMille's manner of showing the early war heroism in which a Naval Reserve doctor maneuvered eight stretcher-confined American sailor casualties through the Javanese jungle to safety while the Japs were hot on their heels. The picture is no doubt as factual as Dr. Wassell says it is, but any fact that is translated into film by de Mille looks like his most ancient movie affectation, and in this case his worst. Dr. Wassell's sailor wards carry on like rowdy prep-school boys on a tear and look silly enough to make anyone think twice before rescuing them. Their hospital in the jungle, which looks like the spick and span and pretty construction of a Frank Lloyd Wright disciple in the midst of a great head of romaine, is jammed with cute nurses—especially Javanese kewpie-dolls, who leave their nurse's uniforms traditionally unbuttoned at the top, and strip them off every third reel as a DeMille premium. In and out of the playful grappling that goes on between the nurses and the sailor-lads is a comic who does all kinds of funny things like getting hit on the head with a coconut or feigning sickness so the nurse will hold his hand. Dr. Wassell is played by Gary Cooper, who has a manner of blinking and gulping shyly and talking about hogs.

According to the ancient DeMille formula, there must always be several intertwining love triangles which untwine through the movie in the simplest beginning-middle-end way possible, no matter what the forces around them. Thus while the heaviest air raid of the picture is going on, with the sailors being jolted and knocked about their hospital ward, it is typical that one of the men should be telling the others the romantic story of how Dr. Wassell found the bug and the girl he was looking for in China before the war. And when the picture moves into the home stretch with about five corners of two triangles still unaccounted for, four of them show up on the same ship headed out of Java for Australia and the other one is heard over the ship's radio. Something else is finished even after the picture ends, when it is announced that the producers have just heard that "Hoppy is alive and a prisoner of the Japs."

"Tender Comrade" is a cloying tribute to a kind of soldier's wife whose
cruel, selfish and over-indulgent love and concept of marriage should cure a lot
of soldier-home-sickness. It presents one supreme example of this type of
spouse, played with unfortunate she-tiger conviction by Ginger Rogers. She is
a possessive, dominating shrew, who goes up in sparks when her husband forsakes her to read a magazine or dance with another woman or do some overtime at the office. Her favorite expression is, "Men are such fools," and her
treatment of the one she is smothering (Robert Ryan) is that of a cocksure, contemptuous mother toward her baby. The author of the picture (Dalton
Trumbo) and its producers (David Hempstead and Edward Dmytryk) feel that
all these attitudes are charming and cute and play them that way. At the end
of the picture when Miss Rogers hears that her husband has been killed, she
picks up his photograph in one hand, her just-born child in the other, and goes
to work on him: "Remember him, Son, remember him as long as you live.
Never forget him, little guy. . . . He only bought you the best world a guy
ever had, and if you dare let anyone tell you different. . . ."

Part of the picture consists of an account of this love-nest, and the rest of
it of Miss Rogers' life with three other soldiers' wives, who share a house while
their husbands are away fighting. Theirs is the ideal wartime behavior for
wives: knitting, gushing over their letters and pictures, and persecuting one of
their members who now and then threatens to go to a night club and is somewhat unenthusiastic about rationing. At the end of the picture one of the husbands has the misfortune to return home on a furlough, and he is devoured
before your eyes, as you expected. The value that the producers place on
drooling, faithful love is incredible. It excuses the embarrassing idiocy of one
member, the bitchiness of three of them and the beaming, pompous satisfaction with which they all sit around like so many hens on eggs.

"The White Cliffs of Dover" is articulated with enough movie sensibility
(Clarence Brown's) to raise it out of the horror category of "Tender Comrade"
and "Dr. Wassell," but it is just about the dullest picture on record. It is an old
shawl of a movie in praise of England and her people, who it feels are an
extremely fine people but on the reserved, mild, snailish side. This leads to
just about the most pooped-out job I have ever seen.

June 26, 1944

Three New Ones

A LOWER-BUDGETED, gimcracked renewal of the gangster films, called "Roger Touhy, Gangster," is more than mildly underdone on a number of its sides. The characterization of the gang is in the one-sentence notation department, and the notations are as indifferently conventional as the invariable fact about cowboy films that the hero's buddy is always comical and decrepit. One member of the gang (Victor McLaglen) has a passion for learning, another (Frank Jenks) for "a girl named Daisy" and a third (Horace McMahon) for alcohol. The one exception in the general void of characterization is an instance of well marked sadism when Touhy (Preston Foster) beats up a henchman for drinking. Documentation about the gang's career seems to have been out of the research department's reach, except for an unaccountably well detailed enactment of their prison break. The acting, aside from Preston Foster's ever reliable surliness, proceeds by fits and starts and as though the performances had been given for different directors and different pictures. Along with some very nostalgic reminders of the old gangster films, such as transportation in careening sedans and communication by snarls, the film has two mild virtues. The first is that though it has very little of anyone's life, none of it is as glorified as the lives of super love, adventure and bravery that Cagney, Muni and Robinson spent in earlier, and better, gangster films. The second is that the director cut in some good, actual film shot at Stateville Prison in Joliet, which is grim and chilling enough to put the fear of prison into any lawbreaker.

"Two Girls and a Sailor" is a sweet-toothed bargain of about 18 vaudeville acts, none of which is very good or very bad but is stuffed for the occasion with cutenesses, to go with a story about two sisters who are in love with the same millionaire sailor. The sisters, Gloria DeHaven and June Allyson, do a lot of grown-up movie things like dancing in night clubs, chasing Latin lovers and holding private servicemen's canteens in their apartment after working hours, which would be about five in the morning, looking all the time as if they should either be home or with Gus Edwards' Kiddie Revue. The people around them, who impersonate sailors, grandfathers and orchestra leaders, are necessarily made to look like kindly fathers or kid brothers. One average sailor, chosen at random, would produce the same effect in this picture as one of these sailors would on a battleship. The quality is a curious one that its producer— Joe Pasternak—gets by having teen-age girls play grown-up roles as if they were playing house, which allows him to hit the cute, wholesome side of sweetness. There is also his ability to interlock vaudeville and story in a nice way, to make them both more humanly palatable than they are in a lot of other musicals, and to turn people like orchestra leaders into actors.

The latest Signal Corps film, "Attack," does a good, important job of showing the technique of invasion as it progressed from the first moment it was decided to obtain a landing place on the western tip of New Britain Island, to a time when the two objectives, Arawe and Port Gloucester, had been captured and American forces were pushing further inland. It is a couple of reels longer than either "Tarawa" or "Memphis Belle," less intense, and has a more polite, manicured look. "Attack" shows the war better than you will find it shown in films of pure entertainment and an amphibious operation better than you will find it in any of the newsreel accounts that have been shown so far of the landings in France. It pictures the thousand and one operations involved in such invasions; there are some grim shots of the destroyer Bronson's survivors being rescued, and some others just as grim when a jungle rainstorm swamped the landing craft. All along there is a good commentary delivered by a good Bogart-like voice.

July 3, 1944

Warners' Boys in the Balkans

THE Eric Ambler novel has been employed rather lightly and playfully by Warner Brothers in "The Mask of Dimitrios" as a playground to exhibit the not-too-related virtuosities of its adventure-story crew of talented male actors, some of whom have been seen doing the same generally evil things about four times a year for quite a while now. The crew in this picture consists of Sydney Greenstreet, Peter Lorre, Edward Ciannelli, Victor Francen and some half-dozen others who are good at making the kind of faces that go with these pictures: cruelty (of the cold, immobile-faced variety), fear (as though the person were taken with cold chills), or a double-take job the others are picking up from Lorre, where the actor's face changes rapidly from laughter, love or a security that he doesn't really feel to a face more sincerely menacing, fearful or deadpan. Among the people in these films are also a number of spectacular pop-eyes, weak chins and hard-as-nail voices to cringe in front of or glower behind revolvers. Many of their set attitudes, like the cat-and-mouse antics between Lorre and Greenstreet, which were originally supposed to express fear, horror, etc., are now played slapstick fashion for laughs.

These actors produce some light, whimsical effects which are generally minor as far as making the plot any more significant, but they are the most intriguing parts of the film and were generally intended to be by the director, Jean Negulesco. Lorre's performance, on the side of the law for once, has a nice tone of humor and distress; Victor Francen does some fancifully fruity things with his voice as a syrupy homosexual spy chief, Kurt Katch injects some funny touches of insinuating eagerness as a Turk named Colonel Haki, a bit player makes the most of another small part as an archives clerk who is a bear for organization. Steve Geray does his usual good job as a meek, frightened-voiced little man who is victimized by the corrupt hero.

Most of these show-off flourishes of acting have about the same effect on the picture as some diverting curlicues of penmanship do on a sluggish, uninspired letter. The story shows the career of a super Turkish scoundrel named Dimitrios Makropoulos (and acted tepidly by Zachary Scott) as it is told in flashback episodes by some of his victims to Peter Lorre—playing a detective-story author who is going to a lot of trouble to find material for a book, and to Sydney Greenstreet—a crook who unaccountably is going to even more to get information he already has so that he can blackmail Dimitrios. For several reasons, Dimitrios and his career are the flattest thing in the picture, psychologically the shallowest, and as dull in an evil way as Irene Dunne's career is in a sweet way in "The White Cliffs of Dover." The flashbacks concerning him are rigorously stunted in order to wring something funny out of the preliminary chats that occur among Lorre, Greenstreet and the people Lorre interviews. His crimes, which are black enough, are brief and dull as movie events. The actor himself looks more like the third violinist in the Philharmonic—or the male lead in an operetta—and about as threatening. The Balkan atmosphere that surrounds him is just as uninspired and is produced mainly by a raucous, smoke-filled dive which is used three times in the film and features either a squirming Oriental dancer, a Gypsy violinist, or neither, depending on which country's backwater it happens to be in at the time. The people run to dark hair, oily natures and mustaches.

The British film called "Forty-eight Hours" is about an imaginary Battle of Bramley End, in which a troop of disguised German parachutists capture a British village two days before the main invasion of Britain, and are defeated a day later by the villagers. It was made more than a year ago and fulfilled a good intent to show Britishers what to be on guard against in pre-invasion tactics and what to do and not to do during them. It is far less flashy than "The Mask of Dimitrios" in its non-use of artificial coloring and excitement, and a dozen times more acute in its perception of people, manners and environments. I still feel it has a dullish, weak-tea quality, the result of making the entire engagement too neat and placid, and the progression of its events too restricted, simple and orderly. There are parts of it less prettily visualized: among them the touching, very realistic reactions of three village women when each kills a German or sees one killed, and a portrait of a tweedy, gay-as-a-lark English biddy, who sings songs about parrot pie, and cherry-ripe, cherry-ripe.

July 10, 1944

Home Sweet Home

DAVID O. SELZNICK's first movie production since "Gone with the Wind" runs on forever like most of his productions (the best of which, to my knowledge, is still his first, "King Kong"), is characteristically crammed with famous movie names from Shirley Temple to Lionel Barrymore, and is described in its foreword as being a story about that "indestructible fortress, the American Home, 1943." The title of the picture is "Since You Went Away" and the fortress in it belongs to the Hiltons, who are a pretty, pie-faced mother (Claudette Colbert), her two pretty, pie-faced daughters, aged 17 (Jennifer Jones) and 13 (Shirley Temple), and their father, who is away at war during all of the film but is seen almost as often as they are—as Neil Hamilton, in the several hundred photographs they have of him around the house. The authors, Margaret Buell Wilder and Mr. Selznick, paw over his family's wartime existence with an idolizing belief and love that should satisfy even the devotion of the husband.

"Since You Went Away" holds religiously to a philosophy consisting in the ideas that only happy, virtuous or funny things happen in the American home, that only the pretty and the brave live there, that any complications should be more than balanced by happy rewards. This is symbolically expressed in the ending, on Christmas Eve, when the mother receives word that her husband, who has been reported missing, is safe and returning home. I suspect that the daughter's fiancé (Robert Walker) was unconsciously made less handsome and less heroic to soften the effect of his really being killed.

In the hands of anyone as scrupulously conscientious about showing *the* American home as Selznick is in this picture the material things that make it up are interestingly accurate. He is finicky enough about almost any object that would go into middle-class life, from the kind of chenille spread you would find on the parents' bed to the kind of sprinkler that would be on the front lawn: but he is fiendishly finicky about mementoes—there are as many of these as there are conceivable places to put them, and among the bronzed baby shoes, the pottery knickknacks, the newspaper clippings, are some more strikingly accurate perceptions, like the kind of poem the husband would write in the kind of handwriting he would have, and the kind of leather family album he would paste it in. These details are good up to the point where their placement in the scene, the amount of wear and tear on them or the way the camera looks at them, are supposed to reveal the nature of the Hiltons' lives. At that point everything turns up either store fresh or, if worn and used, still photographed, posed and lighted to look new and gets the same negative quality pawnshop objects take on when they have been cleaned up and divorced from their old environment.

This denatured realism shows up with an even stranger effect in the story and the uses Selznick makes of it. He has a commendable desire to show all sides of the war on the home front, even the less agreeable. But of all scenes he might have picked in a rehabilitation hospital where wounded men are being taught to use their artificial limbs, he chooses that of the patients being given ice-cream cones—which would have been a neat irony if it hadn't been figured just as a pretty thing to be going on at the moment. In another scene the irony is intended, but again muffled and practically negated: a banker on a delayed train complains of how much the delay is costing him; the soldier next to him holds up the stub of an arm and says he doesn't mind it, he has plenty of time—and then the whole thing is wreathed in the soldier's beatific smile and contentment. There are a number of tours taken through civilian centers like railroad stations and cocktail bars where bits of conversation are caught on the sound track, but cuteness comprises about three-quarters of these fragments of talk.

As a whole, the picture is as doughy and inconsequential as the bread you get in grocery stores, partly for the above reasons and also because of the cautious, narrow level that the people are held at. The older daughter's adolescent agonies are made much of, but only in the form of a cute distress, Joseph Cotten's interest in her, which is supposed to be that of an eternal rake, and ought to cause some poignant sexual difficulties in the girl, remains at a vapid level to preserve the less awkward elements in his personality, the event itself and the general graceful tone of the whole picture. For its length, this is as ineffectual a movie as I ever saw.

July 17, 1944

Hard-as-Nails Dept.

THE most neatly machined movie since "The Miracle of Morgan's Creek," and the meanest one since "The Maltese Falcon" (without being as good as either), is a murder melodrama called "Double Indemnity," which was taken from a James Cain story in which a good-bad insurance salesman and an all-bad Los Angeles housewife figure up a nearly foolproof way to kill the wife's husband and collect his insurance. At the end their crime is so nearly cracked by the insurance company's claims manager (Edward G. Robinson), and the two of them (Fred MacMurray and Barbara Stanwyck) have become so distrustful, sick to death and jealous of one another that they try to shoot each other to death. The whole bloody business is told by MacMurray in a flashback as he confesses into his friend's, the claims manager's, dictaphone.

The film is one in which the only people who aren't deceiving someone are either ferociously soured on life, or as dyspeptic and wry as the claims manager, or too foolish to bother with; the manner of getting on with one another, either in conversation, lovemaking or gunplay, is intended to produce an effect like that of two trains hitting head-on. Their conversation—the joint work of James Cain, Raymond Chandler and Billy Wilder—is as fancy and metaphorical as I have ever heard in a movie, so that sometimes they sound like detective-story writers turned gangster. For instance, when the hero wants to say that he must think something over, he says, "I'll have to drive it around a while," when he feels the conversation is positively finished he says, "That tears it." The motto that the wife and he use to describe how their partnership has to be is "It's got to be straight down the line." This produces some embarrassingly cute, candyish talk, as well as a good deal that is accurately and fatly descriptive.

The film on its own level is a smooth, talented job of writing and directing, with some very bright, realistic perceptions of the kind of people and places that rarely get into American movies, and some adequate playing—especially the monolithic MacMurray, who is less that way than he has ever been, by Tom Powers as the soured husband, and by Robinson, who is a mousy creature, but an aggressive, masterful sleuth. However, it leaves me on the cold side of interested.

It seems to me to be slick, slight, arty and visually synthetic. The first murder is dependent on successfully projecting enough sex between the wife and the insurance agent to make a convincing murderer out of a man who is really too smart to murder anyone; the last two depend on successfully working up enough jealousy between them, hatred and fear of each other's suspected deceit, and concern on the man's part for the woman's step-daughter, to make their foolhardy turning on each other credible. The love affair seems too slight to drive the man into murder and to give the picture the great sense of passion and evil it needs, and which Cain himself often gets. Miss Stanwyck's brand of sulky, aloof coldness doesn't seem big enough, and isn't given a chance to make its evil quality effective. Their falling-out and everything else about the ending has a phony ring.

The characters of the two murderers are in general taken far too much for granted, and the very conscious attempt the picture makes to be bluntly and perceptively realistic, from the hero's match-sucking habit to the way Robinson slobbers his drink when he is excited, is a success to the degree that it is less synthetic than most Hollywood films, but it is certainly not less enough. Without going into the reasons for this for the fiftieth time, I can point out that the Russian film, "They Met in Moscow," is scene for scene more real-seeming and meaningful as realism, without making nearly so pretentious an attempt to be. I recommend "Double Indemnity," though, because the level of the work in it seems to me to be higher than it generally is in Hollywood, for the ingenuity and presentation of its first murder and for a lot of information about an interesting business—insurance.

I recommend also "They Met in Moscow," which does two very common Hollywood preoccupations—the musical films and cuteness—in a much pleasanter, fresher, more natural way than Hollywood does them. The plot of this operetta has a number of standard Sovietisms in it: an honored worker from the north, a swineherdess named Glasha, meets an honored worker from the south, a shepherd named Muzaib, at the agricultural fair in Moscow; and after a year's separation, during which they raise more pigs and sheep than they or anybody ever did before, they get married. Glasha is an example of the Russian felicity for selecting a heroine whose tomboy cuteness seems most diverting and fresh, from her homemade kind of Jackie Coogan haircut to her even more homemade make-up. The acting styles, way of singing, looks and dress of the players are distinct in each case and seem completely natural to them. I was very taken with the teeth-gnashing, passionate style of the hero, the breakneck speed at which he rode his horse home from the fair and the fact that he and his shepherding friends conversed mainly by shouting. His adenoidal singing, the heroine's soprano, the comic's manner, all have an energy, roughness, individuality and charm detrimentally lacking in Hollywood musicals like "Two Girls and a Sailor." These Russian players seem to be genuinely involved in whatever they are doing.

July 24, 1944

The Water's Fine

"Mr. Skeffington" is a hollow kind of film on which Bette Davis, the makeup and costume departments, and Director Vincent Sherman have ganged up to do some excellent things. The film records the career of a great, cold, narcissistic beauty of the early 1900's named Fanny, who lived in New York and was beautiful up to the age of about sixty-five, whereupon she became ferociously ugly. Her ugliness is hobgoblinish and mask-like, but the above individuals and departments have created a spectacularly beautiful woman for the prettier part of her life, and have done a diverting job of showing her change in styles and fashion from period to period. Miss Davis transforms herself with great effect into a girlish, tantalizing prettiness with a high petulant voice that is the best part of the portrait, and then for some reason drops completely back to her old stereotyped self—with the hitched walk, the dance-like business with her arms and hands and the heavy, hysterical voice—for the latter part of the film. "Mr. Skeffington" is dominantly dependent for its interest and suspense on the physical change of its people over a period of time, and to a lesser degree on how they looked and acted in particular events of the time, and it shows an unusual talent for doing this.

It is a good family album, but something less as a movie about Fanny and her Jewish husband, Mr. Skeffington, who masochistically stands by while she collects a horde of admirers, and finally gets the love he has patiently waited for when she is sixty-odd and has grown as ugly as she deserved. It is a meager, somewhat frivolous sketch of their lives, showing you the comic-opera exits and entrances of the various male admirers into the Skeffington mansion, and brief, unimportant chats whose main purpose is to get across some comical lines. You are teased with the idea of a love affair between Fanny and her brother, and the problem of a daughter who has a Jewish father and a Gentile mother, and you are illuminated almost not at all about either fact, just as you are left in a rather suggestive fog about everything else concerning the Skeffingtons.

For all but its last half-reel, the swimming-pool epic called "Bathing Beauty" is a mild entertainment composed of Red Skelton's antics, the kind of situations that usually come up in movies in which a man is caught in a girls' school, and music by a woman named Ethel Smith, who plays quick, corny whirling noises on the organ, and music like Muzak by Harry James and Xavier Cugat's symphony-sized orchestras. At the end, though, there is one of those spectacular chorus numbers, which is performed in its most difficult medium so far, a swimming pool the size of a stadium where the usual human cart-wheels, flower designs, and fountains in the number are made with amazing facility, with no difference at all from the way they are made on land. Then Esther Williams does a wonderful interpretation of under-water ecstasy that is the most aesthetic swimming I have ever seen. The only mediums left to be conquered by the dance directors of Hollywood after this water ballet are lava and quicksand, and I don't think they will be any more difficult than swimming-pool water.

The people who play in another musical, "And the Angels Sing," are bright and brassy enough, the spirit of the piece confident enough that it is the greatest all-out farce in years, and the situations promising enough to cause you only surprise and a mild let-down at the repeated thuds the picture makes. A typical kind of gag is that four people in succession (one of the troubles is that everything is done four times because there are four sisters who are heroines) will walk up to a violently steaming kettle, burn their fingers lifting its lid, and squeal in exactly the same way; not until the third person has done this will you believe that the kettle business is intended as a major gag, and that nothing funnier is going to be done with it, because you have been so taken in by the deceptive brightness. The people in it—like Betty Hutton, Diana Lynn and Raymond Walburn, its desire to jump on anything for a laugh, and the environments it chooses for jumping, remind you enough of Preston Sturges' pictures to make you expect about the same returns. The only places you get them nearly equally are those in which Betty Hutton is allowed to explode to her best capacities. As a human flywheel she produces almost as much emotional effect as she puts in the performance.

July 31, 1944

It Comes Up Corn

THE filming of Pearl Buck's novel, "Dragon Seed," follows a familiar path in occupied-nations films; starting with a good, peaceful folk—those of Nanking, but mainly farmer Ling Tan's family—being subjugated by the Japanese, their learning the nature of the war, the enemy, and their own Quislings, and ending with their guerilla tactics against the enemy. It is full of the right kind of war thought for a brotherhood of nations. Also it is less innocent than most movies about the consequences of war, when its hero finds he cannot kill, nor stomach the fact that so many of his people are becoming as bloodthirsty as the enemy. All of this would be significant, even at this late date, if it came out the kind of life you can generally believe or find in any newsreel shot from Occupied China. Still as a romantic, syrupy picture of China today, I think you will find it more human and effective than many other romantic Hollywood films.

"Dragon Seed" misses creating an intrinsic Chinese existence and people, as well as a convincing Japanese, by as thorough a mile as a nation's character can be missed by a movie, even by one that is spending two million dollars to be accurate. Visually, everything about it is too beautiful and plush. The farming lands of Ling Tan and his neighbors are as idyllic as an Italian landscape in a Renaissance painting, and are made more so by giving the film a golden sheen by shooting it in sepia: the whole effect achieves the splendid, rarified atmosphere of a fairy land rather than of farm land. Even the real Chinese adults who are used as extras to stream across Ling Tan's land carrying factories inland or as Japanese soldiers, and the real Chinese children, are combed and curried to such a fine state that they look no less glamorous, or no more like homemade Chinese, than the main people—Katharine Hepburn, Walter Huston, Aline MacMahon. The sentiment of too many of the events tends toward a similar kind of romantic overstatement: the Japanese officer who is about to rape the young Chinese mother is given a set of those practical-joker's teeth to make him too obviously ape-like; the girl in turn is several steps too prettily dainty; the earth-scorching at the end is done with an arsonist's relish and with enough fire to burn the city of Chicago; Jade's and Lao Er's lovemaking is on the level of newspaper poetry in its stylized winsomeness and plitty-Chinee qualities; Jade's poisoning of the Japanese officers is glamorized to an unreal point. On the sound track is every possible kind of accent, including Akim Tamiroff's borscht tones saying gowernmunt for government, a starched dialogue full of wisdom and about as human as cork, and refined, pretty tunes and marching songs that have their roots in Tin Pan Alley and the Almanac Singers.

"Dragon Seed" still ends up weighing substantially more than is common for a Hollywood epic, having a more compact, definite form and a few things that are very warm and human. For one thing, it covers more existence in less time than usual, getting a variety of feelings, problems and philosophies, from that of the third son (Hurd Hatfield), who turns from a sensitive, faint-hearted youth to a butchering guerrilla, to that of the third cousin (Henry Travers), who is the ineffectual scholar and doesn't turn into anything. And it does this without the tedium produced by too little cutting, or the heavy flow of sentiment you get in a picture like Selznick's "Since You Went Away." Some of the most domestic parts of the film are done very accurately. The love of the mother

(Aline MacMahon) for the other members of the family has enough greed and domination mixed in its fierceness to produce the right insidiousness, while still seeming like a generous kind of love. The relationship between her and the old farmer is lusty enough for all of its ideal prettiness, and the children and babies in the film are grasped, fondled and bounced with a genuine love. The rest of the humanity is contributed by the acting.

Walter Huston's Ling Tan is the one character who seems visually without any kind of artificiality or trace of Hollywood. The role is one of the most common war-movie characters, the good peaceful man who is bewildered and sickened by the war and struggles to understand it. But it is played here probably better than it ever has been before, with a believable amount of pain, puzzlement and goodness. Miss MacMahon's mother has a lot of mother in it, even if it seems grown in Brooklyn rather than the Orient. Miss Hepburn is like a well bred New England razor blade, but strikes many feelings off in a clear, brilliant way. Her mate (Turhan Bey) has a loping walk, the manner of a pampered American college boy, and the misfortune, with Hepburn, to be looked at consistently through the eyes of a director or photographer who should be making Christmas cards.

August 7, 1944

For He's a Jolly, Good Fellow

THE three-and-a-half-million-dollar film about Woodrow Wilson called "Darryl F. Zanuck's Wilson in Technicolor" is as surprising as it is costly, tedious and impotent. Some of the minor events in its life of President Wilson from the year 1908 through 1918 are the First World War, the Versailles Conference and Wilson's first term in the White House; some of its major events include the parade of delegates at the Democratic convention, the Wilsons' singing of "Put on Your Old Gray Bonnet," and the locomotive yells given by Princeton students.

For several reasons, one being that Wilson had a "nice" tenor voice, there are 87 songs blared or sung in the picture from 1 to 12 times and as though the audience left its ears in the cloak room: come in at any time and you will think "Zanuck's Sousa" is being shown. In between musical numbers there is just time for someone to exclaim, "Mr. Baker" or "MacAdoo," for that person to show himself to you, and for Wilson to say something amusing; then the band starts playing again. As important a key to understanding the character of

Wilson as Colonel House is hardly in the film, while two individuals, a cheer-leader and an economics professor from Princeton, who seem of no importance for understanding anything, are given whole hunks of the film to act in. Prob-ably the most surprising thing "Zanuck's Wilson" does is to make Wilson into a congenial, wise-cracking public figure, change his nature from that of a fierce Church father to that of an average business man, and his head from a large horse-head to an oval, doughy one.

The effect of the movie is similar to the one produced by the sterile post-card albums you buy in railroad stations, which unfold like accordions and show you the points of interest in the city. Its views of Wilson and the period are just as sycophantic; the points that it shows can be found for the most part in history books, but it leaves out a whole mass of facts of equal or greater importance, and hides the ones it does show in a kind of atmosphere that Zanuck calls "entertainment." The producers must have known far more about the World War, the peace-making at Versailles, and Wilson himself, but that is kept out of the movie in the same way that slum sections are kept out of post-card albums.

Zanuck and his film author, Lamar Trotti, have a number of pet notions to hang on their biography of Wilson, one of the main ones being the idea that much of American life is like a great, whooping Fourth of July parade, the people rather comical and foolish, but having one hell of a time, and events running the course of a foolish, comical game. The symbol for this is planted in the first scene—after a programme of credits that is a short feature in itself—at a football game between Princeton and Yale, in which the best part of the occasion is clearly indicated to be the yells, singing and excitement of the spec-tators; the game itself is a joke, and the players comic-opera characters. This interpretation of American life as a jamboree is repeated almost beyond endurance through the first three-quarters of the film in showing the jolly, vaudeville kind of home life the Wilsons had at Princeton, the funny Dem-ocratic conventions in 1912 and 1916, and the Wilsons' gay time at the White House; it leaves a minimum of space for the all-important events that came at the end of Wilson's life, and by its noisy, heavy emphasis kills most of the effect of those events. This jamboree interpretation fits in with two other Zanuck notions: it makes for the kind of "entertainment" in songs, dances, and wise-cracks with which he believes a serious picture has to be sold, and it fits in with his desire to recreate Wilson into a genial figure completely lacking in hypocrisy, insensitiveness and imperiousness. By this last transformation he disintegrates a character of the most complicated nature and of terrifying forcefulness into completely unbelievable softness and into the most conventional of screen hero types.

Some of the other notions planted in this film include the lie that the United States' career in the First World War contained only the highest moral aims and actions, any mention of a less noble action is buried in a conversation where its effect is completely obliterated. Another notion it sells is the one that the people of Germany are incurable gangsters who will never get over the idea of world conquest. This is managed by some tricky writing—from the views and feelings of the present war rather than the first one—of a scene in which the German ambassador, Bernstorff, notifies Wilson of the German decision to torpedo all ships without warning. In spite of the evil nature of the scene's idea and the fact that the cards are too obviously stacked to make Wilson look good, it is played into one of the most forceful scenes in the film, with Wilson rising into a great, frightening rage of righteousness and seeming to stomp the not unlikeable, dignified German to death with his voice. The third program of the film is to boil the whole tragic affair of Versailles down to a vague incident showing Wilson nobly arguing—without opposition, as usual—against Clemenceau. The only mistake it attributes to Wilson—in what has often been called a major catastrophe for him—was his choosing the wrong Republican for his delegation to Versailles. A hint made by someone that the Peace Treaty was not the most benevolent and just that could have been written is in the less-than-faint category, and the notion that anyone was sold out isn't even in the picture. It ends on an all-time worst in movie scenes with the Germans coming in to sign the Treaty, while "Deutschland Uber Alles" is played to an idiotic flatness to indicate German depravity.

The creditable moments in the film come during some of Wilson's orations, when Knox turns on a full, brassy voice that makes his Wilson sound as impressive as you expect him to sound. The Wilson dependence on women is moderately attained by showing his courtship of Mrs. Galt (Geraldine Fitzgerald), going forward with a kind of movie determination and strong suggestion that I find lacking in almost every other idea that the film tries to project. There are bits here and there that I liked: for instance, one of a crowd moving dumbly and strangely in a railroad yard as Wilson suddenly collapses in the midst of a speech, then being seen through the train window still moving oddly and trying to find out what has happened. About three-quarters of the way through, a large amount of actual newsreel from the first World War is run off and the strength of it makes the film that comes before and after seem comical.

August 14, 1944

To Be and Not to Be

In "Hail the Conquering Hero" I find that the deficiencies in Preston Sturges' work, which were noticeable enough in his other movies—that is: his unwillingness to alienate anyone in his audience and his equal unwillingness to be a technical innovator or even to say the little he does say in a vital movie way—are present in this new movie to a degree that makes it seem as rotten and confused inside as it seems pleasant and successful outside.

"Hail the Conquering Hero" presents the daring wartime-movie theme of lampooning the American public's worship of returning war heroes, which it does well enough, along with being amusing and pointing up some of the foolishness of small-town politics and civic affairs. It tells how six overindulgent Marines forcibly return a boy (who is afraid to tell his mother that he was discharged after three months in the Marines for having hay fever) home as a disguised hero of Guadalcanal. The people in his home town destroy all the good intentions of the idea by blowing it up into a gigantic celebration that ends with the boy being nominated for mayor. Sturges makes his point about the evils of such hysterical overadulation by the almost automatic device of making his hero the most sympathetic possible kind of boy who suffers terribly from being a failure as a fighter for his country, and who therefore will suffer most from the consequences of undeserved adulation. The more terrible you feel the consequences will be to this boy, who is a very honest Marine Corps worshiper, the more evil the public's demonstration seems to you.

Sturges makes such demonstrations seem more evil by pointing up the brainlessness, hypocrisy, and complete self-indulgence of the demonstrators themselves. He gets wonderful results from his players, his direction of them and his casting, and even though his insights into provincial character and manners are of a meager, stereotyped nature, his people have the look of and exude the small-town soul. There is, for instance, the wonderful actor who plays the perennially defeated reform candidate for mayor; this person presents a masterpiece of patient, stern-eyed virtue with overtones of a horrible inferiority complex from having been beaten so often as a candidate. His rival's campaign manager, played by Alan Bridge, looks as if he had been soaked for twenty years in all the vices and foolishnesses of a small town and endures it with the saturnine triumph of a man who feels vindicated in all his worst judgments. One of Sturges' great abilities is for filling the picture full of this kind of hard, cold, mercenary character, and then making him intriguingly bi-natured by giving him an equal amount of warmth and sweetness.

The picture is funny enough, but less so than any previous Sturges film, partly because it is intentionally more straightfaced than the other Sturges jobs, but also because of its restricted sense of what there is in provincial life to laugh at. The big farce scene, the celebration at the station, is typical of this sparse insight, with its concentration on some hoary laugh formulas—Franklin Pangborn's sissy-britches hysteria, the music which comes in at the wrong time, and the canned welcoming speech the little girl tries to recite from memory. With a station full of small-town Americans, the lack of imaginative satire is striking.

The instinctive proficiency Sturges exhibits in most departments of movie production doesn't hide the fact that he is dead set against evolving a movie style that is basically his own or a cinematic one. His films only express their stories to a subordinate degree out of their visual material, and the feelings aroused by that visual matter are of the shallowest sort. The stories get told by sound track mostly—"Hail the Conquering Hero" is a talking derby—and the motion pictures illustrate the sound track. Sturges, however, peppers these illustrations with inspired acting, diverting secondary business like the campaign manager's lifting the top of his piece of pie to see whether the insides are any good, and then he makes the illustrations appear very real and fills them with activity, so that you get a stuccoing of good surface entertainments which only seems to be related to an inner form and life. The times in this film when the people do something that is emotionally evocative amount to little more than spots on the whole surface of the picture. There is a notable bit when one Marine is brutally beaten up by the other five, one love scene gets just the soft, lovely emotion it should by the way Ella Raines embraces Eddie Bracken (Miss Raines has, by the way, a likable lack of screen-lady forwardness and self-conceit). But even at best the emotional effect of the picture is slight.

After all, Sturges' prevailing interest is in not giving himself away, anywhere. There have been few movies, even from Hollywood, which so confusingly and insistently say one thing and immediately its opposite, so as not to be caught seeming to stand solidly for anything. For instance, at the point where he has a chance to clinch emotionally the theme of his film—when the hero unmasks himself to the townspeople as a phony, by showing the humiliation and lunacy of everyone concerned, Sturges evades the whole issue revoltingly and runs off to a happy ending. One of the most disgusting episodes takes place when Sturges realizes that one possible end to such a fiasco is a lynching, and facetiously has his townspeople go for the boy in a parody of a movie lynch mob; but they aren't going to lynch him, they're going to elect him mayor anyway. In a film entirely devoted to preaching against overadulation of our war heroes, he has the townspeople elect the boy mayor, because, as one character says, "You don't need reasons in politics."

August 21, 1944

Independents' Day

THE chief trend going on in Hollywood at present is toward the formation of independent movie organizations which might be expected some day to make movies that are appreciably less cowardly and commercialized than the present major-studio product. At least a dozen of these companies have been formed in the last two years, but they are as yet only halfway independent, because many of them are partly financed by the large studios and all of them must distribute their pictures through the major studios' chains. The names and owners of some of these new studios are: California Pictures (Preston Sturges and Howard Hughes), International Pictures (William Goetz and Leo Spitz), William Cagney Pictures (the Cagney brothers), Vanguard Films (Selznick), and other units run by Bing Crosby, Sam Wood, Monter and Ripley, Hal Wallis, etc. The reason they were formed, it is said, was to allow their owners to cut down their income taxes: by forming their own corporations, these people can make a few pictures each year on nominal weekly salaries, and report their income-tax returns on the basis of capital gains. According to the internal-revenue rules, capital gains are permitted greater retention of profits than are salaries or fees. This may or may not be the reason for the new units, but many of these people are talented, intelligent and sensible film technicians and they might also want to make more important pictures than the big-studio product.

The trend isn't taken very seriously by the large studios, since a similar one turned up during the First World War and got nowhere; also since they have a strangle-hold on distribution, they will not distribute films that make their own movies look inadequate. But one or two of these new organizations—for instance, International Pictures, which has Nunnally Johnson, Casey Robinson and Gary Cooper under contract, and a box-office hit, "Casanova Brown," to start off with, and the Sturges-Hughes company, which isn't likely, on Sturges' past record, to make unsuccessful pictures—will probably end up as completely independent companies with their own distribution facilities, making pictures that might cause the large studios surprise and worry.

Since many of the people in these new groups have been concerned in the past with making above-the-average films, they will probably turn out even better ones on their own. But I doubt that they will make movies which are frankly original in their styles or independent in their ideas, mainly because they are all Hollywood-bred or, just as important, are working in Hollywood: there are many things about the place that make for a certain kind of movie in the way that a cold climate makes for certain kinds of animals. Put a person to producing films in Hollywood, and he invariably starts thinking in terms of photographed plays rather than movies, of art being separate from entertainment and so not for him, and of not making a movie that will try to change thought or feeling. I would advise all of these independents to go somewhere else in the United States to make their movies. My pessimism over what they can do in Hollywood is prompted by the pictures that have been made so far by the independents: "Casanova Brown," "Lady of Burlesque," "Johnny Come Lately," "Flesh and Fantasy," which have been so little different from the average Hollywood film as not to matter under what conditions they were filmed. The one very different film they have made, "The Voice in the Wind," by Monter and Ripley, is a 1928 version of the kind of movie made today, mixed in with very good intentions and influences from the worst European "art" movies.

The other Hollywood trend—that of making longer and longer movies—may not be so important as the outburst of half-independent producers, but it has already made several films tiresome that didn't have to be, and threatens to do other things like replacing double-feature programs with one picture as long as two. Seventy movies have been produced this year which run for at least an hour and forty minutes; twenty-seven have run for two hours, and six—"Dragon Seed," "Since You Went Away," "Frenchman's Creek," "An American Romance," "Wilson" and "Mr. Skeffington"—average two hours and forty minutes, and at least $3,500,000 each to produce. The chief reason for alarm over such ballooning is that it may cause the producers to cut down on their production of cheap movies, which have always been the most likely entering wedge for new people, the most likely place to find unconventional subject matter and techniques, and things generally more relaxed and human. The movie people say the whole trend is a temporary phenomenon, and the demand for cheap films—and double features—by the public is too great to stop the production of B movies. At any rate, Hollywood seems to be increasingly of the opinion that a major film can't be made for less than a million dollars or shorter than an hour and a half, and once it gets set in that idea, you can generally expect a more academic, conservative major film.

August 28, 1944

The Straight and Narrow

THE British Office of Information has released a competent entertainment, 30 minutes long, about the history of the kindergartenlike song, "Lili Marlene," which became the most popular war song of the Nazi soldiers, was heard in German broadcasts by Allied soldiers around the Mediterranean and became their favorite as well. The song, which was first sung in a Berlin night club by a girlish-voiced entertainer named Lalli Anderson, has had a fairy-tale career. One of its most horrible moments happened when the British substituted some political lyrics of the kind written for music like "Ballad for Americans" for the real ones, and had Lucie Mannheim shriek the song back to the Germans in a propaganda broadcast. The direction of Humphrey Jennings goes incredibly soft at times, with the kind of sentimental overindulgence of the subject matter and the photography that is practised in the still photographs in Coronet Magazine, but does well enough on the whole. The best things have to do with the satire and accuracy of combined sound and visual images: the spectacle and sound of "Lili Marlene" being sung by a horselike opera singer, the accurate, vulgar reproduction of a fantastically elaborate modern-day broadcast, Miss Anderson singing the song in a German night club, symbolically cutting from the sentimentality of that scene to the cacophony of one of Hitler's triumphant entries into a conquered city.

Another British Information short shows equal amounts of Burgess Meredith and life in the British Isles and is called "Welcome to Britain." The two are combined to show American soldiers what English life is like and how to treat it.

"Meet McGonegal," "To the Ladies" and "Resisting Enemy Interrogation" are three recent examples of movie-making by service film units. The main thing about all of them is that they show an increasing ability by their makers to project ideas with genuine movie force, using mainly a greater economy of means, less decorating of the point and the actual visual material, and far less underrating of the audience's ability to stomach or understand most things. The best of the three is the first one, which is a frank, powerfully bare two-reeler that shows disabled war veterans how well one of their members— Charles McGonegal, an armless World War I soldier—gets along with mechanical arms and steel hooks for fingers. The force and success of the film are gained by eliminating everything in the way of patriotism, moral uplift and most verbal explanations and concentrating solely and simply on a visual proof of Mr. McGonegal's skill with mechanical arms: he shaves, ties his shoes, eats, drives his car, types, telephones, plays billiards with facility and good screen presence.

The most likable difference between old recruiting films and the new one, "To the Ladies," is that the new one does only a minor amount of selling you into the service with the idea that you will see the world, live sumptuously, be endlessly entertained and learn the most fascinating trade. "To the Ladies" does its recruiting for the Army Nurse Corps and uses some good, stark film to the best psychological advantage. "Resisting Enemy Interrogation" is an ingeniously worked-out thriller-instruction film that includes an extraordinary number of details for fliers to guard against when they are captured and questioned by the enemy.

Seeing these non-commercial films made me feel more than ever before that there will be an expanded movie world after the war to take care of the thousands of new technicians developed in service units; also to include a documentary-producing industry similar to the one that existed in England before the war. The wartime documentaries have already affected the technique used in almost every fiction film. The one non-comfortable feeling I had on all of them came from their being controlled by a definite political and moral line, which the people making them may or may not agree with. The obvious feeling watching "Meet MacGonegal" and "To the Ladies" is that the same subject matter on war casualties could be used to make the most convincing anti-war movie, which is not likely to be permitted by either this country or Great Britain; "Lili Marlene" presents a history of the war and an attitude toward it which is exactly the same as every other history of the war presented in an Allied documentary; "Welcome to Britain" handles the problem of relations between white soldiers and black ones with a lot of good intentions, but the treatment is that of the most vote-conscious presidential candidate.

September 11, 1944

Against the Grain

IN "Youth Runs Wild," Producer Val Lewton has succeeded in making a very human, neat examination of wartime juvenile delinquency, without showing any very delinquent children or significant examples of their development, hang-outs or behavior. Two extremely good, likable adolescent sweethearts, played beautifully by Tessa Brind and Glenn Vernon, are used for hero and heroine, and get onto the edges of delinquency partly by accidents, partly bacause of their own thoughtful concern for each other. Tessa becomes involved with a "bad" girl (Bonita Granville), who really has the soul of a Marie Dressler type—incidentally, the least convincing character in the picture—and wisely takes her advice and leaves her parents, who have no parental drive and aren't home much of the time anyway. She probably wouldn't have done this if the boy's parents hadn't idiotically stopped him from seeing her. The boy is caught by the police half-heartedly trying to make some money stealing tires in a parking lot; then he is caught again in a night-club brawl trying to get in to see his girl, who has becomes a hostess there. The boy's sister and brother-in-law, who have already started a day-nursery for war workers' children and made many fine suggestions on child guidance and civic duty in wartime, take the girl into their home and make another wholesome suggestion: the girl should become interested in the kind of work Ruth Clifton (Look magazine, May 16) did in Moline, Illinois, which was to make Moline set up play, study and work centers for its youth.

In this manner, and by the vigilant planting of some hints along the outside of the film, "Youth Runs Wild" manages to touch on an adequate number of causes, centers and cures for delinquency, but it runs somewhat pale. As a picture of child corruption, it probably would have gained energy by projecting the personality of at least one adolescent who had been thoroughly educated on Main Street, night clubs, juke boxes, movies and some degree of prostitution; it could at least have used some unbleached examination of life inside or around some of the above institutions. The hang-outs in "Youth Runs Wild" are rendered with accuracy, but they aren't visited enough.

What is generally too mild and too much like school, would have been more so if it hadn't had Val Lewton's production, which includes some adequate realism and some of the only thoroughly acceptable humanity to be found in movies today. Much of this humanity is the result of screen writing that tries and generally succeeds in having characters react with some degree of interest, good faith and intelligence, and of direction and playing which attempt to express characteristics such as dignity or evil in the actor himself as well as through incident. His pictures show a beautiful eye, memory, and a feeling for gesture and attitude—for instance, for the whole visual vocabulary of a group like his high-school kids: their stance and gestures playing handball, smoking, toward parents, and their ways of showing disrespect and superiority at the movies. The best parts of this film are the conception of the girl's parents (Ben Bard and Elizabeth Russell), which exhibits a real knowledge of and love for working-class people, and the performance of the girl (Miss Brind) in

which she presents a touching portrait of thoroughly sincere, trusting innocence. In it there is childishness, a middle-class character and belief that make
the adolescence of a Jennifer Jones seem corny and that of a June Allyson seem
like a pampered midget's.

On the basis of his last three movies, of which the two preceding ones were
"The Cat People"—my idea of the best Hollywood film in about three years—
and "The Curse of the Cat People," I would rate Lewton as the least commercial film maker in Hollywood by about a hundred miles. Whatever spurious
device you can think of for making a movie break box-office records you will
find least present in these three pictures. Each film had a different director and
writing crew, but they look enough alike to make you feel that Lewton controlled the work on all of them. One of their main characteristics is the peculiarly efficient care and good, somewhat pale, sense that moves evenly into
every corner of them. They are about the only Hollywood movies in which the
writing and direction try to keep in front of rather than behind the audience's
intelligence. Also present in all of them is a belief in education (it started in the
middle of "The Cat People" when the hero gave a textbook definition of adult
love, and has enveloped the two later films), actors who seem to be as serious
about their work as the producer, and intelligent realism.

Lewton escapes the corruption of Hollywood by his own integrity and by
skillful practicality such as either making horror films or tackling subjects that
are unlikely to disturb Hollywood's present idea of what movies can handle,
and in staying on the non-volcanic side of their problems and on the mild, conservative side of technique (though this is very promising compared to other
native films). Also, he makes small pictures that don't get in the hair of the
industry or the audience, and being low-budget jobs, they don't have to bring
in enormous returns. In another set-up, I think Lewton would probably make
extremely good movies; he may eventually do that even in Hollywood.

September 18, 1944

More Notes on Newsreels

Along with an unrestricted, more imaginative use of movie technique in
making newsreels, and an emphasis on improving the quality of individual
events rather than the quantity, American newsreels could stand an over-
hauling of their ideas of what makes suitable newsreel material. It seems to me
that the newsreels, as the journalist in movies, should be concerned with

everything that happens around us, rather than restricting themselves, as they do now, to the more spectacular occurrences in human affairs. To get into the lens of an American newsreel camera an event must be as momentous as the first baseball game of the season, the debut of the newest model of anything, or a President's speech. The concern of the newsreels should be to exhibit material that shows to some substantial degree what we are like and what we have done. For this aim, the record of Frank Sinatra's or Harry James's latest performance at New York's Paramount Theatre, and the reaction of the audience to it, becomes a bona-fide newsreel event, since the event has so much importance to the people and indicates what so many of them are like; a camera account of a day spent on a wartime railroad coach is important newsreel material, since it tells us and a future age much more about ourselves than any train wreck, which is the only kind of train news that makes the newsreels now. The straight reporting of any activity on any American Main Street or a detailed examination of that street's buildings should become the most important and exciting kind of newsreel event.

The newsreel producers are too apt to show only the limited, obvious aspects of even their most traditional subject matter. The typical newsreel examination of someone's speech confines itself almost wholly to the speaker, missing all of the effect of the speech as it registers on the audience and all of the character of the event that is defined by the character of the audience. The only part of the event that is shown is the speech part; there is no account of how the people looked as they got ready for the speech, nor is there a post-speech phase—only the speaker's carefully purposeful, man-to-man stare straight into the lens.

The main concern exhibited on newsreel subject matter is less to give you an understanding of the events or the people in them than to give some kind of visual proof that the incident actually occurred and that Fox-Movietone, Paramount or Hearst covered it; the announcer unsuccessfully attempts to fill in with other aspects of the event to make it an understandable, rounded and exciting story. The endlessly repeated way of showing an Allied capture of an enemy-held town follows up a few last-minute examples of the fighting for the town with scenes of the Allies entering and being celebrated, hugged and kissed by the people. All the newsreel audience gets is what is already taken for granted—that the event happened and that everybody there was happy it did. By going behind this obvious center of such an event and doing a straight report about the condition of the people and the town at the moment of its capture, examining homes inside and out, and as much of the life at its most natural as could be got, newsreels would have the most important material about people in war. Where it has approximated this attitude—in scenes coming some time after such a capture, where people are being fed and cheered by the Allies, and in the trying of traitors—it has accomplished its best releases, giving something of the character of the people as it was affected by the Nazis and war: to an audience this is much more interesting (not to mention more important) than the usual spectacular, circus-like aspect of an event such as a fire, where the fearsome, decorative movements of the flames are the main thing shown.

Almost at once, of course, the newsreel people would, with their aim of showing a more abundant and down-to-earth view of human activity, run into all kinds of legal difficulties, the kind of difficulty suggested by the signs you see in various places prohibiting the use of cameras inside them. I can think of all kinds of reasons for shooting the activity inside of an average night club, but I can think of as many reasons why a night-club owner would kick at the idea. The legal point would finally have to be made as to just what the newsreels can look at, and I can't see that their view should be more restricted than that of a daily newspaper. As it stands now, the newsreel's fear of what they can look at is as great as it could possibly be, and their vision almost as limited.

October 16, 1944

Marie the Magician

"To Have and Have Not" is a rather spiritless Bogart movie that shows him as a man named Harry Morgan whose love for minding his own business and having the fewest possible connections with society is overthrown first by a woman named Marie (Lauren Bacall) and then by the cause for which the de Gaullists are fighting. His turnabout in both cases isn't very convincing or exciting though his love affair, which has been advertised as the sex bout to top all sex bouts, has some moments of likable slapstick humor. It consists mainly of verbal grappling that sounds as if the participants—Harry, who understandably calls Marie "Slim," and Marie, who not understandably calls Harry "Steve"—were competing for the chance to fill Oscar Levant's place on Information Please. The love-making is taken further out of the realm of love by Miss Bacall's exaggerated idea of what seductiveness should look like and by her unsure grounding in the art of Katharine Hepburn. The love affair does present the uncommon movie fact of a woman wooing the man, doing it very bawdily, and not getting her knuckles wrapped for it later. But the virtue of this honesty is then more than counterbalanced by the fact that situation and characters are pulled all out of shape, and the writing cheapened, not to illuminate the relationship but to throw the audience some speck-sized erotic thrills. This all takes place on Martinique, just after the fall of France, where Morgan runs a For Hire cabin cruiser, and the film ends with his setting out to rescue a famous de Gaullist from Devil's Island.

I think, though, that the picture has some worthwhile things in it and much entertainment that is easy to take, largely because it presents Humphrey Bogart and his ability to fill a role with a richer response, effect and conviction than a movie role usually warrants. Some of its belligerent dialogue (Bogart's, and that of a character named Johnson, who appears only at the beginning of the picture and is well played, in the Bogart manner, by Walter Sande) is good in a realistic way, and sounds as if it could have been thought up by the characters. Incidents like the first meeting between Morgan and Johnson realize the small animosities and aggressions that ride on every word of some casual conversations. A Howard Hawks film is apt to be very jittery, and this one achieves questionable vitality by not remaining long on any one of a superabundance of scenes. The movie takes place, as do many Bogart films, in a night club, around a piano player who sings and plays tunes from Lucky Strike's All Time Hit Parade with what is supposed to be a genuine jazz quality. Hoagy Carmichael is this piano player, and though both his singing and the atmosphere are overdesigned, he is one of the best popular-song writers and generally worth watching in this picture.

"To Have and Have Not" is nevertheless half-hearted and slight moviemaking, even though one of its screen authors is William Faulkner, its director, Hawks, one of the best for contriving to avoid dull movies, its original novel by Hemingway, and its chief actor, Humphrey Bogart, who seems to me to make a better Hemingway hero than Gary Cooper ever has. It has, for one thing, too many dominant concerns to handle. One of them, which shows the fight on Martinique between the de Gaullists and the Vichyites and the hero's part in that fight, seems completely tacked on. Another, and its most adequately realized one, is its very professional portrait of the traditional Bogart personality. The character is one of the more complicated ones that the movies have tackled, and this picture notes, in an academic, careful way, its main aspects: that he is never weak, affectionate, non-combustible, ineffective, deceitful, cowardly, in need of help, advice or anything else, that he is a man of strong feeling which he rigorously subdues out of his great sense of how to get along in the world. But another thing this film attempts to do is wholly unbelievable and irritating: it tries to change this character from the most determined kind of asocial man into a French patriot. "To Have and Have Not" also has its love bout to exploit, along with all kinds of odds and ends that proved popular in earlier Bogart films, and the result is a picture that has no more structure or unified effect than a string of familiar but unrelated beads.

October 23, 1944

Murdered Movie

"Laura" is a movie exposé of society people that is more awed with them than critical. The ignoble facts it finds—promiscuity, deceit, cowardliness and small-mindedness—are treated with a disinterest that is almost boredom, while it views their wit, fastidiousness, snobbery, splendid clothes and environment with the kind of gaga-eyed reverence that you find in perfume ads. Laura, who is head of a famous advertising agency (acted by Gene Tierney with no other qualities than there are in a fashion mannequin on parade), who is admittedly bound to become the mistress of anybody in pants, who can lie and be as tricky as the next society type in this movie, is nevertheless considered for her gentility as an impossible achievement in glorious womanhood— a career-girl Mrs. Miniver.

The best part of the picture is its description of a Brahmin columnist, named Waldo Lydecker, played with great pleasure by Clifton Webb, whose snobbishness and fastidiousness are about the only facts studied in any detail; his perfumed literary style of talking expresses a lot of auntyish effeminacy and his values get across with some force. But there is the same kind of society-page awe in the way he is treated and a false glorification that is totally impressed with what are actually dime-store book wit and charm, and small-boy behavior. The film is a perfect example of Hollywood's propensity to glorify every kind of character, from the villain to people who merely stand in the background of Laura's cocktail parties and dinner engagements. It has to do, among other things, with a refusal to take any kind of fact about a person plain, but to make the fact more special, perfect and of equal importance with everything else in the picture. It is one reason for the absence of unpleasantness in our films; the pleasant fact, when idealized, is only made more pleasant, but idealizing unpleasant facts changes the entire character of the detail.

"Laura" is also a murder film, but its crime is treated romantically, like its people, only more so. Four days after the murder its supposedly murdered woman, Laura, shows up unmarked, and the New York police, the murderer and the plain-American-guy detective (who is acted with as much wood as he has ever been played by a talented actor, Dana Andrews) discover that some other woman's face was shot off by mistake. Meanwhile the detective has fallen in love with Laura from her picture, and this drives the murderer, who is a former lover and hates to see anybody else handle her, to try shooting off her face again. As a murder puzzle it leaves out most of the clues and hides the rest, which makes the mystery both baffling and boring.

"Laura" has a bareness that is as fabulous as the glass fruit that used to decorate dining-room tables. The heroine is described in a series of moments from her life—getting her hair fixed, having her breakfast in bed, leaning over to say something in a business conference—that are as unnoteworthy as the comments Lydecker makes on each shot (for the one in the business conference, "Laura had an eager mind always"). During the picture she falls in love with four men and out of love with three as unconvincingly as possible, which, compared to the account of the detective's falling in love with her, is rich and moving. The detective's love affair consists of some nervous pacing, interrupted by someone's coming in to say, "MacPherson, you're acting very strange lately. People are going to think you're in love."

Otto Preminger's directing energetically enters into every part of the film and makes it more obvious and more like tin. He underlines attitudes, like the hard-boiled detective's talking through a cigarette, that are already in italics. Characters constantly offer trim summations of themselves for the audience like the society lightweight's, "I don't know a great deal about anything, but I know a little about everything." The players' positions in the scene are often petrified into tableaux, and the few action episodes, like the final murder attempt, are so overtrained that they run off as precisely as ballet-steps. All of this cuts the movie into a minimum of easily recognized ideas and leaves the audience still fewer things to find or judge for itself. As a result it is hard to find anything good in "Laura," or simply anything.

October 30, 1944

The Red and the Black

"The Rainbow," a Russian film adapted from a Stalin Prize Novel written by Wanda Wasilewska, shows as little tolerance, love, mercy, dignity, breadth of understanding or nobility as any work of art I have ever seen. It treats the most common movie story of this war, the one that shows the brutal way Nazis ruled the people in conquered countries (in this case the people of a Ukrainian village), how they failed to get the people to collaborate with them, and their final defeat by soldiers of the people; but it treats it with a mad-eyed simplification unsurpassed in war films.

The Nazis are shown only as craven murderers, who confine their killing to babies, children, mothers and wounded prisoners. In one case the reason given for the murder is the refusal of a Partisan woman to give information; but all the rest of more than a dozen crimes are done completely without provocation. "The Rainbow" suggests that most of these Nazis are fools, but doesn't bother to explain them any further; they are hardly even placed as Fascists. By carefully spreading the outrages throughout all types and ranks of German soldiers shown and implying that there are no exceptions, the movie suggests that all German soldiers are hopeless psychopathic killers, and by carefully planting a sentence at the beginning of the film—"These Germans behaved as Germans"—the movie also implies that their brutality is the trait of a nation. The characters of the Russians are taken just as coarsely for granted: they are given one characteristic—fearlessness, one face—hateful, and one desire—to revenge themselves on the Nazis.

It ends with the most cruel-minded episode since the hero in "Passage to Marseilles" machine-gunned some Nazis who were asking to be taken prisoner. The scene is one in which a peasant heroine stops the other women of her village from clubbing the Nazi prisoners to death, by screaming that they should not give them so easy a punishment as quick death, but should let them see their armies starved and beaten, their cities destroyed, and have them "answer for their wrongs before a People's Court; then kill them." This scene suggests, among other things, that all prisoners be killed, since the prisoners referred to are the total number of those taken in the capture of the town, and would presumably include guilty, less guilty and simply prisoners of war. The woman's speech also implies that the courts for trying war prisoners after the war will simply be places for prisoners' confessions to be heard before the inevitable verdict of death.

Since the Russians and their country have felt Nazi cruelty as much as anyone, it is understandable that their movie makers see the war almost wholly as an affair of killing, cruelty and revenge. But their method, in this film, of showing it only as that is the narrowest possible and one that results for the audience in no understanding of the problem of the Nazis beyond the fact that vengeance must be taken on them. Also, by cutting out of its Russians any response to the war except an unyielding determination to kill every Nazi, the movie leaves its audience with the idea that there is only one thing the

Russians want to do about Nazism—kill the Nazis. And the facts themselves of cruelty, killing and revenge are so oversimplified that one is left with the idea that anybody can become cruel and can kill, given the provocation, without any complication, and without, presumably, experiencing any effects in himself.

"The Rainbow's" way of showing its viewpoint turns up some creditable things but more sterile ones, because of one-trait characterization, an uninspired use of disparate and worn-out movie devices and a basically puerile romanticism. A couple of actors, G. Klering and Natalia Alisova, strain the straitjacket character of their roles (as Nazi Commandant and kept woman) with a likably ham style of acting, which is about all they could use on two roles that were first thought up about the time of Griffith and have been seen ever since in German, Russian and American sex films. "The Rainbow" always has a determination to say something, no matter what, that is more vigorous than is usual in movies these days. This determination leads, midway in the picture, to a couple of situations that are developed in a full, firm way and produce some genuine movie meaning. One is a description of a childbirth that pulls in scenes of the environment and alludes in a crude, pleasant way to the birth of Christ, in a nearly successful, emotionally moving scene. The other expresses the moronic quality of a Nazi by showing his bewildered, ineffectual attempts to communicate with some unpleasant children. It is the one place in the picture where human activity is seen without complete simplification.

November 6, 1944

The Miracle of Morton

PRESTON STURGES' first biography, "The Great Moment," is a comically turned life story of the Boston dentist, Dr. William Thomas Green Morton (Joel McCrea performs in this role almost as naturally as the doctor might, perhaps with even less idiosyncrasy), to whom it credits the discovery of anesthesia. It has as much slapstick as most Sturges films but is likely his least vacillating, tricky and cynical one. Sturges probably wanted to make a biographical film that was more down to earth than film memorials usually are, and he succeeded in some ways. Morton, whose impetus for inventing painless dentistry was, the picture says, to stop his patients from leaping about so he could do neater work, spent the last twenty years of his life trying to make the public believe he had discovered etherization, died without a dime, recognition, happiness or peace

of mind. Sturges makes him even less glamorous but more natural than Hollywood's Wilson, Bell, Pasteur, Curie, Edison, Zola, etc., by giving him little
humor or obvious wisdom, only an average talent for his work, and a wife
(Betty Field) who is on the silly side, ignorant for the most part of what her
husband is doing and anxious for him to make more money rather than dis-
coveries. Most of the public, all of his fellow dentists, and the medical profession give him as little help as possible.

This is Sturges' most humane movie and his least slippery one. There is
much less sharp wavering in his estimation of ideas, and little nose-thumbing.
He seems glad that his hero is not money-mad, that anesthesia was invented;
he is determined in the presentation of the fact that the public is for the most
part uncharitable to inventors or inventions; his people aren't turned so completely and mercilessly into dupes, fools or sadists, but, without oversimplifying them one way or another, he leaves them dominantly mean-minded, silly,
avaricious, kindly, snobbish, and he allows them to move, breathe and reason
with more personal freedom than his characters have had before.

The story and situations, however, are pretty much traditional Hollywood
biography. The film sticks very close to the most successful events of its hero's
life; it is play-like and cardboard-like and somewhat trumped-up. If Sturges
wanted determinedly to make a realistic biographical film, he probably was
working much more than he usually does against the grain of his studio, which,
like all the rest of Hollywood, has firm ideas of what morality and tone should
be in such a picture. This may have produced what seems to me a somewhat
enervated and tight Sturges movie. But part of the tightness must also have
come from Sturges' own fascination with the problem of success, which he has
been gnawing at for some time in his films. Heretofore his answer has been
that the greatest success in terms of money and fame can be had by anybody
with the aid of luck, trickery or something fortuitous which seldom has much
to do with how good or able the person is. In this picture he is definitely interested in the great trouble a man had in achieving success, and in the fact that
what success the man had was followed by twenty years of miserable failure;
and though he says this, his picture is designed to spend almost all of its time,
in the traditional rosy manner, on the more fortunate moments. His knowledge
of and interest in the non-American-dream quality of Morton's career seems to
have been suffocated by his interest in whatever there was in the career that
looked good. This, which is apparently a conflict in purpose (not to forget the
studio), has made the picture less robust and might explain why as much ill fitting slapstick comedy has capped each serious scene.

"The Great Moment" is still very pleasant, on the light side with a few scenes of sharp effect. One is its picture of the epic moment on September 30, 1846, when Morton put his first dental case (William Demarest, still likable but very stereotyped now) under ether after tricking him, in a funny scene, into taking it; following this, much of the suspense, horror and fascination of a mysterious event is projected by the look and walk of his wife as she stares at the operation. Another is the result of some blood-curdling operating-room sounds on the occasion of the first medical surgery under anesthesia. A final one is an aptly dramatic and surprising curtain line. There are also a number of nice perceptions and business, including McCrea's gesture when he says he likes to do "neat work," the damning portrait of President Pierce as an idiot, the entrance of four petty minds of the medical profession into an operating room underneath the outstretched, unstinting arm of a huge plaster statue of Hippocrates, and McCrea's loving attitude toward the decorative quality of a lamp in his dental office. It is not what you would call an important movie, but it is engaging.

November 27, 1944

B-Plus

A MURDER film made by Monogram for $50,000 (a sum considered as money in terms of modern Hollywood production, but just barely; its filming, which took seven days, is close to as fast as a movie director dares go), called "When Strangers Marry," is about as human a movie as I have seen this year. Its best scenes, which express some of the solemn melancholia of being troubled and lonely in a strange city, occur in a story that tells the harassing experiences of a young girl trying to find her husband in New York and what happens when she finds him and has to help him hide from a murder charge. It realizes its hostile environment without using a gingerbread house, dark warehouses or somebody's staircase, and torments its people without starving them or threatening to shoot their kinfolk. The girl and her husband hide out in what seems the kind of desolate apartment building such a couple would get into, the kind that nobody seems to own and in which nobody seems to belong, neat and hard, with a dull, flat, gray light in the rooms where a few heavy pieces of furniture are widely separated. The people do a lot of depressed standing around without saying anything witty, which not only is treating their situation honestly but has a markedly fine effect on the film. Neither of them is considered as exceptional in any way—the girl is as close to small-town innocence as Hollywood gets (even here it is more like finishing-school sensitivity and niceness), and the husband is surprisingly dull, suppressed and frozen. The mood, which is almost the whole picture, even approaches a real sense of alienation.

The movie is as economical as it is human, since its action is on an extremely small scale, with hardly any of the usual suspense mechanisms like hunts, clues or detection. However, it is one of the best mysteries of the year. Aside from the apartment-house scenes it has only a few skit-like moments: at a Share-a-Ride agency (where an unnamed actor turns up one of the few performances of a driver that isn't composed of a mild little Irishman trying to be tough, Brooklynesque and comic all at the same time); at a Harlem jazz dive, as usual; at a Coney Island mental wizard's act; and a few brushes with the police. In all of these there is the common movie mistake of seeing all the people and the environment as equally droll, quaint and productive of an "experience." But even this material seems fresher and less annoying than similar devices used in other films. In fact the whole thing seemed original to me, compared to movies like "Double Indemnity," "Laura" or "Phantom Lady." Though it has certain unsuccessful embellishments that are mainly snatched from German expressionism—such as a face moving almost through the camera, a cross-section of a hotel showing the rise of an elevator from bottom to top, or a scary walk through a park underpass with crescendoing footsteps and the girl's hallucinations dissolving on the walls—it is the least arty of the films mentioned above.

The script is cut down to the bone and a little further, so that it is hard to find any of the villain's character and little more than goodness in the others. But it only stumbles at the dénouement (an old-fashioned stumble so inevitable you take it for granted). Whoever did the casting tried for actors who look as if they belong to some other profession besides acting and to some other income bracket than high middle class or higher, and they act adequately in addition to being credible (the unprofessional stiffness in the leads adds to the frustrated mood that seems good in the film). Bob Mitchum, a sardonic, cold-faced person, is the most interesting. William Castle's direction projects the story as an actuality rather than as something being enacted for a camera, director or audience, and he seldom jumbles a sound image and a visual one at the same moment with the same force. His perceptions don't go as far and are not as original as the early Hitchcock's, but he has much of Hitchcock's light, sharp control of story-telling and technique, which is apparent in how much he accomplishes in this movie's first two or three minutes. That includes the murder, the character of the victim, the motive and the presentation of the problem, plus a degree of terror achieved on almost every shot by irritating sound, cutting or grotesque and surprising image.

"When Strangers Marry" hits just about everything it aims at; as a mystery it puzzled me more than a lot of other movie mysteries have, and altogether it seems to me an intended bunt that scored about a triple.

December 4, 1944

Rich Creamy Lather

"None but the Lonely Heart" is a huge mishmash that tackles the daring and important movie subject of the ugly side of modern society with just about the stalest, trashiest material I have ever seen. It is like setting out to see New York and finding yourself traversing the same old short cut from home to the grocery store.

The film's path—ostensibly pursuing Ernie Mott, a Cockney character played by Cary Grant like Cary Grant, through London's East End slums in "his search for a free, noble and better life in the second quarter of the twentieth century"—actually tells how he comes home to be a good boy to his mother, Ethel Barrymore, when he is told she is dying of cancer. After they are reconciled he becomes so appalled by the poverty around them that he turns gangster, and his mother, in a try to get the money that will keep him from being a gangster, winds up in the penitentiary for racketeering. The picture ends with the son, evidently through as a gangster, meditating on "when the world is going to get off its knees." His wise old buddy (Barry Fitzgerald parodying his Hollywood self) tells him that the job will have to be done by the young people, but agrees with the boy that it will be done and that the bomber flying overhead is the first sign of the world's regeneration. This essential story I think is terrifying.

The film's message that the poor must scrape, thieve or kill to live and have only their own lonely hearts to tide them over, just seeps through at the end, despite the fact that dozens of people have been made sad or bad by that time, innumerable remarks like "The places of the world are empty, the human heart is everything" have been spoken by these people who are all sages, and the melody that the picture was named after has been reminding you of the movie's theme in a number of styles ranging from boozy, weepy piano to the fanciest orchestral sonority. The biggest befogging factor is the situation having to do with Mother, her wandering boy and her cancer, which keeps your mind constantly away from the theme of lonely hearts and social decay and concentrated on the mechanical workings of a tear-jerking plot. Basically nothing has changed in this plot since it began, whenever that was, though Miss Barrymore is probably the most powerful actress ever to play Mother. The most important facts in it are still the violent, melodramatic hurdles, which are supposed to decide everything, including who is good, who is bad, how you should feel inside the theatre and how you should act outside it. The characters' motivations for turning into gangster or loving son still escape you; you have the same trouble liking the good people and hating the bad. Besides, the people are so nice, folksy, exotically talented, strong and wise that it is impossible for *them* to be inhabitants of a barren world. And things like cancer, a noble great lady—especially Ethel Barrymore—in prison for petty thievery, are so spectacular in themselves that you can't feel very grim or mournful.

I felt an essential lack of the evil, hardness, hunger, loneliness and frustration that seem to be what the film was interested in. Instead there is a great deal of lush, pretty lighting, settings, views, events, talk and people. The central material is constantly being obliterated. Either some decoration is too energetic (the halo lighting behind the heroine's head, the double image produced by placing people in front of mirrors); or the structure is clothed in gingerbread (Ernie Mott is made a genius at rifle-marksmanship, music, mechanics, prize-fighting, talking and philosophy when he really needs only a couple of these talents, and he has a ferocious-looking dog which is given about four times the attention necessary); or some element of the production is grotesque enough to step in front of the image (Cary Grant's consciousness of his own acting and posing invariably does; so does the director's interest in what funny things the camera can record). Many entertaining things in the picture, such as a funny scene of a drunk echoing his voice in a tunnel, and much of the film's gangster material still seems to be covering up for what the authors really had to say. Whether or not you agree with their idea of the modern world and people, their use of a dime-store melodrama seems the vaguest, least convincing one to show it with, and the treatment and secondary material look as if they are trying to take your mind off both the theme and triteness of the plot.

It is a very long film and it has some excellent things that should be mentioned. The blunt, journalistic treatment of a scene in which Ernie's gang beats up and robs the pawnshop owner seems to me as accurate as anything I have seen for catching the kind of skilled barbarism the Nazis practise—I don't think the movie calls the victim Jewish but it portrays him beautifully that way. He is played by Konstantin Shayne (whose bit as Karkov in "For Whom the Bell Tolls" was also the best bit performance of last year) with a very exact kind of unbowing dignity, goodness and melancholy. There is a moving scene at the Motts' store, involving a small girl covetously eyeing a caged canary as she pays a fraction of the price on some shoes (here the movie records something very important with the slightest offhand naturalism). Just after this, a strange bit of movie symbolism occurs when a tipsy woman comes in to pawn a canary for liquor money; while she haggles with Ernie over the price the bird dies, and the poor woman goes off hysterically crying. I liked the whole intent and method.

This is one of the biggest hodgepodges Hollywood ever constructed. I doubt that Clifford Odets, who wrote (from Richard Llewellyn's novel) and directed it, would ever have used such a plot or so artificial a folk in a play of his own, but he probably wouldn't have been allowed to make this movie either if he had wanted to change the original novel's material. No doubt he would have preferred actors who looked more like slum people than Barrymore, Grant, Jane Wyatt or June Duprez, but the studio undoubtedly didn't. Nor will studios countenance the ridding of people like Grant or Fitzgerald of their stereotyped screen personalities. The movie is most firm and good when it is dealing with Jews, night clubs, penny arcades and gangsterism, which Odets knows about, and achieves with them a successful, peculiar synthesis of New York East Side and faint Englishness. Technically the film is a stew of literature, theatre, John Ford's, German and modern Hollywood movies. The whole thing, to quote one of the characters, "needs a solid base." It also, to quote the same person in this movie, "fries in its own fat."

December 11, 1944

Flesh and Enamel

"Meet Me in St. Louis" seemed to me a good movie as well as a cloying, callow one. At the same time that I felt a great deal of intelligence, loving care and enormous talent (especially that of Margaret O'Brien) going into the film I was exasperated by the way it restricted so much of itself to the moral level of a high-school play, sweetened and pampered with the modern Hollywood-Broadway formula for making a popular success.

It tells about the year 1903 in the life of a large St. Louis family named Smith. They had a lovely time that year—two parties, a picnic, Hallowe'en and Christmas; the older sisters and a brother were nicely engaged and the father was promoted in his firm; and there was the Louisiana Purchase Exposition which seemed to symbolize for them how perfect life could be and was. It is all genuinely sweet and happy, or colored that way, but the producers hint at far less lovely aspects of life. They point out a spinsterism and coldness in the eldest daughter, a love for power in the middle one, a lot of things in the smallest one—including egotism—and a faded depression in the mother. They don't look very long at these facts, preferring more pleasant things like Hallowe'en, frankly tissue-paper love affairs for the kids, and a good deal of boneless comedy—all of which is talented and quite amusing. I think this should be mentioned, since "Meet Me in St. Louis" is a lot more than Andy Hardy or the average film or stage musical and obviously knew enough to be stronger than it is.

There is a great deal of wonderful perception and feeling in it and the best is in a Hallowe'en hell-raising by the neighborhood kids that is seen through a small girl's eyes and feelings as she carried out her threat to throw flour in the face of the most feared resident of the district—a nice-seeming, blocky German professional type, who is just about the person she would imagine to be the chief poisoner, drunkard and wife-beater in the city. The whole episode is beautifully funny, but is best I think as the child starts away from the gang's bonfire, looking like a vaudeville comic in her brother's pants, and walks, as though toward death, down a street that has a kind of fairy-book lighting, wind and blowing autumn leaves, and ends with a terrified, crying run up to the man's porch. Some other accurately recorded images are the account of the hysteria that hits a family when one of the children is injured (especially how glorious it is for the injured child), a moment when the middle daughter hears that her sweetheart has hit her little sister in the face and rushes at him with a terrifying, sexually driven desire to beat him to death, a similar moment when the little sister rushes at her snowmen and starts clubbing them to bits because she can't take them with her to New York. Many of these scenes are as good as any that have been made this year in fiction films.

The filming of Sally Benson's New Yorker stories will undoubtedly make MGM an enormous amount of money on account of these things, but also because the movie cannily follows the theory that any fact that is plain, inharmonious or less than sweet is neither appealing nor entertaining. Every second of the picture is carefully crammed with cuteness and selling points. It gives you the unpleasant feeling that the family is too talented and practises a tinny kind of humor too much, but there is a more terrifying feeling that the producers figured you out down to your smallest like and dislike and are going to show you your intelligence rating on every foot of their film. The movie also believes that the prettiest state of the detail is the most entertaining, and this leads to décor, hairdos and dresses that are merely candyish, or to photography, like that of Miss Garland, which would be turned down as insipid by film magazines that deal in idealized portraits of stars. The worst thing this attitude does, though, is to doll up the two best scenes by making the Hallowe'en masks and the bonfire too fashionable, and over-sculpting the snowmen mauled by Margaret O'Brien. The movie makes its life too much like the working of a machine. This leads to such overrefined material as Judy Garland's performance, which is choked with effects, schooled into an enameled surface, and left that way; dance routines that are supposed to seem at least half-spontaneous never do; scenes, such as that of the family eating, which are supposed to appear completely impulsive, proceed like circus acts.

I think these latter attitudes override the goodness of the movie, but they don't keep the goodnesses from being startlingly good; and Margaret O'Brien is much too good to miss.

December 18, 1944

To Have and Have Not

"The Very Thought of You" is a Warner Brothers examination of the problem of the soldier-and-girl marriage in wartime that is worth seeing because it is a degree less deceitful and inane than current films have been about sex or the American family. The movie illustrates how adequate war marriage can be, as well as how it should be, with an affair that starts on a Pasadena bus when a parachute-factory worker (Eleanor Parker) who used to be a soda-jerk recognizes a soldier (Dennis Morgan) as a boy she used to make double-rich malted milks for. After she introduces herself to him, their romance goes forward without a hitch (they have some trouble getting a hotel room on their honeymoon night) to marriage two days later and to the end of the film, when the boy returns home to his wife and baby after being discharged for an arm injury. Another happy affair between the girl's friend (Faye Emerson) and the boy's (Dane Clark) accompanies this, which reinforces the movie's thesis by showing that more ruttish soldiers and girls are also serious about their affairs and remain faithful to one another. They provide the film with a lot of suggestive wisecracks, exits, appearances and mugging as a substitute for the sex that the script tries to be constantly involved in. The movie also pays a good deal of attention—too much—to the heroine's irritable family, which it uses to show what some of the attitudes of society are toward soldiers and their girls.

This picture is surprisingly cognizant of sex. For one thing, its nice-girl heroine is shown being moderately aroused during the love scenes, and desiring to be so before them. She is very purposeful about getting the soldier to be her lover and husband, which is probably the most likable and expert touch in the writing because it causes the love affair to go forward less magically than love affairs proceed elsewhere in films and it makes her very lifelike. The energetic acting of Eleanor Parker gives this girl a credible lust at times, though she is apt to be too affected and cagey for the unintellectual, average girl she impersonates and there are too many close-ups of her lusciously opening one side of her mouth in the same manner. The script by Delmer Daves (who also directed) and Alvah Bessie is continually concerned, as it should be, with sex no matter how ersatz the means are sometimes; it seems pretty smart about the subject—very good in a scene at the girl friend's Motel cabin—and is wholesome enough. There is also some down-to-earth writing about the family which includes an ugly dinner-table quarrel that is as painful to watch as it should be, and two characters—a sister who seems to be a little mad but isn't for once over-simplified as a crazy woman, and a sour, ineffectual mother—who are definitely not stock family types though some of the other members are. There is a fine scene when the mother hears that her youngest daughter is pregnant and produces a shattering, forced, stuck-pig shriek and then faints into one of the only convincing and comically awkward fainting positions that I've ever seen in a movie.

The attack, which is best when the picture is trying to show something realistic about soldiers on leave, disperses itself by attending too much to, and not achieving enough with, the girl's family and also by presenting a long stereotyped year after the marriage to show how courageous wives must be when their husbands are at war. The script doesn't get any of the strain, and too little of the detail, that would arise from the lovers' adjusting to each other and simply getting through their three-day event. Dennis Morgan helps to thin this affair further by being unbelievably torpid. It is thinned some more by having to indicate sex by an unending use of two devices—tin wisecracks and pretty kissing—but there is still a lot of unadorned knowledge and feeling.

Since this film is freer with sex than any other around now, you can estimate from it how far Hollywood has progressed toward being less bound by its rules for what can be said about sex in movies. This picture is still playing pretty strictly as the Hays Office says it should play, but it is being more adept and honest. Though the lovers exit and appear indecorously, it is carefully explained after each suggestive maneuver that the people did not have sexual intercourse. The adultress is scolded and made to say she's sorry, the film carefully doesn't advise separation for her sailor husband (when he ought to take nothing less), the morning-after scenes of honeymoon still find the people completely separate, only one of them in bed and both exasperatingly unemotional and made-up. The writing here, though, is skillful at implying sex and then making its refutation much weaker. It gets some robustness just by playing the love scenes less sweetly than usual, so that even if the characters can't love each other until they are married in the film, they still seem to be made of something besides sugar, and seem to be grown-up. You can be just about as lusty as you want these days if you do it by way of a wisecrack and do not directly say that there has been or will be any sex.

December 25, 1944

The Case of the Hidden Camera

LIFE magazine reported last week (about two months after Leonard Lyons had) that sequences were made for "The Lost Weekend" in which the hero, Ray Milland, went about New York's Third Avenue among people who didn't know they were taking part in a movie. They didn't know because, as well as not being able to recognize Mr. Milland realistically made up, they couldn't see the camera crew and equipment, which were hidden in such places as the top of a theatre marquee and inside trucking vans. This hidden-camera maneuver for combining real and fictional lives is as well known as movies, but Hollywood could use it much more than it does—no matter how well the scenes turn out for "The Lost Weekend."

It would be one way of avoiding the unreal, mismated or lifeless details that now occur so often in people, scenery, action and atmosphere of scenes shot in the studio, and it's also a way to find out what the world is like, which Hollywood could use, since it has forgotten most of what it ever knew about the world. Also, it would be seeing the world through the eyes of a camera instead of through those of a novelist or playwright, upon whom it is increasingly dependent for its conception of the world. The movies nowadays turn up fewer and fewer aspects of the world that can be best shown by the camera, and instead get more and more of what novelists like to think about. Besides, they rely too much on their past work for symbols of the real world, though the symbols long ago became stale knowledge to audiences. Making fiction films in a close union with real life and out in the real world isn't the only way to make movies, and it is only a means. Whether a movie is made inside a studio or in the middle of a city street, it is obviously going to be only as good as the skill, intelligence, purpose and honesty of its producer.

Hidden cameras can be used to make actuality serve as the whole material of a fiction film scene or just as environment and secondary material around planned and rehearsed central action. If your plot called for some action inside of a department store the normal activity of the store could be got by sending trained actors into it to carry on a planned business with an actor-clerk. Nobody else in the store need become conscious or self-conscious of this business, since the camera man has been slyly concealed inside an ingeniously made store dummy and is recording everything from there. In this case the fictional business would be provided with the kind of life that ought to go on around it. The sides and backgrounds of modern movie scenes are at rare moments as good as they are in Sturges movies but are generally so dead and vapid and without accident that the action seems to have been played in a bottle.

There are all kinds of tones in an actual event, whereas it is very difficult to get anything but primary effects in studio productions. Also, beyond secondary effects, the marvelous illustrative capacity of the camera could be used at times in fiction films with an effect that would lift you out of your seat. If you wanted a picture of race prejudice you could send a Negro actor into a Southern bus with only one action to perform—he would sit down in a section where only white people are allowed to sit. What followed would be entirely spontaneous and approximately predictable. The value of the material would depend on how, why and where it was used in the movie, and on how well the director understood the situation and what he was about in using it, and even more, perhaps, on how much he knew about the artistic possibilities of the movie medium. Creativity in using the camera is not confined to recording an already created, rehearsed and planned action; film creativity is in the selection of the camera possibilities right for the purpose.

The difficulties involved in photographing with concealed cameras include the problem of hiding oneself and a camera sometimes even bigger. If you are hidden, you can't get around much or fast, so that your view and range are restricted. There would be all kinds of trouble with lighting (but you could hardly do worse with that than Hollywood does right now); there is the problem of sound and getting people's permission to use their stores, trains, homes and selves for movies. However, the solution of these difficulties (and others) requires only ingenuity, and with a normal amount of that, using real-life scenes shouldn't be so hard, expensive or frantic as using some of the dodges thought up in studios for simulating real life.

January 1, 1945

Day of Reckoning

"Tomorrow—the World!" (filmed from the hit play by James Gow and Arnaud d'Usseau) deals with the question of whether the Nazis can be reformed, and does so at a time when its belief that the Nazis can be changed for the better and that the best way is with a minimum of force, will irritate a lot of people and possibly influence some of them. It is most unusual for Hollywood to touch a problem as hot as the one handled by this Lester Cowan film, let alone hedge as little as it does in its judgment. Therefore I would advise you to see the movie because of its courage, decision and the fact that it has been made with a good deal of concern, seriousness and intelligence. Beyond these assets, my liking of the film is confined to a restrained appreciation of the playing of Betty Field and Fredric March, the conception of their roles, a deadly shot of a tardy boy entering a classroom, one of a boy running away from school, and a moment in a kids' fight (generally silly, for one reason because the kids hit with the style of Max Baer and the accurate fury of movie cowboys), in which the camera image of the fight blurs sickeningly the way the fight does to the fighters.

The film presents its "test case" for the treatment of Nazis by showing the experience of a college professor (Fredric March) and his friends when he takes over the training of a twelve-year-old nephew (Skippy Homeier), who has been previously educated in Germany to be a thoroughgoing Nazi. The boy behaves abominably until he finally drives the Americans, who are very progressive-school-minded and believe in sparing the rod, into punishing him. After his fright, pain and hysteria, he wavers for the first time in his addiction to Nazi doctrine. He also shows his first concern for the attentions of those around him; faced with being sent to a reformatory he realizes how nice his room at the professor's house is; the professor's sweetheart (Betty Field) believes that his crying is the first human feeling she has noticed in him. On the strength of all these last-minute indications of change, the professor sends the police, who are waiting to take the boy to a reformatory, symbolically away, and the picture ends with the family happily believing that the boy will not try any more bashing in of skulls, sabotage, teaching Nazi doctrine to his schoolmates, maligning Jews, breaking up his uncle's love affair or trying to divide and conquer everybody in sight. For many reasons this conversion seems highly suspect, but no less so than the rest of the film, whose materials always seem more mamby-pamby than its notions or the intentions of the people who worked on it.

Played with any approximation of what it would be really like if some nice, anemic, emotion-fearing intellectuals bent on doing the right thing took over the training of an adolescent already formed into the terrifying cynicism of the Nazis, the movie's situation could be as devastating a picture of people blunting themselves against one another as can be imagined. If there were any understanding of the squeamish, difficult sorenesses that would arise, you would get a good idea of the enormously perplexing task of re-educating Nazis—dealing, as we would be, with our own incapabilities as well as the Nazis' corruption—and some idea of all the unforeseen traps into which we, not being perfect either, could fall. The evil in the character of this movie's junior Nazi is always produced by stock Nazi attitudes or stock melodramatic ones, each being overweighted and overexplained. There are about a dozen more atrocities and treacheries than are necessary to convince you that he is a Nazi; and he seems too smart to be doing many of them. The villainy is enormous and the situation is one that should be as appalling, difficult and ungainly as they come. But the people's reactions to one another's Americanism, democracy, and to Nazism, are too often only a bemused reaction to quaintness, and they haven't the slightest difficulty in communication or understanding—which would be, it seems to me, in reality the first numbing difficulty. On top of all this, Skippy Homeier's performance as the child is—despite one good cry and a moment of convincing adolescent daydreaming over a lawn-mower—so incredibly insensitive to all of the overcluttered business it contains that you will probably take it as a joke.

The portraits of the college professor and his sweetheart as good, progressive people is the least artificial thing in the film and by far the most interesting. Their constant fear of giving way to any temper or unseemly feeling, their obsession with doing the intelligent thing (which, along with the suppression of emotion, wears them down physically and mentally), their talk, which is so Little Womenish and so limp in its attempts at being witty, colloquial and regular, all seemed accurate qualities of such people and made them just about as silly and watered-down as they usually are. Probably the second most interesting fact is that the heroine is announced to be Jewish. Hollywood does not make a practice of characterizing movie heroines as Jewish, nor does it like to remove all comicalities from the character, nor does it like to marry her to a Gentile. I wish, though, it hadn't been so shy of raising any problems with its Jewish girl. Something else interesting is the unsuccessful attempt of Director Leslie Fenton (who is a good actor and might be a good director, given a good script) to turn a play into a movie. The attempt entails very intimate approaches to indoor action, and excessive leaps into the country whenever possible.

January 8, 1945

Just Plain Folks

"The Keys of the Kingdom" tells an awful story about a Catholic priest, Francis Chisholm, who is helped into the Church by the catastrophic drowning of his parents, someone's seduction of his sweetheart and her death in childbirth, and who lives his life thereafter—in China, from 1878 to 1938—from catastrophe to catastrophe. The movie's attempt to show the actions, character and ideas that are keys to the kingdom is generally waylaid by a number of things; but the characterization of the hero as a self-effacing, kind, slow-witted man, the endless rebuffs by the world that the script writers throw in his face, and the playing of him by Gregory Peck are so likable that you will probably get some feeling of the superiority of humility and tolerance to their opposites.

The film, though, is more concerned with the current religious-movie pursuit, which is to show that the Church does enter, on many occasions, as actively and completely as anybody else into world affairs, and to influence any Church official who may be stuffy to be otherwise. The symbolic scene for this comes, I think, when the curate (Edmund Gwenn), who is supposed to be reprimanding his student, takes him fishing instead and is seen, up to his cassocked waist in brook water, trying to catch fish. After that the hero, who has already got into trouble for some of his behavior (such as befriending an atheist), goes on to behave in an even less orthodox way. I doubt that the movie's championing of this kind of priest will rub anyone else's ideas the wrong way, because for one thing it is zealously careful to over-explain the reasonableness of the Father's actions and then to take the sting out of them. Some idea of the limits it goes to can be had from the difficult, perplexing maneuver it makes to get its priest infuriated at Chinese resistance to his using surgery on a mandarin's child so that he can dramatically ask God to forgive his anger, since he and God know that God and not surgery saved the child. If anybody is upset by the film's idea, it will be in spite of the general softening of a trite story.

Some of the story's outstanding faults are that many of the episodes can be predicted before they start and the rest before they finish; there are several hundred too many and they are too big. The latter overburden everybody: the hero often has to read from letters and diaries as he writes them; the off-screen narrator (Sir Cedric Hardwicke) has to do some hectic explaining to make the sudden leaps in time not seem silly. It makes such areas of the hero's life as his youth seem like a five o'clock subway ride, and leads to embarrassing, hurried explanations (like "My knee had just healed when . . .") for the transitions from crisis to crisis. Situations seem contrived and melodramatic partly because there is little time to make them seem less so. There isn't room here to explain why it is that a Hollywood picture that starts off with a young, kindly priest on his way to China as a missionary is so entirely predictable.

Some good work by Director John Stahl, Writers Joseph Mankiewicz and Nunnally Johnson, and efficient acting by everybody but Roddy McDowall and Thomas Mitchell, relieve some of the doughiness and give the story a humanity that is more dignified than Hollywood's usual treatment of the human race. Its situations are projected with almost as little sentimentality as would be possible without deciding against filming A. J. Cronin's original novel at all, which would have been my advice. There seems to be a general good knowledge of what the people in this story would be like, which is apparent when a young Chinese convert tries to pull (literally) an old beggar into the church. The attitude toward this scene, which is supposed to show the wrong way to do missionary work, is wholesomely comic; the pulling-in is done in an energetic, athletic manner, suitable to the glibness of the boy; the complete, dumb resistance of the ancient seems right; and the people look as they should and talk that way. Such acting as the hero's shaky feather-fingered operation on the child and the interested, neither for nor against, watching of it done by a gallery of Confucianist priests, seems exceptionally subtle in its knowledge of human response. The movie uses ground, trees and buildings that are for once caked, rough and weathered enough to be primitive; the director realizes their beauty sufficiently, and even makes them thrilling. Gregory Peck seems essentially too well heeled, cold and sure for an insecure "peasant priest" but is still very skillful as Father Chisholm, and especially while being troubled and perplexed by his Cassandra-like sweetheart (who knows what's going to happen). He also gives a general impression of slow, dissatisfied thinking, and is best in some physical action like taking an exciting walk through the countryside.

"The Keys of the Kingdom" has as little success in projecting religious or exalted feeling as other Hollywood religious epics that use such devices as overweighted, obvious good deeds and overweighted, obvious rewards, and a too-melodramatic idea of where to find exalted goodness and of what it looks like on people's faces. Probably the most touching and true moments in this film happen when the striking figure of Father Chisholm is shown walking within an equally plain and beautiful landscape; in such scenes purity and reverence come out of the dignity and humility of the figure in its setting.

January 15, 1945

Crazy Over Horses

"National Velvet" tells how a twelve-year-old butcher's daughter, Velvet Brown (Elizabeth Taylor), helped by a vagabond ex-jockey (Mickey Rooney) wins the Grand National steeplechase. It is the best thing to see at the moment, next to another very happy MGM technicolor film, "Meet Me in St. Louis." The subject is likable and unworn (at least when it is dealing with the horse, the girl and her jockey friend and not with the girl's family, which it gets at in the usual movie way), and seems unusually well suited to the screen, since it moves around a good deal in fine, breezy country and has a simple story structure built around one thrilling event, which usually makes for a stronger job than the more snarled plots do.

Pandro Berman, the producer, and Clarence Brown, the director, have made it into a conservatively exciting and engaging film whose chief virtue is its acting, especially a letter-perfect, beautifully felt performance by Mickey Rooney as the jockey. Miss Taylor seemed to me vaporous, though beautiful, either because she is actually a negative screen personality or is made to seem so alongside a particularly virile, smart group of actors, which includes Rooney, Anne Revere and Donald Crisp (who are her parents), a thin-skinned red horse, which appears to be running faster than any horse I've ever seen in the movies, and the child, Jackie Jenkins, who still seems cut off from this civilization and has been wisely left (as Margaret O'Brien and Skippy Homeier have not been) more child than actor.

In the traditional MGM manner, the writing and directing of "National Velvet" seldom tighten onto any of its events objectively or analytically, but stay at a safe level of making everybody and everything indefinitely pleasant, comic or happy. It is typical of MGM's lack of daring that the relationship between Velvet and her jockey friend, which is one of the more interesting in the current movies, is left untouched while the film spends endless time building up your knowledge of what funny, corny things happen in the Brown family. The thing I miss most in the picture is a loving, interested appraisal of the year's training of the race horse; but that is probably the kind of information MGM would feel was too specialized for mass appeal.

This generalized treatment can be especially provoking when it shifts your eye from the center of an event to the edge, where you either can't see it (for instance, a lot of Velvet's rides over the countryside and Rooney's doctoring of the horse), or it is too poor a view to matter, as at the steeplechase, where the film hardly gets in sight of Velvet and her horse. At rare moments the movie turns objectively on a fact and usually comes up with something extraordinary.

There is a drunk scene by Rooney that is actually bewitching (and one of the best scenes I ever saw) because of its marvelous timing and use of hands, voice and eyes. The credits are also recorded against a poetic scene of Rooney walking along an English road that seemed, to me, for the realism of Rooney's walking and the good setting and music, more bona-fide than almost anything that followed it. Then there is a breathtaking moment during a raffle when Crisp manhandles a heckler and is given a chance to be hard and grim, which he can be as effectively as anybody I know of in films.

There are three unusual things in the script. The mother is made a good deal more wise, contented with her ideas and condescending toward the errors of the rest of the family than you'll probably care to see. She is more unbearable than her MGM type usually is, because not only does the film consider her an ideal mother, but she is played with the kind of purposefulness, besides great talent, which seems to mean that Miss Revere also believes seriously in the character's goodness. Velvet's love for horses is written past the usual insipid movie point for such childhood fanaticism and is made to seem, sometimes painfully, like the real thing. Not only does she make you wonder uncomfortably what her motives are when she says she wants to be "the greatest rider in the world," but her favorite pastime is galloping over the countryside as though she were riding a horse and doing some more galloping in bed before going to sleep. Her passion seemed to me at all times more real than Bernadette's. I was rather taken with the moral of the story, which encourages you to be all for "breathtaking folly."

February 5, 1945

Fact and Application

"The Fighting Lady" is a good feature-length documentary about an American airplane carrier and its successful career in the South Pacific, and next to "With the Marines at Tarawa" it is the most chilling, matter-of-fact account of this war that has been shown in American movies. The best part of the film—which was otherwise shot by six navy photographers directed by Commander Edward J. Steichen—is the record of bombing attacks on Marcus, Kwajalein, Guam and Truk and of the Japanese fleet as caught by automatic cameras installed in the bombers. This kind of film, which is affected by every movement of the plane and journalistically records every bullet, evidence of flak and bomb hit, not only gives a violent sensation of dive bombing but records the destruction of a bombing raid as no other means has done so far. The editors wisely refrained from breaking into these records with shots of action inside of planes. Probably no other picture has given the audience a more realistic experience of the crashing force of a plane in combat.

The picture has been edited to include a maximum number of hair-raising incidents, and a number of events—like an exciting refueling of the carrier during a storm and a nerve-wracking fire-fighting job on a burning American plane—have been chopped too close. The only completely shown action is the strangest one: a logy enemy search plane hopelessly trying to evade a swarm of American fighters, and as it goes up in flames, the musical score, with typical Hollywood thoroughness, unnecessarily underlines its defeat with a spot of Japanese music. The destruction of American planes and fliers is almost totally cut out of the film, and even more noticeable deficiencies are the superficial, unimaginative shooting of shipboard life and the non-stop, non-cinematic commentary. This sounds like the heroic stories printed on boxes of Wheaties and is spoken on one grating note by Robert Taylor.

"On Approval" stays within the featherweight, vapid confines of a seventeen-year-old drawing-room farce about Victorians, and manages by amiability and a talented light touch to make its people and their half-assed lives quite lovable. It is the kind of play that is given to rearranging four uninteresting people in marriage for no other purpose than the kind of wit Abbott and Costello might pass up. But Clive Brook (who also directed it), Beatrice Lillie and Googie Withers make out all right with it. They realize how corny their material is and grab every chance offered to kid it, and they are relaxed enough and talented enough quite magically to make the people they are playing human. The film doesn't have the slightest look of modern movie design, which is a good thing. It is thoroughly secure in its kidding, indifferent as to whether or not it is killing its audience—which it isn't—and shows an awareness of the possibilities for achieving humor by a precocious use of the medium. The original play is too weak to stick to as closely as Mr. Brook's movie does, but faint as it is, "On Approval" is more like the work of human beings than you usually get today in films.

Besides the event indicated in the title, "Sunday Dinner for a Soldier" shows the cute existence and habits of a poor, orphaned family living on a Florida house boat, and contains about everything that is found in books like "Mrs. Wiggs of the Cabbage Patch." The problems have to do with scraping enough money together for food and clothes, or whether the girl should marry the rich boy and break up the family, and they get ironed out every minute on the minute by an interminable series of handouts, "miracles" and good deeds.

The humor, which is a major part of every event, has to do with a clothesline's breaking and with six chickens turning up for the Sunday dinner when it didn't look as if any would. The family group is composed of cliché characters for the good ragamuffin family and range from the ventriloquist's-dummy-faced youngest son up through bearded "Grandfeathers." The acting is terrifying, and I felt every action and idea was interpreted so that I was not only shown the fact but told whether I should feel just happy about it or blissfully happy. The movie ruins two or three very good ideas, including the main one of a soldier being the guest of civilians, another having to do with whether "Grandfeathers" will kill the daughter's pet chicken (completely muffed), and another about a moonlight incident when the daughter dances dreamily in an abandoned half-built seaside resort. This movie seems to me as unsuccessful as "Experiment Perilous," "The Unseen" and "Music for Millions," the last of which provides me with the chance to say that I don't think the child star, Margaret O'Brien, is as good as I once or twice said she was.

February 12, 1945

The Gold Rush

Iɴ the usual superficial, gaga Hollywood-biography way, "Roughly Speaking" looks at the life of Louise Randall Pierson, who wrote the movie script as well as the best-seller on which it is based. Mrs. Pierson, who describes herself as "granite" and "New England," is as ambitious as Alexander and "not afraid of anything," and has spent her life, as far as this movie is concerned, mainly in trying to get rich and failing. The daughter of a wealthy New Englander, she was married and divorced by a banker and since then has been successfully married to Mr. Pierson, who has tried a number of ventures, from rose-growing to welding. She feels, so the picture says, that she is one who "breaks rules" and "swims upstream," though her ideas about success, marriage, divorce, America and money fit the conventional concepts even of Hollywood. Mrs. Pierson has had more children than movie wives generally do, but in the film they are typical movie offspring, with, if anything, less to show for themselves than usual. The effect of Mrs. Pierson's "granite" on them isn't noticeable.

The film goes through the last forty years of American history with Mrs. Pierson on "the inside" of its main attractions, which is where she believes in being. But her inside view is as stock and vague as her children. Yale, in the early years of the century, is a singing session of "By the Light of the Silvery

Moon" in a student's room; World War I is a shot of Mrs. Pierson selling a war bond; the money-mad days of the twenties is a shot of a lot of checks being made out; the depression is a comedy scene with Mr. Pierson practising the sale of a vacuum cleaner on his wife; prewar days is someone's remark that they see the lights of the Polish Pavilion going out on the World's Fair grounds; the present war is a shot of Pearl Harbor and a protracted railroad-station scene with the Piersons saying goodbye to three enlisted sons.

"Roughly Speaking" seems to me about as terrifying as it seems useless. It is dealing directly with conventional attitudes about success, money and fame, and all of its people are devoted to these attitudes. Success to the Piersons means getting rich no matter what, ambition is "two of us against the world," "being of a different cut" is coming up from the bottom to win a fortune, money-making is a complete, satisfying existence. The Piersons' blind striving for a fortune, which takes up three-quarters of the film, is seen through a bemused eye as wholesome, virtuous and fun. There is no suggestion of sterility, snobbism or hostility in this money-grubbing. Because they have such a zealous and happy time selling things to people, there is a strong suggestion of the aggressiveness involved and their indifference to everything but the dime they make out of the hamburger. This all seems useless to me because we have been shown it for years, and because once again it sees only these elements in money-making; and it seems to me that such lack of knowledge of what it means to pile up a fortune in terms of personal greed and social evil and the kind of life resulting from it is an anachronism of a particularly frightening kind.

The relationship of Mrs. Pierson to her husband and children is generalized and insipidly vague, though her first marriage is seen a little more sharply and objectively. The banker, who is made convincingly dry and drab by Donald Woods, is a quiet but purposeful conservative with a couple of nice speeches that indicate his character well, and he is the only person in the picture who is allowed to suffer nearly enough from Mrs. Pierson's personality. The best parts of the movie, though, have to do with Jack Carson's ability to make the talent for sophisticated humor and easy sociability of the second husband rich and effective. If some of the less vaudevillian aspects of his marriage had been written into the script, Mr. Carson would probably have created a masterpiece of this particular amiable, insecure rich man's son. I am not a fan of Rosalind Russell, who plays Mrs. Pierson.

The good things that turn up in the picture are inevitably cut to ribbons and compromised by Director Michael Curtiz and his jack-rabbit style. This style, which aims at killing dullness, involves jumping as fast as possible from one aspect of an event to another, gaining the maximum amount of musical comedy and action. A typical example of the way it works is the meeting between Miss Russell and Mr. Carson at a Yale dance, which seems to me quite exciting until it is hurried into a slapstick dive into a fountain. That in turn is hurried into a kitchen conversation, which is then marred by a too quick proposal and the corny, predictable entrance of Miss Russell's four children by her first marriage. The purpose of Mr. Curtiz's style—to get in and around events and keep you awake—is good enough, and he does a lot of convincing things in directing his actors. But as far as I can see, he is totally incapable of shooting a scene without making it seem staged, falsely corny and less interesting than it should be.

February 19, 1945

Crime Does Pay

THE four murder films—"Hangover Square," "The Ministry of Fear," "The Woman in the Window" and "The Suspect"—are clever, entertaining, cynical about murder and the law, and unnecessarily cruel. One of the major drives in these films is to pulverize you with anxiety by putting the hero through an endless number of life-threatening situations. I think this wish to scare the audience and keep it in a constant state of horror has been used in every recent murder film I've seen to an unjustified extent, and with a good deal of deliberate cruelty on the part of writers and directors. Less important than the possible sadism involved is the fact that the movies get overloaded with scare devices to the point where they seem more like comic opera than is good for them. The need to suggest evil at every turn leads to such moments as the one in "Hangover Square" in which a close-up of the hero's hands, innocently cleaning up some stains on his coat, is used to suggest the murder those hands are capable of.

All of these films are dominantly playing at crime as well as dabbling in some questionable moral attitudes. "The Suspect" projects a two-time murderer as a thoroughly good and happy character before, during and after his crimes. Its condoning of his first murder—of an awful, nagging wife—is a radical enough moral attitude to call for more argument than it gets in the film. The second murder—of an ineffectual blackmailer—is also condoned in what seems to me an even more cold-blooded way, and has so little motive that both the action and the leniency toward it seem fruitless. "The Ministry of Fear" tosses off the idea of mercy-killing as lightly as if it were examining the putting of a penny in a nickel slot machine, but its failure to look with any concern at the fact is part of its general lack of love for anything except what is suspense-making. Like all of these films, "The Woman in the Window" presents the murderer as a gentle, well meaning, law-abiding person. It shows him killing in self-defense, having no doubts about it, and worse, attempting to keep the murder secret; the movie then takes it all back by showing that it was a dream. That only adds one more unpleasant trick to the movie's heavy supply, and adds nothing to its puny argument for murder in self-defense and for distrust of the law.

The mystery film is sometimes thought—I think wrongly—to be a form in which Hollywood is more realistic, spade-calling and unrestricted than it is in Westerns, bedroom farces, epics and other forms. The photography in "The Suspect" and "The Ministry of Fear," which isn't watered down or velvety in texture, is good as compared to current Hollywood standards, and the sets are above the average in favoring accuracy over vagueness. The characters, though, are allowed to roll around as incredibly and easily in evil as other movie characters roll around in goodness. All the mysteries that I've seen in recent years restrict themselves to a trashy showing of the murder, the plight of the murderer, a bit of his virility and of his love life. They show much less of the relationship of his crime to his environment and to other people, and less of himself than such films as "I Am a Fugitive" or "Public Enemy," which weren't "American Tragedy's" for thoroughness themselves. The current crime films are far less daring than the old gangster pictures in what they say, and they are alarmingly short on spontaneity or originality. They seem to me very mechanical, cautious and petty.

"The Suspect" is my favorite of these new films because it has tried to create character and to rework its ideas—which have been done before by Hitchcock, von Stroheim and pre-Nazi German movies—with the most vivacity. It does a canny, human job in getting across the purity of the hero's humility and generosity, and does equally well in making his successful marriage to a girl half his age and several times better looking seem both possible and happy in an adult way. The "moods" of the composer in "Hangover Square," which are caused by discordant sounds and lead to his killing people and then burning them, are realized in a good, painful way by some eardrum-cracking music and some good grimacing on the part of the composer, and it deals efficiently enough with the trite material. "The Ministry of Fear" and "The Woman in the Window" are both directed by Fritz Lang, use the same self-conscious, over-emphatic villain, Dan Duryea, and are filled with blank people.

February 26, 1945

Close Shave in Burma

"Objective Burma" is a straight-faced account of a raid by American paratroopers on a Japanese radar station in Burma and of their attempt to walk through enemy-filled jungle after a plan to get them out by plane fails. It is as earnest as Hollywood has been in its attempt to show war and soldiers exactly as they are. The actors still look more like movie people than they should, but they look very soldierly when the camera isn't right on top of them, and when they aren't made to perform to it as though it were a theatre audience. They run and walk like soldiers and the actors who are seen loitering in the background make the backgrounds seem like those of newsreels. Killing the enemy is still given the significance of cutting down clay pigeons at a rifle gallery, and though half the Americans are killed, their deaths are made as little real in movie terms as possible. The acting by Henry Hull, Errol Flynn, George Tobias and others isn't wonderful, but it never tried harder to be naturalistic.

"Objective Burma" has been influenced a good deal by documentary ideas so that its record of the paratroopers' trip takes in more than its melodramatic moments, and it comes closer than usual to telling its story visually. It makes a constant attempt to keep the relationship between people and scene correct and to get as much drama and meaning from this relationship as possible. By the time it's over you have a fair feeling that the paratroopers did travel some hundreds of miles through the jungle, that it took as long as the people said and that (except for the Japs' skill at getting themselves killed) what happened probably would have happened on a real-life raid. The movie not only exhibits Hollywood's usual passion for verisimilitude, but shows some excitement for the look of what it reproduces. There are some wonderful moments, such as a cold, lonely dawn scene during and after the raiders' parachute jump, and an ornate Burmese village they bump into in mid-afternoon, that capture beautifully the mood of the time of day as well as the extraordinary look of an action, some architecture and the grouping of people who are permeated by the particular mood. The movie gets likably excited over the technique of paratrooping and makes its excitement felt. It is especially good at showing the animal-like ability of the raiders to move through a jungle or to work themselves inside enemy territory.

The director, Raoul Walsh, does very little that is original or of any great force, but he can mimic a number of styles with adequate carpentry. The photography is often emasculated D. W. Griffith; the final night battle owes a great deal to "Desert Victory" and also shows some of the admirable naïveté about thrills that used to be in Westerns. The camera is constantly on the move—to good purpose for long shots of the action, but it seems far too intimate and omnipotent, considering both the disconnected nature of war and its aim, which is to be just like war. Max Steiner's music for this film is in the traditional manner that reiterates every idea and act with literary noise poorly related to the scene's visual effect; there are some incredible passages, such as a battle sequence in which every appearance of the enemy is greeted by the drum music used for marching and some head-on collision between the realistic jungle sounds and the musical score doing its interpretation of the jungle. However, there are a few passages when the sound track is dispensed with entirely; at those times the screen seems twice as effective.

The film is admirably objective in its treatment of action and scene, but it is pretty general and soft about its people and has little success in showing the effect of the trip on them. The characters are all the same vague hero. Before a couple of crises somebody turns up with a case of over-emphatic jitters that doesn't develop into anything, and a rickety war correspondent, acted by Henry Hull with a good editorial manner, is sent along with the raiders but contributes too little to the movie to warrant the great trouble that was taken to put him in it. There isn't a sign of a relationship developing along the way between any of the men, and when a response to death, pain, impending attack or to a comrade's character is made, somebody usually explains the response with a big, obvious sentence. Since it gets hardly anywhere into the minds and feelings of its paratroopers, the movie tends to seem a little like a boy-scout hike. But it is an exciting one, and in many ways very genuine.

March 5, 1945

The Brooklyn Dodger

IN the present style of 20th Century–Fox epics, "A Tree Grows in Brooklyn" deals obviously, lushly, safely, respectfully and theatrically with a tenement family named Nolan, who live poorly and indestructibly in Brooklyn during the twenties. It is one of those rare Hollywood films which earnestly endeavors to show the drabness and unhappiness in an American family and in a section of American society. The young mother of the Nolans (Dorothy McGuire) scrapes and goes sour on her life and her husband (James Dunn) trying to get their children (Peggy Ann Garner and Ted Donaldson) through school. Her husband is a drunkard who works off and on as a singing waiter and finally dies of pneumonia and alcoholism. The picture then gets back to Hollywood normal with everybody eating banana splits, the mother about to marry a Gibraltar-like policeman (Lloyd Nolan), the daughter starting on her first puppy love affair, the tree in the tenement court, which was cut down earlier in the film, starting to grow again and somebody announcing that they have certainly had a good time being poor. I appreciate the earlier part of the film for dealing seriously with an unhappy segment of American life, and for trying to find some conflict in the American family (the mother and father falling out, the daughter siding with the father), but I don't like the movie.

The sets have the thin-walled quality of a studio-built Williamsburg and are jammed stagily with people, noise, confusion, quarrels and bric-a-brac, all obviously citified in the same way that Mrs. Nolan is made to be on the go too much. The sets don't matter a great deal, because they are hardly used or seen. The main fact in all of the scenes is that you are supposed to look at the people's faces and listen to what they say, and when they stop talking the scene changes. All of the poetry about the tree in the tenement court, its being cut down and then starting to grow again, is confined to looking at the people's faces as they talk about it, and Francie's rapturous tours of the dime store, the library, and her Sunday walks with her father into a fashionable neighborhood are only as involved with their environment as one street car is in passing another. The most destructive element in the film is its photography, which blankets the poverty in lovely shadows and pearly sentimentality; the least comfortable element is the embarrassing, stiff lower-class speech that sounds like the talk used in old melodramas of the South. I liked the choice of James Dunn as an alcoholic waiter and of Miss Garner as the girl, but Dorothy McGuire looks like a respectable Junior Miss, Joan Blondell is pure fantasy as the adulterous Aunt Cissy, and a good actor, Lloyd Nolan, is awful as the cop. The acting is a theatrical kind that is carefully elaborated and its effects made very round, definite and monolithic.

The movie shows a disarming lack of skill, imagination or daring in telling itself visually. Its material is mostly confined to showing how the life of poor people is dominated by the scrabble for money, and only in a scene of childbirth is there any real terror and hardness in the faces and gestures, any drabness in the photography and any complexity of thought and feeling. It seemed to me the only place where for a time the picture tries to show what the actual life of its people is like, though I liked a glimpse of Francie trying not to step on the lines of a sidewalk, the beauty Miss McGuire manages when she waits up for her husband, and a scene in which Dunn sings "Annie Laurie" and refuses to answer his wife. The life that the mother turns sour over is recorded in one bare instant showing her scrubbing the staircase; the rest of her movie time is spent telling her sister, husband, children, and, mother that she has to be hard to make ends meet, and being told by them that she shouldn't be hard. The characters are narrowed into one or two traits, studied vaguely and unimaginatively expressed—Dunn as a happy, friendly, Saroyan figure, by the easy, unincisive device of having innumerable people say what he is and having him sing "Molly Malone" coming home from work. His trouble getting jobs happens off-screen, and his alcoholism is taken care of by a hurried moment one day when he comes home drunk, and is got through so quickly, pleasantly and neatly that the worrying that is done over it seems silly.

March 12, 1945

Petrified Youth

If there were more effort than there is to tranlate Oscar Wilde's "Picture of Dorian Gray" into movie language rather than that of the theatre and the novel, it would probably equal the horror of a dozen of the kind Universal makes with Boris Karloff. The story credits itself with going through the entire dictionary of pleasure, evil and corruption, and the moral consequences of each act are explored thoroughly either in their effect on Dorian Gray, on the people who are ruined by getting close to him, or on the portrait of him which records the corruption of his soul while he remains young and unblemished. Albert Lewin's new movie (with Hurd Hatfield as Dorian and George Sanders as Lord Henry) is a reverent transference that works much less on the disquieting elements of the story than it does on drawing-room talk, Chopin music and a pretty ballad called "Little Yellow Bird" which is sung by Dorian's first sweetheart (Angela Lansbury) very tellingly. Also, the flavor of it is a corny, romantic one that usually turns up in films about pirates or in woodcuts for the collected works of Edgar Allan Poe.

The movie evades most of Dorian's excursions into "the dreadful places near Blue Gate Fields," but it does make one trip into one abyss, which is a cute, toylike house of prostitution where a nice old broken-down romantic plays Chopin on a grand piano and the prostitutes talk like Inquiring Reporters. Of all the trouble people have when they get with Dorian the movie only works on Dorian's murder of the artist, Basil Hallward (Lowell Gilmore), who helped Dorian into evil by painting such a good picture of him. This scene is pretty good, but the horror is evaporated by your not being able to locate anything in the shadows, and by a chandelier which swings back and forth hysterically but with unlikely energy. MGM treats Dorian's portrait (painted for the movie by the Albright twins), which I think should be examined very closely, and especially so while in the process of corruption, as it treated the steeplechase in "National Velvet"—mostly by looking at its spectators. It is hard to make out the corruption, because there is so much of it and all of the same value; but the main difficulty is that you don't get to watch it grow. You are given a longer view of it in its original state (painted for the movie by Henrique Medina) and a more satisfactory one, so that the corruption has less weight than it should.

Lewin's treatment has the three-times-removed, fancy quality that MGM treatments generally have, but it does some good work, and has, after all, the Wilde story to work on, which is a more exciting, ingenious, cinematic, confusing and witty one than, say, "A Tree Grows in Brooklyn." The notes in it that go against MGM's grain (its esthetic and moral arguing, or the pleasure Dorian gets out of his sins, or all the moral complexities Wilde attached to Dorian's relationship to his portrait) are played very lightly, if at all, and the ones that go with it (the singing and piano-playing) are made too much of. But my impression is that it gives a fair idea of the Wilde story and is well worth seeing. The movie makes an adequate stab at registering the purity of Dorian's youth by a soft lighting of his face and by Hatfield's attempts at radiance, and it makes an exceptional stab at registering the sweetness and innocence of his sweetheart (Miss Lansbury is very fine). The first change that takes place on the portrait seemed to me a very sensitive, judicious bit of painting, and I was impressed by the use of a butterfly to symbolize Dorian's character falling under Lord Henry's domination. But I think this symbol, and the many others that are used—such as a dagger cleaving a boyhood carving of a heart—are employed as if the audience would have difficulty recognizing them, and as though the movie were duty bound to use symbols, being a work of art.

The attempt seems to be to give the sensation of reading the book rather than looking at a movie, and I think it succeeds to a certain extent, anyway sufficiently to paralyze the movie. The characters talk as though they were reading from the novel, in stiff, fleshless voices, scenes are immobilized and edited so that they look more like book illustrations than movie life, faces are made masklike, and there is a great deal of irritating off-screen narration by Sir Cedric Hardwicke that works in the nature of a lantern-slide lecture.

March 19, 1945

Through Thin and Thick

"The Randolphs" is a likable British film that has the lightness the English are better at getting than anyone else, possibly because they are so good at hiding the fact that there are artists at work. Part of it must also come from treating The Family with the nice-as-pie, old-maid sophistication and vacuity of ladies' magazines. The Randolphs are the large, grown-up family that gathers to celebrate the parents' golden wedding anniversary, and the amount the movie has to show of them equals in limpness and generalization its after-dinner speech which explains its conception of the family as a form that "bends but never breaks"—like a "dear octopus." The son gets over his surliness by the second night; one of the daughters has been living adulterously in Paris and expects to horrify her mother, but doesn't (the movie, though, doesn't strain the mother's broad mind by having the daughter still carrying on the affair); there is a bit of a spat between daughter and daughter-in-law, with both immediately apologizing. All of these adjustments, or bends, and the suggestion that some of the characters are either absent-minded, spoiled or "in limbo," are presented and knocked over in a way that makes them seem as formidable as feathers.

But "The Randolphs" shows that the English still make films having a more genuine life than Hollywood movies, and that they treat it with feeling much less dominated by the market. Though there is a pooped-out quality in the most original scene in the movie (one in which the grown-ups watch the children paint in watercolors and then take over the painting themselves), which comes from playing it only for what it could accomplish on the stage and for nothing it could get with the camera, still, what Hollywood would have done with it would have been irritating where this is pleasant. The pace, which here is pretty relaxed, irregular and lifelike, would probably have been stepped up in Hollywood; neither of the parents could have been paunchy, as they are, and unreservedly contented with their portly, parental look; the acting would be a little more trained, the grown-ups would have edged the children out of their chairs with a broader comic quality; the lighting would be less natural; the scene would have ended with a more successful joke and would altogether produce a disquieting cartoon effect. The movie's love affair is very mechanical and predictable but the people aren't so harassed as Hollywood people, and they have a moment at a preparation for a dance in the village that would be too undramatic for Hollywood but here is very touching.

The acting, writing and directing in the film version of the Raymond Chandler novel, "Farewell, My Lovely," that is now called "Murder, My Sweet," are much less repressed than usual, and full of brightness, but it is also by all odds the most incomprehensible film in years. Some of the confusion comes from telling the story in a flashback, from a police grilling of a private detective (Dick Powell), and from having a very similar grilling involving the same people occur within the flashback (to keep straight on these confessions, watch for the eye bandage the detective wears in one of them). Another confusing element is the presence of a green jade necklace, worth about a hundred thousand dollars, which is explained only a little more than it is seen, which isn't ever. Even so, I would say that a green jade necklace is the most uninteresting evidence a movie mystery could use. The main trouble, though, has to do with its detective's working for too many people on too many jobs. Just before the end he says, "There are a lot of things about this I don't know, and a lot of things I'll never know." But the mystery gets solved just the same by killing off everybody but the detective, his sweetheart and the people who grill him in the first scene. I think you could get at the underlying thread of this film the same way you could in "The Maltese Falcon"—by being allowed to take the dialogue home with you to study at length.

None of the cast, who are largely murderers, looks capable of killing, and Powell still looks more like an orchestra leader than a tough detective who is said to be more slot-machine than detective. But they all act as if they were full of understanding about themselves and about what is being said and done to them; also they have a touchy, exploding character that is somewhat theatrical but appropriate enough for people leading lurid lives. The movie does some good work in getting less obvious characteristics into the acting. I particularly liked some nervous giggling and twitching by the murderess (Claire Trevor) when she feels she is getting the better of the detective, and the ability of Miles Mander to make himself convincingly good and doddering, capable of marrying a young, cruel person and defending her to the limit. The movie also makes a nice, unsuccessful try to get inside Mr. Powell while he is being drugged and beaten, and is more exciting just after this when he tries to stand up, walk, go down stairs and carry on as a normal and properly functioning man.

There is a good understanding and enthusiasm about sets that makes the detective's room disordered enough, puts tin cans outside of a hovel for him to trip over one night, and puts the doorknobs in a mausoleum-like mansion chin high. The photography misses a good deal of brutality and grimness, as well as conviction, by being continually as melodramatic as the photographs in detective magazines. The off-screen narration by the detective could be thrown away, and many of the people sound like the same person. The detective's "I was trying it on for size" when he is guessing sounds like the dumb brute saying "She's as cute as lace pants," who sounds like the sweetheart saying "You keep hitting in between tackle and left end," who sounds like the murderess telling the girl, who has lost her temper, "Your slip shows, dearie." The movie has as little interest in uncovering the whole nature of its people and their evil as "The Randolphs" shows in getting at the landed-gentry family. But both films are quite a bit above average. For instance, they are many miles above "The Affairs of Susan" and "Tonight and Every Night."

March 26, 1945

Returning Soldiers

"Practically Yours" is an unusually well aimed, heartless farce having to do with the public demonstration over a pilot (Fred MacMurray) who dives his plane into a Japanese carrier and accidentally comes through alive, and a girl (Claudette Colbert), who gets involved by mistake as his sweetheart. It is mainly an exposure of cynical behavior, also snobbery and foolishness. The girl is immediately grabbed by newsreel and radio, given two mawkish speeches to tell the sweethearts and mothers of the nation, maneuvered coldly and deceitfully into giving melodramatic, ludicrous or completely artificial performances. She and the pilot are taken over just as selfishly and autocratically by their boss, who feels better about having the girl stay at his home when he finds out how amenable she is to the treatment of the radio people and when she seems well mannered. The pilot is ruthlessly tricked into a last-minute marriage by the girl and a Supreme Court judge (Robert Benchley). There is also an earnest bookkeeping clod who is cruelly used and who can be cruel himself. Hollywood criticism is seldom so undiluted and vicious as it is in the portrait of the boss (Cecil Kellaway) as a thoroughgoing tyrant unrelaxed by exaggeration or broadness, and in the way the movie makes everybody foolish and insincere by showing them concerned in something that doesn't concern them but without any of the obvious tags of malice, and behaving more or less naturally, as people will who have no sense of trespassing.

The comedy is adept and economically managed, except for a tacked-on scene with an effeminate photographer who is made fun of in a broad, worn-out way. There is a fine moment inside of a newsreel theatre, where the hero is knocked out by a patriotic spectator for disapproving of a newsreel commentary that praises his own bravery. There are some funny shots of people feeling silly about having to call a dog Porky that they know is really named Piggy, and a contrived but good scene on a crowded subway train when the collapsible raft MacMurray is carrying starts to inflate itself. Like the newsreel scene, it stops before it should, but there is a wonderful last glimpse of an angry woman passenger chasing MacMurray down the platform. MacMurray does a lot of good pantomimic disgust in the theatre, at various hypocrisies and at Miss Colbert for her sentimental suggestion that a wife can will her soldier husband out of being killed. My chief complaint is that the film is visually less sharp, nervy and untraditional than its script. The casting is of smoothed-down, indefinite, overworked people; the visual creation of character is given over to a slight attempt to do Miss Colbert as a white-collar worker; there is almost no interest in locale, and not enough in getting the right kind of janitress, Trans-Lux fan, Central Park kid or bomber crew. I don't think there was really much true concern behind the movie's criticism, which seems evident in its failure to get anybody nearly whole or in any way very touching, likable or important, or to become more deeply involved in what it is about than any other expensive Hollywood comedy.

The David O. Selznick production called "I'll Be Seeing You" tells of an accidental meeting and the love affair that follows it between a sergeant (Joseph Cotten) on ten-day leave from a veterans' hospital, where he is a neuropsychiatric patient, and a girl convict (Ginger Rogers) on a ten-day leave (for good behavior) from prison. The meeting starts with the sergeant hardly able to think, form words or work his hands. He picks up coördination, talkativeness and wit as he falls in love with the girl, who tells him over and over again to believe in his ability to get well; by the end of the leave he is able to perform beautifully in a surprise attack by a mad dog; he hits a lamp post about thirty yards away with a rock; and gets through the one hallucination the film shows in a way that you are supposed to take as a sign of his getting well. The picture ends at the gates of the prison with the sergeant telling the girl he will be there when she gets out three or four years later (she is there because she accidentally pushed her boss through a skyscraper window while defending herself against him).

The movie has most of the unconvincing elements and missing parts of the kind of realistic soap-opera Selznick has been making, in which life flows too obviously, smoothly, melodramatically and toward too many predictable happy endings, and is cast badly, even for films that are obviously box-office conscious—Shirley Temple as an average family's adolescent seems like a misplaced kewpie doll and is still unadjusted to adolescent acting, and Miss Rogers, along with the character she plays, should have been left for another movie. Selznick films do try, though, to put actual American life on the screen. They generally have a good deal of perception, awareness and love or speech eccentricities and visual character, and if the views, attitudes and convictions are those of a suburban housewife, they are still apt to be exact as such. At least Selznick's movies don't get stuck in the living room or over the dining-room table, and they do a fairly good job of fitting people into environments. The best indication of that here is the treatment of the New Year's ball at the "Y," which has the right lack of glitter, does center for once on the crowd and the whole view of the floor and not on the hero and heroine; someone remembered to have a gym enthusiast grimly working out on some tumbling apparatus; and there is a good freezing conversation between a soldier and a civilian seeking the soldier slant. There are a number of good things in Cotten's performance, in that of Tom Tully as the druggist father with the exaggeratedly good-natured voice, and in the conception of the hero's character when he seems very real as a heavy, dull person being light. It seemed to me quite inadequate but very interesting.

April 23, 1945

Sweet and Low

"Colonel Blimp" is a gentle character study of an English army man named Clive Candy (Roger Livesey) that is based on David Low's much less optimistic cartoons and much less admirable cartoon character. In the cartoons Blimp personifies all that is wrong with the English Tory; as Candy in the movie he can hardly make a mistake, and actions he is criticized for—such as wanting to fight the Nazis as a gentleman—are readily understood by him and corrected, causing no trouble.

The film shows Candy, a hero of the Boer War, going rather unbelievably to Berlin to dispel German propaganda that the English treated Boer prisoners badly. A beerhall brawl leads to a duel with a German officer (Anton Walbrook) and ends with both duelists in a hospital, the best of friends, and the German winning Candy's girl (Deborah Kerr). He hunts big game until the First World War, when he is seen as a Brigadier General, humanely questioning some German prisoners and noticing an English nurse who reminds him of his first love. Between the Armistice and the present war he marries her, hunts more game, administers colonies, and in this war he learns that the Nazis must be fought with cruel methods. The story is told in a very leisurely way, mostly talk, with little action by camera or people, few decisive moments, and transitional scenes that seem as costly and long as the main events. It is conservative in technique and about life, but it is a charming, warm-hearted, commendable production, filled with good acting and characterization.

Emeric Pressburger and Michael Powell, who made the picture, show the ability to get character unstereotyped, individualized and definite, and they have constructed their scenes so that consistency and naturalness of character seem more important than what is being said, done or about to be done. Candy seems to me the odd result of starting with Low's pompous fool and trying to make him more commendable. Instead of being rigid and stupid, he turns out lovably boyish and chivalrously half-bright; he is incapable of deception, cruelty or anger, and incapable of recognizing them; he misses a great deal of everything, including his friend's love affair with his girl, his own love for her until it is too late, but he remains true to her for the rest of his life; he goes through war as though it were no more complicated and vast than cricket. The character has some of the naïve gallantry of the old movie comedians like Buster Keaton, and he is played by Livesey with a pure goodness and youthfulness from his handsome days to his walrus period. Candy's wary, complicated German friend has some inexplicable switches to make in his friendship, but he is one of those rare movie people whose nobility and motives are blurred. Anton Walbrook, with a soft, calculating stare and voice, does a good job with the part, especially in his worn-out refugee days. There are a number of nicely twitted lesser people, admirable stretches when people carry on in the most quiet, casual manner, endearing moments, such as the tired, unperceiving way Candy goes through an operetta-like First World War. The two notable events of the film are an unusually full, neat satire of ritual-clamped people and of national character in a duel, and a beautiful picture of old age.

The movie doesn't look with enough wholeness or daring at its life to make it a deeply moving or even mildly complicated experience. Its attitude about its hundreds of almost totally upper-class Englishmen is that they are very good people, and by the casting and treatment are receiving the rewards of a good life. It is ingeniously careful not to brag about them, or make them obviously heroic in the manner of Hollywood, and to be amused by stuffiness, funny looks and conservatism. There isn't a sign of discomfort over them, and nothing to indicate that anybody in England is living insecurely, meanly (there is one cruel South African), much less that the English had anything to do with causing their wars. The hero's endless soldiering, hunting and colony administration probably involved a good deal of character that is not accounted for by the movie. The criticism of the Germans seemed to me to be pleasantly pat, unoriginal and carefully fitted to the popular attitude of the moment toward Germans, and there is something unpleasantly finicky in the treatment of the one good German in the film. The technique is no more daring than what we are accustomed to, but both technique and content are worked to a tasteful, engaging point.

April 30, 1945

Four Flats

"Salty O'Rourke" is energetic in a heavy commercial way, is interested primarily in gags for people who will laugh at anything, and, without any particular wish to be socially satirical or realistic, kids many of the traditional virtues and glorifies treachery, gunplay, lawlessness, an adolescent gangster, drinking, promiscuity and the self-concerned spirit. The quality of its fun is that of erotic drawings on public signs, done with no eye, experience or talent for aping such art. The two heroes are a forging, cynical racing character (Alan Ladd), in the clutches of a rival gangster (Bruce Cabot), and a jockey, who is the script writer's darling; he practises every sin and is the kind of adolescent the movies use to illustrate the early youth of a public enemy or the results of parents who smoked opium. The jockey is played by Stanley Clements, who is probably being rewarded with this trashiest of starring roles for his blood-curdling, humorously intended whipping of a little friend in "Going My Way." He is advertised as "the beloved roughneck." His Dead End Kid strutting, belligerency and show-off mannerisms seem to me graceless and badly accented. If there were a degree of the brutishness in him of the real-life character he caricatures he would be as terrifying as anything you could see on the screen. Most of the picture has to do with the humor of his drinking, cigar smoking, his making a fool of and his being fawned over by more virtuous people, including a heroine (Gail Russell) who is treated with unusual contempt by everyone from cameraman to actors.

"The Silver Fleet" is an English melodrama that shows more desire for visualizing story and character and for making both look more authentic than any of the other movies mentioned in this review. It uses an actual shipyard town, fairly real-life lighting and fairly non-actorish players, and has many of the advantages that usually go with making a good film at small cost. It has the misfortune to be least convincing at the most crucial moments, and it makes a minimum number of not very original observations on Underground patriots and Nazis. Its main interest in the story of a Dutch shipowner and his work against the Nazis is to impress you with his cunning at the expense of showing you anything at all about the people or the Occupation. Like a number of Underground films, it shows lives being unreservedly given up for the hero or for some hardly mentioned patriotic reason, when it is too obvious that the movie takes their sacrifices for granted and is mainly concerned with getting out a reasonable-enough-looking adventure story and in the romantic work of fashioning heroism. The one Nazi who is at all delineated is given an extremely hoked-up ghoulishness of biting his nails, contorting his tic-ridden face and swilling food that is impressive as ghoulishness but not as being about Nazis. The performance by Ralph Richardson as the shipowner is filled with an unusual amount of somewhat self-congratulatory naturalistic pantomime that makes for a rich characterization.

"Without Love" is worthlessly pleasant until it becomes obvious that its people—a "crazy" scientist who marries a society girl on a loveless basis, an alcoholic playboy, a good-natured gigolo, a selfish, spoiled society girl and a brisk, nice career girl—are the ones you saw all those other times, and that there is going to be no problem. It has some good comedy lines written by Philip Barry and Donald Ogden Stewart and the very neat, efficient, shy comedy style of Keenan Wynn as the playboy which enables him to walk off with the picture—for about the fourth time. Another MGM film, "The Valley of Decision," only proves that this company will always be willing to spend a fortune on a movie about a great American industrial family, starring Greer Garson.

"Salty O'Rourke" is dime fiction, with the level of insight, knowledge, feeling and wit about as low as you can go; "Without Love" reminds you of Buck Rogers when its characters are at work on their oxygen mask, of a soap opera when they talk about love and withdrawing from life, and of the old Cary Grant–Irene Dunne affairs when it comes to skirting problems and ending the movie. "The Silver Fleet" is no more important than a Nazi v. Underground comic strip; the Greer Garson film is the circulating-library version of the soap opera. There isn't an original, meant to be deeply affecting, character in them;

they are filled with characterizations, like Ladd's, Clements', Tracy's, Hepburn's, that each has done innumerable times before. The most disturbing element is that in their diluted naturalistic style there is hardly a try at actually affecting the audience emotionally by use of the camera, cutting rhythm, juxtaposition of images, contrast of tone and texture in the photography, or by any other means. Not only is the reality shown weak, untrustworthy or overworked; there is no attempt to make it felt by its audience. Raoul Walsh's directing of "Salty O'Rourke" is completely uninterested in any cinematic standard; there is a moment in the Hepburn-Tracy movie when a meek attempt is made, during the try-out of a flyer's oxygen mask, to use sound with emotional effect. The best you can normally expect from a movie today is that some person or persons may attempt to make hopelessly inartistic, innocuous films just a little less so. This fact is apparent in Tay Garnett's direction of "The Valley of Decision," in which he manages to get some edge and plainness into characters, life and sets that he will hardly be allowed by MGM standards to probe.

May 7, 1945

Dream Furlough

THE fairy-tale kind of soldier's furlough described in "The Clock" starts in Pennsylvania Station when a sweet, pretty office worker (Judy Garland) breaks a heel stumbling over the foot of a corporal (Robert Walker), who has just been driven back into the station by his first frightened impression of skyscrapers. He coaxes the girl into spending the day sightseeing with him, and that night, after they have kissed for the first time in a Central Park glade, they are given a lift into the city by a milkman (James Gleason), whom they eventually have to help through his deliveries. During the next day they lose each other in a subway rush, find each other just as the heartbroken soldier is about to return to camp, decide to marry, manage to do so just before the City Hall closes, and part at the station the next morning with the soldier on his way overseas.

The movie is dominated by the desire to be neatly pleasant and pretty, and truthful only so far as will not basically disturb the neatness, pleasantness and prettiness. The furlough without an empty, disappointing, lonely, distasteful or fearful moment is as hard to believe as is the portrait of New Yorkers as relaxed, daisy-faced, accommodating people who send champagne to soldiers in restaurants. Most of the story is the sensation-filled, laugh-hungry, coincidence-ridden affair a gag writer would invent, and probably the hardest fact to swallow is the film's inability to show anything in its lovers that might indicate that their marriage would ever turn out to be any less blissful than their two-day courtship. Mainly because of the direction of Vincente Minelli, "The Clock," though, is riddled as few movies are with carefully, skillfully used intelligence and love for people and for movie making, and is made with a more flexible and original use of the medium than any other recent film.

One of the most awesome and emotionally accurate scenes in years is the lovers' kiss in the park, which is enlarged with so much suggestion of fatality and importance—in the slowness with which they approach each other, in the heroically stated movement toward each other, in the close-up of Walker's face, sculptured and blocked by a fearful lighting and the grandeur of the sense with which he looks at the girl—that it projects the feeling of their love out of slightness into monumentality. A similar expansion of meaning occurs in a church scene (they have wandered in after somebody else's wedding, and after their own in the City Hall), with the lovers reading in turn from a prayer-book that is still open at the marriage service. The scene is shot in a few protracted, leaden close-ups, and the words are weighted heavily with the lovers' understanding of them. With the exception of some syrupy kissing expressions of Miss Garland's, some equally lush lighting and a great deal of unforgivable music intoning the growing pains of love, the movie is unusually good in its treatment of love, sex, or both. Walker's stroking of the girl's hand at one point is beautifully tentative, ungainly and oppressive; the breakfast scene after the wedding night swims in a feeling of consummation.

The movie continually mixes accurate and far less accurate images—the kind of illumination that operates in the scenes mentioned above with the most academic overexplaining and oversimplifying of movie tradition. The girl makes a nice observation in the park scene, that the city at its most quiet is never completely so, which is proved by exploding the sound track with the noises of New York's entire transportation facilities—the elevated, two railroad systems, a police car, several ships and private automobiles. The City Hall ceremony not only moves over to the window so that the elevated can be seen running outside, but the elevated is used as noise to drown out the ceremony at the two most obvious moments. The grim let-down after the wedding, with the bride and groom trying to eat a cafeteria dinner, is played in their case as much for despair and fright and exactness as possible, while at the same time a comic eavesdropper is placed dead center in the scene and used throughout with a heavy, gag-intentioned hand. Against some of the best work yet done in

Hollywood with extras, there is a scene of a Broadway sidewalk jam with
people hurrying by one another like two opposing schools of fish charging in a
confined space; and in contrast to all the good reactions are some like Walker's
Rip Van Winkle responses to escalators and skyscrapers.

Minnelli's work in this, and in "Meet Me in St. Louis," indicates that he is
the most human, skillful director to appear in Hollywood in years. His films
have been very soft and sweet, with individual sequences tastefully shaded,
filled with sentiment, formed and smoothed to a point where they are without
jaggedness or much strength, and are heavy and lush in a compact way. The
emotional reactions of his characters are elaborated with unusual care and
intelligence, sometimes with great subtlety and always with full roundness
and definiteness. His handling of actors produces people who are unusually
thoughtful, sensitive and innocent, and free of their most limiting or trade-
marked qualities—Miss Garland is relaxed, Walker is less boyish, Jimmy Gleason is sweetly meek (the best acting is by Miss Garland, who is often beautiful
and always up to the most exacting kind of movie role, and by Lucile Gleason, who turns up a wonderful kind of violent robustness and good humor in
the best bit of the year). At his best Minnelli handles crowd scenes so that they
have great reality and interest, and he uses romantic photography to good dramatic purpose.

May 21, 1945

Skin Deep

"The Enchanted Cottage" is not very good but it is likable. The idea that love
makes ugly people appear beautiful to each other is one that the movies don't
work every day, and is generally more distinguished than the ones they work
more often. There is a good performance by Dorothy McGuire as a homely
maid in a cottage she believes is enchanted, and serious, talented ones by Mildred Natwick, the housekeeper who lives in the past, Herbert Marshall, a
blind composer who lives next door, a small boy who is his nephew, and Robert
Young, who rents the cottage to hide his ugliness from society. He falls in love
with the homely maid and finds that love helps both their looks. Next to Miss
McGuire, who not only does her usual skillful and sensitive job, but projects
emotion that seems less muffled and narcissistic, the best part of the movie is
her wedding gown, which is the only completely unconventional and imagi-

native, subtle and beautiful dress ever to appear in a modern American movie. It is designed along Roman lines, for a larger person than Miss McGuire, which is in keeping with the character of the girl who has no talent for makeup or dress and lives away from people and fashions.

"The Enchanted Cottage" seems for the most part overspecialized and oversimplified. The blindness of the composer is constantly pointed at by the dialogue and by centering scenes on his eyes, so that you feel it is constantly being rubbed over your face, and to a greater or less extent so are the house-keeper's enchanted moods, the nitwit destructiveness of the hero's parents, the lovers' kisses, the hero's shame over his ugliness, the acting that seems vacuum-packed and the atmosphere of the room when it is enchanted. The subject of ugliness, the love of two ugly people, and what is involved in each, probably could have turned up less simple problems and been played against more substantial opposition. Here it is mostly a matter of seeing a person sulking or disturbed over his ugliness, being advised by a sensitive friend to have faith in himself, find a hobby or depend on love, and in the final scene showing him telling somebody how wonderful he feels and what did it. The movie ends just as the lovers are about to face the world, which is the point I wish it had reached an hour or so earlier, because the most exciting scene happens when the girl does go through the kind of encounter they are headed for at the end and that they have so much trouble with. It takes place at a USO dance and is the one scene in which the girl's actual feeling about her ugliness and the reaction of others to it is expressed completely believably and with great effect.

"Dillinger" is the work of a Monogram unit made up mainly of the producers, the King brothers, and the writer, Philip Yordan, which is one of the few B-movie units in Hollywood that takes itself seriously. It is further discouraging evidence that the worthwhile work in B films will generally be done in gangster, mystery or horror stories. Yordan and Director Nosseck try moderately hard not to romanticize Dillinger's life. They cast Lawrence Tierney, a malevolent-looking actor with no audience following, as Dillinger, and restrict his acting to heavy expressions of brutality. There are no hair-raising chases or heroic scenes of gangsters holding out against the police. The movie is, in effect, a listing of the various proved ways of holding up a train, breaking out of jail, pulling bank robberies, and of how best to kick, slap, cut, frighten and kill. Tierney's face has coldness, but it is too handsome and actorish to indicate Dillinger's character or the nature of what he went through, and he is never seen in contrast with anyone less hard-faced, kill-minded or vengeful. It is better-made than either of the other movies reviewed here, but I don't think it will tell you more about Dillinger than you could guess and it will tell you almost nothing of what produced him.

"Salome, Where She Danced" is trash, but it is one of the few completely straight-faced gags Hollywood has made, and is pleasantly without talent or worry over the fact. The only possible explanation of what produced the script is that it was made to exhibit a Technicolor special named Yvonne De Carlo. The movie starts near Appomattox with General Lee telling a blond soldier named Cleve and a brunette war correspondent named Steve that "there can be no standing still." This doesn't answer anything discernible at the time, but the film follows the advice as though it did, getting through in the next hour every costume, environment and set that you saw last year. The movie uses at least ten more nationalities than its nearest competitor, a Pathé newsreel I once saw, and mixes them so well that in one scene a gang of Arizona rustlers rows into San Francisco Bay to steal a Chinese junk run by a mandarin who speaks in a porridge-thick Scotch accent and who sits one room away from an Oriental version of Salome's dance done by a Viennese ballerina in Chinese costume who is said to have started the Austro-Prussian war. Most of the affair is a frame-up arranged by a Russian colonel to catch the head cattle-rustler who is the son of Abby Blunt of Virginia, a friend of General Lee's. If Hollywood ever has a Dadaist period, which is unlikely, "Salome" will be its precursor.

May 28, 1945

Signs of the Double-Cross

THE advertising around the entrance to a Broadway movie theatre seems designed to catch the eye of a nearly blind person walking several blocks away, to satisfy bargain-conscious movie fans, to appeal to the mind and wishes of a delinquent, and it is to be trusted as little as you can manage. The signs over the marquees are usually four or more stories high and sometimes as wide as the Gotham's, which extends over the theatre and beyond, to cover stores for jazz records, fruit drinks, magic supplies, men's clothing and cigars. Some of the houses carry two or three of these signs. This advertising creates the illusion that the movie will keep you in an unending state of the most violent emotion, that the show won't have one slow scene and that you won't see a better picture anywhere, any time. The statements of critics who liked the movie or whose reviews can be edited to show liking are generally presented on painted images of gun blasts, or the theatre owner thinks up his own exclamatory sentence. The aim, like a sideshow barker's, is to hold your attention while keeping you from using your own judgment.

The main subjects for exploitation are sex, murder and actors, but it seems that something can also be got out of technicolor, the acclaim of critics and columnists, large quantities of cataclysmic events and the number of weeks the movie has run. There are occasional exceptions, but in general the film's idea is never exploited, and a director or writer only if he had something to do with making "Going My Way" or is as famous as Pearl Buck. As far as I could see last week, the movies that contained moral love affairs and moral people were exploited for having just the opposite; if there was little or no sex, is was suggested that there was lots; details in the posters, such as guns, the fright or cruelty in a character's eyes, the hands of a strangler, the texture and highlights of a dress, were done with the greatest care and emphasis; actors were generally seen in an embrace, or about to kill or be killed. The most popular words were "thrill," "shock" and "suspense." The billboards had exploding, eerie or hallucinatory effects.

Just the deceit practised in these signs is breathtaking. The following are some theatre-front displays within three blocks on Broadway. Underneath the marquee at the Criterion, as an advertisement of "Counter-Attack," is a large shot of the heroine in black negligee, leaf-patterned brassière and pants, chained to a dungeon wall. Nearby she is seen in the costume of a circus bareback rider, lying comfortably on a white satin divan, guarded by a Nazi with a bayonet. This illustrates "The suspense-filled drama of one woman and eight men trapped underground," though the movie is actually without sex, the heroine is never seen in less than the full outfit of a Partisan, and the movie shows how she and Paul Muni guard six Nazis. Two huge billboards over the Astor Theatre are combined to suggest the plot of "The Enchanted Cottage." In the top one is a message that the whole town whispered about these two. The message is enclosed in the kind of balloon used in comic strips for dialogue; the tail of the balloon drips down to the sign below and points to the kiss shown there between Dorothy McGuire, whose head is pillowed on pale clouds, and Robert Young, whose head is shown against a touch of orange sunset. Both seem to be asleep. The kiss is actually in the movie, but there is no whispering or anything irregular enough to be whispered about. The scene that is reproduced in seven or eight places around the Gotham Theatre, advertising "Colonel Blimp," shows the blonde an aged Tory is thought to dream of, a duel, and explanations like "a fighting fool about women," "a lusty lifetime of love and adventure." In the film there is no lust, no fighting over women, no blonde, no fighting fool, and the Colonel's movie lifetime is extremely quiet. The rest of Broadway seems to be covered with posters of people with guns and people running from them or from some nameless horror. It seems to me that even a hopeless delinquent would have a sense of degradation while buying his ticket under these signs.

June 4, 1945

Seven Who Were Harangued

"Counter-Attack" is an interesting movie that takes place some time in 1942 in the basement of a Russian factory that has been sealed tight by shelling. Penned up there together are a Russian paratrooper (Paul Muni), a girl partisan (Marguerite Chapman) and seven Nazis. This situation was created by Janet and Philip Stevenson, who wrote the original play, and it seems an unlikely, canned arrangement that was made with the limitations and demands of the stage much more in mind than those of war. The people are in the basement for three days trying to outwit one another: the Russians are trying to maintain their position as captors and to get important information from their prisoners, while the Nazis are trying to get important information from the Russians and also to talk themselves out of being prisoners. After three days the group is rescued by a Russian battalion which reaches the town by an under-river bridge and is led to the basement by the hero's faithful dog. Building the bridge and the dog's part of the movie have the quality of the Rover Boys, but the basement section is engrossing. It is taken up mostly with good, unlikely conversations between Muni and the Nazis, and has portraits of Nazis that seem wonderful in comparison to the average movie characterization.

The Nazis are, I think, too voluble and extroverted as prisoners, and too comic and light to be studied seriously as Nazis, but they are acted with enormous enthusiasm, are well photographed and are shown generally in an unhackneyed way. The one called the "Professor" seemed to me a subtle combination of buffoonery, sharp-wittedness and excessive cruelty; the "Magician" seemed remarkable for having a genuine middle-class nature and the right degree of above-average—but not too far above—bravery, independence and wit; the officer is acted neatly for elfin cunning and superciliousness. The characterization of the paratrooper is less original and less satisfactory, and Muni's acting, which aims at boyishness and a Russian quality, is in a heavy, emphatic style that could be studied in detail from any distance up to a mile. For a number of reasons the action in the basement has a lot of the quality of a high-school sports event. There is practically no ugliness, obtuseness or lack of communication; the three days are taken up with closely contested talking scrimmages carried on as though there were rooters and sidelines; the Germans occasionally go into decorative huddles; there is one stratagem in which the Russian gives a Nazi an unloaded gun that reminded me of certain faking maneuvers in football, and the one time that a German's request for a scrimmage is refused by the Russian it seems very unsportsmanlike of him.

Due in about equal parts to John Howard Lawson's script, James Wong Howe's photography of the Nazis—which is for once dry rather than silvery—Zoltan Korda's directing, and one of these persons' liking for shots in which subjects are arranged in balanced, stark formation, the Nazis are employed with unusual effect, and the film has a good deal of unconventional movie vitality. The Nazis are seldom seen close up or from a point within the group, but are sharply individualized and given a virulent volubility and energy, so that there is constantly a feeling of a group's cunning, frustrated murderousness and life. The movement of a member away from the group is given grandeur by lighting, and pace and excitement by having the hero fuss over how close a Nazi shall come to ask a question. The following items seem to me ingenious devices for keeping you absorbed: having the magician's performance of magic a hypnotic, dance-like affair with an insinuating pattern of sound supplied to identify the noise cigarettes make hitting the inside of a helmet as the magician throws them; having Muni deliver his orders in a rhythmic, whip-cracking way; and using with morbid effect comic-opera posturing and gestures.

June 11, 1945

Plenty of Nothin'

"Rhapsody in Blue" is an interminable juvenilizing and denaturing of George Gershwin's person, career, friends, relatives and a period from about 1905 to 1937, which sacrifices biography even more extensively than did "Wilson" to indifferent performances of songs. The movie is two and a half hours and what seems like 5,000 song-choruses long, and during great stretches of it you hardly see Gershwin except for an occasional shot of him listening to somebody sing his songs or a close-up of his hands doing rapid two-finger runs over a grand-piano keyboard. The problem of making music eloquent in a movie is as hard as any I know of, and the music in this comes through effectively only by fits and starts. The finest musical intervals turn up in an occasional spot where the music has been subordinated almost to the status of a background, or where the view of the performer—as in Joan Leslie's singing of "You're So Delicious"—remains static, or where the music has been accented rather than destroyed by a violent contrast of action on the screen. For the most part both the image and the music are nullified by being played for maximum effect at the same moment—the most common procedure being to change the screen image as rapidly as the musical image is changed, and obliterating both. The songs are also dulled considerably by performances that are supposedly styled to a period in the twenties or early thirties but are diluted with a pretty, immaculate, lush, modern movie manner of singing, make-up and stage decor, the most destructive element being the hundred-piece Phil Spitalny-like orchestral accompaniment. A number of Gershwin concerts are shown in a conventional way (with mirrors set behind keyboards, players in the orchestra isolated, posed dramatically and lit up like a Hollywood opening), but there is one passage at the end that is likably less ordinary and polished, and almost hysterical. It consists of various nervously changing views of a performance in Lewisohn Stadium, starting directly above the pianist's hands and moving out over the audience to a mile or so behind the stadium and ending up with a shot from the clouds—the purpose being to show that the composer is in heaven and that his music is a product of the people and for the people and now belongs to them.

The music isn't the only element in "Rhapsody in Blue" that is diluted in one way or another. Robert Alda, who plays the Gershwin role, is much less virile, eloquent and Jewish than Gershwin, though he looks like Gershwin in one shot—an ingenious close-up of him with his teacher that is angled to make his face long and narrow and to accentuate nose, mouth and cheeks. Alda's looks, his bland, relaxed manner of acting, and the script's jolly, worshiping portrait of Gershwin which has him smiling at every other moment of his screen career, make his personality resemble that of a musical-comedy juvenile. The script accents two of his characteristics—his egotism and his hurry to compose everything he had to compose—in a way that makes them seem twice as pleasant to live with as they probably were, and uninteresting as characteristics. His love affairs couldn't possibly have been as vapid and predictable as the two shown here, though Joan Leslie uses her Most-Popular-Girl-in-the-Senior Class quality in a way that partially redeems one of them. The Jewishness of the Gershwins is made vaguely evident by fearfully playing an occasional Jewish melody in the background and by using for comedy purposes a limited number of Jewish attitudes, some of which are pretty funny. Most of the scenes are written in the standard biographical-movie way, so that each has its joke, each shows the hero scoring one more victory, and each uses the people around Gershwin (who are acted quite well in most cases) as though everything they ever said or did in their lives was concerned in helping, praising or explaining the composer.

One of the better sequences is a Gershwin party with Gershwin and Oscar Levant kidding a two-piano improvisation in a noisy, flashy, convincing party way; following that, there is a nice group-singing of "Bidin' My Time" that seems just right for the moment and for the tune. Gershwin's taste in homes is realized with skill in at least three different sets: a modern Hollywood number and another closer to the Grauman era, and an earlier Bauhaus-influenced job, all of them stadium-sized, heavily packed with blocky, homely furniture of which each piece is just barely out of relation to its neighbor. There are a number of good things in the final Hollywood sequence besides Ira Gershwin's sports jacket with large brass buttons, and the people who play Broadway characters often get a lot of Broadway into the movie.

July 23, 1945

War Without Glamour

"San Pietro" is an Army Pictorial Service filming of the Allied attempts, late in 1943, to take the town of San Pietro at the head of the Liri Valley in Italy. It is only thirty minutes long and its coverage is sketchy; but it is an absolutely unromantic, depressing account of war, and each of its shots seems to me to create deep and intense emotions. The scenes of the valley are awesome; those of the battle are confused, terrifying, surprising and tragic; and the ending, in which soldiers and villagers cautiously work their way into the town, is one of the most eloquent I have seen. The view of battle is always that of the soldier; the image, taken from flat positions on the ground or on the run, is constantly jumping and cringing from enemy fire, and is always of a small confused area of the struggle. Also the various elements of the battle—the noise, the danger, the task—are shown in the way they affect the soldiers. You are made very aware of the rough mountain terrain and the weather at particular moments, but always in terms of what difficulty the soldiers have in getting over the ground, or of hiding in it or finding the enemy in it. An insistent note is that of the loss of life and of the terrible arduousness of the task, which interacts with the realization that these four or five hills being fought for are backed up by miles of other hills. The treatment of soldiers and villagers in close-ups is warm, loving, adroit in finding the individual eloquence and in getting the most in natural action from a person who knows he is being photographed.

Major John Huston supervised the filming, wrote the commentary, which is used at great length and very well to make the movie more intense, and delivers it himself in a carefully enunciated, unrelenting manner. He uses the medium with a good deal of sureness, and with a skill (similar to Capra's in his Signal Corps films) for molding fairly disconnected material into events that are very dramatic and have a beginning, a middle and an end. He has made San Pietro a melancholy, confused, tragic episode, and has conveyed a greater sense of individual suffering—which is not so much heroism as infinite endurance and dignity—than any other Hollywood director who has made war documentaries. Some of the scenes are edged subtly, and perhaps in some cases unintentionally, with irony: for instance the commentary on the strategy of the battle and its progress is as coherent, all-seeing and military as the movie's view of the battle is chaotic and limited to what the soldier sees. There is a foreword in which General Mark Clark explains the importance of the Liri Valley: the shot of him is strong and unsentimentalized, taken from below and to the side, continually suggesting the decisive, unwavering military man. The introductory glimpses of the Liri Valley show it after it has been thoroughly ravaged by the battle while the commentary describes it as it is in normal times, fertile and beautiful. A typical description is that of the bombed-out chancel of a San Pietro church: ". . . note interesting treatment on chancel." My only reservations are the director's evident satisfaction at having more com- mentary than movie, his use of a number of sequences that have been shot the same way in quite a few documentaries, and the music in the final sequence.

This last episode, which shows the villagers slowly following the soldiers into the town, clearing away debris, being hurt by a last exploding mine, beginning to rebuild their houses, is a beautifully phrased, selected and pho- tographed passage in which every scene is toned with sadness, perseverance and dignity. This section is dominantly made up of views of the town's chil- dren and the various expressions of innocence, shyness and hopefulness they assume while watching the cameraman, expressions overlying the somber and still secret knowledge of what they have been living through during the battle for their village. They are shown moving gently and skillfully, like so many bugs, through the wrecked streets, managing somehow to give this part of the movie a mood of benevolence and joy. The sequence is one of the finest in this war's films, though its ending, which shows a pretty farm land, well fed cows and has a commentary full of conventionally idealistic statements of what the war was about, seems to me out of keeping with the depressing, unromanticized picture that has preceded it.

July 30, 1945

Gag Rule

"Junior Miss" is a mildly funny, thin, comic portrait of a few winter months in the life of an imaginative little girl named Judy Graves (Peggy Ann Garner), who goes to double-features and sees everything in terms of them. The comedy in "Junior Miss" is tried for, in part, by having the children broadly enact attitudes that are supposed to be childish copies of their parents' acting and those of movie people. The children seem unchildlike and unreal because of the heaviness of these actions; they turn several degrees too awkward and unnatural and the attitudes themselves seem neither very real nor funny. Miss Garner is much more natural than the others, but she doesn't strike me as being either adolescent, naïve or much but an ambitious, controlled actress. The children seem too carefully curried and dressed, and you are shown little of their adolescence. "Junior Miss" is—according to people who have also seen the play—a faithful adaptation, but, like the average play, it is talky, is has trouble getting outside the Graves's living room, and every time a child goes off to a movie or a dance or has a date, the event is skipped and you are back in the living room listening to a conversation pretty much like the one that preceded it. There are funny spots—those having to do with the bedeviling of the elevator boy and the scorn of Judy's pal Fuffy for her parents; but I think the film could show more feeling than it does, for instance, some of the very moving, very childlike emotion that is got in a brief scene of Judy playing for the last time with a doll.

The study of adolescence is pallid and theatrically mannered, but the treatment of Judy's parents is less broad and more human and knowing. There is perfect casting in the role of the mother (Sylvia Field), who is less like a movie mother than any I've seen in years but resembles most of the ones I have seen shopping in Junior Miss departments. I liked the apartment building that was used to represent one of the less securely expensive buildings on Central Park, and the Graves's apartment is correctly dull and sterile.

The first of the Gary Cooper productions, "Along Came Jones," is, with a certain amount of good spirits and the desire to do something different in movies, a half-kidding of the kind of cowboy films in which Cooper has acted. But the movie gets awfully snarled (though Nunnally Johnson wrote the script) and talkative, and doesn't seem either funny as a parody or exhilarating as a Western.

Danny Kaye's new film, "Wonder Man," is not less theatrical or inhuman than "Along Came Jones" or "Junior Miss," but it is a much more entertaining, talented one to see. Kaye plays a night-club comic—a mildly irritating one because of his conceit, crassness and passion for goosing—the comic's more likable twin brother, and the comic as a ghost after he is murdered by gangsters. All in all, the three parts allow him to use his talents for mimicry, mugging and screaming probably more than any of them has been used in even a half-dozen films. It is just as well, because the other three actors are Donald Woods and two very similar blonde heroines even more uninteresting than Woods. The production is more decorative and rich than is comfortable, and the dancing is mechanical and boring.

There is a memorable climax in which Kaye, in flight from the gangsters, ends up on the stage of the Metropolitan looking like a goof and doing a crazy operatic parody during which he manages to tell the audience about the murder of a fan dancer named Coochie LaVerne. Kaye's attitude during this song changes elaborately from cringing fear to self-satisfied confidence, and each change is surprising and subtle. A nice diva sings and wrestles with Kaye through the duet, helping to make the duet formations as funny as the singing. There are two other good Kaye episodes: one a volatile argument among four Italians that the comedian breaks into in fake Italian and stops at its loudest with a screaming "Shaddup!"; the other an adroit parody of a jovial Russian baritone singing "Dark Eyes" during a fit of sneezing. Kaye manages each of his effects so that it comes at the best moment, very clear and well, and he is very deft in surprising you with the unexpected, such as repeating a yell even a fifteenth time, or, as in the sneezing act, managing an infinite number of improvisations on a single idea.

I don't think he compares very well with comics like Keaton, Langdon or Chaplin, because the character he presents is somewhat ordinary and dull compared to the imaginative personalities of the best movie comedians, or compared even to those of some of the lesser ones like Charley Chase or Lloyd Hamilton. Also in the night-club style of comedy that Kaye uses there is too little that seems spontaneous and too much that was carefully, doggedly and minutely worked out by gag-writers. All these reservations could be made about almost every modern movie comic, and I mention them about Kaye in the interest of making one more plea for comedies which aren't mainly the work of gag-writers, which allow the comedian to work at least part of the time rather freely, which would be more relaxed and not under the laborious necessity to be foolproof, and which are dominantly film comedies rather than a mixture of the styles of radio, theatre and films.

August 6, 1945

The Hard Way

"Story of GI Joe" is a long, hard, relentless fiction film based on Ernie Pyle's reports of the fighting in North Africa and Italy. Its aim is to show life in the infantry with all the integrity it can—the physical discomfort, the stupor induced by the killing and wounding, the hopelessness, and the malevolence against the conditions of a life that keeps the infantryman constantly humiliated and wretched. It is firmer about its feeling and its concept than any other Hollywood movie has been about anything in years. It has assimilated the whole lesson of the war documentary, which has shown the advantages of truth and some of the techniques for making the truth eloquent in a movie; and as a consequence it differs vitally from any recent Hollywood movie. It is very intelligent about the kind of working-class Americans it deals with. Its director, William Wellman ("Public Enemy," "Wild Boys of the Road," "Oxbow Incident") is very able at getting this American's surface hardness, withdrawal, pride, harshness and independence; and he is especially good when he has a group of men in close contact and speech.

The writing, as well as the direction, constantly shuns the romanticisms that have colored almost every other war film. Nobody talks about the war, either as an aim, or as a matter of beating an enemy; in general they seem too tired to talk, and when they do (about rain, mud, work, sex, discomfort) it is in shorthand, avoiding the obvious, which includes every great question like the danger of death and the separation from everybody they love. The men cast as these soldiers (Robert Mitchum, Freddie Steele and Wally Cassell have the principal roles as Captain, Sergeant and Italian-American private) look literally tough enough to have got through the war and don't look anything like actors. Instead of entertaining you with heroic battle action, the script skips most of the battles in order to show the effects on the men of the stupefying exhaustion, of the death of friends, of the growing hopelessness of surviving the next battle, of the maddening consciousness that nothing they personally endure in battle is going to help their personal situation. One important scene of fighting is shown—that in which two Americans adroitly maneuver a victory from two Nazis in a church—and it is so managed that killing is made a hard, real physical fact, and killing in a church made to hold the entire question of war.

The movie has no plot in the sense of a novel or play or the usual movie, but produces an effect like that of a string of newspaper reports on the career of one company of soldiers during the time they were accompanied by Ernie Pyle (who is played by Burgess Meredith). It is the only Hollywood biography I know that presents the hero in a believable relationship to the events and the other characters. Pyle appears as little as possible, and is shown as a self-effacing unparticipating observer, who talks like the soldiers and as little as they do. Besides his humility the movie manages to convey beautifully his iron-cast refusal to trespass on other lives and especially on the tragic parts of those lives; it also conveys some of Pyle's horror of war (most eloquently expressed in his hostile, exploding manner of typing), and starts to express his fatalism but unfortunately doesn't drive it home. The most moving part of Meredith's acting is his projection of the slight, narrow movements of a frail man who seems by temperament utterly unsuited to infantry life—this is done best during a muddy march when Pyle is shown helplessly sitting in a pool of water, conscious of his own weakness and with his fastidiousness over-whelmed. Meredith on the whole seems to me too cuddly and puppyish, the photography makes him look too cute and toylike, and there is a synthetic note in every word of his slow drawl. Freddie Steele's acting seems to me as good as it could possibly be; I liked the casting and acting of Robert Mitchum and of Dorothy Coonan as a nurse; the characterization of the Italian-American is inspired on all counts, including Wellman's and Cassell's.

"GI Joe" is actually a story-film version of "San Pietro," which was a deeper and more moving film. The first third of "GI Joe" is contrived and synthetic and not very well done, and only in the stretch showing the first activity in a just-conquered village does it achieve the breathtaking reality, fullness of detail and sharp effect from shot to shot that all of "San Pietro" has.

But whatever it lacks in grandeur, depth and tragedy and formal beauty, Wellman's is one of the only movies in years that says just about all it has to say, and drives it home with real cinematic strength.

August 13, 1945

Postwar Movies

THOUGH the Hollywood movie seems to have hardened into a form and a way of seeing life and thinking about it that will never be essentially changed, I look for the following important events to occur in the motion-picture industry during the next century.

A device will soon be invented in Hollywood that will fulfill completely the producers' desire to please every person in the movie-going public. The device will be shaped like a silo and worn over the face, and be designed for those people who sit in movies expecting to witness art. It will automatically remove from any movie photographic gloss, excess shadows, and smoothness, makeup from actors' faces, the sound track and every third and fifth frame from the film in the interest of giving the movie cutting rhythm. It will jiggle the movie to give it more movement (also giving the acting a dance-like quality). To please those people who want complete fidelity to life it will put perspiration and flies on actors' faces, dirt under their fingernails, wet the armpits of men's shirts and scratch, flake and wear down the decor. It comes complete with the final amazing chase sequence from "Intolerance" and the scene from "The Birth of a Nation" in which the Little Sister decorates her ragged dress with wads of cotton, which it inserts whenever somebody is about to conduct an all-girl symphony. The gadget also does away with all audience noise.

Some other powers of the mask are that it gives each shot the quality through solidity of the stereoscope; it colors occasional shots red white and blue for those who go to the movies for political reasons; whenever there is a listing of film credits it changes the director's name to von Stroheim, the title of the picture to "Greed," and uses such actors' names as Charlie Chaplin, Buster Keaton and W. C. Fields. The gadget will absolutely not show any shot in which Charles Winninger or Joan Fontaine appears and it comes complete with the Keaton two-reel comedy called "The Operator." Though it is shaped like a silo it is made of plastic material, and carries on its outer surface a reproduction of the Mondrian painting, "Composition in Black, White and Red." Thus the producers will keep free of all the worries that come from the comments of artists.

In a final, unbelievably patient, energetic effort to corner every possible bit of writing talent for the screen, the movies will start sending scouts through the grade schools looking for remarkable spellers, students who are good at parsing and penmanship, who are already taking historical novels out of the circulating library, and especially for those students who know an easy penny when they see one. These students will be put under contract with a starting wage of $30,000 a year, retroactive from the date of their birth; they will become Junior Members (later on, Intermediate Members) of the Screen Writers' Guild; their parents will be talked into allowing them to go to the movies every night rather than just six out of the seven. Each will be given a 16 mm. version of "The Informer" to take home. At the age of 13 these students will be sent to New York to study Broadway play technique in order to acquire the basic elements of movie writing. Finally, when they are 17, they will be taken to Hollywood and put to work punctuating "Gallant Flicka, Distant Cousin of Flicka."

The day will come when the movie public will not only refuse to see non-color movies but will find it very displeasing to look at the colors of the natural world. On that day a studio will issue the first Techniodor movie—the movie that gives off odors. If "A Tree Grows in Brooklyn" had been made in Techniodor, the actual rancid cooking smells that you find in many tenements would have been projected from the screen. The first odor films, like the first sound films, will be faulty, and long after a particularly evil-smelling person has been got rid of in the movie his smell will still be apparent to the audience. The odors in the first films, like the color in the first technicolor movies, will be very strong and thick. They will dominate everything else about the film and lead to much misrepresentation: for instance, the most mild, well-mannered of heroines will seem to have been bathed in a violent dime-store perfume. The first studio owners will scour the country for sweet-smelling actors, and for people who are skilled in making odors, and for a time there will be 10 of this kind of expert to one of any other kind in Hollywood. There will be some revolutionary movie work done in achieving the best effects with odor, but by one means or another producers will be able to discourage these artists from carrying on their work. After Techniodor, work will go forward on Technitactile movies. The movie customer will then be issued a uniform like a diving suit. It will be synchronized with the screen, so that when an actor puts hand to forehead the suit will touch the customer's forehead with what feels like a human hand.

In order to combat Television, a group of the trickiest promoters in Hollywood will manage to keep airplane-supply stores from handling television sets. Nobody, of course, would go to a movie if he could watch the Lux Theatre of the Air performed on his television set while flying about in his plane. But by the fall of '62 the hold of these producers on supply stores will be considerably weakened. At that moment an exhibitor in Florence, Arizona, will discover a way to keep movies part of American life. He will install in his theatre an opium den, a Madame Tussaud's Waxworks, a Soup Bar, and a library having the best textbooks on welding, calculus and how to use the T-square for laying out rafters. Institutions like the Home, the Scout Meeting and the juke box will quickly go underground in Florence, probably into a lower level of the theater. This theater owner, who will of course show only horror or crime films, has made certain innovations in this kind of film that will make them so painful, so shocking and horrible that movie fans won't be able to afford to miss them. The screen in his theatre will be one that throws actual bullets and tear gas at his audience and when the customer enters the theater he will be given a tommy gun and a horsewhip with which to defend himself. Finally the manager (who will be quoted in *Exhibitor's Weekly* as saying "Don't bother with 'Kill Me Daddy' even with Humphrey Bogart in it. My customers spent most of their time in my library") will hire gunmen, pickpockets, people made up as Zombies, mad doctors and apes to circulate through the theatre plundering, raping and generally making it unlikely that any television performance will keep a movie fan away from his theatre.

Work will soon start on the new Selznick movie, "Wait Until the Sun Shines Through," in order that it be finished by the winter of 1952. It will not be a very unusual Selznick movie, being based, as so many of his films seem to be, on a recipe in *Good Housekeeping*, and having to do with the returning soldier's problems in civilian life. It will take a little under a day to see, but it will have at least 40 of the better actresses in it, in addition to having Joseph Cotten and Robert Walker. The fact, though, that will make this a long-remembered film, will be that Michael Farris who has never acted any role before other than that of the drunk, will be cast for the first time as a non-drunk, the father of a girl played by Jennifer Jones. The idea of a perennial movie drunk playing the virtuous father of the girl who won the Academy Award for her acting of Bernadette will cause most religious movie goers to condemn the film. In order to keep on reaching everybody Mr. Selznick will remake this movie, using Lionel Barrymore instead of Michael Farris. This action also will show producers the folly in breaking a man out of his type.

After all of this has taken place there will be a brief uprising of the few remaining Hollywood haters, who will try to burn Hollywood to the ground. The group, mostly artists, will be led by three men who had tried unsuccessfully for 60 years to raise the money for the filming of a one-reel documentary. The uprising, though, will be put down without the loss of a single makeup kit. The instigators will be punished by being made to watch production on the latest Technicolor movie.

August 20, 1945

Coat of Navy Goo

THE most notable attraction in "Anchors Aweigh"—a long, fairly pleasant film with countless events and musical acts—is Gene Kelly's dancing. I think Kelly is the most exciting dancer to appear in Hollywood movies. He is all dancer, his whole body is involved in the dance, his attitude is lyrical, he seems to be completely transported from everyday existence when he dances and to want to do the best kind of dancing he knows. His dance efforts, like those of his acting, are made precisely, strongly and are seldom blurred or mechanical. All of these talents of energy and spirit enliven routines that are often composed of stock dance steps that build limited and minor designs. He does three carefully rounded, plot-heavy dances in "Anchors Aweigh," which are, like his dances in "Cover Girl," particularly designed for movies. The best of these is a cute, ingenious, unified sequence showing Kelly in a make-believe world of animated cartoon animals. He is good in this at fashioning his movements and employing a high querulous voice to make himself one with the animals and their kingdom; he wears a wonderful variation of a sailor's uniform; the animals are made very appealing, especially the gloomy mouse he teaches to dance; and the scene is played in an unreal, milk-white light that seems right for a make-believe world and gives the event a warm, clean, gay quality.

The most likeable, human and interesting person in the movie is Frank Sinatra, even though he still acts as though he were sticking to what he had just been shown how to do and feels no confidence that he will be able to copy the action. He is cast well as a shy sailor from Brooklyn, named Clarence, who has spent most of his life in a boys' choir and the ship's library, and who hangs on every word of his friend Joe Brady (Kelly), hoping to discover how to be a great lover. He plays the part in an earnest, unpretentious, well-wishing way—like a person trying to show how thankful he is even to be allowed in the movie with the other players—that is exactly right for the role. He also looks as if he was raised in New York, has a good, dry New Yorker's voice, and manages to steal more scenes from Kelly than he loses to this actor, who is one of the most aggressive, unerring players in Hollywood. He does it mainly on his extraordinary face, that is handsome, ugly, tough and commiserating at the same time, but also because he is artless, as most non-actors are in their first movies.

In spite of Kelly's dancing, Sinatra, and some razz-ma-tazz song-and-dance duets performed by Kelly and Sinatra, I think you will find the movie lacks a good song, has a number of long dull stretches and could be a lot less puerile. The puerility is the characteristic of a production by Joe Pasternak, who makes modern fairy tales about lush, very young girls (in this one she is Kathryn

Grayson) seeking musical careers, and getting them by means of a half dozen improbable circumstances. His movies show young women successfully, happily doing everything from bearing babies to running USO canteens, though they look as if they had never seen the outside of a milk bottle. They seem to have been grown by the same process that makes Technicolor, and while they bask through the film in the knowledge of their perfect loveliness the director smears their prettiness over your face as though you were near-sighted. Though the plot generally concerns the career of a young person in serious music, a Pasternak film hasn't to my knowledge ever touched serious music in any sense except the financial. In the interest of making the music entertaining many of the musical sequences end in gags, and performers are given gestures to make during their performances that show they are not only artists but regular fellows. For instance, in "Anchors Aweigh" José Iturbi conducts while holding a pipe in one hand and making a sign with his other hand which, combined with a wink, signifies that the conducting is going o.k.

August 27, 1945

The Hour of Charm

"Bring on the Girls" is a musical, in watery, acid Technicolor, starring Sonny Tufts, Eddie Bracken and Veronica Lake. It is probably the most undernourished, unrewarding expensive movie made in years. The story has to do with the search of a millionaire sailor for a girl who will marry him for love rather than for his money, and is extremely short on incident, action and originality. The movie is blown up to feature length with musical acts—called for even less than usual by the plot—and in all of them, in spite of a certain grace and prettiness of Marjorie Reynolds and a likable, good-hearted quality about Sonny Tufts, the mechanics are overpowering. This is the kind of musical whose songs are as characterless and indistinguishable from one another as whatever comes out of Muzak. The movie is a particularly unsatisfying, jerry-built affair, and I mention it because it is also a particularly crass, tasteless one. It contains more instances of human treachery, meanness, greed and sadism than any movie I've seen recently, all shown to no purpose.

The hero, or fall guy, is the trusting, unselfish, anxiously sincere, mild Sturges character, played again by Eddie Bracken, who is led through one unhappy experience after another because of his virtues and the lack of them in the people around him, and because of the fun that can be got out of spilling him constantly on his face. The sadistic treatment of the character here seems very unpleasant because he is taken lock, stock and barrel from the Sturges movies, and the humiliation of him from second to second seems an implacable, mechanical act; also, whereas in Sturges' movies the sadists seem horrible but important, in this movie they seem just trashy. The script soaks so long and thoroughly in deceit, cruelty and greed that you feel its writers and director are hypnotized by these qualities. This seems most the case when the script gets stuck, purposelessly and for a long time, on the act of one person paying off another for information, or, when in the midst of a silly musical act, you are shown the mildly comic but violently cruel action of two men knocking a boy into the ground by hitting him on the head with sledge hammers. Quite often, the writing of a comically intentioned scene will get sidetracked oddly into a straight, morbid cruelty. This happens during a monologue by a family servant (Alan Mowbray) who, thinking his master has gone deaf, reveals his savage hatred of the hero and the fact that he has put up with him only to fleece the family. The movie ends, after the hero has been taken by at least a regiment of people, with his falling in love, in about one second flat, with a girl as rich as himself; the conclusion being that nobody less rich would be interested in anything about him except his money.

Most of the bearable notes in the movie are struck by Eddie Bracken. He is able to show the sympathy, desire for love and the trust of a kind, meek person in an honestly innocent, believable way. Everything he does, from trying hurriedly to put on his pants to making a suggestion to an officer, is done in a luckless, unheroic, completely sincere fashion that is comic, touching and right for the character. The funniest moment in the movie, in which he tries to locate a nickel that has got misplaced in a fist-sized wad of bills, is due to the beautifully unselfconscious, straight-faced way he plays the scene. Sonny Tufts will be a good actor as well as a good singer of Crosby's type if he can ever give up his unrelenting use of heavy mannerisms. I don't know of any actress who would be less likely to show any trace of humanity in the role of a gold-digger than Veronica Lake. There is one scene that shows Miss Lake moving in on some sailors, in which each glance is monumental with cynicism that is particularly astonishing. Aside from this natural aptitude, her slipshod playing and what seems her total lack of interest are like an exposure of everything behind and in this movie.

September 3, 1945

Renoir on Tenant Farmers

"The Southerner"—directed by Jean Renoir—is one of the least trashy and commercial movies made in years. It tells about the first year spent by a very poor Southern tenant family on a farm whose ground hadn't been worked in years, and whose house is the shabbiest of shed-like makeshifts. During this year all five members of the family (father, mother, two children and grandmother) nearly starve and freeze; the son almost dies of pellagra; a rainstorm destroys the first cotton crop; a depressed neighbor wrecks the vegetable garden and twice almost murders the father. But the life of the family through all this is a rewarding one, because of the goodness, courage and integrity of the people, which seems to be what the movie is trying to show. The farmer and his wife (Zachary Scott and Betty Field) are sensitive, strong, persevering people, who are given a more generous number of emotions and more natural ones than are usually given heroes and heroines; the only two Hollywood disfigurements are that the hero sometimes seems too talented—as when he snags fish out of the water with his hands—and the heroine has a little too much beauty-parlor polish.

I have never been in the South, but the movie doesn't strike me as being particularly Southern. There are one or two Negroes as extras in a limp introductory episode; the characters speak a pleasant, mild approximation of Southern speech and look more like New Yorkers than Southerners I know do; and the movie is so divorced, I think, from an identifiable environment that it seems to be taking place in a generalized American farm country. I still think it is often an accurate portrait of American farming people, with a lot in it that is thoroughly good and sweet. It is especially admirable because it gets about freely into believable locales and, in the case of its men, is extremely well cast and acted.

I particularly liked Zachary Scott's performance, and those parts of the movie in which Renoir has visualised the action so well that you seem to be present in the events as an unseen member of the Tucker family. This happens when the family drives up to the house for the first time and then explores the decayed structure (for once, there is a study of a house that is nearly long and detailed enough, and one in which the director does something as unusual as to use his camera as if it were the eyes of the family as they move into the house and around in it), and during occasional indoor scenes when dialogue is so well handled that there is no feeling that the action is being staged in the manner of a play for an audience. I like the unhoked-up, credible love and hope in a celebration around the first lighting of the stove; the humor in a shot taken from some distance away from the house, of the father pushing a caved-in section of the porch roof into place; the radiant prettiness of an intentionally romanticized dream episode; the reality of a scene at the doctor's office. Much of the humanity in the movie is due to the talented, completely believable playing of Scott; his ability to walk, talk and act as though he had never been to a city, to make small reactions—like a glance, over the dinner table, at his wife showing a sudden respect—count heavily, and his ability to make terrifying moments, like his looking toward the sky and asking God a question, seem natural to a humble, unassuming man.

Director Renoir's idea of a beautiful shot is a prettier, more obviously composed one than I care for, and too often the reason for walking an actor under a large tree, posing his head against clear sky, sending him into the forest to hunt possum, or almost drowning him in a flood, seems to be simply to film some scenery that the director likes. But unlike almost any other Hollywood director, Renoir tries to make every shot count for as much as possible, and the fine, naturalistic work he has done here has turned out some of the only true scenes of American country life that I have seen since films like "Tol'able David." The weight of the movie as a whole is much lighter in effect than I think it should be to be important as a work of art about Southern tenant farmers, but the interest of everybody connected with it is in the direction of art.

Besides "The Southerner," the best of the current movies I have seen are: "Story of GI Joe," "Pride of the Marines," and the documentary, "San Pietro."

September 10, 1945

Dark Victory

"Pride of the Marines" is a tough-minded, intense, skillful movie about the Marine hero Al Schmid (John Garfield), who was blinded in combat on Guadalcanal after he and two other Marines had killed two hundred Japanese. It begins with the year before Pearl Harbor, during which Schmid falls in love and gets engaged, in traditional movie style, shows the battle on Guadalcanal, Schmid's hospitalization in San Diego, and the first days of his return home to Philadelphia. The film is most deeply concerned with showing the good adjustment made by a soldier to a severe war injury, and also with presenting some of the hope and fear with which soldiers look toward their coming civilian life. The events are prolonged to an unusual length, each moment is made to contain a forceful action or statement, and the tone of the event is continually returned to a bitter, ruinous, savage or sour note. In the process a lot that is important and bold is shown or said and a variety of credible action, feeling and idea is packed into each event. A good example of this is a conversation between the hero and his friend on the train going home. Mainly it is good because for once there is a believable feeling of people on a train—the light is garish enough, the atmosphere is warm and sticky and the talk an unending, variegated, exhibitionistic kind in which you feel each person is trying to entertain the other. It is also excellent because it works doggedly through an argument filled with disturbing elements. One of these has to do with the hero's being asked if he would go through the war again if he knew he would be blinded: the movie is honest enough to show him perplexed and unable to answer. Another is an angry description by the hero's friend (Dane Clark) of his trouble in getting work in this country because he is Jewish.

The film is definitely above the current average in every department except that of background music. Movie music could not be written less imaginatively than it was for this one: for instance, there is the scene in which a soldier delivers an unbelievably corny, inflated eulogy of America while the invisible orchestra plays "America." The picture's failings and virtues are strikingly present in the Guadalcanal battle episode, in which three Marines, operating one machine gun from a fairly exposed position, kill what seems like the entire Japanese army. Some of its virtues are that the Marines are given battle emotions that seem entirely credible; their excessively sharpened, frightened, almost panicky reactions and shouting give you a constant, terrifying feeling of how close to death they know themselves; at the beginning they check their gun and ammunition and make their preparations in a very realistic manner; throughout the action they deal with the gun and worry about it in a workmanlike way; and the scene seems to take as much time on the screen as it would in reality. Some of the failures are that the photography in the studio-made scenes (the movie uses shots taken during the actual battle) is an unconvincing, ineffectual, soft kind in which the main high light is inevitably out of place on the hero's helmet or forehead; though Garfield's acting of a very young, frightened, almost hysterical soldier seemed exactly right, the acting of the other two has a make-believe quality; the terrain seems both fantastic and cooked up; and there is always a feeling that the scene is being made to contain more excitement and tension than it should.

There is often a good attempt to project feeling and story solely through an imaginative use of the camera, and unlike the usual attempts in this direction, the effort doesn't seem eclectic, mechanical or fantastically heavy. In the visualizing of Garfield's nightmare about being blind, the first part seemed to me completely convincing and with an odd, wistful quality in the way it showed some of the hero's more anxious moments in battle by combining negative and positive film—the rest of it struck me as being too realistic and banal in symbolism. Another inventive scene is an excellent, tense one in which Garfield's eyes are examined after an operation: it consists in part of an obvious use of blank screen that produces a sharp, correct effect. The script writing of Albert Maltz, which seemed to me the most creditable contribution to the film, has some subtle, very emotional incidents of a kind that is rare in movies—like that of the hero's suddenly going off into an unspoken, sad, loving rumination about his girl. John Garfield, when he is trying to be anything but hard and defensive and is allowed to talk a little less and at a speed slower than his usual imitation of a drill press, becomes surprisingly boyish, somewhat woebegone, nice-spirited and more valuable as an actor than I have ever seen him be.

September 24, 1945

Psychological Melodrama

"Love Letters" has one of the least stereotyped or believable plots in movie history and has almost as much story per second as "Intolerance." It is so weighted with plot that its hero no sooner steps through a door than he is faced with an unexpected, important visitor, and he and the heroine are usually seen between events in a vehicle rushing to make the next sensational development. The story starts with a reserved, mooning, soft-hearted soldier (Joseph Cotten) writing some love letters for a no-good fellow soldier. The letters are so sentimentally bad and dull they should dissatisfy even a D. W. Griffith heroine, but they cause the girl who gets them (Jennifer Jones) to marry the no-good soldier. He is soon murdered with a butcher knife by the girl's guardian (Gladys Cooper); whereupon the guardian has a paralytic stroke and the girl loses her memory. After a year in prison, the girl marries the man who really wrote the letters, and during their first happy months together, she recalls one fact after another from her past until she remembers everything. There isn't one wholly credible development in this story, but in the last half of it, at least, there is a good deal of tension, excitement and real passion.

"Love Letters," which is directed in a scrupulous, well thought-out way by William Dieterle and photographed to the teeth by Lee Garmes, is one of the few current films in which there is an appreciable attempt at eloquence. The scenes are planned and set up with unusual care (to the extent that the transitions are economical, nice and so artful, they are usually the best parts of the movie); the pace is solemn and deliberate; there is the feeling that every last bit of majesty or momentousness is being sought for in a patient, hardworking way; and the playing is a kind in which action and expression are made very full, exact, slow and elegant. Occasional stretches have real grandeur. In a long speech made by the heroine at her trial, the lighting is soft and radiant; the speech is well written and is delivered in a sensuous, slow way that makes the scene very moving and passionate. In several scenes the expression is enlarged by switching suddenly and contrastingly to a close-up of the heroine, who at that moment is in the center of a vivid action. One such scene, in which the heroine is crying, becomes awesome and terrifying through this technique of abruptly changing subject matter and time and making Miss Jones seem almost to overflow the screen, and also by the startling lushness of the acting.

For the most part, though, the movie seems stagy, fancy and wooden rather than expressive. In most scenes there isn't enough action or purposeful conversation, though there will be good occasional effects in a graceful, deliberate gesture, usually of Cotten's, or in a facial mannerism of Ann Richards or Miss Jones. The outdoor shots, in either idyllic or scary English countryside, have a very synthetic quality, and the ones indoors seem not much less cooked-up. Too much of the imagery is like the photography in *Vogue*; however, though Mr. Garmes's photography lacks virility and takes everything at its prettiest, it is composed in light and dark with great handsomeness, is sharp and clear with details, and is consistently more respectable than almost any other photography in Hollywood.

The movie is filled with wistful, vapid, played-out characters, but its heroine is different, very well conceived and acted. She is an innocent, dissociated person who lives for the moment, enjoys it thoroughly, is frank, wise, unconventional, and given to elaborate, affected actions and facial expressions. Miss Jones's playing almost always seems too rich and somewhat amateurish—she stops on a radiant smile or a contemplative look too long to seem not to be acting and there are usually a couple of degrees too much sway in her walk. But a good deal of the affectation is apt for the character; the elaborate style of playing fills the movie, which is often so wooden, with a lot of human emotion and energy; Miss Jones is accurate and exciting enough to give her role a surprising originality and interest. Alongside Miss Jones's lush manner, Joseph Cotten seems to disappear from the screen, but he plays some unusual, very individual actions perfectly—such as a scene in which he is perplexed, surprised and highly pleased when he knocks on a friend's door and is met unexpectedly by the heroine. There is a harmonious, elegantly articulated performance by Ann Richards as a cold, efficient woman who is very concerned for the heroine.

October 8, 1945

Suburban Badlands

THE story of Warner Brothers' movie, "Mildred Pierce," recounts the enormous and unrewarded sacrifices that a mother (Joan Crawford) makes for her spoiled, greedy daughter (Ann Blyth). The mother, whose husband (Bruce Bennett) has left her to live with another woman, starts baking cakes and pies for the neighbors, becomes a waitress in a tearoom, opens a drive-in restaurant, marries a society gigolo for his name, and finally tries to get her business partner (Jack Carson) convicted for the murder committed by her daughter. It ends with the girl being led away to prison and the mother beginning a new, more beautiful existence with her first husband, who has just got work in an airplane factory and whose mistress has married someone else.

So far as the conflict between mother and daughter is concerned, Joan Crawford usually makes the mother's actions credible and forceful, but the relationship between her and her daughter is generally on a trite plane, and it is too sketchy to make all the melodramatic sacrifice seem anything but silly. The origins and the real life of such a situation are practically left out, so that the only question the movie gives you a reason for asking is, Why is the mother such a fool? The daughter—due to Miss Blyth's immobility of face, the fact that she seems always about eighty years too young for what she is doing and that the director trusts her with as little to do as he would an untalented mouse—doesn't seem to be a human or logical part of the picture. Once or twice the mother and daughter are thrown together with some of the impact there ought to be all the way through, and at somewhat greater length than it takes to say "I bought you a car" and "Oh, Mother!" One of these scenes takes place during a good quarrel on a staircase, in which there are some brutal, majestic images by Miss Crawford of hatred, horror and especially a caved-in look of defeat.

The direction and writing, though, in "Mildred Pierce" are less interested in this relationship than they are in showing how lascivious, zealous to make money, untrustworthy, loveless and discontented its Americans are. There is hardly a moment when money is not being haggled over, borrowed, used as a club, waved like a flag, made the reason for marriage, stolen, slaved for or got through blackmail. The movie is full of expressions like "stinker," goes any lengths to show a man grabbing at a dress or ogling a woman's legs, and the most elevated person is considered to be Mildred, whose ignoble actions number only about a dozen. The lack of love, comfort or hope in her marriage is believably done; so is her working, which is hurried, hectic, unquestioning, and something that dominates her entire self; and in its best moments, like that near closing time at the restaurant, people seem dissatisfied, lost, degenerate, frustrated and tense. More often than not, though, the decadence and cynicism are mechanical and stereotyped, and except for Miss Crawford and Mr. Bennett, the acting as well as the characterization is lifeless and unsubtle. So that there is the strikingly unpleasant feeling that the producers were unaware of the extreme immorality of the characters, thought much of the action noble or virtuous, and as a result had nothing to offer either in power in the theme or in alternatives.

The production, mainly because of Michael Curtiz's direction, is unimaginative and badly hoked-up. The most pedestrian note is the way people are arranged for each scene as though at a first rehearsal, all squared off facing the audience. The main variations on this statically balanced arrangement are to show it behind a window or a screen or to have a mirror and its image somewhere in the shot. Most of the actors are the victims of atrocious casting. The only important, pleasant fact in the production is Miss Crawford's performance, which is so honest and good that she looks like everything she is supposed to look like: she is tremendously resolute and forceful, strongly set in the middle class, cold, hard and driven, and has, in addition to the fanaticism of her devotion to her daughter, a soft, lyrical love. Director Curtiz can produce scenes as phony as the one in the police room, in which an attempt to dramatize ordinary noises makes the unfolding of a newspaper sound like a decrepit garage door being opened; and shots as vulgar as the one of a seduction, which moves from an embrace to a mirrored wall, where there is the embrace again. No one else today, save possibly Victor Fleming, could direct a scene to rival dime-store art like the one at the end of this movie, in which Mildred leaves the police station, passes some charwomen arranged as though in a Millet painting, joins with her first husband in a movement suitable to a coronation, and then walks with him toward the outside world, which is composed and painted with dazzling cheapness.

October 22, 1945

Drooping Spirits

NOEL COWARD's English production of "Blithe Spirit" opens with a seance in the home of an English novelist (Rex Harrison) in which appears Elvira, his ex-wife. Elvira, now a ghost, still loves him and plans to have him killed. Her plan misfires, killing instead the novelist's second wife (Constance Cummings). As spirits the two wives bother each other and their husband so much that they request dematerialization and a home on the astral plane. The medium (Margaret Rutherford) runs through her repertory trying to accomplish this, using Irving Berlin's "Always," salt and pepper shakers, bad poetry, a crystal ball, geometry, a ladder and a chambermaid; she fails and advises the novelist to leave home. As he is about to start, he is killed.

These people seem to be stuffed with sawdust; their chief expressions are cruelty, boredom, sick amusement, distaste, limp superiority, fatigue, distrust; often they seem to be trying to laugh. Their voices—which are the only reason for their presence in the film—are metallic, insincere and flaccid; their talk, catty wisecracks and pallid lasciviousness; most of the acting is canned. Though half-convincing as English anemic types, they are just as close to stock drawing-room characters and there is little effort to show anything substantially comic or important about them, to illuminate them for any purpose or to make their dullness bright. The producer seems partially aware of this insipid quality.

Elvira, who is the color of pale green celluloid and acts somewhat crocked, has some softness and freshness. There is a tantalizing, foolish quality about her doll-like movements, some ironic wit about her coloring and the sleazy garment she wears; she uses her childish voice facetiously and well, and occasionally she is photographed in a lustful way. But even she seems incredibly phony at times. The female medium, who looks like a policeman, is loaded with enough mannerisms for thirty-five characters—the least amusing being her use of clichés and the funniest her jolting changes of attitude, such as the extraordinary contentment she expresses when she hears there are going to be dry martinis. She is played with an unusual virtuosity that manages to get in every one of a thousand attitudes clearly and to unify them into a caricature of the middle-aged English woman who is all optimism, tweeds, plaids, bobbed hair, forward progress and bird-books, has the facial structure and outdoor look of an American Indian, can realize snobbery and cynicism, is never down but can be hurt for just a minute. Her first meeting with Elvira has great charm—she fails to locate the apparition by a long mile. When Elvira blows on her neck she goes to pieces.

"Blithe Spirit" just misses being a very dull movie. Its images have the cooked-up look of Lord Calvert whiskey advertisements. There is so little movement that when the husband blows some smoke rings in one scene and fastens the back of his wife's dress in another, the two actions take on major importance. The seances, which have the psychic force of a bridge game, are photographed in a forceful, impersonal way, and are the only scenes that don't consist of theatrically articulated talk between immobilized people. The spirits appear and disappear with as little waywardness or comic purpose as a man pushing a piano into a room. The treatment does achieve a good deal of the pedestrian conservatism of home-cooked spiritualism, but even this variety could stand more supernatural excitement. Aside from its unconvincing, pooped, production of ghosts and the dreariest scratching at marriage, the movie has nothing to say or show about anyone or anything, and after the first half-hour the only remarkable fact about "Blithe Spirit" is that its characters go on talking.

October 29, 1945

Dream Manors

"Spellbound" is a soupy, synthetic movie that will probably hold your attention. For one thing it deals, as few movies have, with the analysis of a man (Gregory Peck) who is said to be suffering from paranoia, schizophrenia and a guilt complex. What is more, it reveals the basic situation in psychoanalysis wherein the patient lies on a couch and says whatever comes into his mind, regardless of the consequences. It is also fairly accurate about some of the questions an analyst asks, some of the things a patient says, and both their reactions. The attitude is always youthful and wide-eyed and the movie as slow-motion and unbelievable as a story in the *Woman's Home Companion*. The plot, which has to do with finding out who murdered the chief psychiatrist at Green Manors, a sumptuous mental home, and the attempt of the female analyst (Ingrid Bergman) to hide the accused while she analyzes him, is worked out with excessive care to give each step some degree of logic, but it is a logic you never believe in and you don't feel that its director (Alfred Hitchcock) does either. Hitchcock's methods of creating tension, fear and obsessive fascination in a character for some threatening or alluring object, have become very mechanical, but he still produces those elements better than most directors. Also he still makes a tight, streamlined mystery. There is a very good bit performance by Wallace Ford as a contemptuous masher from Pittsburgh. He is an integrated character who is above any rebuff, with one of the best drooping lips I've ever seen in the movies, an unusual seediness and loose posture and a wonderful way of talking in a completely done-in style.

The mixture of analysis and murder doesn't come to much, especially for analysis. For one thing, Miss Bergman doesn't look like an analyst. She still seems to believe, and is encouraged to believe, that she should enact the dream girl of a Phi Beta Kappa, which she does better than most Academy Award winners, but it is a role that limits this movie and almost any in which she appears. There is an almost imperceptible amount of characterization of the hero—he has the quality of being less a person than a sharp object. One reason for this is that only one brief instant of his past and little of his present are shown. When he comes into the picture he appears completely misplaced and he always seems to be suffering from the fact of being there. This is partly due to an excessive coldness about Mr. Peck and his look of seeming lost. He is racked almost as much as Lillian Gish was in "Broken Blossoms," but none of his suffering projects any pain, nor do you get any sense of his feeling of guilt. Throughout, Hitchcock and his script-writer, Ben Hecht, imply that the hero is both completely capable and completely incapable of murder. Confusion doesn't seem to be their aim so much as the fact that every time they imply the worst in their hero they are able to build a melodramatic situation.

The movie becomes much more enjoyable and closer to reality when, at the end of the first hour, the hero and heroine go to another analyst (Michael Chekhov). The scene starts off nicely by pointing up the difficulty people in waiting rooms have making their talk and actions seem sensible or unobtrusive. Mr. Chekhov is a cute approximation of Freud's looks and does a good comic mimicking of the popular notion of the foreign analyst. The scene is written well and at length. Chekhov says especially sensible things, for instance that Miss Bergman has been carrying on unlike an analyst—which was noticeable from the beginning, when she flinched at the first thing one of her patients said. I wasn't convinced at all that Mr. Peck himself got cured. It is my belief that the analysis, which takes about three hours and is performed literally on the run from the police, on a Pullman, in a New York hotel room and during a ski jump, was just getting started as the picture ended.

By this time the talent and intelligence that Hitchcock showed in his English movies have been diluted to the point where he no longer seems very talented or intelligent. The first meeting between Miss Bergman and Mr. Peck in the staff dining-room goes over, step by step, one of the most traditional and least sound maneuvers in movie-making—that for showing love at first sight:

the instant in which they see each other is made to seem so long that the movie actually stops, and while it is stopped you are given close-ups of the two faces showing an incredible amount of understanding, love and shock. The average Hitchcock shot today is usually without an effective, provocative or original detail; the photography is an all-soft, warm, harmonious kind in which backgrounds are blurred out; his real efforts at expression now seem extraneous, utterly pretentious and often have a wooden-soldier articulation.

The enactment of the hero's dream, based on Dali sketches, is a pallid business of papier-mâché and modern show-window designing. The moment in which the hero runs in ominous slow-motion down a steep plane has a great sense of the dream—of suspended atmosphere; it also has a quality recalling the kind of geometric distortion of reality that de Chirico practises.

The best movies I have seen recently are "Confidential Agent," "My Name Is Julia Ross" and "The Last Chance"; "This Love of Ours" and "Pardon My Past" are even worse than "Spellbound"; "They Were Expendable" (directed by John Ford) and "And Then There Were None" (directed by Réné Clair) are in "Spellbound's" class.

December 3, 1945

Liquor Flicker

"The Lost Weekend"—a good, freezing movie—covers very specialized subject matter and activity, a long weekend of destructive drinking done by a frustrated writer and dipsomaniac, Don Birnam (Ray Milland). The picture ends when he is saved from shooting himself in front of the bathroom mirror by his girl, who works for *Time*, Inc. It is the kind of movie in which everything seems to be dressed up to look better, which moves diagrammatically and with somewhat dull success, but it seems essentially honest and works up by generally conservative means into a powerful film.

The realism of "The Lost Weekend" is the dogged, broadminded kind the producers, Billy Wilder and Charles Brackett, always manage to overlay with a tinny brilliance. One of the most extreme examples of the latter is the characterization of Gloria (Doris Dowling), who is a hostess in Nat's Bar, where the hero—one of the least heroic of all Hollywood movie heroes—spends most of his time. Gloria is supposed to be dressed to catch a customer's eye, but actually she is dressed like nothing save possibly a chandelier—and especially so for the simple sort of life you get in a workingman's bar like Nat's. Gloria (a vital performer, though one who always seems about to go to pieces) has a phony poetic elegance, a literary manner similar to Birnam's and she is decorated with speech mannerisms and gestures bizarre enough to make almost anyone who happened to be in the bar spill most of his drink.

A more average indication of the showy style is in such a scene as that of Birnam leaving his apartment one morning to go to Nat's; as he comes out he is in a black ensemble that seems calculated to make a striking image against the white walls and white doors of the apartment. Then he is seen outside of the bar and again the image—looking out from the bar at him through piled-up chairs and tables—is the kind of stiff, contrived shot that was prevalent in Orson Welles's movies. The style gives a fake coloring to almost every inch of the movie; it throws melodramatic shadow effects implying a cage behind Birnam in the scene at night in the hospital, makes the noises of the delirious patients sound like those of maddened jungle animals, overspecializes details like the shadow cast by a bottle in the chandelier, drapes ornate mannerisms on characters—like Gloria's "No thanks, thanks, but no thanks," the hero's putting the wrong end of a cork-tipped cigarette into his mouth, and Nat's charades of suicide.

Probably the most successful moments occur when the movie is dealing with something really ornamental—the sequence from "La Traviata," satirizing its slow-motion grand manner and the unjustified happiness everywhere apparent on the stage. It has a dreamy, heavy kind of insanity like Goya's etching, up until the last moment when a discordant, surrealist shot tells you that the hero's mind is on a whiskey bottle in his overcoat, a fact that had been apparent for the previous ten minutes.

This is one of those rare movies in which a small action sometimes seems wonderfully colored by the character of the person and pervades not only the expression of his impulse, but his manner of carrying it out and his reaction to it. An instance of this is the preparation Birnam, like the artist in his surest moment of invention, goes through before a solitary night of drinking in his apartment, particularly his deciding to save time by not turning on the light, his feeling that he has done something brilliant in hiding the second bottle in the chandelier and the pleasure he takes in getting the bottle up there and getting down without breaking his neck, the professional way he takes off his coat. Some of Birnam's other maneuvers, though they are often too neat, unfold as elaborately as a perfect football play, recorded somehow by a cameraman who is never more than a yard away from the hero and always in a position to expose each of his moves in the most dramatic way.

Except for Milland, "The Lost Weekend" is cast with lesser known

Hollywood people and extremely dull ones, though they are seemingly intended to be that way. The plush Hollywood stamp is apparent from the start, when you see Milland, a fluent, handsome, exhibitionistic person in a cramped, mousy building on New York's East Side. At best Milland looks as though he had been out of work and unable to create for about a week and had been on the East Side only as long as it took to film the movie, but he gives a strong impression of a number of other facts about Birnam, particularly his narcissism, gentility and lush romanticism (which operates only when he is degrading himself with someone he considers insignificant—Gloria, Nat, the girl in the night club, the landlady). Milland is a flamboyant player in a movie that is predominantly concerned with his every change of expression, and he succeeds in a spectacular way in making Birnam good entertainment. He is best in those moments when he is portraying Birnam as feeling good with himself or pleased with one of his maneuvers; in general he creates an agitated, actorish character rather than a tragic dipsomaniac. He misses the sorrow of the character, the sunken states—up to possibly the last scene; in his driven moments he seems simply athletic and he often looks as silly with a drink as he claims his brother does. One episode where the directing and acting have themselves a fling involves a male nurse (Frank Faylen) in a provocative, sneering act—one of the only inspired movie portraits of homosexuality I have ever seen.

January 7, 1946

Hamburger Hell

THE movie, "The Postman Always Rings Twice," is almost too terrible to walk out of. It is adapted from the James M. Cain novel (which still brings a gleam to most readers' eyes) and has to do with the mess that a hobo (John Garfield) gets into when he stops at a lunch stand outside of Los Angeles. The mess includes a terror-ridden, blundering love affair with the owner's wife (Lana Turner), their sloppy murdering of the owner (Cecil Kellaway), their attempts to get acquitted and to get along with each other afterward—the idea being to show how unutterably awful life is in lunch stands and law courts. The story has been laundered, comicalized, slowed down in the filming, and evidently made by a crew of bobby-sox characters; and the result has been to take the anger out of the story and make the lunchroom people so grotesque that their rotten life doesn't make you feel anything.

The story calls for particularly feverish, dissatisfied people living in an environment that might well drive them to adultery and murder. Garfield, Turner and Kellaway, instead, look as fresh, upper-class and frozen as tulips, wear Saks Fifth Avenue clothes or better—and lots of them: the hobo, for instance, comes off the highway in a sharp, two-toned affair. The lunch stand is large, too sumptuous for highway hamburgers, and has the dummy look of studio houses. The country around it is dappled with dew. The wife spends her time in what should be a jungle washing the several thousand stunning play suits she wears to wait on tables, going for moonlight swims, dancing stylish rhumbas with the hobo. I think the best bobby-sox touches are the white turban that Cora wears to wash dishes, the love scenes which show Cora in a yum-yum pose and outfit, looking like a frozen popsicle, with Frank ogling her at six paces—and probably the director, in the background, swooning over a hamburger.

Some of the scenes, though, are wonderfully grotesque and unintentionally funny—like the first meeting between Frank and Cora, which amounts to a funny take-off on the appearance of the Virgin in "The Song of Bernadette": in a dramatic silence a lipstick goes trundling down the floor like a trolley car, Frank's face lights up and there, like a vision in the doorway, is the Lady in a white play suit making up her face. When the two lovers decide to hitch-hike to San Diego, Cora shows up for the journey in an Adrian ensemble, high-heeled shoes and all (Miss Turner, though, does a graphic portrait of a lady being bothered by the heat and the dirt and Garfield looks as if he had been on the road his whole life). Underneath all of the white surfacing of the MGM production (in which the main villain must have been Producer Carey Wilson) is a story about two people having trouble achieving some kind of happy love set-up, beating each other's brains in at every turn, and this part of the story makes sense a lot of the time. There is never much indication of love between them; from start to finish it is mostly frustration and anger, and as the affair goes on, their hysteria and fear become more and more convincing, and their straining for love becomes relentless and pathetic, almost solid terror.

I don't think any actress registers the wrong way as constantly as Lana Turner. Since MGM is determined to make a star of her, I wish they would let her go into a movie without the Arabian Nights decoration job, and put her in a part that calls for loyalty, friendliness and lower-middle-class respectability. The things she does best in "The Postman" are ironing, washing the dishes, complaining about someone's wasting electricity; and what she fails at most completely are the Jean Harlowisms that MGM always gives her—the angry walking, looking disdainful, lipstick-ad kissing.

A lot of Garfield's work slides too easily because he has played a slouching, quizzical roughneck too often. Also you can't tell exactly what kind of roughneck he is—soulful, soulless, murderous or not murderous—because by now he is a dull blend of the various shades of tough people he has played in the past. No one, though, has such a store of Dead End Kid mannerisms, and one of the most curious is his suspicion of every conceivable action, even that of a door being opened for him. Cecil Kellaway always strikes me as a monstrous jumble of unrelated bits of business who spends hours on a gesture that shouldn't take any time at all. He makes an auntie out of the hash-house owner, for some reason. The whole movie is picked up by Hume Cronyn and Leon Ames when they take up the murderers' case in court. Their part of the movie, which has to do with showing lawyers and courts to be five times as unprincipled as either of the defendants, is a funny culmination to prove that blackness is everywhere, and is marked principally by Cronyn's beautiful display of calculating crust.

May 20, 1946

Make Mine Muzak

"Make Mine Music" is a program of ten shorts designed by Walt Disney for eighty-three minutes of frothy entertainment, done in a boyish spirit that won't sit well even with the cupids on theatre ceilings. There is no particular tie between the shorts, so that at their end you'll probably wait around for a feature-length movie which you may or may not get, depending on your luck. Each cartoon is based on the very lightest type of music, the average weight being "Roll Along, Blue Bayou," with background singing, recitation or playing by famous people like Nelson Eddy and Benny Goodman, some of whom have tied up most of their careers with music that was lighter than their talents warranted. Half of the cartoons are dreamy fantasies using tango rhythm, realistic subject matter like everglades, cranes, cirrus clouds, Ballet Russe dancers all looking extremely pallid; the pace throughout is sickly. The other acts are in Disney's traditional comic style, somewhat less imaginative and carefree than his average.

In "Casey at the Bat" there is some wonderful satire on rattling the pitcher and peppering the ball around the infield; "Peter and the Wolf" has two animal characters with beautiful souls, one of which—a nervous bird—moves, thinks and feels in the highly integrated way of the best Disney animals;

Disney's skill with cutting and animation keeps the story of the Goodman "All the Cats Join In" moving at an inspired clip; every now and then there is a sequence like the drunken hillbilly's take-off down a hill done with a whimsicality no other Hollywood cartoonists achieve. This Disney, though, is choked almost to death by a bad taste that combines callowness and syrupy sweetness.

The only act that halfway earns the title of fantasy—the one concerned with a whale shaped like a Hoover vacuum cleaner, who has a miraculous, three-register voice and a yen to sing at the Met—is constantly embarrassing, even in its funnier moments. When Willie is first spotted at sea sunning himself, singing "Short'nin' Bread" to a school of porpoise, his hail-fellow-well-met voice is cute, but the singing, supplied by Nelson Eddy, is so unblushingly in the style of Nelson Eddy rather than as Willie might sing it that you feel (1) sorry for Willie, who loses his character as a whale, and (2) that Nelson Eddy is taking advantage of the occasion to show what a whale of a singer he is. The porpoise beat time in a good rocking rhythm, aping revival-meeting Negroes, but their manner makes you ill at ease because it is a white-man's notion of the way Negroes act (just as the first cartoon is based solidly on a phony popular attitude about hillbillies). The shot of sea gulls idling at the top of the Met transfixed by Willie's singing is inspired, but having the people underneath covering their heads with programs is a hoary, embarrassing gag. There are a thousand sticky moments in this short: Willie singing to a packed house of angels; the repeated views of the uvulas in Willie's throat; Eddy's eulogy about what a miracle Willie's and/or Eddy's voice is.

The color and drawing in "Make Mine Music," as in all of the Disney cartoons, are in a bon-bon mode and will satisfy the people who do the printing on wedding cakes, those who invented Mother's Day, the people who write their names with a flurry and end them with flounces and curlicues, those who design theatre interiors, think a James Hilton novel is the way life should be and sometimes is, and dream up the production numbers at the Music Hall. Typical examples of the Disney madness for lollypop color are the Easter-egg uniforms that the Mudville players wear in "Casey at the Bat," the butterscotch backgrounds that are used in most of the shorts, the silvery cottage the last of the Coys and Martins call home, the chi-chi valentines that open each act—the Disney people instinctively turn everything to prettiness, whether or not the purpose is to make a gag on toughness. In lollypop art, forms are made large, full, ovular, as though they were particularly good to eat, and they are finished off so perfectly you feel you can pick them off the screen. To make such forms calls for an artist who is happy, optimistic and uncomplicated beyond belief. Disney drawing is always done with a smile, apes conventional notions of what a shaggy tree looks like, a curtained window, and is made up of one fancy-pants curve after another—even Mickey is a repetition of simple curves that could be produced only by the most blissful taste.

Disney lets himself go into syrupy art more in this movie than the people who select the serious art sold at Kress's. The high moments for this come in "Ballade Ballet" when the two dancers, Lichine and Riabouchinskaya, make like a seesaw on each end of which sits a cupid, and the closing episode in which the cupids embrace, slowly writhe around, and finally come to rest in the shape of a heart.

May 27, 1946

Crime Without Passion

"The Blue Dahlia" is a tight movie about Los Angeles chiselers, coppers, cabaret-owners, peepers, husband-deserters, just discharged Navy fliers who do violence to each other with the dispatch and unconcern of a person stamping an envelope. It is the neatest treatment that has been done on a Raymond Chandler novel and is filled as much with Chandler's smartness (about Los Angeles county, its roads, its lush playgrounds; the looks and manners of high cops and low underworld yeggs; intimate views about gangsters that castrate them, make them weaker but more lovable), as it is with his Adrian-izing of Dashiell Hammett. Chandler makes the mayhem, drinking and talk stylized and arty; never allows his gangsters to lose their suavity, presence of mind, grace, sartorial elegance, wit in every kind of catastrophe; and turns everyone into a sophisticate—even the man in a union suit who operates a cut-throat flophouse.

The story concerns the terrible homecoming of three Navy buddies (Alan Ladd, William Bendix, Hugh Beaumont). Johnny (Alan Ladd), the one the others look up to most, finds that during his war years his wife has become an alcoholic, has killed his son, is in love with a cabaret-owner, so he leaves her. The next day, over a No. 2 with Orange Juice, he hears the police are after him for her murder, decides to avenge her and absolve himself, spends the next eight reels getting bounced around. The murderer turns out to be the person you give the least hang about. The two big notions "The Blue Dahlia" gets across are that (1) people today are living more destructively than ever, and killing, infidelity, hating and being hated all the time have become run-of-the-mill and all but boring, (2) the war veteran has been perfectly schooled to operate in a society similar to the one from which he was discharged. A wonderful example of the way people in "The Blue Dahlia" respond to catastrophe is the final shot of the police chief (Tom Powers) looking a little done in for having blown up the murderer, annoyed in a minor way that he has been the least bit affected emotionally by having to kill the old man.

"The Blue Dahlia" has been hammered down by the director (George Marshall) into a movie that has almost no slack, confusion or ease. Its people think, talk and walk with the greatest consciousness of destruction. They live in unsentimentalized surroundings that show in bas-relief the bleakness, glare, determined, incisive movement, seediness of a city (particularly the way it looks at night). The movie is worthless during its blow-off scenes—when the husband and wife spit at each other, when the flier throws the ceiling at a gangster, when the shell-shocked ex-bombardier goes panicky at the sound of frivolous music (jumping, crazy music that is unusually effective), shoots out a match at twenty paces to prove he wouldn't have to be on top of a person to kill him. But when its people are going through the motions of every-day living—passing in and out of lobbies, motoring to the beach, asking to speak to someone on the phone—"The Blue Dahlia" is beautifully accurate in showing their tension, controlled behavior, suspiciousness and the personalities of people who don't expect to live long or happily. It is perfect on atmosphere. The drive the hero and heroine take to Malibu is gummed with literary chit-chat, but anyone who likes night driving will be pleased with the airiness, the 50-mile-an-hour movement, the lights of roadside drive-ins that flash by, the sense of having been on the road a long time.

The film is well acted from top to bottom and especially in the in-between roles: the acting of a slimy house detective by Will Wright; Tom Powers as a stubborn police captain; Howard Da Silva as Eddie, the miserable hot shot who own a cabaret and loses a trick to every person in the movie because he has more character, sensitivity and good will than his job demands. For some reason he's given a whole world of delicate feeling to put across—the kind that turns up occasionally in old gangster films, more often in French movies: for instance, his realization that he has lost a beautiful woman through his own faults and being frustrated half to death by her easy-as-pie tossing off of his advances. One wonderful episode is when the Navy hero clouts him as though he were swatting a fly; Eddie starts to hit back, realizes objectively he has no moral leg to stand on, having been intimate with the hero's wife, begs his pardon and leaves like a gentleman. Da Silva brings off a remarkable number of sides on the character. Tom Powers has a dyspeptic look that makes him seem completely self-absorbed, and he acts with humorlessness and tenacious earnestness. All of which makes you respect his ability as a bloodhound because you don't expect him to take his work lightly or to be swerved by sympathy for the suspects. He looks incorruptible and substantial, however much you may feel sorry for his suffering and want to help him. Along with his unyielding character, Powers is a fine actor who stands out in any film no matter how good the other players (he was the husband who was choked to death in "Double Indemnity"). Wright, as the voyeur, looks as if he never thought above the level of a filthy postcard, has a dirty voice that seems always to be squirming. He is excellent in showing curiosity over something vile he has done, as though he had completely forgotten having done it; also in portraying a person who only scares a little bit.

June 3, 1946

French Primitive

The French film, "It Happened at the Inn" (made during the occupation and having no political tone, not even an overtone), is so wayward that you feel a new director took over when the plot began to thicken, and from that time on you realize how much more serious the French are in their comedies than the Americans and how much less they roll you around in the aisles. The movie is about a family of peasants who operate a tavern in the French sticks and are as exciting in their own way as the Marx Brothers. The Goupis look as though they were cut out of particularly good turf, have a shopkeeper's mind for money—they spend every waking second trying to earn any kind of penny, honest or otherwise, and finding a safe place to keep it—and are clannish to a fault. The Goupis are dunked in a maze of inter-family farce and melodrama running all of the way from finding out who murdered Ten Drops to locating the family pot of gold, the secret of which lies buried in the dying great-grandfather (a lovable man who goes through the movie asking for a biscuit and a small glass of wine, never getting it, but never getting angry about it).

It is unlikely that you will forget any of the Goupis, even the Idiot who just gets in on the edge of scenes but bears the Goupi stamp of self-approval and has the eyes of a smart doe. Despite their air of unpretentiousness, the Goupis possess enough blood and thunder, individual charm, sense of superiority and moral responsibility (they don't use the police for anything—even murder; they have their own jail, do their own bloodhounding and are their own bank) to take them out of the rut in which most movie characters reside. The director, Jacques Becker, doubtless believes that they are wonderful people, that they typify the average Frenchman and that they will keep France running forever, and he does such a good job he makes you agree with him.

"It Happened at the Inn" is not so much a funny movie as a very understanding portrait of petty bourgeois done with more than average restraint. The best modern Hollywood comedies are a lot funnier but not half as shrewd about people. French directors like Becker point up the bizarreness of human frailty and leave it so close to a natural state that it generally makes you feel sorry for the people. The funniest scene in the picture has to do with three Goupis lugging the paralyzed great-grandfather around the house in a chair, hoping he will give a sign when they pass the treasure. The "Emperor" is not only in a state of stroke, but is large, raw-boned and Lincolnish, the chair is thronelike, the stairways are narrow and the Goupis have as much trouble transporting the "Emperor" as they would a piano on a circular staircase. This takes place at high noon on a hot day and the people are in their Sunday best. An American director would have played it in slapstick until he had covered up most of the movie. As it is, the scene takes a minimum of time and your main feeling is uneasiness—to think that greed could drive these characters to such a project; and worse, you feel sorry for them because they're not going to get anything out of it. The scene is funny enough played straight, the funniest thing being what you already know of the "Emperor," plus his impassive look while touring—it's obvious that he's not going to tell them a thing even if they step on the treasure. Also, his position is one of resting himself in a philosophical way—bent a little forward while the others carry on.

The backbone of the picture is Tonkin (Robert Le Vigan), the most tormented Goupi and the only one who doesn't look capable of living forever. He is constantly burning, suffering, getting angry in a light, narrow way, and is the most tragic person I have encountered in recent movies. Everything about the characterization, from the way he seems poured into his worn-out Legionnaire's uniform to the grace and spring of his movements, is fascinating. Pinchpenny (Arthur Devère) and the Law (Guy Favières) are so intensely and ferociously themselves that, like a lot of peasants, they seem parodies of themselves. Primrose's father, the only serene Goupi, is also the only one that is sufficiently weathered and dusty for a peasant. It is hard to understand, though, how such a household produced a restrained, supercilious daughter like Primrose (Blanchette Brunoy).

June 10, 1946

Olivier's "Henry V"

LAURENCE OLIVIER's spectacle-film, "Henry V," is a sparkling armor-and-woolen-goods movie about a glorious English leader (Olivier), his smashing, upset victory over the French (who had too much armor, too few archers) in 1415, and his lightning courtship—made up of tricky, beautiful talk and vaudeville—of the French princess Katherine (Renée Asherson). "Henry V" is a great deal more than almost any other hell-bent-for-armor movie that you've seen. While definitely athletic, pageant-minded and somewhat recognizable after all of the war dramas that have come out since Elizabethan times, no movie has given a more poignant impression of men in battle or been so cutting about the waste and folly of war.

Its most artistic value rests in the perfection of the portrait of a great medieval leader-type, the kind of power-happy, wily statesman who terrifies people today more than the thought of a subway ride on a hot day. Olivier does an elaborate, wonderful job on Henry. He sends chills down your back as he smiles at an insult; he makes you uneasy, talking in a charming, bland way of how necessary it is that there be just reason for conquering France. When he turns up here and there in battle to pep up his soldiers, you feel that even Joan of Arc couldn't have been so noble and inspiring, but that he is something of a busybody. His transformation during the war into a deeper, greater person is made intensely evident in an almost magical way. Olivier's real feat, though, is in having directed a film that is always as exciting, sometimes more so, than the Shakespeare play. It is basically a word film—every move of the direction is governed by the desire to do the best job possible by Shakespeare's lines. I am sure no one is going to do a better Shakespeare movie of this kind.

The schoolroomish opening (a pokey bird's-eye view of seventeenth-century London and a busy trafficking through a first-act performance of "Henry V" at Shakespeare's Globe Theatre) gives immediate indication of what a knockout this movie will be—poetic, stunning, exquisitely synchronized, fanciful, light and airy in the best Disney manner, bubbling with good spirits and good actors, eloquent but gentle, unpretentious, down to your level. The opening shot of a program swirling airily up to the screen is the tip-off that this is going to be different from all the other Shakespeare films you've seen—breezier and with better scenic effects. The technicolor goes down easily, for once, because the backgrounds are colored in a low, almost natural key and only central figures are occasionally larded with the heavy splashes that you're used to. The irrepressible wit of Olivier's directing shows up in a first wonderful close-up as he is about to walk on the Globe's stage as Henry—it catches him in a look that is a mixture of fear and respect for the audience, the over-worked, bored professional: all in all a very unkingly sight. The costuming of the Chorus (floridly and charmingly played by Leslie Banks) is of a sensible kind that accents rather than hides his skinniness, by sack pants and gigantic white garters.

Olivier's production, though, was aimed to entertain if it had to kill you with charm, to make you understand Shakespeare's thought if it meant inter-preting characters and ideas so well that you get them without half trying, reading the best lines with such care that you feel they're being slyly pressed into your brain to take home with you and chew on till the end of time. But the greatest letdown comes from the realization that so much of it is like what you find in boys' books, the *American Boy,* Disney movies, the action stories on boxes of Wheaties, the paintings of Rockwell Kent or Grant Wood. The pup-petlike Dresden-doll princess would turn up in boys' magazines; so would the quaint comedy and the embarrassing people involved in it, the youthful action backstage and in the galleries at the Globe, and so many of the saccharine land-scapes. You get a big dose of the boys'-magazine spirit when the Globe audi-ence is heard derisively responding to one of the speeches about Falstaff. They are being considered quaint, made to sound youthful, and you feel you're being too carefully instructed about the likes and dislikes of an Elizabethan audience. "Henry V"—because Olivier was so concerned with entertaining on a light plane (a good part of every scene is woven into expert vaudeville), and especially with pleasing middle-brow taste—always looks a bit contrived (stagy and toylike), boyish, and heavy with décor and costuming the way a grade-school operetta is.

July 8, 1946

"Open City"

THERE is a spirit of such depression, leadenness, consuming exhaustion and poverty in every note of the Italian film, "Open City" (which must have been at least partly shot under Nazi as well as Roman noses and was designed to pay homage to the Italian spirit that drove the Nazis out of Rome), that you wonder whether its extreme morbidity was intended. "Open City," made by profes-sionals and amateurs, was meant to show the misery civilians suffered under the Nazis, and the Italian resisters as contrasted to the collaborators (who here com-prise a particularly "Way Down East" type of villain, a dope addict, a 15-year-old prostitute, plus a lot of people on the fringes of scenes who look wonderfully shady and as if they would murder you for carfare). One of the central details of the plot shows the self-effacing heroism of a Catholic priest in the Underground, a detail that tends to be a bit labored in the excessiveness of its relationship to the rest of the picture. "Open City" is the grayest of all war movies.

All of the actors look as if they had fought every round of the actual occupation of Rome. No matter what roles they play—plushy, high-living Nazis, appeasers living the life of Riley, tormented workers—they present one face that drives down your spirit, a mixture of years-long strain, bread-crumb existence, tension and rebellion at their lot. Even the hero, the wheelhorse of the Underground, who looks as if he had grown up at Art theatres showing Gabin movies and is meant to be unbending, incorruptible, indomitable, a holy terror, is so strained, shrunken and starved he reminds you of a wet string. The whole movie has a worn-out look (especially the plot), seems scratched, pockmarked, covered with the dust and grime of war. This is emphasized in physical details—the staircase of the workers' flat that looks as if a good part of the war had taken place on it, the bed clothes, the baby's pot, the fur coat one of the prostitutes gets for informing, all of the varieties of underwear.

"Open City" clings humorlessly and obsessively to a type of life that is seamy enough in peacetime—prostitution, drug addiction, life in two small rooms overflowing with kids, long climbs up badly lighted staircases that look dank, street cars that seem to have limitless capacity, with more people hanging outside than are buried inside. To swell the box-office take the plot sticks like glue to sexy material (but in a way that should teach Hollywood craftsmen plenty, especially about one of their dearest standbys—a woman undressing). In addition to the general seaminess, its other main concern is with the staples of life—like getting in bed, getting out of bed.

About half of this film's burdensome, graveyard quality, though, is due to the fact that there isn't a speck of newness in its plot—no one opens his mouth or takes a step without reminding you of dozens of other movies. There are only flashes when you feel you're out of the melodrama and old movie maneuvers —some of the street scenes, a realistically paced meeting of the hero and heroine on the stairway, some perfect shots of a family getting to bed—and these moments have the effect of a draft in the theatre.

"Open City" shocks you because of its excessively realistic look. Of all the super-naturalistic movies that have been made, this has an appearance of actuality that you used to get in old-time newsreels; if you ran it on the program at your local Trans-Lux, it would make most of the modern news coverage shown there look as stagy, glossy and unreal as the average C-budget musical. But the most graphic scenes in "Open City"—the ambushing of some Nazi trucks, a terrifying shot of a woman being machine-gunned as she runs toward a Gestapo car—develop with the burst and intensity of an oil-dump fire.

July 15, 1946

At Home Abroad

Ernst Lubitsch's "Cluny Brown" shows the adventures of a girl who forgets her place in a society of people who never forget, and kids English snobbism with comic-strip obviousness. It is one of the most ingratiating films around, is free and easy and good-natured the way most movies should be in summertime. Its humor, though, reflects a new Lubitsch touch—it is broad, predictable, monstrously heavy and reminds you of the kind of touch that designs most bank buildings in this country.

Cluny Brown (Jennifer Jones) is a person-who-doesn't-sit-around-and-mope, is sociable, eager to help, a hearty plumber's niece who loves plumbing. She does some of her uncle's jobs in a lucky, slam-bang style that works on the particular sinks in this movie but casts a terrible light on plumbing as a skill. Cluny makes you suspect she doesn't know one end of a monkey-wrench from the other and she whams the pipe that's most accessible to cure any evil from a plugged drain to an Academy Award sink that sounds like a boiler factory having delirium tremens. She not only talks a Hepburn streak but has the rare ability to hold her own on any intellectual level, including communion with dogs. Her troubles come from being so friendly, spontaneous and impulsive in a rigid, custom-bound society. Though her idea of heaven is life with the stuffiest male (Richard Haydn) in the most paralyzed home in that society, she is saved in the last of the ninth, fairy-story fashion, by a not-too-pricipled Czech liberal named Belinsky (Charles Boyer) who by a series of impossible coincidences is generally within shouting distance of Cluny.

Some things about the movie make it seem as artificial as the orange drinks sold on Broadway, but among its virtues is Jennifer Jones's performance, which makes Cluny an unusually sparkling person with more liveliness, intensity, girlish enthusiasm and good nature than a half-dozen average movie heroines. As an actress Miss Jones is one of the most affected, gauche players working at the moment, but the exuberance she gives Cluny seems bona-fide and is of an amount that you usually encounter only in the heroines of Russian films.

There is a great deal of pretension in "Cluny Brown" that it is a critique, however entertaining, of various facets of British life, and I do think it is a little less namby-pamby than the usual Hollywood satire. But you aren't likely to be much affected by the dressing-downs, the puttings in her place and the cruelties that Cluny suffers, nor does the film make you very critical of the silliness and stupidity of the insulated aristocrats she works for. For one thing, the sumptuousness of the production makes everyone's life, even the druggist's, seem rather wonderful. Also while it is obvious that the director and writer feel pretty good about everyone, especially Cluny and her Czech savior, there isn't a non-snob among them. Of all these characters Cluny is the one who luxuriates most contentedly in the various existences she encounters at Friars-Carmel. The director gives her so little the look of a worker when she's plumbing that you are led to think she is slumming when she works on sinks. The hero, Belinsky, who is considered such a charming philosophic person, is actually an unusually snide customer who treats everyone, including Cluny, as stupid, quaint and funny.

Few films have ever had such a country-club air. Every scene—especially the ones in the countryside near Friars-Carmel, which are as lovely as the landscapes in Venetian paintings—gives the feeling that it is not only taking place in the shade but in shade that is air-conditioned. The druggist's living room, which is described wonderfully—"It may not be Buckingham Palace, but it's Wilson's little castle"—has a restful, cool, retreat quality that will undoubtedly drive some people who live in tenements almost out of their minds. Also the sets have been decorated with bric-a-brac and shadows in a tasteful, luxurious style so that they have the same elegance and charm that Lady Carmel's dresses have. The costuming, especially the splendid maid's outfit Cluny wears, would, I think, make the most determined Dead End character yearn for such finery.

July 29, 1946

Hellman's Movietone News

A VACUOUS, journalistic, middle-aged-film called "The Searching Wind" has already achieved the reputation of being the toughest political movie of 1946. Adapted by Lillian Hellman from her play of the same oblique title, it is a sort of March of Time resumé of what seems like the last six hundred and fifty thousand years of international politics. Actually, though, it starts when

Mussolini took over in Rome, moves like an elephant through the crucial events since then and ends, like most educational war films since the First World War, with "America" being played and a grim, disabled veteran denouncing the last generation (particularly his parents) as irresponsible and claiming his type of veteran is not going to be lazy-minded and pleasure-loving enough to get into another mess. (Since throughout the movie he has had the steady face of a man who couldn't understand anything, you don't feel that he is going to be suspicious enough to spot trouble coming.)

The story concerns this boy's father, Alexander Hazen (Robert Young), a no-statement career diplomat who during the thirties becomes No. 1 Ambassador, a symbol of United States foreign policy and, for turning up at critical moments, a lot like Lanny Budd of the Upton Sinclair novels. You suspect he was the only diplomat we had through the twenties and thirties, and there are some wonderful shots of him walking through history sort of tired-faced, like a man who has been used too much by his country. The movie is a slap on the wrist at Hazen's type of statesman. Actually, he is a sort of zero-ball as a dramatic character; he is supposed to be the most traditional kind of statesman, but he says so little and does so little that you don't get enough of an idea about his brand of diplomacy to make him an engrossing or pitiful figure, let alone a tragic one. Especially you aren't given the slightest notion of the forces inside and outside of him that make him so paralyzed in the face of great problems and events. The people around Hazen seem to have been given a postwar view of the prewar events they are living through, and consequently everyone, from his son to his father-in-law, considers him a weak-minded blunderer, and Hazen more or less agrees with them. Most diplomats seem to spend their whole lives justifying their actions, but Hazen's only defense is that he didn't know any better and the people he went with were the wrong sort.

Miss Hellman's characterization generally leads to people with Wheaties in their blood. The casting and the playing are so undistinguished that these people are made even less exciting than you would expect; the only acting that rings true is that of Dudley Digges in his early scenes as a beloved American type, a George S. Kaufman version of Benjamin Franklin. Digges, who in the movie looks like a robin's nest, acts this tired idealist in a hammy way, most of his reactions resembling those of a man with the sun in his eyes. Even when he is sitting still, he's good at making you feel that he is wandering around waiting for something to happen. As the movie goes on, his character turns into a tangle of actorisms. The rest of the people—with the exception of Albert Bassermann's abandoned playing of a Nazi aristocrat—might as well have stood in bed.

It's embarrassing to think that someone thought of Robert Young, who plays the gray stick Hazen, as a leading American diplomat. A lot of the news-reel character of the movie is due to Ann Richards' performance of Hazen's wife Emily. Her portrait of a diplomat's wife is more than adequate, but her attitudes are either too formalized or are played too slowly. Sylvia Sidney is totally miscast.

Director William Dieterle and his staff show embassy life with great savvy. They are so good that the perfect scenes of a glittering Italian social function and the airy, shuttery Italian home of the Taneys have a refreshing effect rather than being overstuffed and heavy as such period scenes usually are. All in all, Dieterle does pretty well by Miss Hellman's script, though the movie always has the look of a stock play. Lee Garmes's photography is responsible for a good deal of the realism—the spaces between people are made concrete and of varying distances so that the movie has not only the three-dimensional but the dispersed look of real life. The average cameraman shows the actors at a monotonous distance—they are generally, aside from close-ups, full size in the middle distance. Garmes's photography makes the people seem bulky and gives you the feeling that you're in the room where the action is taking place.

August 5, 1946

Iverstown Slaughter

THE latest Hollywood film to show modern life as a jungle is titled "The Strange Love of Martha Ivers" and is a jolting, sour, engrossing work. It deals with four people who have lived cataclysmic, laughterless lives since they were babies. There is Martha (Barbara Stanwyck), who likes to steal, run away from home, murder and hammer her victims with clubs; her husband (Kirk Doug-las), who is wracked by guilt because he is made an accomplice in Martha's evil doings, and is further tormented by her promiscuity with life-guard types and lack of yen for him; a gambler (Van Heflin) and a girl just released from the pen (Lizabeth Scott), who act as if there were no evil that hadn't been imposed on them. More and more movies are turning up which show life as constantly hair-raising—an affair of hard knocks, hard drinking, hard smoking, sadism, greed, unhappy marriages, bad parents, bad district attorneys, seedy hotel rooms. They are on the right path in trying to show modern life as a battlefield, but they make each second of living more violent than seems possible. The har-rowing insecurity of people's lives runs to double suicides, gangsterism and blackmail instead of the quieter, more subtle destructions that only drive them to psychiatrists. Too much of "Martha Ivers" seems synthetic; but it is unusual in its power to upset you one way or another—by violent acts conceived with imagination, uninhibited acting, and the fact that it is directed and written so that there are no loose ends or lagging. Its gaudy people are ten times more arresting than those in the average picture.

The movie is concerned with numerous love affairs among the four central characters. The most gripping relationship is the one-sided affair between Martha and her loving, alcoholic husband, in which both Miss Stanwyck and Douglas give successful characterizations of people who suffer inwardly a great deal and are involved in a negative marriage. Kirk Douglas is especially good for his voice, beseeching and miserable, and there is one extraordinary scene with the two of them hurt and shouting at each other at once that is as painful as it is convincing. The chaotic scenes are written with unusual ability and are directed so well that they boil and seethe as movie scenes rarely do.

The hero in "The Strange Love of Martha Ivers" is a character with more personalized details and complexities than any that has turned up in American movies this year; his actions are unpredictable, erratic and impulsive. Basically Sam Masterson is something of a cliché movie character—the cynical tough guy who is on to everything and as pleased as punch with himself—generally played these days by Dane Clark, John Garfield, Zachary Scott. And usually this character gets on one's nerves with his self-pity and the too frequent implication that the world has done him wrong. Van Heflin, in an extraordinary job of acting, gives the role a meatiness and individuality that it's never had before. His Masterson wallows in amazing conceit and scorn. He's not only superior to everyone, but gives the feeling that he must stand apart from them, too. With all of his mannerisms, Heflin makes Masterson an unusually alert person and, strangely enough, a rather sensitive one.

The movie has too much the quality of the sensational stories in the Hearst Sunday Magazine section. The photography (Victor Milner's), which is soft and shiny, is more suited to a wispier, pleasanter subject. It makes every detail seem unimportant because the lighting is so confused and the details so blurred. I don't remember a recent A-budget production that exhibited such indifferent art work. Most of the time the brickwork, billboards, bus-terminal entrance look as if they were whipped up by apprentice carpenters at the studio, and the gingerbread that covers Martha's mansion filched from your nearest theatre. But every now and then some wonderful, bizarre item turns up in a scene—like the regal blanket in the drab hotel room, or the ghost-white Lord and Taylor slip worn by Miss Scott the day she gets out of the pen. Incidentally, I have never seen a movie so given over to people stocking up on cigarettes, lighting them, stubbing them out, throwing them on the floor, studying them. Sometimes it looked like a busy day at the Chesterfield plant.

The whole job is of the punchy type Clifford Odets turns out in which you feel actors, writers, director worked pretty impetuously and felt like trying almost anything to hold your attention. It is a technique that turns out movies with fire and stuff, and generally I'm all for it. "Martha Ivers" is exciting, though it has odds and ends from every non-musical Warners made in the early thirties.

Other recent movies I liked are "The Big Sleep," "The Killers" and "The Stranger."

September 9, 1946

Hollywood Barnum

In the boyishly macabre "The Stranger," which Orson Welles has just beaten out, a dream of a New England village where even the buses seem clean is hit in a quiet way by one nightmarish crime after another. A man looking around a spic-and-span gymnasium is conked on the head by a flying ring; a dog nosing through the woods is given a murderous slug of poison for getting too close to his master's secret; a boy goes fishing and is told his sister has married the Nazi who invented many of the concentration-camp torture devices; some school-boys on a paper-chase in the woods just miss running into their favorite prof choking a lifelong pal to death. Oddly enough, the most horrible events—like that in which the villain dangles his wife from the rafters of a church steeple—go off with dispatch and don't seem terrifying at all, whereas the lazy, cozy, inconsequential scenes—fishing on the lake, checkers at the drugstore, dinner in a secure New England home—hop with excitement; every move the actors make is significant; the scenes are entrancing enactions of everyday activity in an American town.

The story has to do with the location and the all but interminably delayed capture of a fiendish Nazi (Welles) by a detective (Edward G. Robinson) who is working for the Allied War Crimes Commission and who exposes himself to danger with a suicidal detachment and a sense of indestructibility that don't admit of villains hurting heros. Most of the detecting takes place in Harper, Connecticut, where the Nazi is hiding out until the next war as a self-effacing history professor at a plush boys' school. The story goes on forever, with a labored piling up of one bulky event after another. You get the sense of a carpenter at work rather than a writer. But this is as nothing compared to the pervading feeling that the situations of terror and horror are contrivances on a level with Hallowe'en pranks and that the patient and reserved people of Harper would never be involved in such Amazing Story melodrama. This is characteristic of Welles's preoccupation with events (the more sensational the better), his adolescent delight in scaring you, in bowling you over with some knockout notion or other, his use of people as nothing but pawns to carry his fact-laden plots to fruition. The characters are made to fit the event rather than the other way around. Like his plots, his people are conglomerations of showy, unimportant detail rather than the result of curiosity and subtle perception.

But as incurious as Welles is about what makes people tick, he has no such blind spot about the medium, whatever it happens to be at the moment— theatre, movies or radio—and he has turned out a tense and vivid film, the most cinematic to come from Hollywood this year. He has a sense as well as an enthusiasm for movie-making, and particularly in this film, despite the pulp-story plot and the infinitesimal amount of character analysis, he shows remarkable savvy about how to make a movie go. He has given up much of the stagey technique of "Citizen Kane," "The Magnificent Ambersons," "Journey into Fear," and now even hackneyed moments—like the ending—are not unexciting because they are set up in a striking, authentic naturalism and shot at an angle that gives you the hardest impact of the action.

"The Stranger" is beautiful for lighting and textures, and affords an experience of late fall Connecticut landscape that is on the breathtaking side. The most successful and original directing is reserved for casual conversations: here minor actions are made so engrossing and contact between persons so combustible that they seem constantly about to expode. It is as though Welles realized how much his movie was a matter of melodramatic events, and so concentrated on these trivial conversations to give you the greatest possible sense of people thinking, being emotionally affected by one another, and especially of being touchy and distant with each other.

A good deal of the movie's unreality is due to the soggy effect Loretta Young produces as the bride who learns a day or so after her honeymoon that she's married a fanatical Nazi rather than a history professor. She has moments —as in her worried recounting of a bad dream—when she seems in contact with this world, but otherwise she is her usual movie self, a woman whose nerves are shot and who always seems in a totally unnecessary deep study. The greatest force for realism is Robinson as the detective; the most absorbing scenes the conversations he has with the operator (Billy House) of the trick drugstore. Welles deserves a medal for using Robinson in a less sterotyped fashion than has been the case before, and another for showing a reserved, almost sullen schoolboy (Richard Long) who is the only boy I've seen outside of a Val Lewton film who doesn't turn my thoughts to murder.

Recent movies I have particularly disliked are "Night and Day," "The Kid from Brooklyn," "Young Widow," "The Man I Love," "Without Reservations," "Two Guys from Milwaukee" and "The Notorious Gentleman."

September 16, 1946

Journey into the Night

"The Big Sleep" is an unsentimental, surrealist excitement in which most of the men in Hollywood's underworld are murdered and most of the women go for an honest but not unwilling private sleuth (Humphrey Bogart). Coinciding with the special prominence of the private detective in Hollywood movies, he has been tagged with the special name of "shamus." Lest there be friction between thieves and shamuses, script-writers have been equally thoughtful about holdup artists, so that their black deeds have been Disneyfied with the name "caper." The plot of "The Big Sleep," which winds as crazily as a Greenwich Village street and involves so many secondary crimes and criminals that figuring it out makes you faint, starts with the underpaid shamus signing up to stop the blackmailing of a tough millionaire's depraved, thumb-sucking daughter (Martha Vickers) by a dealer in pornographic books. That night two people you and the detective haven't seen before are murdered before they get a chance to show their faces on the screen and a six-year-old unsolved disappearance of an Irish patriot is brought to your already hysterical attention. The rest of the movie puts Bogart through some dozen more exotic and brutal situations until at the end, with unusually refreshing self-effacement, he admits he can tell the police just about all that happened.

There is a fantastic quality about all this excitement due to the apparent lack of integration between crimes, the sudden appearances of bizarre underworld figures and their more sudden, startling disappearances into the murky environment. It all has the feeling of an opium smoker's fantasy, and, incidentally, there's some of that in the film, too. With six murders in the plot, this nightmarish affair becomes less vital as you try to decide what motivates the people, whose chauffeur kills the inept blackmailer, who is having "the big sleep," who the perverted bookseller is—a foppish man with a mustache or a florid old man with a glass eye—what the exact relationship is between the widowed heiress and a classy gambler who operates a crime world by remote control. "The Big Sleep," though, is witty and sinister, and in an odd way is a realistic portrayal of big-city life with "Arabian Nights" overtones.

The detective's job takes him through Hollywood's underworld, which is made up of a classy crook whose cruelty is limitless, and a down-at-the-heel lot with comic faces and angelic souls. The chief impression you get of their world is that the pay is rotten, the people—especially the women—are uninhibited and no one lives to middle age. The locale is particularly seedy and pressed in on all sides by drab concrete. Gangster movies are increasingly coming to be stereotypes. Although the drab, blurred city streets are good, they are too familiar to be arresting. But far more than the usual skill is shown in the way the director (Howard Hawks) handles the human element. He is particularly adept in graphically suggesting voyeurism and other forms of sexuality without running afoul of the Johnston office.

The more inspired work occurs where the exotic subject matter is woven with straight naturalism—one of the best scenes has to do with the hiring of the detective by a tough millionaire. He is an aged individual who looks like a Southern general (writer William Faulkner may have been responsible for this) and who, after a life passionately devoted to pleasure, is living in a hothouse where he grows orchids. The scene is set up in such a super-realistic way it reminds you of an old-fashioned photograph.

"The Big Sleep" would have been a more effective study of nightmarish existence had the detective been more complicated and had more curiosity been shown about his sweetheart's relation to the crime. Lauren Bacall, performing phlegmatically, creates a large empty space in the movie. Though Bogart turns in another jolting performance as well as some good comedy, his detective is a limited, dull person, who seems to have little sympathy with the sub-rosa world with which he must always be associated. A fine bit performance is turned in by Louis Jean Heydt as an incompetent crook who is fully aware of his shortcomings.

Other movies that are worth seeing are "The Strange Love of Martha Ivers," "The Killers" and "The Stranger."

September 23, 1946

Caper of the Week

THE latest in the weekly succession of Hollywood bullet orgies is Mark Hellinger's production, "The Killers," a powerful movie without a relaxing moment. It is concerned with Pittsburgh gunmen and is predominantly a matter of shocking events in great number—avarice, homicide, gunmen being searched for rods, killers being stalked by detectives and rival crooks—with a minimum of concern for personalities. More than other recent blood-bath films, this one pounds home how tenaciously and relentlessly crooks and the people associated with them—insurance investigators, cops, sweethearts—pursue their jobs. Besides its brutality, it has the noise, the jagged, tormenting movement of keyed-up, tough, flashy humanity that you get from a walk through Times Square.

The story, using flashbacks with the abandon and effectiveness that its gunmen use bullets, shows the tortuous route of an insurance sleuth (played in a stiff, breathless way by Edmond O'Brien) investigating the killing of an ex-pug called Swede (Burt Lancaster). Starting with his provoking murder (he is so hopeless about escaping that he waits in his room for the gunmen to get him) by a pair of professional killers who wear heavy overcoats and act as if they had been fed rivets for baby food, flashbacks then show Swede to have lived an exciting life, but one of practically continuous misfortune. In his last prize fight he catches punches that seem like mule kicks, and smashes his hand beyond repair. After that he falls for an icy gun-moll (Ava Gardner), takes a three-year rap to cover up her robbery of an ugly costume jewel, joins a gang that is planning a hat-factory holdup to be near his sweetheart, is double-crossed out of his share of the loot and then murdered.

While there are more tinny notes in this Universal production than in theatre swing bands, Swede is a fascinating, unstereotyped movie tough. He has a dreamy, peaceful, introspective air that dissociates him from everything earthly. This detachment, which gives one the feeling that he's as little concerned with the morals of people as he is with the people themselves, makes him seem capable of any brutality. Lancaster, a hefty actor from the Broadway stage, does an excellent, quiet job that turns Swede into a singularly provocative character. With an almost too polished skill and without losing the basic detachment of the part, he changes Swede's manner to blend with every change of occupation. As a pug he is slow-minded; as an affluent numbers racketeer he is hale, hearty and Broadwayish; as a grease monkey he is something else again.

The underworld people in "The Killers" seem to have been riding subways, scheming, going to prize fights from infancy. The most powerful gangster is "Dum-Dum" (Jack Lambert), who reminds you of Dick Tracy characters (he is four stories high and all muscle, dog-faced, uses a long ciga-rette holder, and it appears inconceivable that the investigator could hold him off with a small revolver, as he does in one scene). This is a surprising film for perfectly cast Scandinavian types. Besides "Dum-Dum," there are a very for-eign maid (Queenie Smith) in an Atlantic City rooming house, Swede's first sweetheart (Gabrielle Windsor) and Swede himself.

Though there is a cheapness about "The Killers" that reminds you of five-and-ten jewelry, its scenes of sadism and menacing action have been formed and filled with a vitality all too rare in current movies. It is a production that is suspense-ridden and exciting down to tiny details in the background. The stolid documentary style; the gaudy melodramatic flavor; the artiness (most noticeable in the way scenes are sculpted in dark and light) are largely due to Director Robert Siodmak, who has made German movies as well as Universal thrillers.

September 30, 1946

Middle-Aged Fling

THE most poignant movie in recent months is a bleak, inactive item called "Brief Encounter," which deals sensitively and decorously with the extra-marital transgression of two solidly married people. This Noel Coward pro-duction could have become soap opera at its worst; instead it is a faithful record of an aborted infidelity occurring between two extremely proper persons. It deals, as few films do, with limp, orderly, repressed, unexciting middle-class people, and carries them through the most exciting event of their lives in a limp, orderly, repressed, unexciting way, the only way of which they would be capable. It is highly unorthodox for movies to handle colorless people and almost unheard of to leave their lives ungilded, yet it is this very naturalism that makes "Brief Encounter" a haunting work.

The lovers in this quiet film are a housewife (Celia Johnson), who has a twitchy manner and a starved face, and a doctor (Trevor Howard), who com-mute on Thursdays to a gray place called Milford Junction. One day on the Milford platform (the producers show a knowledge of railroad stations and the way people act in them that should please the most discerning railroad eye), the housewife gets in the way of a cinder, and the practitioner, in friendly commuter spirit, neatly flicks it out from under her right eyelid. During the next five Thursdays, they entertain each other with canoeing, drives in the country, movies, all of it filmed in a dull way and made as uninteresting as waiting for a street car. Then, because of the shame involved in carrying on an illicit love and because of not wanting to hurt the people involved in their marriages, they decide never to see each other again. In the tradition of the soap opera, he takes a job near the South Pole, and she, from heartbreak but very unrealistically in terms of the personality this movie would convey, comes within an ace of throwing herself under a fast express.

Each of these tepidly warm, melancholy, woodenish lovers is portrayed with unusual insight. The woman, who is not only very proper but a nervous, flighty person, moves through the affair reluctantly, allowing herself to show love in only a few instances, usually when she is away from the doctor. He, on the other hand, is less moral and acts like a very dignified wolf managing a decorous fling. The love affair and marriages of Laura and Alec possibly are made to seem a little too dreary, too much like oatmeal, giving you the feeling that the producers are overly pessimistic on the subject of middle-class love.

This Noel Coward production centers on Laura's actions and morality— the affair is seen mostly through her eyes—and it gets inside of her intuitively. The whole movie takes on the quality of sensitive, dignified femininity. The film sometimes suggests women's magazine fiction, but Celia Johnson's performance, in which she uses a clammy hairdo, little makeup, looks overworked, somewhat undone and all-a-twitter, takes it way out of the *Ladies Home Journal* class. You only get snatches here and there of a sensitive, highly intelligent, aristocratic actress rather than a genuine housewife. She is excellent most of the time, whether appearing airy and energetic in the manner of a wife on her day off, or looking sick and shrunken after her last meeting with Alec, or ruminating happily in a daycoach in a somewhat sheepish, self-conscious way. She has a wonderful, graceful, strong walk.

While Coward's production is sensitive, it is somewhat barren, sketchy, and tends to run to the spareness of current restaurant menus. These defects are not present in the station scenes—where the lovers rush to meet trains, look for each other, walk thoughtfully up and down the platform, give their tickets to a gateman who has seen them a thousand times and yet doesn't recognize them—every detail being accurate, richly defined and extremely exciting.

While the lovers are portrayed naturalistically, secondary characters are drawn unpleasantly with banal, snobbish touches. The refined ostrich (Joyce Carey) who runs the sooty lunchroom shows the pleasure she got from a date in a funny way, but she seems as stereotyped and grotesque as a five-tier wedding cake. The wife's husband, who looks as if he has a passion for all-day lollypops, seems toylike.

October 21, 1946

Maya Deren's Films

THE silent films created by Maya Deren, a young Greenwich Village purist who has the ambition, belief in her own genius, love for esthetic verbalizing, ginger and push of a whole colony of artists, have had numerous screenings at colleges and before art groups in New York, and are scheduled for showings on October 28 and 29 at the Provincetown Playhouse in the Village. Her movies, which she once called "Abandoned Films" and now calls "Films in the Classicist Tradition," are Freudian-toned, lesbianish, freezing, arty, eclectic, conventional and safe. Utilizing real environments and people, they show people who look mesmerized or often ghostly moving through situations that have been contrived to have some Freudian meaning. You are always conscious of a mechanical-mindedness because of the pretense and self-consciousness of the acting, the labored arrangement of objects and people, and Miss Deren's fascination for trick effects with acting, composing and camera. The bleakness of these brief films comes out in the hard, stolid treatment of subject matter. Whether she is filming a perfect stretch of Long Island beach or a mugging esthete, her touch is totally lacking in sensuousness, humor and love, and she seems to petrify the subject until it takes on the character of a museum piece. The lack of sparkle is largely due to a dead eye for photography—she has no feeling for light and dark and is as unable to spot a cliché as a Tin Pan Alley hack.

The program of films at the Provincetown includes "Meshes of the Afternoon," which takes place on a lazy California day in a stucco bungalow and deals with the dreams and objective actions of a stubby girl (Miss Deren) in black slacks, who ends up dead, covered with seaweed, blood and broken glass from the upstairs window. This film, cluttered with corny, amateurishly arranged symbols and mainly concerned with sex, hops too confusingly from reality to dream. The others are "At Land," "A Study in Choreography for Camera" (a lyrical three-minute dance film which might have been a knockout with a more talented masculine dancer), and "Ritual in Transfigured Time."

"At Land," which is fairly typical of the substance of her movies, starts at a lonely postcard-pretty beach where the waves operate in reverse and leave in their receding wash a dead girl in a sarong (Miss Deren)—all of which may be meant to symbolize a birth fantasy. After the inevitable shot of gliding sea gulls, the girl wakens, climbs a miraculously suspended column of beachwood with a South Sea islander's skill and on her face a look of innocence and expectancy, as if she were seeing the world for the first time. Her climbing takes her up to the edge of a long, narrow table in a dismal banquet room (Miss Deren's photography always goes sour on night scenes, where everything becomes too dark and too cold). The girl surveys the banquet table esthetes like a corny Indian, and then starts crawling turtlewise down the stark-white covered table. When she reaches the host, who is working on a chess game, the people leave coldly, suddenly, looking as if they hadn't eaten; the queen falls off the chess board and she follows it down a precipitous slope. There is more to this movie along a similar vein.

This opening stretch of "At Land," shot at Amagansett, Long Island, and at the Great Northern Hotel in New York, gives an indication of how trite and funereal these movies are. The first scene of a clear day at the beach, of breakers washing over a corpse, is such a cliché you feel that you're seeing it for the hundredth time, and when the girl stares up the stand of beechwood you are reminded of arty beach photographs and annoyed by the pansyish composing and lighting. Miss Deren's movements seem unnecessarily mannered and stiff. Her performance in general reminds you of tough leather. With thousands of people from the Fifty-seventh Street art world simulating gayety at a banquet table and Miss Deren crawling the length of the table as though she were paying off an election bet, it is hard to believe that there is not one exciting detail in the whole episode. Instead, there is a seedy, dreary air about the affair because of the barren hall, the bleak lighting and the fact that the guests seem so uncomfortable and unhappy.

October 28, 1946

"The Well-Digger's Daughter"

THE latest attempt on the part of jaded Paris sophisticates to glorify the life and values of people in the sticks is Marcel Pagnol's slow-motion rural opus called "The Well-Digger's Daughter." This movie's ancient story opens with a budlike blonde (Josette Day) clumping across a Renoiresque landscape, bringing her father (the late Raimu) his lunch. Though it is the most vacant sort of landscape, she bumps, as you expect, into her future lover (Georges Grey), standing like an ad for Jantzen bathing trunks in a stream that looks about one inch deep. Inevitable as this scene is, it is surprising to see such an expanse of nakedness, and a tall, plumpish mama's boy, with the smile of a baby kitten, presented as the hero. He rapes her almost before she has inured herself to the pomade he uses on his hair, and then is unexpectedly called to the front. When the girl tells her father she is pregnant, they go to Greasy Hair's wealthy parents to arrange the marriage; they are cast out; the father sends the girl away— and Hollywood never provided a patter ending. The movie is not only sophisticated comedy, but the profession of a faith in the peasant life of outdoor work, fierce self-respect and family love as the most profound way of living.

At least half of this suave job might have been done about twenty-five years ago; for the most part you feel that Pagnol could have done it with his eyes shut: there is a scene with an exploding, swaying 1910 jalopy which jolts down the road with groups of peasants standing around gaping the way people did in Mack Sennett comedies. Half the characters, including the well-digger and his burro-faced helper (Fernandel), are deep-dyed stereotypes; one curious aspect is that Raimu seems miscast and only half involved in his performance. The keyed-up, dynamic, cynical worldly nature he presents would go better in a movie like "The Wolf of Wall Street." Still, the strength of the movie is largely due to Raimu, even though you feel that he is going through it automatically.

There are a few episodes that are surprisingly direct, candid and entirely new. There is a magical scene that combines the qualities of real naturalism and the poise and style of a Seurat landscape. It concerns a message the hero's mother is supposed to deliver to the girl but decides not to at the last minute. Part of its beauty has to do with the setting—a cool country road, the classic movements of the people—and part of it with the fact of how definitely the director gets across each woman's preoccupation with her own emotion. Almost as good is the candid aftermath of the rape scene, and then the girl's sad confession of despairing degradation and her premonitions of love.

The movie seems too obviously contrived to fit the virtuosity of certain ace French players. The two whose acting is least mannered are Charpin and Line Noro, who play the boy's parents, and these are some exciting secondary characters: the talkative, Boweryish waiter and the vase-like aunt. The photography and settings are a kind that are now second nature to Pagnol—gauzy, sun-drenched scenes, like Degas pastels, of people laundering, walking through the fields and handling babies.

November 4, 1946

Very Sweet Sixteen

THE most glamorous current film subject—high-school life in the days of the Charleston, pencil-shaped female torsos, vo-do-de-oh-do and decrepit college dress—is found in "Margie," a gentle, molasses-toned bit of Americana on the order of "Meet Me in St. Louis" and "State Fair." The movie starts restfully in the attic of a high-school principal's dream house, with a self-possessed young matron, Margie (Jeanne Crain, having more trouble looking thirtyish than she does looking sixteen in the flashback), and her bobby-sox daughter going over photographs of the mother's high-school days. As she describes, with a grown-up's boredom, Rudy Vallee, flagpole sitters and goldfish eaters, the movie flashes back to wintry scenes at Central High in 1928 when Margie was a wispy, oppressed romantic, an elevated type who would like to be either a jazz baby or the Lady of Shalott. Margie carries on like an ethereal mouse, envying her hot-cha pal, Marybelle (Barbara Lawrence), who is on a merry-go-round of necking and Charlestoning with a raccoon coat named Johnnikins (Conrad Janis). The person who answers Margie's romantic yearnings is the new French teacher (Glenn Langan—a Nelson Eddy type with all its limitations), a man who studied in Paris. After some soul-torturing incidents with this Mr. Fontayne, involving the broken elastic of Margie's bloomers which causes them to fall down when she gets excited, and also an unfulfilled fantasy that he is going to take her to the senior prom, the movie ends at the prom with Margie making a hit with both Mr. Fontayne and Johnnikins.

While the treatment is sentimental, sophisticated, New Yorkerish and has a cheapened Fitzgeraldian sparkle, it is delicate and sympathetic on the subject of Margie's shy, tortured adolescence and is almost shrewd about the rest of the characters. The direction (Henry King) is sensitive to young girlisms; it tries in a candid and erotic way to express Margie's girlish sensuality by deliberate, youthfully idealized photography of her romantic posturings; her decorous walk is an effective caricature of the ladylike walk of a girl who has been raised too idealistically, and she is constantly wriggling as though her clothes hampered her. The most subtle aspect of the film is the way the romantic quality of both the period and the girl is washed over the screen, particularly in scenes—an ice-skating party, the prom waltz, fantasy-laden moments in her room—where Margie's melting, Victorian dream world seems to transform the people around her.

"Margie" abounds in traditional characters who are made to seem much more significant than usual by shrewdness of writing or acting. The flylike father (Hobart Cavanaugh) is made less mechanical by an emphasis on his passionate reserve and gentility and also by Cavanaugh's ability to make you feel that more is going on inside him than you have been led to expect from this type in the past. Johnnikins is supposed to be the perennial collegiate from *College Humor*, *Judge*, John Held Jr. drawings and Harold Teen, with his pork-pie hat, dirty cords and arrogant slouch, but the performance by Conrad Janis brings him closer to a sort of jiving, energetic lounge lizard with a touch of earnestness and warmth.

The movie is so superficially placed in its Charleston era that if you like the period you'll wait for the copies which Warners and MGM will undoubtedly bring out.

November 11, 1946

Twisted Terry

DEALING with those two side-show delights—murder and mental quirks and jerks—that Hollywood authors imply are as wedded as the Gold Dust Twins, a brisk thriller called "The Dark Mirror" is clinically alert to the differences between a normal and a twisted twin (Olivia de Havilland playing a double-header). It opens on a familiar scene—a plushy suite, a mirror busted, the curtains billowing, some champagne cooling, a clock showing a time to remember, and the boss sprawled on an ankle-deep rug with a theatrical dagger in his back. Operating at a terrific clip, a flat-foot lieutenant (Thomas Mitchell) finds the murderess is one of identical twins, neither of whom will talk against the other. The sisters are weighted with jewelry spelling out their names, but they are clearly distinguishable without the credits on their chests—Terry is sleek, dynamic, always figuring the angles as though she had grown up on the floor of the Stock Exchange; Ruth is Olivia de Havilland. After the coppers flunk the case, an expensively hatted pencil, a twin expert (Lew Ayres), solves the case by throwing a battery of psychology tests at the unaccountably permissive girls.

"The Dark Mirror," in an unsentimental, unpretentious way, is a carefully penetrating portrayal of the paranoid twin, her dominated, subdued, non-psychotic sister, and the psychology prof who projects so effectively an all-knowing air carefully held in restraint. Through most of the film, the paranoid doesn't seem psychotic, and is clearly recognizable as an imperious, restless, unfeminine careerist who appears put together like a jet plane and seems constantly involved in a battle of wits with a threatening world. While the

oppressed sister carries her heart on her sleeve, Terry's affection is always min-
gled with hostility, her conscience is stunted, she's grandiose, and seemingly
content in her isolation. There is an additional interesting projection of the
characters of the three people in their kissing. They are all sort of stodgy and
respectable, but there are wonderfully subtle differences. The Man in the
Adam Hat busses with a custom-built precision and tons of dignity, Terry
challengingly and with little if any effect, and with Ruth each kiss is a new
revelation.

The crisis takes place during the scientific screening of the ink-blot test.
You are prepared so thoroughly by the prof about the blots, and given such a
clear shot of them, that you can have a go at them yourself if you're feeling a
little nervous and rundown. Focusing the movie around these tests makes the
film's scope somewhat restricted and not quite enough for a feature-length job.

While the acting is adroit and more than adequate, the only endearing
performance—the one ray of warmth—is Mitchell's enthusiastic job as the
lieutenant, which is a welcome note in the otherwise rather antiseptic atmosphere. It's heartwarming to find such benevolence, dignity and contemplative
intelligence on the force. Mitchell also employs a sly wit to good advantage.

November 18, 1946

Paranoia Unlimited

In answer to the demand for movies that make you suspect psychopathologi-
cal goings-on in everyone from friend to family dog (yesterday's heroes killed
Indians, today's are associated one way or another with psychiatry), MGM has
reissued a pokey oldie called "Rage in Heaven." This relic starts at a lonely
asylum with a comic-opera escape by an unidentified inmate (Robert Montgomery) who is known to be paranoid only by the asylum doctor (Oscar
Homolka, who gives an embarrassing rendition of a Katzenjammer psychiatrist). The inmate is a prince of a fellow, bursting with paranoid symptoms that
for a remarkable period of time escape detection by his admiring public—he
spies from trees, is afraid of the moon, assumes the name of his best friend
(George Sanders), is suspicious of everybody. As can happen only in Hollywood, after spying on her from a tree and exchanging a few unromantic words,
he becomes married to lovely, dewy, innocent Ingrid Bergman, and is well on
his way to ruining her glowing and enchanted existence and his family's prosperous steel empire. He destroys even Miss Bergman's brand of worshipful

love by his attempts to involve her in a love affair with his best friend. His last act is to arrange his suicide so that it will look as if his friend had stabbed him.

I can't remember any Hollywood effort that pounded so relentlessly on the fact of the hero's insanity. Montgomery makes Philip a fascinating figure as a detached, woodenish, uncertain person whose movements lack conviction because in the same moment he seems both a scared boy and an arrogant person who thinks himself omnipotent. This is brought out beautifully in the one exciting episode, in which some ferocious steel workers crash their employer's office to get at Philip. Philip, afraid of appearing a coward, makes some imperious, tentative, puppetlike moves to control the men and then, in an equally wooden, boyish way loses his nerve and flees. The scene, paced slowly and jerkily, manages to achieve a remarkable projection of fear and the tortured working of a sick mind.

"Rage in Heaven" is crammed with excellent players. Miss Bergman is completely unaffected—charming in her wifely concern as she proudly watches Philip officiate at a director's meeting—without any of the polish and over-ambitious acting of her work in "Notorious" and "Spellbound." With sparkling loveliness, she projects so pure an air of enchanted, yearning innocence that she seems out of place in this picture among so many artful old hands. Lucile Watson, as Philip's adoring, over-protective mother, is brusque and very effective. She is particularly convincing after the suicide, when she seems smaller, shrunken, ravaged and almost hallucinated.

The production is one of MGM's stock-in-trade grandiose jobs. Philip's office at the foundry, appearing rather stunted in the movie, couldn't house more than eight or nine trains.

November 25, 1946

Nervous from the Service

For an extremely sensitive and poignant study of life like your own, carrying constantly threatening overtones during this early stage of postwar readjustment, it would be worth your while to see "The Best Years of Our Lives," even at the present inflated postwar prices.

The sparkling travelogue opening shows three jittery veterans flying home to up-and-at-'em Boone City, a flourishing elm-covered metropolis patterned after Cincinnati. They are too uneasy about entering their homes as strangers to eat up the scenery. The chesty, down-to-earth sailor (Harold Russell), whose lack of sophistication and affectation furnishes a striking contrast to his two chums, is hypersensitive about his artificial hands and is afraid that his girl (Cathy O'Donnell) will marry him out of pity rather than love; the sergeant (Fredric March), whose superiority rests in his being old and experienced, a survivor of the infantry and before that a successful banker and father, feels he has changed too much for his old job and his family; the bombardier (Dana Andrews), who has about him that most-likely-to-succeed look of the Air Forces, got married on the run during training and hardly knows what to anticipate.

After they get through their first night home by painting the town cadmium red, they start civilian life like balky, truculent steers. Their new lives are awfully rocky, particularly the airman's, but after two and a half hours of difficulty that often seems as authentic as a Brady photograph, the air clears considerably. The sailor realizes what you know from the first moment she appeared on the screen: that Cathy with the Sad Eyes worships him; and the bombardier lands a job symbolic of this transition period—turning B-17's into prefabricated houses—and is freed by divorce to marry Teresa Wright.

While the movie bites off more than it can chew (it never has sufficient nerve to hit hardheaded business or toadying clerks as well as it would like to), it is far and away the least sentimental, most human, of current films. The love affair between the married airman and the banker's daughter is handled with rare candor, their every action seeming to arise out of natural, human, instinctual responses that fly in the face of convention. There are wonderful domestic exchanges between these two and the girl's parents.

Fredric March does a superb job in mixing the rebellion and feeling for humanity that he achieved as a sergeant in the Army with the qualities of the solid citizen-banker that he was before the war—reactionary and closemouthed, conforming, respected in the community, a model for the kiddies. Every touch seems exactly right for the hard-bitten successful executive—his knifelike movements, the tight self-control, the ferocity and self-hatred of his type of alcoholic. While she seems too experienced and wise to be playing a daughter role (half the time Myrna Loy looks like her daughter rather than the other way around), Teresa Wright plays so completely from the inside and has so labile a face that some of her scenes—the one in which she quiets a soldier having a nightmare and is painfully affected by the experience—rock with emotion. Hoagy Carmichael gives an adroit soft-shoe rendering of Hoagy Carmichael being genteel, and Walter Baldwin, the father of the boy with articulated hooks for hands, is as authentic as the rest of the production.

I haven't seen a movie with better examples of American housing since

"Greed." This is one of those rare films in which a pose or a gesture stands out so significantly that you feel the cameraman (Greg Toland) has as much to do with the story as the director and writer. The work in every department is so realistic and serious that "The Best Years of Our Lives" doesn't seem at all like a Hollywood job.

December 2, 1946

Never Sharp

"The Razor's Edge" deals in an artificial way with the depressing story of some vital young Chicagoans of the twenties who lead self-centered, destructive, loveless lives while their elders either stand by and watch or work against their happiness. The opening scene, a dinner party for blue-noses in 1919, with a small 45-piece band, introduces all the central figures when they are happy, uncomplicated and looking forward to the future. Larry Darrell (Tyrone Power), a snappy country-club type, deeply distressed by his war experience, is inclined to ruminate profoundly about things like "The dead look so dead when they're dead." He yearns to bum around until he finds out some of the why and wherefore of life. His sweetheart with the clear, metallic voice (Gene Tierney) wants a mink-coated life but is willing to wait a year for him so that he can have his loaf. The parental old guard includes Templeton, a supercilious fancy-pants (Clifton Webb)—a contrasting character to the hero— and Somerset Maugham (played in a disintegrating fashion by Herbert Marshall).

Larry forsakes their upper-crust life to search for a religious faith. He spends the first year in France, mixing with the hoi polloi in his particularly annoying way, looking smug, vacant, never saying anything and seeming rather a bore and a fake in his role as philosophic commoner. When Isabel turns down his offer of marriage, he takes it in his usual carefree, wooden way and goes off to India. There, miraculously, without disturbing Hollywood, he finds God among some artificial-looking mountains and religious folk. Now sufficiently wise and good to cure anything from migraine to dipsomania, and looking like the newest thing in religious leaders—neat, unmarked and well kept as a putting green—he buries himself in the masses to do good deeds and learn even more about life.

The movie, filled with bachelors, widows, loveless and tragically broken-up marriages, is also full of depressing people who are palmed off as good-hearted, generous, wise and constructive. You constantly feel Larry is a man to be pitied rather than a human being who has a corner on virtue. Though he is supposed to be completely gone on exotic, bony Isabel, he doesn't do a thing about it, and his bland forsaking of her to search for wisdom makes him seem extraordinarily self-centered. His search has more the quality of a sickly escape from all problems and human relationships than a pursuit of religious faith, but there is no sign that the director ever considered it that way. The movie actually seems like a vote for people such as Darrell, the snobbish, spinsterish Templeton and the stuffy author who stands aloof from life in a superior, tight-lipped way.

The boyishness, detachment and vacancy projected by Tyrone Power as Larry Darrell seem apt enough for this part. Despite these seemingly unintentional authentic notes and the fact that he moves in a brisk, stylish way, he never plays the role from the inside and he acts with all the earmarks of a drama-school student. Anne Baxter is very moving and strange as a memory-ridden, heartbroken, blousy whore, and Clifton Webb, in a deathbed scene that drips virtuosity, is responsible for one of the outstanding moments of the year. "The Razor's Edge" was directed by Edmund Goulding in a careful, stagey, $4-million style which somehow becomes more like pantomime than real life. The precise, slow, rhythmical movements are often very interesting.

December 9, 1946

Portrait of the Artist

A RECENT French release called "Paris Frills" deals with a new topic for the movies—dress designing for the 16-cylinder-automobile class—and does an intimate, human portrait of an artist, Philippe, the second-best couturier in Paris (Raymond Rouleau). This full-bodied portrayal of a bouncing, effeminate, highly skillful woman's darling, who is constantly breaking out in a rash of abused sensitivity, is the first case in my memory where an artist's life is treated with as much savvy as has been given on occasion to other professions. The movie is another good job by Jacques Becker, whose films are a freakish mixture of unpretentious naturalism and Hollywood's slick glamorizing.

The story opens on a moment of distress in Philippe's dress mill—the seamstresses, who take as much pride as Philippe in his work, think his new designs are turkeys and he is screeching over the texture of some material. The fiancée (Micheline Presle) of a yard-goods tycoon bowls Philippe over with her beauty and he redesigns his collection to go with her personality and figure. His love affair with this girl goes somewhat too quickly over a course that is as full of sudden, shattering break-ups and reunions as a Winchell column; but it is reasonably convincing because the lovers are handled in the honest way of the best French films. The artist, who seems to catch fire only when he has to win the girl from another man, and then is able to get along without her, is driven to a dramatic, if inconsistent, suicide when she rejects him.

This is the only movie I have ever seen in which a posturing, narcissistic personality is shown in the full run of everyday situations and is handled with a matter-of-fact understanding that makes it into a sad, creative, extremely curious and complicated character. This hero's actions in the love affair for once seem to jibe with the complex person that he is. You get a strong impression of the man's incapability of being seriously in love, and one of the most revealing touches is his bouncy, carefree walk just after he has devastated his sweetheart by rejecting her—this after ardently pursuing her through three reels and finally winning her. Rouleau's performance as Philippe is good on most counts. He gives the sense of a person whose nerve endings, by some anatomical quirk, have been exposed to the elements, and at the same time he makes you feel he's truly an artist at his work. The one bad feature of the performance, which he shares with Micheline Presle, is a certain manikin-like facial immobility.

With the efficiency of a good documentary but in a charming, casual, offhand manner, Becker acquaints you with the complicated, caste-ridden business of dress designing. He succeeds well enough to make you feel rewarded in the careful examination of such minor details as the lacquered, spindly chairs that are used at the opening and the tricky, two-way entrance made by the manikins. The nicest group of people I have seen in current movies are the friendly, loyal, unaffected seamstresses whose characters are so different from the dresses they make. Just as well cast is Philippe's partner (Gabrielle Dorziat), a sullen, dignified woman so wrapped up in her loyalty to the business that she seems to be cut off from the people around her.

John Ford's slow-poke cowboy epic, "My Darling Clementine," is a dazzling example of how to ruin some wonderful Western history with pompous movie making. Made almost unrecognizable by this super-schmaltzing by 20th Century Fox, this is an account of how Wyatt Earp (Henry Fonda) and his brothers rode herd on the badmen in Tombstone. Given almost equal billing with the Earps in this version of old Tombstone are cloudscapes which are as saccharine as postcard art. Typical of director Ford's unimaginative, conforming tourist sensibility is the setting he uses—dead, flat country with Picassoesque rock formations jutting dramatically here and there—that has happened in Westerns ever since Art Acord was a baby. "Clementine" is in the new tradition of cowboy films: instead of hell-for-leather action there is concentration on civic-mindedness, gags, folk art. This one goes in for slow, heavy, character-defining shots. There are entertaining, vital performances by Fonda, as the courtly, slow-motion, dead-pan marshal, and by Victor Mature as a tuberculous killer. Secondary roles are filled by good players that you don't see very often—Tim Holt, Grant Withers and Ben Hall.

December 16, 1946

Dixie Corn

THE honey-sweet Dixie presented in Walt Disney's first live-action drama, "Song of the South," shows plantation life as a paradise for lucky slaves. Hattie McDaniel, who will continue to radiate sunshine and warmth until Hollywood gets it from the atom bomb, sings and chuckles over her deep apple pies; old Uncle Remus, looking not a year over 210, sings and chuckles as bluebirds and butterflies frisk through his chicken-feather whiskers; lucky cotton-pickers, straggling home after a carefree 23 hours in the fields, sing and chuckle as the sunset drips gold all over them; the plantation owner pokes Uncle Remus in the ribs as they pass the time all day up to their ears in willows and colonial housing. Despite this hopped-up image of plantation life, "Song of the South" is still the first movie in years in which colored and white mingle throughout, and where both are handled with equal care and attention.

"Song of the South" takes place on a plantation near Atlanta which is—wonder of wonders in this age of movie plenty—smallish and run-down. The hero, Johnnie, is a cute little white boy (Bobby Driscoll) whose father can't spend as much time at home as the little tike demands. Uncle Remus (James Baskett) cheers Johnnie up with tales about Br'er Rabbit until the unpleasant, touchy mother (Ruth Warrick) breaks up the combination. As Remus leaves for Atlanta with Johnnie matching him stride for stride, the plantation bull snags the boy, bringing Remus shuffling back.

In the best scenes Disney gives a vivid sense of child life on a plantation—unlimited space, dirt roads and grassy hangouts that are breath-taking and unfortunately long forgotten; kids moving with the effortless, coördinated manner of children. But even here there is the annoying Disney ickiness—the colored boy grins too much, the Easter-egg color sugars the otherwise genuine sets; the Dead End Kids of the plantation are hardly a step removed from the sweetness of choir boys.

As Uncle Remus, James Baskett is so skillful in registering contentment that even the people who believe in the virtues of slavery are going to be impressed and want to know his secret. He's just as slick at his story telling. The three cartoons which are used when Remus tells his stories aren't top-drawer Disney, but as much as anything else make the movie worth seeing. Br'er Fox is a beautiful example of cartooning genius—a fox with a strongly drawn, original personality, a modish skinniness and the breathless loquaciousness of a Holy Roller. The rabbit is a watered-down Bugs Bunny and funny in the same way.

The latest Hollywood effort to wrestle with diseased minds and their Fu Manchu machinations, a two-hour waste of high-priced Hollywood talent— "Undercurrent"—shows you and a feverish, cultured, somewhat slap-happy chemist (Katharine Hepburn) that life can be horrendous under its placid surface. This is first revealed to the chemist the day after she weds a chromium-plated, ambition-rid industrialist (Robert Taylor) who lets her show up at a Washington cocktail party in an old rag of an $80 dress. The day after this shattering, unbearably humiliating experience, she learns what a twist-brain it was who thought up such an outrage—her seemingly perfect husband with the unruffled exterior is obsessed with a maniacal hatred of his brother (Robert Mitchum), whose whereabouts has been unknown for five years. This destructive hatred arises out of the garden variety of sibling rivalry—everybody goes for the selfless, gentle, artistic brother, while even the dogs growl when Taylor enters the room.

Because there pop up some creepy characters who have in common a hatred for her husband, the wife suspects husband killed brother and snoops to substantiate the fact. This enrages husband, who becomes twice as enraged, and well he should be, when the wife falls in love with the brother whom she has never seen. A funny thing happens during the terror-ridden ending which tends to alleviate the horror somewhat. Katharine Hepburn, so ravaged by fear, opens her mouth but remains speechless. This you may want to see.

December 23, 1946

Stranglers and Toreadors

A RARE type of big-theatre movie is the cheerless British film, "Wanted for Murder," made on a shoestring by Marcel Hellman and using a great deal of unposed action in London streets, parks and at a fairground. The film doesn't come off too well—its portrait of a compulsive strangler is thin, and the adaptation from an English play has many static, stereotyped moments—but it has an interesting, home-made newsreelish look that few movies have today. The players move curiously at a quicker, more hectic pace than those in studio films; when a Hyde Park crowd surges against a police line or the villain crosses a street, they seem to hurl forward dangerously in dramatic movement. Shot without artificial lighting, the architecture looks cold, bleak, forbidding, and it accentuates the smallness, forlornness and vulnerability of the people. The trickiest item in a low-cost production is the sound recording, and in this respect "Wanted for Murder" slips up. It is another of those rattling movies in which a weak old mother opens her mouth and lets go a blast that reminds you of a subway train.

Hollywood is queasy about showing any but the most ghoulish gangster as an out-and-out killer, and often makes dangerous criminals softer than they should ever be. There is much less romanticizing of this film's gentleman-strangler. He is a beefy businessman (Eric Portman) who pretends to befriend pretty working girls and then strangles them in lonely spots in the park. As this worried, introverted, somewhat childish businessman eyes a toothsome girl near a Punch and Judy stand, you get a strong impression of morbid, fear-ridden existence. But you aren't shown enough of the maniac's grisly career picking up stray girls, puzzling them with his fancy-pants manner and then snuffing them out.

Portman is particularly effective through his bulkiness and moody, introverted silences, but he goes very blank and amateurish in the scenes that count the most. He is extraordinarily wrong with a meek Cockney girl. As the strangle fever starts possessing him, he looks like a tabloid poet wrestling with a verse about cloudy skies, and you feel his victim probably choked to death watching him mug. It is too bad that this movie, which at its best reminds you of Graham Greene's *Brighton Rock*, fails generally by being so sketchy in its portrait of the murderer.

Even moviegoers who detest Hollywood's slickness will feel that "Carmen"—an item about Spanish gypsies, played by French actors, using English titles, Italian scenery and Second Avenue hock-shop clothes—could stand some polishing. The editing is so crazy that each time some swooning Spaniard starts the climb to Carmen's second-floor love nest you can expect the next shot to show him buying bananas in the village square or having a knife fight with a hairy character named Garcia on top of Mt. Etna. The screen is generally half-covered with English titles, but even so the love affair between Carmen and Don Jose is hard to grasp.

If you like to keep warm in your neighborhood theatre these days or have to review movies for a living, you can find something good in any film, and so it is with "Carmen." It has an unusually eerie dagger fight, a long sequence on bullfighting that is very instructive except that the bull and the toreador slink past each other as though they were imitating Hollywood's idea of a Negro's walk.

The movie, essentially a cowboy film in serapes, has to do with the smooth love affair between a gypsy (Viviane Romance, who is too sophisticated and mellow for the part), and a soldier (Jean Marais). To win Carmen's love, the soldier has only to kill his commanding officer, turn traitor, take up banditry and rub out another of Carmen's lovers, the most feared of Spanish killers. As soon as he has performed these harrowing feats, she leaves him for the first and worst toreador that whistles at her. This one dies and the unhappy soldier, who seems destined to frustration, must kill her on her orders. This he does in a good smoky scene on top of Mt. Etna, while mission bells clang nearby.

"Till the Clouds Roll By" (which makes a better title for a biography of Jerome Kern than some of his other song titles like "Who" or "Bill" or "Kalua") is a strange biography that credits much of Kern's success to a Tin Pan Alley arranger named James Hessler (Van Heflin). As far as I know, this is complete fiction. The movie reproduces the several musical-comedy scenes in which Kern's songs were first sprung, and the Metro stars who do the singing generally have small voices and go in for excessive mugging to cover up that fact. The good moments turn up when Lucille Bremer sings the exciting "Who" and when Frank Sinatra performs a well phrased job on "Old Man River."

Flashback.—Despite a hackneyed script, the Italian film "Open City" seems to me the best movie released in 1946. The six I liked next best were "It Happened at the Inn," "The Best Years of Our Lives," "Henry V," "Brief Encounter," "The Killers" and "The Strange Love of Martha Ivers." Anna Magnani's performance in "Open City" as the full-blooded, vital Pina, who was so completely the middle-class Italian under the Nazi regime, is the most perfect job by an actress in years and years. Robert Montgomery in "They Were

Expendable" is excellent as the efficient, officious naval officer. Robert Le Vigan gives a poignant performance of Toncan in "It Happened at the Inn."

Best supporting performances: Renee Asherson's virginal, Dresden-doll princess in "Henry V"; Walter Baldwin in "The Best Years of Our Lives." Best directing: Roberto Rossellini ("Open City"). Best photography: Ubaldo Arata ("Open City"). Best musical score: Miklos Rozsa ("The Killers"). Best Western: "Canyon Passage." Best musical: "State Fair."

Worst Movies: "Undercurrent," "The Harvey Girls," "Pardon My Past" and "The Postman Always Rings Twice."

December 30, 1946

Mugging Main Street

Frank Capra, Hollywood's Horatio Alger, fights with more cinematic know-how and zeal than any other director to convince movie audiences that American life is exactly like the *Saturday Evening Post* covers of Norman Rockwell. "It's a Wonderful Life," the latest example of Capracorn, shows his art at a hysterical pitch. Capra's moralizing, which is driven home in films packed with absurdly over-simplified characterizations and unbearable whimsy, is presented with great talent and almost wholly through visual detail. It has never been told so frantically as in this expression of how kind, innocent and happy the "little" people are on Main Street.

The postwar Jimmy Stewart looks a shade more mellow and works much harder at his acting, but he's still stuck in "It's a Wonderful Life" with his traditional character grown flat with usage—unassuming, a bit shy, sincere as a Boy Scout, a passionate spokesman for the little people. His George Bailey is a golden-hearted small-town businessman forever thwarted by his ties to family and friends. Year after year he scrapes along in the small-town rut he hates, doing a good deed here and a better deed there, selling houses with his golden heart instead of his head.

One day Bedford Falls's meanest man (Lionel Barrymore, who in other years at this time has played Scrooge) steals money for which George is responsible, and George, faced with disgrace, works himself up into a first-class tizzy. His character changes so drastically—he becomes a whimperer, a mean drunk, suicidal—that you wonder where this side of him has been hiding. It seems reasonable to suspect that Jo Swerling, who is credited with doing additional scenes, got in an additional character too. An angel (Henry Travers) comes down, cures Jimmy by showing him the good he did in Bedford Falls, and Jimmy goes home to find his friends have given him a laundry basket full of dollar bills. Admirers of this honest, hard-working, self-sacrificing character Stewart has played since he left Princeton are going to be uneasy when they see Jimmy's face light up like a Christmas tree at getting all this free dough.

Capra is an old-time movie craftsman, the master of every trick in the bag, and in many ways he is more at home with the medium than any other Hollywood director. But all of his details give the impression of contrived effect.

To make his points he always takes an easy, simple-minded path that doesn't give much credit to the intelligence of the audience. In characterizing the grasping, hateful banker he evades criticism by admitting indirectly that he is painting this hobgoblin with absurdly black strokes, but even a child would find this excuse unpalatable. Capra's attempt to show the town as it would have been if George hadn't been born leads to another hurried, unimaginative simplification. Main Street would be lined with dance halls; its citizens would be greedy and mean; there would be a Negro barrelhouse piano player in George's favorite saloon; the people close to him would be in institutions, in the gutter, under the table, running flophouses. A regiment of good fairies couldn't have worked the wonders in Bedford Falls that George did.

The few unsentimental moments here and there are usually contributed by Stewart. One of these is a scene on a railway platform in which he gets across the pain of his frustration. The charming moments—when he is courting Donna Reed—come off because of his soft-spoken, perfectly timed delivery. The most surprising performance is that of Miss Reed, for her self-possessed dignity and intelligence. There is an army of good supporting players like Frank Albertson, who get nowhere because they have to play such impossible parts.

No one has made a Western recently as good as "The Overlanders," Harry Watt's Australian hell-for-leather movie which uses the technique of the British documentary. Watt made the exceptional "Target for Tonight" early in the war and his new Australian film is in the same informative, somewhat slick, documentary manner.

"The Overlanders" deals with an extraordinary event that took place at the time the Japs were threatening to invade Australia and Aussies in the north were scorching the earth. A small group of cattlemen, made up principally of a Gary Cooperish drover (Chips Rafferty), a baby-faced sailor who has never been on a horse before, a rancher's family and a five-by-five English aristocrat who bounces in the saddle like Humpty-Dumpty, drives 1,000 head of cattle across 1,600 miles of the most dismal wastelands and begins a string of such cattle migrations.

Even if you've been seeing cowboy movies since the days when it cost only a nickel to get into the theatre, you'll find some new thrills in this quietly realistic job. Watt is apt to get a scene too neatly packaged and prettily composed, but he avoids this in one beautifully shot sequence of drovers attempting to turn a herd from stampeding toward a bog. The players are somewhat restrained, but very earthy and real, particularly the cool, hard-riding heroine (Daphne Campbell), who manages to ride a horse well and look glamorous, too.

The following films were awarded grand prizes at the recent Cannes Film Festival. It's too bad America is seeing so few of them.

Czechoslovakia	Men Without Wings
Denmark	Red Earth
France	Pastoral Symphony
Great Britain	Brief Encounter
Italy	The Open City
India	La Ville Basse
Mexico	Maria Candelaria
Sweden	Torment
Switzerland	The Last Chance
USSR	The Turning Point
United States	The Lost Weekend

January 6, 1947

1949–1954

Fight Films

THANKS to Rocky Graziano's infamous fame, and the box-office killing of *Body and Soul*, the studios have been turning out fight films as fast as they could steal each other's material: though tightly humorless and supersaturated with worn-out morality, they remain pure fantasy in so far as capturing the pulse of the beak-busting trade is concerned. You go to this type of movie expecting to see plenty of good prize-fighting and the atmosphere that surrounds the trade. You come out on the street feeling like a sucker, having been frustrated by a jittery cameraman who is always in the wrong place, double-crossed by editing that switches you continually away from the fight, tricked by actors who couldn't fight their way out of a subway rush. These actors, with bodies attuned by years of acting to comfortable, easy, relaxed movement, foolishly try to ape a trade they may have studied for a month, instead of relying on their own imaginations to convey boxing technique. Occasionally an aggressive actor turns up, like Cagney or Mickey Rooney, who loves to act and move in his own way, which results in a style as unique and worth watching as the technique of the average pug.

The scenarios seem to have been written by a gossip columnist—they concentrate on spanking the hero for the un-Christian way he breaks training by smoking, the mean treatment he accords his friends, and, most of all, his crude, ugly approach to women. He goes with disreputable females, mistreats his mother and the girl back home waiting for him; but the fact of the matter is that he, more than any other movie hero, is swamped by a prize collection of boring, freakish women. While the gangster, cowboy, ballplayer are lauded, the boxer is never presented as anything but a bad nickel.

The romanticism of the script is quite restrained, compared to the peculiar business that goes on in the ring. Whereas real fighters actually hit each other about one-sixth of the time, the fearless "phenoms" of the cinema are hitting every second—and never anywhere but flush on the chin or in the stomach; in spite of this, the hero is usually looking around the audience for someone he knows. Hatred can propel a fighter who looks like a spent, squashed herring to heights that always surprise his opponent. There are no decisions, fights are never stopped, there are plenty of fouls, which the hero is above recognizing even when a blow tears his knee half off; it seems incredible that in-fighters, counterpunchers, "cuties" are never characterized—only one type is presented, a creaking version of the mauling club-fighter.

The two latest fight films, *Champion* and *The Set-up*, return to the movie-for-

313

movie's-sake technique of pre-1935 B films, but they are dehumanized by an effort at newsreel realism and a compulsion to grind away at a message. Attempting to describe the sadism of the ring, the directors exaggerate the savagery inherent in prize fighting, dragging in enough peripheral mayhem to scare the officers of Buchenwald. The basic quality of these scripts seems to be a pure imaginative delight in the mangling of the human body: tired fighters inhale with the frightful expression that leaves one with the feeling the air is filled with needles rather than oxygen, while, outside the arena, people are thrown from trains, smacked by canes, bricks, and blackjacks—in *The Set-up* this builds into the overwhelming impression of a nightmare. What results is a double distortion—the effect of oversmearing brutality and the lust for ultrarealism—which strangles the actual movement. The action, mimicking reality, moves too fast to convey its meaning through the medium of the camera; unless realistic pace is transformed into the slower rhythm that movies can handle, it tends to jumble action. The hard, crassly clear photography of *Champion*, which aims at spotlighting reality, actually produces a metallic stage set, while the bitter moral realism which *The Set-up* aims at produces another type of overstatement which has the flavor of lurid melodrama.

Champion is hung on the weariest formula in boxing films—the success story. In the original Ring Lardner version, success is only a minor strain in a theme devoted to depicting a morosely malevolent pug; the movie reverses emphasis so that the hero (Kirk Douglas) exhibits above all things a flagrantly lucky, talented, bewitching adaptation of Hollywood's pet ideal that all amoral, egocentric behavior possesses an endurable charm and fascination. Douglas, as a windmill of activity on the screen, portrays a hard, quartzlike, malevolent show-off, yet maintains a smooth inner serenity. The movie's voltage is chiefly a tinny, quick wit displayed through the virtuosity of Douglas's performance and the director's strained vague realism. In an unbearably moving death scene, in which the hero throws himself over the moon of emotion, and the camera spills an oatmealish atmosphere around him, the style is a cross between Hawks and Euripides, and the visual details are magnificent. Except for this cinematic episode, *Champion* pivots on a vaudevilleish technique, which consists of strategizing scenes to the last detail before the actors go before the camera, thus saving the time and money that go into excessive reshooting. They rely on the self-sufficiency of their characters for movement rather than on expensive movement from locale to locale. Actors appear, as in no other film, loaded with material and perfectly trained. The result is a new esthetic in which every effect is the $64 one, perfectly executed and dehumanized.

The Set-up—its fighters aren't champions but the derelicts, beginners, old men who fight four-rounders in arenas that have more trash on the floor than seats—is a rhetorical Robert Wise film, overstating the malice in ordinary people (repeated near close-ups of a blind fight fan yelling "go for his eyes"), but often good in the intermediate nonbrutal scenes in a penny arcade and a cheap hotel room. Alan Baxter is good in a bad all-black fight-fixing role; whatever strength comes second-hand from the unity of a 1920's poem on which the film is based; but Wise's direction (not nearly as quietly authenticated as his *Curse of the Cat People* and *Body Snatcher* for Lewton) schizophrenically moves from hyperbole to its opposite, from the tabloid geekery of the arena crowd to a standout shot of a soured ring wife throwing her torn-up ticket off a bewitching bridge into the smoke of a passing train. The movie's honesty comes from the ruminating, suspicious performance of Robert Ryan, a prelim fighter one punch away from punch-drunk, and the same distanced performance of his wife, Audrey Totter. A lot of intelligent in-fighting acting technique seeps in around the edges of what seems a static approach: don't act, move a muscle, or smile.

May 7, 1949

Home of the Brave

IN the static atmosphere of Hollywood film production, the appearance of Screen Plays Corporation, a peppery little band of young esthetes as hard and profit-minded as Du Pont, should cause more upheaval than any incident since the Santa Barbara earthquake. Hollywood has never experienced anything as brainy and volatile as this ant-hill organization, which has managed not only to shake the foundations of the elephant studios but to leave them standing still in their own race for the fattest loot. The curious aspect of this new company is that it blends the creative artist's imagination with the Sammy Glick talent for peeling cash off of nothing. Its aim seems to be to kill two birds by turning out a five-cent *Gone with the Wind* and introducing technique and ideas that are a few levels above the IQ of the average moviegoer, according to the superstitions prevailing in the industry. But Screen Plays is not the Prince on the White Charger, for, underneath, as is seen in its new movie, *Home of the Brave*, beats the heart of a huckster, a heart that has grown its tissues in the theatrical atmosphere of middlebrow and sentimental Broadway.

The irrelevantly titled *Home of the Brave* is a war film which starts with some good shattering shots depicting the brutality and destruction of battle but suddenly changes into idle, muddy psychiatric double-talk and a tepid display of the Negro problem. A Negro GI named Moss (James Edwards) returns from a dangerous mission traumatized and half-paralyzed; in this weakened condition, he is put under the care of a noisy psychiatrist (Jeff Corey) with the face of a manic hawk and a bellicose, exasperated attitude that should complete the ruin of Moss but instead puts him on his feet in a couple of days and gives him a lot of difficult thoughts to play around with for the rest of his life. After all this psychotherapy, Moss is told he suffers from discrimination chiefly because he is too sensitive. This gets a big laugh, particularly from Negroes in the audience who doubtless think of all the jobs they didn't get because of their oversensitivity.

The script-writer (Carl Foreman) plants some bold dashes of prejudice but never grounds the movie in the street-level type of incident that would illustrate the Negro situation in all its bulging ugliness. The bite has been taken out of the problem by constructing the black GI as a thoroughly passive creature who is ceaselessly tormented by his enemy, continually soothed by friends, who plays a meek guinea pig for the psychiatrist but scarcely makes an impression on anyone else; he is so suavely mute that this pioneering movie about antiblack prejudice unreels itself oblivious of the fact that the whole film does not contain a black (Moss is actually the man who wasn't there). James Edwards plays him as a bland, unmarked, self-possessed, and graceful character, very little different from the other players, although he is supposed to have been a long-standing victim of their conscious and unconscious prejudice. The character in the original play by Arthur Laurents was a Jew, and, in making the change, the producers simply lost sight of the fact that the black has suffered from a different, more violent kind of prejudice here; Moss appears to have neither offered nor suffered any kind of violence.

Home of the Brave is infused with a sophisticated technique that turns an essentially thin and artificial script into a clattering, virile movie with deeply affecting moments. The sophistication appears everywhere: instead of seeing the Jap sniper fall, as in any other war movie, all that you see in this movie is a broccoli jungle, accompanied by a slithering sound and a mild clonk to inform you that the sniper is done for. The script is so basically theatrical that it has to be acted almost entirely from seated or reclining positions, but the director works more variations on those two positions than can be found in a Turkish bath. The actors talk as though they were trying to drill the words into one another's skulls; this savage portentousness not only forces your interest but is alarming in that the soldiers are usually surrounded by Japs and every word can obviously be heard in Tokyo. The actors are never balanced within the picture frame; often a head is half cut by the top of the screen or, for no reason, some secondary figure will walk straight through a shot, knocking out your view of the principal figures, but giving an effect of careless spontaneity to a scene that is actually no more active than the inside of a can of sardines. This energetic technique has several limitations: the repetition of close eye-level shots practically puts the actors in your lap, but, after a few reels, I would have liked a long shot of all of them on top of a mountain; the cameramen are so enamored of shadows in outdoor scenes that the actors often seem afflicted by leprosy. Dimitri Tiomkin's background music only comes on in crises, adding extra heartthrobs where the action is as swollen with emotion as a Faulkner river.

Well-played and punchy, *Home of the Brave* is not quite clever or ingenious enough to conceal its profit-minded, inept treatment of important issues.

May 21, 1949

John Huston

HOLLYWOOD's fair-haired boy, to the critics, is director John Huston; in terms of falling into the Hollywood mold, Huston is a smooth blend of iconoclast and sheep. If you look closely at his films, what appears to be a familiar story, face, grouping of actors, or tempo has, in each case, an obscure, outrageous, double-crossing unfamiliarity that is the product of an Eisenstein-lubricated brain. Huston has a personal reputation as a bad boy, a homely one (called "Double-Ugly" by friends, "monster" by enemies), who has been in every known trade, rugged or sedentary: Mexican army cavalryman, editor of the first pictorial weekly, expatriate painter, hobo, hunter, Greenwich Village actor, amateur lightweight champ of California. His films, which should be rich with this extraordinary experience, are rich with cut-and-dried homilies; expecting a mobile and desperate style, you find stasis manipulated with the surehandedness of a Raffles.

Though Huston deals with the gangster-detective-adventure thriller that the average fan knows like the palm of his hand, he is Message Mad, and mixes a savage story with puddin'-head righteousness. His characters are humorless and troubled and quite reasonably so, since Huston, like a Puritan judge, is forever calling on them to prove that they can soak up punishment, carry through harrowing tasks, withstand the ugliest taunts. Huston is a crazy man with death: he pockmarks a story with gratuitous deaths, fast deaths, and noisy ones and, in idle moments, has his characters play parlor games with gats. Though his movies are persistently concerned with grim interpersonal relationships viewed from an ethic-happy plane, half of each audience takes them for comedies. The directing underlines a single vice or virtue of each character so that his one-track actions become either boring or funny; it expands and slows figures until they are like oxen driven with a big moralistic whip.

Money—its possession, influence, manufacture, lack—is a star performer in Huston's moral fables and gilds his technique; his irony toward and preoccupation with money indicate a director who is a little bitter at being so rich—the two brief appearances Huston makes in his own films are quite appropriately as a bank teller and a rich, absent-minded American handing out gold pieces to a recurring panhandler. His movies will please a Russian audience: half the characters (Americans) are money mad, directly enriching themselves by counterfeiting, prospecting, blackmail, panhandling.

His style is so tony it should embarrass his threadbare subjects. The texture of a Panama hat is emphasized to the point where you feel Huston is trying to stamp its price tag on your retina. He creates a splendiferous effect out of the tiniest details—each hair of an eyelid—and the tunnel dug in a week by six proletarian heroes is the size of the Holland Tunnel.

Huston's technique differs on many counts from classic Hollywood practice, which, from Sennett to Wellman, has visualized stories by means of the unbroken action sequence, in which the primary image is the fluid landscape-shot where terrain and individual are blended together and the whole effect is scenic rather than portraiture. Huston's art is stage presentation, based on oral expression and static composition: the scenery is curiously deadened, and the individual has an exaggerated vitality. His characters do everything the hard way—the mastication of a gum-chewing gangster resembles the leg-motion in bicycling. In the traditional film, life is viewed from a comfortable vantage point, one that is so unobtrusive that the audience is seldom conscious of the fact that a camera had anything to do with what is shown. In Huston's, you are constantly aware of a vitaminized photographer. Huston breaks a film up into a hundred disparate midget films: a character with a pin head in one incident is megacephalic in another; the first shot of a brawl shows a modest Tampico saloon, the second expands the saloon into a skating rink.

The Huston trademark consists of two unorthodox practices—the statically designed image (objects and figures locked into various pyramid designs) and the mobile handling of close three-figured shots. The Eisenstein of the Bogart thriller, he rigidly delimits the subject matter that goes into a frame, by chiaroscuro or by grouping his figures within the square of the screen so that there is hardly room for an actor to move an arm: given a small group in close quarters, around a bar, bonfire, table, he will hang on to the event for dear life and show you peculiarities of posture, expression, and anatomy that only the actor's doctor should know. The arty, competent Huston would probably seem to an old rough-and-ready silent-film director like a boy who graduated from Oxford at the age of eight, and painted the Sistine Chapel during his lunch hours.

Aside from its typical compressions and endless padding with perspiration, mad scenes, and talking, the chief fact about the tempoless, shapeless *We Were Strangers* is that Huston doesn't know where the movie's going or how long it's going to take to get there. Played largely in interiors and demanding lightness rather than philosophic noodling, his Cuban picture is divided between two huge white figures: Jennifer Jones, who wears a constant frown as though she has just swallowed John Garfield. Garfield acts as though he's just been swallowed.

The Asphalt Jungle, directed for MGM with a surface vivacity and tricky hucksterish flash that earlier Huston doesn't have, sums up a great deal about his work and adds a freakishness that isn't far from Camp. Almost all of his traits, the strange spastic feeling for time, lunging at what he feels is the heart of a scene and letting everything else go, the idea that authority is inherent in a few and totally absent in everyone else, a ticlike need for posh and elegance, are funneled into this film, which describes the planning, organization, specialization, and cooperation surrounding a million-dollar jewel heist. At best, it is a trade-journal report of the illegal acquisition of jewels, its most absorbing stretch being the painstaking breakdown of a professional robbery, recalling the engineering details of the mine operation in *Sierra Madre* in which huge men seem nailed in front of mountains, or the tunnel-digging in the Cuban film, the tunnel ending up slightly smaller than the ones entering Grand Central Station.

Apparently influenced by French 1930's films like *Port of Shadows*, with their operatic underworld portraits getting lost in the gray trashiness of back rooms, *Asphalt Jungle* is just as inventive as Huston's other job-oriented films in its selection: a top-flight safe-cracker wears a magician's coat honeycombed with the tools of his trade—monstrous crowbar for prying open a manhole cover, three-eighth-inch mortar chisel for separating bricks, lapel-anchored cord for safely suspending the bottle of nitro (no jostling, as any student knows), extra bits for his electric drill. Few directors project so well the special Robinson Crusoe effect of man confronted by a job whose problems must be dealt with, point by point, with the combination of personal ingenuity and scientific know-how characterizing the man of action. Two exquisite cinematic moments: the safe-cracker, one hand already engaged, removing the cork from the nitro bottle with his teeth; the sharp, clean thrust of the chisel as it slices through the wooden strut.

Throughout this footage, Huston catches the mechanic's absorption with the sound and feel of the tools of his trade as they overcome steam tunnel, door locks, electric-eye burglar alarm, strongbox. It is appropriate that the robbers dramatically subordinate themselves to their instruments and the job at hand, move with the patient deadpan *éclat* of a surgical team drilled by Stroheim.

Huston unfortunately betrays the documentary invention of the robbery by clumsy stratagems for making his gangsters something more than human. Borrowing *Battleground*'s racy technique of divulging character by idiosyncratic tabs, actors are distinguished unto extinction: as in a masquerade, red, yellow, blue harlequin costumes urge contrast while withholding identity. The safe-cracker (Anthony Caruso) worries over a wife and kids; the hunchbacked driver (James Whitmore) loves cats; the mean-faced murderer (Sterling Hayden) jabbers nostalgically about the horses on his father's farm; the mastermind (Sam Jaffe) leers at young girls in the flesh or sprawled on calendars. These traits are so arbitrary and unilluminating that Huston's effort to show the Criminal as Human Being deteriorates into humorless Damon Runyon. Like Runyon's gunsels, Huston's thugs terrorize shopkeepers by night, but morning returns them to their homes, gentle-faced and clean-shaven, again to defend the dispossessed (cats, etc.) from the citizenry who terrorize by day.

The citizenry of Huston's movies, like Robin Hood's opponents, are dreary, anemic souls who fail every crisis through constitutional deficit of the courage of which every gangster worth his salt has an abundance. When the hoodlum slowly bleeds to death through the last third of the movie as he tries to reach the old farm, Huston has the attending physician say admiringly, "Anyone else would be dead after bleeding that much!" Victims of hemophilia have bled for years without comparable eulogy. It is really this laboring of the outcast's courage that raises a point which seems to turn Huston's blood to water; isn't it *fear* of the citizenry's ordinary responsibilities that provokes the criminal to crime and makes him unequal to the citizen unless he is fortified by gun and gang? By his evasion of the criminal's central cowardice, Huston is unable to countenance the possibility of every gentleman being a murderer at heart, preferring instead every murderer being a gentleman at heart.

The consequence of his evasion is an endless piling up of mawkish footnotes on how the gangster passes his time between jobs. The safe-cracker's apartment ($20,000 per caper?) is standard Italian-tenement decor: narrow hallway, beaten-up four-poster bed, harassed mother with her arms protectively outstretched toward her weeping child. With equal banality, the hunchbacked driver, Whitmore, pitifully explains his deformity, "I didn't grow this, I was born with it," belying the whole previous impression of his being an eager, cheery, indomitable assassin. Sterling Hayden begins credibly enough as an unthinking, prideful brute, meeting every remark with uncomprehending surliness, yet, twenty-four hours later, he is so intoxicated by the mastermind's charm that he is willing to forgo his fee for the unsuccessful robbery, wishes Jaffee godspeed with the wistful comment "That little squarehead, I can't figure him."

While it is Huston's talent to untype the familiar character actor by blowing up a particular physical gesture, he seems also to incapacitate actors with anticipated, summarized characters. Hayden, mostly a curled lower lip and hick sullenness, is practically stapled to what must have been a one-line comment, "stoic but sentimental farmer," in the shooting script. Jean Hagen's stylized jerkiness as a debauched gangster's moll, while eye catching for a few seconds, incapacitates her in terms of credibility for the materialism asked of her at the end of the picture, when she tends the bleeding Hayden.

With the end of the movie, Huston's faults—working against his adventurous self by telegraphing punches: 90 per cent of *We Were Strangers*, everything but the gray bit player going mad, is taken care of in written compressions—combine with MGM's postcard elegance in a scene almost unequaled in vulgarity: on the ripe green meadow of his father's farm, Hayden breathes his last, while colts gently lick his face in bucolic farewell. The ending suggests that Huston may not have the simple underworld courage to withstand MGM's glossy impositions.

June 4, 1949, and July 15, 1950

♦

THE weariest myth of critics tabs Hollywood for the formularized movies and foreign studios for the original ones; actually the worst Hollywood B has more cinematic adrenaline than most English or French movies, and no one is more eclectic than the English director Olivier, reactionary than the Frenchman Pagnol, victimized by easy sensibility than the Italians De Sica and Rossellini. The art of these prize-plastered directors washes like a waterfall over their movies so that you feel common for paying only $1.50 for your ticket to culture, they are more dispiritedly indebted to pre-1935 Hollywood technique than Sturges,

Huston, or Korda. The decadence of the French film, dominated by pooped-out aesthetes, is somewhat belied by "Devil in the Flesh," which has almost the weight and fulness of a "Madame Bovary" (more than can be said for the Radiguet novel on which it is based). This film's decadence—its novelistic approach; the smooth, velvet finish of ten-year-old MGM films, time-worn images like fire for passion, raindrops on water for sadness—does not keep it from being the best movie condemned by the Legion of Decency since "Monsieur Verdoux."

The love affair in "Devil in the Flesh"—a restless, bored young wife (Micheline Presle) bed-locked with an unstable charmer (Gérard Philipe) who doesn't yet shave—is a staple as old as the French novel but never realized so well on film. This disastrous affair moves with an inexorable logic the love film hasn't had since psychiatry took over Hollywood, the inexplicable last shot (sky breaking into V-formations of airplanes) is a minor disturbance.

Director Autant Lara creates a tapestry of unemphasized details; density and depth, currently ignored by directors in favor of the one-thread effect, are produced here by some old-fashioned ideas of what makes a beautiful movie. Trying as Griffith did for the serenely articulated image drenched in sentiment, he sinks his actor into a perfectly ordered environment emptied of discord (sunlit scenes glow without heat, rain is soft and warm, family scenes are as unhectic as a Childe Hassam canvas). The impression of profusion comes from the bountiful detailing of each shot and of the central characters; like the treatment of the Chaplin figure, these two roles are loaded with expression and gesture and seen from all sides. The attempt to imbed the story like a pearl in a period (World War I) and a milieu (suburban Paris) results in the use of some banal devices: figures are back-lit with halo-like contours, viewed obliquely behind grillwork, lace curtains, flowers; the last shot of a scene is cemented in time by a lingering camera. But the over-all effect is of being submerged in and idling through a self-contained world.

The solidity of this movie, as of current French films, is partly a gift from the past gods of art. In a Hollywood movie each event is seen for itself, without cultural overtones; events in Lara's movie are unconsciously burdened by the painting, literary, and movie tradition of the preceding century. Both in subject and treatment (boating scene, François's home) this movie recalls Seurat and Manet; the movie would not have been so laden if Proust had not created such a dense atmosphere; with decades of precedent to draw upon, directors like Pagnol, Lara, Clouzot do impeccable funerals and walks through the streets with their eyes shut and both hands behind their backs. The wry treatment of incidental people, waiters, school teachers, mothers, is an old snobbery that should have been given up before it was started. It would be nice to see a French movie free of its academic albatross.

Gérard Philipe, a new, momentous figure in European films, is an original actor, so absolutely the ill-starred creatures he plays—the glum, impudent adulterer in this, an over-sweetened but near-perfect Myshkin in the excellent "The Idiot"—that his performances are less magical for being so real. French movie actors (Raimu, Barrault) have tried for an absolute naturalism based on theatrical expression, and the spectacularly gifted Philipe is the $64 end-product of this tradition. The average player presents a threefold personality—the script character, the type he represents in the public mind, and his private-life personality. Philipe presents one whole different character in each movie, no carry-overs. His François—arrogantly sensitive, disaffected, histrionically bad-tempered, a social sneerer but indolently dependent—seems to have walked into the movie from an art-colony garret bringing no acting baggage with him. His performance is as rich a characterization as any in Tolstoi and one bound to amuse people who think of the boudoir hero in terms of physical beauty and bourgeois virtues; François lies, tricks, wilts at the tiniest obstacle, flees, and is generally a whirlwind of unsavory attitudes. Philipe seems to live on the screen rather than perform; he manages to be three-dimensionally in action so that the cubistic effect is of seeing from all sides. Compared with this fresh, realistic performance, the Boyer-Cooper-Stewart lover seems to be built out of the old nuts and bolts of romantic acting.

June 18, 1949

THE film industry has moved with a scythe and a prayer into a golden period of civic uplift, sparked by soul-savers bent on a joyless excision of every social wart—Jew-baiting, Jim Crow, philistinism in art, bookmaking, dope addiction, non-democratic administration, euthanasia. The bloodlessly earnest psychiatry movie is another sleep-making example; like a busy St. George, it hacks away at everything from destructive parenthood to Bedlam asylum conditions. Through its primer-simple, roseate presentation Hollywood has sold psychiatry to an audience which only a few years ago rated it as phony as wrestling and as dangerous to mankind as a loaded cigar butt.

The static conditions of real-life psychoanalysis—couch-pinned heroes, plot buried in the patient's subconscious, expensive free associations—are not a hot subject for an action-hungry medium. Realizing this, screen writers have

linked psychiatry to the violent story—murder, war, catastrophic insanity—
thrill-exploited everything from shock treatment to extra-sensory perception,
melodramatically juiced therapy for as much terror as possible: the hypodermic
needle is always aimed at the audience's heart. While seeming to accept the
fact of scrambled psyches and their scientific rearrangement, the movies have
concentrated only on spectacular symptoms like paralysis and on patients too
severely disturbed to fall within general experience—in the filming of a street-
common ailment like alcoholism psychiatry never shows its rehabilitating face.
Hollywood might succeed in distressing its audience if it filmed the suffering
of an everyday neurotic (a few early films like "Now, Voyager" went in that
direction); as it is, the sensational collapse-therapy-cure cycle works like a bar-
biturate. The average fan is no longer surprised when the movie Horowitz
freezes on the Polonaise, expects him to be chucked into a new and photogenic
device like the Orgone Box, awaits impassively the flashback to a fateful day
when the hero was lashed to the piano to make him practice.

Of the currently fashionable movie characters—morally inflamed cowboys,
unprincipled athletes, the Holy Ghost of a psychiatrist—the last is the most
oafishly glamorized. Even directors like Hitchcock, Robson, Huston, Litvak,
Meyers of "The Quiet One" lose their nerve when the irreproachable analyst
angel-flaps onto the screen: at these points the story looks like a paid ad for the
American Psychoanalytic Association. The movie psychiatrist—haunting the
ward at 3 am to cheer up his patients!—rates higher in the film firmament than
the Catholic priest or the FBI agent. The role of this Dr. Ingenious Bland is
played by a "square" actor like Ingrid Bergman or Leo Genn, who habitually
performs with ponderous self-consciousness and both feet on the Oscar. Only
Chekhov (a slapstick Freud in "Spellbound") and Corey (the noisy, sickle-like
doctor in "Home of the Brave") have shown any glee in the part; the others
have all been stuffed so full of heavy, dull, unparticularized virtues that they
have the constricted look of people doing a public service, like air-raid wardens. Yet compared to his real-life counterpart, the movie therapist has a
soft snatch: where he sees only a few troublesome traits that have to be
scrubbed off the patient, the real analyst knows that the analysand's everything
—posture, wife, type of tie—will have to go; the screen genius has a deadline
two days hence, while the other finds himself in the situation of Magellan still
in Portugal; Dr. I. Bland is only called on to ferret out one big childhood
trauma, but Dr. Central Park West flounders in a lifetime's dirty laundry of personal data.

The formularized psychoanalysis in current films is a product of the *Popular Science* mentality: the director goes overboard for gadgets and a drugstore

version of Freud. Mechanical procedure is the whole battle, once the patient, juiced by electricity, drug, or doctor ("Think, think, you've got to remember!") starts recalling his one trauma—straining like a man lifting the Woolworth Building—the cure follows immediately. The documentary filming of machinery—loading the hypodermic needle, identifying the ink spots, turning the knobs of the shock machine—produces the most effective scenes. Stripped of emotional difficulties and subtleties, unpredictable consequences, analyst-patient realignments, the therapy you are shown is a dull memory game. Subjective material—dreams, free association, unconscious imagery—which the shiny instruments are a means of getting at, is concretized and made immobile by these Boy-Scientists. The dreams in "Spellbound" are turned into little surrealistic maps, those in "Blind Alley" (refilmed as "The Dark Past") are just as arbitrarily represented by what looks like the linear version of a film negative. It is disconcerting that the director always credits the patient with total cinematic recall, instead of showing the blurred, spotty, personalized texture of spontaneous recollection. The psychiatry film looks like the kitchen of tomorrow, lined with labor-killing devices, in which the patient's poor addled soul is pressure-cooked into a functional, flavorless stew to fill the stomach of respectable society.

July 9, 1949

A QUIETLY dignified fame attaches to Producer Louis De Rochemont who developed his pseudo-documentary style—real life stories reduced to streamlined banality—in "March of Time" and three fact-packed movies* stuffed with sober, official hot air. The DR style is easily spotted: its sanitary realism is midway between Norman Corwin and Walker Evans, it avoids the problems of human relations and glories in objects, job-routines, and skills (how to fall on one's head without breaking it). Its Hero is an institution like the FBI, and its trademark is the dignified, know-it-all narrator whose voice drips with confidence in an America that is like a Watson Business Machine. His terrain-conscious titles spotlight De Rochemont's managerial outlook in which the postoffice, Parish House dance, time-honored remark ("Some fighting man may lose his life because of this, Miss Richmond.") are the determinants that shape, protect, and dominate Americans, lucky cogs in a golden social machine.

13 Rue Madeleine, House on 92nd Street, Boomerang!

Aiming at spontaneity, his writers dote on the actions, remarks, and facial expressions made most often by Americans; in no movies do characters spend so many serious moments and such concentrated energy on pedestrian actions like parking a car and walking to a telephone, the implication being that a commonplace culture is full, rich living. Unlike his other films, De Rochemont's latest, "Lost Boundaries," is mildly poignant, has a simple, direct honesty (Director Werker had a much smaller budget), and tells a good story dedicated to the idea that silence about being a Negro is golden if you can get away with it. Though it is over-populated by creamy people, friendly smiles, the least exciting real-life talk ("You'll have to excuse me, I'm not the ballroom type."), it has a homespun, non-Hollywood plainness unmatched in current movies, even by "The Quiet One."

It is based on the fascinating biography of New Hampshire's Dr. Albert Johnson—twenty-eight years a Negro, twenty years a white, then colored again by courtesy of the Navy—and is the second round in the movie battle with the Negro problem. The benevolent writers—working in studios where as far as I know there are no colored directors, writers, or cameramen—so far have placed their Negroes in almost unprejudiced situations, presented only one type of pleasant, well-adjusted individual, and given him a superior job in a white society. The light-skinned Negro couple (played like Mother Hen and Young Lincoln by Beatrice Pearson and Mel Ferrer) are passive, innocuous, duty-happy creatures totally unscarred by discrimination except for an anxious flutter in the mother's voice and the melancholy stare of the father who looks as though he had just remembered getting a parking ticket that morning. They are mournfully stoical, quietly dignified, and custom-built for upright citizenship; they personify as Moss did in "Home of the Brave" the current movies argument that the Negro will be accepted if he lives according to the rules of the stuffiest white gentility.

A few scenes with authentic bite—a Goya-like view of Lenox Avenue highlighting grotesque faces, ambling Dead End Kids, clusters of suspicious Negroes—are inserted to show the results of brutal segregation. Next to the sticky depiction of the folksy, respectable characters in Keene, New Hampshire, these shots tend to make the audience feel that the macabre position of the Negro is due to mysterious factors that have nothing to do with small-town America and probably stems from the fact that the Negro on his own does not know how to live. After all of these demi-tasse versions of the Negro problem are filmed, none of them will come close in cinematic power to the greatest of all films, the unfortunately anti-Negro "Birth of a Nation"; the movie progressives as yet seem frightened of authentic emotions and to lack the nerve to deal with prejudice at its primitive, ugly level.

"Lost Boundaries" is an affecting, wholesome affair held down by De Rochemont's belief that the documentary should be safe, artless, and free of variety. The photographer's head evidently comes off if he tries anything but the orthodox, group-portrait composition: central details a little above screen center, neither close to nor far from the camera. The prime concerns in composition are that there shall be no exercise of taste—either good or bad—and that every detail shall be crystal clear and easily understood. This, plus the spontaneous energy lost through reconstructed realism, leads to compositions as spineless as vanilla pudding and a non-atmospheric movie that seems to have been scrubbed with Spic 'n Span. There is a Henry Ford-like passion for traditional American architecture, all of it looking mended and polished, and the people carefully devitalized so that they don't steal the scene from the decor. One of the exceptions is a casually constructed scene between teen-aged sweethearts in a river-side setting where everything—clumsily sincere talk, troubled movement, flexible camerawork and directing—is geared beautifully to a rustic landscape and an intense, adolescent grappling with prejudice. These smooth, even-paced documentaries are a catch-all for actors from grocery stores, straw-hat circuits, and Broadway, but most of the actors behave as though they were being watched by the FBI for any outrageous display of individuality. A few scenes in which the movie comes to life occur when it deals with the doctor's daughter (Susan Douglas); Miss Douglas is busy being her intense, sober-mouse self, poignantly and credibly touched by the ramifications of discrimination. All the others—hawk-faced New Englanders and silky Negroes—act as though they were on a two-day furlough from real-life to create a poster-like portrait to show the virtues of the Democratic Man of Tomorrow.

June 30, 1949

WHILE "The Great Gatsby" is a limp translation of Fitzgerald's novel about the tasteless twenties, magical mid-Westerners on Long Island, and the champion torch-bearing hero in American literature, it captures just enough of the original to make it worth your while and rekindle admiration for a wonderful book. Its characters are like great lumps of oatmeal maneuvering at random around each other, but it tepidly catches the wistful tragedy of a jilted soldier (Alan Ladd) who climbs the highest mountains of racketeering and becomes an untalented socialite, trying to win back his Daisy (Betty Field) from a hulking snob and libertine (Barry Sullivan). Etched in old MGM-Renaissance style Fitzgerald's panorama of the twenties takes on the heavy, washed-out, inaccurate dedication-to-the-past quality of a Radio City mural. Save for an occasional shot—the rear of a Long Island estate studded with country-club architecture and bulky town cars—that shrieks of the period, the movie has little to offer of Fitzgerald's glory-struck but acrid perceptions of period, place, and East Egg society. The cottage scene, with an added touch of Booth Tark-ington, talks and moves, as little else of the movie does, with some complica-tion and emotional development.

Director Nugent's forte is the country-club set tinkling delicately against each other amidst stupified living-room furniture, but it only appears in the scenes at Daisy's and the Plaza, which have a timeless aura and show the leisure class at customary half-mast—summery weather, a glitter due to Betty Field's delight with her role, and tasteful, knee-waisted dresses. The crucial lack is that Gatsby, Daisy, the cynical Jordan, don't have enough charm to explain the story; in fact, they don't have much more than the weary hulks that are currently beached on Long Island. Owing to a tired director who, however, knows the book with uncommon shrewdness, and Fitzgerald's inspired dia-logue combined with slow, conservative movie images this peculiarly mixed movie draws the most vociferous, uneasy audience response.

It would take a Von Stroheim to cast Fitzgerald's characters, each as fabu-lous as Babe Ruth, but rendered with the fragmentary touches of a Cezanne watercolor; the cast is routine for Paramount (Ladd, Da Silva, Macdonald Carey—Frank Faylen, a studio perennial, must have been sick) and inspired only in the case of Betty Field, whose uninhibited, morbid-toned art blows a movie apart. Ladd might have solved the role of Gatsby if it had consisted, as his normal role does, of shocking, constant movement, no acting, and trench coats. An electric, gaudily graceful figure in action movies, here he has to stand still and project turbulent feeling, succeeding chiefly in giving the impression of an isinglass baby-face in the process of melting. He seems to be constantly in pain; and this, occasionally, as in the touching cottage scene, coincides with Gatsby's. As a matter of fact, he gives a pretty good impression of Gatsby's depressed, non-public moments. Barry Sullivan streamlines the aging (30) football player ("if we don't look out the white race will be—will be utterly submerged. It's all scientific stuff") into a decent, restless gentleman whose nostrils constantly seem horrified. For a dismal C Western star, Sullivan is surprisingly deft and subtle in a role that has become meaningless without the sentimentality, fears, and shockingly comic scenes with Myrtle's circle (probably dropped because they were too cinematic).

Betty Field is no more marked by Southern aristocracy than a cheese blintz, but she plays Daisy with her usual incredible daring and instinctive understanding. She hits the role (compulsive, musical voice; scared sophistication) so hard, giving Daisy a confused, ineffectual intensity, missing some of the scintillating charm, that her creation is a realistic version of the character Fitzgerald set up simply as a symbol for Gatsby to dream about. The music of the period, when it is played right, is heartbreaking, and Elisha Cook captures this nostalgia for a few minutes at Gatsby's grand piano.

Academic Broadway veteran that he is, Elliot Nugent implies in his direction that the period and terrain—so consistently primary and wondrous to Fitzgerald—are simply a backdrop. In place of the wasteland of ashes that surrounds Wilson's garage, morbidly counterpointing the story's death-ridden conclusion, there are fleeting glimpses of a humdrum dumping ground. The huge, chaotic parties are a dispiriting blur of Arthur Murray dancing, Muzak orchestrations, stock drunks with one individualized detail (the stridently sequined stage twins) in place of the dozen needed to build the atmosphere that draws New York's night life to Gatsby's door. Fitzgerald's broken story structure has been straightened so that the movie flows slowly without break through routine stage sets. In the occasional place where a contrasting shot is slashed into the "Old Man River" development, the strategy, because of its rarity, produces more excitement than the image warrants—the oculist's billboard, with the enormous spectacled eyes, steals the movie.

August 13, 1949

The Third Man

THE most depressing movie irony is that American longhairs—raised on the nonliterary naturalism of Barthelmess, Fairbanks, and movies like *The Crowd Roars*, along with the revolutionary Griffith, Sennett, Keaton—continue to coddle and encourage European directors in their burnt-out sentimentality and esthetic cowardice. Carol Reed's *The Third Man* (the short happy life of Orson Welles, who, having killed or crazed half of Vienna by black-marketing diluted penicillin, evades the police by playing dead) is one import in which the virtuosity is tied in with some (not much) of Reed's *Odd Man Out* talent, the musically sensitive ear for middle-brow talk, the fractional, almost surreptitious, revelation of character through gestures, quietness, modulated voice. Though there is an unfortunate alliance here, as in *Fallen Idol*, with Graham Greene's glib incapsulation of people, and the feeling here that Reed is deserting intelligence for a lyrical-romantic kick, the precocious use of space, perspective, types of acting (stylized, distorted, understated, emotionalized) and random, seemingly irrelevant subject matter, enlarges and deepens both the impression of a marred city and a sweet, amoral villain (Welles), who seems most like a nearly satiated baby at the breast. But it bears the usual foreign trademarks (pretentious camera, motorless design, self-conscious involvement with balloon-hawker, prostitute, porter, belly dancer, tramp) overelaborated to the point of being a monster-piece. It uses such tiresome symbol-images as a door that swings with an irritating rhythm as though it had a will of its own; a tilted camera that leaves you feeling you have seen the film from a foetal position; fiendish composing in Vuillard's spotty style, so that the screen crawls with patterns, textures, bulking shapes, a figure becoming less important than the moving ladder of shadow passing over it.

The Third Man's murky, familiar mood springs chiefly from Greene's script, which proves again that he is an uncinematic snob who has robbed the early Hitchcock of everything but his genius. Living off tension maneuvers that Hitchcock wore out, Greene crosses each event with one bothersome nonentity (a Crisco-hipped porter, schmoo-faced child) tossed in without insight, so that the script crawls with annoying bugs. While a moony, honest American (Joe Cotten) unearths facts of Welles's death, Greene is up to his old trick of showing a city's lonely strays blown about the terrain by vague, evil forces. Greene's famous low sociology always suggests a square's condescension and ignorance. He sets Cotten up for quaint laughs by characterizing him as a pulp writer, having the educated snipe at him in unlikely fashion ("I never knew there were snake-charmers in Texas") and the uneducated drool over him; every allusion to Cotten's Westerns, from their titles to their format, proves that no one behind the movie ever read one. Greene's story, a string of odd-sized talky scenes with no flow within or between them, is like a wheelless freight train.

But Reed manages to turn the last half of this tired script into a moving experience of a three-dimensional world in which life is sad, running simply from habit, and ready to be swept away by street-cleaners. In Reed's early films (*The Stars Look Down*, *Kipps*, *Night Train*), sordid domesticity was scored in a poky, warm, unbiased way; in the daylight scenes of *Third Man*, his paterfamilias touch with actors is tied to a new depersonalizing use of space that leaves his characters rattling loose, like solitary, dismal nuts and bolts in vaulting landscapes. A beautiful finale—Welles's girl Valli, returning from his burial down a Hobbema avenue of stark trees—picks up the gray, forlorn dignity of a cold scene and doubles the effect by geometrically pinpointing the figure and moving her almost mechanically through space and finally into and around the camera. Reed has picked up a new toy-soldier treatment of conversations, where the juxtapositions and movements are articulated like watch cogs, each figure isolated and contrastingly manipulated till the movie adds up to a fractured, nervous vista of alienation in which people move disparately, constantly circling, turning away, and going off into their own lost world. But the movie's almost antique, enervated tone comes from endless distance shots with poetically caught atmosphere and terrain, glimpses of languid, lachrymose people sweeping or combing their hair, and that limp Reed manner with actors, which makes you feel you could push a finger straight through a head, and a sweater or a hat has as much warmth and curiosity as the person wearing it.

Always a soft director, Reed turns to chicken fat on night scenes, where his love of metallically shining cobblestones, lamps that can hit a face at eighty paces, and the mysterious glow at every corner turns the city into a stage set that even John Ford would have trouble outglamorizing. For instance, endless shots of Cotten and Welles sliding baseball-fashion in rubbled wastelands that look like Mount Everest touched up by an MGM art director. Both are seen only momentarily in these wastes because it is obvious that no human could make the descent without supplies. Reed is seldom convinced that anything artistic is being said unless the scene looks like a hock shop. Scenes are engulfed in teddy bears, old photographs, pills; a character isn't considered unless he is pinpointed in a panorama of baroque masonry, seen bird-fashion through bridge struts or rat-fashion through table legs; like most current art movies, Reed's are glued to majestic stairways.

The movie's verve comes from the abstract use of a jangling zither and from squirting Orson Welles into the plot piecemeal with a tricky, facetious eyedropper. The charm, documentary skill, and a playful cunning that fashioned this character make his Morse-code appearances almost as exciting visually as each new make-believe by Rembrandt in his self-portraits. The cunning is in those glimpses—somewhat too small shoes, a distant figure who is a bit too hard and resilient, a balloon man, not Welles but flamboyant enough to suggest his glycerine theatricality in other films—that seem so Wellesian, tell so much about him, yet just miss being Welles. Through camera tricks and through a nonmobile part custom-built for this actor (whose flabby body and love of the overpolished effect make any flow in his performance seem a product of the bloodiest rehearsing), Welles achieves in brief, wonderful moments the illusion of being somebody besides Welles. Two of these—some face-making in a doorway, a slick speech about the Borgias that ends with a flossy exit—rate with entertaining bits like Paul Kelly's in *Crossfire* and the time Bob Hope tried to hide behind a man taking a shower in a glass cubicle. Reed's nervous, hesitant film is actually held together by the wires of its exhilarating zither, which sounds like a trio and hits one's consciousness like a cloudburst of sewing needles. Raining aggressive notes around the characters, it chastises them for being so inactive and fragmentary and gives the film the unity and movement the story lacks.

April 1, 1950

Frank Capra

Having won more prizes and recorded more hits in thirty years than any other Hollywoodian, Frank Capra is rated a "cinemagician" whose "masterful comedies" reveal a "tender sense of humor, a quick sense of social satire, and a glowing faith in human nature." Since he is always for the little man (Mr. Smith, Mr. Deeds: helpless, innocent, likable, gawky) against such populist bogies as the Corrupt Politician, Hearstian Newspaperman, Big Tycoon; always in favor of copybook maxims (Be Kind, Love Thy Country, The Best Things Are Free); and spices his sermons with equally stereotyped sentiment and humor (a mild tap by a car salesman and the headlight falls off), Hollywood's best-loved preacher should please anyone who goes for obvious social consciousness, character-building, and entertainment. Actually the only subtle thing about this conventionalist is that, despite his folksy, emotion-packed fables, he is strictly a mechanic, stubbornly unaware of the ambiguities that ride his shallow images.

Riding High (from riches to nags with Bing Crosby) catches some of the jumpy, messy, half-optimistic energy seen around race tracks, but leaves you feeling that you've been taken in like a carnival sucker. For instance, the movie drools democratic pride in Crosby's sugary relationship with his colored stable-boy, displaying a sashaying Negro named "Whitey" whose happy slave personality, Sambo dialect (hallelujah), rapid expressions of unctuous love are derived from an old stencil cut out of the deepest kind of prejudice.

Capra's nervous films skip goat-fashion over a rocky *Satevepost* terrain. In

Riding High, Crosby throws over a dollar-plated job and fiancée to make a stakes-winner out of an underprivileged beast called Broadway Bill (characteristically cast with a gentle, trick-performing horse who doesn't look "diseased with speed"). As in all Capra films, the world is given to the underdog (the 100-to-1 entry, two-buck better, brat daughter—all win over the big, pompous, and rich), but the sleek, pampered technique, the grandiose talk, and eating habits of his down-and-out characters, and even the names (Imperial City, Pettigrew, Brooks) make for a plush, elegant movie that subtly eulogizes the world of powerful wealth. Capra's poverty boys are royalists in ratty boarding houses and leaky stables; when they eat at a hamburger stand, they treat the owner like a witless palace scullion. The gags always revolve about large sums of money, often rib a character for not being a liberal spender, delight in scenes that resemble a busy day at the Stock Exchange. Actually Capra only hates and attacks the humdrum plodder made humble by necessity; his smart-aleck jibes at artless, hard-working waiters or farmers invariably win sympathy where Capra intends you to snicker.

Capra's career-long punching bag has been smug respectability (one of the key lines from *It Happened One Night* was "Twenty millions and you don't know how to dunk"), but he characteristically double-crosses his social criticism. Although Crosby stands for the beautiful freedom of the gypsy (against job slavery, punctuality, table manners, neatness, and bathtubs), he suggests a spoiled little boy more than an anarchic vagabond. Surrounded by male and female sycophants who giggle violently at his jokes and turn up at a crisis with money, food, and good cheer, Crosby looks like a well-kept seal, generally compromises his role with self-confident affectations (he knocks out a cop with a neat, powerless punch) and the secure, aloof expression of one whose mind is on a treasure buried twenty feet from every scene.

The chief sensation in *Riding High* is of a slick, capricious, overtrained life that holds one completely out of the movie as though there were a glass pane between audience and screen. The interesting details have an idiotic element because the director's hand is constantly showing, and the effects are obviously dictated by formulas for keeping an image active, holding the eye, manufacturing excitement in a slight, predictable plot. The idiocy is apparent where Capra energizes static scenes by having Crosby chew gum with jet-propelled jaws, or by photographing the burial of Broadway Bill, who dies crossing the finish line, in a small tornado. Capra is always getting into foolish, capracorny corners and almost edging himself out by suddenly reverting to stark journalistic shots (the horrifying close-up of Broadway Bill in a ground-piercing nose dive), and carefully anatomized melodrama. One trick scene is the ultimate in surrealism; an extended mid-race examination (the race is so expanded by drama-building close-ups that a camel could have won) of a crooked jockey slyly throwing the race by standing upright in the stirrups and pulling the bit so hard the horse's nose is practically skyward. Despite the exaggerated villainy, the fact that the cameraman should have been trampled to death, and that the jockey is a different, even taller one than the rider who started the race, this is one of the few scenes that pulls you into the movie—as much by spontaneous acting and newsreel photography as by its weirdness.

June 10, 1950

◆

THE unhappy fact is that movies are *worse* than ever. Against the menace of television and a dwindling box-office even the best directors and producers have over-reacted into artistic catatonia rather than expected conservatism. Val Lewton, only non-commercial B producer, has disappeared from the scene; folksy Nick Ray ("They Live by Night") is wholly confused by his efforts to be both slick and arty; iconoclast Sturges stereotyped a musical after Paramount butchered one film and Hughes another; Huston and Wyler have glossed their War II documentary style; Zoltan Korda ("Sahara") hasn't been heard from for several years; hard-bitten Wellman decided grime doesn't pay when he signed an M-G-M contract; and the wonders of Negulesco (after "Belinda") haven't materialized.

Hollywood's lost art—present-tense realism through low-budgeted, off-the-cuff, on-location technique—is timidly pursued by the religious pep talk "The Next Voice You Hear," Hollywood's suburban answer to "The Cocktail Party." In six transworld broadcasts God the Psychiatrist exhorts Joe Smith (James Whitmore) to count his blessings, straighten up and fly right, and above all control his temper about the house. Writer Charles Schnee seems to feel that suburban existence, sufficiently well-regulated, shouldn't necessitate any further interference by God. Any movie directed by Bill Wellman ("G.I. Joe," "Oxbow Incident") will be poetically masculine, with geometric groupings and uncluttered surface emphasizing actors' physicality, the screen dominated by American gesture, timed and obsessively watched so that the camera seems to ride freshly on top of movement. "Wild Bill" has become a very mild character since moving to M-G-M, judging from such usual Hollywoodisms as mousey wife Nancy Davis waking from kempt sleep with the languor and well-being of a mattress advertisement. Whitmore, genius for appropriating other actors' mannerisms, blends Bendix, Tracy, L. Barrymore, and George Murphy into a babyish Joe Smith; Miss Davis, an effortless disembodied wisp, gets through her role by osmosis.

While more ambitious directors produce the terrain-dull "Asphalt Jungle," studio landscapes of "Battleground," laundered suburbia of "The Next Voice," Ted Tetzlaff finds a new textural way to see and hear nature, crawling up a Swiss mountain called "The White Tower." A simple mountain-climbing story that turns into a quest for reality, the movie flogs its stars with national neuroses which spoil their climbing, acting, and eventually the movie. The Nazi (Lloyd Bridges) postures like Superman and moves his limbs like a goose-stepping soldier; the decadent Frenchman (Claude Rains) suddenly becomes a puddle of affected spinelessness; the aimless ex-G.I. (Glenn Ford) relaxes into inauthentic cat-naps. Despite sleazy characterizations, the movie flows cinematically, particularly when studying climbing techniques, and best of all contains some affection for nature. In addition to a rather ordinary feeling for scenery, Tetzlaff is gifted with a sculptor's touch that molds sounds, colors, surfaces into a tactile rather than visual wonderland, so that one feels the sting of snow, the rain-soaked heaviness of canvas, the luminous sponginess of color.

This month the only cinematic bop appears in the pugnacious "Crisis," which gleefully jazzes a thousand clichés while pondering whether a kidnapped Johns Hopkins surgeon will kill or cure a South American tyrant: will Hippocrates or Jefferson win the day? Overtrading on the possibility that a ruthless *caudillo* would support endless conversation with his captive, the script deteriorates into slow prolix exchanges always terminated with some self-righteous remark or grimace from the surgeon orating for democracy. But a blizzard of documentary touches, sprung by belligerent show-offs like Signe Hasso and wild direction bent on nastily punching up the melodrama, makes the movie better than comic opera. Some hackneyed images are improved by moving furiously in riot scenes, vulcanizing extras to hide their Hollywood faces, authenticating details like coach-car washrooms so that a credible poverty weighs on the studio production. A stock scene with elegant diners on a veranda is saved by a Rossellini-minded director who takes advantage of Paula Raymond's camera fright and affected mouth twitchings. Visual journalism like Grant's drawings of Ferrer's skull and his sensitive manipulation of a giggly-saw makes for the sharpest surgery on Hollywood celluloid. Ferrer's neat changes of Spanish intonation to fit different social situations reward the spectator for putting up with a strenuous actor who expresses evil by gnashing his Bugs Bunny teeth.

"The Duchess of Idaho" is a lacquered musical (stilted Cinderella story spiced with vaudeville acts and stock sports shots) that pays off some mysterious debt owed the Sun Valley resort by M-G-M. Saturated with water ballets that prove Esther Williams is still only a fair club swimmer with one trick—swivel-hipping her behind into the camera while effortlessly changing direction—the only curiosity is an anatomy-hating camera man who emphasizes Williams's bulk, Connie Haines's stubbiness, Lena Horne's toothy mask, Eleanor Powell's Gibraltar-solid thighs, and the seamstress's-dummy shape of Paula Raymond.

August 12, 1950

◆

HOLLYWOOD's move from studio-built to on-the-spot productions has led to well regulated rather than raw realism ("Lost Boundaries" vs. "Open City"), and judging from recent films even more unexpected developments are on the way. Marlon Brando's "throw-away" tactics in "The Men" may swerve naturalistic acting from "dead-pan" to florid, and produce a new tribe of instinctual fire-balls who explode only during the actual shooting in order to circumvent every theatrical point on which the director had planned. Elia Kazan distills the corn out of the city documentary in "Panic in the Streets." The photography in "Edge of Doom" (in a shrewd attempt to mix the physicality of theater with the journalistic aspect of films) gets so close to the action that any further intimacy will put the camera inside the actors. In fact, this close-up style—huge bodies, faces hypnotically looming from the screen—gets very close to painting: the flat, massive envelopment of space found in Matisse or in painters like Kees and Baziotes.

"The Men"—a dull, over-designed primer on paraplegia—rehabilitates a sullen introverted patient (Brando) and then drops him into soap-opera. The script concentrates on the savage wit and dull pain of spinal cases, with an unhappy talent for making slick stereotypes of a cast largely made up of patients from Birmingham Veterans Hospital. Of the Hollywood players, Richard Erdman does a kind-hearted clown with the cocky insensitivity of a child star; a prima donna M. D. is done with hard conceit by Everett Sloane, who makes a stage business even of sucking a milk shake. Brando, however, nearly script-worshipped into a prig, gives his role a likable amateurishness by brilliant underplaying, delaying on cues, slouching through his lines.

Although "The Men" is excessively composed, abstract visual effects are

achieved at the expense of naturalness of action. Zinneman's cold craftsmanship and somewhat innocent view of Americans leads to a basketball scene
(Brando deploying down court with an ending close-up of him hooking in the
winning basket) made up of diagrammatic moves, staccato editing, and an
understanding of sports that must have come from reading Frank Merriwell.
Zinneman sometimes tones down his artiness and with Brando's help gets
poetic effects in which the tragedy is in the space that divides people.

Kazan's New Orleans manhunt, "Panic in the Streets"—a forty-eight-hour
journal of a diverted plague—needs more medical curiosity and less vigorous
gab. The discovery of a hapless, unidentified victim of two bullets and a deadly
contagious disease sets the city officials (Richard Widmark, Paul Douglas) on
a race to nab the murderer (Walter Palance) who is unwittingly touching off a
slight epidemic of pneumonic plague. Kazan, the true New Yorker, cuts movie
life down to virulent conversation between suspicious opponents, who, like
the average Broadwayite, hide character under an easily read appearance and
demeanor. All that one gets from Widmark & Co. is a frustrating surface of gesture and grimace. This type of melodramatic travelogue is fun because the
writer (Richard Murphy) dodges the places haunted by tourists and corny realists, stumbles into scenes that are already in motion and need no build-up, and
disguises folksy insights by a cold sophistication. While two thugs growl at each
other, one is munching Nabisco wafers; a brief look at the kitchen of a Greek
cafe reveals a hopeless cook cutting her way through a fog of grease. But for a
story about such things as rat fleas, bacilli pesti, and coughers, the script misses
scientific excitements. The bullying tactics of Widmark and Douglas are
watched on board a tanker, but not the doctor, below deck, ferreting for rats.
The camera is usually one room removed from plague victims, looking the
wrong way on autopsies, and forsaking the careers of germs left by Palance on
various coffee sacks, Bendix washers, and scratch sheets.

September 2, 1950

◆

"Sunset Boulevard"—the story of Hollywood movies draped on a depressing
sex affair—is an uncompromising study of American decadence displaying a
sad, worn, methodical beauty few films have had since the late twenties. Its
creators—pseudo-sophisticated Charles Brackett and Billy Wilder, a mean
director with telescopic eyes—are dispassionate observers rather than artists
who dig inside their characters, and they make the melodrama even shallower

by top-casting it with the superficial Gloria Swanson. My guess, though, is that this contrived but essentially uncorrupted journalism will live longer than a "great human" job like "The Bicycle Thief," a film that hides the worst type of cheating sentimentality beneath its "untouched" surface.

The story, parading an unadmirable hero (William Holden) through ugly affairs with his best friend's fiancée (Nancy Olson) and a rich neurotic of fifty (Swanson), amounts to morbid liaison between the "talkie" and silent film world, with Swanson doing a lot of ear-bending with a voice like a hollow stone wall, while Holden does an unemphatic version of the best silent-film pantomime. The tragedy inherent in his gigolo setup with the ex-star is largely muffed because the Brackett-Wilder combination—vague about the sunset period of an actress's life—entwines Holden with a cliché of the frustrated middle-aged artiste and drenches them both in gimmicks and weird atmosphere. Holden occasionally escapes into a more accurately observed world of young Hollywood talent, before the Swanson character clobbers him with three incredibly well-placed bullets which skillfully nudge him to his final floating place, the swimming pool recently dredged for the body of Alan Ladd, the late star of "Gatsby."

The cold, mean "Sunset Boulevard"—a beautiful title, though I suspect it was shot on another boulevard—is further proof of the resurgence of art in the Hollywood of super-craftsmen with insuperable taste. American film makers have suddenly learned how to make movies work as plastically as Mondrian paintings, using bizarre means and gaucherie, with an eye always on the abstract vitality produced by changing pace, working a choppy sentence against a serene image, extravagant acting against quiet. In this gimmick-ridden "Sunset" a corpse talks. The improbability bothers me less than the fact that he over-talks, explaining action—when Holden is delicately beached by the cops—that explains itself with a morbid realism about American scene. But his lines—spoken with a nice, trapped, Midwestern twang—work as wise-guy counterpoint to scene, building up each audience perception like a good tail-gate trombonist. Study the silent close-up of Holden being needled by a lecherous clerk, and you must respect skill that compresses so much of the kept man's malaise into a fraudulent secondary bit. This scene, with its lingering focus on a nauseated countenance, is a small horror movie that not only starts with an improbable, hammy cruelty by the clerk but uses it to magnify Holden's unhighlighted anguish. The upsetting fact about craftsmanship that always finds a way to out-maneuver criticism is that it is putting movies beyond the tastes of an audience that heretofore has judged films for elements— morality, sociology, message—no longer primary in such form-conscious art.

Save for one devilish axis, this would be a stiff, obsessively detailed record of corruption. Holden is one of the most quietly charming hard-luck guys a movie ever watched for his pin-point reactions, which give the film its endless silent perceptions of the way an average studio worker thinks, moves, worries, day-dreams. As the murdered narrator, he spreads a dense poolroom pallor over the imagery (his lines operate like silent film titles), but the Hollywood tone of his tight gestures and pantomime—the bound-in floridity, jumpiness, and showy crispness—is what gives this movie its virulent snap. The load is entirely upon him because the other portraits, while blistering, run from good comic strip (Fred Clark's safe-playing producer) through soggy urbanity (DeMille playing himself) to stereotyped abandon (Swanson).

The movie is stultified by spectacle, novelistic development, and a slow dismemberment of the human beings that are strictly from Von Stroheim's day. It is hard to find any logic or life in Swanson's grotesque because the director is too busy building baroque furniture for both her and her ménage. The illogicality of her mausoleum-like mansion, moldering outside while one butler keeps the inside jungle of rococo spotless, is less stultifying than the eclectic worship of forebodingly cluttered shots and dated insights about contaminated life. Where John Huston cuts a face into a mosaic of analytic shots, "Sunset," without any short cuts, standoffishly views a butler descending eighty stairs, crossing acres of beefy carpet, to open a door. Just as laborious and frightful is the old single-alley focus on character. Save for one poignant, relaxed scene in bed, Swanson stays exactly as directed, and very like Theda Bara, within a nasty stereotype: she sinks talon-like fingers in her lover's arm, telephones his other girl with a voice dripping demoniac evil, piles up straight gestures and exclamations that are the stock notions of the undersexed neurotic. This dated technique would sink the movie under minutiae if Wilder's inveterate meanness didn't turn every shot into a shocking, mad, controlled chewing of assorted twentieth-century cuds.

September 23, 1950

Ugly Spotting

Hollywood has spawned, since 1946, a series of ugly melodramas featuring a cruel esthetic, desperate craftsmanship, and a pessimistic outlook. These supertabloid, geeklike films (*The Set-up*, *Act of Violence*, *Asphalt Jungle*, *No Way Out*) are revolutionary attempts at turning life inside out to find the specks of horrible oddity that make puzzling, faintly marred kaleidoscopes of a street, face, or gesture. Whatever the cause of these depressing films—the television menace, the loss of 24 million customers since the mid-1940's—it has produced striking changes in film technique. Writers overpack dialogue with hackneyed bitterness, actors perfect a quietly neurotic style, while directors— by flattening the screen, discarding framed and centered action, and looming the importance of actors—have made the movie come out and hit the audience with an almost personal savagery. The few recent films unmarked by the new technique seem naïve and obsolete.

The new scripts are tortured by the "big" statement. *All About Eve* (story of the bright lights, dim wits, and dark schemes of Broadway) hardly gets inside theater because most of the movie is coming out of somebody's mouth. The actors are burdened with impossible dialogue abounding in clichés: "Wherever there's magic and make-believe and an audience—there's theater"; timely words: "We are the original displaced personalities"; and forced cleverness that turns each stock character into the echo of an eclectic writer. The new trick is to build character and plot with loaded dialogue, using hep talk that has discolored cheap fiction for years. In *The Breaking Point*, the environment is a "jungle," the hero a morose skipper "with only guts to peddle," who decides after a near fatal gun battle that "a man alone hasn't got a chance." His spouse comes through with, "You're more man than anyone I ever knew."

The stories, parading success-seekers through a jackpot of frustration, are unique in that they pick on outcasts with relentless cruelty that decimates the actor as much as the character. As a colored intern moves through the *No Way Out* blizzard of anti-Negro curses, everything about him is aggressively spiked so that a malignant force seems to be hacking at him. When the cruel estheticians really click on these sadistic epics, foreboding death lurks over every scene. Cameramen dismember the human body, accenting oddities like Darnell's toothpick legs or Pat Neal's sprawling mouth, to make them inanimate; faces are made up to suggest death masks, expanded to an unearthly size, spotlighted in dark, unknown vacuums; metaphorical direction twists a chimp's burial (*Sunset Boulevard*) into an uncanny experience by finding a resemblance between monkey and owner. Under the guise of sympathy, these brutally efficient artists are sneaky torturers of the defeated or deranged character.

Directors like Wilder and Mankiewicz mechanically recreate the unharnessed energy and surprise of great silent films with an elegantly controlled use of the inexplicable. In the jitterbugging scene of *Asphalt Jungle*, Huston delicately undresses the minds of four characters and gauchely creates a sensuous, writhing screen, though his notion of jive is so odiously surrealistic it recalls

Russian propaganda against the United States. The first glimpse of the faded star in *Sunset*, using Bonnard's suede touch on Charles Addams's portraiture (a witch surveying her real estate through shutters and dark spectacles) is lightning characterization with a poetic tang. Brando, in *The Men*, commands a GI troop into battle like a slow, doped traffic cop wagging cars through an intersection, but his affected pantomime electrifies the screen with the hallucinatory terror of an early painting by di Chirico. Movies have seldom if ever been as subtle as these scenes, or as depressing in the use of outrageous elements to expedite ambiguous craftsmanship.

To understand the motives behind the highly charged, dissonant acting employed today, one has to go back to the time-wasting, passive performance of an early talkie. No matter how ingenious the actor—Harlow, Garbo, Lee Tracy—effectiveness and depth were dissipated by the uninterrupted perusal of a character geared to a definite "type" and acted with mannerisms that were always so rhythmically and harmoniously related that the effect was of watching a highly attenuated ballet. Directors today have docked the old notion of unremittingly consistent, riverlike performances, and present what amounts to a confusion of "bits," the actor seen only intermittently in garish touches that are highly charged with meaning and character, but not actually melted into one clear recognizable person. Darnell's honestly ugly characterization of a depressed slattern is fed piecemeal into *No Way Out*, which moves her toward and away from malevolence, confuses her "color," and even confounds her body. Her job—like the recent ones of Nancy Olson, John MacIntyre, Hayden—shouldn't be called a "performance," because it is more like a collage of personality, which varies drastically in every way to create the greatest explosion and "illumination" in each moment.

October 28, 1950

◆

In "Ways of Love" three vignettes directed by three top film makers add up to the year's best foreign release. Marcel Pagnol's "Jofroi" is about a senile farmer (Vincent Scotto) who shams suicide thirty times to protect some lovingly nurtured trees. This director feels that there is nothing more delightful than pondering the virtuosity of character actors—earthy types who immobilize the screen with chattered wisdom and time-wasting mannerisms. In Jean Renoir's "A Day in the Country," a pretty Parisian (Sylvia Bataille) is seduced while the camera fastens on the countryside in tender mimicry of Papa

Renoir's paintings. As usual Renoir maneuvers his motorless plot into splendid landscape to press home the idea that man is a handsome spot in nature. Rossellini's controversial "The Miracle" is a powerful, messy slab of life, starring Anna Magnani as a talkative idiot made pregnant by a silent stranger she believes to be St. Joseph. Rossellini, thirsting for brutality, filth, misery, attacks his actors with an innocent technique. His people are always sent out to face uncontrollable crowds, unpredictable weather, or unconquerable terrain— victims of a half-written script and a carefree photographer. The effect of this masterpiece is like walking into a hail storm; Magnani's intense, sullen jabbering and gesturing paralyze the brain; the chaotic editing of unbalanced images captures existence in its most unrelated, disheveled state.

"Oliver Twist" is a mood-saturated version of Dickens's novel about slighted childhood, slowed down by a contrived million-dollar reproduction of London's nineteenth-century slums. Replacing adventure with threatening atmosphere, the movie carries its sparrowish waif (John Howard Davies), starved, beaten, corrupted, from workhouse to the underworld of Fagin (Alec Guinness). The actors can barely grimace under mask-like make-up, but Guinness amuses occasionally with some oily virtuosity. Davies runs and fights with a furious talent, and Francis Sullivan works a lot of subtle discomfort into the role of Bumble. The skill of director David Lean ("Great Expectations") comes through in spots that have the traumatic feeling and movement of vivid reality—scenes darting between knees, zooming up with someone's fist as it explodes in Oliver's face, moving with a murderer's gaze the morning after his dark, wild deed. However, Lean's attack on a situation congests and blurs the action by detouring all over the landscape for tricky views. This approach —different from the Hollywood method of gluing the camera to action and getting through it fast—makes an unimportant walk upstairs seem like a detailed report on slum staircasing by an over-zealous building inspector. With unnecessary sadism Lean has built a badly lit film, cluttered and confused with precious effect—filthy dens tattered by expensive arc lighting, Sykes's brutish mugging, sloshing rain—that makes the plot seem ten hours long and anything but absorbing.

"Manon" is a hard-boiled version of Prévost's bedridden novelette, with a creaking, improbable script job waylaying director Georges Clouzot. Manon Lescaut (Cecile Aubrey) is now a baby-faced siren, her incredibly faithful lover is a *maquis* fighter, and their unswerving passion—shared with any willing and wealthy fat man—lights the way from Paris black markets to the sands of Palestine. The cold, frank Clouzot ("The Raven," "Jenny Lamour") is a perverse craftsman who casts incongruous creatures (half-pint Aubrey) and contrives unnecessary obstacles. On a jammed train where there is no room for moving-picture apparatus and crowds are unwieldy, he threads his heroine through every aisle for a masterful analysis of life on the level of canned sardines. In an abandoned farmhouse with no constricting conditions for the director, the impassioned teen-agers neck in the dark, search the rooms with a flashlight that digs the past out of the worn-out décor. Clouzot's best talent is for clawing behind camouflages with a candid camera. He achieves the lonely, unglamorous feeling of a junky movie theater by working only in the basement and manager's office. His detailed pictures of a high-class bordello, a frenzied jive cave, a dress salon, unearth the provocative nuances of its people—usually from the waist down. "Manon" is halted and conventionalized by its hack plotting, enlivened by its ludicrous pornography, and is, otherwise, a painful study of Parisians at their peculiar worst.

As an anti-climax to the Critics' Awards, the following are my choice of the best films that didn't appear on other "Ten Best" lists.

"Union Station." A famous depot kidnapping reenacted by Rudy Mate for all the remembered thrills of a game of hide-and-seek; Mate revives an all but lost film style in which excitement springs from the crisp, moving patterns made by players on a carefully controlled surface.

"Mystery Street." Its scientific crime detection makes better use of documentary technique than any other fiction film; an intelligent, unsentimental rendering of American citizenry by Betsy Blair and Bruce Bennett.

"Crisis." Director Richard Brooks's clever, explosive blend of documentary and melodrama casts a revealing light on the inside of a dictator's brain: elegantly acted by Cary Grant.

"Broken Arrow." A preachy western; it shows Director Delmar Daves's unique talent for moving lone figures through dangerous terrain and gaining the suspense of an early Hitchcock without using gimmicks.

"Winchester 73." Anthony Mann's arty western; a striking example of how to humanize an overworked genre with natural dialogue, acting, and a director's original "film eye."

"The Winslow Boy." The best adaptation from the stage. Roughly equal to sitting in a library of thick carpets and padded chairs, reading a familiar, beloved English classic.

"Captain China." The second-best thing for landlubbers who have a desire to experience the sights, skills, and smells of life on a tanker.

"Macbeth." Orson Welles's orgiastic rendering of Shakespeare, co-starring my nephew, Jerry Farber.

January 13, 1951

◆

THE current Hollywood releases are mostly virtuoso pieces tailored to show off the florid craftsmanship of some expensive actors. The recent turn to slow, close-up presentation has brought about a measured, theatrical type of acting in which daring, often anomalous touches supply the interest that once came from large-scale action, environmental situation. The total effect of the films mentioned below makes me yearn for the tough, plain, understated acting that appeared in "The Set-up" a few years back, and before that in films like "The Ox-Bow Incident" and "The Clock." With the exception of a few underrated players (Ann Sheridan, Robert Ryan, Grable), actors today give the impression of social workers improving movie characters with a liberal-minded, educated attitude and an elegant, flamboyant acting technique.

For instance, Judy Holliday in "Born Yesterday." Satirizing a ritzy gradu-ate of the Bronx who moves into Washington circles on the arm of an unprin-cipled roughneck (Crawford), the begirdled blonde provides a noisy, overlong farce with all its speed and fun. But her performance is always too trained and intellectualized for a delicatessen type with the toughness, vulgarity, and gar-rulousness one encounters on the New York subway. Her Mae West walk is the mechanical maneuver of a university-educated mimic; her statuesque bearing in tight, gaudy gowns produces a ludicrous effect but also a feeling that the actress has never really liked tasteless clothes. Holliday's rescue from illiteracy and sin by a gallant bookworm (Holden) in shiny spectacles is a predictable event in a film that squeaks with a do-good spirit and brainy, democratic-looking actors. The success of the picture is due to direction (Cukor) that makes one hyperconscious of visual gags and wastes little time authenticating the brassy Kanin play.

The story of the Supreme Court's Holmes (Louis Calhern) starts in his sixty-first year and so caricatures old age that I advise sensitive old folks to forgo "The Magnificent Yankee." The theatrical Calhern mauls the process of growing old into a picturesque joke of rheumatism, fatigue, diminishing powers. The script periodically cues Calhern to pluck a flower from a small fenced garden, and each time Calhern loads the screen with creaking motion and strained humor. Endless scenes show a silly fascination with rickety physique: Holmes's feebly bent posture before the Lincoln Memorial, his bouncy-kneed strolls with Brandeis in Rock Creek Park, the laborious attempt to straighten his spine for a meeting with Roosevelt. For crafty virtu-osity Calhern is a bag of admirable tricks—he greets each of thirty birthday well-wishers with a different grimace of affection—but because he loves to flaunt urbanity and skill, he turns "the great dissenter" into a gay old dog.

"Branded" is a wordy but tightly edited western; among Hollywood cowboys Glenn Ford is the trickiest horseman, Randy Scott has a lonely, weather-worn façade, Cooper is the handiest with six-shooters, but the star of this film, Alan Ladd, is an anachronism, from his crisp, pavement glide to his well-bred sneer. Ladd, seldom forfeiting a character for comic showboating and fancy style, is sold out by direction (Mate) that pins his deceptive, slight build under tablecloth shirts, loses his impenetrable face in the shade of ten-gallon hats, and takes little advantage of his quick, efficient movements. When he isn't flexing or bending over backward to see his biceps, he is wandering up and down the Rio Grande—"like a ferry-boat"—verbally unfolding the complicated plot.

The antidote to all this baroque acting is offered in "Operation Disaster," a submarine documentary anchored by a theatrical script but made seaworthy by its underplaying cast. The sailors were obviously recruited from Rank, Inc.: a grimy face always bears the tell-tale smudge on the cheekbone; the forthright, confident eyes are those of battle-hardened actors; Captain Armstrong's (Mills) tapping of signals to a diver is the cool, crisp action of an officer who knows his listener has read the script. But these British players live inside their characters as though they owed a debt to real life; their fiddling with pen-knife, dice, or soiled cards amounts to more than just a move against a static script. Few moments are squandered on clichés like the sight of seagulls ascending heavenward as the submarine Trojan submerges. The movie sticks to its business of educating the audience on the week-long business of salvaging sub and crew, despite the tiny message at the beginning which announces that the British use a different salvaging technique from the one disclosed in the film.

February 3, 1951

THE crisp journalistic technique introduced in "Home of the Brave," which transformed a low-priced movie into a box-office hit, has become an official style for radical young crusaders. Specializing in candid emotions and views with the steely photography used in OWI films, this new approach differs from old-time journalism like "They Won't Forget" in its incessant emphasis on preaching and florid use of documentary ideas. Like a machine, the precision and intricacy of the recent "Teresa," "The Steel Helmet," "The Sound of

Fury" put so much spin, phrenetic editing, and unending misery into life that the spectator can never relax.

"The Sound of Fury," an indignant, twisted parody of the 1933 San José, California, lynchings, leaves the audience as limp as its two strangled kidnappers. With a zest for pointing out the worst aspects of average folks, the script studies an unemployed worker (Lovejoy) who tries to provide for a poverty-scarred wife and child by chauffeuring a vain hoodlum (Bridges). An amateurish abduction goes wrong and the captive's skull is bashed in; the last movie hour pounds through the crackup of the piteous Lovejoy, the mob-siege of the county jail, incited by a sensationalist reporter, with a housewife yelling, "We're going to save the taxpayers' money!"

The case of the Brooke Harte kidnappers and "those fine patriotic San José citizens"—Governor Rolph's description of the lynchers—warrants a less contrived reconstruction. It is commendable as a thoroughly angry work—no cute or chucklesome bit players, no inevitable rescue from evil—but in its determination to wreak havoc, tension effects are cruelly piled on by an ingeniously tricky mind.

Even before the listing of film credits, the theme is stated—"The world is going to the devil"—in a tempestuous prologue of Main Streeters fleeing a mysterious danger, while a blind sidewalk evangelist exhorts and the sound track makes like a bombing raid. Sound, camera, and actors settle down to an ominous snarl at American life. As Lovejoy careens home with a truck-driver, there is talk about burdensome wives in that loquacious vein that has gripped truck-drivers ever since talkies came in. Their headlights suddenly pick out an eerie image—the "inflammable" sign on the truck head, an unknown hitchhiker at the roadside. On the street a murmur of the grocer's wife—"Did you ask him about his bill?"—hits the sound track with a thud. At home Lovejoy's son nastily makes ratchet-like noises with a butcher knife. When the two murderers are seated in a cafe, heckling data—a raw steak being pounded, a girl too pretty to sling hash, the tedious ritual of deciding what to eat—emphasize the trying job of simply existing. The views mix figures and terrain in a tortuous bond where the décor obtrudes, slows down, and evaluates the characters so that they seem to carry a civilization on their shoulders.

Mercilessly lunging at small-townisms, the film finds the motive for the lynching everywhere, in everyone. Emulating the mad-dog journalism that it denounces, "Fury" raises audience emotion with shame-ridden maneuvers, twisted freakish sounds, relentless crowds, the murderers' frenzied terror, and wrings sentiment from farewell letters, pitiful kinfolk. However, in searching out odd tidbits of reality, the director (Endfield) deserves a TV set for trying valiantly. Like a slow ferret he hunts out human beings in private places, trysting sheds, a wallflower's bedroom, and fastens on them while they are hiding girdles, sparring with mirrors, buying sexy shoes for the wife. Although movies seldom stick with inane, irrelevant, everyday talk that reveals personality, Bridges tells Lovejoy about everything, from his girl friends in Germany to his collar size.

Much of the acting, which underlines pantomime with exaggerated psychology, should have cracked the camera lens. But midway in the film Katherine Locke sneaks in as a leaden manicurist on a blind date and by compressed understatement creates a new type of movie caricature. Packing silent, vacant, colorless qualities into a character who is sophisticatedly kept within the unsophisticated Bronx middle class, Miss Locke creates a feeling of hopelessness that overpowers the sloppy animation around her.

February 24, 1951

◆

Hollywood, which once poured hope and happiness into studio-built stories about poor devils in tenements, now sends its crews to mingle in common life and embroider it with more troubles than a psychiatrist hears about in a month.

"Teresa," a rather warm love story about a war bride (Angeli) orienting herself in a new country, busily poses more problems than its tyro scenarist (Stern) and speedy director (Zinnemann) can cope with. The two-part script details the war experiences of a panicky G. I. as he quickly woos and wins a pretty Italian, a sparrow version of Ingrid Bergman, and cracks up on his first combat patrol. Back home, in an East Side tenement, a dominating mom tries to maladjust the marriage, and the ex-G. I. runs away from so many things—jobs, picnics, rehabilitation clinics—that he literally suggests a heavy-gaited fullback getting into condition on New York sidewalks. This rather simple story of a son snarled in his mother's apron strings and a smart girl-wife trying to untangle him is hopelessly complicated by a writer who seems to know about every uncomfortable thing that is bothering mankind, and spells it out in neon lights. Fortunately the mishmash has some refreshing talent working for it in the way of uninhibited non-actors and a poetic director; so the result is as perversely enjoyable as a Third Avenue El excursion with stops in derelict rooms and sauerkraut-odored hallways to show you what terrifies the average New York visitor.

Sometimes the director forgoes his documentary tricks to assist the writer in squeezing a morbid fact until it shrieks. The opening scene in a state unemployment office tingles with the bald accuracy of unhurried, depressed faces, a stark gymnasium-like room, an incredibly mean-faced clerk pounding out questions to the roar of a drum beat—and the conscious lining up of clients like a neatly spaced chain-gang takes all the dejected straggle out of the scene. When the cavernous-eyed hero bolts in fear from his line and start hoofing through a jittery Bowery, caught wonderfully by a hidden camera, a mysterious narrator pops into the picture for a single deathless announcement: "His occupation is—running away!" Just in case this hasn't been nailed home, the hero keeps running into and out of various places. In a mental clinic his neurosis is glibly tied with a Freudian knot: "My father, he's nowhere, that guy. He never made me feel safe." This over-explaining is less objectionable than the clutter these fractional scenes contribute to a script that gets lost in an unending flashback.

However, no M-G-M crew in years has been so inventive in making nonactors behave naturally as they flounder about in existence. Much of the film's intricacy and intimacy comes from Angeli, who is given mannerisms and speech so cloying that she is literally forced into cunning impetuousness to bring them off. Ericson gets as close to the oafish insecurity of a perennial adolescent as a movie lead ever managed, partly as a result of the trying situations Zinnemann arranges in order to play on his very lack of acting experience. Out of this extended hodgepodge Zinnemann gets the traumatic accidents he wants, and a brutal study of that pet New York game of harassing the unsophisticated underdog.

The Italian sequence in Scasoli, a town in the Apennines that M-G-M redestroyed to film its war-torn look, shows the handiwork of some G. I. advisers and two new explosive personalities, Bill Mauldin and Ralph Meeker; the soldiers are good realistic versions of the Mauldin cartoons. There is also the kind of fight between G. I.'s, with its tiny heartbreaking evidences of cowardice and surprising accidents, that hairy-chested directors like Huston have been mismanaging for years. On the other hand, the makers of this film might well have studied Huston's superior "San Pietro" before they got around to pretentiously sentimentalizing war waifs, printing a war scene on glossy stock, and using a fearless camera man cool enough to make a poetic study of a sparkling stream in mid-battle.

Other new releases include "The Magnet," which will draw inaudible chuckles from people who never tire of psychiatrist jokes and invented childish antics. Save for some exciting, unpredictable, gravel-voiced slum kids, the British actors are as easily read as the carefully wrought production, which makes skilful use of editing and photography in the questionable project of kidding a ten-year-old's conscience.

"I'd Climb the Highest Mountain" missed the path when script-writer Trotti decided to exploit the folksy charm of a young backwoods preacher. Susan Hayward's robins'-nest coiffeur, not quite realistic impressions of deep country mustaches, attractive children, and red-clay roads may make the picture worth seeing—on a double bill in the 50-to-85-cent price range.

March 10, 1951

◆

"Fourteen Hours," based on Joel Sayre's story of a hesitant young suicide (Basehart) whom a persuasive cop (Douglas) tries to talk in from a Fifth Avenue ledge, teeters between life and death before falling flat on its celluloid face. The least of the film's faults are flaws of authenticity, many having to do with New York cops, who call each other "flatfoot," wear the same shiny uniform whether on emergency or traffic patrol, and locate stray citizens all over Long Island with weird technological methods. The "poor loony's" last act (reconstruction of John Warde's leap from the Gotham Hotel in 1938) is padded with so much contrived wit, mush, camera gymnastics, and self-conscious "natural" acting that it seems to be a hapless toying with facts by semi-documentarists building a case against suicide.

To start with, the film was not directed by an artistic genius but by Henry Hathaway, usually a sound journeyman on not quite factual suspense films ("The House on 92d Street"). He believes in gleaning characterization from pantomime, visual detail, realistic décor, so that his scenes seem to pull at one's eyeball; these are like a huge kaleidoscope made of splintered bits of New York. The views are beautifully varied to give the effect of a thousand eyes watching the ledge incident from all levels of a skyscraper scene. Part of the fun happens because he dares things with a camera that are considered frivolous by soul-searching directors—like the prolonged shot of the jumper's cigarette floating down to the crowd.

Hathaway has removed some of Barbara Bel Geddes's custardy sweetness, pushed Agnes Moorehead so fast she hardly has time to mug, rid Robert Keith of some flexibility, so that he is just about right as the dull, ineffectual Middle European father. However, the director is not nearly good enough with actors—in conveying the boy's abnormalities, or showing some degree of the "stinking life . . . rat-race" that drives Basehart out the window.

Of all the people who reason with him, the boy's mother (Moorehead) projects the most credible ugliness, but she has done her type of morbid hysteria so often before that it is hard to associate her with this particular trouble. Basehart seems totally confused by his role, either over-acting pathologically or simply standing in his nook like a neat, misplaced actor waiting for direction. After two hours he is no more convincing than in the first moment with the hotel waiter (Frank Faylen), in which Faylen tries to act a bit part into the Academy Award league and Basehart twitches out messages from his subconscious.

This spellbinder script by John Paxton is crammed with tricks and messages the size of dinosaur bones. The seven-point story is cleverly composed to put legs on a one-locale movie. While Douglas coaxes Basehart with conversation—baseball, fishing, picnics—dear to every "human" script, the camera dallies among hotel and sidewalk spectators and adjacent buildings, picking up six subplots that explain why the guy is contemplating suicide. Somehow these distracting vignettes only indicate the studio's realization that the morbid subject is mighty hard to tilt into a plea for better living. The patchwork continuity first pounces on a sidewalk romance played on the level of "the flowers, how sweetly they bloom." Then a cabbies' betting pool on the hour Basehart will jump tries to define cynical existence, but gives way to twinges of conscience almost before it is under way. A woman in the throes of a divorce suit sees the would-be suicide and changes her mind. Finally, the psychiatrist's explanation of the family's destructive role in Basehart's life pushes the suicide even farther out of the film.

The man on the ledge appears to be there for the visual image he offers to movie cameras; he is pinpointed dramatically against gray city-scape with the teetering, wall-hugging, tic-like movements that lead to a pre-climactic fall. His ordeal, made to order for the Special Photographic Effects department, is glimpsed with every lens maneuver and camera gimmick, and cast from every reflection known to trick cinema. The petulant blonde struggles with divorce attorneys and the window pane reflects the ledge incident; a TV room shows Basehart on six small screens; the final shot is seen in a bedroom mirror. These precious compositions produce the effect of a guy already wounded by existence being cornered by an indomitable camera man. After a few reels his actual situation is so confused by the machine-gun volleys of still-life compositions that one feels he has been inclosed in a coffin by the photography long before he decides whether or not to jump.

March 31, 1951

Val Lewton

THE death of Val (Vladimir) Lewton, Hollywood's top producer of B movies, occurred during the final voting on the year's outstanding film contributors. The proximity of these two events underlines the significant fact that Lewton's horror productions (*Ghost Ship, The Body Snatcher, Isle of the Dead*), which always conveyed a very visual, unorthodox artistry, were never recognized as "Oscar" worthy. On the other hand, in acclaiming people like Ferrer, Mankiewicz, and Holliday, the industry has indicated its esteem for bombshells who disorganize the proceedings on the screen with their flamboyant eccentricities and relegate the camera to the role of passive bit player.

Lewton always seemed a weirdly misplaced figure in Hollywood. He specialized in gentle, scholarly, well-wrought productions that were as modest in their effects as his estimate of himself. Said he: "Years ago I wrote novels for a living, and when RKO was looking for producers, someone told them I had written horrible novels. They misunderstood the word horrible for horror and I got the job." Having taken on the production of low-cost thrillers (budgeted under $500,000) about pretty girls who turn into man-eating cats or believe in zombies, Lewton started proving his odd idea, for a celluloid entertainer, that "a picture can never be too good for the public." This notion did not spring from a desire to turn out original, noncommercial films, for Lewton never possessed that kind of brilliance or ambition; it came instead from a pretty reasonable understanding of his own limitations. Unlike the majority of Hollywood craftsmen, he was so bad at supplying the kind of "punch" familiar to American films that the little mayhem he did manage was crude, poorly motivated, and as incredible as the Music Hall make-up on his Indians in *Apache Drums*— the last and least of his works. He also seemed to have a psychological fear of creating expensive effects, so that his stock in trade became the imparting of much of the story through such low-cost suggestions as frightening shadows. His talents were those of a mild bibliophile whose idea of "good" cinema had too much to do with using quotes from Shakespeare or Donne, bridging scenes with a rare folk song, capturing climate with a description of a West Indian dish, and, in the pensive sequences, making sure a bit player wore a period mouth instead of a modern lipsticky one. Lewton's efforts not infrequently suggested a minor approximation of *Jane Eyre*.

The critics who called Lewton the "Sultan of Shudders" and "Chillmaster" missed the deliberate quality of his insipidly normal characters, who reminded one of the actors used in small-town movie ads for the local grocery or shoe store. Lewton and his script-writers collaborated on sincere, adult pulp stories, which gave sound bits of knowledge on subjects like zoanthropia or early English asylums while steering almost clear of formula horror.

The Curse of the Cat People, for instance, was simply for the overconscientious parent of a problem child. The film concerns a child (Ann Carter) who worries or antagonizes the people around her with her daydreaming; the more they caution and reprimand, the more she withdraws to the people of her fantasies for "friends." When she finds an old photograph of her father's deceased, psychopathic first wife (Simone Simon, the cat woman of an earlier film), she sees her as one of her imagined playmates; the father fears his daughter has become mentally ill and is under a curse. His insistence that she stop daydreaming brings about the climax, and the film's conclusion is that he should have more trust and faith in his daughter and her visions. Innocuous plots such as these were fashioned with peculiar ingredients that gave them an air of genteel sensitivity and enchantment; there was the dry documenting of a bookworm, an almost delicate distrust of excitement, economical camera and sound effects, as well as fairy-tale titles and machinations. The chilling factor came from the perverse process of injecting tepid thrills with an eyedropper into a respectable story, a technique Lewton and his favorite scriptwriter, Donald Henderson Clarke, picked up during long careers writing sex shockers for drugstore book racks. While skittering daintily away from concrete evidences of cat women or brutality, they would concentrate with the fascination of a voyeur on unimportant bric-a-brac, reflections, domestic animals, so that the camera would take on the faintly unhealthy eye of a fetishist. The morbidity came from the obsessive preoccupation with which writers and cameramen brought out the voluptuous reality of things, such as a dangerously swinging ship's hook, which was inconspicuously knocking men overboard like tenpins.

Lewton's most accomplished maneuver was making the audience think much more about his material than it warranted. Some of his devices were the usual ones of hiding information, having his people murdered offstage, or cutting into a murderous moment in a gloomy barn with a shot of a horse whinnying. He, however, hid much more of his story than any other filmmaker, and forced his crew to create drama almost abstractly with symbolic sounds, textures, and the like, which made the audience hyperconscious of sensitive craftsmanship. He imperiled his characters in situations that didn't call for outsized melodrama and permitted the use of a journalistic camera—for example, a sailor trying to make himself heard over the din of a heavy chain that is burying him inside a ship's locker. He would use a spray-shot technique that usually consisted of oozing suggestive shadows across a wall, or watching the heroine's terror on a lonely walk, and then add a homey wind-up of the cat woman trying to clean her conscience in a bathtub decorated with cat paws. This shorthand method allowed Lewton to ditch the laughable aspects of improbable events and give the remaining bits of material the strange authenticity of a daguerrotype.

The Leopard Man is a cleaner and much less sentimental Lewton, sticking much more to the suspense element and misdirection, using some of his favorite images, people moving in a penitential, sleep-walking manner, episodes threaded together with a dramatic sound. This fairly early peak example of his talent is a nerve-twitching whodunit giving the creepy impression that human beings and "things" are interchangeable and almost synonymous and that both are pawns of a bizarre and terrible destiny. A lot of surrealists like Cocteau have tried for the same supernatural effects, but, while their scenes still seem like portraits in motion, Val Lewton's film shows a way to tell a story about people that isn't dominated by the activity, weight, size, and pace of the human figure. In one segment of the film, a small frightened señorita walks beyond the edge of the border town and then back again, while her feelings and imagination keep shifting with the camera into sagebrush, the darkness of an arroyo, crackling pebbles underfoot, and so on, until you see her thick dark blood oozing under the front door of her house. All the psychological effects—fear and so on—were transformed by Tourneur into nonhuman components of the picture as the girl waited for some noncorporeal manifestation of nature, culture, or history to gobble her up. But, more important in terms of movie invention, Lewton's use of multiple focus (characters are dropped or picked up as if by chance, while the movie goes off on odd tacks trying to locate a sound or a suspicion) and his lighter-than-air sense of pace created a terrifically plastic camera style. It put the camera eye on a curiously delicate wave length that responds to scenery as quickly as the mind, and gets inside of people instead of reacting only to surface qualities. This film still seems to be one of Hollywood's original gems—nothing impure in terms of cinema, nothing imitative about its style, and little that misses fire through a lack of craft.

Unfortunately, his directors (he discovered Robson and Wise in the cutting department) become so delirious about scenic camera work that they used little imagination on the acting. But the sterile performances were partly due to Lewton's unexciting idea that characters should always be sweet, "like the people who go to the movies"—a notion that slightly improved such veteran creeps as Karloff, but stopped the more pedantic actors (Kent Smith, Daniell) dead in their tracks. Lewton's distinction always came from his sense of the soundly constructed novel; his $200,000 jobs are so skillfully engineered in pace, action, atmosphere that they have lost little of the haunting effect they had when released years ago.

April 14, 1951, and September 27, 1952

◆

"The Thing (from Another World)" is a slick item thriftily combining a heavy science story with a pure adventure yarn for better than ordinary entertainment. This story of an intellectual carrot who delivers a flying saucer from Mars might have taken years and millions to make; instead, the problem was solved by setting the film at the uncomplicated North Pole, hiding the saucer under ice, and keeping the ferocious vegetable for an hour from the audience's eyes. Before its appearance there is little more than imaginative science talk and off-screen howling from the Thing, but the dialogue is a flashy, interesting, erratic jumble reminiscent of disc-jockey chatter. Despite its indulgence in the cliché of the Mad Scientist—a vaguely Russian-type "Nobel Prize winner"—and the final letdown when the Thing turns out to be merely the familiar Frankenstein monster *fines herbes*, the film almost convinces you that its imaginative predictions may some day all come true.

"The Brave Bulls"—concerning a frightened *torero* who mysteriously loses his fear in the last five minutes—is an exercise in powerful photography if not in lucid story-telling. Its first scenes in the Plaza Mexico—an ancient *paso doble* blasted forth out of battered trumpets—provide the year's most spine-tingling footage. The rest is an arty, confused attempt to show what's so special about "da bools, da muzik, da beeg crowds in da hot afternoon." Robert Rossen, its producer-director, is an ex-pugilist with proletarian proclivities who uses newsreel and editing devices with a pummeling effect. Rossen breaks his story into three plots so that he can admire the quaint nobility of small-town Mexican breeders, impresarios, and other walk-on figures. Somehow, the incidental crowd has always had a great importance for Rossen, and in this film he has loaded his stations, streets, and patios with the same "little people" who jittered in the foreground and background of "All the King's Men"—only now they are *paisanos*. For all this, "The Brave Bulls" turns up an endless thread of visual treats, and it is probably less un-Mexican than some of its lines.

The under-dogs have their day again in "The Scarf," a disjointed, monstrously affected psycho-mystery freak show. This time the producer-directors are Dupont and Goldsmith, two European aesthetes who have been snarling at the rich and drooling over the poor ever since the days of Emil Jannings. Here they glamorize a singing waitress, a turkey-raising hermit, a jaundiced metaphysical barkeep, and a morose amnesiac fugitive from a desert asylum. These types are set up against a Berlin's-eye-view of the American scene: Greyhound buses, hitchhikers, cactus, flourishing analysts, prison breaks. Dupont and Goldsmith turn their tinny proletarians into sententious talkers, dubbing them with names like "Level Louie" and "Cash-and-Carry Connie" and having them oscillate their eyeballs in a sophisticated version of Griffith's pantomime. It sounds awful but it's kind of interesting.

Back to bulls. "The Bullfighter and the Lady" is produced by actor John Wayne and suggests his own personality and career by its simplicity, its spaciousness, its complacent trust in cagy brawn. A Yankee skeet-shooter (Robert Stack) quickly learns the matador's trade—*faena, veronica, et al.*—from Mexico's head bull-slayer, thus reminding us of Wayne's quick rise to stardom after a mediocre discus-throwing career at the University of Southern California and his close student-master relationship with John Ford. Ford's inclination to glorify rugged masculine fellowship also comes through—but in a surprising and sticky way. The audience is besieged with handsome male anatomy—nearly nude matadors flexing their muscles in a steam room, matadors bulging out of their skin-tight pants, endless close shots of Stack's platinum curls and toothy grin. However, Wayne makes bullfighting clearer than Rossen does.

"Appointment with Danger" is a fascinating textbook on the Average American Flop—his speech, mien, sage misanthropy, doubt. It is also a well-done report on the geography of Gary, Indiana, a place that seems crowded with failures. There are only two really weak actors in it: Alan Ladd and his co-star, Phyllis Calvert, who like many English players always looks ready to keel over from lack of orange juice, exercise, and sunshine. Still, it's about time the critics stopped jumping on Ladd. This emotionless splinter has one real virtue: his incessant numb bravery often inspires the rest of the cast to outdo themselves in the opposite direction. So in this mail-robbery movie, the more Ladd outguns and outslugs a gang of white-collar thugs—most of whom seem instinctively sure their fool-proof scheme will backfire—the more Henry Morgan, Jack Webb, and the other thieves inject subtle trouble into their traditionally tough characterizations. These understated shades of dejection are so perfectly articulated that Ladd fans are growing restive—not from the monotony of his heroics but from seeing their own pessimism revealed in grainy, gloomy honesty.

May 26, 1951

◆

Iɴ "A Place in the Sun"—the latest and glummest re-re-remake of "An Amer-ican Tragedy"—there is enough gimmicky, pretentious footage to keep one's eyes glued to the screen while one's common sense and muscles beg for respite. For all its flash, occasional power, and streaks of frighteningly natural acting, this extra-earnest Paramount production is one long, slow, hyperbolic attack on ordinary American existence—an attack whose renewal in one recent film after another is obviously part of Hollywood's strategy to jerk its audience back from the ingenuous attractions of television.

We are given, for instance, the oh-so-languid rich; the pious, magisterial M. D.; billboards that out-Petty Petty; distant sirens playing a counterpoint of doom to ordinary phone calls; the beefy, hysterically shrill D. A.; a thick undergrowth of portable radios everywhere the camera goes; juke-box joints sprawling with drunks. And I am getting very tired of stock shot 32-B, which feeds us the myth that all the windows in depressed urban areas face out on huge, blinking neon symbols of wealth and achievement.

The script by Harry Brown is remarkably faithful to the plot of Dreiser's bleak novel: the complicated love life of a not quite bright social climber (Montgomery Clift) puts him finally in the electric chair. But Brown's dialogue is so stylish and unalive ("You seem so strange, so deep, so far away") that it appears to drift out of the walls and furniture rather than the twisted, jittery, or guppy-like mouths of Clift and his two ladies—Elizabeth Taylor and Shelley Winters. An even more troubling factor is Brown's determination to modern-ize a tale that is hopelessly geared to an outdated morality and a vanished social set-up. ("An American Tragedy," published in 1925, was based on the Chester Gillette case of 1906. By its contortionist avoidance of the *verboten* subject of abortion—or less drastic alternatives—and its black-white demarcation of the worlds of luxury and drudgery, this "modern" version cuts the ground from under its own feet.)

But Producer-Director George Stevens turned Brown's arty, static non-sense into something almost as visually interesting and emotionally complex as "Sunset Boulevard" or "The Asphalt Jungle"—one more key example of Hollywood's recent desperate commitment to misanthropic expression via elegant, controlled, mismated power effects. Ordinarily a soft-hearted poetic realist, Stevens is particularly good at getting natural performances out of his actors and at putting across the gauzy, sentimental *Gestalt* of a popular song, a kiss, an important dance, a ritualized seduction. Here he has blown such elements larger than life—building them into slow, parabolic choreographies of action and camera movement in which you are more dazzled by the incredible control and purposefulness than repulsed by the schmalz of the whole thing. The Clift-Taylor kiss—repeated in three double exposures—is a huge, intimate, extended business that practically hammers an erotic nail into your skull. It is preceded by Taylor's curious Tin Pan Alley line: "Tell Mama—tell Mama all!"

Stevens squeezes so much of their "real" personalities out of his actors that the story is congested with discordances. Most of the honors go to Miss Winters, who at long last gets to show that she can do a Mildred—just like Bette Davis; but a far more complex one-man show is that of the non-aging late adolescent, Montgomery Clift. To some spectators his performance expresses the entire catalogue of Greenwich Village effeminacy—slim, disdainful, active shoulders; the withdrawals, silent hatreds, petty aversions; the aloof, offhand voice strained to the breaking point. To others he is a sensitive personification of all those who knock themselves out against the brick wall of success. Clift can stare at a Packard convertible or slump down on his spine with fatigue and by simply not acting make you aware of every dejected, mumbling success-seeker on a big city street. Finally, for the more perceptive he is a childish charade on all the fashionably tough, capable outcasts who clutter up "hard-boiled" fiction: cigarette dangling from mouth, billiard cue carelessly angled behind his back, Clift makes a four-cushion shot look preposterously phony.

The exploitation of a talent like this goes far to prove that ace directors no longer make movies as much as tight-knit, multi-faceted Freud-Marx epics which hold attention but discourage understanding in a way that justifies Winchell's name for their makers—"cinemagicians."

June 30, 1951

◆

"The Frogmen," in which Richard Widmark wins the latter part of World War II under water, is a new type of movie experience roughly equivalent to reading "Tom Swift" in Braille at the bottom of a well. While examining the strokes, breathing apparatus, and demolition tactics of the navy's warfaring bathing beauties, it unwinds a boyishly heroic tale beneath the Pacific-in-middle-distance shots that make the story as hard to see as a recent dillie called "The Long Dark Hall," which was shot without electric lights in a dark walnut court-room. One virtue of 20th-Century-Fox films is that they are cast with manly males of the advertising-executive type who reject the kind of pansy-brained, masochistic, floor-walker's poetic technique that has become a lauded acting style in most Hollywood films.

"Ace in the Hole"—an ex-G. I., crazy for Indian relics, is pinned down in a cave fall-in, with sand dribbling in his face, while a sensationalist reporter keeps him there for the sake of a gaudy news story—is built chiefly round the acting of a tough, corrupt newshound by Kirk Douglas. Douglas plays it in the worst style of the Yiddish theater, bursting with self-pity, slowing everything with a muscular, tensed-up technique, and ranting as though he were trying to break the hearts of people blocks away from the theater. His conceited hamming is pretty typical of the whole show, in spite of a well-cast Albuquerque contractor, a reasonably well-cast floozy (Jan Sterling) who makes a nice nasty thing of riffling some currency in Douglas's face, a few beautiful long shots of the carnival that blossoms at the scene of the tragedy. These last make up in very small part for Producer Wilder's dreadful, misanthropic, corny depiction of the rubber-neckers gathered for the kill and of "hicks" whose provincialism consists of not being hep to chopped liver or Yogi Berra.

Joseph Losey, the left-wing naturalistic director of two excitingly candid films, "M" and "The Prowler," is an ambivalent citizen who loathes the cupidity, sadism, and prejudices of his fellow-men, and lovingly borrows the best things they have done with a camera. In his remake of "M" the discriminating Losey makes good use of, among other things, Lang's morose camera set-ups and lighting, the architectonic design and subjects of Walker Evans's photographs, and the eerie handling of carnival freaks, last seen in a good "B" called "Woman in Hiding." "M" provides a sensitive if unimaginative evening, whose major asset is David Wayne's somewhat over-harassed acting of an elegantly hysterical psychopath. However, in "The Prowler," which catalogues a cop's hot pursuit of a frightened wife and his disposal of her disc-jockey husband, Losey has perfected his taut, dry naturalism to the point where he has turned out a near "sleeper" held down only by its mimicries, all less snappy than the models from "Double Indemnity," "Greed," and so on.

"He Ran All the Way" is an old-fashioned gangster film (no message or Freudian overtones; fairly intense and exciting) about an inept hooligan (Garfield) who shacks up, unwanted, with a tenement family. This family, generalized with dull virtues, never tries to find out what makes the gangster tick but just stands around scared to death. The locale, dialects, architecture are a puzzling mish-mash of Bronx, Venice, Cal., and Group Theater. The film takes place entirely in a railroad flat, where, despite the fact that the ceilings seem to have been removed and the doors left off all rooms so as to allow for camera movement, the energy comes entirely from emotionally congested acting which appears to have worked its way down through a hundred plays and movies from "Awake and Sing," an earlier and better Garfield show.

July 14, 1951

◆

"A STATE of uncertainty, generally accompanied by a feeling of anxiety or fear; indetermination; indecision." This, according to Webster, is the meaning of suspense—probably the best single theme for movies in an anxious era like this, when we are all sweating out something—from A-bombs, bullets, or furloughs to pregnancies, ironclad marriages, or high prices. But this theme has been misconstrued and bastardized by both Hollywood and its critics. One director in particular has made his living by subjecting the movie audience to a series of cheap, glossy, mechanically perfect shocks, and for this he has been hailed as the High Boojum of Suspense. The name of this artist is, of course, Alfred Hitchcock—who has gone farther on fewer brains than any director since Griffith, while cleverly masking his deficiency, and his underlying petty and pointless sadism, with a honey-smooth patina of "sophistication," irony, and general glitter.

Having vented this long-pent-up gripe, I hasten to add that Hitchcock's latest film, "Strangers on a Train," is fun to watch if you check your intelligence at the box office. It is too bad that this director, who has the observing eyes of a Dos Passos and the facility of a Maupassant, does himself the disservice of intercutting rather good naturalistic scenes with so much old hoke. His forte is the half-minute visual uncertainty—a murderer's hand straining through a sewer grating for a symbolically decorated cigarette lighter. Hitch not only shows the fingers straining forward with slow, animal cunning but throws a white, metallic light over them, thus turning a dirty black hole into Grauman's Chinese on opening night. The whole thing is done in a boxed close-up, so that one can't help feeling the camera man could have cut the nonsense short by handing the Ronson up to the villain. The late-twenties Hitchcock, devoted to the fairly credible style of John Buchan and Belloc Lowndes, would have rejected all such intrusive, romantic, metronome-timed schmalz and no doubt fired the script writer for lifting the gesture and locale from a film—"The Third Man"—made by his former shadow, Carol Reed. However, like so many transplanted foreign aces who consider American audiences more childish, gullible, and slow-witted than those in the Marshall Plan countries, Hitchcock has gone so soft that he makes even the average uninspired native director look comparatively non-commercial. His only really punchy Hollywood job was "Lifeboat." "Strangers on a Train" ranks somewhere between that effort and mushy gab-fests like "Sabotage," "Under Capricorn," "Spellbound," and—though it had its merits—"Rope."

Because chases and homicides and Pearl White escapes clutter his pictures, no one notices the general emasculation Hitchcock has perpetrated on the thriller. Brittle, soft-cheeked, petulant pretty boys (Dick, Dall, Todd, Donat, Cummings, Granger) are projected into high melodrama. These characters seem to disappear like clothes dummies within their tweedy, carefully unpressed Brooks Brothers jackets and slacks, thanks to a director who impregnates costume and décor with so much crackling luster, so much tension and latent evil, that the spectator expects a stair corner or tie clasp to start murdering everyone in sight. Hitchcock did a lot of harm to movies by setting off a trend toward investing backgrounds, architecture, and things like cigar bands with deep meaning. Finally, he takes all the bite out of his stories by whipping quickly but delicately down various "artistic" détours. In "Strangers on a Train" he cuts away from a brutally believable strangulation to the concave image cast up by the lens of the victim's fallen spectacles. At once the onlooker loses interest in the murder as such because he is so entranced with the lush, shadowy choreographic lyricism with which Hitchcock shows the life being squeezed, fraction by fraction, out of a shallow, hateful nymphomaniac.

The movie, by the way, is built around the travestied homosexuality of the murderer. Robert Walker provides the role with a meatier, more introverted, unhealthier savor than the stars usually give a Hollywood production. This is partly the result of Hitchcock's mechanical and spurious use of the new close-up style of camera work, which is evidently aimed at fetishists who like to study pores. Here he has given Walker an oily, puffy face and made him skitter his tiny eyes back and forth horizontally until it appears that the actor looks at everybody as if he were reading a book. But somewhere in the past two years Walker has picked up an aggressive jump style of acting; so that he seems to bull his way through the action—even when quietly waiting around a carnival for the sun to go down—like a thoughtless, savage two-hundred-pounder about to plunge for a touchdown. The heavy blanket of twisted melancholia which Walker spreads over this film is beautifully counterpointed by the work of Laura Elliott in the role of the victim. She seems to swish up into the picture like a sexy bespectacled baby whale. All the best things in "Strangers" have to do with the playing of these two.

July 28, 1951

◆

Using the *Time* cover-story technique of puffing and petrifying an unlikable individual, "Bright Victory" shows a gabby, over-eager, self-satisfied young Floridian winning his soul—and a pretty workin' girl, a better job, a home in the North—by losing his eyesight in the North African campaign, then his passion for the security represented by a semi-pretty lifelong sweetheart, and finally—ten seconds before the movie ends—his addiction to the epithet "nigger." (Negro here, as in "Home of the Brave," "Steel Helmet," and who knows how many films to come, means willowy, highstrung James Edwards.) Racing out one lunch hour to string some wire in the busiest patch of terrain east of Bizerte, the eager-beaver infantryman (Arthur Kennedy) gets clipped alongside his right eyeball by a sniper's bullet. From there on Kennedy contributes a solid, feverish, consistent characterization full of incredibly shrewd perceptions about both Southerners and the sightless.

Aside from his performance, this mixture of "The Best Years of Our Lives" and "The Men" is so unimaginatively perfect and so well-barbered by its cutters that it is a little like being caught on a fast assembly line. And wherever it takes a chance on real pathos or ugliness, it goes far enough overboard to be deeply offensive: by suggesting, for instance, that those with eyes are so stupid as to hand a blinded vet six lit matches as soon as he pulls out a cigarette.

Good citizenship and good box-office sense are for the umpteenth time cheesily mortised together in "The Well," as are the two hottest themes in cinema today—the Negro problem and the problem of trying to get somebody (and the movie itself) up out of a hole or down from a ledge. This one begins with a spanking-cute Negro tot, her bright, happy eyes glued firmly on the director, zigzagging across a very handsome meadow as if on trolley wires and suddenly plunking down an unseen well—thus probably disappearing from films until the early 1980's, when she will emerge in "Under the Knife," the hard-hitting pro-Puerto Rican epic, as the enlightened nurse who finally persuades the chief surgeon of Harlem Hospital (James Edwards) to seat the chief surgeon of Harlem Hospital (James Edwards) to seat the young Puerto Rican interne (José Ferrer, Jr.) at the same table with his duskier colleagues.

The first three-fifths of "The Well" is a discordant symphony of overstated angry banalities: a race riot padded with extra-awful extras who accidentally snatch up clubs all cut to one size by the factory that makes Louisville Sluggers; a thundering Tiomkin piano cascading bass notes into critical moments in case you should miss them; a progressive waitress peppering the salad of a bigot; some elegant but unidentified Negro students sitting around in the high-school library self-consciously chirping civics-course stuff on the ramifications of race prejudice. The last two reels, however—drilling for the imprisoned little bit player—are an extraordinary education in the use of a rotary drill and a night-time camera. Here, in a shimmering, oscillating phantasmagoria of lights, faces, and machinery, all the white supremacists—who have, to a man, abandoned the error of their ways—turn up in key technological roles to dredge the missing waif up out of the ground.

"Take Care of My Little Girl," clobbering the sorority system with a ton of bobby pins, abuses old Tri U so surrealistically that any freshman with verve would join U³ at the drop of an arch. The inmates, watch-pocket replicas of Phil Spitalny's second cellist, dash for the porch to sing a different song every six minutes, drink Kleenex-wrapped cokes all day long, never see a classroom, are always in secret session hashing out the proposed blackball of poor Lynn Heppenstahl. After a semester of this, sister Jeanne Crain hands in a variety of pledge pins and walks off toward the dormitories on the arm of an earnest, leather-jacketed veteran who has wised her up as follows: "I don't think you're a heel—but I don't think you're Eleanor Roosevelt."

Another film with a slightly more credible collegiate setting is now sliding imperceptibly through the neighborhood circuits. Not credible, but *more* credible. This is "Night into Morning," a very old-fashioned Louis B. Mayer–type movie, without kikes, Negroes, fascists, proletarians, or psychopaths. It is even gently anti-psychiatric, while often poking rather realistically into unimportant corners of California University's Wheeler Hall and the miseries of a suddenly widowed professor of English (Ray Milland, somewhat miscast). It's just well-handled soap opera, but compared to "Victory," "Well," "Girl," and dozens of even more pretentious recent films like "The River," "Ace in the Hole," "A Walk in the Sun," it goes down like Flaubert or Fielding.

August 11, 1951

◆

THE grimmest phenomenon since Dagmar has been the fabulous nation-wide success of Jerry Lewis's sub-adolescent, masochistic mugging. Lewis has parlayed his apish physiognomy, rickety body, frenzied lack of coordination, paralyzing brashness, and limitless capacity for self-degradation into a gold mine for himself and the mannered crooner named Dean Martin who, draped artistically from a mike, serves as his ultra-suave straight man. When Jerry fakes swallowing a distasteful pill, twiddles "timid" fingers, whines, or walks "like Frankenstein," his sullen narcissistic insistence suggests that he would sandbag anyone who tried to keep him from the limelight. Lewis is a type I hoped to have left behind when I short-sheeted my last cot at Camp Kenne-kreplach. But today's bobby-soxers are rendered apoplectic by such Yahoo antics, a fact that can only be depressing for anyone reared on comedians like Valentino, Norma Shearer, Lewis Stone, Gregory Peck, Greer Garson, Elizabeth Taylor, or Vincent Impellitteri.

"That's My Boy" has to do with the transformation of an inept sissified bookworm (Lewis) into a halfback as sterling as glamour-boy Martin, a man who nonchalantly slaps off tacklers the way most of us shoo away mosquitoes. (For his part, Martin has modeled himself so carefully on Crosby and Como that he seems to jiggle like a mannered skeleton inside his heavily padded suits.) The film is almost saved by Eddie Mayehoff, a lantern-jawed bruiser with practically no mouth and a funny way of overemphasizing his role of an ancient Bronko Nagurski; I figure him for a terrible-tempered tuskless mastodon who never actually went to college but knows enough to despise this puerile TV-style pigskin parody. If I am right, he supports my opinion that the American public is now ready to laugh at lepers and gas-chambers.

Almost every Italian film trickling into the "art" theaters these days has been awarded a prize by a foreign film festival. They also have in common a flux of odd-angled shots of thighs and heaving bosoms; a quantity of daring propaganda against such ogres as warmongers, pimps, non-leftist priests, prison wardens, Lesbians, and petty government officials; and an all-around frenzied unkemptness in cutting, lighting, make-up, and underlying purpose. Such a movie is "Women Without Names," a detention-camp melodrama which won the Selznick award in Venice and will probably play here to an almost solidly male audience—aesthetic to the core—drawn in by such ads as "women trapped by intrigue . . . and the heartless passion of ruthless men!" Not to mention stills like the one of Simone Simon languishing in bra and shorts on a mattress of hay in order to tease the fat pervert who sits nearby, ogling her in a torment of frustration. With sharp Italian sense of irony and realism, the director has stuck a donkey into one corner of the frame and scoured the brassière industry for a spectacular zebra-striped number—just what you'd expect a prisoner to wear on off-hours in the camp stable. The story behind this sly scene is that a gold-hearted hoyden is trying to seduce a fruity ice-cream vendor into marriage so that she can promote herself and her pal, Valentina Cortese, out of this corral for women without passports. The plan fails; the pal dies in childbirth while the camera, by way of no change, dollies down a line of sulky, dowdy onlookers. In Cortese, my favorite actress of the moment, the film has at least one undebatable asset: no tricks, quiet grace, and a sensitive beauty which must have seen and lived wisely and well.

Just in case you've run out of sodium amytal for the week-end, here are a few substitutes with which I've just caught up. They've been floating around for some time. "Fabiola": Christian tribulations in the time of Constantine. A two-hour chaos of disconnected sequences snipped more or less at random from a much longer French production. English dubbed in; livestock by Barnum; male and female costumes by Claire McCardell; lighting by Mr. Moon. "Tony Draws a Horse": Cecil Parker and all the gang in a sophisticated British psycho-comedy. Very intelligent movie in which the heroine swaths her head in a bandana, pulls her dress over her head, and then takes the bandana off. Perhaps, this is the English way of distracting your attention from obvious cheesecake. "The Secret of Convict Lake": Battle between the sexes, somewhere north of Carson City in 1871. Five escaped convicts drop in on eight temporarily unattached lady pioneers of the sort you might meet in Lord and Taylor's any day now: Gene Tierney, Ethel Barrymore, Richard Hylton. A grotesquely overcivilized Western larded with small talk about decency and indecency, peace of mind, kindness.

"Force of Arms," the only likable film I saw last week, deserves a longer review than I can give it here.

September 1, 1951

THE design of "Force of Arms" is rather simple-minded. This World War II tear-jerker starts off with Bill Holden fighting in the trenches behind some lush mountains, and then, with hardly more than a transitional line of dialogue, comes to a loquacious love scene between Sergeant Holden and WAC Lieutenant Nancy Olson, the girl he bumps into one midnight during a jaunt through a military cemetery. Thereafter, this structure repeats and repeats—a bit of war, a bit of love—to form the checkerboard cast up by script-writer Orin Jannings, whose cinematic naiveté is matched only by his idealism. In his version of the Italian campaign, there is a jeep waiting within elbow-reach of any infantryman worth his fighting weight; and beatific romance, Errol Flynn heroics, and brotherly affection geyser up like Old Faithful.

The sergeant-hero is a sensitive, moody, kindly one-man army who does the thinking for his platoon, writes letters to the parents of deceased buddies, plays poppa to the drunks, throws strikes with hand grenades, and looks frequently off into the cloudcast mountains while murmuring that it's going to be tough tonight for some poor doggies somewhere. (There are some very frightening battlefront clips from Huston's San Pietro, sandwiched in with pictures that always seem to be slanted to give a glamorous impression of combat. When a soldier is hit, he always goes into a graceful half gainer; slotted carefully into every composition is a glistening olive tree freshly dipped in black syrup for poetic imagery.) Holden's sweetheart is even more noble, high-minded, wholesome, and intellectual, although she does seem singularly addicted to battlefront romances. When the sergeant first meets her, in the potter's field of a Flanders Field designed by some Grant Wood disciple, she is laying a wreath on the grave of her last boy-friend. She rejects Holden's first rather interestingly truculent advances in a manner becoming to an officer and gentlewoman—an obstacle the film expediently and disappointingly hurdles in the very next sequence by having Holden hustled off to see General Mark Clark and receive a battlefield promotion to second looie. (Nice shot of Clark; ingenious montage trick by the special-effects people.) All succeeding problems are handled in the same nimble fashion, which means you can stop worrying about the plot and concentrate on the items of greater interest: the flashy, schmaltzy vigor injected by Director Michael Curtiz, who showed in "Casablanca" that he knew a movie had to move and that its players should bounce against each other democratically; the Cézanne-like sculptural realism of cameraman Ted McCord, an artist whose atmospherically accurate work I am forced to admire in spite of my distaste for the self-conscious; and especially the gifted acting of the team of Holden and Olson.

This ladies' magazine facsimile of "Farewell to Arms" is really a startling, intimate show-window displaying the talents of two unheralded young dramatic dynamos: the girl with more subtleties than Hollywood has seen in several decades and the guy with more controlled and potent American grace than it may have ever seen before. Miss Olson fills the slightest requirement for a change of mood with a compacted intensity of technical razzle-dazzle and the astuteness of an actress who is about 150 points smarter on the Binet scale than the 4-H character she is portraying. One begins to realize presently that she is editing the role as she goes along—and the idea also begins to dawn on you that this flat-eyed starlet is a diamond-hard sophisticate, full of hidden crossness, the icy ambition of a Hepburn, and the determination to play a traditionally pure and lofty role in such a way as to reveal the sterility, stubbornness, and rigidity of the middle-class American heroine. Her most powerful weapon here is her voice—a flexible carillon that pierces into a scene like a knife and cuts it into a frame for her words. Like that vocal magician, Mercedes McCambridge—who came up the hard way, through radio—Olson can wind her voice into an ambiguous composition of ferocious, haunting, demanding elements that captures the ear and refuses to relinquish it until the moment has been milked dry. Holden does the same thing in a different manner— disclosing the self-righteous stupidity of the awkward, charming Jimmy Stewart type of hero, but doing it less intricately, less pretentiously than his co-star. He's at his best when laying it on thickest, as when he asks a sentry the way to town, takes in the answer, and then spins off in the opposite direction. Or when he pouts viciously because his light o' love has caught him with his defenses down.

There are other ingratiating or interesting things: a good, driving trio playing "Ain't She Sweet?" in the Mamma Mia dive; a pragmatic WAC major, so obviously intended as the one ugly note in an otherwise optimistic film that she stands out like a Turpin fan on Lenox Avenue; the two usual Bronx-Brooklyn comic riflemen who this time put across a certain smutty aroma of both homosexuality and the real thing; and a furloughed officer (Frank Lovejoy) who, having picked up a girl without much front, darts a hopeful backward glance at her behind. But there's also a tidal wave of tedious bright talk, including all sorts of visually unproved references to the beggared peasantry, Hershey-bar prostitution, and the glories of Italian architecture. "Can you hear my heart beat?" Olson asks during one typically gabby embrace, and Holden, who is forever answering such difficult questions, replies: "I thought it was mine."

September 15, 1951

◆

THOUGH "People Will Talk" is basically only a Dr. Kildare story about "good" medicine and "bad," it has been precociously adult-erated into the toniest film of the year. It tells the tale of a miraculous gynecologist (Cary Grant) who embodies all the fortunate attributes of the well-analyzed, well-to-do, liberal know-it-all, and may very likely speak symbolically in defense of well-analyzed Hollywood millionaire-liberals like Joseph L. Mankiewicz, who wrote and directed the movie for Darryl F. Zanuck. We meet this Hippo-democratic whiz-bang at a stormy moment in his career, when he is being attacked by a jealous pip-squeak professor of anatomy (Hume Cronyn) who, driven by resentment, accuses the great Dr. Praetorious of resorting to unorthodox methods of therapy—methods which are never clearly defined to any greater extent than that they include a chummy, considerate attitude toward patients. Working on the broad-minded doctor from another quarter at this particular instant is the pregnant but unmarried Miss Higgins (Jeanne Crain), a fainting, crying, fearful, charming drifter. After missing herself at zero range with a pearl-handled one-shooter, she seduces Dr. P. into an elegant marriage.

The spectator learns a lot of highfalutin nothings about these troubled characters, and even less about the practice of medicine, eccentric or otherwise, since never more than for the briefest moment does the camera quit the lips of the protagonists in order to examine the real business of doctoring. There are, however, a good many daring cracks about such things as illegitimacy, impotence, infantile toilet habits; as a result, the naive and impressionable may be led to believe that this daredevil, Mankiewicz, is raking the medical profession—and certain other American institutions—over the coals. Well, I have no doubt that such was the intention, for "People," like so many other films in the past six years, contains that disguised, free-wheeling leftist attack on American manners and morals that Senators are always looking for but wouldn't recognize if it bit them.

The good doctor is presented by Mankiewicz as a new faith healer surrounded by all those small-minded, cantankerous, inefficient little cogs who make our boring capitalist system run. An eminently successful man who does nothing according to Hoyle, he moves pompously and talkatively through the world, finding something wrong with everything and everyone and showing us, with tired but unflagging urbanity, the way of the truth and the light. He scolds a heartless nurse ("Don't ever let me hear you say that about a patient again!"), looks down his nose at over-conscientious note-takers in anatomy class, makes epigrams about our obsession for packaged foods, twitches all over when he visits a prosperous farmer who has a fondness for television and chicken every Sunday. (Mankiewicz has outdone Wilder and Stevens at creating nasty caricatures of minor "representative Americans.") Meanwhile, he takes in Miss Higgins, her misfit poet father (Sidney Blackmer), and a slow-witted giant of a murderer (Finlay Currie), who in gratitude becomes the hero's constant companion and valet. These adoptees, unequal to the demands of our vicious competitive society, find a cosy paradise with Praetorious, his Brahms records, and his Lionel electric trains—so help me. Out of this holocaust of black-white contrasts, overstatements, and simple blind misstatements comes the message —stylistically bootlegged from Wilde, Shaw, F.D.R., anybody—that until we begin living in some mysteriously friendly, understanding, noble relationship with one another, we're pretty far up the creek.

*

A movie made with considerable more insight and cinematic know-how about its subject matter—though no less biased—is "Saturday's Hero"; putting the blast on college football with all the subtlety and flexibility of Fordham's Seven Blocks of Granite, it sees greedy sadists everywhere except among the gentle, brotherly workers in coal mines and dyeworks. The Millard Lampell story shows a scrapping scatback (John Derek) from the New Jersey proletariat being pursued, landed, and then manhandled by an obsessive coach, a big-wheel alumnus (Blackmer again), and one particular All-American end whose apology to the injured Derek goes like this: "I'm sorry, Novak, I really needed the dough, the $150 they offered me if I could put you out of the game." Lampell has constructed his script in brief, active scenes which jolt past the eye like telephone poles seen from a Pullman window. For instance, about five minutes of his script parlays the following shots: Derek's "I love you" to Donna Reed over milk shakes, picture of speeding train, newspaper shot of alumni banquet in Norfolk, spread on Novak in national magazine, speeding train, letter from home ("Poppa not feeling so hot"), close-up of forever troubled Novak, speeding train, distant view of football practice in Jackson Stadium. The more extended scenes are also pretty unimportant. They spit out shots of Donna Reed, a hollow actress with jittery, camera-shy eyes, and of Derek faking most of his acting by a facial expression fraught with intensity because the scriptwriter apparently forgot to write any dialogue for him.

But this gridiron exposé is probably the toughest sports film since "The Set-up." Someone in the crew was hep to certain football types: the rangy, shy, and almost moronically incurious end; the lanky frosh coach, full of pepper, who is himself a perennial freshman; and the ex-paratrooper fullback who has about ten years in toughness and worldliness on his mates. Having done a good job of casting the team around Novak, the director quietly keeps you aware of each player in the scrimmaging without establishing a special little scene of comedy or glory to make him memorable. The football action approximates the appalling speed and business-machine efficiency of the modern game, while an electrically precise camera man (Lee Garmes) manages to make Derek into a fairly credible pigskin ace. Garmes button-hooks his camera at a swift speed from the forward-passing Derek to a point just behind the receiver, an often-repeated tactic that immeasurably speeds up the play and allows some unlisted Otto Graham to throw the bullet pass for Derek. The movie is spotted with things as nostalgically barren in design as the freshman rooms and as nearly right in poignance as the distant view of a blanketed halfback hobbling forlornly down the sidelines to the dressing room. But all in all the film thrusts so much message and quick fame at its audience that you can almost hear the high-school spectators drooling about all those dollars that are within tackling distance of their ham-sized hands.

September 29, 1951

◆

Everything that kept the Broadway "Streetcar" from spinning off into ridiculous melodrama—everything thoughtful, muted, three-dimensional—has been raped, along with poor Blanche Dubois, in the Hollywood wood version, so that the drama takes place completely in the foreground—all clamor, climax, and Kazan. The movie opens characteristically with cabs zooming in an arc toward the camera and then cutting sharply into the New Orleans depot. With "impact" thus established, Warner Brothers takes us into the station for an artistic tip-off on what's to follow: a herd of crinolined bridesmaids jounce gaily off the Seaboard Limited while away to the side the shabby-genteel figure of Blanche (Vivien Leigh) emerges through a cloud of engine steam. A chirpy sailor interrupts his whistling long enough to give Miss Dubois directions to her sister's house. A streetcar named DESIRE, in white block letters a mile high, lunges in another vicious arc before our eyes, and there we are in Stanley Kowalski's serene, sexful, squalid little flat in the French Quarter. From here on, the story proceeds as Tennessee Williams first wrote it, except that all the frankest—and most crucial—dialogue has been excised and the last scene has been churned disastrously to satisfy the Johnson office but confound the spectator. These changes bothered me less than the fact that screen writer Williams thought he could turn his play into a movie by merely running the cast "outdoors" to a bowling alley or waterfront cafe whenever the dramatic structure of the original work permitted such a maneuver.

However, if the author surrendered without firing a shot, the actors and directors certainly did not. Marlon Brando, who on the stage gave a revolutionary head-on portrait of the rough-and-ready, second-generation American Joe, has upped the voltage of every eccentricity by several thousand watts. The performance is now more cinematic and flexible, but the addition of a lush physicality and a show-off's flamboyance to the character of Stanley makes him seem like a muscular version of a petulant, crazily egotistical homosexual. Brando, having fallen hard for the critics' idea that Stanley is simply animal and slob, now screams and postures and sweeps plates off the table with an ape-like emphasis that unfortunately becomes predictable.

As the ex-school-teacher-harlot-belle in this study of social-sexual disinte-
gration, Miss Leigh injects a bitter-sweet fragrance and acrobatic excitement
into the role, but the effects are freakish, too ambitious and endless. All this
inchoate electricity helps sustain Kazan's record of directing nothing that is
boring or insipid. The morning bed scene with wholesome Mrs. Kowalski
(Kim Hunter) shows her as smug and contented as movie wives usually are in
that situation. But Kazan gives the audience a rough shove with his candid
view of the lady's legs widely spread under a disheveled sheet that never saw
the inside of a laundry. Still, by activating all the characters to a pitch where
they seem one comic-opera step away from lunacy Kazan has obliterated
Williams's more delicate gradual revelation of the fact that Blanche is a rotten
old Dixie apple fated for squashing by that raw, instinctual, 100 per cent industrial American, Stanley Kowalski.

Among the less arty but more enjoyable movies I have seen are "The
People Against O'Hara," "The Day the Earth Stood Still," and "The Red
Badge of Courage."

October 20, 1951

THOUGH "The Red Badge of Courage" is a thin study, overdirected and
underwritten, about the havoc war plays in the souls of common citizens, it is
also the most sharply focused view of soldiering yet presented by Hollywood,
and, in the pure sense, one of the most uncompromisingly artistic films ever
made in this country. (In my opinion, this is not especially to its credit.) Writer-
director John Huston tells his story of the great death as it appears to an average American farm boy, suddenly plucked out of his peaceful Ohio
adolescence and thrown into the terrible annealing-vat of battle against the
Johnny Rebs. This soldier-hero (Audie Murphy), who is worried sick over the
prospect of not being as brave as he wants to be, is tossed up and down like a
cork during his first skirmish near the Rappahannock, the main part of which
is actually fought and won far from the picture-postcard grazing-land where the
boy evolves through much pain and humiliation into a ferocious, inspiring,
foolhardy warrior. Murphy's infantryman is a more worrisome, innocent version
of the deft, resilient handyman-hero of all the earlier Huston films. Like his
forerunners (Spade, Dobbs, "Dix"), the young soldier is an emotionally snarled
man of action, the bitter, confident pessimist, who was first revealed in "The
Maltese Falcon" and has since virtually splashed the chaotic diary of his inner

life all over the American screen. Murphy, the genuine article as men of action go—he won a carload of medals in the war—is hardly the type to project so much hot, florid perplexity and despair at what the world is doing to him. Neither is his cinematic comrade in arms, Bill Mauldin. Both of these baby-faced veterans are obviously suited to getting things done in life without fuss or feathers, and their agitated quiverings in "Red Badge" make you feel that here, more than in any previous Huston film, the actors have been harried and pushed into great, baroque, disproportionate demonstrations of feeling.

But if Huston torments his actors as one might torment a fly with a pin, he still knows the ways of self-conscious, thoughtful, hard-rock individualists better than anyone else in movies; and this shows through in his casting, which is invariably precise and subtle: discounting the emotional ejaculation they have to go through, Murphy and Mauldin are right out of Stephen Crane's cold furious brain; the boyishly shy, pristine, elegant Douglas Dick is even more accurate as an earnest, romantic, somewhat effeminate lieutenant; the quiet, huge-boned John Dierkes—a man you will be seeing more of—exactly por-trays the tall farmer-soldier whose death is as awesome as that of a falling oak tree; while for bit players, Huston has somehow derricked from central casting a whole regiment of men who might well be the uncouth, unaware recruits from the Ohio villages of 1862. A past master at working a performer away from any pet manner of acting, Huston has done such things in this film as make Dick abandon the deadening, inflexible seriousness with which he always in the past tried to counteract his all too apparent effeminacy; here Dick is merely a tender, perplexed, surprised boy to whom things happen in unexpected vio-lent ways. And then, surrounded by his men in the smoking battle area, he shows the toughening effects of combat in one split-second look of un-believing astonishment, the same look seen on the faces of halfbacks or steel-workers who have come through what seemed like a hopeless, endless orgy of hard work.

In spite of virtues like this, "Red Badge" is one of the least warlike films ever made. The chief trouble seems to be that it was put together by a direc-tor and a photographer (Hal Rosson) less impelled and excited by Crane's story of war than by the untouched natural setting they found to shoot it in—a low, flowing, pastoral plot of ground that inspired them to make one of those styl-ish, Renoir-ish studies, all delicacy, poetry, beauty, trees, bark, sunlight, eupho-ria. The terrain, in fact, is the true hero of this production, which is proved in a number of Steinbeckian scenes, including the falling-oak business and a wonderful sequence in which a dying Confederate flag-bearer squirms up a little hillock like a broken-down ant. Every composition seems cast in the character of the land, which in real life forms part of Huston's ranch; the result is to make the soldiers, their drums, flags, muskets into little more than handsome adjuncts of nature. There is something wrong with any picture that must rely for climax on straight-up views of sun-drenched foliage; and in this particular case, the fancy camera work seems far out of line with the essential drama of small-time figures caught on the darkening plain of battle.

November 10, 1951

Detective Story

Detective Story spends a day in a precinct squad room, making it jump with hokum, "business," and the acrobatic mugging of a horde of aggressive actors, all of whom have wonderfully sculptured faces. Though the station house is realistically crummy—as any New York set should be but almost never is—the cameraman, Lee Garmes, in an effort to instill some outdoor excitement into an indoor stage play, has pumped it full of a curious gray mist. Mist or no mist, the squad room is the most credible thing you're going to see in this high-powered, entertaining piece of histrionic schmaltz. Through the station door—which bangs back and forth, back and forth, until, at last, exactly as anticipated, it bangs some poor cop in the behind—swarm riffraff, the mulcted, mouthpieces, and minions of the law, each a walking caricature in physiognomy and mannerism of certain familiar Manhattan types.

Among this traffic is a string of recent Broadway exiles: Lee Grant as a man-hungry shoplifter with a sinuously unfeminine wriggle, a parrotlike head thrust, and some other not quite hilarious tricks, which she moiders with her East Side dialect; Joseph Wiseman, a degenerate cat-burglar who sweeps into the familiar Jewish palms-up gesture as no man ever did before—yet he seems to have genuine pool-hall cynicism and chilling scorn for the "artists" with whom he is working; Michael Strong, Wiseman's dumb crony, who crosses the affectations of a slack-jawed delinquent with those of a hep cat, doing this with a glib exaggeration that makes actor seem more confused than character. While these evil-doers are booked and printed by grumbling detectives, they are jumbled into a mass of lively movement designed to make you laugh —sentimentally—at Bronx-Brooklyn-East Side deficiencies.

The central figure in the crew of suffering, sweating cops is Kirk Douglas, a one-man army against crime who, in the course of the day, third-degrees a lot of crooks, discovers his beloved wife is not so immaculate, goes off his rocker, and dies walking into the bullets of four-time loser Wiseman. Douglas's mad-dog style of acting is bound to make any character into a one-sided surface of loud-pedaled ugliness. In this instance, his stiff-lipped biting off of dialogue, his muscle-bound strut, his grotesque posturing complicate a character already cluttered with the snapping documentary facts that Sidney Kingsley has dredged from three years of research in New York precinct stations.

The casting of gymnastic-minded Douglas for the rigid, unmerciful cop's role is a puzzling one, since both Kingsley and the producer-director, Wyler, are trying, in a wrangling hit-or-miss manner, to give some understanding of the psychology of an authoritarian sadist. And yet it isn't puzzling at all when you remember (a) that Douglas is top box-office these days and (b) that he has been built by Hollywood, film by film, into the cine-symbol of the Hollow Man who flies high, blind, and arrogant above the rest of us until the poison vapors of our rotten society at least reach his innards and bring him, too, cringing, crumbling, squirming to earth. (Question: Is our society rotten because there are too many honest cops running around? Is it the honest cop, as a matter of fact, who has been blowing his brains out lately? Question: Could misanthropic film-makers peddle this nonsense without a Douglas—or, before him, a Widmark, or, before that, a Muni—to serve as chief huckster? I wonder.) The cop dreamed up for us by Douglas, Wyler, and Kingsley is developed no more than one inch below the surface. For no other reason than that he has been uncharitably tough and just, he suddenly starts screaming and doing silly things like wanting to cut out his brain, take it in his hand, and examine the "dirty pictures" put in it by his wife. (The emptied skull is one of Kingsley's many images of hollowness; others are bells, graves, ticking meters, and, gaudiest of all, the cop's stomach, in which, according to Douglas, there stands some "pore little guy"— that is to say, his criminal father—laughing and crying with scorn and pity.) What all this "meaningful" color adds up to is total confusion, even unto the hammy death scene when you are finally given to understand that Detective McLeod, if he had it all to do over again, would have gone about it more like one of Harry Gross's friends and less like Johnny Broderick.

The movie's big item is the crack-up of Douglas's marriage to Eleanor Parker, a tremulous actress with a genius for finely shaded whimpering, bawling, tense-legged walking. Kingsley bears down on the emotions, words, and thoughts of these two as sadistically as his belligerent hero pursues the criminal abortionist, who, it turns out, once did a small favor for Mrs. McLeod. With stricken face and trembling lips, Douglas will mention that he's afraid to go home armed if his wife isn't there, while Parker, with her insidiously flexible lips, talks constantly of being unable to go to sleep without Douglas's arms around her. Then he learns the awful truth about her. There has never been anything, for theatrical agony, like the stricken faces, clenched hands, and agonized hate-poetry that ensue between the two.

Detective Story is far more absorbing than some equally lurid message melodramas (*A Place in the Sun*, *A Streetcar Named Desire*) now being touted for the Academy Award. But it plays the same hoax on its audience, transforming a sordid locale with full-color effects that seem so wrong one suspects a writer and director of selling out everything they know in order to dislodge the spectator's eyeballs—and reason.

November 24, 1951

"Best Films" of 1951

LET Stevens or Kazan win their Oscars; *The Nation*'s Emanuel—a life-size drip-celluloid statue of Kirk Douglas, ranting and disintegrating in the vengeful throes of death—goes to the man or men responsible for each of the following unheralded productions of 1951.

Little Big Horn. A low-budget western, directed by Charles Marquis Warren, starring John Ireland and Lloyd Bridges. This tough-minded, unconventional, persuasive look-in on a Seventh Cavalry patrol riding inexorably through hostile territory to warn Custer about the trap Sitting Bull had set for him, was almost as good in its unpolished handling of the regular-army soldier as James Jones's big novel. For once, the men appear as individuals, rather than types—grousing, ornery, uprooted, complicated individuals, riding off to glory against their will and better judgment; working together as a team (for all their individualism) in a genuinely loose, efficient, unfriendly American style. The only naturalistic photography of the year; perhaps the best acting of the year in Ireland's graceful, somber portrait of a warm-hearted but completely disillusioned lieutenant, who may or may not have philandered with his captain's wife.

Fixed Bayonets. Sam Fuller's jagged, suspenseful, off-beat variant of the Mauldin cartoon, expanded into a full-length Korean battle movie without benefit of the usual newsreel clips. Funny, morbid—the best war film since *Bataan*. I wouldn't mind seeing it seven times.

His Kind of Woman. Good coarse romantic-adventure nonsense, exploiting the expressive dead-pans of Robert Mitchum and Jane Russell, a young man and a young woman who would probably enjoy doing in real life what they have to do here for RKO. Vincent Price is superb in his one right role—that of a ham actor thrown suddenly into a situation calling for high melodramatic courage. Russell's petulant, toneless rendition of "Five Little Miles from San Berdoo" is high art of a sort.

The Thing. Howard Hawks's science-fiction quickie directed by Christian Nyby; fast, crisp, and cheap, without any progressive-minded gospel-reading about neighborliness in the atomic age; good airplane take-offs and landings; wonderful shock effects (the plants that cry for human blood as human babies cry for milk); Kenneth Tobey's fine, unpolished performance as a nice, clean, lecherous American air-force officer; well-cast story, as raw and ferocious as Hawks's *Scarface*, about a battle of wits near the North Pole between a screaming banshee of a vegetable and an air-force crew that jabbers away as sharply and sporadically as Jimmy Cagney moves.

The Prowler. A tabloid melodrama of sex and avarice in suburbia, out of Cain by Joe Losey, featuring almost perfect acting by Evelyn Keyes as a hot, dumb, average American babe who, finding the attentions of her disc-jockey husband beginning to pall, takes up with an amoral rookie cop (nicely hammed up by Van Heflin). Sociologically sharp on stray and hitherto untouched items like motels, athletic nostalgia, the impact of *nouveau riche* furnishings on an ambitious ne'er-do-well, the potentially explosive boredom of the childless, uneducated, well-to-do housewife with too much time on her hands.

The People Against O'Hara. An adroit, scholarly example of sound story-telling that every Message Boy should be made to study as an example of how good you can get when you neither slant nor oversimplify. Also highly enjoy-able for its concern about a "static" subject—the legal profession as such—and the complete authority with which it handles soft-pedaled insights into things like the structure and routine of law offices; the politics of conviviality between cops, DA's, judges, attorneys; the influence of bar associations; the solemn manner of memorializing the wrench caused by the death of a colleague; the painful "homework" of committing to memory the endless ramifications of your case, as well as the words you are going to feed the jury in the morning.

The Day the Earth Stood Still. Science-fiction again, this time with ideals; a buoyant, imaginative filtering around in Washington, D.C., upon the arrival of a high-minded interplanetary federalist from Mars, or somewhere; matter-of-fact statements about white-collar shabby gentility in boarding houses, offices, and the like; imaginative interpretation of a rocket ship and its robot crew; good fun, for a minute, when the visitor turns off all the electricity in the world; Pat Neal good, as usual, as a young mother who believes in progressive education.

The Man Who Cheated Himself.   A lightweight, O'Henry-type story about a cop who hoists himself on his own petard; heavyweight acting by Jane Wyatt and Lee J. Cobb; as a consequence, the only film this year to take a moderate, morally fair stand on moderately suave and immoral Americans, aged about forty. An effortlessly paced story, impressionistically coated with San Francisco's oatmeal-gray atmosphere; at the end, it wanders into an abandoned fort or prison and shows Hitchcock and Carol Reed how to sidestep hokum in a corny architectural monstrosity. Cobb packs more psychological truths about joyless American promiscuity into one ironic stare, one drag on a cigarette, or one uninterested kiss than all the Mankiewicz heroes put together.

Appointment with Danger.   Tough, perceptive commercial job glorifying the P-men (Post-Office sleuths), set in an authentically desolate wasteland around Gary, Indiana, crawling with pessimistic mail-robbers who act as though they'd seen too many movies like *Asphalt Jungle*. Tight plotting, good casting, and sinuously droopy acting by Jan Sterling, as an easily had broad who only really gets excited about—and understands—waxed bop. Interesting for Morgan-Webb bit playing, such sidelights as the semi-demi-hemiquaver of romantic attachment between the head P-man and a beautiful nun.

And, for want of further space, six-inch Emanuels to the following also rans: *The Tall Target, Against the Gun, No Highway in the Sky, Happiest Days of Your Life, Rawhide,* Skelton's *Excuse My Dust, The Enforcer, Force of Arms, The Wooden Horse, Night Into Morning, Payment on Demand, Cry Danger,* and a Chuck Jones animated cartoon—the name escapes me—about a crass, earnest, herky-jerky dog that knocks its brains out trying to win a job in a Pisa pizza joint.

January 5, 1952

◆

"Miracle in Milan." A sententious documentary fable about loving that neighbor, set in a hobo jungle beside the Milan railroad tracks; a grubby, inventive "My Man Godfrey" that came to America late in the year but walked away with most of the best-foreign-film awards and will doubtless delight every filmgoer who seriously believes he loves his fellow-men. It is a De Sica treatment of a Zavattini novel, featuring Francesco Golisano—a grinning, bull-like mixture of Burt Lancaster and Mussolini—as a naive orphan who turns his shanty town into a haven of fine emotions, simple pleasures, and modest comforts. Highly unenjoyable for its moronically oversimplified pantomime and symbolism, its fragmented and ragged structure, its exhaustive sentimentality:

to wit, the forlorn thread of a dirt road (loneliness); marble-walled interiors (the idle rich); fried eggs (what the poor dream about); the falsetto operatic voice (art is pompous and pansy-like); high hats and mink coats; little capitalists being chased down the street by angry mobs; buttocks-rich shots of pseudo-Grecian statues; bums kissing bums; people counting (charmingly) on their fingers; white flags of surrender; sunsets; parades; angels. Though it has been called "the freshest movie in years"—by those who very likely applied the same phrase twenty years ago to the René Clair films which served as prototype (in the matter of high hats being blown across a lot, for instance)— "Milan" really burglarizes the repertoire of those suave, altruistic C-men (Cartier-Bresson, Chaplin, Clair, Capra) who treat the spectator as a child to be guided, taught, and disciplined.

"Rashomon." A torpid, stylish Japanese study in human frailty, like nothing so much as a tiny aquarium in which a few fish and a lot of plants have delicately been tinkered with by someone raised in Western art-cinema theaters and art galleries. Five characters, two unfrequented real-life sets—a ruined temple and a forest—and a script which is probably the first to describe a highly contrived sword-fight-and-seduction through the biased eyes of four different people. The villain is a conceited, slothful, bug-ridden bandit (Toshiro Mifune)—a type now familiar in Hollywood adventure-comedies about Mexico—who has a hard time pulling himself away from a good nap to ravish the wife of a traveling samurai. Makes its play for posterity with such carefully engineered actions as one in which the dozing barbarian scratches his crotch while the sword across his knees somehow rises (Maya Deren-fashion) as though it had just had a big meal of sex hormones. "Rashomon" is supposed to get down to the bedrock of such emotions as lust, fear, and selfishness, but actually it is a smooth and somewhat empty film whose most tiresome aspect is the slow, complacent, Louvre-conscious, waiting-for-prizes attitude of everyone who worked on it.

"I Want You." The Goldwyn stock company (Granger, Andrews, McGuire, Keith, etc.) drafted away from their side of the railroad tracks—the other side from De Sica's—for the duration of the cold war. Written by *New Yorker* writers Irwin Shaw and John Cheever. Much too talkative and taken up with the sad departures of drafted men; nothing more momentous in it than Mildred Dunnock sweeping all her pseudo-hero husband's war mementoes off the wall. Yet good—as all Goldwyn's soap-operas are—for its sad, cautious desire to get at the haggard side of Americans by being exactly right about the stained wall-paper around picture frames, the sexless bathrobe of Mrs. Suburbia, the sullen pooped-out expression on her face, the chenille His-Her towels in the bathroom, and the fact that most of the conversation consists of tired nothings: "What'll it be? . . . I want to say hello to George Kress. . . . Why, I'm making you rich; what're you complaining of? . . . Oh, wait a minute. . . . Why doesn't Landrum mind his own business? . . . How are things in Washington? Scary." Not even Goldwyn can keep Farley Granger from his obsequious, frightened, liver-lipped manipulation of a smile or a drag on a cigarette, but the others almost break your heart with their pinched-faced "bravery," their frozen pantomime, their ability to talk without opening their mouths.

"Behave Yourself." A tasteless, paceless, surprisingly good farce, spoofing the "Thin Man" idea of having cops, robbers, a dog, a mother-in-law, keep a young married couple (Granger again, with Shelley Winters) from going to bed together. Crammed with ultra-modern buildings, furniture, statues; shot mostly through leaves and incidental bric-a-brac. Cameraman James Wong Howe, usually an earnest documentarist, shoots a crucial murder here as if he'd been bribed by Florence Knoll. The humor is either strictly from Minsky or tied up with the décor, or both (as when the dog finds himself in a jungle of plastic mannikin legs). Best funny moment of many months is provided by the scene in which a silly egg-skulled cockney gangster (with a bullet wound in his forehead that may have been painted by Piero della Francesca) slides down like a well-oiled banana into a colossal bubble-bath.

"The Racket." This movie had everything—Mitchum, Ryan, and today's most-talked-of subject matter. But it came out a junky, impossible bore.

"Another Man's Poison." The elevation to co-stardom (with wife Bette Davis) of the over-energetic Gary Merrill in a psychotic melodrama that left me limp, incredulous, and baffled.

"Westward the Women." Two hundred women and Robert Taylor. This is a Western?

January 19, 1952

◆

"My Son John," the story of a traitor out of Anytown, U.S.A., goes across the screen dodging its point with all the deftness of a suspense yarn. The point was to show you the heart of a home-grown Communist as well as his day-to-day scurryings in the red network, but all you get is generalized bombast in his folks' idealized democratic household and familiar tear-jerking situations. Plot-wise, a bright shy boy goes into government work and, reversing "Mr. Smith

Goes to Washington," becomes a top Soviet spy. Back home for a rare visit, he mentions a speech he is to make to the graduating class of his old Alma Mater, and the content of that speech gets him into a dozen angry arguments on communism with his folks, who are charter members of the church and the Legion, and inspire each other with lingo from the gridiron ("Take the ball, John!"). An amiable FBI agent keeps poking around the neighborhood, and pretty soon the mother discovers the truth about her favorite son, leading to tear-duct scenes as she teeters on the edge of insanity and soul-stirring shots of the son's face as he begins to see the democratic light (in one silent stretch, shadows play over the face, changing it back and forth from Judas Iscariot's to Abe Lincoln's). The rest is mechanical fireworks: the flight from his co-spies, his bullet-ridden car spinning up the steps of the Lincoln Memorial, and the tape-recorded recantation of the dead ex-Communist played back to the empty faces of the sweet, innocent graduates.

With Helen Hayes, the late Robert Walker, and director Leo McCarey—the latter a social philosopher who makes platitudes boom like the truth—heavily involved in "My Son John," no one is going to fall asleep for want of effervescent dramatics. McCarey tries to stop United States youth from falling for the party line with the same formula he used in the past to get the kids off the street and into church—that is, tears, faith, and solid red-blooded Americanism. It is done with such earnestness as to be slow-moving, but the actors are masters of intricate timing and intonation and have the easy spontaneity and control to put across a story that is mostly talk in parlor, bedroom, and bath. Walker, with his unhealthy face and blunt sincerity, plays the traitor in a way that makes you marvel at how much this craggy, solemn-toned actor learned about his business and the people outside it in the last few years of his life. He was, I think, the first great actor to turn up in decades of films, one who reminds me only of silent geniuses like Conrad Veidt, Keaton, or an awkward, sour, dissipated version of Barthelmess. Helen Hayes plays the manic mother with all the eccentric wallop of Eleonora Duse doing a Krafft-Ebing rewrite of "Mrs. Wiggs of the Cabbage Patch." With Frank McHugh making you feel happy that he is back in films and McCarey working powerfully in the new style of close-ups, disembodied faces, and immobilized groupings, the movie is worth seeing, if only to dig Hollywood's latest political orientation.

Two Works of Art that reek with social therapy and old-fashioned technique —everything from grainy photography to sentimental curlicues—are in the neighborhood, occupying the bottom half of double bills. The quaint adolescent study called "The Big Night" is so slow, murkily lit, and incoherently involved with the meek pantomime of John Barrymore, Jr., that it might make more sense if the reels were run backward. However, "On Dangerous Ground" almost achieves a success in spite of itself. In the first place, it has to worry over the old chestnut about reform of the incorrigible by sweetness and trust—personified this time by a blind, tottering Ida Lupino who inspires cop Robert Ryan to mend his brutal ways. In the second place, it is tied to the idea that anything that moves makes a good motion-picture. The movie is a tread-mill of stumbling, fumbling, smooching, hurtling movement, and by the time it reaches the run-down of an adolescent murderer over half the snow-covered hills of northern California, the customer is as fed up with motion as the panting actors. But the story is told with a camera and a rather unorthodox one, though it is often late to the scene and not sure of what is about to happen. Some of the support—Ward Bond and Anthony Ross—is good, but the chief virtue of the film is the fascinating jumble of action that results when two awk-ward, determined characters (Bond and Ryan) try to outclaw each other at the job of detecting.

March 22, 1952

ALONGSIDE "Boots Malone," a race-park drama executed in a relaxed and mobile fashion, most of the current films appear to be moving on club feet. The story in capsule form shows a track-struck rich kid being adopted by a jaded jockey's agent, put through an intensive training, and turned into an expert bug-boy. The necessary problems are provided along the way by a quiet, matter-of-fact, grim syndicate that muscles the agent, who is for a hero surprisingly timorous; also there is a snobbish mother who probably learned her acting trade at the rodeo—she practically throws her eyebrows off her face. It is fashionable these days to show corruption in the United States; so the story has all but one of the jockeys, trainers, and so on merrily finagling with horses and mutuel prices. All this corruption is probably exaggerated but treated with remarkable plausibility: the techniques and documentation obviously derive from a thoroughgoing knowledge of the sport of kings and bookies. The only possible moral is that horse-racing is a fascinating sport but don't place too much confidence in your scratch sheet.

There has been so much blowing on what is stale in this movie and what is wonderful—paddock lingo and lore—that I won't swell its volume, except to suggest that kid athletes are not likely to learn their profession via the ABC instruction meted out by the agent to his apprentice rider. I suspect that if basketball coaches told the rookie players to dribble in zigzags, keep their eyes on the basket, or imparted any other kindergarten knowledge, there would be an outbreak of assassinations in American athletics: Ninety-nine per cent of American athletes learn their trade in their own way, and I see no reason why jockeys should depart from the norm. Such instruction ("Cock your knees, grab a handful of mane . . .") is there to please the critics who like educational movies and the chalk-sniffers who want to peep into the bowels of their favorite sport. As for the authentic racing talk ("fourteen-karat slow-bones," or "You don't make a claim on a one-horse owner"), quite a bit of it is sensitive, accurate, and illuminating. I remember with delight a race-track scrounger chortling with glee and using his winning mutuel tickets as blinkers, and the stark sentences: "All horses respect is force. They are mere brutes who have had all the intelligence bred out of them." And the entire handling of a fat, rich "win-crazy" owner is one of the most accurate examples of greed that I have seen this year. But a good deal of the fancy talk is contrived, and it hangs between people like tiny, misshapen dirigibles.

Milton Holmes, a movie specialist who writes only horse epics, is a born story-teller even if his stuff runs to pulp. His script treats the actuality of working for a living and does it without those short cuts that chop current movies into static fragments. The kid is shown learning how to ride on back-to-back chairs, a bale of hay, a chalk drawing, and finally race horses; this variety of mounts is obviously a gimmick for avoiding monotony, but it makes for a genuine movie atmosphere in which you see figures involved with racing and nothing else from dawn to midnight. This type of continuous and untightened narration gives actors room for small natural movements which never seem to get into a movie like "Detective Story," where close perspectives and absence of action force the actors into slightly hysterical business with eyes, lips, and hands. Holden, as the tarnished agent, is a dour sort who usually muffs the climactic scenes that demand big emotion (the pocket-picking in the beginning), but he is masterful in these realistic stretches—doing some relaxed coaching in the starting gate or galloping along with the boy telling him how to whip his mount (the best working shots I've seen in recent films). Holmes knows and likes the sights of a race track well enough to waste footage on the trip to the diner, motel life near the track, and the unrelated wanderings of a racing troupe stuck on the highway. This last scene, with its credible terrain and each shot connected into a line of actions that lead easily and logically from one thing to another, seems rather wonderful when compared to any of the vulgar settings and crazily viewed scenes of such over-touted masterpieces as "Streetcar" and "A Place in the Sun." "Boots Malone" is no world-beater, but it does show professional men actually working; the surface of their lives is almost real; and thanks to Holden, the story tells you a good deal about the grace, recessiveness, and quiet discernments of a moderately gifted man going nowhere.

A word or two further about the acting. However he does it, Holden seems in constant motion standing still; his posture, coloring, and disinterested technique are so perfectly adjusted to a natural setting that he appears to be a worn, moving part of the air currents in a scene. Basil Ruysdael's kindly trainer is so full of lofty spiritual feeling and the visual qualities of a daguerreotype that he could be a farmer who wandered off the set of "Tolable David" into this picture of corruption at the tracks. The rich kid, done in a controlled, over-trained Broadway style by Johnny Stewart, is just this side of revolting.

Also recommended: "Five Fingers," "The Captive City," "Los Olvidados."

April 5, 1952

◆

My list of top pictures made in the last five years ("Red River," "He Walked by Night," "Act of Violence") has now been expanded to include a titleless documentary of street life in Spanish Harlem, shot entirely with a 16-millimeter sneak camera by Janice Loeb, Helen Levitt, and James Agee. The technique of documenting life in the raw with a concealed camera has often been tried out, in Hollywood and in experimental films, but never with much success until this small masterwork turned up. One problem was finding a camera either small enough to be hidden or made in such a way that it could be focused directly on the scene without being held to the operator's eye. The "Film Documents" group used an old model Cine-Kodak which records the action at a right angle to the operator who gazes into his scene-finder much as was done with the old-fashioned "Brownie." The people who wound up in this movie probably thought the camera-wielder was a stray citizen having trouble with the lock of a small black case that could contain anything from a piccolo to a tiny machine gun. For dramatic action, the film deals with one of the toughest slum areas extant: an uptown neighborhood where the adults look like badly repaired Humpty Dumpties who have lived a thousand years in some subway restroom, and where the kids have a wild gypsy charm and evidently spend most of their day savagely spoofing the dress and manners of their elders. The movie, to be shown around the 16-millimeter circuit, has been beautifully edited (by Miss Levitt) into a somber study of the American figure, from childhood to old age, growing stiffer, uglier, and lonelier with the passage of years.

Let me say that changing one's identity and acting like a spy, or a private eye, are more a part of the American make-up than I'd ever imagined before seeing this picture. This not only holds for Levitt, Inc., who had to disguise their role of film-makers to get the naked truth, but also goes for the slum people who are being photographed. The film is mostly concerned with kids who are trying to lose themselves in fake adultness by wearing their parents' clothes and aping grown-ups' expressions; even the comparatively few adults (at a war-time bond rally) go in for disguises—Legionnaire uniforms, etc.—and seem afraid to be themselves. The chief sensation is of people zestfully involved in making themselves ugly and surrealistic, as though everything Goya's lithographs indicated about the human race had come true. This mood is established right off in a wonderful shot of a Negro tot mashing her tongue and face out of shape against a windowpane. This private bit of facemaking is followed soon by a shot of a fat man leaping up and down and chortling with glee at the sight of a neighborhood kid carrying another one on his shoulders, solemnly impersonating a new two-bodied grown-up. And this scene gives way to a macabre game of gypsy kids making like maniacs by clubbing each other with flour-filled stockings swiped from their mudders.

Every Hollywood Hitchcock-type director should study this picture if he wants to see really stealthy, queer-looking, odd-acting, foreboding people. Even the kids, whose antics make their elders look like a lost tribe of frozen zombies, act a bit like spies from the underground. Enigmatic and distrustful, a small boy watches the little colored girl (mentioned above) smear her features on the window; an older smart-alecky one slyly bats a flour stocking against the back of a teen-aged princess—the Mary Pickford of the neighborhood— carefully watching her every move to see if she's getting erotically excited. It is this very watchfulness which makes one part of the picture so brilliant: these kids must jeweler's-eye everything, and when the camera man (Agee) reveals himself, the space in front of the camera fills up with every kid in the neighborhood staring at the now bared camera like one Huge Eye.

To see what these kids will be like when they grow up, all we have to do is look at the shots of their parents. The watchfulness of youth has now become a total preoccupation—an evil-faced pimp, a Grant Wood spinster, a blowsy Irish dame picking at her teeth, are all forever staring at the world as though it were a dangerous, puzzling place filled with hidden traps. The great American outdoors, once a wide-open prairie for adventurers, is here, in one shrunken pocket of New York City, a place of possible terror to people who spend their time looking at it with 100-per-cent distrust.

"High Noon." A deftly fouled-up Western, starring Gary Cooper as a disillusioned marshal enforcing law and order in Hadleyville where everyone else is happily barricaded within his own avarice and cowardice. Carl Foreman's attempt to do an original cowboy script consists in starting the story at 10:40 a.m., ending it just after noon, and limiting the dramatic action to one situation: Gary Cooper walking silently and alone down the deserted streets looking for volunteer deputies. The contrived result: a movie which does take you into every part of the town and features Cooper's beautiful rolling gait, but which reveals that someone spent too much time over the drawing board conceiving dramatic camera shots to cover up the lack of story. Moral: the Kramer gang ("Champion," "The Men") is making too many films for its own good.

"The Marrying Kind." The story behind a sad little divorce suit told by the cut-back method, with the director (Cukor) using a sneak camera without putting any heart or belief into it. Cukor is a fine technician who has lately been imagining himself as an American Rossellini. The actors make Anna Magnani seem soft-spoken and even-tempered. Every camera set-up indoors shows you a person in a bathrobe, brassière, or long underwear, poking his or her behind into the camera lens to prove that this is a candid movie. And there is the uncomfortable spectacle of Judy Holliday, a cautious and intelligent highbrow, squeezing herself into the dumb role of a Bronx *yenta*.

"The Fighter." Herbert Kline's romantic fight drama about an unpolished Mexican bolo-puncher, who earns five dollars a day as a sparring partner and works feverishly at night for the revolutionary cause of Zapata and Villa. An inexpert mixture of politics and hokum, set in the Rio Grande towns of 1910, which look as unreal as the backdrops on the old Keith circuit. Conte, the silky Italian star of bare-chest films, is a Mexican fizzle.

April 26, 1952

◆

HOLLYWOOD films were once in the hands of non-intellectuals who achieved, at best, the truth of American life and the excitement of American movement in simple-minded action stories. Around 1940 a swarm of bright locusts from the Broadway theaters and radio stations descended on the studios and won Hollywood away from the innocent, rough-and-ready directors of action films. The big thing that happened was that a sort of intellectual whose eyes had been trained on the crowded, bound-in terrain of Times Square and whose brain had been sharpened on left-wing letters of the thirties, swerved Holly-wood story-telling toward fragmented, symbol-charged drama, closely viewed, erratically acted, and deviously given to sniping at their own society. What Welles, Kanin, Sturges, and Huston did to the American film is evident in the screen version of Dreiser's "Sister Carrie," which is less important for its story than for the grim social comment underscoring every shot.

You first see Carrie Meeber, rural and naive (Jennifer Jones), rushing to get off a daycoach while a drummer tells her she is making a mistake: "South Chicago? That's the slums." The remark, which makes a 1909 masher sound like a 1952 social worker, is full of meanings that the movie audience by now is wise to, and the writers need only touch on Carrie's first threadbare months in the city. The next few scenes are also immersed in social significance and accomplish the same kind of half-implied story-telling. One of them shows a crabby foreman driving Carrie so relentlessly that she runs a needle through her finger and loses her job as a shoe-stitcher. Since the foreman is played by a spidery bit player always type-cast as a mean "pinch-penny," and since his dialogue runs to sentences like "Here's a dollar, a whole day's pay," the spec-tator has picked up a quick course in non-union labor in no more than two min-utes of screen time.

The most important aspect of all this social significance is its prejudice against Americans, who are being ridiculed in films as completely as they were in the writings of Mencken. In this movie, the bias is managed, Mencken fash-ion, by treating people as "national" or "local" types rather than ordinary fig-ures, and then casting the roles with actors who love to over-act uncharming traits. Carrie's first amour is played by Eddie Albert, whose portrayal of an American "go-getter" consists of flashing a big, lopsided grin, twirling a heavy gold watch and using his voice like a loud musical instrument. Somehow the heroine, whose strong point is her essential gentleness, puts up with this cari-cature who opens every conversation with either a belch or a couplet: "Charley's the name, charm's the game!" When Carrie and her second lover, the sleek restaurant owner Hurstwood, skip to New York with his partner's money, they are tracked down by a detective from the Western Bonding Com-pany. The acting of this leering, gum-chewing slob is rendered by Ray Teal, who has a penchant for using one eye as though it belonged to a cruel pig and working a rich, sneering sound into his voice. Hurstwood's decline takes him into a Third Avenue hash house run by the sort of confident, ruthless Irishman Barry Kelley has been enacting since he entered films. The cameraman helps Kelley to look repugnant and slovenly with floor-shots that exaggerate his huge belly and the lazy, tyrannical way in which he lolls in a chair. And finally, Hurst-wood's wife, rich shrew that she is, turns up near the end to trade him a divorce for the rights to their Chicago home. Miriam Hopkins plays the scene by holding her mouth in a single grim line and keeping a rigid, buzzard-like look in her eyes.

One of the cardinal elements of the Times Square technique introduced in the era of "McGinty," "Citizen Kane," "A Man to Remember," and "The Maltese Falcon" was the use of very close, snarling presentation which put the actors practically in a nose-to-nose relationship with the movie spectator. The entire production of "Carrie" is thrown at you in shallow scenes, the actors arranged parallel-fashion and statically on the front plane of the scene so that their physical presence is overpowering. The film was fortunate in having Lau-rence Olivier as the high-powered Hurstwood, all delicacy, intelligence, and high style up to his last weakened whispers on the Bowery. But after an hour of close views Olivier becomes less a figure than a formidable mustache, a mouth that has a tendency to flap, and poignant hands that sometimes mimic the gestures of madonnas in medieval painting. In one of the last views of the pitiable Hurstwood his ravaged face is exposed to Carrie as she turns a lamp on it. The fact that Hurstwood is ashamed to show himself seems next to ludi-crous after an hour spent watching his face disintegrate over most of the screen.

"Carrie" is also fortunate in having a handsome production all around, but in the deliberate and magnified style to which Hollywood has turned, lightness of touch is impossible. When the camera dollies slowly over the cubicles of a flop-house (the big "art" scene) one has the feeling that the director is working with material that is as heavy and dignified as a Steinway grand inlaid with precious stones.

"Outcast of the Islands." A lesser Conrad story, showing the evil conse-quences of a tropical environment on a chivalrous, well-meaning leech. Star-ring Trevor Howard, who is surprisingly credible as a feverishly bored ne'er-do-well getting hot over a native girl who confines all her acting to moving her eyes. Despite some bad casting (Robert Morley and his daughter), Director Carol Reed has created an exceptional film that entangles the spec-tator in tropical textures and worries him with the shame and guilt of a hero who betrays only his friends. Alongside Reed's film, "African Queen" looks as if it had been shot in Palm Beach.

May 17, 1952

◆

"The Sniper"—the story of a sweet-faced laundry driver who compulsively murders pretty brunettes because "someone did something mean to him when he was a kid"—is a smooth, technically astute, 100 per cent dull melodrama. It was made by a progressive producer, Stanley Kramer, whose films often fight prejudice with all the usual antiquated prejudices. For example, he has gone to unusual lengths to build sympathy for the underdogs of society—the oppressed Negro, mother-fixated tenement kid, or paraplegic—while sniping at publishers, business men, government officials, etc. Here, he has cast the role of a sex offender with an actor (Arthur Franz) whose nice manners and muffled personality make him appear to be the movie's most wholesome American. The only thing interesting about the figure is that he is so unlikely as a "maniac." He has a neat way with guns, cars, baseballs, and laundry deliveries. When he spots a likely victim, he picks himself out a rooftop, calmly removes a telescopic carbine from a briefcase, efficiently puts it together, and puts one bullet cleanly through the girl's temple. Then he goes home, locks the carbine in the top bureau drawer, and writes a note to the police begging them to capture him ("Stop me—Find me and stop me—I'm going to do it again."). Aside from the fact that Franz is an expert driver and takes his laundry truck into picturesque San Francisco locales, his behavior is pretty colorless in a movie where the more normal citizens knock themselves out acting angry, cocky, pompous, or mean.

Though Kramer never tires of exposing ugliness in society, his movies are peculiar for an absurdly well-organized look: they move well, have a laundered kind of slate-toned photography, and never get tangled up in any event. It is typical of his Business Machine style that when the boy is finally spotted by a painter working a block away on the top of a factory chimney, the kid brings him down with a single bullet (the body slides down so photogenically on a pulley contraption that it must have been engineered by a Phi Beta Kappa in movie stunt shots). Another interesting example of Kramer's efficiency is the way his females act when the bullets hit them. They go into a cyclonic version of Leon Errol's rubber-legged walk before smashing into a brick wall or table; this is a difficult thing to do, but it is managed with fascinating skill by otherwise wooden females. Finally, there are the scenes between aroused civic leaders and police officials, in which "liberal" and "anti-social" remarks turn up with perfect timing and placement. A newspaper publisher, played by a stock Republican type, says some asinine thing ("We want this fellow caught, and punished, punished, punished."), and is immediately put in his place with a remark that sounds like it hurried in from a Barry Gray disc-jockey show ("Your paper slants the news, exploits killings."). Because of his spic-'n-span technique and the predictable left-wing slanting of characterization, "The Sniper" is a movie that you'll have to fight to enjoy.

"The Pride of St. Louis," another ultra-civic-minded work, manages to kill the idea of baseball as the national pastime. The script-writer (H. Mankiewicz) decided that Dizzy Dean is a democratic Ozark peasant, more important for his clean habits and civic behavior than for his fast ball. He has confined the movie to shots of Dizzy (Dan Dailey) glad-handing customers and developing, via talk, into a good citizen, while his career is described by radio announcers and newspaper headlines. When the movie occasionally gets around to baseball, it shows Dailey doing a hammed-up burlesque of pitching—so intricate that he doesn't seem to be throwing the ball. Odd note: Dailey, in certain profile shots with his hair dry and bushy, looks a bit like Dean's old-time rival, Carl Hubbell.

May 31, 1952

The Gimp

SOMEBODY once told me, no doubt inaccurately, that lady golfers in the Victorian era used a certain gimmick that went by the name of "Gimp." It was a cord running from hem of skirt to waistband; when preparing to hit the ball, you flicked it with your little finger and up came the hem. Thus suddenly, for a brief instant, it revealed Kro-Flite, high-button shoes, and greensward, but left everything else carefully concealed behind yards of eyeleted cambric. Something like this device has now been developed in Hollywood. Whenever the modern film-maker feels that his movie has taken too conventional a direction and is neglecting "art," he need only jerk the Gimp-string, and—behold!—curious and exotic but "psychic" images are flashed before the audience, pepping things up at the crucial moment, making you think such thoughts as "The Hero has a mother complex," or "He slapped that girl out of ambivalent rage at his father image, which, he says, he carries around in his stomach," or "He chomps angrily on unlit cigarettes to show he comes from a Puritan environment and has a will of iron."

Over the past couple of years, one movie after another has been filled with low-key photography, shallow perspectives, screwy pantomime, ominously timed action, hollow-sounding voices. All this pseudo-undershot stuff, swiped from any and every "highbrow" work of films, painting, literature, has gone into ultraserious movies that express enough discontent with capitalist society to please any progressive. In these beautifully controlled Freud-Marx epics, the only things that really move are the tricks and symbols designed to make you think, "God, this is sensitive!"

Somehow the nature of this new mannerist flicker has been misinterpreted by critics, by the good ones as well as the merely earnest publicists. With their preconceptions, their ennui, and their formularized responses to stimuli, the critics go their complacent (or disgruntled) ways, finding movies better (or worse) than ever, but never noticing that movies *aren't* movies any more. Not so long ago, the movies, whatever their oversimplifications and distortions, still rested on the assumption that their function was to present some intelligible, structured image of reality—on the simplest level, to tell a story and to entertain, but, more generally, to extend the spectator's meaningful experience, to offer him a window on the real world. What are they now?

Well, icebergs of a sort, one-tenth image, action, plot, nine-tenths submerged popular "insights" *à la* Freud or Jung, Marx or Lerner, Sartre or Saroyan, Frost, Dewey, Auden, Mann, or whomever else the producer's been reading; or they are Dali paintings, surrealist fun-houses with endless doors leading the spectator to inward "awareness" and self-consciousness, and far away from a simple ninety-cent seat in a simple mansion of leisure-time art and entertainment, or they are expressionistic shotguns peppering the brain of that deplored "escapist" with millions of equally important yet completely unrelated pellets of message—messages about the human personality and its relations to politics, anthropology, furniture, success, Mom, etc., etc. The trick consists in taking things that don't belong together, charging them up with hidden meanings, and then uniting them in an uneasy juxtaposition that is bound to shock the spectator into a lubricated state of mind where he is forced to think seriously about the phony implications of what he is seeing.

Most readers will remember the calculated moment in *Sunset Boulevard*— the kept man in the fashionable men's shop, ashamed of buying the vicuña coat with the ex-star's money. Up to a certain point, this scene was unfolded in a straight narrative line, and then Director Billy Wilder pulled his Gimp-string. The camera moved in for a very close close-up, the atmosphere became molecular and as though diseased—and there was a sleek clerk whispering to the slightly ill gigolo: "After all, if the lady is paying. . . ." Thus Wilder registered spiritual sickness and business-world corruption in an ad-libbed shot that had all the freshness of an old tire-patch, consisting as it did, under the circumstances, of naïve moral gibberish that no adult in his right mind would mouth.

This indirect shot, with its leaden overpantomiming going back to and beyond Theda Bara, offers a classic example of what the Gimp can do for a director, helping him avoid monotony (by switching from storytelling to symbolic "pseudoaction"), explaining hidden content, and ensuring his position in movies as a brave, intransigent artist.

One of the most confusing films of all time, *People Will Talk*, dealt with an unflaggingly urbane gynecologist, a liberal-minded doctor, who cured patients with friendliness, played with electric trains, scoffed at ration programs and packaged food, and generally behaved like a Lubitsch portrait of an enlightened college professor. One scene showed him making vague epigrams and looking down his nose at overconscientious note-takers in an anatomy class. Obviously all this suavity needed some excitement, and so Director Mankiewicz jerked his string and provided the well-analyzed doctor with a weird trick that you'll never see again in a movie. The doctor undrapes the corpse on the slab before him, and—surprise!—you are looking at a naked brunette, not only the most ravishing person in the movie but the whitest and least dead-looking. While the doctor talks on about heartless people and gracefully does things with the corpse's Godivalike tresses, the audience is so shocked by the beauty and lifelikeness of the corpse that it starts thinking all sorts of things about how society nags the individual, even unto death. (Visually, in the best Gimp tradition, this scene was bewitching for its pure unusualness; Cary Grant's classy erotic playing with the dead girl evokes a compound of evil, new kinds of sex, and terrific grace.)

The Gimp is the technique, in effect, of enhancing the ordinary with a different dimension, sensational and yet seemingly credible. Camera set-ups, bits of business, lines ("They don't make faces like that any more") are contrived into saying too much. Every moment of a movie is provided with comment about American society. "Original" characters are sought, the amount of illogical and implausible material is increased, to such a point that movies which try to be semidocumentary actually seem stranger than the Tarzan–Dracula–King Kong fantasy.

We are getting such characters as the abortionist in *Detective Story*, a close-mouthed Dutchman dressed like a low-paid respectable clerk from an early Sinclair Lewis story about department-store life in the Midwest. To make him look as though he has emerged from the bowels of common life in America, he is given a pinched, deathly pallor and a sickly personality that hardly allows him to breathe, much less talk. The apparent intention was to set up a significantly ordinary, true-to-life, entirely evil, grass-roots American; the result was a surrealistic creature who seemed ready at any moment to throw up. Thanks to the canny acting of George Macready, possibly Hollywood's most impressive character actor, this sour figure provided the film with its only good moments.

Two recent pictures have made especially adroit and unrelenting use of the Gimp. In *A Place in the Sun*, Director George Stevens, not content with letting a climax of violence follow naturally upon an inevitable train of events, treats us constantly to macabre darkenings of the landscape, metronome-timed hootings of a loon, and about six other sensational effects reeking with recondite significance. The story is about a not-quite-bright social climber, and Stevens so buries him in symbols of money, dominance, and sex that every last member of the audience must become involved with the vague meanings of the boy's daydreams. Wherever he walks, there is sex or wealth—usually both together—written out so big that no one can miss it: billboards that out-Petty Petty, languid and sophisticated aristocrats, a Gus Kahn love lyric coming from a midget radio. And of course his dingy furnished room in a depressed urban area must have a window facing on a huge neon factory sign standing for wealth and achievement.

In one protracted example of contrivance, a luscious babe in a Cadillac flashes by the boy as he hitchhikes on some spacious highway, and then comes a broken-down truck chugging straight out of *The Grapes of Wrath* to pick up the disappointed hiker. Immediately, the audience was saying to itself one or all of these things: "This is about the unfair distribution of wealth in the United States," or "His spirit is crying out for joy, ease, and love," or "He has a complex about being raised in a poor, harsh, confined neighborhood." Whenever any particularly delectable symbol crossed the boy's line of vision, he would freeze up with yearning, refusing to act, not answering questions for minutes on end, his wispy shoulders almost but not quite jerking, and occasionally one dead word straying out of his twisted mouth. There were eccentric scenes in which the boy met up with a deputy cop and a suspicious boatman, who—with the help of acting that was probably coached by Emily Brontë, and camera angles that gave the actors height and took away width—looked like ominous scoundrels from the Dark Ages and showed you Society intimidating the Outcast, American Justice breaking the Common Man on the wheel.

Symbols are a dime a dozen in Hollywood's storehouse, and Stevens bought up the stock: police sirens, train whistles, double shots of a boy's face and a remembered kiss, the lame leg of the sadistic district attorney (which makes him more formidable), a shadow going over a face to indicate an evil thought. Such things may seem to come from real life, but actually they are the products of medieval imaginations capable of grasping glaring features of contemporary life only in cliché terms. These creators have entrenched themselves within a vicious circle of decay: having helped to create and foster the world of lurid wealth, romantic love, and Big City glamour, they now express despair and chaos by exaggerating the same corny symbols they originally invented.

It has always been obvious that the movie camera not only reflects reality but interprets it. This fact used to imply the deepening and enrichment of an intelligible structure of plot and character. What is happening now is the complete disappearance of reality in the fog of interpretation: the underground "meaning" of every shot displaces the actual content, and the moviegoer is confronted with a whole crowd of undefined symbolic "meanings" floating entirely free. Shove the camera up against the pimple on an actor's face, and you automatically produce an image of immense importance: it will mean *something*—no matter if you don't know exactly what, and no matter if you have made it impossible to tell your story. Just as comedians now manufacture their humor out of immense card indexes of gags, so directors dip into their mental gag file of disconnected bits of social significance, amateur psychiatry, and visual shock effects.

In *A Streetcar Named Desire*, Elia Kazan pulls the Gimp-string so mercilessly that you never have one plain character or situation, but vast bundles of the most complicated sociological phenomena. For example, the hero, a sharp-witted Polish mechanic, conveys heavy passion by stuttering the first syllables of his sentences and mumbling the rest as though through a mouthful of mashed potatoes, a device that naturally forces the spectator to sociological speculation; disgusted with the fact that the hero has apparently been raised in a pigpen, the spectator is impelled to think about the relation of environment to individual development. Tennessee Williams's hero is getting ahead in his work, is a loving husband, makes "those colored lights" with his sexual genius, and is possessed of a delicate moral sensitivity. But all these bourgeois attributes have to be matched with their opposites for the sake of excitement, and so Kazan pulls his string and you see the Polack slobbering, licking his paws, howling like a troglodyte, hitting his wife so hard that he sends her to the maternity hospital, playing poker like an ape-man, exuding an atmosphere of wild screams, rape, crashing china, and drunkenness. And to make sure every two-year-old will understand how bad life is in this Grimm's fairy-tale hovel, Kazan hammers his point home with continual sinister lights, dancing shadows, gaseous oozings.

With its freakish acting, nightmare sets, and dreamy pace, *Streetcar* may seem like traditional, Hollywood poeticism, but looked at more closely, it becomes very different from movies of the past, and in the same odd, calculated way as *A Place in the Sun*, *People Will Talk*, etc. For one thing, the drama is played completely in the foreground. There is nothing new about shallow perspectives, figures gazing into mirrors with the camera smack up against the surface, or low intimate views that expand facial features and pry into skin-pores, weaves of cloth, and sweaty undershirts. But there is something new in having the whole movie thrown at you in shallow dimension. Under this arrangement, with the actor and spectator practically nose to nose, any extreme movement in space would lead to utter visual chaos, so the characters, camera, and story are kept at a standstill, with the action affecting only minor details, e.g., Stanley's back-scratching or his wife's lusty projection with eye and lips. On the screen, these grimly controlled gestures appear huge, florid, eccentric, and somewhat sinister. Again, there is nothing new about shooting into incandescent lights and nebulous darks, but there is something new in having every shot snotted up with silvery foam, black smoke, and flaky patterns to convey decay and squalor. Never before has there been such a use of darkness in masses as we find in the new films (at least not since the Russians, who probably didn't have any lights). All this to jazz up a pseudodrama in which nothing really happens on the screen except dialogue in which you see two faces talking, then a close-up of the right speaker asking, then a close-up of the left speaker answering, then back to the two, etc. The spectator is aware that a story is being told, but mostly he feels caught in the middle of a psychological wrestling match.

Though there has never been so massive a concentration on technique, the fact is these films actually fail to exploit the resources of the medium in any real sense. Kazan, Stevens, and their colleagues have been shrinking films down to an almost babyish level in situation and grouping. With slumbrous camera movement, slow choreographies of action, sustained close-ups of enigmatic faces surrounded by areas of gloom, and drifting dialogue that seemed to come out of the walls, Stevens in *A Place in the Sun* had time only to unreel in grandiose terms a kiss, a seduction, and a drowning that would have taken him all of five minutes to examine with the straight story-telling technique he used in *Penny Serenade* and *Alice Adams*, both of which he made in the 1930's. *Streetcar*, for dramatic action, shows one big character—a neurotic Southern girl on the last lap to the mental ward—in one main situation: talk, talk, talk with an uninhibited couple in a two-room apartment. *The African Queen* was shot entirely in the Belgian Congo, but the characters do almost nothing that couldn't have been done on one studio set with the aid of some library shots.

Movies have seldom, if ever, been so physically overbearing in their effect. The scenarios are set up so that the story can be told with a small cast, little movement, and few settings. The camera fastens itself on the actors with such obsessive closeness that every moment becomes of overwhelming importance and threatens to disclose some terrifying psychic or emotional fact. The effect becomes even stronger and more curious when the actors occasionally move across the room and this all-revealing eye just barely moves to keep them in focus—as in *Something to Live For*, when a worried advertising ace paces his office, while the camera seems to move back and forth no more than a fraction of an inch. One has the feeling that nothing is any longer of importance except a magnification of face, gesture, and dress, and that these can tell you all you need to know about life in our time.

All this seems to have started in an exciting, if hammy, 1941 picture called *Citizen Kane*. This grim mixture of suspense thriller and tabloid obituary, in which most of the surface facts paralleled events in the career of William Randolph Hearst, combined the thunderous theatrical trickery of Orson Welles with a reckless use of darkish photography and funny angles by a top cameraman named Gregg Toland. Toland threw into the film every device ever written into the accomplished cameraman's handbook—everything from undercranking (to make the people in "newsreel" clips jerk and scuttle) to craneshots, two-shots, floor-shots, and his favorite perspective shot in which figures widely spaced and moving far off down long rooms were kept as clearly in focus as the figure closest to the audience. This stuff helped make an exciting film, though marred by obvious items of shopworn inspiration: camera angles that had been thoroughly exploited by experimental films, and the platitudinous characterization of Kane as a lonely man who wanted love from the world but didn't get it because he had no love of his own to give. This unpeeling of a tycoon was clearly the most iconoclastic stroke in major studio production since the days when D. W. Griffith and his cameraman, Billy Bitzer, were freeing movies from imitation of the stage. Orson Welles's bold jumbling of techniques from theater, radio, and film led inevitably to a shock-happy work that anticipated everything that has since become fashionable in American films.

Oddly enough, this film, which had the biggest cultural build-up before release since Eisenstein's Mexican film, made little impression at the time on Hollywood's veterans. Only in the 1950's did the ghost of *Citizen Kane* start haunting every A picture out of Hollywood. Before the advent of Orson Welles, the most important thing in motion-picture technique had been the story, the devising, spacing, and arranging of shots into a plot line that moved easily from one thing to another. Welles, more concerned with exhibiting his impudent showmanship and his deep thought about graft, trusts, yellow journalism, love, hate, and the like, fractured his story all along the line, until his film became an endless chain of stop effects. At every instant, the customer was encouraged to pause over some Kublai Khan setting, some portentously lit floor-shot of an actor, or some symbol (the falling-snow toy, the bird screaming in escape), and think in the terms of what it had to tell about a publisher's immoral pursuit of love-power-respect. The plot was simple enough: a famous man said something ("Rosebud") just before dying in his castle on a mountain, and "March of Time" sent out an inquiring reporter to make a story out of it. Eventually we did get the answer, not through the flashbacked memories of those interviewed—Kane's oldest friend, his newspaper manager, the girl, the butler in the castle—but in a final nerve-tingling shot, privy to the director and audience, of the "Rosebud" sled of Kane's lost, barren childhood. The story was presented in such complicated ways and made so portentous with the shadows of meaning cast off by a hundred symbols that you could read almost anything into it, including what Welles had put there. There were certain dramatic high points like the rough-cut in the "March of Time" projection room, the kid outside the window in the legacy scene, and the lurid presentation of an electioneering stage. But in between these was a great deal of talk, much less action, and almost no story.

Welles bequeathed to Hollywood, which had grown fat and famous on hurtling action films, a movie that broke up into a succession of fragments, each one popping with aggressive technique and loud, biased slanting of the materials of actual life. He told his story backward—which was nothing new—and slowed it even more by breaking it into four situations that didn't flow together but settled stiffly and ambiguously into a sort of parallel construction. He also complicated and immobilized each shot with mismated shock effects that had never been seen before in Hollywood. For example, the ominous figure of Kane was shown in the dark alongside a clearly lit pseudo-Grecian statue and a vast undone jigsaw puzzle that the cameraman had cleverly shot so that it seemed strewn over a marble floor. The spectator had trouble arranging these disparate items into a convincing visual whole, but his brain was mobilized into all sorts of ruminations about avarice, monomania, and other compulsions. Even the devices for moving the story along were complicating and interrupting: again and again, you went from the first part of a sentence spoken at one time and place to the last part of the same sentence spoken years later; this made one less conscious of time passing than of a director stopping time to play a trick on reality.

Welles also showed the Hollywood craftsmen how to inject trite philosophy, "liberalism," psychoanalysis, etc., into the very mechanics of movie-making, so that what the spectator saw on the screen was not only a fat, contrived actor screaming down a staircase, but also some exotically rendered editorializing contributed by everyone from the actor to the set designer. The movie opened and closed on the iron fence around Kane's castle. In between this repetition, which spelled out the loneliness and baronial character of a tycoon, were similarly meaningful images: Kane in his castle among the boxed accumulations of his collecting; hopeful and innocent Kane gesticulating in front of a huge electioneering poster that showed him as a sinister demagogue. And always, practically on top of the cameraman, his unreal figure suggesting a blown-up cue ball adorned with the facial features of Fu Manchu, with nothing inside him but a Freudian memory giggling around in the fumes cast off by Welles's ideas about how an American big shot goes wrong.

The hidden meanings and the segmented narration were the two most obvious innovations of this film. Toland's camera provided the third, and it was anything but what you'd expect from a film that was advertised as using an unbound camera. Toland's chief contribution was a shallow concept of movie space. His camera loved crane-shots and floor-shots, but contracted the three dimensional aspect by making distant figures as clear to the spectator as those in the foreground. To accomplish this, Toland had to arrange his actors in widely spaced, parallel arrays across the screen. He also had to immobilize them and cut them off from the natural obscurations of scenery and atmosphere. His powerful lens did the rest. The spectator was faced with an image that exaggerated the importance of the figures it showed to a point where the deep space between them seemed to have been negated. The chief visual effect was the microscopically viewed countenance, one into which you could read almost anything. Almost as important was the static grouping of figures, amounting to a reversal of everything Hollywood had previously perfected in the creation of fluid groupings in unbounded space.

Citizen Kane and its Gimp-effects were generally laughed off by high-brows in Hollywood and elsewhere. Their opinion of the film was that it was too obviously theatrical and exhibitionistic to be linked to the main journalistic path of cinema. But one had the feeling, during the war years, that, as Hollywood turned out dozens of progressively more realistic action films—Western, war, detective—it was more than a little concerned with what Welles had done in the symbolic enriching of a movie through florid mannerisms. For Hollywood directors and actors couldn't forget that *Citizen Kane* was crazily three-dimensional in the manner of a psychoanalytic hour and that it did start you thinking at every moment of ambiguous drives hidden inside each character. *Citizen Kane* seems to have festered in Hollywood's unconscious until after the

Wylers and Hustons returned from their government film chores; then it broke out in full force.

In the acclaimed films of the early postwar years (*The Lost Weekend, The Best Years of Our Lives, The Treasure of the Sierra Madre, Champion*), one began to see Welles's theatrical innovations effectively incorporated into certain films that otherwise tried to look like untouched records of reality. There still had to be a long training in what is known as "semidocumentary" technique (movies shot in real streets with nonstudio make-up, natural lighting, spontaneous pantomime) before Hollywood could link Welles's florid symbolism with enough of the appearance or actuality to make it appear moderately reasonable. But by now the lesson has been learned, and the ghost of *Citizen Kane* stalks a monstrous-looking screen. The entire physical structure of movies has been slowed down and simplified and brought closer to the front plane of the screen so that eccentric effects can be deeply felt. Hollywood has in effect developed a new medium which plays odd tricks with space and human behavior in order to project a content of popular "insights" beneath a meager surface.

Thus has a revolution taken place in Hollywood, probably unbeknownst to the very men—directors, actors, and critics—who have led it. If the significance of the New Movie is understood, it may well be that Hollywood will never be able to go home again. Any attempt to resurrect the old flowing naturalistic film that unfolds logically and takes place in "reasonable" space seems doomed to look as old-fashioned as the hoop skirt. For better or worse, we seem stuck with an absurdly controlled, highly mannered, overambitious creation that feeds on everything in modern art and swallows it so that what you see is not actually on the screen but is partly in your own mind, partly on the screen, and partly behind it. You have to read these pictures in a completely different way from the one you've been accustomed to. They are no longer literally stories or motion pictures, but a succession of static hieroglyphs in which overtones of meaning have replaced, in interest as well as in intent, the old concern with narrative, character, and action for their own sakes. These films must be seen, not literally, but as X-rays of the pluralistic modern mind. But the popular ideas deliberately half-buried in them have the hard, crude ring of Stone Age tools, though most of them come out of psychoanalysis and the Popular Front morality plays of the depression. The most ambitious of the current film-makers got their higher, and highest, education in the New York of the latter 1930's and have never lost the obsessive need to "improve" the world through art. They are by now too sophisticated and weary really to believe that this will work, but the hangover of conscience, regret, guilt, and frustration still produces in their movies the new Worried Look. They have lost the spirit and convictions of the radical 1930's, but the characteristic feelings of these years remain expressed vaguely in a bleak, humorless, free-floating, and essentially pointless misanthropy—social significance gone sour. There may be nothing wrong with misanthropy as a working viewpoint, but when, as in *A Place in the Sun*, it takes its conception of workers, tycoons, and debutantes from a world of ideas fantastically unrelated to current American experience, it is merely a negative sentimentality. The emotional impact of a technique committed to elegant, controlled, mismated power effects is as modern as ammoniated toothpaste; but the popular ideas to which this technique is wedded seem almost as dated and provincial as those in *Damaged Goods* or *A Fool There Was*.

June 1952

THE fourth instalment of de Rochemont's perusal of New England character, "Walk East on Beacon," plods through a leisurely-paced action story vaguely based on the Judy Coplon and Klaus Fuchs espionage cases. The de Rochemont film is always dedicated to lauding a certain American type which blends the qualities of a model Sunday-school student with the talents of a mad industrialist. The central character is a refugee scientist (Finlay Currie) revolutionizing everything from dinghies to flying missiles with a theory he has worked out on high-speed calculators. Looking like a huge Edam cheese topped by a flowing Jean Harlow hairdo, the scientist fits the de Rochemont formula for heroes in that he is pure and innocent and spends his time lifting the lids from high-powered machines and reading numbers from them with a mysteriously joyous tone. Before the film settles down to a series of chases on land and sea, a Communist-spy ring tries to blackmail the scientist with threats against his son being held in Germany's Soviet zone. The movie is against Communists, but it pays a lot of respect to the shrewd, tortoise-like crafts-manship of the spies. Besides being so dedicated to their jobs that they tap their fingers, or sit down to lunch with a mechanical and somewhat hypnotized air, they are seldom seen doing anything except their daily jobs as taxi-driver, florist, or photo finisher. The idea is that they are too clever to expose their devilish skills. Occasionally the movie stops and hovers happily over a tiny electric fixture for blowing up a safe or a set of skeleton keys to lockers in the air terminal or a wristwatch that rings likes the chimes in Moscow, all of which symbolize the hard-plugging talents of the spies. By the time the FBI smashes the gang with a flurry of gadgets and techniques, the movie has been turned into a crushing bore by a producer who is so dryly factual and absorbed with mechanical wonders that his movies would ring like an anvil if you bounced them.

Since the first March of Time short de Rochemont produced for Luce, Inc., he has placed a peculiar restraint on the realistic skills of his movie crews. It consists of locking his films halfway between the total naturalism of a newsreel and the well-scrubbed, obviously reenacted realism of the old March of Time film which was almost methodically stripped of everything but dull facts. Here, as always, he uses an eye-level camera shot that seldom moves in any direction, so that his true story has to be arranged rather stiffly in hundreds of tiny shots accompanied by masses of explanatory dialogue. For example, a Russian agent on his first day in this country is glimpsed on a stroll through a Boston park; the camera catches him briefly in a middle-distance shot but that is all you get because the casual documentary quality would be destroyed if the cameraman followed him around in a normal movie fashion. The movie's speed is dissipated everywhere in brief, head-on shots of inconsequential stuff: a blonde courier getting out of a taxi, a suave Russian dummy hurrying to a telephone, a fat dowager carrying stolen information on to a Pan-American plane. It takes de Rochemont about thirty leisurely minutes to get to his plot (the blackmailing of the scientist) and by that time the movie has settled down to the crawl of a Hawaiian travelogue.

De Rochemont's helpers can set up a scene that bristles with excitement and shows a sharp eye for the personalities of headline figures tried as traitors. The characterizations are never pure mimicry, but it is obvious that Hiss, Coplon, and Elizabeth Bentley are in the film in slightly disguised performances by little known actors. These actors are at the top of their skill when de Rochemont is trying for stark realism (as in the FBI film shots taken of suspects) and at low tide on the sort of inauthentic reenactment he used on March of Time. One of the actresses, Virginia Gilmore, turns up on the FBI screen as an efficient runner for the spies, with a loping stride, a nervous headachey appearance, and a dedicated manner in everything from snubbing out cigarettes to kissing. In these newsreel-type shots, she is realistic in the manner of neo-naturalistic Italian actresses, with a jerky, erratic vitality that seems to belong in the rough gray atmosphere that is caught on location around Boston. However, when she is not being watched by a hidden FBI camera, Miss Gilmore consciously oversimplifies and overstates the mannerisms of a determined but somewhat unhinged neurotic (in line with de Rochemont's theory that a semi-documentary should be controlled and manipulated by its artists, resulting in a more expensive and studied-seeming film than the pure news-reel). Throughout the film the scenes that have an authentic look and the tangled energy of real life (the scientist's midnight walk to the church on Beacon Street, the Coplon figure snapping at her FBI questioner) are balanced by shots in which the movie crew deliberately plays to the audience in thriller fashion. The combination of styles gives the film its peculiar fugue-type composition as well as a certain kind of grotesque and schizophrenic effectiveness.

June 21, 1952

◆

"Clash by Night," a passable movie about sexual unrest on Cannery Row, is like a blues number given class by a Stokowski arrangement and a hundred-piece symphony orchestra. Barbara Stanwyck returns to her clapboard home-stead near a sardine cannery after ten years of romantic misery in the city. Working around San Something, California, are Paul Douglas, a dumb fisher-man whom Stanwyck decides to marry for security, and Robert Ryan, a movie projectionist who not only speaks in the hard, poetic language of Stanwyck but has the kind of left-handed charm that causes the lady to stay up nights gazing at the most costly sky-and-sea shots ever to grace a Howard Hughes-RKO production. Ryan is fine "for a ride on a roller coaster," but after a cata-clysmic affair—their "last shot at happiness"—Stanwyck finds she can't forsake her year-old child and hurries back to the fishing boat where Douglas is busy fixing the baby's formula. This old-fashioned sex drama is supposed to hit you in the belly with its candid shots of men and women screaming, yearning, fighting, and suddenly coming together in rib-cracking embraces. But what was intended as a hot James Cain type of shocker was cooled considerably in the making by a hundred classy devices for making clichés look important and artistic. For instance, that old gimmick in which the man mouths two cigarettes at once is dragged in for kicks and then neatly twisted around. When Ryan hands Lady Stanwyck her cigarette she throws it away as though she thought it unsanitary. Several reels later, after Ryan's excitement has wormed its way into her torn and twisted little bitch's heart, Stanwyck is lighting Chesterfields two at a time just like her boy friend.

Stanwyck has occasionally been thawed out—by Sturges and Wilder—but here she is up to her old trick of impersonating a mentholated icicle. With his mellifluous broadcaster's voice and cafeteria manager's body, Douglas just seems out of place as a Sicilian fisherman and silly in a turtleneck sweater that outlines every pound of his C-shaped stomach. Marilyn Monroe, who is supposed to be burning up the screen with her size-36½ bosom and horizontal walk, has several scenes custom-built to her measurements. Someone holds her upside down on the beach—to shake the water from her ears; she gets out of bed in a tricky hip-length shirt—designed by Adrian for cannery workers; she walks around in dungarees which must have been broken in by a midget cowboy. Nothing happens because Monroe is still a tight amateur presented as a spectacle. Given four-word sentences and simple actions like eating a candy bar, she seems to break them up into dozens of little unrelated pieces paced in a slow, sing-song fashion.

"Clash by Night" doesn't have too much to offer outside of two good actors (Ryan and J. Carrol Naish) and fluid, flexible direction (Fritz Lang), but they make it worth your time. Ryan is supposed to be enacting a "sort of imitation," "the Kingfish of Buckman County" run down and out of luck, a cynical guy who plays every word and gesture halfway into paranoia and with hard-bitten pathos. The role has been played by everyone from Widmark to Mitchum, but Ryan is the first one to give you the sense of an ordinary citizen being destroyed by a neurotic urge to act and admire himself at the same time. With pantomime that gives the sensation of a clock ticking away inside his skull, he is almost always caught in the process of observing himself while seeming to be observing and philosophizing about his friends.

Starting with a talkative script that offers nothing more active than a "tight two" set-up between talkative characters, Director Lang moves the story around a Monterey village with the space-devouring glide of a seagull. One of his neatest tricks is to keep the central fact of a scene at a tantalizing distance, so that he forces you to use your own eyes and imagination on something the average director would wear out in a minute of screen time. He takes you to the beach with Monroe and her boy friend and then watches their antics from a block away as they affect a cynically interested onlooker. He plays through the first Stanwyck-Douglas date at a movie house without ever showing the action on the screen that draws at least five revealing comments from the mismatched love birds. The script, like so many adaptations of Broadway plays, consists of endless exits and entrances, but Lang makes you so familiar with the architecture that one of the minor pleasures of the movie is trying to guess which stairway, door, or hallway will pull forth the next action.

June 26, 1952

◆

THE only pastime that seems to bewitch citizens lately is game-playing—quiz programs, gambling, big-time athletics—and so to please the customers Hollywood has glutted theaters with sports films. The latest crop ("Pat and Mike," "The Ring," "The Winning Team") proves that the industry continues its childish treatment of golf, tennis, and the like by concentrating on Success, casting unspectacular athletes, and using stationary camera set-ups on games that thrive on split-second relationships of movements that are a mixture of technique, personality, and accident. Of the above-mentioned films "Pat and Mike" is a Hepburn-Tracy starrer apparently created to prove that Hepburn is in a class with the Marbles and Didricksons. (With her cautiously orthodox form, Hepburn is not an explosive, highly individualized athlete whose games one enjoys watching in a two-hour film.) The second film, "The Ring," is an unpretentious job built around the novel twist of a young Mexican fighter who does nothing but lose to the rankest small-club lightweights. "The Winning Team" is about the reprobate pitcher, Grover Alexander, as rendered by a lamb-like actor, Ronald Reagan.

"Pat and Mike" is an almost charming fairy story about two subjects that give most sports writers the creeps—a female athlete and the more mercenary type of language-mangling, underworld-haunting manager. Its chief trouble is that it is packed with such long-drawn-out scenes as golfers lining up for crucial putts and carefully tapping a ball that is predestined by the script either to drop in or not to. These scenes are supposed to have you on the edge of your seat, but they look so well rehearsed and are so lacking in the unpredictable that the spectator loses interest. At one point only does Hepburn display some spontaneous sport activity: when she bangs out about six balls in one continuous blur of swinging. The story, by the Kanins, is geared to the suave, exquisite by-play of the two stars, who have done their act—the frisky, spinsterish woman in love with a lackadaisical wolfish fat man—so often they are like a romantic version of the Hope-Crosby team. Both teams depend a lot on charming the customer by acting as though they were charmed to death with each other's talents, but Hepburn and her partner tend to curdle their performance by behaving like elderly bobbysoxers who have just been necking in the rumble seat.

"The Ring" follows the dismal career of a young Mexican from a bar-room brawl by Mexican baiters to the moment a year later when he tosses his boxing togs into a neighborhood incinerator. Between the two points is an unkempt yarn that depicts a good deal of the painful effort, misdirected wilfulness, day-dreaming, and heartache that go into the athletic record of a character who shouldn't be an athlete. The movie is worked out mostly with a counter-attack technique that uses all sorts of conventional movie situations but simply turns them inside out. The hero (Lalo Rios) loses his girls and his friends when he takes up fighting; he falls in with a flashy manager who handles him with pru-dence and kindness; his first fight is with a poignantly untalented youngster rather than a broken-down pug; his ring earnings are offered to but turned down by his impoverished parents; he gives up fighting and then makes an inglorious comeback. The movie would seem more unique if it were not so apparent that the directors and actors were reversing clichés wherever they traveled. Well worth seeing for such episodes as dreary bus trips to small Cal-ifornia fight towns, the educational depiction of a trainer's chores, the tired rou-tine that goes on after a losing fight. The film misses a lot of punch because of an amateurish, petulant performance by its star and certain glaring mistakes: the youth is supposed to be a welterweight, but he is usually put in the ring with someone too heavy or too light for his division.

Although "Shadow in the Sky"—not a sports film—is feeble-minded on its main subject of a war psychosis, it is needle-sharp on the ambivalent behavior of kindly, primly sensitive middle-brows trying to be nice to deranged war vet-erans. The movie, a low-budgeted M-G-M job from the pen of the studio's most talented scripter, Ben Maddow, often looks like an ad for a surburban housing development—it is set in the clean bungalow section used in "The Next Voice" with the same wholesome couple, James Whitmore and Nancy Davis, whose acting is as standard and square as the décor. The story—whether or not an occasionally daft brother of Miss Davis should be taken out of the demoralizing atmosphere of a veterans' hospital and allowed to hallucinate under Davis's tables—pays only a stereotyped nod to the cause and character of the brother's (Ralph Meeker) illness. Somewhat like the hero of "Blind Alley," Meeker is a rugged type with a rain phobia: he turns to quivering protoplasm at the first unfavorable weather report and rushes for the pro-tection of the nearest table. Meeker performs this business as though he were having a hard time with an embarrassingly silly parlor game, and afterward he starts shrieking with Whitmore about some vague trouble the two of them had in the war on a South Pacific isle during a rainy season. If you can make any sense out of their drivel, you have the key to Meeker's psychosis. The rest of the film is confined to nice people being catty to each other in ordinary situations, and doing it so that it is almost imperceptible—a rare accomplishment for an M-G-M movie.

August 9, 1952

◆

It is perfectly safe to see "Don't Bother to Knock," which is a little more different from a Marilyn Monroe peepshow (as advertised) and a lot closer to the portrayal of the atmosphere of a second-class New York fleabag than the critics mentioned. Constructed like a stage play, with no more motion than can be found in a hotel restaurant between meals, it concerns a small-town Alice in the Wonderland of the "Franklin Hotel," a place so dull and quiet that it is hardly able to wake itself up to the sordid problems of violence, suicide, and insanity that the girl brings in. She seeps through its revolving doors with a blank, questioning look, and is led out about three hours later wearing the same stare by two cops who handle her like an expensive glass figurine that might disappear into thin air. Her uncle, the elevator jockey, has put her on to a baby-sitting job, unfortunately for the baby—for she takes to the occupation in a way that should scare even tabloid readers. First, she dons her employer's black negligee, jewelry, and perfume; next (no surprise) she invites a lonely pilot in; and then she really goes to work until all her crazy little dreams tumble down around her bobbysocks. For some unfortunate reason this story is split between the baby tender and a stock love affair (the pilot and the Dinah Shoreish canary in the lounge), but it is nevertheless a relief to find a new movie that hasn't been foreshortened, polished and sensationalized out of all relation to its middle-class scene.

The matter-of-fact treatment (Zanuck must have been looking the other way) makes for an old-fashioned movie with a nearly dormant pace, a greedy curiosity about small hotel matters, and people who fit in with the antiquated cigarette stands and radio outlets in their rooms. They all have a degree of unsophistication that has been missing for some time in American films, the kind of bourgeois sincerity which causes the housewife to look puzzled when Monroe aggressively tells her to have a good time, and which starts Widmark quaking and back-tracking almost before he gets to work as a seducer. Monroe, with her unconcerned dreaminess and ability to make any garment look as if it came from a bargain basement, generally seems to be working upstream as far as life is concerned, being nonplussed about everything except getting her own way and doing what she wants. She can also be shrewdly coy, as when she lures Widmark in from across the way by wigwagging the Venetian blinds and then turns with a cocky expression toward his inevitable phone call. It is the most direct and plaintive job of acting a hot, lost, peace-wrecking female since Keyes in "The Prowler." Widmark has the lesser role (his bosses are trying to bury him in near "B" films), but he stands out as probably the only literate, salty-talking he-man who would play a fast pick-up with some embarrassment, doubt, and compassion.

The director (Roy Baker) keeps everything prosaic, leveling all incidents —including the baby-sitter's steady maltreatment of her ward—and lulls you into always believing the girl is more normal than she is. Baker's passive version of the Graham Greene type of controlled understatement keeps his people, and the audience, captives of hotel machinery, a trick that brings out all the jittery yearning for excitement that lies beneath the lack-luster surface. The film does have a studio-type face or two (Widmark and his girl) and occasionally there is a heavy touch in the middle of its naturalism. The story comes together too neatly at the end for a *Daily Mirror*-type yarn, but compared to "Fourteen Hours," which dealt pretentiously with a suicidal castaway in a New York hotel, it is far from a turkey.

"Glory Alley" is also around but not worth looking into, primarily because of a preposterously cluttered script bent on making angels of the shake-down artists, grifters, and crackpots of skid row. It deals mainly with the endless ups and downs in the life of a swaggering fighter (rather well played by Ralph Meeker) who wants to be the biggest man on Bourbon Street, but even the author of "Moll Flanders" couldn't have dreamed up a more involved, melodramatic biography. The whole picture might have come off better if Director Raoul Walsh had tried to counter the plot's sensationalism (the hero runs out on a championship fight because he is afraid to show his stitched skull in public) with a more factual portrait of the street where jazz was born. As it is, he gives you soggy moments, overripened characters, and a swell assortment of such clichés as the nostalgic fighter wandering around the empty fight auditorium and the sawed-off scrounger pounding the change box on a telephone to save a dime (repeated five times for laughs). Then there are ill-advised moments with Louie Armstrong making faces in the style of the 1930's cinema Negro and Jack Teagarden so busy swinging and swaying that you wonder how he is able to blow his trombone. Leslie Caron makes a good-enough cabaret dancer (though she smiles even more than Eisenhower) who forgoes a ballet career to take care of her blind poppa, Kurt Kasznar, who piles up Teutonic dulness until it is knee-deep and sits in his easy-chair throne in the middle of the fight gym. Poppa has a super-hatred for Meeker, but warms up when

Meeker hires his childhood friend, now a famous Minneapolis doctor, to save his sight. Gilbert Roland is a likable bar owner, if not a flexible screen player, who is also Meeker's manager, and who tries to take Meeker off the skids by giving him a fighter to manage and a job in his bar. As I was saying, Walsh and his crew should have been paid double time to work on a script as involved as this.

It's not news that newsreels have been going nowhere for years, but they outdid themselves in dulling the impact of the record-breakingest Olympic Games. One of the "musts" of photographing track and field events is to clarify the race if it takes every trick in the camera man's handbook (slow motion, stop camera, more than one camera set-up, etc.). The two-seconds screen time allotted to each event neither showed anything about the individual performers nor gave a sense of the continuity and vastness of the affair, making you wonder why the filmers traveled all the way to Helsinki just for a blitzkrieg coverage. Even Paramount, most dedicated and serious of the newsreel concerns, did a good job of missing the point. The shot of Les Biffle's near-record broad jump, caught head-on from the ground, makes him look as if he were jumping all of six feet. Mathias was shown only in those decathalon events that took place around sunset, so that you got an illuminating glimpse of a lot of stadium shadow; the fantastic 100-meter dash (four runners hitting the tape simultaneously, with the chunky, barreling winner, Remigino, resembling no one else in sprinting history) seemed to have been glimpsed by a chance sparrow; Moore's hurdle journey was photographed from a distance that made it impossible to discern which one was Moore and what kind of hurdles he was taking. Except for some good work in the walkathon—which the newsreelers think is "*funny*"—sportscasting companies can now go back to filming bangtails and skiers with the happy knowledge that, in comparison, they made Leni Riefenstahl, the Nazi photographer of the Berlin Olympiad, seem like a camera genius.

August 16, 1952

Parade Floats

By way of the characteristic reticence of John Ford, you probably know that he considers *The Quiet Man*—which, given Ford's influence, should produce some awful offspring notable for female pratfalls, fistfights, and every person a Macy's balloon—to be the best of his 108 pictures. An old-fashioned confection idealizing the scenic beauties and quaint customs of Ireland, it is no better than the supersentimental landscapes and editorial-ridden life in *Grapes of Wrath* (probably the most-bloated-yet version of vocation-oriented films, without any of the looseness of *Slim* or *They Drive by Night*) and a bit worse than the potboiler *When Willie Comes Marching Home*, which was somewhat less hampered by Ford's bellicose barroom sentimentality, the promiscuous dumping of actresses, or falsified by the unstinting use of picturesque, ethnically slanted scenes. Often during *The Quiet Man*, the audience finds something laughable (the town drunkard and gossip muttering when he is offered buttermilk instead of whisky, "The Borgias would do better"), but mostly the moviegoer has to put up with clumsily contrived fist fights, musical brogues spoken as though the actor were coping with an excess of tobacco juice in his mouth, mugging that plays up all the trusted hokums that are supposed to make the Irish so humorous-sympathetic, and a script that tends to resolve its problems by having the cast embrace, fraternity-brother–fashion, and break out into full-throated ballads.

In the midst of it, is the formless love story of two champion poseurs, one of them a strong, silent ex-boxer from Pittsburgh, Massachusetts (gag), who returns to the thatched cottage of his birth and spends the film wistfully lapping up luxurious scenery around Galway; the other, a hot-tempered, shy country wench who runs through streams clutching her broad-brimmed hat or compulsively glancing over her shoulder as she backs off to the very bottom of the screen. The characters are paper-thin types with traits taken from pulp stories, nineteenth-century novels, and a dozen British films starring members of the Abbey Theater. The noble close-mouthed hero developed his tungsten muscles in Pittsburgh's mills, learned about Ireland's beauties at his mother's knee, and lost his urge to fight when he killed a ring opponent. All this is revealed by way of dialogue, so that there is nothing for John Wayne to impersonate except John Wayne. Maureen O'Hara plays the windlike heroine out of *Wuthering Heights*, and the Ford stock company (Arthur Shields, Ward Bond, Victor McLaglen, Mildred Natwick, Barry Fitzgerald) goes through the dated mimicry of such stereotypes as the tippling village cabby, the thick-headed, bellicose squire, and the jovial village priest, who curses, jokes, and fishes from start to finish of the film.

Some of the technicolor photography is pretty original—a dense, gray atmosphere takes most of the hue and intensity out of the scene and makes for a curious picture that takes place in daylight yet has some of the sunless, remembered look of a surrealist painting. Ford's ability to lyricize a movie with scenic effects is manifest wherever the camera moves: Barry Fitzgerald driving his sidecar beneath a little bridge as the train passes over it, the old business of the wedding photograph burlesqued like a quaint valentine, wind delicately whipping a pile of sweepings. But all this padding of what is supposed to be an illusive, impressionistic study of a land and its people is disturbing because it becomes the underlying motive for the scenes, revealing the limited significance of every pub brawl, horse race, or pastoral event almost before the scene is under way.

September 13, 1952

A 1961 cavalry film that is like an endless frontier-day pageant, *Two Rode Together* has the discombobulated effect of a Western dreamt by a kid snoozing in an Esso station in Linden, New Jersey. Two wrangling friends, a money-grubbing marshal (Jimmy Stewart) and a cavalry captain (Richard Widmark, who has the look of a ham that has been smoked, cured, and then coated with honey-colored shellac), seek out a Comanche named Parker and trade him a stunningly new arsenal of guns and knives for a screaming little Bowery Boy with braids who's only bearable in the last shot when the camera just shows his legs hanging limply from a lynching tree.

The movie's mentally retarded quality comes from the discordancy and quality of the parts: it's not only that they don't go together, they're crazy to start with. Each woman and Indian is from a different age in operetta and a different part of the globe. The Indians include an overdeveloped weight-lifter, a sad Pagliacci trying hard not to let his flabby stomach show, plus the above Leo Gorcey tough with his histrionic impression of a monkey on hot coals. The movie wobbles most with Widmark, embarrassed but strangely submitting to courting scenes with Shirley Jones that are filled with temerity and wide-eyed hopefulness. His tomboy sweetheart, a fraulein out of *The Student Prince* with two thick long yellow braids and enough make-up to equal Widmark's, has a fixation on a music box and runs to it at every chance.

The movie is a curious blend of modern blat and a senile impression of frontier culture that derives from the cheapest and oldest movies about pre-railroad days in Indian territory. There is a wild, non sequitur quality about the courtship, frontier dialogue, and spitting, thin-skinned, stupidly stubborn Indians taking place in a free-for-all atmosphere in which not one detail or scene goes with another. In general, it is Widmark and Stewart, like two Pinter characters, separated out from a stiff (despite the yelling and flouncing), corny TV-styled production going on behind them. Throughout, these actors barely listen to each other, and, affecting a curious, dragged out, folksy dialect, they take up great amounts of space with words that are from Dimwit's Land. "No!

She didn't kill herself, ladies and gentlemen. Not because she was a coward, but because her religion forbade her. Sometimes, it takes more courage to live than to die." Facetiously delivering this speech, Stewart is operating here in a feeble, tensionless mock-up of an officers' cotillion at the local fort. (I kept wondering, Why are they dragging in a dance? Could it be to squeeze that white hypocrisy speech into the remains of a script previously taken up with removing the normal skin tone, stealth, dignity, and clothes sense from Indians?)

It is filled with cliché conceptions: of an Indian camp, a Texas Guinan seenioreeta who owns the saloon and the town, slow-witted people, an innocent tomboy heroine throwing a barrel of flour over the two Cleggs who come courting her, country bumpkins having a fight in the woods. These one-dimensional impressions could embarrass any actor, but what is staggeringly insensitive about the treatment is the way an actor is made so ridiculous by the camera treatment, either being locked, sliced in two, or frittered away in golden shoe polish by pictorial set-ups. A fine TV soap-opera actress, very good at shading womanly intelligence into irony, showing much more range than Agnes Moorehead in Lady Macbeth–type roles, Jeanette Nolan is murdered long before the Me Comanchah kid gets her by compositions which turn her into unpleasant pleading, cropping her at the hips and hardening her flat, angular face and voice. Mae Marsh, whose frenzied vivacity enriched many Griffith films with improvised, energy-spilling effects, is similarly waylaid, not so much by her corny "I had a white husband once" speech and a make-up job midway between a clown face and Molly Drunk All Night, but by a wigwam composition in which, bent over, she cringes out of a sea of blue ink.

The fascination of the director with lines of action in deep space adds ten lethal minutes here and there of illogicality, to a script that is already overloaded with fat items: capitalist law enforcers, matricide, overbearing mothers. For instance, the Widmark-Stewart team leads a wagon train into the wilderness through bogs of bumpkin comedy and tinsel wooing. Later, after a brief moment at a campsite, all these people are mysteriously back in the fort as though they'd never left it.

It's incredible, the amount of leeway that is allowed. If a prop man locates a bench from an antique store next to a tree in a just-set-up campsite, the scene stays in, though the film for the preceding five minutes has been insisting on formidable wilderness. This is studio moviemaking at its slackest.

All these gauche, careless skills—the uglification of actors (padding a buxom barmaid, Annelle Hayes, so that her bust line starts angling out from the collarbone and doesn't turn in till it reaches her waist), the jerky progress from melodrama to bathos to camp, the TV-Western feeling of no flow, outdoors, or sense of period (Stewart is wearing a jacket from Abercrombie, all Indians and their tents are from a psychotics' Halloween Ball)—are the responsibility of John Ford, a director generally noted for making movies with a poetic and limitless knowledge of Indians, ranging farthest across the landscape of the American past, and being the moviemaker's Mr. Movie.

1969

◆

"The Leopard Man," a reissued "B" (1942) showing with the rickety "King Kong," is a nerve-twitching whodunit giving the creepy impression that human beings and "things" are interchangeable and almost synonymous and that both are pawns of a bizarre and terrible destiny. A lot of surrealists like Cocteau have tried for the same supernatural effects, but while their scenes still seem like portraits in motion, Val Lewton's film shows a way to tell a story about people that isn't dominated by the activity, weight, size, and pace of the human figure. In one segment of the film a small frightened señorita walks beyond the edge of the border town and then back again, while her feelings and imagination keep shifting with the camera into the sagebrush, the darkness of an arroyo, crackling pebbles underfoot, and so on until you see her thick dark blood oozing under the front door of her house. All the psychological effects—fear and so on—were transferred to within the nonhuman components of the picture as the girl waited for some non-corporeal manifestation of nature, culture, or history to gobble her up. But more important in terms of movie invention, Lewton's use of multiple focus (characters are dropped or picked up as if by chance, while the movie goes off on odd tacks trying to locate a sound or a suspicion) and his lighter-than-air sense of pace created a terrifically plastic camera style. It put the camera eye on a curiously delicate wave length that responds to scenery as quickly as the mind, and gets inside of people instead of reacting only to surface qualities. This film still seems to be one of Hollywood's original gems—nothing impure in terms of cinema, nothing imitative about its style, and little that misses fire through a lack of craft.

"My Man and I" is a flag-waving love story; one of the worst. It has a multiplicity of themes, situations, and hokums that have been around in Saroyan-type writing since the first issue of *Story*, but it is generally about a Mexican field worker (Ricardo Montalban)—his-pure-in-heart character, his set of the "Encyclopedia Britannica," and his simple desire for a foothold in the U.S.A.

The story, by Jack Leonard and John Fante, hews to an after-laughter-come-beers-and-then-tears routine: there is a comic-opera scene between his Mexican cronies, then a sentimental one in a bar with Montalban trying to reform his dypsoid girl friend (Shelley Winters), and finally a scene with a double-crossing farmer (Wendell Corey); and the whole thing is repeated. Director William Wellman wastes plenty of footage (each embrace knocks off the hero's homburg, and we follow its journey on the floor), but sometimes he gives the nostalgic feeling of wandering back in memory trying to find the special streets, embittered characters, and cold lighting effects that probably made him the best hard-rock director of the thirties. Add the quiet acting (by Corey and Claire Trevor) of two spectacularly worn, unhappy meanies, and you find a reason for seeing the film.

It is no secret that the brightest and screwiest movies being made today are around the eight-minute subject of "eternal enmity" by some smart-aleck artists named Avery, Quimby, and McKimson. I will take up their animated cartoons ("Bugs Bunny," "Tom and Jerry," dogs, cats, tweedybirds) in a subsequent issue, but in the meantime the closest approach to their cheerily sadistic style and sharply timed humor can be found in Mitch Leisen's movie "Young Man with Ideas," which is quite a lot of fun because it searches in an unmerciful fashion for the same unique booby traps to make unsuspecting persons indignant, embarrassed, obsessive, or destructive. It opens on some negligible nonsense at a small-town country club (the spouse of the poorest and least appreciated law desk gets drunk and tells off the firm's big shots) with Ruth Roman mauling her mimicry of drunkenness and Glenn Ford energetically over-acting as her Milquetoast husband. But then the story starts down an uncharted path that takes up the studying habits of law students, the fight of some Los Angeles dead beats against a vicious bill-collecting outfit, and the mistake of answering phones in a bungalow just vacated by a betting syndicate. Leisen never misses an opportunity to dispatch his movie into another street, office, or apartment in order to find one more locale to satirize (Leisen is a sort of slapstick decorator) and one more crass character trying for an illegal foothold in a foolish city. Except for Sheldon Leonard (in his favorite portrayal of a dismally inept Little Caesar) the actors are not funny; but the movie's humor is derived from Leisen's knowing how to keep his people fairly smart in dumb situations, sensitive in slapstick scenes, and just selfish enough when they are being their most virtuous.

Those of you who are sucked into theaters by the encomium-studded ads in daily newspapers will probably rush to see the following films. "Sudden Fear" ("one of the screen's all-time thrillers") is a garish tale of homicide with such original, unemphatic items as yowling cats, cars teetering around San Francisco's hilly streets, and Joan Crawford acting as if she were pushing her tormented psyche through the thickest mud. "The Big Sky" ("in a class with 'Mutiny on the Bounty'") shows a whiskey-laden keel boat being poled and pushed up the Missouri River. Cast with some amiably fearsome stars who act as if they had been coached by Al Capp, and saddled with a talkative Western plot, this film is not up to the talents of its director, Howard Hawks. "Ivanhoe" ("a rich, dramatic, action-filled picture") is informative on the subject of fighting with a mace and pike, but its polished actors are a bore, and the remnants of Scott's story are lost in the care that went into handsomely mounting the panoramas at the jousting fields and on the battlements. "The World in His Arms" shows how Alaska and Ann Blyth were maneuvered away from the Russians by Gregory Peck. It proves that director Raoul Walsh never makes routine melodrama dull, and never fails to fill it with handsome scenic bits and fast action scenes. "Monkey Business" sputters along with a lot of actors, monkeys, and humor in general becoming literally juvenile. "Dreamboat" is in the running with "The Washington Story" and Zsa Zsa Gabor for the sorriest movie mess of the year. "Just for You" betrays the ten-year-old secret that Crosby has lost his hair, most of his crooning voice, and any pleasure he once took in relaxing into the laziest and most easygoing actor in Hollywood.

September 27, 1952

THE Kinesis films, produced by a group of little-known San Francisco experimentalists, are mostly animated "cartoons" that have the glitter and bang-bang sort of interest of Pollock-Motherwell-Hoffman paintings, and practically drug you with their quick, even-cutting pace, lush over-scoring of music, and shallow richness. The idea of most of the Kinesis group is to take something that is practically nothing (thick swirls of lavalike paint, etc.), make it march, expand and fade, relate it to Mozart or Dizzy Gillespie, and hope that it takes wing like music. My own feeling is that if you put as much music into films as do Gordon Belson and Hy Hirsh, you won't have a picture so much as a repetitious exercise in rhythm. Belson's new animations give the impression of a Jackson Pollock kaleidoscope set in motion to mamba sounds; the over-all effect is morbid and thick. Hy Hirsh puts on a stunning display of tricky neon-colored evolutions, but her film—Arp-like ovals deploying across the screen like a formation of airplanes through three symphonic movements—almost sent me to sleep.

Weldon Kees's "Apex Hotel" (not animated) steals the Kinesis show, partly because the camera work and cutting are as primitive as the drawing of "Moon Mullins" but principally because it is such an aridly neat and unbiased picture of architectural debris. Kees's camera takes you through a crumbling two-story dwelling, a completely unilluminating tour that keeps you guessing about where the house is, what shape it originally had, and who lived in it. The movie crawls down a steam pipe at the pace of a half-dead bug, sits on a busted light socket for four seconds, stares down a toilet bowl, examines the MacArthur headline of an old newspaper. Kees may never threaten Gregg Toland or James Wong Howe as a lensman, but he has a wonderful eye for accidental composition—shapes, lines, and textures lock together as though they were set in concrete. The effects he gets are sometimes quite jolting, as though things were appearing as they are, without any evidence of mood, or participation.

"This Is Cinerama" is a series of pedestrian travelogue ideas (a ride on a roller-coaster, bagpipers skirling around Edinburgh Castle, Niagara from a helicopter) showing what the new three-lensed camera and cycloramic screen can do. To judge from the audiences' reactions, the movie industry some day will throw its old camera equipment in the ash can and start rebuilding movie theaters with fifty-foot-long curving screens and three projection booths midway in the orchestra section. Fred Waller's invention is a device for widening the screen image to take in periphery impressions seen from the corners of the eyes; three synchronized images joined at the edges are thrown on the screen, which seems to half-surround the spectator. The impact of this presentation will probably open the pores of the movie industry, and I am all for it, partly because it will bring into power the panoramic shots and documentary photography originally basic to the medium, before the theatrical people took over talkies. There are some disappointing things that Cinerama's backers (Lowell Thomas, Mike Todd) failed to mention. The big, deep screen is much too large for comfortable viewing, and the sound is roughly equivalent to being at the center of a volcano. You frequently look at an image that offers some of the distortions of a concave or convex mirror—it is apparently not yet possible to show a perfectly straight line across the screen. The three-dimensional effect is strictly an illusion; it would be interesting to see the result of an alliance between this invention and a stereoscopic device.

So much for the out-of-the-ordinary movies. Now the problem is how to enjoy such pillars of platitude as some of the following releases. "What Price

Glory?" owes its spark and vitality to the Cagney-Dailey acting team, which doesn't seem bothered by having to shoulder the oldest luggage of slapstick and pathos. Going along with modern Broadway ideas, someone at Twentieth-Century–Fox got the notion to do this War I play and movie (which had guts, explosive energy) as a snappy, overdecorated semi-musical, with soldiers on motor cycles running smack into haystacks, tough officers choking up at the sight of a wounded youngster and cursing the horrors of war, and every so often the oh-so-cute Corinne Calvet being maneuvered by a crowd of drunken friends into a position where you can either look up or down her dress. The rivalry between Captain Flagg and Sergeant Quirt is worked out with a ballet-like synchronism between its two leads, both of whom seem to have ripened in recent years and to have become curiously uneasy and eccentric, even verging to the slightest degree on madness—Cagney, with a crazy waddle and ferocious decisiveness, and Dailey with a loose-tongued delivery and the signs of frenzy in his Gary Cooperish face. Their befuddled digressions into man-nerism give the film the sharp accents and jagged rhythms of silent films, and lessen the romantic distortions of director John Ford, who derived his shapes and colors from Thomas Benton's paintings.

"The Happy Time" takes a sweet look at a twelve-year-old being indoc-trinated into the mysteries of life in 1910 in Ottawa; it stars Bobby Driscoll, a juvenile whose strident ambition to get ahead in films has gained him some of the indigestible qualities of Betty Hutton and Jerry Lewis. "The Snows of Kil-imanjaro" is mainly lacking in a sense of when enough is enough; the hero is a great-lover-writer-hunter-soldier who has lover's quarrels and reconciliations with everyone but Ethel Barrymore and daydreams endlessly. Its only actors who manage to combine fire and grace are an eerie hyena and the alto saxo-phonist Benny Carter.

October 11, 1952

"Limelight" gives us something different in Chaplin, who barehanded has produced, written, directed, starred in, and scored the entire picture. The film deals quite dourly with the joys and sorrows that go into seeking theatrical suc-cess and is an ideal subject for the world's first funny man, whose naivete is such that he must always have the center of the stage—whether as Chaplin the private citizen or Chaplin the great panto. It is not coincidental that the movie is a portrait of a famous tramp-clown at the end of his career, and that the waif whom he rescues from suicide and paralysis bears a striking physical resemblance to Oona O'Chaplin. What is new and good about the film is Chaplin's acting: he has given up the travesty of characterization and is doing a wonderful parlor game of charades—pantomiming, among other things, drunken walking, a tiny man trying to carry an unconscious girl up a narrow flight of stairs, left-handed violin playing, the flight of two trained fleas, a rock, a Chinese tree, and crazy-ballet dancing. For once, Chaplin's powerful personal traits don't conflict with his screen role, since at best he is playing a sort of neutralized version of himself.

The movie opens on a bit of Sennett-type business with the kind of mat lighting found on dignified English Christmas cards: A tipsy has-been clown named Calvero teeters down a London street and has trouble hitting the keyhole with his apartment-house key (the drunk act continues through the first three reels though he never takes a drink). Once inside the coldly lit flat, the "age makes way for youth" tale becomes laughless as Chaplin attempts to inspire the beautiful, chalky, hysterical paralytic (Claire Bloom) to go on living. This portion of the film suffers most from overwriting, dividing it from subsequent action, and manages only to keep pace with current politicians in its use of unrelieved exhortation and big, empty words. Lines like "I must have truth, Truth, TRUTH—and, if possible, a little dignity" come out as though they had brackets around them, giving the mechanical, bridging effect of old silent film titles. All sentimental stops are pulled out; but the whole is toughened by a succession of vaudeville skits which turn up whenever the clown snoozes. In these you see Chaplin playing a new, devilish tramp with nasoid singing voice and a frisky, aggressive dancing style.

The second half of "Limelight" moves into a London theater where the best ballet dancing recorded on celluloid (Melissa Hayden) alternates with some primitively grouped shimmy acts that go straight back to the veiled dancing in "Intolerance." Meanwhile the story hits climax after climax as the clown sinks into oblivion and the girl rises to the heights of Markova and Danilova.

Throughout, Chaplin's comedy-drama doesn't produce one belly laugh, but hardly a gesture in it lacks grace, point, or perfection. A master at getting the effect he wants into the camera's eye, he can conquer you with anything from a throttled, straining sound in his throat to a silly smile. While I've never been convinced of the humanity in the pathetic tramp, the krauty dictator, or the dapper murderer Chaplin enacted in earlier films, here pleasure and warmth spread a likable emotion over his pantomime, so that you accept things as hackneyed as the flower-eating, or as dim-witted as the burlesque gags. Even with the over-wise-human flavor, there is a mixture of glee, pomp, absurdity, and power adding a knife edge. Chaplin has a greedy, mean way of cracking a whip that seems the end in foolish cruelty; he can gasp and slip under the burden of lifting a girl so as to rib the entire business of doing a kind deed; and he charms you out of your seat with anatomical details: a wide, loose grin or the Mephistophelean eyebrows of his tramp mask.

For the sophisticates who want to find fault with the film, many errors lie in the vaguely primitive technique. You can start with the cutting (much too little in the first half) and end with the background music (a tenderizing of Tchaikowsky, Gershwin, and Jolson), finding the same naive technique operating in most of the departments. The process-screened backgrounds are stiff; the camera man takes no short cuts. But the chances are that you will be more delighted by "Limelight" than by any of the other Chaplin films. In the interim between his earliest two-reelers and the present movie the artist has traveled a complete circle, finally arriving back at his first and best medium, vaudeville.

October 25, 1952

◆

"Come Back Little Sheba," Hal Wallis's high-priced entry for the Academy awards, is not so much a good picture about a dismal, twenty-year old marriage as a somewhat funny and touching play that someone failed to make into a movie. With a crawling pace of events, an unusually bulky cast, and great displays of vivid Theater Guild acting that is almost always consciously perpetrated, it sits around kitchen and parlor revealing—in dialogue—the blundering and wastage of life. Meanwhile its two main figures—a shiftless housewife and a temporarily reclaimed stewbum—watch the love affair of a college-girl boarder and think of all they are missing. It is crowded with plaintive touches (the wife's vicarious participation in radio soap operas, her aimless conversations with anyone she can pull off the street) that are the bulk of the show, while the only cinematic trait lies in its concentration on trivia.

When the movie clicks, it is always on something tiny and pedestrian: Lancaster's gingerly pouring of grapefruit juice, for the boarder, from can to glass; the dependable little kiss when he goes off each morning to his chiropractor's office; his newspaper reading being broken into by the wife's need for companionship. At times it creates a large sense of American domesticity at its warmest and most intertwined. However, Miss Booth gets into her part of the female "schlump" with such an upwelling of enjoyment that she threatens to become Anna Magnani; Lancaster goes at his role of the long-suffering hus-band as if he were resolved to be an undertaker. You will half-enjoy the film, but its realism is more effective than convincing, and it tends to reiterate the twisted sentimentality of left-wing writing that tries to be very sympathetic toward little people while breaking its back to show them as hopelessly vulgar, shallow, and unhappy.

Since most directors these days have neither the time nor the interest for filmic inventions, we should make the most of the new team of Rouse and Greene which leaps after strange devices to set their films off from the aver-age run. Their "The Thief" is almost as boring as the spy thriller "Saboteur" which it recalls, but it has some dynamic scenes done with a hidden camera and (ah, bliss) no talk. The movie is Ray Milland's, who, throughout this latest milking of the Klaus Fuchs case, is a friendless, mild-tempered nuclear scien-tist who photographs secret atomic data, hides his tiny packets of microfilm in books at the Smithsonian Institute, where they are picked up by a Russian courier (Martin Gabel), intercepted by a half-dozen decoys (wooden actors), and eventually sneaked off to the Kremlin. After an hour of jangling tele-phones, spastic eye movements, and Milland's panicky chain smoking, the movie comes to a *déjà vu* Hitchcock climax with the hero trying to shake off an F.B.I. agent on the observation platform and stairways of the Empire State Building.

This rather puny chase film, however, is not so pat as it sounds. Milland, no pantomimic genius, manages to breeze through his silent role with much of the real distaste and embarrassment of a quiet guy caught in the lurid machi-nations of a super situation. You expect the usual anguish, guilt, and patriotic misgivings—and you get them—but in inspired moments Milland also plays the practical spy who believes "any job worth doing is worth doing well." It is a show in which the camera, the framing and handling of scenes, is the major concern. The Rouse-Greene team figure out their camera shots to hold back the unexpected until the right split second; they approach problems in the intellectual fashion of latter-day Eisensteins, such as using ceiling shots when the hero is cornered and low shots when he is free. The lofty camera study of a spy hemmed in by the walls of his furnished room is in a class with the ear-liest Hitchcock inventions in psychological film work; the panoramic angles of Griffith Stadium offer the most particular qualities of a ball park with the fewest effects. And when you see Milland blend convincingly with a Times Square atmosphere, scene after scene of actors being spotted in just the right place to catch the character of a real-life setting, you get the idea that R-G did a lot of looking at windows, signs, and crowds before they even hired an actor.

During Howard Hughes's reign at RKO a number of good movie ideas and artists were stopped in their tracks by the boss's slutty taste and inveterate kibitzing on every production. "The Lusty Men," one of Hughes's last jobs, however, has a refreshing story idea (about wild men who work the rodeo Big Apple from Tucson to Pendleton) with a more humanized version of the Hughes formula, which includes cheesecake, climactic and fast events, spare somewhat salty dialogue, and a copy-book exercise in splitting up two pals with wine, a practical-minded redhead, and quick money. What *is* good about it is the occasional imaginative scene; as when the has-been bronco buster searches under the old ranch house for a boyhood cache, with the camera taking you on a treasure hunt under the rotting beams, and the treasure turning out to be a broken sixshooter and a purse with two pennies. Arthur Kennedy brings to the male lead—the glory-seeking contestant—a mixture of sweetness and wildness, with some exquisite touches, like the shy, guilty smile of encouragement just before his rival takes off on his last Brahma-bull-riding turn. Mitchum is the most convincing cowboy I've seen in horse opry, meeting every situation with the lonely, distant calm of a master cliché-dodger.

For a fairly good movie you can see "Kansas City Confidential," which in general burglarizes another burglar movie, "Asphalt Jungle," adds a few wrinkles picked up from the Brink robbery, and passes over probability faster than any movie in memory. But unlike any of the above films, it tells a story without gimmicks or short cuts, and all the people involved—director Karlson, actors Elam, Van Cleef, Brand—were not only concerned with the best way to express the material on hand but obviously enjoying themselves. Stanley Kramer's "The Four Poster" is a domestic saga that shrieks for clean directing, less claustrophobic situations, and two stars who are a bit less conceited about their own charm and wit than Rex Harrison and Lilli Palmer.

November 8, 1952

◆

"The Promoter" is a good example of an efficient but not very stimulating comedy that gets seen and liked because the critics admire it. The plot is an impudent reworking of the Horatio Alger type of picaresque story, in which an ordinary jerk, eager to help everyone, manages to do it for a fat profit. The idea of a twenty-dollar-a-week solicitor's "clark" moving through the complications and coincidences of a fairly lightweight comedy until he winds up rich, mayor of the city, and favored by all the girls reminds you, in its neatness, of the early

Sturges satires. But where the Sturges films moved easily and deftly from one situation to another and took a great delight in making everyone look like a chump with the wild dream of success motoring him through slapstick, "The Promoter" is definitely stiffened by a stodgy novelistic style and made sort of dull by its insistence on "normalcy." One of the hero's money-making activities has to do with collecting rents and a "rake-off" on each collection. The episode is recorded in a staccato series of documentary shots which gives you the bare facts and a glimpse of urban ugliness, but there is no zany movement through the shops, streets, and around the chimney pots in search of fun. When slapstick is employed it is done with a dry crotchetiness, and dropped so quickly that you feel the director was embarrassed about having a donkey go berserk in the market place with the players being buried in lettuce, cabbage, and carrots.

Audiences find good reason for roaring with laughter through Alec Guinness's farces—but I keep hoping that, with his knack for making an ordinary fellow bizarre, those silly little smirks, eccentrically timed expressions, and that unexpected demoniac light in his eye, he will some day fill out a role with more than virtuosity. But then I tell myself that compared to Jerry Lewis, Hope, or Skelton's pebbly characterizations, Guinness's roles are imaginatively conceived and like rocks cast in the sea.

"Park Row" is possibly aspiring to be a sort of poor man's "Citizen Kane," but this story of the street which in the late nineties was the most famous newspaper yard in the world can be put into one sentence: a two-fisted editor didn't like the policy of America's first woman journalist; so he started a rival sheet named the *Globe* and after an hour of misunderstandings they lived happily ever after. It was produced, written, and directed on less than a pursestring by the talented Sam Fuller, who made "Broken Bayonets" last year, but from the opening shot Fuller jams his entire cast of newcomers—Mary Welch, Bela Kovacs, the choleric Gene Evans—into a two-by-four room and has them juggle lines that have to do primarily with listing famous names like Greeley, and defining things like "that's thirty" and "printer's devil." As a director, Fuller tries for epic overtones in every frame. Someone offers the just-fired editor a chance to start a new paper, and immediately the screen goes heavy with effects while the editor munches savagely on a cigar and looks off into the distance as though he were visualizing the entire history of man's fight for a free press.

The discouraging thing about this not-unspirited work is that it is another signpost marking how far the easygoing "B" film has back-tracked in recent years—from something which opened windows and let air into the industry, to an arty business full of died-in-the-wood characters and solemn actors who weigh down the floor with their theatricality. With its absence of fluidity—two huge faces usually dominate the screen—and a cast that is all wrong, the only virtue the movie has is a certain brazen rashness.

It's hard for me to dislike an Alan Ladd picture, but "Thunder in the East" is one of the slowest, most gruesome distortions of Asian existence since "Lost Horizon." Since Ladd has to his credit such films as "This Gun for Hire," "The Blue Dahlia," and "Appointment with Danger," nothing shall be said about the new effort beyond the fact that Deborah Kerr finally manages to turn in a half-human, fairly warm performance and Charles Boyer plays a Nehru type in a way that makes you painfully conscious of his wig, make-up, and stagy personality.

"O. Henry's Full House" offers four meager, tired short stories filled with tenderness for the hapless, and worked out by a few dozen proficient but over-confident artists. Each vignette is introduced by a short talk by John Steinbeck, and as evidence of the movie's high-powered technique, he uses an unctuous bass voice dubbed in by Ward Bond. Of the various rolling stones that bound through the movie, David Wayne is pretty interesting to watch, and Gregory Ratoff shows that he is a subordinate player who can handle any line thrown his way.

November 22, 1952

"The Turning Point" is a throwback to another gangster era in movies, when the director knew the difference between a movie and a play, the writer confined his dialogue to short, sharp chunks, and bit players were telling you all that you needed to know about the affectations and preoccupations of mean pool-room types. Like the movies of that "Little Caesar" era, this film masks a thin story—stealthiness, stalking, subpoenaing—with numerous smart tricks for making screen life seem like a more taut and colorful version of activity in the drab corners of a big city. Unfortunately, it is halfway between the old and a new era which shelters an epidemic of wicked ones—gangsters, molls, and fight-arena types—mixed in with Romantic Notions of the good people. For example, Edmond O'Brien is so exuberant in demonstrating the self-sacrificing, hard-hitting traits of a district attorney that he overburdens the screen even when he is just walking through an empty hall; Bill Holden plays a reporter who seldom has to do anything unromantically ordinary like showing up at the newspaper office.

The good quality of the movie comes from its crisp handling of a few action sequences in which the main idea seems to be to make movement as colorful as possible with a vast variety of purely cinematic contrasts. The big scene has a syndicate killer trying to draw a bead on Holden from the catwalks above the boxing stadium. You get the delectable visual contrast of the easy, graceful Holden turning up with a pet underworld spy, a slick, slinky mixture of the Bronx and anyone you have seen holding up the wall outside the neighborhood ginmill. Meanwhile, the stalker moves with the speed and deftness of one who has spent his life playing hide-and-seek with the law. The wonder of his performance is that he does all this delicate, intricate weaving through crowds and over arena chairs in spite of a body that is thick and awkward and a glib conceit that insists on making everything appear nonchalant. Director Dieterle, all the while, swings his camera over set-ups where the actors are static and talking, pries with his lens into the least-noticed corners of the stadium to evade the cliché shots of boxing situations. He not only produces a tingling entertainment but gives you an encyclopedic knowledge of character types as they build themselves out of the movements of their job of the moment.

The next item on the agenda is a poetic pantomime that is supposed to glow with the fulfilment of childhood desires, but probably because it cost four million dollars, took three years to create, and goes about an hour overboard in length, it takes on a faint glitter of grown-up ambitions. Up from fairyland comes "Peter Pan" replete with crocodiles that have swallowed clocks, children who can fly through the air, pirates who fight Indians, and a Walt Disney treatment that may leave a nauseated smile on your face. Being a veteran anti-Disney leaguer, I expected the extravaganza literally to put me in dreamland, which it did. But before falling asleep, I found that the picture moved rather well, in the pleasant fashion of British domestic comedies. Also, I discovered that Disney, who has always had trouble making a human figure realistic, intermittently tries out a new drawing style and a more hectic type of animation and timing. As usual most of the central figures are coated with a sticky charm. Peter, the boy who wished never to grow up, can be touching and funny at times when the people in charge keep their attention on unorthodox visual effects. But Disney gets so much syrup into the first realistic scenes that the later fairy-tale stretches somehow don't seem quite right. Doll-like Wendy's brothers are done with a sissified touch, and give the feeling that someone has pinned the sign "Kick Me" on the back of each one.

After the picture moves from the chattering nursery of the Darlings, it almost reaches the borderland of laughter with Disney's new way of caricaturing figures. In place of the ovular features and symmetrical rhythms that make Peter and friends so insipid, Disney draws his pirates and crocodiles with an angular, hacking, cutlass stroke, and he puts the frenzy of a Widmark gangster into their personalities. In the best scenes you will see an unbelievably misshapen crocodile working through a beautiful lagoon in weird animation. It is somewhat like a jet-paced hiccuping, and all the while there is an evil pirate trying to escape the animal's jaws and making some of the nicest prickly patterns to be found anywhere in drawing art. All in all, the fantasy runs thin, and as Disney feeds it rich technicolor, sweet songs, and such candy-box items as pixies and mermaids in tiny Maidenform undies, he seems to tell us once more that he is one Hollywood adult who refuses to grow up.

Bad pictures have been piling up to a record thickness that exceeds even that of 1929, the first big year of talkies. One of the most romantic is "The Iron Mistress," a slightly hysterical attempt to clear up conflicting accounts about a large, outwardly peaceable pioneer who left his name on an unliked county and on a favorite weapon of the border. The picture about Jim Bowie's young manhood has a few good individual scenes like a sword-and-dagger fight in total darkness—the screen lights up a couple of times to show the duelists floundering in opposite corners of the room—and reveals the steady hand of producer Henry Blanke in the endless handsome technicolor shots that might serve as landscape paintings but make for a rather stilted adventure film. "The Steel Trap" was bound to be called a "sleeper" by numerous critics, since it is a modest-budget thriller with great stretches of silence, underplayed acting, and a James Cain-type story of young married love up against the husband's desire to embezzle all the currency lying around his bank job. The story is repetitious; so you can forget it and concentrate on the sad plight of Teresa Wright, who once played her quiet, vaporous style without tricks but, cast with actors too tall and overbearing for her, seems to have turned into a straining, obstreperous glamour girl. "Babes in Bagdad," a backroom study of harem love, seems to have been produced during a lunch hour on a single Monogram set by a couple of celluloid butchers.

December 6, 1952

Blame the Audience

WHILE Hollywood, after all, still makes the best *motion* films, its 1952 products make me want to give Los Angeles back to the Conquistadores. Bad films have piled up faster than they can be reviewed, and the good ones (*Don't Bother to Knock, Something to Live For, The Lusty Men, My Son John, The Turning Point, Clash by Night*) succeed only as pale reminders of a rougher era that pretty well ended with the 1930's. The people who yell murder at the whole Hollywood business will blame the current blight on censorship, the star system, regimentation, the cloak-and-suit types who run the industry, the dependence of script-writers on a small group of myths, TV, the hounding of the Un-American Activities Committee, and what I shall laughingly call montageless editing.

There is plenty of justification for trying to find what is causing this plague, and I point my thumb accusingly at the audience, the worst in history. The present crowd of movie-goers, particularly the long-haired and intellectual brethren, is a negative one, lacking a workable set of values or a sense of the basic character of the medium, so that it would surprise me if any honest talent in Hollywood had the heart to make good pictures for it.

Their taste for preciously styled, upper-case effects and brittle sophistication has encouraged Hollywood to turn out some of the most smartly tooled art works of the times—films like *Sunset Boulevard* and *The Bad and the Beautiful*, stunning mixtures of mannerism, smooth construction, and cleverly camouflaged hot air. While I find these royal creations pretty good entertainment, I keep telling myself that the audiences craving for costly illusion (overacting, overscoring, overlighting, overmoralizing) may produce total confusion in Hollywood. The industry is still turning out movies that are supposed to be moderately naturalistic, but it must grow puzzled by having to make plain simple facts appear as special and delectable as the audience demands. So what we have to deal with now is a spectator who has Tiffany-styled esthetics and tastes in craftsmanship, and whose idea of good movies is based on an assortment of swell attitudes.

If some stern yearner makes a movie full of bias for the underdog, or a clever actor crowds his role with affectations picked out of real life, or the script-writer sets up innumerable situations wherein the camera can ponder over clocks, discarded cigar bands, and assorted bric-a-brac, the audience responds as though it were in the climate of high art.

Faced with such an audience—half tory and half culture bug—Griffith, with his practical genius, or Sennett, with his uninhibited improvising talents, would probably have passed up moviemaking for something more virile and exciting.

The reason movies are bad lies is this audience's failure to appreciate, much less fight for, films like the unspectacular, unpolished "B," worked out by a few people with belief and skill in their art, who capture the unworked-over immediacy of life before it has been cooled by "Art." These artists are liberated from such burdens as having to recoup a large investment, or keeping a star's personality intact before the public; they can experiment with inventive new ideas instead of hewing to the old sure-fire box-office formula.

Such pictures are often made in "sleeper" conditions (sometimes even the studio hotshots didn't know they were being made), and depend, for their box-office success, on word-of-mouth approval instead of "colossal" ads. But since there is no longer an audience response to fresh filmic trends, this type of movie is being replaced, by most of the big Hollywood factories, with low budget jobs that emulate prodigious spectacles, foreign-film sentiments, or best-seller novels, until you can no longer tell the "B" from an "A".

In the past, when the audience made underground hits of modest "B" films, Val Lewton would take a group of young newcomers who delighted in being creative without being fashionably intellectual, put them to work on a pulp story of voodooists or grave robbers and they would turn $214,000 into warm charm and interesting technique that got seen because people, rather than press agents, built its reputation. After 1940, a Lewton, Preston Sturges, Sam Fuller, Allan Dwan, or Budd Boetticher finds his best stride in a culture-free atmosphere that allows a director to waste his and the audience's time, and then loses himself in the culture-conscious conditions of large-scale work.

The low budget appears to economize the mind of a director, forcing him into a nice balance between language and what is seen. Given more money and reputation actors, Sam Fuller's episodic, spastically slow and fast film would probably dissolve into mouthy arrogance where characters would be constantly defining and apologizing for the class separation that obsesses Fuller and burying in words the skepticism and energy which he locates in his 1949–52 low budgets. The structure that Fuller invented in *I Shot Jesse James* depends on close-ups of large faces and gestures, combustive characters in close face-to-face confrontations where they seem bewitched with each other but where each one is actually in a private, lightly witty rumination about the wondrous information that springs up from being professionals pursuing highly perfected skills. In *Steel Helmet*, the weight of too many explanations about race-class-position seems to leaden Fuller's work, drives him into a pretentious strain that is not apparent in the totally silent *Jesse James* opening.

Sturges's turning point occurs in *Hail the Conquering Hero*, when he begins patronizing, caricaturing his small towners with patriotic sentimentality. The Eddie Bracken hero—no energy, desiring isolation, trying to free himself of responsibility—is a depressing symbol suggesting the spiritual difficulties Sturges must have been under, trying to psych himself into doing culture-conscious work. The last good Sturges occurs in *Sullivan's Travels*, which is not low budget, but its best sections—the hobo material, rudimentary slapstick, an expensive cross-country bus trying to stay with a kid's homemade motor tank, Veronica Lake's alertness within leisure—are elemental "B" handling.

In 1943, William Castle, the director of the Monogram melodrama *When Strangers Marry*, could experiment with a couple of amateurs (Robert Mitchum and Kim Hunter), try out a then new Hollywood idea of shooting without studio lights in the sort of off-Broadway rented room where time seems to stand still for years and the only city sounds come through a postage stamp opening on the air well. The movie was a hit with perceptive moviegoers, made a fair profit, and prepared audiences for two new stars and some of the uninvented-looking cinema later made famous in *Open City*. All this was possible because Castle wasn't driven to cater to cliché tastes.

Once, intellectual moviegoers performed their function as press-agents for movies that came from the Hollywood underground. But, somewhere along the line, the audience got on the wrong track. The greatest contributing cause was that their tastes had been nurtured by a kind of snobbism on the part of most of the leading film reviewers. Critics hold an eminent position, which permits control of movie practice in one period by what they discerned, concealed, praised, or kicked around in the preceding semester of moviemaking. I suggest that the best way to improve the audiences' notion of good movies would be for these critics to stop leading them to believe there is a new "classic" to be discovered every three weeks among vast-scaled "prestige" productions. And, when they spot a good "B," to stop writing as though they'd found a "freak" product.

December 19, 1952

I DON'T understand the belt people get out of overwrought, feminine pictures, but "My Cousin Rachel" must be regarded as a skilful blend of suspense, romantic acting, and infallible middle-brow direction. The first hour of the picture—which recalls "Rebecca," which in turn recalls "Jane Eyre"—tells us that a naturally sulky boy could be upset by a woman who seems to have poisoned the boy's beloved guardian after driving him crazy, spending his money, and carrying on with an Italian lawyer. After that, the boy falls in love with the Wicked Woman, and the second hour finds him living through a small-scale hell. The picture happens to be a mystery, but because it is tied to the wispy conventions of romantic fiction, it never gets on the road. There is a reliance on candlelit scenes which probably made for thrilling literary descriptions, but it means that the actor has to wade through a choppy filigree of lights and shadows before he can steal a crucial letter or jealously peer up at a boudoir window. The situations are of a type that could be rehearsed in chairs, the few active ones having a tendency to seem silly in a medium that depends so heavily on authenticity. For instance, the meatiest romantic sequence shows the hero climbing to a balcony at midnight, throwing a ton of the family jewels at the siren's feet, and then kissing her with such force that the camera lens begins to perspire and the scene fades off into a blur. Richard Burton, in the anguished hero's role, has an active grace, and can do anything Montgomery Clift invented—looking and listening with the wide-awake surprise of a woodpecker who has just happened into an oil field—with more style and masculinity. Olivia de Havilland does not seem either charming or wicked, but now that she has been through Shaw-Shakespeare, she can musicalize every sentence, without seeming to know what she is saying, and move with the firm, cold conviction of an actress who has finally overcome an inferiority complex.

"Above and Beyond" stalks a real-life hero named Paul W. Tibbetts, Jr., in a picture that is interesting despite its lack of filmic virtues. The history it simplifies begins at the atom-bomb proving ground and goes on to Hiroshima, and I suppose part of the entertainment lies in watching M-G-M make a valiant attempt to dodge the reverential clichés of shrines-to-the-living. At the start Tibbetts's wife is worrying over whether her marriage is on the rocks, and then via a two-hour-six-minute flashback we see her husband tangle with the big brass, B-29's, and security agents, acquire a reputation as a swelled-up perfectionist disciplinarian, neglect his marriage, and generally worry-frown his way through the difficulties of running the bomb tests at Wendover, Utah. Robert Taylor ushers in the atomic age with a good, negative performance that consists of trying not to look too communicative, handsome, or triumphant.

At no point does the camera tell the story; the film is done in clear, sunny shots with the main fact always anchored firmly in the center of the screen. Anyone who remembers early air films like "Only Angels Have Wings" is bound to miss the loose-jointed animation of a Grant or Cagney, the climactic excitement of watching a box-kite plane take off in a storm from a postage-stamp air-field, such visual inventions as a hawk smashing through the glass of a plane, and the unforgettable tempo of the crash ending in "Ceiling Zero." This script is on the mild side all the way ("Dimples eight two from north Tinian tower"); when the first shock wave from the bomb hits the Enola Gay, a white light fills the plane—the camera seems to have snapped suddenly—and then the movie settles back into its precise treading of general facts. It might have been more interesting if someone had been more faithful to trivia—like showing the human side of the fateful crew that started chomping on ham sandwiches and no doubt wondered whether radioactivity would make them sterile. But the script skips from the newsreel record of Hiroshima back to Tinian, where you see Tibbetts walking toward a four-star general and another decoration. Also, there is a remarkable reluctance by M-G-M to credit anyone (Truman, Stimson) but Mr. Tibbetts for the terrible decision of killing so many Japs with one efficient maneuver.

Though no one can make a certain kind of tragical-comical-pastoral picture like the French, "Jeux Interdits" is the only one I have liked since "Goupi Mains Rouge." The story—about the morbid entertainments of a five-year-old girl whose parents have been machine-gunned in an air raid and an eleven-year-old peasant boy who takes her home—has been managed by René Clément in the shocking but convincing style of the "Red Hands" film. The most remarkable performance is that of a peasant father (Lucien Hubert) who seems to be created out of unfertile country earth. His manner—the cigarette that drips off the front of his lip, the way he beats up his kids with a mellow brutality, his way of wasting through the hours between supper and sleep—is achieved with the most frugal type of pantomime. Yet it tells you all that exaperates him about his family and all that he has picked up in wisdom through a lifetime. The homely settings are photographed in crude darks and lights so that the scenes of children fleeing down a country road at night give the scary, bleak, adventuresome feeling of country life to a degree that must be recalled from childhood experience.

Most of my reservations are small: there is a cartoon quality about the farmers' feud, and at least three of the teen-agers think it is right to play country kids as morons. The only major dislike has to do with Director René Clément's glibness with difficult effects. As a result the movie goes precious in those places where it should be plainly and simply terrifying, as when the five-year-old starts down a long, completely vertical ladder and later when she reacts to violence with the cheek-clawing hysteria of an over-protected spinster. Nevertheless, his best effects are quite simple and original; these usually have to do with showing the fleeting emotions of small children when their games are a sort of startling mimicry of what is going on in the adult world. The two stars, Brigitte Fossey and Georges Poujouly, manage to be natural, comic, and utterly moving in a hair-raising way without even trying. You should see this film, even at art-theater prices.

December 20, 1952

◆

The only way to pull the vast sprawl of 1952 films together is to throw most of them in a pile bearing the label "movies that failed through exploiting middle-brow attitudes about what makes a good movie." This leaves me with the following box-office stepchildren to list as my "ten best" films. It is difficult to say whether I liked or disliked a number of films that will appear on most other lists, since it was usually a case of being impressed with classy craftsmanship and bored by watching it pander to some popular notion about what makes an artistic wow. One such film, "Come Back, Little Sheba," went all out for sympathizing with underdogs; another, "Member of the Wedding," stuffed itself with odd "characters" of Dickensian proportions; "Forbidden Games" rubbed amateur acting and untampered rural surroundings in your eyes. In each case, I felt I was supposed to applaud the "crutches" that are currently leaned on in cinema, and that, for me, negated some good things about the films.

"The Strange Ones." A macabre melodrama about incestuous adolescence; rates top honors in every film department for its tough-minded, unselfconsciously clumsy but delicate treatment of a subject a movie crew could easily have murdered. Turns up one fascinatingly grotesque image after another; set in the small, special world of a fantastically disordered bedroom, it works with a sick brother and his sister who wander about in bathrobes seeking some new gadget or ritual for kicks; crowds the whole tremulous desperation of two deeply affectionate, anarchic little beasts into the performances of Stéphane and Dermithe, whose acting of the queer and fantastic should be studied by the overrated Julie Harris–Shirley Booth–Marlon Brando academy of overplaying.

"Oh, Amelia." A fifty-year-old French bedroom farce refashioned by Claude Autant-Lara with split-second timing, extreme gaiety, and ingenuity in repeatedly compromising a heroine without actually corrupting her; though it may have been slapped together by a group of aloofly amused actors during their lunch hour, it has the ridiculous charm of a Punch and Judy show and the innocent, pell-mell vulgarity of a Sennett comedy.

"The Turning Point." A tingling, rather moving example of the half-serious gangster film that Hollywood does better than anything else in its repertoire; particularly good for its unsentimental handling of cutthroat competitors in moments of duress, when their ambitious careers are about to crumble around them; also casts a touching spotlight on New York-type friendships: a cop turning virtuous but trying to play fair with his gangster friends; an attorney's girl friend methodically setting up a romance with his best chum but being very concerned about not losing the attorney's affections; a triumph of crisp acting (Edmond O'Brien, Tom Tully), vigorous camera work, lean writing.

"Don't Bother to Knock." An unpolished, persuasively written little melodrama about a blonde baby sitter drifting in cuckoo-land in a big-city hotel; Richard Widmark's acting of a grousing, ornery, efficient individual waltzing into a pick-up romance and then finding himself unable to cope with the personality of the girl; Monroe's amateurish manner and childishly blank expression used without the usual glamour treatment in the character of a paranoiac refugee from a small town; the best naturalistic photography on a drab American hotel since "When Strangers Meet" and a job of direction (Roy Baker) that seems to dig its way into stale hotel atmosphere through room radios, between plastic Venetian blinds, and over ugly ashtrays.

"Something to Live For." A soap opera that started with a story that was practically nothing and ended up as a strangely disturbing, clean, uncluttered picture of alcoholism; mark up another score for the camera magic of Director George Stevens, the only genuine pioneer working in current films; he evokes a rich lather of romance with his slow, imaginative use of looming close-ups, overlapping dissolves, filtered camera effects, and oddly contrived compositions; story-telling images bring out the inner problems of characters in a purely cinematic way: two members of Alcoholics Anonymous trembling through a party, with the camera insistently hovering over trays of Martinis and highballs; creditable acting by Milland and Fontaine.

"Five Fingers." In its literate, satirical way, this spy melodrama was the most unusual thriller since Hitchcock's first low-budget films; almost totally a product of witty scripting, it built up incredible tension and speed with elegantly comicalized dialogue, neatly turned portraits of war-time diplomats with their brains at half-mast, and practically no outward violence; a great job of perfectly controlled, suave acting by James Mason; wonderful bits of unscrupulous carrying-on: the slow awakening of Countess Danielle Darrieux to the possibilities of being a valet's mistress once she finds out he has a priceless pair of safe-cracking hands.

"Limelight." A sentiment-ridden tragi-comedy with enough of Chaplin's grace and absurdity as a funny man, and Raphael-like taste for visual qualities to compensate for the slow, rumpsprung style of story-telling.

"The Sell-Out." A fast thriller off the top of the news, with perceptive atmospheric bits of barroom drama that fall quietly into place, two plausible performances (Audrey Totter, John Hodiak), and the feeling throughout of something chanced upon rather than confected.

The following also placed: "Room for One More," "Boots Malone," "Brandy for the Parson," "House Across the Street," "Young Man with Ideas," "Casque d'Or," "Scaramouche," "Wait Till the Sun Shines, Nellie," "Beauty and the Devil," "Apache War Smoke," "Pennywhistle Blues," "Jour de Fête."

January 17, 1953

◆

Though "The Member of the Wedding," Carson McCullers's prize-winning play about the last days of childhood, betrays its stage origin on the screen, it has been made into a somewhat amusing, and moving, sometimes improbable picture. Stanley Kramer has a trick way of opening his productions with a pastoral scene followed by a sustained shot of the star walking toward the camera: this one starts at a fishing wharf, follows Julie Harris home, and anchors itself in an ugly Southern kitchen where a small social circle—a tomboyish girl, her seven-year-old cousin, and the family cook—is viewed battling loneliness in a way that sometimes harks back to Saroyan or Tarkington types of humor. One of the funnier scenes has to do with a three-handed bridge game; they sit around the table with much concentrated clumsiness and dreamy domestic relaxation, with two of the players moaning about the "rotten hands" until it develops that the solemn little boy cut up the picture cards because they were so "cute." Eventually, melodramatic things begin to happen—the boy dies, the cook's nephew is sent to the pen, the girl runs away from home—and then, for no reason at all, the movie ends.

An interesting feature of the film is that it makes use of a television-type shot—the very close close-up of an active breathless face against a blacked-out background such as turns up in Gillette's prize-fight programs. With intimate, revealing image-maneuvers like this, the movie attempts both to break its bondage to the play and to penetrate a visual sphere new to movies. It starts drifting in a strange sea made up simply of motion and anatomy on a super-realistic level; you are practically on top of the human figure when, trapped in the most intense motion and feeling, it is cut off from the surrounding things that make life seem ordinary and fairly secure. And you are devoured by a rather plain twelve-year-old girl, her bound-in misery, her perspiring intensity, her boniness and impulsive hair cut.

This is a good example of a "director's picture," crammed with vivid details none of which falls quietly into place. The main character, the gawky girl, is an unspectacular sort who suffers from every stigma known to childhood, and Director Zinnemann allows Julie Harris to play the role in the manner of a cannibal chewing up a rare hunk of beef. Along with her flexible voice, which blends Baby Snooks with a sour, muted violin, she has an elegantly active pair of hands which clutch, pluck, drum, and posture in a rhythm that is peculiarly out of key with the rest of the acting, talk, and atmosphere. While Miss Harris eats a bit of stew like Marlon Brando playing an eccentric Bennington College student, Zinnemann brings out a small, select group of weird people. Among them are a smooth Harlem-type dresser who doesn't feel conspicuous carrying an unboxed silver trumpet through a small town and a silly child who minces about the room like the most professional Mae West impersonator.

When the more normal characters encounter abnormal behavior (the girl's determination to go along on her brother's honeymoon), they provocatively shift into the unreasonable—that is, the father brutally yanks the girl out of the car and throws her on the sidewalk, where she is stared at unmercifully by queasy neighbors. It is as though Zinnemann, along with a lot of his sensitive colleagues—Kazan, Wilder, *et al.*—tried to show only the oddest members of the human race.

January 31, 1953

◆

I<small>N</small> "The Little World of Don Camillo" a serious subject—the conflict between Christian principles and Communist dogmas—is treated with a tolerance and whimsy that made my skin crawl. Yet this extended serio-comic brawl between a godless mayor and a militant priest has some qualities that set it off from the French movie franchise—a crisis in the life of a small town which happens to be running over with simple, excellent people and cute situations. It is a surprisingly white film, with hardly a shadow in it; and it features distant views from steeple, sky, and ceiling that make an earthy affair confined to the monumental irritations of two characters into an exceedingly elastic film—a village chronicle that has the open spaciousness of a county. There is also a drugged, novelistic pace that must have been difficult to achieve in a format of sketches each of which has a separate plot, twist, and point.

Most French comedies are filled out with the personal traits of townsfolk, but this one impresses you with the degree of it rounded characterization. The priest is an ordinary fellow who far outshines the crooning, ball-playing priest in "Going My Way." Along with his piety and good humor he has an addiction to carrying a tommy-gun, and on occasion he is capable of lying, poaching, attempted bribery, fist-fighting, and scoring the best mark in the carnival games testing physical prowess. Fernandel gives the priest another talent—a clever ability to make oily self-satisfied faces that put across a point with exquisite timing. "Don Camillo" has already taken Europe by storm, but unless you are amused by apple-polishing in place of sharp realism and enjoy the idea of a statue of Christ saying, "You're telling me!" you can postpone seeing this one.

On their visit to the Falls the "Niagara" movie crew must have got into difficulties not usually associated with the manufacture of action-thrillers. Between stereotyped chases up dizzy heights and shots of Marilyn Monroe tossing in bed, the movie breaks up into a choppy assemblage of fragments that just barely tell the bickering, homicidal story of a trampish blonde and her deranged husband. Director Hathaway, the Richard Halliburton of the Fox directing stable, is not one to lose his thrills in complications of the terrain, but he seems to have been overpowered by this locale—to such a degree that he settled for telescopic shots of a body being fished out of the water, a chase on the sightseeing stairs that is almost obliterated by spray, and scenes that have nothing more momentous than a technicolored rainbow. Usually you see Joe Cotten, wedded as always to a hangdog expression, at about six in the morning, when no one was around to trouble the camera crew, worrying, plotting against his wife, or trying to stash a damned corpse in the roaring vicinity of the falls. It is my impression that Miss Monroe has now arrived at a style of breathy mumbling, sloppy posture, and physical self-consciousness that is boring as well as silly.

"Taxi" is a slender, highly unlikely comedy that you might catch on an off night. The film cruises for fourteen hours through New York's boroughs while a taxicab driver (Dan Dailey) makes deprecating remarks, argues, and tries to disillusion a genteel, pretty colleen who has one day in which to find her long-missing husband. The story is too sweet for my taste, but it is one of those infrequent occasions on which Danny Fuchs, one of Hollywood's more gifted penmen, gets a chance to display his ear for Brooklyn speech. Dailey anchors the vanity-sized sentimental comedy in some sufficient kind of reality with an unbuoyant walk, a blatant voice, and an uncomprehending, almost goofy expression. But despite the contributions of the two Dannys, you see less New York life in "Taxi" than the subject offers. For instance, the cab moves easily through parkways, tunnels, and streets, as if Manhattan weren't the bent-fender city, and Dailey's supporting cast of traffic cops and fellow-cabbies generally turn out to be decent, lovable hams like Wallace Beery.

Though it is on the jerry-built side, "Curtain Up" is the kind of movie the ads call a "murderously funny" example of high British comedy. Those highly stylized comedians Robert Morley and Margaret Rutherford weave a web of frustration and cheerful irresponsibility around a morning's theatrical rehearsal, but the action generally drags so badly that it elicits no more than three audible laughs. Director Ralph Smart has managed to get some fun into the film with fresh stuff about flubbing of lines, ham acting, and stale writing in a provincial repertory theater. It starts out leisurely and wastefully: the ingenue taking a nap backstage, a harried producer trying to find the plot in a new script, someone else unsuccessfully rallying the group on stage. Then, as the rehearsal turns into a nightmare, the people work up the energy of hungry tigers. You don't see such amiable, unglamorous faces on the screen every day; and quite outside the hackneyed sub-plots (a faded character actress ruminating over a brief early London success; a stage-struck ingenue having to be fired) there is a certain know-how in the central matter of showing the ambivalent pleasure (confusion, mock anger, hysterical displays of ego) that can be worked into a trivial situation by little people with time on their hands.

February 14, 1953

◆

Huston's "Moulin Rouge" is packed with crunchy songs, French taste in clothes, and picturesque people, but the quality of its color is its most striking attribute. The dramatic use of filtered camera effects and off-key tonalities re-creates on film the heated, hazy quality of French Impressionist painting. When the dwarf Toulouse-Lautrec painfully picks his way out of a Montmartre bistro, the scene is the studied abyss of a blue-green interior, with hot accents (geranium red, acid yellow) in the foreground and scrub-women carefully spotted for a dash of human content. In some instances actual paintings are "staged," reproducing everything but the vein of casual objectivity that lay at the core of Lautrec's work. Other shots capitalize on canvas-worthy things like Zsa Zsa Gabor's spun-glass skin next to the starchy texture of her white and orange costume, the paint-spattered derby Lautrec wore while painting, the ambling grace of a Negro dancer who seems to move on nothing more solid than space, and the can-can girls who dance with their whole bodies instead of just their legs. In this fascinating visual arena the heavily blurred atmosphere seems to have drained the characters of realistic personalities, leaving the decorative details of the composition to compete for interest. In fact, Huston has crowded such an attractive world around the subject of this biography—such surging impressions of Parisian activities—that you never get a good line on the artist himself.

Mainly, this is the fault of an unworkable script in which the double dose of romance given Lautrec fails to become credible before reaching a sudden and definitive conclusion. It fumbles past its hero as a real figure to feed him such explicit literary dialogue as "The streets of Paris have taught you to strike fast and draw blood first," and moralizes on the topics of love, alcoholism, and appreciation of art.

Lautrec was a wealthy nobleman, grotesquely misshapen and a chronic drunkard. After his first affair with a prostitute (Colette Marchand) who is too warped to value Lautrec's love but who wields a devastating power over him, the crippled count takes up with a virtuous dress model (chinless beauty Suzanne Flon). You see them sightseeing in Parisian settings until, incomprehensibly, she decides the smitten Lautrec will never love her and leaves him with a torch to carry the rest of his days. Meanwhile, the picture of Lautrec as an artist has been built up by such disintegrated maneuvers as having the camera travel down to his flying pencil on a cafe's tablecloth, dance over the paintings that cover his studio walls, document the production of a poster, dart about kiosks, and peer over shoulders at his *vernissage*.

Lautrec's personal drama might have been more absorbing if Ferrer had not been incarcerated in his make-up, which involved the binding of his legs to make him as short as the four-foot-eight painter, as well as elaborate facial changes. On those occasions when the camera digs into his face it unearths nothing more informative than a highly inscrutable expression. Certainly Huston as director and co-author compensated for the fact that his main character couldn't zip around on his stunted legs with avid camera movement and prodigious exuberance on the part of the other performers. Marchand, for instance, literally dances through her role—jerking, slouching, making eccentric patterns with her arms as though she were playing to a spastic nickelodeon piano. As for Miss Flon, I've seldom seen an actress with greater presence or stature in a role remarkable for its unimportant activity.

The big bone I pick with all this entertainment is that it attempts to idealize Lautrec for his deficiencies and to simplify the tale of the artist by implying that genius in painting is a by-product of painful experience. And despite the iron discipline of Huston's direction, it frequently becomes too brightly emphatic; one feels that the charming groups of blondes and redheads who bounce about with such hilarious gaiety are afraid to relax for fear the movie will run down like a clock that needs winding.

February 28, 1953

◆

THE directors of two new films—"The Naked Spur" and "Jeopardy"—having worked on a number of low-budget thrillers, claim space this week for a notation of their talents. John Sturges, director of "Jeopardy," is a deft mechanic who has turned out such pictures as "Mystery Street" and "The People Against O'Hara." He has almost Defoe's talent for creating circumstantial detail, along with the ability to make hard-to-do things seem easy. Interested in the problem of how "people like you and me" express ourselves at work, Sturges steers his films away from melodrama into literate, semi-documentary studies of such subjects as law-office routine or sleuthing in a college laboratory. He has a restrained hand with actors, a moderately realistic camera style, and a remarkable talent for letting us know what goes on in the minds of people faced with a scientific or mechanical problem.

Only as individual a director as Sturges could have concocted anything worth seeing out of "Jeopardy," with its picture-postcard settings, ragged dialogue, and Pearl White-type thrills that have been guidebooked by a dozen other hair-raising films. The story, which could have been worked out for a radio play, has Barry Sullivan trapped under a jetty, with only his wife (chief desperate star Stanwyck) to save him from drowning in the incoming tide. The help she finally gets turns out to be a sex-starved killer (Ralph Meeker) who commandeers her car to escape from his crime. Some of the dialogue sounds as if it came from a *Collier's* gangster: "Is there anything your husband has that I could use?" leers Meeker. However, Sturges has lowered the temperature of this frantic story by turning it into a kind of examination of wild landscape, car problems, and how one can outwit nature on a holiday trip along the coast of Lower California. By searching with the lens into every corner of a late-model Ford convertible and creating interest in such things as lug-wrenches, spinning wheels, and raising a car without a jack, Sturges made a fine study in car mania, one that speeds along at a fast clip and would be clear and suspenseful even to a deaf person.

Anthony Mann, director of "The Naked Spur," is good at making action films come to life after the sun sets, when in delicately underlighted episodes he demonstrates that nothing is more fascinating than an objective study of nihilistic evil, death, and destruction. The Marquis de Sade of the Metro directing crew, Mann not only gives genuine form and style to his cruel-toned works but has almost vindicated Hollywood's technique with mountain slides, Indian fights, and shooting matches by showing how a deluge of violent scenes can create striking visual rhythms that are like powerful if devastating music. Mann did a careful and artful job with the ingredients of "The Naked Spur," but he got some of his material—the theme of human greed—distinctly third-hand via the Huston "Sierra Madre" epic. Just five people—a cagy desperado, a merciless pursuer, an old prospector, a dishonorable cavalryman, and an attractive blonde—go along on the hoked-up ride through the rocky hills of Colorado.

Each of the roles, except Millard Mitchell's slow-witted prospector, is played as if the actor thought he could do this job blindfolded at the bottom of a well. For a while Robert Ryan and his companion in flight, Janet Leigh, are as mean a couple of coyotes as you will find in a Western, but then Leigh casts off her unglamorous disguise, and Ryan starts in with his oily Iago-type expressions of self-assured evil. Perhaps there is too much predictable plot complication here to please old Anthony Mann fans, but his particular gifts are evident anyway: the unique love scene that is cut in against the eerie patter of rain on outdoor eating utensils; the three-way shooting match around a rocky cliff that builds up a frightening chorus with the ping of bullets on rocks. A laudable achievement, too, is the way all that Technicolor landscape is kept under control, seeming to be as plain and solid around the cowboys as in any good black-and-white horse opry.

March 23, 1953

IN earlier days Director Robert Wise revealed an interesting talent for working with dispiriting situations, keeping the story of their progress mounting to a maddening climax. He made a number of "sleepers" in this vein, so called because they had somehow turned out to be believable, skilful feature films, though made on little more than it now costs to feed the lions in "The Greatest Show on Earth." These films are evidence that it is quite possible to make movies on less money and more skill. Wise learned movie-making by working in various jobs on the lot, he edited some Lewton-produced horror films and directed "The Set-Up." So it is somewhat disturbing to find that he, like some other artists who started out on good "sleepers," has progressed to making rather pointless "A" pictures.

His new film, "Destination Gobi," is such a step in the wrong direction. But while it is not first class, it is a workman-like job of film-making that flows like sand in an eggtimer and has some funny situations and adequate settings. It is an adventure story with Richard Widmark, in a customary frenzied role, establishing a weather station in the Gobi Desert. Its best quality is its rugged visualization of an eight-hundred-mile trek through enemy soldiers and suspicious Mongols, to the accompaniment of thirst, hunger, and all the usual trappings of a "never say die" movie. Well composed out of a succession of panoramic shots and fast action scenes, the film suffers from Wise's loss of contact with realism in acting. The characters of the weather observers are bombastic or comic swaggerers, and the Mongolian horsemen act like Western movie regulars.

Another director who has overreached his earlier talents is Alfred Hitchcock. As a movie pioneer, Hitchcock introduced imaginative sounds, fine character effects, and fleet economy. He brought you an everyday world that was as real as it was ominous ("The 39 Steps"). However, Hitchcock's new melodrama, "I Confess," has negated the realism to settle for the "effects." His mystery story is peopled with familiar suspense-film types—a sadistic detective, a suave prosecutor, an amoral scoundrel with a tidy but vapid wife—and laid among the crooked, elevated streets of Quebec. It does get a certain dramatic punch through the sensitive underplaying of Montgomery Clift as a young priest who, learning the identity of a murderer in the confessional booth, plays the remainder of the picture with sad compassion and locked lips. With a line like "We can do nothing," he spreads his hands with a quiet weariness that expresses the feeling of people caught in a rotten jam. For the most part, "I Confess" is a problemless piece of stagecraft in which the suspense, except for a quick twist at the end, is just so much decoration.

In the American spectacle class, frontiers division, "The President's Lady" is a studiously dull picture about wild young Andrew Jackson and the trouble he had with the divorce laws of his time. It is a triumph of histrionics over history, starring Charlton Heston and Susan Hayward. The only real contributions were made by an over-particular set designer, and by Leo Tover, director of photography.

Howard Hughes's "Angel Face" is a congested thriller that kills off all its actors with modern sports cars. Unlike many of Hughes's hard-working murder films, this one is too often verbal instead of visual, with a lot of time spent in a dimly lit boudoir where Robert Mitchum and Jean Simmons mutter forlornly and wear dressing gowns.

April 11, 1953

◆

"Off Limits" has Bob Hope horsing and miming like a Mack Sennett employee. The story casts him as a prize-fight manager in the army who smart-talks the most inept pug (Mickey Rooney) into winning the lightweight title. The part disproves the idea that Hope's comedy lies mainly in his fast verbal satire, for here he creates a many-faceted character who is as boastful as Falstaff, as unmanly as Lloyd Hamilton, and as good-humored, in a misanthropic way, as Bugs Bunny.

An example of Hope's flexible characterization is in the scene where he cons his fighter at a 200-word-a-minute speed, and while the terms "Hook him," etc., seem apt for the situation, they are delivered with a dreaming fool's mien and mismated connections that hint the manager is not only contemptuous of both battlers but not even watching. Sometimes Hope gets feelings of deep distaste, disdain, into a single keen-eyed stare, a haughty quiver of his body, or a jutting of his leaden underslung jaw a fraction of an inch in the direction of his victim. But always his malevolence is so mixed either with comic self-debasement or utter selflessness as to make him seem precariously vulnerable.

Although the audience is treated to the entire range of great silent comedies—violence, exchange of insults, intense humiliation and embarrassed apology, ludicrous mix-ups, and Don Juan love-making—somehow Hope never creates the laugh that kills. It is not that he refuses to milk or build a gag but possibly that he just looks too normal and prosperous to evoke the delighted rush of relief—"Gee whiz, that guy's worse off than I am"—that the pathos of Chaplin, Keaton, and Langdon achieved. Or possibly Hope's style, which combines precision of timing with intellectual suppleness and finesse, puts too fine an edge on all this sort of foolishness.

In one sequence from the dark ages of situation comedy he scratches and paints a general's mile-long black sedan, believing it belongs to a loathed gangster. For ten minutes of screen time he gets your thoughts away from the ancient heaviness of the gag by doing an elf-child's display of grace and roguish self-delight. He paints fetching abstract patterns with broad calcimine strokes, while giving you the footwork of a sissified Nijinsky. It is really swell, but you are reacting not to humor but to cleverness.

In the hands of director George Marshall, a sort of Studs Lonigan distant cousin of Sennett, the film emerges as an uneven work that often hugs bad gags and zooms past promising situations. Marshall has an uncommonly good eye for hard-boiled harried types; he turns Marilyn Maxwell into a classic figure of brassiness. The list of assistant laugh getters—Rooney, Stanley Clements, Eddie Mayehoff—promises more than it achieves. Making brief personal appearances are some muscular fellows—Dempsey, Tommy Harmon, Art Aragon —who seem almost gentle in the midst of the pratfalls and mad activity.

April 25, 1953

◆

In a seventy-minute feature called "Bright Road," M-G-M has refashioned the story of "The Quiet One," a Levitt-Loeb prize-winning documentary that dealt with the rescue of a blocked, bewildered colored boy, new methods of education, and common-sense therapy. Here, in Emmett Lavery's script, a pretty Alabama school teacher—demure, devoted, glowing with Christian endeavor—breaks through the shell of a perverse juvenile named P. T. ("It don't stand for nothing"), the shame of Vinedale school.

While the tale leans rather heavily on the idea that all becomes well when the wand of modern psychology is waved, and the view of boyhood is forcibly patterned to make this outcome possible, the movie has a surprise gift of humor and humanity. Negro actors, not unlike others, have too frequently fitted themselves into a stereotype that makes them either caricature or figures of sentimentally sterling worth. The newcomers in "Bright Road"—a dozen kids plus two adults (one of them Harry Belafonte)—cause one to be more acutely aware of the burdened propagandist portrayals of Canada Lee, the exquisite clichés of Ethel Waters, the oversensitivity of James Edwards, and the servility of Hattie McDaniels. What I'm trying to say is that this all-colored cast does not accommodate itself to an audience's ready-made ideas and so brings to the screen a fresh spontaneous life.

Some artful scenes reveal the boys' classroom behavior, a mixture of swagger and glee. A small spectacled kid stalls on the trip from blackboard to seat to run his hand across each student as though he were a slat in a picket fence. A born cynic throws tipster comments at a chum having trouble with long division. Another shrugs through a ridiculous description of his vacation experience. This is all enacted with an air of special and private knowhow about humor and an easy grace that make the teacher's correct manners and speech seem hopelessly wrong.

But for the rest, too much of the film is idealized out of reality. The teachers are up on all the latest trends in child psychology and dish it out in globs. The songs are done in the calculatedly intimate, mink-soft voices used by so many popular singers; the delicately chiseled profiles seem too universal. The only apparent sufferer is the new teacher, Dorothy Dandridge, who goes in for worried pantomime and mumbles such things as "Oh Lord, let me say the right words for once." Since Miss Dandridge offscreen is one of those quick bright songstresses who rely less on voice than on an ability to tell a story with a sensitive and emotional face, this is rather nice to watch.

May 30, 1953

It is a custom among professional pipe smokers to offer romantic estimations of American moviegoers. The latest evaluation appeared in the *New Leader*— a tongue-in-cheek description of the action-movie fans who attend shabby theaters west of Times Square. It was a classic case of what happens when a critic turns sociologist. Mr. Markfield found that the largely male audience for action and horror pictures was made up of a desperate crew—perverts, adolescent hoodlums, chronic unemployeds, and far-gone neurotics—who possessed an impeccable taste in good, unpretentious off-beat films. These moviegoers shuddered or tittered, snored or shrieked obscenities. But somehow, while unable to control their bodies and emotions in the slightest degree, they were movie critics who simply couldn't be fooled by the expensive or pretentious. "Marvelous" was the word used to describe the infallible instinct of this *Lumpenproletariat* which causes Hollywood to shake in its assorted beach sandals.

It is a dangerous thing to lump a whole audience under general labels. The writers who did this in the twenties—during the era of Griffith, Sennett, and other silent-film "greats"—convinced a world-wide reading public that American moviegoers had low standards of appreciation and were to be treated like unintelligent children. Today, it has become fashionable for intellectuals to pretend to the same level of responses as the average member of the average audience. Every day another intellectual goes "popular" with a poetic, gaga dissertation on Mickey Spillane, "Moon Mullins," Ray Robinson, or Teresa Brewer. People everywhere are now encouraged to consider the audience for pop-artists infested by aesthetes looking like roughnecks and behaving like slobs.

As a steady customer in male-audience houses, I've never seen anything odd or outstanding in the clientele. Finding interest and excitement in almost any type of film filled with brawny men, destruction, and fights, a steady procession of people fill most of the seats from mid-morning until almost dawn, lapping up the bad with the good, the merely pretentious with the unheralded realistic gems. My reason for citing a difference with Mr. Markfield's illusions is to encourage moviegoers to look at the screen instead of trying to find a freak show in the audience.

"The Moon Is Blue" is a small comedy that seems to sparkle, sound monotonous, look machine-made, and appear smartly guided at the same moment. For a while it merely irritated me. A blatantly calculated actress named Maggie McNamara trades jokes with a miscast William Holden in the observation tower of the Empire State Building. The girl is supposedly a wittily open-minded ingenue actress being picked up by a "terribly sweet" and personable young architect. They both talk in empty little sentences that suggest only the psuedo-teen-age characters in popular magazine romances. After hearing innocuous things like "Oh, this is terrific" or "You're nice, I like you" in an observation tower that has been used to death by movie-makers there seems little reason to expect anything daring or smart from "The Moon Is Blue." Nevertheless, when the pair shift to the young man's bachelor apartment, the dialogue shifts to a steady drumbeat of better-than-average epigrams, and though people come through doors and answer phones as constantly as in television comedy, the movie seems to get more flexible and interesting. How this happens is a little intangible, but it may be because Miss McNamara looks natural acting a proper little pop-off and because the director, Otto Preminger, can set up a modern apartment scene that seems as shrill and phony as Broadway living actually is.

While its sex is strictly antiseptic, this Preminger project has been tagged as too "blue" in story, action, and dialogue by Joe Breen's industry-censorship department. Everybody remains idyllically pure, but the risqué lines caused the Breen office to condemn the picture. It will therefore be kept out of several thousand theaters.

July 4, 1953

◆

"Stalag 17" is a crude, cliché-ridden glimpse of a Nazi prison camp that I hated to see end. Rather than a story, this version of the Broadway hit comedy is a loosely linked succession of spots featuring amusing ideas picked up from a hundred different sources. The film gets under way through the clumsy device of a recollection by an American airman who, stuttering for movie realism, has a story to tell about his years as a war prisoner in a squalid camp. According to the narrator, there was a mysterious stoolie sneaking information about secret tunnels, hidden radios, and Allied troop placements to the Nazi commandant.

The story has to do with the unmasking of this informer. Thanks to one sharp, informative portrait—a Sammy Glick type of enterprising heel played by Bill Holden—the yarn has some suspense. And the various bits of Broadwayish entertainment—the character who skulks around like an exile from Hoff's union-suit cartoons, a human bulletin board with a high electric-saw voice ("all men from Texas will meet behind the north latrine"), a wonderful gag about the you-won't-believe-this letter-writer—are exploded with skill and humor. The camera work is bold. The direction gets an enormous amount of detail and vitality into the crowded hut, which may remind you of a static New York subway car. Though it tells you little about prison camps, Nazis, or American fliers, the film gives you your money's worth of entertainment.

Billy ("Sunset Boulevard") Wilder directed, and as usual he plays high, wide, but not very handsomely with the realism of the picture. Sometimes, as in the exchanges between the camp's "operator" (Holden) and a millionaire flying hero from Southampton (Don Taylor), Wilder can make the talk caustic and real. Most of the time he is simply clowning around with the truth. The gross ape from Brooklyn who creates most of the laughs because he is supposed to be an ugly near-illiterate happens to move in the graceful patter steps that have been around vaudeville for years. In fact, most of the disheveled, quarreling prisoners act like night-club entertainers. One of them does a Jimmy Cagney impersonation; another looks very smooth strumming a primitive one-string instrument; even the barracks' "crazy Joey" acts demented in perfect rhythm.

According to "Stalag," the prison camps were run by petty, ambitious fools and inhabited by American prisoners who were almost all glib, tough city boys. This is a typical Wilder view of the human race. While he has a reputation for making "downbeat" movies, he impresses more with his knack for getting a quality of "plenty" into everything. Taking a crass character like the one Holden plays, Wilder builds him up in all directions. The fellow has a little clock in his head which tells him just how tough he can act without getting into a fight. He refuses to be insulted and can be pushed around indefinitely. When Wilder shows you something about this opportunist, you always recognize it as something you've seen or heard. It doesn't seem important that in this picture Holden has a long skeletal head and does a lot of oily talking with his hands. But Wilder presses these details into your consciousness. By rounding out a character here and a gag there he ends by giving you the feeling of having participated in an unusual amount of disreputable, noisy movie life.

Except for a few grainy, wintery shots of the prison compound, the photography is all close focus. Usually you are looking over someone's shoulder into a tight little clump of prisoners, the camera acting like a kibitzer nosing himself through a crowd into the center of every event. In one telling picture the lens is practically up against a soldier's lips as he kisses a pin-up of Betty Grable. Another shot that stuck out reminded me of Mantegna's foreshortened painting of Christ—the beat-up figure of the supposed stoolie, Holden, glimpsed from around his shoes as he convalesces in bed. In other words, Wilder keeps the pressure on with a camera that is hard up against the actors.

The current movie scene includes these pictures:

"Shane": an incredibly slow Western with a Paul Bunyan type of hero, a pro-homesteaders theme, and the silliest of all child characters.

"Julius Caesar": an overrated play about political assassins, helped no end by James Mason's poetically human rendering of Brutus and Greer Garson's effective performance as a conqueror's wife.

"The Desert Rats": an intelligently handled film about the Tobruk siege, injured somewhat by the fact that there is more noise than warfare in the battle scenes.

"Crash of Silence": an unheralded British film that takes a realistic journey into the brain and feelings of a deaf child; a good, shocking film.

"Scared Stiff": a haunted-house comedy which has some fair nimble-grotesque dancing by Jerry Lewis and nothing else.

"Rome 11 O'Clock": a multi-plotted handling of an actual newspaper headline, one want ad that drew an enormous number of applicants, a building crash, and the feeling of being jammed-up in a city are well captured with a documentary technique.

July 25, 1953

◆

It would be silly to underrate Hollywood's current battle with stereoscopic film technique. The conversion to 3-D or its alternative, the wide screen, is not any overnight occurrence dreamed up as a counter-attack against television. Hollywood's move toward "giant screen" effects and a three-dimensional look about the actors has been going on in earnest since the period of "The Best Years of Our Lives." In fact, it has been the chief drive in the work of every important American director except De Mille, who never changes, and Huston. The basic objective in "new vision" films seems to be the same as that of "flat" films—a more accurate and natural image.

What you usually see on the new aluminized screen is a picture in which the actors' contours are extremely sharp and there is little building up of the figure with dramatic light effects. The 3-D director, in order to make you aware of the depth factor in a scene, tries to lead your eye quickly past the actors. Along with sharpening the outline of bodies, there is an effort to clarify the "feeling" of negative spaces—the spaces in a composition that are more or less unfilled. One of the most overworked images in the new 3-D's is a view through a frame made of an animal's legs, the boughs of a tree, or the opening between the wheels of a wagon. The frame intensifies the feeling of space behind it, making a sort of hole between the front plane of the screen and whatever is seen in the background.

The result of this three-dimensionalism is a more exact impression of masses. Flat cinema tended to put so many pounds on the actors that the rarest sight in a Hollywood film was a small wiry figure. Now for the first time a lot of lean or close-knit shapes are showing up in films—such as those of Guy Madison and Frank Lovejoy in "Feather River"—and some actors who were getting too bulky for the screen, like Mitchum, seem to have suddenly shrunk.

Unfortunately, working in a 3-D film does not seem to improve the acting of stars. "Second Chance," the first 3-D with stars in the leading roles, amounts to a sort of hurried tour through Cuernavaca and Taxco. The characters are all chasing one another and fleeing from some dreadful thing in the United States.

Jack Palance, an incredibly hardbreathing gunman, is trying to get as far from a crime investigation as possible, Linda Darnell is trying to shake Palance along with her past as a famous gun moll, and Bob Mitchum, also pursuing Darnell, is a prize-fighter drifting down hill from a fight in which he killed an opponent. These unhappy expatriates are not far from the characters in any Hemingway short story, but the actors, except Palance in his familiar "burning coal" performance, drift through the story as if it were a bad dream. Darnell's one effective scene is the product of a carefully planned shock—after thirty minutes of being clothed to the neck in black she is suddenly sprung on the audience in a gay, low-cut job. The three-dimensional expanse of Techni-colored flesh is all but dazzling. Mitchum always shows good sense in his self-consciously indolent portrayals. He acts unpretentious as a celebrity in a Mexican town, is frankly lascivious the moment he sees Darnell, and manages to look agile and crafty in the prize ring. But that prize-fight scene is the only one in which he seems to be awake.

The actors apparently lose heart when they are shrouded in bad to fair photographic effects. Every actor before he operates must be placed in an awk-ward composition that carefully defines the front, middle, and back planes of the picture. The shot that made the greatest impression on me was the very first—the back of Palance's head coldly cutting into the bottom of the screen while one of his gangster enemies parades unknowingly before him in the foyer of a hotel. This rigid composition repeats itself almost as often as the "trick" shots—the gun blasting straight at your eyes, the rocket showering sparks on your head, Mitchum dangling Jack Pickford-fashion from a rope attached to a busted cable-car.

Something should be said about the dark, confining spectacles one wears at 3-D films, the multiple sound tracks that give the impression of voices com-ing from the side of the screen, and the wide screen with all the compositions "masked" top and bottom to fit. However, movies like "Charge at Feather River," "Arena," and "Second Chance" are mainly notable for their simple-minded stories in which there is always a chase after some prize, quarry, or goal as though movement—almost any kind of movement—were the key to depth.

"The Band Wagon" is a unique musical that takes place mostly backstage and shows how a sagging revue was "saved" by a fading star dancer. Nanette Fabray steals a picture that runs through enormous amounts of scenery, as only Director Minnelli can make it do.

"Night Without Stars" is a nicely handled story of Riviera intrigue dealing with a nearly blind English lawyer and a power-crazed French lawyer. It has no substance whatsoever.

"From Here to Eternity" is a somewhat truncated and not very bold version of the famous Pearl Harbor novel: intelligent and enjoyable but with too many schmaltzy touches like Clift's beautiful trumpeting on just a bugle's mouthpiece. Except for Sinatra's angry, precocious Italian, the soldiers remind you of Hollywood stars. The girls—Kerr and Donna Reed—are realistic, worn-out, and quite disturbing. More later about this one.

August 8, 1953

◆

"From Here to Eternity" must have seemed like a chore to its director, Fred Zinnemann. He is inspired by experimental films in which the actors are new to movies and the story has an amateurish ring, while this picture is based on a best-selling novel and carries a load of famous "name" players and a budget, $3,000,000, that has to make the final product look slick. It held my interest until the final reel, when the bombing of Pearl Harbor suddenly turned up, but I don't think its success is due either to Zinnemann, who sentimentalized a lot of James Jones's story, or to Taradash, whose adaptation moves too quickly through the various love affairs, feuds, drinking bouts.

The laurel wreaths should be handed out to an actor who isn't even in the picture, Marlon Brando, and to an unknown person who first decided to use Frank Sinatra and Donna Reed in the unsweetened roles of Maggio, a tough little Italian American soldier, and Lorene, a prostitute at the "New Congress" who dreams of returning to respectability in the states. Sinatra plays the wild drunken Maggio in the manner of an energetic vaudevillian. In certain scenes —doing duty in the mess hall, reacting to some foul piano playing—he shows a marvelous capacity for phrasing plus a calm expression that is almost unique in Hollywood films. Miss Reed may mangle some lines ("you certainly are a funny one") with her attempts at a flat Midwestern accent, but she is an interesting actress whenever Cameraman Burnett Guffey uses a hard light on her somewhat bitter features. Brando must have been the inspiration for Clift's ability to make certain key lines ("I can soldier with any man," or "No more'n ordinary right cross") stick out and seem the most authentic examples of American speech to be heard in films.

The story is supposed to give you the lowdown on the professional soldier —it is about the thirty-year men in Company G at Schofield Barracks, Honolulu. Taradash juggles a number of plot threads—a clandestine romance between a smart top sergeant and the captain's sexy wife, the brutal treatment of a new transfer who refuses to box on the company team, the feud between Maggio and a sadistic captain who operates in the "stockade"—in such a concise way that they seem to be bouncing off one another. In one crucial section a love affair on a lonely beach and another in a crowded brothel are wound together like the strands of a rope. The shift from one to the other is somewhat too abrupt, but it is a minor defect in a highly professional job of writing.

What you are supposed to get is a sour, violent, sometimes funny portrait of the character who makes soldiering his business. It was my impression that the performances were often too fancy and the camera work too arty for a convincing study of tough Americans. The "big" performance is turned in as usual by Clift, as Private Prewitt, a character who has every talent (boxing, bugling, soldiering) except an ability to conform to army pattern. He does an ingenious job of acting a plain, slow-thinking individualist, but he is often working with an actor like Lancaster who does everything with a glib, showy Tarzanism. Then there are Deborah Kerr, a fluent actress who never lets you forget she is acting, and a number of supporting players like Ernest Borgnine, whose sadism has a Broadway glitter.

"From Here to Eternity" happens to be fourteen-carat entertainment. The main trouble is that it is *too* entertaining for a film in which love affairs flounder, one sweet guy is beaten to death, and a man of high principles is mistaken for a saboteur and killed on a golf course. When the soldiers get drunk, the scene is treated in a funny, unbelievable way. When Clift blows his bugle, it is done with a hammy intensity that tries to mimic Louis Armstrong at his showiest. When Lancaster and Kerr are being passionate on the beach, it is done in patterned action that reeks with a phony Hollywood glamour. The result is a gripping movie that often makes you wish its director, Zinnemann, knew as much about American life as he does about the art of telling a story with a camera.

Eric Ambler had the almost hopeless task of adapting "The Cruel Sea," a long novel made up of clichés taken from English war movies. His solution was to drop most of the corny plots that told of various sailor lives ashore and to insert in their place a record number of camera shots of the sea and close-ups of sailors reacting to a torpedoing. The movie version of Monsarrat's 500-page book seems, curiously, hardly to move, though it is based on the history of a corvette's crew which is moving almost from the moment you see it on its first trip through U-boat-infested waters. On the other hand neither the sea nor the turmoil of abandoning ship has ever before been rendered with such meticulous camera realism. And I doubt whether any other actor has equaled the realistic suffering, fatigue, and nervous strain of Jack Hawkins in the only role that matters to the film—a captain who molds a green crew of lawyers, reporters, bank clerks into first-class seamen.

August 29, 1953

◆

THE Paramount crew that worked on "Roman Holiday" reminded me of expert marksmen who had made "charm" their target and seldom if ever missed it. The ancient buildings and streets of Rome are used as an unobtrusive backdrop, and I doubt whether architecture and sculpture have ever been tied in so tenderly and humorously with what the characters are doing at the moment. In the leading role of a bored princess who steals away from dull court routine for a day of street adventures with an American newspaperman, Audrey Hepburn has enough poise and looks for seven princesses. She also has an affected tom-boyish delivery. But Gregory Peck, Hollywood's master of all shades of the thoughtful expression, manages by his varied throw-away movements to keep the film from stopping on Miss Hepburn's affectations. While "Roman Holiday" is too succulent for my taste, I enjoyed Wyler's switch to romantic comedy more than the heavier art style he used in directing "Carrie," "Detective Story," and "The Heiress."

Wyler sometimes seems to be operating here with one eye on "The Bicycle Thief." He is moving a well-scrubbed new movie face—Hepburn's—against the worn face of the Eternal City, and doing a lot of other photogenic things borrowed from De Sica. When his princess is pacified with a drug by the royal doctor, both the camera and Miss Hepburn start acting in an innocent-dreamy De Sica-ish way. When the heroine leaves the palazzo in the back of a laundry truck, the palace gates float up and away as though Lewis Carroll had given them life. Instead of simply crossing the street, Miss Hepburn walks into and out of a carriage and then dreamily down the street—in what *Variety* would call a boff bit of business.

If I enjoyed Wyler's new work more than De Sica's famous comedy-drama, it is simply because Wyler is a sharp-shooting technical wizard compared to the Italian neo-realist. Wyler is working strictly in the magically postured and timed idiom of Chaplin comedies when he starts Peck homeward with the doped Hepburn tagging behind. The main gag in this stretch is funny enough—Hepburn circling the winding stairway while Peck ascends it—but the wonderful things are the small bits of ballet work engineered by Peck and

Hepburn. Peck's movement with his arm leading the sleepy girl back to the stairway is a masterful piece of grace-note acting.

Wyler does noble work getting his princess away from the inhibiting palace and into the reporter's bohemian quarters, but the adventures he arranges for the pair during the day are neither natural nor amusing. She gets a haircut, which is all to the good because of Paolo Carlini's oily-gigolo acting of the barber. After that she takes a wild motor-scooter ride, gets arrested, and escapes from a dozen plain-clothes detectives—and nothing works because it is all stock movie zaniness.

Unfortunately, the entertainment values of the picture make you constantly aware of someone's maneuverings. Miss Hepburn often startles you with perfect impressions of England's Princess Margaret Rose, even in her slow way of giving forth with a toothy, uncomplicated smile and that pale little hand wave to the crowd. You are always conscious of Wyler's cleverness—the way he times his jokes, puts sentiment into the laughs, or points up a silent stretch of story-telling with a funny photographic trick. Though I suspect the movie is aimed at an extremely gentle audience, it strikes me as a welcome, if eclectic, throwback to the beautifully acted, suavely directed comedies turned out in 1935 by Cary Grant and his zany tribe.

Laurence Olivier acts the role of an amorous, fast-moving bad man with a sort of smoldering, stuffy distinction, but otherwise Warner's has a loser in "The Beggar's Opera." Most of the bows for the artistic failure should be taken by the technical advisers. The technicolor is made up largely of hot emerald, scarlet, and a surprising amount of black to keep the film as indistinct as possible. The story consists of a few basic items from Nelson Eddy-type operetta—a dashing highwayman having fun holding up stagecoaches, escaping from jail, falling in love—raced through in stagy, skittery fashion. Besides Olivier's swashbuckling, there are two interesting crowd scenes and some half-intelligible lyrics that sound talented and racy.

September 12, 1953

"Martin Luther" is a nice, well-behaved little movie about a religious thunderbolt. The title role is played by an Irish actor named Niall MacGinnis. While he seldom suggests the phenomenal force of the Reformation leader, MacGinnis makes the most of a pugnacious face and a clever, if somewhat fancy, theatrical voice. Occasionally his eyes bulge too much and he tries to make his tones too clear and firm—as in that fateful speech which starts "Unless I am convinced by the testimony of the Scripture"; but otherwise he seems a good modest version of Luther. The rest of the movie, a Louis de Rochemont production, is interesting, since it is possibly the first religious movie to sidestep sensational violence of any kind and concern itself with items that might be used by a debating professor. The closest de Rochemont comes to conventional movie fury are a few rocks heaved through a church window and a Wittenberg bonfire scene which must be a pale duplicate of that famous incendiary attack on the papacy.

The "plot" takes the practical reformer through his decisive years, from his unexpected entrance into a monastery at Erfurt to a happier moment when the German princes have been won over to his cause and a former Bernardine nun has wooed him into marriage—according to the film Luther was the pursued. The script, by Lothar Wolff and Allan Sloane, is constructed in the bric-a-brac manner of art films like "The Titan." On a screen that often goes in for odd-angled camera shots and dark-toned compositions you are given a cultural grab-bag of everything from an etching of St. Peter's before the dome had been built to a view of the actual castle where Luther translated the Bible. When you aren't looking at lithographs, old books, the Medici coat of arms, the film offers brief reenactments of famous Lutherian moments. The whole thing is unfolded somewhat stiffly and in the manner of a packet of attached photographs.

An army of commentators—sounding like pupils of Laurence Olivier—supply the cement that holds these fragments together. When the pictures are generalized and close to cliché—two monks trudging in silhouette over rolling hills—the commentator fills in with information on, say, walking trips to Rome. When the camera man goes off on an arty excursion—a totally obscured view through foliage of the heads of some horsemen—the commentator lets you know that a friendly kidnapping is taking place in the Thuringian Forest.

In scenes emphasizing character Luther is shown as a brooding, melancholy figure struggling to find a "gracious rather than a punitive God," a practical reformer who finally arrives at the notion that ecclesiastical vestments, pilgrimages, mortifications, and so on are of no avail to the soul. Ex-Professor Pichel, the director, opens up Luther's arguments in a clear, entertaining way and works in nice touches having to do with the dialectical skill, unruffled temper, and phenomenal memory of good disputants. A typical bit of professorial humor makes an illiterate loafer the key figure in that famous moment when Luther nails the Theses to the church door.

Any similarity between "Luther" and the religious works made by De Mille, Dieterle, Dreyer, or D. W. Griffith seems to be confined to the fact that the producer's name has the same first initial. While de Rochemont's film may be somewhat tepid as biography and motionless as a movie, it is unique in its class in that it makes its play more to the mind than to the eye.

"Island in the Sky" is a heavy John Wayne drama revolving around an A.T C. plane crash in the Labrador wastes. Aerial photography in shivery weather provides some thrills but not enough to make up for Wayne's dreary monologues addressed to himself, the faulty use of stereophonic sound, and the waste of some good actors like Lloyd Nolan and Bob Steele.

"99 River Street" is another energetic, semi-realistic gangster film by the group that made "Kansas City Confidential." The plot is routine, but the direction, which seems to dislike anything that smacks of the phrase "don't get excited," makes the picture worth seeing. Its worst feature is Evelyn Keyes over-emoting; its best, the opening prize fight that exhibits the dexterity of actor John Payne.

September 26, 1953

◆

THIS is the age of elephantine, humorless films that show little if any artistic endeavor. The latest example of gigantism, "The Robe," deals with a Roman counterpart of Lanny Budd who gets around to all the important Biblical events. The story, however, is less important than the fact that it is presented on the new CinemaScope screen, probably the widest and largest in existence. The screen is exploited here chiefly for spectacular mural-type photographs in which every detail is clearly defined: the movement of the camera lens is usually a slow sideways one, giving you the impression of looking at the world through a slot-in-the-wall.

These overpowering views have been colored and composed with some of the skill that went into "Moulin Rouge," but they exist as great static blocks of scenery, with the characters—from Lloyd C. Douglas's enormously popular book—squeezed in between in an unintentionally funny way: the camera seems to bump into a leading character standing in the middle of a street, open plain, or mountain top with nothing to do but gaze off into the distance. If he is played by a hammy actor like Mature, the fellow's face can be seen moving like mammoth plates of steel. But no matter who the actor, the character is usually a forlorn figure who looks as if he had stumbled into the center of a Music Hall set on the wrong cue.

"The Robe" tells the story of a young tribune (Richard Burton) who annoys an evil, effeminate prince regent to the point where he is sent into the worst spot of the Roman Empire. In Jerusalem he starts out as indolent play-boy, falls under the spell of the new religion, and eventually operates like Douglas Fairbanks spreading the gospel in Rome itself. There has been so much effort on Twentieth Century–Fox's part to put this first CinemaScope production over that about all you notice is the dull competence strewn into a hundred and one corners of the film. Only a few actors really individualize their roles. Someone named Jay Robinson enacts the petulant prince regent with a weird wobbling walk in which he invariably teeters off to the side before moving forward—he reminded me of both Leon Errol and an untalented Charles Laughton. On the credit side there are Frank Pulaski, Jr., as a tough, taunting Roman commander, as hard as anyone I've seen in movies, and a humanized bit by Richard Boone, who as Pontius Pilate has only to wash his hands in a distracted way.

Director Henry Koster and script writer Philip Dunne may have tried to spark up the movie by making the non-believers more manly and the Chris-tians less obviously saintly than is usual in Hollywood journeys through the Bible. In the case of the Cana Christians—Dean Jagger as Justus and Michael Rennie as Peter—the characterizations come out insipid anyway. Jagger talks and acts as if he were a colored preacher in a 1930 Hollywood musical, and Rennie just moves around making you conscious of the shoulder padding under his toga. The other actors—most of them British (Burton, Simmons, Thatcher)—are adequate in a one-dimensional way. Burton plays the proud, hot-tempered, somewhat cocky hero with an angry set to his mouth and an impetuous way of moving and talking.

Some of the usual faults of Biblical melodramas have been avoided in "The Robe." There is less sadism and sex of the glamorous, freely brushed-in type that De Mille has used so often, but what there is, is definitely corny. In a clanking sword fight around the dusty main street of Cana the sound-effects crew steals the show with its phony noise-making while the swordsmen slice away in rhythmic patterns. The thrills are mild and invariably the prod-uct of the spectacle scenes. One of the best of these, Christ's entrance into Jerusalem a week before the Crucifixion, handles a swirling line of marchers in deep space with the skill of an old master. But the whole intent in such scenes—to produce static pictures that are breathtakingly big and colorful—

seems as philistine as anything I've seen recently, reminding me of nothing so much as the worst examples of calendar art.

October 17, 1953

◆

HOLLYWOOD, often scolded by the critics for exploiting a child's cuteness until the spectators are ill from sugar-poisoning, has seldom gone so far as the "amateur" film "Little Fugitive." The movie sends a seven-year-old (Richie Andrusco) "on the lam" via BMT to Coney Island's amusement park, the victim of a practical joke which made him think he had murdered his older brother. At the end of the subway line he suddenly doffs his dependent character and becomes a pocket-sized version of Robinson Crusoe operating on a crowded beach—calmly and ingeniously carving out a new life for himself, making a living off soda-pop-bottle deposits, and sleeping wherever his tired body slumps. The film pleased me for about five minutes, even though the plot seemed manufactured to permit yet another documentarist to shoot his favorite run-down American environment, then it disintegrated into a compromise with the truth about the world of a small-fry Brooklynite.

The producing team (Orkin-Engel-Ashley) obviously feel Andrusco is an acting fire-ball, a kid Brando, but they are probably wrong. His chief traits are provoking enough—a phlegm-inclosed Brooklyn dialect that makes him sound as if he were talking through a tin can, a purposeful expression achieved by searching eyes and sullen mouth, and a style limited to those childish mannerisms that make fatuous mothers squeal with pleasure. Moreover, his personality seems to lack a core: the more the camera searches for a miniature Chaplin, the more vague and boring Andrusco becomes. He is best as a sort of incidental figure—playing with a pail and shovel, drifting out of the subway with a crowd of adults.

"Little Fugitive" has been a money-maker on the art-theater circuit. It pleases the people who go for "Rashomon," Rossellini, and Cocteau because it offers a modern view of a child's psyche, plus the preciously naturalistic technique of a European film. This camera man is too skilful and sincere to be branded a mere eclectic, but his contribution is unhealthily close to what is generally popular in avant-garde films. The camera work on Andrusco is always "significant" and "creative" in that it is constantly telling a story of New York at the same time that it fastens on the drooping lines of the boy's face or the lonely wiggle of his walk. The view of his ball game in the street is "canyonized" by an angle shot from the roof top; his lonelier moments on the beach are played against patterns that shriek Big City—the cracks of the boardwalk, the wired garbage cans on the empty beach, lovers' silhouettes on the sand.

The film's idea is to show how easily a child throws off the emotions of a tragic situation, and how he out-adults adults in a new and trying experience. This point, along with the ultra-sensitive photography, makes the film seem too refined and optimistic for the subject it deals with. The consistently fortunate turn of events makes life around Brooklyn unrecognizable, particularly, no doubt, to the kids who live there.

October 31, 1953

◆

T$_{\text{HE}}$ last few years in Hollywood have been a sort of mopping-up act on the assembly lines. Some six or seven directors the public recognizes as artistic have been reworking old skills perfected long before the onslaught of wide screens and 3-D glasses. Big pictures like "Roman Holiday" (which I liked) and "Mogambo" (which wasn't good enough to dislike) are typical examples of rehashings on the part of a couple of old masters, Ford and Wyler, who have been temporarily frozen into academic entertainers by the TV threat. A step down from the big pictures and the big-name people, we find that the honest low-budget film has been eliminated from Hollywood's output. The sensitive, unadorned actors—Widmark, Dan Dailey, Basehart, Wendell Corey, Glenn Ford, Ireland—are either drifting away from Hollywood or being wasted in the rankest pot-boilers. One reason for considering the following movie odds and ends is that they give an immediate picture of the entire recapitulation period.

"The Joe Louis Story." A slow, plodding journey back through the ex-champ's career. For a while it captures the simple, good-hearted quality of the younger Louis but then turns into a shapeless, predictable glad-handing of the hero and everyone connected with him—Marva, Chappie, Roxborough, Jacobs, *et al.* Coley Wallace, performing as the Brown Bomber, tries to be smooth and nonchalant but his slow, unassuming walk and business of switching from dead pan to face-covering grin become tiresome. The real villain of the production—it is hard to believe anyone directed it—is the *Daily News* columnist whose screen play seems determined that the colored hero is a touchy subject and therefore should be "sold" as a sort of saint who did nothing worse than play hooky from his violin lessons and eat too much cake before the Schmeling upset.

"The Big Heat." A compelling crime show. Sydney Boehm's story contains unexpected explosions of sadism at the end of long, tightly constructed dialogue sessions but manages to give off sparks even though it is based on nothing more substantial than several dozen cops-and-robbers films. A crime syndicate, which has half the city on its pay roll and is operated by a sex maniac (Lee Marvin) and an oily, Seagram's-ad type (Alexander Scourby), is broken up by an ex-cop (Glenn Ford) and a few of his war buddies who turn up to help him in crucial moments. The characters seem to be wrapped thinly around steaming amounts of vengeance, avarice, or cruelty, but Marvin and Ford make it a well-acted movie that offers interesting impressions of how a practical-minded American male operates in crises—marring a girl's face with scalding coffee, pulling a woman's body out of a bombed automobile.

"Mogambo." A half-interesting safari adventure, meant as a sequel to "King Solomon's Mines." It is inflated with at least one authentic thrill (a gorilla family charging the camera of an annoying anthropologist), a few tastelessly staged excitements (Ava Gardner playfully loving up a baby elephant), and some dated romancing. It suffers less from its silly dialogue than from the fact that the stars (Gable, Gardner, Grace Kelly) have large blank features and a dull spot in the center of their personalities. Because of Ford's genius for mobilizing the screen with off-the-cuff notions of glamour, Gardner acts for the first time as if she were half-interested in the film, and the African terrain—a big-game hunter's sprawling animal farm, the lush landscape as it is crossed by a line of marchers—seems as authentic as in the jungle films of the Merion C. Cooper era.

"The All-American." Tony Curtis as a halfback from the wrong side of town at a snob college is as convincing as a line plunger as Joe Palooka is as a heavyweight boxer.

"From Mainstreet to Broadway." It took a rare amount of greed and insensitiveness to entice so many Broadway celebrities into such a slipshod tribute to "today's American theater." Lester Cowan managed the feat in a Samuel French-type production that has to do with the troubles of a callow playwright who has written a first play called "Calico and Lust."

"The Actress." M-G-M in a mellow mood, which means the folksy acting by Tracy-Simmons-Wright is full of mugging and around-the-home comedy. Its main trouble is that it underrates the intelligence and talents of the rather impoverished New England family: the seventeen-year-old stage-struck girl moons over the performance of an absurdly stereotyped road-company queen; father tries to put on a nice comedy act but fails because he loses his pants.

November 21, 1953

◆

"The Living Desert" is a full-length color film on locales familiar to cowboy and foreign-legion films; only here treatment of them has been refreshingly reversed. All these places—Death Valley, Monument Valley, Salton Sea, Yuma's sand dunes—have usually been pictured as uninhabited, quiet regions that run to sandy tints and encourage peaceful contemplation. Disney's desert is a wild, forbidding land swarming with antagonistic animals, violent loves, seductive dances, oddly matched fights, weird victory celebrations, and enough terror stuff to unnerve any city-bred animal lover. The unusual thing about Disney's photography is that it is so close to the various creatures that you get, in clear jewel-like tones, the incredible ugliness of animal parts—a thin, hairy rat's leg, the pugnacious and grotesquely shaped head of a wild pig, the worm-like contour of a centipede's body.

This documentary drama fascinates but at the same time arouses suspicion. It is hard to believe in some of the shots. In one episode the camera is some- how wheeled into the network of underground tunnels built by a kangaroo rat, where it watches a mother rat struggle to save her offspring from a visiting snake. The camera must have been pulled through those tiny passages with a sewing thread. Most of the episodes are put together with bits and pieces of photography in which the character of the lighting changes enough to make you wonder about the consecutiveness of the action, and there are so many varying shots within each episode that you can almost hear the echo of the edi- tor's scissors.

In all, Disney's picture has its thrilling moments—as when it shows a tor- toise moving like a bulging, clanking intruder from medieval times—but it tends to repeat itself in savagery and reveal too many animals who move around in the sentimental dance rhythms of a Hollywood musical.

The second Cinemascope production, "How to Marry a Millionaire," is a mildly amusing comedy about three girls using an elaborate Sutton Place trap to catch millionaires. The very wide screen in Cinemascope may prove to be a death-trap for Hollywood stars, since it brings out every physical and personality trait. In this case it emphasizes some unmanly aspects of the leading male actor, shows up the excessive make-up on Miss Monroe, and makes it clear that Grable hated the picture. The wide screen also encourages Hollywood directors to traffic in panoramic shots. The film has more stock shots of highways, bridges, and mountain landscapes than intimate shots of the stars. And unlike Cinerama, the new Zanuck technique adds little if any three-dimensional excitement to the vast shots of terrain; so that this film amounts to one well-acted gag (Marilyn Monroe's near blindness) and a few bright lines surrounded by dead landscapes and uninteresting masses of interior decoration.

"The Man Between" is a classroom example of suspenseful British movie-making, replete with fuzzy, smog-colored photography, actors who look as if they could use a more robust way of life, and a choppy story line. Carol Reed's man hunt in post-war Berlin is more entertaining than any other current film, but it seems a case of a good director standing still, relying a bit too much on clichés. The scratchy photography of wintry European streets has become an accepted synonym for good naturalistic lens work.

Reed saves his melodrama with innumerable tricks that give "The Man Between" a certain amount of sentiment, humor, and photographic interest. Mason's thin body and dental work are made into touching items, as though they were brought on by impoverishing war conditions. His brief affair with Miss Bloom, carried on over rooftops, in fleeing automobiles, and up and down a ragged-looking construction job, is constantly turned away from the mechanics of a chase melodrama into something more tender and interesting. It is done with techniques that remind you of "The African Queen." All the miss-matching qualities in Bloom and Mason are emphasized in ways that add schmaltz and a bit of truth to their love affair. Where Bogart was forever being comically expert with his broken-down steamboat, Mason shows off in various ways as a Berlin gadabout. To the long-winded conversations that recall Huston's film Reed adds his own pattern-happy talent with a camera and a light comic touch that he has not used since his low-budget days. All in all, an ingratiating movie.

December 26, 1953

◆

THE past movie year will probably be generally remembered as the one in which three-dimensional gimmicks—multiple sound tracks, polaroid glasses, masking, wide curved screens, and other flashes in the panoramic craze—just about displaced the importance of content and quality. For me 1953 was the year in which Hollywood almost lost me as an irritable non-paying customer. The simple reason for my disaffection with H-movies—I ceased to be a foreign-movie fan when foreign films became so pretentiously unpretentious—is that there were few pictures last year in which the "human element" wasn't swallowed up by production values. In this era of hard, tight semi-documentaries embroidered with fancying-up touches that seem controlled almost to rigidity, only an occasional "Roman Holiday" turns up with enough individual flourish to make one interested in any craftsmen but the lead actors.

Wherever you look today, you find the movie artist subordinating himself in order to glorify a mechanical process. There was the wildly energetic dance scene in "Moulin Rouge" in which the speed, grouping, and rhythm of the dancers seemed indebted to the piston and lever. Even in "Shane" you found gimmicky stuff going on in every frame: the hero's name was repeated so often in affected voices that it was like listening to a bird in a clock which instead of saying "Cuck-oo" gave out with a metallic nasal "Shane!" In Disney's "Living Desert" actual mud puddles in the Salton Sea were made to burp, writhe, turn themselves inside out, and even spit in time to classical music by means of mechanical tricks.

Mechanization of the artist has become the rage in other arts besides movies. In juke-box ballad-singing tiny voices like those of Como and Joni James are stretched, made earthy, sometimes even doubled and tripled, by the use of sound boxes and tape recorders. The most talked-of realistic painter—Wyeth—does a surrealistically touched-up imitation of the camera image. Most of the important American abstractionists drip, scrub, or bleed paint on to canvas with an impersonal skill that makes it hard to believe human hands had anything to do with the painting. But it is particularly irritating to find movie artists over-indulging in mechanical tricks because the medium is so dependent on the immediate kinship set up between spectator and characters. How do you connect with the people in a movie like "From Here to Eternity" if their very brains and emotions seem ensnared in the delicate camera contortions that fuzz up the surface of a Zinnemann-directed film?

This department saw nothing last year that deserved a Best Film award. Here, but not in any preferential order, are the seven films that gave me the most pleasure.

First there was Alfred Hitchcock's "I Confess," a suspense yarn with too much talk and some polished semi-documentary photography (by Robert

Burks) that was too obviously chopped up with symbols and oddly arranged angles for my taste. However, it had the most interesting acting of the year—by Anne Baxter, Roger Dann, and particularly Clift, involved in a methodically directed murder story in which the chief suspect is a young priest. Clift won the year's acting award for his ability to project states of mind and feeling with a kind of repressed toughness that became too obvious in the "Eternity" film. The movie was also noteworthy for the skill with which Hitchcock exposed the raveling out of a romance without wasting a motion, moving from the most romantic movie styling to the uncolored quality of a police report.

Next there was "The Young Wives' Tale," a domestic comedy that seemed to have a screw loose and featured Joan Greenwood, the woman with a fog-horn voice and the manner of a slightly drowsy, kittenish narcissist. It was a fresh little British movie that gave you the sense of all hell breaking loose in a two-family house, while Miss Greenwood, a rather gawky Audrey Hepburn, and some others had fun in the manner of unregulated acting virtuosos.

The next three spots go to three substanceless Hollywood movies—"I Love Melvin," "Inferno," and "The Big Heat"—that seemed to be perfect second features on neighborhood double bills. "Melvin" was the only musical I saw that had any genuine liveliness or youthfulness in its choreography; "Inferno" used the Robinson Crusoe technique of dreaming up realistic details to draw you along on a fantastic journey and was more fun to watch than any of the American comedies. "The Big Heat" was excitingly acted by Glenn Ford and Lee Marvin—in spite of the lush décor and sentimental writing.

Sixth, George Stevens's "Shane," though it often seemed ridiculously arty and slow as its precise director attempted to give ballad-like stature to the ordinary ingredients of a cowboy story. But it is a movie that takes its own measured, deliberate time finding ways to increase your pleasure. Its key method was to provide an endless number of visual treats through the color photography of Loyal Griggs, who seems to have a genius for dramatizing moody stuff like the approaching shadow of a rain storm or the eerie night light on a porch. Unfortunately the spectator had to put up with some unbelievable fights, the overaged-child acting of Brandon de Wilde, Palance's phony cowboy costume, and the nasal delivery of Jean Arthur.

Seventh, William Wyler's "Roman Holiday," a completely pleasing comic travelogue that seemed close to the first Garson Kanin comedies in its ability to inject heart and zip into zany human situations. It starred a rather cold and facile actress who turns on charm with a kind of trade-marked affectation. On the credit side it sported a clever rebelling-princess script, the tough stooge acting of Eddie Albert, good Cary Grant-type mugging by Gregory Peck, and direction that was masterful in its ability to manufacture small humorous details to delay the cliché twist in each segment of the story.

My honorable-mention list includes "The Man Between," "The Naked Spur," "Jeopardy" (for the tension-heightening direction of John Sturges), "Stalag 17," "Bellissima" (Magnani was the year's best actress), Martin and Lewis's "The Stooge," "Blowing Wild," "The Moon Is Blue," "Split Second" (an unusually good performance by Stephen McNally), and "Sky Full of Moon." In the worst-film category, "I, the Jury," "From Mainstreet to Broadway," and "Return to Paradise" were tied.

January 9, 1954

Preston Sturges: Success in the Movies

By all odds, the most outstanding example of a successful director with a flamboyant unkillable personality to emerge in Hollywood during the last two decades has been that of Preston Sturges, who flashed into the cinema capital in 1939, wrote, produced, and directed an unprecedented series of hits and now seems to be leaping into relative obscurity. Hollywood destiny has caught up with Sturges in a left-handed fashion; most whiz-bang directors of the Sturges type remain successes while their individuality wanes. Sturges seems to have been so riddled by the complexities, conflicts, and opposed ambitions that came together to enrich his early work that he could not be forced into a mold. Instead of succumbing to successful conformity, Sturges has all but ceased to operate in the high-powered, smash-hit manner expected of him.

It is a peculiarly ironic fate, because Sturges is the last person in the world it is possible to think of as a failure. Skeptical and cynical, Sturges, whose hobbies include running restaurants and marketing profitable Rube Goldberg inventions, has never publicly acknowledged any other goal but success. He believes it is as easily and quickly achieved in America, particularly by persons of his own demoniac energy, mercurial brain, and gimmick-a-minute intensiveness. During the time it takes the average American to figure out how to save $3 on his income tax, Sturges is liable to have invented "a vibrationless Diesel engine," a "home exerciser," the "first nonsmear lipstick," opened up a new-style eatery, written a Broadway musical, given one of his discouraged actors his special lecture on happiness, and figured out a new way to increase his own superhuman productiveness and efficiency.

In fact, Sturges can best be understood as an extreme embodiment of the American success dream, an expression of it as a pure idea in his person, an instance of it in his career, and its generalizer in his films. In Sturges, the concept of success operates with purity, clogging the ideology of ambition so that it becomes an esthetic credo, backfiring on itself, baffling critics, and creeping in as a point of view in pictures which are supposed to have none. The image of success stalks every Sturges movie like an unlaid ghost, coloring the plots and supplying the fillip to his funniest scenes. His madly confused lovers, idealists, and outraged fathers appear to neglect it, but it invariably turns up dumping pots of money on their unsuspecting heads or snatching away million-dollar prizes. Even in a picture like *The Miracle of Morgan's Creek*, which deals with small-town, humble people, it is inevitable that bouncing Betty Hutton should end up with sextuplets and become a national institution. The very names of Sturges's best-known movies seem to evoke a hashish-eater's vision of beatific American splendor: *The Great McGinty*, *The Power and the Glory*, *The Miracle of Morgan's Creek*, *Hail the Conquering Hero*, *The Great Moment*, *Christmas in July* reveal the facets of a single preoccupation.

Nearly everyone who has written about Sturges expresses great admiration for his intelligence and talent, total confusion about his pictures, and an absolute certainty that Sturges should be almost anything but what he nakedly and palpably is—an inventive American who believes that good picture-making consists in grinding out ten thousand feet of undiluted, chaos-producing energy. It is not too difficult to perceive that even Sturges's most appreciative critics were fundamentally unsympathetic toward him. Throughout his career, in one way or another, Sturges has been pilloried for refusing to conform to the fixed prescriptions for artists. Thus, according to René Clair, "Preston is like a man from the Italian Renaissance: he wants to do everything at once. If he could slow down, he would be great; he has an enormous gift, and he should be one of our leading creators. I wish he would be a little more selfish and worry about his reputation."

What Clair is suggesting is that Sturges would be considerably improved if he annihilated himself. Similarly, Siegried Kracauer has scolded him for not being the consistent, socially-minded satirist of the rich, defender of the poor, and portrayer of the evils of modern life which he regards as the qualifying characteristics of all moviemakers admissible to his private pantheon. The more popular critics have condemned Sturges for not liking America enough; the advanced critics for liking it too much. He has also been accused of espousing a snob point of view and sentimentally favoring the common man.

Essentially Sturges, probably the most spectacular manipulator of sheer humor since Mark Twain, is a very modern artist or entertainer, difficult to classify because of the intense effort he has made to keep his work outside conventional categories. The high-muzzle velocity of his films is due to the anarchic energy generated as they constantly shake themselves free of attitudes that threaten to slow them down. Sturges's pictures maintain this freedom from ideology through his sophisticated assumption of the role of the ruthless showman deliberately rejecting all notions of esthetic weight and responsibility. It is most easy to explain Sturges's highly self-conscious philosophy of the hack as a kind of cynical morality functioning in reverse. Since there is so much self-inflation, false piety, and artiness in the arts, it was, he probably felt, less morally confusing to jumble slapstick and genuine humor, the original and the derivative together, and express oneself through the audacity and skill by which they are combined. It is also probable that he found the consistency of serious art, its demand that everything be resolved in terms of a logic of a single mood, repugnant to his temperament and false to life.

"There is nothing like a deep-dish movie to drive you out in the open," a Sturges character remarks, and, besides being a typical Sturges line, the sentence tells you a great deal about his moviemaking. His resourcefulness, intelligence, Barnum-and-Bailey showmanship and dislike of fixed purposes often make the typical Sturges movie seem like a uniquely irritating pastiche. A story that opens with what appears to be a bitingly satirical exposition of American life is apt to end in a jelly of cheap sentiment. In *Hail the Conquering Hero*, for example, Eddie Bracken plays an earnest, small-town boy trying to follow in the footsteps of his dead father, a World War I hero. Discharged because of hay fever, Bracken is picked up by six Marines who talk him into posing as a Guadalcanal veteran and returning home as a hero to please his mother. The pretense snowballs, the town goes wild, and Bracken's antics become more complicated and tormenting with every scene. After he has been pushed into running for Mayor, he breaks down and confesses the hoax. Instead of tarring and feathering him, the townspeople melt with admiration for his candor and courage.

This ending has been attacked by critics who claim that it reveals Sturges compromising his beliefs and dulling the edge of his satire. "At his beginning," Mr. Kracauer writes, referring to *The Great McGinty*, "Sturges insisted that honesty does not pay. Now he wants us to believe that the world yields to candor." Such criticism is about as relevant as it would be to say that Cubists were primarily interested in showing all sides of a bottle at once. To begin with, it should be obvious to anyone who has seen two Sturges pictures that he does not give a tinker's dam whether the world does or does not yield to candor.

Indeed his pictures at no time evince the slightest interest on his part as to the truth or falsity of his direct representation of society. His neat, contrived plots are unimportant per se and developed chiefly to provide him with the kind of movements and appearances he wants, with crowds of queer, animated individuals, with juxtapositions of unusual actions and faces. These are then organized, as items are in any art which does not boil down to mere sociology, to evoke *feelings* about society and life which cannot be reduced to doctrine or judged by flea-hopping from the work of art to society in the manner of someone checking a portrait against the features of the original.

What little satire there is in a film is as likely to be directed at satire as it is at society. The supposedly sentimental ending of *The Conquering Hero*, for example, starts off as a tongue-in-cheek affair as much designed to bamboozle the critics as anything else. It goes out of hand and develops into a series of oddly placed shots of the six Marines, shots which are indeed so free of any kind of attitude as to create an effect of pained ambiguous humanity, frozen in a moment of time, so grimly at one with life that they seem to be utterly beyond any one human emotion, let alone sentiment. The entire picture is, indeed, remarkable for the manner in which sequences are directed away from the surface mood to create a sustained, powerful, and lifelike pattern of dissonance. The most moving scene in it—Pangborn's monumentally heartfelt reactions to Bracken's confession—is the product of straight comic pantomime. The Marine with an exaggerated mother-complex sets up a hulking, ominous image as the camera prolongs a view of his casual walk down the aisle of the election hall. The Gargantuan mugging and gesturing of the conscience-stricken Bracken provokes not only laughter but the sense that he is suffering from some mysterious muscular ailment.

Such sequences, however, though integral to Sturges's best work, do not set its tone. The delightfulness, the exhilarating quality that usually prevails is due to the fact that the relation to life of most of the characters is deliberately kept weak and weightless. The foibles of a millionaire, the ugliness of a frump are all projected by similar devices and exploited in a like manner. They exist in themselves only for a moment and function chiefly as bits in the tumultuous design of the whole. Yet this design offers a truer equivalent of American society than can be supplied by any realism or satire that cannot cope with the tongue-in-cheek self-consciousness and irreverence toward its own fluctuating institutions that is the very hallmark of American society—that befuddles foreign observers and makes American mores well-nigh impervious to any kind of satire.

Satire requires a stationary society, one that seriously believes in the

enduring value of the features providing its identity. But what is there to satirize in a country so much at the mercy of time and commerce as to be profoundly aware that all its traits—its beauties, blemishes, wealth, poverty,
prejudices, and aspirations—are equally the merchandise of the moment, easily manufactured and trembling on the verge of destruction from the moment
of production? The only American quality that can conceivably offer a focus for
satire, as the early moviemakers and Sturges, alone among the contemporaries,
have realized, is speed. Some of the great early comic films, those of Buster
Keaton, for example, were scarcely comic at all but pure and very bitter satires,
exhausting in endless combinations of all possible tortures produced as a consequence of the *naif* belief in speed. Mack Sennett was less the satirist of
American speed-mania than its Diaghilev. Strip away the comic webbing, and
your eye comes upon the preternatural poetic world created by an instinctive
impresario of graceful accelerations. Keystone cops and bathing beauties mingle and separate in a buoyant, immensely varied ballet, conceived at the speed
of mind but with camera velocity rather than the human body as its limit.
Sturges was the only legitimate heir of the early American film, combining its
various methods, adding new perspectives and developing the whole in a form
suitable to a talking picture.

Since Sturges thought more synoptically than his predecessors, he presented a speed-ridden society through a multiple focus rather than the single,
stationary lens of the pioneers. While achieving a more intense identification
of the audience with the actors than in the earlier films (but less than the current talking pictures, which strive for complete audience identification with
the hero), Sturges fragmented action, so that each scene blends into the next
before it comes to rest, and created an illusion of relative motions. Basically, a
Sturges film is executed to give one the delighted sensation of a person moving
on a smoothly traveling vehicle going at high speed through fields, towns,
homes, and even through other vehicles. The vehicle in which the spectator is
traveling never stops but seems to be moving in a circle, making its journey
again and again in an ascending, narrowing spiral until it diminishes into
nothingness. One of his characters calls society a "cockeyed caravan," and
Sturges, himself, is less a settled, bona fide resident of America than a hurried,
Argus-eyed traveler through its shifting scenes, a nomad in space observing a
society nomadic in time and projecting his sensations in uniquely computed
terms.

This modern cinematic perspective of mobility seen by a mobile observer
comes easily to Sturges because of his strange family background and broken-
up youth. He was the son of a normal, sports-loving, successful father and a fan-

tastic culture-bug mother who wanted him to be a genius and kept him in Paris from the age of eight to about fifteen. "She dragged me through every goddam museum on the continent," he has rancorously remarked. Glutted, at an early age, by an overrich diet of esthetic dancing, high-hatted opera audiences, and impressionist painting, Sturges still shows the marks of his youthful trauma. The most obvious result of his experience has been a violent reaction against all estheticism. He has also expressed fervent admiration for his father's business ability and a desire to emulate him. The fact that he did not, however, indicates that his early training provoked more than a merely negative reaction in him and made him a logical candidate for Hollywood, whose entire importance in the history of culture resides in its unprecedented effort to merge art and big business.

As a moviemaker, the businessman side of Sturges was superficially dominant. He seems to have begun his career with the intention of giving Hollywood a lesson in turning out quick, cheap, popular pictures. He whipped together his scripts in record-breaking time, cast his pictures with unknowns, and shot them faster than anyone dreamed possible. He was enabled to do this through a native aptitude for finding brilliant technical shortcuts. Sturges tore Hollywood comedy loose from the slick gentility of pictures like *It Happened One Night* by shattering the realistic mold and the logical build-up and taking the quickest, least plausible route to the nerves of the audience. There are no preparations for the fantastic situations on which his pictures are based and no transitions between their numberless pratfalls, orgies of noise, and furniture-smashing. A Capra, Wilder, or Wellman takes half a movie to get a plot to the point where the audience accepts it and it comes to cinematic life. Sturges often accomplishes as much in the first two minutes, throwing an audience immediately into what is generally the most climactic and revelatory moment of other films.

The beginning of *Sullivan's Travels* is characteristic for its easy handling of multiple cinematic meanings. The picture opens abruptly on a struggle between a bum and a railroad employee on top of a hurtling train. After a few feet of a fight that is at once a sterling bit of action movie and a subtle commentary on action movies, it develops that you are in a projection studio, watching a film made by Sullivan, a famous director, and that the struggle symbolizes the conflict of capital and labor. As Sullivan and the moguls discuss the film's values and box-office possibilities, Sturges makes them all sound delightfully foolish by pointing up the naïve humanity of everyone involved. "Who wants to see that stuff? It gives me the creeps!" is the producer's reaction to the film. When Sullivan mentions a five-week run at the Music Hall, the producer explodes with magnificent improbability: "Who goes to the Music Hall? Communists!" Thus, in five minutes of quick-moving cinema and surprise-packed dialogue, a complex situation has been set forth and Sullivan is catapulted on his journey to learn about the moods of America in the depression.

The witty economy of his movies is maintained by his gifted exploitation of the non sequitur and the perversely unexpected. In nearly every case, he manages to bring out some hidden appropriateness from what seems like willful irrelevance. In *The Miracle of Morgan's Creek*, a plug-ugly sergeant mouths heavy psychiatric phrases in an unbelievable way that ends by sinking him doubly deep into the realm of the psychotic. With nihilistic sophistication, Sturges makes a Hollywood director keep wondering "Who is Lubitsch?" till you are not sure if it is simply fun or a weird way of expressing pretentiousness and ignorance. Similarly, in *The Conquering Hero*, the small-town citizens are given a happy ending and a hero to worship, but they are paraded through the streets and photographed in such a way that they resemble a lynch mob—a device which flattens out success and failure with more gruesome immediacy than Babbittlike satires.

What made Sturges a viciously alive artist capable of discovering new means of expressiveness in a convention-ridden medium was the frenetic, split sensibility that kept him reacting to and away from the opposite sides of his heredity. These two sides are, in fact, the magnetic poles of American society. Accepting, in exaggerated fashion, the businessman approach to films, he nevertheless brought to his work intelligence, taste, and a careful study of the more estimable movies of the past. He also took care to disappoint rigid-minded esthetes and reviewers. Although it has been axiomatic among advanced movie students that the modern film talks too much and moves too little, Sturges perversely thought up a new type of dialogue by which the audience is fairly showered with words. The result was paradoxically to speed up his movies rather than to slow them down, because he concocted a special, jerky, spluttering form of talk that is the analogue of the old, silent-picture firecracker tempo. Partly this was accomplished by a wholesale use of "hooks"—spoken lines cast as questions, absurd statements, or explosive criticisms, which yank immediate responses from the listener.

Sturges's free-wheeling dialogue is his most original contribution to films and accomplishes, among other things, the destruction of the common image of Americans as tight-lipped Hemingwayan creatures who converse in grating monosyllables and chopped sentences. Sturges tries to create the equally American image of a wrangle of conflicting, overemotional citizens who talk as though they were forever arguing or testifying before a small-town jury. They speak as if to a vast, intent audience rather than to each other, but the main thing is that they unburden themselves passionately and without difficulty—even during siesta moments on the front porch: "I'm perfectly calm. I'm as—as cool as ice, then I start to figure maybe they won't take me and some cold sweat runs down the middle of my back and my head begins to buzz and everything in the middle of the room begins to swim—and I get black spots in front of my eyes and they say I've got high blood pressure. . . ."

As the words sluice out of the actors' mouths, the impression is that they teeter on the edge of a social, economic, or psychological cliff and that they are under some wild compulsion to set the record straight before plunging out of the picture. Their speech is common in language and phrasing, but Sturges makes it effervesce with trick words ("whackos" for "whack"), by pumping it full of outraged energy or inserting a daft idea like the Music Hall gag. All of this liberated talk turns a picture into a kind of open forum where everyone down to the cross-eyed bit player gets a chance to try out his oratorical ability. A nice word-festival, very democratic, totally unlike the tight, gagged-up speech that movies inherited from vaudeville, radio, and the hard-boiled novel.

Paradoxically, too, his showman's approach enabled Sturges to be the only Hollywood talking-picture director to apply to films the key principles of the "modern" revolutions in poetry, painting, and music: namely, beginning a work of art at the climax and continuing from there. Just as the modern painter eschews narrative and representational elements to make his canvas a continuum of the keenest excitement natural to painting, or the poet minimizes whatever takes his poem out of the realm of purely verbal values, so Sturges eliminated from his movies the sedulous realism that has kept talking pictures essentially anchored to a rotting nineteenth-century esthetic. In this and other ways, Sturges revealed that his youth spent "caroming around in High-Bohemian Europe" had not been without a positive effect on his work. Its basic textures, forms, and methods ultimately derive from post-Impressionist painting, Russian ballet, and the early scores of Stravinsky, Hindemith, et al. The presence of Dada and Surrealism is continuously alive in its subsurface attitudes or obvious in the handling of specific scenes. Sturges's fat Moon Mullins–type female, playing a hot tail-gate trombone at a village dance, is the exact equivalent in distortion of one of Picasso's lymphatic women posed as Greek statues.

Sturges's cinematic transpositions of American life reveal the outsider's ability to seize salient aspects of our national existence plus the insider's knowledge of their real meaning. But the two are erratically fused by the sensibility of the nostalgic, dislocated semiexile that Sturges essentially remains.

The first impression one gets from a Sturges movie is that of the inside of a Ford assembly line smashed together and operating during a total war crisis. The characters, all exuding jaundice, cynicism, and anxiety, work feverishly as every moment brings them the fear that their lives are going to pieces, that they are going to be fired, murdered, emasculated, or trapped in such ridiculous situations that headlines will scream about them to a hooting nation for the rest of their lives. They seem to be haunted by the specters of such nationally famous boneheads as Wrong-Way Corrigan, Roy Riegels, who ran backward in a Rose Bowl game, or Fred Merkle, who forgot to touch second base in a crucial play-off game, living incarnations of the great American nightmare that some monstrous error can drive individuals clean out of society into a forlorn no man's land, to be the lonely objects of an eternity of scorn, derision, and self-humiliation. This nightmare is of course the reverse side of the uncontrolled American success impulse, which would set individuals apart in an apparently different but really similar and equally frightening manner.

Nearly all the Sturges comedies were centered with a sure instinct on this basic drive with all its complex concomitants. Using a stock company of players (all of a queer, unstandard, and almost aboriginal Americanism), Sturges managed to give his harrowing fables of success-failure an intimate, small-town setting that captured both the moony desire of every American to return to the small world of his youth and that innocent world itself as it is ravaged by a rampant, high-speed industrialism. The resultant events are used to obtain the comic release that is, indeed, almost the only kind possible in American life: the savage humor of absolute failure or success. Sturges's funniest scenes result from exploding booby traps that set free bonanzas of unsuspected wealth. In one episode, for example, two automat employees fight and trip open all the levers behind the windows; the spouts pour, the windows open, and a fantastic, illicit treasure trove of food spills out upon a rioting, delightfully greedy mob of bums, dowagers, and clerks. In *The Palm Beach Story*, members of the "Ale and Quail" club—a drunken, good-humored bunch of eccentric millionaires—shoot up a train and lead yapping hounds through Pullmans in a privileged orgy of destruction. This would seem the deeply desired, much fantasied reward of a people that endures the unbelievably tormented existence Sturges depicts elsewhere—a people whose semi-comic suffering arises from the disparity between the wild lusts generated by American society and the severity of its repressions.

Sturges's faults are legion and have been pretty well gone over during his most successful period. Masterful with noisy crowds, he is liable to let a quiet spot in the script provoke him to burden the screen with "slapstick the size of a whale bone." A good businessman believes that any article can be sold if presented with eardrum-smashing loudness and brain-numbing certitude. From a similar approach, Sturges will represent hilarity by activating a crew of convicts as though he were trying to get Siberia to witness their gleeful shrieks. To communicate the bawdy wit of a fast blonde, he will show the tough owner of a lunch wagon doubled up like a suburban teenager hearing his first dirty joke. The comic chaos of a small-town reception must be evoked by the use of no less than four discordant bands. Sturges has been accused of writing down to his audience, but it is more probable that there is too much of the businessman actually in his make-up to expect him to function in any other way. The best of his humor must come in a brash flurry of effects, all more or less oversold because there is nothing in his background that points to a more quiet, reasonable approach to life.

But even these vices are mitigated somewhat by the fact that they provide an escape from the plight of many intelligent, sensibility-ridden artists or entertainers of his period whose very intelligence and taste have turned against them, choking off their vitality and driving them into silence or reduced productivity. The result is that artistic ebullience and spontaneity have all but drained down to the very lowest levels of American entertainment. Even in the movies these days, one is confronted by slow-moving, premeditated affairs— not so much works of art or entertainments aimed by the intelligence at the glands, blood, and viscera of the audience as exercises in mutual criticism and good taste. The nervous tantrums of slapstick in a Sturges movie, the thoughtless, attention-getting antics combined with their genuine cleverness give them an improvised, blatant immediacy that is preferable to excesses of calculation and is, in the long run, healthier for the artists themselves.

As a maker of pictures in the primary sense of the term, Sturges shows little of the daring and variety that characterize him as a writer and, on the whole, as a director. He runs to middle shots, symmetrical groupings, and an evenly lit screen either of the bright modern variety or with a deliberately aged, grey period-finish. His composition rarely takes on definite form because he is constantly shooting a scene for ambivalent effects. The love scenes in *The Lady Eve*, for example, are shot, grouped, and lit in such a way as to throw a moderate infusion of sex and sentiment into a fast-moving, brittle comedy without slowing it down. The average director is compelled to use more dramatic composition because the moods are episodic, a completely comic sequence alternating with a completely sentimental scene. Sturges's treatment is fundamentally more cinematic, but he has not found a technique equal to it. Fluent as a whole, his pictures are often clumsy and static in detail, and he has not learned how to get people to use their bodies so that there is excitement merely in watching them move. In a picture like Howard Hawks's *His Girl Friday*, Cary Grant uses legs, arms, trick hat, and facial muscles to create a pixyish ballet that would do credit to a Massine. But, when Sturges selects an equally gifted exponent of stylized movement, Henry Fonda, he is unable to extract comparable values from a series of falls, chases, listings to portside, and shuddering comas. Stray items—Demarest's spikey hair, Stanwyck's quasi-Roman nose—clutter up his foreground like blocks of wood. Even dogs, horses, and lions seem to turn into stuffed props when the Sturges camera focuses on them.

The discrepancies in Sturges's films are due largely to the peculiar discontinuities that afflict his sensibility, although such affliction is also a general phenomenon in a country where whole eras and cultures in different stages of development exist side by side, where history along one route seems to skip over decades only to fly backward over another route and begin over again in still a different period. What Sturges presents with nervous simultaneity is the skyrocketing modern world of high-speed pleasures and actions (money-making, vote-getting, barroom sex, and deluxe transportation) in conflict with a whole Victorian world of sentiment, glamour, baroque appearance, and static individuality in a state of advanced decay. In all probability, his years spent abroad prevented his finding a bridge between the two worlds or even a slim principle of relating them in any other way than through dissonance. A whole era of American life with its accompaniment of visual styles is skimped in his work, the essential problems thus created being neatly bypassed rather than solved.

But his very deficiencies enabled Sturges to present, as no one else has, the final decay of the bloated Victorian world, which, though seemingly attached to nothing modern and destined to vanish with scarcely a trace, has nevertheless its place in the human heart if only for its visual splendors, its luxurious, impractical graces, and all too human excesses. From McGinty to Harold Diddlebock, Sturges gives us a crowded parade of courtly, pompous, speechifying, queerly dressed personages caught as they slowly dissolve with an era. His young millionaires—Hickenlooper III (Rudy Vallee), Pike (Henry Fonda), and rich movie director Sullivan (Joel McCrea)—a similar type of being—are like heavily ornamented bugs, born out of an Oliver Twist world into a sad-faced, senile youth as moldy with leisure and tradition as an old cheese. Incapable of action, his obsolete multimillionaires gaze out into a world that has passed them by but to which they are firmly anchored by their wealth.

A pathetic creature in the last stages of futility, Vallee's sole occupation consists of recording, in a little black book, minute expenditures which are never totaled—as though he were the gently demented statistician of an era that has fallen to pieces for no special reason and has therefore escaped attention. Fonda as Pike, the heir of a brewery fortune (*The Ale That Won for Yale*), is the last word in marooned uselessness. A wistful, vague, young, scholarly ophiologist nicknamed Hoppsey, Pike's sole business in life consists of feeding four flies, a glass of milk, and one piece of white bread to a rare, pampered snake. In between, he can be seen glumly staring at a horde of predatory females, uncooperatively being seduced, getting in and out of suits too modern for him, sadly doing the oldest card trick in the world, and pathetically apologizing for not liking beer or ale. Oddly enough, his supposed opposite, a fast, upper-class card-sharp (Barbara Stanwyck) is no less Victorian, issuing as she does from a group of obsolete card Houdinis with an old-fashioned code of honor among thieves and courtly old-world manners and titles.

If Sturges has accomplished nothing else, he has brought to consciousness the fact that we are still living among the last convulsions of the Victorian world, that, indeed, our entire emotional life is still heavily involved in its death. These final agonies (though they have gone on so long as to make them almost painless), which only Sturges has recorded, can be glimpsed daily, in the strange, gentle expiration of figures like Shaw, Hearst, Jolson, Ford; the somewhat sad explosion of fervor over MacArthur's return (a Sturges picture by itself, with, if the fading hero had been made baseball czar, a pat Sturges ending); and the Old World pomp, unctuousness, and rural religiosity of the American political scene.

Nowhere did Sturges reveal his Victorian affinities more than by his belief in, use, and love of a horde of broken, warped, walked-over, rejected, seamy, old character actors. Some of these crafty bit players, like Walburn, Bridge, Tannen, made up his stock company, while others like Coburn, Pangborn, Kennedy, and Blore appear only in single pictures. They were never questioned by critics, although they seemed as out of place in a film about modern times as a bevy of Floradora girls. They appear as monstrously funny people who have gone through a period of maniacal adjustment to capitalist society by exaggerating a single feature of their character: meekness, excessive guile, splenetic aggressiveness, bureaucratic windiness, or venal pessimism. They seem inordinately toughened by experience, but they are, one is aware, not really tough at all, because they are complete fakers—life made it inevitable. They are very much part of the world of Micawber and Scrooge but later developments—weaker, more perfect, bloated, and subtle caricatures—giving off a fantastic odor of rotten purity and the embalmed cheerfulness of puppets.

They all appear to be too perfectly adjusted to life to require minds, and, in place of hearts, they seem to contain an old scratch sheet, a glob of tobacco juice, or a brown banana. The reason their faces—each of which is a succulent worm's festival, bulbous with sheer living—seem to have nothing in common with the rest of the human race is precisely because they are so eternally, agelessly human, oversocialized to the point where any normal animal component has vanished. They seem to be made up not of features but a *collage* of spare parts, most of them as useless as the vermiform appendix.

Merely gazing at them gives the audience a tremendous lift, as if it were witnessing all the drudgery of daily life undergoing a reckless transmutation. It is as if human nature, beaten to the ground by necessity, out of sheer defiance had decided to produce utterly useless extravaganzas like Pangborn's bobbling cheeks, Bridge's scrounging, scraping voice, or Walburn's evil beetle eyes and mustache like a Fuller brush that has decided to live an independent life. It is all one can do to repress a maniac shriek at the mere sight of Harold Lloyd's companion in *Mad Wednesday*. His body looks like that of a desiccated 200-year-old locust weighed down by an enormous copper hat. Or Pat Moran's wrecked jeep of a face, and his voice that sounds as if its owner had just been smashed in the Adam's apple by Joe Louis. These aged, senile rejects from the human race are put through a routine that has, in one minute, the effect of a long, sad tone poem and, after an hour, gives a movie a peculiar, hallucinatory quality, as if reality had been slightly tilted and robbed of significant pieces.

No one has delineated sheer indolence as Sturges has with these characters. When one appears on the screen, it looks as if he had wandered into the film by mistake and, once there, had been abandoned by the makers. When a second one of these *lumpen* shows up, the audience begins to sit on the edge of its seat and to feel that the picture is going to pieces, that the director has stopped working or the producer is making a monkey out of it. After a few minutes of lacerated nothingness, it becomes obvious that the two creatures are fated to meet; considerable tension is generated, as the audience wonders what build-up will be used to enable them to make each other's acquaintance. To everybody's horror, there is no build-up at all; the creatures link arms as the result of some gruesome asocial understanding and simply walk off. In *Mad Wednesday*, this technique yields a kind of ultimate in grisly, dilapidated humor, particularly in the long episode which begins with Harold Lloyd meeting the locustlike creature on the greasiest looking sidewalk ever photographed. The two repair to a bar presided over by Edgar Kennedy, who slowly and insanely mixes for Lloyd his first alcoholic potion. This entire, elaborate ritual is a weirder, cinematic version of the kind of "study in decrepit life" for which

e. e. cummings is famed; certainly it is at least comparable in merit and effectiveness.

Sturges may not be the greatest director of the last two decades; in fact, it can be argued that a certain thinness in his work—his lack of a fully formed, solid, orthodox moviemaker's technique—prevents him from being included among the first few. He is, however, the most original movie talent produced in recent years: the most complex and puzzling. The emotional and intellectual structure of his work has so little in common with the work of other artists of our time that it seems to be the result of a unique development. Yet it is sufficiently logical and coherent to give it a special relevance to the contemporary American psyche—of precisely the kind that is found in some modern American poetry and painting, and almost nowhere else. Nothing is more indicative of the ineptitude of present-day Hollywood than its failure to keep Sturges producing at his former clip.

with W. S. Poster; Spring 1954

1957–1977

Hard-Sell Cinema

ONE of the major weapons against boredom these days is the joyless rumination one can expend over the success in the "culture underground" of efficient, hard-working mediocrities who threaten to wipe out the whole idea of "felt," committed art. I am referring to the revolution that is occurring simultaneously in jazz (Brubeck, Guiffre, Getz); painting (Rivers, Kline, Hartigan, Brooks); the novel (Salinger, Bellow, Cheever); and films (Chayefsky, Delbert Mann, Kazan). The revolution that has introduced a "new" type into what is known as advanced, radical, experimental, progressive, or, simply, avant-garde art. The figure who is engineering this middle-class blitz has the drive, patience, conceit, and daring to become a successful nonconforming artist without having the talent or idealism for rebellious creation. The brains behind his creativity are those of a high-powered salesman using empty tricks and skills to push an item for which he has no feeling or belief. Avant-gardism has fallen into the hands of the businessman-artist.

The similarities between a Rivers diary-type abstraction, a Brubeck jazz record, and the Lumet-Rose film *Twelve Angry Men* are startling. Each work presents a clever, racy surface, peppered with enough technical smash and speed to make any spectator suspect he is in the presence of a disturbing original talent. However, nothing is explored in depth: Washington does not cross the Delaware in Rivers's famous painting; in fact, this badly composed work barely makes it to a stage of tasteful *joie de vivre* (tentative cobwebby lines, messy water color, and open canvas) that every painting crosses in its early, more facetious moments. By removing the soul from creativity and leaving an easy-to-read exposé of modernity, Rivers paints what amounts to a come-on for every clerk who dreams of greatness in a more romantic occupation. Anyone with necessary brass, drive, restlessness, and lack of taste can not only play the game but become a champion.

An interesting thing about these artists is that they are wonderfully neat and quick technicians. The new jazzmen—Guiffre, Getz, Brubeck—are unbelievably deft and crisp in their run-on gimmicks with instrument and composition. But, by removing everything in accomplishment that gets in the way of technique, they have landed a long way from that which had been planned for progressive jazz by its founding fathers. Without the human involvement and probing of Parker's sax-playing—the pain-wracked attack, as well as the playfulness and sudden spurts of wildly facetious slang—Getz turns the baritone sax into a thing that can be easily mastered, like a typewriter.

It is a mild pleasure simply watching TV director Sidney Lumet's control in *Twelve Angry Men*, bringing a hundred tiny details of schmaltzy anger and soft-center "liberalism" into a clean mosaic. His pointed control and swift exploitation of the beadlike detail is dazzling compared to the slow, camera-milked style of a more perceptive and meticulous Huston, who takes an age of screen time to get across the idea of a stomach growl. In *Giant*, the ponderously traditionalist craftsman George Stevens deliberates through reels of finicky realism to build a slum background for Mexican peons, while Lumet works the same sentimental route to a do-gooder's heart with one line of Reginald Rose dialogue. Within the Stevens triteness (Elizabeth Taylor descending like Miss Nightingale on the poor little adobes of Poker Flat), there are a hundred minor thrills of coloring, tone, texture, time, sunlight, and architecture that are far beyond Lumet's moderate Philco-Hour technique. Nevertheless, it is the shrill tingle of Lumet's counterfeit moviemaking that is helping to drive the Stevens type of architectural craftsmanship into obsolescence.

The most morbid fact about the "revolutionists" is that their leaders are *made* artists, basically blacksmiths who have acquired expedient techniques through long hours of insensitive hard work. Obvious examples of the deadly hand with craft are the current champions of avant-garde fiction whose near best sellers are basically the products of a stale, conservative charm camouflaging an immeasurable vacuity of thought. This *"New Yorker–Partisan Review* axis" writer has built an impressive and odious style that has the solemnity and emptiness of a small-town library room. It features words that are anchored to the page by lead weights, characters who are wobbly, unrecognizable reconstructions of chic art attitudes, and ideas impossible to understand because they come out of a fog of stupidity.

It is hard to say where the business mind first entered the door of modern American creativity. Tracing its antecedents is like working backward across a terrain of quicksand, but one fact keeps thrusting forward: in the rise of cold, short-stack, grounded Macy's artistry, there is an aroma of mean commercial competitiveness.

The new ultrasmooth "radicals" have succeeded on no art front as quickly as they have in films, where fourth-rate talents in compressed flurries of artiness have made the crucial films of the giant screen. The crews responsible for these films are mostly exiles from Broadway, who developed a rigid, eclectic movie technique to go with mean-spirited "liberalism" that always pretends it is being wonderfully kind, curious, and civic-minded about people from the Upper Bronx, Lower Manhattan, and Piggott, Arkansas. The group discussed here (writers Serling, Chayefsky, Willingham, Schulberg, Rose, Lehman and directors Delbert Mann, Ritt, Mulligan, Lumet, Frankenheimer, Cook, Garfein) started its rise in 1955 with *Marty*, a souped-up, genteel counterfeit of the quaint Preston Sturges–Sam Fuller B-film technique, and continued through a string of successes, each a slightly rougher snap version of something that was controversial in the art of the 1920's and 1930's.

The most immediate effect in each of their hits is that of seeing a fast copy of some art image from the past. In Kazan's *A Face in the Crowd*, there is a preciously knitted shot of two distant silhouette figures walking up a lonely rural road through an atmosphere that suggests barley-textured sunlight, a stock exit that has been a pet of many semigenuine artists (including Chaplin). In the new eclectic style, familiar angles engulf the entire story structure. The social conscience ping-pong in *Twelve Angry Men* is heavily indebted to Steinbeck's tender concern for infinitesimal underdogs. *A Face in the Crowd* makes a lunging sophomoric attempt to show up the boobs and crackpots connected with "jes' plain folks" programs, recalling Sinclair Lewis's caricaturing and Henry Miller's candid, slapstick sex. The Broadway vultures in *The Sweet Smell of Success* plot each other's destruction with fancy dialogue that bounces Clifford Odets into Damon Runyon and Molly Goldberg. The slick-magazine psychoanalysis of a lonely traitor in *The Rack* and a deranged ballplayer in *Fear Strikes Out* take you back to the late 1930's, when movies like *Blind Alley* were bringing Freud to proletarian art.

The most painfully amusing thing about this devotion to "ancient" modern art is that it also borrows from the big era in TV drama, the early 1950's, which gave the world Chayefsky, Reginald Rose, and many other businessmen "radicals." The scripts that are fed into the noisy films about New York employ concision and coercion maneuvers that were invented so that a full-scale drama could be squeezed in between the commercials of such hour shows as the Kraft Cheese program. By using these same maneuvers in full-length films, the picture-makers have invented a new type of play-movie and also managed to produce the most vertical movies in film history.

The story is unfolded by savage emotionalizing and trouble-injecting dialogue while two people are in between the events of life (i.e., walking from the cloakroom of the 21 Club to the table of the big-shot columnist). As in the Dr. Rex Morgan comic strip, life is a horrible mess that transpires in the speeches of upright citizens who seem to be glued against a gray backdrop that is always underlit and hard on the eyes. Their run-on speeches ("I don't know what's the matter with me, I keep getting so depressed. I'm going to quit night school. My nerves are shot") invariably touch some trouble that is supposedly bothering each spectator in the theater. For this reason, many people, including the critics of *The New Yorker* and *Time*, think the movies are full of "ideas"—"disturbing," "offbeat," and even "three-dimensional."

Nevertheless, the basic fault of the New York film is that it has no living at all. Though the screen is loaded with small realities—flickering hands, shadows, grunts, squirms, spinal sag, lip-clenching, an old brassiere in a bum's suitcase, homely first names like Sidney and Charley repeated endlessly—the New York films seem to shriek for one ordinary casual action, realistically performed, such as Bogart's succinct repairs on the overpopulated tank in *Sahara*.

No matter how hard the actors try to hide under a mantle of ordinariness, an extraordinary conceit pours from them in timing, emphasis, posture, and mood. It shows up in the smirking, overcooked accent of a pregnant wife in a housing project. It even creeps into the unusually humble acting of Henry Fonda, who, as a tender-hearted intellectual on the jury of *Twelve Angry Men*, knocks off his Nero Wolfeian crime analyses as though he were swatting flies. The actors and directors of these New York films tunnel through problems as though they were made of paper. In *The Sweet Smell of Success*, the dialogue spills out of realistically mannered mouths before you expect it. The "dumb-blonde" cigarette girl minces and whines in a quick unfolding as though she had been cranked like a toy. Newspapers are read and flung away in a violently stylish way and the frozen-lipped delivery of repartee makes the columnist look like a pompous orangutan. It is inconceivable that this high-glossed, ultra-sophisticated drama hinges on a dope-planting act in a nightclub that is carried on with as little difficulty as water has finding its way through a sieve. The self-confidence of these new picture-makers is of a kind that feels the audience's eye will accept anything, no matter how dull or unconvincing, if it is dressed up in some sort of trappings borrowed from "Art."

The characters in New York films are usually nonentities, the kind that have been filmed only occasionally, as in Preston Sturges's earliest low budgets —a meek old man whose only individuality is a horrible glint of self-satisfaction in his eye, an untalented baton-twirler who has nothing except a determined leg kick and a hawklike opportunism in her limply pretty high-school face. Starting with something in their favor, these faceless characters remind you of the dried-up, joyless atavisms inhabiting the great comic strips of middle-class defeat: "Out Our Way," "Boarding House," "The Bungles," "Colonel Hoople." After being mauled by what *Life* and the *New York Post* call "New Talent," these average characters are the most schmaltzed-up, pushy group of unlikables to cross the screen, far worse than the money-soaked glamour that traipsed up and down the Georgian staircases of MGM and Irving Thalberg.

The New York films, which make an almost useless item of the camera, are carried to popularity by their pop-pop-pop type of masochistic acting, which is usually in the hands of Strasberg-influenced performers. The idea behind their florid act is to exploit the worst in people until the effect is like spit, pus, or garbage. The idea of intense character criticism is all right, but the way the New York films do it is close to sickening. No matter how modest or quiet the acting seems—Paul Newman's traitor in *The Rack* or Pat Hingle's hard-rock plebe in *The Strange One*—there is a priggish, superior-smart feeling underlining the performance and making it unbearable. When these actors put a character under the light, the result is apt to be a comic-strip characterization rather than a movie figure. The bulges, bumps, and bubbling in Newman's doubting, worrying, unaggressive soldier are like the short-stroked venom that is scratched into the form of a Colonel Hoople. Though the figure is in constant play, there is no movement or characterization. Newman's job is made up solely of torment, much of it interesting and all of it irrelevant to the idea of a continuously developing, forming personality.

Except for a few interesting situations like the delicately drawn web of secretarial malice, jealousy, and insecurity around a water cooler in *Patterns*, the most obvious ruts are followed to expose types that have been victimized in American art as far back as Horatio Alger. It is actually a comic-strip world for stereotyped victims—the domestically hounded bookkeeper, slug-headed football star, pimple-brained ball fan, oily fixer—with acting clichés piled on top of a stock character. In sparking two films with his baseball-rowdy bit, Jack Warden does fascinating things with scorn and world-weariness, but his basic attack is so rancidly corny as to kill the mobility of the role. There is only one word to describe such inverted acting that whipsaws nothing but triteness, the word being "corrupt."

Also, the acting has so much pitch and roll that there is overflow with each performance. From Pat Hingle (mild smirking), Ben Gazzara (facial showboating), Tony Perkins (coy simpering fragility), Don Murray (boyish earnestness), Anthony Franciosa (well-oiled glibness), E. G. Marshall (superiority), John Cassavetes (aggressive conceit), and Paul Newman (surreptitious modesty), the spectator gets a load of self-consciousness along with the piles of role-bitching sawdust. Thus, one of the neatest jobs in New York films, Lee Remick's ungifted, eye-wandering baton-twirler in *A Face in the Crowd*, is marred by a slight knowingness that surrounds an otherwise unpolished sex-bomb miniature living in a small-town nowheres. Another good effort, the non-actorish playing of academy troublemakers in *The Strange One*, is nearly ruined by Gazzara's self-satisfied pantomime and three bit players who use banality to plug up the slapdash generalizing of Willingham's script. The result: there hasn't been a dumber "dumb tackle," a more weasely crawler, a snottier mamma's-boy snot. For people who like the taut, life-worn fluidity of Dailey-Nolan-O'Brien-Marvin-Cagney-Bogart-Armstrong-Darro-MacLane acting, the New York film portraiture, which made its debut in some early Judy Holliday films, sweats too much around the edges.

The Kazans and Schulbergs of the "Talent Revolution," who glory in their grasp of American ordinariness, are incapable of touching any figure or locale with warmth, charm, or respect. Where modestly skillful Pat Neal is ground into tightness by the Kazan-Schulberg brass knuckles in *A Face in the Crowd*, the fate of newcomer Andy Griffith, who plays a cute hillbilly crashing his way to the top of TV and then falling off, is more like massacre. Off his comically "hick" records of a few years back, Griffith should be a close fit for the soft-shoe backwoods joker, a-wailin' and a-wanderin' Rhodes, who is supposed to be the hero-villain of this barrel-house epic. Instead, Griffith is put in a hyperbolic strait jacket by Kazan's predilection for "mean-animal" acting; only one scene—Rhodes's first encounter with the camera—is played close to the truth of the Ernie Ford type of left-field TV entertainer.

In that scene, as Griffith cuddles with the technicians, makes obvious jokes about the complicated TV machinery, and likens the camera eye to his uncle's drink-soused orb, he scores the only troubling notes in a boringly seething film. In mid-stride, the scene then crumbles into a Capraesque carnival of hokey "documentary shots"—little Americans throwing coins at the needy; Negroes in silent gawking at Rhodes's democratic "dare" and sure-shot confidence. The professionally sly fumbling and stop-go improvising of the hayseed smoothie is never again seen in a film that is supposedly dedicated to revealing the hypnotism of such performers.

These new ambassadors to Hollywood concentrate on the fleetingly seen situation and itinerant figures that must supply most of the immense backlog of material that feeds into dreams. The situations are like stray bits of nothing picked up out of the corner of the eye: the party of drunken office workers at the largest table in a crowded Italian restaurant, a mysterious conversation amongst jazz buffs in the dark alley behind a nightclub, an attempted pickup in the center of a jammed subway car, the jazz-infected body of a slim delinquent stretched across the stairway in a precinct station-house, a tourist couple seen at the end of a hotel hallway, evidently teetering on the edge of some problem. Each film has one or two expanded episodes that break the rhythm of these veiled impressions, a big scene that usually involves a complicated attempt at prostitution, promiscuity, or, as in *A Face in the Crowd*, some long-distance wooing that transpires between a judge and contestant in a baton-twirling contest at the local football stadium. It is in these big-deal moments, where the movie suddenly switches from quickly gimmicked sketches to a fully developed event, that the New York film technique shows up in all of its rickety melodramatic thinness.

Though the New York films like the side-of-the-eye perception, each director makes sure that his film is cluttered with classy examples of "self"-expression. Thus, it is not hard to locate those effects that show the director breathing hard on the story. In each film, one notices that the handling—Delbert Mann's use of spongy acting in an otherwise stiff nighttime scene, Mackendrick's svelte, speeded-up stylizations of the "money-mad American" cliché, Garfein's heavily ironic direction of actors, which seems to stretch characters to a stock Greek-tragedy size—is as sleek as glass, and that it differs from old-fashioned Hollywood direction in that the style parades in front of the film instead of tunneling under a seminaturalistic surface. In other words, from Mulligan's ethereally delicate ballplayer to Mackendrick's mannered columnist, the salient effect is preciousness.

In each story, a marred character stumbles heavily over most of the hurdles, eaten up by a fashionable sickness, like megalomania, a hunger for great financial security, a cowardice brought on by the absence of parental love. An Iago-type hipster, in *The Strange One*, runs a military academy as though it were an easy game of sadistic checkers. A ballplayer breaks down under an unbearable perfectionist load placed on him by a demanding father. A shrewd personnel manager rises like helium in a Wall Street firm while despising the tactics of his patron saint and boss. One doesn't mind the crawling acceptance of cures, motives, troubles that have been rubber-stamped by endless usage in fiction and plays as much as the mechanical feints made at the idea of human complexity.

The most consistently used maneuver in these scripts is the one that throws a switch on characterization. It is predictable that the hard, sure, convoluted sadist in a Southern academy will at some point show a small-scale worry, cowardice, and need for friendship; that the malevolently biased cop will be switched to simply an overworked humanist; that the outspoken "gee-tar" player, who befriends a homeless Negress at 2 A.M. on the corner of Beale and Handy, will end up shouting incredibly written filth—"dressed-up black monkeys"—at his help.

But the most tiresome of all Chayefsky-Willingham-Rose maneuvers is the voyeurlike use of supposedly daring material. Manhattan types are always tiptoeing towards a seamier LIFE but never opening its green door. Prostitutes, lesbians, bathroom culture, sordid bedroom setups, strippers, pornography, and immoral cops move into the orbit of the central characters so that the production team can mince, tickle their toes in the kind of subject that is supposed to give an enormous boost to those who want to reach the avant-garde circle. The peak of movie-script boredom is reached when, in the long *Bachelor Party* funeral through Greenwich Village, a groom's sex trouble is taken up every stair of a prostitute's walk-up, through tons of fear, nausea, and doubt and finally taken downstairs, without encountering one detail that could "realistically" occur anywhere in the world. In terms of all-around inflexibility and genteel observation, the whole scene is reminiscent of the insipid, stiff jerkiness of Charley Chase boxing in two-reel comedy with Jim Jeffries.

Although the new TV exiles to Hollywood are cagey and deft in their social-conscience sell, the New York films, at their best, do a cold deviling of the middle class. Chayefsky creates an unbearably cute prison camp in which pale-gray New Yorkers are humiliated intellectually, shrunk in courage, robbed of wit and grace, given a variety of Freudian pimples and scars, and generally misused in a tender way. There is a half-minute bit in *Twelve Angry Men* in which the halo-wearing minority vote on the jury, a pinch-faced architect (Henry Fonda), is seen carefully drying each fingernail with a bathroom towel. It is a sharply effective, stalling-for-time type of adverse detailing, showing the jury's one sensitive, thoughtful figure to be unusually prissy. Unfortunately, this mild debunking of the hero is a coldly achieved detail that sits on the surface of the film, unexplored and unimportant. After being exposed to such overplanned thrusts at a host of enemies—prejudice, stupidity, Madison Avenue affectation, sadism, meek conformity, perfectionism—the spectator leaves the theater feeling mildly entertained by clever craftsmanship, and slightly ill from swallowing rancid education in good citizenship.

The same type of repetition that drives TV fans crazy during the commercial is used in "New Talent" films. One trip to the market of trouble isn't enough for Chayefsky's Little Fear character; he keeps cutting back, circling, returning to the same trouble, until you feel he's caught in a series of revolving doors. In *The Young Stranger*, the handsome bowlegs (James MacArthur), who punches a movie-owner and ends in a police court, keeps renewing the experience. A worried indigestion (Begley) in *Patterns* keeps swallowing pills for heart sickness and feeling guilty about not taking the kid to see the Giants. The peculiar note in this repetition, which gives a treadmill effect to the scenario, is that it is played with the overstated vehemence of a TV spieler. The actors—Begley, MacArthur, Tony Curtis, who, as Sydney in *The Sweet Smell of Success*, breaks the Olympic record for fast acting—don't chew their roles so much as storm past them, like a train going through a nightmare tunnel that never ends, and with a grating monotony about the forward-motion performance, in which actions and words seem hardly to affect the acting. One leaves these films with a buzzing head, plus a feeling that the jingle-jangle of hard-sell cinema is a long way from the complicated art of simple picture-making, as it has been employed by the unrecognized Hawks, Walsh, Anthony Mann, and John Farrow.

The worst TV play has more on-the-spot invention than the best hard-sell film, and occasionally on TV one notices a Hollywood oldie that is haunting for the fact that it is completely the product of quiet improvisation in the face of a miserable, pulpish story. In such TV "repeats" can be seen the amount of natural, uncompromised picture-making that has been displaced by the new hack saws of artiness. One of the fixtures on TV movie shows, a lovely Raoul Walsh film called *The Roaring Twenties*, journeys with niggling intricacy and deceptive footwork in a lot of grayed rice pudding, capturing the most poignant aspects of the twenties' background and movement. One pounds along with a broken gun on walks and fights that are tensely coiled with forlorn excitement. They are not walks so much as anatomical probings of densely detailed backgrounds that give a second level of formed life to a movie about the last throes of Capone-type gangstering.

Watching the detailing and steering in Walsh's most minor shot of a worn-out *chanteuse* singing "Melancholy Baby," the viewer can estimate the damage of the Kazan-Chayefsky tribe. These newcomers, in being so popular and influential, have all but destroyed background interest, the gloved fluidity of authentic movie acting, and the effect of a modest shrewdie working expediently and with a great camera eye in the underground of a film that is intentionally made to look junky, like the penny candies sold in the old-time grocery. In place of the skillful anonymity of *Pickup on South Street*, *The Lusty Men*, or *The Thing*, there is now a splintering and caterwauling that covers gaping holes with meaningless padding and plush.

The mess we are facing in movies and other media promises to be the worst era in the history of art. Not even the ponderously boring periods, similar to the one in which Titian and Tintoretto painted elephantine conceit and hemstitched complication into the huge dress-works affair called Venetian painting, can equal the present inferno of American culture, which is so jammed with successful con men. One can only glance back in wonderment at those sinkings in each art form where the "shrewdster" gained a decisive entrance. In painting, it occurred in the late 1940's, when certain eruptions combined to bring about a glib turning in avant-garde painting (art-dealer Putzel's death, stylistic hardening of the introsubjective leaders, arrival of businessmen appreciators like Soby, Sweeney, Kootz, Janis, and backing of the entire radical school by all kinds of high-powered critics and publications).

In movies, the Ice Age started to set in with another weird combination of forces (giving up the experimental "B," the ultraconservative turn of big shots like Huston, the decline of the action directors, and explosion of the gimmick: big screen, the "liberal" insight, Freudian symbols, arts-and-crafts Wellesian photography). In the case of each medium, the crucial moment occurred when immense popularity became an important factor in the field of difficult, naturally talented expression. At that moment, the businessman-artist appeared with his quick formulas for achieving "daring," the "original look," and his skills for maneuvering into, and holding, favorable corners in the world of high culture.

Now that the middle class has found serious art, it is almost impossible for a natural talent—good, bad, or in between—to make any headway. In other words, if you are wondering what has happened to the tough, impersonal, against-the-grain innovator in our times—the type of artist who has the anonymous strength of a Walker Evans, the natural grace of a James Agee, the geographic sense of an Anthony Mann, the bitingly exact earthiness of a J. R. Williams, the suavely fluid humanism of a Howard Hawks—he has been hidden by a fantastic army of commercial fine-artists, little locustlike creatures who have the dedication of Sammy Glick, the brains of Happy Hooligan, and the joyful, unconquerable competitive talents of the Katzenjammer Kids.

November 1, 1957

Underground Films

THE saddest thing in current films is watching the long-neglected action directors fade away as the less talented De Sicas and Zinnemanns continue to fascinate the critics. Because they played an anti-art role in Hollywood, the true masters of the male action film—such soldier-cowboy-gangster directors as Raoul Walsh, Howard Hawks, William Wellman, William Keighley, the early, pre-*Stagecoach* John Ford, Anthony Mann—have turned out a huge amount of unprized, second-gear celluloid. Their neglect becomes more painful to behold now that the action directors are in decline, many of them having abandoned the dry, economic, life-worn movie style that made their observations of the American he-man so rewarding. Americans seem to have a special aptitude for allowing History to bury the toughest, most authentic native talents. The same tide that has swept away Otis Ferguson, Walker Evans, Val Lewton, Clarence Williams, and J. R. Williams into near oblivion is now in the process of burying a group that kept an endless flow of interesting roughneck film passing through the theaters from the depression onward. The tragedy of these film-makers lies in their having been consigned to a Sargasso Sea of unmentioned talent by film reviewers whose sole concern is not continuous flow of quality but the momentary novelties of the particular film they are reviewing.

Howard Hawks is the key figure in the male action film because he shows a maximum speed, inner life, and view, with the least amount of flat foot. His best films, which have the swallowed-up intricacy of a good soft-shoe dance, are *Scarface*, *Only Angels Have Wings*, *His Girl Friday*, and *The Big Sleep*. Raoul Walsh's films are melancholy masterpieces of flexibility and detailing inside a lower-middle-class locale. Walsh's victories, which make use of tense, broken-field journeys and nostalgic background detail, include *They Drive by Night*, *White Heat*, and *Roaring Twenties*. In any Bill Wellman operation, there are at least four directors—a sentimentalist, deep thinker, hooey vaudevillian, and an expedient short-cut artist whose special love is for mulish toughs expressing themselves in drop-kicking heads and somber standing around. Wellman is at his best in stiff, vulgar, low-pulp material. In that setup, he has a low-budget ingenuity, which creates flashes of ferocious brassiness, an authentic practical-joke violence (as in the frenzied inadequacy of Ben Blue in *Roxie Hart*), and a brainless hell-raising. Anthony Mann's inhumanity to man, in which cold mortal intentness is the trademark effect, can be studied best in *The Tall Target*, *Winchester 73*, *Border Incident*, and *Railroaded*. The films of this tin-can de Sade have a Germanic rigor, caterpillar intimacy, and an original dictionary of ways in which to punish the human body. Mann has done interesting work with scissors, a cigarette lighter, and steam, but his most bizarre effect takes place in a taxidermist's shop. By intricate manipulation of athletes' bodies, Mann tries to ram the eyes of his combatants on the horns of a stuffed deer stuck on the wall.

The film directors mentioned above did their best work in the late 1940's, when it was possible to be a factory of unpretentious picture-making without frightening the front office. During the same period and later, less prolific directors also appear in the uncompromising action film. Of these, the most important is John Farrow, an urbane vaudevillean whose forte, in films like *The Big Clock* and *His Kind of Woman*, is putting a fine motoring system beneath the veering slapstick of his eccentric characterizations. Though he has tangled with such heavyweights as Book of the Month and Hemingway, Zoltan Korda is an authentic hard-grain cheapster telling his stories through unscrubbed action, masculine characterization, and violent explorations inside a fascinating locale. Korda's best films—*Sahara, Counterattack, Cry the Beloved Country*—are strangely active films in which terrain, jobs, and people get curiously interwoven in a ravening tactility. William Keighley, in *G-Men* and *Each Dawn I Die*, is the least sentimental director of gangster careers. After the bloated philosophical safe-crackers in Huston's *Asphalt Jungle*, the smallish cops and robbers in Keighley's work seem life-size. Keighley's handling is so right in emphasis, timing, and shrewdness that there is no feeling of the director breathing, gasping, snoring over the film.

The tight-lipped creators whose films are mentioned above comprise the most interesting group to appear in American culture since the various groupings that made the 1920's an explosive era in jazz, literature, silent films. Hawks and his group are perfect examples of the anonymous artist, who is seemingly afraid of the polishing, hypocrisy, bragging, fake educating that goes on in serious art. To go at his most expedient gait, the Hawks type must take a withdrawn, almost hidden stance in the industry. Thus, his films seem to come from the most neutral, humdrum, monotonous corner of the movie lot. The fascinating thing about these veiled operators is that they are able to spring the leanest, shrewdest, sprightliest notes from material that looks like junk, and from a creative position that, on the surface, seems totally uncommitted and disinterested. With striking photography, a good ear for natural dialogue, an eye for realistic detail, a skilled inside-action approach to composition, and the most politic hand in the movie field, the action directors have done a forbidding stenography on the hard-boiled American handyman as he progresses through the years.

It is not too remarkable that the underground films, with their twelve-year-old's adventure-story plot and endless palpitating movement, have lost out in the film system. Their dismissal has been caused by the construction of solid confidence built by daily and weekly reviewers. Operating with this wall, the critic can pick and discard without the slightest worry about looking silly. His choice of best salami is a picture backed by studio build-up, agreement amongst his colleagues, a layout in *Life* mag (which makes it officially reasonable for an American award), and a list of ingredients that anyone's unsophisticated aunt in Oakland can spot as comprising a distinguished film. This prize picture, which has philosophical undertones, pan-fried domestic sights, risqué crevices, sporty actors and actresses, circuslike gymnastics, a bit of tragedy like the main fall at Niagara, has every reason to be successful. It has been made for that purpose. Thus, the year's winner is a perfect film made up solely of holes and evasions, covered up by all types of padding and plush. The cavity-filling varies from one prize work to another, from *High Noon* (cross-eyed artistic views of a clock, silhouettes against a vaulting sky, legend-toned walking, a big song), through *From Here to Eternity* (Sinatra's private scene-chewing, pretty trumpeting, tense shots in the dark and at twilight, necking near the water, a threatening hand with a broken bottle) to next year's winner, which will probably be a huge ball of cotton candy containing either Audrey Hepburn's cavernous grin and stiff behind or more of Zinnemann's glacéed picture-making. In terms of imaginative photography, honest acting, and insight into American life, there is no comparison between an average underground triumph (*Phenix City Story*) and the trivia that causes a critical salaam across the land. The trouble is that no one asks the critics' alliance to look straight backward at its "choices," for example, a horse-drawn truckload of liberal schmaltz called *The Best Years of Our Lives*. These ridiculously mal-treated films sustain their place in the halls of fame simply because they bear the label of ART in every inch of their reelage. Praising these solemn goiters has produced a climate in which the underground picture-maker, with his modest entry and soft-shoe approach, can barely survive.

However, any day now, Americans may realize that scrambling after the obvious in art is a losing game. The sharpest work of the last thirty years is to be found by studying the most unlikely, self-destroying, uncompromising, roundabout artists. When the day comes for praising infamous men of art, some great talent will be shown in true light: people like Weldon Kees, the rangy Margie Israel, James Agee, Isaac Rosenfeld, Otis Ferguson, Val Lewton, a dozen comic-strip geniuses like the creator of "Harold Teen," and finally a half-dozen directors such as the master of the ambulance, speedboat, flying-saucer movie: Howard Hawks.

The films of the Hawks-Wellman group are *underground* for more reasons than the fact that the director hides out in subsurface reaches of his work. The hard-bitten action film finds its natural home in caves: the murky, congested theaters, looking like glorified tattoo parlors on the outside and located near bus terminals in big cities. These theaters roll action films in what, at first, seems like a nightmarish atmosphere of shabby transience, prints that seem overgrown with jungle moss, sound tracks infected with hiccups. The specta-tor watches two or three action films go by and leaves feeling as though he were a pirate discharged from a giant sponge.

The cutthroat atmosphere in the itch house is reproduced in the movies shown there. Hawks's *The Big Sleep* not only has a slightly gaseous, subsurface, Baghdadish background, but its gangster action is engineered with a suave, cutting efficacy. Walsh's *Roaring Twenties* is a jangling barrelhouse film, which starts with a top gun bouncing downhill, and, at the end, he is seen slowly pushing his way through a lot of Campbell's scotch broth. Wellman's favorite scene is a group of hard-visaged ball bearings standing around—for no damned reason and with no indication of how long or for what reason they have been standing. His worst pictures are made up simply of this moody, wooden standing around. All that saves the films are the little flurries of bulletlike acting that give the men an inner look of credible orneriness and somewhat stupid mulishness. Mann likes to stretch his victims in crucifix poses against the wall or ground and then to peer intently at their demise with an icy surgeon's eye. Just as the harrowing machine is about to run over the wetback on a moonlit night, the camera catches him sprawled out in a harrowing image. At heart, the best action films are slicing journeys into the lower depths of American life: dregs, outcasts, lonely hard wanderers caught in a buzzsaw of niggardly, intricate, devious movement.

The projects of the underground directors are neither experimental, liberal, slick, spectacular, low-budget, epical, improving, or flagrantly commercial like Sam Katzman two-bitters. They are faceless movies, taken from a type of half-polished trash writing, that seem like a mixture of Burt L. Standish, Max Brand, and Raymond Chandler. Tight, cliché-ridden melodramas about stock musclemen. A stool pigeon gurgling with scissors in his back; a fat, nasal-voiced gang leader; escaped convicts; power-mad ranch owners with vengeful siblings; a mean gun with an Oedipus complex and migraine headaches; a crooked gambler trading guns to the redskins; exhausted GI's; an incompetent kid hoodlum hiding out in an East Side building; a sickly-elegant Italian barber in a plot to kill Lincoln; an underpaid shamus signing up to stop the blackmailing of a tough millionaire's depraved thumb-sucking daughter.

The action directors accept the role of hack so that they can involve themselves with expedience and tough-guy insight in all types of action: barnstorming, driving, bulldogging. The important thing is not so much the banal-seeming journeys to nowhere that make up the stories, but the tunneling that goes on inside the classic Western-gangster incidents and stock hoodlum-dogface-cowboy types. For instance, Wellman's lean, elliptical talents for creating brassy cheapsters and making gloved references to death, patriotism, masturbation, suggest that he uses private runways to the truth, while more famous directors take a slow, embalming surface route.

The virtues of action films expand as the pictures take on the outer appearance of junk jewelry. The underground's greatest mishaps have occurred in art-infected projects where there is unlimited cash, studio freedom, an expansive story, message, heart, and a lot of prestige to be gained. Their flattest, most sentimental works are incidentally the only ones that have attained the almond-paste-flavored eminence of the Museum of Modern Art's film library, i.e., *GI Joe, Public Enemy*. Both Hawks and Wellman, who made these overweighted mistakes, are like basketball's corner man: their best shooting is done from the deepest, worst angle. With material that is hopelessly worn out and childish (*Only Angels Have Wings*), the underground director becomes beautifully graphic and modestly human in his flexible detailing. When the material is like drab concrete, these directors become great on-the-spot inventors, using their curiously niggling, reaming style for adding background detail (Walsh); suave grace (Hawks); crawling, mechanized tension (Mann); veiled gravity (Wellman); svelte semicaricature (John Farrow); modern Gothic vehemence (Phil Karlson); and dark, modish vaudeville (Robert Aldrich).

In the films of these hard-edged directors can be found the unheralded ripple of physical experience, the tiny morbidly lifeworn detail which the visitor to a strange city finds springing out at every step. The Hawks film is as good on the mellifluous grace of the impudent American hard rock as can be found in any art work; the Mann films use American objects and terrain—guns, cliffs, boulders, an 1865 locomotive, telephone wires—with more cruel intimacy than any other film-maker; the Wellman film is the only clear shot at the mean, brassy, clawlike soul of the lone American wolf that has been taken in films. In other words, these actioneers—Mann and Hawks and Keighley and, in recent times, Aldrich and Karlson—go completely underground before proving themselves more honest and subtle than the water buffaloes of film art: George Stevens, Billy Wilder, Vittorio De Sica, Georges Clouzot. (Clouzot's most successful work, *Wages of Fear*, is a wholesale steal of the mean physicality and acrid highway inventions in such Walsh-Wellman films as *They Drive by Night*. Also, the latter film is a more flexible, adroitly ad-libbed, worked-in creation than Clouzot's eclectic money-maker.)

Unfortunately, the action directors suffer from presentation problems. Their work is now seen repeatedly on the blurred, chopped, worn, darkened, commercial-ridden movie programs on TV. Even in the impossible conditions of the "Late Show," where the lighting is four shades too dark and the porthole-shaped screen defeats the movie's action, the deep skill of Hawks and his tribe shows itself. Time has dated and thinned out the story excitement, but the ability to capture the exact homely-manly character of forgotten locales and misanthropic figures is still in the pictures along with pictorial compositions (Ford's *Last of the Mohicans*) that occasionally seem as lovely as anything that came out of the camera box of Billy Bitzer and Matthew Brady. The conditions in the outcast theaters—the Lyric on Times Square, the Liberty on

Market Street, the Victory on Chestnut—are not as bad as TV, but bad enough. The screen image is often out of plumb, the house lights are half left on during the picture, the broken seats are only a minor annoyance in the unpredictable terrain. Yet, these action-film homes are the places to study Hawks, Wellman, Mann, as well as their near and distant cousins.

The underground directors have been saving the American male on the screen for three decades without receiving the slightest credit from critics and prize committees. The hard, exact defining of male action, completely lacking in acting fat, is a common item *only* in underground films. The cream on the top of a *Framed* or *Appointment with Danger* (directed by two first cousins of the Hawks-Walsh strain) is the eye-flicking action that shows the American body— arms, elbows, legs, mouths, the tension profile line—being used expediently, with grace and the suggestion of jolting hardness. Otherwise, the Hollywood talkie seems to have been invented to give an embarrassingly phony impression of the virile action man. The performance is always fattened either by coyness (early Robert Taylor), unction (Anthony Quinn), histrionic conceit (Gene Kelly), liberal knowingness (Brando), angelic stylishness (Mel Ferrer), oily hamming (José Ferrer), Mother's Boy passivity (Rock Hudson), or languor (Montgomery Clift). Unless the actor lands in the hands of an underground director, he causes a candy-coated effect that is misery for any spectator who likes a bit of male truth in films.

After a steady diet of undergrounders, the spectator realizes that these are the only films that show the tension of an individual intelligence posing itself against the possibilities of monotony, bathos, or sheer cliché. Though the action film is filled with heroism or its absence, the real hero is the small detail which has arisen from a stormy competition between lively color and credibility. The hardness of these films arises from the esthetic give-and-go with banality. Thus, the philosophical idea in underground films seems to be that nothing is easy in life or the making of films. Jobs are difficult, even the act of watching a humdrum bookstore scene from across the street has to be done with care and modesty to evade the type of butter-slicing glibness that rots the Zinnemann films. In the Walsh film, a gangster walks through a saloon with so much tight-roped ad-libbing and muscularity that he seems to be walking backward through the situation. Hawks's achievement of moderate toughness in *Red River*, using Clift's delicate languor and Wayne's claylike acting, is remarkable. As usual, he steers Clift through a series of cornball fetishes (like the Barney Google Ozark hat and the trick handling of same) and graceful, semicollegiate business: stances and kneelings and snake-quick gunmanship. The beauty of the job is the way the cliché business is kneaded, strained against without breaking the naturalistic surface. One feels that this is the first and last hard, clamped-down, imaginative job Clift does in Hollywood—his one nonmush performance. Afterward, he goes to work for Zinnemann, Stevens, Hitchcock.

The small buried attempt to pierce the banal pulp of underground stories with fanciful grace notes is one of the important feats of the underground director. Usually, the piercing consists in renovating a cheap rusty trick that has been slumbering in the "thriller" director's handbook—pushing a "color" effect against the most resistant type of unshowy, hard-bitten direction. A mean butterball flicks a gunman's ear with a cigarette lighter. A night-frozen cowboy shudders over a swig of whisky. A gorilla gang leader makes a cannonaded exit from a barber chair. All these bits of congestion are like the lines of a hand to a good gun movie; they are the tracings of difficulty that make the films seem uniquely hard and formful. In each case, the director is taking a great chance with clichés and forcing them into a hard natural shape.

People don't notice the absence of this hard combat with low, commonplace ideas in the Zinnemann and Huston epics, wherein the action is a game in which the stars take part with confidence and glee as though nothing can stop them. They roll in parts of drug addicts, tortured sheriffs; success depending on how much sentimental bloop and artistic japery can be packed in without encountering the demands of a natural act or character. Looking back on a Sinatra film, one has the feeling of a private whirligig performance in the center of a frame rather than a picture. On the other hand, a Cagney performance under the hands of a Keighley is ingrained in a tight, malignant story. One remembers it as a sinewy, life-marred exactness that is as quietly laid down as the smaller jobs played by the Barton MacLanes and Frankie Darros.

A constant attendance at the Lyric-Pix-Victory theaters soon impresses the spectator with the coverage of locales in action films. The average gun film travels like a shamus who knows his city and likes his private knowledges. Instead of the picture-postcard sights, the underground film finds the most idiosyncratic spot of a city and then locates the niceties within the large nicety. The California Street hill in San Francisco (*Woman in Hiding*) with its old-style mansions played in perfect night photography against a deadened domestic bitching. A YMCA scene that emphasizes the wonderful fat-waisted, middle-aged physicality of people putting on tennis shoes and playing handball (*Appointment with Danger*). The terrorizing of a dowdy middle-aged, frog-faced woman (*Born to Kill*) that starts in a decrepit hotel and ends in a bumbling, screeching, crawling murder at midnight on the shore. For his big shock effect, director Robert Wise (a sometime member of the underground) uses the angle going down to the water to create a middle-class mediocrity that out-horrors anything Graham Greene attempted in his early books on small-time gunsels.

Another fine thing about the coverage is its topographic grimness, the fact that the terrain looks worked over. From Walsh's *What Price Glory?* to Mann's *Men in War*, the terrain is special in that it is used, kicked, grappled, worried, sweated up, burrowed into, stomped on. The land is marched across in dark, threading lines at twilight, or the effect is reversed with foot soldiers in white parkas (*Fixed Bayonets*) curving along a snowed-in battleground as they watch troops moving back—in either case, the cliché effect is worked credibly inward until it creates a haunting note like the army diagonals in *Birth of a Nation*. Rooms are boxed, crossed, opened up as they are in few other films. The spectator gets to know these rooms as well as his own hand. Years after seeing the film, he remembers the way a dulled waitress sat on the edge of a hotel bed, the weird elongated adobe in which ranch hands congregate before a Chisholm Trail drive. The rooms in big-shot directors' films look curiously bulbous, as though inflated with hot air and turned toward the audience, like the high school operetta of the 1920's.

Of all these poet-builders, Wellman is the most interesting, particularly with Hopper-type scenery. It is a matter of drawing store fronts, heavy bedroom boudoirs, the heisting of a lonely service station, with light, furious strokes. Also, in mixing jolting vulgarity (Mae Clarke's face being smashed with a grapefruit) with a space composition dance in which the scene seems to be constructed before your eyes. It may be a minor achievement, but, when Wellman finishes with a service station or the wooden stairs in front of an ancient saloon, there is no reason for any movie realist to handle the subject again. The scene is kept light, textural, and as though it is being built from the outside in. There is no sentiment of the type that spreads lugubrious shadows (Kazan), builds tensions of perspective (Huston), or inflates with golden sunlight and finicky hot air (Stevens).

Easily the best part of underground films are the excavations of exciting-familiar scenery. The opening up of a scene is more concerted in these films than in other Hollywood efforts, but the most important thing is that the opening is done by road-mapped strategies that play movement against space in a cunning way, building the environment and event before your eyes. In every underground film, these vigorous ramifications within a sharply seen terrain are the big attraction, the main tent. No one does this anatomization of action and scene better than Hawks, who probably invented it—at least, the smooth version—in such 1930's gunblasts as *The Crowd Roars*. The control of Hawks's strategies is so ingenious that, when a person kneels or walks down the hallway, the movement seems to click into a predetermined slot. It is an uncanny accomplishment that carries the spectator across the very ground of a giant ranch, into rooms and out again, over to the wall to look at some faded fight pictures on a hotel wall—as though he were in the grip of a spectacular, mobile "eye." When Hawks landscapes action—the cutting between light tower and storm-caught plane in *Ceiling Zero*, the vegetalizing in *The Thing*, the shamus sweating in a greenhouse in *The Big Sleep*—the feeling is of a clever human tunneling just under the surface of terrain. It is as though the film has a life of its own that goes on beneath the story action.

However, there have been many great examples of such veining by human interactions over a wide plane. One of the special shockers, in *Each Dawn I Die*, has to do with the scissoring of a stooly during the movie shown at the penitentiary. This Keighley-Cagney effort is a wonder of excitement as it moves in great leaps from screen to the rear of a crowded auditorium: crossing contrasts of movement in three points of the hall, all of it done in a sinking gloom. One of the more ironic crisscrossings has to do with the coughings of the stuck victim played against the screen image of zooming airplanes over the Pacific.

In the great virtuoso films, there is something vaguely resembling this underground maneuvering, only it goes on above the story. Egocentric padding that builds a great bonfire of pyrotechnics over a gapingly empty film. The perfect example is a pumped-up fist fight that almost closes the three-hour *Giant* film. This ballroom shuffle between a reforming rancher and a Mexican-hating luncheonette owner is an entertaining creation in spectacular tumbling, swinging, back arching, bending. However, the endless masturbatory "building" of excitement—beautiful haymakers, room-covering falls, thunderous sounds—is more than slightly silly. Even if the room were valid, which it isn't (a studio-built chromium horror plopped too close to the edge of a lonely highway), the room goes unexplored because of the jumbled timing. The excess that is so noticeable in Stevens's brawl is absent in the least serious undergrounder, which attains most of its crisp, angular character from the modesty of a director working skillfully far within the earthworks of the story.

Underground films have almost ceased to be a part of the movie scene. The founders of the action film have gone into awkward, big-scaled productions involving pyramid-building, a passenger plane in trouble over the Pacific, and postcard Westerns with Jimmy Stewart and his harassed Adam's apple approach to gutty acting. The last drainings of the underground film show a tendency toward moving from the plain guttural approach of *Steel Helmet* to a Germanically splashed type of film. Of these newcomers, Robert Aldrich is certainly the most exciting—a lurid, psychiatric stormer who gets an overflow of vitality and sheer love for movie-making into the film. This enthusiasm is the rarest item in a dried, decayed-lemon type of movie period. Aldrich makes viciously anti-Something movies—*Attack* stomps on Southern rascalism and the officer sect in war, *The Big Knife* impales the Zanuck-Goldwyn big shot in Hollywood. The Aldrich films are filled with exciting characterizations—by Lee Marvin, Rod Steiger, Jack Palance—of highly psyched-up, marred, and bothered men. Phil Karlson has done some surprising modern Gothic treatments of the Brinks hold-up (*Kansas City Confidential*) and the vice-ridden Southern town (*The Phenix City Story*). His movies are remarkable for their endless outlay of scary cheapness in detailing the modern underworld. Also, Karlson's work has a chilling documentary exactness and an exciting shot-scattering belligerence.

There is no longer a literate audience for the masculine picture-making that Hawks and Wellman exploited, as there was in the 1930's. In those exciting movie years, a smart audience waited around each week for the next Hawks, Preston Sturges, or Ford film—shoe-stringers that were far to the side of the expensive Hollywood film. That underground audience, with its expert voice in Otis Ferguson and its ability to choose between perceptive trash and the Thalberg pepsin-flavored sloshing with Tracy and Gable, has now oozed away. It seems ridiculous, but the Fergusonite went into fast decline during the mid-1940's when the movie market was flooded with fake underground films—plushy thrillers with neo-Chandler scripts and a romantic style that seemed to pour the gore, histrionics, decor out of a giant catsup bottle. The nadir of these films: an item called *Singapore* with Fred MacMurray and Ava Gardner.

The straw that finally breaks the back of the underground film tradition is the dilettante behavior of intellectuals on the subject of oaters. Esthetes and upper bohemians now favor horse operas almost as wildly as they like the cute, little-guy worshipings of De Sica and the pedantic, interpretive reading of Alec Guinness. This fad for Western films shows itself in the inevitable little-magazine review, which finds an affinity between the subject matter of cowboy films and the inner esthetics of Cinemah. The Hawks-Wellman tradition, which is basically a subterranean delight that looks like a cheap penny candy on the outside, hasn't a chance of reviving when intellectuals enthuse in equal amounts over Westerns by Ford, Nunnally Johnson, J. Sturges, Stevens, Delmer Daves. In Ferguson's day, the intellectual could differentiate between a stolid genre painter (Ford), a long-winded cuteness expert with a rotogravure movie scene (Johnson), a scene-painter with a notions-counter eye and a primly naïve manner with sun-hardened bruisers (John Sturges), and a *Boys Life* nature lover who intelligently half-prettifies adolescents and backwoods primitives (Daves). Today, the audience for Westerns and gangster careers is a sickeningly frivolous one that does little more than play the garbage collector or make a night court of films. With this high-brow audience that loves banality and pomp more than the tourists at Radio City Music Hall, there is little reason to expect any stray director to try for a hidden meager-looking work that is directly against the serious art grain.

November 1957

Nearer My Agee to Thee

JAMES AGEE was the most intriguing star-gazer in the middle-brow era of Hollywood films, a virtuoso who capped a strange company of stars on people's lips and set up a hailstorm of ideas for other critics to use. Of all the ham-on-wry critics who wrote for big little magazines, Agee had the prose and ad-libability to handle the business-craft from all sides. He gave any number of unsung creators their only "deep" coverage; certain key images like "gentleman director" (in the case of Howard Hawks) spotlighted a peculiarly mellifluous soft-shoe type.

While his Tol'able Jim classic, *Let Us Now Praise Famous Men*, disclosed that he was an unorthodox, unsure left-fielder, Agee was able to build skyscrapers in art out of cross-purposes and clay. Even at his worst, in reviews where he was nice, thoughtful, and guilty until he seemed an "intellectual" hatched in Mack Sennett's brain, Agee was a fine antidote to the paralyzing plot-sociologists who hit the jackpot during the 1940's. His great contribution was a constant emphasis on the individuals operating in what is wrongly supposed a "mass art" that assembly-lines the personal out of existence.

The writers who flowered in 1939–47 movie columns of liberal middle-class journals had the same kind of reader-employer freedom that encouraged good sportswriters in the 1920's—i.e., they served an undemanding audience that welcomed style and knew hardly anything about the inside of movies. Agee wrote reasonable exaggerations, beautifully articulated, about dull plodding treacle that stretched from Jean Simmons to Ingrid Bergman. (Olivia de Havilland, he once wrote, "has for a long time been one of the prettiest women in movies; lately she has not only become prettier than ever but has started to act as well. I don't see evidence of any remarkable talent, but her playing is thoughtful, quiet, detailed, and well sustained, and since it is founded, as some more talented playing is not, in an unusually healthful-seeming and likable temperament, it is an undivided pleasure to see.")

Thus, Agee built a Jim-dandy fan club almost the equal of Dylan Thomas's. Given this terrain of Ageephiles (Auden's rave about Agee in a *Nation* fan letter included the proud "I do not care for movies and I rarely see them"), it was predictable that Agee's contradictory, often unlikable genius would be distorted, simplified, and dulled by an ever-growing hero worship.

Even where he modified and showboated until the reader had the Jim-jams, Agee's style was exciting in its pea-soup density. As in his beloved films (*Treasure of the Sierra Madre*, Olivier's work), his criticism had an excessive richness that came from a fine writing ear as well as cautious hesitancy, ganglia, guilt. The sentences are swamps that are filled with a suspicious number of right-sounding insights. Actually, Agee's appreciations stick pretty close to what the middle-brow wants to hear, as when he accused Mel Tormé of being out of a jar, and raptured about the unequaled "poetry" of Huston's Mexicans (who were closer to a bottle—spirits of hammonia—than Tormé). His three-dimensional use of "I" constructions, which seldom aroused the reader to its essential immodesty, was buttressed by a moralism that hawked the theater looking for the "sellout" in art. The Hollywood technicians were put through a purgatory: a new angle—the artist's soul—was added to movie criticism, as Agee, borrowing words from God, decided whether the latest Hollywood sex-pot, in *Blanche of the Evergreens*, was truthful, human, selfless, decent, noble, pure, honorable, really good, or simply deceitful, a cheat, unclean, and without love or dignity.

As he shellacked the reader with culture, Agee had one infallibly charming tool in his kit: an aristocratic gashouse humor that made use of several art centuries, a fantastic recall of stray coupons—like old song lyrics and the favorite thing people were saying in February, 1917—and a way of playing leapfrog with clichés, making them sparkle like pennies lost in a Bendix. The funniest passage Agee wrote had to do with a fairly deadpan description of a movie discussion in a *Time* elevator, humor coming from his capacity to capture an elevator's sociology in the fewest words. But more often he indicated great comic timing, winding up the top-heavy *Lost Weekend* review with one flashing line: "I undershtand that liquor interesh: innerish: intereshtsh are rather worried about thish film. Thash tough."

Agee built slow reviews with his pet multiplications: "It is unusually hard, tense, cruel, intelligent, and straightforward. But I see nothing in it that is new, sharply individual, or strongly creative." The humor, which came strictly in spots, acted as an oasis: "Otherwise, the picture deserves, like four or five other movies, to walk alone, tinkle a little bell, and cry 'Unclean, unclean.'"

At least half of the growing Agee legend—that he had a great camera eye, writing equipment, and love for moviemakers—is fantasy. Agee's visual recall, so apparent in *tour de force* pieces on Sennett's gang that hit like a cold shower of visual needles, is always wedded to a blindness to chic artiness. His humanity has a curious way of leveling performers with flattery, and over-competing with directors by flooding their works with a consuming sensibility. His journalistic manner in the smaller *Time* reviews is flawless, but, unfortu-nately, Agee's reputation is based on heavier writing which has a sensitively tinctured glibness (as in this pontifical stretch: "In these long close-ups, as in much else that he does, Dreyer goes against most of the 'rules' that are laid down, even by good people, for making genuine and good motion pictures. In a sense I have to admit that he is far out at the edge rather than close to the center of all that I think might be most productive and original. But there is only one rule for movies that I finally care about. . . .")

Agee's *Time* stint added up to a sharp, funny encyclopedia on the film industry during the 1940's. Though he occasionally lapsed into salesmanship through brilliantly subtle swami glamour (*Henry V*, the Ingrid Bergman cover story), Agee would be wisely remembered for quick biographies and reviews, particularly about such happy garbage as June Haver musicals and an early beatnik satire *Salome Where She Danced*, where his taste didn't have to outrun a superabundant writing talent. But this is the writing that has been shrugged out of *Agee On Film* by too shrewd editing that is conscious of the art-minded and carriage trade. Other evidences of the book shortchanging Agee's richness: (1) no sign of those extended journeys on Luce limb for a box-office hero, and (2) no evidence of his conflicting reviews on the same picture for the power (*Time*) and the glory (*The Nation*).

Suffering from happy-plexis and booming emphasis, Agee's deep-dish crit-icism in *The Nation* was motivated by a need to bridge Hollywood with the highest mounts of art. Like Gilbert Seldes, he had a dozen ways to move films into the museum. For instance, Agee was a master of critics' patter, the num-bers racket, and the false bracket. He used other critics' enthusiasms ("Win-sten and McCarten think it is one of the best ever made. I don't care quite that much for it, but. . . ."), expanded petty courage into infinity (Wilder's courage in making *The Lost Weekend*), and maneuvered in a pinch with the one-eyed emphasis. "June Allyson, who seems incapable of a superficial performance" is a typical Agee periscope of an actress's one trait, a minor sincerity, at the expense of an immobile, rangeless cuteness.

If Agee had struggled more with the actual material of the popular nonartist, it is inconceivable that he could have missed the vapidity of so much "good" film art. With his incurious response to super-present-tense material in films, he could praise the stuffed-shirt timing in Olivier's "Crispin's Day" speech or the academic woodchopper's emphasis on that leer in *Sunset Boulevard*. A great segment of fine Hollywood work isn't interested in Big Art, but in making a contemporaneous "point" that, by the nature of its momentary truth, dies almost the moment the movie is released.

In certain abrupt *Nation* reviews (Kazan's anonymous realism in *Boomerang*, Ford's smoglike *They Were Expendable*), there is a mild struggling with the awareness that the movie is talking not about art but of the necessity of placing itself in a likable position with the furthest advances in currency— whether that contemporaneity has to do with nonchalance (*Good News*), a manner of shorthand phrasing (early parts of *The Ox-Bow Incident*), or a way of looking at "hip" folk (*The Big Sleep*). Agee was a brick wall against pretense in small movies, but, on Big Scale work, where the Boulevard is made of National Velvet and the Limelight's as stunning as the Sierra Madre, Agee's reviews suggested a busy day at Muscle Beach: flexing words, bulging rumps of talent, pyramidal displays of filming cunning.

Agee is perhaps as bewitching as his bandwagon believes, if his whole complexity of traits is admitted in the record. Seldom has more personality walked through American criticism with such slyly cloaked overpossessive manners. The present Hollywood film, in which a mishmash knowledge of faintly old modern art is presented in show-biz language, owes part of its inauthentic soul to a fine critic, who even felt obliged to place pictures he disliked in a company with "all the good writing of this century, the films of Pudovkin and Pabst, and some of the music of Brahms."

November 8, 1958

Bathroom Mirror Sinceratease

WHEREAS the early silent film developed quickly into a director's medium, television has become the happy haunting ground for actors, particularly those closer-my-face-to-thee actors who are adept at bathroom mirror sinceratease.

The actors own television, partly because TV's best directors are mired in Hollywood's 1930s and the writers (S. J. Perelman's script for a recent "Omnibus" disaster) are logging semi-unconscious Marxist protestations, using the foghorn style of the depression writers. Despite its dated construction, the average TV effort is saved by a type of acting that is ruthlessly unsuccessful in either Broadway or Hollywood. TV's consistent victors—Martin Balsam, Jack Klugman, Jack Warden—are technicians who, having grown up with the living-room medium, now create mundane rocks in plays that are obsessed with mobility and never able to achieve it. Where Julie Harris's cunning comes through the TV set as a reek, Klugman's unforgettable bartender in Saroyan's *Time of Your Life* succeeded by being believably flat, colorless and gripping, something like the rug near most TV sets.

Until the production crews can create an authentic plasticity on a screen that looks like a thumbnail, televised emoting would wisely follow the tough-flat projectionist and forget about any acting that resembles salesmanship. There is a *negative* salesmanship about Joey Bishop's sensitive dead-panning on "Keep Talking" which recalls the infectious hopelessness of the "Out Our Way" comic strip, where the wrinkle of a boy's sloppy knickers seemed possessed by a dead octopus. Bishop, accusing the spectator with every despondent flick of his face, displays a type of toughness rarely seen in allied arts, where the stakes have become so high that acting has taken on a heavily over-refined effect. This drugged, on-the-job vitality, which appears even in the pantomiming of TV's non-actors, is a curious throwback to the 1920s, the Sennett actor as well as the proletarian cartoonist.

TV acting, seen in rear view only in the burlesque walk-off that cheese-cakes the well-acted "Bob Cummings Show," is plopped, inescapably, front-faced, halitosis-close before an audience in an intimacy new to popular art. Unfortunately, many thespians try to close this close relationship further with a wealth of inside chicanery that oversells the actor and over-befriends the viewer. Within a short video span, Jackie Gleason has done some smiley-genial face popping on "Playhouse 90," Jack Lemmon has over-explained a neurotic barrister by rubber-faced communion with his audience. And in the non-actor shows, narcissistic meanderings have become the juice-hiding basic material. The songs of Perry Comotose are overpowered by slowly straying eyes and a wandering forefinger: "What's My Line" is another example of the real thing hidden by pantomime, such as smiles that walk on elephant's paws.

Finally, TV's acting freshness is needlessly sapped by casting ideas picked up from the Goldwyn-Selznick mentality. The most imitable is the all-star cast: sinking reputable pillars in focal points, so that the play is anchored and squared with carefully nurtured tiresomeness. Another clammy notion is that familiarity breeds excellence: During one decade Selznick used the Joseph Cotten–Jennifer Jones–Shirley Temple cast on the American movie audience as though it were a brand. Seeing Nina Foch (ladylike jitters), Keenan Wynn (humorless plodding), or E. J. Marshall (hangdog burrowing) has become a divertissement as predictable as Tiger Jones on the weekend fightcast. Logical casting is another theory that should have been left to fester in the movie bosom. For instance, there is enough stately ennui in Henry James's writing without actors (James Donald, Dana Wynter, John Baragray) bred on the hot-house manners of a Jamesian story. A few Odets types or some of Preston Sturges's dyed-in-evil plebian gypsies might have pushed "Wings of the Dove" into a spectacular mediocrity.

TV's gift to this age is an actor who, neither deadened by style nor inter-ested in making the space nimble, amiable, hopeful or poignant, admits all lim-itations of his locked position looking straight at the spectator. Sterling Hayden's convict stranded with a pregnant woman in Faulkner's flood story, Ralph Meeker manacled to a detective in a Pullman thriller on the "Pursuit" series, James Witmore as a racketeer-fixer hemmed in a boy's camp by a forest of sentimental progressives, are examples of TV's best acting which, repeating notes like a woodpecker, uses the mirthless, narrow range of the TV camera to present a savagely As Is portrait.

Sucked dry of sentiment, ungiving, tightly closed to any spectator's ready insight, the finest TV acting makes any current theater attempt at forbidding individuality seem as soft as custard. Like the subway rider forced to explore a co-rider's impassive face, the spectator gets a performance of a consistently unreadable hard note. There doesn't seem any doubt that Dick Stark's sand-paper directness delivering a Remington Rand commercial packs more intrigue and vitality than the caricatured Critics' Award performance of David Niven as a perverted doilie in *Separate Tables*.

February 2, 1959

Hollywood's New Peepshow Naturalism

NOT since movie patrons of the early 1900s glimpsed *What the Bootblack Saw* through a kinetoscope cranny have movie moguls invested so in Peepshow and come up with such counterfeit magic. While Europeans have taken the high road, using plot and subject matter to make gee-whiz disclosures, lately arriving at high-class pornography (*Smiles of a Summer Night*) only a halter away from *Vogue* fashion ads, Hollywood has gone underground into technique. Its inventions have led to a preposterous, self-conscious naturalism that, in the wilder works (*Cat on a Hot Tin Roof*), betrays small truths with enough around-the-edge sensuosity to circle the theater labyrinth and plunk like pellets of vaseline.

The new thrill-glutted, Penny-Arcade film style first appeared in the late 1940s but was hard to grasp because it used past movie tradition as a free-lunch counter. An audience accustomed to films with structure felt startled and thwarted by dream-like garbling of graphic exotica, such re-heated metaphors as Ray Milland's disrobed eyeball in a vein-ridden close-up (*The Lost Weekend*), the decadently banal sadism of a district attorney's limp as he stalks Monty Clift (*A Place in the Sun*), and that Thomas Wolfe moment of a war veteran enjoying a ghostly junket as he daydreams in the cockpit of an interred DC654321 (*The Best Years of Our Lives*). Actually, the image-mongering of these late 1940s films brought a new stance into movie-making: a knothole vantage-point on life, a ruthless leisureliness that disregards the naturalist's regimen of responsibility, and the trick of jazzing up a dull truth with pseudo-documentary shrubbery.

For the first time, producers are less interested in exploiting environment than in examining the concentrated existence that goes on in a keyhole view of life. While the outside world, dying as a major screen novelty, is given only token identity, there is a feeling of zeroing in on a target of extraneous details, obviously magnified and filled with wimmen and vigor. An over-cunning keeps the viewer in contact with the super-nervous sensuosity of items, exotic surfaces; the clings, tugs, stretch involved in the well-sexed costumes of an unbedded wife (*Cat on a Hot Tin Roof*). But, more notably, the overtrained technique that occurs in pop-jungle (*The Bridge on the River Kwai*) or post-card Gulf Stream (*Old Man and the Sea*) is another example of Hollywood's drift from trek or frieze-like progression of events toward a succession of sensational moments, simplifying the screen, locking the story in place.

With the telescoping of interest on singular surfaces, emphasis on sexual contraband becomes the biggest box-office trait. Marlon Brando's Nazi lion rising from a drunken sprawl to give a Prussian tug to the rear of his officer's coat, is an example of average gesture being loaded with sensual concentrate (and then played, unforgivably, as ballet). The most likable "major star" has to be Paul Newman: his self-admiring nonchalance—drooping his hands, like reserve weapons, from his rear pockets—startles the audience, not with sexual frankness, which is already old-hat, but with a simple confrontation of sensual reality.

The fooler in Peepshow is that its jolts are conspicuous waste effects: the beguilement comes from a combination of chicanery and crochet-like precision. A counterfeit graphicness—the fact that Orson Welles storms a plantation in a jeep, talks fast in a clogged-mattress Southernese and carries a lapel-pocket filled with a Japanese garden of choice Eversharps—is obvious in every scene of the likably precious *Long Hot Summer*. The fantastic note is not in the hokey naturalism, but in the exquisite speed-writing that arranges the spots and collides them with steel-string clarity.

The orgiastic tempo of director Stanley Kubrick is exciting, but his work leaves the vacuous feeling of having seen a filmed collage. The spectator has to work through a smoke-screen of irrelevance in a brilliant scene from Kubrick's long-forgotten *The Killing*; the scene, which involves Tim Carey as an underworld weirdie flourishing in the rustic pleasures of a pastoral vacant lot, is a Spike Jones clatter of inanities banging off each other; but, because of its detachment from all logical moorings, the contrivance acquires an eccentric vitality that is the special glory of authentic peeperism. The unkempt improvisations of Carey's slavering gives a stinging sense of haphazardly grasped character and of reality echoing beyond the bonds of the film's sequence. This ephemeral vitality hasn't been honored in films, except in an accidental way. Whatever this new tic-technique loses in substance and credibility, it almost supplements with a plasticity, a marginal life that intensifies subliminally as it slips from the audience's attention.

February 16, 1959

"That's It, Boy. I Mean, That's It."

BEARING little relation to the music heard on radio and discs, TV's version of pops and jazz is Operetta, either full-scaled agony like *Hans Brinker*, or a one-song picture story: the balladeer adrift in an eerie vault spotted with display furniture and flying chorus boys. The various movements that pass through juke boxes appear only as shadows on TV's screen, usually in hammering satires such as Dick Shawn's athletic take-off on Elvis Presley, Bob Hope's wonderful beatnik skit, Sid Caesar's zooter blowing tenor sax. Dodging the more frightening areas of Tin-Pan culture, TV serves a production-wise thing,

filled with decorous types, lethargic pace, and tasteless jazz propaganda starring "Looie" Armstrong as the end, Man!, in triteness.

Hit records and dance bands comprise an eccentric province, photogenically uncouth and troublesomely alive with corners, brashness, wild dishon-
esty. TV's facile approximation of this wild-woolly universe is the Hank
Mancini score for *Peter Gunn*, a private-eye funhouse that provides the correct
photographic clatter while keeping camera off the relaxed ensemble work of a
slick group that includes Shelly Manne. Much closer to the heartbeat of jazz
were the extraordinary swinging duets between Stuff Smith's middle register
fiddling and Maxine Sullivan's muffled gamin voice on the now defunct Art
Ford show. But generally, there is less agility or inspiration in TV's song shows
than occurs in the fine syncopation of Johnson & Johnson's Band-Aid ad.

Since the product is dismal, the baffling question is: why so many song specialists in front of costly evening shows? When a high-pressure show is in its
normal stride, the costly apparatus is being carried by a fairly vacant personage
slipping self-consciously through a fine oldie ("Goodie, Goodie"), backed by
the most typical of all TV sounds, ten or twelve horns playing the same note
with a rhythmic deficiency that recalls Muzak. The impossible relationship
between mild baritone and huge band brassiness hardly matters in a setup
where the singer, like the medium itself, is congenitally a con-artist: genial,
unhurried, ready to please. Even in the hands of a shrewd pseudo-jazz
singer (Pat Suzuki) the music idles, simpers, waiting for the insertion of self-
salesmanship out of the cute Doris Day drawer.

"Don't be a stick in the mud," "It doesn't hurt to smile" are the pep songs
that lie buried in the back of TV musicianship. While TV sophisticana likes to
imply that Liberace or Lawrence Welk are the ultimate in musical clichés, it
is only a-won-anna-two steps from Como (the end result of the "make a good
impression bit") to Welk's show, where endless soloists doing one-fingered
melody and wearing a gripped-by-nausea concern take dead aim at TV's older
audience.

Somewhere in the era of Frank Sinatra's rise and Bing Crosby's fall the
coolness that fogs televised music came into being under the aegis of some
specialists in exaggerated suaveness. Shouting his "talent" for phrasing with
flagrantly bent notes, Sinatra helped invent the idea that show-biz superiority
can be branded on American entertainment through a consistent, deadpan performance of "extra" effects. King Cole (adding several Oxfordian syllables to
every song word on a raydeehoh) and Lena Horne (great at implying sex with
throat chords and gums) gave the cool revolution impetus. Thanks to these and
such early TV "actors" as Billy Williams, there is a fine web of hokum in TV

music that disappears only under the onslaught of a giant (Ella Fitzgerald), or a newcomer with a flair for invention (Ruth Olay, the new George Burns).

TV addicts have to find their kicks in the grace notes that evolve from building a "personality act." For instance, Diahann Carrol (on Jack Paar's show) does a snide, lattice-y dramatization with nostrils and eyes that makes the average face seem a wasted organ. On the Timex jazz show, Dizzy Gillespie's great power and authority somehow disappeared as the documentary cameraman examined his phenomenal cheek expansion, and the curious bend in the horn of his trumpet. Probably the funniest grace note occurred on a recent Bell Telephone broadcast, with Woody Herman reaching an impossibly corny stance, while working on the inspirational symbol "Saints Go Marching In."

Television could use some of the innocence that pervaded vaudeville in the days of big-band swing. The joy of catching Louis Prima, Lionel Hampton or Ella Fitzgerald came partly from the rampant giving that poured into each performance, partly from the fact that the audience, having grown up in the neighborhood of popular music, was considered tough and knowledgeable. This fever of jamboree and hard work that made the Paramount an all-hours delight is a long mile from Fred Astaire pointing his professionalese finger at Jonah Jones' tight, mechanical trumpeting saying something idolatrous like "That's it, boy. I mean, that's it."

February 23, 1959

Three Art-y Films

THANKS to a climate rife with tax loopholes, crumbling censorship codes and a wandering sickness that drives film citizenry from island to island, each new film presents a melting-pot dilemma: The independent reigns, but individuality drains out of his mixed-nations productions. Except for bits of Robert Siodmak's dryly amusing portrait of an impervious mass killer, the following films are all products of the same drag, an élite intellectual whose ideas on fascism (*The Devil Strikes at Night*), religious experience (*He Who Must Die*) and psychiatry (*The Black Orchid*) came to a halt around the Spanish Civil War.

They are stamped with an aimless liberalism, as though the Oscar headhunter, having escaped the chauvinistic chains of home studios, finds himself gasping for breath under the weighty blanket of freedom. Each work is victimized by an attitude—the muddlebrow's mock-serious pride in creativity—

that places little tension on ex-studio slaves, allowing them to function far below the form shown in big studios, where commercialism and censorship often force a subterranean inventiveness.

Having made a black film (*Rififi*) of burglaring, bosom shots and acid-y dark tones, Jules Dassin now changes stride with a white one: pleasant to look at, with a delicate, if stale artistry, but, nevertheless, not much to think about. The plot of *He Who Must Die* (from a novel by Nikos Kazantzakis) has as many links as its author's name, but it is a good one about some Greek peasants, the cast of a Passion play, enacting their Biblical roles in a "real" event having to do with helping a refugee band or siding with a "fatbellied Pope."

Always corny in its broad conception of villains (a miser who's patterned after an anteater), this allegorical whatsis makes most of its effective strokes with heroic whiteness—two blondes (Melina Mercouri, Pierre Vaneck) whose goodness is evolved with a taut, worn athleticism; a sun-blasted landscape caught handsomely in shadowless photography. However, by the time the movie completes its whitewash, making the lowly villagers seem like beeau-teeful stones and high-and-mighty "capitalists" like disagreeable custard, a lot of untidy laundry has been sagging an interesting story line.

At their deepest level, all of Jules Dassin's films are involved with brotherly love, and everything else is a be-kind-to-laborers spray that covers the film's windshield, giving a fake impression of "ideas." When his films hit a provoca-tive moment, two men (father and son or old political cronies or Young Turks) are as close as two front teeth, finding communion in such strong pulls of Depression-era fiction as "militant goodness," "one world," "down with money-grubbers." Producing soggy spots through his pictures, Dassin's buddy-buddy obsession is interesting in that the plot, messy and over-threaded, is only sub-ordinately involved with The Duet, which, appearing as erratically as it disap-pears, knocks the story construction completely out of shape.

Via his two bullseyes in art theaters, Dassin has become a leader in the creamless movie and coffee circuit, a cloaked figure whose mixture makes films that are easy to dislike and hard to categorize. Filled with animalistic touches, too black or white manliness, events that start well but end up in Marxian ruts, Dassin's films recall early Steinbeck novels, except for one dif-ference that makes them more interesting.

Where Steinbeck is a free and obvious plotter, Dassin, after years at the bottom of Hollywood's barrel, is a lightningly facile technician. Like a pirate in his scavenging of classics and in his swashbuckling manner of evolving sen-suous imagery, Dassin sinks his directing fangs into pink-liberal hoke and makes it far more puzzling and sinister than any of Steinbeck's undubious battling. Much of his imagery casts a tang of propaganda, but it has a devilish under-effect produced with what seem like decorative nothings: inserting countrified ambulation (the eccentric path of action) in everything from a scar to a peasant's stutter, and working soft lecherous exercises with skin-hair-clothes textures.

In *The Devil Strikes at Night*, Robert Siodmak (*The Killers*) is working at second speed on an unglossed Vuillard-plain image of a women-strangler whose fifty or more murders cast a dreadful spot on the inferiority of Aryan police. Most of Siodmak's comment on Hitler's *Reich* is a dated recall of Hitchcock-Reed thrillers, plus an even sadder use of West German "politics" (as in *The Young Lions*, *The Enemy Below*, which shows the *Reichland* overrun with anti-Nazis and infected with a murderous disaffection for war. However, it is almost worth the admission price to follow the portrait of a hummingly normal looney, which starts on the infantile "science" level of *M* and becomes a more interesting picture of violence, played suicidally as far into gentleness as credibility allows.

Using a wonderful roughened stone (Mario Adorf) as the shambling killer and shifting between a curious lack of technique and gymnastic inventiveness out of the old experimental film kettle, this ghoulish portrait accomplishes a feat that is rare in current mixed-goodies film. Where Dassin's international potpourri has a helpless discomfort about its Potemkin mimicry, as though he were trying to change a diaper in midstream, Siodmak's best moments, flexibly relaxed or tight, seem comfortably inventive. In the movie's peak scene, the village idiot (always on the hunt for food, always eating) wanders into a pick-up meal with a spinsterish Jewess, and the movie settles down, as though forever, as idiocy meets hopeless loneliness in a drifting conversation played as silently as any Vuillard painting of inverted domesticity.

The Black Orchid, filled with dark intensity and the dullness only Sophia Loren can generate when she sinks her nose into a solid acting part, shows a sullen Italian-American widow doing very little but somehow driving people into states verging on madness. After gloomy gus-undheit's husband is in a gangster's grave, the low-budget gem starts table hopping, from card table to breakfast table, skipping the most visually promising scenes (husband's murder by brother rats, boy caught tampering with parking meter).

Sailing wham into a bocce-balled-up production by the Girosi-Ponti team, the movie presents a mismatched crew of non-conformist actors given complete freedom to exploit their flair for neuroses. Only Anthony Quinn, a cheerful widower whose grown daughter locks herself in bedrooms like Dickson Carr victims, rides through this production, handling his one note (burp-gun masculinity) with style and bravado. Almost rubbing his hands off to energize table-bound scenes, Quinn has many exciting scenes between grins, such as ruminating over a widow's delights while going through a neatly timed job of tie-shirt-coat sprucing.

Director Martin Ritt, who engineers the nice positive in-the-scene vitality while showing a curious disregard for the niceties of composition, uses sex energy everywhere, moving freely or against itself, even in underdone material involving the ordering of a sundae. Ritt here orgone-izes his minority couplets so that they seem to be in supercommunication with each other; his Reichian direction forcing actors into impossible situations—Mark Richmond assaying a premarital smile of contentment with pork sausage filling his mouth.

Ritt's good movies (*No Down Payment*) deal with smart cynicism circa 1962, handled by intellectual zipguns (Tony Randall). When Ritt brings his bruising, unstylish close-two technique to bear on working class goodness (*Edge of the City*), the film's grimacing goes from bathos to worse.

March 9, 1959

Home Screen Jabberwocky

W<small>HILE</small> TV's community of talkers has succeeded (to a point where one New York channel is solid jabberwocky), the semi-snobbism that caused quick success may lead to quicker demise. Rugged individualists are a rare sight on flip talking shows which have cashed in on the public's current hunger for *haute culture*, an appetite that settles for anything—non-stop flattery, inside comments, half-baked opinions—suggesting a trash collector in the lively arts. Occasionally, Bob Hope, a refreshingly private talker (free of caste) who shuns artiness like the plague, appears on talk marathons taking a back seat, talking perceptively of the Los Angeles Rams, casting a vaguely critical eye at the presumptuous artiness of TV's ad-lib stars.

Unless television opens its corral to other types and brows beside the semi-intellectual hotshot who wings through pretentious inside topics on a prayer and a flypaper memory of a hundred cocktail parties, the smoking mouth of midnight may end in TV's Boot Hill, buried beside Jerry Lester and under tombstone punchlines created by Jack Paar: "Here lies a real chomp, a delightful warm sound, one of the most fascinating, attractive, unusual voices in entertainment history."

"Are you the devastatingly beautiful Lena Horne?" is an average bouquet from TV's electric talkers (Arlene Francis on "What's My Line"), who operate an interpersonal machine of flattery, the big compliment that is supposed to stop all debate and bounce back in the first return sentence. Jackie Gleason's straining delight in Gleason (Arthur Godfrey's show) is easy to understand and dislike, but most of TV's conversation deals in Kiwanis palsmanship and cheery-cheery-being that should, but never does, drive the audience to the Late Show or to bed.

The following programs, notorious entries in TV's talkalong, are built to a surprising extent around an immodestly modest device, in which a big wheel, being gracious, spreads compliments over a neighbor, whose humorless acceptance of same is now a trademark of "Open End," several hundred Paar shows and countless Mike Wallace interviews in deep smoke.

"Open End" is a successful New York tedium with interesting moments and angles, involving at times actors, authors, statesmen, directors, in a two-hour group discussion that adds up to propaganda for the Liberal blab ticket. Run by an interesting elegant, David Susskind, a Renaissance charmer with an unctuous tightness, Susskind's casts discuss such rum topics as "live vs. kine," "to Beat or not to Beat," or "the female, should she baby-sit or walk alone." Familiar answers come encased in tons of complacency and the deeply serious sincerity that points a thoughtful, crucial finger and then repeats a familiarism that has been bouncing around since the first commercial.

The Henry Morgan Show, attempting to combat the agreeableness of Paarlor talk, putters nowhere, thanks to Morgan's hilariously unfunny mixture of hovering waiter and the buffoon sage out of stale avant-gardism. With no curiosity and a grandiloquent assumption of wit that always seems tongue-tied, Morgan's interviewing (now fearfully taped) leads to ping-pong, in which the guest —Dali (incoherent), Shelley Berman (victimized), Martin Gabel (scornful)— barely dents tensely brittle chatter with his name, occupation, serial number. While Morgan is capable of a funny malevolence when taken by surprise, radio's brash rubber-voice is still trying to equal his first stunning victories, through preciosity, high boorishness, anti-ing the highbrow by exaggerating the lowbrow, and a masterful grasp of old *PM* editorials.

As it did on radio's disc-course jockey shows, spontaneous jabber scored in early Mike Wallace interviewing by offering an item that drugs the current population: middlebrow art talking about itself—showboat, opinions and, particularly, chat-chat-chat about the artist's newly-won hedonistic life. Occasionally, the conversation ventured into less predictable areas: William Carlos Williams waging a battle for his anti-Semitic theories. But, generally, the talking was remarkable for its belief that the TV audience was fascinated in following the intramural activities of art-showbiz people as they moved from sports cars to the cover of *Life* to expenses-paid vacations on some distant Hilton shore. Goaded by Wallace's fluid questioning middle people appeared to be flying, showing up in all their motley glory. Whether a creased brow or an itinerant actor unseating himself with Brando's mannerisms, TV's hot talker was a joy to behold, always in the market place, but, somehow, acting the pure artist in all of his impersonations as oddball bohemian, conversation-wrecker (Jack Kerouac) or repugnant Mahatma (Norman Mailer).

Reincarnated on a local New York channel, Wallace's show has lost its smoky backroom spell, though its winning numbers are still in evidence: life-in-raw pore-studying photography, garrulity, breezy fare, cigarette smoke patterns. Supplied with bountiful but vulgar researching, and addicted to spraygun editing that blends half-digested psychiatry, "blue" mongering and a likable thirst for "color," Wallace is still a chameleon with a remarkable fluidity, but no longer absorbing.

TV has uncovered talkers by the carload (and one uncut gem, May Craig), but a good listener who can encourage conversation is pretty hard to find. Except for Paar and Susskind, the listening is phony (Godfrey), half-involved (Wallace), or nervously inattentive (Morgan). An inability to listen killed Ben Hecht's nightly spiel, despite the fact that his jaded interviewing was garnished with the most suspensefully unbalanced sentences on TV. Until recently, the most expensive chit-chat has been engineered by a tin ear interviewing the at-home celebrity: Answers fell through Ed Murrow's disinterest like coins in a gum machine.

Though the Jack Paar Show is finally treadmilling itself to death, Paar has made ad-lib conversation a hot TV commodity by bringing pretentious spontaneity into channeled conversation, preserving a plain get-together surface with a firm Madison Avenue grip. Despite a charming personality (far-right in politics, suburban square in art, a poor sport in human relations), the Paarlerist "built" an interesting sound: happy applause and buoyantly agreeable talk, that suggested a party in wild flight.

Except for an original such as Dino Panzini (syncopated country-club charm, post-war Italian style), Paar's regulars are deadly familiar semi-intellectuals who bloom under Paar's clever, if low, curiosity. With its anonymous manner and shrewd spurring, Paar's listening adds interest to acts that would otherwise fall flat from hack vaudeville (Charley Weaver), too much ego (Peggy Cass) or too little talent (Genevieve). Paar runs the only entertaining talkfest: his Club doesn't ask much or give much, but a bit of entertainment is not to be disdained, considering.

March 23, 1959

Underground Magic, Eccentric Vitality and Artful Direction Salvage Banal Stories

Since every film is the product of an agglomeration of technicians who are situated in different spots of the universe in relation to art, business and talent, the *real* fascination of a movie isn't the sum total of esthetic effects, but the underground channels created by each artist pursuing his path. When considered only as whole works somewhere between dud and masterpiece, the following films not only shrink in interest but are too easily pigeon-holed:

Rio Bravo is a big version of *High Noon* (four law defenders cornered inside a cowardly town by a brother team that has untold hired guns to sacrifice in a harvest of in-town violence), a pleasant disappointment with bits of graceful, semi-humorous American dead-panning as only Howard Hawks can spread on a screen.

Lonelyhearts turns a revered novel of pessimism into a semi-optimistic newspaper story, confused in casting, rigid in story-telling, but mildly gripping because of its TV-style intimacy and drive.

Forbidden Fruit details the short and unhappy infidelity of a Milquetoast doctor, a perfect "French film," but, except for some talented James Cain-type pornography and honest comments on listless afternoon bar life, only moderately interesting.

The Eighth Day of the Week (filmed in the bombed-out slums of Warsaw) and *The Sound and the Fury* are opposite sides of the same film coin: banal stories of decadence inside crumbling architecture, supposedly starring sexually frustrated youth, but actually highlighted by elaborate (*Sound*) or dirt-cheap (*Eighth Day*) production jobs.

Fortunately, each movie has an iceberg's hidden resources—the continuity of interest represented by each technician's following or veering from a battle-scarred path that has been "long abuilding" and seems more crucial than the generalization of any single picture. Often a movie's mistakes are inconsequential beside the seemingly picayune contributions of a bit player (Jackie Coogan in *Lonelyhearts*, a colored teenager in *Sound and Fury*) scoring his usual victory in modern bitterness.

An exquisite pleasure in movie-going is to watch a long-time debit (George Simenon, Dore Schary), whose hand has been like a mechanical claw on films, suddenly appear in work that is technically unpredictable, almost human. Perhaps the most satisfying of underground pleasures is to see the fantastic technician (Walter Brennan in *Rio Bravo*) building with suicidal force within a stale, corrupt, losing proposition. Finally, there is the familiar figure from another medium, turning to films with expected results: Mike Kellin, a fine actor in TV pot-boilers, projects a convincing low-brow garrulity in *Lonelyhearts*, a film that is otherwise plagued by talent over-riding roles that should be buried almost from sight in plebian mediocrity.

Rio Bravo is a soft, slack, not very rousing Western by a man (Howard Hawks) who knows better, having supervised a nearly endless chain of masterful journey films. Many things have slowed Hawks' skill besides an inability with color (*Rio Bravo* is photographed through a piece of seaweed) and an aging lead athlete (John Wayne) who still moves well in fast action but in standing around, like latter-day Henry Fonda and Clark Gable, seems nailed together.

Most importantly, Hawks and Jules Furthman (a fine, unnoticed scriptwriter) unsuccessfully excluded the motorcycle-corvette-cattledrive gimmick that makes Hawks' films "go" (while Hawks and his whimsically tough scriptwriters are fooling around, improvising in soft-shoe far beyond the borders of the actual plot). Where Hawks' best films (*Big Sleep*) are surrealistic caravans that never pass the same street corner twice, *Rio Bravo* is mostly ambushed in a jail where a sheriff, a drunk and a cripple are holding a prisoner against a gang of miserably unconvincing hoods.

From the moment that the town derelict (Dean Martin) tries to fish a half-dollar out of the saloon's cuspidor, the movie's emphasis is less on pumping lead into the audience than on exploiting Hawks' movie birthright—the building of abstract ploys based on a high-toned, Social Register notion of grace, decorum, even wholesomeness. Occasionally, in Martin's shuffling, easy movements, so fluid as to be imperceptible, the movie catches Hawks' nonchalant tone with actors. But most of *Rio Bravo* is recall, a sign of decline that still reveals Hawks' genius with placement, his ability to build a symphony based on diversions having to do with the landscaping of action.

Unlike any other experience to be gained in films, *Rio Bravo* leaves the spectator with a touching memory, consisting entirely of plastic effects produced with choreographed action, the route from stable to bar taken by a fleeing criminal (done mostly with words), the path taken by a rifle as it whips diagonally across a face, and countless other "maps" of humanity—of hands, reclining body in relation to stairway, doors to other doors—that produce a curiously poignant effect in a film that is supposedly without message or mind. The wonder of Hawks' underhand style is in scenes that have a silent, ticking explosiveness, where his tricky figure deployment and slightly off-center characterization steer the film out of what seems like $3 million of cliché Westernism.

Lonelyhearts has the same eccentric interest and awfulness of *Some Came Running*, but it still packs more vitality than anything Schary conceived as MGM's production boss. Schary's big studio creations (*The Next Voice You Hear, Battleground*) were regulated for the family trade and filled with cheap soap opera about the civic health of American guys named Joe, mechanical constructions that were the furthest remove from *Lonelyhearts*, which, if nothing else, is human: a collection of pretentious actors who seem unleashed, a weird script in which the normal out-hallucinate the crack-pots, TV-style direction that ends many scenes on a face staring straight ahead, waiting for the camera image to change.

In the story, Montgomery Clift shoulder-shudders through a role that is nipped by everything but bloodhounds: as a fledgling lovelorn columnist, Clift is driven nearly crazy by the misery that writes for advice, is lectured by editor Robert Ryan (archly overjoyed monosyllabic overacting), mothered by Ryan's wife Myrna Loy (mummified and breathy) and, finally, in the movie's best stretch, is seduced by a stranger with a wildly mean tongue (Maureen Stapleton). Despite the facile tone of Stapleton's acting, this series of scenes in hotel and taxicab have the zig-zag authenticity of hot tabloid stuff, where the people change face with an unpredictability that leaves the reader gasping. The ending is the most electric example of movie magic: the finest cab scene since *Waterfront*, thanks to Stapleton's acting and a rare reading of taxicab culture, particularly its cockeyed composition of figures.

After his cheerful American chauvinisms for MGM, it figures that Schary's first determined attempt at an ugly subject and somber feeling is confused by his old MGM sickness. For no discernible reason, *Lonelyhearts* counters the ugliness of newspapers and their clientele with "healthy" scenes—the family huddled around a TV set is supposed to carry itself as propaganda without the slightest injection of magic.

Not even Nathanael West, an expert in making emptiness surrealistically horrible, can equal Schary's horror when he is showing the fine constructive life: Pa mowing the front lawn, Buster flipping a football and Sis, a soaped-up version of D. W. Griffith's sweet unguided Missylles, dating Clift in the family limousine. When Schary contacts something familial, even a father who's resting in the pen for murdering mother, the screen goes rigidly antiseptic, like a toothpaste commercial censored by the State Department before being sent to a crisis spot in the cold war.

Apart from the central palace of its story, Jerry Wald's *The Sound and the Fury* is a voluptuous de Mille-cunning production filled with "extras." Not even George Stevens (*A Place in the Sun*), nor Joshua Logan (*Picnic*), nor Elia

Kazan (*East of Eden*) has been able to enclose a contemporaneous scene so completely, producing a Within Naturalism that is massively silent and contained, like a good Edward Hopper painting, and that offers shrewdly observed material to satisfy any town-o-phile.

The straw hats in a cavernous general store, a hungry theater wall across the village square, the worn-out patterns on carnival grounds, particularly the touching material that is parlayed from open fields, a battered station wagon— this bric-a-brac of American desolation is caught in good phlegm-green harmonies, the best use of large-screen composing that has been seen in Vista Vision; and, in this day of corruptly directed crowds, this film has inordinately skilled direction of nobodies languoring or shuffling off to nowhere.

In many ways, *Sound* is a bad joke: Its main story drags; its central players are frighteningly bad mannerists, each with a "special" walk and a wide assortment of shakes, toupees and mumbles; the main ideas are cornier than the stains that fog the doors and walls of the old plantation house. However, everything outside the story (which isn't Faulkner's as advertised, but actually Tennessee Williams' castration nonsense wrapped in a slick-magazine guise) is sharply etched and fairly gripping for an opulent movie.

April 20, 1959

Big-Studio 'Supers'—Monumental Art Baked in a Pittsburgh Blast Furnace

THE last month has turned into a victory parade for distinguished tonnage, a new type of big-studio "Super" that seems conceived at the top of Wall Street by an art board recruited from *Time*, *The New Yorker* and *Partisan Review*, and then baked in a Pittsburgh blast furnace so as to outlast the Easter Island sculptures as monumental art. Hard to pin down by the old critical processes, these new blockbusters are more than massive esthetic complications. With their high-powered craftsmanship, curious efficiency as art and a Genius-bug that insists on making the "listing of credits" more costly than an old-time "B" film, these films demand a far-out criticism that is more like bead-reading than esthetic evaluation. *The Diary of Anne Frank*, *Compulsion* and *The Five Pennies* are throwbacks to early silent film-makers whose idea of a great movie—even in the case of a Chaplin feature—suggested a hulking, solemnly evolved Gothic building rather than a mere "flick."

However, unlike the big-studio films of yesteryear, which were supervised by romantic dreadnaughts (D. W. Griffith) or Dreiser-type realists (Erich von Stroheim), these new blockbusters are usually steered by a surprisingly hip craftsman. *Compulsion* lists a directing unknown (Richard Fleischer), who, in comparison to a George Stevens or John Huston, is an ingenious fireball in composing the huge horizontal screen. Fleischer's miniaturist technique often floods a tapestry-like richness across the Cinemascope surface; at other times, in an intimate change-of-pace, his actors practically walk out of the powerful semi-slick chiaroscuro image.

Room at the Top, an admirable (if not likable) study of a rake's progress in small-town society, owes its solid, engrossing effect to a director (Jack Clayton) making his first feature film—and it is interesting how well Clayton uses an Old Master (Carol Reed) when he needs a morosely bitter "bourgeois" effect to bring his film down to cinematic earth. Each of the above films presents a garrulous youngster (Dean Stockwell, Laurence Harvey) brilliantly involved in an unrelentingly difficult role. Even the vapid "girl-next-door" role is played with neurotic-toned ambitious cunning: Both *Compulsion* and *Room* are helped by ingénues (Diane Varsi, Heather Sears) who, compared to the former habitués of young-love roles, project a disturbingly skillful innocuity.

Compulsion is a smart, terse study of a notorious team of kid killers, but, in choosing to charm its audience in every particular (the various wallpapers in Leopold's palatial home rank with the sensuous stuff Matisse painted), the producer (Darryl Zanuck's son) has forfeited every awkward individuality of a dreadful, amateurish crime. The most idiosyncratic things may be the "beauty" of lighting in interior scenes or the irritating high camp style of Bradford Dillman's Loeb performance.

However, the movie's star is Richard Murphy, a master of compression, whose screenplays, somewhat like Katherine Hepburn, have a beautifully hinged, lean look, plus a chronic Quakerish decency that forbids any kind of violence or vulgarity. A typical Murphy maneuver presents most of the Bobby Franks murder by indirection: In a country undertaker's parlor, where, as the camera works in a tight "map" around the shrouded corpse of a 14-year-old schoolboy, finally arriving at a reporter's nauseated expression as he kneels to pick up "a pair of hornrimmed glasses," the spectator learns "by intelligence" about the murderer's strategy and cruelty but hardly anything about the actual homely event. Murphy's scenes always play with a unique educational vigor (objects, economy, give-and-go action, an undertaker's flat, business-as-usual voice) but his architectonic story-telling euphemistically masks an inability to handle dirt, cruelty, sensationalism.

After 105 minutes of Murphy's socio-psychiatric hop-scotch, in scenes that are deeply personal yet social as all outdoors, the "crime of the century" ends up without any feeling of crime (a boy's head beaten with a chisel), loneliness (an open bit of prairie with a body half-wedged into a culvert's mouth), sickness (Leopold's droopingly sad goggle eyes) or punishment. Murphy is finally forced into a messy gimmick: adding an arbitrary scene of cruelty during the listing of credits so as to stamp his script and its thrill-killers with violence.

Despite some trying items such as Dillman's pronunciation of "Mumsie" and endless patronizing of Clarence Darrow's famous "summation" (honestly cornballed by Orson Welles), *Compulsion* has surprising power, the feeling of a new intellectualism being poured into the handsomely mounted "liberal" juggernauts Sam Goldwyn once produced. Most of its whiplash intensity is produced by Dean Stockwell, playing the Leopold role with a style—brusque stylishness, unpredictable bitchiness, sanded-down clarity—that recalls Robert Walker's last triumphs. Unlike Orson Welles or E. G. Marshall, who turn in static "voice" performances as opposing lawyers, Stockwell is always a mobile Full Figure, whose intelligence, inward bound rather than (as in Dillman's method-styled, happy-joe acting) following in all directions, makes every scene play three-dimensional, with a neurotically sad honesty.

As happened throughout most of *Double Indemnity* and those parts of *Sunset Boulevard* which carried a corrupt scriptwriter away from his cracked, aged legacy, Billy Wilder's cold *Some Like It Hot* is successful only where there is no official middlebrow viewpoint—usually when Wilder is working with the trashy realism that makes the worst pocketbooks tick. His slapstick comedy picks up warmth and dramatic interest when its jazz pair try for a job in the cutthroat atmosphere of a booking office, and later in a Pullman washroom, where Marilyn Monroe (employing a poor-folks schlump she seldom allows herself) describes the life and times of a mediocre torch singer.

As the two musicians (Tony Curtis, Jack Lemmon) don female costumes (evidently using Maggie of the "Bringing Up Father" comic strip as a model) and head for Florida, the movie flattens out into a stiff vulgarization of Hollywood fame and fortune—stretching from the cabin-jamming scene in a Marx Brothers movie to Preston Sturges-type millionaires and the mirthless face-stretching of Joe E. Brown.

While the female impersonations have a meager, cartoon-y interest (particularly Curtis' spinster, whose mouth and nasal voice seem spiked by lemon juice), the Lemmon-Curtis musicianship is terrible and the odd characters met in Florida are worse. For instance, Lemmon's drunken antic with Latin music is a mercilessly repeated irritation, but, as a movie toothache, it is often surpassed by Wilder's tasteless parodies on famous movie gangsters. To flesh out these impoverished conceptions (mostly gimmicks: coin-flipping, hearing aid, spats) Wilder brings back some revered hobgoblins from Chicago films (Pat O'Brien, Mike Mazurki, George Raft, George E. Stone, plus familiar plug-ugly bit players)—but, unlike Sturges' loving reincarnation of old acting shoes, Wilder murders his repertory group.

Some Like It Hot is a real weirdie: Wilder gets no laughs at all out of his siz-zling, fast wedding of female impersonation to 1929 thrills, but, from a non-entertainment angle, his movie has a not-quite-real surface that is worth examining. Wilder's surface (hard, tense, straightforward, like those in Stuart Davis' equally jazzy abstract paintings) is as hard to shrug off as it is to enjoy. Endless leg shots that seem cut with a razor, transitions that move on a fast Mack Sennett line *via* bicycle-motorboat-wheelchair, lewd dialogue in which the key vulgarities are spiked to the spectator's attention, a Model-T flivver flipped around by a gangster's careening car—all these skins of objectivity have a brazen electricity, a staccato truth and sharpness that is one of the unlikable achievements in Hollywood motion pictures.

Unfortunately, this frenetic surface is allied, as in all of Wilder's cold showers, with a tragic obeisance to the crowd's opinion. Most of Wilder's impressions of the '20s are up-dated to sit well with the middle audience, and, worse, his use of Marilyn Monroe shows a decided fear of mobilizing her new pudginess. As the dumb blonde center of Wilder's film, Miss Monroe is stiffly posed, long-shot, blacked out, all but rubbed out, to uphold the popular con-ception of a movie doll's dimensions.

In contrast to the over-cautious cunning that inches a spotlight up and down Miss Monroe's bosom during a night club act, *Room at the Top* is a British blizzard of improvisation, in which Horatio Alger's rags-to-riches story of an aggressive social climber is played backwards with chic bitterness. From the opening on a handsome young clerk (Harvey) fondling his one elegance, a pair of shoes, to the closing shot of his honeymoon car traveling the same wistful avenue that finished *The Third Man*, *Room* has a tricked-up impressiveness that holds the spectator's mind long after the movie's windup.

Actually, the movie is closer to *The Best Years of Our Lives* than to upside-down Alger, an ironic, more literary British cousin to Goldwyn's slightly sour sweetness and light. In the film, the ex-flyer from a factory slum has his mar-ried woman, tangles with small town mores, wins the daughter of the town's richest man—but loses all along the line. Despite the basic shallowness of the plot, there are endless consolations in dialogue (wonderfully natural, foul-mouthed, etc.), acting (Signoret's performance of an unhappy married woman on her last affair) and directorial magic (particularly in off-moments when the story is in the streets, or fastened on clerk friends of the infamous hero).

Watching this slow, interesting film in which endless, corny literary dodges (the jilted woman driving to her death, her mean-spirited lover drowning his guilt in a bar-room floozie) are saved by a felicitous "shot-in-the-dark," the spectator has to cast a tear for the solemnity that makes so much of Hollywood's recent masterpieces seem "canned." Even a schmaltzy jazz delight like Danny Kaye's hot cornet film, *The Five Pennies*, has a solidity and thoroughness that belongs in an Encyclopedia Britannica discussion of post-Dixieland music.

May 18, 1959

Getting Inside 'Inside Humor'

THOUGH "Sergeant Bilko," "The Honeymooners" and the first Ernie Kovacs vaudeville showed traits (lonely, abrasive, lower-than-lowbrow, morose, not too energetic) that predicted a comedy of desolation, TV's most recent comedians have done an about-face. An Elegant Ego has taken over: In a medium that discourages physical comedy and robs experienced clowns (Jackie Gleason, Red Skelton) of fantasy and finesse, turning them into realistic rogues-gallery personalities, the newest stars consider tasteless any movement more earthy than Shelley Berman's dainty crossing of legs while reaching for a make-believe telephone, Mort Sahl's waving of a rolled-up newspaper, or Jack Benny's princely, slow double-take.

The greatest assist to the new Ego is an ugly invention, Inside Humor, which allows the comedian to buddy-buddy his humor without actually committing himself in action or idea: *i.e.*, chuckling at hidden jokes, playing snob-balls with names like "Needleman," aiming words ("cool it, cool it") and ideas at a mysterious group of superior characters who claque on cue.

While the professional funnyman still reaps the highest price and best TV time, the news in humor is being made by the satirical monologist, whose home is the chi-chi nightclub and whose goal is a place somewhere in the suburbs of High Art.

In its most likable form (the Canadian low-think team of John Wayne and Frank Schuster doing a faintly Jewish, contemporary blabbering of Great Works like "The Scarlet Pumpernickel"), egghead comedy is a revolt which starts by insulting audience intelligence with a contrived gag, and then, through semi-skilled pantomime (Skelton, Lou Costello) builds a hectic atmosphere that could be called laughably energetic, if not funny. At its worst, the cerebral, cruel or freethinking talker, in trying for trenchant comment on the current scene, uses words, tastes, dialects and subjects that have long been the ego-supports of Bohemian intellectuals and are now the property of bank-safe middlebrows.

As self-admitted as a guy who thumbs his nose at the tide, the make-them-think monologist is actually the most ferocious belonger and sect-worshiper in a business engulfed by mystic brotherhood stuff. Lenny Bruce, whose Beat Generation specialties are wrathful anti-bourgeois humor and self-devotion ("I find most of my satires on 42nd Street"), devotes part of his routines simply to listing passwords in upper Bop: "Nat Hentoff, Ralph Gleason, Jules Feiffer, Herb Caen, Miles Davis" (and manages at the same time to apple-polish the pop-art critics). When Mort Sahl's raspy voice is in normal jet repulsion, the audience is inundated by generalized hates, loves, gambits that add up to stale anti-American swing.

The most celebrated of Serious-Blooming wits, Sahl has an interesting delivery, a rapid outpouring in which words are used for abundance, beat and ripple. The most curious gimmick (plagiarized by Lenny Bruce) is Sahl's fake laugh, which sounds like genial surprise but is used as a fraternity button, to show that Sahl is inside the Group with a cynical word ("Right, it's wild"), opinion ("The Man Upstairs, Henry Luce") or topic ("We have Utopia with Byrd, Eastland, Faubus, all the Southern senators who want to hang the world").

Despite a talent for swinging doggerel and brashness that probably developed in college bull-sessions, Sahl is only a slight improvement on Will Rogers' safe political iconoclasm. Sahl's flooding speech does occasionally turn up an insight, usually about night people—his picture of a restless figure who wanders out at 4 A.M. just "to see if Kantor's Delicatessen is open," and then the real confusion of Western Man: "Do I want a hamburger or fried eggs?"

The most engaging egghead comedian is Shelley Berman, an essayist usually found with imaginary telephone in hand, working with intimidation (an airplane passenger), badgering (delicatessen owner deflating his son's acting ambitions), and small annoyance (the pornographic look of an emptied glass of buttermilk). Berman combines a number of unlikely comic talents: a writer's knack for small-word humor ("I'm fine thenk you and how are you . . . fine, fine, thenk you very much"), an acting flair that indicates training in The Method and keeps the spectator glued to outrageously dramatic tricks of timing and correct tone, and a conceited-needling voice that creates a suspenseful mood that almost strangles the audience.

Berman's essays, which play like Mozart with infinite control of rests, elongations, and tiny pointed notes, have brought TV audiences some enormously beguiling relationships, particularly a frustration-on-the-telephone skit involving a man badgering a Dennis-the-Menace child to call his mom to the phone ("If you put the telephone down, lightning will strike you, I'm God"). Though Berman is a persuasive, interesting, elegant raconteur in Jewish-toned anguish humor, he stays too far within average sensibility to escape sentimentality, backslapping, preciosity.

Despite a few stunning moments on TV spectaculars, the Mike Nichols–Elaine May team is often undone by a cheerless, frightened presence and a shallow dialect that backfires, suggesting Nichols-May are themselves as untough and pretentious as their victims in look-Ma-no-rehearsals conversation ("maybe you could be a boss and his secretary in a cocktail lounge"). While poking about populating their spontaneously created scenes with plagueable types such as the jazz-accompanied Beat poet ("You did it, you son of a gun . . .") or the Trevor Howard dentist in an English movie abscess ("When you looked in my mouth and said it's rotten . . ."), their humor soon sags in midstream of consciousness and Nichols-May become the two sad bunnies tracking through the darkest interior of David Reisman's lonely crowd.

Their real talent, however, is in the delicate craftsmanship of fantastically light voices that seem spooked by inhibitions, a trick of building each dialogue to a pin-point of passion ("Oh Riba, Oh Riba, when you looked at me as if I were me . . .") and a suspenseful comic format (faucet-drip dialogue of clichés in which the comedy never shows its face).

In its early period, TV hit roads which few in pop-comedy thought to travel: impressions of empty treadmill existence done with unbeguiling humor, created by an immobile, charm-robbing medium, and hack writers such as Nat Hiken ("Bilko"), who can anchor a story in the center of commonplace life without making philosophic promises. For the first time, the large audience saw a murderously dry infantry life ("Bilko"), a morbid, bickering slum series ("Honeymooners"), and a driveling Mr. and Mrs. ("I Love Lucy"), all of which were funnier in their depiction of the mirthlessness of daily existence than for their expected comic embroidery.

Recently there has been another turn in the direction of desolate, anti-chic humor. Where an Inside comedian (Jack Paar) spends a lot of time simply in boasting, *savoir faire*, explaining his comedy, and cementing himself with the esoteric flock, his opposite is a modern version of Buster Keaton playing into social outcast comedy, bucking the current with a negative streak that balances his artistic sophistication. While the chain of Insiders has been growing rapidly from Tom Poston to "Guido Panzini" to genial smiler Dave King, it is surprising to find lonesome (unpopular?) humor turning up in a variety of forbidden shades.

Joey Bishop (calculated) and Jack Douglas (madly wooden) are two fair examples. Perhaps the most authentic examples reside on TV's outskirts— Howie Morris (in last summer's "Pantomime Quiz"), Morey Amsterdam (a long-time horror who somehow lights up the "Keep Talking" panel), or Kaye Ballard (on a recent "One Night Stand")—uncontrollable clowns who work within several levels of sophistication without the slightest pretense of belonging to the mysterious group of cohorts that succeed in alienating at least this reviewer.

June 22, 1959

Hollywood's Plot Against the Plot

SCRATCH any Hollywood film and you'll probably find a skyscraper of complicated craftsmanship mounted on a plot that seems to be used simply from theatrical habit.

(The last year in new TV drama could be separated into three types of afflicted fiction: stories in which a wry, arbitrary ending replaces the usual denouement—much of Playhouse 90; thrillers which are impossible to follow because an enormous amount of climactic occurrence has been crammed into endless, sluggish, unvaried dialogue scenes—"Perry Mason," "77 Sunset Strip"; message plays in which the big anti-something notion is sprung from a wild string of corny, pulpish incidents—any of the "award-winning" dramas of Rod Serling.)

Recent works of elder-statesman movie directors show that even they have changed to an anti-plot kick, placing their blue chips on secondary aspects of production, such as the beautiful silhouette made by an Army brigade riding across the Cinemascope horizon.

Alongside the old granite constructions that appear on TV's "Late Show" under John Ford's name, *The Horse Soldiers* is the disaster of the month, an uneventful canter in which Ford, without any plot to speak of, falls back on boyish Irish playfulness (played by a rigor-mortified John Wayne, an almost non-existent Bill Holden, and a new gnashing beauty named Connie Towers) to fill a several-million-dollar investment. The "comedy," which includes Wayne's troubles with a drunken top sergeant, a soldiering doctor and a captive Southern belle, is interspersed with Ford's stolidly evolved, beefy, Rosa Bonheur-ish "pictures." It all takes place on a plodding journey, which sends 1,700 Union cavalrymen into the Confederacy on what turns out to be an unsuccessful search for a screenplay.

In *The Nun's Story*, Fred Zinnemann, the strong story-weaver of *High Noon*, barely squirts a romantic woman's-magazine story between great slabs of educational footage, mostly of the prettily photographed regimen in a strict Belgium convent (brown-black-white harmonies, reminiscent of the more delectable Cubist paintings). When the plot turns up—corny scenes of a noble nursing nun (Audrey Hepburn) flunking an exam on orders, curing the Congo with a genius surgeon, working in the Belgium underground—Zinnemann reduces each heroism to kernel size and then resumes his tasteful but rather insipid documentation.

The anti-plot development is perhaps the final signpost in the decline of scenic-action story telling, the mode which started the movie madness and which, since the rise of the Orson Welles type of Lindy's-Toots Shor intellectual, has been a dying parody of its original silent-screen self.

As yet, no one of D. W. Griffith's stature has appeared with a substitute form. But there are always middlebrow rebels, usually from the neighborhood of the New School in Greenwich Village, with a technique that sneers at Hollywood practice, breaks records for grinding out hysterical boredom (*The Goddess*, *Paths of Glory*), and, unintentionally, looks like an antiquated version of the material which old silent directors left on the cutting-room floor.

The story of *Middle of the Night*—an elderly widower rejuvenating himself with a lost, neurotic tootsie—is exposed in the first shot, and the following two hours are an evasion consisting of Paddy Chayefsky's intense interest in dialogue-character-idea clichés. Only two scenes are allowed to be played out instead of small talking the spectator into a visit to the pop-corn machine. And both scenes—a Poconos weekend tryst and a panting-around-the-apartment seduction—are crippled by a characteristic Chayefsky ploy, such as the extended one-note misery of an amateur drinker having a hangover. Assisting Chayefsky in his scorn for Hollywood's old story-through-action technique, the director, Delbert Mann, does a clichéd grim realism with backgrounds, weather, faces. The two miscast leads, Fredric March and Kim Novak, are a sometimes effective but generally square approximation of garment district miserables.

That the plot has become a vestigial part of the screen practice is due at least partly to the fact that scenery and fast action are practically dead issues in the naturalistic film. There hasn't been a convincing fight on the screen since the 1940 heyday of masculine directors. As for scenery, *The Young Philadelphians* is like a *Ladies Home Journal* illustration. *The Five Pennies* uses a noisy, tourist-y, musical comedy substitute for native scenery, and *Pork Chop Hill* offers another generalized nothing, without any feeling of a particular war, period or state. Given a dodging attitude on sets and action, it is to be expected that each film (the best being *Five Pennies*) turns into a dull fantasy in which the plot whirls around in a vacuum, free, foolish and unattached to anything except a memory of slick-magazine fiction.

July 6, 1959

Compromise in a Closed Medium

ON a Sunday when TV normally turns cultural with a deep frown, New York stations recently offered 65 summer repeats and old films, plus a few live shows that ranged from uncreative radio technique ("What's My Line") to a confused, slowed-down version of Busby Berkeley production numbers in Depression-era musicals (the Chevy show). Even the day's best event—the U.S.–USSR track meet—was marred by a torrent of corn-flake commercials and a Movietone newsreel style that partially lost several events, including the best race (the 400-meter hurdles) and most exciting leap (a Greg Bell broad jump).

And given a day's program that was either dead or a compromise from its opening "highlight" (golf lessons in a fake country club set; Guido Panzini doing stale Henry Armetta humor on the sidelines), a TVer's mind naturally turns to the as yet closed medium, in which the most committed direction (John Frankenheimer) uses camera set-ups resembling those in Wyler-Huston films of the late 1930s.

Ruled by the snobbish, pin-stripe mind of Madison Avenue advertising, TV art has departed drastically from the script usually followed by pop-artists, who, in the case of movies, jazz and comic strips, started in vigorous, somewhat brainless experiment, and then descended onto a plateau of thinking man's art—most of it dry rot (like the monologues of Sicknik comedians). TV's prog-ress has been strictly horizontal, from the tastefully unkempt work of the first Sid Caesar hours to the tastefully chi-chi Andy Williams hour, which cranks along through DeMille-silly ballets, bamboo poles receding into silvery air, tons of gently blown fish net, and its star's insipidly relaxed but accurate singing. The tragedy is that TV, which has yet to pass through an honest exper-imental stage, offered its only example of deep style years ago in a James Agee film for "Omnibus."

What TV dispenses is a bastard form of movies, burlesque, and RKO vaudeville. Every effort is made to transform the basic commodity, make it more amiable, poetic, plastic than it actually is. A typical example is the Dave King half-hour, starring a British import in fairly funny skits about a cute, dev-ilish fellow being mangled by the routine of clinic, barber shop, department store. King is an interestingly square Hal Roach comic who glides and fidgets "comfortably" instead of punching jokes.

But Madison Avenue's practicality has seen fit to pour his low-keyed act into a Radio City Music Hall bonbon production. Surrounded by both cheese-cake and space-devouring dancers, King shudders his way through an ama-teurish version of Astaire's dancing and strained high-voice singing in the Perry Como manner. Even King's "showmanship"—brisk rubbing of hands, a glass smile—seem to be tics worked up to charm a basically homely medium.

A rare example of creative TV occurred recently on ABC, when a British rock-'n'-roll program was re-run to disturb American meditation. While the hybrid jazz was mostly dismal, the visual production had some of the jaggedly cut, bang-bang plasticity of first-rate primitive art. The British show revived cutting as a plastic effect, dared to depart from the vanilla lighting of Ameri-can TV, used dissolves, and managed to do without those slow, gliding approaches and exits that paralyze every song hour, particularly Dinah Shore's.

The real point of the rock-a-billy show is that it stayed well within the mor-bid confines of TV's set-up, turning the curse of its limitations (harsh lighting, cameras that hardly move but make a case history of every face, push-button direction, a studio space that is usually the size of a small hangar) into a stri-dent nightmarish work. Energy seems to pour from the TV screen when the production is stripped. While the telethons and Channel 13 talk shows are basi-cally escapes from the TV problem, they point up the fact that TV comes alive when it gets down to its skin.

However, there is always an attempt to hide somehow the cheerless, stricken facts of TV life. A summer reliable ("Pantomime Quiz") destroys itself by turning into unmodified Minsky burlesque. A reasonably quiet actress suddenly reverts to the wild, eyelid-flapping pantomime of prehistoric films (June Havoc in a "U.S. Steel" disaster).

Any year now, TV may realize that little help is needed from neighboring arts, and not too much brain power from interior decorators. Working well within the restrictions of the medium, TV could shake the now muscle-bound audience out of its easy chairs.

August 3–10, 1959

Wild 'Wild Strawberries'

Since Ingmar Bergman is now considered a Swedish assembly line of masterpieces, it may seem sacrilegious to bracket his eighteenth wonder, *Wild Strawberries*, with *Anatomy of a Murder* (a tempo-less 160 minutes, involving Otto Preminger competence and one fine lawyering performance by George C. Scott), *North by Northwest* (the first hour is fun, despite senility catching up with Cary Grant's charm technique), and *The Devil's Disciple* (a trivial, syncopated Western, sparked by some of Bernard Shaw's dialogue).

Each one of these films uses a precise, currently popular photography, in which details protrude with an icy, magic realist clarity that once ruined most surrealist painting. The fact that Bergman is always photographically in style doesn't quite destroy his new film, which numbers among its assets a fine feeling for highway travel and an appealingly muted performance of old age by Victor Sjöström.

Like most of Bergman's films, *Wild Strawberries* has a wild scenario built on the most indifferent event: a pleasant run through the countryside in an old, elegant boxlike car that resembles its owner, an eminent physician (Sjöström) traveling to a university where he is to receive an important degree. In transit, the unemotional doctor talks to his daughter-in-law about her marital bust-up, picks up a trio of happy kid hitchhikers, has a close shave with a passing Volkswagen, and stops at lunchtime to visit his ancient mother. Most importunately, too, he moves in and out of dreams and daydreams that suggest the old man is "dead though alive," and that his trip through life has been victimized by a cold heart.

In its less complicated moments, the film is one of the most natural car films on record, being kept free of both meatball melodrama (as happened in *The Hitchhiker* and *Wages of Fear*) and high-powered folksy humor (Gene Kelly's *The Happy Road*, plus several films with the word "night" in the title). Though the travelers do an immense amount of cute, coy metaphysical and psychiatric talking, the journey is kept fluid by a wonderfully succinct, evocative treatment of car items and roadside effects. One shot of the physician's chalky face against the darkly blotted car windows is almost worth the price of admission.

However, as the movie purrs along with a sure-handed grace, it becomes obvious that Bergman the Dream Merchant is often practicing stock riffs. Bergman shows the doctor caught in dreams that are a web of dated maneuvers from the scarier wing of museum art. In one dream that is fictionally rigged, as well as a *potpourri* of arty effects, the old man is seen attending his own funeral in an empty, shuttered street, where, among other rickety horrors, the doctor is almost dragged down into a casket by his own corpse.

The old man's dreams of childhood are even more mired in fantastic landscaping that should be a finger exercise for any competent Swedish director. "As believable and profound as any ever filmed," these tender reveries involve a small army of burstingly healthy blond kids having the giggles, pouts and tear jags around a landscape that Sweden's film colony foolishly stole from an Auguste bore named Renoir.

One of the tiresome academy tricks (Renoir used it to death) consists in making triplicates of the children, matching the kids to the same prettily insipid physical mould. The scenes sparkle and silver in leafy arbors, then move to a perfectly still lake shore, and finally, in one tremendous snooze, do the famous Renoir bit at a heavily populated luncheon table where everything is a smash of vivacity, provincial bounce and domestic perfection. They are conceived with little more than esthetic shoe polish, are no more profound than the circus-candy charm that Joe Pasternak once created for Deanna Durbin.

Despite its blast of eclectic charm, Bergman's film picks up excitement everywhere from a "demoniacally creative" style that hasn't been on the film scene since the silent era. A fountain of tricks, the auto trip prospers from a parallelism that keeps the car interior populated with opposing tandems. The three hitchhikers are a mugging, chorus-boy irritation; however, they give the film some of its cold, surfacy jazz, and, for contrasting music, are rubbed against a jarringly neurotic husband and wife (whose Volkswagen turns over in one of the many piquant roadside images), forced to accompany the doctor as symbols of degradation.

As is the case with the three Hollywood films mentioned above, the descriptive "slick" seems like gross understatement in discussing *Wild Strawberries*. An eerie, felicitous opportunism steered this film—just enough Freudian bitters, modern marriage, supernatural overcast, and "smashingly beautiful" postcards to provide a full matinee of culture for the expanding middlebrow-highbrow audience. It probably is unnecessary to add that there's a happy ending—with his reunited son and daughter-in-law watching over him and the hitchhikers serenading in the yard outside, the doctor slumbers off with a warm, pleasant, self-assured smile creasing his *papier-mache* face.

August 31, 1959

Corny Anti-Philistinism

A CAREFULLY rigged yak from *Look Back in Anger*—"It's pretty dreary living in the American age, unless of course you're an American"—might well be said of this film and a new item from France, *Back to the Wall*, which are hopelessly and rather sadly indebted to such American stylists as the underrated Michael Curtiz.

Edouard Molinaro's *Back to the Wall* is a dully inactive throwback to the last days of Hollywood "B" crime films. In those films, tone-deaf technicians had little to offer except a cynical story and a religious low-budgetism that consisted of bad lighting, a cast of stiff-faced studio actors marking time between bigger jobs. At least half of those movies were taken up with a dead-handed college movie course treatment of free material (cars cruising through dark streets, people necking in the park, sitting at bars, or standing in post office lines).

Of all the foreign stylists who murder the tough crime technique invented by Dashiell Hammett, no one does a more ruthless, witless variety than the young French director trying for a quick art score. For instance, Molinaro's film starts off with a crime (a cuckold gunning down his wife's lover in a crowded apartment house, hauling the corpse through the lobby and into a car, and then entombing the body in a concrete wall that might go without a hitch in a Hitchcock moonless desert but hardly seems possible in its crowded Paris set-up). Needless to mention, the concrete wall chosen by the murderer is thick enough to secrete a rug-encased corpse, and the trying job of concrete-mixing, shoveling and hod-carrying is managed without doffing, or even unbuttoning, the traditional trenchcoat.

The movie version of John Osborne's hit play about a social rebel husband who talks endlessly about the monotony of life is a reminder of the teeming, cluttered social studies that once flowed from Warner Brothers, dedicated to capturing the smear of lower depths life. The *Anger*-class movie nostalgically recalls Curtiz's schmaltzy epics in which dialogues were constantly joined in mirrors, crowds were usually glimpsed in a hazy blur, and outdoor action either had to contend with a heavy rain or a gaggle of slum brats swarming over a parked Cadillac.

As a movie about a snarling rebel who is spiritually immobilized by wanting everything and nothing, and constantly in eruption, criticizing wife, friends, Mummy and Edwardians in general, *Look Back in Anger* suffers from a common affliction of angry young writing: It lambasts the forces of philistinism while gilding its hipsters with the corniest maneuvers of square art.

This film's relentless fault-finder (Richard Burton) waxes heroic through the reels by blowing the same tiresome Dixieland trumpet that has loused up a lot of New Orleans films. The worst part about Jimmy (Burton) Porter's terrible trumpet sound (which spots the film like measles) is that it is joined with romantically bleary nonsense: a duet in the midnight streets with an answering horn that seems to be coming from outer space, and a number of jazz society sessions in which an army of beat generation customers react in tempo to Jimmy's "12th Street Rag," as though they were purposely corning it up only to impress a photographer from *Coronet* magazine.

Freed of his trumpet, Jimmy Porter is often glimpsed in a glistening wetness that has enclosed other irritating heroes such as Kirk Douglas' *Champion*, somehow casting a burning silver halo around the fellow's artfully messed-up locks. At home, Jimmy is a jangle of sexual histrionics, a faint tremor of lust working the lower eyelid, his wooing (which at low ebb includes some hard-to-believe Pooh Corner antics, mimicking affectionate animals around the living room floor with his wife) being only a mess of grasps, lunges and lip-tracking which seems to come from a decade of hot-kiss films.

As conceived by Director Tony Richardson and tortured by Burton, Jimmy Porter's wrath ("being alive you know, just being alive") is bound to score well in art theaters where the worldly clientele may perceive the bi-sexual brocade that nestles in and around the Porter characterization. While Jimmy knocks his women over an ironing board and spews a steady flood of cheap Broadway jokes, he pursues a fine, flawless, high-minded friendship with his pal, Cliff (Gary Raymond), who practically lives in the very center of Jimmy's marital horror.

Despite every golden impurity, Richardson's film is somewhat of a spellbinder, thanks mostly to its solid pictorial "memories" of the archaic Warner Brothers clutter style. Though its sociological bric-a-brac is often either dull (the Porter dwelling) or over-pointed in the direction of irony (the shots of

Salvation Army churchgoers moving through the rain, Edwardians wisping in the garden), *Look Back in Anger* bulges with a good deal of marred but interesting visual detail.

October 5, 1959

Culture With a Price Tag

A STANDARD type among Hollywood movie makers has been the fairly sensitive producer whose yearning for a huge cultural audience is coupled with a knack for inflicting a price-tag sheen on every actor, wisecrack or furniture item in his "altruistic" films. Today, the rich thumb that belonged to Irving Thalberg and Sam Goldwyn has become a catastrophe in TV, where the self-elected thinker and artist (producer Robert Allen Aurthur or writer Budd Schulberg, always heard in Sunday supplements and on TV panels pleading for more truth and less claptrap) has been pasting play after play with a peculiar quicksilver schmaltz. Such "stamp-of-quality" creativity has been turning fall TV into chandelier art: Most of the specials and showcases are similar to the *nouveau riche* smartness that can be seen any day exiting clumsily from a mile-long Chrysler and then doing a parody of dignity and grace, dragging a mink stole toward the Four Seasons restaurant.

What has been turning up in more ambitious TV is the safe-playing conservative producer who is invariably haloed in public prints. Try as he may, and though he is always near the target, this quality-stamp artist turns out work notable for languor and over-padding that is usually acclaimed as "handsomely mounted" and belongs on the air Sunday evenings, when the audience is naturally overstuffed and half-asleep.

What's he up to, this lofty artist? First, he is a great believer in proven art, being almost incapable of moving without a sure shot from fiction (*Turn of the Screw*), movies (*The Fallen Idol*) or theater (Robinson Jeffers' luncheonette-talk version of *Medea*). Second, he has a knack for finding deep-dish name stars and cramming them into the one vehicle in which they are bound to lose their offbeat potential.

Next, he is a fall guy for dialogue that has a brassy message ("They wouldn't sell a gun to a spick. I have to steal it") or a sophisticated death-rattle that is out of line with either character or period ("The woodwork's full of zombies" is the plaint of a Puerto Rican pug). Finally, this producer, obsessed with the need for plays that make a challenging statement, seems to infect his actors and directors with a destructive positivism that leads to moralizing ballads rather than credible drama.

None of the opening plays this fall had directing style so much as collisions, shotgun marriages of fate and death (in *What Makes Sammy Run*, a celebration for the hero's latest movie feat is interrupted by an announcement that he has failed to attend his aunt's funeral) that beat a bongo on the picture table. Adding to the sing-song was a jabbing dialogue track (fast cracks in which a character frequently set himself up to be knocked down as a symptom of the nation's crassly commercial ailment) and a simplistic acting style that worked with one-note conviction, as though its script were a Congressional report on corruption in movies or boxing. In *Body and Soul*, Ben Gazzara's overly gentle minority boxer had to contend with a Cassandra-like mother; a Puerto Rican friend whose goodness had the conviction of a soft, soggy handshake: a Negro ex-champ whose big punch-drunk scene at night in a training-camp ring (accompanied by that trite movie fixture, a distant train whistle) demotes Kirk Douglas as champ of space-devouring emotionalism.

Except for the *Deputy* Western series, which is directed by an alumnus (David Butler) of Bob Hope films, the new action items evidently learned to walk watching the latest false innocence from the Talent Associates Ltd. factory. Each *Bonanza* face is a battleground for goodness, gentleness and show-biz cunning. The plots of *Riverboat* are dedicated to overcoming as much congested immorality as swarms in a Hieronymus Bosch painting; rich framing bloats each installment, which boasts such production intricacies as Darren McGavin's bravado laugh and a Debra Paget dance over bales, crates and stray deckhands that Cecil DeMille might have designed. Happily, at least two crime serials, including a sedate version of last year's Desilu pilot for *Untouchables*, have been considerably improved by the flexible acting of Nehemiah Persoff.

An odd rivulet of extreme amateurism has started up, almost as a protest against the suave productions of mature artists. Some of these bowlegged productions—Steve Allen's broadcasts from Hollywood, an ABC midnight comedy show, the first photographed play on a New York channel dedicated to immobility—have the uncorseted fascination of TV wrestling. Also, ABC's *Everything Goes* Paar-ody offers miles of Dayton Allen comedy, which is almost bruisingly funny. On the whole, TV seems committed to the questionable ceiling and garment-district touch of a David Susskind, whose idea of artistic heaven is a big audience soaking up the sure-thing culture practiced by DeMille, Darryl Zanuck or Elia Kazan.

October 26, 1959

A Director's Skill With Terror, Geography and Truth

WHILE the New Wave (*The Lovers*—from France) and Nouvelle Vague (*The Magician*—from Sweden) have been hatching record-breaking lines in front of art theaters, a touching drama goes on alongside, involving numerous old Hollywood pros who are trying to keep pace, or at least regain their youthful vigor. One of these pros is Robert Wise, the director. Wise has fared better than most as Ponce de Leon trying for a new Hollywood youth. Wise has evolved an elongation of the Fritz Lang expressionism that he used briefly in the grimy, brutal 1949 sleeper, *The Set-Up*, and never again. He uses a trip-hammer technique that is fun to watch and brings into play his rather odd talents, which mostly have to do with shock-connections inside and between episodes.

From his earliest and best study of middle-class mediocrity (*Born to Kill*), Wise has had trouble giving his inflexibly acted, shrewdly terrored films an "identity." Now, in a late stretch drive against the anonymity that has piled around his career as a hard-boiled specialist on the shabbier seams of life, and an economical director of dowdy, middle-aged derelicts (such as the nearly punch-drunk prelim fighter in *The Set-Up*), Wise has thrust himself so far into style that on a clear screen almost anyone in the last row of the balcony can recognize the film as his.

Before his new film, *Odds Against Tomorrow*, springs its trap too quickly into a pat ending and a last staccato note (a shot of a street sign that reads, "STOP— DEAD END"), Wise has run through a catalogue of sadism including wild contrasts, odd transitions (a rabbit's nose twitching before a menacing rifle), and a camera that does a rhythmic up-and-down jabbing. He has such strange effects as a diesel train honking through the center of a head-on argument, cruel weather reports, a James Cain type of romantic meeting shot mostly around the hips, and a zooming camera that carries on a "dialogue" of white supremacy between two people spaced a block apart. The result is a tricky but tough movie about a bank robbery that has a lot of insights into the decrepit, nearly hopeless life, and, like all Wise films, needs only a good story.

The robbery involves an integration-among-criminals dispute between a chronic Negro-baiter and a tough colored singer who has trouble with the jungle outside his door—with most of Wise's comments on the Race Problem too easily come by. While he does some credible by-play with an embittered colored wife and her playboy husband (Harry Belafonte), these domestic strife scenes in a neat "project" apartment are much too tepid for Wise's virile, anger-spun art. Nevertheless, throughout this quick, heated story of a crime arranged by three amateurs, there are moments of exciting accuracy.

The main point in all Wise films is that the human being is a luckless, often furious, figure in an imprisoning city which, unlike its inhabitants who seem almost rigid with frustration and broken hopes, is shatteringly alive, interesting, complicated and, in its more sordid areas, unbearably photogenic. With his orthodox notion of an offbeat cast (Shelley Winters, Robert Ryan), a passive handling of actors that makes for stone-like people or strangely neutral ones, and a quiet wizardry in connecting technical gimmicks with a shrewdly selected environment, Wise is inordinately suited to bringing his pessimistic impression of mankind into credible shape.

Even with a pro-arty cameraman who makes every blast of sunlight on white clapboard, every stiffness in an aging ex-cop's walk, seem a bit rich and special, Wise is almost unequaled in post-silent films for his brooding around ugly Eastern city hotels and rooming houses. Perhaps the best Wise trait is his unshowy respect for unimportant scenes. Whether it is the lights of a main street turning on, a sad hallway wrapping itself around a tightly elegant singer, or a heavy-fisted punk reacting with meager, ungiving admiration to someone else's ingenuity, Wise gives the effect a chance to exist with all of its sensitivity intact and without the wild pointing found in most films of decadence.

Part of the trouble with Wise's films is that he is unable to break the cage of conservative casting and imitative stories. Here he has Harry Belafonte, who is a bit too comfortable and unmarked for a man caught in a soul-shaking financial bind. As Harry's nemesis, Robert Ryan is somewhat more persuasive, at least when Wise bridges Ryan's thoughtfully static acting approach and grooved responses with some silent, near-newsreel documenting. In these fine moments, a homely obscurity seems to sag from every crevice of Ryan's face, and sometimes, when he is musing grimly on his gigolo life with a waitress (Shelley Winters), it is hard to tell where the homely environment stops and Ryan starts. The fact that this film is at all commendable is the result of Wise's ability to transform a melodrama into something that mixes terror, geography and truth.

November 23, 1959

White Elephant Art vs. Termite Art

Most of the feckless, listless quality of today's art can be blamed on its drive to break out of a tradition while, irrationally, hewing to the square, boxed-in shape and gemlike inertia of an old, densely wrought European masterpiece.

Advanced painting has long been suffering from this burnt-out notion of a masterpiece—breaking away from its imprisoning conditions toward a suicidal improvisation, threatening to move nowhere and everywhere, niggling, omnivorous, ambitionless; yet, within the same picture, paying strict obeisance to the canvas edge and, without favoritism, the precious nature of every inch of allowable space. A classic example of this inertia is the Cézanne painting: in his indoorish works of the woods around Aix-en-Provence, a few spots of tingling, jarring excitement occur where he nibbles away at what he calls his "small sensation," the shifting of a tree trunk, the infinitesimal contests of complimentary colors in a light accent on farmhouse wall. The rest of each canvas is a clogging weight-density-structure-polish amalgam associated with self-aggrandizing masterwork. As he moves away from the unique, personal vision that interests him, his painting turns ungiving and puzzling: a matter of balancing curves for his bunched-in composition, laminating the color, working the painting to the edge. Cézanne ironically left an exposé of his dreary finishing work in terrifyingly honest watercolors, an occasional unfinished oil (the pinkish portrait of his wife in sunny, leafed-in patio), where he foregoes everything but his spotting fascination with minute interactions.

The idea of art as an expensive hunk of well-regulated area, both logical and magical, sits heavily over the talent of every modern painter, from Motherwell to Andy Warhol. The private voice of Motherwell (the exciting drama in the meeting places between ambivalent shapes, the aromatic sensuality that comes from laying down thin sheets of cold, artfully clichéish, hedonistic color) is inevitably ruined by having to spread these small pleasures into great contained works. Thrown back constantly on unrewarding endeavors (filling vast egglike shapes, organizing a ten-foot rectangle with its empty corners suggesting Siberian steppes in the coldest time of the year), Motherwell ends up with appalling amounts of plasterish grandeur, a composition so huge and questionably painted that the delicate, electric contours seem to be crushing the shalelike matter inside. The special delight of each painting tycoon (De Kooning's sabrelike lancing of forms; Warhol's minute embrace with the path of illustrator's pen line and block-print tone; James Dine's slog-footed brio, filling a stylized shape from stem to stern with one ungiving color) is usually squandered in pursuit of the continuity, harmony, involved in constructing a masterpiece. The painting, sculpture, assemblage becomes a yawning production of overripe technique shrieking with preciosity, fame, ambition; far inside are tiny pillows holding up the artist's signature, now turned into mannerism by the padding, lechery, faking required to combine today's esthetics with the components of traditional Great Art.

Movies have always been suspiciously addicted to termite-art tendencies. Good work usually arises where the creators (Laurel and Hardy, the team of Howard Hawks and William Faulkner operating on the first half of Raymond Chandler's *The Big Sleep*) seem to have no ambitions towards gilt culture but are involved in a kind of squandering-beaverish endeavor that isn't anywhere or for anything. A peculiar fact about termite-tapeworm-fungus-moss art is that it goes always forward eating its own boundaries, and, likely as not, leaves nothing in its path other than the signs of eager, industrious, unkempt activity.

The most inclusive description of the art is that, termite-like, it feels its way through walls of particularization, with no sign that the artist has any object in mind other than eating away the immediate boundaries of his art, and turning these boundaries into conditions of the next achievement. Laurel and Hardy, in fact, in some of their most dyspeptic and funniest movies, like *Hog Wild*, contributed some fine parody of men who had read every "How to Succeed" book available; but, when it came to applying their knowledge, reverted instinctively to termite behavior.

One of the good termite performances (John Wayne's bemused cowboy in an unreal stage town inhabited by pallid repetitious actors whose chief trait is a powdered make-up) occurs in John Ford's *The Man Who Shot Liberty Valance*. Better Ford films than this have been marred by a phlegmatically solemn Irish personality that goes for rounded declamatory acting, silhouetted riders along the rim of a mountain with a golden sunset behind them, and repetitions in which big bodies are scrambled together in a rhythmically curving Rosa Bonheurish composition. Wayne's acting is infected by a kind of hoboish spirit, sitting back on its haunches doing a bitter-amused counterpoint to the pale, neutral film life around him. In an Arizona town that is too placid, where the cactus was planted last night and nostalgically cast actors do a generalized drunkenness, cowardice, voraciousness, Wayne is the termite actor focusing only on a tiny present area, nibbling at it with engaging professionalism and a hipster sense of how to sit in a chair leaned against the wall, eye a flogging over-actor (Lee Marvin). As he moves along at the pace of a tapeworm, Wayne leaves a path that is only bits of shrewd intramural acting—a craggy face filled with bitterness, jealousy, a big body that idles luxuriantly, having long grown tired with roughhouse games played by old wrangler types like John Ford.

The best examples of termite art appear in places other than films, where the spotlight of culture is nowhere in evidence, so that the craftsman can be ornery, wasteful, stubbornly self-involved, doing go-for-broke art and not caring what comes of it. The occasional newspaper column by a hard-work specialist caught up by an exciting event (Joe Alsop or Ted Lewis, during a presidential election), or a fireball technician reawakened during a pennant playoff that brings on stage his favorite villains (Dick Young); the TV production of *The Iceman Cometh*, with its great examples of slothful-buzzing acting by Myron McCormack, Jason Robards, et al.; the last few detective novels of Ross Macdonald and most of Raymond Chandler's ant-crawling verbosity and sober fact-pointing in the letters compiled years back in a slightly noticed book that is a fine running example of popular criticism; the TV debating of William Buckley, before he relinquished his tangential, counterattacking skill and took to flying into propeller blades of issues, like James Meredith's Ole Miss-adventures.

In movies, nontermite art is too much in command of writers and directors to permit the omnivorous termite artist to scuttle along for more than a few scenes. Even Wayne's cowboy job peters out in a gun duel that is overwrought with conflicting camera angles, plays of light and dark, ritualized movement and posture. In *The Loneliness of the Long Distance Runner*, the writer (Alan Sillitoe) feels the fragments of a delinquent's career have to be united in a conventional story. The design on which Sillitoe settles—a spokelike affair with each fragment shown as a memory experienced on practice runs—leads to repetitious scenes of a boy running. Even a gaudily individual track star—a Peter Snell—would have trouble making these practice runs worth the moviegoer's time, though a cheap ton of pseudo-Bunny Berigan jazz trumpet is thrown on the film's sound track to hop up the neutral dullness of these up-down-around spins through vibrant English countryside.

Masterpiece art, reminiscent of the enameled tobacco humidors and wooden lawn ponies bought at white elephant auctions decades ago, has come to dominate the overpopulated arts of TV and movies. The three sins of white elephant art (1) frame the action with an all-over pattern, (2) install every event, character, situation in a frieze of continuities, and (3) treat every inch of the screen and film as a potential area for prizeworthy creativity. *Requiem for a Heavyweight* is so heavily inlaid with ravishing technique that only one scene—an employment office with a nearly illiterate fighter (Anthony Quinn) falling into the hands of an impossibly kind job clerk—can be acted by Quinn's slag blanket type of expendable art, which crawls along using fair insight and a total immersion in the materials of acting. Antonioni's *La Notte* is a good example of the evils of continuity, from its opening scene of a deathly sick noble critic being visited by two dear friends. The scene gets off well, but the director carries the thread of it to agonizing length, embarrassing the viewer with dialogue about art that is sophomorically one dimensional, interweaving an arty shot of a helicopter to fill the time interval, continuing with impossible-to-act effects of sadness by Moreau and Mastroianni outside the hospital, and, finally, reels later, a laughable postscript conversation by Moreau-Mastroianni detailing the critic's "meaning" as a friend, as well as a few other very mystifying details about the poor bloke. Tony Richardson's films, beloved by art theater patrons, are surpassing examples of the sin of framing, boxing in an action with a noble idea or camera effect picked from High Art.

In Richardson's films (*A Taste of Honey*, *The Long Distance Runner*), a natural directing touch on domesticity involving losers is the main dish (even the air in Richardson's whitish rooms seems to be fighting the ragamuffin type who infests Richardson's young or old characters). With his "warm" liking for the materials of direction, a patient staying with confusion, holding to a cop's lead-footed pacelessness that doesn't crawl over details so much as back sluggishly into them. Richardson can stage his remarkable seconds-ticking sedentary act in almost any setup—at night, in front of a glarey department store window, or in a train coach with two pairs of kid lovers settling in with surprising, hopped-up animalism. Richardson's ability to give a spectator the feeling of being There, with time to spend, arrives at its peak in homes, apartments, art garrets, a stable-like apartment, where he turns into an academic neighbor of Walker Evans, steering the spectator's eyes on hidden rails, into arm patterns, worn wood, inclement feeling hovering in tiny marble eyes, occasionally even making a room appear to take shape as he introduces it to a puffy-faced detective or an expectant girl on her first search for a room of her own. In a kitchen scene with kid thief and job-worn detective irritably gnawing at each other, Richardson's talent for angular disclosures takes the scene apart without pointing or a nearly habitual underlining; nagging through various types of bone-worn, dishrag-gray material with a fine windup of two unlikable opponents still scraping at each other in a situation that is one of the first to credibly turn the overattempted movie act—showing hard, agonizing existence in the wettest rain and slush.

Richardson's ability with deeply lived-in incident is, nevertheless, invariably dovetailed with his trick of settling a horse collar of gentility around the neck of a scene, giving the image a pattern that suggests practice, skill, guaranteed safe humor. His highly rated stars (from Richard Burton through Tom Courtenay) fall into mock emotion and studied turns, which suggest they are caught up in the enameled sequence of a vaudeville act: Rita Tushingham's sighting over a gun barrel at an amusement park (standard movie place for displaying types who are closer to the plow than the library card) does a broadly familiar comic arrangement of jaw muscle and eyebrow that has the gaiety and almost the size of a dinosaur bone. Another gentility Richardson picked up from fine *objets d'art* (Dubuffet, Larry Rivers, Dick Tracy's creator) consists of setting a network of marring effects to prove his people are ill placed in life. Tom Courtenay (the last angry boy in *Runner*) gets carried away by this cult, belittling, elongating, turning himself into a dervish with a case of Saint Vitus dance, which localizes in his jaw muscles, eyelids. As Richardson gilds his near vagrants with sawtooth mop coiffures and a way of walking on high heels so that each heel seems a different size and both appear to be plunged through the worn flooring, the traits look increasingly elegant and put on (the worst trait: angry eyes that suggest the empty orbs in "Orphan Annie" comic strips). Most of his actors become crashing, unbelievable bores, though there is one nearly likable actor, a chubby Dreiserian girl friend in *Long Distance Runner* who, termite-fashion, almost acts into a state of grace. Package artist Richardson has other boxing-in ploys, running scenes together as Beautiful Travelogue, placing a cosmic symbol around the cross-country running event, which incidentally crushes Michael Redgrave, a headmaster in the fantastic gambol of throwing an entire Borstal community into a swivet over one track event.

The common denominator of these laborious ploys is, actually, the need of the director and writer to overfamiliarize the audience with the picture it's watching: to blow up every situation and character like an affable inner tube with recognizable details and smarmy compassion. Actually, this overfamiliarization serves to reconcile these supposed long-time enemies—academic and Madison Avenue art.

An exemplar of white elephant art, particularly the critic-devouring virtue of filling every pore of a work with glinting, darting Style and creative Vivacity, is François Truffaut. Truffaut's *Shoot the Piano Player* and *Jules et Jim*, two ratchety perpetual-motion machines devised by a French Rube Goldberg, leave behind the more obvious gadgetries of *Requiem for a Heavyweight* and even the cleaner, bladelike journalism of *The 400 Blows*.

Truffaut's concealed message, given away in his Henry Miller–ish, adolescent two-reeler of kids spying on a pair of lovers (one unforgettably daring image: kids sniffing the bicycle seat just vacated by the girl in the typical fashion of voyeuristic pornographic art) is a kind of reversal of growth, in which people grow backward into childhood. Suicide becomes a game, the houses look like toy boxes—laughter, death, putting out a fire—all seem reduced to some unreal innocence of childhood myths. The real innocence of *Jules et Jim* is in the writing, which depends on the spectator sharing the same wide-eyed or adolescent view of the wickedness of sex that is implicit in the vicious gamesmanship going on between two men and a girl.

Truffaut's stories (all women are villains; the schoolteacher seen through the eyes of a sniveling schoolboy; all heroes are unbelievably innocent, un-believably persecuted) and characters convey the sense of being attached to a rubber band, although he makes a feint at reproducing the films of the 1930's with their linear freedom and independent veering. From *The 400 Blows* onward, his films are bound in and embarrassed by his having made up his mind what the film is to be about. This decisiveness converts the people and incidents into flat, jiggling mannikins (*400 Blows, Mischief Makers*) in a Mickey Mouse comic book, which is animated by thumbing the pages rapidly. This approach eliminates any stress or challenge, most of all any sense of the film locating an independent shape.

Jules et Jim, the one Truffaut film that seems held down to a gliding motion, is also cartoonlike but in a decorous, suspended way. Again most of the visual effect is an illustration for the current of the sentimental narrative. Truffaut's concentration on making his movie fluent and comprehensible flattens out all complexity and reduces his scenes to scraps of pornography—like someone quoting just the punchline of a well-known dirty joke. So unmotivated is the leapfrogging around beds of the three-way lovers that it leads to endless bits of burlesque. Why does she suddenly pull a gun? (See "villainy of women," above). Why does she drive her car off a bridge? (Villains need to be punished.) Etc.

Jules et Jim seems to have been shot through a scrim which has filtered out everything except Truffaut's dry vivacity with dialogue and his diminutive stippling sensibility. Probably the high point in this love-is-time's-fool film: a languorous afternoon in a chalet (what's become of chalets?) with Jeanne Moreau teasing her two lovers with an endless folksong. Truffaut's lyrics—a patter of vivacious small talk that is supposed to exhibit the writer's sophisti-cation, never mind about what—provides most of the scene's friction, along with an idiot concentration on meaningless details of faces or even furniture (the degree that a rocking chair isn't rocking becomes an impressive substitute for psychology). The point is that, divested of this meaningless vivacity, the scenes themselves are without tension, dramatic or psychological.

The boredom aroused by Truffaut—to say nothing of the irritation—comes from his peculiar methods of dehydrating all the life out of his scenes (instant movies?). Thanks to his fondness for doused lighting and for the kind of long shots which hold his actors at thirty paces, especially in bad weather, it's not only the people who are blanked out; the scene itself threatens to evaporate off the edge of the screen. Adding to the effect of evaporation, disappearing: Truf-faut's imagery is limited to traveling (running through meadows, walking in Paris streets, etc.), setups and dialogue scenes where the voices, disembodied and like the freakish chirps in Mel Blanc's *Porky Pig* cartoons, take care of the flying out effect. Truffaut's system holds art at a distance without any actual muscularity or propulsion to peg the film down. As the spectator leans forward to grab the film, it disappears like a released kite.

Antonioni's specialty, the effect of moving as in a chess game, becomes an autocratic kind of direction that robs an actor of his motive powers and most of his spine. A documentarist at heart and one who often suggests both Paul Klee and the cool, deftly neat, "intellectual" Fred Zinnemann in his early *Act of Violence* phase, Antonioni gets his odd, clarity-is-all effects from his taste for chic mannerist art that results in a screen that is glassy, has a side-sliding motion, the feeling of people plastered against stripes or divided by verticals and horizontals; his incapacity with interpersonal relationships turns crowds into stiff waves, lovers into lonely appendages, hanging stiffly from each other, occasionally coming together like clanking sheets of metal but seldom giving the effect of being in communion.

At his best, he turns this mental creeping into an effect of modern misery, loneliness, cavernous guilt-ridden yearning. It often seems that details, a gesture, an ironic wife making a circle in the air with her finger as a thought circles toward her brain, become corroded by solitariness. A pop jazz band appearing at a millionaire's fête becomes the unintentional heart of *La Notte*, pulling together the inchoate center of the film—a vast endless party. Antonioni handles this combo as though it were a vile mess dumped on the lawn of a huge estate. He has his film inhale and exhale, returning for a glimpse of the four-piece outfit playing the same unmodified kitsch music—stupidly immobile, totally detached from the party swimming around the music. The film's most affecting shot is one of Jeanne Moreau making tentative stabs with her somber, alienated eyes and mouth, a bit of a dance step, at rapport and friendship with the musicians. Moreau's facial mask, a signature worn by all Antonioni players, seems about to crack from so much sudden uninhibited effort.

The common quality or defect which unites apparently divergent artists like Antonioni, Truffaut, Richardson is fear, a fear of the potential life, rudeness, and outrageousness of a film. Coupled with their storage vault of self-awareness and knowledge of film history, this fear produces an incessant wakefulness. In Truffaut's films, this wakefulness shows up as dry, fluttering inanity. In Antonioni's films, the mica-schist appearance of the movies, their linear patterns, are hulked into obscurity by Antonioni's own fund of sentimentalism, the need to get a mural-like thinness and interminableness out of his mean patterns.

The absurdity of *La Notte* and *L'Avventura* is that its director is an authentically interesting oddball who doesn't recognize the fact. His talent is for small eccentric microscope studies, like Paul Klee's, of people and things pinned in their grotesquerie to an oppressive social backdrop. Unlike Klee, who stayed small and thus almost evaded affectation, Antonioni's aspiration is to pin the viewer to the wall and slug him with wet towels of artiness and significance. At one point in *La Notte*, the unhappy wife, taking the director's patented walk through a continent of scenery, stops in a rubbled section to peel a large piece of rusted tin. This ikon close-up of minuscule desolation is probably the most overworked cliché in still photography, but Antonioni, to keep his stories and events moving like great novels through significant material, never stops throwing his Sunday punch. There is an interestingly acted nymphomaniac girl at wit's end trying to rape the dish-rag hero; this is a big event, particularly for the first five minutes of a film. Antonioni overweights this terrorized girl and her interesting mop of straggly hair by pinning her into a typical Band-aid composition—the girl, like a tiny tormented animal, backed against a large horizontal stripe of white wall. It is a pretentiously handsome image that compromises the harrowing effect of the scene.

Whatever the professed theme in these films, the one that dominates in unspoken thought is that the film business is finished with museum art or pastiche art. The best evidence of this disenchantment is the anachronistic slackness of *Jules et Jim, Billy Budd, Two Weeks in Another Town*. They seem to have been dropped into the present from a past which has become useless. This chasm between white-elephant reflexes and termite performances shows itself in an inertia and tight defensiveness which informs the acting of Mickey Rooney in *Requiem for a Heavyweight*, Julie Harris in the same film, and the spiritless survey of a deserted church in *L'Avventura*. Such scenes and actors seem as numb and uninspired by the emotions they are supposed to animate, as hobos trying to draw warmth from an antiquated coal stove. This chasm of inertia seems to testify that the Past of heavily insured, enclosed film art has become unintelligible to contemporary performers, even including those who lived through its period of relevance.

Citizen Kane, in 1941, antedated by several years a crucial change in films from the old flowing naturalistic story, bringing in an iceberg film of hidden meanings. Now the revolution wrought by the exciting but hammy Orson Welles film, reaching its zenith in the 1950's, has run its course and been superceded by a new film technique that turns up like an ugly shrub even in the midst of films that are preponderantly old gems. Oddly enough the film that starts the breaking away is a middle-1950's film, that seems on the surface to be as traditional as *Greed*. Kurosawa's *Ikiru* is a giveaway landmark, suggesting a new self-centering approach. It sums up much of what a termite art aims at: buglike immersion in a small area without point or aim, and, over all, concentration on nailing down one moment without glamorizing it, but forgetting this accomplishment as soon as it has been passed; the feeling that all is expendable, that it can be chopped up and flung down in a different arrangement without ruin.

Winter 1962

The Decline of the Actor

THE strange evolution of movies in the last ten years—with the remaining studios ever more desperate, ever more coordinated—has brought about the disappearance of something that reviewers and film theorists have never seemed to miss: those tiny, mysterious interactions between the actor and the scene that make up the memorable moments in any good film. These have nothing to do with the plot, "superb performance," or even the character being portrayed. They are moments of peripheral distraction, bemusement, fretfulness, mere flickerings of skeptical interest: Margaret Sheridan's congested whinny as a career woman sparring with Kenneth Tobey (Christian Nyby's *The Thing*); Bogart's prissy sign language to a bespectacled glamour girl through the bookstore window (Howard Hawks's *The Big Sleep*); or Richard Barthelmess's tiredly defiant dissolute slouch when he enters the *cabaña* in *Only Angels Have Wings* (also by Hawks). Such tingling moments liberate the imagination of both actors and audience: they are simply curiosity flexing itself, spoofing, making connections to a new situation.

Even so-called photographed plays—for instance, George Cukor's *Dinner at Eight*—could once be made to produce that endless unreeling of divergence, asides, visual lilts which produce a vitality unique to the movies. With the setting and story of a Waldorf operetta, Cukor was able to get inflections and tones from the departments that professional cinematicians always class as uncinematic: make-up, setting, costumes, voices. Marie Dressler's matronly bulldog face and Lee Tracy's scarecrow, gigolo features and body are almost like separate characters interchangeable with the hotel corridors and bathtubs and gardens of Cukor's ritzy and resilient imagination. Cukor, a lighter, less sentiment-logged Ernst Lubitsch, could convert an obsession or peculiarity like Jean Harlow's nasal sexuality, or Wallace Beery's line-chewing, into a quick and animating caricature—much as Disney used mice and pigs in his 1930's cartoons.

Lately, however, in one inert film after another, by the time the actor moves into position, the screen has been congealed in the manner of a painting by Pollock, every point filled with maximum pungency, leaving no room for a full-regalia performance. No matter what the individuality of the actor may be—an apprehensive grandstander (Jeanne Moreau) with two expressions: starved and less starved; an ironing board (Gregory Peck) who becomes effective in scenes that have been grayed, flattened, made listless with some domesticity; a defensively humble actress (Anne Bancroft) who overvalues her humanism and eloquence—and no matter how fine the director's instincts may be, the result is invariably almost the same. In a situation where what counts is opulence and prestige—a gross in the millions, winner of the Critics' Award, Best Actor at a film festival—the actor has to be fitted into a production whose elements have all been assembled, controlled, related, like so many notes in a symphony. As a full-blooded, big-wheel performer rolling at top speed, the actor would subvert this beautiful construction, and so the full-blooded, big-wheel performance has become an anachronism.

Item: David Lean's *Lawrence of Arabia* is almost a comedy of overdesign, misshapen with spectaclelike obtrusions: the camera frozen about ten feet in front of a speeding cyclist, which, though it catches nice immediate details of his face, primarily shows him fronted on screen for minutes as a huge gargoylish figure; the camels, by far the most exciting shapes in the movie, photograph too large in the "cineramic" desert views; an actor walking off into fading twilight becomes the small papery figure of an illustrational painting; Jack Hawkins's General Allenby, so overweighted with British army beef, suggests a toy version of a Buckingham Palace guard. While the other technicians are walloping away, the actors, stuck like thumbtacks into a maplike event, are allowed—and then only for a fraction of the time—to contribute a declamatory, school-pageant bit of acting.

Item: Another prime example of this sort of thing is Serge Bourguignon's *Sundays and Cybele*, whose two leading players are made to resemble walking receptacles for the production crew. The story (Patricia Gozzi, a twelve-year-old, goes on little outings to the park with Hardy Kruger, an amnesiac) is made into a rite of style consisting mainly of layer-on-layer compositions in which the actors become reflected, blurred, compartmented, speckled, through some special relation with apparatus, scenery, a horse's body, windshield wipers. Such things as the tilt of a head or a face reflected in a drinking glass become so heightened, so stretched, that they appear to go on echoing, as if making their effect inside a vacuum. Yet all this is in the service of the kind of role that consists of little more than being delightful with a sniffle or looking transported while walking through trees carrying a child who is cutely imitating a corpse.

The new actor is, in fact, an estranged figure merely jiggling around inside the role. Sometimes he seems to be standing at the bottom of a dark pit, a shiny spot on his pomaded hair being the chief effect of his acting. Or he may be a literate fellow riffling the clutter on his desk. But, in either case, performance is invariably a charade: the actor seldom makes his own sense. He is no longer supposed to act as close to credible as possible; he is a grace note or a trill; he is a dab of two-dimensional form floating on the film surface for photogenic purposes.

Item: Keir Dullea's acting of the psychotic student in Frank Perry's *David and Lisa* is broad, swingy, without a moment that suggests either curiosity or the macabre homeliness, jaggedness, that might be expected in a disturbed kid. The set-piece handling of each scene usually finds Dullea's Frank Merri-wellish, chalk-white face in the empty stillness, holding to an emotion for an unconscionable time. His tantrum when a doctor pats him on the back takes so long in evolving that the performance of it (crying, a face rigid with intensity, a stiff-handed wiping at his clothes to get rid of germs) seems to be going backward in slow motion.

The only good acting in recent films has been lavished on the role of the eternal sideliner, as played by John Wayne (the homesteader in John Ford's *The Man Who Shot Liberty Valance*) or by George Hamilton (as the liquescent juvenile in Vincente Minnelli's *Two Weeks in Another Town*). These actors salvage the idea of independent intelligence and character by pitting themselves against the rest of the film. Standing at a tangent to the story and appraising the tide in which their fellow actors are floating or drowning, they serve as stabilizers— and as a critique of the movie. Mickey Rooney's murderously gloomy, suspicious acting in Ralph Nelson's *Requiem for a Heavyweight* is another case of superior sidelining, this time among the lunatic effects of apartment scenes that are pitch black except for a 40-watt bulb, a huge hotel sign blinking on and off, actors photographed as eucalyptus trees being ogled from the ground by tourists.

While today's actor is the only thing in the film that is identifiably real, his responses are exploited in a peculiar way. His gaucheries and half-hitches and miscalculations are never allowed their own momentum but are used self-consciously to make a point—so that they become as inanimate and depressing as the ceaseless inventories in Robbe-Grillet novels. Jean-Paul Belmondo, the cool cat car thief in Jean-Luc Godard's *Breathless*, is seen standing before the stills at a theater entrance, doing a smeary Bogart imitation that leans on false innocence instead of developing spontaneously. Monica Vitti, a frightened erotic drifter in Antonioni's *Eclipse*, does a scene-hog's cheerful reaction to a dog's trick walk, full of "meaning" that upstages the characterization.

Falling out of the film along with the actor as performer are other related devices that once had their value. Compare, for example, the heavy, weighted masks of the actors in *Lawrence* with the caricatured features of William Powell, Cary Grant, or Edgar Kennedy, features that served to offset and counterpoint what might otherwise have been precious, sour, or effete about them. Powell, an artist in dreadful films, would first use his satchel underchin to pull the dialogue into the image, then punctuate with his nose the stops for each chin movement. He and Edgar Kennedy, who operated primarily with the upper torso, were basically conductors, composing the film into linear movement as it went along.

Another loss is the idea of character that is styled and constructed from vocation. In Kurosawa's *Yojimbo* (a bowdlerized version of Dashiell Hammett's *Red Harvest*, with a bossless vagabond who depopulates a town of rival leaders, outlaws, and fake heroes), the whole superstructure of Hammett's feudal small town is dissolved into an inchoate mass of Goyalike extras whose swarmings and mouthings are composed with naïve pictorialism. Swarming, moreover, seems to be the full-time occupation; you never see interiors, work, or any evidence of everyday life. The exposition of character through vocation has completely evaporated and been replaced by a shorthand of the character's daily habit, jotted into a corner of the role by set-designer, costumer, author. Jean Seberg's journalistic career is merely wedged into appropriate notches of *Breathless*: a *Herald Tribune* sweat shirt, a quick question to a celebrity novelist at the airport. The source of Monica Vitti's well-tended existence in *Eclipse* is snagged in a one-line footnote about her translator's work. The idea of vocations is slipped into the spectator's acceptance without further development.

The idea of movement per se has also lost its attraction to moviemakers. The actor now enters a scene not as a person, but like a Macy's Thanksgiving balloon, a gaudy exhibitionistic fact. Most of those appurtenances that could provide him with some means of animation have been glazed over. The direct use of his face as an extension of the performance has become a technique for hardening and flattening; and the more elliptical use of his face, for showing intermediate states or refining or attenuating a scene, has vanished, become extinct. In fact, the actor's face has been completely incapacitated; teeth—once taken for granted—or an eyeball, or a hairdo, have all become key operators. They front the screen like balustrades, the now disinherited face behind.

The moving body, too, in its present state of neglect has become a burden —particularly on foreign directors, who seem to realize that their actors might be mistaken for oxen, pillars, or extensions of a chaise longue and, so, give each of their films a kind of late, sudden, jolt. Toshiro Mifune suddenly comes alive toward the end of *Yojimbo*, throwing daggers into the floor of his hideout. Before this, he could usually be seen in one of those compositions Kurosawa prizes of three heads sticking out of their respective potato bags watching one another's faces while waiting for the lunch whistle to blow and break up the photography. *Eclipse* has a parody, very exciting, of people using their arms and hands in a stock exchange scene; most of the time these actors working on telephones, sandwiches, penciling, seem to be trying to fling their hands away. The *Lawrence* ensemble travels over literally half a continent with almost no evidence that any legs have been used. No actor is ever trusted with more than a few moves: a thin path having been cleared for him to make his walk down a dune, or to pontificate around porch furniture, he is then choreographed so that each motion, each bit of costume creaks into place.

Item: The lack of athleticism in *Requiem for a Heavyweight* is, under the circumstances, peculiarly comical. The cast seems made up of huge monolithic characters being held in place, incapable of a natural movement—particularly the overrated Anthony Quinn. Walking down a lonely street sparring at the sky or mumbling while he puts on shirt and tie, Quinn plays the role as though the ground were soft tapioca, his body purchased from an Army-Navy store that specializes in odd sizes.

The late work of certain important directors—Cukor's *The Chapman Report*, Huston's films since *The Roots of Heaven*, Truffaut's *The 400 Blows*—shows a drastic change into the new propulsive style. Every element of the film has been forced into serving a single central preoccupation, whether of character (gelatinous frigidity), metaphysic (elephants are the largeness and mystery of life), or situation (the kid as misunderstood delinquent). A key, symbolic feature of the new style is the transformation of dialogue into a thick curtain dropped between the actor and the audience. The words spoken by Alec Guinness in *Lawrence* (prissily elocutionary), by Montgomery Clift in Huston's *Freud* (mashed, faintly quivery), by Laurence Harvey's Washington journalist in John Frankenheimer's *The Manchurian Candidate* (girlish, whispering) sound like valedictory speeches coached by Archibald MacLeish or the way Indians talk on TV Westerns. The peculiar thing is that each word has been created, worked over by a sound engineer who intercepts the dialogue before it hits the audience. There is no longer the feeling of being close to the actor.

Joan Crawford—despite the fact that each of her roles was played as if it were that of the same dim-witted file clerk with a bulldozer voice—always seemed hooked up to a self-driving sense of form which supplemented exactly what the movie couldn't give her. The current population of actors must probably be said to have more real skills than Crawford, but they don't come off as authentically. Geraldine Page, for instance, an actress of far greater sensibility and aplomb, must go through an entire glossary of mouth-shifting, sinus-clearing, and eye-blinking to make her character in *Sweet Bird of Youth* identifiable as anything. The difference between Crawford's tart in *Grand Hotel* and Page's obsessed ex-star is as great as that between George Kelly and William Inge. The effect of Miss Page's increased power and leisure, which expects no resistance from the movie, is to eviscerate the entire film. The same is true of Gregory Peck's pious Lincoln impersonation in *To Kill a Mockingbird* and of Angela Lansbury's helicopterlike performance in *The Manchurian Candidate*, in which every sentence begins and ends with a vertical drop.

The first sign of the actor's displacement could be seen in a 1952 Japanese film whose implications were not made clear until the New Wave, Antonioni, and others incorporated them into that special blend of modern-art cliché and Madison Avenue chic that now makes such good business. Just about every film aimed at American art theaters has come to be a pretentious, misshapen memory of *Ikiru* that plays on the double effect of the image in which there is simultaneously a powerful infatuation with style and with its opposite—vivid, unstoppable actuality. The fantastic clutter and depression of a petty government office; mouthed-in tepid talk that dribbles endlessly (as in John O'Hara's fiction, where dialogue now devours structure, motive, people, explanation, everything); the poor ghosts who crawl in trying to push a request for a playground in their spot of a slum—each of these items in *Ikiru* seem overrun by a virus of creativity without concern for its direction, everything steaming together into an indictment of drudgery that finally muffles the actors.

The same funguslike creativity and narcissistic style appear in an almost dead-handed way in *Freud, Lawrence of Arabia*, and *Eclipse*. Here the actors show up as rugs, or an entire battle scene is converted by artful lighting into an elongated shadowy smear. Just as *Ikiru* moves from a white emptied abstract death ceremony to a jammed city scene, *Lawrence* employs the split between desert and crowded Cairo to accent the peculiar density of each, and Antonioni juxtaposes the frenzied stock exchange with inarticulate lovers in emptied streets. Even in the crudely constructed *Divorce, Italian Style*, a din of diverse technical energy moves over streets, trains, the very bodies of the acting team. Mastroianni's face, sleep-drenched and melancholic, stares out of a dining car at the flat, parched Sicilian fields; and few actors have looked so contaminated by sleaziness, a draggy kind of living: it is the whole movie that is sitting on him. *Divorce, Italian Style* is like a parody of the realism in *Ikiru*; there is nothing to touch this unfunny farce for the sheer jarring effect of eager-beaver technicians charging into one another, trying to put in *more*—more funny stuff, more realistic stuff, more any kind of stuff.

Most directors have been pushing Kurosawa's invention to the extreme of treating actors with everything from the fancy tinker-toy construction of *Lawrence of Arabia* to the pure sadism of *The Manchurian Candidate*. One of the wildest films in its treatment of actors, *The Manchurian Candidate* is straight jazz all the way through—from the men who are supposed to be brainwashed to the normal ones in army intelligence. When Sinatra, for instance, moves in a fight, his body starts from concrete encasement, and his face looks as though it were being slowly thrown at his Korean houseboy opponent, another freak whose metallic skin and kewpie-doll eyes were borrowed from a Max Factor cosmetic kit. Janet Leigh seems first to have been skinned and stretched on a steel armature, and then compelled to do over and over again with hands and voice things supposed to be exquisitely sexual. The audience is made to feel unclean, like a Peeping Tom, at this queer directional gamboling over bodies. And Sinatra's romantic scenes with Miss Leigh are a Chinese torture: he, pinned against the Pullman door as though having been buried standing up, and she, nothing moving on her body, drilling holes with her eyes into his screw-on head.

In one advanced film after another, we find an actor being used for various purposes external to him—as a mistake, a pitiful object, a circus sight. The most troublesome aspect of Peter O'Toole's Lawrence is that the story moves faster and further than the actor, who is not unlike the Tin Woodsman of Oz (O'Toole starts with a springing outward movement, to walk over the world, and then turns into a pair of stilts walking in quick, short strides). Consider also the squashy ineffectual performance by Peter Ustinov in *Billy Budd* (which he himself directed) or the pitiful ones by Jeanne Moreau in Orson Welles's *The Trial* and Truffaut's *Jules et Jim*. A frightened actress, Miss Moreau is never there with enough speed, sureness, or grace, but her directors realize that her inadequacies can be exploited photogenically. Watching her stretch out in a sexy bed pose, or teeter on a diving board, or climb up a bridge abutment, stand poised, and then leap off, you get the feeling that her feeble creaking is intentionally being underlined as something to sorrow over.

THE DECLINE OF THE ACTOR ◆ 549

*

What we have, then, is a schizoid situation that can destroy the best actor: he must stay alive as a character while preserving the film's contrived style. Thanks to this bind, there are roughly only two kinds of acting today. With the first, and the least interesting, type, the actor is hardly more than a spot: as in Antonioni's films, where he becomes only a slight bulge in the glossy photography; or, as in the endless gray stretches of Truffaut's, where his face becomes a mask painted over with sexual fatigue, inert agony, erosion, while his body skitters around weightlessly like a paper doll. Huston's work, too, has moved in a progression from the great acting of, say, Bogart and Mary Astor in *Across the Pacific* to no acting at all: in *Freud*, the actors do not escape for one moment from the spaces Huston has hacked out of the screen for them in order to make an elegant composition.

The second style of acting turns up in fairly interesting films. Here the actor does a movie-full of intricate acting by turning his back to the camera. He piles a ferocious energy and style into sorrowful characters who have lived through dismal orphanages, or alcoholism, or life membership in Alcatraz— precisely the characters who should have nothing in common with his kind of joy in performing, happy animal spirit, all-out vigor. The result is that there is no communication at all between the setting—which is flat and impressively accurate—and the actor, who splatters every second with a mixture of style and improvisation. Blake Edwards's *Days of Wine and Roses* drags unbelievably while Jack Lemmon kicks in a liquor store door or stares drunkenly at the dirty sea water. Lemmon in this movie is a blur of pantomimic skill, though with enough cynicism in his performance to cut the mechanical writing of the role. However, inside all the style, the actor seems to be static, waiting around sourly while the outer masquerade drags on.

There has, finally, never been worse acting nor more mistakes made by actors being given impossible things to do. A fan's memory gets clouded by these weird performances: a jilted intellectual (Francisco Rabal in *Eclipse*), who goes through an entrance gate as though he had learned to walk by studying an airplane taking off; a U.S. Senator imitating Lincoln at a costume ball (James Gregory in *The Manchurian Candidate*), picking up his didactic acting from several garbage heaps left over from the worst propaganda films of World War II. The poor actor today stands freezing, undone, a slab of beef exposed to public glare as never before. Clift's Freud may be hidden behind a beard, buried in a tomb (his walk to the cemetery must be pulled by earth-movers), but he is still unmercifully revealed as an unused performer. Some actors, like Jackie Gleason in *Requiem for a Heavyweight*, haven't yet moved into their act.

And Kirk Douglas, as a gesticulating, angry ex-actor in *Two Weeks in Another Town*, is a body on display, one now shrinking in middle age while the mind of his employer is fixed on other things. Criticism of acting has always been quick to cover a performance with a blanket word, but trying to consider today's actors as auxiliaries of the story in the pre-1950's sense is like analyzing post–Jackson Pollock painting with an esthetic yardstick that esteems modeling.

July 1963

Nearer My Agee to Thee

UNBEKNOWN to most moviegoers, the saddest story in films concerns the emergence of brutal scorekeeper critics, led by Susan Sontag and Andy Sarris, an odd duo, hard and soft—a Simone de Beauvoir and a boneless Soupy Sales—whose special commodities include *chutzpah*, the ability to convert any perception into a wisecrack or squashed metaphor, and the mobility of a Hollywood sex queen for being where the action is. The protean, ubiquitous Miss Sontag is catlike at showing up in influential gatherings, panel shows, magazines, taking over the show with a matter-of-fact attitude, a flat voice, and a confidence that her knowledge is all-purpose (if contracted, she'd show up in Vietnam).

These writers may be a mystery to the average reader, but one or the other has initiated or firmed up every recent murmur in the American scene: camp as a new estheticism based on distance between art and audience; the placing of Jean Luc Godard, an imitation American, at the top of modern art films; and Alfred Hitchcock, who is a sort of Francophile, at the peak of the pre-1960s films. Particularly they've torn down the selections of the '40s critic, who was a prospector always repanning and sifting for buried American truth and subconscious life. The American landscapes bewitched James Agee and his fellows, but their biggest realization was to give the sense of the Hollywood film as "corpuscular," in constant flux.

Sarris and his mimic, Peter Bogdanovich, have shrewdly suggested that the American critic in the '40s was a philistine compared to those in *Sight and Sound* and the French film magazines. The only trouble with this deviling of Agee and company is that the shadowy conditions of all this now overrated Hollywood art had long ago been accurately spelled out by Otis Ferguson's columns in *The New Republic*, and, to a lesser extent, by Agee's own columns in *The Nation*. Agee, who never noticed Robert Aldrich or Raoul Walsh and hardly mentions Howard Hawks, is always committed, centered in the least important film. Sarris, whose oft-repeated brand for older American criticism is that it was isolated, provincial, in love with poor people, and anti-Hollywood, is seldom inside the film. Using axiomatic statements, working in short paragraphs, incorporating a French journalist's taste, he appears to remove himself, in the most inanimate voice, from the film.

One of the favorite modes of expression of the new blackboard critic is an "of course" construction implying an authority that it is useless to challenge. "Of course, all the spies" in Hitchcock's earliest films were fascist. Untrue: the Cecil Parker, George Sanders villains are never more than grim, tactile evil, undefined in politics and nationality.

Godard is the preferred modern for the new critic. He has their eclectic style, never letting you forget he is of a select yet catholic estheticism. In Miss Sontag's canniest, most extended analysis of a film—Godard's *My Life to Live*— the film is a "beautiful, perfect" work without one reference to acting, scenery, or any other aspect of the movie image.

The trouble with this new criticism, at its most nimbly exact (Miss Sontag) or pointlessly sniping and arrogant (Eugene Archer in the Sunday *Times*), is that it appears to sift through the film's problem, depersonalizing as it goes. Sarris can rub out an accurately savage despair (Fredric March's banker in *The Best Years of Our Lives*) simply by listing other performances (Bogart's defectively mannered Sam Spade), carrying the authority for his put-down of March in his voice. He is forced into the same illusiveness building Godard as a genius: All of Godard's limitations are rubbed out in paradox which ends with the unspoken thought that isn't it funny Godard, the most realistic director, is self-conscious?

Another trouble is that the new critic—a genial combatant, doing a free-fall parachute jump onto stray truths, then leaving a critical puzzle for someone else—simplifies the Hollywood past into chaos. In one small Richard Schickel paragraph, *The Informer*, a film of garbled Irish rhythms and speech and badly lit like early Carol Reed, becomes "one of the best films"—"unrelenting in is realism," the first example of John Ford's covert, rebellious, antistudio genius. *The Informer* is a typical Model T Ford: German expressionism in an early talkie, made "cinematic" by having the talkers take short strolls to nowhere; except for Joe Sawyer's subtlety as an Irish tough, the realism runs to the "Irish mist" turtleneck sweaters sold in 1940 department stores, barroom and death scenes in which the actors move in Disneyish packs and formations.

The idea of John Ford, an iconoclast sneaking shots past his fond patron, Darryl Zanuck, brutally rearranges the facts about a conventionalist who went to sleep inside the mannered reflexes of Fox studio style. Ford ended up (*The Searchers*) doing a glumly humorous, elephantine, Melville-type spoof of a movie pattern he helped establish along with the two Henry's—Hathaway and King. The style of this pattern, which amounts to a broadening, deepening and swirling arrangement of Zanuck pace (episodic, zippier than MGM's), character (balloon-like Americana), and space (exotically prettied Rockwell Kent), was antedated long before the hard-to-bear *Informer* in the lyrical *Young Mr. Lincoln*, *Mohawk Trail*, and the Mudd biography.

The ironic fact is that, while these critics rip away at Agee's antebellum taste, they are his direct descendants. They have taken over his tensionless, hypnotic language effect and his success as a gambler (*Man's Hope* on a level with Homer; *GI Joe* almost out of sight for greatness) gives these scoreboard critics the courage to gamble with every word.

Agee's criticism was actually the start of a major detour from hawking the image to verbal stunting. The great Agee defect, apparent in the deadly dull, humorless prep-school letters to Father Flye, was a ravishment with bard-type giant artist. Pinned down by this maniacal yen for perfect craftsmanship, Agee operated on his writing until it took over his criticism.

A monster technique became the critic, while the enormous IQ became pigmyized by the devious things he found he could do with pure skill. He used a dozen public-voiced mechanisms for pumping up or deflating actor or film: There is no great courage shown in the love scenes of *Nightmare Alley*; beneath the cat's cradle of sensitive things he could wrongfully say about *Sunset Boulevard* Agee was a fall guy for candor, the honestly corny (Billy Wilder films) or the honestly archaic (*Monsieur Verdoux*). Agee's reviewing progressed through the years into simplification, taking the cunning artist exactly as he hoped to be taken, but the writing ear and sense of timing are such that he strikes fear in the reader with his arrogant, omnipotent decisions in unbeatable prose.

What we have now in the new criticism is a semi-pro, speeded-up version of Agee's additive, tensionless language with its flagrant escalations. Agee at his most famous is a simplifier impersonating a zealously objective writer operating with tons of passion: "Buster Keaton's face ranked almost with Lincoln's as an early American stereotype, it was haunting, handsome, almost beautiful, yet it was irreducibly funny." Keaton's face has a French quality, like the famous "weeping Frenchman" photo or Fernandel; it is closer to a caricature of handsomeness, the body was funny and important for positional geometric comedy, the face came in a slow last for humor.

The big story in film criticism is a two-part serial: The first involves the persistence of the sentimentalized, misread Agee review, and the second concerns the arrival in power of the Sarris-Sontag classifier, who can pack so much authority into a subordinate clause. Like so many unhappy art events, the second envolvement might not have happened had Agee's writing in *The Nation* been correctly assessed for what it was—the first important film criticism to show a decided variance between the critic's words and what actually went on in the film.

December 1965

DESPITE the fast-fading charm of *Breathless* and the poignant travelling effect Godard gets in *My Life to Live* (by giving his pimp-prostitute characters a stucco-like flatness and then mobilizing them in awkward, slow, stop-go motion), Jean Luc Godard has created a near desert of complex boredom. With its uninventive, listless, strewing about of actors, and insistence on improvisation which, allowing for no tension between actors and film, produces a kind of mindlessness, *The Married Woman* arrives at its love-is-fleeting bromide. Its route follows no story and no evolving form but is sprayed like grapeshot at the audience through a melange of quotes, texts, monologues, and confidences from characters faced straight on to the audience as though the film's basic situation (a wife finding married and illicit love are exactly the same) is worthy of nothing so much as dismissal.

There is always in Godard the desire to distend the medium without breaking it, mostly through the approach of (1) flattening characters into the thinness of rolled-out cookie dough, (2) inflating these envelopes of dough with closeups, extended views in various locations, and, most of all, with words. It doesn't really matter whether they are the character's words or Godard's and in fact it is impossible to tell, because they speak a common language of foamy pseudo-philosophizing, filled out with hesitations, pauses.

A child turns bluntly to the camera and delivers an awkward, halting, portentous description of the 10-step process involved in an impossible-to-identify assemblage. One of Godard's less blocked-out events, the scene shows his desire to ingest the world through little spigot mouths, as well as certify the validity of vacuous, coffee-urn characters. This maneuvering with mouths and the questionable sententiousness of what's being said emblemizes the masturbatory quality of Godard's work, trying to call forth seminal freedom, redundant energy in lifeless, self-accepting faces. Godard's oratorical afflatus, which first showed itself in a blighting, self-advertising scene (*Breathless*) in which a sage-like celebrity in sunglasses fielded sex questions from sopho- moric reporters, worked more plausibly in *My Life to Live*, the only Godard steeped in documentary tactics, in which the dialogue springs from a certifiable coffeehouse, late hours situation.

The Married Woman is another heavy installment in a career-long attempt to somehow bring a man and woman together, despite an attitude that is more strangely covetous and voyeuristic than Antonioni's behavior with Monica Vitti. The Charlotte of Macha Meril spends this film chewing up time, slowly posturing, listening in rooms intentionally dulled of any interest (one dead bedroom at the airport is faked up with a Moliere portrait) while two men, off- camera as in Antonioni, glide their suppliant hands over her anatomy. Nothing happens in this hollowed anti-movie: It is as though an obscenely dim-witted perfection were being set before male actors and spectators by a perverted husband. Godard's struggle is fantastic: Besides the studied Mondrian setups with parts of the body that imply lovemaking, a small tiresome movie is spent listening to erotic laughter on a pop record, a scabrous description (Celine) has a maid fronted so long she seems embarrassed; and, when Charlotte is forced into street dress, a self-fondling goes on in which her hand is patting, raking, smoothing, it's like a dead cobra sent in by Greyhound bus to visit the woman.

Godard has a distrust of the physical that leads into endless hiding— turning faces away from the camera, sinking the body in a roadster until it is almost hidden, treating the figure in street scenes as a weightless, distant acci- dent hardly worth watching. His pedestrians are always flitting towards or away from events that never happen unless the scene can be blotted out by re- versing the film to negative; in his latest, *Alphaville*, these pedestrians are crab- like, faced to the hallway wall, trying to erase themselves into the masonry.

The fear of open, natural behavior makes his film one that is disinclined to use closeups, which nevertheless eventually over-run, embalm the film. In any setup—a middle-distance perspective of Charlotte's clammed-up face below a huge Triumph brassiere billboard; two-shot with Charlotte kissing Robert's temple, a nauseatingly frozen hour in which her mouth, a ruminant animal, alternates "Je t'aime" between nibbling kisses—bodies seem to fade, while the faces, which may not even be in the shot, become a swelling, fronted importance. It doesn't help matters that cameraman and everyone else is shov- elling something, Cultural Importance, against the shot, so that besides the feeling of a big empty countenance with a greedily linear mouth, the story is hidden further in a dense sinister excellence made up of the silver-ish sick-woman effects found in Dick Avedon's photography, plus the kind of delays that suggest hidden psychosis used in James Purdy's novel.

Thus, Godard has made himself Mr. Big in coolness by subverting what could be much more than a skimpy, journalistic technique, answering the acclaim of critics and festival supervisors with poetic free association and types of dervish creativity that show his obvious music-hall gifts. Something approximating self-conscious dance turns up on any occasion. A girl in bikini walking diagonally across a flat roof, stopping to make a windmill motion signifying nothing; a detective flying in a sloppy ballet move towards a disappearing car thief; Belmondo's karate slice in a bathroom; Eddie Constantine gunning down *Alphaville* agents with a greased, soft-shoe effect; Karina's persuasive dance, teasing a new boyfriend who plays billiards as ineptly as Constantine shoots; a magical scene at the airport with a child doing figure-eight moves amongst the adults (which survives Miss Maril's squeezing her chin between fists, a pet gesture meaning indecision). The worst part of this outre fever in Godard's work is that it is sprinkled onto film with the hidden notation that it be taken as no more than the haphazard words heard in drifting conversation.

January 1966

The Wizard of Gauze

WHEN did movie directors decide that boredom was part of the game? The first mushrooming took place long before *The Red Desert* in a steady parade of overrated classics made in France: the metaphysical masquerades of Julian Duvivier, the under-visualized blues ballads of Marcel Carné.

Punctuating his films with tremolo effects, using voices like flute music, and turning shootings, escapes, flights into echoes, Carné (in the 1930's) created movies that eluded a direct gaze like the light from a subway train. What he did was grayer, less battering, with more romantic longueurs than the new Bondishness of *Ipcress File*. However, many of his techniques, such as using Arletty as a public image rather than an actress, are not too different from Sidney Furie's scaled-down work in *Ipcress File*.

This is a Chandleresque thriller that has no thrills, with an antihero who is more like a sugary flavor than an actor doing a Philip Marlowe. For his ticket, Furie's customer tries to pretend that set designs in chic colors are adding up to a movie. Actually, the only suspense is how slowly an effeminate knight (nonplayed "superbly" by Michael Caine) can put dimes in a parking meter, crack eggs in a skillet, or flatfoot his way through a library. This is something like watching Rod Steiger in *The Mark* trying to substitute a prop coffeepot for a decently written part.

Alfred Hitchcock, one of the most dogged of entertainers, hit a fallow period in the 1940's when he anticipated the kind of humorless playfulness we now find in such French prizes as *Zazie* (comic strip techniques) or *Breathless* (satires of acting styles, self-conscious parodies of Cagney-Bogart films). Trying to make the studio film pliable again, Hitchcock hit on esthetic accidents that aroused queer sensations: for example, an elusive sense of size (how large is the lifeboat in *Lifeboat?*); the claustrophobic sensation of being caught for two hours in the deadly orange-peel harmony of *Rope*; a speeding car in which the only thing moving is Ingrid Bergman's overteased coiffure; a scene fastened to the back of Michael Wilding as he walks through a ballroom; a succession of shots in which actors pop into and out of the frame, like shooting-gallery figures; the spooky-looking guests being introduced to Miss Bergman at Claude Rains's party; Cary Grant appearing upside down to the morning-after perspective of a sobered heroine.

Somewhere on the road between Hitchcock's cumbersome *Lifeboat* period and the latest glutted diversions, there has been a general desire among directors to (1) feed their vulgarity on the material of old Hollywood films, (2) replace tempo and form with unfunny satire, and (3) surround the spectator by film, as by a volley of buckshot, attacking him from all sides.

Using a Ziegfeldian chorus with nudes in classic Mr. Clean poses and reviving the chiclet colors that didn't work for George Sidney when he directed MGM musicals, Federico Fellini tyrannizes the audience in *Juliet of the Spirits*. The apparent idea, if it isn't to prove himself a cinematic Bellini, painter-director of overstuffed masquerades, is to provide the spectator with an additional stomach, a gastric passage that imbibes the billows of fake chatter and color without the mind having to contend with them. Like Godard-dammerung's chatter, Fellini-Bellini doesn't focus one's attention on unnoticed reality, but dissolves the spectator's capacity for noticing. Before his Pillow Case Special has moved past the scene in which an oversaccharine Joan Blondell type has been chopped (hidden with Curtiz's mirror and Orson Welles's trick of unspooling ticker-tape dialogue from unopened mouths), the spectator feels he is being pushed through an endless, unexciting crowd.

Any film that starts out with Giulietta (one-expression) Masina as a devoted wife beginning to doubt her husband's fidelity is in trouble. Her sexless acting is a parlay of Bambi's stiff motion, Harry Langdon's large ball-bearing eyes, and Spring Byington's ability to exude goodness, patience, and

domestic cleanliness with a raspberry valentine smile. The movie leaks entertainment as this tender smile under an inverted soup-tureen hat falls half
asleep at the beach (in harmony with the spectator) or flies to the wall in terror when a Liberace in mint-green toga gazes at her in minuscule eroticism.

A Jack-the-wrapper director, who grabs the spectator's throat in the first
shot and doesn't let go until he has used every sexual-fantasy item from a
leatherette boa constrictor to stiffened tongues, Fellini has boldly, willfully
transformed a single idea (wife in a torment of phantasmagorical thoughts) into
a hundred cliché-packed scenes. Every night scene employs an excruciating
cricket noise to imply Country. The key scene in Spencer Tracy cycles—a
gliding fox trot through admiring ballroomites while someone plays Their
Song—is stylized into glassiness, made creepy by lengthening the moves,
deadening the husband (Mario Pisu), who wears more eye-mouth make-up
than his wife and holds her in the angelic no-touch embrace that is standard
for Fellini antiquarianism.

Fellini is the only enthusiast for old Hollywood Muzak who doesn't
believe in syncopation or its absence. A sort of mentholated accordion sound
(like rain with dead raindrops) is bent forward and moved fast, but it doesn't
have any beat.

He is also afflicted with a sort of equalism that makes every object as loudly
important as the people. At least a tenth of the film takes place above, below,
or in the neighborhood of an oversized baroque hat which has no life but out-
acts the glazed face beneath. While people are walking under these chic Barney
Google creations, everything is stationary, and the spectator wanders under the
tentlike brim, pursuing time.

Such lidded echoes of the floats in Pasadena New Year's Day parades are
only one of the many cotton bandanna devices for diminishing people. Dead
skin, feet that don't touch the ground, kids expanded and overdressed. A simple walk from a front gate to a doorway suddenly becomes a Big Scene (any
older director would have skipped it). An iron bellpull carries as much import
as the whole clutter around a decayed mansion.

Fellini reverses the old Warner Brothers theory in which a talented bit
player provided a great deal of the scenery, built the pace, and served as a foundation for the movie's structure. The bit players here are used as wasteful clutter. Instead of individuals, they become wiggles, clown effects: e.g., an expanse
of fiendishly concentrated enthusiasm on a face posed artfully against a bright
orange umbrella.

Fellini's own distaste and ennui creep into the film in the form of a Gauze
Wonderland of meaningless decor. Objects, transparent stuff, a basketwork lift

for getting customers to a tree platform for minor orgies are brought forward actually to degrade, lessen the actors who have to cart them around. This personification of objects and depersonalization of people was fairly serviceable in *M. Hulot's Holiday*—or, for that matter, in Keaton's *Navigator*—but all it does for Fellini is to suggest some failure of moral intelligence. He can't seem to distinguish between the importance of a dark blue wickerwork lift and the actress who's riding in it.

The antithesis of these globular confections can be found in *What's New, Pussycat?*: especially in its handling of supporting cast (Capucine's tense nympho, Paula Prentiss's suicidal stripper). Clive Donner's direction gets a hardness of line, a whiplike individuality by compressing his actresses into a murderously confined space. Keeping the tempo fast, Donner has them almost on tiptoe, with no time to overpromote their Hollywood traits.

Woody Allen's writing, too, often appears as the obverse (funny) side of the bed-sheeted surrealism of Juliet in Remorseville. Despite too many Sennett chases in an overlong finale, Allen and Donner between them manage a punched-up college-humor style which really is funny. When they are not merely kidding the old two-reelers but trying hard for real Sennett or Keaton, they give us such moments as the Siegfried funeral with Sellers (wrapped in a flag) planning to launch himself out to sea.

Fellini's characters, on the contrary, generally look as though they were operating under the same ideological burdens as their director: Valentina Cortese, piled high with romantic garbage, a wig that ends in daisies, huge frilly chokers, Billie Burke's chattering gaiety. It is impossible to have all this and a Bergman Festival, too. Actresses staggering under this amount of trickery are not at their best while diving ecstatically through the morning dew.

Fellini's best image in recent years is still the opening of *8½*, a berserk Madison Avenue type hopelessly trying to climb through a cab window while life and/or the movie business streams past. This at least had dramatic meaning, which is not found in *Juliet of the Spirits*. Even the images have a kapok-padded puffiness that Claes Oldenburg gets in his pop-art sculptures of fried potatoes. For pure uninspired nothingness, openness within pacelessness, this *shtick* may be the closest meeting between the commercial art film and the Andy Warhol idea of shooting buildings or real-life situations with a stationary camera, not trying to make a movie.

The result: A film that surrounds the spectator with canned beauty and surprisingly indicates that the New Cinema is in one sense a kitchy-coo throwback to that old convention in painting, now abandoned—a windowlike opening on a scene of pillowy shapes representing Nature. Fellini's circusy image, remarkable as it is for luminosity and seamless continuity, offers the eye and mind far less than *International Showtime*, a Saturday TV fixture with foreign clowns and gymnasts.

February 1966

Pish-Tush

SOMETHING died in the movies when TV, wide screen, and the New Wave film made the bit player expendable. Watching Rita Tushingham or Jeanne Moreau makes one think wistfully of Frank McHugh's eyebrows, Eugene Pallette's humpty-dumpty walk, Edgar Kennedy's mad wounded-bull heavings, and all the others. Whatever happened to Eric Blore?

The great strength of the movies in the 1940's was the subversive power of the bit player. Movies that have become classics, rightly (*The Lady Eve*) or wrongly (*Casablank*), are never more savage and uninhibited than in those moments when a whirring energy is created in back of the static mannered acting of some Great Star.

Casablanca shifts into high gear as soon as Bogart's glum face hits the surrealistic Yiddish energy of Leonid Kinskey. *The Lady Eve* is charmingly acted by Stanwyck and Fonda, but that looney Dickensian spirit that was Sturges's trademark came from brief moments with people like Blore, Pallette, and Demarest. Most of these subactors were short on range, but the explosiveness of their Brief Moments more than made up for it: Frank McHugh, using his hands, eyebrows as though they were wings; Edgar Kennedy, mixing drinks like a barker playing a shell game; the electric-fan velocity with which William Demarest counteracted the monotony of his voice.

As opposed to these midget giants, we find something more nearly the opposite today. Tushingham, Moreau, and especially Giulietta Masina—three tiny women—swell their proportions to giantism with gestures and decor. Moreau, for example, in *Bay of Angels*, piles herself with outsized boas, eyelashes, cigarette lighters, corsets, wigs. This is supposed to prove that she's psychologically doomed.

There is good acting today, but it is very different from the Tushingham-Moreau approach, in that it stays within the modesty and infiltrating of good bit-playing: Oskar Werner's precise melancholia in *Ship of Fools*; James Fox's toughness immersed in a soft-sweet intellectualism in *King Rat*; Robert Shaw's scene-stealing in *From Russia with Love*, which is done alongside Sean Connery, who is a master in his own right in the art of sifting into a scene, covertly inflicting a soft dramatic quality inside the external toughness.

Thus, the current movie, like the current cocktail party in which one or two cultural Big Shots take over, tries to get along with a few big actors doing star turns. *Repulsion*, a Mittel-Europa case history modeled on Hitchcock's *Psycho*, is often convincing and horrific, but the star, Catherine Deneuve, is a too glamorous actress, incapable of blending herself into the street scenes, which lack bit players to make them credible. Just as the best thing in *The Hill* is the hill itself, so the best things here, substituting for the old bit performances, are background minutiae such as wall cracks, dripping faucets, distant views of a playground.

A good actor is usually one who has picked up the tricks that made Lee Tracy better than Spencer: a talent for (1) retreating into a scene, (2) creating an effect of space, and (3) becoming a combination of fantasy figure and the outside world, but always a fragmental blur. For the same reason, a good straight man is nearly always a better actor than the star comic: Dean Martin, George Burns.

A bad example of an actor who has nothing of Tracy's sifting is Simone Signoret, Werner's partner in the *Fools* film, a female Lionel Barrymore sullenly encased in a blocklike girth. She shows nothing but perspiration to pull herself into the scene. An even worse example of the megalomaniac star who can make the simplest action have as many syllables as her name is Rita Tushingham.

The myth that a director breaks or makes a film is regularly disproved by this actress who does a sort of Body Unpleasant act of turning herself into a Duck Bill Blabberpuss (*The Leather Boys*) and carrying on a war of nerves against the other actors. In a somewhat gentler vein (*The Knack*), she adds a gratuitous spookiness, which makes every gag seem to last forever. While this film has been accused of having too many jokes, the fact is that the actress smothers every joke with a goonish nasality and by peering overlong at the grown-ups.

Similarly, it is not the director's fault if she Tushinghams everything up with her particular brand of pathology: being sullen when she should have been airy, simulating the fevers of lust with a wooden body. She injects a grotesquerie into her love scenes, which has more to do with dirty Puritanism than with real sex. In *A Taste of Honey*, Tony Richardson's direction was unfairly blamed for this: he was accused of being too "moralistic" to bring out the "lyrical, childlike, *gamine*" qualities of his heroine. But Tushingham's lyricism is always more gamey than *gamine*. For example, the scene with her unlovely aging mother in the bathtub is made unnecessarily cruel and embarrassing merely through the daughter's appraising stare of distaste.

Actors, too, have been unjustly accused of a certain crudity when playing against Rita (and "against" is the word). Peter Finch has never looked more like a marooned dirigible than in *The Girl with the Green Eyes* when he either beds down or drinks tea with this hard-eyed adolescent. (Olivier, in a similar situation, was allowed by his fellow actress to gain sympathy for his Entertainer.) It's not that Tushingham hogs the screen exactly, but she does chew her way through another actor's scene with bulldog incisors.

The difference between good acting and the Tush treatment is evident in that Richardson film, *The Entertainer*, where Olivier and Alan Bates are working typical Tushingham material: ugly faces, a cesspool existence, meandering narrative, and a grainy *Breathless*-style photography. Here the tawdry beach resort picks up something of the wonder of Chaplin's *Gold Rush* cabin or the dentist's quarters in *Greed*.

There is no moralizing in Olivier's low-comic treatment of a lower-depth character, as there always is in Tushingham's overplaying. In other words, the actor is not always pinning placards on himself explaining: "This is a Bourgeois, this is a Proletarian, this is a Lovable Child." Olivier avoids every stereotype of the tawdry show-biz has-been in order to give his Entertainer some of the magical complexity of a real-life Chaplin. In fact, Osborne's "liberal" clichés that were thrown away by Olivier were overplayed by Tushingham in *A Taste of Honey*.

Like Richardson in *Taste of Honey*, Sidney Furie has never been a more luckless director than in *The Leather Boys*. The best thing about this film is the performance of Dudley Sutton, who plays the homosexual with real old-fashioned elegance, like a bit player. Compared to this, Tushingham plays her lower-class sex kitten with a wild inappropriateness which might look better in a comic strip than in a movie.

Tossing her head about like a basketball and nasally, toothily spewing scorn at her high school teacher, she seems a cross between an adolescent Maggie Jiggs and a delinquent Orphan Annie. A few shots later, abed with her teenage lover, there is the same wild improbability about her sexuality. No one, except possibly Anne Bancroft, can outdo her in a bed scene.

It may be unfair to expect a young and relatively inexperienced actress to exercise her own discretion on a bad script. But actors such as Olivier are flexible enough to improve on the author's intention; others make a bad intention worse.

Furie, a Martin Ritt–type director, who works with submiddle-class people in overstrained wrangling situations, sets up one Tushless situation in an early winter boardwalk that serves as a chaser for Miss Tushingham's presence. The scene involves a potential (Colin Campbell) and committed homosexual (Sutton) picking up a pair of unsentimentally sexy blondes, who have a rowdyism the movie needs and a convincing manner at Ski Ball.

The matter-of-fact presentation of these birds—who recall Howard Hawks's birds of passage in *The Big Sleep*—gives the feeling of a 1940's film made twenty years too late.

The scene moves about with a roughed-in, wind-blown looseness, fanning out into several corners of Coney Island. The comic-strip sexology of Miss Tushingham reappears, and the film veers back into didactic acting and working-class scenes shod or shoddy with leather.

There were moments in high 1940's films—Elisha Cook in *The Big Sleep*— when a supporting player hit his peak and managed to dry out whatever juicy glamour and heroics were in the film so that it took on a slatelike hardness. The art in this Cook-type acting—played from left field—is miles beyond the studiously ill-mannered Reo Rita, who is not only old-fashioned, but who, with her special brand of pushing and ham, manages to rob the film of its space, background, and the effect of being made with a camera.

March 1966

The Cold That Came Into the Spy

What is interesting about the Cultural Exposition is that, while the public has become cognizant of the geniuses in each art form, the works themselves have been losing their separate identity as painting, TV comedy, or film.

As Abstract Expressionism moved into history, it became glaringly evident that its brand names, De Kooning & Co., were involved in a dilemma which dated their works without resolving the problem: a hang-up between no-environment painting and a much thinner wall-covering that shuns all the mannerisms of the Masterpiece.

Similarly with TV. The only original brand of humor in this medium was developed on the late-night talk shows from Jerry Lester to Johnny Carson. By turning its back on the more obvious TV possibilities (probably a good thing) and concentrating, like *Pussycat*, on the format of a nightclub routine, Don Adams's *Get Smart* is one of the few half-hour shows which manage to be both funny and successful. As a klutz version of James Bond and the U.N.C.L.E. agents, Adams's comedy is at once lower (the voice of a canary spieler), faster (the razzing one-liner of the night-clubs), and higher (originally geared to fewer people) than anything except the more inspired ad-libs of the Allen-Paar-Carson-Griffin variety shows.

In the last five years, movies have reached the point achieved in painting some ten or fifteen years ago. No moviemaker wishes, in other words, to be caught dead making a movie. If you compare *Life at the Top* with its parent, *Room at the Top*, you can see how much ground has been covered in a hurry. Instead of the corny, old, candid scene of adultery in the earlier film, we now have that floor-walker's inventory of "camp" objects (Good Godard!) plus a cockeyed notion of how a husband reacts to being cuckolded. Adultery is neither represented nor symbolized in traditional terms; it is rather triggered like Pavlov's dog by a series of associations which remind us of earlier movies.

Instead of plot or characters—in place of old-fashioned acting or directing—all the film-maker needs to do now is exhibit a string of objects reminiscent of old cinematic love affairs: the discarded shoes, the half-eaten remains of what passes for a champagne supper, the "telly" rolling an old Astaire film and (most nostalgic of all) one punchy shot of the cuckolded Laurence Harvey wearing a child's mask of Disney's dog Pluto and holding the lover's discarded tie.

Jean Simmons's total feminism, faultlessly played, is the one redeeming reality in the drifting, witless dramatization in an Englishy version of O'Hara's Country: hapless married people ensnared, sort of scratching around in superfluous plumbing, croquet sets; Antonioni's morbid strip-tease, done twice without cuts; and, mostly, car scenes that are nearly pointless whether the inevitable Rootes product (the movie's hero) is moving or parked. Oddly enough, what all this emphasis on decor at the expense of people suggests most is the social realism novel that appeared before Edison invented the camera.

This is particularly apparent in *The Spy Who Came in from the Cold*, which is also a striking example of a bookish movie issuing from a cinematic book. Less a routine spy story than a novel, the fascination of Le Carré's book was precisely in a filmlike quality which managed to combine the complexities of *Herzog* with the mobility and eyewitness technique of Hitchcock at his *Vertigo* best. Ten years ago, any reader would have thought, "What a great movie this would (will) make." But today all this cinematic quality is wiped out in favor of something else.

Although Martin Ritt has done an interesting job of bringing out the dull, pudgy side of Le Carré's hero, this is at the expense of Leamas's equally important other side, which is one of great physical and spiritual strength. Burton's big face is not too well cast as the "faceless hero," and the pulverizing attempt to get rid of all his box-office glamour seems to have shriveled the actor considerably beyond the author's intention.

Despite this handicap, Burton has some memorable scenes with whisky bottles, drunken talk, and particularly in one final courtroom close-up when he realizes he's been sold out by his own superiors. Burton and Ritt deserve a good deal of credit in going against the actor's grain here—he is not even allowed to use his biggest asset, his voice. And even though they don't quite manage to make Le Carré's character come through, it still remains a powerful projection of something so rocklike and stubborn in Leamas's character as to be good in its own right.

What is more interesting, however, is the manner in which current techniques succeed in turning a slow filmlike book that grips the reader into a "terse, swift" screenplay that is solemn and often dull. For one thing, the script is condensed like an accordion, with scenes either dropped out or briefly suggested in a manner which destroys any subjective identification.

Hitchcock, for example, got his subjective effects from using normal time: The spectator is there, living through a scene and seeing only what he would see as an eyewitness. The new vogue does just the opposite. Although the plot flashes by with almost meaningless rapidity, there is no impression of speed or movement—of many different scenes being compressed, as in *Tom Jones* or *The Knack*.

It's more like reading a five-page precis of *War and Peace* while sitting in a handsomely decorated library. The camera lingers interminably, like a Winslow Homerish version of the nineteenth century, on some studiously squared detail of emotion or decor, but there is such an absence of identification with the actor as to suggest the word "objective" in its worst scientific sense.

The cold that's now in *The Spy* was put there by a writing team (Guy Trosper and Paul Dehn) who have the notion that Leamas is an up-to-date Cold War version of the burnt-out figure who infests books by Arthur Koestler and Graham Greene: always demoralized and dehumanized by a rotten system.

The film's most telling frame shows Burton, humiliated by the East German head of counterespionage and manacled hands-to-feet in a bare cell. Ritt has prepared this shot as though it were the Last Supper, yet Burton manages a surprisingly truthful effect of middle-aged discomfort and defeat, like a sort of grounded, misshapen sea monster. What is dropped from the script here is a brilliantly worked out scene in which Leamas—far from being the sodden depressed cipher so often portrayed by Charles Boyer or James Mason in Graham Greene movies—maneuvers one of his captors into a dark room and, outthinking him with a wonderful chair gimmick, destroys him with his own brand of superjudo.

It is typical of the new-style film that any scene so actable as this is automatically too melodramatic or corny and must be dropped. Instead, we get innumerable beginnings and endings of scenes (like the above), all done in a slow friezelike genre style, which makes it impossible for the actors to get any complication inside their roles.

Leaving out so much self-explanatory action makes it necessary to explain the plot with a good deal of improbable dialogue. Even when the dialogue comes verbatim from Le Carré, it must be encircled with traffic lights to make sure the audience gets every plot idea from the loaded speech. The chief device for tying these fractional views and mobilizing the continuity is a door that flaps people in and out with a constancy recalling an old-fashioned play.

The book opens with a chase-and-kill scene in which Leamas's prize agent is gunned down cycling towards Checkpoint Charlie. Anyone reading this was hooked by Leamas's view, which becomes Dostoyevskian in its realization of all the pigeons, all the cheating, and hopelessness involved in a mucked-up operation.

The movie has scrubbed this viewpoint, which would have filtered Leamas's personality into the event. In its place is a perusal of the storefront scenery and an enthralling music-hall enactment of the bicycling, but the movie loses its one chance to identify Leamas as not merely depressed but as also a subtly talented technician in a squalid Looking Glass job. After Burton has been squeezed into his role, the same undercutting goes on with Claire Bloom and Oskar Werner, who never get to act themselves into the Cold War scene.

When the bearded East German intelligence official (Werner) asks Leamas for his forged signature, a typically Hitchcock moment is set up with two professionals absorbed in the intricacies of handwriting. This scene, the kind that can be acted into a killing bit and realized best with a subjectively used camera, is not milked at all.

As Leamas disintegrates according to a fantastic plot arranged by his Control, he moves through a London underworld, employment office, crackpot library, prison. Le Carré made these moments into great bouts of acting. A fussy librarian gets tangled in his stubbornness as a bum, his garbage and smell, even the problem of spelling his name on pay checks. Burton could have acted this highbrow Bowery comedy into the area of Falstaff's humor, but it has all been displaced or tersed up by obsessive need for a dour, relentless movie.

An actor who can defeat this chilling style has to be a master at working in needlepoint. There is a tantalizing stretch when Burton reports back to his prissy, devious boss, and the actor (Cyril Cusack) gets more inflection with his glued-together lip motion on "Quite so" or "mental fatigue" than Errol Flynn does in the whole underrated movie about Gentleman Jim Corbett.

Werner, as the tough Jewish questioner, does a weirdly clever job of being just what he should be (like a terrier, slight and agile). Most of his virtuoso-ish hocus-pocus is done by obliterating one word to emphasize a raised syllable or accented laugh, and it is managed within a whiskery mask that should deaden his talent for eloquence.

The Spy may not be as stylish as *Eva, Help!*, or *Giulietta of the Syrups*, but it has an aftereffect that is surprisingly pungent and more provoking than the other movies. Despite the cold literary treatment of *The Spy*, a few of the fragments are so precisely verisimilitudes, both in relation to Le Carré and to life, that they succeed in themselves in making this a hard movie to forget.

April 1966

Day of the Lesteroid

THERE has no doubt been an upheaval in films during the 1960's, but almost nothing has been said about the Department Store styling or Modiste's Sensibility which seems to be causing the upheaval. Near the beginning of *Help*, the Beatles are seen walking up paths to identical red-brick houses, which, inside, turn out to be one long arcade of opulence, most of it vulgar and on display at any department store. It is typical of Beatledom that, while the spectator gets a distinct impression of modern goodies—an electric organ complete with comic books, a lot of food dispensers, a sunken bedroom for John Lennon—the scene itself is hardly touched.

During the night, Ringo does a funny crawl and talk when he is thrown from his bed by a ring-removing device, and later John Lennon does some dead-pan phoning, but on the whole their wild talent for goonish comedy is scarcely tapped by their director, Richard Lester.

Although there is a critical notion about Lester, a poor-man's Prospero showing us our wilder dreams, the fact is that he has been getting farther away from fantasy in any stereotyped sense and closer to a rather depressing comic-strip world of his own.

It is a world of Display Cases in which—like the old-fashioned Harold Teen or Katzenjammers—the humor is melancholy and the zaniness forced. Despite the frenetic postures, there is no real movement, and the chief effect is a sad, gray, frustrated technology. There is hardly a smidgeon of fun in any of these "cool" scenes (as in *The Knack*) where the actors have an embarrassing lachrymosity and limpness like drooping flowers or candles.

Lester's trademark is a kind of thickness of texture which he gets purely with technique, like the blurred, flattened, anonymous, engineering sounds which replace actors' voices, plus the piling up of finicky details, as in the scene of the Beatle shaving his friend's image in the mirror. A Harold Lloyd would have milked this gag by lengthening it; Lester goes to the opposite extreme of such radical foreshortening that the spectator is in danger of losing the scene.

In his exploitation of camera-editing devices, Lester has used his advertising-film background with such intensity that he leaves the idea and feeling of movies. What he creates is a new, assertive, hard-pushed Nowness that makes one feel out-of-it with a syntax of restlessness, cacophony, Gothic toys, gadgets as gadgets rather than plot mechanisms, and, most of all, a Fu Manchu feeling that comes from heavy costuming-cosmetic jobs that hardly allow an actor to exist.

Master of the Erector Set effect, Lester is a compendium of tricks and traits used by other Macy's directors who give a movie experience that veers between a catalogue of posh-vulgar items for licentious living (*Thunderball*) and a wildly imaginative Cecil Beaton notion of the twenty-first century in which Mastroianni, with his French's mustard skin and hair, manages to be the only decent actor despite a puckish notion that he is as doll-like as the mechanical porcupine that he uses for skin massager, gun bearer, and pet (*The 10th Victim*).

Louis Malle, in *Viva Maria*, shares with Lester the notion that any item, from the brass bedstead which Lester's unclowns push across the spectator's dormant spirit to a bronze horse in Malle's Mexican courtyard, can be turned into a causeless sight gag. Laboring under the delusion that he is Mr. Malleable, the director takes dozens of implacable items, including a miscast Jeanne Moreau, and piles up toothless slapstick effects. A typical priceless moment: a priest beheaded by a grenade, the pay-off being a shot of the torso descending the stairs, the head lodged in the man's hands while smoke issues from his cowl.

Thunderball never lives up to its prologue special, a water ballet involving silhouetted nudes in strawberry punch, a fishbowl effect that has some authentic eroticism and sets the Commodity tone of the ensuing mess. Lesterizing the Bond movie, the director has achieved something even Malle doesn't quite do in his *House-and-Garden* version of a 1912 banana republic: A marriage of the tinker-toy and the human in which the very air seems to turn into high-priced leather.

When Bond flies off via a missile corset, the interesting item isn't the stiff take-off, as though he had been ascending into the air by way of an escalator, but the dead-air effect behind him. It is exactly the same non-air that is used in the Alpine high jinks with the Beatles, the interesting difference being that the far-from-gilt-edged Bond director intentionally stops far short of credibility so that the spectator, like a buyer, can study each construct: the clipped square eyebrows that Sean Connery shifts in a placard effect, the frothy bubbles that spin up from an underwater love act.

The 10th Victim is by far the best neo-Lester film in that it totally accepts the idea of a department-store film and in certain nonplot scenes comes close to the perfumed eroticism that is always promised in painting by Rothko or Jasper Johns but never delivered. The good scenes are those that move away from the one-plot idea of legalized murder into a burnt-color madness in which the male is not only emasculated but turned into a sort of Vogue-designed vapor that the Amazon female lugs, hauls, shoves.

Lester's idea basically is a film that doesn't grow organically, but is postbuilt and prebuilt by a team of design specialists who are only bothered by the fact that they have to use actors inside their blue-white gauzemanship and painter's-dream sets. The Italian combine behind *Victim* actually blasts this Group-Ther-wrappy notion into disturbing poetry that is only grounded by the plodding and oddly arranged musculature that Ursula Andress exhibits as a female Mr. America.

Lester's syntax involves a relentless enterprise with photography (zoom, helicopter view, hand-held camera, changing the speed by removing frames) worked against a careful compartmenting. In this schizoid presentation, the actor is only a ploy in a program where the audience's ordinary view of a scene is constantly destroyed while he is held stationary against a maniacal engine which may be a bus-station storage locker (Lester's worst sight gag) or a black-white image of the Beatles at work which serves as a target for colored darts.

The bounciness and terrible rigidity is found in all the sub-Lester works, the most schizoid being *The Chase*, an America-stinks number written by an old-time specialist in that area, Lillian Hellman, who here turns one small Pan-handle town into a manic-depressive hell of lechery, Frugging, car-madness, Sin-town shakes and quivers à la Beatledom: At peak moments the streets get piled up with hell-raisers in new Chevrolets, all heading in different directions.

In the queen bee of vignette scenes, in which two or three moralistic scolds bitch each other in interesting dialogue, Miss Hellman has caught the Lester sickness: she has borrowed the kaleidoscopic effects in *Help* and chopped her script into a mass of Small Town filigrees, miniature versions of *The Little Foxes*. Some of her 100 per cent masochists and sadists drive in from the most distant reaches: the stray gum-chewers and Coke-drinkers who idled around gawking at the lynch scene in *Fury*. The weirdest borrowing: one beaten up wagon from the Our Gang comedies and the fake piety Negress, who discolored so many 1920's films, telling her child to pay no attention to those white folks and their criminal acts.

This diced conglomeration Middle Class Theater that forces its director to mimic scenes from *On the Waterfront* and *Ice Palace* is pure department store. Where Malle uses two actresses to play one starved role, Miss Hellman has written three and four of everything: Two near ghosts who walk uninvited into anyone's office or living room just to kibitz the action; three Robin Hoods in reverse who beat up anyone who looks lawful; two sexpots who have little flesh but manage to divide the good and bad males between them; three huge revels that go on simultaneously. The only nonduplicate is an escaped convict who sneaks home one night and is played with sneaky movie-stealing cheeriness by Robert Redford.

The chase, near the end, suddenly gives up the Lester ghost and becomes a wonderfully sinuous inside depiction of a fire in a car dump that leads into a perfectly timed version of the Lee Oswald murder. Swatchlike characters who automatically move into place (as a Miserable Drunken Bag, Martha Hyer at her lowest as an actress) give way to a complicated unfolding in which there is an unpredictable exit and entrance of shockingly beautiful images. One fiery moment with Brando working his way toward Redford penned in by thugs in a lakelike inferno is a stunner. No one has died more perfectly or surreptitiously than Redford, but hardly anyone in this Day of the Lesteroid has been allowed to act, i.e. to sift his way within a panoramic unfolding. In the Commodity program which Lester Help-ed engineer, every situation has a beginning-middle-end development that murders an offbeat actor (Marlon Brando) who thrives on working away from Systems and has based his throwaway talents on being able to grab attention from any Chevrolet or sequin gown that the lower technicians throw in his way.

May 1966

Lambs Without Mary / Lumet Looms Again

In the current criticism, where the goal is building bronze Central Park statuary out of minor talents—Joe Losey, Jerry Lewis, Sidney Lumet in the L category—a great deal that is of peripheral interest is never mentioned.

Every review tends to become a monolithic put-down or rave, as in Richardson's *The Loved One*—the closest Hollywood has come to showing a film the way it is created in bits and pieces by a motley assortment of technicians, few of whom know the script in its entirety—which was handled by critics as a 100 per cent assault against taste and form.

Rod Steiger's intricate lacy performance of a mother's boy veering in and out of fantasy was forgotten, and also the funny original scene with a house teetering on a sliding cliffside high above a Los Angeles freeway. This one scene—with its climate, view, the girl-in-swing eroticism flipped at the spectator like fast dealt cards, the dangerous drops, sags and jumps that go with life in a sliding house—is far superior in movie technique to at least three W. C. Fields feature-length frauds.

Sidney Lumet? A reasonable question, since, despite the publicity that piles up around his prolific career, he is still a shuttling blur to the public and is generally mistaken by critics as a junior follower of the more arrogant Elia Kazan or as an honorary conscript of the Actors' Studio.

In *View From the Bridge*, Lumet stages a knife fight at midday in Sheepshead Bay, in which, aside from the weird lack of onlookers, the spatial relationships are such that the fighters need a crosstown bus to achieve contact. Another sign of his weird spacing is the locale in *The Pawnbroker* with no sign of the clutter, old golf clubs and used auger bits to hinder movement or keep Steiger from suggesting the volcanic energy, towering mythic character that appeal to the smallish retiring Lumet.

Lumet is usually downgraded as a dated Warner Bros. type because, along with making a sort of fascinating movie with a built-in Ida Lupino gloom and distrust, he appears to be chained to the script. His obligation to keep the story moving contains a fear about boring the spectator that comes allied to a commando-type drop in which he darts in and out of a conversation after circling it.

Thus the chief sensation in the acting is of being hurried, almost lunatically, and an esophagus effect in which the figure—Anna Magnani in *The Fugitive Kind*, still one of his best works—appears to have trouble getting her fiery feeling from chest into mouth. The constricted style reaches one peak with Henry Fonda in *Fail Safe*—alone with white walls, a translator, and a telephone—creating enormous tension as he tries to talk Russia out of an atom-bomb retaliation, the ominous well-chosen words barely getting through Fonda's mouth which has never been large, but, under Lumet's pressure, appears to shrink and dry up to the size of a guinea pig's.

Ossie Davis' unexpectedly inspired clumping as a walrus-y prisoner in *The Hill* is one sign that Lumet's breaking out into a stronger comic director, but most of his traits—people being throttled by time, their own weight, the arena-like attitude of actors, the drops into conversation, elephantiasis in the com-position—are at their worst in his new film about eight Vassar classmates heading into suicide, lesbianism, unhappy childbearing, helped along by the most flaccid, gross, middle-aged boyish characters in modern fiction.

The Group is bad Lumet for the simple reason that the movie involves an unlikely coupling: Lumet, whose idea of a prolonged conversation times out to a half second, and Mary McCarthy's polite murmur, which is like cramming and has no movement beyond that of her voice which piles up deanimating details, not about character but something on the fringes of personality, such as errors, gullibilities, habits, possessions. Lumet, who, save for the bombed New York shots in *Fail Safe*, is too frightened to shoot in real life and hasn't much locale curiosity anyway, must have caved in when he read Sidney Buch-man's script: A New York-less storyline that loses the weight and flavor of Miss McCarthy's book and almost any movie Lumet's done.

Wasting its comments about Spain, being blocked in analysis, and barely workable as a mashed-together series of biographies, Buchman's screenwriting gives the director a two-hour-plus example of a *New Yorker* magazine short story. A luncheon next to a billiard table in a Village restaurant, the sign in a hallway lavatory are the miserably inadequate substitutes for Miss McCarthy's spotting, which has no movement and doesn't know how to stop.

Candice Bergen, as the group's one lesbian, gets some of the book's men-tal rapidity: imperiously putting-down someone's cliché; like quick silver, leaving a taxi. Again, with Joan Hackett's humor-enclosed, too-clever acting—the glistening tricks in which her elegant elbows go one way at different speed from her eyes and voice—Lumet moves in towards the book's endless defining and observation.

In her deflowering and pursuit of a pessary, Miss Hackett catches the McCarthy not-quite-believable objectivity, but the film short-circuits the pileup of observations about birth control, clinic pictures, an afternoon in a sticky dress, undressing, etc. When the Hackett-Bergen characters drop out early, Lumet loses all chance to do a monstrous deadpan takeoff on an inter-esting book in which the pages don't turn.

The film script concentrates somewhat safely on Joanna Pettet's nerves and opportunism in a failing marriage with Larry Hagman, but the material—a webbing of details about the number of mink coats at a cocktail party, whether Hagman's been true to his humble origins in his play—is thin to the point of vanishing. Lumet pushes this fraction of McCarthy journalism like Jane Austen gone berserk: Besides the shoved-along pace, the fake anguish and fake cheer pile up on the year's noisiest sound track, and Miss Pettet does an agonizing face-wrenching that is talented but spreads repetitiously.

Buchman didn't welsh on any of the classmates. He also concentrates on Jessica Walter, who does a lot of smiling and phoning (a born Fellini-type actress who uses face powder to torture the spectator), and there are several chapters involving Shirley Knight who brings punch home from parties for her neighbor (Lumet's father) and listens to her vacillating lover discuss his analysis and Sundays with little Gus. These discussions feature Hal Holbrook who, aside from his flat face, talks in a flat, grating, superearnest style that makes him the squarest character to appear outside of a McCarthy male-hating story.

Part of the trouble is that the love affairs aren't much without words like pessary which are the only ones in McCarthy stories that move and seem to come from on-the-spot perception. Other than the fact that Miss Bergen's stylishly moving lesbian gets the least footage, the trouble also is that Lumet does nothing with Manhattan (no surprise) and that the pony-ish actresses haven't the undulatory motion, hips, or any Harold teen-ish ideas of how to make the '30s dresses count (no one dreams of wearing less than a complete outfit). A big nothing-shot shows the whole cast arm-in-arm walking towards nothing at an East Side intersection, a distant Ford in the background.

Giganticism is, of course, the main Lumet contribution. When Holbrook grates on about his faltering analysis or when the girls' "Who'd a thunk it" pet remark is used, the words dig out a Grand Canyon importance. Miss Walter's sundae-whipped-cream face gets larger and larger as her deadly chatter increases in speed and decibels. Hackett's fling with a shambling-in-all-directions painter takes place in air pockets the size of a ballroom. Miss Knight, in a contented post-coitus scene atop Holbrook's chest, has a head the size of a watermelon. Lumet's looming differs from the old escalation in De Mille in that it has little to do with splendor impressing the spectator. Like a bowl of thin oatmeal overturned and spreading in all directions, the scenes appear to sprawl, to have no sense of boundaries.

Whatever attracted Lumet to McCarthy's most readable book, a wild effect takes place in the meeting of a writer whose prose has no sound, little feeling for the spoken word, and a director who passion-tatters the screen, who expands simple sounds into shrieks. Normal Lumet is Rod Steiger sweating, eyeballs rolling, every sentence moving upwards in ascending hysteria (the closing anguish in *The Pawnbroker*).

Miss McCarthy and Lumet share one trait that may have attracted the director, whose images often suggest the old post office WPA mural: big shambling bodies, vacuity inside a weak outline of a scientist. Beneath the McCarthy crenellated descriptions, the characters are little more than archetypes, and Lumet, given a speck of mythic information, can sprawl a character through two hours of self-contented gush (Walter), hacksaw ambitiousness (Pettet), lower-class "heart" (Knight).

Even in this shambles with a writer he doesn't get, Lumet suggests his talent for hauling-shoving-interpreting scripts. There are snips of scenes that are perfect translations of McCarthy's page, one scene (extended for Lumet) of a wife-beating that is the most explicit, awesome, sadism-at-home image. The fact is that *The Group* has its Lumet guarantee—a bit of fascination—and in certain moments with the Hackett-Bergen duo there is Miss McCarthy's dry caustic effect that is almost humor embedded in something approaching her flat-heeled verisimilitude style. Had Lumet-Buchman tried for the kind of density, webbing, the blend of Edmund Wilson and *The New Yorker* that goes into her literary non-stop, the superdescriptions piling up, the film might have been an inspired Howl.

June 1966

The Subverters

ONE day somebody is going to make a film that is the equivalent of a Pollock painting, a movie that can be truly pigeonholed for effect, certified a one-person operation. Until this miracle occurs, the massive attempt in 1960's criticism to bring some order and shape into film history—creating a Louvre of great films and detailing the one genius responsible for each film—is doomed to failure because of the subversive nature of the medium: the flash-bomb vitality that one scene, actor, or technician injects across the grain of a film.

The Ultimate in a Director's Film, *Strangers on a Train*, now seems partly due to Raymond Chandler's talent for creating erotic eccentrics like the quarrelsome sex bomb who works in a record shop. Nothing in Hitchcock's file of female portraiture has the realistic bite of this Laura Elliott role, nor does any other Hitchcock film show the shady Los Angeles eye for transportation and suburbia.

Inside Daisy Clover, a thoroughly soft Hollywood self-satire, has one scene that is dynamite as anti-Hollywood criticism and the only scene in which Natalie Wood, snapping her fingers to get in time with a giant screen image of herself, is inside the Daisy role with the nervous, corruptible, teenage talent discovered years ago by Nick Ray.

The crassest film, *The Oscar*, has a bit performance by Broderick Crawford, in which he creates his boillike effects of degeneration, vileness. Crawford's corny lolling performance of a small-town sheriff suggests a career of hard-won professionalism, the kind of inside movie technique this Sammy Glick film is supposed to exude but never touches.

King and Country is generally credited as a Joe Losey film, one that is stained with his loathing and casts the spectator in the center of a rat-infested muddy horror known as trench war. It may be a "very good movie," but, within its didactic, humorless images that seem to brood themselves out of a Rembrandt darkness, there is almost nothing that is fresh for Losey, the actors, or Larry Adler, who did the lachrymose music. From the opening harmonica solo, which is pure bathos and standard for little characters crushed by their superiors, to the final Freudianism in which a gun is placed inside the deserting soldier's mouth to finish off what the firing squad started, this is a photo-graphed play with overtrained bits, particularly from Losey's catalogue of male-female symbols.

Just as *Paths of Glory* is indebted to Tim Carey's smart-alecky performance and Calder Willingham's talent for edgy words, obscenity-skirting dialogue, Losey's new films are given a great lift by Dirk Bogarde and the tepid intel-lectuality he inflicts by dragging back on his lines, going silent before quietly spacing his words, in a manner that suggests some fear or sensitivity pulling the words down his throat. Bogarde is woodenly interesting, and, to a lesser extent, so is Tom Courtenay repeating his specialty, a face that has the stiff, convicted homeliness of a wanted criminal on the Post Office bulletin board, plus a chewing, swallowing dialect in which every fourth word gets home to the spectator.

However, aside from the acting, there is a small reward in Losey's ability to bring out a suffocating intimacy, apparent long ago in Hollywood films Losey made about a prowler, wetback, and green-haired boy. Nobody gets such a feeling of worshipful hovering, but it is the disconcerting coldness of a Losey that he doesn't touch his doomed material but just polishes the surfaces.

The Flight of the Phoenix has as its dominant image a group of unstinting character actors strapped like horses to a small airplane or pieces of a larger one. This repeated shot and another fine one of the same hard-working line of actors resting against a plane's fuselage, each one choked with realistic gimmicks and fervor, suggest that almost any Robert Aldrich film is based largely on the wild, sloppy life that a Dan Duryea ensemble player can ply around the edges, trying to budge a huge, flabby movie script.

Aldrich's movie is not only built on the idea of subversive acting, it is pure entertainment that balances the director's shortcomings as a highly personal technician against an unerring instinct for the type of filigree electricity that makes a film but never gets discussed in the *Cahiers* interviews with great directors. The major project—flatly recounting the building of a small plane from bits of a larger one—is flubbed in faulty coloring, *Lawrence of Arabia* shots of the desert, some miscasting with two French actors who lack the hard, antimovie approach of a typical Aldrichite, and the curious fact that Aldrich, who can sift the landscape into the faces and emotions of his actors, goes dead on anything strictly involved with setting.

The film's excitement comes from baroque latticework, unimportant bits of action that seem to squeeze through the cracks of large scenes: The freakish way in which Hardy Kruger's Germanic gabble works over a sun-cracked lower lip; the job-type sensation of watching work procedures from the perspective of an envious, competitive colleague; Ian Bannen doing a monkeyish prancing and kidding around the German; a great deal of letter-perfect hatred of authority by Ronald Fraser as a butterball sergeant; the weird effect of Jimmy Stewart veering back and forth between the slow Charley Ray affectations that made him an unbearably predictable star and a newer Stewart who has a middle-aged doggish look and threads his way along a complicated moment in a peering tricky fashion unrelated to script or acting.

Watching Duryea quietly pin down his Milquetoast role without the usual Duryea aggression of a corny trumpet effect in his upper palate, enjoying the queer pogo-stick jumps of Fraser when a dead engine slowly comes alive, a critic might hope for a new award at the year's end: Most Subversive Actor. This is possibly the only way that justice can be afforded the real vitality in film.

Instead of the overreported people in faulty projects—the Lumets, Steigers, Claire Blooms—the moviegoer is pointed toward the fantastic detailing of Ian Bannen as a toadying liberal officer in *The Hill*; Michael Kane doing a forceful amalgam of silent cunning and subofficer deviousness as the "Exec" in *The Bedford Incident*; Eleanor Bron's mugging, put-on acting that just skirts sickening cuteness as the fake Indian girl in *Help*.

One of the joys in moviegoing is worrying over the fact that what is referred to as Hawks might be Jules Furthman, that behind the Godard film is the looming shape of Raoul Coutard, and that, when people talk about Bogart's "peculiarly American" brand of scarred, sophisticated cynicism they are really talking about what Ida Lupino, Ward Bond, or even Stepin Fetchit provided in unmistakable scene-stealing moments.

July 1966

Rain in the Face, Dry Gulch, and Squalling Mouth

THE obvious fact about any movie image is that it can be read for any type of decisive, encapsulating judgment. A library has been poeticized about Keaton's diluted Sitting Bull face, the horizontal hat, and the rigid sags of his clothes, an automatic "personality" which fades from view as the real Keaton works inside the frozen "armor." Regardless of the occasion, Keaton uses the tar drop eyes, the discouraged fish-mouth (held closed by an act of will) like a slot machine to make a viable situation out of whatever lemon turns up in the scene. Critics sentimentalize Keaton into a wish-fantasy of poetic comedy— superimposed upon what they cannot help observing. They thereby attempt, also, to separate this intensely pragmatic, though original, craftsman from the movies in which he appears, and from the kind of crass opportunism which these comedies, the best of them at that, represent.

Keaton, a re-enactment of the silent film era by a crude writer, is a joy to read when Rudi Blesh is setting the scene at Keaton's studio, presenting a clown who is a clutter of versatility (bridge shark, third baseman, lover) and directly opposite to the deadpan artist eulogized in film books. This is a fabulous book, but, when Blesh starts analyzing the comedies as great laugh machines, the pages become stiff, hard to assimilate. Much of Keaton isn't meant for laughs, and what has been said about his sad, motionless pantomime, the famous frozen kisser, now is irrelevant. The shingle face, at the rare times when Keaton uses it in place of his angled body, is used as an efficient florid syrup, an acting weapon much beloved by its owner.

Blesh's images of these comedies as a roller coaster of energy, a machine gun of perfectly manipulated gags, doesn't have anything to do with Keaton's normal zigzag. *Sherlock Jr.* is a slow scroll, a coiling together of short movements in which Keaton's native fixation on mechanics and slow-witted concern for his own talent works as a drooping agent on the action. The prefabricated Sennett slapstick, which may have been energetic before it became worked into automatic maneuvers by constant repetition, appears to be moving in slow halt-go rhythm; in fact, the pavane-like motion sometimes is standing still. The disappointment now produced by Keaton comes from the fact that there is no real victimization from the disasters. Also, this world that has breathtaking reality and nowness—Santa Monica in the 1920's—is hardly touched by the action, which is faded, automatic, overdecided.

There is a dreadful notion in criticism that movies, to be digested by esthetes, must be turned from small difficulty into large assets and liabilities. James Agee, who always paid out tribute like a public-address system, is never precise, but his fastidious pricing of a Lauren Bacall gave the reader the secure feeling that Bacall could be banked at the nearest Chaste National.

Henry Fonda, during a recent run-through of his films in New York, doesn't add up as "one hell of an actor" (as Bill Wellman declared in a *Cinema Magazine* interview), but he is interesting for unimportant tics: the fact that he never acts one-on-one with a coactor.

When Glenn Ford is a boneless, liquidy blur as a cowboy dancer in *The Rounders*, Fonda fields Ford's act by doing a Stan Laurel, suggesting an oafish bag of bones in a hick foxtrot. Again, in *The Lady Eve*, Sturges kids this Fonda-ism of opposing his playmates in a scene: Fonda's Hoppsy is a frozen hopsicle, a menace of clumsiness, while Eric Blore and Eugene Pallette are clever acting dervishes playing scintillating types.

Fonda's defensiveness (he seems to be vouchsafing his emotion and talent to the audience in tiny blips) comes from having a supremely convex body and being too modest to exploit it. Fonda's entry into a scene is that of a man walking backward, slanting himself away from the public eye. Once in a scene, the heavy jaw freezes, becomes like a concrete abutment, and he affects a clothes-hanger stance, no motion in either arm.

A good director must chop Fonda out from his competition: John Ford isolates Fonda for a great night scene in *Young Mr. Lincoln*, communing with himself on a Jew's harp; there is another one, in *The Ox-Bow Incident*, where Fonda explodes into a geometrical violence that ends in a beautiful vertical stomping. Left on his own, Fonda gets taller and taller, as he freezes into a stoical Pilgrim, sullenly and prudishly withdrawing while he watches another actor (Lee Tracy in *Best Man*) have a ball.

Fonda's man-against-himself act was noticeable in his first films during the 1930's, when his twenty-year-old Tom Joad–Slim-Lincoln were aged into wizened, almost gnomelike old folks by an actor who keeps his own grace and talent light as possible in the role. During the 1940's, in *Daybreak* and *Ox-Bow*, Fonda starts bearing down on the saintly stereotype with which writers strangled him. In a typical perversity, he edges into the bass-playing hero of *Wrong Man* with unlikable traits: nervousness that is like a fever, self-pity, a crushing guilt that makes him more untrustworthy than the movie's criminal population. Almost any trait can be read into his later work. From *Mr. Roberts* onward, the heroic body is made to seem repellently beefy, thickened, and the saintliness of his role as an intelligent naval officer–candidate–President shakes apart at the edges with hauteur, lechery, selfishness.

The peculiar feature of these later Fonda performances, however, is that he defeats himself again by diminishing the hostility and meanness—so that they fail to make us forget the country-boy style in which they are framed.

In his best scenes, Fonda brings together positive and negative, a flickering precision and calculated athleticism mixed in with the mulish withdrawing. Telephoning the Russian premier, desperate over the possibility of an atomic war (*Fail-Safe*), Fonda does a kind of needle-threading with nothing. He makes himself felt against an indirectly conveyed wall of pressure, seeping into the scene in stiff, delayed archness and jointed phrasing—a great concrete construction slowly cracking, becoming dislodged. It is one of the weirdest tension-builders in film, and most of it is done with a constricted, inside-throat articulation and a robot movement so precise and dignified it is like watching a seventeen-foot pole vaulter get over the bar without wasting a motion or even using a pole.

Before it reaches its two strippers at midway point, *The Rounders* shows Fonda in urbane-buoyant stride, but, even a second-team bit player, Edgar Buchanan, outfences him during a funny exchange in which Fonda explains the name Howdy. Eugene Pallette (*Lady Eve*), a buoyant jelly bowl moving skyward as he goes downstairs, is a magical actor, and nothing in Fonda's divested vocabulary is equipped to produce that kind of spring-water bubbling and freshness.

The decisive encapsulating opinion in movie reviews comes usually from reading a plot that is all but hidden by molecular acting and direction. *Who's Afraid of Virginia Woolf?* is an example of Kaleidoscopic Limited, an ordered mélange with not too many pieces but each of them colliding against its neighbor, and all of them hitting like flak into the famous Albee play. The most famous scene is an erotic nondance, which is neither erotic nor dancelike, in which Elizabeth Taylor suggests a gyrating milk-bottling mechanism. Part of the problem here is that the view is top-heavy, and, while her pinchy face and Orphan Annie hairdo are very noticeable, there is no feeling of fatness in action. All the little effects—the acorns in her cheeks, cushion bust, tiered neck—mitigate against the story idea that this is a Bitch Wife drawn to an impotent Science Boy.

That the all-important George name is screamed, belched, panted at a non-George shows once again that movies must not be read as stories. The mangled name (even Miss Taylor yowls or jowls it, seeming not to know who it belongs to) is never acted by its supposed owner, a cyclonic acting-machine named Richard Burton. Burton is pleasing, but the emerging character is not Albee's, or Martha's, George.

This is not to say that Burton, who is far ahead of his co-workers in this movie, doesn't add up to intensely absorbing, complex terrain. Alongside the mushy Taylor performance, Burton is without self-consciousness as a drinker, and, unlike his wife, who moves like a three-dimensional playing card, he fills a scene with body, talk, face. Everything flows around Burton, though at no point is he a masochistic, mediocre ultimate in soft, ineffectual husbands.

Miss Taylor's Martha is also a perfect example of the error in trying to surround a performance with an imprisoning judgment. The role has been castigated as crude, monotonous, prankish, but there are at least two scenes in *Woolf* where she's close to humor and uses the fat lips and lines enclosing them to fill the screen with credible humanity. Her opening mimicry of Bette Davis reacting to a messed-up bedroom should become an unforgettable movie bit, probably because it suggests Burton's mentoring. The bit involves the expression "Wha-ta dum–puh!" said with a complain-y, whine-y little girl effect in which Miss Taylor ends up handing you the puh sound in dump; Miss Davis, a blatant blend of Sophie Tucker and Eleanor Roosevelt, should be jealous. Miss Taylor is even more haunting later in the film, when, after sleeping with the visiting professor (George Segal), she suddenly starts using the kitchen as a workable locale. Moving from counter to fridge to sink, her hips become a hub around which the kitchen appears to be moving.

Shifting Albee's play into a Warner Brothers movie brings on a curious ambivalence. There is a need to make every surface intensely touchable or realistic in the manner of every rackets-film photographed by James Wong Howe. At the same time, opposing this old Warners trick is an abstract theatricalizing, a negation of scene and scenery when the play moves outdoors and into non-scenes: yards without neighbors, streets without cars or people, and a juke joint without customers. Yet the surfaces are intensely specific as air, bark, skin—even moon surfaces. A movie about intellectuals, sophistication, high verbosity, rattles with images of blindness, papier-mâché settings out of children's operetta, streets ridden with street lamps and blinking signs that don't light, and people staring into these fake lights without seeing anything, à la Orphan Annie and her blank circle eyes.

Thus, the movie loses reality by disallowing terrain, but picks up interest when people are treated as terrain. The movie's pivotal scene is a long mono- logue, Miss Taylor weaving back and forth, using the word "snap" to suggest the final disruption of her marriage. Her weavelike motion, the lights moving kaleidoscopically on her face, a hairdo like a great tangled bird's nest—the whole effect is a forest of tangled nasoid speech and crafty motion that doesn't record as talk, but makes insidious impact as shifting scenery.

October 1966

◆

USING unrealistic dialogue, de-emphasized story line, and what often seems a mosaic of disconnected actions, foreign directors have arrived at an inter- esting station in which Scene is more important than plot or characters.

An early instance of this burrowing inside a scenic fragment: Antonioni's *Red Desert*, a silly film in which there is a continual shift away from murky char- acterization to take advantage of the director's suavity with color, his knack for suggesting decay-apathy-strain by doing a photographic doodling with stiffness and stillness in modern landscape. Antonioni's message, his mordant feelings about the New Class, is always filtering into kinds of puffed-up color, scenery which seems to be pulled apart from inside by a highly abstract Mondrian-ish sensibility. A fruit vendor done in one melancholy gray tone, a whole town in wistful pinkishness, a toy man wheeling across a nursery floor and then the dis- traught mother looking toy-sized as she wanders around the same apartment.

Each of these moments shows a massive effort to squeeze a portentous effect out of decorative elements, while the characters and/or actors are left out in space. One of the unforgettable mistakes in modern films is the queer orgy (that never happens) inside a shanty, with its curious recall of a beautifully engineered scene in a shepherd's hut during a rainstorm in *L'Avventura*. Using a documentary that is always Inside Landscape, Antonioni creates a vividly tac- tile feeling of modern hedonists almost glued to a dour island with its fantas- tic impact of air and spray. Then, in a weird turnabout, he makes the same drifting types appear to be embedded within a shack that is like a dark match- box in the center of a terrifying vastness. The photography within this cramped hut is perfect both in terms of realistic space and the nearly lost moderns who wander in from all corners of the island.

In the repeat of this scene in *Red Desert*, Antonioni has abandoned story line, and is doing a sort of wishful esthetics in which the scene gets moved in arbitrary directions towards a hoped-for psychic tie or pictorial tic. Between *L'Avventura* and *Red Desert*, his characters—the new industrial rich—have been steadily losing will as an important part of their characters. In the slowed up action of the *Red Desert* shanty, the actors have a papery unreality while the walls, painted surfaces, and odd jumbling of people have almost human impact. Besides Monica Vitti (a toy: possessing neither will nor self-control), there is a non-acted husband and Richard Harris who dissolutely trails after both. Harris's queer impact comes from the fact that his engineer's personality is built out from the skin in haute monde elegance which includes an orange bob and, from having enormous shoulders atop inadequate legs, an odd weaving stance.

Thus, in removing the insides of characters, the foreign director has suddenly arrived, without realizing it, at a scene built mostly with the appurtenances of Chic. To understand this current flooding of High Fashion calls for a memory of *The Gunfighter*, a fine Western in which there is a deliberate severity, a turning away from all types of brocade in setting-camera-acting.

That movie gets all of its intellectual movement and subtlety from Gregory Peck's miming of quiet self-knowledge, stoicism—the quality of a man standing absolutely straight while being depressed by a hopeless state of affairs. Any recent film from the European avant garde seems, by comparison, to be plunged in *couture*, the materials of the Handsome Life, and the feeling of de-brained characters happy to be wafting about in an atmosphere of constant diversion.

With its crawling pace, witless use of phallic symbols, and a shady treatment of French peasant women falling for an itinerant woodcutter, *Mademoiselle* is a visual nightmare rather than an entertainment.

Jeanne Moreau, a schoolteacher who is the prize citizen in a French village, is set on the road to madness by unrequited love for an Italian woodcutter. The problem—making this pyromaniac an interesting character—is dodged rather than solved. Supposed to be as deeply involved with country character as James Agee's first book about itinerant farmers, the movie becomes a curious case of Hidden Chic. Miss Moreau's sickness is dissolved by a painful repetition in which she seems to be magnetically pulled towards a series of mirrors in her bedroom. In front of triple mirrors, the actress does a slow motion version of her favorite movie technique: running her short fingers over a dry flattened mouth, using an eye pencil on her unseeing eyes, and, at those rare moments when she can draw herself away from her likeness, gazing fondly at the snappy items to be worn to the next fire-flood-poisoning.

Miss Moreau has one marathon lovemaking scene around the entire Correze countryside in which she occasionally seems to move (the big moment: an item Richardson picked up from *Morgan* in which the actress imitates a hound while her boyfriend makes the noises and gestures of a hunter). Otherwise, she creates statue effects: asleep in the woods, staring at a snake worn belt-fashion around her boyfriend's waist. It is no wonder that Richardson must force his sound, dramatizing a scene that is often simply a block of dark-on-dark photography. Miss Moreau's voice (an alienated sound that she achieves without moving her lips) appears to journey around room, wheatfields, before it registers and some of the phallic effects (an axe buried in lumber) seem to crash into a deadened film.

The lack of motion in *Mademoiselle* is brutally shown up by Claude Lelouch's *A Man and A Woman*, with its marvelous tinted color, feeling for pace, and know-how about the racing car scene. A widow and widower keep getting in and out of a Ford Mustang as the rain pelts down; this repeated image forms the basis for a modern romance that suffers from cuteness and the feeling that the racing driver (Jean-Louis Trintignant) and his film studio friend (Anouk Aimée) are the less-than-charming people always seen away from jobs in the more dismal TV commercials.

The Kennedy influence asserts itself here through images that could have been taken out of an album from the family's scenes of young lovers and their two children, long walks along gray beaches, endless stunning shots of Cape Cod sunsets, boating. Much of the Kennedy impact comes from Anouk Aimée's self-assured, slightly frozen performance: a Jackie Kennedy appearance in which she wears a wistfully urbane smile and keeps raking at her dark hair with a model's gesture meant to be captivating and stylish. She seems not only outside the film but as though the love story of a stunt man's widow were being acted straight at her stiff countenance.

Lelouch is registered in this film as writer-director-editor-cameraman. Actually, he is an insatiable doodler of mobile, easily crafted images which get strewn through the film in a mosaic of Affluence. For instance, the Good Life is exemplified in one long dinner table scene in which the love duo does an impossible-to-sustain chuckling over the widower's son, a John-John type with a cute Spanish pronunciation of Coca Cola. For long stretches, all that are seen are the accoutrements of some attractive commercial. One long wrestle in bed, rendered in hot custard yellow with a deadly ballad singer replacing the voices of the actors. The only interesting item in this section are Aimée's perfectly groomed fake eyelashes.

Lelouch is obviously not a top director, but he is (1) a surprising scene creator, and (2) a colorist. A veteran of Scopitone movies, his talent is for tiny Klee-like light reflections and tinier refinements in dry tints.

Lelouch's movie is worth the admission price for a car-driving scene on the edge of the surf, a kind of skater's drift and slide, using an expert driver and getting a car movement never attained on film. Later he gets the same delicacy with gesture: a father playfully tripping his small boy in a misty beach set-up, Trintignant applying a soccer player's side-of-foot motion to spill his son. The peak achievements: Boudin-type effects of bleakness-fog-grayness in tinted blue-gray beach scenes.

Masculine Feminine is a clever follow-up for Godard of the technique he used in *A Married Woman*: almost no plot, often a fixed camera, and a narration that seems to be Godard's own thoughts fed haphazardly through posters, interspersed titles, conversations heard above or behind the Godard serious-ness they mouth. The chief difference between this and any other Godard: Jean-Pierre Leaud, a feverish actor with big head and small body who gives the film a smouldering dark effect, something like the cigarettes he keeps trying to pop into his mouth. Leaud plays a boy just finished with military service, falling in love with a pop singer, and spending most of his screen time trying to be a committed socialist.

The movie is broken into "fifteen precise actions," each section shot in one locality with no beginning or end and no apparent relationship to the sur-rounding actions. The subject—the Children of Marx and Coca Cola during a particular political December in 1965—gets vaguely covered. But mostly it is a matter of ballooning an incident arbitrarily: Leaud writing "U.S. Go Home" on S.H.A.P.E. cars, interviewing a Miss Nineteen about the various devices for birth control.

Godard's sociological interests are endless and he ticks them off with his pet interviewing technique, a sometimes endless verbal ping pong in which Leaud is seldom seen talking but the girls he gets involved with, the stray people who sit-eat-work near him, never stop proclaiming. Somehow, Godard manages to kill the interest of any item he contacts: Bob Dylan and why he is called a Vietnik, homosexuality, brassieres, suicide, etc.

Lelouch, in *A Man and A Woman*, gets exciting motion through his ease with gesture, glances, and particularly the persimmon-pistachio-sepia color. In Godard's film, there is a similar dumfounding virtuosity and it comes through in the sporadic, jazzy actions of Leaud: an aggressive, sometimes hammering use of pantomime in which self-consciousness is balanced by a pathetic daring reminiscent of the clowns who hopped-jerked-raced through Mack Sennett. His declaration of love in an instant recording booth should live longer than the movie itself: an inventive stop-go affair with Leaud backing away, glancing nervously to the side, trying to affect the precise intensity, gesture to fit the doggerel poetry Godard wrote for this scene.

Thus, the directors with old and new reputations are involved in an Absolutely Now cinema in which the scene before you becomes the all of a film, an insatiable monster that blots out the old plot-character-flow elements of a movie. Some good work is still being done in the old style: a straight narrative unfolding within a hopelessly commercial project. The first twenty minutes of *Wild Angels*, an atrocity about fascists on motorcycles, is surprisingly somewhere in the neighborhood of Orson Welles' *Touch of Evil*. A desolate, sun-baked California scene captured with an ingenious documentary camera and a neat trick: using very distant and very close detail shots to hide the substandard script and cast.

December 1966

New York Film Festival: 1967

IF any symbolical figure appeared at the film festival in New York, it was the emergence of the Flat Man, a central character structured like a vapor, a two-dimensional hat salesman, telephone-operator, or decrepit dirt-farmer who doesn't appear to come from any relevant Past, and, after aimless reels of time, there is no feeling that any Future is in sight.

The only one who could be remembered with any clarity, with any sense of physical impact coming from the screen, was a sportscar fanatic, a late adolescent (Jean-Pierre Léaud) who gives shampoos and delivers wigs throughout *Le Départ*. With his crimped manner, a darkly impassioned face, and intensely clear definition of some vigorous act that makes him suggest a pair of scissors gone angrily out of control, Léaud is somewhat less frenetic than he was in last season's *Masculin-Féminin*, where his innocence was more apparent than the exhibitionism that is all that's present in Léaud's other festival appearance, a sort of shadowy sidekick whose main occupation is entering and exiting in *Made in USA*.

Jerzy Skolimowski's *Bariera* is a gentle infant-asy of monumental contrivance, such as a scene in which students tumble onto their faces from a kneeling position on a table, having had their hands tied in a competition, the object being to mouth a matchbox which is held just tantalizingly out of reach by the outstretched hand of an anatomy-class plaster model.

On the order of *Mickey One*, this film is a Surrealistic maze about a man named He, astir in the new Poland. He, picked arbitrarily from the four students who are involved in the quest for the matchbox in the opening *tableau semi-vivant*, is almost too boring to describe. Sort of handsome in the Ricardo Montalban, dark, muscular style, with Vittorio Gassman's down-pointing nose and chin, his indecipherable career is aborted by a series of Bauhaus compositions that shunt him into corners and tie him into square knots—at one point a gauze-draped horse chases him into a bathtub.

There are street scenes on top of street scenes, like a club sandwich of masonry, in which crowds stream while street lights march backward across the screen in perfect alignment into space. Later on in this convoluted Odyssey, we enter a dead-white ballroom (the "dead" here is used advisedly) in which youthful He and She come face to face with "capitalist opportunism," a featured star in this festival. Skolimowski's idea of capitalist wreckage: no one on the dance floor, waiters seated like last year's autumn leaves at tables, the one other important detail being a few palm trees, suggesting the old Poland, or the old Coconut Grove in Hollywood in the era when a ballroom scene meant literally twenty minutes of uninterrupted laughter with Harold Lloyd wearing a magician's jacket and its zoo of hidden animals.

In most of the festival films, particularly the limp, pale grey ménage of *Puss & Kram*, where the theme is a smooth, muscleless gliding in and out of love, a definite disassembling of people and events takes place. Eva (Agneta Ekmanner), as a free-swinging sex cat, takes on lovers in a quick, deadpan, indiscriminate way that makes Julie Christie, the dip-lipped Diana of *Darling*, seem erotically stodgy. The peculiarity of Eva's most uneccentric body and her democratic style is that she is amazingly mellifluous, almost unobservable, and her languid nothings seem to take place in an amphitheater of dead space and dead time.

At the center of this new European entertainment—no pace, a desertlike evenness—is a threadbare, condescending treatment of the individuals: the character who is no deeper, no more developed, prepared, explained than the people in fashion advertisements. In the limpidness, the anemic charm of *Puss & Kram*, the haberdasher Max and his statuesque wife appear transplanted from *Elle* magazine. Repeatedly, the classic Richard Avedon fashion-shot appears (the kind of image that also opens and closes *Le Départ*). It shows a large photograph of the antelopelike wife, in bellbottom pajamas, legs akimbo, seated in white space. This blow-up appears above the movie's central bric-a-brac, a bed, and it consumes an enormous amount of silly footage.

First you look at this dark silhouette of the wife framed with a finely etched contour, then the movie image slides with cliché chic down the wall, onto the two cute heads barely perceptible beneath the sheets. Again, it's more white and a more deadpan sophistication of a type that seems to go back to Cary Grant–Carole Lombard–Topper humor: sunshiny, well heeled, contrived.

Too often, the movie character has been stripped of many of his functions: not so much the victim of a totalitarianism (the smileless boys boarding school in *Young Törless*) or a paternalistic Japan (Toshiro Mifune fighting the clan in *Rebellion*) as a puppet in the hands of his director. The actor, the incredibly passive Törless, a young Audrey Hepburn in military uniform simply bystanding in esthetic fashion, has been sacrificed to the self-interests of the director, while the modishly leaden scene moves around him.

For instance, the *Puss & Kram* scene is supposed to be carried by an interesting looking actor, Hakan Serner, a bowlegged star with a Popovlike face, whose Pinteresque mission is to defleece his school-day pal of house and hold. His puckish mimicry becomes pointless—trying to sustain slight sophistications whose purposes in the new movie syndrome are to belittle him and keep his world trivial. The wife's need for sunglasses before she can breakfast in bed sends him to retrieve the errant glasses: nothing must weigh down or slow up the general buoyancy of the situation. The trouble with this movie program is that, in the effort to keep out any complication that might gum up the works (the message about a decadent laissez-faire world), the Serner character is forced into moves that are insipid.

One of the elements scalping the New Actor is a simpleminded contrariness to the old story-telling film. An amazing complacency allows any arbitrariness as long as it reverses-mocks traditional expectations.

During the festival, there was a steady rain of names and erudition, calculated to score instantly with the In segment of the audience. This eclecticism —someone gets murdered on Preminger Street, a character runs off in mocking ecstasy to catch a showing of *Hatari*, over the loud-speaker in a swimming pool comes a deadpan "Will Ruby Gentry please come to steam bath 67," two girls cavort with the giggling innocence of the Gish sisters in a scene that has the wintry desolation and spareness of a Dovschenko—is too blatant to be bothersome. What is unsatisfying is that this snickering appeal to the sycophantic spectator takes over the forefront of the movie which the actor used to have.

Actually there were peaks at the festival where the actors were given opportunity to Go. One of the great scenes in *The Battle of Algiers* is the besieging of an FLN hideout, a frantic scrambling in a wet clammy Arab house. It's a perfect scene of shock and terror constructed with a multiplicity of detail, a palpable tremor working through the inner court of a four-story building. But the real hammer in *Algiers* is its vengeful, ferocious women, who seem to go on their own: three Arabs, dressed as Europeans, planting bombs in a crowded *café* and dance hall, a fifteen-year-old bride whose incredibly thin-limbed body projects a flower's delicacy blended with suicidal courage.

Le Départ, a conventional New Wave film, balances a cheeky, flake-type actor against the French notion that outdoor telephone booths or tunnels are—bang!—nerve-centers of the modern psyche. Léaud's acting trademark is a passionate decision that peaks his frenzied exasperation, quizzical compulsiveness. His taunted, berserk, exhausted moods are not unlike Julie Harris's Frankie Adams in *The Member of the Wedding*, the same sense that everything around them is insipid, banal, and what they need, crave, is a release to some glamorous scene. With Léaud, the release never comes; he's a sort of Lilliputian given a streak of go-go energy, trying to keep from sinking in the middle-class sloth, a near paranoid who's dead if he ever slows down.

There is a surrender being played out in many European films, a decision to forgo any apparatus of pleasure (any groping in the acting that will make the role transitory and human) in order to show the deficiencies of modern man.

In *Made in USA*, there is a joke amongst the actors that each is to act below his normal talents. Thus the image is truly contrary: in a scene of total artifice, surfaces covered with an enamel version of nighttime Times Square color, the actors are pinned down in curious angularities and stiffnesses. Unusually small-sized even for French actors, all looking as though they were dressed by Ohrbach's (the Junior Dept.), the general impression is of the Ken and Barbie dolls, a cardboard lower-echelon Madison Avenue group maneuvered into cramped setting and held there.

A typical image presents a man named David Goodis, seated at a tiny table squashed between bed and window. His uncle lies bruised on the bed, spot of red paint on each cheek. Meanwhile the woman he loves sits in a bathtub, scrunched up, shell-shocked, singing plaintive Rock and Roll on the guitar. Choked with people and no movement at all, the scene is so disconnected that every word, person, decoration presents itself as a solitary unit. The over-all effect is a pastiche of fakery, a day in the life of a hotel room, Atlantic City.

Midway in *Far from Vietnam*, this same contrariness and condescension is repeated: a long dull dissertation by a French actor reviewing Herman Kahn's book *On Escalation*. Explaining the war to his wife, he is a man drowning in a no-technique film. The only relief he gets in this static situation is an occasional glimpse of his wife, her eyes glued to him, dripping melancholy, plus a heavy sense of art objects in his vicinity. This cultural surface—pontification, name-dropping, the appurtenances of High Art—is one of the chief dilemmas that is vaporizing the movie actor. The actor in effect is being flattened by erudition.

This is probably the hidden message of the festival: the notion that a surface rich in suggestions of high culture is becoming more the character in movies than life itself, whether the life comes through characterization or a vital use of the medium. It is as though the movies were acquiring the character of the place itself: Philharmonic Hall, with its overwhelming sense of worthy endeavor, posh program notes, a cheerful club-room atmosphere for critics, plus a special aroma of Money Being Spent.

November 1967

Cartooned Hip Acting

THE kooky thing about film acting is its uncontrolled, spilling-over quality. The meat of any movie performance is in the suggestive material that circles the edge of a role: quirks of physiognomy, private thoughts of the actor about himself, misalliances where the body isn't delineating the role, but is running on a tangent to it.

Burt Lancaster's stationmaster in *The Train*—a semireluctant fighter in the Resistance stationed in Nazi-occupied France—is an interesting performance because it has almost no center. Seven-eighths of his time is spent occupied at work tasks, scrambling around the countryside. The basic information of his role is impatiently dispatched to the audience: a man pissed off at the absurdity of total sacrifice to save a carload of Van Goghs and Picassos, the "glorious French heritage." The overtone in a Lancaster performance is that of a man who seems to disappear into concentration when he has to work with his hands. The amount of work, involvement, that goes into a Lancaster action is fairly ravishing: he seems perversely committed to sidetracking quietly (no one's going to notice this) the fantastic leonine head, the overrated nimbleness of his body. Lancaster half ruins his performance with innocent sincerity, but at that point where the script stops and Lancaster has his task before him, he sinks into it with a dense absorption. His energy of concentration is like a magnet that draws the atmosphere into the action of his hands.

The opposite of Lancaster's energy-expending performance is everywhere in *Bonnie and Clyde*. Where Lancaster's *Train* performance is filled with small bits of invention to entertain himself while the movie progresses, Faye Dunaway glides, drifts like a vertical sashay. She goes into the movie at one end, comes out the other, leaving a graceful, faint, unengaged wake behind her. (Lancaster, at movie's end, has left behind him a map of zigzagging tracings and small clusters of intense activity.) The idea that this pastel dream of the Depression days is "perfectly cast and edited" is nonsense, and the proof of it is Miss Dunaway. She could have been folded neatly and quietly by the real Bonnie Parker (a very tough ex-waitress), slipped gently into an envelope, and posted to the Lincoln Center Repertory Company from whence she came. If movies were dependent on an "intelligent," exact rendering of a believable character, Miss Dunaway's vanilla charm would be a single-handed blight. At her best, she is too clean, blossoming. Catherine Deneuve-ish, nurtured in luxury, she'd shrivel up in the dirt crumbiness of the 1930's. (For perfect casting you'd need the butch short-order cook at Howard Johnson's: "Hey, Clyde, come pick up your A.C. on toast!")

The movie starts with the aroma of a French Agnes Varda bedroom scene: Miss Dunaway lying belly down on a bed, in heat, restless, with no action in town, West Dallas. "Hey there, that's my momma's car you're stealing!" She flies down the stairs, the camera staring up her billowing skirts. The movie picks up now that it's out in the open air, an authentic small town street with covered sidewalks: pseudo-folk conversation, spiffed-up Warren Beatty doing that coy shuffle in which his face loses itself inside a boyishly fake half-grin.

The fluke of Dunaway is that her body moves uncannily in harmony with the film's movement. While Beatty-Pollard-Hackman are muscular, earthbound, scurrying and plodding in skitlike business that is both entertaining and synthetic, she is almost air.

The point is that, in both Lancaster's and Dunaway's acting, there is little center, i.e., deep projection of character. Though a great deal of interpretation can be plied into the written role of a kid uneasy and bored in West Dallas, trying to become a celebrity through bank robbery, the center of the role, just a step from the sexy, flamboyant gun-moll role in *White Heat*, is a static, negligible thread.

The only kick in *Reflections in a Golden Eye* comes also from extras: Taylorisms and Brandoisms that shoot the film away from Carson McCullers's story and into the careers of two stars: his mulishness, her shrewishness. According to the daily newspapers, this is a "dirty movie" but "magnificently acted." When you meet the "gross, termagant wife" and her "pompous, purse-lipped major," the major is building his chest measurements by lifting weights, his wife is on her way to another ride into the hay with her next-door neighbor.

Mostly what is seen is girth, the inert mass of Brando's elmlike body, the eye-brows moving in a slat face. Then cut to the stable area: much material about Taylor's riding gig and how she gets on a large white stallion.

Reflections is a clawingly bland movie about two army officers and their wives: amongst their quiet routine are such diversions as horse-beating, clothes-sniffing, nude bareback-riding, nipple-snipping with garden shears, masturbation fantasies with the beloved's discarded Baby Ruth wrapper, daily adultery in the woods. Given these In-gredients, this story of a seldom seen Army camp is Stalesville, due to the neuterization of the locale, the dated use of symbols (a close-up straight into the pupil of an eye to sink home the voyeurism of a young soldier standing outside a living room looking at a nude female). The people here are treated with a symbolic scorn that has cobwebs on it: a bobbing behind on an army saddle to suggest that Weldon (Brando) is Major Impotence.

Then there is the corny literalism of the color to go with the Golden Eye of the title (every word of McCullers's title is insultingly reiterated). The movie's color is that of caterpillar guts, and its 14-karat image is a duplicate of the retouched studio portraits that could be obtained in Journal Square, Jersey City, in 1945. Here and there, the color is vulnerable to rose pink. For instance, during the scene in the stables, there are any number of people, horses, buildings, but the local color that registers in the all-over yellowed monochrome is the rose pink of Liz Taylor's shetland wool pullover and a faint flush of the same pink in her cheeks.

The tough ad for *Point Blank* is misleading. An Andy Warhol silk-screen effect, Lee Marvin's Planter's Peanut head is seen alongside a gun barrel pointed at Times Square. This smashing blue-red-black-white ad suggests Action, in the Hammett-Chandler tough-cop tradition. You sort of expect to see Sleet Marvin and Angles Dickinson. They're there in recognizable form only.

Whatever this fantasy is about, it is hardly about syndicate heist artists, nightclub owners, or a vengeful quest by a crook named Walker (Marvin) for the $93,000 he earned on the "Alcatraz drop." The movie is really about a strangely unhealthy tactility. All physical matter seems to be coated: buildings are encased in grids and glass, rooms are lined with marble and drapes, girls are sculpted by body stockings, metallic or velour-like materials. A subtle pornog-raphy seems to be the point, but it is obtained by the camera slithering like an eel over statuesque women from ankle across thigh around hips to shoulder and down again. Repeatedly the camera moves back to beds, but not for the purposes of exposing flesh or physical contact. What are shown are vast expanses of wrinkled satin, deep dark shadows, glistening silvery highlights. The bodies are dead, under sedation, drugged, or being moved in slow-motion stylistic embraces. Thus, there's a kind of decadent tremor within the image as though an unseen lecherous hand were palming, sliding over not quite human humans. It's a great movie for being transfixed on small mountains which slowly become recognizable as an orange shoulder or a hip with a silvery mini-skirt.

In a sickening way, the human body is used as a material to wrinkle the surface of the screen. Usually the body is in zigzags, being flung, scraped over concrete, half buried under tire wheels, but it is always sort of cramped, unlikely, out of its owner's control. At one point in the film, Marvin walks over to a public telescope at Pacific Palisades and starts squinting at a whitish skyscraper. It is one of the mildest scenes since the births of Sam Spade and Philip Marlowe, but after the endless out-of-control cramping of bodies, the serenity of the composition and the reasonable decorum make for a fine blissful moment.

The fact that Academy Award Lee Marvin is in the film hardly matters. His blocklike snoutlike nose makes itself felt, also the silvery snakelike hair that doesn't look like hair, and the implacable, large-lipped mouth. Particular parts of his body and face are used like notes in a recurring musical score. His body stays stiff, vertical, very healthy and sunburned, but he is not actually in the movie. The syndicate is ripped apart by a psycheless professional who never moves except in a peculiar way—like a mechanical soldier quick-stepping through a Bauhaus corridor; a memorable mystical moment has him flying slow-motion through a bathroom door, his arm waving a blasting Colt 45.

Point Blank is an entertaining degenerate movie for its bit players: Michael Strong as a used used-car dealer, Lloyd Bochner and his sharkskin style of elegant menace. There are fine tour-de-force action compositions: a woman berserk with rage, beating a man from head to toe, a car salesman being tortured in his own used Cadillac as it is bounced between concrete pillars (a take-off on the Huston-Hawks gangster beating in which the victim is jabbed back and forth between two people in black).

However, with all its visual inventions and dreadfully fancy jazz, the movie really belongs to a composite image of look-alike actresses. As the dawn goes further down over the old notion of acting as a realistic portrayal, Angie Dickinson's flamingolike angles can be seen one-half foot away from the despised Mal, all debauched beef-cake. They are seated on an orange chaise, like two book ends; his left hand reaches over two acres of sumptuous material and starts descending down the buttons of Angie's mini-dress. It is a surprisingly delicate scene (considering the camera-made massiveness of the two figures), and it has almost nothing to do with the actors.

If one's mind focuses momentarily on any of the acting personnel in the abovementioned films, one's reaction is not in terms of over-all evaluation, the role played. The movie experience is a magical, intimate recognition of some small intimate trait or traits that are unique to the actor. In the current papers, some blazing performances have been credited to actors whose persona is an imperceptible excrescence that bubbles up alongside the role: Elizabeth Taylor (spunky shrillness), Warren Beatty (natty dreamer), Rod Steiger (sweaty know-it-all), Alan Bates (bucolic shrewdster).

The actors, in other words, are erroneously built up as migratory statues, but in reality their medium has the blur, the shifting nonform of a series of ant hills in a sandstorm.

December 1967

How I Won the War

How I Won the War, a neither admirable nor contemptible altruism about the villains who coin money making war films, has enough material to stock several war films. Basically, it's the war story of the fictitious Third Troop, Fourth Musketeers. Among its luminous personnel are a sweating coward digging himself into holes and hiding under pots and pans; a working-class mocker in steel rims played by the Beatles's John Lennon; a mad clown who prates Falstaffian brain-dulling lingo; and two zombies—a pink and a green man returned from the dead.

The exploits of the boy leader, Michael Crawford, and his dotty Musketeers, dragging a heavy roller across sand dunes, building a cricket pitch, and so on, are hard to follow on screen but funny to recall. The movie starts with a public-schoolboy type in a yellow rubber raft, presumably on a night patrol across the Rhine. It is one of the only humanistic moments: a palpably left-alone scene with one little peppermint stick of a man having believable trouble staying inside a raft which thwarts his every attempt to stay aloft. The raft's action suggests a bar of soap squirting out of a soapy hand. This is the one scene where Crawford is allowed a margin of gallantry: he is a scissors in this raft trying to remain upright. Everywhere else he is a forlorn figure locked up in a unit of action: the little boy trying to cut a snappy militaristic figure, trying to be a dandy good guy to the men he commands.

Visually the movie is quite impressive, something like a confetti storm in which the spectator never gets to rest. The Moon Mullins comic strip is more realistic than the average shot, a scene on a desert that suggests an old used-car lot without cars. The Musketeers—a gaggle of quirks and quacks always bitching about their pontificating, but out-of-it, leader who gets each one predictably killed—are antlike, scurrying around in this mediocre B-movie scene. Before the spectator can get his bearings, there is another disturbingly hollow scene: old newsreel shots, given density with inserts of reallife actors. Not too interesting as visual images, these actor-newsreel bits have a ferocious, scabby humor: a wife suddenly appearing on the battlefield to comfort her nearly dismembered husband, saying in a cold, platitudinous voice, "It's impossible to tell the million tragedies that happen in wartime." Meanwhile, her soldier spouse, in pain, murmurs, "They hurt, Flo, they hurt," and his wife breaks her stilted officialese with: "Run 'em under the tap luv." The whole situation, with a soldier bloody from waist down, contrasted to the wife's blitheness, is a real shock for its callousness.

The first question to ask of this not unfunny Surrealism is "Why is it so weird?" Save for the opening bit of old-fashioned knockabout comedy, apparently inserted to make the spectator feel normal before he gets confused, the movie employs enough technique (collage tricks, non-sequitur inserts, oblique satire, a sound track that keeps most of its jokes to itself) to take care of the five films that are crammed into its flashback-choked two hours.

The mucky sound track is the first major weirdness in this film. The movie is built on the complacent notion, held by young British cinéastes, that the most artistically meaningful voice is one so deeply colloquial that it just escapes understanding. In this particular movie, the voices seem filled with a slurring machine or an electric amplifier, with the ends of sentences being either swallowed or lifted.

One of its buzzing, electrocuted, nonstop sounds belongs to an ex-cavalry colonel, played in a possessed, Mad-Hatter vein by Michael Hordern. In one scene this Super Idiot, leaning forward in his tank, symbolizes victory like the figurehead on an old schooner. Conducting an insane court-martial, surveying the land from a desert tower, climbing from underneath an overturned jeep ("Damn, damn, damn"), his whole face seems bloodshot, always cocked toward the sky as though he were listening to some private demon that was feeding him ideas and lines. As his voice constantly jaws on about the wily

Patton or the common soldier ("Tend to their feet, Goodbody, they're no good to you without feet"), it becomes fairly clear that he is putting down the genius of sand and tank, General Montgomery, as a snobbish fantasy-obsessed Officer Nut. But this parrotlike battering ram is a grating agony.

In one part of the fluxlike plot—a boring stretch kidding (?) the cultural butcher's idea of *River Kwai*—Crawford says to a noncommittal Nazi: "You're the first person I've been able to talk to in this whole film." This Fauntleroy Jack Kennedy, whose voice spirals metal Cheerios into the atmosphere, talks bales of words. At the peak of heroism, killing off his patrol, sending up signals to bring down a barrage of bombs, he becomes a titillating figure, not through comic style, but because an apparatus of technique has been slipped between the character and his material. Everywhere, there is this Svengali jamming apparatus between soldiers and their war activities.

Actually, this is the film's key effect: the cross-references from the small activities of the troop to the hallowed image of large consequential Dunkirks. The misalliance makes strange wit out of a fat man's last words as he is about to be bayoneted in the chest: "Ah, 'ave a 'eart." A guy can't even die without being metamorphosized into and out of newsreel footage before he draws his last breath. Sometimes, Crawford's nerve-scratching voice circles above him, as though it were carried in a cartoon balloon, while his body unrelatedly goes about its business.

Secondly, the movie's weirdness comes from its inept image: the movie actually gets into the area of hallucinatory art through the malapropisms of people and locales. Just after the troop has been chopped up in a sortie against a Nazi patrol dump, the furious boy-leader lines them up for a bayonet drill to correct their courage. It's hard to forget this bungled composition: The Musketeers look like a cast of characters from a greasy spoon near the docks—a smart-aleck dishwasher, a fat and unkempt short-order cook, and an angrily anxious owner who thinks he can get more work by worrying his help to death. An ultrabright scene, everyone squinting: it is a demoralizing time of day—high noon after a brief defeat—to be taking part in a savagery drill.

Finally, along with the freak accents on a jazzed-up sound track and the misanthropically crude scene, the movie gets its weirdness from cowardliness. It scatters its energy, never staying with any scene enough to exploit it.

Why is this not quite up to the loathesomeness that Lenny Bruce fed, funkwise, into his excrementlike social conscious humor? At its best, it has a crawling-along-the-earth cantankerousness and cruddiness, as though the war against fascism were being glimpsed by a cartooned earthworm from an outhouse on a fake hillbilly spread somewhere in the Carolinas.

But genuine funk is a pretty rare item, at least as exemplified, say, in Sam Fuller's vulgar, belittling directing style, W. C. Fields's two-reelers as a sleazy-souled barber or store owner, Jack Oakie's suggestion of pigskin hide encasing a sneaky conceit and cheapster's malevolence. It occurs where the insurgent artist views his subject matter from a position so far down on the ladder that his work is knee deep in muck, misery, misanthropy. Situating himself in the Bowery reaches of technique and exposition, the artist can take pot shots at the accepted notions of Style, Beauty, Gentility. The debased position allows a desperate film man to hold onto his wit and dignity while creating a richer surface through crudity than he could achieve through niceties, skill, taste.

Since the mid-1950's, funk was discernible in the TV shows of Sam Peckinpah, in a scummy Siegel remake of *The Killers* that far outclasses the Siodmak epic, in parts of Frank Tashlin, Burt Kennedy, and in the young French wizards —Godard-Truffaut-Malle—who apparently breathe funk but are never unpretentious enough to stay in it.

This movie is as far into funk as anyone has gone in 1967 in the major leagues. When Crawford slips into a kind of reverie, he achieves a human effect that is half funk: he gets the qualities in the old English version of the word (fear, cowardice, anxiety) but misses the part that comes in the Negro jazz term (slangy, sweaty, low-down) which his colleagues embody. An agony takes over Crawford's performance, as though he were moving beyond the wooden, cut-out cartoon figure that is supposed to be synonymous with satire in this film. There is one scene in which he seems to be flying through space, like a mad eagle, as he shows his men how to signal an airplane down. The unmatched toothpick legs never touch the ground, his voice is like metal filings spraying the air. And then, when he cozies up to one of his men to bare his soul, the performance gets lunatic and hypnotic, losing itself in its Jack Kennedyish elegaic heartfulness.

However, the film is filled with estheticisms that pad it out and make it insipid: documentary shots, corny references to *Lawrence of Arabia*, slapstick that is within the reach of Jerry Lewis and not contaminated or unique. In its scabrous, unrefined attack on the Establishment, the movie suggests Lenny Bruce, with one glaring difference: it is limited in its tasteless jokes and material to the mentality of a bright schoolboy. Like *Help* and the Zero Mostel *A Funny Thing Happened on the Way to the Forum*, it suggests an overaged boyishness almost incapable of relating to the hard-nosed, dry, sardonic war films supposedly under attack here. There is little connection between these soft-cheeked near-baby Musketeers with petulant voices, and the underplayed leanness that makes up the background of *Air Force*, or *They Were Expendable*.

To cover up the puerility of acting, wisecracking, and imagery, everything has to be partially hidden by racing past the jokes, which pile up like cordwood, swallowing any gag that threatens to make itself known as a tiresome gentility.

January 1968

Experimental Films

THE theaters of the Underground—often five or six docile customers in an improbable place that looks like a bombed-out air shelter or the downstairs ladies room at the old Paramount—offer a weirdly satisfying experience. For two dollars, the spectator gets five bedraggled two-reelers, and, after a sojourn with incompetence, chaos, nouveau-culture taste, he leaves this land's-end theater feeling unaccountably spry.

In the cliquish, subdued atmosphere of the New Cinema Playhouse or Tambellini's Gate, there is more than an attempt to dump the whole history of films. One glance at the pock-marked terrain and the placid spectator suggests a new concept of honesty and beauty based on beggarly conditions. Tambellini's paradise, the Gate, on Second Avenue, starts as an entrance to an old apartment house, moves through a 1920's marble hallway, and engulfs the customer in a black chamber. God help him. The big sensation here is the ancient unreliable floor, which, like the ceiling in this blitzed miniature cathedral, is indescribable. Sometimes, the shredded carpeting, with its patches of masking tape, feels as spongy and sandy as the beach at Waikiki. Actually, it is an old room of murky origins, painted flat black, no two dimensions the same. There is a bombed-out area in the front half, which houses the screen, and a number of wooden constructions that have been started by a nonunion carpenter and then thrown up as a bad job.

A respectable uncle of the Gate Theater, the New Cinema is located dead center in the basement of the Wurlitzer Building. This likable chamber has filigree woodwork, flat dove-gray walls, and a legitimate cashier's window that belongs in front of Carnegie Hall. The theater, only somewhat larger than the Gate, sits behind the cashier's booth, and has these piquant walls, which epitomize the ancient Stonehenge character of the Underground. Alongside the seats are little arches scalloped along the wall, each one with its own recessed ledge on which the customers sit, when they're not asleep in the aisle or sitting with trademark lassitude in the seats.

The Undergrounders with the quickest talent—Warhol's virile close-

close-up, George Kuchar's homely family humor with pixyish use of a roly-poly flirt, Bruce Baillie's *Castro Street*—are involved in what seems like a sentimentality but is much better than that. The apparent sentimentality: the idea that a shrunken, impoverished film is necessarily purer, more honest than a highly budgeted studio film. Actually, the Kuchar-Warhol is so impoverished that it gives a spectator the kind of disenchantment, sordidness, feverish wastage that no other movie even suggests. The films of late Bergman-Godard-Penn, like a private elevated paradise in lovely waltz-time, are based on ideals in acting, camera work, and story technique that have become absurdly removed from the spectator's experience.

Right now, the Head Chef is a bland pastry with bangs whose newest film, *Four Stars*, is almost a *Ulysses* of non sequiturs dished up with the most galling largesse. Warhol's latest is a sort of jaded valentine in twenty-eight flavors, in which he salaams, butters up, betrays, and fondles the three female exhibitionists he favors: a 1967 Theda Bara, whose chief feature is a deep kohl line; a nymphet, who is boyishly slender, short-haired, gaminlike; and, finally, the female Falstaff of his company: a grotesque who suggests the underworld of drugs and dissipated, humiliated flesh.

With its rich gemlike image and its elegance, this sinister movie is dedicated to exposing people as far from their life functions as possible. From its opening shot of Nico chanting (a primitive sound in which the notes are sucked in and rasped out), the audience is disengaged. The actors are continually in non-acts: they sit in bathtubs with no thought of bathing, couples are in bed boring themselves to death, endless application of cosmetics for no apparent purpose, a hungerless face eats an apple, a slender body rolls his Chinos down and up.

Devoting about twenty minutes of droning improvisations to each of its "stars" (Ultra Violet, Viva, International Velvet), the movie offers a violently physical image. It's as though the whole of Genet's perverted world were funneling into the shot, from every inch of the frame, by way of the rawest close-up technique and those Drool colors—sherbet, bonbons, marzipan, icing—now fashionable in Leo Castelli's, Capezio's, Schrafft's.

This image is basically the *Harper's Bazaar* photo set in motion, most of the motion coming from superimposed sounds and scenes. For example, in one rapid-jawing segment, a female Lenny Bruce comes on in a silvery boutique, doing a stand-up monologue sitting down. Wearing knee-high silver boots, a blond wig (a big bouffant job, every lock like a banana), fondling and twirling gadgets made of tiny mirrors arranged in mosaics, this human poison-pen letter is seen and heard in triplicate. Her big joke about a twelve-year-old and his erection keeps returning, so that, like the horse race in Kubrick's *The Killing*, every line returns three or four times. Despite the hopped-up monologue, the cliché-lurid-lamé-on-lamé setup, the scene is weirdly cozy.

One real problem today is the fecund quality of Warhol's image. There are dragging sections: a gang of lymph nodes wrapping themselves in bands of yard goods. Even this scene picks up incredible vegetation of vitality when a hirsute honeybun describes his rape by an adorable Puerto Rican "Golden Gloves type" and his three uncles named Sammy. This dreadnaught extrovert, detailing his quadruple "sex" ("It was disgusting. . . . I just lay there and let it happen") is wearing a red satin mantilla, the scene is like a pajama party, with everyone lying around the floor. An outrageous ham actor steams with life, due to Warhol's parlay of indolence, who cares, fun, and a largesse eye which seems to lap shots, sounds, into a unique multiplied vivacity.

Ribald, inexplicable, *Hold Me While I'm Naked* (Kuchar) is a hit-miss funny film, because, like the Gate Theater, it seems a mockery of the detailed movie courses now taught in every university. For the Kuchars, Edison has just invented the movie camera, and the industry is getting ready for its infancy. Even the various themes that come back like a belch in Underground film— the big party or orgy, lyricism in the bathroom, the body beautiful or ugly, genre work around the film-maker's home, exotic clutter—are all present in any Kuchar two-reeler.

In a lunkish comedy about two marriages gone flat, the cornerstone of humor is anything that can be exaggerated, bushwacked, so that it is fashionably out of kilter, gruesome. The most toothsome of its actors—a grotesque bratwurst played by Bob Cowan—has such funny factors as straight-cut long hair parted in the middle, skinny legs, a pillow beneath his shirt. His comedy, a sluggish, witless version of a type of goon comedy kids sometimes use in their play acting, is built around a bent-kneed walk that suggests his body is a heavy flour sack.

The sad thing about George Kuchar's soured talent is not so much the confusion, the skidding around in old movies, Jewish Mama humor, do-it-yourself Rabelais, but the curious assumption that the audience—particularly the In Society segment—are enthralled with the very smell of his rambunctious, galumphing Bronx personality.

February 1968

One-to-One

Besides being a brazen movie with a built-in sneer, particularly for the older denizens of Coin Flats, Beverly Hills, *The Graduate* is another in a series of Sandwich Specials. Clyde wins Bonnie over hamburgers; Perry and Dick, the *In Cold Blood* murderers, relax with hamburgers before and after the Clutter massacre; in *Bedazzled*, Dudley Moore and Eleanor Bron are a cook-waitress team in a Wimpy Bar. All this chopped steak is a give-away on the new tone in films; unless the material is thoroughly banal, it isn't considered chic.

A life of innocuousness marches over the spectator and greenhorn hero. A little stump of a man, dragging himself around with weighty reluctance (he walks toward something as though going away from it), Dustin Hoffman is laid out like an improbable menu. People are always darting into his periphery to point him out as a boy wonder, from captain of the track team to debating captain and literary editor. Benjamin, as it turns out, is Bill Bradley crossed with Denny Dimwit.

The most literate sound Benjy makes is a short pup's whimper, which is overplayed in the same way as his panicky rabbit's expression, whenever a demanding or threatening adult hovers in sight. The simplest sentences have trouble surfacing through this lipless mini-man, who, despite Hoffman's intelligence-within-contrivance acting, adds up to a facile, hardly original put-down of the whole affluent class. If vulgarity is being shown up in *The Graduate*, it's on both sides of the camera.

Resembling George Segal's sculptures of a banal Everyman, generalized and locked in a few trademarks of his job, Benjy the Ordinary is the direct opposite of the eclectically hopped-up movie he inhabits. Goalless, not possessed of much wit or intelligence, lacking stature or bearing, he is a champion of the Lacklustre, along with the simple-minded, gullible nurse, Sister Alma, in *Persona*. This chunky tomboy (Bibi Andersson) is morbidly grounded in the commonplace. In a two-character movie, it is Alma's not too bright, undeveloped gush that holds the screen, does all the talking.

Andersson's Jean Seberg face has always been a slightly awful fixture in Swedish cinemah for button-featured beauty. In this film, it becomes a curtain to compose the Acropolislike screen, while the zealous miss gets button-hooked to the pedestrian task; she props up pillows, turns on radio, gets into bed, carries a tray. And undercutting the role further is an X-ray image (perfected through a string of late Bergman films) that denatures her face of its health, lustre, and, at the same time, gives it a formal elegance.

The irony of these movies, which cherish ordinariness, not allowing a speck of glory to their earth-bound characters, is that the activities dull while the syntactic invention shoots skyward. In a vast expanse of ultramarine, the parents—Mr. and Mrs. Gruesome—present their prize graduate ("who is soon to continue his studies as a John H. Alpington scholar") to the adult world. The father is a goggle-eyed irritant, the mother is a shrill veteran of beauty parlors, and both are acted with shattering glibness. Yet the factor that dominates these son-parent collisions is the Image: a whole scene of clean, glistening, expensive materials.

It would be hard to overestimate the ultrafluorescent image and its involving power. The hero is usually grounded, Antonioni fashion, silhouetted against a canvas float, some shutters in a darkened hotel room, the wall of a swimming pool. The movie takes on a near science-fiction excitement and presence, half today, half a year from tomorrow, an uncluttered cube of overpowering color and glowing cosmeticized skin.

There has been little or no attempt to keep up with the syntactic development in such imagery. While critics analyze the Sturgeslike satire of *Graduate*, the cheap fictional moves of *In Cold Blood*, the puzzling psychology of *Persona* (are the two characters halves of one schizoid personality?), the screen is being designed into one that has more grip per inch than ever before. One to one haunts the screen today, a condensing of persons, places, those one-prop compositions in *Graduate*, everything boiling down into a single symbol of itself. Given these symbolic units (all four Clutters flattened into one stretch of pseudo-Kansas cloth), the screen gets manipulated into a dynamite-laden rectangle of superreality.

With its strong performance by Bibi Andersson, *Persona* is an obvious example of a one-to-one syntactic conception. The opening, like a quick run-through of the old Ingmar Bergman, is a penny arcade of one shots: a man's hand being spiked to the table, shots of people's heads in the manner of Mantegna's dead Christ, a spiked fence, the countdown of numbers that precedes an amateurish movie, the ripping sound of film flying around the sprockets. Everything that follows this surreal Ensorish gallop is its clean, cool white, unpopulated reversal. And within this section, which is the movie proper (two seemingly opposite women in a forced, highly-charged confrontation with each other), the screen is a march of bare, stringent compositions.

Perhaps this composition should be detailed, because it appears in film after film: *Red Desert*, *Le Départ*, *Knife in the Water*. Antonioni must have invented it: the human figure as an island silhouetted against a sharp drop of unsympathetic scenery. There are two or three delineated elements, none of which act as support for the other. Antonioni uses a wall or building as a menace; in *Persona*, the background is a disinterested one; in *The Graduate*, the subordinate detail is manipulated into placards of American vulgarity.

In these oned-up scenes, the design play becomes as important as the story theme. As seldom happened in pre-1960's naturalism, the movie is constantly drumming a pattern in which dominant and subordinate are contested. The most fascinating pornography springs out of a low-keyed, lackluster setting: a nurse and her ward lounging in a darkened summer place. The camera, desultory in its moves, shuttles between the two women, each in a sort of Whistler's Mother pose. The nurse's verbal description of a four-way sex act between two young women and two boys on a sunny, vacant beach springs into flagrant physicality. On screen, there is nothing but a dry interior.

In Mike Nichols's film, there is a studied effort to make everyone exotic and nutty, like walking fish tanks. A coarse deadening and simplification goes on, so that a whole string of aged, overdressed people march through a hotel as one gingerbreaded gaggle. A cookie-cutter is used on Benjy, cutting away all ambiguous edges, fixing him in place. Grown-ups, wherever they appear—at Benjy's welcome-home party, around a hotel lobby, in a campus boardinghouse—seem eight feet tall, misshapen, bolted to prefab versions of themselves. Hoffman and his plaguing environment of adults are indented into the screen with a diamond drill, glistening and hollow at the same time.

A total agnosticism permeates all the above films: a disbelief in the romantic life, institutions, children; a jaded view of sex; a tired feeling that nothing will come up on the horizon to save a lost character. The synthesized technique which gets so little critical attention is burdensomely keyed into portraying *angst* at its most enervated. It seems significant that both Anne Bancroft and Bibi Andersson, in roles that are worlds apart—a stale John O'Hara captain of the fleet and a hard-working blonde dumbshell—are exposed with similar morbidness by a Pat and Mike team: Bergman and Nichols. (Another weird case of two directors inflicting the same treatment: Godard and Antonioni with their perennial mug-vamps, Anna Karina and Monica Vitti.)

Nevertheless, the critics go on with their old ploys on a movie in which editing, camera moves, acting have been preconcentrated, mostly done "in the mind." It seems irrelevant to compare *In Cold Blood* with the best-seller and find 80 per cent or more of it to be an exact duplicate in terms of cheapness. Or, in the case of Anne Bancroft's female shark, middle-aged and middle stream (you're never told what she'd be puttering at, if not Benjy's manhood) to make out a case for her acting far above the movie.

"Go to the bar and order yourself a drink." Giving directions on clandestine love to a boy who suggests Mary's lamb, embarrassed by her every move,

Bancroft acts like a traffic cop. Except for a two-minute stretch in the Taft lounge where she glows with a chilled humor, education, that the role demands, her whole performance—steely and disengaged—is done by camera set-ups.

It is a funny love affair, strange rather than ha ha. All the piquancy has to do with (1) the difficult sketch-class poses, age-revealing and impossible to act, that pin down Bancroft, (2) the curious split and distance between the two supposed bedmates, with the woman always being turned away, as though she were a disgrace.

With all its overtrained acting and nonsense (Perry's daydream before a mirror, fantasying himself as a Vegas star), *In Cold Blood* is a somber, slablike, all-of-a-piece inclemency that bears little resemblance to the open, cheap-knit style of Capote's writing. All the puzzle is created by the Conrad Hall image, incredibly dense, a concretelike block of Kansas scenery, damp climate, that is almost impossible to enter. With the semivirtues of a John Vachon photograph, the real curiosity is how so much pictorial movement and variety could be rerouted so that it is contained within a scene that is always fronted and classically static.

March 1968

Clutter

THE movie scene: crawling with speciousness; one type of clutter examining, reporting, publicizing another. The dictionary defines clutter as a confused mass, untidy collection, crowd (a place) with a disorderly mass of things, litter. Just to go near the art theater district on Third Avenue is to be jostled by the definition, a cattle drive that includes the little pink plexiglass sign with $2.50 printed into it (if you're lucky; sometimes it's $3), and a character, tenacious as Epoxy resin, guarding the sanctuary with red velvet hose and an unswervable litany: "There will be no further seating for the present showing. Buy your tickets now; seating will begin at 7:50 for the 8 P.M. show." A customer comes out of *The Graduate* saying, "Finally, I've seen it," and you realize a hysteria has been built up by a thousand-headed ghoul named Advance Press.

This involves a jangle of affirmations and pronouncements by critics, raging controversies that follow and overlap one another (Bonnie-Titticut-Jason-Graduate-Tell Me Lies-Fox), crazy lines—a critic's quote or a line from a movie ("I think you're the most attractive of all my parents' friends, Mrs.

Robinson") stamped on every subway rider's brain, Sunday supplement interviews in sensation prose by Flatley Rex detailing Sunday morning with a Saturday night hero in the Royal Suite of the Plaza.

And this festering, knickknacky swarm doesn't stop when the lights go out.
For example: *China Is Near*, a beehive film in which a dozen digitlike, turned-
away people, mostly unlikable (they seem small even in the bed scenes) suggest a kind of ratty elegance within a humid, *Marienbad* structure of boredom,
deeply dimensioned pieces of nothing, somber suavity. The plot, criss-cross or
mixed doubles, centered around an innocuity running (who knows why) for
local office, has been likened to Stendhal and genius. Some of it is fun, particularly two lower-class lovers with a cynical snap to them, but most of the time
you just sit there and watch.

Each of the characters (a ninny professor who happens to have two aunts
who are nuns, a teenaged brother who is a raging Maoist, a sister who is a beautiful fullback) represents a different segment of society. The professor, besides
being a dead loss as an actor—immobile, cowardly, puddlelike—stands for the
effete dregs of played-out aristocracy (a superior actor in this role: the James
Fox architect in *The Servant*). His sister travels this film with incredible self-
love, as though the other actors were Little Leaguers: she gets her ennui, dis-
temper from Jeanne Moreau in the Antonioni role of a woman who is Lost
because men have disintegrated. Then there's a Joe Lampton–*Room at the Top*
type (he suggests a sneaky buck private, *faire savoir*, after impregnating two of
the film's disgusted women). He chills it through the film and moves in on the
professor as a political adviser.

In one scene, which shows Bellochio's talent for getting multiple angles on
a locale, the director backs the Italian Fernandel into a village square where
he's to give his first man-of-all-parties speech. Chilled by the lack of turnout
for his debut, scared to address even the three straggling locals, infuriated by
a kid who bicycles off with his speech notes, beaten down by villagers who
attack him for cuffing the kid around, the professor is squirted in and out of a
nice shuttling action filled with familiar ideas about little people, losers, and
small-time politics. This is a readable scene, also an atypical one.

For the most part, this prize film is comprised of hard-to-relate skits, composed in a puzzling staccato manner, creating an ambiguous feeling of high
modern skill in Renaissance-style scene sculpting. Scenes of a bird-shooting
range (mindless sadism of the rich), cherubic boys clustered around an old
bedridden monsignor (ravishing charm of child muggers), girls and boys
together in dark rooms (lack of proper lighting). The sex scenes, rather than
ideal love or great passion, suggest pleasurable passing of time, second-rate

opportunism. Underneath is the insinuating esthetic idea that texture, technique, and subject should be dedicated to how lousy, discordant, an average day is when it isn't sharpened and cleaned by an orthodox script-writer.

The Fox (bleak outlands, two forbiddingly lonely women trying hopelessly to make a go of a chicken farm, an extremely willful hunter-soldier wants the stronger of the two girls) is always in a middle area between decorum and sensationalism: a rough-stuff movie dished up in the most insipid, uniform, uptight manner.

The movie has the piddling, top-of-a-cookie-tin look of a painting over a motel bed. Nothing unstaged ever enters the chicken farm. No woodchuck, no birds, but a great army of tensed-up technicians trying to charge up a scene with the sense of sexual obsession. So a fox—quivering nose, piercing stare, head jutted out—performs admirably. He moves up to a chicken coop just like a little train, well behaved in the manner of Brandon de Wilde acting Shane's kid idolizer.

One of the problems is the landscape: a dry, coldless snow setting, in which everything has the feel of pieces of glass, with no sense of nature. Because of the lack of pliability in handling this snow scene, delay (not Dullea) becomes a major actor. The scene stays simple—calendar scenes of winter woodsiness —but it takes an eternity to look through those damn crystallized twigs at a gabled house sticking out of a woodland thicket.

Indoors, Lawrence's earthy, work-ridden story is transformed magically into a silent, ersatz psychodrama. In a quiet evening after pitching hay, chasing a cow, the movie gets hung up on a trolley wire, journeying between three faces lushed up with color. Sandy Dennis, doing her homework in the farm book, is quivering like a baby rabbit ("We would have come out even this month, if we hadn't lost those chickens to the fox"). An empty weight is in the room as her loneliness sinks home and the movie trundles over to the solid, self-sufficient partner, Anne Heywood, an actress who has an up-down fence-post quality, reading in a chair. After a short-long stop over her rigid and slack face, the movie crosses the room to Primeval Male, cleaning a rifle Step by Step. The movie is stolid, patient, but Dullea gets it to a plod by his mystical enunciation, penetrating features (he did the same stretching job in *David and Lisa*, another psychoticdrama).

The thing about *The Fox* is that it needs Clutter, i.e., distraction from its deadly adherence to a coarsened Lawrence theme (seething earth, the dark enveloping force of sex). The smart people in films—Satyajit Ray, Godard, Warhol, George Kuchar (now and then)—realize that the scene today is one of Clutter and the problem is finding the disarray technique to fit the discordancy.

*

   The Museum of Modern Art, the Fort Knox of film footage, has recently had major retrospectives of the following closely related giants: Michel (salt of the French earth) Simon, the Charlie Chan conceptions of Sidney Toler, some third-rate Japanese pornographers, and Middle European animated films. Relating these four entities would be a trial; but actually the juxtaposition makes sense if the Museum is considered as a notions counter: bathing caps, steno pads, combs. Under Iris Barry's tutelage, the Museum's library had the feeling of a camphorized chamber; now the film department suggests the work of a Lon Chaney curator, a man of many faces, a Tinker's tinker. Unbeknownst to the savants above the E and F trains, the Museum has osmotically picked up the idea that film is clutter as much as it is a multi-driven vehicle that can be simplified to the point where it can suggest any philosophical content, stylistic acumen.

   The element of debris, disconnection, has been in most finished films, but it's obliterated by Mr. Clean critics who need antiseptic design the way some people need catsup. Tons of criticism have been written about Hitchcock: the Catholicism, talent for directing viewers, cosmic homicides—a Lewtonish conception, in which environment, a shower curtain or telephone booth, is inclement and capable of unleashing the most violent destruction on a mild clerk or schoolmistress. More tons have been offered about his overrated knowledge of cheap thrillers, his synthesizing of diverse events into a pathlike visual event, compacting a whole Gulliver's adventure into a silent linear pattern that takes five minutes.

   It beggars such uneven films to keep pressing in on them with more and more analyses, favoring the film as a one-man operation, pure genius. As late Hitchcock passes into history, his bashful cleverness ("I used the high angle; I didn't want to cut; I insisted that the audience . . .") becomes less apparent than the feeling of pulpishness, a mostly unbelievable woman's mag thriller. Spotted throughout are those much celebrated stretches, frittery and arty, where the director's hand is obvious: the berserk carrousel, the feet going this way and that into a Pullman encounter, the bloodthirsty crows on a jungle gym (OK, send the next bird out).

   To put Hitchcock either up or down isn't the point; the point is sticking to the material as it is, rather than drooling over behind-the-camera feats of engineering. *Psycho* and *Strangers On a Train*, respected films in the Hitchcock library, are examples of good and bad clutter, though the first third of *Psycho* is as bare, stringent, minimal as a Jack Benny half hour on old TV.

   Seeing *Psycho* today is disturbing for the amount of suppositional material.

Why is taxidermy necessarily a ghoulish hobby? Are stuffed birds in a motel's back parlor dead giveaways of an aberrant mind? First, a passing motorist, then a wily detective, takes one glance at seven stuffed heads and becomes either queasy or intrigued by the psychological significance ("What kind of a warped personality is this?"). The great supposition is that the haunted house, California Gothic, is going to scare people. Having picked such a Casper the Ghost, turretted antique, a cliché before Charles Addams stamped it to death, his choice isn't justified by anything more daring, unexpected, against the grain than the Abbott-Costello rudimentary Eeeeek. Forget the faky mother-mummy down in the wine cellar, a-rocking with one hand on each knee, a stock old lady wig on a stock skull (the viewer is supposed to faint), the most contrived scene is the head-floating-backward of a stabbed detective falling downstairs. Hitchcock and his devoted auteurists have sewed and sold this time-expanded scene a dozen times.

Taking this "classic" apart, scene by scene, is pointless because the horror elements have dried up (with the exception of the shower scene) like mummy's skull in the cellar. The most striking material is the humdrum day-in-the-life-of a real estate receptionist: Godardlike, anonymous rooms, bare, uncomfortable. Except for the World War II armor-plated brassiere, the opening of a girl having only her lunch hour to be in bed with hardware swain is raunchy, elegant. The scenes later are even better: packing the bags (there's something wonderful about the drabness), and the folks from her office, off to lunch, passing in front of the embezzler's car: the little smile and wave, and then, nearly out of the camera's range, the doubletake.

The point is: why deal with these films nostalgically as solid products of genius? *Strangers* is medium-superior to *Psycho*, right through the murder in a pair of fallen spectacles: a ravishing wooded island with a pavilion, a balmy dusk air that can actually be felt. If "pretty" in a good sense can be used about film, it's usable here. There's nothing handsomer than the calm, geographic scything through Time, from the moment of the feet going through a railroad station to Robert Walker's head back-foot out promise of sex in an open-air carnival, the unbeatable elegance with which he rings the bell in a hammer-and-ball concession.

Nothing, even the pristine engineering of the bashful, uncomplaining Master, is sustained here (how many movies since *Musketeers of Pig Alley* have been sustained?). Walker's contaminated elegance, which suggests Nero Wolfe's classy, intricate hedonism, with omelettes in a brownstone, dissolves into momma's boy brocade. Alongside a pretty block of husband-wife bickering in a record shop, its unusual use of glass partitions, sexual confidence and bitchiness in a girl with glasses, there are literally acres of scenes in elegant homes and tennis stadiums which could be used to stuff pillows if there were that many pillows in the world.

One of the best studio actresses (Laura Elliott: a sullen-sexy small-town flirt with ordinary, nonstudio glamour) gives a few early sections extraordinary reality, eating up the sexual tensions created by a posh character who tails her around an amusement park, while she juggles two local louts. Then, like a homing pigeon, the movie goes back to the old Hollywood bakery, dragging out those supposedly indispensable ghastly items: Senator rye bread, daughter egg twist, and little Babka. Hitchcock has always been a switch-hitter, doubling a good actor with a bad one, usually having the latter triumph. It takes real perversity murdering off Elliott and settling for Ruth Roman, a rock lady in Grecian drapery, plus Pat Hitchcock, who, aside from her clamped-on permanent wave, carries an open-mouthed expression from one dull blocklike scene to another.

Charlie Bubbles is the first movie about a cool-sleek 1968 artistic success: an ennui-ridden, spoiled-rotten writer who can hardly breathe from the fatigue of being an acclaimed artist. It is for the most part an irritatingly stinting film, even though the photography's pleasant, the apple orchard color is cheery, and there are two fairly good female performances by Liza Minnelli, an extraordinarily willing no-veneer actress, a gnomic, quaint, slight girl with enormous eyes, and Billie Whitelaw as Bubbles's casual, leathery ex-wife.

It's also a single-minded film. Bubbles, in Albert Finney's puritanical, sucked-in ungiving performance, is not so much a man as a particular stage when life has lost its zing and there are no more visible goals on the horizon. It's a unique performance of a Bully who sullenly recedes: Finney keeping his acting technique below a dead flat surface, acting as a foil for the other actors, in the one-note role of a washed-up, limp prick. No matter how far back and under Finney plays, he is like a bull trying to hide. Every time the camera works around a stiff scene, the one outstanding fact is not so much the obnoxiousness of the role (even ordering some prime roast beef is an imposition; he makes a point, offensive manner and all, of flashing five-pound notes as tips, with the recipients being obsequiously grateful, never showing the slightest resentment) but the fact of Finney's bulk. His deliberate sulks not only spring him in front of scenes, but suggests a self-centered soreness.

Part of the fascination is that *Bubbles* is so singularized. It's beyond simplification into a Chaucerlike parable of Ennui, each section of the journey illustrating one or two explanatory sentences about the Writer's Life ("And on the road he met a friend from his youth"). The opening fiasco sequence sets Bubbles up as a puzzled Personality, appalled at the vacuity-complacency-greed in an upper-class restaurant (nowhere else does Finney score so heavily with his pancake make-up and posh clothing); the rest of the film continues as a wooden march through stock situations. There's an awareness that these situations (the fact that a guy, no matter how rich, still has to deal with nagging intrusions: bullying servants, a wife who doesn't think Bubbles the hot shot that the public does—in her eyes, he's the guy who wrecked her life—a son who is contemptuous and distant) are stock, but the film stands on the belief that any given person, successful or not, is involved continuously in the Banal.

Bubbles is beset by parasites of all types: inbetween men, aspiring neo-phytes, crocodiles who work in cafeterias and at gas pumps, snotty lower-class types who watch enviously, seething on the sidelines while Bubbles fills up his Rolls with premium gas or views a football match from a glass-enclosed booth. There's the implicit fact that Finney's male seconds give him little competition in acting or physical attractiveness in these scenes. But more interesting is the weird notion of how much obeisance is given a Famous Writer.

The chief effect is of a constipated actor hooked onto a trolley line. The first half is comprised of programmed, rigid segments, holding on to scenes which, to begin with, are of questionable if not zero interest. The low point: Mrs. Noseworthy and her relentless kvetching over the chore of having to prepare a cheese-cracker snack for Finney. The only occasions where the paralysis works are situations where the action would be normally run down: the creepy, dazed, don't-bother-me mood of an expressway stop and its waitress at about postmidnight. Even here the situation crumbles with the arrival of some hedonists out of late Fellini. Who the hell are these lacquered zombies who seemingly bring an assortment of vapors into the scene and also work magic on the image, which begins to tilt and get giddy? Everything's a mystery: where they came from, the insidiously familiar way they begin addressing Bubbles, the dialogue from *L'Avventura* by way of Outer Space.

After all this mannerism, the back door is opened near the end and the work becomes a memorable fresh air film starring Billie Whitelaw, as the sharp-tongued Mrs. Bubbles, no time for anything except her son and animals. A straggling Julie London hairdo on a packed frame, she is unimaginable as a health-food nut or a byway hideaway (what's that broad doing so far out from the Action?). But she goes well with a living room, and is very likable feeding livestock, a cigarette dangling from her lips, crouching down to chuck some grain, still dispensing acid around the funny-fishy Finney farm; barnyard animals all over the front yard, but perfect grass?

This last twenty minutes suggests a flower suddenly blooming out of a wooden box. Compared to the strongly typed symbolic parable style of every other actor, Miss Whitelaw is loose, relaxed, attractive inside a taut, bitter portrayal. The whole section blooms, due to her unpretentious act and the fact of the house, how it's conceived in movement, credibility, exact timing: the way that even the up-to-now wooden Finney is made easy by the fulsome-calm house, turned off from the I-love-Finney isolationism. It's one of the richest twenty minutes to be found in current film. There's good casting: the whole undertone of negativism in the boy's regard of his father (the parental wrangling over his upbringing, the dead-look-alike down to the short neck and broad face). The peak of this magical treatment is at the very end, with its Dylan Thomas exuberance and scenery. A film that starts as Big Finney seems to end up as Little Finney floating away over a devastatingly lovely countryscape in an aerostatic balloon.

A consistent minus in deep-dish foreign films has to do with a jog that occurs in mid-film (the hour of the woof), about the time Monica Unvital or Jeanne Morose is turning green with jadedness. It usually involves a peanut-butter orgy and a contaminated group of upper-class people who are supposed to stand for muck, sordidness, disillusionment. A police line-up turns up, people who look like they issued from a vacuum cleaner that serviced the set of a Theda Bara movie. Even before they're overdressed in vampire movie costumes, gone-to-seed Victorian elegance, these fusty ensembles apparently have been hired for the stale dumpling look of their skin and the effect of super dullness, as though they came from a Transylvanian employment office for decrepit domestic help.

A large section of *Hour of the Wolf* is devoted to this Instant Horror, a preachy chastisement to suggest that this decay can happen to anyone in the audience. Someone pushes a computer button and out pours another variation of these Fag Ends of life, a more solemn, stonelike, Northern version than the ones you find in *L'Avventura* (shallow and gossipy), *La Notte* (grossly commercial), or *Juliet of the Spirits* (fatty, with rancid makeup). *Hour of the Wolf* tries to solve the mystery of a half-mad, all-bad slick Baskinish symbolist, who disappears mysteriously while breaking apart on a craggy isle off the coast of old Frizzled. Almost from the start, an Arklike scene of a giant rowboat (a deathboat, as opposed to a lifeboat) creaking into and then out from shore, the feeling is old, old, old, as though the color (a grailer shade of angst), faces (syphilitic), and obsessional idea (the danger of pursuing art to its furthest extremity?) had been dug up from an abandoned mindshaft.

There's this self-centered Swede (Max Von Sydow) who stares morbidly between his cupped hands at a flickering candle, peeks furtively behind curtains to see if the dawn has arrived so that he can finally go to sleep, or studies his wrist watch as it ticks out sixty seconds. What's bothering smileless Max? His wife (acted with fine patience by Liv Ullmann) waits with the spectator for Max to Sydow, but he just glums it.

The painter, supposedly a combined Munch and Bosch, is obsessed by Night Creatures (big idea, *circa* 1832) who poke out of the landscape to bedevil his painting and peace of mind. One by one, they turn up, minus footsteps: an ancient aristocratic Isak Dinesen lady, meticulously dressed in the style of 1918, and a couple of pallid, bodyless Undertaker types.

One of the most disgusting relics of Bad Living is an executive's wife, totally useless with a dyed hair, eyebrowless face put together at a beauty parlor. Supposedly the essence of Beef Broth in its most sexually rapacious form, this woman produces a disgusting movie effect everytime she appears: bragging about the bruise near her crotch, all the while talking nonstop of the delicious bedtime excitements shared with a cold-faced husband (one of the Undertakers).

The banality of Max's visions should make him unhappy. His ghosts, the emissaries from his past, are like an empty day in New York's Forty-second Street bus terminal. Occasionally a spare *nebbish* with very thick lenses in his horn rims asks for a light, and what happens? Getting a sadistic pleasure out of letting people know about their intrusions, Max responds with a fantastic indignation, his bowling-pin face going very cold and hard.

Actually, before it gets involved with the castle creeps, the movie reveals Liv Ullmann as a unique perpetrator of humanistic depth and female presence. Like a sharp knife going through old cheese, she opens up the entire first third of this film: natural, perhaps even homely, shunted to the side, she portrays an accommodating frump. This whole off-actress treatment is remarkably different from her Elizabeth Vogeler in *Persona*, where she is decidedly intellectual, willful, and controlling. She is one of those rare passive Elegants in acting who can leave the screen to another actor and still score.

The Big Eat is another growing factor in films, an effect probably invented by Finney in his *Saturday Night*. In his case, it was a combination effect, involving a big chomp, heavy breathing, slashes of braggadocio, a side swivel, and baring of his teeth. This emphasized eating has been fined and slowed down in his latest work, but within the time span of four Finneyfilms, it has taken hold, cementing a new convention for giving an underside, the animalistic traits, to character. The same message-laden eat has appeared in

Pumpkin Eater (James Mason steals it with his putrid, lecherous teeth and mouth work), *Accident* (a symphony in Bogarde-Baker nuances around the cooking and eating of an omelette), not to mention the current indigestion examples: Henry, a yellow sweater in *La Chinoise* who keeps cutting away to talk while buttering and jamming sixteen pieces of bread; in *Hour of the Wolf*, there is a crucial scene where Ullmann goes on in an inspired sadness about the household expenses (she's just read about her husband's infidelity), and Von Sydow inexcusably kills the scene with a wrong note of silent arrogance.

In other words, Specialized Eating has become a pocket for arty effects, but more importantly it is one of three new maneuvers which scriptwriters are using to get the movie into an undertone area and away from overt dialogue. This tangentialism—taking off at an angle from the movie's plot self—also includes athletics and pop music overloads. Benjamin the graduate, as he floats in his pool, or races in his red sports-car, is enmeshed in an endless grid of wire sounds, back and forth nasality, a dreamy blanket of Garfunkel simon or semen. *Hatari, Live for Life, Darling, Bonnie and Clyde*—in so many films, there is a scene of a mod type in jeep, car, airport lobby, with the celebrated music by Miles Davis or the Yardbirds stamping chicness on your temples.

Up the Junction is a love paean travelogue in which Suzy Kendall, free living and free loving, takes music-engulfed walks, looking like a blah-sweet version of Julie Christie. Whenever Kendall starts her philosophical, Marxian-toned sight-seeing, the image takes on the misty pretty color of Tulip Week in Rotterdam. Swans are seen through weeping willows, smiling eighty-year-old lovers stroll by. While she drifts in a molasseslike park scene, the music track is the dregs of sweet folk rock.

It is a conglomerate of up-shot stray scenes in which there are three inevitable presumptions: (1) a good British sound track consists of giggling, jeering, well-aren't-you-the-cheeky-one; (2) the coolest movie is one jammed with blotched skin, snarled hair, grease; (3) good acting is the automatic result of a deep, uncritical, tough, saccharine grubbiness.

The Wild Bunch has a virile ribbon image, often an aerial view, of border life in 1914 Texas, stretched across a mottled wide screen in which there are so many intense, frontal details—five kids marching in a parade with their arms linked, a line of bounty-hunters riding straight at the camera—that the spectator's store chest of visual information is constantly widened. Someone seems to have studied all the frontal postures and somber-sharp detailing in Civil War photographs, as well as the snap-the-whip, across-the-page compositions that Homer often used as a perfect substructure for the spread-out, pastoral, early

1900's. There is a lunatic intensity in exploiting this archaic photography, getting the inside effect of life in movement, having people in rows, the pride and uprightness of a pose, emphasizing dishevelment in peasant huts or the dry-dusty exit from a Mexican walled city.

From this pulverizing attempt at photographic beauty, the movie becomes a bloated composition. There is an unpleasant feeling of expense, of enormous amounts of money being spent, tons of footage being shot in order to get one slow-motion instant that will stamp home Peckinpah's obsessive theme: that man's propensity for cruelty and self-destruction is endless. This expanding and slowing gets unbelievable effects: a bridge blowing up with nine men on it, all sinking in a row, facing the camera. They drop at the same time and rise up again out of the water in unison, only to sink again, and, with ebbing force, bob gently up and down while floating downstream. Probably the best second ever filmed showing fumbling ineptitude in the face of ungraspable horror: a young sergeant's instant realization that a quarter of his troops are going to be crushed to death.

What is unique in *The Wild Bunch* is its fanatic dedication to the way children, soldiers, Mexicans looked in the small border towns during the closing years of the frontier. An electric thrill seems to go through the theater when Lucien Ballard's camera focuses on groups of kids: two pale blonde children, straight and sort of stiff, holding on to each other in the midst of a gun holocaust. There are others crouched down next to buildings, staring out and cringing. It is remarkable enough to focus on kids in a shoot-'em-up, but the Ballard-Peckinpah team, without condescending to the Amishlike children, gets this electricity with positions, the coloring of hair, hats. These rough Pershing uniforms have been in Westerns like Rossen's *Cordura*, but here there is a crazy fanaticism woven into the cloth and shapes.

With all its sensuous feel for textures, the engineering of events that take place from three different points of view, the movie is ridden with a flashy, Rubenslike virtuosity. Even the dry, fantastically unified, visual characterization of Robert Ryan's Deke Thornton doesn't escape the *éclat* of Peckinpah's hectic drive. Part of Peckinpah's love of gusto and bravura involves repeated scenes of raucous belly laughter—by kids watching a scorpion devoured by red ants, by a badly acted young sadist making a production of holding three prisoners in a bank, by paeans to camaraderie built through the laughter of five buddies—that are an outright case of bad judgment and poor observation.

Very close to the end a beautifully vehement exchange between two squarish, beyond-the-pale criminals creates the mood for the unbelievable ending. William Holden, his face clammed up and looking as battleworn as it should, says in defense of Robert Ryan, who has betrayed him: "He gave his word." Borgnine, with great contempt: "He gave his word to the *railroad*." Holden replies: "It was his *word*." And then Borgnine: "It's not your word that counts but *who* you give it to."

This mind-stopper is of the genre of Burt Lancaster's explanation in *The Gypsy Moths*, for his career as an exhibitionist sky diver: "A man can choose his way of dying as well as his way of living," or the young German student-turned-junkie in *More* who says: "I wanted the sun and nothing was going to stop me. If I had to die to discover life that was okay too."

With Ryan's remarkable deathlike portrait and some good spontaneous-combustion acting by other old Hollywood war-heroes, *Wild Bunch* is an old style action film filled with these modern non sequiturs that suggest an effort to find some deeper purpose or point for the travelogue that goes on elsewhere. They serve only to highlight the drifting content and the weird alternations in current films between an obsession with death and situations in which the people strain for some point over which they can do some willful, extended, fake laughter.

Easy Rider, a sparsely written cross-country movie with a Don Quixote and Sancho Panza on extravagant motorcycles, is marred by draggy, romantic material: chunks of time spent on glinting handlebars, hippies solemnly sprinkling the earth with seeds at sundown, ghastly Bachrach portraiture. Dennis Hopper's lyrical, quirky film is better than pretty good in its handling of death, both the actual event and in the way the lead acting, like Ryan-Holden's in *The Wild Bunch* and Shirley Knight's in *The Rain People*, carries a scent of death. The death scenes, much more heartbreaking, less programmed than Peckinpah's, come out of nowhere, involve an explosion of grief-stricken acting (Fonda and Hopper), and are snipped off. The finality and present-tense quality of the killings are remarkable: the beauty issues from the quiet, the damp green countryside, and a spectacular last shot zooming up from a curving road and burning cycle.

There's quite a portrait dead-center of *Easy Rider*: a young Southern lawyer, ex-athlete, town drunk, good-natured and funny. Practically a novel of information, this character's whole biography is wonderfully stitched from all directions (a lawyer's son with a shaky but established position in the town, with an unbiased scorn for his own mediocrity), sprung in short time without being obviously fed. Jack Nicholson's acting of "George" is done with dishevelment, squinty small-town gestures, and a sunniness that floods the performance.

More is the oldest of movie stories: down the sluice with a poor duck who has fallen into the hands of a heroin heroine, Mimsy Farmer. The film is a voyeurish, fondling showcase for two new beautifully tanned nonactors, a nice unpretentious boy and a blonde slim animal who barely accompanies her clothes through a whitewashed Antonioni island. It's encyclopedic on rich hip clothes.

A Place for Lovers, a De Sica concoction in which Faye Dunaway knows she's dying from the first reel and is unable to act one speck of disease, has zero credibility or interest, although scripted by a team of six writers. At any given moment, she is an icicle version of Mimsy Farmer posing for another fashion spread in *Harper's Bazaar*. Mastroianni's performance suggests a compassionate chauffeur or else a slightly overweight poodle following the mysterious lady around. One of the best laughs is watching Dunaway working on the subject of despair.

The ridiculous idea in *The Gypsy Moths* is that Deborah Kerr, an unhappy small-town wife, should run off with a parachute trickster. Like a frozen food, glummer and slower than Robert Stack, she has trouble crossing the street— and Lancaster wants her to travel with his parachute troupe. A singularly square movie for this period, more stolid than Frankenheimer's last coin waste, *The Fixer*, it still has the pretension of presenting the "real America." Every other shot is a preciously done insert that some assistant director achieved after the main shooting was over (a poison-pen portrait of the high school band warming up for July 4th) followed by a pointless Inge-type scene of a typical family wake featuring Lancaster's red-puffy face about to explode from acute decency. Gene Hackman and Scott Wilson just weather the cape dance and are the film's only half-assets.

The Rain People is a fine example of acting and writing that exploits modern dislocation, the mulling, glumness, and revery of people in tight places. One of the countless current films that are basically travelogues, this one is made up of Warhol-type monologues in telephone booths and motels along the turnpike. Actually, if Francis Coppola's film had something stronger than the pastel Lelouche image and a more intense identity in its grim, preoccupied Long Island heroine, it would be harrowing as well as touching, because James Caan and Shirley Knight must think about acting twenty-four hours a day, and are good at drawing the spectator inside the mournful textures and grotesque-sad moods of turnpike life. There are some excellent scenes in one of those masonite-monstrous motels and in the home of a 100 per cent real and idiotic Virginia family, with Shirley Knight doing the keyed-up New Yorker trying not to believe what's going on around her.

Paul Mazursky's *Bob & Carol & Ted & Alice* comedy treads skillfully on a questionable, overworked subject: the all-round crassness, eyesore appearance of anyone who lives around Beverly Hills. It's amazing that it keeps such a questionable cast (Natalie Wood, Robert Culp, etc.) absorbing despite the fact that every inch of the film is intentionally played in a quasi–abstract-clever area generally hailed as "satire." This is a very self-contained movie. Charles Lang's hot-hollow camera hawks the bodies and faces as closely as the one in *Faces*, but the put-down acting at every moment is a half-snobbish Elaine May mimicry of middle-class patois that is both an abstraction and a generalization. The script stays right on top of its subject, which isn't the wife-swapping scene or the sensitivity institutes, but gullibility: how easy it is to get sucked into the latest turn in fashionable mores, and the humiliation of resisting or going along. A crucial part of the tight structure is the patient, unpretentious playing through of a scene: each segment, like a Nichols-May bit, is a dialogue played long and shot in one take.

I sort of liked and admired Mazursky's handling: inside the dialogue is the gracious, savvy-filled shrewdness of a Burns-Martin second banana who knows how to set up his partner, keep the dialogue moving, and amiably swallow mistakes and crassness. Someone has to be a small genius to even make palatable such a Weird Bunch cast, less than a genius to use them in the first place, and a genius to rig their normally loud personalities with mile-long eyelashes, oxblood suntans, and underwear made of daisies sewn into shaving cream froth.

The most interesting scene: a psychiatrist, a cynical Buddha with a velvety cogent voice, goes through an hour with patient Dyan Cannon. Just the registering of her embarrassment, and geyserlike involvement on his face, soft as a cloud and enormously sensitive as well as half asleep, seem to soften and wipe out the loudness and instant-compromised modernity that threatens to sink the movie.

April and May 1968; October 1969

La Chinoise and Belle de Jour

La Chinoise concerns a summer shared by four to seven youths intoxicated with Maoist Communism: a humorlessly vague, declamatory crew made up of Jean Pierre Léaud (taut, overtrained, exhibitionistic), Anne Wiazemsky (girl intellectual), Juliet Berto (girl ineffectual with a year of prostitution behind her) and a sensitive tapeworm with steel rims, always dunking his bread and butter in coffee. Reclusive, never penetrating or being penetrated by the outside world, they study, debate, never seem to converse but try to out-fervor one another, while the camera images suggest a scissoring motion, shuttling back and forth, giving equal billing to the doors and shutters, rough-brushed with red-blue-yellow, and large blackboards covered with measured handwriting.

What has to be made clear is that this is an infuriating but cagy film. Why? There is such a wide swath of rhetoric, dogmatic rights and wrongs, employed or deployed through replicas of the pop media, pamphleteering, TV interviews, slogans, and protest march placards, as well as in the mechanical recitations of the adolescents, escapees from a local nursery school.

What is maddening is not the facile manipulation of modern communication devices, but the hollow shaft between the hot-shot imagery and cunning rhetorical jam-up. Scene after scene has a gaping hole, as well as, admittedly, a kind of piquancy: the hollowness seems to result from a number of curious policies: (1) limiting actors to one trait, like Wiazemsky's single-minded zeal, plus one maddening repeated tic, lip-pulling, shifting the eyes dreamily, fingering the hair, (2) pre-editing scenes into anagrams, talking news-photos, pettily pedantic debates, (3) flashing the screen with a Pepto Dismal of modern painting devices (Marvel Comics heroes), which seems as peculiarly out of date as the supposedly hip clothes.

Given the stunted bloom on their faces, the parrot talk, as though they're reading a news report, and the With It air, these Marx-Lenin jabberers come across with enormous dairy-fresh impact. Living surprisingly cleanly on a Paris top floor, always fresh new 1957 prol clothes to wear (palish yellow and red cardigans and pull-overs), these kids seem to be pushing out with intolerable talentless mugging. Véronique (played with hard-to-say blandness by Ann Wham) stands smack in front of the screen and does Nothing. Pushing her innocuousness into a virulence, she and her buddies turn the Cubistic Mary Poppins set into a nursery, a French primary school called Notre Gang. Scenes are set up like a first-grade primer: Dick and Jane drink tea, Dick-Jane-Jasper-Max do morning exercises on the veranda, the kids take an afternoon nap, looking like happy little mummies, no reaction, like zombies.

It is hard to get this sealed-off Communist cell as a shrewd portrait of youth protesters: Berkeley-Tokyo-Paris. While seeming to patronize these foolishly idealistic fishlike girls, green-garrulous boys, the film actually sees itself as being part of the movement to shake up the Establishment. Bomb the Sorbonne, bomb the Louvre, "Donnez-moi un bombe" incanted endlessly. The film is summed up in the pathetically slack-faced amateur presence of the second-girl lead, an aimless player who acts out a series of talking newsphotos.

In one, she is a Vietnamese peasant cringing with terror as cardboard bombers buzz around her like gnats. In another, she's a Viet Cong soldier with a plastic machine gun, behind a barricade of firecracker-red books. Each one of these bits of play-acting is rawly, offensively puerile. The use of amateurs who play their ineptness to death is a deliberate, effectively gutsy move, but, nonetheless, it can make your skin crawl.

Unlike the sliding-door effect of *Chinoise*, *Les Carabiniers* has a surprisingly wet, fluid mossiness: its people seem beautifully wan, primeval, murky, little woodchucks camouflaged by nature. Forget the allegory about war: this is a topsy-turvy series of pastoral gambols, with so many throwbacks to Sennett, etc., that it suggests a Movie-Lover's Diary. The movie takes place on an interesting piece of real estate—it's flimsier than dilapidated—a cropless farm in Southern Question Mark. Four mysteriously demented ragamuffins exchange their brother-daughter-mother roles like demented kids, bundled up and waddling on this dusty D. W. Griffith plot. (Those girls are some tomatoes, like the Gish sisters, skipping around the back yard. The mother (?) is named Cleopatra and thus wears Egyptian-gypsy make-up). The two male clods get conned into an anonymous war, which ranges around the two hemispheres. Much of the battlefield looks like the Marseilles suburbs, but is referred to as Santa Cruz.

Michel-Ange and Ulysse have a hard time getting into the area of human beings. One of them is skinny but is covered with old rags, old Potemkin costumes, so that even he looks bloated, limp, and lymph, unable to act in any way except sort of cruising through events. They move through this war amazingly uncognizant. The supposedly comic hubcap, Michael Jello, is a little rubber duck, a banal actor who keeps pushing a curds-and-whey, soppy milk effect. Raking his hair across his forehead à la Buster Langdon, using his limbs like club feet, this actor embodies the stupidity, sadism, and salt of the earth in one compressed shape.

One of the most haunting passages is that of Mike pawing, in Neanderthal fashion, two immobile customers before finding his seat in the Cinéma Méxique. (What's that neon sign about? Your eyes travel up and down for ten seconds trying to locate the hidden political association or anagramlike reference in it.) Buffeted about, climbed over, they never twitch (the effect is the same as the evil-face Kirilov marching over his sleep-paralyzed pals in the *Chinoise* bedroom). More extraordinarily, they don't move, as Michael, now up on the stage, slowly and stupidly and wondrously runs his hands over the screened image of a naked woman, and jumps up and down trying to see over the bathtub rim.

A thing you notice as the movie goes by is that this mid-film passage is the first in which there is a sense of buildings and streets being four-square to the earth. It comes after a swell of off-kilter scenes, lilting girls, and tilting soldiers. This mysteriously poetic effect is of a whole movie funneling into a stillborn chamber where a slow somnambulist pace takes over. It should be said about now that *Carabiniers* (French for "Shoot 'Em Naked") is beautiful, the nicest bleak photography since *Wretched Orchard* or *Bleak Blouse*. Rather than being ominous or warlike, this worn-torn allegory is likable and terrestrial: frozen rivers, empty squares with van Gogh trees, the feeling of boy scouts on a Saturday morning hike, the men uncover their enemies, partisans, like kids would uncover slugs in the undergrowth.

The beautiful people in *Belle de Jour*, a queerly pseudo-Hollywood film, include a wife, pale blond from head to foot, her beefy male-model husband, an urbane Iagoish friend on the sidelines who cynically nudges the wife out of purity and the husband into cuckoldry. A singular trait in this coolly deadpan comedy is the sinister equilibrium in the alignment of these figures with their furniture and possessions.

In *Belle de Jour*, the viewer is apparently directed towards perverse eroticism of the standard types and a modernized *Bovary* story: a pair of patent-leather pumps (Catherine Deneuve) takes a two-to-five job as a prostitute, supposedly because she wants to try some new moves but feels either shy or uninclined to try them with her Boy Scout doctor husband. This sunlit story, pampered wife driven into prostitution during the hours usually reserved for piano lessons and housework, is filmed with a linear concision, Daliesque clarity, and, like that painter's works, it works well within conventions forty or fifty years old. In the case of the pornography, the conventions are Victorian and earlier: a woman walking the corridor of a grand chateau, naked except for black transparent veils and a lily-of-the-valley wreath, heading for a necrophiliac encounter with a Count (an aged, stretched-out Jean-Pierre Aumont). The count has her lie down in a coffin, and begins an incantation about his deceased daughter before climaxing below the casket. This little pageant, as well as many others, is so well rehearsed and costume-oriented that there is little sexual bite.

"There's one wonderful *maison* that has such marvelous *ésprit de corps*," enthuses Michel Piccoli, the Iago, murmuring in syphilitic sibilants about Madame Anais's fancy brothel. Truth to be, it's a very stuffy, furniture-cramped apartment, but Catherine Deadnerve, who plays the wife, flourishes as Carmen-Bite-Me-Daddy until she runs into a possessive jealous client, an international dope-pusher with provincial brass-knuckles teeth. This never-ending thin ingénue is fantastic, the only element of 1968 post-*Blow Up* hip. Sulking, a lot of lip and gnashing, he seems to be on the wrong movie set, pushing through the rooms, trying to find his place in the film.

For such a clear, carefully styled film, *Belle* is a consistently jarring film, one put-on after another. Starting with the mezzotint color, a kind of sallow sunlight which throws every shot off kilter, off the realistic, the movie keeps knocking askew each character-actor-situation, going off a little or a lot into the *outré*. What seems like a Who Knows cut, a broadly caricatured death, a standardized fetish, a dreadful gag about geisha credit cards, a lead actress who gets happy at the strangest moments, turns out to be one deadpan twist after another.

The clientele and the staff at the whorehouse, on the surface, seem like mismatches and questionable movie solutions. Séverine's two cowhores, Anaïs's ninnies, are like two sides of the same dismal, unappetizing working-class woman: hard and soft, straight hairdo and Ann-Margaret tease. With each Joker Card client, these two merge and fade out, creating a solid background for Deneuve's golden-girl figurine effect. Unlike these two, who are simply reversed from the expected Mercouri effect, dropped back without causing any excitement at all, the men are an endless run of assorted sordid weirdos.

The inch-from-convention bedroom innocuities of Séverine and Pierre Serizy have to be a pun on all Hollywood movies: Spencer Tracy and Joan Bennett in neat, expensively sheeted twin beds, the man always wearing white rayon pajamas with blue piping, a pair of white slippers alongside, in between the beds a little table with lamp, clock, and a cup of hot Bovril. There's no blood: when young handsome Meatface asks his wife if he can get in her bed, she says *Non* (Scram, buster, go fuck someone else).

How does one get passionate about a perfection piece like *Belle*?

A few things I left out so far are:

(1) A recitation scene in *Carabiniers*, with a partisan blonde reciting Mayakovsky's poem before the riffraff, the same way she would be doing an oral exam in Russian 1A. Without enumerating the queernesses of this blasé blonde May Queen in a car coat and old slacks, she picks up the film's hollownesses. When her friend gets knocked down, she runs for shelter in the most amateurish, no-ferocity manner. The effect that the movie is trying for: to fill her with a frenzied saintliness, like a witch about to be burned.

(2) The swift, expedient, doesn't-make-it carpentering, which still has a great deal of shambling charm. The first set starts out as a small farmhouse with an assortment of chicken coops, a bathtub, tall fences. While this dazzling Gothic single-room house, foundationless, shifts around the plot (the better to

photograph you, my dear) the movie also finds a new focal point, a mailbox at shoulder height which is the only manmade item for desolate miles. The two left-behinds skip to it and home again, the mailbox drips postcards.

(3) It wouldn't be legit to describe the contaminated spirit in *Belle de Jour* as being similar to the raunchy, down-and-out decadent expression normally on the face of a Rolling Stone. In fact, the movie's studied canterlike pace, its nicely staid-static images, the complete lack of emotion or drama in its star, or its photography, are actually the furthest reverse of Mick Jagger's cruddy, carefully nurtured degeneracy. But this *Eau de Clean* movie, its actors doused in deodorants and after-shave lotions, harbors decadence. Also its casting suggests the *Fleurs du Mal* put-downs that are inherent in a Rolling Stone production.

(4) Deneuve is so objectlike: even as a beauty she is lacking. From head to foot, she's like a porcelain dummy, probably the most evocative shot of her mechanical-doll act shows her walking along the edge of a tennis court, forcing herself to be jaunty, walking with a forced stiff-legged jauntiness. Deneuve keeps achieving a curiously intriguing detachment, as though she's on drugs. What's so infuriating about her is actually her contribution: that she's content to be all surface. Her very unrebelliousness, the fact that she stays in place, a contained element among other contained elements, is a large part of what makes this film so precisioned and polite.

(5) Compared to the nice dappled, three-dimensional impressions of *Les Carabiniers*, *La Chinoise* has a suspicious sideways movement: the actors and/or cameraman can't retreat or advance one inch. Watching it is like being forced into an insidious, abnormal work that, sliding sideways, crab fashion, bars progress to its inhabitants, keeps turning the actors whirligig fashion without revealing anything about them.

September 1968

Carbonated Dyspepsia

A BIG sour yawn pervades the air of movie theaters, put there by a series of tired, cheerless, low-emotion heroes who seem inoculated against surprise, incapable of finding any goal worthy of their multiple talents. The yawn is built into people who seem like twins though they are as various as the teetering scriptwriter in *Contempt*, the posh master crimester of *The Thomas Crown Affair*, and that ultimate in envy and petulance who is the philosophy professor approaching middle age in *Accident*. Each of these three heroes (Michel

Piccoli, Steve McQueen, Dirk Bogarde) shifts constantly in a voluptuous way between mobility—driving trickily in flashy little cars, making fast-cut repartee while rushing into an airport—and its opposite, the most deadening kind of innocuous living.

The disenchantment that sweeps over the theater is also caused by a series of technicians who are quite literally emptying the screen of conventional tension and rules. These technicians, who range through a realistic cameraman (Raoul Coutard) whose ability for candidness seems mercurial, a master of concision in scriptwriting (Harold Pinter), and a bite and bitterness director (Luis Buñuel), seem totally cynical about the pre-1960's notion of good and/or profitable movie creation. The Coutard-Pinter technician has contrived a lighter-the-better film, in which the attack is on the industry and the middle class, and the method includes turning the action toward the spectator, using people as walking-talking editorials, making positional geometry of the most mundane, piddling actions.

Accident is filled with positional constructs, one centered around an omelette whipped up at midnight, a nice kitchen crisscrossed with anger, embarrassment, brutal rudeness, as well as paths of action. Similar geometry, exercises in movement using the screen as a floor, are set up around the packing of a suitcase and hedge-clipping. *Band of Outsiders*, a parody of a sex triangle, its people not real, but more like fleas, is also crammed with ricochet movements; a Madison danced in a two-bit bar with its nonsense trio led by Sami Frey, building a spacious rectangle over and over, punctuating the construction with a witless hop and clap at one corner, and a foot stamp at another.

One of the funnier scenes last year involved a zinged-out Albert Finney, comatose on the living room sofa, blearily looking at the Telly. "Charlie, you look awful. Don't you get any sleep?" Charlie, hangdog, gets up, heads for the bedroom. The seedy-sexy Billie Whitelaw says: "Charlie, come back here and sit down." He returns just as docilely as he left. This is a very low-key, high-humor scene; the bemusing things come mostly from positioning, the automatic moves that Charlie perpetrates every time his tough, all-woman ex-wife goes into her top-sergeant act. There is also something perversely sardonic about the lush-sour woman, an incongruous health addict wearing satin on a zoo-farm in the country, appearing more spent and ravaged than the city-corrupted Charlie.

Charlie is one of the many reputedly gifted and successful he-men who, poleaxed by the ironies and vagaries of life, appear for most of their screen life with a creased and deflated expression. This face, which might seem to be thinking of Black Power, McCarthy's chances, or what they mean by "the art of the Real," is more likely chewing on the question: "What can I do with myself for the two hours between now and dinner?"

The Stare has devoured a great deal of screen time in movies. Benjy the Graduate, ex-college-magazine editor and track captain, leads a split life on screen; half the time he's hung up between Mrs. and Miss Robinson, the other half he's at half mast: a flattened silhouette, descending an escalator, staring at a fish tank or lying on a raft silhouetted against the pool.

The Stranger, a man who takes quick naps on his feet while eating, sitting vigil over his mother's coffin, is a handsome office worker in Algiers. Bereft of ambition, there's always the definite feeling that this escapist intellectual, as torpid as they come, is working and living below his mental structure. This is one of the most interesting performances, so filled with the materials of sensuality and lassitude. Mastroianni not only does the curious, innocuous routines that now make up the life of the Inactive Hero, but he gets the most intense sybaritic pleasure from simply a smoke after lunch, a swim, the dozing-off ride on a bus, or the slow movement of the street below his beaten-up hotel room. He is a snake, slowly, luxuriously unwinding. But in the midst of this tantalizingly sensual, pleasure-driven acting, and below the staring, is the frightful aspect of bottomless emptiness, aimlessness.

Actually, it could be said that the whole riverbed of films shifted somewhere in the early 1960's, at the time of Antonioni's rise, when the rudiments of nausea, apathy, jaundice, heart soreness were examined by actors. Movies suddenly changed from fast-flowing linear films, photographed stories, and, surprisingly, became slower face-to-face constructions in which the spectator becomes a protagonist in the drama. In 1961, while actors like Jeanne Moreau in *La Notte* were sinking into self-absorption, miserable doubts about their past careers, the movie became determinedly psychological and, more important, the face of the screen as well as the actors emptied, flattened out. Now, whole characterizations, like those of the active-passive duo in *Persona*, tied together in an identity struggle, are based on a kind of prolonged staring, not only at life but into oneself. What is more exciting is that the movie has almost accidently arrived at the beauties, handsomeness, of banalized emptiness. A whole book could be written about the exquisite beauties of the one scene in *Persona*, comprised of Bibi Andersson in a 1950's bathing suit, a sunny courtyard scene, and not much action. The whole drift of the scene is based on flat, yawning stretches of skin, silence, sunlight, and, behind it all, particularly, is The Stare.

Although used to put a virtue-wins-out pulp story, like *Graduate* or *Band of Outsiders*, in the area of sensitivity and conscience, the stare is much more interesting for what it means in movie technique. When this pensive, larger-than-life profile, back of the head, or full face, fills the screen with a kind of distilled purity, the image becomes purified abstract composition, a diagram, and any soul-searching is secondary. The movie, in a mysterious fashion, diverts at this moment from the clutter and multiplicity of story-telling, naturalism, to a minimal condition. The screen is reduced to a refined one-against-one balance, and the movie's excitement has shifted strictly into a matter of shape against shape, tone against tone.

Prior to the 1960–62 outburst of debut films, the material of the screen—shadow, people, the sound, too—gave the comforting sense of a continuous interweave of action in deep space. Today, an elementalism has taken over. When the pointed starkness of a Greek statue is moving slowly against a flat, bludgeoning stretch of blue sky (*Contempt*), it is similar in syntax to the flat eroticism of Faye Dunaway's silky stride and body as it is seen as one all-over matlike shape against the loneliness of a 1920's Dallas street. In both cases, a kind of primitive block-against-block composition is being worked for a singing, coloristic impact.

The movie today has been turned around, flattened out, the most obvious sign of this re-arrangement being the prevalence of pictures within pictures: instead of one continuous image, the scene appears to fragmentize: an evil husband watches witchlike activities on a TV screen; his wife worries about the shadow-rimmed square on the wall where a portrait once hung; a revenge-driven bride, camouflaged by make-up and wrong wigs, appears to come together in drawings and paintings; the teenaged careers of an intellectual circle are recounted in still photographs; an unconfident husband mimics and discusses the brashness of the Dean Martin gambler in *Some Came Running*; a homely peasant wife plasters a fashionable brassiere ad against her body. In effect, this image-within-image marks the advent of a movie that is no longer an evolving scene but singular confrontations between actor and spectator (a psychological effect that is not a great deal different from the question-answers confrontation that goes on in therapy between psychiatrist and patient).

There is now a distrust of unity, continuity, and it shows itself in what appear to be calculated thrusts at the spectator. These synthesized fragments, placards of propaganda, are often precious editorials that seem isolated, self-contained, aimed at the audience's soul. Groups of decaying Kiwanis types displayed in fancy hotels like a Natural History exhibit, motel rooms loaded with vulgar energy-savers, computers and IBM machines, highways that are diseased and sign pocked with modernity, material (nuns, wigs, orgiastic discothèques, splendiferous luggage) that has a built-in scene-satirizing point, bloody sports events, all-night supermarkets, the carrying of unlikely mirror-bed-tuba objects through crowded streets, an alienated person wandering in an industrial wasteland, standing against an empty wall.

Sometimes, these dislocated items represent the Muck of the Establishment, sometimes they are Escapes from it, but they are always treated as a kind of magic.

In one film, the image slides from sports cars and their owners in Esquire clothes into an idol effect: a Negro in white coveralls who tends cars in an underground garage. This somber, statuesque attendant is examined as though he held some crucial message: seated in a chair against a wall, looking somewhat like an electrocution victim.

Julie Kohler's scarf and Bubbles's balloon are escapes from the labyrinth; in structural terms, they are film-within-film segments in which the movie abandons story progression and talks directly to the spectator. A white scarf billows over a French seacoast town, a pastel journey, overextended and precious, that ends when the straight line of a jet crosses the soft-focus image. Prefigured in some wall prints earlier in the film, an aerostatic Goya balloon comes to rest at the end of a film. The mesmerically improbable object, plus the perfect pastoral landscape, draws the gutted hero out of his lethargy into a more promising life.

Nausea is everywhere in movies today. Yet, there is a great distance between this negative feeling on screen and the anti-Establishment nihilism that has made such thought-provokers as a clean, grace-filled sort of gorgeous, cartoony, facetious film (*Contempt*), a beautifully grainy, intimate, limpid survival fight (*Persona*), and another movie of real suffering (*Accident*) that is clever, delicate, and urbane with the most elegant infighting in acting between Dirk Bogarde and Stanley Baker.

For both the nullity rampant in movies today as well as the simplistic image, the most advanced and volcanic are the latest from the Warhol factory. Behind *Nude Restaurant*, *Bike Boy*, and, particularly, *4 Stars*, is a morbid, flesh-bound, self-reviling vision: the films crawl with an obsessional pursuit of rancid pleasures. By just presenting rambling Ondine or National Velvet as isolated, spoiled fruits, stripping away their connections to personal drama or outside world, and by languidly exposing jig-acting situations (tangled bodies on a mattress, gargantuan make-up scenes, a crazy telephone scene with a witchlike gypsy, her maddening horsey smile flashing on and off like a neon sign), the picture becomes a drum-beat of the film concept that the Moment's the thing, and, also, that what's Now is pretty sickening.

There is no story-telling form imposing its pressure on the screen. When Brigid Polk, hippopotamus of sin, sprawls in a bathtub in white bra and blue jeans, and talks to someone just outside camera range about the drug-curing scene in different hospitals, the image is free, for itself, and wide open: the spectator, as well as the actor, can almost vegetalize inside the frame. Everything is stopped as the movie engulfs itself in a fuck-off atmosphere. With giggling hysteria, fag expressions, the most pathetic bravado voice, she explodes the screen outward by giant abandon and cravenness. The camera milks the paleness of her slack flesh, a cheap cotton brassiere cuts into the doughy torso, the image is the most underrated phenomenon in films: a blast of raw stuff.

It's not only Brigid Polk or her counterpart Jason in the underground film firmament, but their flesh-obsessed self-exposure (both diarylike and diarrhetic in that bits of decaying self are flung out) has become a standard role in films everywhere. This confessional acting is abetted by a voyeur camera which does not enhance, but feeds on, every flaw: the actor stands crucified in front of the camera. A detective's wife turns a seduction scene into a flat head-on encounter with the audience: a pinched and dried Lee Remick under a humiliating light, seems disrobed for a flagellation rather than a love scene. Truffaut's Bride, supposedly a male-gobbling Mata Hari, is tortured by an insensitive wig-maker and her own recalcitrant, slipping flesh. She becomes a series of static parodies filling the screen, stark presentations, almost processed before your eyes, of someone's middle-aged aunt. Good or bad doesn't matter in a screen presence that comes across like an Easter Island sculpture: the Dread C. Scott performance of a kook-hooked brain surgeon isn't actually a performance: a tortured larger-than-life face seems to be dazed as it moves occasionally right or left.

As soon as these versions of the Underground Man and Oblomov start reviling and revealing themselves, the spectator is hooked. While bathing him in remorse, the picture cathartically immolates him in a new kind of connection to the screen. What happens is that everything becomes open ended: time is untempered and boundless; characters are left enigmatic, full of the complexities of a single moment; photography is deliberately raw, uncentered, violently push-pulling against the confines of the screen.

September 1968

Jean-Luc Godard

Eᴀᴄʜ Godard film is of itself widely varied in persona as well as quality. Printed on the blackboard of one of his Formicalike later films, hardly to be noticed, is a list of African animals: giraffe, lion, hippo. At the end of this director's career, there will probably be a hundred films, each one a bizarrely different species, with its own excruciatingly singular skeleton, tendons, plumage. His stubborn, insistent, agile, encyclopedic, glib, and arch personality floods the films, but, chameleonlike, it is brown, green, or mudlark gray, as in *Les Carabiniers*, depending on the film's content. Already he has a zoo that includes a pink parakeet (*A Woman Is a Woman*), diamond-black snake (*Contempt*), whooping crane (*Band of Outsiders*), jack rabbit (*Carabiniers*), and a mock Monogram turtle (*Breathless*).

Unlike Cézanne, who used a three-eighths-inch square stroke and a nervously exacting line around every apple he painted, the form and manner of execution changes totally with each film. Braining it out before the project starts, most of the invention, the basic intellectual puzzle, is pretty well set in his mind before the omnipresent Coutard gets the camera in position. He is the new species creator, related directly to Robert Morris in sculpture, in that there is an abhorrence of lethargy and being pinned down in a work, alongside a strong devotion to Medium. Travel light, start clean, and don't look back, is the *code du corps*.

Each of his pictures presents a puzzle of parts, a unique combination of elements to prove a preconceived theory. Some of his truculently formulated beasts are:

A Woman Is a Woman ("I wanted to make a neorealistic musical, which is already a contradiction") is a monotonously scratching, capering version of a hack Arthur Freed musical, perhaps the most soporific, conceited, sluggish movie of all time. The crazy thing about this movie is the unrehearsed *cinéma verité* feeding on littleness, love of the Real slamming against the Reel, the kind of studio-made pizzazz that went into *My Sister Eileen*. The elements include deliberately artificial Times Square color, humorless visual puns, each scene pulled out like taffy, the action told so slowly it paralyzes you, awful mugging that is always fondling itself while the bodies are dormant.

My Life to Live. The fall, brief rise, and death of a Joan of Sartre, a prostitute determined to be her own woman. The format is a condensed Dreiserian novel: twelve near-uniform segments with chapter headings, the visual matter used to illustrate the captions and narrator's comments. This is an extreme documentary, the most biting of his films, with sharp and drastic breaks in the continuity, grim but highly sensitive newsreel photography, a sound track taped in real bars and hotels as the film was being shot and then left untouched. The unobtrusive acting inches along in little, scuttling steps, always in one direction, achieving a parched, memory-ridden beauty. A film of extraordinary purity.

Les Carabiniers. A rambling, picaresque-piquant war film, seen through the exalted, close-to-earth vision of a Dovschenko. As a bitter against-war tract, the film is a gruesome contradiction, played as deadpan slapstick with two murderously stupid rustics for its heroes. Since war is a grand mistake that sweeps across borders, the movie leans heavily on mistakes, vulgarity, around-the-globe and around-the-calendar hikes.

Each new movie is primarily an essay about form in relation to an idea: a very deliberate choice of certain formal elements to expostulate a critique on young French Maoists; a documentary report on prostitution, poetic style; or a gray, somber, sophisticated portrait of an existential hero of confused commitments. *La Chinoise*, for instance, is incredibly formalized, a doctrinaire syntax to go with a doctrinaire group of modular kids. The movie's not only in one classroomlike room, but the actors are in an uptight acting arena in the manner of fervid teachers in front of a blackboard, and the camera and the actors never move except in a straight left-right motion.

However, there is a huge gap between the purported intention of the films and their actuality. And it's the undeveloped space between intent and end product that gives them their nutty, Dr. Kronkite character. In front, the movie is the most ponderous undertaking: in *Le Petit Soldat*, an assessment of the political climate after the Algerian war is the theme, but the actual film time is taken up with a dull day in Geneva: one driver ineptly trying to get in front of another, a photographer shooting rolls of film, a mock torture scene. Certainly Anna Karina and her usual inept, little-girl exhibitionism is a Grand Canyon away from the point of *My Life to Live*, which is to document the short career of a spunky, self-educating Heart of Gold able to go through a phase of prostitution without losing decency or chipping her soul. There is so little sex in the movie that she could be pure High School, 1950 version, acting cute with her lollipop Louise Brooks hair, if the narrator didn't tell us she was a risk-all prostitute. There is something so far fetched about Anne Wiazemski, in *La Chinoise*, solid lassitude inside a girl's fastidiousness and politely controlled snobbery, living communally, murdering coldly, plotting a bombing of the Louvre.

The overlapping constants of his cerebral, slapdash movie can be summarized in the following seven points:

(1) Talkiness. His scripts are padded, coruscated with Chatter in all its

forms, from lecture hall to afterdinner talk. His actors become passive billboards for a mammoth supply of ideas, literary references, favorite stories. That he is a man of verbal concepts should never be forgotten; his visual image is an illustration of an intellectual idea, and often his lists, categories, rules, statistics, quotes from famous authors come across with pictorial impact.

(2) Boredom. This facetious poet of anything-goes is the first director to reverse conventional film language in order to surround the spectator with long stretches of aggressive, complicated nothingness. There is a contrary insistence on outrageous lengths, lassitude-ridden material, psycheless acting, the most banal decor, a gesture that is from left field.

(3) Ping-pong motion. The heartbeat of his vocabulary is the pace and positioning of a slow Ping-pong match. Marital couples compose themselves and their wrangling into a symmetrical ding-dong. One of his pet systems has a couple seated opposite one another, between them a dead lamp, ornate teapot, or a train window opening on a travelogue French countryside. Why should the most intellectual director employ such a primary one-two, one-two rhythm? His is basically an art of equal emphasis: it's against crescendos and climaxes. Violence becomes a boring, casual, quickly-forgotten occasion. *La Chinoise*, his most controlled film, is also his most equalized, and behind all of its scenic plays is the regular, slicing motion of a pendulum in a narrow area.

(4) The Holden Caulfield hero. Inside every character is a little boy precocious who resembles one of Salinger's articulate, narcissistic dropouts.

(5) Mock. Rather than being a mocker, a real satirist, Thackeray or Anthony Trollope, he makes mock versions of war, a Maoist cell, a husband-wife fight, strip acts. He even makes mock profound conversation, and, in those Greek statue shots in *Contempt*, he is doing a mock-up of beautiful photography. Mockery suggests an attitude of being against; invariably this director is in a middle position, finding it a more flexible, workable situation not to take sides. The role of pseudospecialist allows his movies to go where they will go, with no feeling of clampers on the material.

(6) Moralizing. An urban Thomas Hardy, he sees the world as a spiky place, the terrible danger of brassiere ads, the fierce menaces of Coca Cola and Richard Widmark, the corruption implicit in praising a Ferrari when in the character's heart-of-hearts it's Maserati all the way. Just as Tess, the once-laid milkmaid, is a landscape-consumed figure, the idiot children in *Band of Outsiders*—waferlike, incubated snits—are beset by, and get their meaning from, the darkling air around them. The moralizing is always a tone that sneaks in despite the ambivalence that keeps his surface brittle and facetious.

(7) Dissociation. Or magnification of the molehill as against the mountain, or vice versa. He's a thing director, though he doesn't imbue articles with soul in Polanski's manner. Mostly he goes in the opposite direction, free-wheeling across the scene. He dissociates talk from character (a tough secret agent in a freak-boring-weird discussion of conscience), actor from character (Bardot is often flattened, made into a poster figure rather than the spunky-shrewd wife in *Contempt*), action from situation (two primitives in a Dogpatch kitchen holding life-size underwear ads against their bodies), and photography from scene (a mile-long bed scene, the cheapest record-cover color on a Petty-posed, baby's-flesh nude.)

It is easy to underestimate his passion for monotony, symmetry, and a one-and-one-equals-two simplicity. Probably his most influential scene was hardly noticed when *Breathless* appeared in 1959. While audiences were attracted to a likable, agile hood, American bitch, and the hippity-hop pace of a 1930's gangster film, the key scene was a flat, uninflected interview at Orly airport with a just-arrived celebrity author. The whole movie seemed to sit down and This Thing took place: a ducklike amateur, fiercely inadequate to the big questions, slowly and methodically trades questions and answers with the guest expert. His new movies, ten years later, rest almost totally on this one-to-one simplicity.

This flat scene, appearing at points where other films blast out in plot-solving action, has been subtly cooling off, abstracting itself, with the words becoming like little trolley-car pictures passing back and forth across a flattened, neuterized scene. This monotony idea, which is repeated in so many crucial areas, in sculpture (Bollinger), painting (Noland), dance (Rainer), or underground film (Warhol), has practically washed his film away from all of its eclectic old movie moorings.

At the *Breathless* station, fourteen features and ten shorts ago, he had not yet perfected his idea of the actor as a mere improvising face which pops in and out of a carnival curtain while the director throws verbal baseballs at it. This is a strange elaboration of the ping-pong effect, which had the ball bouncing erratically back and forth, first one face talking, then the other, while the top of the screen appeared to curl over in the sagging atmosphere. During the next years, he perfected this abstractionism into a shooting gallery effect, first one face moving into range, then another, while the bodies diminish into strings and their owners recede behind the words.

But this ping-pong technique has impelled a minimalizing that gives a pungent tactility to his worst (*Made in USA*) and best (*My Life to Live*) films.

When Anne Wiazemski, *La Chinoise*, is talking about serious things (and a lot of the audience to sleep), plucking at her lip, showing her two middle teeth, the image is pure, spare, reduced, and rather wondrous.

Boredom and its adjuncts—lack of inflection, torpor, mistake-embracing permissiveness—get his movie to its real home: pure abstraction. When he is just right, his boredom creates kinds of character and image that reverberate with a clanking effect in one's mind and gets across that morbid nullity which is so much at the heart of his work. In the last analysis, it is just the amount of deadness that gives the film a glistening humor: Véronique and her partner, seated in cardboard Victorian elegance at opposite ends of the table, a fancy tea service between them. The whole scene picks up the lovable gimmick of children's books, the stand-up illustration that goes into three dimensions as you open the page, and then dissolves into flatness as you close it again. Looking blankly across the table, she says "et cetera" and Guillaume repeats the word with the same deadpan inflection, so that each syllable carries a little, sticking, Elmer's glue sound.

Behind the good (*Band of Outsiders*), bad (*Woman Is a Woman*), and beautiful-bad (*Carabiniers* is visually ravishing at any moment, but nearly splits your skull) is the specter of an ersatz, lopsidedly inflated adolescent, always opposed to the existing order, primitivistic either in his thinking or in terms of conscience and feelings. In all the film's expressions is the feeling of a little boy drifter, a very poetic and talented self-indulgent Tom Sawyer, who can be a brainy snot throwing doctrinaire slogans or coyly handling books so that the hip spectator can just barely make out the title. Every one of his actors, with the exception of Michel Piccoli in *Contempt*, has been shifting his performance around this Salinger adolescent as a grown-up: few of these people—Seberg (tinny, schoolmarmish), Belmondo (outlandishly coy and unfinished; squiggly little grimaces with his mouth), Bardot (coarse, spunky shrewdness), Brialy (old-fashioned egotism, stolidly sissified), Jack Palance (fiercely elegant, better silent), Sami Frey (whiplike), Macha Meril (fairly human pug-noise), Jean Pee Loud (vigorous rodent), Brasseur (chunky, mock methodical), Michel Sémi-anko (nicely unpushy; high school clarinetist type), Fritz Lang (businesslike self-effacement and warmth)—seem less than obnoxious or escape the flattening technique of a director always present as a shadow over each actor. Actually his actors are halves, and it is only our awareness of the director's dramatic presence behind the camera that gives the character a bogus completion.

Ordinarily the character is queer, sawed off, two-dimensional, running the gamut from brainless brutish in *Carabiniers* to the shallow, disgustingly cute Belmondo-Brialy-Karina triangle that worries about getting a stripper pregnant in *Woman Is a Woman*. There's one last variant of this type, the politically sensitive boys in *Masculin-Feminin*; also the narrowly smug clique in *La Chinoise*, who are loaded with sophistication and act as self-contained units (or eunuchs). Obviously these new, stark, cool characters have a closer kinship with the director than Nana, a prostitute who is hung up on personal freedom. Secret, Ban, and Fresh, his new product, come off the screen strong willed, determined, passionately committed, and they give his movie a new decision and affirmation that can make a spectator feel flabby and drifting by comparison. With its shallow space, shadowlessly antiseptic surfaces, and photography that shoots from the waist up as though the camera were resting on the counter, *La Chinoise* is like a modern diner employing a summer waitress (Wiazemski), busboy (Léaud), a skulled scullery maid (Berto), and a toast boy (Sémianko, who dispenses intelligence despite a sitting-still position and a scene that sinks him up to his blue eyeballs in words).

Had he done nothing else, Godard should be remembered for having invented an army of graceful, clumsy, feeble oddballs. With foot-loose acting in the most sketchily written roles, these figures come across like Chin Chillar in Dick Tracy or Andy Capp, defined to their teeth, exposed in space from the awkward feet to their crazy heads (which are always punched up with some caricaturing element: mostly hats and wigs, occasionally an obscenely large eyeball).

One of these, Arthur (*Band of Outsiders*), memorable for his woolen stocking cap pulled down over most of his malignant Jim Thorpe face to his nose, is an argyle-sweatered sweetheart to forget. As the chosen beau in a triangle, he implacably keeps his eyes, like a hungry airedale, glued to the curb, while Claude Brasseur acts him with the unyielding sneakiness of a furtive fireplug.

Another, as poetic in a different but equally crazy way, is a bunchy, layered concoction of vamp make-up and thrift-shop clothes acted as a latter-day Gish sister by Catherine Ribeiro in *Les Carabiniers*. Cleopatra is a primping, prancing, real primitive, the mistress of a dinky one-room house that shifts around a dirt plot and a mailbox that spits letters the way old movie calendars once dripped leaves.

Lemmy Caution (Eddie Constantine, in *Alphaville*), known as Richard Johnson to his enemies, a bullfrog whose face has been corrugated by a defective waffle iron, has the flexibility of an undistinguished low-income "project" building. His role consists of walking through hallways, rooms, and up and down staircases, either pinching his nonexistent lips or blinking against the torrential onslaught of lights.

Compared to the soft-shoe nonchalance of a Hawks war hero as played by

Cary Grant, the moronic warriors, Michel-Ange and Ulysse in *Carabiniers*, are heavy, stillborn bricks falling off a building. Why does a celebrated artist devote so much time to inane time-wasting cockiness, the showboating of a character so limited he's close to a wisp? Karina's little fawn, eyes blinking and hair shaking, limbs used like stilts, hasn't anything of reality or good acting, but she has a robust, complacent ego that presumes her one-note acting is tireless. A collegiate little girl, a partisan captured in the forest in *Carabiniers*, has this same unchallenged *chutzpah*. There's an inner sureness that he's going to score, no matter what he does, that is repellent in Albert Juross's dumpling Michel-Ange. The director is like a street vender who has a suitcase of windup dolls, which he sends out to do their little, cranked-up turns.

One of his personal gambits is the cocky fun that he gets into these scuttling figures: his fake Bogarts and Mary Pickfords shoot, slide, and trot in a bizarre carbonated fashion on a semiabstract screen constructed like a pinball machine. It's a trademark of his landscape work that he cuts against the newsreel image by formalizing the shot: a diagrammatic line of action, a syncopated stop-go sound track, someone yapping tick-o-tick, tick-o-tick. A funny, waistless chick in cute cotton pants embraces her nude breasts in a defiant X formation and marches outdoors and indoors like a football referee stepping off the yards; a car chase shot backward in rigid, linear patterns; Bardot pacing diagonals on a roof, using her arms like the guy who signals an airplane down to a carrier (did he do this because the villa roof is the size and shape of a ship's landing field?). Cleopatra, waltzing out into a dusty yard, does a couple of big-footed pirouettes and, with a melodramatic shove, sends an aging lover packing in a Sennett Essex.

He gets the most singular acting response, probably with a magical dishwater command like "That's OK for now." The response he gets is supreme slackness, seemingly without worry or prethought about the role, and a sublime confidence in the director's unerring genius. The result is a mindless drifting, in which reactions come mystifyingly late. Brasseur's desultory, undistinguished dance style in *Band of Outsiders* is peculiar in that it is so self-absorbed, out of sync with his two partners; occasionally something beautifully sinuous suggests itself amongst his mock absorptions.

Since the role is almost invariably a reference to an image or actor out of film history, the clothes, basically unpretentious and everyday, are supplemented with misaligned *outré* items: an unnecessarily heavy overcoat and prol cap from *Potemkin*, a trench coat and Sam Spade lid from Dashiell Hammett. The gestures also seem tacked on. A blob-faced actor (Juross in *Carabiniers*) dressed in dirty swaddling clothes fatuously and hammily pats his hair into place. Kovacs and Véronique at pensive moments, one every two minutes, pass a thumb in slow motion across their lips, a gesture that is a flagrant pun on mouth tricks, from Bogart through Steve McQueen. Instead of being unobtrusive, these tics are applied like thudding punctuation.

He just doesn't care whether any of these actions carry conviction. There is no antiwar scene more strained and irritating than a kid soldier methodically terrorizing a female hostage by raising and lowering her skirt, delicately, with the tip of his rifle. Meant as a real raking-under of the military, it's a slow, crude, visual metaphor for rape, ending in a house being burned. The oddness about the scene is that the havoc is played so deadpan: a lot of emphasis on the dopey way he orders her to "unbutton," the Rembrandt self-portrait on the wall underlined. Instead of the atmosphere of outrage, the sentiment is reversed and the scene played as though the next-door neighbor had come in and demanded a cup of sugar. This severe dissociation of tone from content spreads the scene with grotesquerie, a fantastic comic-strip feeling coming off the screen, discordant bits of ungodliness like Juross's glazed leer, the fact that the skirt is raised at a point dead-center on her person. He is a master of the brusque and angular. He'll play along with Juross's booby incompetence because it brings him an antiheroic oafish bayonet-pointing line of action. This kind of jabbing, off-balance virulence is at the very heart of his brilliantly diseased message.

Godard's legacy to film history already includes a school of estranged clown fish, intellectual ineffectuals, a vivid communication of mucking about, a good eye for damp villas in the suburbs, an ability to turn any actress into a doll, part of the decor, some great still shots that have an irascible energy, an endless supply of lists. I think that I shall never see scenes with more sleep-provoking powers, or hear so many big words that tell me nothing, or be an audience to film-writing which gets to the heart of an obvious idea and hangs in there, or be so edified by the sound and sight of decent, noble words spoken with utter piety. In short, no other film-maker has so consistently made me feel like a stupid ass.

October 1968

New York Film Festival: 1968

THERE is nothing so funny in the recent New York Film Festival as the Romanyesque overland coach in *Lola Montes*, a blood-colored Pullman on wheels that belongs to Franz Liszt, and serves as a major trysting nest for the scandalous heroine. A love affair on wheels is a nice idea but this over-decorated vehicle is the hub for eight minor events which are nothing but crazy make-up, improbability, and an ordeal of graceless acting. Martine Carol, an hourglass made out of stale golden cupcakes, is a mock George Sand, locked on a chaise longue; her boyfriend has a goofy smile, silken curls, and stumbles about putting the finishing touches to "The Farewell Waltz." The real nutti-ness is the feeling of hometown operetta around them. Lola's getaway wagon, which follows behind, is operated by a husband-wife servant team who run out from behind the wheels, carrying bird cages and carpetbags, shouting "spa-ghetti." Some other fake elements: a painted backdrop of the Italian country-side and one of those villas which once housed Ricardo Cortez, a domineering mother, and a raging river, the wildest in 1920's melodrama.

The oozelike structure about a Garboish woman of affairs played by a non-Garbo as stupid, not very classy, and two shades from pure ugly, is a perfect Festival film, steeped in attitudes. The theme, from *Naked Night*, through three festival films, has the director as a ringmaster, magician, lion-tamer, vul-nerable to man's foibles but knowing everything about life. There is a gran-diose attempt at cosmic embrace, pro-life and pro-love, with the requisite number of peculiar bosom shots: the breasts are pushed up and then bounced, always a couple of fleshy folds around the armpits. Any Ophuls movie is sup-posed to be fluid magic, but after the first five minutes of circus, it is like hauling an old corpse around and around in sawdust.

The truth about a film festival is that it is a parlor of myths, a dilemma bound to overrun a place that is supposed to be exhibiting only the best blue-chip films. Some of the very clear myths are (1) that Renoir is deadly accurate on "human passions," hard-working folk, and the plight of the poor, (2) that there is a torrent of important films washing through Czechoslovakia, (3) that Ophuls made better films in Europe than in Hollywood, (4) that American moviegoers want and need the taunts directed into films by Franco-Italian mandarins and mad-dog labelers.

What a queer sensation to be face-to-face with a causeless film that can draw a "my God, I like it" remark. Mailer's *Beyond the Law* has a zillion little irritations, but it has authentic scurrility and funk before it goes sour with Mailer's Irish brogue monologue. *Faces* is a real break-through in movie acting, despite the wrong stamping of Americans as compulsive laughers; it also goofs such motivations as a husband cheerfully clicking his heels and greeting his wife after spending ten hours with a high-priced whore, and a squad of elderly males, who are just rancid hams with facey leers.

Bresson's *Mouchette*, by about three-hundred miles the most touching and truly professional film in the festival, is about a fourteen-year-old girl of the peasant class, living in a small French village, the daughter of two alcoholics. The film has apparently melted down to a short story, being adapted from a Bernanos novel, but it moves on about five levels. It has to do with the surpassing beauty of a girl who is in a state of excruciating physical discomfort. On another level, it is about difficulty, an almost pure analysis of its sides and, in this case, the way it multiplies when luck is out. (Mouchette has some luck in a bumper-car concession at the amusement park, but it doesn't last long—only long enough to create the most poetic action sequence in years.) Other levels deal with a particularly bitter village and its inhabitants (the snare theme, Life chasing the human being into extinction); the conception of people as being so deeply rooted in their environment that they are animallike: the simple effect of a form briefly lit by a truck's headlights.

Mouchette, played by Nadine Nortier, has a touching toughness, the crushing sense of not expecting anything from anybody, and a harrowing know-how about every niche of village life. Unlike Frankie Darro, who got the same desperate shadow effects in *Riding High*, Nordier's singularity is tied to painful appearances: apathetic about her well-being, hair uncombed and probably lice-ridden, a large part of the painfulness has to do with large lumpy legs, stockings that won't stay up, big shoes. Despite all these humiliations, she is never cartoony and gets enormous somber dignity into her walking tours, combats with other girls, and a terrific moment when she climbs into bed, wet from a rainstorm, and then goes into some slovenly chores for the baby.

Some of the most important things movies can do are in this film. The barmaid, for instance: a queer and singular girl, as muscular as she is narrow, her character, which has tons of integrity and stubbornness, is just barely caught: through a crowd of locals, from an offangle, pinning up the top flap of her apron, drying the glasses. The role is backed into through gesture and spirit, rather than through direct portrayal. Then there is the great device of placing Mouchette's house on a truck route, and milking that device for the most awesome, mysterious wonders. Also, for a film that is unrelievedly raw, homely, and depressed, it seems a wild perversity to bloom for five minutes into sudden elation with Mouchette and a likably acted boy riding some dodgem cars at a fair. After so many misused amusement parks in films, it is remarkable to come across one that works.

In the category called Bloody Bores, the Festival offered *Capricious Summer*, *Hugo and Josefin*, and *Twenty-Four Hours in a Woman's Life*. Orson Welles's little orchid, *The Immortal Story*, missed by being only minutes long and having but four audible lines ("Take back your five guinea piece, old master." The next line—"In one way or another, Miss Virginey, this thing will be the death of him"—is repeated at least four times. What makes Eilshemus Levinsky so sure?)

Capricious Summer features three middle-aged crocks hanging around a 1920's bathhouse doing their thing. An ex-athlete gone to girth swaggers, brags, and plays dull largesse. An army officer is an irritating, strutting performer doing worldly cynicism. The third, a minister, works on timid innocuousness. A slender, owlish magician (acted in fey, fond-of-itself mime style by director Jiri Menzel) comes to town with a threadbare tightrope act, and, after his blond assistant diddles the three dullards, this rerun of dozed-off acting, Renoir color, and Bergman soupy philosophy winds up with the notion that a circus invariably leaves whistle-stop town sadder and wiser than it was in the first reel.

The most interesting work always occurred outside the self-conscious languor acting that grips French and Italian films. Jacqueline Sassard and her Lesbian owner in *Les Biches* sit on this veneer act so hard that it becomes possible to decide how much cosmetic art has been planted on an eyelid, or the number of small elegances that transpire in getting one bite out of a chicken leg. There is a strain of this nauseous elegant withdrawal in the two dozen conceited stiffs who make up the young Parisian middle class in Godard's *Two or Three Things I Know About Her*, led by Marina Vlady, a project-dwelling housewife who daylights as a prostitute when she isn't haughtily walking through a dress shop, sniffing the air, discussing her inner life with the audience. It's amazing how Raoul Coutard's camera can transform this puerile conceit into a singingly crisp image.

In *The Red and the White*, a swift, fresh-air war movie about Czarists, Red Russians, and a band of Magyars who get tangled within the scythelike moves of both armies in a Hungarian border locale that has a grandiloquent sweep, there are a dozen actors with amazing skin tone, sinewy health, and Brumel's high-jumping agility in their work with horses. These actors have an icy dignity—they never mug, make bids for the audience's attention, or try for the slow-motion preening that still goes on in cowboy films. (Jack Palance in *Shane*, hanging over his saddle iron, spitting tobacco juice, menacing poor townfolk, relating to his horse as another part of his stylist's costume.)

As far as acting goes, though, *Faces* is a far more important case. Lynn Carlin is near perfection, playing the deepest well of unexplored emotions as the wife of a rubber-faced business wow who seems like a detestable ham walk-on until he surprisingly lodges into the film's center for good. This Carlin style starts as soap-opera face work, a camera intimately registering the melancholy of an American woman, but it builds velocity and possibilities for itself by working into the area that Warhol has pioneered. It's amazing how far Carlin swings her role as a middle-class wife: she's so deep into the events that, after one night out or in with a gigolo swinger, she seems to have expanded the role out of sight by the time her husband returns from a bored-with-job whore.

Faces is a Loser Club movie, the theme being about people straying into brief sexual relations, or wanting to stray and not being able. The strength of the movie is the depth to which it dives into a particular situation: four middle-aged women, uncomfortable with themselves, awkwardly trying to be swingers, entertaining a blond hustler who does some sexy dancing around the living room. The movie—no rush and plenty of time—sits and stares at each. It stares at a pair of blazing eyeballs in a woman who is scared, out-of-practice. It's very good on a woman nearing sixty, greedy, and nearly out of her mind at the possibility of making it with a young cat: she palpitates with suicidal abandon and blatant lust. There's a sweating excitement in the work with Carlin, a decorous young wife full of twitches, stiff postures suddenly dropped, and prissy lips that never stop working into nervous moods. One of the movie's unspoken themes is the disparity between this unworldly woman and her husband, an oily actor (John Marley) who suffocates the movie with he-man sophistication. The top moment is a profile shot catching this actress at the end of a marathon, teasing evening of too many cigarettes, lousy drinks, and faded chances. The movie ricochets from a drunken semicomic dance to the coldest close-up of Carlin's frazzled side of the face, an innocent mouth that exudes the feeling of a long night's journey into deafening defeat.

November 1968

New York Film Festival 1968, Afterthoughts

"Manny, how are you holding up? How's your Festivalitis? Oh well, Lola Montes will do it to the best of us. ('What film did you like best?') Definitely The Nun. *I liked the whole projection of the period. But my favorite director is Jancso; he's a great stylist. ('Didn't you like anything about that German film,* Signs of Life?*') Good God no. When the Germans deal with minutiae, they leave me."*

—Film critic

"What a corny coincidence that both the husband and wife manage to get laid in the same night. I just can't stomach that kind of unbelievable coincidence in a film which pretends to be raw realism."

—Director of a film department

"It's just a shitty film. These North American sincerists call me up all the time. I caught your film: simply fantastic or terrific. But I know it was nothing but a shitty film, just shit. I didn't delude myself for a minute. I didn't like the French entries, the Bach thing was a bore, Mouchette *was a piece of shit, the German film was rather nice in a crude sort of way. Couldn't seem to get an image, could he?"*

—Canadian film photographer

People talk a lot about the star glamour, action, straight-ahead drive that the old Paramount film used to have, but one thing it didn't have is even a fraction of the talk that goes on outside of theaters today. This drone, which starts the moment the *Times* informs you that *Pretty Poison* is a bang-up job à la Hitchcock and doesn't stop until sleep rubs out an important comment about Jacqueline Sassard ("She looks slim, but I'm sure that when she has her first kid her ass will spread"), goes on everywhere, all the time, until life is one long, steep ramp leading upward to a classy double bill at the Elgin Theater. This hum, which could occur driving down the West Side Highway, over a phone to a friend in Brooklyn, in a roadside college bar where Janis Joplin and Aretha Franklin are soul-shouters just barely audible over "Jean Vigo was a master at street scenes complicated with a lot of cross-currents," is compulsive, decisive, scrofulous, flapping about, and completely engulfing once it gets under way.

One of the desperate facts about being part of movies today is that every thirtieth word might be "Truffaut-Moreau-Godard," a depressing, chewed-over sound, and that a heavy segment of any day is consumed by an obsessive, nervous talking about film. This is often a joyless sound that couldn't inspire anybody, but it suggests that modern moviegoers are trying to possess the film or at least give it a form or a momentousness which it doesn't have.

Godard's *Weekend* is the handsome, maddeningly long pilgrimage of a jaded, fascinating, wrinkle-faced woman (Mireille Darc), which gets more and more barbaric while the actress shows a sexy, haunting talent for withdrawing, going blank when she hasn't anything to say. It is a soul-shouter movie which often devours the violence it wants through a spoiled rotten, rich-man's technique, a toylike presentation of highway cannibalism, sexual expertise, capitalism at its hate-consumed dead end. Sometimes the web of words builds into a good funny speech and there is a growling display-room color, a vehement moving from one grotesque, humorous texture and setup to another.

There is a scene in a gas station, after a sports car smashes up against a trac-tor, that has a dizzy, blunt, Mel Frank momentum. Odd, wonderful stray faces are flashed on screen, and the actress's unconvincing rhetoric somehow becomes menacing and real as she prods herself, trying to charge herself up into more and more vituperation. It builds into a jelly-apple shrillness, with a last terrific shot of stray onlookers banded together in a we-are-the-French-nation camaraderie, soul brotherhood. Through her last words, "You crumby Jew bastards," the idea gets implanted that these onlookers and the victim her-self can only get together when they find a common enemy: a possibly Jewish couple in another sports car who won't give the girl shouter a lift.

For its Cubistic pace and garishly cruel throwaway dialogue, this scene in a gas station has a wild, daring, hit-and-miss excitement. The rich girl, whose boyfriend is killed, screams at the farmer driving the tractor: "You filthy unwashed peasant, you killed the man I loved and ruined my car. He was handsome and he was rich and now he's dead and you're stupid and ugly and you don't even care. You hate us because we screw in Saint Moritz. You prob-ably don't even know how to screw. You just get screwed by the union. You probably don't even own the tractor. [She kicks the tires.] Cheap tires? My car was beautiful. It had a Chrysler motor. I got it because I screwed the son of General Motors."

It's a film which loves its body odor. A husband and wife sit on the side of the road. She says, "I'm fed up," climbs down into a ditch to take a nap. Hus-band lights a cigarette. Tramp comes along, asks for a light. Husband says: "Haven't got one." Tramp spots the wife in the ditch, says, "Hey, that's a bird down there. Is that your bird?" Husband doesn't answer, just looks bored. So the tramp climbs down into the ditch and rapes the wife. The treatment, with the motionless camera, far back and across the road, is offhanded, antiformal, so slight and slack that the spectator feels, "Well, OK, what's next?"

What's next is a scene with two garbage collectors who give the couple a lift. The garbage men, a white and a black, lean against the truck, eating sub-marine sandwiches. The ravenously hungry husband asks for a bite, and the Negro gives him a small section, saying: "If this sandwich were the American budget, what I gave you represents the portion the U.S. gave to the Congo this year." Movies like *Weekend* show the spectator how to run off at the mouth and keep a sense of self-importance at the same time.

In yet another scene, there is this delighting in far-fetched spuriousness. Mireille Darc takes a bath, and, while the camera watches her washing her neck, her husband, not seen on screen, tells a story about a hippopotamus: "The hippo goes to the master of the animals. 'Please let me live in the water.'

The master says, 'No, you'll eat up all the fish.' The hippo answers, 'If you'll let me live in the water, I promise that when I shit, I'll spread it out with my tail and you'll see that there are no fish bones in it.'" This story (most of it is Darc in the bathtub, plus cuts to previous material) has charm and piquancy, but in the recounting there is the uneasy feeling of a director moving unresisted material that he knows backward and forward from one end of a film to another without snarl or conflict.

Czech films, Underground films, Hollywood films. Now people who take films seriously study skin flicks, TV commercials, scopitone. In the days of Wrath or Raft, there were just Hollywood films, "B" or "A," Arthur Rank, and a few art directors like Renoir. The sheer bulk of what is known as film, plus the equal cheers for so many different types of film, has loosened everyone's bowels. Everyone's in the cat-bird seat casting out rambling comments.

A smarmy, navel-rubbing movie like *Zita* shows this instant aging process with its pretentious and precocious facility by a crew of movie-world teeny boppers. The film's point is that the circle of life goes on in a delectable, heartfelt slow motion, as this French Debbie Reynolds, whose beloved aunt is dying, finds earthly love at the same moment that her aunt passes into the hereafter. The main presumption is that skill permits any amount of goo to run into a film: a blue-ribbon ram on a tear through Paris streets, a little red toy auto taken as a memento, lovers coyly eating peach preserves out of a jar by the spoonful.

Among the visual gimmicks is an embarrassing bedroom scene, a wispy prancing *pas de deux* in slow motion as the two lovers undress. Imagine Bogart, in a haze of spring blossom color, pantomiming ecstasy as he drifts around the bedpost, tearing off his shirt, a flower opening to the sun. Or standing with such fey charm in the middle of a highway at dawn, playing a bass fiddle.

Signs of Life (three Nazi soldiers on a cushy detail, on an island near Crete, pass the time making fireworks, dozing, eating in the yard at a small card table) has been the subject of a typical noisy dismembering: "A modern Don Quixote, apathetic and inhibited, is at last stung into rebellion against society, and reveals the first senseless signs of his humanity only in insanity." Very ephemeral in its charms, *Signs* has some of the casual goodhearted zaniness that Gassman injects into *The Easy Life*: playing up meandering activity over dialogue, getting all the times of day, the feeling of friendship in its inactive-silent aspects. The meals at the table are perfect: dramaless, engrossed in eating, an unemphasized graceful Greek wife who comes across as a war bride who doesn't know the language or the people she's living with. The hub of this sly, dry, truly comic movie is a cranky-bitching soldier, a butcher of insects, so serious working away in the corner or on the beach trying to devise Rube Goldberg traps to devastate the "cookalockers."

The Nun is a young girl in a Chardin pose doing needlepoint. A maid comes in with a message: "Your mother will see you." The camera, an undistinguished onlooker, doesn't move, and the perfumy scene doesn't develop until there is a cut to another stagy setup with people in chalk-marked confrontations.

Les Biches, *Secret Ceremony*, and *Negatives* are psychologically oriented movies about fetishes in which the subtlety consists of playing perversion very close to normality, unlike Huston's *Golden Eye* movie, which goes sour because of the "oh-look-at-that" attitude about soldiers riding bare ass or playing with a Baby Ruth wrapper.

With a constant lacquered barrenness, from its stylized acting to its setting, Saint Tropez in December, *Les Biches* is an exploitation-doesn't-pay film. Two women meet in the middle of a bridge where the younger one, "Why," earns a living doing chalk drawings of does on the sidewalk. Frédérique (Stéphane Audran), a droll and spicy sybarite, circles around Why, flamboyantly throws her a large sum of money, and, after moving indoors and putting one too many sugars in her coffee, seduces her. In this seduction scene, Jacqueline Sassard has just bathed and is standing around, a pretty girl with a strange neuter manner and the walk of a dull penguin, her head always down, constantly in need of a good nose-blowing. The whole scene plays as though it were inside a mattress: Audran slowly rearranges Sassard's shirt, and, in the corniest of hushed close-ups, the camera frames itself around her hands as they start to unzip the girl's blue denims.

The movie depends on Audran's willingness to lay it on in a pure baloney performance. One of her slow, succulent moments takes place in her stadium-sized kitchen where the frazzled cook is whipping up some veal and brussel sprouts, the favorite dish of two dull-acted pansies who live off Frédérique. Looking as though someone rubbed berry dye on her face, using a slow catlike walk, making one small name, Why, sound like three bars of an organ piece, she addresses the cook: "Vio-let-ta! Ça va? Ici Mademoiselle Wh-y-ee."

Tropics, a fictional documentary about a Brazilian dust-bowl family on the road, is a lukewarm muddy river. There seems to be a film over the film: no blacks or whites, nothing emphasized, a limp-vague father moving through villages bereft of script and money, even the air and trucks evidently needing a Geritol pick-me-up. ("You know, I didn't really mind it. I couldn't bear the first half, but in the second half, I got interested in those crabs they were pulling out of the mud. I thought it gave a true projection of what it means to be poor. You know what I mean: standing out in the mud all day long, reaching down for those ugly things.")

Hugo and Josefin is life as seen through the eyes of people in a Kodak camera ad. There is the sense of a hummingbird or apple orchard just around the next bend in this clean-fresh-buttery movie. ("It could be called something like a preadolescent *Elvira Madigan*, impossible to resist.") Their Breck-shiny hair, photographed through lichen, pine trees, and spotless windowpanes, has an equal importance with Hugo's little tooled Tyrolean suspenders and Josefin's beautifully pressed microsmocks (there is an obsessional effort to get the gray flannel pinafore above her tiny white drawers). It's the epitome of a Blonde Is Beautiful and Best film, a proper bourgeois mentality and relentless wholesomeness that should further madden the already maddened Stokely Carmichael.

December 1968

Canadian Underground

THE best film at "Canadian Artists '68" is a study of a room not unlike the basement room at the Art Gallery of Toronto, where the films were privately shown. A bare and spare room with the simple construction of a Shaker-built outhouse, the gallery room had an austere charm, a continuing dignity, even after twenty films had been seen. Exactly like the interiors of schoolrooms in Winslow Homer, it has a magical plain gray color and an equally magical pattern of woodwork on the side walls, four-inch boards running horizontally from floor to ceiling, divided by four-inch studs spaced two feet on center. The back wall is brick, but it has the same transfixing green-tinged gray paint plus that eye-level line of coat hooks that American architecture should never have given up.

Michael Snow's *Wavelength*, a pure, tough forty-five minutes that may become the *Birth of a Nation* in Underground films, is a straightforward document of a room in which a dozen businesses have lived and gone bankrupt. For all of the film's sophistication (and it is overpowering for its time-space-sound inventions), it is a singularly unpadded, uncomplicated, deadly realistic way to film three walls, a ceiling, and a floor. Maybe if all moviemakers worked as directly and simply, leaving out the literary and commercial hangovers from the days of Cecil De Mille, other film content than this one white room would possess a startling freshness.

Probably the most rigorously composed movie in existence, Snow's film is a continuous zoom toward the lineup of windows and the complex of signs, tops of trucks, second-story windows outside the loft. So integrated, taut, fully realized, not like an idea-suggestion someone could pick up and use, in one aspect, the minimal project picks up the *Blow Up* theme. An unexplained murder occurs, the camera dissolves itself into a moody, turbulent photograph that is obsessively present but not immediately discernible. This photograph is the target for the relentless, oncoming zoom, which is an abstract corollary of photographer Hemmings's concentrated gazing at the print mutations on the *Blow Up* murder photos. There is a marked similarity in the choice of photographs in both films.

Good as the darkroom episodes are in Antonioni's hit, Snow's working out of the idea is more abstract, and, by being so, gets to the uncomfortable bones of the theme: the overpowering, indestructible reality of the physical world alongside the wispiness of the human presence. This kind of paradox is hardly original, but Snow brings off the horrible largeness of the idea by doing it austerely, in the right cold, objective tone and with unusual balances between the unpretentious acceptance of room objects and severe abstractions of time-space techniques.

The zoom, always at eye level, is almost imperceptible and goes from the widest view of the field to a particular point between the windows, ending up inside the sea photograph. The journey—accompanied by exactly syncopated natural sounds from street and people plus an electronic sound, which comes up to an unbearable point when the camera is six feet away from the wall and then depreciates—is broken into four equal time-space intervals by human entries. There is nothing fey about these incidents: they are quick, realistic, and lightweight. The film opens with the first human event, a cabinet being moved into the loft, while an alert, rotund woman directs two movers, and ends with a young girl making a telephone call. She says, "Could you come over right away, I think there's been a murder." These events happen as the camera determinedly presses forward, slowly ingesting every possible fact of place and light, and, like Fate, sees every wall-person-light detail as equally important.

If a room could speak about itself, this would be the way it would go. The movement of the camera is almost nonmotion, or a room's movement. The people—very small, never filling the room, their feet making slipping sounds—are seen as light, impermanent guests. The color-light, which is so multiple and unpredictably changing, is really ravishing. One stretch of the journey has the field in reversed negative colored with sepia and burnt-sienna tones. The street, which has been a changing, shadowy backdrop, goes in an instant explosion to pure tone when all the complementary color is removed. The middle section is an assault of abstracted color, but the compositional elements, the tall rectangular windows, are still those of the room. It's like flushes of color in the consciousness of a room: a green shudder, a sort of visceral perception of the walls and windows.

The best quality is that the rigorous, high-level diary of a room is so itself, so unlike anything a moviegoer might imagine. Suddenly, with these exciting but soothingly balmy color-light variations in a worn interior, what had seemed a tabby-cat movement, the Underground film, takes on the profundity and sophistication, austere dignity and inventive wit of a major art. It is hard to believe that a film could be more taut or intelligent.

The actors who star in the Canadian films—desultory, lacking in intensity, numbed and ominous—never win awards in the category of either the beautiful or the damned. There is no passion about the casting. It is usually the guy next door, a girl friend, or the family pet who are willing to work free and have an inert boldness in front of a camera. The funniest is the sort of likable kid who does nothing in *On Nothing Days*. With a colossal mindlessness, a body in which no part strikes a harmony with another, and too embarrassed to breathe, he shuffles around downtown like a coat sleeve looking for an arm to stick in itself. The first time you see him he's in bed debating with himself (Guess I'll get up. What's there to get up for? You don't have to get up, you know.) and examining his fingernails. Forty minutes later, after he's bummed around town, ridden the subway, had a fantasy about the girl across the aisle, he comes home, lights a cigarette, sits on the windowsill, and this adolescent-frustration movie ends.

This is a draggy, heavy-footed movie: the air is heavy and hanging, he walks as though pulling up molasses with each step, and the scenes never come to anything. A spectator going through such a day would be ready for suicide.

The horror film of the Festival, *Slow Run*, is about free love amongst the enlightened in some tenement of New York. A young man's misadventures in a Manhattan that has never been photographed in more depressing tones, a continuing sluggish gray with interior scenes that are mordantly airless and street life in which the people are slow, stoned, and silly. This is a film about a girl undressing and a folk-rock group type with bangs over his eyes, sort of delicate and vague, who sits collapsed in a stuffed chair or stands naked in a shower soaping himself with a zonked-out expression on his face. Between these two repeated incidents there is some mysterious *schlepping* around the living room, some going-nowhere playfulness in bed. All this determinedly minor material is ridden over by a willfully pretentious narration, forty unclear words a second, that keeps pounding home the theme that this movie is a run-down version of Joyce's *Ulysses*. In effect, this ode to freedom and youth is a profoundly grim and depressing film.

Right now, the two polarities of the independent scene are the Static Field film (*Wavelength*; Mekas's stunning study of swelling tides and shooting sail-boats in the French seaport of Cassis; Andy Warhol's films, which, for all their overlapping, are basically static field; and some of Bruce Baillie's "haiku") and Nudity. *Soapy Run* has all the signposts in this latter film: (1) the touching is scant and sort of paternal, considering the amount of nudity and the hot-blooded bragging of the narration, (2) the eroticism is played out singularly with the man completely dressed, gazing with a blank face, (3) the moony-faced nudes treat themselves like illustrations in a science lecture, unveiling as though they were performing a social service, (4) the film heads for the bath-tub as though it were the altar of love, and, when there, the activities consist of plastering each other with soap suds.

Joyce Wieland had three entries: the first, *Cat Food*, studies the eating habits of a luxuriously furred cat devouring separately five fish just arrived from the market. The viewpoint is always as though the camera were held at the edge of a table while the cat operates on top against a black backdrop. It is filled with supreme succulent color, sometimes recalling Manet in the silvery glints of the fish scales, and, as in the *Rat Life* picture, getting the deep, ovular splendor of a Caravaggio. The second entry, *1933*, is a slight exercise which alternates the numerals of that year when Miss Wieland was born with a speeded-up street scene shot from a window. The third and most ambitious, *Rat Life and Diet in North America*, proves that she's been looking long and affec-tionately at animal life and is a sort of whimsical Evelyn Nesbit, never corny and creating with an intense femaleness.

A band of revolutionary gerbils escape their cat jailors and journey up the Hudson, where they hide out at a millionaire's estate and perfect their tactics as guerrilla fighters. It has some hard-to-forget, singular images: One, cap-tioned "Skag Mitchell was the first to escape," shows a grimly bare section of floorboards with the tiny gerbil hovering against the wall furtively waiting for the moment to make his escape. Another, with incredible color shots of fruit, rolls piled on paper doilies, cut-glass goblets, a lavish spread on which the hun-gry rodents eat their full, is overpowering for its recall of Spanish still life, and the animals are pretty charming. The third is the earliest shot in the film, the actor rats jumping up and down against a screen while the huge cats guard them with fixed attention. Just the glinting texture of grass against pitch black night and her use of black burgundy gem color in the cherry festival sequence suggest that Miss Wieland is more than a diary-like recorder of domestic enthusiasms.

R34, the name of a cadmium red dirigible which appears in a cartoony-loud color painting by Greg Curnoe, is the name of a movie documenting the life of this Ontario painter. The documentary reeks with the idea of this artist, a cool and industrious Gideon of Scotland Yard (no neuroses, just a lot of industry), as a good-guy-husband-worker. Always in a steady metronome-pace production, Curnoe *schlepps* the garbage back and forth, sits at a drafting table cutting-assembling-pasting little collages from a welter of commercial labels, magazine ads, bits of type, colored paper (he seems to command his pile of elements like a Red Army ant). The one quality the film shows is that there's hardly any wavering, missteps, backtracing in his production.

One of the questions provoked by *R34* is why are these moments—three shots of a blonde combing her hair, Curnoe grazing the top of a mannikin's wooden bald head with his palm, wetting his moustache with a glass of milk, repeated shots of his and his wife's smiles filling the screen—considered salient in the life of a creative person? These lackluster, haphazard moments are obviously intended to counter the heroic garbage that goes into a *Lust for Life* painter's biog. Chambers's selection doesn't come any closer to the creative process than shots of Kirk Douglas feverishly fighting inner voices and the mistral of Provence. There is one fascinating stretch: Curnoe applying opaque lilac with an absorbed certitude to a serpentine, hard-edged picture.

The great acting of the festival is done by a white loft room, some rodents up the Hudson, and a forest of small industry-made "sculptures" that make up a personal, eccentric pair of films by Gary Lee-Nova. Hinges, toggle bolts, gauges, dials, bolts, an all-yellow map of the United States drawn in 3-D, a cartoon drawing of the Bomb's mushroom cloud, roadway signs, railroad and shipyard iron fixtures, a lot of pipes, cable patterns, spools, capstans. The thing is that Lee-Nova's is a discriminating, coherent choice of Pop, utilities, hardware: a cartooned cloud, a toggle, and a huge, flat giant next to a roadside stand are equalized in scale, all become kin, like the way Léger paints scaffolding, clouds, and workers so that each has the same weight and texture.

January 1969

Films at Canadian Artists '68
Art Gallery of Ontario

THE film side of *Canadian Artists '68*—an open competition that started with 120 entries and ended with 20 finalists and four prizewinners dividing $6,000— leaves strong impressions, stronger say than those of *Secret Ceremony* or the latest film featuring acting by a one-movie nymphet whose playing of a little girl parasite (Zita, Joanna, or Cenci) is being memorialized at this moment in Sunday supplements by Rex Reed or Guy Flatley.

Some of these impressions would obviously include (1) an austere "Loft To Let" space overlooking Canal Street in Manhattan, which is examined for 45 minutes in Michael Snow's *Wavelength* as no room ever has been, outside of Vermeer paintings, (2) the nasty blankness of a prefab room in Clarke Mackey's *On Nothing Days* and the poignantly dispirited way the lacklustre teenager walks to the window and stares at a scene of children jumping rope—as though he were going through a tunnel that stretched across seventeen cheerless years, (3) an amazing shot of rats eating their way through luscious apples and pears, expensive rolls piled high on paper doilies in a scene from Joyce Wieland's funny, personal studies in which she brackets a nostalgic high life song from the Thirties with the incredible darks, pristine whites, and velvety coloring of a Caravaggio painting, (4) the deep-in-the-woods, Waldenesque spirit of Gary Lee-Nova's *Magic Circle*, (5) the Olympic track star's speed with which Lee-Nova gets right into a phenomenologically jolting presentation of hardware, shipyard fixtures, roadside art, and Eastern meditational paintings, and (6) Lee-Nova's dinky but roseate cartoon of an atom bomb in *Steel Mushrooms*, suggesting a cream puff drawn in Moon Mullins style shot upside down and backwards, so that the mushroom cloud is seen first, and then, folding inwards, extinguishes itself.

All these films seem very private, made for the artist's sake rather than a Cinema I audience. A girl who has the homely beef and push of a carpenter's thumb seats herself on a window ledge and does some bereft mugging, trying to please the unseen cameraman. Larry Kardish's *Slow Run* female and her leaden gesticulating doesn't have a fraction of wit, but the glaring point of this and other entries is that they're not after glamour and seem completely minus in show-biz chutzpah, which is a fixture today in every film from the Mod of *Blow-up* to Godard to the tasteful, Europeanized Hollywood feature, such as *Pretty Poison* and *Bonnie and Clyde*.

Thus this first of what should become a yearly institution was really grey when it was grey, running through the homely (*On Nothing Days*), sluggish

(*R34*), dryly cerebral (*Maltese Cross Movement*), stale air (*Slow Run*), and densely wispy (*White Noise*). And, occasionally, the Festival broke into the crisper works of Snow, Wieland, and Lee-Nova; at those sudden moments, the effect was like the reverse side of greyness, a kind of clear, strongly defined formfulness.

R34 is John Chambers' collage film about a collage maker: spliced together are shots of his mustache and smile, his studio and family life, the texture of his paintings, and his wife's long flaxen hair. Like a steam table at Horn and Hardart's, this compartmented documentary is set up with little deep dishes, in which there are steaming, disconnected evidences of an industrious artist's life in London, Ontario. The theme is the interweaving of an artist's personal life with his oeuvre; but there is a sly sardonicism suggesting that "all is not heroism and romance" as Irving Stone and Rolland imply in biographies of painters. To prove this, the artist is seen taking out the garbage four or five times, getting his mustache wet when he drinks a glass of milk, and sitting inside one of his painted sculptures with his child on his lap.

Joyce Wieland's *Cat Food* is about a rotund cat and how he eats a fish. An explicit movie and an exercise in simplicity, it has three elements: well-fed, insatiable cat, pretty-but-dead fish, all on a table top with a flat back background.

1933, an even harder haiku-like movie to examine in depth, has the numerals of the title on a blank screen alternated with a street scene of quick walkers, who suggest the least-funny actors in old movies. Wieland repeats the recipe six times and that's it.

Her *Rat Life and Diet in North America*, which uses the scurrying and furtiveness of rodents to tell a parable about modern day revolutionaries, is marred by pretentious over-reaching. Using chapter headings ("some of the finest were lost"), inserted new photos of Cuban political heroes, the Canadian flag and anthem to make heavy statements about world politics, this Aesop's fable has the merriness and warm domesticity of a Beatrice Potter children's book, and some of the strong images and puerile construction ideas of a Godard.

Clarke Mackey's *On Nothing Days* is a Celine-like travelogue into the exasperation and distraught boredom of a teenager who bums around downtown, rides the subways, and sits on a park bench, looking for something to happen, and finding the inevitable: that everything is so flat. This is sort of a truthful epic about Poking Around, gained with the unseeing stare of depression and inertia, a monotonous capture of very muggy weather, and a touchingly homely job of acting in which there's not a moment's release from the feeling of numbed frustration of an adolescent who hasn't yet located "his thing."

Les Levine's *White Noise* has the feeling of an image made out of moonbeams: a camera endlessly roams in a fairly large but claustrophobic studio room that has a bed built on stilts, no colour, shadowy people, stuff stacked against the wall. With the poorly exposed effect of the first Polaroid cameras and the whirr of a movie projector, Levine arrives at a movie that is shadowy, thin, and ungraspable. It's a film that brings up questions about aesthetic intent. Unlike Levine's sculptures which have lucidity and form, this mock experimental work is a sort of tone poem to feverish, restless gazing, as though a director, bedridden, were compelled to memorialize an uninteresting convalescence.

You hear the hollow sounds of footsteps on a bare wood floor, the door closes, and then you see this large, empty space with four tall rectangular windows at the far end of the room. You're aware immediately that this isn't a dwelling: industrial neon lights on the ceiling, no curtains on the windows, no decoration or utilities of any kind. This brisk, athletic woman in a raincoat enters with two people carrying a metal office cabinet and, in a voice dominated by the room, gives them a brief direction: "Put it there."

In a slight, snap-of-the-finger way, with a decided and reduced indication of a high stoical intelligence, begins what could become the sternest reproof to the commercial film as we know it. *Wavelength* is a 45 minute diary of an empty room, spaced into sequences by four human intrusions so quick and deft that they suggest the theme: that the individual is a short-lived negligible phenomenon and that it is the stability of the inanimate that keeps life from flying away. This kind of forbidding, animistic statement about life—the indestructible, Moby Dick qualities of Nature and Objects as contrasted with the slip-and-slide transitoriness of Man—in terms of art is as old as the Bible. The book on Alabama sharecroppers by Agee and Evans and Faulkner's *Light in August*, can be seen in the same topography-loving area as this minimal movie that is bound to shake anyone with its rich color and visual curiosities in a basically empty, unvaried, static field.

Snow's movie is built around a surprisingly ingenious device, a stationary zoom that is always head-high, all but unnoticed, and goes from the widest view of the loft to a pinpoint in the center of the four windows. The movie is always focused on the four splendid rectangles of the windows and the clutter of signs, roofs of buses, and street architecture framed by the window panes. The first two segments are serene, mainly composed of dry-soft morning light moving towards the afternoon. The middle sequence is composed of violent changes of color in which the screen shudders from intensities of green, magenta, sienna; a virtuoso series of negative and positive impressions in which complementary colors are drained out so that the room, undergoing spasms, flickers from shrill brilliant green to pure red to a drunken, gorgeous red-violet. The final segment settles down to a sombre night lighting in which a lemon yellow kitchen chair, practically a bit player stealing the picture, is very important.

The joy of *Wavelength* is in seeing so many new actors—light and space, walls, soaring windows, an amazing number of color/shadow variations that live and die in the window panes—made into major aesthetic components of movie experience.

Kardish's *Slow Run* is the mundanely shot, narcisisstically narrated story of a not very convincing young sybarite, his friends and lovers in an anonymous Manhattan apartment. Pat, Ramona, George, and the nameless drab face who is the center of the movie's erotic scene (people constantly get undressed before him, enter baths and start soaping themselves, and talk to him while the soundtrack is restricted to a garrulous, non-stop Molly Bloom-like monologue by a voice which is presumably his) move through the days in an uninspired, lax, pre-hippy Bohemianism. What holds people to this monotonous image? A pinched and nervous face with false eyelashes who is constantly pulling off her T-shirt and revealing a tightly muscled dancer's body; the intimacy of seeing people in off moments; and the unbashful way that talentless acting and scene-setting are exhibited—as though encircled with haloes.

Lee-Nova's *Steel Mushrooms* is a devotional William Carlos Williams poem on the common comicality of roadside art. What's so winning is the enthusiastic swiftness: this movie about the beauty of little-industry-made objects is paced in the joint-churning mobilism of a champion 3-mile walker and somehow gets into the modest, lovely stupidity of a bolt, spike, or lonely pipe crawling up a factory wall.

Maltese Cross Movement is a whacky-whicky cabala of the mind, one man's "own personal hieroglyphic." Whatever this Dadaist poem is about, various puns and visual games are made around words like frog and knife, intermittently there is an image of a slender, Pre-Raphaelite Bronte-like teenager walking through the glen in her mother's Victorian cambric nightgown, and equally often and awful, a little moppet, illuminated in a deep Renaissance darkness, asks: "Are you ready yet?"

This critic, who didn't get see John Hofsess' *Palace of Pleasure*, a dual projector job, came away convinced that it's not easy to break "Frontiers in Cinema." But the Festival in Toronto's Fogg Museum-like set-up had one film, Snow's pure and rigorous masterpiece about a room, that did astoundingly break with tradition, underground or overground, and film after film as well

that insinuated themselves into the mind. What impresses is the private quality of the filmmaking; there's no school in Canadian filmmaking, similar to the
Italian neo-realists, but a grouping of personal technicians who plug a deadpan, nerveless, un-neurotic industry—a beaverishness that is not greedy.

February 1969

Shame

It's about 6:30 in the morning, and this pair, the woman all efficiency, trying
to keep to a schedule, the husband always lagging behind, are loading lingon-
berries into a station wagon that has a funny brinelike crust on its discouraging
surface. The mood that encases these two—the wife trying to make a go of a
failing farm operation, the husband becoming more and more of an isolation-
ist (first he doesn't want to get out of bed, then he wants to discuss his dream,
finally he figures out that neither the radio nor the telephone needs to be
fixed)—is of one tiny exacerbation scraping against another. It's a very nice
scene: the scale is perfect; the fact that a dusty car, two crabby people, and an
unflourishing farmyard are in perfect alignment is only part of the feeling of
serenity. There are no camera gimmicks or script dramatics to distract from the
small chafings between a husband (before he takes a big dip in this picture,
Von Sydow is an attractive, crotchety guy without the cocky sternness that narrowed his previous work) and a tough-practical farm wife (Liv Ullmann, very
sophisticated but achieving an un-self-consciousness that makes her more
woman than a movie can bear).

Shame is a thematically grim movie about a nonpolitical couple, both vio-
linists, who have been forced into farming by a civil war and the husband's bad
heart. Stranded by their lack of commitment, as the war moves into the front
yard, they sink first into a drunken, slothful existence, and then into the furthest reaches of despair and dishonor, until these quiet, decent, and sensitive
people become caricatures of misery; Von Sydow is now a calculating murderer
and his woman a numb beast of burden.

Shame is a complicated, crazily plotted film that loses most of its development in a slot between the time that the Rosenbergs are rounded up as suspected collaborators and a Millet-like scene with exasperated Ullmann and her
spouse digging for potatoes and being real bitter ("When this is all over, we'll
leave each other"). During this slot that you don't see, months in duration, the
wife has become hopelessly miserable, estranged, and a compulsive drunk. The

head man of the district (you guessed it: Gunnar Bjornstrand) is showering the couple with gasoline, special wine and cheese, his life savings and an heirloom ruby, and a speechless neighbor, who is on screen no more than thirty seconds, has metamorphosized from a kindly fisherman to a Resistance leader so powerful that in one crazy scene he has his men methodically break, slash, and blowtorch every inch of the farmstead searching for a wad of money that was in Von Sydow's pocket all the time. Even allowing for war working drastic changes on people, the two protagonists are never credible again: a man who couldn't kill a chicken to fill his pot becomes a shrewd killer who carries around a tommy gun and a knapsack full of stray knives; his wife, who started out in the movie as the most fetching body-face-spirit since Ann Dvorak, develops a droopy mouth, a Neanderthal forehead, and the piggy, sunk-in-mud features of a sow.

There's great tact and spareness in the way the Rosenbergs are initially presented: a still room at dawn, a woman with a beautiful volume to her body walks with her pajamas opened to the waist to the kettle, moving with an exciting, brisk, hard walk. Between this episode, where everything is quiet except the woman's energy, and the scene on the ferry as the Rosenbergs head for their customers, a serenely satisfying cadence sets up as two large, entertainingly intelligent bodies chafe against each other.

No one has concentrated so hard as Ingmar Bergman on the principle of push-pull as it is worked out by two people dependent on each other because of a lack of diversion or support from their surroundings. In *Persona* and *Hour of the Wolf* (a bomb), as well as in *Shame*, a fated duo is isolated on a craggy island, far away in the country. In *Silence*, a strangely sexy and physical movie with no male lead, a haggard fight for approval and love goes on between two sisters in a foreign hotel where no one speaks their language. In *Winter Light*, a snowbound rural district and a congregation that has its own problems are the purgatory for a stolid, uncommunicative minister and his plain, morbidly loyal mistress.

This setup, with two people inextricably bound together, both lovers and bitter enemies, at the same time each other's sustenance and downfall, is similar to the one that characterizes Bergman as a moviemaker. His played-down naturalism has picked up grace and elegance in his latest films, but each one presents a bleak arena, with two Bergmans entwined in a battle that never resolves itself. There's so much lust for naturalism that it's puzzling how he keeps being seduced into a soupy, pretentious symbolism where characters become anonymous in a charred landscape and sink leadenly into the pathos of a Kathe Kollwitz "despair" drawing.

February 1969

Howard Hawks

Scarface (1932) is a passionate, strong, archaic photographic miracle: the rise and fall of an ignorant, blustery, pathetically childish punk (Paul Muni) in an avalanche of rich, dark-dark images. The people, Italian gangsters and their tough, wisecracking girls, are quite beautiful, as varied and shapely as those who parade through Piero's religious paintings. Few movies are better at nailing down singularity in a body or face, the effect of a strong outline cutting out impossibly singular shapes. Boris Karloff: long stove-pipe legs, large-boned and gaunt, an obsessive, wild face; Ann Dvorak: striking out blindly with the thinnest, sharpest elbows, shoving aside anyone who tries to keep her from the sex and excitement of a dance hall. Besides the sulphurous, extreme lighting and so many feverish, doomed types, like Osgood Perkins as Johnny Lovo, top hood on the South Side until his greedier right-hand man Tony Camonte takes over, the image seems unique because of its moody energy: it is a movie of quick-moving actions, inner tension, and more angularity per inch of screen than any street film in history.

Crisp and starched where *Scarface* is dark and moody, *His Girl Friday* (1940) is one of the fastest of all movies, from line to line and gag to gag. Besides the dynamic, highly assertive pace, this *Front Page* remake with Rosalind Russell playing Pat O'Brien's role is a tour de force of choreographed action: bravado posturings with body, lucid Cubistic composing with natty lapels and hat brims, as well as a very stylized discourse of short replies based on the idea of topping, outmaneuvering the other person with wit, cynicism, and verbal bravado. A line is never allowed to reverberate but is quickly attached to another, funnier line in a very underrated comedy that champions the sardonic and quick-witted over the plodding, sober citizens.

The thing you remember most about Cary Grant's sexy, short-hop Lindbergh in *Only Angels Have Wings* (1939), a rather charming, maudlin Camp item, is his costume, which belongs in a Colombian Coffee TV commercial: razor-creased trousers that bulge out with as much yardage as a caliph's bloomers and are belted just slightly under his armpits. Except for a deadpan, movie-stealing performance by Richard Barthelmess, this movie about a Zeta Beta Tau fraternity of fliers in a South American jungle is a ridiculous film of improbability and coincidence, the major one being that Bat McPheerson, the blackest name in aviation, the man who betrayed Thomas Mitchell's kid brother and married Grant's old flame, should show up years later broke and in need of a job in Barranca, where buddies Grant and Mitchell are busting up planes on the strangest stalactite mountains.

Red River (1948), as a comment on frontier courage, loyalty, and leadership, is a romantic, simple-minded mush, but an ingeniously lyrical film nonetheless. The story of the first trip from Texas to the Abilene stockyards is a feat of pragmatic engineering, working with weather, space, and physiognomy. The theme is how much misery and brutality can issue from a stubbornly obsessed bully (John Wayne, who barks his way through the film instead of moving), while carving an empire in the wilderness. Of the one-trait characters, Wayne is a sluggish mass being insensitive and cruel-minded on the front of the screen; Joanne Dru is a chattering joke, even more static than Wayne; but there is a small army of actors (Clift, John Ireland) keyed in lyrically with trees, cows, and ground.

The very singular compact names that beat like a tom-tom through the above films are as eccentric and Hollywoodish as the character who makes them. They're summing up names, they tie a knot around the whole personality, and suggest the kind of bravura signature that underlines itself. Jeff Carter, Tess Millay, Mathew Garth, Guino Rinaldo, Buck Kennelley, Johnny Lovo, Molly Malloy, Cherry Valance are dillies of names that indicate a Breughel type who creates a little world of his own, outfitted in every inch with picturesque hats, insensitive swagger, and good-natured snobberies.

Howard Hawks is a bravado specialist who always makes pictures about a Group. Fast dialogue, quirky costumes, the way a telephone is answered, everything is held together by his weird Mother Hen instinct. The whole population in *Scarface*, cavemen in quilted smoking jackets, are like the first animals struggling out of the slime and murk toward fresh air. *Only Angels*, a White Cargo melodrama that is often intricately silly, has a family unit living at the Dutchman's, a combination bar, restaurant, rooming house, and airport run by a benevolent Santa Claus (some airline: the planes take off right next to the kitchen, and some kitchen: a plane crashes, the wreck is cleared and the pilot buried in the time it takes them to cook a steak; and the chief control is a crazy mascot who lives with a pet donkey and serves as a lookout atop a buzzard-and-blizzard-infested mountain as sharp as a shark's tooth). The wonderfully dour reporters in *His Girl Friday* and the mawkish cowboys in *Red River* are also strangely pinned in place by the idea of people being linked together in tight therapeutic groups, the creations of a man who is as divorced from modern *angst* as Fats Waller and whose whole movie-making system seems a secret preoccupation with linking, a connections business involving people, plots, and eight-inch hat brims.

The Mother Hubbard spirit gives the film a kind of romance that is somewhat WASP-ish with a Gatsby elegance and cool. Both the girls in *Scarface*, like Zelda Fitzgerald, would fling themselves away over a Russ Columbo recording of "Poor Butterfly." Ann Dvorak, dancing with a big, bland-faced clod who is bewildered by all her passion and herky-jerky cat's meow stuff, is so close to *Tender Is the Night* in her aura of silly recklessness. The sophomoric fliers of Barranca, like Fitzgerald's expatriates in Paris, are ravished with each other's *soignée*: Bonnie, playing real jazzy "Peanuts" with a whole saloon jammed around her piano cheering her on, is an embarrassing square version of supersquare Chico Marx. The feeling of snobbery in any Hawks work is overpowering, whether it is a Great White Father (Grant) patronizing a devitalized native with a gift watch or the female Jimmy Breslin (Rosalind Russell) breezily typing a socko story. This romanticism, which wraps the fliers-reporters-cowhands in a patina of period mannerism and attitude, makes for a film that isn't dated so much as removed from reality, like the land of Tolkien's Hobbits.

It is interesting how many plots are interwoven into a scene. The whole last part of the *Front Page* remake is a fugue in fast humor, peculiar for the way each figure touches another in ricochets of wild absurdity. Molly Malloy, the killer's lady defender ("Ah come on fellahs, he didn't even touch me, I just gave him some tea, and he was shaking all over") jumps out the window and is forgotten; her boyfriend, who has been entombed forlornly inside a rolltop desk, is dragged to his cell, presumably to be hung the next morning; Hildy Johnson finally gets maneuvered back to the *Morning Star* by her arch-heel editor; the mayor and the sheriff are politically destroyed for trying to bribe a fat Baby Huey, who turns up with a reprieve for the convicted killer. Then there's Louie, a terrific heist artist who steals a mother-in-law and gets mangled by a police car which was driving in the wrong lane. People who talk reams about great film comedy never mention this version of Hecht's play with its one twist, an elegantly played, pragmatic girl, sharp and immediately aware of everything in the ace reporter's role. It is a prime example of Hawks's uncelebrated female touch: the light flouncy foot, the antipomposity about newspaper problems, and the Mother Hen way of setting up family relationships. The ingenuity of its pragmatic engineering is that every gesture (she picks up the phone, it's funny) contributes to the plot, is laugh-provoking, and adds up to a supply of intricately locked humor so large that there's hardly time to relish any one gag.

The films have a musical comedy hokeyness joined to a freedom, a mellifluous motion, which is summed up in the line "Wherever they roam, they'll be on my land," spoken as a couple of cows—the start of a mighty herd: the man's bull and the boy's cow—wander off into a nice, sparse landscape. But the deep quality in any Hawks film is the uncannily poetic way an action is unfolded. Sometimes this portrayal of motion is thrilling (the cattle going into Abilene), funny (Abner Biberman's harmless hood: "Everybody knows Louie"), gracefully dour (Karloff's enigmatic cockiness in a bowling alley, like a Muybridge photograph), or freakishly mannered (Karen Morley sizing up Scarface's new pad: "It's kinda gaudy, isn't it"), but it is always inventive, killingly expressive, and gets you in the gut. One blatantly colloquial effect is slammed against another. The last section of *Scarface* builds detail on detail into a forbidding whirlwind. As the incestuous duo shoots it out with the cops, slightly outnumbered eighty to one, the lighting is fabulous, Dvorak's clamoring reaches an unequaled frenzy ("I'm just like you, Tony, aren't I, I'm not afraid"), and there is an authentic sense of the primeval, life coming to smash the puny puffed-up egos.

Not many moviemakers have gone so deeply into personality-revealing motion, the geography of gesture, the building and milking of a signature trait for all its worth. Hawks's abandon with his pet area, human gesture, is usually staggering, for better or worse. Why should Cary Grant get away with so much Kabukilike exaggeration, popping his eyes, jutting out his elbows, roaring commands at breath-taking speed in a gymnasium of outrageous motion? Sometimes Hawks's human-interest detailing falls on its face: the beginning of a cattle drive with Wayne a tiny speck moving down a channel of earth, the Knute Rockne of Cattledom, and, then, those endless ghastly close-ups of every last cowboy, one after the other, giving his special version of a Yahoo.

Scarface, as vehement, vitriolic, and passionate a work as has been made about Prohibition, is a deadly grim gangster movie far better than *White Heat* or *Bonnie and Clyde*, a damp black neighbor to the black art in Walker Evans's subway shots or the Highway 90 photographic shot at dawn by Robert Frank. Nowhere near the tough-lipped mentality or hallucinatory energy of Hawks's only serious film, *His Girl Friday* is still better than a clever, arch, extremely funny newspaper film. It's hard to believe that anything in Chaplin or W. C. Fields has so many hard, workable gags, each one bumping the other in an endless interplay of high-spirited cynicism. But rating these close camaraderie films, teeming with picturesque fliers-punks-pundits and a boys' book noble humanism, in the Pantheon division of Art and giving them cosmic conceptions is to overweight them needlessly.

A director who's made at least twenty box-office gold mines since 1926 is going to repeat himself, but the fact is that Howard Hawks's films are as different as they're similar. In each action film, he's powerfully interested in the fraternal groups that he sets up, sticking to them with an undemonstrative camera that is always eye level and acute on intimate business, and using stories that have a straight-ahead motion and develop within a short time span. The point is that each picture has a widely different impact: from the sulphurous lighting and feverish style of *Scarface* to the ignorant blustering of John Wayne in a soft Western that doesn't have any pace at all. Within the devil-may-care silliness of his *Angels* picture, the difference in acting between Barthelmess (crafty and constipated), Thomas Mitchell (maudlin, weepy), and Jean Arthur (good grief!) is so violent as to suggest the handling of three directors.

Hawks, a born movie-manipulator who suggests a general moving little flag pins around on a battle map, is not very fussy about the pulp-story figures nor the fable-ized scenery into which he jams them. The opening shots of his Andes airline movie are supposed to "vividly create Barranca, the South American town" in and around which the "completely achieved masterpiece" is set. This operetta seaport, with boas of smoke hanging in swirly serpentines and pairs of extras crisscrossing through the fake mist, might be good for a Douglas, Arizona, high school production. In the next "vividly created" scene, Jean Arthur is being dim and blithe, snapping her fingers (the first of the block-headed swingers) in time with some fairly authentic calypso dancers who are being unbelievably passionate at ten in the morning. In such movies, where a broken-down Englishman or a drunken rubber planter is seated in the corner muttering "Only two more months and I get out of this godforsaken place," a Rhonda Fleming or Brian Keith (in something called *Jivaro*) is far classier than the dopy inner-tubes who so seriously act characters getting the mail through for seven straight days in Hawks's corny semicatastrophe.

Hawks gets exhilarating situations: the stampede in *Red River* is great, maybe because everyone shuts up during the panic. He can be very touching, as in Harry Carey Jr.'s death with four or five cowboys standing in straight-line silence in a strangely hollowed out terrain that suggests Gethsemane. Yet no artist is less suited to a discussion of profound themes than Hawks, whose attraction to strutting braggarts, boyishly cynical dialogue, and melodramatic fiction always rests on his poetic sense of action. It would be impossible to find anything profound in Rosalind Russell's Hildy, but there is a magic in the mobile unity of the woman: her very mannish pinstripe suits, the highly stylized way she plants a hand on her hip, and her projecting of the ultimate in sophisticated swagger, taking off her hat and coat and showing how a real reporter sets up shop. The genius of such action engineering is that Hawks is able to poeticize dialogue as well as faces and costume, making a 100 per cent ordinary line—Hildy's parting shot to Earl Williams in his death cell: "Good-bye Earl and good luck"—seem to float in an air of poignant, voluptuous cynicism.

April 1969

◆

Two Rode Together, a 1961 cavalry film that has been holed up this winter at a campsite in the Museum of Modern Art, has the discombobulated effect of a Western that was dreamt by a kid snoozing in an Esso station in Linden, New Jersey. Two wrangling friends, a money-grubbing marshall (Jimmy Stewart) and a cavalry captain (Richard Widmark, who has the look of a ham that has been smoked, cured, and then coated with honey-colored shellac), seek out a Comanche named Parker and trade him a stunningly new arsenal of guns and knives for a screaming little Bowery Boy with braids who's only bearable in the last shot when the camera just shows his legs hanging limply from a lynching tree.

The movie's mentally-retarded quality comes from the discordancy and quality of the parts: it's not only that they don't go together, they're crazy to start with. Each woman and Indian is from a different age in operetta and a different part of the globe. The Indians include an overdeveloped weight lifter, a sad Pagliacci trying hard not to let his flabby stomach show, plus the above Leo Gorcey tough with his histrionic impression of a monkey on hot coals. The movie wobbles most with Widmark, embarrassed but strangely submitting to courting scenes with Shirley Jones that are filled with temerity and wide-eyed hopefulness. His tomboy sweetheart, a fräulein out of the *Student Prince* with two thick long yellow braids and enough makeup to equal Widmark's, has a fixation on a music box and runs to it at every chance.

The movie is a curious blend of modern blat and a senile impression of frontier culture that derives from the cheapest and oldest movies about pre-railroad days in Indian territory. There is a wild non sequitur quality about the courtship, frontier dialogue, and spitting, thin-skinned, stupidly stubborn Indians taking place in a free-for-all atmosphere in which not one detail or scene goes with another. In general, it is Widmark and Stewart, like two Pinter characters, separated out from a stiff (despite the yelling and flouncing), corny, TV-styled production going on behind them. Throughout, these actors barely listen to each other, and, affecting a curious, dragged out, folksy dialect, they take up great amounts of space with words that are from Dimwit's Land.

"No! She didn't kill herself, ladies and gentlemen. Not because she was a coward, but because her religion forbade her. Sometimes, it takes more courage to live than to die." Facetiously delivering this speech, Stewart is operating here in a feeble, tensionless mock-up of an officers' cotillion at the local fort. (I kept wondering: why are they dragging in a dance? Could it be to squeeze that white hypocrisy speech into the remains of a script previously taken up with removing the normal skin tone, stealth, dignity, and clothes sense from Indians?)

It is filled with cliché conceptions: of an Indian camp, a Texas Guinan seenioreeta who owns the saloon and the town, slow-witted people, an innocent tomboy heroine throwing a barrel of flour over the two Cleggs who come courting her, country bumpkins having a fight in the woods. These one-dimensional impressions could embarrass any actor but what is staggeringly insensitive about the treatment is the way an actor is made so ridiculous by the camera treatment, either being locked, sliced in two, or frittered away in golden shoe polish by pictorial setups. A dependable TV actress, Jeanette Nolan, is murdered, long before the Me Comanchah kid gets her, by compositions which turn her into an unpleasant portrait of pleading, cropping her at the hips and hardening her flat, angular face and loud voice. Mae Marsh, formidable in silents and early talkies for her gentle, underscored beauty, is waylaid, not so much by her corny "I had a white husband once" dialogue and a make-up job midway between a clown face and Molly Drunk All Night, but by a wigwam composition in which, bent over, she seems to cringe out of a sea of blue ink.

The fascination of the director with lines of action in deep space adds ten lethal minutes here and there of illogicality, to a script that is already overloaded with fat items: capitalist law enforcers, matricide, overbearing mothers. For instance, the Widmark-Stewart team leads a wagon train into the wilderness through bogs of bumpkin comedy and tinsel wooing. Later, after a brief moment at a campsite, all these people are mysteriously back in the fort as though they'd never left it.

It's incredible, the amount of leeway that is allowed. If a prop man locates a bench from an antique store next to a tree in a just-set-up campsite, the scene stays in though the film for the preceding five minutes has been insisting on formidable wilderness. This is studio moviemaking at its slackest.

All these gauche, careless skills—the uglification of actors (padding a buxom barmaid, Annelle Hayes, so that her bust line starts angling out from the collarbone and doesn't turn in till it reaches her waist), the jerky progress from melodrama to bathos to camp, the TV Western feeling of no flow, outdoors, or sense of period (Stewart is wearing a jacket from Abercrombie, all Indians and their tents are from a psychotics' Halloween Ball)—are the responsibility of John Ford, a director generally noted for making movies with a poetic and limitless knowledge of Indians, ranging farthest across the landscape of the American past, and being the moviemaker's Mr. Movie.

There's no question that there's a new crowd-pleasing movie around that has to do with a disenchanted cop, a city in which no corner is untainted, and an artichoke plot. Wrapped around a heart that is just a procedural cop story, police routines in Washington (*Pendulum*), San Francisco (*Bullitt*), Phoenix (*Coogan's Bluff*), and Manhattan (*Madigan and the Detective*), is a shrubwork of *Daily News* stories, the whole newspaper from beginning to end: the sensationalism, sentimentality, human interest, plus some liberal editorials. Each film has its mini-version of the drug scene, investigating committees, philandering wives, some of it as wrong as the psychedelic dance orgy in *Coogan's Bluff*, the weirdness there being the thousand equally frenzied participants, or the two senators (Robert Vaughn in *Bullitt*, Paul McPrissy in *Pendulum*) who are played odiously and with heavy messages.

Superficially, it's a straight Bogart story with Sinatra (interestingly mediocre), McQueen (you could buy back Manhattan for the Indians with his blue eyes), or Peppard (unfulfilled, slightly sedentary) playing the ace detective role, but playing it less mythically and with much more defeat. The real juice of the films is their ranginess, that they give you a lot, the zest for what a city contains, and the flatness.

These movies work partly because they are exploiting the fairly unplumbed field of pessimistic observing rather than action, or, for that matter, acting of the traditional or method variety. The work often goes overdone, as when Bullitt is shown waking up and McQueen, trying for a bent-over feeling, does a St. Vitus dance while suggesting a wave of nausea spreading across his face. But in a long, near-silent and very good stretch in U.C. Hospital, which is almost excessive in the way it sticks like plaster to the mundaneness of the place, the movie hits into about seventeen verities: faces looking out as though across the great divide of 20th-century lousiness.

These movies use Hollywood bodies in a new way which could be called city physical: unglamorous, a lot of self-contempt (although I don't see Jean Seberg as anything shy of complacency), naturalness emphasized or pushed to the front of the screen without losing its ordinariness (both Peppard and McQueen have great rooted-to-the-earth stances). The boy rapist in *Pendulum*, the young cop who gets shot in the beginning of *Bullitt*, Lee Remick (too nice and too frail for a nympho), Don Stroud's very ungraceful, unused to running in *Coogan's Bluff*—all these actors seem to work towards an ideal of anonymity through a kind of unweighted gesture and great stretches of silent resistance to the material around them. There's nothing better in these films than Peppard rifling the yellow pages for the telephone number of his wife's beauty parlor, or McQueen eating a sandwich and drinking a glass of milk, very tense and guilty about having lost his prize hood to a pair of hired killers.

The scripts are written with the lore of a taxi driver, his head filled with routes, the difficulty of getting through crowds, and the cold, confusing congestion to be expected at any monument, terminal, or bedroom. These are not stingy films. If Jimmy Stewart were playing the gassing stage manager in *Our Town*, 1969, he might have this to say about Sinatra's effulgence: "Take Joe Leland, The Detective. He's one part Sam Spade, one part middle-aged and just plain tired, and, here and there he sounds like Norm Mailer ('You're full of crap, Doc,' or, 'The people of Harlem are living in garbage cans, the job of the police is to hold down the lids.'). He has a lot of angles, Joe: a hidden appreciation of O'Casey and Shaw; trouble with his wife, his boss too." And the biggest angle is the way Sinatra plays him: clamped down, non-violent and passive-ized, as though he's swallowed more than he can take of a dull office.

There's so much particularity that the film goes from bad to good to smashing and back to good in the briefest quarters, and the excitement of each film is that it does. A police commissioner, acted stiff and lofty by Henry Fonda, is having an affair with a redhead who is performed like a dress dummy. A Negro rookie, in a so-so performance by Al Freeman Jr., vomits over the mutilation of a homosexual. A young long-haired wife looks out dazedly over the body of her shotgun-blasted rookie husband: her realistic shock and bitterness is too good for a movie. Some material gets into these frenetic films that suggests misplaced footage left over from another film, but the largesse about particularity turns the non sequitur material into something curious (Jacqueline Bisset painting a rowboat with the shortest, most ineffectual arms in movies) or wonderfully rich (McQueen and his partner ripping through some suitcases, accompanying their machine-gun search through the luggage with some curious litany-like dialogue).

The catchy impact of these sordid, philistine cop films comes from curiosity and a high degree of transience inserted into movies that are really rather rhythmless and not much for old-fashioned give and go. Playing the characters so hyper-observant, and suggesting through acting that each person is a conflict of pulls in all directions, makes the hollow, TV-styled *Pendulum* seem almost mobile, and sort of intelligent. This jangle and sharp attention occurs even in a virtuoso, Madeline Sherwood, cranking herself into self-pitying hysteria, or Bisset, so dewy and out of key in her alliances with Sinatra and McQueen.

A pylon-like Peppard, who has nothing horizontal in his acting vocabulary, seems to replace the lack of spring in his personality and the telephone-drenched stasis of the plot with a curiosity that roams all over the nation's capital setting. The final chase in each cop epic should be ho-hum after a thousand Hitchcock-type films that end in a chase through Albert Hall or across the Mt. Rushmore sculpted horror. Nevertheless, the scenes at the end of *Bullitt*, by emphasizing the pursued's and pursuer's stiff running style and making the most of the unpleasant (the freezing night, the two non-athletes uncomfortably at work), keeps a shriek ascending through the last reel.

May 1969

Luis Buñuel

His glee in life is a movie of raped virgins and fallen saints, conceived by a literary old-world director detached from his actors but infatuated with his cock-eyed primitive cynicism. It's this combination of detachment and the infatuated-with-bitterness viewpoint, added to a flat-footed technique, that produces the piercingly cold images of *The Exterminating Angel*.

Buñuel reveals a kinship to other moderns: to Godard (the basic feeling that the audience needs educating, and he is just the one to do it), Bresson (they share an absorbed interest in the peasantry and the role of religion in rural life), and the Renoir of *Toni* and *The Lower Depths* (what it is like to be poor). Often he seems to be duplicating Renoir, decades later. The same choked, peeling, dank courtyard through which Louis Jouvet walked in *Lower Depths*, like a halt-footed, bowlegged, giant rooster, is recreated in *Nazarin* long after Renoir's version of Gorky's tale. In *Nazarin*, the setting is characteristically comicalized with three cruddy whores fighting with caricatured abandon over a set of buttons, suggesting stock-company Carmens or Yvette Guilberts painted by a cross-eyed Toulouse-Lautrec. The Spanish workers who try to fix up the estate in *Viridiana* are brothers to the men who live at Marie's boarding-house in *Toni*. They fit into their village milieu with the same vitality, as natural as animals. Renoir's Spaniards, less wacky by far than Buñuel's, are always in the grip of a human passion, either happy or grief-stricken as lovers, when they're not giving the feeling of hard, conscientious workers.

But more than any other modern, Luis Buñuel is a pariah, locked off by himself, stitching a sort of dank, bitter grotesquerie into a backhandedly charming movie that has an overpowering, haunting involvement with Catholicism. Just as Westbrook Pegler, in his newspaper columns, overpowered his incessant barbs and rancor with a deep love for classy journalism, Buñuel's antichurch movie just seems to give off the wonder and sweetness of being a member of the fold. His slow-cut scene, which stresses a pet Gabrielle Figueroa shot of two sentimental characters standing on a hill with the twilight backlighting them, distressingly suggests the passion plays put on year after year by R.C. parishes the world over: the scenery suggesting the least talented of Murillo's street scenes, the same costumes worn by the same insurance agent who pridefully and possessively takes his role each Lenten season. These cold movies—the way the shot is framed and the airless edges, flaccid lighting—are redolent of religious calendars and the small booklets on the life of Saint Catherine for sale in the back of the church.

From early in his career—a powerful skin shot, in which a widow washes her feet while a brash punk, Jaibo (*Los Olvidados*), languorously leans against the doorway and takes in the act—his characters have suffered a nightmarish lack of privacy in all their domestic setups, with no refuge from gossip, prying eyes, nosiness. No secret can be cherished, no man or woman is allowed to singularize himself for long. The rancor and malice of the neighbors act to break down their resolves. In *The Exterminating Angel*, his most personal film, the characters exist in an agony of exposure. All his population, even the fashionable professional class in *Belle de Jour* or the powerfully rich in *Exterminating Angel*, bear the poor man's feeling of being a prey for anyone who wants to harass him.

In these *danse-macabre* films, it's shocking to see a character alone, or one, like Catherine Deneuve in *Belle*, who seems to respect the institution of doors (a wonderfully unexotic hallway and sequence of embarrassed, fearful moves, suggesting the horror of applying for an unwanted job). One of the funniest gimmicks in *Nazarin* is the stream of odd occupations and types that flows through Padré Nazario's open window, either to look for money, curse him ("You better clear out, Father"), snoop around, ask him snidely personal questions, bring him tortillas, and eventually burn his room down to get rid of a whore's stinking perfume (of all the arson in films, this perfume-destroying motive is the silliest).

Buñuel's central characters—a happy-go-lucky priest on the bum, a saintly figure on a platform in the desert—have a yearning to separate themselves, to live a more exalted life than those around them. They're fervently idealistic and adore making sacrifices of worldly comfort, while their pals, kinfolk, and enemies conspire to bring them to heel. It's an expected denouement that a girl sighs, lets down her bunned-up hair, and surrenders herself to the mob, "Here I am."

Most of the stories—they're about fall guys; it's Buñuel's theory that if you try to be good, watch out: if a person wants to spread cheer, wealth, or virtue, the whole community views him as a sore hangnail they have to amputate— have to do with complicity, the fact that everyone is the devil whispering "Do it" in a pal's ear. A sort of preposterously dry comedy goes on in each shot, having to do with the quick way evil little plots are hatched: people fall into league with one another as often as cowboys jump on and off horses in an Allied Artists' Western. Working for his dinner, Padré Nazario gets a chance to put four shovels of dirt into his wheelbarrow before his colaborers murderously gang up on him for horning in and undercutting their wage rate. Most of the movie seems to be retelling old anecdotes, but all these sudden conspiracies, partnerships, and deals give the moral-cynical-mocking episodes a ridiculous surprise and wildness. Every Buñuel film has one elegant actor moving at a different pace from the others, and, in *Viridiana*, it's a wonderful maid acted by a stately-modest Spanish Jane Greer (this is an overdue plug for Jane Greer). She lubricates a tedious movie that needs all the mobility it can get by repeatedly dealing herself into the nearest available plot.

Each movie is a long march through small connected events (dragged out distressingly to the last moment: just getting the movie down the wall from a candle to a crucifix takes more time than an old silent comedy), but it is the sinister fact of a Buñuel movie that no one is going anywhere and there is never any release at the end of the film. It's one snare after another, so that the people get wrapped around themselves in claustrophobic whirlpool patterns.

When it's good—as in *Robinson Crusoe*, where he magically harmonized with a normally outrageous overactor, Dan O'Herlihy—a Buñuel movie has a heady, haunting effect, like an exquisitely enjoyed meal, the weather of a foreign country, something private and inexpressible: a favorite pornographic book. The musky quality comes from a variety of sources, from the all-round oldness of his lighting and buildings, to the old-fashioned literary quality that flows over each episode: Rabal fishing through his inherited heirlooms, coming across a pearl cross that has a switchblade hidden inside. There's a lot of the dirty old man, a rotting lasciviousness in all Buñuel films. In *Un Chien Andalou*, a man and a woman are having a go at each other. He produces an army of ants out of a deep hand wound, whereupon she retaliates by growing a luxurious patch of hair on her armpit.

Los Olvidados, a turgidly heavy tract on hideous childhood, hasn't enough of the above Daliism (he unfortunately gave up the Dali-type line work early on and didn't revive it until *Belle de Jour*), but it has a heavy aromatic quality, due to Figueroa's tiresomely velvety photography, an occasionally biting image like the one of two performing dogs with some raunchy band music going on, and another scene where he goes light on the standard leftist tract work: Pedro's dream of raw meat. Within a wretched Mexican city of slums, hovels, and street fights, reigns an unforgettably repugnant, corrupt-to-the-core bully—with an irritatingly sparse moustache and languid mannerisms—named Jaibo. Like all Buñuel's villains (Pinto in *Nazarin*, the eyeless beggar in *Viridiana*), he flag-waves his evil, terrorizing children, in particular a spunky twelve-year-old whom he frames with a theft after laying the kid's mother.

Viridiana is a lush, pretentious Jane Eyre story given a heavy illustrational style and sentimental, parasitic characters that are not like Charlotte Brontë at all. The theme, the silliness of virtue, is implanted with a heavy hand, through conventional types like Silvia Pinal's Snow White, a pure-minded virgin who tries to create a camp for beggars and ends up being raped by two of her more loathesome boarders. She and the syphilitics and unwed mothers, who cut her down when the chance comes, seem slow and drugged as though they were compulsory creations. These are explosions of truly independent work: the ferociously poetic dance done by a transvestite beggar, and a perversely experimental stretch where Buñuel varies a church-art impression of beggars praying in the fields with hard factual shots of construction work going on around the outside of the mansion.

Buñuel has always been a man of fits and starts, and his later career veers back and forth, from the preoccupation with so-called iconoclasm that seems very aware of the Yankee moviegoers (a dextrous, competent movie like *Simon of the Desert*, which is all surface), to more poetic work. *Belle de Jour* is one of his more straightforward films, giving play to his tight, narrow, provincial preoccupation with bondage, subservience. *Exterminating Angel*, a looser, less pretty film than *Belle*, seems the first occasion on which he doesn't attack himself to some convention.

In *Exterminating Angel*, an after-opera party finds itself unable to move out of the sitting room in a Frick Museumlike residence. Very tense, puzzling, sinister, and yet extraordinarily stodgy, this is the least anecdotal Buñuel and the most redolent of the Barrier effect that seems to murmur through his films. Once it is anchored inside the spellbound chamber, the movie becomes increasingly desperate, festering, pock-marked with strange crowdedness, bedding conditions, and particularly with powerful images—a Goyaesque scene of people in soiled, crumpled evening clothes, huddled around a fire built of smashed violins and eighteenth-century furniture, in the center of an elegant sitting room, and gnawing on mutton bones. A young bellowing bear, who makes a sound like a foghorn scraped against a blackboard, careens around the front hall, climbs a pillar, and swings on a chandelier with hard-to-identify menace. What powers these scenes is a new, more modern, Buñuel esthetic. The moral lesson is no longer encircled, and the tone is no longer so obvious: instead of criticizing outward conditions, it points inward. Excoriation is the point, but, as in all Buñuel at his best, the movie goes in a linear, imaginative direction, picking bits of subject matter that have been in his movies before but now seem encrusted with doubt, suspicion, and what amounts to creative self-torture. The same material poked out of other movies as far back as *El* when the jealous, envy-ridden husband zigzags up an elegant stairway knocking his cane in a tormented way against the stairs and balustrade.

One slant into his limitations is through his cutting, which, in each event, is delayed to the last possible moment but produces the only actual movement in the film. In *Nazarin*, he does as much as he can within the frame, but there isn't much action within any single shot (inept actors talking), and the frame itself becomes an enclosure within which he pays obeisance to a familiar "liberalism" and certain story-telling conventions favored in church art. Until his show of independence in *Exterminating Angel* and Gallic works (*Belle de Jour, Robinson Crusoe, Diary of a Chambermaid*), where he gives rein to an elegance and handsomeness that had been suppressed in consciously "unpretentious, profound" work (*Viridiana*, etc.) that made him a great favorite in America, he is irritatingly submissive to a moral narrative style. Buñuel translates his material through a leaden pedanticism that hides the narrow, provincial quality of his talent with underlined sentimental evidences of depravity, cruelty that shouldn't dismay any traditionalists in the church.

In a sort of entertaining old-Buñuel film, strong images occur only as a kind of explosion from the orthodox, sedentary way he moves through slime and crime. This kind of orgasmic burst of poetic styling after socioreligious conventionalism happens in *Nazarin*, when a limpid goody type, who might be Betty Compson playing Peter Pan, reacts erotically to the intermural fight between two whores. This imaginatively choreographed hallucination, from a weird eyelid fluttering to an orgiastic backbend on the bar floor, has a crushing dynamism compared to Buñuel's stodgier, normal style with sex: a seduction in an attic crowded with broken furniture. Buñuel typically overexplains the halting, sluggish mystery of this *Viridiana* scene, with its dirty old man feeling of not really being with it, by capping it with a mattress shot of a cat leaping on a rat. The symbol is as pedantically stitched in as the limply overstated facial work between Rabal and the maid.

The tremendous reputation that has accrued from exoticism and religious-toned "primitivism" mimics the safe route Buñuel has taken as a celebrity, from working in Franco Spain through a long span as an easily identified leftist. His bizarre films, airless and dank, a lot of perverse, festering plants in them, give the feeling of a hothouse. The best way to suggest this hothouse is to describe his handling of some of his actors; the princely Hotspurish Rabal, the puzzlingly inexpressive Pinal, whose mystery, like that of the miscast Deneuve in *Belle de Jour*, comes from a clogged effect of a passive surface, a blond beauty who moves like a grandmother. These main characters (there's a good, more hesitant one playing the transvestite uncle in the *Viridiana* opening) are blander, cleaner, more straight up and down than the excessively picturesque bit players: Father Nazario's cell mates, the beggars in *Viridiana*. Buñuel, who always seems in a dark closet of privacy, like a nobleman sitting back and watching his vassals climb all over each other, hardly directs these conceived-in-sentimentality actors who don't punch so much as crawl and fester.

However, the fancy people holed up in the music room of *The Exterminating Angel*—professional society types; the women, crushed in boned evening gowns; the men, a little too old, paunchy Don Juans in opera clothes; the very outfits that would be most insufferable if you were forced to keep them on for two months—literally give off a steam of sweat, ill temper, physical disgust, a remarkable intensity of discomfort that hasn't been seen before in movies. The standard leftism is nowhere apparent in these shots where Buñuel doesn't try to gloss his vision and imagination, where he exposes himself in relation to Franco Spain, the Church, whomever he worked for. He seems to admit his stylistic limitations, the past compromises, in powerful images where often three look-alikes are in a strange shot, grousing at each other, sort of escaping cognition. The people lined up in the doorway, staring out as though across a great expanse of empty, messed-up existence, while all types of garbage is piled up outside their escapeless room, suggest that the director has finally departed the obvious, weary, message-laden work that made him more of a commercial-minded director than anyone suggested.

Summer 1969

Samuel Fuller

THOUGH he lacks the stamina and range of Chester Gould or the endlessly creative Fats Waller, Sam Fuller directs and writes an inadvertently charming film that has some of their qualities: lyricism, real iconoclasm, and a comic lack of self-consciousness. He has made nineteen no-flab, low- or middle-budget films since 1949, any one of which could be described as "simple-minded corny stuff . . . but colorful," a bit of John Foster Dulles, a good bit of Steve Canyon, sometimes so good as to be breathtaking. *Pickup on South Street* is a marvel of lower-class nuttiness, Richard Widmark as a pickpocket working with a folded newspaper in the subway, almost all of it at night and each all-libido character acting uncorked, totally without propriety checks. Besides being a slow, awful movie, *Steel Helmet*, with its insane hero, a big-faced character, fighting a war against everybody but a little Korean boy, exemplifies the way Fuller touches everything with iconoclasm, turning it into black comedy. *Run of the Arrow*, one of the two movies that still embarrasses Rod Steiger (a mulish Confederate with a mysterious Irish accent and a hatred of Yankees that drives him into joining the Sioux nation), is totally unpredictable and always fresh.

The simplest way to describe his best film, *Pickup on South Street*, is to talk about his movie eye. A blunt melodrama about microfilm, stoolies and Soviet agents (Fuller's scripts are grotesque jobs that might have been written by the bus driver in *The Honeymooners*: "OK, I'll give you five minutes to clear out. If you're not out, we're going to burn the place down"), its quite long segments in a subway have a devilish moodiness, spareness, quietness. While Widmark's Skip character goes to work in a crowded subway car, there is this light touch and satisfying balance between build-up and attention to the moment. Bresson in his own *Pickpocket* film doesn't get close to the directness or the freshness: the ability to keep a scene going without cuts or camera tricks, fastening on enormously pungent faces, Widmark's fine-boned and tight-skinned youthfulness, the way he moves through the car, approaching his victim, Jean Peters, and, in one of the most unexpected detail shots, his hand becomes like a seal's sensitive flipper, dropping down below a newspaper and into a pocketbook. Part of the fun is the not-sure consternation on the faces of the two FBI agents who are following the girl and have no expectation of seeing an expert pickpocket at work.

The movie is filled with good images (the girl walking across the avenue, Widmark standing in his river shack drinking beer) that are always dependent on a trademark coziness to draw the spectator's attention. Little nests or lairs instead of apartments, a hammock instead of a bed, a box lowered into the river in place of a refrigerator, violence that is never interrupted and includes Widmark's friendly grin after nearly decapitating Jean Peters. Fuller's concentration has the curiosity of a kitten: the fine thing about Peters is that her nervous defiance, her guileless and garrulous jabbering seem the pensive, unfortunate traits of a private person rather than an actress's tricks.

Fuller is typically enthralled by material that George Stevens or Capra would consider hopelessly drab. He makes great scenes out of an aged woman's talk about her fatigue. A conventional scene of spies questioning an unwitting accomplice becomes the meanest hotel scene, reminiscent of Diane Arbus's camera eye, her obsession with picking up the down side of American life. The hub of the scene is its directness, the lack of fastidiousness with setting, people, dialogue. The stolid furniture is Moscow, 1940, the three men are square *sauerbraten* types, and Peters is a keyed-up, frenzied dame working through a debris of untalented dialogue: "Boy, you'll never believe it. You know what he thinks we are: Commies. Can you beat that? There sure are nuts walking around."

Once you've seen any of the uncut scenes or heard the blunt cartoon names (Short Round, Lucky Legs), it is impossible to forget the grotesque artist, the wackiness of his films. *China Gate* is sincere about inexplicable mush: Nat King Cole at a crossroads in Asia, expending lavish concern shining a rifle, overpowered by his GI costume, singing about lost love at the China Gate. For a movie that is inordinately white supremacist, it is wild seeing Cole's ecstatic grin at being an American soldier in a torn-up Asian battlefield.

All of his war films, loaded with fatuous brotherhood, show this unstomachable condescension of whites toward blacks, Orientals, and Sioux, plus Cole's type of demented happiness at being part of the white man's inane projects, such as capturing a pointless pagoda in endless, scrubby woods. Apart from the madness for Oriental art work that has an undressed look and has been dropped onto an unlikely spot from a helicopter (after being constructed overnight by a single blind carpenter), the craziness of these propagandist films is that the white hero is such trash: unprincipled, stupid, loud-mouthed, mean, thinking nothing about mauling women or any man a foot shorter. Zack, who starts *The Steel Helmet* as a helmet with a hole in it, a bit like a turtle until the helmet rises an inch off the stubbled field to show these meager, nasty eyes slowly shifting back and forth, casing the area, is like someone born on Torment Street between Malicious and Crude. Brueghel has a study of a peasant on crutches, drawn from behind, that suggests the sunk-in-earth, tired squatness. One of F. M. Ford's descriptions of Tietjens, "his body seemed to be constructed of meal sacks," gets close to the soft leadenness, the rancidness with which he's portrayed by Gene Evans, one of the most raucous guys in films. Evans plays the hot-headed showing off, the endless chewing on a cigar stump, with the blast effect of water issuing from a whale's spout, bestial and grotesque as a charm spot in a film dedicated to the U.S. infantry.

With its mangy, anonymous sets, lower-class heroes who treat themselves as sages, and the primitivism (the lack of cutting, rawness with actors, whole violent episodes shot in one take), *Steel Helmet* antedates Godard's equally propagandist work. From the bald and bereft sets to the ponderous, quirky messages that are written on small bits of paper and mailed out of the film like little newspapers (Please help Baldy to grow some Hair), his mangy characters are stubborn cousins to the similarly blocky ones that fight a war near Godard's Santa Cruz. The countries involved are just as unknown, and below both careers is this obsession with renegades, people straddling two worlds, the sane and insane (*Shock Corridor*), the bourgeois and the revolutionary (*La Chinoise*). What's good about his films is lovable; the daring, uninhibited use of semi-documentary techniques that save the movie from Fuller's mind, an unthinking morass at best. Against so many insane scenes (Cameron Mitchell standing in a fake teahouse and screaming, "I'm your Itchi-ban, not him! I always sat next to you!") there is a straight technique that seems all movie, with no tie-ins to other media. No one has been so sly at inserting an animated cartoon into a fiction screen: showing the trajectory of an arrow through drawing when, if photographed, the arc would have been invisible. Blunt and abstract, he often measures a scene into stylized positions and chunks of time.

There are two instances of this nonillustrative composing in *Run of the Arrow*. A whole town stands on a bridge looking into the river, while a counterpoint conversation goes on between Rod Steiger and his mother, building a slow, pastoral effect and a haunting time sense. Another third into the movie and this classical scene almost repeats itself: Steiger and Brian Keith sit at right angles to one another, staring into the prairie, neither party looking at the other. Keith says, "You can't turn your back on your own people," while Steiger is locked in his nursery-rhyme verbal incantation, "I don't like Yankees," etc., etc. It's a lovely scene: Steiger repeats this jingle in fifteen quiet, solidly stubborn ways, just as Godard has it done at a service station in France in *Weekend* ("You killed my boyfriend, he was beautiful and you're ugly," etc., etc.).

Fuller is one of the first to try for poetic purity through a merging of unlimited sadism, done candidly and close up, with stretches of pastoral nostalgia in which there are flickers of myth. The opening scenes in *Run of the Arrow* establish one man's bitterness toward the North, his vision of the South and a maximum heart-throbbing romanticism about General Lee (seen from a blacksmith's shop on a prancing white horse), and it's all done with lines and masses, a correct positioning of woods and fields and the decorum of Corot. There is so much of this offbeat visual posturing, but the question remains: how much of it occurred accidentally?

Fuller has no aptitude for foreign milieu, but, with his lingering passion for the exotic, he can't stay away from it. It's touching and ludicrous to see him lingering over bric-a-brac until he mauls the pagoda or the Buddha out of shape. (His Buddha, the highest one ever built out of wood, should have been sold to Macy's for its Thanksgiving Day float.) There are a few other traits: a fixation about children, blunt violence, the lurking feeling that he'd like to do a movie all in close-ups. *China Gate* is so absurd that it becomes an enchantment to the camp taste. The whole opening is impossibly nutty: an adorable tot and his puppy run through a ruined city, being chased by a figure in black silk pajamas and ballet slippers who is ready to butcher the boy's flop-eared pup for breakfast. A voice over all this says, "In this ravaged city where people are starving, all the dogs have been eaten except one."

September 1969

New York Film Festival: 1969

IN the type of multisensation circus that is the New York Film Festival, it is difficult to pin down the precise intellectual tone and incredible grace of Eric Rohmer's *Ma Nuit Chez Maud*. What makes it so special is that it's involved with a whole stratum of European culture that's totally ignored in films: the intellectual Catholic living in the provinces. Constructed on the encounters of a single person in a new town, its pleasure comes from specificity: of time (Christmas), locale (a bustling job-prosperous town of narrow streets), geography (a wintry, sparse landscape), cast (an unimposing man leading a deftly ordered life meets a bristlingly alert charmer who seizes opportunities and is a hard loser when they dissolve; these two are brought together by an interesting old friend whose specialty is conversational fencing). The most important specific is that the movie is centered on the private intellectual and emotional areas of the very civilized, educated, believable French professional class, and, moving along through small, unpointed, often unconnected events, it gets to the component parts of this class's life. The tone of their conversation, their bookstores, food markets, how they might meet in a bar or go on outings is sensitively phrased, spaced out, observed. Such consistently undramatic material is extraordinary in films today and needs tempered lightness to bring it off. And, actually, Rohmer's film, in its last third, begins to run down, as its good Catholic finally effects a date with a girl who meets all his qualifications.

One obvious fact about this *auteur*-minded festival is that it contained only one rich, satisfying, hard-to-accomplish performance: Jean-Louis Trintignant's indirect, intelligent acting, which fleshes out Rohmer's cerebral, problematic script. An older version of the shy, rather lonely, poignantly vulnerable student in *The Easy Life*, Trintignant keeps the movie elastic, droll, and dryly exciting through a mastery of slightness: he's slightly prissy about his Catholicism, slightly awkward defending himself against accusations of Jansenism, slightly graceful as he dashes across a snow-covered street in pursuit of a pretty blonde he's been sizing up in Mass as a future wife. It's a fascinating idea for a movie—a young man's undramatic settling into a new town and job, structured around a long philosophical discussion in the rooms of a sexy, taunting divorcee—and, though it is immaculately written, it depends on taut smudges of elegant acting to keep it afloat.

While criticism gets hung up on old problems of taste, right and wrong, history in the making, the New York Festival at its simplest is an unweeded garden of mixed delights and endurance tests. Most of the interesting work—the BBC anatomy of Sternberg's unfinished *Claudius*, *Le Gai Savoir*, *Ma Nuit Chez Maud*, and Bresson's transposing of a murky, believable Dostoevsky story into an afternoon piece for clavichord—were far from traditional movies. The BBC *The Epic That Never Was* is appetizingly special for the collage effect, but it's no movie. Godard's uncompromising stab at the story film is one of the few occasions when English subtitles under French-speaking voices are a positive design element.

What is good about Bresson's *Une Femme Douce* is the mulishness: the direct, resolute, obsessional artist always driving after the idea of exalted suspension and ascetic rigor in small, quiet phenomena. The movie works despite the spooky queerness of its three inhibited, sleepwalking actors and the silly verbatim use of Dostoevsky's lines, which are rescued from total silliness in the film by a blatant throwaway quality. Bresson, trying for a kind of Cubistic misalliance, doesn't care if the lines are understood or whether they fit in with the image. As storytelling, the movie is a brain-twister in which few sentences connect to the image they accompany. A young bride jumps up and down on her new bed, and her husband, the ultimate in prissiness and mundaneness, says, "I threw cold water on her ecstasy." Also: "I knew she had behaved honorably, there was no question about it." This blank, icy man has just seen his wife passionately necking in a roadster.

Through movies about hand-task-oriented social outcasts—a poacher setting his traps, an imprisoned man weaving ropes and making hooks for his escape, an apprentice pickpocket learning the trade—Bresson's vocabulary has been honed over the theme of humility as nobility. He likes a face to be as free from reflection as an animal's: his sensitive-faced outsiders do what they do without the face making any comment on the action. Before speaking, eyes methodically drop in nervous, hopeless abjectness. People turn away from the camera, assume prayerful or meditated poses, pass one another as though on a private procession.

On one level, the film is a geometric ballet of doors opening and closing, people exiting and entering, husband or wife turning down the bed covers, of objects or people moving into and out of range of the stationary camera, a young wife's dazzlingly white fresh face against the sharp, crotchety profile of her black-haired husband, TV sets turned on and off, bathtubs filled and emptied. Despite the stylized repetitions of gesture, the rigidly held camera angle at stomach height, the uninflected voices speaking desperate, passionate lines, *Une Femme Douce* is an eerie crystalline work, a serious affirmation within a story of suicide.

The Epic That Never Was is a British TV documentary about the making of an unfinished movie called *Claudius*. Narrated by a strangely stiff, schoolboyish Dirk Bogarde, the movie gets sparkle and dimension from intercutting candid interviews with a few completed segments from the elephantine Korda production that mysteriously smashed up after a month. A lot of the sparkle comes from smart-aleck remarks by the writer, Robert Graves, and the costar, Emlyn Williams. There are pathetic-exciting shots around the abandoned Dedham studios, and, along with the funny, uncut rushes of *Claudius*, the flubs, nervous wisecracks, false starts, Charles Laughton's strong, emotional turmoil turns up like a ghostly giant in anachronistic crowd scenes. At moments, this BBC document reaches a poetic peak above its witty gossip: somehow the material becomes layered, recapturing a moment in time, through the mind of a costume-designer still puzzled at this date by Sternberg's giantism ("I want sixty naked vestal virgins dressed in white gauze on the stage by tomorrow morning"). Or the oblivious, quivering voice of heart-faced Merle Oberon: "Korda wanted to make the film to make me a real big star, to really make me shine." (She has the same naïve-vain expression thirty years earlier when she answers Caligula's "Wouldn't you like to marry my Uncle Claudius, Messalina?" with a helpless "My family has other plans for me.")

In Godard's *Le Gai Savoir*, which looks for the most part like a funny, daring, remarkably lighted, neon-colored rehearsal on an empty stage, two bright-faced Parisians, aged twenty, get together each night between midnight and dawn, to examine the meaning of words and their relationship to the phenomena they describe. Practically all of the movie is structured on one static frontal image in boundaryless black depth, the edges of the two seated figures picked out by a powerful floodlight. This mysteriously inky-hot lighting is hypnotic, slowly joining usually unseen nooks and crannies in the sullen Léaud-Berto faces with some sense of the young Leftists' purpose and youthful energy. To describe its content (silhouetted faces alternating with Tom and Jerry cartoons, newsreel footage of Paris students rioting, illustrations, ads flashed on the screen with words or parts of words scrawled over them, flashes of colored photography of city streets that are as deep as the rest of the film is flat) fails to convey the exhilarating goofiness. As always, Godard's sound track is distinctive: sporadic, unsettling, and, as with the visual material, apt to issue from any source. Does anyone else use sound as a totally filmic weapon?

Pierre and Paul is an eccentric film with a headlong self-involved propulsion. Wry and affectionate, it never managed to get inside the young working couple, a stocky, self-made builder and a nicely acted slender typist. The subtheme, the extent of the inroads into Paris life of plastic modernity, is sort of amusing and skillful in its details. Bergman's *The Ritual* is a self-indulgent film with one good actor, and some good writing about people defiling each other. The good actor is a Richard Basehart type with funny embedded-in-fat eyes and a crisper style than Thulin and Bjornstrand. The movie probably evolved when a David Susskind Swede made a phone call: "Mr. Bergman, would you be interested in writing an original play for TV? There'll be no censors and no cutting to save time. You'll have complete control. Would you be interested in that kind of a project?"

Susan Sontag's *Duet for Cannibals* looks and feels like skimmed milk. An airless, room-locked, unusually adroit drawing-room comedy. A young man with the style and dress of an avant-garde painter is employed to catalogue the life work of a political refugee. There is nothing convincing about his task, his employer's career, or the reason he and his girl are swallowed up by the powerful personalities of the two urbane, pompous vampires in an ultrabourgeois house. The combination of a gutless spirit and sadomasochistic games (I kill you, you kill me, and then we all get up and walk out the door) kills the film midway, when a suicide, with unbearable playfulness, hides herself and her lover behind a windshield that she covers with shaving soap. What is amazing is how little juice there is in the inventions and characters, yet this gray coagulation keeps going forward in a half-entertaining way.

Sifting through a Festival experience, a madness, 100 hours sitting in a dark chamber, brings back a half-dozen vulgar, terrific, enervated images that are anything from piercingly poetic to whorish. Norman Rockwell's vignettes of adolescent rural life, full of obsessively researched and accentuated-beyond-realism detail (buttons a little larger than life, suspenders filled with folksy charm), were never more fastidious than the nostalgic redo of the early 1930's in *Adalen '31*. It is the craziest picture of people out of work and on strike: an intensely lyrical evocation of slender boys in caps and trousers, flowering meadows, delicately patterned wallpaper and summer heat. Two big scenes in *Bob & Carol*, played on a slow-curving Spanish stairway, have squirts of hard, modern patois ("Why didn't you call me first?" "I couldn't call and ask you, 'Bob, can I have an affair?'") calculatingly poised together, while a vulgar camera reveals old hard-core Hollywood physiques in long-forgotten Edith Head costumes.

November 1969

Don Siegel

CONSIDERING the automatic high coloring of his vermin, the anxious hopping around for the picturesque, the hokey scripts with worn-out capers and police-routine plots, why write about Don Siegel? Having made a few good modest-budget films—*Baby Face Nelson, Flaming Star* with Elvis Presley, *The Invasion of the Body Snatchers*—that aren't shown in art theaters, he has been wrongly deified by auteurists, though he's basically a determinedly lower-case, crafty entertainer who utilizes his own violence to build unsettling movies with cheap musical scores that leave in their wake a feeling of being smeared with bilge. Not as good as Hawks before *Red Line 7000*, probably better than Blake Edwards (*Gunn*), another manipulative sock-bam director, not as gutty or lyrical as the Sam Fuller of *Pickup on South Street*, he is interesting only if he's left life-size and unhaloed.

What is a Don Siegel movie? Mainly it's a raunchy, dirty-minded film with a definite feeling of middle-aged, middle-class sordidness. Every cop, prostitute, and housewife is compromised by something: the pimp in *Madigan* is compromised by his connection to the police; the police commissioner keeps company with the society matron when her husband is on a camping trip with her son, and so on. There are elements of the *Brighton Rock* Graham Greene (the suspension between melodrama and farce in *Baby Face Nelson*), Robert Louis Stevenson (the odd feeling for desert grayness and squalor in *Flaming*

Star), and Al Capp (cartoon exaggeration in the Daisy Mae, who services Coogan of *Coogan's Bluff* in a Mojave shack's wooden bathtub). With these elements and the fact that Siegel's a commercial director who's good at his job, the movie works out so that it has something more than push and slime.

Siegel's movies are spiritually as opportunist and crafty as the grafting cops, cheating wives, and winged hoods who make up the personnel. They are also zesty, hard-working entertainments with good nervy second bananas (Don Stroud, Steve Inhat) working alongside the wooden, sat-upon Widmark (Siegel normally discourages his expensive actors from becoming anything but wooden replicas of themselves), unsettling camera work with a lot of zooms, high-angle shots, zigzagging action scenes that make devastating cut-away material. (The last thing heard in a police station is the line "I know it was him, Officer, because this is his shoe.")

While using as his movie basics the same ingredients that rattle around in a TV crime drama—a twenty-minute wait for a decent Stirling Silliphant line, two stiff-brainless-righteous cops who are like Hoboken lawyers, with everything being played for its sensational value—Siegel gets at least one scene, in *The Lineup*, as sensitive as Robert Frank's still shots. What is so lyrical about the ending, in San Francisco's Sutro Museum, is the Japanese-print compositions, the late afternoon lighting, the advantage taken of the long hallways, multi-level stairways in a baroque, elegant, glass-palace building with an exposed skating rink, nautical museum, and windows facing the sea with eye-catching boulders. It's a minor masterpiece of preplanning by an assistant director and an extensively structured pictorial tour by Siegel, expediently using Hitchcock's *Foreign Correspondent* (the interesting, relaxed use of girls from a convent school, a dummybody carefully described in its three-story drop) and Welles's *The Lady from Shanghai* (nice glass cases with miniature boats). The Siegel touch is always apparent in the excessive number of viewpoint shots, the nice feeling for an eroded structure with awkward angles, a sad reliance on edgy Broadway acting (Eli Wallach overworking his nervous-leering eyes) and especially the fascination with a somewhat mannered athleticism seen from above, in which the body is poised or moving against background action that is a violent contrast in space, tone, movement.

Siegel is a director who stays strictly outside of people, away from their ideas, emotions: the scripts from the bottom of a TV-office barrel concern impulsive, nervous-energy types who live strenuously and usually die fast in scenes that are cluttered with their cronies and enemies. Individually rather shallow creations, they pick up color from contact with one another. It's symbolic that Dancer, main criminal of *The Lineup*, becomes hysterical when faced with a noncommunicative stone-faced hawk in a wheelchair who is supposed to receive the cache of heroin. The man's absolute refusal to be familiar drives Dancer to shove man and wheelchair off the balcony into a somersault that ends three floors below on an ice rink. (If someone won't talk to a Siegel character, the effect is literally a mortal insult.)

Though Siegel doesn't let his star actors seek their own level of expression, Betty Field and Don Stroud, mother and son in *Coogan's Bluff*, can literally tear the screen apart with ribaldry while being squashed. "That wasn't nice, that wasn't nice at all. I show you the coat my son bought for me and you say things like that. You talk like that to a mother." Always surprised, strident, Field here is a great comic caricature trying to rid her territory of a hostile intruder. Stroud has this evasive, rabbity quality, as though people were harassing him and he's had just about enough. "Leech off," the old high school expletive for shrugging off a pest, has never been varied more ways than in Stroud's writhing-lifting maneuvers. Siegel's lopsided discourse on the cantankerous New Yorker has sweetness, kookiness, and, behind its stiffly parodied face, enough lyrical humor to almost cover the roughed-through feeling of a TV production.

Siegel has a way of suggesting chains of rapport and intimate knowledge, from a police commissioner down to the pimp and teenaged thrill addict in the hinterlands of Brooklyn. Much of the interest comes from the swift connection between weirdly separated types. A tough Manhattan prostitute walks into the hotel room of a just arrived Phoenix cop: "Hi, sugar, will you zip me up?" The opening of *Coogan's Bluff* is a slambang parody of Kubrick's *2001* start: space-devouring images, a sheriff's jeep whipping across the desert floor, and a ravaged-faced Indian hopping around in the hills, setting up his arsenal to destroy the world as the jeep approaches. The first line of dialogue has a funny intimacy that establishes the sheriff's snide antihero character in seven small words: "OK chief, put your pants back on," and the pants fly into the shot, landing at the feet of a most eccentric Apache—very stocky, battered face, hair cut with a tomahawk.

Siegel's concept of what a secondary player can do is more idiosyncratic and inventive than Peckinpah's boisterous use of Strother Martin and Warren Oates in *The Wild Bunch*, who always stand for earthy, beer-guzzling, whoring health of life. The real humor in Siegel perhaps stems from his putting second leads into roles that reverse their real natures in compositions that have a rowdy off-kilter vigor: sensitive-gentle-practical Betty Field as a popeyed bat out of Hell's Kitchen. How does one explain the wild fun in the scenes between Lee J. Cobb, a New Yorker with not one minute of patience left in his harassed body, and Clint Eastwood (Coogan), a cunning non-verbal actor who makes most of his acting scores by going cool-faced while others talk at him. ("Look Tex, you're not a cop here. How many times have I got to tell you? There's a plane leaving for Phoenix in three hours. If you're not on it I'm putting you in jail.") The real punch comes from the strange intimacy: this precinct cop uptown on the West Side acts as though he's been putting up with the annoyance of Eastwood's stubbornness and clear blue eyes for a lifetime. He acts tired of Coogan from the moment Eastwood, totally polite and civilized, enters his office.

December 1969

Michael Snow

THE cool kick of Michael Snow's *Wavelength* was in seeing so many new actors—light and space, walls, soaring windows, and an amazing number of color-shadow variations that live and die in the window panes—made into major esthetic components of movie experience. In Snow's *Standard Time*, a waist-high camera shuttles back and forth, goes up and down, picking up small, elegantly lighted square effects around a living room very like its owner: ordered but not prissy. A joyous-spiritual little film, it contains both Snow's singular stoicism and the germinal ideas of his other films, each one like a thesis, proposing a particular relationship between image, time, and space. The traits include rigorous editing, attention to waning light, fleeting human appearances (which suggest a forbidding, animistic statement about life: that the individual is a short-lived, negligible phenomenon and that it is the stability of the inanimate that keeps life from flying away), a rich-dry color so serene as to be almost holy, and a driving beat that is like updated Bach.

Standard Time is an astute, charming exercise compared to the other Snows, which are always steered into purposefully intolerable stretches: tough, gripped snarls of motion which have to be broken through to reach a restful, suave, deltalike conclusion. In his sternest film, titled with a ⟷ sign for back-and-forth motion, a specially rigged camera swings right, left, left, right, before a homely, sterile classroom wall, then accelerates into an unbearable blur (the same frenzied scramble, as though the whole creative process was going berserk, that occurs three quarters through "Abbey Road"). In *One Second in Montreal*, ten stray photographs, culled from the library, all of them of little drab parks connected to public buildings, are turned into a movie that has a special serenity and is pungent with a feeling of city, snow, unexcitement, the mediocrity of public buildings and parks (no fresh air). Despite the dirgelike sonority, I question the length of time that Snow holds on each park to create a majestically slotted ribbon composition.

When the electronic sound in *Wavelength* reaches an ear-cracking shriek, the one-shot movie, a forty-five-minute zoom aimed at four splendid window rectangles, burns hot white, like the filaments in a light bulb. This middle section is composed of violent changes of color in which the screen shudders from intensities of green, magenta, sienna: a virtuoso series of negative and positive impressions in which complementary colors are drained out so that the room, undergoing spasms, flickers from shrill brilliant green to pure red to a drunken gorgeous red-violet. Despite the grueling passage, which always comes three-quarters through a four-part construction, his two major statement films, *Wavelength* and ↔, are liftingly intellectual. Besides his Jeffersonian mien, Snow's films are filled with the same precision, elegance, and on-the-nose alertness that went into Jefferson's slightest communiqué to a tailor or grocer.

His film career, a progression from austere painterly to a more austere sculptural style has peaked into this queer "double-arrow" film that causes a spectator to experience all the grueling action and gut effort of a basketball game. Just listing the ingredients doesn't sound like a real night out at the films. This neat, finely tuned, hypersensitive film examines the outside and inside of a banal prefab classroom, stares at an asymmetrical space so undistinguished that it's hard to believe the whole movie is confined to it, and has this neck-jerking camera gimmick which hits a wooden stop arm at each end of its swing. Basically it's a perpetual motion film which ingeniously builds a sculptural effect by insisting on time-motion to the point where the camera's swinging arcs and white wall field assume the hardness, the dimensions of a concrete beam.

In such a hard, drilling work, the wooden clap sounds are a terrific invention, and, as much as any single element, create the sculpture. Seeming to thrust the image outward off the screen, these clap effects are timed like a metronome, sometimes occurring with torrential frequency.

The human intrusions in *Wavelength* and *Standard Time* are graceful, poignant, sensitively observed: a fair-sized turtle walks on a line through the camera's legs straight toward the right-angled corner of a studio bed; at another point, a cat does an arching, almost slow-motion leap onto the bed; then a woman walks briskly by with a towel over her shoulder on her way to the bathroom. There's no eclecticism to these events, which show a good touch for the tactile quality of 1969 loft existence. Formularized and stiffened, the humanity in the double-arrow movie is a bit dried up. Things are done on cue: a man and woman self-consciously play catch, a cop cases the joint, a mock lecture is given to three students, a gawking and hodgepodge group is seen uncomfortably standing around.

The movies are utterly clear, but they get their special multimedia character from Snow's using all his talents as painter-sculptor-composer-animator. Obviously a brainy inventor who is already a seminal figure and growing more influential by the day, there is something terribly different about this Canadian in the New York sharp scene. Incapable of a callow, clumsy, schmaltzy move, he's a real curiosity, but mostly for the forthright, decent brain power that keeps these films on a perfect abstract path, almost always away from preciosity.

January 1970

◆

THE ten best: 1) *Black Girl* 2) *Ma Nuit Chez Maud* 3) *Tom, Tom the Piper's Son* 4) ⟷ 5) *Chronik der Anna Magdalena Bach* 6) *Le Gai Savoir* 7) a tie among three Hollywood eccentricities, *The Wild Bunch*, *Easy Rider*, *The Rain People* 8) *High School* and *La Raison Avant La Passion* 9) *Coming Apart* 10) *They Shoot Horses, Don't They?* and *La Femme Infidèle*.

One. *Black Girl* could have been sentimental pro-African anti-white (a very quiet, particular, personal story: an obstinate, naive Sengalese, taken to France as a mother's helper, finds that she has no freedom of movement when she gets there. Thrilled to begin with, anticipating high life and parties, she is made into a full-time maid, baby-watcher, chef, and, quite soon, a bathtub suicide), but instead Sembene's perfect short story is unlike anything in the film library: translucent and no tricks, amazingly pure, but spiritualized by a black man's grimness in which there is not an ounce of grudge or finger-pointing. The whole movie, echoing flawless acting of an inarticulate who hasn't broken out of an adolescent self-absorption, holds an even, equilibrated, spiritual tone. Within a spiritualized braille art, Sembene catches perfectly the terrible thing about irreconcilable disjointedness: an illiterate village girl employed by an educated, advantage-seeking French couple; servant-boss; lonely-secure; ritual as against lack of ceremony, the materialistic domesticity of a family circle as opposed to the adventure-seeking of a romantic in a foreign place. With marble cool visuals and one marble cool actress, the spirit of loggerheads is caught in the most minimal conditions. The most charming image: a very long-legged girl teetering around the kitchen on foot-long high heels and a dust rag in her hands.

Two. *Ma Nuit Chez Maud* is civilized work, beautifully spaced out and observed. Very straight, not pretentious in any way. Rohmer has conceived a potential love affair that doesn't take, by way of a 24-hour verbal sparring match that is magically phrased by Trintignant and Françoise Fabian. A very atmospheric movie—dry, cold snow, both outside, in the forest-y suburb and inside, in the minds of two people who can't be totally happy. It's unusual to center a film inside an encounter of hesitance, either-or moments; his resolve wavers, then he catches himself, the girl goes through a lot of changes from understanding, then sympathy, to miffed and final resignation. Trintignant's drying out technique for suggesting vulnerability is that of a lean-exquisite miniaturist in a very private, intelligent ground-covering act. Within Fabian's taunting, flamboyant role is the pathos of a confused intelligence at loose ends. She's very exciting.

Three. *Tom, Tom the Piper's Son* is a shockingly different reconstruction film in which Jacobs, a combined historian-painter-camera nut, too endlessly reshuffles the parts of a rustic 1905 film about two boys and a piglet being chased around one-sided barns and cottages. The major part of an hour-long film is of not-totally abstract shapes in which there is enough of the specific pig-beret-fold to make for the movie's trademark spiritual richness. Jacobs' image of the wide black-white crumpled stripes in a boy's pants or the goose-like neckline and upswept hair of a Chardin maid not only ravishes the eye but moves the spirit, much like a Seurat conté sketch on rough, pebbled paper. All of his pioneer moves—matting out whole areas, blurring, using the closest close-up on an elbow crease—are for going beyond illusionism, illustration, into a spirit world: what should be pure picturesque because of the quaint-corny material is really a turbulent experience of an analytic sensibility. By jamming the spectator right against the substance (a little boy rolls around with a pig in his arms, then rolls into the fireplace and is sucked up the chimney) and looking for the essential-irreducible elements of film, he is in the forbidding Serra-Snow area where the concepts of all his contemporaries are challenged.

Four. ←→, which caused fists to fly and eyes to roll when last shown at MOMA, is a frantically-paced, eccentric, hard-to-take pendulum movie in which Mike Snow's high-tensile mind is perhaps too poised over the film idea of a charmless classroom projected as sculpted rather than pictured time. The camera, on a special gig that restricts its movements right and left, swings like a guillotine, a hard wooden clap registers on the ear like a butcher's mallet, as

Snow, in his most unsensuous movie so far, concertedly tries for a spiritual realism inside a minimal image. The beauty is in the hardness.

From beginning to end of a resolute three-part musical form of perpetual motion, Snow has mobilized a mirthless, lonely subject, a classroom wall, into an expressive weapon that is made up of all-but-unstomachable ingredients in their purest form: jar, jerk, frenetic motion over space. As the back-forth image speeds up to a hair-raising, psychotic clip, light appears to filter off the sides of a horizontal cube of greenish whiteness. All literary connections in a film image have been junked and a forbidding subject—sculpted in-motion space —has been made the jump-off point of a film design that doesn't rely on any behavior-sensory patterns of the spectator. The one conventional point in the film, a greenish board choked with chalked information about the film stock, actors, the setting in Fairleigh Dickinson College, comes between the back-forth, up-down section and a hypnotic lyrical coda: this fulcrum-like effect re-emphasizes quite logically the physical conditions of a film that swings right-left, left-right from a fixed spot.

When Snow is at his best, he seems to know first-hand the historical grain of a loft room or renovated artist's studio. In this hectic, neck-taxing film, he's very aloof: except for a cop who drives up and cases the unreal activity inside the room, the people are out of place, and there is no curiosity about the fixtures or construction that give this pre-fab room its sterile mechanistic flavor. The asymmetrical design is much harder to take than *Wavelength*, from the long-short relationship of an unendurable opening and the much shorter mash of repeated shots in the coda to the misery-provoking effect of a camera that is pouring over a space that seems lopsided because the camera is much closer to one wall than to the other.

Five. Straub's *Chronik der Anna Magdalena Bach* is full of reflective, icy beauty, which demonstrates that designing a Bach movie and J. S. Bach's own job-clogged career were equals in hard work. Nothing is made up, no embroidering of the facts (a la *Lola Montes*). What the film is about—a wife's life of subservience, discipline, restraint, and a composer engulfed by work, maddened by humiliating jobs, incessantly involved in conning more money out of his patrons—is poured through a minimalist movie apparatus, producing a timeless, classical, boring work in which every shot comes across with super clarity and poignance. There's no pretense at naturalism and the hollow images of wigged actors who don't act playing harpsichords and choir singing, suggest a touched-up super-real grisaille, like Ingres' black-white *Grande Odalisque*. It looks very staged, the fixed camera angle never pans or zooms, and the basic material—the Bach music used throughout in solid chunks, alternating with silence or the wife's intense-mellow voice reading passages from her diary—creates the silvery resonance of a Vermeer coming to life, but not too much: no one ever runs, breathes hard, or laughs.

Six. *Le Gai Savoir* has the same mix, fanatic estheticism, and outrage at the Establishment of an anti-form piece at Leo Castelli's warehouse. A fresh-faced girl and boy spend the post-midnight hours on a TV stage reviewing the state of world affairs, in a potpourri of advertisements, Tom and Jerry, Magic Marker scribbles and glaring newsreels of street crowds that come on like lantern slides and flicker off quickly. The raucous, exhilarating track hasn't a soporific note in it. The Berto-Léaud actors are curt, impatient cartoon characters, more extremely cartoons than the Parisian red guardists in *La Chinoise*. Coutard's face-slapping photography is robust and throws itself completely into every moment. Every Godard has a new form; this one, with its burning light, gem color, and scarring discordancies, image-sound-titles-handwriting sometimes all at one time, is the meanest and least lulling, a not-too-pure, sprawling attempt to stay politically committed while trying, impossibly, to keep up with the minimal Straub-Warhol-Snow film which is racing out of sight.

Seven. My reservations on *The Wild Bunch* are almost balanced by the passion for the period (1916 near El Paso). Lucien Ballard's Winslow Homer-like compositions, and the two warring personalities of Peckinpah's movie art: a scholarly care with details and a braggart *Machismo* complex. The trouble is that his writing is sometimes pulp (how did one Tommy Sands *muchacho* from a little village become a badly-acted explosives ace?), sometimes romantic (a jammed fortress of soldiers and camp followers all gunned down by four bank robbers who become Bunyan-esque heroes at the end), and often keeps the movie 1945 in sentiment. It's often a lovely movie: a shot of baby-faced soldiers slouched around in a coachcar or the slow motion of bounty hunters, like little logs, going down the river.

The whole movie is out of shape; what is good comes from a tender, nostalgic, patient detailing of the period, always counteracted by the silly, school-boy Peckinpah philosophy and what it leads to: raucous fellowship is more important than anything, the worst cheat-thief-mercenary is OK as long as he's true to his mate.

Easy Rider is naive in suggesting that Captain America and Billy could survive one day, not because of redneck Texans or the silent majority, but from being menaced off the road by real Hell's Angels. The film doesn't work until these two clichés wake up in jail and meet Jack Nicholson, a Villon in rumpled seersucker. What had been a simplistic, sentimental lament for drugs, dropping out, the road, becomes specific, rhythmic, and abrupt. Comradely scenes between the three are so well set up that when each one is torn out by death the effect is shocking. Hopper, especially, is good, more contemporary than *Wild Bunch* acting, aware that he's in a movie, and, through an underhand private technique, keeping the movie alive with weak-ish bluster.

February 1970

◆

Dᴇsᴘɪᴛᴇ many good things (the first notable eyes since Per Oscarrson's in *Hunger* in Segal's sodden performance, Eva Marie Saint's intelligent and tense mimicries emphasizing a hungry, tensed-for-disaster face, the dress shop scene which has a compassionate pessimism but stops before all the material is exploited), *Loving* at times looks disturbingly like the "two together" cigarette commercials. Actually, the movie is a fifty-fifty movie: it shows a sensitive touch for a man who is a complete mess, whose habits are wrong from the ground up, and, along with a sharply acted wife, creates this pain inside tepidly filmed scenes.

Most hemmed in, domestic, tidy, and not put down hard by parts of the New York press, *Loving* deals with survival on a middle class level rather than eroticism or affection. Compared with an ingenious scene in *Topaz*, a silent long shot with a brilliant actor, Roscoe Lee Browne, maneuvering in Harlem's Hotel Theresa, or with the teen-age dance in a mirrored hall in *Au Hasard Balthazar* in which Bresson creates a powerful psychology having to do with youthful sadism, *Loving* has a staid, pedestrian image.

Yet the more sensitive critics go strong for this small-gauge movie about a rather talented craftsman who, despite his youth, is a confirmed malcontent taking hidden pleasure in messing up other lives. The reasons for its success must reach beyond its ingratiating gag-a-scene format to the fact that it has a perfect combination for American box office: a well-groomed Hollywood style and a joking pessimism. It shows Connecticut life as a sloppy, painful experience, without an exalted moment to justify or bring some relief to the formlessness of Brooks Wilson's existence, a shambling modern malaise in which everything—wife, mistress, job, children—runs together into a distasteful routine which he can hardly focus, never mind resolve.

Loving is the foolproof blend: no technical breakouts and an anti-hero whose nihilism is beyond Camus' Algerian clerk who, unlike Wilson, insists on a measure of dignity in his daily life. George Segal's Wilson is the third example of Director Irvin Kershner's invention, a husband of doomed ambition who expends tons of energy promoting himself, a muddle-brained slave who is always in passage around the city looking for stakes, projects, a killing. The crux of the boulder-pushing character is the relationship to success: he's not exactly hungry for it but on a treadmill that doesn't yield any—even momentary—satisfactions but gives the moviegoer a vision of an endlessly hurrying wage earner who never hits the same spot twice. Segal's competent hack, who must be the most mindless, blurred character in film history, is performed almost entirely with an unfocused fatigue around the eyes and a hulking weight in his head and shoulders which lead to endless comedy, lurching toward the camera, stumbling forward in bars, construction sites, and the lavish Connecticut party that abortively ends the movie and solves nothing.

Absolutely, the key to the movie's interest is the extent of Wilson's soddenness and Segal's slurring ability to swim in abasement. Not only is the face a puddle of guilt and woefulness, but the devastating portrait of a weak man depends on Segal's stalling, on the fact that he can never eliminate, be decisive, or turn down a possibility, be it girl, job or joke. From *Brother Rat* profiteer to the only employed member in the *Bye Bye Braverman* band of Jewish writers, Segal's instinct is to insert himself obliquely so that he's neither Segal nor role but a supremely devious lurking presence: he has a great pantomiming instinct for the intentional fuck-up. Pre-arranging the psyche of his roles, Segal spends an entire movie on shifting: any wave of energy in his vicinity draws him in its wake. He scores heavily in unpromising exits and entrances, planting a heavy aura of mindlessness and destructive sociability. Comics since Arbuckle and Snub Pollard have been knocking accidentally into waiters and carefully arranged dinner tables: with his sliding, floating technique for soaking in shameful behavior, Segal gives the familiar situation a grotesque realism and the sense that these slapstick moments have real consequence in the hack illustrator's life.

So most of Wilson's day is spent in floating, scurrying, innocuous activity; and a good part of the time it's not far from the truth of New York life. It's curious how the imaginative texture of this conception is stuck to a stiff, unfulfilled script. There's no real mystery, excitement, or curiosity in anything concerning the tragic Segal marriage with Eva Marie Saint. Every scene appears to be stretched out and aborted at the same moment—events are arranged out of forgettable dialogue and arty pieces of photography—so that the feeling is of a movie moving toward the beginnings of events.

The opening razzmatazz scene seems endless: all padding and a strangely cast, uncompelling mistress. The camera pans down and across the window of an inexplicably ritzy apartment, finally taking in Segal in a nothing pose, having a morning cigarette while his mistress, all industry, walks out in a huff. The movie's squareness is indicated before the credits finish: the over-complete decor for a low-salary museum clerk, and all that photographic romance, spotting the pair through fences, traffic signs with varied camera angles to imprint a decidedly chic New York flavor.

Forget the time ambiguity (she's going to a morning job and he's rushing to Westport to arrive late at an evening performance of his small daughter's school play about tin men and fairies), Kershner's movies, from the sensitive naturalism in *The Luck of Ginger Coffey* onwards, have been terribly unconscious of the formal and syntactical aspects of filmmaking. This very decent, observant, socially concerned director is pulled along by conventional scripts and when there is an attempt to spike a modest realism with the broad satire used in *The Graduate*, the director goes for gimmicks and types.

The script could be enumerated scene by scene by listing the gags. A kid from the school operetta—a little prig dressed in a tin suit—upbraids Segal in the boy's room; the key thing is the self-righteous crack, "You can't smoke here," and he picks up the cigarette when Wilson leaves. A grouchy neighbor arrives at eight in the morning with a garbage pail smeared with Wilson's name, coyly asks "Is this yours?" A tireless female buttonholer interrupts scenes at school, railroad station, and party, to flirt with Wilson. And, finally, a whopper gimmick: an estate with a TV hookup to all its rooms, particularly a child's play-house where Wilson's drunken infidelity is revealed to the whole community. Kershner's movies, filled with earnestness and situation comedy gags, are kept in a status quo area: his dismal marriage—a job-obsessed husband and a decent wife trying to keep the household going—is hamstrung by the neat middle class instincts of a director who sees all problems of dignity and self-respect in American life as being tied to economic survival, earning a good buck.

The limitations in density and tragedy are always suggested by the way Kershner handles wives, thoroughly domestic creatures who are fearful that their homes are falling apart and, more important, that their fantasy-possessed men are drifting into private worlds. Through no fault of their own, they find themselves in a barren position. The real horror of the film is that while dealing with psychosis it is short-circuited by the cut-rate dialogue, the dabs of impressionistic material that are used as inserts to impress certain labels about a wife (hungry for attention, bitching about petty matters, absorbed with the children). Eva Marie Saint comes across as a telling face rather than as a whole figure understood, developed, brought to fruition by the movie's material.

The fairly conventional betrayed-suffering wife is a Kershner staple and a limited view of a woman (strictly a husband's slant), but something remarkable always happens in these movies: an intelligent actress turns a cliché role into high art, playing it for limitless bitterness. Saint is too well-groomed to top Mary Ure's Mrs. Coffey, but there are scenes which have a morbid honesty, the first occasions on which she has tangled with lack of self-esteem. This is the first role in which she exploits timid awkwardness and the facial qualities of maturity. In fine scenes, like the one in a dress shop where she's trying on party dresses for a couldn't-care-less husband, the actress's terribly moving candor is both better and deeper than anything written or directed.

Zabriskie Point. Slugged by critics, this continuous photographic lyricism shouldn't have been treated as a realistic portrait of America. Among the things excoriated were a non-actress (Daria Halprin) with great legs, tan, and sleeveless suede-colored dress, a dustbowl section with a perfectly chosen location and imaginatively used kids, and a handsome lyrical view of America right through the fantastically photographed shots of 1970 culture floating and shooting into the air.

Topaz. Pretty good entertainment with a number of standout scenes involving either Roscoe Lee Browne or Michel (always good) Piccoli. It is an unusual, logical Hitchcock spy film in that it deals with so many faces, nationalities, global locations, and portrays the American-French espionage geniuses as devitalized, all the others as witty and passionate. There are a lot of details—a woman's death glimpsed in a slow spiral—that belong in a defunct movie drawer called "Hitchcock touches," but the movie stays alive.

The Damned. A fascinating film, complexly conceived and composed in chiaroscuro color, melodramatic space, extravagant held-on poses. In a movie that has the compelling power of Géricault's *Raft of the Medusa*, all the good sections seem to be dominated by Helmut Berger's silent-film acting and plastered down hair. Visconti's remembrance of the Third Reich has ridiculous images: a trumped up marriage scene and a mother-son bed scene, but it also has a great birthday party with an unexplained scream and a very intense broad image study of a daringly acted depraved hysteric in a small furnished room. A rotten musical score by Maurice Jarre.

Au Hasard Balthazar. A rich catalog of mythology and symbolism about donkeys squeezed into a queer script that wanders and doubles back, detailing the varieties of evil and self-destruction that Bresson seems to be saying is Human Nature. Anne Wiazemsky is exquisitely and movingly beautiful, both willfully perverse and strong in character (a standout scene: eating spoonfuls of honey while practically trading her body for a night under a miser's roof). I think this is a superb movie for its original content, exhilarating editing and Bresson's Puritanistic camera work, belt-high and wonderfully toned, that creates a deep, damp, weathered quality of centuries—old provincialism.

May 1970

◆

Oɴᴇ of the strongest images in Ozu's *The End of Summer* (1961) is the crematorium smokestack at the top of a bland, inexpressive landscape, symbolizing the end of an old rake, who sneaked a day at the bicycle races with his mistress and died of overexposure. The sinewy sturdy old man (Ganjiro Nakamura, who looks like Picasso himself with his cockiness and golden sturdy vigor) is the only rambunctious member of a very restrained, duty-conscious family— the invariable cornerstone around which Ozu constructs his pared down home drama perfections. The tactics of the long lead-in to the crematorium shot (besides the smokestack aimed at heaven, some equally sobering, numb landscapes shot nearly from sand level of two peasants washing clothes in the river, and three crows pacing very nervously, waiting for the old man's cremation, plus a few moments with the querulous, self-concerned family, impatiently put out) smacks a little of an over-obvious crossing of t's and dotting of i's.

Ozu's rigidly formalized, quaint hominess, a blend of Calvin Coolidge, Blondie, and Mies's neo-plastic esthetic, is like coming into a beautifully ordered home and being surrounded by respectful manners. It doesn't quite reach the pedestal of being "utterly Japanese," or "an unusually profound presentation of character." Simply poised linearism is probably closer to the truth. The simple-minded Jane Austen script (who's going to marry whom) shows a Fifties image of Japanese life in which there is often a bland proper face with a spectacular keyboard of gleaming white teeth. "Profound characterization" seems to be a minor concern of the director compared to that of creating a delicately poised domestic panorama and in the process making workable some of the oldest tools in movie construction. Two people standing, sitting, kneeling, always amazingly decorous, deciding whether the family's brewery will have to merge with "big capital," their conversation spaced out in one-shots of each speaker. Ozu is much more formalized than this 1930s early talkies technique suggests. Where Hawks is matter-of-fact and eye level at the two speakers, Ozu hieratically shuttles one-two-shots, the camera always on speaker, never on listener, and autocratically dismisses anything (no dolly, fades, punctuation) that smacks of movement or congestion. Ozu uses big still-life shots—the barrels outside a brewery—as chapter divisions between the little heartaches of the Kawamild family: should Number One sister marry the owner of a small steel mill? Must father embarrass his three grown daughters by renewing an early infidelity with an innkeeper?

The whole story moves towards the serene, ironic death of a lecherous father, unlike any other movie, in a kind of Morse code line. You see a little segment of family drama, then silence, followed by three shots of the brewery's wide tubs lined against a wall just outside the omnipresent doorway, which is Ozu's most consistent compositional device, and then another piece of middle-class soap opera. This scene-silence-bridging routine (sometimes wildly emotional music is played against the chapter division landscapes) repeats until the last of the three shots of black crows on a very blue-serene shore ends the graceful dot-dash parade and leaves the Ozu message: all is transitory, but the family remains.

Ozu's shorthand syntax most resembles Bresson's in his attention to the beauty of restricted movement, ritual-like repetitions, a human emphasis that is either agonized (Bresson) or sunnily benign (Ozu). This film, the September song for a cheerful old rascal, makes any Bresson seem the darkest dungeon of morbidity and sexual obsession. Lighting, theme, acting: you'd never find a row of white teeth fronting Bresson's graffiti-like shadowy imagery.

Ozu seems dedicated to that three inch doll whose head bobs up and down in the rear window of a philistine's automobile, but there's something likable, possibly profound, about these decorous, doll-like people. A hypnotic goodness pours out of restricted actors in coupled compositions.

Ozu's long career, which started in Snub Pollard-type silent comedies, never outgrows the Hal Roach idea of a movie image being naive and making you feel good. From start to finish, it's benevolence day with a family of short people who are short of every possible neurosis except an infinite capacity to sit still and grin happily at each other. Funny compositions: the two speakers are parallel rather than facing each other and they're boxed in by a vertical-horizontal order that is more emphatic than the tranquil pair. A person gets a little bored watching this family worry over its future, but, despite all the linear ploys, the use of up-down views in which there is a sense of a person looking straight ahead from a repose position on a mat, the movie stays light, airy and fresh because of its rigorous abstract style. As it travels across a nearly empty landscape of precisely poised static compositions, the film leaves no doubt of being in the hands of a masterful housekeeper who has both sympathy for his family and a deep belief in his Morse code style of moviemaking.

"You haven't got any real body, any dark sensual body of life. What you want is pornography, looking at yourself in mirrors." This frothing philosophizing causes Eleanor Bron, a fiercely self-conscious actress of smirks and mincing, to come down on Alan Bates's passionately yammering head with a lapis lazuli paperweight. This blow to kill an elephant produces the funniest response to sadism. "Oh no you don't Hermione, I don't let you," and, instead of rushing for a doctor, Bates runs straight through all kinds of Nature, thickets-turfs-clumps, pulling off his clothes, ending up in a grass-squirming act where he tries to cleanse himself of Hermione's hothouse corruption and culture mongering. Like *Isadora* and *Charge of the Light Brigade*, *Women In Love* is a lush decorator's job split between spurts of steaming, whipped-up acting and longer amorphous stuff where a whole production crew immerses itself in scene setting: a yearly picnic for mine workers jammed with choreographies, cows moving like Rockettes, and the double drowning of two young lovers—a treat for necrophiliacs (their naked bodies are discovered entwined in the mud after the lake is drained).

This sprawling period reconstruction is not as florid a production as *The Damned*, but it's in there, and much more of a multi-auteur product. The script (Larry Kramer) is carefully collaged D. H. Lawrence, the direction (Ken Russell) is an extravagant rouge job, each scene an operetta with its own private mahogany-to-hayseed yellow color, and the movie is further pushed out of whack by four actors who loom and bulk like Maillol sculptures, but have the quirky idiosyncratic faces of a Lautrec. All these people pushing the film in personal ways are really dominated by Lawrence and his apocalyptic vision. So the movie ends up like a gaudy chariot pulled by twelve furious stallions who have been nibbling on locoweed.

Lawrence wrote about restless people, of quick irritations and tenacious wills, more involved with the idea of love than the act. The exact scenes of his self-nominated "best novel" have been cheapened because they now echo a hundred films. Glenda Jackson in *Nighttown* has been rendered by conventional romanticists, Carol Reed style, with the same hulks of necking couples in chiaroscuro alleyways; two Joe Sawyer types washing themselves in their backyard watch Jackson's hard-eyed glitter pass them by, and they hit her with the same over-centered, bragging crack that might appear in Ford's *Informer* sculpture or even Richard Lester: "I'd give a week's wages for five minutes of that." Oliver Reed, the only character with enough script time to make his brute-strength-under-a-stiff-collar character halfway understandable, is in one formalized action film cliché after another, spurring blood from his horse's flanks in a race to the crossing with a freight train. Kramer's script cuts out all the quiet spots, particularly the inner thoughts and Lawrence's favorite image, the always-changing emotions of conversation.

June 1970

Introduction to
Negative Space

Sᴘᴀᴄᴇ is the most dramatic stylistic entity—from Giotto to Noland, from *Intolerance* to *Weekend*. How an artist deploys his space, seldom discussed in film criticism but already a tiresome word of the moment in other art, is anathema to newspaper editors, who believe readers die like flies at the sight of esthetic terminology.

If there were a textbook on film space, it would read: "There are several types of movie space, the three most important being: (1) the field of the screen, (2) the psychological space of the actor, and (3) the area of experience and geography that the film covers." Bresson deals in shallow composition as predictable as a monk's tonsure, whereas Godard is a stunning de Stijlist using cutout figures of American flag colors asymmetrically placed against a flat white background. The frame of *The Wild Bunch* is a window into deep, wide, rolling, Baroque space; almost every shot is a long horizontal crowded with garrulous animality.

Jeanne Moreau, always a resentful wailing wall, works in a large space, which becomes empty as she devastates it with scorn. Ida Lupino, an unforgettable drifter in a likable antique, *High Sierra* (1941), works close and guardedly to the camera, her early existentialist-heroine role held to size: she's very unglorious, has her place, and, retracting into herself, steals scenes from Bogart at his most touching. Whereas Moreau is a sensibility ember burning from beginning to movie's end—there's no specific woman inside all the emotion—and Lupino is a specific woman in a cliché pushed-around-gal role, Laurence Olivier's Archie Rice is a specific man as well as a flamboyant type. In the *Entertainer* role, which is part burlesque and part pathos, he works from small nuances of exchange with his daughter to broad gestures, while brazening his way through cheap, humiliating skirmishes with his creditors.

One curious fact about 1969 acting—Jane Fonda's jugular wisecracker silencing everybody in *They Shoot Horses, Don't They?*, Michel Bouquet's meek-murderous husband trying to hold his domestic status quo in *La Femme Infidèle*, a gentle *Black Girl* performance that goes from glee to silent misery and is very much like sleepwalking—is that it inhabits a much smaller space than the ball-room-museum-golf-course that Katherine Hepburn treats as her oyster in *Bringing up Baby*. The attitude is all different from Hepburn's egotistical-bitchy "Oh, Davids!" Both Audran (*Infidèle*) and Jane Fonda appear to own every inch of a small principality that extends about six inches to any side of their bodies, and anything else on the horizon is uncontrollable, unattainable, and therefore hardly concerns them. Where Roz Russell in *His Girl Friday* and Hepburn are swashbucklers running everyone in sight, particularly men, Audran's skillful niggling act of undulating sensuality or Fonda's stubborn life-loathing is very inside, grudging, thoughtful, always faced toward the situation—nothing escapes their suspicious cool observance. It is heroic acting, but it is also enclosed, inclement, and battle ready.

Since the days when Lauren Bacall could sweep into a totally new locale and lay claim to a shamus's sleazy office, a world in which so much can be psychically analyzed and criticized through the new complex stare technique has practically shrunk to nothing in terms of the territory in which the actor can physically prove and/or be himself. In pre-1960's acting, a Bogart could swing in indeterminate space: his selfless hurt dignity overpowered, practically ran kingdoms set up quickly, half-authentically, across the U.S., in *High Sierra*. The solid thing about Trintignant in Rohmer's *Chez Maud* is that he's incapacitated, on guard, defensive, in a sexy divorcée's threatening living room. Delphine Seyrig, an elegant blonde wife of a shoe-store owner in *Stolen Kisses*, enforces this same restricted psychology. Guarded, knowing, exact estimations are going on all the time: she's very aware where she's at, a middle-aged beauty unable to sustain a shoe-clerk's dream of her for more than an afternoon. She knows exactly how much she can commit herself.

Because it's the uniting style plus the basic look of a film, the third kind of space controls everything else—acting, pace, costume. In *La Femme Infidèle*, Chabrol's completely controlled horizontal moves—arch and languorous, picking up an insurance exec's paralyzed existence of posh domesticity—set the tone, almost blueprint the way actors eat, like a paper cutout family, the distanced politeness of their talk. *Virginia Woolf*, an American marriage of 1960, seen for all its vicious, despairing, negating features, is middle-aged academe flagellating in a big, hollow, theatrical space. The George-Martha shenanigans, hokey and virulent, are designed, grand-opera-style, as though the curtain were going up or down on every declamation. *In a Lonely Place*, a 1950 Nick Ray, is a Hollywood scene at its most lackluster, toned down, limpid, with Ray's keynote strangeness: a sprawling, unbent composition with somewhat dwarfed characters, each going his own way. A conventional studio movie but very nice: Ray stages everything, in scenes heavily involved with rules of behavior, like a bridge game amongst good friends, no apparent sweat. A sad piece of puff pastry, Demy's *Model Shop* (1969) comes together in a lazy open space: overblown, no proportions, skittering, indulgent. The scene is an absolutely transient one—drive-in bank, rock and roll group, J. C. Penney houses—that saunters lackadaisically in the most formless imagery. *The Round Up* (1966), a stark overhead lighting from beginning to end, geometric shadows, hard peasant faces, stiff coats, big sculpture hats, is a movie of hieratic stylized movement in a Kafka space that is mostly sinister flatness and bald verticals. Sometimes there is violent action, but Jancso's fascinating, but too insistent, style is based on a taut balance between a harsh, stark imagery and a desolate pessimism. In all the movies mentioned here, the space is most absolutely controlled, given over to rigidly patterned male groups.

The emphasis being given to space by today's leading directors forces a look backward at what has been done in movie space. In *What Price Glory?* (1926), space is used innocently for illustrational purposes, which is not to say that it isn't used well. Raoul Walsh's film is still an air-filled, lyrical masterpiece: the haphazard, unprecious careers of two blustery rivals who swagger around trench and village exquisitely scaled in human terms to the frame of the screen, suggesting, in their unhesitating grace, the sweet-tough-earthy feeling that is a Walsh trademark. This is a very early example of Walsh's special aptitude, getting people from place to place gracefully, giving an enchantment to bistro or barracks through repetitions in which the engineering slightly alters each trip, jump-cutting his movie into and out of events with unabashed shorthand and beautiful detail.

Whereas Walsh bends atmosphere, changes camera, singles out changes in viewpoint to give a deeper reaction to specific places, *The Big Sleep* (1948) ignores all the conventions of a gangster film to feast on meaningless business and witty asides. Walsh keeps re-establishing the same cabin retreat; Hawks, in another spatial gem, gives the spectator *just enough* to make the scene work. One of the fine moments in 1940's film is no longer than a blink: Bogart, as he crosses the street from one bookstore to another, looks up at a sign. There is as much charm here as Walsh manages with fifteen different positioning setups between Lupino and Arthur Kennedy in a motel cabin. All the unbelievable events in *The Big Sleep* are tied together by miserable time jumps, but, within each skit, there is a logic of space, a great idea of personality, gesture, where each person is. Bogart's sticking shirt and brain-twisting in front of a princely colonel, which seems to have present-tense quality, is typically out of touch with other events and probably dropped into its slot from a facetious memory of Faulkner.

Touch of Evil (1958) is about many things: murder, gang rape (an American blonde marries a Mexican attorney, and all her fears about Mexicans come true), a diabolic sheriff, and a dozen other repellent figures. Basically it's a movie about terrorizing, an evil-smelling good movie in which the wildly Baroque terror and menace is another world from Hawks-Walsh: an aggressive-dynamic-robust-excessive-silly universe with Welles's career-long theme (the corruption of the not-so-innocent Everyman through wealth and power) and his inevitable efforts with space—to make it prismatic and a quagmire at the same time. Welles's storm tunnel has always the sense of a black prankster in control of the melodrama, using a low-angle camera, quack types as repulsive as Fellini's, and high-contrast night light to create a dank, shadowy, nightmare space.

Basically the best movie of Welles's cruddy middle peak period—when he created more designed, less-dependent-on-Hollywood films (*Arkadin*, *Lady from Shanghai*)—*Touch of Evil* is a sexual allegory, the haves and have-nots, in which the disorienting space is worked for character rather than geography. An amazing film, the endless bits of excruciating black humor are mostly involved with illogical space and movement, pointing up some case of impotence or occasionally its opposite. A young Mexican lawyer jumps around jack-rabbit fashion while a toadlike sheriff floats away in grease; a whacky episode has the lawyer stuffing an elevator with old colleagues while he zips up the stairs ("Well, Vargas, you're pretty light on your feet"). The funniest scenes, spatially, revolve around a great comic grotesque played by Dennis Weaver, a motel night man messed up with tics who is last seen clinging to a leafless tree, and, before that, doing woodpecker spastic effects at the sight and thought of Janet Leigh on a motel bed.

His allegorical space is a mixture of tricks, disorientation, falling apart, grotesque portraits. A deaf-mute grocery clerk squints in the foreground, while Charlton Heston, on the phone, embarrassed over his wife's eroticism from a motel bed, tries to suggest nonchalance to the store owner. A five-minute street panorama develops logically behind the credits, without one cut, just to arrive at a spectacular reverse zoom away from a bombed Cadillac. Just before the car goes up in fire, the car's blonde has given a customs agent one of those black speeches that dislocate themselves from the image: "I've got this ticking noise in my head."

Those who blew their cool in the 1960's were shipwrecked on spatial problems, among other things. So much is possible or acceptable in photography-acting-writing now that films expand with flashy camera work, jazzy heat flutters, syrupy folk music, different projection speeds, and a laxity about the final form that any scene takes. *The Gypsy Moths*; *Goodbye, Columbus*; *The Arrangement*; *The Swimmer*; *The Graduate*; *Pretty Poison* are caked with glamour mechanisms.

Winning and Polonsky's *Willie Boy* seem the perfect examples; the former an auto-racing film with no action, but inflated with slow motion, slight and oblique acting, a leaky savvy about marital dalliance, and the latter a racial Western with affected photography and ambiguous motivation. Though there is smugness, neither film comes to a head, because of the vague, approximate way in which events are shown, the confusion about being spatially sophisticated.

Polonsky's invective against the crushing of the Paiutes, a disappointing but hardly loathsome movie, loses itself behind the unwieldiness of the very wide scenes. There's a fiesta going on at Willie's reservation, and the point of any shot is gracefully ignored while a lyrical snowstorm of camera shots occurs. In a scene of big heads and upper torsos, an interesting crowd of Indians are involved in something interesting, but what is seen is tinted coloring and Willie, a heavy jerky wave moving through a crowd of shoulders and hats. Seen between two of the sententiously parted shoulders is Willie's Lola, an ambiguous solitary gardenia in an otherwise maidenless tribe. The movie implies no Indians can act: Katharine Ross is the only Paiute maid, and the only actual Indians are bit players.

A film cannot exist outside of its spatial form. Everything in a good movie is of a piece: Joe Calleia, scared out of his wits, is a grey little bureaucrat fitted perfectly into *Touch of Evil* with the sinister lighting and tilted scenes in which he's found, buglike at the end of hallways and rooms. Godard doesn't start a project until it is very defined in its use of space: *La Chinoise* is an indoor picture with primary colors to look like Maoist posters and stiltlike, declamatory actors to go with a didactic message. Space seems so dramatic and variable in *Weekend* (1968); this exciting shake-up movie is made up in progressive segments, each one having a different stylistic format, from the fixed camera close-up of a comic-porno episode (". . . and then she sat in a saucer of milk . . .") through the very Hawkslike eye-level dollying past a bumper-to-bumper tie-up on the highway, to the Hudson River pastoralism at the end, when Godard clinches his idea of a degenerate, cannibalistic society and a formless, falling-apart culture. At least half the moviemakers are oblivious to the space excitement that is front-center in *Weekend*; the other half are flying off in all directions.

It's very exciting to see the stylistic unity that goes into *Weekend* or *Fellini*

Satyricon, where a stubborn artist is totally committed to bringing an idea together with an image. After a whole year of varied films, it's pertinent that *Weekend* seems to increase in resonance. These hopped-up nuts wandering in an Everglades, drumming along the Mohawk, something about *Light in August*, a funny section where Anne Wiazemsky is just sitting in grass, thumb in mouth, reading a book. Compared to the podium-locked image of *They Shoot Horses*, *Weekend* is a rambling mystery not unlike the long, knotted tail swirling under an old dime-store kite.

What does one get from the vast sprawl of film reviewed in this book? That the spatial threads seamlessly knit together for the illustrative naturalism that serviced Keaton's *Navigator* through *Red River* simply broke apart. When the 1960's directors became fascinated with the formal excitements that could be gotten through manipulation of space, each film became a singleminded excavation in a particular type of space. Pasolini, in *Teorema*, places the figure as though it were sculpture in deep space. His movie becomes an ecstatic, mystical, hortatory use of mid-anatomy: Terence Stamp, languid silence and superior smile, his crotch exposed in tight, spiffy jeans, exuding compassion for all the flipping-out individuals around him. From *Breathless* through *Teorema*, the path is strewn with singularized vocabulary. *L'Avventura* is like a long serpentine through desolate environments: the human figure isolated, posing in a vast, anonymous, sinister space. Godard's career, a movie-by-movie exploration of one image or another, always involves a philosophical proposition matched by a pictorial concept, i.e., an unraveled bleak image serves as a metaphor for the brutalizing, rag-tag conditions of war.

Most of what follows involves a struggle to remain faithful to the transitory, multisuggestive complication of a movie image and/or negative space. Negative space, the command of experience which an artist can set resonating within a film, is a sense of terrain created partly by the audience's imagination and partly by camera-actors-director: in *Alexander Nevsky* the feeling of endless, glacial landscape formed by glimpses of frozen flatness expanded by the emotional interplay of huge-seeming people. Negative space assumes the director testing himself as an intelligence against what appears on screen, so that there is a murmur of poetic action enlarging the terrain of the film, giving the scene an extra-objective breadth. It has to do with flux, movement, and air; always the sense of an artist knowing where he's at: a movie filled with negative space is always a textural work throbbing with acuity.

Criticism can subjugate the bestiality of the screen image by breaking it down into arbitrary but easily managed elements—acting, story logic, reasonableness, the identifiable touches of a director—that bring the movie within the doctoring talents of the critic. Suggesting where a film went wrong and how it could have had the logic of an old-style novel or theater piece seems a pedantic occupation compared to the activity in modern film, which suggests a thousand Dick Cantino accordionists in frenetic action, heaving and hawling, contracting and expanding. Because the space in film has been wildly and ingenuously singularized into cool (*Judex*), charted (*Rio Grande*), schematized (*Pickpocket*), jagged (*M*), or graceful (Satyajit Ray's *Two Daughters*), it doesn't seem right that the areas for criticism should be given over so completely to measuring.

Most of what I liked is in the termite area. The important trait of termite-fungus-centipede art is an ambulatory creation which is an act both of observing and being in the world, a journeying in which the artist seems to be ingesting both the material of his art and the outside world through a horizontal coverage. The Senegalese *Black Girl* is a series of spiritual odysseys: through a kitchen; a ceremonial procedure before the bathtub suicide; a small boy, holding an African mask over his face, following his sister's employer across Dakar; in which the imagination of Ousmane Sembene appears to be covering all the ground that his experience can encompass. *La Femme Infidèle* is often antitermite in its backward idolatry of the Hitchcock murder plot and old-movie formulas for showing cuckoldry, lustfulness, the way a sheet-wrapped body sinks in pod-covered water. Aside from its central murder-cops plotting, the movie is quite different when the material gets into straight business-living and the acting, Chabrol's strong suit in this film, becomes mobile, whether anyone's moving or not, charged with watchfulness, frankness, purity. The measured flow that Chabrol has perfected—a world of forms observed, acts performed without flubs or awkwardness—is hypnotic, suggesting the tension of an embarrassed subordinate saying yes-sir-no-sir, getting his drama through the pasty, worried heaviness of an unblinking face.

It is not likely that any esthetic system can enclose all the art ever made—fetishistic, religious, decorative, children's, absurdist, primitive. Why even invent two such categories: white elephant and termite, one tied to the realm of celebrity and affluence and the other burrowing into the nether world of privacy? The primary reason for the two categories is that all the directors I like—Fuller's *art brut* styling; Chuck Jones's *Roadrunners*; the inclement charm Godard gets with drizzly weather, the Paris outskirts, and three nuts scurrying around the same overcast *Band of Outsiders* terrain—are in the termite range, and no one speaks about them for the qualities I like.

1971

Raoul Walsh

OFTEN during the heyday of the Zanuck-Cohn-Mayer studio warlords, metaphorical approximations of the studio setup appeared in film after film. In the depression highlife movies—*Holiday* and *Easy Living*—the studio is a corpulent rich man's silvery baroque mansion, the studio employees are a giddy loquacious parasitic family that chews up his wallet. In the *Shane–Red River* mythic westerns a cattle baron, chairbound Ryker or Tom Dumbson, functions as though he's running a movie studio by driving men and cattle into broken-willed obedience. Half of the Capra-Sturges library is involved with family-town-legislature made up of two-faced Edward Arnold smoothies or bombastic bosses, notable in Sturges for incompetence and pudgy cheeks, who mislead a population of angling gullible eccentrics. Raoul Walsh is one of the most enigmatic directors to unconsciously play around with this metaphor about the sick compromising situation of working inside a big studio monolith. In Walsh's world there's no omnipotent kingpin character, but the bustling studio environment is recreated in a script that moves around a lot through rooms, cars, streets.

Unlike the evangelistic hymns or hums in which a Shane, Congressman Smith, or Matthew Garth acts as a savior figure, standing for the director, who frees the prisoners from the institutional behavior, Mad Dog Earle and his director are ostriches with their heads buried deep inside the System; they'll never "crash out." This director never walshes out, but stays inside a disingenuous script, accepts the inflexible requirement of at least three big stars acting out a measly story, also the stable of boisterous, bathetic, Irish Soul bit players (Frank McHugh, Hale, Bond, Arthur Shields, Joe Sawyer) who appear the same debilitating way every Walsh picture, and the all-purpose Warners backlot, like Nervi trying to reach the sky, with mysterious, all-white, slanted abutments, which could be a brewery, Nazi munitions factory, chemical plant, or penitentiary wall.

Reflecting the suffocating, man-under-a-toadstool relationship with Warners, he uses family-institutional-industrial frameworks for his stories, emphasizes the burden of team responsibility and loyalty, tightly frames the space covered by plucky, full-bodied actors. The meat-and-potatoes of a Walsh film is the sense of a busy day at the factory, where the workers hustle this way and that as in a Walsh scene in a prison jute mill, a sweatshop place which would madden an Upton Sinclair: the frenetic, boxed-in crisscrossing of paths and the corrupt clamor, hellish Hale of prol types.

Safe, trend-conscious producers (Hal Wallis, Robert Buckner) wouldn't dream of hiring Walsh to handle their prized Oscar-race entries, metaphysical bog-raphy (*The Story of Louis Pasteurized, Juarez*) starring Paul Money. Walsh, a Peter Pan perpetual boy scout, did unsophisticated, boyish, swaggering movies for six decades. Well within Walsh's sweet-natured, high schoolish value system are the poignant, just buddies, untactile relationships (co-workers, the *Strawberry Blonde* dentist and his father), enduring love for a wholesome icon family, the neighborhood conceived as a family unit, lead characters played as Dandies (the *Strawberry Blonde* dentist loves the town beauty for her style; Gentleman Jim Corbett has a lustful admiration for the upper-class elegance and style of the Olympic Club and its members; Danny Dolan has an aspiration for stylish garments, the right hats). A possible MOMA retrospective of boyish Hog Walsh: Cagney, strangely soothed and thoughtful as though he's just read James Joyce for the first time, returning from the dark woods where he's been quietly communing with his deceased mother: "I liked it out there. M-m [savoring the memory of it]. Nice feeling out there talking to Ma." A mad-dog killer returning to his mountain hideaway to find his two punkish assistants have had a silly spat; one is hiding sheepishly in the woods, the other is barricaded inside a cabin. Edward G. Robinson performing an aerial act amidst live electric wires, plummeting 30 feet to the ground through sparkling electrical jolts, dying in his buddy's arms with the final comment, "I was out of line, way out of line."

A miniaturized, shrunken version of Walsh's "little big shot" position in the studio caste system might be any of the following handymen: Earl Morrall, Don Knotts, Howard Cosell, Hubert Humphrey. Like the dancing, caroming scrappers who populate his movies, Walsh moved around a lot, spiking any sick-slow scene the studio had, while turning out a preposterously prolific number of his own films per year. *The Roaring Twenties*—a young man who distinguishes himself in war trenches comes home to unemployment and a boot-legging career—follows predictable plot patterns but is acted-directed in such a feisty, snub-nosed, tight-britches fashion that it occasionally soars. *High Sierra*, a half-likable struggle between the dated, moralistic Burnett-Huston script and Walsh's dry burning touch with Lupino, a cunningly aged, tired Bogart and a squashed, bedridden Donald MacBride who springs Bogart from the pen for one last caper, annoyingly jumps back and forth between the gangster's loathsome partners in crime and a white picket fence area inhabited by mawkishly played Steinbeckian Okies. It's somewhat like a Brueghel (the over-populated scene has some deadly stereotypes including a jinx mechanical Hugh Herbertish pooch, environmental sweep, and a slow, non-shortcut type of detailing) but Walsh's environmental imagination is countered by the heavy moves that the script makes. *White Heat* is an alternation of one spectacular Cagney scene for every dud involving Ed O'Brien's sloppy telegraphed reactions, especially for a gang infiltrator whose specialty is nerveless conning. Walsh goes to sleep when he handles Decency, the wooden lawyer who works for the DA's office in *Roaring Twenties*, the four bland T-men tendrils in *White Heat* who possess one remarkable idiosyncracy, a baton-like cigarette holder, the banker stiffs in *Gentleman Jim*, colorless insipid blonde who jilts Cagney in *Roaring Twenties*, Ward Bond's inflated chest and mustache chewing as John L. Sullivan ("I can lick any man in the world"). *Gentleman Jim*, a distinguished singularity in movies, is a non-pious-pedantic biography in which Errol Flynn's mocking overconfidence is cleverly employed in the role of a shameless social climber who maddeningly maintains poise and balance through endless rowdy Irish family bashes and heavyweight bouts.

Why dig up this "great action director" whose enormous progeny includes such clunkers as *Saskatchewan*, *Distant Trumpet*, whole scenes devoted to the art of spitting and to an obscenely acted, scene-hogging drunk, whole films carbonated with ironic bawdy jokers or miserably maudlin weepers? It's a rank understatement to say that Walsh's personality has never been properly identified. Either he is lauded as a pure, uninhibited pagan who found formula action stories to be an ideal, uncompromising framework in which to celebrate the spirit of adventure, or else he is rudely put down as an unworthy, featureless assemblyman of invariable Warners pulp. Actually Walsh is at his most stale stereotyped when he handles compulsory action-adventure situations, whereas his position deep within the studio served to inspire his treatment of earthy, bread-and-butter human conditions, where the spirit as well as the body is yoked, burdened, slack, unassertive.

Walsh deserves to be re-seen through a modern looking glass, but to dissolve the studio influence from any discussion of his films leaves him a fantasy figure of this or that rating system, dated, easily read. It's easy today to rate Sturges as a stinging satirist of American myths by ignoring the image's desperate pushing and shoving and constrictedness. Hawks's films can be read as moral tales of danger-defying professionals only by deleting the studio conditions which appear visually as cliquish characters enjoying a pampered security and insulation. Walsh's stagnant, no-promotions role as a Warners factory hand led him inevitably to undercut purportedly Good Thoughts (pro-family, pro-working crew, pro-fidelity and trust) with homely congestion and bitter dailiness. He insists on keeping people away from the center of the event, using endless plays for separating two pals or a married couple, increasing loneliness, the feeling of doom, so that hope is sucked out of the character. Walsh's inclusion of scenes of daily human pathetique should separate him immediately from American mooring, and especially from the action specialists, Hawks, Farrow, Curtiz, with whom he's usually classed. A good director of homeliness, innocence, vulnerability, Walsh can be amazingly direct, forthright, clear, rhythmic, a dedicated-to-folk cousin of Renoir's *Toni*, Vigo's *L'Atalante*, Brassaï's street-life photographs, with more brisk jocularity than his French counterparts.

Manpower, about emergency repairmen who work on high-voltage power lines in ferocious pseudo storms, is a very strange somber movie. The sadness of its triangle lovers, scenes of the most homely daily order, the amount of material on sexual ignorance, impotence, and hysteria make this a primitive movie with subtle directing. A convict's first day out of prison is usually a number one stumble in movies (e.g., the *High Sierra* opening with the prissy editorializing in Huston's script: one contrived, structured, informative fact after another about the rediscovered wonders of fresh air, sunlight, park foliage, plus a stray newspaper with the convict's public enemy face punctured in the left nostril by a trash collector's pedantic paper-sticker). In the feverish *Manpower*, the First Moment Out, acted awesomely straight by the least statuesque Marlene Dietrich, takes a surprising, abrupt right-angle turn to a little local drugstore, very quiet and sidestreet drab; the ex-girl-con says "Stop here" and she heads with a fierce resolve to the cosmetic counter, where she buys cream-lipstick mascara and defiantly paints away while Raft glowers his once-a-tramp-always-a-tramp philosophy.

Both this scene and one in Honeymoon kitchen are photographed-acted with a great chasm of tension between a man and woman. Walsh is always angling out of a familiar movie situation by doubling and tripling the environments and splitting the people apart with terrifying, unmodified Pathos. Robinson, drunk and passed out on his wedding night, wakes up and panics when his wife's not in bed the next morning. This is a cliché image, but Walsh then travels into hopeless disparity of man and wife. He layers misery—the deepest naive optimism of a husband, a wife's despairing realization of not hitting the Marital Jackpot in any sense—into unglamorized scenery. Robinson's beer joint hostess wife is in the kitchen whipping biscuits from scratch. Robinson's ecstasy is funny—pathetic: "Did you make these?" then rushing off to show his crew the biscuits, the proof of his wife's true-blueness. ("Fay, my wife, made these, the best biscuits you'll ever eat.") In *Roaring Twenties*, Cagney takes a show-biz beginner home on the last train to New Rochelle. It's probably one of the best familiarizing locale scenes; it is so strict, clean, shrewd about positioning people and camera. The cunning—a quiet intimate first date zeroed in from the end of a train car over the head of a passed-out drunk—is in doubling the pathos and humor of a scene that is instantly stationary and enclosed.

Walsh seems inspired primarily when poeticizing a glum, unsunny, lower-middle-class milieu that's miles from the graceful, dauntless life-styles pictured in expensive, expansive, dream-factory fabrications by Cukor, Wyler, or Hitchcock. Pinball machines and cigarette smog provide essential atmospheric details for an unbuttoned society with no prohibitive admission requirements —grace, wit, or effervescence—where the typical man's outfit includes a tight-fitting hat with a narrow turned-up brim and a zip-up waist-length jacket that makes the wearer look chubby or puffed. A director whose feel for small-time, scrappy wage earners possibly came from his own cooperative, energetic function in the movie industry, Walsh made a mistake when he misread his own strengths (he was insistently touted as a flexible master of swift-moving adventure epics) and abandoned stagnant, suspended scenes of truckers resting up at an all-night roadside café before tackling the next leg of the truck route, of a bedraggled dame (Gladys George) consoling a deposed rackets chief mourning his lowered status over beer after beer, of the petty, racy banter passed around with waitresses, chorus girls, and hat-checkers. His later movies tend to look like *Captain Horatio Hornblower*: stiff swashbuckler costumes pushing a sweeping, episodic narrative, glued together with look-alike shots of handsome vessels plowing like logs through the water.

The great traffic cop of movies, keeping things moving, hustling actors around an intersection-like screen that's generally empty in the center, Walsh's style is based on traveling over routes which are sometimes accomplished by bodily movement, the passage that a gaze takes, suggested or actually shown, and the movement of a line of dialogue, the route indicated by a gesture. The fact that spitting is often used in very early Walsh suggests how important Paths figure in his syntax. Birthed in films as a Griffith actor and the director of Fairbanks films, his no-shortcut style is steeped in the silent film necessity for excessive, frantic visual explication, taking nothing for granted.

The usual route for Walsh is to slow the development by increasing specificity. It is very cunning: by the time his gangster comes apart, is shot down, or shoots his way through an ambush, Walsh has slyly doubled and tripled every move that the gangster makes in terms of height, texture, path, angle, and sound. Cagney's psychotic break in the penitentiary dining hall involves a messy noisy tantrum after he hears his beloved Ma has been gunned down. Every move Cagney makes has been counterpointed and varied. His incredible frenzy literally swimming through cutlery and china down the length of a table has twice been anticipated with a slow camera dolly down the table and back, picking out each diner who gets splashed and shocked by Cagney's tantrum crawl across the table. Cagney's running battle through a half-dozen guards spaced at crucial spots around the hall has been anticipated by a quiet over-the-hall long shot as the prisoners file in and angle off into the various aisles. The battle itself is frenzy improvised with perfect Cagney instincts: characteristically it is a mesh of variations on pace and height, ending with Cagney being carried by the guards down the aisles and out the hall, above their heads like a frantically struggling fish on a tray.

The melancholic fact about this natural, unsophisticated humanist is that he is often alone in playing straight rather than cynical (Hawks), surrealistic (Farrow), or patronizing (Huston) with genre material. Walsh, who wrote some scripts as bald copies of hit films he directed, and probably entered each new project with "Christ, it's not bad. It reminds me of my last movie," never fights his material, playing directly into the staleness. He is like his volatile, instinctive, not-too-smart characters, who, when they are at their most genuine, are unreclaimable, terrifying loners, perhaps past their peak and going nowhere.

In 1931, he directed his best film, *Me and My Gal*, an unpredictable jauntiness built around a dubious theme: "Life is sunny, if you don't stir it up." A suspended moment of grace for Walsh and Tracy, when newness and budding maturity were clicking for them, Tracy banters back and forth over a beanery cash register with a Harlow-ish sass machine (Joan Bennett): "Haven't I seen you someplace?" Packing flaunty and insolent earthiness into a challenging act, Miss Bennett's waitress answers: "Maybe, I've been someplace." This did-I-hear-right crack, early vaudeville style, is fleshed out with typical Walsh-engineered acting: mock documentary—full bodies in full space—that sifts into material that is innocent, anachronistic, quietly amoral. Despite the inevitable expectoration, truculent drunk, talentless slapstick, this primitive oh-you-kid effervescence is inspiring for its balmy innocent actors: J. Farrell MacDonald, as an Irish father whose leering-winking face, in screen-filling close-ups, comes off as blunt Godard put-on commentating; Bennett, the least lockjawed and haughty version, as a slinky, don't push me around toughie, chewing gum ("You're a pretty tough Beezock; why don't you park that gum?"); the youngest, most buoyant Tracy usually freeloading off someone's table, combining outrageous swagger with a self-mocking he enjoys to the hilt. His favorite move: he pushes out his cheek with his tongue, does a pleasantly sociable leer, mouths an automatic sarcasm, "Let me see if you have a hat fit for a detective," that hardly parts his lips.

It is only fleetingly a gangster film, not quite outrightly comic: it is really a portrait of a neighborhood, the feeling of human bonds in a guileless community, a lyrical approximation of Lower East Side and its uneducated, spirited stevedore-clerk-shopkeeper cast. There is psychological rightness in the scale relationships of actors to locale, and this, coupled with liberated acting, make an exhilarating poetry about a brash-cocky-exuberant provincial. Walsh, in this lunatically original, festive dance, is nothing less than a poet of the American immigrant. Certain scenes—the hoods trying to trick a passionate vulnerable sister into intoxication and collusion on a bank job; a clandestine embrace in a drab narrow hallway; a fabulously arrogant bank heist that starts from an over-the-bank living room; a joyfully fresh prelim to courtship on a parlor sofa that includes Bennett's provocative swaggering dance from sofa to victrola—are terrifying exposures for the actors. Bennett's provocative room-crossing is that of a snake, half-falling apart, trying to ambulate a room vertically and nonchalantly.

The movie has a double nature, looking exactly like 1931 just after the invention of sound, and one that has queer passages that pop out of the story line, foreshadowing the technical effects of '60s films. These quirky inclusions, the unconscious oddities of a director with an unquestioning belief in genre who keeps breaking out of its boundaries, seem timeless and suggest a five-cent movie with mysterious depth. A crowd of neighbors swilling unbelievable amounts of food, a big sea captain, rhino face and figure, eating whole herrings in one gulp, are less contrived versions of the expressionism in *Leo the Last, The Servant, Goodbye Columbus*. "That's my son-in-law Eddy; he's a nice lad even though he does look like a runaway horse." This dark comedy scoff is backed up with shots of a shockingly homely, foolishly grinning simpleton, a total butt of the family's jokes.

If hardwares sold a house paint called Gusto, the number one customer would be Walsh: six decades in film using a jabbing, forthright crispness to occasionally vitalize the crudest hack fiction.

November 1971

The Venice Film Festival

THE great octopus, the Venice Film Festival, whose tentacles pull in every film except the Baillie-Gehr-Snow structuralism, which is just too radical, takes place in a building as bland and depressingly familiar as Volker Schlondorff's *Strohfeuer*. Neither the film palace nor the film (a young woman's bid for freedom from her marital grind, but Schlondorff doesn't give her a fighting chance) has a hint of Venice's eccentric grandeur. There's nothing Italian about the brand new two-story mausoleum which has to be perked up with massive free-standing bouquets of gladiolas (visiting sex bombs like Gina Lowbridge are posed in front of these bouquets) and Don Jose cops with swords that start under the armpits and reach the ankles. That's metal-clanking nonsense: the only crime in the city is committed inside on multiple screens in works like Samy Pavel's narcistic drivel *Les deux saisons de la vie*, and Carmelo Bene's intensely vulgar free form adaptation of the Oscar Wilde play *Salomè*, clearly the two dogs of the festival; the two directors also starred without reservations in their films as versions of Jesus Christ. One of the bewildering charms of any festival is that some revered critics, Dilys Powell for *Les deux saisons* and John Francis Lane for the Bené color spin with flashing nude behinds, will champion the flagrant pretenses; immediately someone else comes up with "What an abomination, don't you agree?" A person keeps running into the same two types: a bus-crash of commuters going all of eight blocks, every other one Alain Delon or Catherine Deneuve, a teenager's slender body in skinlike garments that are spotless, wrinkleless, perfect. The second most common face at Venice is a hard working maestro who runs a similar festival in Trieste-Sydney-Chicago, spends every year on an unenviable festival grind, partaking of "hospitality": plane fare, plus bed and breakfast at a stripped down Edwardian spa.

Like the Whitney Annual and its arbitrariness, the festival is a pointless hodgepodge, mostly box office films; a stalled adolescent film, in which a supercilious ambulance assistant roams around the city, moving between his separate lives as dutiful son and secret father (*Mein lieber Robinson*: pleasant, lackadaisical, and low key); a recall movie in which a massively sensitive lover goes into his past to piece together his identity (*Sindbad*); or a tourist sensibility film that combines postcard camera expertise with bicycles and the first day in an exotic turreted city (*Klara Lust*). A lot of sincerity seeking and professionalism goes into a single person's private experience of the world, but just a murmur comes out.

It's a drag to write about mediocre movies. *Sindbad* (Zoltan Huszarik), the penultimate of lush turn-of-the-century reminiscing, suggests fat rich soups. *The Ragman's Daughter* (written by Alan Sillitoe, directed by Harold Becker) is an established way to make a film less flexible and fresh than its Billy Liar-Saturday Night progenitors. It's the Nottingham ash can school, castrated by a stupid, incongruous Truffaut love affair, daring pranks, and unbelievable law breaking for kicks. Nothing rings true about the small-time Bonnie and Clyde pair, especially the white horse and long blonde hair on a stilted actress,

Victoria Tennant. But the hero grown-up and his wife are acted well with grit and the movie itself is closely knit and holds the eyes. *The Harder They Come* (Perry Henzell) is the first line of a hit tune sung by an ambitious Jamaican from the country (the very agile Jimmy Cliff), a classic rise and fall from choir boy to pop singer-pusher-killer-public-idol-bullet-riddled corpse. The movie has snappy pace and a thousand disparate views of Jimmy Cliff's antelopelike, long-limbed swagger as he makes his zap zap way through the underworld, always sinned against in a funny newsreel shot in which the camera illogically goes anywhere to get a smashing focus on the hero. Cinderella as a jive killer, everyone a corrupt citizen fleecing his neighbor, and the main corruption being a cute camera. It's fun to watch, which Ken Russell's *Savage Messiah* isn't. Deadly arabesques.

Searching for scraps of surprising art in the white warehouse, a critic can feel as unnecessary, shunted to the side, as the small, hunched Venice cat with his absorbed, haunted gazing, a remnant looking for a remnant pizza crust. The hodgepodge here is about one third of the film spray shown in the modern, blocky building which houses five or six theaters, featurelessly impersonal despite the human Sala Dreyer, Sala Volpi titles. An antifestival, supposedly the operation of more advanced, leftist Bellochio-Bertolucci directors runs concurrently several canals away in two unrepaired 18th-century cockpits. Lit by two yellow bulbs, the interior shaped like a dilapidated three-tier wedding cake, filled with cigarette smoke and fierce, irreverent customers armed with coke-cigarettes-comments, the Moderno and Margaritta twins are next door to Manhattan's Thalia for mad singularity and setting up obstacles between the spectator and screen. How incongruous are the sleek cult films, *La Cagna* and *La notte dei fiore*, with glamour stars in full St. Laurent couture, in these abandoned, pockmarked remnants of austere regality.

It is hard to convey the layered experience which is the Venice Festival: a German film about a tempestuous Goya, played by an actor in bronze pancake, dubbed with Italian voices, possessing French subtitles, engineered in the polished rococo kitsch of a Tijuana iron-leather shop; a press conference moderated by an expatriated, slightly worn Henry James type, awkwardly translated into three languages by the Swiss director of a paralyzed Dracula film, the main speaker being a Munich *enfant terrible* whose mock boredom permits only a snide yes or no to long questions, or an occasional "Why are the Venice press conferences so boring? I have beautiful conferences other places."

Feeling humiliated, like Bresson's enduring donkey harnessed to a fruit cart, a henpecked boob beats up his wife in a bedroom tableau which stays on screen without camera change until the remorseless ending, the husband rolling over in a drunken stupor. The agonized, frustrated drunk beating up his selfish, penny-pinching wife is the oldest scene in movies, going back to *Greed*, but this fully lit futile explosion in a 1971 Munich movie is a remarkable blend of charm and ferocity. Aimed against prissy, middle-class taste, the purple overstatements of *Written on the Wind* and *Splendor in the Grass*, the camera work (straight recording), lighting (shadowless, very bright), and sound (the film has no musical score) stay cool on a melodramatic scene: a grunting husband beating up the screaming, flailing wife while their golden-haired tot tries to separate them. In movies of marital angst, the camera inevitably milks facial reactions; here the removed camera stays quiet and what's recorded are three figures intermeshed around a narrow bed, their awkwardness, and the out-of-control momentum. Anyone should look clumsy being beaten and this movie doesn't welch on dreary but touching gracelessness: the wife's legs thrashing in the air with a brazen vulnerable exposure of her crotch in spotlessly clean cotton underpants. (The whole film, with scenes juxtaposing hygienic neatness with raw physicality, expresses a droll, whiplashing temperament.)

After five days at the Venice Film Festival, Rainer Werner Fassbinder's *Der Handler der Vierjahreszeiten* is the single antidote to thoughts of suicide in the Grand Canal. It's a supersimple fable about bourgeois defeat, the awkward despair of a chunky fruit peddler, for whom events move too quickly to grasp, told in panellike tableaux of similar length. Hans Epp (Hans Hirschmuller, one of the festival's most pungent actors) is seen as a victim in a modern Matisse image of four orchard-fresh colors. He is Sturges' bumbling, well-meaning conquering hero at the mercy of others' machinations (these standing for the middle-class status quo), given no relief from miserable frustration in an intense shadowless image that's miles more personal than Sturges'. Where the 1940s' Sturges is sexless and censors out mean details, Fassbinder adds a lot of unpleasantness, frankness about the body (like Warhol, all shapes and sizes are given their due as sexual creatures), and petty shopkeeper's ambition to a fable of drudgery with no end in view. Deliberately giving a primitive innocent turn to the peddler's stubborn retreat from the venal ambitions that surround him, Fassbinder makes a wholesome frontal image in many ways like small Fra Angelico panels: a man in a crisp blue and white plaid shirt hawking the pale green pears filling a rectangular cart, a humble action frozen in a shallow-still composition.

Like a cat burglar feeling out the combination lock on a safe, Fassbinder keeps turning the knob on a character, working parsimoniousness with lustfulness in the same pinch-lipped housefrau (Irm Hermann), compassion and coldblooded frankness in a marvelous sister (Hanna Schygulla) who sticks by the peddler against his disapproving family and stands for integrity in the film.

The clear individualizing and silhouetting of each character are emblematic of Fassbinder's tough decision-making about style. His intense, shadowless image is disarming: though the story is about a fruit pushcart and its discontented couple, there are no shadows, dirt, or squalidness anywhere. To see the spinster-wife's transformation in mid-movie is never to forget it: she has been straight hypocrisy and stinginess, but, after crucifying her inept Epp husband into the hospital, there is a jump cut that has incredible impact. She turns up with a stranger in one of the most robustly staged sex acts in film: a woman who had heretofore been all tightness is suddenly exposed in all her white length, abandoned to pleasure. Blatantly head-on sex with no coy-tease covering up sections of the body: as in the fight scene, the blunt impact comes from the impersonal lighting and head-on camera (imagine this scene in the Turkish bath lighting of *The Godfather*). An unmistakable decorative modernity and human savagery are gained through anti-sentimental cunning working inside the oldest kitsch narrative.

Fassbinder's American neighbor is obviously the Warhol of *Bike Boy*, *Chelsea Girls*. There is the same painterly ability to hit innocent, insolent colors, using flat, boldly simple formats; Warhol's image is more porous, coarse grained, while Fassbinder's has a sardonic fairy tale look. The Tartar-faced writer-director has done five films in 1971, which is up to the early Warhol pace, and, in the background of Fassbinder's image, there is the sense of grifters and bootlegging, plus the effect in early Warhol of being tough and able to control such anarchy. Probably the most important revelation is that Warhol innocence needn't be unraveled at the edges: Fassbinder's Marxist world unchained is compressed and delineated; you know where each form-idea-narrative-sequence starts and stops. While the Munich director moves inspiringly into the structural area of Godard and Straub, the Warhol-Morrissey film is tamed, made respectable in *Heat* (shown in Venice), the closest that they have come to the Harvard *Crimson* collegiate spoof. Morrissey's make of *Sunset Boulevard*, with Joe Dallesandro in Bill Holden's role, is close to Russ Meyer's and Roger Ebert's *Beyond the Volley Balls*, having fun with clichés. A very raucous film. The crazy quilt set-up reaches its peak in late afternoon with the Chaplin reruns—the all-ages audience covering every seat-aisle-wall, kids tumbling around the stage, hesitantly fingering the screen. Hotels, buses, different theaters, patching a film segment seen one day with its mate, seen the next day in another theater, watching one film in the red plush grand salon and the next one outdoors in a handsome red brick amphitheater, banked by twenty-foot trellises and even taller poplars. A sea of umbrellas goes up and down through intermittent showers, while the outdoor arena audience is unforgettably combative: the main thing is to get the whole family seated together.

The festival hits one human stretch, pure joy, each time the "Little Fellow" appears in the *Il tutto* Chaplin retrospective. The massive audience formally applauds every scene change, the iris shots used in *The Kid*, any deft example of Chaplin's balletic footwork, or exquisitely timed malice. Most of the adults react with an explosive, joyous certainty as though no time had elapsed since 1917 and the herky-jerky egotist is still their spokesman, a perfect fit for every thought process and feeling. This instantaneous reading in which the audience knows immediately whether the sweet, cloying smile like a baby's ass is true or trick, gets its best rewards in *The Kid*, a marvelous film, one of the rare Chaplins where another actor shines. The whole screen is activated, and the primitively staged exits and entrances are comparatively bare of biased competitions in which a devious pest inevitably wins (the Arbuckles are great for the same reasons). How all of a piece Jackie Coogan is: four years old, with copious good humor and resourcefulness, he moves across screen like a buzz saw. Breaking glass for Chaplin's window-repairing business, Coogan unites all the lovely features of the '20s comic strip: its amalgam of spirit, cheerfulness, and guileless perfect design. He is a perfect tension-building counter to Chaplin's Irish neighborhood strutting and lifelong insistence on the truisms embroidered and framed on 1914 walls.

One esthetic development of the '60s, from the jump cuts in *Breathless* to Straub's use of unbroken Bach scores in the diary of Anna Magdalena Bach, is the discovery of ways to keep a movie from being engulfed by anecdote. There's been a steady parade of movies in which some director finds a new area in which to assert the element of distance, keeping either actors, sound, or image from being numb integers in the storytelling continuum. Godard, who's tried this Brechtian attitude about art in so many ways, and extracted his *Tout Va Bien* (codirected with Jean-Pierre Gorin) from the festival at the last moment, is symbolically buried every hour by such a regressive daydream as *Klara Lust* (pastoral optimism in soft focus), *Les deux saisons de la vie* (seven different camera angles each time the director and star, Samy Pavel, moves from one narcistic position to another), and *Le grand sabordage* (two self-admirers moving nude across cotton clouds at a tormentingly slow pace, finally proving their Juliet-Romeo kinship by scoring each other's breast with matched daggers). What makes the festival hard going is the sparsity of work like that of Fassbinder and Duras in which there is the attempt at removed self-enclosed abstract-structure.

Nathalie Granger (Marguerite Duras in French with Italian subtitles, an easy film to understand) is Hamlet done through a feminist domestic metaphor(?), a hexagonal portrait in which each resident in a French country house and its single visitor are sides of the same character in retreat from the outside world(?), a feminist tract about ceaseless monotony in a woman's daily routine(?), all these possibilities suggested by movements that barely crack the surface: somnolent clearing of dishes, silent raking in a long neglected pool, burning of dried leaves, sewing of name labels into a child's wardrobe. Official story: one afternoon in the civilized, tasteful Granger home, from which the young daughter is to be sent to live in a school for disruptive children. Official verdict: a didactic, puzzling movie which uses apathy as a unifying structural force in the film, its star actors like furniture, and produces an exciting equilibrium, as well as black humor, with two actresses (Jeanne Moreau, Lucia Bose) who move to a secret metronome with a grand presence.

A high-toned Resnais-ish film for this festival in a large blockhouse run by a small silvery blockhead, Gian Luigi Rondi. Like Mozart's *Cosi Fan Tutte*, an endless rearranging of symmetrical alliances is done somnambulistically, slowly, and deliberately. There's pleasure seeing these two majesties becalmed, moving like chess pieces in an elegantly photographed (Cloquet) de Hooch-like interior. Bose, a statuesque giant in black velvet, paces abstractly from room to room, starts a task and drops it. Mostly Moreau picks up and does the chores, has ironic humor, but, together with Bose, is in an elegant marathon of noncommunication.

All the subject matter seems to resonate suggestions of broader societal facts: Nathalie's boarding school (concentration camp), an intrusive door-to-door salesman (the worker left out on a spiritual limb by the callous commercial world), the absence of a male figure in the household (the daily isolation of women), the house itself (the apathy inside the boundaries of existence). Duras is not the most nimble director: too much stasis, excessive and ponderous mystification, and an excitingly tasty scene (two completely humorless dames looking stony and never at each other, doing mannered exits and entrances) has been familiarized by *Marienbad-Femme Douce* work. It's a likeable movie: precisioned, private, totally mysterious.

Random pleasures of the 33rd Mostra Cinematographia. *The Baddest Daddy in the World*, a documentary cashing in on Cassius Clay, doesn't threaten Vertov but gets quite a few of Clay's sides: his puckishness, good heart, pious naiveté. A perfect bit takes place at a restaurant breakfast, as Clay four times steals big mouthfuls of his tiny daughter's cornflakes by focusing her attention on an imaginary big dog out the window. Each time she suspects what he's done, the charming gagline being how he outfences her mounting suspicion. Morrissey's *Heat*, dirtied-up Wilder minus the Gothic element, has some funny whiny unique-to-Warhol sounds ("Look, you're not a Lesbian. I want you and her to stop going to these gay bars; the word is getting around. You can't do things like that in Hollywood.") and a craven unisex daughter, "one of those kids who come out of Hollywood High," who brings back the Warhol sting. Never seen convincingly or full face, her head is ducked and a craven voice comes out of a corner of her streaked blonde hair.

with Patricia Patterson; November 1972

Werner Herzog

MOVIEMAKING today divides into two main bodies of work: (1) the genre films that are so public a hermit couldn't escape the omnipresent *Nashville-Jaws* hype; and (2), a less observed film (*Death by Hanging, Not Reconciled*, et al.) that leans heavily on the traits of other art forms, is strongly concerned with structure, and mightily taxes the brain with motivations and ideas well worth the dredging that it takes to find them. There are good films in both worlds, but they don't feed each other in any framing-language-narrational way. Mike Snow never touches a Hollywood ticket and Coppola's never heard of Fassbinder. This latter Oshima-Guerra-Duras film lives a limited existence: once a year at Berkeley's Film Archive, then a gypsy route: The VA188 class at Colenzo College in Milwaukee, the once-a-month meeting of the Goethe Club, etc. It shouldn't surprise anyone that the people who create-criticize *Mean Streets* shun *Serene Velocity* as though it were invisible.

Right now, a key figure in the less-exposed film is a Munich native, Werner Herzog, a key figure not only because he lives in an irrational movie area only distantly touched by early Buñuel-Franju-Browning, but because of his odd-man-out posture even for Munich, which, thanks to government-owned TV and script grants, is the subversive-film capital. Herzog occupies a left-out role, with no seeming contacts with Fassbinder-Schroeter-Straub and their strong bonds with Brechtian theater.

Herzog, who has carried a film from Munich to Paris by foot and lived in a beaten VW van gathering mordant exotica from all California corners save Hollywood, is a music-addicted gypsy who is a specialist on the limited people (cripples, dwarfs, the blind and deaf) and has an outsized rage as extreme as his odd *outré* technique. A closed-on-himself artist who'll never give up, Herzog is weird on distance: His camera, always far away from people, finds strange locations, such as shooting Pizarro's search for El Dorado, the city of gold (*Aguirre, the Wrath of God*), mostly at water level in mid-Amazon. The one film where his unpredictable camera views show any interest in the actors is in his magnificently un-artful movie about deaf mutes in German hospitals (*Land of Silence and Darkness*), where his hand-held camera nuzzles its way close to people who can't see or hear it. This uncompromising movie—every image shows Fini Straubinger, a German Helen Keller, eyes shifting sideways, or raising her fervent face toward the ceiling, her gaze anywhere but at the camera, since her spatial-sound sense differs from the people shooting the film— is unusually obsessive and awkward, even for a director who has yet to construct a frame that isn't off-kilter.

All the Munich films are grounded in a Leftist version of present-day society as a maze of cruelty, captivity and frustration. For instance, Fassbinder's operatic family movie bases itself on the silent group pressure that causes people to come through with philistine passions and behavior: His wurst-shape siblings and shopkeepers take turns being mean and exploitative in a musical chairs of victor and victim. Unlike Fassbinder and Schroeter, who insert an insinuating, outsized Kabuki acting into movies that get a lot of animal sensuality, hedonistic camping, Herzog is a scattered buckshot phenomenologist, who doesn't give a damn about actors. His movies are compassionate but you won't find any box-office potatoes (they're not about human relations: there's no love theme, anything resembling a genre situation, no family problems, no Altman-ish thrills and defeats).

Herzog can go in a number of film directions—*Signs of Life* is low-key fiction, *Fata Morgana* is a didactic poem, and *Aguirre* often suggests a bad Raoul Walsh adventure, an episodic paceless film in which you're wondering "will they make it or not"—to inflict his vision: a droll, macabre, romantic, zestful wrathfulness at God's work. Though he tends towards big themes (normality and mental disorder, the destiny of the Western world, power and conquest), his touch with the medium is unpretentious and he puts awkwardnesses together rather than going for the big, detailed performance, like De Niro's Johnny Boy in *Mean Streets*. In place of a ten-minute acting triumph filled with self-assurance, a physical performance no one, square or otherwise, can miss,

Herzog creates a perverse world, but one which feels peculiarly truthful, by joining odd-angled small perceptions of events to create a different space than the one with which he started. In this manner, he has done beautiful work with tasks-laborers-hands, i.e. a long tracking shot in *Fata Morgana* which flows past two construction workers standing in a shanty town. Puzzled by Herzog's half-directions, they wave at the camera crew, and, then, for some bravado-ish thing to do, they start running parallel, with the tracking camera, each one angling off into a different direction. The last you see they are far back, tiny figures in the distance, shading their eyes and looking dispirited. Herzog's persistence leads to a queer unfolding poignance in deep space.

Most of *Fata Morgana* is a catalog of dead colonialism in the Sahara: the abandoned debris from World War II, the mad-magical strain in both the blacks and German tourists digging for ethnic information. It would die were not Herzog a shrewd gambler-manipulator with material often no more lively than a *National Geographic* display of dunes, etc. With his cache of expressionist ploys (recostuming native blacks into anti-colonial posters, forcing black urchins into stylized poses of combat and postures that somehow escape being cruel, mocking fellow German tourists into witless obsessional panting after scientific facts), Herzog has turned a placid and lyrical desert-landscape image for the travel-folder trade into a spacious gliding visual-aural circus. There is nothing quite like *Fata Morgana*!

His mordant, bleak style in this breathtaking mirage of space, speed and quirky events made in 1970 could be outlined in four steps:

(1) Endless horizontal tracks like a briskly moving line in a cafeteria; he keeps his camera detached, emotionally as well as actually distanced.

(2) Objects and people are like flotsam, used coffee grounds on a flat, brown desert strewn with military debris, shack houses, animal carcasses, barbed wire, displaced blacks living within the remnants of World War II.

(3) Herzog half directs his actors: It's clear these confused puzzled tourists and natives don't know what the mischievous director is doing. His blank-gaze camera stays on them while they become progressively more perplexed.

(4) A shock sound track, one that you're always questioning: What does the drippy Leonard Cohen have to do with a 1940s bus letting off passengers in a heat haze? Herzog not only vegetates his sound (all types of music, Couperin to Cash) but he razzes it as well. In one fierce Swiftian section, which is devilishly presented as the iconic image of civilization's Golden Age, a husband-and-wife dance band play on a brothel's box-like stage, creating jaundice by the excessive amplification and their comatose expressions. The goggled Don

Juan on drums and dyspeptic matron at the piano rap out their endless dance tune for no audience amidst tired paper decorations and a resounding hollow echo.

In *Even Dwarfs Started Small* (1968), all the players are midgets and dwarfs of widely disparate personas and heights. The mostly nonverbal helter-skelter takes place in a reform school built for normal-sized hoods on a lava-like burnt-out island in the Canaries as scarred as the passionate shrieking of the gypsy girl whose song keys the movie's fiery emotion. The director of the reformatory has gone; the deputy barricades himself in his office with the revolt ringleader as a hostage; as the day goes on, the inmates turn more chaotic and destructive. The deputy becomes more the traditional liberal pleading for reasonable behavior. The two smallest and meekest are practical-joked into the director's bedroom "to have a go at it"; the blind dwarfs, stand-ins for the Status Quo, are tormented out of a Peaceful Life by the others. The institution car is set in motion to drive in a continuous circle, furniture is smashed, the deputy is bombarded with stones and live hens, and the dwarfs finally march in a procession through smoking flower pots ("the flowers are in bloom, let's burn them"), holding aloft a pet monkey tied to a cross.

It is an hallucinatory attack on half-baked revolutions, and has most of the anti-culture bric-a-brac that fills a Herzog movie: stormtrooper goggles, rusted barrels and oil drums from past military debacles, long tracks that are like a slow train going through landscape accompanied by a vitriolic or facetious sound track, the ferocious sound of mad laughter, diabolic mistreatment of animals by other animals or humans.

Herzog's nightmares are speckled with a kind of dormant, lazy, motiveless cruelty: two dwarf women, out of boredom, giggle in comradeship over the killing of an enormous white sow who had been nursing nine piglets. An earlier focus of great friendship was directed against the plant world. "Let's burn down the director's favorite palm tree"—this accompanied by the most intense, delighted laughter.

Along with cruelty, a big Herzog item is enslavement. One of the most touching, wistful moments: a high shot down on a woman with her two-story, cigar-box apartment house, an extraordinary miniature of Madame Tussaud's occupied by two dozen insects dressed in elaborate costumes. The inmates perform this inspection once a week with total delight, and there's extreme consternation if any tiny convict has had a wing damaged or lost his top hat. Each view of the bride evokes, "Ohhhh, how lovely!"

Herzog's film—the awkward framing, the jagged pace, a deep space that spreads beyond the edges of the screen—hinges on his being a real German gypsy, an Outsider whose movies sing with sunlight, a keen sensitivity to the beauty of motion, rush of water, bird flight, the trajectory of an arrow, etc. The portrait in *Signs of Life* of Meinhard, a German soldier on the fringes of the war with nothing to do, is a catalog of restless-grumpy poking around a sun-blasted foreign place. Meinhard, the amiable roach trapper, with his constant questions about animal behavior ("Have you ever seen a caterpillar procession . . . do you know how to hypnotize a chicken . . . what does a kangaroo look like on Sunday?") is enveloped by space, literally swallowed by sunlight, save for a Herzog trademark: his unflagging determination and physicality.

The only roof Herzog admits to is the sky; even the indoor shots of a dwarf prisoner, roped to a swivel chair, are unenclosed, chaotic, spacious. Herzog perversely subverts any potential drama, always opting for a spontaneous activity over a pre-thought plan. One of his most rambunctious examples of history erupts in *Aguirre*. The Spanish are making an assault on a cannibal village. They push in front of them an improbably acquiescent black slave on the proposition that he'll scare the savages to their knees. As they move forward, the ground turns at an angle, the stalwart Castilians roll around like marbles, and the spectator wonders why, where and what the director and his camera are doing. Where are these Indians? Where are these countless arrows coming from? You can image Herzog whipping his frazzled actors before him with some of his movie's frazzled dialogue: "Move, you sons of ducks, *la pudre duh madre*, keep the cannon out of the water!" His beautiful, immaculate star, Helena Rojo, changed into her best Balenciaga for this gala chaos, walks into the forest in disgust, preferring a cannibal stew to the company of her noble (no-bull) defenders who are rolling around the ground in various states of slovenliness. "There she goes, never to be seen again." Could such dishevelment be strategy, or did the jungle heat do them all in?

From the witty observations of the eccentric Meinhard in his seminal debut, *Signs of Life*, a seedbed of images and themes which appear in every other Herzog, to the disturbing and very moving moments with the deaf-and-blind in *Land of Silence*, Herzog has been in a perverse situation: He doesn't want to deal with actors but is obviously fascinated with people as phenomena. His camera is evasive and recessive when the time comes for character-building (with the ironic, above-noted exception of the Fini Straubinger story), he feels people's relationships are their own business, and could care less about person-to-person situations: His two-shot setups are mostly stiff. A person in relation to his obsession-passion-hobby is where Herzog turns on: Walter Steiner, Swiss ski-jump champion, and his ecstatic ski-flights; Straubinger's travels spreading the language of touch; a mad lizard worshipper ("you can't imagine how long it takes to catch them if they run away"); the intensively private experience of a thin hospital patient fingering her dress, making a sign of the cross incessantly and feverishly in a hand ballet that never stops . . . her face delicately befuddled and poignant.

The overwhelming isolation of every mortal in the human kingdom is the sensation of any Herzog frame. When two types of loss-alienation can be split apart within one frame, the movie inevitably is at its most hurtful and associative. Perhaps his entire oeuvre defines itself around the miracle scene, utterly dirty, of a wiry Algerian hammering stones into gravel. His clenched doggedness is suddenly matched by an equally weathered intruder who takes a stiff, belligerent stand toward the camera. It catches a whole area's existence, dry mid-Sahara, and the outsider's impotent relation to it. Over this image is a rasping incantation: "The gates of paradise are open to everybody . . . there works are inspected which no one would do . . . you slake lime and are chosen for this by the rich."

Herzog is one tough guy with an ability to be pliant, gentle. But he's undivertable, insisting on this seething passion that washes over every frame of *Aguirre, Fata Morgana*. There's no moaning in such work, but also there's no Pollyanna glossing: They're often fiercely funny, pleasurable, naturally energetic. But always there is this disturbing statement: "This is a treacherous world and there is a considerable amount of dementia in all of us." His message: "When things become irreal, this is the moment which moves me most."

with Patricia Patterson; July 13, 1975

The New Breed of Filmmakers: A Multiplication of Myths

THE difference between the two obsessive quests in *The Searchers* (1956) and *French Connection II* (1975) is one of quantity: Popeye Doyle's one goal, revenging himself on the hedonistic narcotics king, Charnier, to hell with everything else! involves more staccato cuts, more bits of cheerful Mediterranean color, more focus changing, and, especially more mobility and paranoia in Hackman's acting than occurs during the entirety of Ethan Edward's (John Wayne) endless Monument Valley search for little white Debbie (Natalie Wood) who, unthinkable for a Wayne-Ford adobe epic, has been cohabiting rather sensibly with a Comanche chief named Scar.

Effulgence, luxuriance . . . the new Hollywood film multiplies everything, trying to get the mythic aspect as well as a very contemporaneous attitude about candidness, what does candidness mean as a way of life? Old studio works like *Double Indemnity* (1944) stick to one hard-boiled attitude about the Forties in the L.A. suburbs: the camera-lighting-acting-language is dry, deadpan, and along with its clipped, blunt pace, adds up to a unified experience. Why does the new film try for so much within the genre system? Scorsese's movie (*Alice Doesn't Live Here Anymore*) about a woman's search for fulfillment is an updating of an old Stanwyck tearjerker in which a gutsy woman isn't going to give up; Scorsese's movie surrounds this Stanwyck structure with down-to-earth feistiness, mythic glamour, and a fairy-tale quality. *Godfather II* is a gangster movie that's come a long way since *Scarface*; the production is grander than that of *Gone with the Wind* and its gangsterism becomes a portrait of America, from the hopes of Ellis Island to the unspeakable obscenities of Las Vegas.

The mushroomed technique and attitude in *Godfather-Alice-Jaws-Night Moves* is talking about a bountifulness that has to do with a new grasp of the entertainment film, a new belief in speaking to a mass audience. There's a tremendous euphoria and confidence banked into *California Split*, even the puzzling Mike Nichols comedy, *The Fortune*. From editor to writer, the crew making these films is young (at least in spirit), educated, and composed of a Quiz Kid student of film who has spent vast amounts of time just studying the poster of *Forty Guns*, or what Ferguson wrote about the iron fence in *Citizen Kane*. With such box office-prestige winners as *Last Picture Show* and *Godfather*, this group of mutual supporters have taken over the Seventies.

French Connection II comes from a financial structure in which all the chips are riding on a dozen blockbusters per year instead of the fifty-two annually turned out by a Darryl Zanuck and fed into theaters Fox once owned. Where Walsh-Capra-Wellman created prolific oeuvres cranking out movies each tailored to the dimensions of a Warners or Columbia film, the new directors often speed from one studio-genre-producer to another, creating a *Four Musketeers* one-for-all, all-for-one atmosphere.

In place of the Jim Thorpe versatility which generated so many Forties-Fifties films where one Sturges-Welles-Fuller did all the jobs, the vibrations today in the cutting rooms are Happy Days Are Here Again, and perhaps something of the feeling that it can't be true: "Could we really have won all those Oscars? Is it really me who dashes off a high-priced script in thirty hours and flies to Rome for a Dino de Laurentis confab? Only yesterday I was an usher at The New Yorker and trying for a Howard Hawks autograph."

"Now that we've run off those Sixties punks (Godard, Jim McBride, the first Truffaut films, Rocha, the ass-poking Kuchar brothers) who tried to crumb up the genre movie," a Bogdanovich director says to the world, "we can really have some fun, wear some fancy summer linens, and screen *Young Mr. Lincoln* every night in our own bedroom . . . with our own classy chick beside us."

Comparing the image of *The Thing* (1951) with any frame from Scorsese's *Alice* is like comparing a clean, neat square to a luxuriant garden which might turn upside down, where one portion is hard to see but one or two bewitching flowers are in sharp focus, and where a till-now benevolent gardener may turn into a frenzy of sadism and jeering. Scorsese's movies are about youth's dream squelched-by-the-adult-verities, the charismatic fullness of a jungle cat punk, a feisty ten-year-old, a vulgar and good-natured veteran waitress, and a visceral apprehension about an eager-messy world, a reaction he transmits through a saucing, glamour technique. He has a romantic appreciation for Life, which remembers an actor's best moves and generously supplies the time for full-scale exposition.

Using a nervous-generous hoopla of real to camp techniques, the makers of *Alice* set up Harvey Keitel's country-boy stud so that his every move is repellently slick but excitingly canny and detailed. All of Keitel's scenes are contrived but stick in the brain, particularly the one in which he tries to pick Alice up after a singing turn. Ben is a man with a funny trade (he fills bullet cases with gun powder) and he plays a little boy game, disarming by persistence and a refusal to recognize a brushoff. The exhausted and irritated Alice can hardly look at this pest, "God, not another one." Keitel's careful improvising gradually breaks Alice down and seems to throw the actress, Ellen Burstyn, off stride, springing her into what she does best: a gutsy and undisguised presentation of a woman who's lived a lot, lost a lot, and who throws all her scars at you. The scene sinks into itself and becomes its own time and place. A great plus for the Alice movie is that it does have these quiet pockets.

So what's being said here is that Hollywood has leaped into a new studio saddle, long after the studio system is supposed to have expired. The studio now is one large, pliant, amicable structure run by a group of Squire Allworthys rather than Jack Cohn or Warner Mayer. These chesty optimistic nomads—writers, set designers, editors—move fast and comprise a large familial network behind the scenes. The importance of this gemütlichkeit phenomenon is that it is creating a new type of film, a sort of hybrid, which crosses a mythicized genre film with a mushroomed aestheticism. Like any film since 1959, it has been indelibly touched by the process-oriented innovations which began with *Breathless*. The process element in Godard's mercurial, never pat soundtracks or Bertolucci's sumptuous color and grandiloquent camera motion have by now been domesticized. The result: a cheerful, full movie fleshed out with TV's audience-grabbing mechanisms, inflected by an omnipresent, overwhelming showboat technique, and, whether the subject is an illusive menace haunting Amity (*Jaws*), an heiress being fleeced by two bumbling losers in a totally actionless frame (*The Fortune*), or an introspective Sam Spade tossed around by a case that starts with a cliche aging actress and ends with several cliche water shots in the Florida Keys (*Night Moves*), the movie is unconsciously talking about the familial triumph and mass appeal philosophy of the new filmmaking alliance based in San Francisco and L.A.

From one angle, these movies are about the cheerful possibilities of being sheltered, covered, having a buddy ethic, etc. The population being depicted in *The Fortune* (a mock family), *California Split* (pals), *The Passenger* (two women pushing their man into Commitment), *Jaws* (buddies), and *Night Moves* (instant intimacy with anyone Harry Moseby meets) is mostly asserting family values as being above criticism. Each movie takes its own route into this theme. Coppola's family (*Godfather II*) finishes by eating itself up. The structure is a series of family events, past and present, in which the technique (slow tracking shots through crowded space, setting up scenes that have the sentiment and color of old postcards, giving his De Niro–Brando characters a statuesque stillness that suggests power, setting up two-person scenes which create the sense of a Boss-serf relationship) often involves the humiliation of someone who has strayed from the family. Scorsese never divulges the reality of Alice's day-to-day survival process. Alice is continually acquiring substitutes for a family, while the technique (a spotty lighting system, an overly dramatic camera conveying a lot of movement and mood, the glamourizing of non-star types) has the effect of spicing up the material. In *The Fortune*, three people without a past or future are doomed to be buddies all the time: the whole film is about bumbling and incompetence, in which the rote-like procedure (a classic cooking scene like the one in Hitchcock's *Frenzy*, hardly examined or entered) suggests that the three incompetents are in a perpetual primitivism.

In *French Connection II*, Frankenheimer's ease in France reveals itself with fast day-to-day talk in a police station, a great second knife (Philippe Leotard) in constant lean motion like an efficient stiletto, and his allowing Renoir's rhapsodic camera to go on, never stopping him. The movie is one cheerful, snappy family in a town that seems incredibly fast and rough.

Finding Frog I in *French II* is cued to Hackman's motion and malice slob persona (no friends, a ratty hotel, dowdy clothes, and, except for P.J. Clark's blood-oozing burgers, he wouldn't know good from bad food) the way the Lana Turner film was cued into her still shot glamour. Hackman's Popeye is physically active to a point where, like Keitel-Nicholson-Burstyn in full momentum, he is visually ungraspable. Just what kind of a body does Popeye have (Hackman's Harry Moseby in *Night Moves* is another story: he's laid back, looking tall, sexy, with a Newmanesque grace) when he's scrunched-to-running as a three-week junkie in a crummy Marseilles basement, clammy with massive stone walls out of *Les Miserables*. If they really want him to recover, why couldn't Frankenheimer get him a less TB-arthritis-infested room. He's always scrunched up, sweating, often in a tantrum, running madly through the streets: like Pacino in the *Needle Park* film, he's a darting performer who inflects off the gag's center, falling away from the action.

My favorite scene: a very vulnerable Popeye, nearing the final stages of his cold turkey, is taken for an around-Marseilles ride to locate the fleabag where he was shot up. The subdued, quiescent, enfeebled Popeye is neatly countered by the jangle of Marseilles streets and Renoir's jerky camera shots. As a handsome girl goes by with an ice cream cone, Hackman answers from the rear: "I'd like some of that." His French counterpart, a sluggish Bernard Fresson, warns, "It would kill you right now." Popeye answers: "I mean the ice cream," and the windup is a quiet, meditative eating of the ice cream. Unlike the pointed embarrassment of a cellar speech explaining baseball, "the dandy southpaw Whitey Ford," to an uncomprehending Fresson, the car scene is played-photographed off-center, creating space that's not dependent on virtuosity but lets in a sensually complex world.

The danger of genre movies is the tyranny of the plot, the domination of the male hero (Alice Hyatt is an exception), and the fact that, despite the yen for rack focus, dusky lighting, sun-blanched backgrounds, and tunnel vision, the movie is still tied to the hero's upper torso, or two bodies clamped dead center in an empty wide screen. Good improvisation and an actor who lets it all hang out hide these dangers, but are also ironically the cause of them. The idolatry and dependence on the hotshot actor leads to total contradiction. Alice Hyatt's trial run in a sparsely populated Tucson bar should be a desperate occasion. Her voice has no resonance, there's no phrasing, and at no point is she working to improve vocally other than in her repartee with her upstaging kid. The scene gets a one hundred percent glamour treatment. In these films centered around one or more hotshots, both the environment and the feeling of process withers. When the new hybrid film is at its best (Hackman's ice cream act), its reality seems to be about waiting, spending time: there is the sense of the plot being off frame, happening next door.

with Patricia Patterson; July 20, 1975

Rainer Werner Fassbinder

I⊤'s interesting that the true inheritors of early Warhol, the Warhol of *Chelsea Girls* and *My Hustler*, are in Munich, whereas the new Warhol-Morrissey film has gone west, i.e. *Heat* is a Zap comic book *Sunset Boulevard* and *Frankenstein* is a salacious child's version of the James Whale classic. Warhol's idea of a counter-mainstream has to do with reversing the conventions of high-low art: rejecting with a giggle Greenberg's edicts formerly considered on a par with the Ten Commandments: the artist as a moral superior, integrity of the painting surface over illusion, the relationship of the picture's inside to the edge, the high-vs.-kitsch polarities.

Like Genet's polemical stand for the beauty of crime and perversity, Warhol proclaims the wondrousness of monotony, banality, machine-made art, expedience, and an easy mobility from one medium to another. He's a great mover towards facetiousness and flexibility: it's not that he doesn't work like a bearcat at his dozen professions, but that he tries to imprint a not-that-taxing air into each new painting-print-film-interview.

By osmosis, Warhol's kinkiness made a big dent in the Bavarian beer-bratwurst-Bach film capital, Munich. Probably few of the Munichers have seen any Warhol, but the latter's *Bike Boy*, *Chelsea Girls* are neighbors under the skin to some of the reel wheels in TV-supported Munich films, particularly Fassbinder's anti-cinema. There is the same painterly ability to hit innocent, insolent colors, using flat, boldly simple formats; Warhol's image is more porous, coarse-grained, while Fassbinder's has a sardonic, fairytale look. The Tartar-faced writer-director-actor has done one film a week (practically) since 1971, which is up to the early Warhol pace, and, in the background of Fass-binder's image, there is the sense of grifters and bootlegging, plus the effect in early Warhol of being tough and able to control such anarchy. Fassbinder's Marxist world unchained is compressed and delineated; you know where each form, idea, and narrative sequence starts and stops.

A henpecked boob beats up his wife in a bedroom tableau which stays on screen without camera change until the remorseless ending, the husband rolling over in a drunken stupor. The agonized, frustrated drunk beating up his selfish, penny-pinching wife is the oldest scene in movies, going back to *Greed*, but this fully-lit, futile explosion in a 1971 Munich movie is a remarkable blend of charm and ferocity. Aimed against prissy, middle-class taste, the purple over-statements recall *Written on the Wind* and another Sirk, *All That Heaven Allows*, which he draws on more explicitly in the 1974 *Fear Eats the Soul*. But the cool and very contemporary candidness suggests Warhol's deadpan on the androgynous underworld.

A minor example of Fassbinder paralleling Warhol: the presence of Viva's cloying, nasal whine in Irm Hermann's startling portrait of a peddler's sneaky wife in Fassbinder's *The Merchant of Four Seasons*. In this portrait, which moves back and forth from thin-lipped petty conventionality to moments of sensuality and spunk, the mocking drawl of Warhol's superstar combines with the lower-class traits out of another world. It's like joining the "liberated" Soho with the corner-cutting uniformity of J. C. Penney. Hermann's squinty eyes behind dowdy glasses, her spectacularly lean body inside frumpy, printed housedresses. Fassbinder is not the only member of Germany's re-awakened film scene to be in a curious congruency with Warhol's filmic investigations: his gorgeous hermaphrodites (Schroeter), put-on freakiness (Herzog), the precisionist long takes on a seemingly unseductive scene (Straub), but he's the one we're going to deal with here.

Fassbinder's a mixture of enfant terrible, burgher, and pimp, whose twenty-four features (since 1967) are mainly sprung out of a camp sensibility. All of his appetites (for the outlandish, vulgar, and banal in matters of taste, the use of old movie conventions, a no-sweat approach to making movies, moving easily from one medium to another, the element of facetiousness and play in terms of style) are those of camp and/or Warhol. The point—to dethrone the serious, to make artifice and theatricality an ideal—is evident in an amazing vivacity, re-introducing Fable into a Hollywood genre, while suggesting a tough facile guy manipulating a deck of cards. Warhol's ace move, taking anyone and making her a superstar, draping her in glamour and incandescence, is also Fassbinder's. The same three leggy females appear in most films; Hanna Schygulla, a halo around her in every frame, is the ravishing beauty, the trump or tramp card in his films.

Merchant of Four Seasons (the down-path of a family black sheep, who goes through a Dreiser-ian list of humiliations, and then, as he's beginning to make some headway and breadway as a fruit-and-vegetable hawker, he methodically drinks himself to death) is a luminous, inventive movie that is so damn clear about its aims and means. The basic idea—the silent group pressure which causes people to come through with conventional emotions and behavior, so that every moment gets compromised and discolored—has never before been pinned down so subtly and constantly. It's not the sodden story of a downtrodden, henpecked husband but a hard portrait of middle-class ritual, circa 1972. People take turns being mean and exploitative in a musical chairs of victor and victim. As in all his films, Fassbinder is pushing melodrama to absurd limits to show how its cliché attitudes and emotions discolor normal situations.

The Merchant is the work of a medieval illuminator who has a command of visual ornateness, suggesting the most famous of hand-painted books: the Duc de Berry's *Book of Hours*. Its radiant people are faced close to the camera, in what always seems a peak moment. The scene is shadowless, intensely lit. It has the ecstatic tenderness of Fra Angelico but the archetypical characters (the greedy wife, generous sister, the innocent daughter, mean-stingy mother, a sychophantic brother-in-law) are played by an acting troupe of vivid dynamic hipsters. Fassbinder makes a wholesome frontal image, in many ways like small Fra Angelico panels: a man in a crisp blue-and-white-plaid shirt hawking the pale green pears filling a rectangular cart, a humble action frozen in a shallow-still composition. This unconquering hero sells only three bags of pears during the movie.

Like a cat burglar feeling out the combination lock on a safe, Fassbinder keeps turning the knob on a character, working parsimoniousness with lust-fulness in Irn Hermann's wife, compassion and cold-blooded frankness in Schygulla's sister, who sticks by the peddler against his disapproving family and stands for integrity. The clear individualizing and silhouetting of each character are emblematic of Fassbinder's hermetic formalism, even when there is a reverse twist in every major character. A woman who had heretofore been all tightness is suddenly exposed in all her white length, being serviced from the rear by a stranger whose tiny smirk is hung on until its meaning is in your brain.

His tough-tender vision is expressed through ritual, whether the film is a *Death in Venice* story (*Petra von Kant*) or a working-class Babbitt gone berserk (*Why Does Herr R. Run Amok?*). Whether the filmed event is Petra's hypocriti-cal phoning, Herr R.'s pompous tutoring of his little son, the Ali-Emmi dance that opens and closes *Fear*, these rituals serve to keep the world in place; other rituals—Hans's evening round of drinks with his buddies—freak them out.

His ritualized syntax could be outlined this way:

(1) He inserts violence and tension beneath stupefyingly mundane talk in *The Merchant*: "Gee Hans, what a success you are now," or extreme sentimen-tality in *Fear*: "Emmi, you not an old woman, you a big heart," or the chest-beating Susan Hayward–style in *Petra*: "I can't live without her, I can't bear it," as she rolls around on a terrycloth rug, hugging a Jack Daniels bottle to her breast. She also screams at her daughter and mother: "Go home, you bores, I can't stand the sight of you, I want Karin!"

(2) Acting in the *Petra* film is feverishly singular. As in Noh theater, it's proto-artificial and always trying for the emblematic joined with the rich effect of a sausage bursting its casing. Petra and her monosyllabic assistant, in black Edwardian gowns, are pugnacious with their personas.

(3) From the endless yammering of Petra, who runs a dress career from her bed, to the tense, spoken opera in *Fear*, it's always musical incantation. "Come home, Hans, please come home," and he throws a chair at his wife's poised body half-hidden behind the saloon door. Hermann's porcelain skin, ruby lips, tightly curled hair has the same iconic impact as her pleading intonation. His whole acting team—Hirschmüller's peddler, Carstensen's designer-heroine, Brigitte Mira's Emmi—use language for the same taunting purpose, as in the arch fox-trot by the two long-gowned women in *Petra*. Dancing to "Oh Yes, I'm the Great Pretender," they never look at each other, which points again to his trademark belief in power struggles incessantly waged.

(4) He and Kurt Raab ("the design is done for me by Raab, the guy who plays Herr R. I tell him what I need; every color is carefully thought out, each image is worked on.") are extraordinary inventors with captive settings—furniture, décor, people have a captured-inside-a-doll's-house feeling. The prime factor in his syntax: the pull between characters and their diminutive, dollhouse environment. Wife-child-husband around table eating baloney-cheese is a scene out of Beatrix Potter, people too big for tidy-tiny repetitive existence.

(5) Dress and decor: each character has his own type of clothes; Hans wears plaids, Erna dresses like a Hawks heroine, Petra's mute assistant (played as a studied slow dance by Irm Hermann) is always in black, a sepulchral creature whose incredible curtain scene (slowly suitcasing her wooden mannequins and taking off in a tense, extended silence) is a lovely example of power infighting between two deity-like personages. Fassbinder's very eclectic: his people stand before beautiful wallpaper like Xmas lights, mixing styles and eras within the same tableau.

A P. T. Barnum using workers and shopkeepers for his entertainers and making them as luminous and exotic as candelabras, he is actually all over the map with a playful larceny. He has taken a number of tactics from the Sirk melodramas (the flamboyant lighting, designing décor and costumes that indelibly imprint a character's social strata, being patient with actors and playing all the movie's elements into them, backing your dime-store story and soap-opera characters all the way) and stapled Sirk's lurid whirlwind into a near silent film style which is punctuated with terse noun-verb testiness. A good example is Ali's terse response to a sultry hellcat's proposition: "Cock's bust."

Bresson's visual economy (the delayed reactions by the camera and actor, hanging on walls, doorknobs, or a peasant's numb expression) is turned into very prominent rituals.

After having said all this, the fact is that Fassbinder's intense shadowless image is not like anyone else's, and his movies have installed the workers' milieu—their homes, love affairs, family relations, the wallpaper, knickknacks, the slang, food and drink, the camaraderie—as a viable subject for the Seventies. Whether the filmed event is a fruit vendor yelling downstairs for his departed wife, or the fascistic business calls that transpire on the outsized brass bed where a yammering dress designer eats, works, and loves (the only males in sight being the gigantic nudes on the mural behind her bed), the scene most often plays in one take, without development, so that his trademark, *saftig* feistiness, the up-front pugnacity, always hits with more meat than you expect, it claws you with churlish aggressions.

A nosy neighbor spitefully watches the middle-aged Emmi and the handsome black Ali go up to her apartment. In this typical tableau a rack-focus shot suggests all three, like all Fassbinder's denizens, are caught in a shifting but nevertheless painful power game of top dogs and underdogs. The scene is dominated by aggressive decisions about décor and motivations; the camera, positioned directly behind the neighbor's helmet-like black hairdo, pins the Emmi-Ali lovers behind an ornate iron screen that points up a tasteless magistrate and two rather gentle rule-breakers. The methodically worked-on event displays Fassbinder's radical mix of snarl and decoration.

His strategies often indicate a study of porn movies, how to get an expanse of flesh across screen with the bluntest impact and the least footage. With his cool-eyed use of Brecht's alienation effects, awkward positioning, and a reductive mind that goes straight to the point, he manages to imprint a startling kinky sex without futzing around in the Bertolucci *Last Tango* style. Style is everything in these blunt, motionless tableaux: there is a cunning sense of how much space to place between the candid sexuality and the camera, how much lurid, ersatz color needed to give the act a kinky rawness. He seems able to cue you into the licentious effect of a Thirties film, and still hold the scene in the Seventies by the stylized abandon of his ruthlessly installed temptresses. The lustfulness of Hermann's long scrawny *Hausfrau*, the blow-job on Hans, and particularly Hanna Schygulla's lazy opportunistic lesbian in *Petra von Kant*. She walks with her hips stuck out in a slow insinuation as drawling as her talk. There is nothing more kinky than her love scenes in a sheet-metal slave costume.

Fear Eats the Soul: the marriage between a sixty-year-old charwoman, the widow of a Nazi, and a splendid Moroccan column of muscle is endangered because Emmi won't make couscous for Ali. Given all the possible problems that such a marital miss-match could incur, it shows Fassbinder's perversity that he drives them apart with a cracked wheat stew. Emmi, becoming chauvinistic and complacent, tells this catch of the century to go get his couscous elsewhere. The circular structure evolves back and forth between the Asphalt Pub, a hangout for Moroccan pals, their bosomy gals, and Emmi's cozy flat, subjecting the pair to endless prejudice bouts with the grocer, maître d', that bitch who patrols the hallway, her gross beer-drinking layabout son-in-law (played by the snarling camp-elion himself: Rainer Werner F.). This endless series of trivia gates overlorded by bigoted high priests causes Ali's stomach to rip. Fassbinder, who looks like a Vegas blackjack dealer, knows how to get the effects he wants: he turns this sweet-sauerkraut into a double-edged enthralling movie.

In *Why Does Herr R. Run Amok?*, the light is blasting, the sound of people conversing is early TV play in its grating, granular stridency, and the plot develops an accurate catalog of comment in the daily round. A draughtsman, Herr R., dully moves through a measured tedium, until one night while his glazed eyes are on the TV and his wife and a friendly neighbor chatter along with the TV sound, he picks up an alabaster vase, kills wife-child-neighbor. The next morning his amenable colleagues find him hanging from a latch in the office lavatory.

Scenes like the two friends talking of school songs on a funny little sofa look like comic strip: the Katzenjammers, Major Hoople. This crackup of a petty bourgeois done in raw presentation catches most of what Fassbinder is about.

(1) Humiliation; daily, hour by hour, in the shop, at breakfast, humiliation everywhere.

(2) The shopkeepers of life treated without condescension or impatience.

(3) Physical and spiritual discomfort: The essence of Fassbinder is a nagging physical discomfort.

So Fassbinder has two sides, the operatic and the forthright brash. In moving from the low-budget, avant-garde movie to large TV-financed films ("I am a German making films for the German audience"), he has always retained a hatred of dubbed dialogue and holds to a theatrical premise, a few characters interacting in a stage space, which keeps his image shallow and makes it easier to do sync sound. What an image! His is the precision of a painter with space and color: he has a fantastic painter's eye (he's Mondrian with a sly funk twist) and knows how to angle a body, how much space is necessary to set it off. But his movie sails home on its lighting-color-pattern, a frontal, geometric poise that should make any hip painter envious. Someday we should love to see the early grainy black Fassbinders—*Katzelmacher*, *The American Soldier*, *Love Is Colder Than Death*, etc.—which have come to this coast only once via Tom Luddy's single-handed championing at the Archive.

with Patricia Patterson; July 27, 1975

Nashville: Good Ole Country Porn

By now there can't be any film buff who doesn't know that two dozen actors sing their own songs, contributed last-minute dialogue, filled out their own characters, and that Altman, a Svengali of surface funk, has a slight hit on his hands. One obvious fact is that *Nashville* isn't authentically structured by sound, Country/Western or otherwise, as is Losey's *Accident*, where the thin, dissatisfied sound is precisely keyed into the film's hyper-refined decadence and summery atmosphere, or Glauber Rocha's *Antonio das Mortes*, where a very passionate combination of African and Portuguese sounds creates a sense of people connecting with their history via music. Unlike Godard, who revolutionized sound tracks, rhythmically punctuating stretches of silence, streets sounds, spoken voices, cafe noises, all used as music, Altman is saying that the media has corrupted and dulled Americans with a sound track that is one continuous flow of noises.

It's true that there's always some noise going on, a lot of it garbled, symbolized by Opal of the BBC (Geraldine Chaplin) and her pestiferous gushing as she interviews celebrities in Nashville . . . looking at the gospel singers: "It's so exciting, you can see the throbbing pulse of the eons . . . can't you just imagine them naked?" She'll interview anyone; seeing a Viet Nam vet on the stage of a fake show boat: "What did it feel like?" There's always a car roaring by, a half sentence drifting in the air, the loudspeakers of a hollow fascist candidate, all of it mixed into a cacophony that's supposed to be natural or exciting. The fact that it all sounds contrived is less pertinent than that it's enough to drive you around the bend, like BBC's Opal jamming her mike and frantic face everywhere. That awful telephoto image, a bird's-eye view onto an automobile graveyard where she's roaming along, blabbing into her tape recorder: "It's eerie, like some prehistoric graveyard. . . ." Very florid, she's always about to faint from the overwhelming significance of her preconceived generalities about the South, gun-owners, the American death wish. She's a one-line joke—a daffy foreign intellectual determined to find everything marvelously typical—who won't go away. Her canned emotion ("I can't bear it, the maimed limbs" at a farcical auto wreck without a damaged hubcap) is supposed to suggest that if Nashville is a nuthouse, other countries produce worse nuts, who are also intellectual parasites and who can't recognize the most blatant putdown.

There is a lot of mule-headed persistence. You ask yourself: "What is it about?" Nothing can stop Shelley Duvall, a preening stringbean from California trying to get closer to the action, from appearing in another trendy outfit. Along with this character, totally inside her fantasy about the music scene and her conquest of it, there are other hiccups: Gwen Welles, endlessly practicing her sexy moves for her debut number; a priapic rock singer, a monster of vanity (Keith Carradine), who beds every other female in Tennessee; a runaway wife (Barbara Harris) running for fame as a hit singer: she's always dropping things, getting runs in her stockings, sneaking backstage. They are the movie's idea of the American success urge. Aside from being hobnailed boots instead of grace notes, they're devices who create a smug, pat predictability.

Nashville is an *Airport* or *Grand Hotel* structure pretentiously convoluted so that it is an epic poem about disillusioned Americans. Two dozen characters are moved through five days of discordant fetes, from one banality (a welcome home for Barbara Jean, Tennessee's darling singer, in which the movie does the stale symbol of the majorette, the baton twirler, as the unaware sex object) to a final fixture out of Busby Berkeley, where an assumed no-talent (Harris) who's been hanging around the fringes for six reels suddenly blossoms in Ruby Keeler fashion as a show-stopper. She quells a disturbed crowd which has just witnessed an assassination with her slick Broadway style, her voice always rising: "You may say I'm not free, but it don't worry me."

It isn't unusual for movies to do weird things with the music of a place (New Orleans in "Birth of the Blues"), a singer (Diana Ross's Billie Holliday), or a composer (Cary Grant's Cole Porter), but the infuriating *Nashville*, busily criticizing the music world of Country/Western, hasn't even bothered to investigate the best sounds of the place: Hank Williams, Jimmy Rogers, Minnie Pearl. The cheap-shot quality is that the happiness of the Altman family takes precedence over a real Nashville portrait. This family—a 27-year-old L.A. cat, Richard Baskin, who scored the film and admits owning only one C&W album at the time he was hired, and an assortment of actors from "Laugh In," etc. whose song solos appear at regular intervals as in an old Paramount Theater vaudeville show—is amateurishly delighted at all times. "Gee, I can write a hit tune about being easy, little Lorelei, we must be doing something right to last two hundred years." Along with the schmaltz, Lily Tomlin moving her lips in mechanical Gospel ecstasy, the music is orchestrated immediately into a melody, which means a cold-hearted stud, with fake tenderness, using two words, "I'm easy," every eighth and ninth word.

Nashville is a promiscuous movie that will go for anything to make a sensation. Its director is supposed to be dedicated to kaleidoscopic images and sounds, the fringe aspect of an event, improvisatory structuralism. Part of Altman is modern, but his movie, like Heinz 24 Varieties, has a character representing each area of society. The promiscuity is everywhere but its most nagging phenomenon is a group of nonentities who appear at every bash: a husband who is like a mountain man and too old for his goofy runaway wife, a beribboned soldier, a mysterious black who runs an airport coffee shop, an obvious oddball cyclist with enormous goggles, some magic tricks, but no words. Their tick-tock, checking-in quality is irritating, but, for a director famous for fluidity and glancing effects, these inevitables seem cold and horribly conventional.

Talk about sensation mongering: The movie is chameleonesque, skipping around for excitements, flip-flopping attitudes towards the material, switching its way through Godard-Tashlin-Fellini-Jewison-Spielberg, and, especially, doing turnabouts with single note stereotypes. A key figure, like a young Ozzie Nelson, is an aspiring young musician with an omnipresent fiddle case and a puzzling, un-divulged interior. At each event, he falls into a different movie atmosphere and its built-in message. The first half hour is a staged casualness which starts with an aborted Tashlin gag about all the celebrities hurrying to leave the airport, becoming locked together, knocking down the gate opening device allowing a car into the parking lot. This situation develops into a huge traffic jam where characters who had been manicly daffy in the Jerry Lewis manner abruptly switch to the facetiously brutal characters of *Weekend* and Fellini's claustrophobic genius sweating in an *8½* car. The boy with the violin case slams down the hood of his smoking sedan and storms off: abandoning his car with the don't-give-a-damn spirit of a Godard rebel. Midway in the film, he becomes a meek Mother's boy during a crucial phone call, then a heavy mourner at a classic movie funeral (deep mist or rain, a distant shot of dark shapes, like Grant Wood's solemn Americans, huddled around a grave), and, for the big assassination scene in bright sunlight during the same afternoon, he is Kazan's *Face in the Crowd* ready to go berserk.

This mush from the man who made *M*A*S*H* hinges on its last crowd scene, a new roots third party rally in which twenty-four cast members appear (each one gets equal time) for Altman's inevitable punch ending. His cemetery now includes bird-like Bud Cort crashing on the Astrodome floor in *Brewster McCloud*, boaster Beatty as a snow-covered corpse in *McCabe*, a proper Rene Auberjonois husband knocked off the road by his schizoid wife in *Images*, the double-crossing Bouton playboy gunned down by Marlowe in *The Long Good-bye*, Keith Carradine's anti-capitalist gunsel ambushed by cops in *Thieves Like Us*, plus a raft of spiritual deaths: the astronaut James Caan in *Countdown*, dope-smoking Julie Christie in *McCabe*, the big winning gamblers in *California Split* who lose their life-giving friendship.

"This isn't Dallas!" shouts *Nashville*'s bleeding poet laureate (Henry Gibson) after Barbara Jean's been gunned down by a dented pistol that's been bouncing around in David Hayward's empty violin case. The ending works through symbols: a screen-covering American flag with an engineered wind swell, an audience that changes on cue from polite and stiff through a dozen-plus songs into a slow-building affirming chorus, close-ups of babies and dutiful parents; and some lower-case symbols, a female somnambulist out for a stroll in her fire department uniform, a soldier-defender smothering the assassin. The suggestion that a crackpot America is re-sealing itself winds into the emptiest of mechanisms: a slow reverse zoom shooting diagonally down on the Barbara Harris solo, gradually enveloping the whole crowd, the flag, and the Nashville Parthenon before panning into the sky.

Altman's godlike camera view, combined with the demagoguery-to-democracy soundtrack (from Gibson's pompous ode through a melting-pot of country-folk sounds to a massed chorus), creates a Fifties idea of enduring America. This latest improvisation, "the biggest, most complex movie family Altman has ever assembled," is not about Nashville, Country-Western sounds, but about group endeavor: the cure for a fucked-up America—hysterical, filled with grotesquerie, hooked on celebrities—is something on the order of Altman's collaborative, everyone together art. "At the start of a typical day Bob would communicate the feeling, 'what kind of fun are we going to have today. . . .'"

with Patricia Patterson; August 3, 1975

Nicolas Roeg

"It's something that obsesses me: the idea of where, how we approach, and where we finally reach our personal death scenes. Nowadays, when people talk of the Gothic cinema, they're really talking about camp. It's very sad, because the Gothic is a tremendous cultural influence, not a funny thing at all."

—Nicolas Roeg

A LONG-TIME cameraman (since 1947) on some unique projects, *Petulia* for Dick Lester and *The Masque of the Red Death* for Roger Corman, Nicolas Roeg is an elegant if arty director with an imposing record: a fast, brutal, junked-up action film about perverted sexuality as the key to violence (*Performance*, a collaboration with Donald Cammell: "It's impossible to sort out who did what"); a shrewd reading of child behavior done with a documentarist's eye, proving his career-long idea that the world, whatever its faults, is visually breathtaking (*Walkabout*); and his most complex film to date, a Henry James-like maze built around Donald Sutherland's brilliantly sombre acting of a careful, practical man in an uncontrollable city ("Don't expect too much, Mr. Baxter," says the police inspector of Venice's ancient maze, which finally destroys Sutherland and his willfulness in *Don't Look Now*).

Always involved with this against that, the co-existence of contradictories, Roeg's very athletic films are filled with baroque strategies—jumpy and jazzy editing, a topsy-turvy scale, an aquarium-like space in which hush is a major effect along with the sense of people floating dreamily toward the front of a stretched out, sinister vastness—and the feeling that people don't love life enough; they're either too rigid or willful to get as much out of life as they could.

His extremely faceted film is very ingratiating, but the charm—the cute animal shots, impeccably trim cosmopolitans and pretty sunsets—counts much less than the astute use of the medium. Each film starts with a minimal plot idea—three children adrift on the Australian outback; a gangster hiding from the syndicate in an erotic manipulator's haze of drugs, transsexuality and literary references; a church restorer receiving a message from the grave that his life's in danger ("My daughter does not send messages, Laura . . . she is dead, dead, dead!")—and then is built into an intricate, semi-slick, absorbing blend of the ominous and lyrically sensual.

While the radical Germans were picking up the transsexual banner and facetious attitude from Warhol, it would seem that England's big three—Losey,

Boorman and Roeg—were fastening on *Muriel*, its princely craftsmanship and Leftist fervor. Talking about the way the French handled themselves in Algeria and World War II, Resnais's movie about Boulogne, a city split by its bombed past and reconstructed postwar present, shows the marks left on its citizens by the sordid or disillusioning parts they played in two wars.

The counter-narrative devices of *Muriel* turn up repeatedly in the baroque British film, particularly the rapid cutting that produces a ripple of shots for each event, the disjunctive soundtrack that is situated at odd angles to the people's presence, and the feeling of civilized, middle-class people caught in the midst of corruption that set in without their noticing it. Most of all, they respond to a landscape-person synthesis, the effect of people momentarily tied together in a subversive milieu. Terrain, potently present, becomes the main event, and the camera becomes the brains of the operation, the chief weapon for exposing social corrosion in the sterile, plastic L.A. nightmare of shiny office buildings, used-car lots and over-sized billboards (Boorman's *Point Blank*), or corrosion being overturned in Roeg's three films, where exotic terrain points out the deficiencies in a tidy miss, macho gangster, and a too sensible architect.

In Roeg's surreal strangeness, there is always an eerie message that London, indoors and out (*Performance*), the desolate Australian wilderness (*Walkabout*) and the Gothic corridors and waterways of Venice (*Don't Look Now*) existed before his people were born and will be there after they die, which happens often in three films bracketed by deaths, fore and aft. This last film, which starts with a church restorer's daughter chasing a rubber ball into a lake and drowning, and ends with her father killed by a hook-faced dwarf wearing his daughter's shiny red raincoat (pretty strange), creates an authentic adult terror. As the Baxter couple (Sutherland and Julie Christie) becomes entwined with a British psychic and her sister who are touristing in Venice, Daphne Du Maurier's addlepated writing is toughened by an interesting portrait of Venice in winter, putting the spectator in contact with the city's surfaces, heights, dampness, rats, hallways, canals.

"Oh, don't be sad. I've seen your daughter sitting between you and your husband . . . and she's laughing, she's very happy you know." Sutherland's church restorer, who's prescient himself but resists it, doesn't pay attention to Hilary Mason's messages from daughter Christine. But Roeg's use of this blind, dowdy English spinster shows Hitchcock's ability to milk terror from enigmatic secondary characters, plus his own geographic cunning for entangling a character's possibly sinister traits in a deep, threatening space. Roeg is very inventive and likably hokey (in Hitchcock's false-clue style) using her eerie moon-face and large halt-stepping body to animate his city's unpredictable, unfavorable terrain. Sporting her mischievously into backgrounds, choreographing her into the most awkward relationships with beds, choir stalls, mantle mementos, bringing out her rabid, maiden-aunt benevolence with a jack-rabbit camera, Roeg's Gothic movie has a scene-by-scene richness unique in films.

More than just a pretty, camera-minded director taking on offbeat subjects (drugs, transsexuality, the will and the supernatural), Roeg is an animist of the first-run theaters. He implies that a medieval statue, a flock of ducks flapping in a mucky canal, a red stain on a slide, a pair of white rats struggling to get out of the water, the tiny mosaic tiles stomped by a bishop's shoe, are as alive with sinister possibilities as the forbidding city and the questionably motivated people.

Cutting sharply on people in mid-action, covering each event with one camera focus after another, from extreme deep space to a closeup, *Don't Look Now* is a very active film employing the stretched effects, operatic lighting and stylish people of Mannerist art. In each shot, the blind psychic is presented differently: she is variously seen from below, as a closeup of her blue irisless eyes, or as a disturbing tiny figure running her hands across the rails of a choir stall. The look of Roeg's cinema is wedded to extreme changes in scale and point of view. He threads every part of the medium into each situation, using such suspect devices as slow motion, zooms and stop frames to create an aquarium's density.

If not the best scene, *Don't Look Now*'s showiest set piece is a Sutherland-Christie sex act, all surface and no insides, that barely skirts fashion-magazine snobbery, but illustrates how far Roeg will move off the central content of a scene to expand its ideas and give the sense of lurking trouble. The scene is not the most lovable: its sex could be performed only by the most svelte, agile and well-heeled . . . the actors are given the full glamour treatment: shadows, elegant serpentine effects with their torsos. It is interesting that Roeg's extrapolated material invariably toughens up the event, suggesting threat from the underworld, either spiritually or psychologically. In this case, a dot-dash sequence of shots, in which the serpentine motion of the coitus is alternated with vertical mid-torso shots of one or the other person getting dressed, (1) becomes more elegantly viewable; (2) places the people more firmly in a posh, selected social strata, and (3) underlines their ruminative, worried, even fragile connection to Venice's ungraspable landscape.

Roeg's attracted to tank tactics, such as fish-eyed focuses, convex reflections and skittish movement. As often as not, his people are in deep or middle space, but there is an unpredictable approaching and receding toward the camera, the way a fish moves toward an aquarium's viewing glass. When Jagger, a bankrupt *Performance* singer living out his time in exotic decadence, sings his "Memo from Turner," challenging the syndicate's idea of masculinity, his taunting thrusts his face close to a convex lens, which splays and demonizes his features. This same lens maneuver on the children's nap in *Walkabout* is supposed to suggest pulverizing desert heat.

The amount of detail and complicating delays that are woven into a single flowing line of action is astounding, probably unique in the history of action films. Resnais's elliptical editing becomes much more aggressive and pyrotechnical through a doubling back, reassessing attitude and a Hitchcockian desire to throw you off the main forward moving plot. A simple action, Sutherland positioning a statue, three people meeting on a quay, goes forward by an infinite number of asides (you're not sure what these signify, but you feel it's something). A simple situation breaks up into subterranean aspects: why should the closeup of an elegant Rex Harrison–type bishop opening his overcoat to reach for a handkerchief have such an unsettling impact? Cutting across the normal flow of a mundane meeting with an enigmatic gesture that fills the whole screen adds to the growing malevolence that surrounds Sutherland. Following the overcoat gesture, the murmured words of the low-key bishop, "considering it's the house of God, he doesn't take care of it . . . perhaps he has other priorities," elicit the same did-I-hear-right, did-I-see-right response.

Three events—the fall from the scaffold, the placement of the statue on the church's outer wall, Sutherland's interview with the suspicious, ambivalent police inspector (a strange, insolent, very effective performance)—are at the heart of this cubistically spiraling style, in which there is always the sense of an event being excavated for any potential intrigues. Sutherland is on an amateurishly built, creaking scaffold three floors up, checking some new mosaics against the originals in a wall picture. A plank breaks loose high above him, crashes down, breaking the scaffold. Sutherland and the tiny mosaics are sent flying. The smoothness of this accident is constantly sliced, so that the event is recorded cubistically from various sides. Along with the tenuous, poignant, moment-in-time quality, there is the sense of a movie spiraling on itself, revealing a great deal without appearing hokey. The scene finally ends on a canal far away from the church: the police dredging a murder victim from the canal, lifting her humiliated form by crane out of the polluted water. The grim tableau, seen from the distance, suggests a shameful, upside-down crucifixion; Sutherland, barely recovered from his fall, can hardly take in this new evidence of waste and horror lurking in the city.

Roeg's complex Gothic style also involves:

(1) putting his handsome characters on a disorienting trampoline: the trampoline's sensation is one of dislocation, of being in a rising-falling suspension with no secure sense of ground. The scaffold's creaking slowly back and forth: each move to the right reveals a giant Byzantine eye staring between Sutherland's ankles; far below, the baleful bishop watches a tense situation about to explode.

(2) screwing up the scale of the universe: when the two *Walkabout* children, miss clean and master cub scout, begin their test in the outback, her schoolgirl oxfords float past an eight-inch reptile; the camera zooms in to reveal a hissing, fork-tongued creature out of Bosch with a mane like a dinosaur.

(3) suggesting the quality of hush: the style constantly emphasizes the intervals between people, parts of events and sounds. The hush takes place in the no-man's-land when the character and/or spectator are trying to digest different experiences. Two kids are sleeping peacefully alongside a waterhole. As they sleep and the night passes through five light stages, an enormous snake slithers along a branch close to their bodies, a wombat waddles past sniffing at them, neither awakening nor frightening either one, particularly the towhead zonked out and smiling in the middle of this animal crossroad.

(4) using a distinctive cutting rhythm for each section: the suspenseful opening of *Don't Look Now* starts with rain on the lake and ends with Christie's abrupt scream, at the sight of her daughter's corpse in her husband's arms; it is a crisscross of shots, each one slightly to the right or left of the preceding one. When the Aborigine boy first appears in *Walkabout*, a tiny silhouette on the horizon, advancing in a snake-like zigzag down the hill toward the exhausted brother and sister, this left-right strategy follows a slower expressionistic route (closeup of a large lizard swallowing a smaller one, stop frames of the triumphant hunter, Lucien John's eye-blinking wonder at the black's whirling approach) into a trademark lushness.

In *Muriel*, the overriding quality is the cool ecstasy about the old-new city's physicality and the sad transience of the people, their delusions and obsessions. *Walkabout* is filled with sadness, in this case the divorce of Sydney's middle-class people from Nature. Their brittle isolation is swiftly condensed in a sinister set-piece of card-like shots. This strange synthesis has Resnais's aristocratic precision and cool: an eager-to-conform girl practicing breathing exercises in a voice class, a child standing with charming self-confidence among pedestrians at a busy corner, a shot of a brick wall that pans right to expose the desolate outback, a Hockney-esque image of the father, with cocktail in hand, gazing dyspeptically at his two kids capering in a magnificent pool fronting the sea. This staccato section is so like a sharp knife . . . as though the buildings were sucking the life out of the people.

Walkabout, which starts with one type of suicide, the children's crazy father trying to shoot them ("come out now . . . it's getting late, we've got to go now, can't waste time") and hitting only the boy's tin soldiers off a boulder before killing himself, and ends with an Aborigine youngster's ritualized willing of his death, makes you think of the basic knitter's formula: one stitch of charm, one stitch of cruelty. The story: an antiseptic teenager (Jenny Agutter) and her toy-hoarding brother (Lucien John) are left adrift on the edge of an immense desert by their father's suicide. A cheerfully stoic Aborigine (David Gumpilil), a whirling hunter of animals on a solitary tour to prove his manhood, discovers them at the edge of exhaustion, and guides them back to civilization, where the girl retreats back to her Bold and Ajax persona, and the black, reading her sexual fear as a death sign, hangs himself.

The movie shows its director as a sentimental R. D. Laing psychiatrist creating a wonderful enchanted kingdom of snakes, spiders, wombats . . . with an anti-capitalist twist and a sentimental back-to-Nature solution to the problems of civilization. A sort of Hansel and Gretel fairy story: cast out in the woods by parents, coming to the crone in the gingerbread house, throwing the witch in a boiling caldron, etc. The Gothically underlined, rather swank movie not only vouches for Laing's idea that that society-perversion the nuclear family is the surest road to misery, but has the authentic exhilaration of an adventure story. It is half heartbreaking magic, like a *Jr. Moby Dick*, and half Kodak cloying.

Inside its sun-struck pace, lush landscape images and associative editing, *Walkabout* is a pessimistic impression of two Sydney children civilized to death by an alienating city, schooling and family, almost zooming to freedom through their odyssey but not making it. One of the last words the clench-faced father tells his son, chewing on a butterscotch in the VW's back seat: "Don't eat with your mouth full son." Later, during their desert trek, his uptight sister reprimands him: "Look after your clothes, people will think we're tramps." The kid, game and willing to believe, looks around the Australian emptiness: "What people?" Where the family is all rules, the Aborigine responds directly to the need of the moment. The movie's all about gifts: the black boy's gift is teaching the Sydney children survival know-how, practicality, as opposed to law-abidance.

One of the movie's gifts to an audience is a Fourth of July display of camera tricks, childhood insights, a zany piling on of details in a jammed frame.

The young boy seeing the Aborigine in the distance blinks his eyes, which don't stop popping through the next three minutes. The Aborigine is hunting a giant desert lizard: as he swirls closer, you realize his waist, encircled by a ring of dead lizards, is aswarm with 50 flies and their buzzing on the soundtrack: bzzz . . . bzzz . . . bzzz. The movie's soundtrack is filled with many such non-human sounds mixed with silence, voluptuous music and sometimes a human voice. The little boy is often imitating car motors, airplanes: "bam . . . bam . . . ," aiming a green plastic water pistol at an imaginary airplane, whereupon his fed-up father, in the VW, stops reading his geological report, debarks from the car, and uses his hunting rifle on the boy. Again, Roeg gives us one stitch of charm, one stitch of cruelty.

An average scene is a wondrous deep-focus experience that goes forward in a meticulous crisscross of free associations. Passing some camels (or cameras —the movie has a dozen operating on each event) in the distance, the amenable, on-his-toes kid envisions a caravan of 1900 prospectors riding the camels. The scene alternates between his daydream and his sister's fantasy which is riveted on the tight, muscular buttocks of their Aborigine savior. The undulating, sun-struck scene is filled to brimming: vista shots of the camels that bend around the three youngsters, closeups of the children's feet showing the difficulty of walking through the heat and sand, the boy carrying on an imaginary gallantry with his fantasized fellow travelers, by doffing his school cap each time the caravan scene catches up with him.

One thing that the movie is always saying is "be open, be open." It's rigidity that keeps Jenny, short for hygienic ("you've got to make your clothes last") locked in her mother's world of jobs, time, and kitchen gadgets. The director is always available to the possibility of evil. The teenaged Jenny's authority and coolness is monstrous from beginning to end. It's not that the girl is cruel but that she's insensitive to anything but the world as it's defined by radio commercials. She's the quintessence of beauty and health, plenty of calcium and good fruit, but, despite her lush beauty, she's rather cranky, incurious and fanatically conventional. She sits enthralled at a radio lesson in how to use a fish knife. Roeg, who believes the world's become health-crazy, that the ideal of perfect health has replaced religion, family, consequences, paradoxically loves beautiful bodies, animals, foliage. His movies are extra sweet because of their luxury: beautiful skin, flowers, near-naked buttocks.

His forbidding, grandiloquent work rests rather precariously on a sweet-and-sour sword's edge: on the one hand, a predilection for dealing only with the beautiful people and *National Geographic* photography (right now, he's working with David Bowie in New Mexico) side by side with a talent for expressing the primordial depths erupting in the modern world. His film is that of a savoring, thoughtful, idealizing sensualist who can gunk up a movie with sex-tease nonsense and florid sunsets that drive you up a wall. At the same time, as with Resnais, he is not coercive: he doesn't insist that you see things, people or events through his eyes. His labyrinthian movie, which keeps you entangled in its every moment, is a protest against the smooth, harmonious existence, the grayness of neighboring films. From the aggressive, propagandistic *Performance* (make love, not war) through the serious attempt to make *Don't Look Now* a modern Gothic movie, Roeg's message has been: the most fulfilled life is the one that advantages itself of all the signs-gifts that life throws into the individual's path. There is more peripheral richness in the scaffold sequence than in the entire *Night Moves*, with its old-fashioned hawking of actors' faces, or *The Passenger*, where landscapes divulge their handsome identity in an instant.

with Patricia Patterson; September 9, 1975

Badlands, Mean Streets, and The Wind and the Lion

"It occurred to me as I looked through my father's stereopticon that I was just a little girl from Texas and I had only a certain number of years to live." As the acquiescent, slack Holly (Sissy Spacek) muses out loud about the limitations of life, wondering what her future spouse is doing at this moment, "is he thinking about me somehow even though he doesn't know me," the screen fills with haunting images of the world's past. These images jump around in terms of geography and culture: the sphinx, two Victorian harlots leaning on a piano, a sentimental picture of a farm boy and his sad girl.

Along with Warren Oates' lean performance of a billboard-painting loner and the modernized Tom Benton view of Midwest Americana, Malick's *Badlands* is often into the most artist-bewitching strategy of the '70s. Conceptual artists like John Baldessari, Yvonne Rainer in her two films, Eleanor Antin and Martha Rosslet in their postcard diaries, Fred Lonidier, Phil Steinmetz and Allan Sekula in their photo-fiction narratives are all using visual images and verbal texts in which the alignment isn't exact, so there is a space or jar created by the disjunct. In that space, the irony, humor, absurdity or message resides. The electricity created by the jar between text and visuals, words and pictures, has become the favorite technique for pinning down the madness of the human condition. It's also a strategy that allows for an exhilarating freedom, opening up the film, photo, painting format formerly closed to the possibility of informational facetiousness.

One of the earliest, surpassing examples: Godard's grainy, brusquely edited, stark antiwar film, *Les Carabiniers*. Throughout the mordant fable, two cretinous brothers, Michelange and Ulysses, send home postcards describing their adventures in the king's war, appended with terrific messages presented in longhand on the screen: "We can break old men's glasses, we can steal juke-boxes and slaughter innocents." The climactic scene: promised the world, the soldiers come back with a suitcase filled with postcards which voluptuously pin down the variety and beauty of civilization in a nearly ten-minute scene. Godard's idea is that this pictorial catalog—a 1920s Maserati, Durer's rabbit, the Taj Mahal, the technicolor works in Hollywood, the Chicago aquarium—represents the mad disparity of image and reality. The double-time biography of Liv Ullmann, which used actual snapshots of the actress to prove a feminist point, was the least trumped-up section of Bergman's otherwise soapy *Scenes From a Marriage*, Rainer's very interesting *Film About a Woman Who . . .* has a postcard-narration sequence, and the home-movie sequence in *Mean Streets*, including the typewritten credits, is vivacious and electric.

All these artists are turning their backs on '60s formalism in favor of a crossed-media art involved with biography, myth, history. Cliche is super pop-ular ("cliche is in a sense the purest art of intelligibility: it tempts us with the possibility of enclosing life with beautifully inalterable formulas, of obscuring the arbitrary nature of imagination with an appearance of necessity" is a Leo Bersani quote which appears twice in Rainer's *Film*) as is the gritty, nervous teasing of the *Scarface* genre in *Mean Streets*, the broad parodying of a swash-buckler in Milius' *Lion* film, the slyly drained version of the Bonnie Clyde spree through flat, dull American towns in *Badlands*.

No survey of American films could route itself around two 1973 films, *Mean Streets* and *Badlands*, ambivalent milieu films about frenetic NYC punks and a Mr. Cool mad-dog killer, which are ebulliently lit from inside by a stored-up desire to make a personal statement. If these two oddballers, still intellectu-ally interesting in 1975, are linked with a more recent writer-director film, *The Wind and the Lion*, they spotlight various postures that make the New Holly-wood film so different from its forerunners, i.e., a facetious attitude about his-tory, an automatic distrust of cops-soldiers-presidents, and, along with the bent for or against bizarre Americana, a jamming on the idea that people are inex-tricably influenced by myths, cliches, media, postcards, diaries, home movies, letters, etc.

From its jived, happy credit sequence, segments of a home movie with Keitel's Charlie mugging a church christening, *Mean Sreets* is uniquely keyed to the small, off-center improvising of a snapshot. *The Wind and the Windy, The King and I* crossed with Brecht and a ton of anti-American roundhouse swings, is constantly teasing the official photograph. *Badlands* is the Bonnie-Clyde bloodbath done without emotions or reactions, plus a suave, painterly image (the visuals resemble postcards with the color printed twice) that bespeaks a near-comatose Dakota life. The lethargy of S. Dakotans is joined with a girl's (Sissy Spaced) deadpan, rosy-sided diary on the soundtrack. It takes this blood-less chick eight murders to figure her ex-garbage slinger with Nat Cole in his heart as not only "trigger happy," but, in fact, "the hell-bent type." "Hi, we're on the run, we'd like to hide out here for a few hours." A frozen-with-fear rich man, a paper doll chastized by gentility, says: "Of course, go right ahead." Holly, educated on fan mags and pop lyrics, tours the man's gothic mansion, deter-mined to normalize pure terror. Meanwhile, her industrous lover (he was the handsomest boy I ever saw . . . he looked just like James Dean), always on the prowl between emotionless murders for useful items, has dug up a silver loving cup, an old football and a dictaphone for some studious Norman P. Veale messages for straightening potential Dakotan screwups: "Listen to your par-ents. They usually know best. Don't look down on the minority opinion, keep an open mind. But when the minority becomes a majority opinion, pay atten-tion to it."

The deliberate mismatch of what you see and what you hear puts *Badlands* in the surreal neighborhood of a Thoreau nature study crossed with Lewis Car-roll. One choice small event occurs near nightfall on the prairie. The still faith-ful and gullible Spacek is reporting Kit's latest plan to organize their outlawed life. "Kit said we had to get rid of that football because it was excess baggage." On screen, Sheen is in the middle of a prairie nowhere, repeatedly shooting a worn-out football, then trying to sqoosh out the air with gun butt and cowboy boots. He does it with the seriousness of a chem major. All this takes place about three minutes after her bland sing song reports: "Kit hits cows with the Cadillac to save ammo."

One thing that stands out is the way that many of the new demons in Hol-lywood and Marin Co. lived their youth in the Eisenhower '50s, hid out in film schools and Corman-ish B films during the heyday of Godard and Snow, and exploded in the '70s as impatient Prousts in an attraction-repulsion syndrome with the pious, smug Americanism that pummeled their teenaged years. These 30-year-olds, who are on a kick investigating myths, cliches and auto-biography, were educated in an era that was unforgettable, not only for the sponge mop, Pat Boone and Korea, but for sincerity, chastity and the drabbest clothes of the 20th century, charcoal gray being the big color. The main point being made here is that each movie, plus a dozen semi-tortures like *White Line Fever*, gets its bite from being a backlash against the solemnity of the '50s.

The viewpoint in each film is from the outside looking in on a milieu that may seem as askew and perverse as Alice's Wonderland. From Sheen's angry moments in *Badlands* (disappearing behind a barn, where he starts kicking the ground, furiously jerking his shoulders, flinging his head around to rid himself of a pathological malice) to the Roosevelt vignettes in Milius' *Lion*, with Brian Keith's enactment of a middle-aged boy scout promoting America and himself as the quintessence of manliness, there is a quality of quaintness. The past is treated with an indulgence that expects idiocies.

Milius' film is a languid, cheerful portrait of the American as a beamish blunderer squandering lives and energy in the third world. It takes place alternately around Morocco and wherever Teddy Roosevelt's sporting performances occur. A robust, deep-chested Teddy (Keith) is clean, sure of himself, optimistic, and the movie implies that such conceit, naivete, and shallow comprehension has led in time directly to Selma, My Lai and Kent State. A rich American widow is kidnapped by Raisuli, the last of the Barbary pirates, whereupon Roosevelt creates a campaign catch phrase (Pedecaris alive or Raisuli dead) and some whacky moves to get her back.

Mean Streets, one of the classiest 1970s films, talks about the '50s in an immigrant neighborhood from an ambivalent viewpoint, that of a writer-director who is now an outsider looking in but still yearns to be part of the neighborhood. Scorsese, who is the voice-over for Charley's conscience in the opening church scene and plays the small, retiring gunman (to perfection) who shoots up the three leads in the final Brooklyn Bridge scene, doesn't know whether to say hurrah for Little Italy or let me out of the place. His stand-in, Keitel's Charley, everybody's guardian, "everybody likes Charley, a regular fucking politician, this guy," is reminiscent of Brando's Terry Malloy in *On The Waterfront*, a big '50s hit. Keitel's weight-lifter's showy grace, his nervous-tiny fidgets, is stationed, like Scorsese himself, between Teresa who wants out in the worst way, "who needs this place," and his taunting pal, Johnny Boy (De Niro), who's totally out of control and caught up in the neighborhood, like a whirlwind.

Mean Streets is a terrific example of intricate, tough filmmaking. Like Renoir's *M. Lange* gem, Scorsese's whip-like style moves his ensemble with incredible vivacity in an opening disco scene and later in a remarkable car scene with a funny queen screaming at every cute guy who passes in the street,

"Wait for me, honey," mortifying all the tough hoods with him in the car. The poignant street film is a once-in-a-lifetime work: his own neighborhood, talented actors before they've scored and all the same age (nothing to lose), it's an intensely autobiographical work.

Scorsese's gritty, small imaged, nervous epic is a lower-case study of petty hoods who are more a problem to themselves than to the police or rival gangs. Grandiosity, paranoia and saving face are the movie's subjects, rather than real crime. Still, it is the small lower-case touch that sets the movie off from its Caesar-Scarface forerunners. The oldest of gangster-film violences, one car's gangsters shooting up another car's trio, is cashed for a dozen small-time points. The two hoods are not only stunned that they butchered Charley-Teresa-Johnny, but they park nearby like amazed grandstanders with a stricken curious look on their faces. An over-choreographed bash in a poolroom is at least crossed by an uncanny surprise note: a feisty fatty in tennis shoes who turns into a Toshiro Mifune. A possible dull stretch while moving the lovers from hotel tryst to elevator is cunningly spiced with a credible racist crack: one minority picking on another.

This shot-in-the-dark film that paid off shows a gut connection to the '50s on Mott St. The crude use of earthy language to make strong contact: "Where the hell you been, Johnny? Your cousin's been worried sick." The rejoinder ("I've been out, taking a walk, what's the big deal, can't I go for a walk?") comes from the all-stops-out, suicidal Robert De Niro, who's just casually come through the fire-escape window after ferociously and furtively beating it up and down the East Side pavements. The show-biz gesturing, vacillating between raging and supplication, reeks of the '50s: hiding the fact of caring for a girl from pals, horrified about a girl's obscene language ("boy, Teresa, you've got some mouth"), looking good to other guys ("I don't want Johnny Boy making me look like a jerk-off"). Scorsese understands these touchy bonds.

From one angle, *Mean Streets* is another glorification of the hood as a glamorous energy force. At least, Scorsese has injected a rare lower-case vision, from the concept of the area as small figures in a threatening, congested darkness to the murky, musical, prowling camera. Scorsese's grasp of the hilarity, finely tuned camaraderie and in-fighting that can happen in a car adds a recurring and unique element to this film, the final scene beginning with De Niro's charming, bravado dance around the car, when his life's hanging by a thread, and proceeding through a ride that is cunningly detailed just for its mapping and geography. "You're sure you know where you're going, Charley?" Charley answers: "You're asking me, do I know Brooklyn? Does Livingston know Africa?" The movie's ragged, vitriolic image is a high '70s point, and it has a razzing sound track that is great for juicy NYC timing and emphasis, the way a single word like moog or Joey Clams surfaces out of a sandpapered garble. This final ride, with a willowy, gritty Amy Robinson and the incautious, self-destructive De Niro slicing perfectly in and out of Keitel's intricate put-on piety, "What's this, Chahley, Yuh talkin' to yuhself now," is beyond perfect ensemble acting into exhilaration.

with Patricia Patterson; September 23, 1975

New York Film Festival: 1975

NEW YORK's press knows without a doubt how movie elements should behave, and it excoriates those films which dare to rearrange formal conventions. It tells us (1) music should never be an aggressive, dominant element (as it is in *Moses and Aaron*); (2) voices over the film should explain and correspond with visual material and never create a contradiction to the image (*India Song* blasts this law); (3) an image should hold the screen no longer than it takes a quick New Yorker to digest the point (*Kaspar Hauser* has its own passionately held notion of pace and its purpose); (4) an image should never be blocky, sculptural, and anti-flow (*Moses and Aaron* promulgates these Cézanne-esque qualities) or airlessly compacted, flattened into close frontality (the homosexuals in *Fist-Right of Freedom* are often profiled toward each other, close to the camera, filling most of the frame). Above all, a movie should progress fluidly in a rhythm and length that are comfortable and familiar to audiences (which applies to none of the above films, our favorites at this year's New York Film Festival).

Yvonne Rainer, a Manhattan dancer and filmmaker, describes one of her dances with an iconoclastic humor unknown to the righteous, reproving New York movie critic, who not only knows every point at which an artist goes right or wrong, but knows it conclusively within twenty-four hours. Ms. Rainer talking about *Parts of Some Sextets*: "Its repetition of actions, its length, its relentless recitation, its inconsequential ebb and flow all combined to produce an effect of nothing happening. The dance went nowhere, did not develop, progressed as though on a treadmill or like a ten-ton truck stuck on a hill: it shifts gears, groans, sweats, farts, but doesn't move an inch. Perhaps next time my truck will make some headway; perhaps it will inch forward—imperceptible—or fall backward—headlong."

Ms. Rainer is a saturnine independent who makes jokey, unkempt, opinionated films ("Well, you know, Shirley, I've always been a pushover for sweeping statements about society by deep thinkers"). None of her films are shown in this year's turn of Roud's Roulette Wheel at Lincoln Center.

"Is it Ms. Duras's intention to bore the audience, and, if so, does she feel she has succeeded?" This question, which is asked Duras every time she brings the festival another of her talented cryptic movies of beautiful people trapped in rituals, is typical of New York's daily-weekly press, treating anything other than illustrative storytelling as the act of a witch. This brings up some subdued, plotty filmmaking: *The Wonderful Crook*, a Swiss world in which all emphasis is on tidy landscape, décor, and props. The movie stays far away from its subjects, lingering on small people, shopkeepers and workers, in pleasant outdoors décor that contradicts the reality of their trade; the few closeups remain decorative and reveal little in a soft, all-the-way Thirties storytelling that made many critics anything from comfortably happy to ecstatic.

With its gentle, fresh landscapes and towns, laundered to pristine perfection, and a *tout va bien* attitude that expresses itself in the diluted, rhythmic pace, the movie's design involves keeping the figures small inside the landscapes and being tidy and/or whimsical with each event that might otherwise become sordid. The hero's first robbery, to pay the wages of the carpenters in his failing furniture factory, ends quickly with his shooting a vase of wildflowers. An ugly fight is made piquant by the Robin Hood hero throwing a portly businessman's spectacles into a sprawling oak tree. You barely see the factory or the all-important handmade furniture which furnishes the motive for the entire plot. Everything is muted and decorous: a half-nude cutie pie (Marléne Jobert) in a half-lit room, in a pose-y private moment; she runs the bath, pensively waits in bed for the bath to fill, her feet on the wall. It's terribly photogenic for a supposed private moment, but, in its stiff juicelessness, it's like everything else in the film: tepid and decorous.

In the modern Swiss films, a good character actor has to be repressed, filled with propriety, in no-energy scenes that don't develop and hardly expose the actor beyond a decorative prettiness. A small patrol of talent has been obscured here: Labourier, a firecracker with a solid Thirties toughness in Rivette's cute gripper; Léotard, a swiftly efficient villain, now you see him, now you don't, in *French Connection II*; Depardieu, whose washing-machine salesman in *Nathalie Granger* was a memorable vaudeville turn. These second knives are dropped into this film's fastidious landscapes with an eyedropper. Heaven forbid there should be some excess—acting, dialogue, anything.

The rage against radicalism went on in the press and perhaps exhibited itself behind the scenes in the selection of short films which, with the exception of Straub's *Introduction to Schönberg's Accompanying Music for a Film Scene*, were, across the board, mediocre, philistine. Is it possible that Ernie Gehr hasn't made a brilliantly lit, ghost-image short good enough for this festival?

While some critics talk about the wit and movie legerdemain in *F for Fake*, a tour de force on the pomposity of art dealers, this cleverly edited, fast-cut movie is a crude attack on what is obtainable in painting and how it is read. At the base is François Reichenbach's dismal footage about the art master faker Elmyr de Hory: repeated shots of de Hory, wooden palette perched on his left thumb, squashing his brush into the paint, mixing the color without ever looking at the palette, and then smashing it onto the canvas in an unintentional parody of the inspired artist at work. This image of the modern artist is as misleading silly as the kid in Bresson's *Four Nights of a Dreamer* brushing three strokes before walking back to his tape recorder.

Reichenbach's chit-chat footage has been smartly re-edited by Orson Welles, the main gag being a staccato three- or four-shot interview which ends in a stop frame of the gleeful con artist with a fake conviction and enthusiasm on his face. A typical laugh is gained from Clifford Irving's story that de Hory painted two Modiglianis and one Matisse before lunch and sold all three. De Hory, a natty and rather petite man who wears ascots and wide belts in jet-set bohemian fashion, runs about Ibiza like the island's official host, kibitzing with anybody he meets in outdoor cafés, inviting them to his next party: "Don't forget now, I'll be looking for you." He presides over forced jolly dinners in restaurants, with a glib, stage-center garrulity, as he tells his guests of his most outrageous coups against those fools, the art experts, and brags that every major museum in the world has a de Hory hanging in it.

Throughout, the artist is presented as one who puts something over on others, and the communicated material of painting is only the various insignia that superficially denote a Matisse or van Dongen (de Hory's not bad at a Matisse *conté* crayon drawing, but he paints a lousy van Dongen oil). It is not the joyful effervescent experience indicated by Welles's narration and the chief actors: de Hory, Irving, and the mad zoomer, Reichenbach. Along with its vulgar idea—the concept of art as a conspiracy of greedy, pompous people in collusion to create an image that will make them look like big shots—the actors seem to be pushing the most tiresome hedonism; and beneath some razzle-dazzle editing and insert shots of an editor's paraphernalia, there is Reichenbach's society-reporter's sensibility: celebrities bragging through some flimsy anecdote, walking toward and away from the tipsy, hand-held camera.

Along with the above film, there were two other self-indulgent hand-held camera ramblings. In *Grey Gardens*, a smug crew, liberal and complacent as to its motives, swims toward and around two compulsive, painfully poignant performers, a pair of recluses trying to play up to and not let down this movie crew which is putting them in the spotlight. The camera in *Milestones* is even more A-B-C desultory, jiggling around, tagging after the actors, not very interesting people babbling their lives away. An interesting idea—the student radicals of the Sixties, five years later—weighed down by tons of desultory encounter therapy talk.

Derivative, taking from everywhere, *Black Moon* opens quite wonderfully: damp and romantic early morning light, the image is of a badger sniffing around on the highway. It's in lush countryside, not quite light yet; tension builds as a car is heard approaching. It becomes clear that the badger will be killed, and, after this happens, a slender adolescent in a Tyrolean hat steps out of the small car, traumatized but expressionless, staring back to where the badger lies crushed. From that point, the porcelain-faced English beauty, revealed to be a young girl, is relentlessly tormented and undergoes one unimaginable reversal after another.

After some exquisitely engineered tracking shots which follow the adolescent's orange Honda rippling through woods, across fields, the girl ends up in a Lewis Carroll country house inhabited by kinkiness and multiples. First, she's immersed with Thérèse Giehse, an old lady (not unlike the complainer in *Grey Gardens*) propped in a vast bed littered with food, newspapers, animals. She converses in jabberwocky with her grumpy bosom-buddy rat, checks up on the surrounding male-female war via a large short-wave radio, and eats by suckling her daughter's breast. Lily, the young girl-woman, is then terrorized by a brother and sister who look alike and will tolerate her presence, but won't speak to her. Instead they run their hands slowly over her face and make little pressure with the tips of their fingers on her shoulder. "Oh, your name is Lily," says Cathryn Harrison to Joe Dallesandro; "so is mine." The handsome, muscular Joe, wearing a white ruffled shirt and a golden necklace of two wings around his neck, symbolizes the movie's sensation of being encrusted in rich appurtenances.

Black Moon is prodigiously inventive but in a way that is a rather heartless pastiche of films made with passion and vehemence. The hand-touch communication (bed-ridden Thérèse Giehse running her hands over the contours of Harrison's delicate adolescent face) is a shocking echo of Fini Straubinger's efforts to communicate with other deaf mutes in Herzog's *Land of Silence and Darkness*. A snake crawls over the virginal sleeping teenager in *Walkabout*; another smaller snake crawls up the skirt of the virginal sleeping Lily. In Herzog's *Signs of Life*, the movie comes to a halt, observing some quiet animal behavior, a school of fish causing a paper to twirl in the water; *Black Moon* similarly stops and becomes silent, watching an animal . . . The animals in this movie are fancifully good actors: the wonderfully dumpy unicorn whose slangy talk is mostly comprised of bitchy advice-giving, and a terrifically independent rat who talks like a querulous Moog synthesizer.

We didn't see everything, but it was no surprise that the Munichers (including the Straubs, who have been in Rome five years) provided the intensity and uplift, the sense of crackle, anticipation, that sets their films apart from a work like *Conversation Piece*, a cavernous space inhabited by one interest: Helmut Berger's sinuous, outrageous freeloader. *Fist-Right of Freedom* is less about various types and classes in a dated image of the gay world than it is about the passing snits that lead to petty cruelty, every moment against the nearest person. What seems like a Joan Crawford melodrama (a gentle, unprepossessing guy who has a side-show act—"Fox, The Talking Head"—Fox makes a bundle on the lottery and is slowly fleeced of it by a foppish lover) is really a gutty, pessimistic indictment of the constant treacheries between the closest lovers, friends, and family members that arise out of the minutest provocations.

The Festival's most deceptive movie is loaded with standard clichés (the suave predatory aristocrat in the ascot; Fassbinder, himself, in a cunningly pliant portrait of the rough-trade hustler); the acting is theatrical to lugubrious; the framing is all tight space, little distance between front and back, the people uncomfortably within a tiny box composition (suggesting the claustrophobia of being pinned, forever, with a certain class). The sense of the plot is of a five-line news shocker from the back page built into theater with the focus and framing kept lowercase.

The final scene—Fox lying dead in a garishly lit subway, his pockets being rifled by a pair of twelve-year-olds—is appallingly unremarked. Two of his ex-lovers passing by trying not to notice, the cobalt-blue tiled station, combine to stamp Fox's unimportance. Ironically, the scene is the first since the opening in which the ill-equipped, emotionally vulnerable Fox has been allowed enough room in the frame to feel a bit free and comfortable.

Every Man for Himself and God Against All—the awkward framing, unpredictable camera positions, the flow of light that meanders in and out of the frame—is the droll, zestful, looming work of a filmmaker still on the prowl, making an exploratory work each time out. The work of a self-propelled artist who'll never give up, the movie uses the Kaspar Hauser mystery, "the sole known case in human history in which a man was born as an adult," to take you into an anti-rational as well as irrational movie area previously inhabited by Buñuel, Franju, and Browning. It gains this lovingly crafted anarchism through (1) the intense estrangement of the lead actor, Bruno S.; (2) joining odd-angled inventions and disparate actions choreographed within the same scene; and, especially, (3) giving the sense that the filmmaker has ferreted out (Bruno S. and the prosperous peasant town of Dinkelsbühl, which has tremendous charm in its colored shapes) or made all the elements which appear in the movie. With its unpredictable joins, off-kilter shots, it's a lyrical affirmation that resonates one main idea in the mind: the beauty and loss involved in adjusting to society.

While *Kaspar* is involved with ideas of Access to and Deprivation from expression and communication, *Moses and Aaron* addresses itself to the problem of the space between idea and image in the most materialist of films. "I want the actors to sing as they act, to sing in the desert; in other words to do the Schönberg opera in the most materialist way possible." The movie is exalted, rough-hewn, multifaceted. The *Moses* style (bare décors, minimal camera, actors as passive vessels doing an exact singing of the abrasive and seductive music) is conveyed through an uncompromising concern for Thingness over illustration. This is a theater costume, this is wool . . . Ultimately there is only examination of cracked walls, parched ground, wool, paralleling the same intense physicality of the musical sounds. In the past, its forbiddingly austere filmmakers—who have found a way in films to illustrate the conflict between the necessity to understand one's own time in social and economic terms, and the infinity of silence toward which great art tends—have made the sound track the major element in their films. The delicious and joyful *Moses and Aaron*, however, is a very sensual experience, from its voluptuous 360-degree pan around the oval-shaped Roman arena in the Abruzzi mountains to the Cézanne-like sculptural insistences which make every crack in the arena's walls seem extraordinary, a physical reality that reverberates in the mind.

Both *Moses and Aaron* and the Kaspar Hauser film are apart from the other Festival films, given the ecstatic intensity of their weather. In the exact reading of Schönberg's opera, the *mise-en-scène* has a dry, parched air and a light that produces the sensation of a new sculptural world. The sense of air resounding with music is not only a rare movie experience; this is one of the few times when weather, sound, and physical setting have been united with such tactile objectivity. The movie's anti-flow nature, the scrupulous insistence that each element be accountable for itself, leads to a weird sensation: every item is a concrete phenomenon that has to be read for the first time.

The movie about Kaspar—a grunting, lumplike figure raised in a dungeon-like cellar from infancy—has the sense of fragrance, plus the very delicate motion of rustling, the small effect of flapping bird wings. Whether two sodden, aging creatures are seen in a pauper's prison watching Kaspar's first introduction to words and anatomy ("Kaspar, das ist die hand . . . das ist der arm"), and grousing about it ("What kind of a place is this, anyway?"), or the movie is outdoors on a misty hilltop, Kaspar being back-packed into civilization on the shoulders of his black-caped jailer, the film in terms of light has an awakening, ethereal effect. Like its strange foundling who is a just-born grown man, the movie seems introduced to the world for the first time.

Granted that it looks homemade (one of its wonderful essential qualities), the great quality of the Kaspar movie is its entry into the poetry of the unadjusted and unaligned. Kaspar's appearance in 1828 in the Nuremberg streets has been examined from every possible literary direction; this totally passionate job of direction, an attempt to penetrate details of what Kaspar's reactions might have been, brings together an actor's (Bruno S.) own real-life estrangement and a director's career-long obsession with the awkward and unacclimated, those who are not harmoniously part of society's mainstream, and a sense of pace and composition that is unusual in its music-poetry orientation. The first scene—Bruno S. chained to his cell floor, rapidly shuttling a toy horse on wheels back and forth, abruptly mouthing the word "horse" in rhythm with each movement—symbolizes every other scene in this Rousseau-like mystical experience. The figure of Bruno S. has the clarity and stark innocence of a Rousseau portrait, and each part of his world (Mr. Daumer's living room, his garden) has the same earnestly portrayed presence.

Kaspar's progress from cell to autobiographer is peculiarly paced: it doesn't move by cinematic flow or any approximation of normal movie progress. Each scene is not only involved in itself, but the actor's trance-like stare, sucking an egg in a queer shed scene, finds its own space in a musical development. One of the key qualities in this stubborn film is its off-balance list (a list: an inclination to one side, as of a ship; a tilt) through time, a lyricism that won't be hurried for box-office or plot convenience.

Where Fassbinder works with close two-shots and the effect of two people butting against one another, Herzog's favorite images not only involve Separation but the effect of two stubborn people, kids or adults, involved in different realities. A young girl tries to teach a complex nursery rhyme to Kaspar, who's lunking along in his own rhythm, completely unable to accommodate her speed. While the schoolmarm-ish, insistent girl rattles off her rhyme about a little white cat, Kaspar can best achieve single hard-won words. The very physical feeling of Herzog's films derives partly from double action scenes: an ingratiating kid with a memorable trilling voice teaching the rigid Kaspar anatomy while some squashed prisoners grumble nearby; a lieutenant reading Kaspar's letter while a flea-like town scribe is recording the document, making the officer stop over every word, setting up a rhythmic mismatch of sounds that has the enthusiastic humor of a Preston Sturges scene.

Herzog gives the sense of a director without ambivalence, fantastically concentrated on building his movie by piece. There are qualities in the above scenes—the world is full of marvels, it's stupid not to know there are venal capitalizers and those with pure vision, the A-B-C enactment of education: how do we learn to talk, the difference between deprivation and accomplishment—of a very joyful, uplifting, erratic movie that gives the sense of not being preplanned.

A bit like *Moses and Aaron*, the foundling's education starts and stops, progressing fitfully through blocky, self-enclosed units. The film will stop to observe phenomena: a quiet peasant couple in a second-story window watching Kaspar, standing transfixed with a letter of introduction in his hand. A close shot: Kaspar's name written in cress and flowing script in Mr. Daumer's garden. It was planted by Kaspar and then negligently trampled by some visitor to the garden. This surprising interstice—nothing leads into or away from this garden scene—suddenly lifts into a focus on a nearby stork, just that movement having caught a frog, and tossing it around before swallowing it. Whereupon the camera returns to Kaspar's name in cress. The movie, which gives the sensation of being handmade, filled with its own constructs, always seems charged with enthusiasm: unenclosed, fluid, spacious.

The one film that approached the German films in dedication, the feeling of artists trying things, is the mysterious *India Song*, a leftwing work fascinated with rituals. Using actors who have a nightmarish sensuosity, choreographing near stasis theatrically and with a heavy Freudian quality, lingering like Bertolucci on the Past, beautiful people dancing in a beautiful setting, *India Song* is very polite, intellectual, and smells of polished leather, fine tobacco, and spices. Its great attraction: a sound track that works off Godard's layering voices, overcrowding the language, creating a film that acquires much of its excitement in the mixing room. While the iced, frozen visual film suggests a barely mobilized Dewar's liquor ad, another movie parallels the visuals, permeated with every sound from unearthly whisper to a chattering Laotian beggar woman and man's shriek that is like a culture's death pangs.

While the sinuous, off-screen movie ravishes itself with talk, about the forbidding heat, great love affairs, the defeat of Leftist Movements in the Thirties, the visual side of *India Song* is a slow ballroom dance with Delphine Seyrig in hypnotic movement with one of five male dancers. Some of its stylistic moves:

(1) Movements that barely crack the surface;

(2) A hermetically still, glazed scene: no bit players, few props;

(3) The camera behaves like one of the detached languid characters;

(4) Creation of stasis and order. Waiting;

(5) Constant doubling: in casting; staging the work against a giant mirror; having the look-alike actors in operations that hug the border of the screen; everyone but the beggar woman talks in aesthetic monotone.

Most of the formal qualities in *India Song* seem motivated by the filmmaker's language, her talent for cryptic writing: the elegance, ironic humor, women's-magazine sentimentality, the excessive control. The whole affair trembles between the fiction in third-rate women's writing—"what bliss, what heat" (and what perfect spun-silk trousers)—and a slow-moving horizontal structure in which tempo, silence, pause, repetition, modulation are stressed. A sort of fine-laced acerbity and irony cut through the *Gatsby*-like acting and scene. The film has mysterious ponderousness, and one wonders about the importance of elegantly held cigarettes, a Venetian-red gown which is possibly held in place by adhesive tape, and the over-dosage of a Thirties fox-trot, "Blue Skies," re-phrased and played 300 choruses.

One thing about the Festival: it didn't overturn, or even begin to contest a five-year-long fascination with the films of Herzog, Straub, Fassbinder, and Duras. The Kaspar film perhaps overruns into its ironic autopsy with doctors poking Kaspar's brain, the camera holding on the limping clerk's fadeaway exit. There are scenes in *Moses* where the documentary approach, the severe clarity, approaches illustration more than in *History Lessons*, the Straubs' meditation on didacticism or political discourse. Shots of the golden calf, a bad dance, the erotic moments, are closer to De Mille and Rossellini's late history films than to Schönberg's mind and music. Still, to sum up, there were no films that even touched the fervent, uncompromising starkness of the *Moses*, the snarling energy and frankness of *Fist*. You would have to be blind not to realize the responsibility for movies as a medium, the energy, and ideas, in any of the above films.

with Patricia Patterson; November–December 1975

The Power and the Gory

Taxi Driver has a lot of negative aspects, but it would be silly to shrug off its baroque visuals and its high-class actor, Robert De Niro, whose acting range is always underscored by a personal dignity. He's very good at wild manic scenes and better at poignant introversion: a man watching TV in a trance and eating while not looking at his food, or giving the sense of tense repression. Every scene combines the frantic and the still, almost simultaneously. The film has a good sense of modern paralysis, people flailing about energetically but not moving an inch ("twelve hours of driving a taxi and I still can't sleep"). The visuals are almost constantly bold, covering a scene from all angles; a scene like the transaction of guns, even the pimp-cabbie verbal duels (in which Michael Chapman's funky but somewhat slick photography is nearly static), are interesting scenes for the odd way the nearly catatonic cab driver (De Niro) is at an angle to some juicy spielist. He's hypnotized and puzzled by Harvey Keitel's razzle-dazzle pimp act. The queer oblique positionings of the scene, buzzing with star-turn acting, reveal a subtle insight: when any person feels tapped off-balance by ridicule, it often has a paralyzing effect. De Niro's uneducated taxi driver freezes on the spot, not quite sure whether Sport, a big smile, is putting him down. He keeps saying "but I'm not a cop" as he gets the nice quality of a literal-minded person not knowing how to react to a hipster.

De Niro's Travis Bickle, wanting to be "a person like other people"—to be a pair with the wondrous purity of his political campaigner blonde (Cybill Shepherd)—joins Alice Hyatt and *Mean Streets'* always-repenting Charlie in Martin Scorsese's angst oeuvre. His movies are about youth's dreams squelched by the adult verities, the charismatic fullness of a jungle-cat punk (Keitel, trapped in Sport's coded character), a feisty twelve-year-old whore (Jodie Foster, who has the shiny complexion, hair, and bright eyes of neither Lower East Side nor a baby prostitute), a vulgar and good-natured cabbie (Peter Boyle, who, like a Thirties character actor, tells Manhattan versions of tall tales to his buddies at the Belmore Cafeteria).

The apprehension about an eager-messy world is transmitted through a saucing technique in which Scorsese's unique effect is the number of optical moves that are made in a tight space, seldom using a character's point of view for his camera position. He has a romantic appreciation for Life which remembers an actor's best moves and generously supplies the time for full-scale exposition. With its nervous-generous hoopla of techniques (including the tic of flicking suddenly to a ceiling shot directly down on a seduction, gun sale, or bloodbath episode), almost every moment of a lumpen figure's hellish career has an assaulting quality, like a gnat banging suicidally against the light fixture.

When sensing danger to their young, small groundbirds with brains go off on a diversionary path, pretending to have a broken wing; in a pure case of bird theater, the female limps away from her nest to divert the attacker from her young; as the stalking fox or coyote gets close, the pretend invalid simply takes off. Just as diversionary to the always-interesting visuals as the pounding, illustrative music which grinds you, are the spike words which stud the *Taxi Driver* soundtrack. "Pussy" and "fuck" have never been harvested so often; the black race is mauled by verbal inventions spoken with elaborate pizzazz styling, "a regulah fucking Mau Mau land down there."

One showy stopper seems a blue landmark for the R-rated movie. The pimp Sport, who is dressed with more mannerisms and gingerbread than an Xmas tree, is talking about his teenaged bankbook Iris: "If I wanted to save money, I wouldn't fuck her, man. Because she's only twelve years old. You've never had a pussy like that. You'll be back here all the time. You can do anything with her you want. You can come in her face, you can put it in her ass, she'll get your cock so hard, you won't believe it man." Lots of things in *Taxi Driver* are diversions keeping the audience's mind from the fact that it's not getting the Promised Land: the inner workings of a repressed, ignorant fantasist, the mind of a baby whore, the experience of being a taxi driver twelve hours a day in the incredible New York street noise and jostle.

The movie starts a lot of material and then abruptly cuts it off, giving the sense that much of Bickle's life, particularly his cab work, is reposing on the editing floor. No other Checker cab seems to be operating at night in Manhattan except De Niro's cab, which never stalls, needs gas, or runs into the delays and quick decisions which are the cabbie existence norm. New York street noise is replaced by a writhing, intense Bernard Herrmann music track, saxophones and a pulled-taffy Muzak sound that almost buries the visuals. The hero's taxi is mostly seen in abstract effects pulling up or taking off, the windows awash with ingeniously engineered colored lights; in one quick spray of inserts, there is a rhythm series of the same stop light, seen close by a camera crew that must have been stop-light high at midnight with its equipment almost hugging the light fixture. With its nearly abstract shots of the cab slowly moving like the *Jaws* shark through liquidy situations, the use of lush-soft, often reddish lighting for the effect of New York's street jungle, and a floating camera style that finds funny angles of perception, the movie is filled with a spooky, exploratory beat.

Par for a Scorsese film is the jamming of styles: Fritz Lang expressionism, Bresson's distanced realism, and Corman's low-budget horrifics. After making a quotation, using the refracted light effects that appeared in so many Sixties European films, the movie adds one more shot inside the slick action. De Niro's cab almost collides with the two child-whores—just as Janet Leigh's fearful *Psycho* thief nearly overruns the man from whom she's stolen a bundle—but in this film a long tracking shot is added to the gimp effect. When De Niro stares at his Alka-Seltzer glass, there is a tiny sneak zoom into the bubbling water, which adds one more shot to Godard's rapidly spoken philosophizing in *Two or Three Things* in which the camera frames the coffee cup from above.

Basing its tortured hackie hero vaguely on the pasty-faced Arthur Bremer, who, frustrated in his six attempts to kill Nixon, settled on maiming George Wallace for life, *Taxi Driver* not only waters down the unforgettable (to anyone who's read his diary) Bremer, but goes for traditional plot sentimentality. Bremer, as he comes across in his diaries, was mad every second, in every sentence, whereas the Bickle character goes in and out of normality as the Star System orders. The number one theme in the Arthur Bremer diary is I Want to Be A Star. Having dropped this obsession as motivation, the movie falls into a lot of motivational problems, displacing the limelight urge into more Freudian areas (like sexual frustration) and into religious theories (like ritual self-purification). The star or celebrity obsession is a Seventies fact—the main thing that drives people these days—compared to the dated springboards in Paul Schrader's script. Instead of Bremer's media dream, getting his name into the *New York Times* headlines, this script is set on pulp conventions: a guy turns killer because the girl of his dreams rejects him. The girl of his dreams, a squeaky-clean WASP princess, is yet another cliché assumption: that the outsiders of the world are yearning to connect to the symbols of well-washed middle-class gentility.

Busily trying to turn pulp into myth, the movie runs into all kinds of plot impossibles:

(1) A shy guy converts himself into a brutal killer after scenes in which he is a smart-ass with an FBI agent, a near matinee idol with his Miss Finishing School, and an unsophisticated, normal Lindbergh type with a teen prostitute. The latter girl similarly goes from street-hardened and cynical to open and cheerful, well-nourished and unscarred, in one twelve-hour time interval.

(2) The cabbie, after having readied himself with push-ups, chin-ups, burning dead flowers, and many hours of target practice, guns down a black thief in a Spanish deli. The brutality, which is extended by the store-owner golfing the victim's corpse with a crowbar, is never touched by the police.

(3) A taxi driver who's slaughtered three people, been spotted twice by the FBI, and has enough unlicensed artillery strapped to his body to kill a platoon, is hailed as a liberating hero by the New York press.

(4) A Secret Service platoon, grouped around a rather minor campaign speech on Columbus Circle, fails to spot and apprehend a fantastic apparition: a madly grinning young man who is wearing an oversized jacket on a summer day, sunglasses, and has his head shaved like a Mohawk brave, with a strip of carpeting for the remaining hair.

Although *Taxi Driver* is immeasurably more gritty, acrobatic, and zigzagging than the *Jeremiah Johnson* mythicizing of mountain men, the two films (one moves blandly forward on snow shoes, the other sets a grueling pace) are remarkably similar in their linear structure and ideology. Both are odes to Masculine Means in which a mysterious young man appears out of indistinct origins; learns the lore of survival warfare in a hostile land; after a heartbreak, lashes out in a murderous rampage; fades into a mythic haze. The lore Jeremiah-Travis learns has to do with manly self-reliance: the first learns to kill a bear, catch a fish barehanded; the "hackie in Hell" becomes a one-man commando unit. Both inhabit a world—an unpeopled wilderness and a callous jungle—where no one can be counted on for help. Women are the spurs to the climactic bloodbath: Jeremiah's Indian wife is murdered, while Travis's efficient blonde tease rejects him, confirming him in his conviction that blood is the only solution.

The character of the Loner, which dominates American films from Philip Marlowe to Will Penny to Dirty Harry Callahan, has seldom been given such a double-sell treatment. The intense De Niro is sold as a misfit psychotic and, at the same time, a charismatic star who centers every shot and is given a prismatic detailing by a director who moves like crazy multiplying the effects of mythic glamour and down-to-earth feistiness in his star.

From Michael Chapman's opening camera shot of De Niro's almond-shaped dark eyes filling a giant screen with a lizard-like stare, this movie's aim is to turn a supposed nobody that no one sees into a glamourous giant who's bigger than all New York. The presidential candidate, in his scenes with the lonely cabbie, is a vague, tissue-paper figure in the background, playing it safe. The cabbie, full of energy and verbally exhilarated, becomes movie dynamite with a speech about flushing New York down the toilet. While De Niro is dramatically lit and upshot in a powerful near-closeup, the earnest candidate (Leonard Harris) is pale and wooden in the back, caught offguard by the verbal passion flooding in from the front seat. With its punching-ahead style, the movie typically explodes another Bickle persona at the spectator. Spreading out his features and smiling, De Niro suggests a slow-witted hick, which is at complete variance with the lean, intelligent face that he mostly wears as a cabbie. The yokel is really excited: "Everybody who comes in my cab is going to vote for you, Sir."

Though De Niro rarely changes speed inside a scene, from scene to scene his Bickle figure is a whirligig with his IQ and sophistication shifting and sliding all over the place. At one moment, not knowing the meaning of the word "moonlighting" or how to react to the "how's it hanging" query, at another he uses such words as "venal," "morbid self-attention," and muses to himself: "I cannot continue this hollow empty fight." At one moment, he is indistinguishable from Robert Ryan's truculent *Odds Against Tomorrow* bigot; at another, he ravishes his blonde princess like a new Cary Grant: he spreads his hands debonairly on her desk, looks into her eyes, and says "*You* are the most *beautiful woman* I have *ever* seen." Later, asking the Wizard (Boyle) for advice, he becomes an inarticulate Jimmy Dean mumbler. The point isn't that people don't have many sides to their character, but that the filmmakers, going for hot and heavy scores, bend the material for spiking effects.

This changing hero is a deceptive opportunism hiding the movie's polemics about superman and guns, plus a raft of prejudices that float through the two genres (vigilante and he-man loner) that are blended by the script. Every frame is awash with the prejudices of take-the-law-into-your-hands fare: the idea of sex as transaction, in which all the barely differentiated women are professional manipulators of men; black people as animalistic sinisters who get the sexual goodies and call the sexual shots; the lower class patronized as animals feeding on each other.

What's really disgusting about *Taxi Driver* is not the multifaced loner but the endless propaganda about the magic of guns. The movie's pretty damn cunning *mise-en-scène* is a mystical genuflection to The Gun: what a .44 Magnum can do to woman's face and pussy, the continuous way in which male brotherhood is asserted by one man pointing his pistol finger at the other and saying "pow." If the male population isn't exchanging this payoff gesture, they're addressing each other with "Hyah, Killer. How's the killer, today." The film's funky, insinuatingly ripe surface comes from a steady litany of "I'll kill you" shrieks, a collaging of sinister inserts, anal allusions, so many references to the sewer, "wiping the come and sometimes the blood off the seat," a giant lotus of steam enveloping a cab like fumes from Hell. Each item of this mélange is used as metaphor for the destructive blasting of a gun. Even the cab, moving forward with ominous slowness, is felt as either death machine or coffin.

"Isn't that a honey, that'll stop anything that moves" is the repellently glib remark of a traveling salesman, dealing in guns, dope, and Cadillacs. He looks like a choirboy turned bad, and is talking here about a .38 Smith and Wesson nickel-plated, snub-nosed Special in a tour de force scene in which the underground man is sold a $900 arsenal. Our salesman, earlier, on a .44 Magnum: "I could sell this to some jungle bunny in Harlem for $750 today, but I just deal high-quality goods to the right people." This scene opens with a swift lower-case zest, when Bickle is picked up by a cab buddy and taken with the salesman to an anonymous hotel room. As the guns are taken out, one by one, the camera settles into a meticulous interweave that combines some of Vermeer's patience for illuminating smallness (the rich dark handles, the bewitching highlights of a gun barrel displayed against soft black cloth) with the salesman's fast talk, Bickle's silent concentration on choosing his weapons, and a textbook of small sneak-moves of the camera going across furniture, shiny guns, and respectful hands.

De Niro, inscrutably going through a repertoire of gunman stances, seems directed to act a Bresson isolate: disclosing little of his interior, emphasizing the ballet of gestures (like the poacher laying down traps in *Mouchette*). The movie has entered a new stylized world; the spaces between people are calmer and the black hallucinatory street images have dropped away. The character is in a more methodical world of information and religious ritual; the mood is the one that prevails in Travis's one-room sanctuary: no sheets, TV propped on a wooden crate, a printed admonishment "I Must Get Organized" tacked to a wall incredibly layered with cheap, cracking enamel paint.

Seldom since John Ford's epics of Joad and Lincoln in the 1939–40 period has there been such oily, over-definition of the lower classes. How colorful these workers are: a one-man compendium of champion jazz drummers studied for three minutes ("now Gene Krupa's syncopated style"); or Keitel's incredibly garish pimp, decked out with tight-muscled mannerisms, the weirdest clothing, an appetizing voice that tries to score on every word. One standout example of an over-detailed shtick: a snarling, aggressive guy who hires cabbies and overreacts wildly to Travis's small attempt at a joke with a ferocious "Are you going to break my chops? . . . If you are, you can take it on the arches right now." Twenty seconds later, he melts with brotherhood and warmth, learning they're both ex-Marines. The spectator is asked to digest a lot, given an excess of muscle and colloquialism, but there is yet another small feistiness out of Brueghel going on over the hiring boss's shoulder. Behind him is a window in which two cabbies are gesticulating in another rich slice of street ham, starring Peter Boyle or his domed-forehead brother.

The movie relishes getting blacks off as malevolent debris that proliferates on the streets. Everywhere the cab moves there is a black marker representing the scummiest low point of city life. A muscular black walks through a barely noticing crowd on a narrow sidewalk; he's muttering loudly "I'll kill her, I'll kill that bitch." A gang of black teenagers bursts out of an alley hurling garbage at Travis's Checker. Three little black kids torment a black whore, who, seeming used to such defiling, lashes back with her shoulder bag. There've been tons of media explication about the bigotry and sexism in Travis's head.

The fact is that, unlike the unrelentingly presented worm in Dostoevski's *Notes from the Underground*, this handsome hackie is set up as lean and independent, an appealing innocent. The extent of his sexism and racism is hedged. While Travis stares at a night world of black pimps and whores, all the racial slurs come from fellow whites. In fact, Travis tries to pick up a mulatto candy seller in an interesting porno-theater scene. He tries to joke with this bored, rather pretty but definitely uninterested popcorn girl who's reading a fan mag, and she calls the manager. De Niro, giving up quickly and furtively switching to buying candy, creates a telling poetic ambience ($1.87: "gimme some Chuckles . . . and some Jujus, they last longer . . . some popcorn and some Coke").

There's dubious indication that the cabbie is a woman-hater, but the film is a barrage of cheapened sex washing over a graceful nobody who is basically a receiver rather than a giver. It's not Travis who talks about blowing a woman's pussy with a .44 Magnum; nor is it Travis who speaks as the patently insincere voice-over in a porno flick ("Ooh, that's a big one, I'd like some of that"); nor is Travis talking about a hot customer who changed panty hose on the Triborough Bridge.

Taxi Driver is a half-half movie: half of it is a skimpy story line with muddled motivation about the way an undereducated misfit would act, and the other half is a clever, confusing, hypnotic sell. End to end, behind as well as in front of the camera, is the sense of propagandists talking about power, scoring, and territory. The movie's ad campaign (the poster of De Niro as a looming presence, the interviews with crew members almost before the final mixing, the terrible schlock novel now sold in every supermarket which takes Bremer's diary and Schrader's script to an unbelievably trashy depth) is revelatory of what the filmmakers feel it takes to move, score, and hold your territory in a competitive U.S.A. society.

Reconstituting pulp is central to both the movie's writing and filming, always juicing up or multiplying a cliché notion so that the familiar becomes exotically humorous. Pumping up clichés runs inevitably into moral problems.

A scene that's been grooved a thousand times on TV crime shows, not to mention late *film noir* like *Hustle* (a store heist recorded with the camera on an unexposed customer who then guns down the surprised marauder), is supercharged out of the cliché by showing the store-owner brutally beating up the black corpse. Are there any moviegoers left who aren't fed up with personal reform through Atlas physical exercises? The hero suddenly stops "mistreating his body," goes into a regimen of musclebuilding, target practice, and health food. This situation is juiced up with a comedy scene that throws audiences in the aisles. Bickle, strapped up with his special equipment and guns, faces himself in the mirror: "You talkin' to me, You Fuck! You must because I'm the only one here." The sneering monologue refurbishes two or three clichés, it sneers at anyone who isn't a gunsel or muscle boy, and puts a glamorous sanction, a good gunman seal of approval, on the movie's future holocausts.

A chief mechanism of the script is power: how people either fit or don't fit into the givens of their status, and the power they get from being socially snug. Travis's dream girl has power because she has a certain golden beauty and doesn't question or rebel against her face or her position as political campaigner. Various pimps are shown as editorialized icons of illegal power. The cabbies, more or less at peace with themselves, are glimpsed as a gang not fighting job or status. The movie shows the facts of being in or out. Everyone plays this power game but Travis—he can't figure what kind of game he wants to play. While this misfit moves toward his massacre in a Twelfth Street bordello, the movie's heart is an ensemble of chesty people jockeying to score points. The script sets up a world where people constantly score off each other, releasing petty hostilities. Little Iris's professional command: "You better get to it, Mister, because when that cigarette goes out, your time is up." Some sexual invitation; the guy's just payed $25 for Iris's briskly dispensed time and at least ten smackers for the use of the beads and candle-filled room. The jittery pimp, a big grin, gestures off De Niro toward his fifteen-minute session: "Go ahead, go on, enjoy yourself, have fun."

The importance of humor is one of the movie's trumps, as well as one of its bad cards. When people try to jokingly tease De Niro, he can't throw it back. He tries to joke with the cab employer and the guy explodes. Betsy doesn't get his "organized" joke. This sealed-off guy's problems with humor—his crestfallen, embarrassed, or shamed responses—are always poetically right; and the movie is almost always good when it's dealing with his communicative impotence. Each class here has its own way of trading quips. The slick, TV-influenced razzing between Betsy and Tom (Albert Brooks) is repellently smug; the tall-tale sex stories the taxi drivers trade are more inventive, and Peter

Boyle's timing ("Shoot, they don't call me the Wiz for nothing . . . well, I'm not Bertrand Russell, I'm just a cabbie") is tantalizing.

Through the use of red- or brown-toned darkness and the feeling of closed space (in which, despite the sneak camera moves, down shots, and weird angles, the focus is narrowly on players), the movie is often zeroed in to womb situations. The spectator is focused on some territorial claim. Tom, the indispensable hack, is upset about Travis's entering the campaign quarters, which is his turf. The hiring boss at the cab depot is immediately suspicious, all territorial muscle, when an unknown intrudes. When Bickle squires Betsy to a porno house, she makes it clear the skin place is not her turf, she's a high-class girl. A suffocating dance presses home the fact that Iris is Sport's real estate. At times, the movie seems to be about worried landlords protecting their property. Perhaps the movie's central speech is the Wizard's: "You have to find your niche and fit into it. It'll be awkward at first, but you'll get used to it." Travis, seldom relaxed in any territory except his animal-lair room, works his way through a violent landscape which is curiously pluralist in its technique. One frame isn't promoted over another, there is no favored composition (as there is in every Bresson film), there are constant changes of style, pace, and arrangement. The only constant is that the hero, in crowds or alone, in broad daylight or total darkness, appears to be alone in a dense funnel or cave of space.

All the elements in *Taxi Driver*—from the steam which billows from street openings enveloping the screen to the incredible army of technicians who had to engineer the fortissimo reverse tracking shot through the bordello's bloody hallway—are aggressively self-assertive. *Taxi Driver* is always asserting the power of playing both sides of the box-office dollar: obeisance to the box-office provens, such as concluding on a ten-minute massacre, a sex motive, good-guys vs. bad-guys violence, and casting the obviously charismatic De Niro to play a psychotic, racist nobody. (Some nobody—like casting another neurotic-role star, Helmut Berger, to impersonate Kaspar Hauser. "OK Helmut, look as though you had no education at all. Pretend you're not handsome, no social graces at all.") On the other coin side, it's ravishing the auteur box of Sixties best scenes, from Hitchcock's reverse track down a staircase from the *Frenzy* brutality, through Godard's handwriting gig flashed across the entire screen, to several Mike Snow inventions (the slow *Wavelength* zoom into a close look at the graphics pinned on a beaten plaster wall, and the reprise of double and triple exposures that ends *Back and Forth*).

One thing that stands out is that many of the new demons in Hollywood are flourishing inside a Bastardism. They are still deep within the Industry and its Star-Genre hypocrisies, and at the same time they have been indelibly touched by the process-oriented innovations which began with *Breathless*. The result: a new hybrid film that crosses a mythicized genre film with a mushroomed aestheticism which (while skimping the material of psychosis, prostitution, taxi work, the celebrity urge) shows a new sophistication about pace, camera, and organizing. It's revealing that the *Taxi Driver* political scenes—from the office comedy between Shepherd and Albert Brooks to the speech in Columbus Circle—are very bland and stock. Why should a movie that is so anti-American go so dull when it hits a glib phony populist running for President? Busy building the old loner character who never asks for anything, N.Y.C. as a dead sea of garbage in the Fritz Lang manner, the girl-boy gag charm from the Screwball era, the crew's mind comes up empty on the movie's one area that rises above the working-class milieu, that's free of the city-as-a-sewer metaphor. Empty politics are more of a US tragedy than the lone assassin. Why is all the attention going toward the De Niro charm as a displaced country boy who is out of his depth, unless the authors are obsessed by Industry staples?

How did they get those colored shapes of light to swim around the nighttime heads of De Niro and his passengers? Was that overhead shot, of De Niro's hand and arm sweeping over the blond campaigner's cluttered desk, shot at the same time as their conversation? In the final moments, the furtive panic of Travis, glancing to right and left, washes into a long corridor of multi-layered street impressions. When were the decisions made to go for slow motion in this tumultuous irresolution that ends *Taxi Driver*? Did the final track out of the death chamber move under or above the ceiling's paper lantern? And what about De Niro's succulent scene ("Are you talking to me? . . . you must be talking to me . . . I'm the only one in the room") in which the mole usually on his right cheek shows up on the left cheek? The amount of twisting questions that are thrown at a spectator highlights its director's boldness on intricate visuals.

Taxi Driver is yet another glorification of the hood as a glamourous energy force; at least its director has injected a rare lower-case vision (the *Godfather* movies being uppercase filmmaking) into the threatening congested darkness.

Scorsese is clearly an original force in films. Some of the best things come from the sense that the director and lead actor know what it is "to be poor," to live in a N.Y. walkup, the tormenting lethargy of depression. The overhead shots of De Niro lying on his grimy cot, fully dressed, totally riddled with discomfort, lap the hollowness of the room that doesn't nourish its owner with Travis's desperation. *Taxi Driver* is actually a Tale of Two Cities: the old Hollywood and the new Paris of Bresson-Rivette-Godard. More importantly, its immoral posture on the subject of blacks, male supremacy, guns, women, sub-verts believability at every moment in favor of the crucial decal image that floats around the world—a lean, long-legged loner in cowboy boots who strides down the center of a city street, knowing he cuts a striking figure. This De Niro image, looming over his vague environment, is voiced everywhere in the script: "Around his eyes, in his gaunt cheeks, one can see the dark stains caused by a life of terror, emptiness, and loneliness." The next line is great: "He seems to have wandered in from a land where it is always cold."

with Patricia Patterson; May–June 1976

Kitchen Without Kitsch

THE lay of the land, in the Seventies film, is that there are two types of struc-ture being practiced: dispersal and shallow-boxed space. *Rameau's Nephew, McCabe and Mrs. Miller, Céline and Julie Go Boating, Beware of a Holy Whore* are films that believe implicitly in the idea of non-solidity, that everything is a mass of energy particles, and the aim, structurally, is a flux-like space to go with the atomized content and the idea of keeping the freshness and energy of a real world within the movie's frame. Inconclusiveness is a big quality in the Sev-enties: never give the whole picture, the last word. A distinctly different struc-ture and intellectual set—used in films as various as *In the Realm of the Senses, Katzelmacher, Nostalgia* (the Hollis Frampton film in which a set of awful pho-tos are presented and destroyed on a one-burner hot plate), the various short films of minimalist sculptors and painters—is to present a shallow stage with the ritualized, low-population image squared to the edges of the frame. Facing a fairly close camera, the formal-abstract-intellectualized content evolves at right angles to the camera, and usually signifies a filmmaker who has intellec-tually surrounded the material. In both cases, the strategy is often encasing a strikingly petty event: a nonviolinist scrapes away on a violin in a Richard Serra film; the limp Laurel-and-Hardy high jinks beginning Rivette's *Céline and Julie* has one mugging charmer chasing another through Paris to return a book left on a park bench; *Rameau's Nephew* creates linguistic/filmic systems using avant-garde types in low comic dress; and in Fassbinder's *Katzelmacher*, two indolents gossip their way toward a reverse tracking camera—a startlingly handsome image encasing absurd, inane conversations. Each film picks up the current fas-cination with keeping things a little bit amateurish, as though that were an automatic connection to drollery and wit. In all the above-mentioned films, grandness and pettiness are blended in skeptical visions that significantly go against heroic careers.

The thing that strikes one about the early-Seventies Fassbinder *Beware of a Holy Whore* is the movement of both camera and actors, a kind of lurching serpentine of petulant drawling sounds, inside jokes, and minute-long temper tantrums. They're all like flicks within a flux of sexual liaisons. Everyone is distracted, anxious: they're weeping, betraying, at the level of two cents. Kurt Raab collapses onto the bar, exaggerated and whining, very melodramatic, "I can't bear it!" The circular, 360-degree pan of a hotel lobby picks up bits of decadence from strays around the room: one girl saying she likes a Spanish light technician sitting nearby, another member of this desultory film crew saying to his new acquaintance, "I could help you if you came to Rome."

Central to the Seventies dispersed movie is the lack of big statement (as there is in *Citizen Kane*, *L'Avventura*). It is a profoundly rhythmic filmmaking, with a lot of lowercase observations, a brusque, ragged movement in *Mean Streets* and a ballad-like rhythm in Altman's *McCabe* with its clutter of ideas about frontier life, starting with the individual-vs.-the-corporation problem, the bewildered love of a foolhardy romantic for a practical down-to-earther, etc. etc. What is picked up about the trudging, muttering McCabe character, with his derby and long overcoat, is a half sentence ("got poetry in me—ain't gonna put it down"), a suspicious and balky glance. Centering upon a person or event is not involved. *Céline and Julie Go Boating* is a new organism, the atomization of a character, an event, a space, as though all of its small spaces have been de-solidified to allow air to move amongst the tiny spaces. A bit like a Cézanne watercolor, where more than half the event is elided to allow energy to move in and out of vague landscape notations, Rivette's slap-happy duo in a musical without music can't be defined. Each is a series of coy and narcissistic actions. They appear out of nowhere, no past profession or character traits: at one moment Céline is a sober librarian, and at another she is a stage magician, suddenly a fantastic extrovert. Who are those people in the large Gothic establishment? A shaft of air encircles each bit of information about the two mysteries; things are deliberately kept uncircled.

The Straubs—Danièle Huillet and her husband—are the penultimate exponents of shallow-space filming: a very hard presentation of minimal visual information with the one major difference, that the composition is angled diagonally into the shallow space. While they move back and forth between grand spatiality (*Moses and Aaron*) and movies in which the subject matter is tight to the surface (*History Lessons*), the Straubs are always major spade-and-shovel workers in framing that places the material close to the surface, whether they are doing classical theater on a sun-baked Roman terrace or a long tracking on the Landsbergerstrasse in Munich's red-light district, or staging a telescoped filmed play. Their Bach film is a breakthrough in filming an un-dramatized act: underlining the editing rhythm, a very programmed camera, and the geometry of groups: adding a documentarian's respect for the subjects and asserting the most rigorous respect for a movie's text ever perpetrated. The Straubs' upfront framing is interesting in that it creates both a feeling of cement blocks and extraordinary poetry at the same time.

It's also interesting here to mention Ozu's far-earlier-than-Seventies work with shallow-boxed frame innovations, using still-life interstices to do the work of an establishing shot, framing the most jagged husband-mistress con-flict across railroad tracks as a two-dimensional emblematic design, playing out entire episodes in bars and modern "project" rooms so that every door frame, every crossover move by a snotty six-year-old, is schematized and abstracted into a perfectly poised, becalmed world view. Ozu, without drawing a heavy breath, predicted many of the conditions in upfront boxed movies: a limited cast, very domestic situations, abstract placements, the sense of people trying to break-out of or living within the rules, super-controlled direction.

The images of the wife and daughter waiting at the dinner table for Hans to come home in Fassbinder's *The Merchant of Four Seasons* had the same visual stillness and handsomeness containing suppressed nerves at the dinner table as the scenes with mother and son in Chantal Akerman's *Jeanne Dielman, 23 Quai de Commerce, 1080 Bruxelles*: the same sparsity of dialogue, phrases like "Isn't the beef better this week than last, I added less water this time" or "Don't read at the table" or "I've received a letter from Aunt Fernande in Canada." Each of Jeanne's isolated remarks is responded to by a *oui*, a grunt, a nod, and each one preceded and followed by an uneasy but unaccented silence. This is Bressonian territory. But unlike the dinner-table scenes in *Mer-chant*, in this film one gets the entire meal: its purchase, preparation, con-sumption, the cleaning up of the table and washing of the dishes, all this conveyed through images of terrific clarity. Each step in this meal's progress necessitates passages from kitchen to hallway, through doorway rectangles of flower-printed wallpaper and painted woodwork, the figure of Jeanne framed over and over as she moves from room to room, putting lights on and off, changing into and out of her work smock, her cardigan sweaters, her street coat.

A marginal life away from the progressing mainstream, with all the tradi-tional forms and strictures, is chronicled with a static wide-angled lens, using structural traits first found in Warhol's fixed-frame film (early Sixties) and developed in other repetitive films (Ernie Gehr, Michael Snow, et al.) in which the space becomes spiritualized and proliferates ideas. The *Dielman* film—in which the spectator peculiarly becomes a coolly curious voyeur and jurist watching a case history—is often a breathtaking, crisp, and luminous example of shallow-boxed framing.

The drily pugnacious title (*Jeanne Dielman, 23 Quai de Commerce, 1080 Bruxelles*) is a giveaway on the movie's politics and mental set. It suggests that Chantal Akerman, a shrewd young Belgian who is bridging the gap between the commercial film and the structural (every part, every shot is representative of the movie's shape), has a passion for the factual, is not going to make the heroine, a field marshall of the kitchen (Delphine Seyrig), any more or less than what she is; has a contemporary yen for a blunt presentation of objects, spaces, proper names, and geography; and is concerned with defining a puritanistic and routinized woman in her space, describing her existence, how she moves from sink to table, her daily rounds in a one-bedroom, fusty flat. There is a definite respect for surfaces; a lot of this is Babette Mangolte, whose dead-straight cinematography, impeccably framed, is responsive to the cool hardness of a tile wall, the flat light cast by one ceiling fixture, the crisp whiteness of bed linen, light changing on a casement window. The movie is thoroughly a product of Seventies sensibility: the integrity of things as they already stand, the presentation of a text as a concrete object, and out-front admission of the means of production.

This still-life film—a genre painting by a Seventies Chardin (to quote Babette Mangolte: "a Forties story shot by a Seventies camera")—is vivified by a welter of louder than natural noises on the sound track. What an inspired idea, to treat the sounds of the kitchen as music: sounds of pot covers, ladling, a kettle hissing, water running, splashing, sponge against pot, sponge against plate, plate against table. And in the image, there is the incessant turning on and off of lights by the penny-conscious Jeanne, the small intricacies of housekeeping, opening and shutting drawers, handing up scrub brushes, returning dish towels to their place, and replacing lids on pots. It's a movie in which neither the heroine nor the director cuts any corners, except on dialogue. The only line spoken in the kitchen: "Did you wash your hands?"

She's a logician who turns firm material into brilliantly sound equations: an industrious loner living a static existence is equaled by a space filled with noises; a life of routines going right, clicking, turn midway in the film into the same life of routines misfiring in little ways. The perfect symmetry of Akerman's constructions operates also in the plot, in which an everywoman's life is glued to a flashy red-light-herring idea.

A forty-year-old widow, mother of a dour son (obedient but pampered, like a fifteen-year-old De Gaulle) runs a matriarchal household without a wrinkle on the few bucks she makes from turning one trick a day. One might think that the luridness of the Simenon-like plot—that Jeanne Dielman is a prostitute, conducting her business in her tidy uptight bedroom once each afternoon, and that she scissors to death one of her clients on a mysterious postcoital impulse—came out of a pragmatic desire for more audience by a director whose heart belongs to the structural film but who wants more audience than a Gehr-Frampton-Sharits film gets at stray film clubs and college dates. But it's just as likely that the sex-gore material is an extreme expression of the director's radical feminism. Analysis of the luridness issue is further complicated by the fact there is an offscreen murder in which a near-corpse staggers into the frame in *Wavelength*, which has to be a big item in any structuralist's background.

Jeanne Dielman is the persevering woman's film, a conscientious mom forced into "the life" for the sake of son and s-income (before Seyrig's performance: Ruth Chatterton, Dietrich, Bankhead, Constance Bennett, and Garbo), reconsidered by three sophisticated women of the Seventies. The three-pronged effort: a purified performance (Delphine Seyrig's) sustaining one suppressed note; a mesmerizing colored image (Babette Mangolte's) that uses the troublesome wide-angle lens to suggest the entirety of Seyrig inside each frame, from her chaste pumps to the flat lighting of a single ceiling fixture; and, using some of its heroine's obsessive control on traditional detail, a feat of recall and engineering (Chantal Akerman's) which rearranges this second-by-second tragedy so that it has a bold, electric frontality, very close to the effect in Mike Snow's *The Central Region*.

Whatever image one has of Delphine Seyrig is bound to be involved with her haute-couture sinuosity, her graceful undulating body and voice. But the Seyrig of *Last Year at Marienbad* and *India Song* doesn't even resemble the straight-up-and-down puritan, Jeanne Dielman: seduction is out here. The A-1 intent of this fugue-like movie is to divulge the molecules of moment-to-moment existence, the repetitious conditions of life: eating, sleeping, cleaning. Both Seyrig and Akerman nail this single-track woman into her condition of doing and redoing; her elevator trips, dishwashing, rising from bed in cold pre-dawn are magnificently fulfilled by a performance that doesn't obfuscate the movie's routinized, repetitious *mise-en-scène*.

It's a resolute film that knows exactly what it wants. Its three makers are seemingly in perfect accord as to what they want to say about a tradition-bound treadmill whose back-forth, up-down existence is the phenomenological stuff of this movie, what other movies leave out. The hallway scenes—which take on a shoving force and awkward angularity as Seyrig's one-track woman goes over the same tasks, errands, exits, and entrances—convey her driven state of mind. With its sculptural capture of hallway surfaces and the unchanging gaze of the factual camera, Seyrig's force as a human metronome hits the spectator with the monotony and poignance of such a life. When this movie's going right, it makes the spectator aware not only of repetitiousness but of the actual duration of a commonplace act. What's wonderful is that we are made to *feel* the length of time it takes water to filter through in coffee-making, the length of time a sponge bath consumes, the number of spoonfuls it takes to eat soup, the number of steps from the kitchen stove to dining-room table, how many floors it takes the elevator to move Jeanne from her flat to the ground.

In the morning Seyrig-Dielman awakes to the alarm. She is buried inside the voluminous, white, linen-encased comforter which is like a tidal wave across the entire lower half of the screen. Next to this arctic white mass is a dark-looming wardrobe, and at the foot of the bed a window opens up into the room. Jeanne throws off the covers in one gesture, gets up and stands at the open window, looking out as she puts on her pale-blue flannel robe. She stands abstracted, still groggy, buttoning her robe. A hard, minimal space, with early-morning air wafting through a modern composition, thrusts each shape at the audience as though the surface of the form had been flattened and weighted.

Within this sharp, cold dampness (it is one of the few moments of distinct climate in a largely indoor film), Jeanne moves to the kitchen, beginning the elaborate start of the daily ritual, grinding the coffee, putting on the kettle, polishing her son Sylvain's shoes, setting the kitchen table for his breakfast. The kitchen is like a shallow stage of black and white tiles and green curtains, a stage that has a peculiar still-shot-shallowness and seems estranged, cut off from neighbors, the rest of the city. As in Vermeer's equally bounded painting, pettiness and grandness are blended in a seamless domesticity in which every item carries precise information and registers within a color that looks both slow and full.

Her traits are those of a monumentally efficient housewife, totally routinized, detail-obsessed. (A great example: she searches all over Brussels to match a button for a jacket.) Jeanne Dielman is brought up to a certain point of portrayal and then left an abstraction, a symbol of the repressed woman. Repressed in many ways: she can't express herself in anything but formularized paths. She doesn't know how to use language personally, and can only say things like "My son is a wonderful boy. I don't know what I would do without him." She serves the same meals in the same sequence each week.

Jeanne D., locked within her three-room flat existence, fits the conditions of a structural film to a T or a D. Her life unfolds in perfect mathematical inhale-exhale clarity, first running well and then at midpoint falling apart over the same routines. The conditions of a minimal underground classic—that the shape of a film be discernible in any single frame; that a single-camera strategy be the basis for the movie's metaphysic and any situation within the film; that the repetitions of the camera, which is always obviously present, creates a spirituality; and that the field of examination be more or less static, durational, and unromanticized—couldn't have found a better narrative than the one in which a life dedicated to perfection breeds its opposite, an apocalypse of sinister results.

The movie's key is that it presents one full day as the handy heroine's norm, and then shows it spinning out of control midway in the tragedy when the wooden Jeanne is jolted. Her attention, which till now has been exclusively focused on timing (her paid coital encounters are timed to fit into the act of boiling potatoes for her momma-regulated son's dinner), is distracted by a new bedroom experience with her second day's customer. Only after having seen a normal twenty-four-hour cycle does a spectator discern the signals of Seyrig's distress. The potatoes burn because she's washed the tub before taking the spuds off the fire; her hair is allowed to escape from its helmet-like perfection ("Your hair's all tousled" is her son's flat, Bressonian remark); she forgets to turn on the radio after dinner, and can't concentrate on a letter to her sister Fernande. "No inspiration," asks Sylvain from the couch.

With its still-shot vision and durational attitude toward recording chores in full, Seyrig's ladylike stylization stimulates speculations of all types. Akerman's probable reaction to such spectator-psychology work would probably be boredom: "O.K., if you want to find a polemic against the nuclear family, go right ahead." But the fact is that the movie proves itself by generating intellectual action. It is no minor plus, the wealth of questions that are thrown up (Is this a diatribe against housework? Is it a Marxian examination of the isolated individual in an every-man-for-himself society?) to keep earnest eggheads ruminating long after its handsome image and flat sculpted shapes have disappeared.

In the background of its three artists are such prestigious Manhattanites as Robert Frank, Annette Michelson, Yvonne Rainer, Mike Snow, P. Adams Sitney, ad infinitum. These and other voices echo through this acute and impressive work: the look of the film, its geometric clarity (Ozu, Straub, Snow), the heroine's psychology and behavior (Buñuel and Bresson), the script's coexistence of respectability and prostitution (*Belle de Jour* and Godard's *Two or Three*

Things): As in Buñuel's *El*, the fetishistic handling of items that resonate sexuality gives a movie that is closemouthed and dour a lot of humor, intentional or not. Basically, three women are insisting that the conventional world of a woman be seen straight in a film that is stylistically somewhat domesticated, being a delta of the most influential style-content moves in the less straight film world—the one called variously as radical, visionary, avant-garde, or underground.

Partly it is the early Warhol gig: almost like a silent movie, no music, very little dialogue, a self-willed woman's working is pinned by one unbudging four-to-five-feet-high camera. As in Warhol's *Nude Restaurant* or *Bike Boy*, a movie that is stylized from first to last moment makes a theater of the mundane act of Jeanne's every chore. The final long extended glimpse of a staring Jeanne seated at the dining-room table suggests the final Warhol shot freezing an image of his sleeper.

The same strategy which presents Gustav Leonhardt playing an entire harpsichord piece within one diagonal camera setup in Straub's *Chronicle of Anna Magdalena Bach* is used to present Delphine Seyrig making a meat loaf. In both cases what is presented has complete documentary integrity within a self-contained frame. A virtuoso of the harpsichord or mixing bowl is being allowed a full imprint or registration without types of filmic spicing (fancy mimicry, seductive camera shots, editing for impact or psychology).

Though somewhat pat in comparison to its fiercer influences, the Akerman revelation is a political thrust against the box-office hype of the straight press, which has convinced audiences that it needs Vito Corleones, Johnny Guitars, or Carries, constant juicing, dramatic rises and falls for its satisfaction. The audience has been brainwashed to believe it can't stand certain experiences, thanks to the Mekas propaganda wheel as well as the media hypesters. Watching the luminously magical space of a washing-smoothing-cooking-slicing-kneading near-peasant is particularly provocative in that it suggests a workable parlance between the structural and commercial film.

with Patricia Patterson; November–December 1976

Munich Films, 1967–1977:
Ten Years That Shook the Film World
Guggenheim Fellowship Application

In the last ten years, it's towards the Munich-based film industry that anyone interested in innovatory stylistics and polemical statement has had to turn. This renaissance, all the more interesting in that the German film industry had been almost wiped out as a national entity by the war against the Nazi regime, was triggered in the early Sixties by the Marxist film essays of Jean Luc Godard and Jean-Marie Straub, the latter a Frenchman who spent his early years in German-occupied Lorraine and made his first austere, minimal films in Munich. The coming of age of a new generation of leftist filmmakers, whose particular concern is the weave of formalist inventions with political dimension, has been amplified from the start by funding from the government and the attention of German TV producers. There is now a Munich school of film-making, according to the critics ("More people have read about the young German directors than have seen their spooky films"), but its interest lies more in its diversity than in its unity. Filmmakers like Fassbinder, Wenders, Herzog, and Schroeter share in common the same kind of financing, and low budget techniques (the biggest budget to date: Wim Wenders' $800,000 "The American Friend"), but vary greatly in their anti-establishment content and abstract styling. Another interesting fact is that the American critics, for lack of precise information on the Munich situation, have been unaware of an incredible increment of young filmmakers (Hauff, Sanders, Syberberg, Boehm, Sinkel, Kluge, Reitz, Raben, Schlondorff, Ucicky, and Verhoeven).

The book that I propose, "Munich Films, 1967–1977: Ten Years That Shook the Film World," inspects the visible tip of the iceberg, but also plunges underwater to try and show the bulk of the German phenomenon. The book examines the ongoing renaissance in terms of politics, economics, and art, paying particular attention to its progenitors, such as the haunting exoticism of F. W. Murnau, and those emigrés (Von Sternberg, Wilder, Lang) whose expressionist techniques and cynical outlook strongly influenced the dark, suspenseful Hollywood thrillers known as Film Noir.

From "Katzelmacher" to "The American Friend" is a remarkable passage in film history, an unusual conjunction of Marxist polemics with formidable use of graphic-oral inventions. That the odyssey of Herzog, Wenders, and Fassbinder has moved away from its first anti-establishment positions in "Not Reconciled" (1965), "Fata Morgana" (1971), and "Katzelmacher" (1969) is symptomatic of the massive entrance and infiltration of media values into

Seventies art. A major act of the book is to explain this encirclement and containment without downgrading the vital nature of the films under discussion.

The preparation for this book has been underway since 1970 when I began teaching film and painting at UC San Diego. During this 1970–77 period, a series of three-hour lecture classes paid attention not only to the films of the above filmmakers, but centered each semester on a particular area: politics, issues of the Seventies, the relationship of these works to other movie types made at the same historical moment, elements of form such as lighting, framing, sound, and narrative. A large volume of notes and research material accrued from the twelve classes, which served as reading matter for the students. These notes built the lectures given throughout the state and elsewhere (Southern Methodist, NYU, Illinois Wesleyan) as well as a series of articles that were written in 1975 as I served as regular film critic for CITY of San Francisco magazine and later as a frequent contributor to FILM COMMENT. At this writing, half of the final work on Fassbinder, Herzog, and the introduction has been done. About one third of the research is accomplished on Straub, Wenders, Schroeter, and Kluge.

I've worked a great deal in close collaboration with the Pacific Film Archive in Berkeley, California, and its director, Tom Luddy. Through him I've been in close contact with many of the crucial filmmakers in Europe, such as Rossellini and Godard, the Straubs, Herzog, and Wenders. A lot of the proposed work is going to be done at the very active, pertinent archives. My experience as a critic for Coppola's CITY magazine gives me a good access to Hollywood screening rooms. My connection to the abstract film scene in America has been a long-standing one: so a segment of the study in New York will be done in cooperation with Jonas Mekas and Annette Michelson. But I'll also be working with Adrienne Mancia, the film curator at the Museum of Modern Art. In London, I'll be working with David Wilson, Jonathan Rosenbaum, and other critics of the German film, most of them based at the British Film Institute. In Munich, my base of operations is the Filmverlag der Autoren which distributes many of the films in which I'm interested and has also asked me to do some lecturing.

I am singularly placed in relation to most of my colleagues in movie criticism in that I have deep experience as a practicing painter and as an instructor in painting. Added to this is a sort of odd union of popular magazine criticism (a ton of this) and teaching large lecture classes (350 students) and small seminars in film, where the drive is always towards probing and dense analyses. These types of persuasion allow me to move more freely into serious music, performance, and art history to understand the forces that have helped radicalize the Munich films. With this background, I am equipped to work back and forth between the audience film and the traits of other art forms, which form the basis for a Merchant of the Four Seasons or The Chronicle of Anna Magdalena Bach.

My work has been very publishable. This is the second time that it has involved such wide ranging research. My first book, "Negative Space," deals largely but not totally with American and European films that are easily seen in the neighborhood theaters. My second book, a collaboration with my wife, Patricia Patterson, is in its final revision stage, a study of the Seventies film which ranged from the highly public genre films into a huge underground of less exposed radical work, from Serene Velocity to Death by Hanging. The texture of my criticism has changed considerably since 1941 in The New Republic, and takes a lot longer to write. A number of publishers have expressed interest in the project, and, as the work is fulfilled, there will be little trouble finding a publisher. As of now, no contract has been negotiated.

The publications that have the greatest relevance to my proposed study are the following:

> Werner Herzog, CITY magazine, 1975
> Werner Fassbinder, FILM COMMENT, Nov. 1975
> Article on the Venice Film Festival, ARTFORUM, Sept. 1972
> Fassbinder, CITY magazine, 1975
> New York Film Festival, FILM COMMENT, 1975
> The interview published in FILM COMMENT, 1977
> The New Breed of Hollywood Filmmakers, FILM COMMENT, 1975

1977

APPENDIX

Mrs. Parsons, etc.

L OUELLA ("I have always had a gift for creating a great deal of confusion in otherwise normal lives") O. Parsons has written a Hollywood gossip column in Hearst papers for around thirty years, and "The Gay Illiterate" (Doubleday, Doran, $2) is her own gabbling tribute to that fact. Mrs. Parsons' gossip column has always been an unincisive, undiscerning cliché-ridden portrait of Hollywood affairs, and her book doesn't confuse the record. Only the most famous stars get into Lollie's gallery, and only if they bring two of Mrs. Parsons' adjectives with them: "gay, bronzed Doug," "honest little Mary," "vivid little Bebe," "impish little Dorothy Gish," and "unhappy little Rita." Mrs. Parsons, who hates Henry Luce because Mr. Luce's Time Magazine describes her as "plump, pompous and prattling" and then runs a cut of her taken when she was ill and looking her worst, is apt to describe anyone but Primo Carnera as little. Long, worn-out Hollywood stories like the Fairbanks-Pickford break, or Mabel Normand's narcotic addiction or Valentino's passion for Pola Negri are resurrected once more to prove Mrs. Parsons' savvy, and are buried after little clarification with a typical Parsons' deathblow, like "I could not help but feel that at least she [little Jean Harlow] had found peace," or, "It is one of the great personal tragedies of the industry that this girl [lovable little Mabel Normand] lost her way," or "Would it have been a real love story or were they just two artists playing at an emotion at which both were past masters?"

Mrs. Parsons is extremely contented with her accomplishments, referring to her life as "fabulous, the gayest success path, a popular fable," and it is touching to see her describe with such throat-catching pride her most magnificent triumph—Louella O. Parsons Day in Dixon, Illinois (which Time claims she staged to offset a Hedda Hopper Day in a nearby town). Her autobiography is equally affecting when a certain regret gets into the mother's voice that her daughter, Harriet, brilliant as she is, hasn't been as successful as she might have been with a less disliked name. "The Gay Illiterate" is generally a testimonial banquet to Mrs. Parsons and her immediate family, with a few close friends of the family—Marion Davies, William R. Hearst and Bebe Daniels—getting some good plugs in that unbelievable style Mrs. Parsons calls chatting.

Simon and Schuster's latest collection expansively titled "A Pictorial History of the Movies" ($3.95), though it includes shots from American movies only, is a book to spend several days in with the same fascination, curiosity and interest that you give to the Montgomery Ward catalogue or Radio City Music Hall. It includes stills from most of the important American films and from apparently all of the unimportant ones, and since the attitude of the compilers —Deems Taylor, Bryant Hale and Marcelene Peterson—has been that of amused, tolerant adults looking at a quaint, disreputable but likable child, your response to this particular collection is apt to take in the same grades and qualities of feeling. For it seems that the one standard for selection has been to get a still from each movie in which all of the main performers' faces are turned to the audience, and the comment on each, by Deems Taylor, to consist mainly of telling you who they are. There are few stills here that sum up the effect of the entire movie, or have a perfect realization of a special personality, or are simply a fine piece of photography, and as a result those from favorite or memorable or important movies often turn out to be disappointing. The shots are preponderantly medium ones, and the lack of close-ups or long shots is dulling and lessens the importance and interest of the whole thing. The incapable eye and attitude that chose these pictures (the general arrangement and design are as clear and coherent as a Macy's Christmas crowd) compiled an edition that is not what it could well have been—a guide to what is artistically possible in the movies and what has been most significant in them. But in spite of its mediocrity there is a world of enjoyment in it that comes from the pleasant and amusing recognitions, associations and remembrances that go with any album. And now and then you come across a scene that is marvelous—Buster Keaton in "The Navigator," or Barthelmess in "Tol'able David."

Miss Lillian Hellman's master script for "The North Star" has now been brought out in book form (Viking, $2). The picture did not do, I think, as well with this script as it warranted, and Miss Hellman's accusations that someone—she says Director Milestone—tinkered it in the filming seems borne out by a reading of the original. But it is still too quickly and purposefully a pat on the back for the Russians, without being at the same time even close to an important experience of them.

January 10, 1944

The Hidden and the Plain

SINCE ending his early duets with Godard, Jean-Pierre Gorin has been doing investigations of anonymity in innocuous places: the twin kids with their private language, the swaggering Samoan street gangs of an L.A. suburb, model-train obsessives ensconced in an off-season fairground hangar. His subjects—pockets of intense activity off the geographic mainstream—echo his own life. A ferocious intellectual, a Paris-born son of the Sorbonne, he works a mundane California plot for all it's worth. He has built a filmic world on the Hidden and the Plain. Gorin, he's something, with crescendos of wild, inventive wit that build to precise penetrations of what makes a particular movie tick. An uncompromising critical predator, he will circle his subject until he nails it. As a film-maker, critic, teacher, he has a brilliant, deep grasp of moviemaking.

September 2004

TIMELINE

SOURCES & ACKNOWLEDGMENTS

NOTES

INDEX

TIMELINE

1917–24   Manny Farber born February 20 in Douglas, Arizona. Parents and family, Russian immigrants to Southwest, own succession of dry goods stores. Two older brothers, Leslie and David, both later psychiatrists.

1925   Begins copying photos and cartoons of sports stars from Douglas *Daily Dispatch*.

1931   Forms jazz orchestra with brothers and Corporal Adams, saxophone teacher from African-American army camp on outskirts of Douglas.

1932   Sportswriter and illustrator (Mickey Mouse and pals are motif) for *Copper Kettle*, Douglas High School annual, and is elected sophomore class president. Family moves to Vallejo, California, in fall.

1934–35   Enters University of California, Berkeley. Becomes sportswriter for *Daily Bruin* newspaper and plays freshman football. Enters Stanford as sophomore and takes first drawing class.

1936–37   Moves to California School of Fine Arts where fellow students and friends include Hassell Smith, Janet Terrace, and Carl George; then enrolls at Rudolf Schaefer School of Design, San Francisco.

1938   Marries Janet Terrace, figurative painter and writer. Works as guard and Saturday morning children's art instructor at San Francisco Museum of Art. Begins apprenticeship in carpenters and joiners union; builds tract homes and participates in construction of World's Fair held on Treasure Island.

1939   Relocates to Washington, D.C., where his brother Leslie is a psychiatric resident at St. Elizabeths Hospital. Through Les and his wife, Midge, meets future film director Nicholas Ray, a resident psychodramatist. Other friends include Ahmet and Nesuhi Ertegun, future founders of Atlantic Records. Teaches painting; finishes carpenter's apprenticeship on Bethesda Naval Hospital, Jefferson Memorial dome, and Army and Navy barracks in area.

1942   Moves to Greenwich Village, New York. Begins career as critic for *The New Republic*, writing first about art (February), then also movies (March). Work brings him into contact with writers and artists such as Isaac Rosenfeld, Seymour Krim, Willy Poster, Alfred Kazin, Edmund Wilson, Saul Bellow, David Bazelon, Walker Evans, Jean Stafford, Robert Warshow, F. W. Dupee, James Agee, and Mary McCarthy.

1943–44   Moves to 219 West 14th Street. Becomes friendly with painters Jackson Pollock, Robert Motherwell, and William Baziotes. Meets artists around Hans Hoffman School such as Nell Blaine, Virginia Admiral, Robert De Niro, and Larry Rivers, who influence a move to brighter color and push-pull brushwork. Other close friends include James and Mia Agee, Weldon and Ann Kees, Willy and Connie Poster, Betty Huling.

1945   Farber and wife separate. Begins painting semi-abstractions with Matisse-like coloration and iconic, striped figuration. Paintings will be included in early group shows organized by Clement Greenberg, Peggy Guggenheim, and James Johnson Sweeney.

1947   Publishes last review for *New Republic*, when Henry Wallace becomes editor. Tries to get job back, but Wallace refuses.

1949   Begins to write about films, art, jazz, and furniture for *The Nation*; first review published May 7. Takes over as *Time* film critic from James Agee on August 18.

1950   Discharged by *Time* January 24. Returns to write about films and art at *The Nation*, where he becomes friendly with subeditor Jerry Tallmer, later a founder of *The Village Voice*. Marries Marsha Picker.

1951–53 Resumes carpentry. In a "tactical switch" from *Nation* film columns starts to write "long position articles" including "Movies Aren't Movies Anymore"—later retitled "The Gimp"—for *Commentary* (June 1952); "Blame the Audience" for *Commonweal* (December 19, 1952); and a collaboration with Willy Poster, "Preston Sturges" (*City Lights*, Spring 1954).

1954   Last *Nation* column on January 9.

1957   Daughter Amanda born. First solo exhibition at Tibor de Nagy Gallery, New York, featuring words-and-straw paintings. Publishes "Underground Films" in *Commentary* (November) and "Hard-Sell Cinema" in single-issue magazine *Perspectives*. Writes multimedia criticism for *The New Leader*, first column November 8.

1959   Last column for *The New Leader* on November 23.

1960   Works on construction crew around Manhattan's eastern perimeter and in Roslyn, New York. Carpentry work on 40 Lefrak apartment buildings in Forest Hills leads to sculpture phase: hundreds of wooden constructions made of three-quarter-inch decking recycled from construction project's garbage.

1961   Works on canvas parallel sculpture and break with Abstract Expressionism.

1962   Publishes "White Elephant Art vs. Termite Art" in *Film Culture* (Winter). Group and one-person sculpture exhibitions at Kornblee Gallery, New York. Over summer months, gallery converted into single environment created by Farber, including ceilings, walls, and floors.

1963   Publishes "Fading Movie Star"—later retitled "The Decline of the Actor"— in *Commentary* (July), analysis of emerging director-oriented auteur cinema.

1964   Prepares "bit player article" which is never printed. Takes carpentry job at Corning Glass and commutes between Manhattan and Corning, New York, on weekends.

1965   Marsha Picker and Farber separate. Shares apartment with writer Chandler Brossard. Begins writing monthly column for *Cavalier* in December.

1966   Helen Levitt, photographer and poker partner, introduces Farber to Patricia Patterson, artist and teacher for Catholic Archdiocese of New York. Farber and Patterson co-rent loft at 20 Warren Street, near City Hall. Last *Cavalier* column in December.

1967   Begins film column under editor Philip Leider for *Artforum* in November, jointly written with Patricia Patterson. With Patterson also begins abstractions using format, character, and three-dimensionality of sculpture, and develops process of bleeding acrylic paint through Kraft paper. Patterson's close involvement in both Farber's criticism and painting will continue throughout his career. Receives Guggenheim Fellowship to complete *Negative Space*, a collection of his critical writing. One-person exhibition at Warren Street studio.

1968   Writer Donald Phelps, a close friend, devotes issue of magazine *For Now* (Number 9) to short Farber anthology. One-person exhibition at Bard College, Annandale-on-Hudson, New York. Begins to teach script writing and art history at School of Visual Arts, New York. Receives painting grant from National Endowment for the Arts. With Patricia Patterson and friend Jeremy Lebensohn, renovates 1815 Federal House, where all three reside.

1969   Runs writing workshop at School for Visual Arts, where he meets film critics and future friends Greg Ford and Duncan Shepherd. Solo exhibition at 20 Warren Street sponsored by O.K. Harris Gallery.

1970   Joins University of California, San Diego (UCSD), visual arts faculty, which includes artists Michael Todd, Ellen van Fleet, Newton Harrison, Gary Hudson, and Harold Cohen, as well as critics Amy Goldin and David Antin and art historian Jehanne Teilhet.

1971   *Negative Space: Manny Farber on the Movies* published by Praeger in the U.S., and by Studio Vista in England. One-person exhibitions at O.K. Harris, New York; San Diego State University; and Parker Street 470 Gallery, Boston. Meets Tom Luddy of Pacific Film Archives; contact results in interactive film programs between Berkeley and San Diego.

1972   Final *Artforum* film column in November. One-person exhibitions at O.K. Harris, New York, and San Diego State University. Spends two weeks at Venice Film Festival on first European trip. Sees films by Rainer Werner Fassbinder and other young European directors and builds "Radical Film" course at UCSD around experiences. Gives two lectures at Pacific Film Archives on Jean-Marie Straub and Fassbinder, as well as seminar at New York University, which marks change of critical concern with Hollywood action films to experimental New York filmmakers and radical directors outside U.S. Meets filmmaker Jean-Pierre Gorin, who later joins UCSD faculty.

1973   One-person exhibitions at Parker Street 470 Gallery, Boston; Suzanne Saxe Gallery, San Francisco; David Stuart Gallery, Los Angeles. Juries American Film Festival, Dallas.

1974   *Negative Space* is reissued in paperback without Farber's permission by Hillstone under the title *Movies*. Abbreviated Spanish translation of *Negative Space* published by Anagrama as *Arte Termita contra Elefante Blanco*. Commences narrative-type paintings using bird's-eye viewpoint and small objects to explore ideas about composition; backgrounds replaced by stagelike platforms; projects combine concerns and materials allied to experience in movie theaters. One-person exhibition at Jack Glenn Gallery, Los Angeles. Teaches painting at Art Center College of Design, Pasadena.

1975   Farber and Patricia Patterson co-author six articles for *City Magazine* (some reprinted in *Film Comment*) which define divisions between traditional box-office films and other cinema by Straub, Nagisa Oshima, Michael Snow, among others. Visits Mexico City, Oaxaca, and New York Film Festival.

1976   Article (with Patricia Patterson) about *Taxi Driver* for *Film Comment* in May-June issue. Marries Patricia Patterson. Begins "auteur" paintings, adding to narratives by using allusions, puns, and cues that refer to subject matter of actual films along with painted notes from his own movie criticism. Teaches course on films of Werner Herzog, Oshima, Jacques Rivette, and Budd Boetticher at New York University. Included in UCSD faculty exhibition. One-person exhibition at Illinois Wesleyan, Bloomington.

1977   Final film article (with Patricia Patterson) in *Film Comment* in November-December issue. One-person exhibitions at Seder/Creigh Gallery, Coronado, California, and O.K. Harris, New York. Awarded fellowship by National Endowment for the Humanities. Interview with Rick Thompson appears in *Film Comment*, explaining style and content changes in Patterson-Farber collaboration.

1978   Awarded Guggenheim Fellowship to write book on Munich films; book is never published, but research leads to numerous paintings. One-person exhibitions at Converse College, Spartanburg, South Carolina; Ruth Schaffner Gallery, Los Angeles; Hansen-Fuller Gallery, San Francisco. Group exhibition at P.S.1 Contemporary Art, Long Island City, New York. First retrospective exhibition at La Jolla Museum of Contemporary Art, San Diego (now MCASD), accompanied by lectures on films *Katzelmacher*, *Christmas in July*, *Me and My Gal*, and *History Lessons*. Paints second "auteur" series, discarding silver color harmony and increasing intensity, items, and scale changes for more Baroque-style effects. Gives lecture series at Pacific Film Archives, Berkeley, on works of Boetticher, Anthony Mann, and Fassbinder.

1979   Teaches film lecture course that contrasts films from 1930s with those of 1970s. Uses material for lecture at Museum of Modern Art, New York.

1980   One-person exhibition at Temple University's Tyler School of Art, Philadelphia; included in UCSD faculty exhibition.

1981   One-person exhibition at Mira Costa College, Oceanside, California, and group exhibition "19 Artists: Emergent Americans" at Exxon National Exhibit, Solomon R. Guggenheim Museum, New York.

1982   Interview with editors and Jean-Pierre Gorin published in April edition of *Cahiers du Cinéma*; Farber painting "A Dandy's Gesture" (1977) appears on cover. Accidentally sets fire to wife's studio and is incarcerated in campus police station after altercation with campus policeman. Incident results in conviction for resisting arrest; sentenced to teach 40 hours of writing classes to pre-freshman students. Concurrent exhibitions at Oil and Steel Gallery in New York; Diane Brown, Washington, D.C.; and Janus Gallery, Los Angeles.

1983   One-person exhibition at Larry Gagosian Gallery, Los Angeles. Awarded plaque for film scholarship by Los Angeles Film Circle. Work included in California Current at L.A. Louver, Venice, California. Car journey through northern Spain; visit leads to three weeks of intensive Madrid–Barcelona street drawings.

1984   Exhibits at Quint Gallery, San Diego, where works juxtapose cutouts with intricate narratives.

1985   Commences lecture series at UCSD dealing with domesticity in all cultures, much of which is absorbed into diaristic paintings. One-person exhibition at The Museum of Contemporary Art, Los Angeles.

1986   Gorin makes film *Routine Pleasures* about Farber. Farber and Patterson take car trip from Barcelona to Rome looking at everything from Catalonian Romanesque murals to the "Piero Trail."

1987   Retires from teaching at UCSD in order to concentrate on painting.

1988–91   Has series of one-person exhibitions in the late 1980s and early '90s, including shows at the Texas Gallery, Houston (1988); Krygier-Landau Gallery, Los Angeles (1990); Susanne Hilberry Gallery, Birmingham, Michigan, (1991); and Quint Gallery (1990 and 1991). Spends time drawing in Paris and Brittany in 1989. Begins to develop series of black-and-white paintings. Receives Telluride Film Festival award for contribution to film (1990).

1992–96   First exhibition of Farber's black-and-white paintings at Mandeville Gallery, University of California, San Diego in 1992. Major museum exhibition at Rose Art Museum, Brandeis University, featuring work from 1984 to 1993. New work is shown at the Carnegie Museum of Art, Pittsburgh in 1994. Paul Schrader makes short film, *Untitled: New Blue* (1995), an introspective look at Farber's painting of the same title. Farber is honored with award for his body of work in criticism by PEN Center. Trip to Italy with Patterson to visit Lombardy and Po Valley. From 1993 to 1996 Farber has important series of gallery exhibitions in New York at Rosa Esman Gallery (1993), Frumkin-Adams Gallery (1994), and Charles Cowles Gallery (1996).

1998 *Negative Space* reissued by Da Capo Press with a preface by Robert Walsh and new material, including collaborative reviews written with Patterson, triggering revival of interest in both Farber's paintings and criticism. Continues showing new paintings at Quint Contemporary Art, with schedule of one exhibition per year. Returns to exploring black-and-white backgrounds, looser paint handling.

1999 Chris Petit releases short film *Negative Space*, a documentary about Farber's way of looking at movies, which is shown on BBC and at film festivals. Texts by and about Farber are featured in *Framework: The Journal of Cinema* and *Media* in April. Receives "Special Award for Distinguished Contribution to Film Criticism" from New York Film Critics Circle, and is introduced by J. Hoberman.

2000 Eleven essays by Farber reprinted in *Cinema Nation*, a compendium of the best film criticism published in *The Nation*. Work included in Los Angeles County Museum of Art exhibition "Made in California: Art, Image, and Identity, 1900–2000."

2001 Painting "Cézanne avait écrit" (1986) used as poster art for 39th New York Film Festival. "A Tribute to Manny Farber" organized by *Artforum* and the New School Graduate Writing Program, with talks and commentary by Jonathan Crary, Kent Jones, Jim Lewis, Greil Marcus, Robert Polito, Luc Sante, Robert Walsh, and Stephanie Zacharek.

2002 Feature article in *Artforum* by Robert Polito addresses connections between Farber's paintings and criticism; excerpts from previous year's tribute also reproduced.

2003 "Two for the Road," first-ever joint exhibition with Patricia Patterson at Athenaeum Music and Art Library, La Jolla, California. Farber honored with Mel Novikoff Award "bestowed annually on an individual or institution whose work has enhanced the filmgoing public's knowledge and appreciation of world cinema" at the San Francisco International Film Festival, where he is interviewed onstage by Robert Polito. Publication of French edition of *Negative Space* as *L' Espace Negatif* by P.O.L., whose journal *Trafic* has previously printed translations of Farber's articles. Opening of Farber's major retrospective "Manny Farber: About Face" at the Museum of Contemporary Art San Diego. Solo exhibition at Quint Gallery, La Jolla.

2004 "About Face" moves to Museum of Contemporary Art, Austin, Texas, and then to P.S.1 Contemporary Art, Long Island City, New York. Lectures with Patricia Patterson on Maurice Pialat at Film Society of Lincoln Center. Speaks at symposium on *L'Espace Negatif*, Centre Pompidou in Paris; other participants include Patrice Rollet, Raymond Bellour, Robert Walsh, Brice Matthieussent, Chris Petit, and Patricia Patterson. *On Detour with Manny Farber*, film by Paul Alexander Juutilainen, is shown on public television.

2006 "Manny Farber and All That Jazz," a tribute to Manny Farber, at University of California, San Diego, organized by Jean-Pierre Gorin, with appearances by Gorin, Tom Luddy, Robert Polito, Edith Kramer, Kent Jones, John Mark Harris, Sheldon Nodelman, Robert Walsh, and Jonathan Crary. Solo exhibition, Quint Gallery, La Jolla.

2007   Featured in American Academy of Arts and Letters (New York) Invitational Exhibition of Visual Arts.

2008   Solo exhibition, "Drawing Across Time," Quint Gallery, La Jolla. Manny Farber dies at home in Leucadia, California, on August 18.

SOURCES AND ACKNOWLEDGMENTS

It was Manny Farber's wish that reviews, essays, or columns that were collected in *Negative Space* (expanded edition, New York: Da Capo, 1998) should be printed from the revised texts included in that volume. For Farber's uncollected essays and reviews, this volume prints the texts of their original periodical appearances. These publications used distinct house styles and employed different conventions regarding titles, capitalization, punctuation, and other editorial matters; the extent of their fact-checking of names, dates, and titles also varied. In preserving these texts the present volume does not regularize or otherwise standardize the conventions used in the original texts, or alter irregularities, inconsistencies, and certain incidental errors. In substantive instances in which a mistake might become an impediment to the reader's comprehension some small errors have been silently corrected.

The following is a list of these pieces with the publications in which they originally appeared (sometimes in more than one installment), along with original title if any and if different from that used in *Negative Space*:

"Short and Happy": *The New Republic*, February 2, 1942.

"Fight Films": *The Nation*, May 7, 1949.

"Home of the Brave": *The Nation*, May 21, 1949.

"John Huston": *The Nation*, June 4, 1949, and July 15, 1950.

"The Third Man": *The Nation*, April 1, 1950.

"Frank Capra": *The Nation*, June 10, 1950.

"Ugly Spotting": *The Nation*, October 28, 1950.

"Val Lewton": *The Nation*, April 14, 1951, and September 27, 1952.

"Detective Story": *The Nation*, November 24, 1951.

"'Best Films' of 1951": *The Nation*, January 15, 1952.

"The Gimp": *Commentary*, June 1952 (as "Movies Aren't Movies Anymore").

"Parade Floats": *The Nation*, September 13, 1952.

"Blame the Audience": *Commonweal*, December 19, 1952.

"Preston Sturges": *City Lights*, Spring 1955 (as "Preston Sturges: Success in the Movies," with W. S. Poster).

"Hard-Sell Cinema": *Perspectives*, November 1, 1957.

"Underground Films": *Commentary*, November 1957 (as "Underground Films: A Bit of Male Truth").

"Nearer My Agee to Thee": *The New Leader*, November 8, 1958 (as "Stargazing for Middlebrows").

"White Elephant Art vs. Termite Art": *Film Culture*, Winter 1962.

"The Decline of the Actor": *Commentary*, July 1963 (as "Fading Movie Star").

"The Wizard of Gauze": *Cavalier*, February 1966.

"Pish-Tush": *Cavalier*, March 1966.

"The Cold That Came into the Spy": *Cavalier*, April 1966.

"Day of the Lesteroid": *Cavalier*, May 1966.

"The Subverters": *Cavalier*, July 1966.

"Rain in the Face, Dry Gulch, and Squalling Mouth": *Cavalier*, October 1966.

"New York Film Festival" (1967): *Artforum*, November 1967.

"Cartooned Hip Acting": *Artforum*, December 1967.

"How I Won the War": *Artforum*, January 1968.

"Experimental Films": *Artforum*, February 1968.

"One-to-One": *Artforum*, March 1968.

"Clutter": *Artforum*, April 1968, May 1968, and October 1969.

"*La Chinoise* and *Belle de Jour*": *Artforum*, Summer 1968.

"Carbonated Dyspepsia": *Artforum*, September 1968.

"Jean-Luc Godard": *Artforum*, October 1968.

"New York Film Festival" (1968): *Artforum*, November 1968.

"New York Film Festival 1968, Afterthoughts": *Artforum*, December 1968.

"Canadian Underground": *Artforum*, January 1969.

"Shame": *Artforum*, February 1969.

"Howard Hawks": *Artforum*, April 1969.

"Luis Buñuel": *Artforum*, Summer 1969.

"Samuel Fuller": *Artforum*, September 1969.

"New York Film Festival" (1969): *Artforum*, November 1969.

"Don Siegel": *Artforum*, December 1969.

"Michael Snow": *Artforum*, January 1970.

"Introduction to *Negative Space*": *Artforum*, March 1970 (as "Film [Space]").

"Raoul Walsh": *Artforum*, November 1971.

"Werner Herzog": *City*, July 13, 1975.

"Nicolas Roeg": *City*, September 9, 1975 (as "Gothic Lives!").

"New York Film Festival" (1975): *Film Comment*, November-December 1975 (as "New York Film Festival Review: Breaking Rules at the Roulette Table").

"Rainer Werner Fassbinder": *City*, July 27, 1975; *Film Comment*, November-December 1975 (as "Fassbinder").

"The Power and the Gory": *Film Comment*, May-June 1976.

"Kitchen Without Kitsch": *Film Comment*, November-December 1976.

The bulk of the essays and reviews reprinted here (except for the items listed above) are taken from the periodicals where they first appeared:

From "With Camera and Gun" (March 23, 1942) through "Mugging Main Street" (January 6, 1947): *The New Republic*.

From the review of *Devil in the Flesh* (June 18, 1949) through the essay on movie gimmicks and seven films of 1953 (January 9, 1954): *The Nation*.

From "Bathroom Mirror Sinceratease" (January 2, 1959) through "A Director's Skill With Terror, Geography and Truth" (November 23, 1959): *The New Leader*.

From "Nearer My Agee to Thee" (December 1965) to the review of *Red Desert*, *Mademoiselle*, *A Man and a Woman*, and *Masculine Feminine* (December 1966): *Cavalier*.

"Films at Canadian Artists '68": *Artscanada*, February 1969.

The reviews of *Two Rode Together, Coogan's Bluff, Bullitt*, etc.; the ten best films of 1969; *Loving, Zabriskie Point, Topaz, The Damned, Au Hasard Balthazar*; Ozu's films; "The Venice Film Festival": *Artforum*.

"*Badlands, Mean Streets*, and *The Wind and the Lion*"; "*Nashville*: Good Ole Country Porn"; "The New Breed of Filmmakers: A Multiplication of Myths": from *City*.

"Munich Films, 1967-1977: Ten Years that Shook the Film World" (Guggenheim application): Typescript as submitted to the foundation.
"Mrs. Parsons etc.": *The New Republic*, 1944.
"The Hidden and the Plain": Typescript; written for J. P. Gorin at Vienna International Film Festival, October 15–27, 2004.

Portions of the editor's introduction were previously published as "The Farber
Equation" in the exhibition catalog *Manny Farber: About Face* (La Jolla, Calif.:
Museum of Contemporary Art, San Diego, 2003).

Following Manny Farber's wishes, this book does not include his unsigned
short reviews for *Time*, written during late 1949 through early 1950; because his
copy was so often extensively rewritten by editors, usually to comply with *Time*
editorial style, he did not consider them among his own film writings. Farber was
hired as a writer in the *Time* cinema department on August 18, 1949, and discharged on January 24, 1950. No Farber *Time* drafts exist, but reviews as ultimately
printed are accessible by film title at TIME.com. The annotated bound volumes
in the Time Inc. Archives indicate that Manny Farber is the author of the reviews
of the following films:

Sept. 12, 1949: *Sword in the Desert* (George Sherman); **Sept. 19, 1949:** *White Heat*
(Raoul Walsh), *That Midnight Kiss* (Norman Taurog), *Saints and Sinners* (Leslie
Arliss); **Sept. 26, 1949:** *Germany Year Zero* (Roberto Rossellini), *The Secret Garden*
(Fred M. Wilcox); **Oct. 10, 1949:** *Pinky* (Elia Kazan), *Thieves' Highway* (Jules
Dassin); **Oct. 17, 1949:** *I Married a Communist* (Robert Stevenson); **Oct. 24, 1949:** *The
Heiress* (William Wyler); **Oct. 31, 1949:** *Beyond the Forest* (King Vidor), *Father Was a
Fullback* (John M. Stahl); **Nov. 7, 1949:** *Red, Hot and Blue* (John Farrow), *Tokyo Joe*
(Stuart Heisler), *Christopher Columbus* (David MacDonald); **Nov. 14, 1949:** *Battle-
ground* (William Wellman), *Everybody Does It* (Edmund Goulding), *That Forsyte
Woman* (Compton Bennett); **Nov. 28, 1949:** *They Live by Night* (Nicholas Ray),
Adam's Rib (George Cukor); **Dec. 5, 1949:** *Always Leave Them Laughing* (Roy Del
Ruth), *Tension* (John Berry), *All the King's Men* (Robert Rossen); **Dec. 12, 1949:** *The
Bicycle Thief* (Vittorio De Sica), *Intruder in the Dust* (Clarence Brown), *The Story of
Seabiscuit* (David Butler), *The Doctor and the Girl* (Curtis Bernhardt); **Dec. 19, 1949:**
The Great Lover (Alexander Hall), *Oh, You Beautiful Doll* (John M. Stahl), *Holiday
Affair* (Don Hartman); **Dec. 26, 1949:** *Bride for Sale* (William D. Russell); **Jan. 23,
1950:** *And Baby Makes Three* (Henry Levin), *Tell It to the Judge* (Norman Foster), *The
Lady Takes a Sailor* (Michael Curtiz).

Editor's Acknowledgments

Farber on Film is inevitably a collective venture, and I'm happy to say the book
discovered many friends along the way. Manny Farber approved the individual
contents of the essays, reviews, and columns during my frequent discussions with
him over the years, and my greatest debt here is to him—not least for teaching me
how to look, how to see—and to Patricia Patterson, herself also a daring, beautiful artist and writer, and of course co-author of all his writing starting with the *Artforum* columns in 1967. For introducing me to Manny and Patricia I wish to
celebrate Tom Luddy, and for their spirited conversation and abiding support in
all matters Farber I'm immensely grateful to my confederates, companions, and
confidantes: J. P. Gorin, Kent Jones, Edith Kramer, Alice Waters, and Robert

Walsh, gifted editor of the expanded edition of *Negative Space*, and a resourceful and tireless participant in the creation of this book.

I wish to signal my appreciation to the staff of The Library of America for their signature skill, dedication, and care. I want to thank my remarkable agents, Glen Hartley and Lynn Chu. For his role in an earlier conception of this project I thank Lindsay Waters. My gratitude to John Radziewicz at Da Capo Press for his timely and generous ministrations. At the New School, I wish to honor my research students, Peter Drake, Elizabeth Schambelan, Benjamin Birdie, Michal Lando, Yotam Hadass, Justin Taylor, and Brent Kite.

Years ago *Artforum* and *Bookforum* kindly asked me to speak on Manny Farber's film criticism and paintings, and I want to express my indebtedness to Knight Landesman, Andrew Hultkrans, and Eric Banks for that crucial occasion en route to this book. Similarly, I want to thank Stephanie Hanor and Hugh M. Davies of the Museum of Contemporary Art, San Diego for asking me to contribute to the catalog for the retrospective *Manny Farber About Face*.

I wish to dedicate my part in *Farber on Film* to my wife, Kristine Harris, and to my friend, Patricia Patterson.

Robert Polito

page **xv**   All quotations from Manny Farber in the Introduction, except when indicated otherwise, are drawn from conversations with Robert Polito. The epigraph is taken from "Farber on Farber" by Leah Ollman (*Art in America*, October 2004); this is also the source for Manny Farber's recollections of teaching and UCSD. The remarks on criticism, writing, and mimesis in the opening paragraphs are from "Manny Farber and Patricia Patterson Interviewed by Richard Thompson" from *Negative Space*, expanded edition (New York: Da Capo, 1998). The quotes by William Gibson and Paul Schrader are from *Negative Space*; by Susan Sontag, from "Against Interpretation" in *Against Interpretation and Other Essays* (New York: Farrar, Straus and Giroux, 1966); by Pauline Kael, from "I Still Love Going to Movies: An Interview With Pauline Kael," *Cineaste 25*, no. 2 (2000); by Duncan Shepherd, from *San Diego Reader*, May 25, 2006.

page 138   "Movies in Wartime": An accompanying note indicated that this was the "third of a series of articles on American civilization in wartime." Other wartime topics included architecture and science.

page 460   The original opening of "Preston Sturges: Success in the Movies," by Manny Farber and W. S. Poster (*City Lights*, Spring 1955):

> While Hollywood, in its post-silent period, has produced many directors of unusual skill and competence, it has only developed a handful with enough temperamental endowment to establish themselves as individual artists. To be successful and strongly individual in the present-day industry is only possible to artists of a peculiar, cross-grained character, who combine instinctive resistance to fashions with personality that is naturally prominent and popular. As the result of such a combination, about thirty or forty Hollywood players (stars and minor actors) have been most responsible for keeping movies alive, for preventing the industry from disintegrating through sheer slavery to its own conventions. By virtue of their skill and because of the peculiar tensions and ambivalence of their situation, they have also manage to project more of contemporary life than is delineated in nearly any other art, more of the violence, morbidity and confusion than can be evoked in genres dominated by traditional moral goals.
>
> It is a different matter when one comes to consider the situation of Hollywood directors. They are, by and large, subjected to such crushing, box-office generated pressure that it is nearly impossible for them to survive as individuals except through an almost psychotic integrity, some deep-rooted idiosyncrasy of character which cannot be eradicated. By all odds, the most outstanding example . . .

William S. Poster, aka William Shakespeare Bernstein (1916–1960), published poems, reviews, and essays in *The New Republic, Commentary, Poetry, Partisan Review, Nation, New York Times*, and New York *Herald Tribune* during the 1940s and '50s and was a film critic and editor for the *American Mercury*. Usually identified as "a poet and critic," he was born in the Brownsville section of Brooklyn and attended City College and Columbia University. Reviews for *Commentary* include Ezra Pound's *The Pisan Cantos* (November 1948), J. D. Salinger's *Catcher in the Rye* (January 1952), and Kenneth Fearing's *New and Selected Poems* (August 1957). According to Janet Richards, Farber's first wife, "Willy was thin and frail, tallish, and bent into a permanent hipster slouch. His face was gaunt, with high cheek bones, thick lips, a pointed chin and beautiful pale blue eyes luminous with intelligence and hilarity." After two years in a psychiatric sanitarium, Poster committed suicide.

page 550   Farber started writing a "movies" column for *Cavalier* in December 1965. His first piece, "Nearer My Agee to Thee," is not the essay that appears under that title in *Negative Space* (see p. 497). *Cavalier* introduced his debut with this note: "We are proud to present Manny Farber in this new department. Mr. Farber is renowned for some of the finest film criticism of the '50s and early '60s and has been published in *The New Republic*, *The Nation* and *Commentary*. For his first column, he has chosen to assess the present state of film criticism."

page 584   After their meeting in the summer of 1966, Patricia Patterson, although initially uncredited, collaborated with Manny Farber on all *Artforum*, *City*, and *Film Comment* essays; however originally published, these should be considered joint Farber-Patterson writing productions. An interview with Manny Farber and Patricia Patterson by Richard Thompson published in the May/June 1977 issue of *Film Comment* (and subsequently printed in the 1988 edition of *Negative Space*) throws light on some aspects of their collaboration:

RICHARD THOMPSON: *When you began writing with Patricia in the late Sixties, what did she bring into the process?*
MANNY FARBER: Patricia's got a photographic ear; she remembers conversation from a movie. She is a fierce anti-solutions person, against identifying a movie as one single thing, period. She is also an antagonist of value judgments. What does she replace it with? Relating a movie to other sources, getting the plot, the idea behind the movie—getting the abstract idea out of it. She brings that into the writing and takes the assertiveness out. In her criticism, she's sort of undergroomed and unsophisticated in one sense, yet the way she sees any work is full-dimension—what its quality is rather than what it attains or what its excellence is; she doesn't see things in terms of excellence. She has perfect parlance; I've never heard her say a clumsy or discordant thing. She talks an incredible line. She also writes it. She does a lot of writing in her art work; she gets the sound related to the actuality in the right posture. It's very Irish. You don't feel there's any padding or aestheticism going on, just the word for the thing or the sentence for the action. I'm almost the opposite of all those qualities: I'm very judgmental, I use a lot of words, I'm very aesthetic-minded, analytic.
PATRICIA PATTERSON: If it were up to me I'd never dream of publishing anything—it always seems like work in progress, rough draft. But he'll say, "Just leave it at that." I'm more practical than he is. Manny is willing to stay up all night long, take an hour's nap, and then do another rewrite, retype, collage. He's the workhorse of the pair of us; he does the typing. He will initiate many, many rewrites, come up with new tacks to explore when we're way beyond deadline and patience.

MF: I'm unable to write at all without extraordinary amounts of rewriting. The "Underground Movies" piece took several years to write. An article on bit players was stolen from the car—a funny thing to steal on Second Avenue and Second Street, but it was stored in the lid of an Underwood at about the fifth year of its evolution. I'm not a work-ethic nut, but the surface-tone-composition in everything I do—painting, carpentering, writing, teaching—comes from working and reworking the material.

PP: Maybe we could paint a little picture of the writing process. Also, I'm a little more scrupulous. I'm less willing to let the statement be made: I'm always saying, that's not exactly true, or that's not fair, or look at this other side.

MF: They go together—to get the sounds right and to get the idea attached to it. She cannot be unscrupulous. We have ferocious arguments over every single sentence that's written.

RT: *What are the arguments about?*

PP: For example, *India Song* has never been resolved and boils both of us. I still balk at the languor, the fashion-model look, and I have no patience for the slow tango pace Duras sets up with camera and actors. It's beautiful but it offends me.

MF: Straub was wrong when he said *India Song's* soundtrack interested him but not the image. The image, a tracking shot through the grounds and across the building of the consul's residence, is determined by the music. The music was played constantly on the set to regulate the way the camera and actors move. Even though it's slow action, the people are never still: action has been slowed down and stasis speeded up. There is barely a difference in the two; as in late Snow, Altman, Rivette, everything has been pushed to the periphery, characters constantly entering and exiting a movie that is mostly at the edge of the frame. What about the deep plum glowing color—what would you call it, Victorian? Like Caravaggio, but softer than that.

PP: I have the same difficulty reading Duras. I don't quite buy the leftist politics. Marxism with a silver spoon in your mouth, Marxism expounded while lolling in an exclusive Alpine health spa. Although I liked *Nathalie Granger* very much. What troubles me is the pampered droning voice. There's so much narcissism in these rebellions against capitalism.

MF: No one sticks to Duras's difficulty enough. It has to do with the emptying out, the willingness to have bare stretches: the time it takes a washing-machine salesman to move from a car, up the path, and into the suave company of two elegant women. That's the kind of thing I like in Duras. It's the join between persistent, drawn-out time passing and the fact that life is at a standstill. It's cut itself off from active life as it was lived in the colonial past and is waiting for some utopian state of affairs. But the movie is going to remain stubbornly implacable until that time. Duras should direct a Continental Op story: two grudging, monosyllabic writers.

PP: It occurs to me that a difference between us is Manny's pull toward Minimalism, whereas I've never been able to do abstract work. It usually comes down to a difference on Herzog's cruelty, say, or the safe-playing in *History Lessons*.

RT: *So it doesn't come down to this verb or that noun?*

MF: No. I like to get an opinion, and Patricia's obsessionally against opinions. There's always another side to every fucking movie or painting; there's always an assuaging side.

RT: *Often you two resolve that through multipurpose sentences. You run the idea through the first half of the sentence and then reverse it through the second half, but you don't end up canceling out the meaning: you end up getting both meanings.*

PP: If you ever saw us at the end of writing an article, it's . . .

MF: It's death. It's like a cemetery.

PP: It's unbelievable, having sat through this sedentary thing of fighting, eating junk food, not washing your clothes—oh, it's awful.

MF: Except she sleeps.

PP: I sleep. I haven't Manny's stamina, and I don't have his dedication, at all.

MF: For one thing, Patricia doesn't have a history as a critic, or a love of criticism.

PP: That's not true. What do you mean?

MF: What I meant was that she disbelieves, I think, in judging the work.

PP: I like seeing creeps get their just due.

RT: *But you two seem the opposite of that with your advocacy pieces. The* Taxi Driver *piece (Film Comment, May/June 1976) is carefully balanced—but some of the pieces for* City! *The corner turns so suddenly. In the first article about Hollywood's hotshot young directors, the first two paragraphs read like a recruiting poster for the new Hollywood, then in the next few paragraphs it goes through a corrosive tone change. So many of the references, like referring to Ferguson's citation of the iron fence in* Citizen Kane, *I take to be references to Coppola's own Charles Foster Kane lifestyle.*

MF: I'm very proud of that first article for *City* on the New Hollywood.

PP: I kept saying, "Unnhhh"—not because I was afraid of Coppola, but because I thought we weren't covering each film enough, and that to write this provocative a piece, you really have to back it up.

RT: *Are there things in common in painting and criticism as you practice them?*

MF: The brutal fact is that they're exactly the same thing. American criticism doesn't take cognizance of the crossover of arts, and American painting doesn't take cognizance of it either. It's always very provincial. I don't get why other critics don't pay more attention to what's going on in the other arts, because I think the Godard-Straub-Herzog-Fassbinder moviemakers do; the styles are so pertinent. The kind of photography you see at any point is that way because of what's being written in novels and painted in pictures. Like the crossover from Hopper into writers like McCoy and Cain, the film noir movies—scripters like Furthman and Mainwaring—all over the place at the same moment. You couldn't have had that kind of imagery that directors and screenwriters were trying for, unless it were the most important thing for painters to be doing. It's as if there were a law in film criticism that you're not supposed to get involved in the other art forms.

PP: My first experience with Fassbinder's *Merchant of Four Seasons* was a painter's reaction, shock and envy that someone had gotten there first. Specifically the scene in which Irm Hermann, the wife, bustles around the kitchen with the daughter doing her homework, dejected Hans staring out the window. Visually, the scene has to do with the wallpaper, patterned oil cloth on the table combined with the enamel-like color, shadowless Fra Angelico lighting, with everything both ecstatic and ordinary at the same time. Straub and Fassbinder in 1972 were far in advance of what representational painters were doing then. Pearlstein was doing the studio thing, the photo-realist Estes-Goings were doing a single item Americana, a pickup truck or a close-up of an escalator.

The first impact Straub had was visual. I even made a small painting of a still from the tense dining-room encounter between two old political enemies— "Would you trust a Nettlinger"—Schrella and Nettlinger. *Not Reconciled* is terrifically interesting, visually. The curious motif: a bird's-eye view of a two-shot, the soberness of the people combined with the black/white richness, the kind of rigor and integrity with which the documentary shot is heightened. The fact is that visually the Straubs are so beautiful. *History Lessons*; the scenes in the garden with the big flowers. I always liked the oversized stage with tiny actors in *The Bride-Groom, the Comedienne, and the Pimp*; it's such a misreading to say that he's only about dry intellectualism.

MF: To go back: I think what I set out to do with criticism in the Forties—it was always the same goal, I had about 800 words, a column-and-a-half in *The New Republic* —was to set out the movie before the reader's eye in as much completeness as I could, in that topography. I had to develop a picture which could pull the audience in and give them these sights without their realizing it, and which would divulge the landscape of the film as accurately as I could get it. That involved a lot of color work in the language and in the insights—color work in the sense of decorative quality. Topography changes every decade. Now we're into a new topography.

In the same issue of *Film Comment*, Manny Farber and Patricia Patterson defined their critical principles as follows:

OUR CRITICAL PRECEPTS

(1) It's primarily about language, using the precise word for Oshima's eroticism, having a push-pull relationship with both film experience and writing experience.

(2) Anonymity and coolness, which includes writing film-centered rather than self-centered criticism, distancing ourselves from the material and the people involved. With few exceptions, we don't like meeting the movie director or going to press screenings.

(3) Burrowing into the movie, which includes extending the piece, collaging a whole article with pace changes, multiple tones, getting different voices into it.

(4) Not being precious about writing. Paying strict heed to syntax and yet playing around with words and grammar to get layers and continuation.

(5) Willingness to put in a great deal of time and discomfort: long drives to see films again and again; nonstop writing sessions.

(6) Getting the edge. For instance, using the people around you, a brain like Jean-Pierre Gorin's.

(7) Giving the audience some uplift.

page 680   The essay on 1969's ten best films as it appeared in *Artforum* ends with *Easy Rider* and does not include any discussion of several films on Farber's list at the beginning of the piece.

page 691   In 1970 Farber also published "Film (Space)" (*Artforum*, March 1970), a shorter version of his introduction to *Negative Space*. Because that introduction is so crucial to *Negative Space*, his original column is reprinted here:

> Space is the most dramatic stylistic entity—from Giotto to Noland, from *Intolerance* to *Weekend*. How an artist deploys his space, seldom discussed in film criticism but already a tiresome word of the

moment in other art, is anathema to newspaper editors, who believe readers die like flies at the sight of esthetic terminology.

If there were a textbook on film space, it would read: "There are several types of movie space, the three most important being (1) the field of the screen, (2) the psychological space of the actor, (3) the area of experience and geography that the film covers." Bresson deals in shallow composition as predictable as a monk's tonsure while Godard is a stunning de Stijl-ist using cutout figures of American flag colors asymmetrically placed against a flat white background. The frame of *The Wild Bunch* is a window into deep, wide, rolling, Baroque space; almost every shot is a long horizontal crowded with garrulous animality.

Jeanne Moreau, always a resentful wailing wall, works in a large space which becomes empty as she devastates it with scorn. Ida Lupino, an unforgettable drifter in a likeable antique, *High Sierra* (1941), works close and guardedly to the camera, her early existentialist-heroine role held down to size: she's very unglorious, has her place and, retracting into herself, steals scenes from Bogart at his most touching. While Moreau is a sensibility ember burning from beginning to movie's end—there's no specific woman inside all the emotion—and Lupino is a specific woman in a cliché pushed-around-gal role, Laurence Olivier's Archie Rice is a specific man as well as a flamboyant type. In an *Entertainer* role that is part burlesque and then pathos, he works from small nuances of exchange with his daughter to broad gestures, while brazening his way through cheap, humiliating skirmishes with his creditors.

Since it's the uniting style plus the basic look of a film, the third kind of space controls everything else—acting, pace, costume. In *La Femme Infidéle*, Chabrol's completely controlled horizontal moves, arch and languorous, picking up an insurance exec's paralyzed existence of posh domesticity, set the tone, almost blueprint the way actors eat, like a paper cut-out family, the distanced politeness of their talk. *Virginia Woolf*, an American marriage, 1960, seen for all its vicious, despairing, negating features, is middle-aged Academe flagellating in a big, hollow, theatrical space. The George-Martha shenanigans, hokey and virulent, are designed grand opera style as though the curtain were going up or down on every declamation. *In a Lonely Place*, a 1950 Nick Ray, is a Hollywood scene at its most lackluster, toned down, limpid, with Ray's keynote strangeness: a sprawling, unbent composition with somewhat dwarfed characters, each going his own way. A conventional studio movie but very nice: Ray stages everything, in scenes heavily involved with rules of behavior, like a bridge game amongst good friends, no apparent sweat. A piece of puff pastry, Demy's *Model Shop* (1969) comes together in a lazy open space: overblown, no proportions, skittering, indulgent. The scene is an absolutely transient one—drive-in bank, rock-roll group, J. C. Penney houses—that saunters lackadaisically in the most formless imagery. *The Round Up* (1966), stark overhead lighting from beginning to end, geometric shadows, hard peasant faces, stiff coats, big sculpture hats, is a movie of hieratic, stylized movement in a Kafka space that is mostly sinister flatness and bald verticals. Sometimes there is violent action, but Jancso's fascinating but too insistent style is based on a taut balance between a harsh, stark, imagery and a desolate pessimism. Of all the movies mentioned here, the space here is most absolutely controlled, given over to rigidly patterned male groups.

The emphasis being given to space by today's leading directors forces a backwards look at what has been done in movie space. In *What Price Glory* (1926), space is used innocently for illustrational purposes, which is not to say that it isn't used well. Walsh's film is still an air-filled lyrical masterpiece: the haphazard, unprecious careers of two blustery rivals who swagger around trench and village exquisitely scaled in human terms to the frame of the screen, suggesting in their unhesitating grace the sweet-rough-earthy feeling that is a Walsh trademark. This is a very early example of Walsh's special aptitude, getting people from place to place gracefully, giving an enchantment to bistro or barracks through repetitions in which the engineering slightly alters each trip, jump-cutting his movie into and out of events with unabashed shorthand and beautiful detail.

Where Walsh bends atmosphere, changes camera, singles out changes in viewpoint to give a deeper reaction to specific places, *The Big Sleep* (1948) ignores all the conventions of a gangster film to feast on meaningless business and witty asides. Walsh keeps re-establishing the same cabin retreat; Hawks, in another purely spatial gem, gives the spectator *just enough* to make the scene work. One of the fine moments in forties film is no longer than a blink: Bogart, as he crosses the street from one book store to another, looks up at a sign. There is as much charm here as Walsh manages with fifteen different positioning setups between Lupino and Arthur Kennedy in a motel cabin. All the unbelievable events in *The Big Sleep* are tied together by miserable time jumps, but, within each skit, there is a logic of space, a great idea of personality, gesture, where each person is. Bogart's sticking shirt and brain-twisting in front of a princely colonel, which seems to have present tense quality, is typically out of touch with other events and probably dropped into its slot from a facetious memory of Faulkner.

Touch of Evil (1958) is about many things: murder, gang-rape (an American blonde marries a Mexican attorney and all her fears about Mexicans come true), a diabolic sheriff and a dozen other repellent figures. Basically it's a movie about terrorizing, an evil-smelling good movie in which the wildly Baroque terror and menace is another world from Hawks-Walsh: an aggressive-dynamic-robust-excessive-silly universe with Welles's career-long theme (the corruption of the not-so-innocent Everyman through wealth and power) and his inevitable efforts with space—to make it prismatic and a quagmire at the same time. Welles's storm tunnel has always the sense of a black prankster in control of the melodrama, using a low angle camera, quack types as repulsive as Fellini's, and high contrast night light to create a dank, shadowy, nightmare space.

Basically the best movie of Welles's cruddy middle peak period, when he created more designed, less dependent on Hollywood films (*Arkadin*, *Shanghai Lady*) mostly about perverts, *Touch of Evil* is a sexual allegory, the haves and have nots, in which the disorienting space is worked for character rather than geography. An amazing film, the endless bits of excruciating black humor are mostly involved with illogical space and movement, pointing up some case of impotence or occasionally its opposite. A young Mexican lawyer jumps around jackrabbit fashion while a toad-like sheriff floats away in grease: a whacky episode has the lawyer stuffing an elevator with old colleagues while he zips up the stairs ("Well, Vargas, you're pretty light on your feet"). The funniest scenes, spatially, revolve around a great comic grotesque played by Dennis Weaver, a motel night man messed up with tics who is last seen clinging to a leafless tree, and, before that, doing woodpecker spastic effects at the sight and thought of Janet Leigh on a motel bed.

His allegorical space is a mixture of tricks, disorientation, falling apart, grotesque portraits. A deaf mute grocery clerk squints in the foreground, while Heston, on the phone, embarrassed over his wife's eroticism from a motel bed, tries to suggest nonchalance to the store owner. A five minute street panorama develops logically behind the credits, without one cut, just to arrive at a spectacular reverse zoom away from a bombed Cadillac. Just before the car goes up in fire, the car's blonde has given a customs agent one of those black speeches that dislocate themselves from the image: "I've got this ticking noise in my head."

Those who blew their cool in the sixties, shipwrecked on spatial problems, among other things. *Winning* and Polonsky's *Willie Boy* seem the perfect examples, the former a race track film with no action but inflated with slow motion, slight and oblique acting, a leaky savvy about marital dalliance, and the latter a racial Western with affected photography and ambiguous motivation. Though there is smugness neither film comes to a head because of the vague, approximate way in which events are shown, the confusion about being spatially sophisticated.

So much is possible or acceptable in camera-acting-writing now that films expand with flashy camera work, jazzy heat flutters, syrupy folk music, different projection speeds, and a laxity abut the final form that any scene takes. *Gypsy Moths*, *Goodbye Columbus*, *Arrangement*, *The Swimmer*, *The Graduate*, *Pretty Poison* are caked with these glamour mechanisms. Polonsky's invective against the crushing of the Paiutes, a disappointing but hardly loathsome movie, loses itself behind the unwieldiness of the very wide scenes.

There's a fiesta going on at Willie's reservation, and the point of any shot is gracefully ignored while a lyrical snowstorm occurs. In a scene of big heads and upper torsos, an interesting crowd of Indians are involved in something interesting, but what is seen is tinted coloring and Willie, a heavy jerky wave moving through a crowd of shoulders and hats. Seen between two of the sententiously parted shoulders is Willie's Lola, an ambiguous solitary gardenia in an otherwise maidenless tribe. The movie implies no Indians can act: Katharine Ross is the only Paiute maid and the only actual Indians are bit players.

A film cannot exist outside of its spatial form. Everything in a good movie is of a piece: Joe Calleia, scared out of his wits, is a grey little bureaucrat fitted perfectly into *Touch of Evil* with the sinister lighting and tilted scenes in which he's found bug-like at the end of hallways and rooms. Godard doesn't start a project until it is very defined in its use of space: *La Chinoise*, an indoor picture with primary colors to look like Maoist posters and stilt-like, declamatory actors to go with a didactic message. It seems so dramatic and variable in *Weekend* (1968); this exciting shake-up movie is made up in progressive segments, each one having a different stylistic format, from the fixed camera close-up of a comic-porno episode (". . . and then she sat in a saucer of milk . . .") though the very Hawks-like eye-level dollying past a bumper-to-bumper tie-up on the highway, to the Hudson River pastoralism at the end when Godard clinches his idea of a degenerate, cannibalistic society and a formless, falling-apart culture. At least half the moviemakers are oblivious to the space excitement that is front-center in *Weekend*; the other half are flying off in all directions.

It's very exciting to see the stylistic unity that goes into *Weekend* or the new Fellini, where a stubborn artist is totally committed to bringing an idea together with an image. After a whole year of varied films, it's pertinent that *Weekend* seems to increase in resonance. These hopped up nuts wandering in an Everglades, drumming along the Mohawk, something about *Light in August*, a funny section where Anne Wiazemsky is just sitting in grass, thumb in mouth, reading a book. Compared to the podium-locked image of *They Shoot Horses*, *Weekend* is a rambling mystery not unlike the long, knotted tail swirling under an old dime-store kite.

page 770   Farber received a fellowship from the John Simon Guggenheim Memorial Foundation for a project titled *Munich Films, 1976–1977: Ten Years that Shook the Film World*. The application refers to another book, on the subject of "Seventies film," in collaboration with Patricia Patterson. The Seventies film study would have combined their already-published essays with revised class notes and lectures from Farber's film courses at the University of California, San Diego. Both books remained unfinished.

INDEX

LINCC

Plant City